Valentin Vydrin

Dictionnaire dan de l'Est–français avec une esquisse de grammaire et un index français-dan

3e édition

Dhɪ̋wȍgā klɔ́ɔ̏pɤ̏gɯ́ sʌ́ʌdhɛ̋bȅ kwɪ̋wȍ wāa dànwȍ gɯ́ wāa dànwȍ yʌ̋n-bhɔ̄-sɯ̏ sʌ́ʌdhɛ̋

Paris — Man — Québec

Mandenkan —Päbhɛ̄nbhäbhɛ̏n

2021

Vydrin, Valentin. *Dictionnaire Dan de l'Est – Français avec une esquisse de grammaire et un index français-dan.* Paris— Man — Québec : Mandenkan— Päbhɛ̄ nbhäbhɛ̏n, 2021. 410 p.

Ce travail a bénéficié partiellement d'une aide de l'Etat gérée par l'Agence Nationale de la Recherche au titre du programme "Investissements d'Avenir" portant la référence ANR-10-LABX-0083. Il contribue à l'IdEx Université de Paris - ANR-18-IDEX-0001. Cette édition parait grâce au financement de l'Institut universitaire de France.

MEABOOKS Inc.
34 CH. DU BOISE
LAC-BEAUPORT
QC G3B 2A5
CANADA

info@meabooks.com

ISBN 978-1-988391-10-6

à la mémoire de mes amis disparus
Kességbeu Mongnan Alphonse
Margrit Bolli

Préface de la 2e edition (2021)

La nouvelle édition diffère considérablement de la première, publiée il y a douze ans.

D'abord, le dictionnaire est désormais présenté en nouvelle orthographe du dan de l'Est, élaborée en 2014 et adoptée par l'assemblée des alphabétiseurs en décembre 2018. Cela permettra de l'utiliser comme support dans l'enseignement pour les adultes et, éventuellement, à l'école, à côté des matériaux pédagogiques et des livres de lecture.

En second lieu, cette édition est d'environ 50% plus volumineuse que la première : elle comporte plus de 4000 entrées (y compris des entrées de renvoi), tandis que l'édition de 2008 n'en comptait qu'un peu plus de 2600. Bien évidemment, cela ne me permet toujours pas prétendre à ce que le dictionnaire représenterair la richesse lexicale de la langue dan d'une façon exhaustive ; on est encore loin de là. J'espère qu'on serait plus proche de ce but avec la troisième édition.

Les nouvelles données lexicales incluses dans la 2e édition ont été collectées pendant une période de 12 ans d'une collaboration fructueuse avec tout d'abord Kességbeu Mongnan, mon co-auteur de la première édition, puis après sa mort en 2011, avec Gama Hubert (Gué Nestor) que je tiens à remercier ici pour sa coopération et patience. J'ai profité des consultations ponctuelles de mes autres amis dan, avant tout Zeh Emmanuel.

Je tiens à exprimer ma gratitude à Gérard Dumestre et Paulette Roulon-Doko qui ont fait la relecture finale des traductions et textes français.

Préface de la première édition (2008)

Ce dictionnaire et l'esquisse grammaticale du dan de l'Est (dialecte de Gouèta) sont adressés en particulier au peuple dan et ont pour but de promouvoir l'alphabétisation et la scolarisation en langue dan. Cependant, ce livre peut également servir à ceux dont la langue natale est autre que le dan, et qui désirent l'apprendre, aussi bien qu'aux linguistes qui s'intéressent à la langue dan.

L'élaboration du présent dictionnaire a été réalisée dans le cadre d'un projet commun suisse-russe, en coopération étroite avec des collègues ivoiriens. Il s'insère dans un projet qui a pour finalité la description grammaticale et lexicographique des langues du groupe mandé-sud parlées en Côte-d'Ivoire. Ce projet a été soutenu par deux subventions du Fonds National Suisse de Recherche Scientifique (SUBJ 062156.00 et SUBJ 062156.00), ainsi que deux subventions de la Fondation Russe des études en sciences humaines (04-04-00262a et 08-04-00144a). Ce projet a également bénéficié d'un inestimable support financier, moral et organisationnel de la part de Margrit Bolli et Eva Flik, deux chercheuses de la Société Internationale de Linguistique, et d'un sponsor anonyme. Notre gratitude s'adresse également à Thomas Bearth, le coordinateur du Projet côté suisse, dont la persévérance a rendu possible l'aboutissement de ce travail.

Le dictionnaire et la grammaire sont basés avant tout sur la compétence linguistique d'un des auteurs, Kességbeu Mongnan. Cependant, là où cela s'avérait nécessaire, d'autres locuteurs du dan-gouèta ont bien voulu élucider nos nombreuses questions. Dans ce contexte, nous tenons à remercier Gama Hubert et Diomandé Vassiafa, tous deux de Santa, ainsi que Vassa Jonas de Tokpapleu. Nous exprimons aussi ici notre gratitude à tous nos autres interlocuteurs : amis et parents qui ont, d'une manière ou d'une autre, contribué à ce travail de longue haleine.

Nous tenons également à mentionner le nom d'Alyona Tcherdyntseva, une étudiante russe de St-Pétersbourg, qui a entamé le travail portant sur ce dictionnaire en 2001.

Nous remercions Klanniégbeu Gongblin, professeur de lycée en service au Lycée Moderne de Duékoué, de l'important travail éditorial bilingue accompli sur l'ensemble du dictionnaire. Nous exprimons enfin notre gratitude à Chantal-Nina Kouoh (traductrice, Neuenhof, Suisse) qui a assuré la relecture finale des traductions et textes français.

Esquisse de grammaire du dan de l'Est
(dialecte de Gouèta)

1. Informations générales

1. La langue dan de l'Est est parlée dans les départements Biancouma, Sipilou et Man de la région Tonkpi, district des Montagnes, dans l'Ouest de la Côte-d'Ivoire. Le dialecte gouèta (*dân gwɛ̂ɛ̀tàa*) dans la sous-préfecture de Santa a été choisi comme base de la langue littéraire dan (yacouba) pour la zone nord-est, tandis que le dialecte de l'ancien canton de Blo a été sélectionné pour la norme linguistique de la zone sud-ouest. La zone d'habitation relativement homogène des Dan s'étale au-delà la frontière libérienne, où les Dan sont connus sous le nom de Gio; leurs dialectes sont assez proches du dan du sud-ouest de la Côte-d'Ivoire. Il existe aussi une enclave dan dans la préfecture de Touba, près de la frontière guinéenne (y compris 4 ou 5 villages du côté guinéen) ; on y parle le dialecte kla, qui est assez différent des autres variantes du dan.

Le dan est une des langues du groupe linguistique mandé-sud. Les langues les plus proches génétiquement sont le goo (parlé au nord de la ville de Man), le mano (parlé au Libéria et en Guinée) et le toura. Les autres langues de ce groupe sont le gouro, le yaouré, le mwan, le wan, le gban, le beng et le ngen ; toutes ces langues sont parlées en Côte-d'Ivoire. Une parenté linguistique plus éloignée lie les Dan avec les autres langues de la famille mandé, comme le manding (dioula, bambara, maninka, mahou, etc.), le kpellé et le looma (toma), etc.

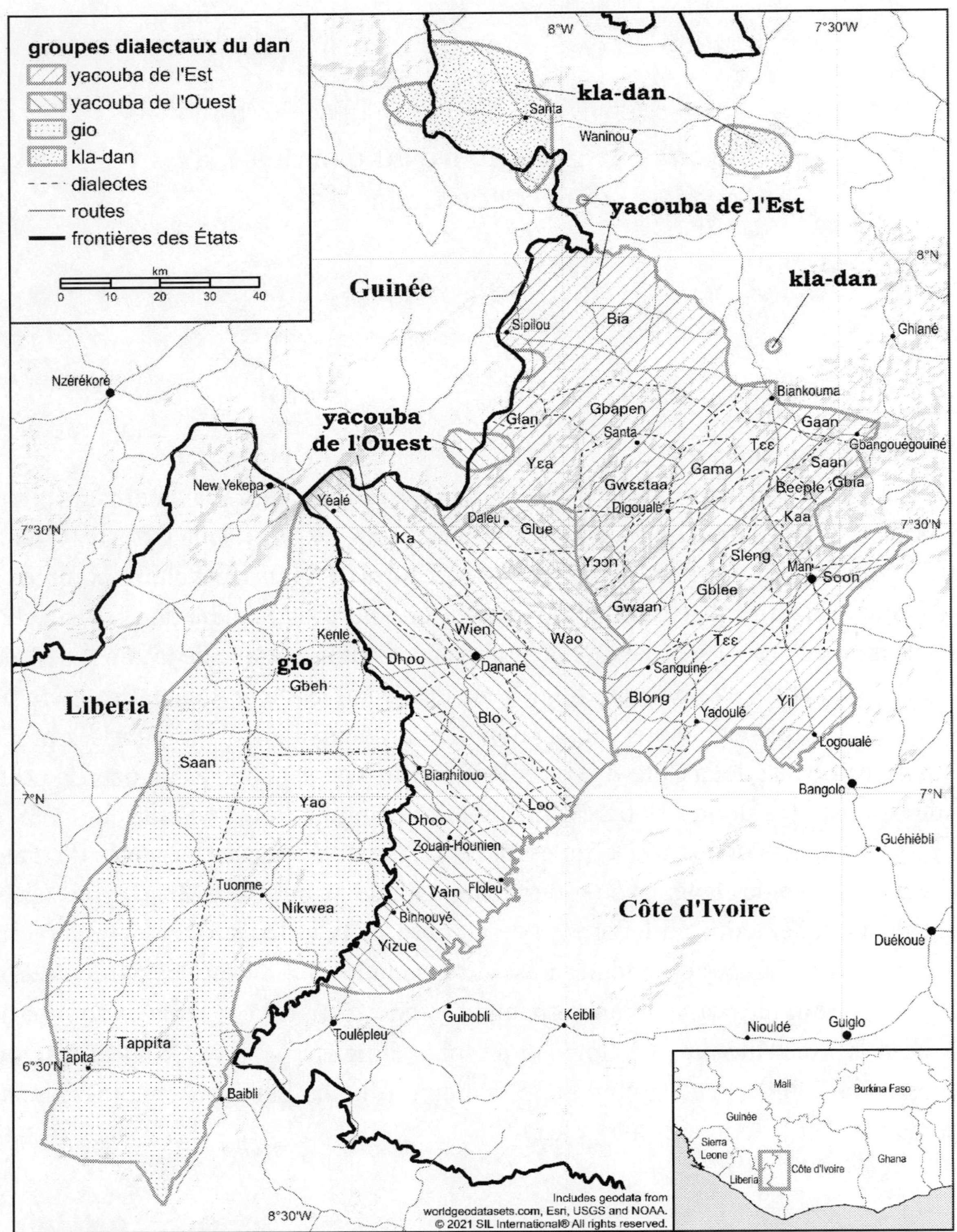

La langue dan et ses dialectes

La plupart des Dan pratiquent des croyances traditionnelles (cultes des masques, fétichisme, animisme), bien qu'aujoud'hui le christianisme se répande petit à petit, aussi bien que, dans un moindre degré, l'islam.

Le nombre des Dan en Côte-d'Ivoire est d'environ un million trois cent mille, dont à peu près la moitié vivent dans la zone Est.

Il y a des émissions en dan à la « Radio des Dix-Huit Montagnes » à la Mission Catholique à Man, aux radios, « ONUCI FM » et « Tonkpi FM ». Il y a aussi une émission hebdomadaire d'un quart d'heure en dan à la télévision ivoirienne. Le dan est utilisé dans les offices protestants. Le Nouveau Testament a été publié en dan-gouèta en 1991. Il existe aussi des livres d'alphabétisation. Un journal *Pȁbhɛ̄nbhȁbhɛ̏n,* 'Le Réveilleur', paraît irrégulièrement depuis 2005.

2. Phonologie

2.1. Phonologie segmentale

2.1.1. Voyelles

Le système vocalique du dan-gouèta comporte 12 phonèmes oraux et 9 phonèmes nasals (en alphabet international phonétique) :

Tableau 1. Voyelles du dan-gouèta (symboles phonétiques)

Orales				Nasales		
anté-rieures	postérieures non-arron-dies	postérieures arrondies		anté-rieures	postérieures non-arrondies	postérieures arrondies
			ŋ			
i	ɯ	u		ĩ	ɯ̃	ũ
e	ɤ	o				
ɛ	ʌ	ɔ		ɛ̃	ʌ̃	ɔ̃
æ	a	ɒ		æ̃	ã	ɒ̃

Sous le ton extra-haut, mais aussi après le ton extra-haut, les voyelles *e, ɤ, o* se réalisent comme semi-fermées, respectivement [ɪ, ɣ, ʊ]. Ces allophones étaient désignés par des graphèmes séparés en ancienne orthographe (celle de 1982); dans la nouvelle orthographe, ils ne se distinguent pas.[1] Les voyelles nasales *ɛ̃, ɔ̃, ʌ̃* portant le ton extra-haut ont des variantes libres semi-fermées : *dhɔ̋ndhɔ̋n* [nɔ̃̋nɔ̃̋ ~ nʊ̃̋nʊ̃̋] 'lait', *bhʌ̋nŋ* [mʌ̃̋ŋ̋ ~ mɣ̃̋ŋ̋] 'néré (Parkia biglobosa)' ; cependant, cette différence n'était pas introduite même dans l'ancienne orthographe. Ainsi, le système vocalique se présente de la façon suivante **en nouvelle orthographe** (la nasalisation de la voyelle est rendue par *–n* après la voyelle : *an* /ã/, *ɛn* /ɛ̃/, etc.) :

[1] Dans certains dialectes dan de l'Est, les voyelles *ɪ, ɣ, ʊ* apparaissent pas seulement sous le ton extra-bas, on peut donc dire que dans ces dialectes *ɪ, ɣ, ʊ* sont des phonèmes à part. Les lettres *ɪ, ɣ, ʊ* peuvent donc être utilisées pour transcrire les dialectes en question.

Tableau 2. Voyelles du dan-gouèta (la nouvelle orthographe)

Orales				Nasales		
			ŋ			
i	*ɯ*	*u*		*in*	*ɯn*	*un*
(ɩ)	*(ɣ)*	*(ʋ)*				
e	*ɤ*	*o*				
ɛ	*ʌ*	*ɔ*		*ɛn*	*ʌn*	*ɔn*
æ	*a*	*œ*		*æn*	*an*	*œn*

L'élément nasal vélaire *ŋ* est considéré comme une voyelle (à aperture zéro) à distribution limitée. En orthographe, il est désigné par la lettre *ŋ* à la fin du mot (ou d'une partie de mot), et par *n* pour le pronom non-subjectif de la 1ère pers. du sg.

Les voyelles longues se comportent, en ce qui concerne la distribution des tons, de la même façon que les séquences des voyelles différentes, elles sont donc interprétées comme des combinaisons de voyelles identiques. Ainsi, la forme *bhɛ̄ɛ̋* ‘prière’ a deux voyelles identiques *ɛ* et est donc constituée de deux syllabes, *bhɛ̄* + *ɛ̋* (de la même façon que *bhīʌ̋* ‘corde’ = *bhī* + *ʌ̋*).

Les voyelles *æ* et *œ* /ɒ/, *æn* /æ̃/, *œn* /ɒ̃/ représentent un cas spécial. Ces voyelles proviennent historiquement des combinaisons *ɛ* + *a* et *a* + *ɔ* (orales ou nasales) respectivement. Elles posent deux problèmes :

1) Dans de nombreux mots en dan-gouèta, on observe une variation libre entre *ææ* et *ɛɛ, ææn* et *ɛɛn, œœ* et *ɔɔ, œœn* et *ɔɔn* : *gæ̀æn* ou *gɛ̀ɛn* ‘veuvage’, *dhœ̄œ* ou *dhɔ̄ɔ* ‘cloche métallique’, etc. Une question se pose : est-il vraiment nécessaire de distinguer ces phonèmes, ou s’agit-il simplement des variantes automatiques de *ɛɛ, ɛɛn, ɔɔ, ɔɔn* ? Cependant, il s’avère que la variation en question n’est pas automatique ; par exemple, le mot *bhɛ̋ɛ* ‘chemise longue’ n’a pas de variante **bhæ̋æ* (cf. *bhɛ̄ɛ̋* ou *bhǣæ̋* ‘prière’ qui a les deux variantes), ou encore *dœ̄œŋ* ‘dimension’ qui n’a pas de variante **dɔ̄ɔŋ* (cf. *dɔ̋ɔ̏n-* ou *dœ̋œ̏n* ‘araignée venimeuse’). La variation en question n’est donc pas prévisible, ce qui veut dire que les phonèmes en question doivent être retenus.

2) Dans la grande majorité des cas, ces deux voyelles apparaissent comme longues : /ææ/, /æ̰æ̰/, /ɒɒ/, /ɒ̰ɒ̰/. On peut se poser la question suivante : s’agit-il, dans ce cas, de « vraies » voyelles longues (plutôt que de suites de voyelles brèves identiques) ?

Cependant, les voyelles brèves existent tout de même. /æ/ apparaît dans la position devant une voyelle nasale *–ŋ* : *dhæ̏ŋ* ‘étranger’, *sæ̋ŋ* ‘touffe de queue de porc-épic’, etc. *œ* bref est attesté dans quelques formes redoublées : *zœ̏nzœ̏ndhē* intensif pluriel de *zœ̏œndhē* ‘rouge’. La présence des voyelles brèves en question est limitée, mais elle permet d'établir pour ces phonèmes le même type de correspondance entre les voyelles brèves et longues que pour tous les autres phonèmes.[2]

2.1.2. Consonnes

Les consonnes du dan de l'Est sont représentées dans le Tableau 3. Les allophones apparaissant en contexte nasal figurent entre parenthèses. Dans l'orthographe, /ɓ/ et /ɗ/ sont désignés par *bh* et *dh* respectivement, même pour les allophones nasals devant les voyelles nasales : on écrit *dhʌ́n* 'enfant' pour /ɗʌ̃́/ [nʌ̃́], *bhɔ̏ɔn* 'souris' pour /ɓɔ̏ɔ̃/ [mɔ̏ɔ̃]. Dans l'ancienne orthographe, /ɓ/ et /ɗ/ devant voyelles nasales étaient rendus par des lettres *m* et *n* : *'në* 'enfant', *-mɔɔ* 'souris'. *m* n'est plus utilisé dans l'orthographe de 2014 (on peut quand même l'utiliser, à titre d'exception, pour quelques rares emprunts, comme *mōtô* 'moto').

Tableau 3. Consonnes dan-gouèta

	Labiales	Alvéolaires	Palatales	Vélaires	Vélaires labialisées	Labio-vélaires
Occlusives sourdes	p	t		k	kw	kp
Occlusives sonores	b	d		g	gw	gb
Fricatives sourdes	f	s				(h)
Fricatives sonores	v	z				
Implosives	ɓ	ɗ				
Sonantes		l, (rr)	y		w	

Le phonème *l* se réalise à l'intérieur du pied métrique comme [r] après une consonne dentale ou palatale (*t, d, s, z, ɗ, y*)[3] et comme [l] dans tous les autres contextes. À l'écrit, on ne distingue pas ces allophones : *tlōo* [trōō] 'jeu', *dlɑ̋* [drɑ̋] 'pont de lianes'. Cependant, il est permis d'utiliser la lettre *r* dans les idéophones, là où cette pronociation n'est pas conditionnée par la consonne précédente, mais sert pour

[2] Dans l'ancienne orthographe, ces phonèmes étaient désignés par des digraphes (*εa* et *aɔ*), ce qui rendait impossible la distinction entre les voyelles simples et doubles.

[3] Plus précisement, les séquences /zl/ et /sl/ en dan gouèta se prononcent respectivement comme [ɮ] et [ɬ], mais dans certains autres dialectes, les prononciations [zr] et [sr] sont possibles également.

l'expressivité, ex. : *krrɔ̏ɔdhɤ̄* (crépitement des os quand on s'étire), *krrɤ́ɤdhɤ̄* (son de rongement).

Le phonème *h* est très rare, il n'apparaît que dans quelques interjections : *hāá* 'ouff!'

L'alphabet dan-gouèta (en orthographe de Côte-d'Ivoire) se présente comme suit :

a, æ, ʌ, b, bh, d, dh e, ɛ, f, i, g, h, k, l, n, ŋ, o, ɔ, ɤ, œ, p, s, t, u, ɯ, v, w, y, z

Les lettres supplémentaires sont: m, r, ɩ, ʊ, ɏ.

2.2. Tons

Le dan-gouèta a cinq tonèmes simples, essentiellement réalisés comme tons unis :

1) extra-haut : *ka̋a*[4] 'gale' ;

2) haut : *káa* 'vous' (marqueur prédicatif négatif du présent) ;

3) moyen : *kāa* 'vous' (marqueur prédicatif du prospectif) ;

4) bas : *kàa* 'gratter' (dans la construction « conjointe », cf. ci-dessous) ;

5) extra-bas : *kȁa* 'roseau'.

S'y ajoute trois tons modulés :

1) haut – descendant : *gbân* 'fourmi grosse noire' ;

2) moyen – descendant : *dı̄ı̏* 'faim' (un ton rare) ;

3) extra-haut – descendant : *tö* 'arbre à bois très mou', *zīizïdhȅ* 'très-très ancien', *bhëbhë* 'extrêmement bon, excellent' (un ton rare, sans doute inexistant dans de nombreux dialectes du dan de l'Est hors gouèta).

Le ton joue un rôle grammatical très important en dan-gouèta. Le ton extra-bas sur le verbe marque l'aspect neutre (cf. la section 9. Verbes); le ton extra-bas sur le nom marque la fonction de tête syntaxique du nom dans une construction génitivale ; des modifications tonales marquent le pluriel et l'intensif des adjectifs, etc. Le suffixe tonal (un ton extra-bas final), désigné par une apostrophe après le mot, peut représenter un pronom élidé de 3ème pers. du sg. de la série non-subjective (*ȁ*), par exemple : *… yɤ́' pɤ̄' dhȅ* 'Il le lui a dit.' Il sert de marque pour l'infinitif (*Ā dhɔ̏ dhūn' dhı̄a̋.* 'Je viendrai demain') et le prohibitif.

Il faut donc retenir l'idée qu'un mot en dan peut apparaître dans des contextes différents avec des tons différents et que ce changement de tons n'est pas arbitraire. On peut toujours rétablir le ton lexical du mot puisque les modifications obéissent à des règles bien précises.

---

[4] Selon les principes de l'orthographe de 2014, quand deux voyelles qui se suivent ont le même ton, on ne met la marque du ton que sur la première. Ex., *ka̋a* (se prononce ka̋a̋), *kàa* (se prononce kàà), etc., voir 2.3.

2.3. L'organisation rythmique : pieds

Dans les langues du monde, il va de soi que les mots se subdivisent en syllabes. Normalement, le noyau d'une syllabe est la voyelle ; tant de voyelles dans un mot, tant de syllabes. Ainsi, le mot *gʌ̏nŋ̏gʌ̄nŋ̋klȍȍ* 'espèce de liane (Paullinia pinnata)' a 6 voyelles (*ʌn, ŋ, ʌn, ŋ, o, o*), donc 6 syllabes.

Il s'avère cependant que la seule subdivision en syllabes ne permet pas de bien comprendre le fonctionnement du système phonologique du dan. En fait, certaines syllabes sont beaucoup plus fortement liées entre elles que d'autres. Par exemple, dans le mot *bhánŋ́glō̄ō* 'mangue' la liaison entre les syllabes *bhán* et *ŋ́* est plus forte que celle entre les syllabes *ŋ́* et *glō*. Les séquences comme *bhánŋ́* et *glōō* sont des **pieds**, unités intermédiaires entre les syllabes et les mots ; leur rôle en dan (comme dans les autres langues du groupe mandé-sud) est prépondérant.[5]

D'après leurs structures, on note les types suivants de pieds rythmiques en dan-gouèta :

a) pieds légers, consistant en une syllabe : V, ŋ, CV et ClV[6].

b) pieds lourds, consistant en deux syllabes chacun : CVV, CVŋ, ClVV, ClVŋ

c) pieds extra-lourds, consistant en trois syllabes : CVVV, CVVŋ

Un pied rythmique se caractérise par

– l'harmonie de nasalité : dans le cadre d'un pied, toutes les voyelles peuvent être soit nasales, soit orales; une combinaison des voyelles orales et nasales est impossible.[7] En orthographe, la marque de nasalisation (*-n*) porte toujours sur l'ensemble du pied, plutôt que sur une seule voyelle : *pɔ̏ɔn* 'hernie' (/pɔ̏̃ɔ̏̃/, et non pas */pɔ̏ɔ̏̃/ !), *zīaan* 'route' (/zī̃ā̃ā̃/, et non pas */zīāā̃/ ou */zīā̃ā̃/ !) ;

– des restrictions concernant les combinaisons tonales. Naturellement, un pied léger ne peut porter que les tons énumérés dans la division 2.2 (les cinq tons unis et les trois

[5] Dans les travaux linguistiques sur les langues mandé-sud, ces unités sont traitées tantôt de « syllabes », tantôt de « syllabèmes », ou encore de « monèmes ». Le terme « pied » pour les langues mandé est discuté dans la littérature linguistique depuis environ 20 ans (Leben 2002; Vydrin 2001; Weidman & Rose 2006; Kuznetsova 2007; Vydrine 2010; Green 2015; Vydrin in print). Il est évident que le type de pied qu'on observe dans les langues mandé est différent de celui dans des langues à accent (« le pied métrique »). Le type mandé peut être défini par le terme anglais « featural foot », proposé par Green (2015) ; en français, on peut traduire ce terme par « pied caractéristique ».

[6] C représente une consonne, V représente une voyelle (autre que *ŋ*).

[7] La voyelle ŋ est hors du système de l'harmonie de nasalité ; elle se combine avec les unes comme avec les autres.

tons descendants). Mais dans les pieds lourds et extra-lourds, beaucoup de combinaisons tonales, théoriquement possibles, ne sont pas attestées. Les règles des combinaisons tonales dans un pied lourd peuvent se résumer comme suit :

a) toutes les combinaisons de tons unis identiques (Haut-Haut, Moyen-Moyen, etc.) sont admises ;

b) tous les tons initiaux se combinent avec le ton final extra-bas (*bhɔ̋ɔ̏n* 'marabout', *gbáȁ* 'une sorte de banane plantain, grosse et longue', *gɔ̄ɔ̏n* 'homme', *kèŋ̏* 'après') ;

c) le ton moyen initial du pied se combine avec les deux tons plus élevés à la finale (Moyen-Haut : *bhɔ̄ɔ́* 'espèce d'abeille' ; Moyen-Extra-haut : *bhīa̋a̋* 'piège à singes') ;

d) dans quelques rares cas, dans les pieds composés originellement (résultant de la fusion de noms avec des postpositions), on trouve la combinaison Extra-haut-Moyen (comme *sı̋āā* 'par terre', le cas superessif du *sɛ̋* 'terre') ou Haut-Moyen (*bhláā* 'au champ', le cas locatif du *bhláȁdhɛ̏* 'champ') ;

– des restrictions concernant les combinaisons vocaliques. Ainsi, dans les pieds du type ClVV les deux voyelles sont toujours identiques. Dans les pieds des types CVV et CVVŋ les deux voyelles sont soit identiques, soit la première voyelle est la plus fermée (i, u) et la deuxième est postérieure non-arrondie et non-fermée (ɤ, ʌ, a). Dans les pieds de structure CVVV, les deux dernières voyelles sont toujours identiques, mais différentes de la première voyelle, qui est pratiquement dans tous les cas *i* ou *u*.

Il convient de souligner que le pied métrique est différent du morphème : il y a des morphèmes qui comportent plus d'un pied (comme *dlȁȁká* 'petit-déjeuner' ou *gbʌ̋ʌ̋lȍȍ* 'serpent rouge'), et il y a des pieds qui résultent de la fusion de plus d'un morphème et qu'on peut donc considérer comme comportant deux morphèmes (comme *gɛ̄ɛ̄n* 'avec le pied', historiquement **gɛ̏n+ ká*).

Selon les règles de la nouvelle orthographe, si les syllabes d'un pied lourd ou extra-lourd ont des tons identiques, la marque du ton n'est mise que sur la voyelle de la première syllabe : *glő̋o* 'trace' pour /glő̋ő/, *klȕu* 'louche' pour /klȕȕ/, *kpı̋ʌŋ* 'joue' pour /kpı̋ʌ̋ŋ̋/. L'absence de la marque tonale sur la deuxième voyelle ne veut pas dire que cette voyelle n'a pas de ton ; ce n'est qu'une convention pour rendre l'écriture moins lourde.

Dans les pieds extra-lourds dont les tons ne sont pas homogènes, le changement du ton est noté :

- si le pied se termine par un *ŋ* (qui est considéré comme une voyelle, voir 2.1.1), le deuxième ton est marqué sur cette lettre, ex. : *sı̋ʌŋ̏* 'emprunt', *tœ̋œŋ̏* 'homonyme' ;
- sinon, le deuxième ton est marqué sur la deuxième voyelle du pied, ex. : *pīɤ̏ɤ* 'douleur', *sūʌ̋ʌ* 'orgelet'.

3. Morphologie

3.1. Parties du discours

3.1.1. Critères de subdivision en parties de discours

Les parties de discours[8] sont des classes de mots (plus précisement, de lexèmes) qui se distinguent par des critères formels : morphologiques (le type de flexion ; l'aptitude à accepter des auxiliaires) et syntaxiques (les fonctions syntaxiques que le mot peut assumer). En établissant la liste des parties de discours, le critère sémantique (donc le sens du mot) n'est pris en compte que secondairement. Chaque langue a son propre inventaire des parties de discours.

3.1.2. L'inventaire des parties de discours

En dan de l'Est on obtient l'inventaire suivant des parties de discours :

Noms (substantifs). Ils peuvent assumer (sans aucune marque morphologique supplémentaire) les positions syntaxiques de sujet, de complément d'objet direct et de complément oblique lorsqu'ils sont suivis d'une postposition. Dans le cadre d'un groupe nominal, le nom peut occuper les positions de déterminant et de déterminé dans la construction génitive, et du déterminé dans une construction attributive.

Les noms locatifs se distinguent des noms « propres » par le fait qu'ils ont une catégorie morphologique de cas ; autrement dit, ils se déclinent. Ils peuvent donc, à la différence des noms, apparaître dans la fonction syntaxique de circonstant ou de complément d'objet indirect sans être suivis d'une postposition.

Les pronoms personnels sont proches des noms par leur comportement syntaxique ; ils assument les mêmes rôles syntaxiques, sauf celui de déterminé dans une construction du type génitival. Ils se distinguent radicalement du nom par un critère morphologique : les pronoms personnels ont un paradigme flexionnel très riche. Dans le cadre de ce paradigme, des valeurs grammaticales différentes sont opposées : le cas, les statuts pragmatiques…

Les marques prédicatives pronominales (MPP) sont des mots auxiliaires qui apparaissent après le sujet et expriment des valeurs grammaticales différentes : l'aspect, la négation, la mode, etc. Elles expriment conjointement la personne et le nombre du sujet de la phrase. Les marques prédicatives sont les têtes syntaxiques des propositions verbales. Certaines séries MPP peuvent apparaître également dans des propositions non-verbales où elles servent de copules.

---

[8] Dans la tradition linguistique française, le terme « catégories grammaticales » est souvent utilisé pour les « parties de discours ». Je ne l'utilise pas en ce sens à cause de son ambiguïté.

Les adjectifs se distinguent des autres parties du discours à la fois par leur morphologie (ils modifient leurs formes pour exprimer les valeurs de pluriel et d'intensif, d'ailleurs assez irrégulières) et leur syntaxe (les fonctions attributive, prédicative sans postposition et avec la postposition *ká*, voir section 3.6.1).

Les numéraux sont proches des adjectifs en ce qui concerne leurs fonctions syntaxiques. Leur différence principale est morphologique : d'une part, ils n'ont pas du pluriel flexionnel ni d'intensif (ce qui est compréhensible, compte tenu de leur sémantisme) ; d'autre part, ils produisent par une dérivation régulière des ordinaux (adjonction du suffixe *-dhȁan*). En plus, les numéraux se distinguent des adjectifs par leur aptitude de former des numéraux composés.

Les déterminants n'ont pas de flexion ; ils occupent la position après un groupe nominal. Si un groupe nominal comporte un adjectif ou un numéral, le déterminant ne peut jamais le précéder, il ne peut que le suivre. Les déterminants constituent une classe fermée.

Les verbes ont les caractéristiques suivantes : ils assument la fonction du prédicat à valeur d'action, d'événement ou d'état en combinaison avec les marques prédicatives pronominales (MPP) de toutes les séries qui existent dans la langue. À la différence des adjectifs, ils changent leurs tons lexicaux à extra-bas suivant l'MPP de la série existentielle.

Les copules. Une classe peu nombreuse. Ce sont des mots qui apparaissent en fonction de têtes des propositions non-verbales ; ils n'ont pas de flexion. À la différence des verbes, elles ne se combinent pas avec des MPP à l'affirmatif.

Les adverbes assument la fonction syntaxique du circonstant sans être suivis d'une postposition. À la différence des noms locatifs (dans leurs formes des cas obliques), l'adverbe ne peut pas avoir un déterminant nominal à sa gauche.

Les postpositions sont des marqueurs de la fonction syntaxique de complément oblique. À la différence des adverbes et des noms locatifs, ils ne peuvent pas remplir seuls ces fonctions, ils doivent forcément suivre un groupe nominal. Les postpositions peuvent également servir de marques de liaison syntaxique entre les noms.

Les particules phrastiques n'ont pas de flexion. Elles occupent la position à la fin d'une phrase et expriment des valeurs modales. Elles se distinguent des adverbes par leur comportement syntaxique lors de la nominalisation des verbes.

Les conjonctions marquent la liaison syntaxique entre les mots ou les phrases.

Les interjections sont des mots-phrases, donc des mots équivalents de phrases entières. Elles expriment les valeurs modales.

3.1.3. Conversion

Par conversion on comprend le passage d'un mot d'une partie du discours à une autre sans aucune modification de sa forme, c'est donc une « dérivation zéro ». Elle existe en dan de l'Est, mais elle est beaucoup moins fréquente que dans certaines autres langues mandé. On peut mentionner des relations conversionnelles suivantes :

1) verbe ↔ nom, la direction de la conversion n'est pas toujours claire : *gœ̄œ* 'donner cadeau' – 'cadeau', *glòo* 'se réposer' – 'répos', *gblɜ̋* 'crier' – 'cri', *sɯ̋ɤ* 'avoir peur' – 'peur', *wɛ̋* 'parler' – 'son', etc.;

2) verbe → adjectif : *blʌ̋* 's'user' → 'pourri', *sɛ̄ɛ̀* 'gâter, se gâter' → 'gâté', *tlɤ̄ɤ* 's'assombrir' – 'sale', etc. ;

3) nom → postposition : *dhɯ̋ɤ* 'bord, sommet' → 'devant', *gɔ̄̀* 'tête' → 'à', etc. ;

4) déterminant → nom : *bhá* 'autre' → 'beau-frère cadet' ;

5) adjectif → adverbe : *dèe* 'nouveau' → 'récemment', *gbéɛ̀* 'important, difficile' → 'très', etc. ;

6) adjectif ↔ nom, la direction de la conversion souvent n'est pas claire : *pɪ̋ʌʌnpɪ̀ʌʌn* 'mous et rares' (cheveux) → 'barbe de plume', *sæ̀æ* 'frais' (temps) → 'fraîcheur', *sʌ̋nŋ* 'or' → 'de l'or', etc.

Passons maintenant à une analyse plus détaillée des particularités de chaque partie de discours.

3.2. Noms

3.2.1. « Noms relationnels » et « noms libres »

Les noms en dan se subdivisent en deux classes : « noms relationnels » (une autre appellation pour « noms inaliénables ») et « noms libres » (également appelés : « noms autosémantiques », « nom aliénables »). La différence entre ces deux types s'exprime formellement comme suit : lorsqu'un nom libre apparaît comme le déterminé (possédé) dans une construction génitivale, une postposition connective *bhȁ* (souvent réduite à *ȁ*) doit être intercalée entre ce nom et le nom précédent (le déterminant) : *dhēbʌ̀dhʌ́n bhȁ wʌ̄ʌ̀gā* 'l'argent de la femme' contrairement à l'absence de connectif dans le cas d'un nom relationnel : *dhēbʌ̀dhʌ́n wʌ̄* 'le visage de la femme'.

Les noms relationnels forment deux groupes sémantiques :

a) noms des parties du corps (noms inaliénables proprement dits) ; il s'agit ici des relations « partie d'un ensemble » ;

b) termes de parenté et le vocabulaire limitrophe comme *yœ̄œ̀* 'ennemi', *tɛ́bhɜ̋n* 'camarade d'âge', les noms relationnels proprement dits : le sens d'un tel nom n'est valable que par rapport au nom déterminant. Ainsi, la personne désignée par la construction *Yɔ̄̀ dʌ̄* 'père de Yo' ou *Tɔ̀kpȁ yœ̄œ̀* 'ennemi de Tokpa' n'est père ou ennemi que par rapport à Yo ou Tokpa, à part ces relations la personne en question n'est ni « un père », ni « un ennemi ».

Il convient de dire qu'en dan, les limites de ces groupes sémantiques sont floues, dans le sens où il y a des noms qui, d'après leur valeur sémantique, devraient se trouver parmi les noms relationnels mais ne s'y trouvent pas. Ainsi, le mot *wūn* 'chevelure' ne se trouve pas dans le groupe des noms relationnels (on dit *ȁ bhȁ wūn* 'sa chevelure', et non pas **ȁ wūn*), tandis que *kāȁ* 'poil' (y compris le poil de corps humain) s'y trouve (*dhēbʌ̏ kāȁ* 'poil de corps d'une femme'). Les termes de parenté *bɛ́ɛ̏* 'neveu, nièce' (enfant de sœur) et *dhʌ́n* 'enfant' ne sont pas des noms relationnels, tandis que *dhūʌ̏ʌ* 'oncle maternel cadet' et *bhāŋ* 'enfant' le sont : *Gbȁtȍ dhūʌ̏ʌ* 'l'oncle de Gbato', mais *Sítȁ bhȁ dhʌ́n* 'l'enfant de Sita'.

Une autre précision importante est qu'en dan la différence de comportement entre noms relationnels et noms libres ne se manifeste que si le nom déterminant désigne une personne. Ainsi, nous avons :

bhɛ̄n gɛ̏n 'jambe d'un homme' vs. *bhɛ̄n bhȁ kɔ́* 'maison d'un homme';

bhȁan gɛ̏n 'patte d'un oiseau' vs. *bhȁan kɔ́* 'nid d'un oiseau'.

Cela nous permet de dire que les noms d'humains et de non-humains forment en dan deux groupes qui se distinguent formellement (bien que d'une façon indirecte).

3.2.2. Pluriel

3.2.2.1. La marque standard du pluriel est un déterminant *dhȕn* qui suit le nom (il s'écrit séparé du nom précédent avec un trait d'union). Si le nom est suivi d'un adjectif, *dhȕn* peut être placé après l'adjectif (ce qui est le cas de loin le plus fréquent) ou après le nom, et parfois il peut être répété deux fois en occupant les deux positions. Ainsi, nous avons trois constructions qui ont le même sens, 'enfants bêtes, abrutis' :[9]

dhʌ́n-dhȕn bhɔ̋ɔnbhɔ̏ɔn

dhʌ́n bhɔ̋ɔnbhɔ̏ɔn-dhȕn

dhʌ́n-dhȕn bhɔ̋ɔnbhɔ̏ɔn-dhȕn

Le pluriel peut également être exprimé par la flexion de l'adjectif (voir 3.6.2).

Le plus souvent, le déterminant *dhȕn* n'est pas utilisé si la pluralité est déjà exprimée par un autre moyen (un autre déterminant quantificateur ou un numéral). A part ça, l'utilisation de la marque du pluriel *dhȕn* dépend du sémantisme du nom déterminé : il est plus ou moins obligatoire avec les noms désignant des êtres humains ; il est plutôt facultatif pour les noms des gros animaux et rarement utilisé por les noms des petits animaux, insectes, objets inanimés.

Il y a des noms qui ont une valeur collective et ne prennent pas la marque *dhȕn,* ex. *zlūu* 'fourmis magnan' (**zlūu-dhȕn* ne se dit pas). Il faut cependant admettre que l'aptitude de se conjuguer avec la marque du pluriel est souvent lexicalisée ; ainsi, les

[9] Il y a des restrictions d'ordre lexical concernant la position du déterminant *dhȕn.*

noms des autres espèces des petits insectes l'acceptent : *zɛ̀* 'termite maçon' (à valeur plutôt collective) – *zɛ̀-dhʉ̀n* 'termites maçons'.

3.2.2.2. Il y a un groupe de noms, désignant soit les représentants masculins des professions soit les parents cadets ou du même âge, qui forment leur pluriel de manière plus compliquée. En plus du déterminant *dhʉ̀n,* ils prennent le suffixe *-zʌ̀*. Dans le cas des noms de représentants de profession qui portent le suffixe *–bhīn,* ce suffixe est remplacé par *–zʌ̀* :

yɛ̄ɛbhīn 'griot' – pl. *yɛ̄ɛzʌ̀-dhʉ̀n* (mais aussi *yɛ̄ɛgɔ̄n-dhʉ̀n*),

bɛ́ɛ̀ 'neveu' – pl. *bɛ́ɛ̀zʌ̀-dhʉ̀n.*

Cependant pour certains d'entre eux, le suffixe *-zʌ̀* est facultatif :

zőobhīn 'chasseur de sorciers' – pl. *zőozʌ̀-dhʉ̀n* ou *zőo-dhʉ̀n* ou *zőobhīn-dhʉ̀n ;*

gwʌ̄ʌ́bhīn 'factotum' – pl. *gwʌ̄ʌ́zʌ̀-dhʉ̀n* (cependant, la forme plurielle *gwʌ̄ʌ́bhīn-dhʉ̀n* existe aussi) ;

Quelques rares mots de ce type peuvent désigner les personnes des deux sexes :

tɛ́bhʌ̋n 'camarade d'âge' – pl. *tɛ́bhʌ̋n-dhʉ̀n, tɛ́bhʌ̋nzʌ̀-dhʉ̀n* 'camarades d'âge' (des deux sexes).

3.2.2.3. Le mot *dhēbʌ̀* 'femme' a, à côté d'une forme régulière *dhēbʌ̀-dhʉ̀n,* une forme irrégulière *dhōo-dhʉ̀n* (avec une variante facultative *dhōŋ-dhʉ̀n*). Celle-ci est moins usitée ; elle apparaît dans quelques expressions figées, et aussi dans des mots composés, comme un analogue féminin du suffixe pluralisant *-zʌ̀* susmentionné : *gwʌ̄ʌ́dhōo-dhʉ̀n* ou *gwʌ̄ʌ́dhōŋ-dhʉ̀n* (mais aussi *gwʌ̄ʌ́dhēbʌ̀-dhʉ̀n*) 'servantes' ; *bɛ́ɛ̀dhōo-dhʉ̀n* ou *'bɛ́ɛ̀dhōŋ-dhʉ̀n* 'nièces' (mais aussi *bɛ́ɛ̀dhēbʌ̀-dhʉ̀n*).

3.2.3. Dérivation des noms

Il existe plusieurs suffixes dérivatifs des noms en dan-gouèta.

1) *-dhʌ́n,* le suffixe diminutif, provient du nom *dhʌ́n* 'enfant' et peut suivre le nom comme l'adjectif : *dhʉ̋dhʌ́n gbʌ̂gbʌ̀* ou *dhʉ̋ gbʌ̂gbʌ̀dhʌ́n* 'petit arbre rabougri'. Avec certains noms désignant des êtres animés, le suffixe n'a plus de sens diminutif et sert plutôt de marque de singulatif, ou encore fait partie de la base nominale : *gɔ̄ndʌ̄dhʌ́n* 'homme mûr', *dhēbʌ̀dhʌ́n* 'femme', *bhʌ̏andhʌ́n* 'oiseau', *gwʌ̋ndhʌ́n* 'chat', *sʌ̄ndhʌ́n* 'lapin'.

2) *–bhīn,* suffixe d'agent masculin ou de membre masculin d'un groupe ethnique ou professionnel, cf. 3.2.2.2.

3) *–dʌ̄,* suffixe désignant le propriétaire, maître (masculin) : *yídhʌ̋n* 'génie' → *yídhʌ̋ndʌ̄* 'magicien', *pɤ̂* 'village' → *pɤ̂dʌ̄* 'notable', etc.

4) *–dhē* un suffixe d'agent féminin, il est lié étymologiquement au nom *dhē* 'femme ; mère'. Il est homologue des aux deux suffixes « masculins » susmentionnés : *yídhʌ̋ndhē* 'magicienne', *gwʌ̄ʌ́dhē* 'servante'.

5) *–dhē,* suffixe du nom de résultat d'action : *sʌ̄ʌbhōdhē* 'fatigue'.

6) *–bʌ̀* (dans certains dialectes, *-bɔ̀*), suffixe peu productif à valeur obscure, dérive des noms désignant des gens ou des objets personnalisés : *dhē* 'femme' → *dhēbʌ̀* 'femme', *gèe* 'cadavre ; masque' → *gèebhʌ̀* 'fétiche' ; *bhlàa̋nbʌ̀* 'amant', *dhɔ̋nbʌ̀* 'amante' (les deux derniers mots n'ont pas des noms correspondants sans le suffixe).

7) *–dhɛ̀* suffixe à valeur abstraite, dérive des noms à partir d'autres noms et à partir d'adjectifs (s'écrit avec un trait d'union) : *sànbhű̋nzʌ̀* 'partenaires du cousinage de plaisanterie' → *sànbhű̋nzʌ̀-dhɛ̀* 'cousinage de plaisanterie' ; *dhùʌŋ* 'esclave' → *dhùʌŋ-dhɛ̀* 'esclavage' ; *gblɛ̀ɛn* 'longue' → *gblɛ̀ɛn-dhɛ̀* 'longueur', etc. Il s'agit probablement du même suffixe que celui du masdar (cf. 3.8.2.3.).

3.2.4. Composition nominale.

C'est un procédé très productif pour la formation des mots. Le modèle le plus courant est la construction génitive : *táàgbɔ̄* 'pipe' (pot de tabac), *sɯ́ɤ̄tɛ̄ɛ* 'fumée' (vent du feu), etc. Il est souvent difficile de définir la limite entre un nom composé (une séquence qu'on écrit en un seul mot) et un syntagme (écrit en deux mots) : *gɛ̏ndhɛ̋* ou *gɛ̏n dhɛ̋* (jambe + feuille) 'pied' ? *ya̋n kɔ́* ou *ya̋nkɔ́* 'orbite' (œil + maison) ?[10]

On peut considérer comme une variante du même modèle la construction basée sur une phrase relative « de gauche » (cf. la division 20.2, p. 81-82) comportant un nom verbal : *dhű̋súgɔ̀* 'grumier' (« voiture qui prend l'arbre »), *tɯ̋nbhōbhɛ̏n* 'chanteur' (« personne qui fait cueillir chanson »), etc.

Le troisième modèle assez fréquent est la construction attributive (nom + adjectif), comme *glɛ̋ɛnpű̋u* 'liane Canthium venosum' (« épine blanche »).

3.3. Noms locatifs[11]

On peut dire, en simplifiant dans une certaine mesure, que les noms locatifs résultent de la fusion de noms avec des postpositions. De telles fusions sont attestées dans beaucoup de langues mandé, mais il semblerait qu'en dan de l'Est le processus soit beaucoup plus avancé qu'ailleurs, au point d'engendrer un système de déclinaison.[12]

---

[10] J'ai choisi l'écriture collée pour le premier cas (*gɛ̏ndhɛ̋*) et l'écriture séparée dans le deuxième cas (*ya̋n kɔ́*). Malheureusement, faute de critères formels, ces décisions relèvent de l'arbitraire. Ce sujet demande des réflexions supplémentaires.

[11] Pour davantage de détail, voir (Vydrin 2011).

[12] La déclinaison est un ensemble des formes morphologiques du nom (ou du pronom) qui distinguent des fonctions syntaxiques différentes. Chacune des formes en question représente un cas.

Les noms locatifs ont donc normalement plus d'une forme morphologique. L'une de ces formes, celle utilisée en position de sujet, de complément d'objet direct et en position non-finale dans les groupes nominaux, est considérée comme représentant le « cas commun » ; les autres (provenant de la fusion avec les postpositions) sont des formes de « cas obliques ».

À la différence des déclinaisons bien grammaticalisées (comme en latin, grec ancien ou polonais), la déclinaison en dan de l'Est, qui n'est encore qu'en formation, est fort irrégulière. On peut établir six cas morphologiques dans cette langue, avec une réserve importante : il n'y a aucun nom locatif qui aurait les six cas, le plus souvent il n'y en a que deux ou trois, avec un maximum de quatre cas pour un même lexème.

3.3.1. L'inventaire des cas

Les cas commun et locatif sont le plus souvent (mais pas toujours !) formé avec les suffixes *–dhɛ̏* (le cas commun) et *-dhɤ̄* (le cas locatif). Ces suffixes s'adjoignent à une base qui résulte souvent de la fusion de la racine avec une postposition.

Les cas obliques (autres que le cas locatif) proviennent de la fusion avec les postpositions *bhà, tà, gṹ, ká* (certaines formes peuvent être décomposées par les locuteurs en un nom et une postposition ; ces formes décomposées sont le plus souvent considérées comme des « formes du langage enfantin »). Chaque cas est nommé selon le sémantisme de la postposition en question.

Voici l'inventaire des cas en dan-gouèta.

1) Le cas « commun » (CMM). Dans la majorité de cas, cette forme est dérivée du nom correspondant avec le suffixe *–dhɛ* ; très souvent, cette dérivation s'accompagne d'une modification de la base :

sɛ̋n 'flanc, côte' – *sɛ̋nŋ̏dhɛ̏,*
bhɔ̄ 'cou' – *bhɛ̄ɛ̋dhɛ̏,*
kɔ́ 'maison' – *kɔ́ɔdhɛ̏* (mais aussi *kɔ́gṹdhɛ̏*).

Les formes facultatives des noms locatifs comme *kɔ́gṹdhɛ̏* 'maison' nous indiquent que la modification de la base résulte de la fusion avec une postposition qui a été intercalée entre la base et le suffixe *-dhɛ̏.*

Il existe toutefois un certain nombre de formes sans suffixe *-dhɛ̏* mais qui peuvent cependant être interprétées comme des formes du cas commun : *tő* 'oreille', *sɛ̋* 'terre', *yɤ̋n* 'œil', etc.

2) Le cas « locatif » (LOC). Il y a deux modèles de formation de ce cas :

a) A partir de la forme du cas commun, on substitue le suffixe *-dhɤ̄* au suffixe *-dhɛ̏,* ce qui s'accompagne parfois d'une modification tonale de la base : 'paillote' CMM *gɔ̄nŋ̏dhɛ̏* — LOC *gɔ̄nŋdhɤ̄* ; 'pied/jambe' CMM *gɛ̄nŋ̏dhɛ̏* — LOC *gɛ̄nŋdhɤ̄.* Le suffixe

–dhɤ̄ ne correspond à aucune postposition du dan-gouèta,[13] mais il revêt la même forme que le suffixe des adverbes. Bien évidemment, il s'agit historiquement des deux fonctions du même suffixe.

b) Plus rarement, la forme du cas locatif n'a pas de suffixe *–dhɤ̄* ; elle se dérive par l'élimination du suffixe du cas commun ou/et par une modification de base : 'champ' CMM *bhláàdhɛ̏* — LOC *bhláā*.

3) Le cas « superessif » (SUP) vient de la fusion avec la postposition superessive *bhà* 'sur' : CMM *kó* — SUP *kwʌ́ʌ̀* 'l'un sur l'autre', CMM *kɔ́* — SUP *kœ́œ̀* 'sur (le mur de) la maison', CMM *gɛ̄nŋ̄dhɛ̏* — SUP *gɛ̀ɛn* 'aux pieds, sur les pieds', CMM *kɔ̏* — SUP *kwɛ̀ŋ̄* 'sur les mains'.

4) Le cas « adessif » (AD) vient de la fusion avec la postposition superessive *tà* 'sur, au-dessus de' : CMM *kɔ̏* — AD *kɔ̀ɔ* 'sur les mains', CMM *zīaan* — AD *zīàan* 'sur la route'.

5) Le cas « comitatif » (COM) vient de la fusion avec la postposition comitative et instrumentale *ká* 'avec; par' : CMM *yɑ̋n* — AD *yɑ́an* 'devant les yeux', CMM *sɔ̋n* — AD *sɔ̋ɔn* 'avec les dents', CMM *kó* — COM *kwʌ́ʌ* 'l'un avec l'autre, ensemble'.

6) Le cas « inessif » (IN) vient de la fusion avec la postposition inessive *gṹ* 'dans' : CMM *yɑ̋n* — IN *yʌ́nŋ̀* 'dans l'œil', CMM *kó* — IN *kőo* 'l'un dans l'autre', probablement CMM *sɨ́ɤ* — IN *sɨ́ɤɤ* 'dans le feu'.

Parmi les cas obliques, c'est le locatif qui est le plus fréquent, tous les autres étant nettement plus rares. À cause de la rareté relative des cas superessif, adessif, comitatif et inessif, il est difficile de formuler les règles strictes de leur formation, on ne peut parler ici que de tendances.

3.3.2. La composition de la classe des noms locatifs

Le nombre des noms locatifs est limité. Le dictionnaire, à l'état actuel, en contient presque 60. Ce sont, quasiment sans exception, des noms de parties du corps, de parties de la maison, ou des noms de lieux et d'emplacements. Il faut souligner que la fusion d'un nom à valeur locative avec une postposition (même s'il s'agit des postpositions *bhà, tà, gṹ, ká*) n'est pas du tout automatique, elle ne se produit que dans des contextes les plus typiques. Un exemple très révélateur est la combinaison du nom locatif *sɔ̋n* 'dent, dents' avec la postposition comitative *ká*: la fusion ne se produit que dans l'expression *kṹn sɔ̋ɔn* 'mordre' (lit. : « attraper avec les dents »). Dans tous les autres contextes, la fusion n'a pas lieu, cf. (1).

---

[13] Cependant, dans le kla-dan, une autre langue du groupe dan, il y a une postposition locative *lɤ̀* (Makeeva 2017: 653) qui se rapproche par son sense au suffixe *–dhɤ̄* en dan-gouèta. Ce fait sert d'argument de l'origine postpositionnelle du suffixe *–dhɤ̄*.

(1) *Yà* *wlɯ̋ɯ̋* *sɯ́ɯ́* *ɤ̄* *sɔ̋n* *ká.*
3SG.PRF mortier prendre REFL dent avec
'Il a soulevé le mortier avec ses dents.'

3.3.3. Les noms locatifs relationnels et libres

Tout comme les noms « proprement dit », les noms locatifs se subdivisent en « relationnels » et « libres ». La seule chose remarquable, dans cette relation, est l'accord de cas de la marque possessive. Un nom locatif en cas commun est connecté avec son possesseur par la postposition *bhȁ.* Toutefois, lorsqu'il est employé dans un des cas obliques, c'est la postposition *gɔ̏* qui apparaît au lieu de *bhȁ* :

(2) *Bhán* *dhó* *n̄* *gɔ̏* *bhláā.*
1SG.PRF aller 1SG.NSBJ POSS.OBL champ.LOC
'Je suis allé dans mon champ', 'Je suis sur le point de partir à mon champ.'

(3) *Yà* *séŋ̏* *zīɤ* *Yɔ̏* *gɔ̏* *kɔ́ɔ̄.*
3SG.PRF charbon passer Yo POSS.OBL maison.SUP
'Il a laissé des traces de charbon sur le mur de la maison de Yo.'

3.3.4. Pluriel des noms locatifs

D'une façon générale en dan-gouèta, le pluriel des noms locatifs en cas obliques est plutôt rare, certaines formes n'en ayant pas du tout, par exemple le comitatif *gɛ̄ɛn* 'avec le pied/avec les pieds'.

Cependant, la formation du pluriel de certains noms locatifs en cas obliques est possible. Pour le cas locatif, la marque du cas commun *-dhɛ̏* se rajoute par-dessus le suffixe du cas locatif *–dhɤ̄,* et l'auxiliaire du pluriel *–dhɯ̏n* suit celui-là. Cette forme perd la faculté de remplir la fonction du complément d'objet indirect ou du circonstant sans postposition, elle est nécessairement suivie de la postposition *gɯ́ɯ́* :

(4) *Wɔ̏* *dɔ̄-sɪʌ* *blɛ̋edhɤ̄.*
3SG.EXI arrêter-DUR bord.de.champ.LOC
'Ils sont arrêtés au bord du champ.' →

(5) *Wɔ̏* *dɔ̄-sɪʌ* *blɛ̋edhɤ̄-dhɛ̏-dhɯ̏n* *gɯ́ɯ́.*
3SG.EXI arrêter-DUR bord.de.champ.LOC-CMM-PL dans
'Ils se sont arrêtés aux bords des champs.'

On trouve parfois des formes avec l'une ou l'autre marque de cas omise, qui sont en variation libre avec les formes « complètes » : *blɛ̋edhɛ̏-dhɯ̏n gɯ́ɯ́* ou *blɛ̋edhɤ̄dhɛ̏-dhɯ̏n gɯ́ɯ́* 'aux bords des champs', *bhláȁdhɛ̏-dhɯ̏n gɯ́ɯ́* ou *bhláȁ-dhɯ̏n gɯ́ɯ́* 'aux champs'.

Le pluriel des autres cas obliques, là où il est possible, suit à peu près le même modèle, avec la « restauration » de la postposition : *zīȁan* 'sur la route' AD — *zīaantȁdhɛ̏-dhȕn gú* 'sur les routes'.

3.4. Marques prédicatives pronominales (MPP)

Les marques prédicatives pronominales (MPP) sont des mots auxiliaires qui occupent la position après le sujet (quand il est exprimé) et devant le verbe (dans une construction intransitive) ou devant le complément d'objet directe (dans une construction transitive). Les MPP forment des « séries », chaque série exprimant des valeurs grammaticales comme l'aspect, le mode, la négation, voir Tableau 4. Elles apparaissent également dans certains types d'énoncés non-verbaux où elles fonctionnent en tant que copules.

La présence des MPP dans un énoncé verbal est obligatoire en dan-gouèta, même si le sujet est déjà exprimé par un groupe nominal. Précisons tout de même que les pronoms de la 3ème pers. du singulier (et même du pluriel) des séries existentielle, conjointe et subjonctive peuvent être omis, mais il s'agit ici bien d'une omission, c.-à-d. qu'ils peuvent toujours être rétablis (ils laissent souvent des traces tonales).

Les marques prédicatives du dan-gouèta distinguent quatre personnes au singulier (1e, 2e, 3e et logophorique), une personne au duel (1e inclusif, « moi et toi ») et cinq personnes au pluriel (1e inclusive, « moi et vous », « nous et vous », « nous et toi » ; 1e exclusive, « nous sans toi » ; 2e, 3e et logophorique). Les MPP plurielles de la 3ème personne sont également employées avec une valeur impersonnelle (à peu près comme le pronom français *on*).

L'MPP logophorique apparaît dans la position du sujet d'une proposition subordonnée et se réfère au sujet du verbe *pɤ̄* 'dire' (ou d'un autre verbe de parole ou d'activité mentale) de la proposition principale : *Yȁ' pɤ̄ ɤ̄ kʌ̄ dhȍ.* 'Il a dit qu'il (lui-même) était parti' (*ɤ̄* est une MPP logophorique) vs. *Yȁ' pɤ̄ yɤ̏ kʌ̄ dhȍ.* 'Il a dit qu'il (personne autre que celle qui parle) était parti.'

Considérons les séries une par une.

I. Série existentielle

Les MPP de cette série proviennent sans doute de la fusion d'une série de base avec une copule d'existence.[14] Les contextes principaux où les MPP de la série existentielle apparaissent sont :

[14] Il s'agit ici d'une reconstruction historique, parce que ni la série de base en question ni la copule n'existent plus en dan.

Tableau 4. Marques prédicatives pronominales

Séries	Singulier				Duel	Pluriel				
	1 pers.	**2 pers.**	**3 pers.**	**Logoph.**	**Incl.**	**1 incl.**	**1 excl.**	**2 pers.**	**3 pers.**	**Logoph.**
Existentiel	*ā*	*ū ~ ī*	*yɤ̏~∅*	*ɤ̄*	*kō*	*kwā*	*yī*	*kā*	*wȍ*	*wō*
Conjoint	*á*	*ú ~ í*	*ɤ́~yɤ́~∅*	*ɤ́*	*kó*	*kwá*	*yí*	*ká*	*wó*	*wó*
Parfait	*bhán*	*bhá*	*yȁ ~ yà*	*yá*	*kó*	*kwá*	*yá*	*ká*	*wȁ ~ wà*	*wá*
Prospectif	*bhāan*	*bhīi (yīi)*	*yɤ̄ɤ*	–	*kōo*	*kwāa*	*yīi*	*kāa*	*wōo*	–
Impératf	–	*∅ ~ bhɤ̏*	–	–	*kȍ*	*kwȁ*	–	*kȁ*	–	–
Subjonctif	*á*	*ú ~ í*	*yɤ̏*	*ɤ̋*	*kó*	*kwá*	*yí*	*ká*	*wȍ*	*wő*
Présomptif	*bhāȁn*	*bhāȁ*	*yāȁ*	–	*kōȍ*	*kwāȁ*	*yāȁ*	*kāȁ*	*wāȁ*	–
Négatif imperfectif	*bháan*	*bháa*	*yáa ~ áá*	–	*kóo*	*kwáa*	*yáa*	*káa*	*wáa*	–
Négatif gnomique			*áan*							
Négatif perfectif	*bhíin*	*bhíi*	*yíi*	–	*kóo*	*kwíi*	*yíi*	*kíi*	*wíi*	–
Négatif subjonctif	*bhán*	*bhá*	*yá*	–	*kó*	*kwá*	*yá*	*ká*	*wá*	–
Conséquence négative	*bhín*	*bhí*	*yí*	–	*kwí*		*yí*	*kí*	*wí*	–

— un énoncé non-verbal affirmatif à valeur locative, dans un sens large (*Gbȁtȍ yɤ̏ sȍȍ wlɤ̏ɤ.* 'Gbato est sous le cheval'), équative (*Dūū wɔ̏n ɤ́ bhā yɤ̏ tæ̏æ̏n ká.* 'L'affaire de la sorcellerie, c'est la vérité') ou qualitative (*Gbȁtȍ yɤ̏ dhɛ̏ɛnsȕȕ.* 'Gbato est sévère') ;

— la construction verbale à valeur durative (l'action ou l'état qui est en train de se produire) ; le verbe adjoint le suffixe *–sīʌ* : *Bhɛ̄n bhā yɤ̏ zɔ̀ɔ-sīʌ.* 'Cette personne est en train de bégayer' ;

— la construction verbale de l'aspect neutre (voir plus en détail dans la division consacrée au verbe) ; le ton lexical du verbe est ramplacé par le ton extra-bas : *Gbȁtȍ yɤ̏ kɔ́ dɔ̏.* 'Gbato bâtit les maisons' (Gbato est un constructeur de maisons).

Les MPP de la 3ème pers. fusionnent le plus souvent avec les pronoms non-subjectifs : *yɤ̏ + ȁ → yȁ, yɤ̏ + ȁ-dhȕn → yȁa-dhȕ, wȍ + ȁ → wȁ, wȍ + ȁ–dhȕn → wȁa–dhȕn.*

II. Série conjointe

Ces MPP remplissent plus ou moins les mêmes fonctions que les MPP existentielles (elles apparaissent dans les énoncés non-verbaux, la construction verbale à valeur durative, la construction verbale « conjointe »), mais elles signalent, de plus, une liaison de la situation ainsi désignée avec le contexte précédent ou suivant. Les MPP conjointes apparaissent dans la proposition relative, dans une proposition où un groupe nominal est focalisé et mis en position initiale, dans un contexte narratif pour marquer des actions consécutives ; dans quelques types de propositions subordonnées (surtout introduites par la conjonction *yɤ̂*).

Le verbe dans la constuction « conjointe » change son ton lexical selon une formule présentée dans la section « verbe ».

III. Série du parfait

Les MPP de la série du parfait se conjuguent avec les verbes qui apparaissent dans leurs formes de base. Les variantes tonales de la marque de la 3ème pers. (à ton bas et à ton extra-bas) semblent être véritablement facultatives et interchangeables.[15]

La MPP de la 3ème personne du sg. du parfait fusionne avec le déterminant *gbàn* 'tout, entier' : *gbàn + yȁ → gbàan.* Dans l'orthographe, la séquence de cette MPP avec le pronom de la 3ème personne du sg. non-subjectif s'écrit comme *yȁa* (au lieu de *yȁ ȁ*), même s'il n'y a pas de raison de considérer cette forme comme véritablement fusionnée.

IV. La série prospective

Cette série sert à la formation de la construction prospective (« action qui va s'accomplir dans la perspective la plus proche, et les conditions de son

[15] Il semblerait que certains locuteurs préfèrent la forme *yà,* d'autres préfèrent *yȁ.* Il est probable aussi que les préférence peuvent varier entre les locuteurs des dialectes différents.

accomplissement sont réunies ») ; ces MPP se conjuguent avec le verbe dans sa forme lexicale. La MPP prospective de la 3ème pers. du sg. *yɤ̄ɤ* fusionne facultativement avec la conjonction *kɤ́* 'même si' : *kɤ́ + yɤ̄ɤ → kɤ́ɤ.*

V. La série impérative

Cette série est incomplète, ce qui s'explique par son sémantisme : seuls les MPP impliquant la 2ème personne y sont présentes. À la 2ème pers. sg., la MPP peut être absente, mais on peut aussi utiliser une MPP spéciale : *Dhūn !* ou *Bhɤ̏ dhūn !* 'Viens!' (la construction avec la MPP *bhɤ̏* est considérée comme légèrement plus polie). Le verbe ne change pas son ton dans la construction impérative.

VI. La série subjonctive se conjugue avec la formes de base des verbes. Les formes des MPP subjonctives de la 3ème pers. sont les mêmes que celles des existentielles, et sont pour les autres personnes les mêmes que celles des conjointes ; cependant, les contextes de leurs emplois sont nettement différents de celui des deux séries en question.

Les MPP subjonctives du singulier fusionnent avec la conjonction *kɤ̄* (à valeurs différentes) : *kɤ̄ + á → káa, kɤ̄ + ɯ̋ → kíi* ou *kɯ́ɯ, kɤ̄ + ɤ́ → kɤ́ɤ.*

VII. La série présomptive

Les formes de cette série des MPP coïncident en partie avec les pronoms des séries coordinatives simple et liée, mais le contexte d'emploi les distingue indubitablement. Ces MPP forment la construction présomptive avec l'opérateur *dhùn* et l'infinitif du verbe notionnel (marqué par un préfixe tonal extra-bas).

VIII. La série négative imperfective

Cette série provient historiquement de la fusion avec une copule existentielle négative **wá* 'ne pas être', 'ne pas exister'.[16] Elle apparaît dans tous les types des énoncés négatifs non-verbaux et verbaux ; le verbe garde son ton lexical.

IX. La série négative perfective

Cette série est d'emploi beaucoup plus restreint que la série précédente ; elle se limite aux constructions verbales à valeur du passé, où le verbe maintient sa forme lexicale.

X. La série gnomique négative

Cette série est représentée par une seule forme, celle de la 3e personne du singulier. Cette MPP apparaît dans les constructions négatives à valeur universelle, ex. : *Bhʌ̄nŋ́ áan bɔ̏ bhɤ̏.* 'Les Dioulas ne mangent pas le porc'.

XI. La série subjonctive négative

Ces MPP se conjuguent avec le verbe auxiliaire *dhó* et l'infinitif du verbe notionnel ; cette construction exprime une interdiction : *Wá dhó bȉaŋ sɯ́!* 'Qu'ils ne courent pas'.

[16] Cette copule est maintenue dans les langues apparentées, comme le mano.

XI. La série de la conséquence négative

Apparaît dans les constructions de la conséquence négative, ex. : *Bhíi yī zʌ̄, bhí dhɤ́ ū tɛ̋ɛ pā'.* ‘Si tu ne dors pas, tu ne te réposeras pas’.

3.5. Pronoms personnels

Les pronoms personnels ont les mêmes personnes que les marques prédicatives pronominales, seulement, aux MPP logophoriques correspondent des pronoms réfléchis qui font référence à un participant de la situation qui est déjà mentionné dans la phrase, le plus souvent au sujet. Ex. : *Yȁ dhūn ɤ̄ pɪ̋ɤ.* ‘Il$_i$ est venu chez lui$_i$’ (*ɤ̄* est un pronom réfléchi, donc la personne vient dans sa propre maison) vs. *Yȁ dhūn ȁ pɪ̋ɤ.* ‘Il$_i$ est venu chez lui$_j$’ (*ȁ* est un pronom 3 pers. sg., donc la personne vient chez une tierce personne).

Les pronoms personnels expriment la personne et le nombre, mais en plus, ils servent à rendre d'autres valeurs grammaticales, comme la fonction syntaxique ou pragmatique. Selon ces caractéristiques, ils s'organisent en dix séries, cf. Tableau 5.

I. Série non-subjective

Ces pronoms apparaissent dans toutes les positions syntaxiques sauf celle du sujet.

Le pronom pluriel de 3ème pers. est dérivé de la marque régulière du pluriel du pronom singulier ; c’est l’unique cas dans tout le système pronominal. Le pronom *ȁ* a une forte tendance à s’élider en laissant une trace tonale, un suffixe tonal extra-bas. Si le ton final du mot précédent est déjà extra-bas (ce qui est souvent le cas), cela ne laisse aucune trace (pourtant, une convention orthographique demande d'y mettre un apostrophe). Ex. :

(6)	*Yȁ*	*kʌ̄*	*dhɤ̋,*	*wȍ*	*wȅ'*	*bhȁ.*
	3SG.PRF	faire	ainsi	3SG.EXI	parler-3SG.NSBJ	sur

‘Quand cela sera fait ainsi, ils l’accepteront.’

L’élision de ce pronom ne se produit pas en position initiale d’un énoncé, ex. :

(7)	*Ȁ*	*kplàagā*	*yɤ̏*	*gbɛ̋ȅ.*
	3SG.NSBJ	jambe	3SG.EXI	difficile

‘Ses jambes sont fortes’.

II. Série possessive

Cette série est dérivée de la série non-subjective par la fusion avec la marque possessive *bhȁ.* En fait, la fusion concerne les formes du pluriel, tandis que les pronoms singuliers restent non-liés (le pronom de 3ème pers. du pl. présente un cas intermédiaire : c’est la marque du pluriel *–dhȕn* qui fusionne avec la marque possessive). Il faut noter que la marque possessive qui se conjugue avec les noms locatifs en cas obliques, *gɔ̏,* ne fusionne pas avec les pronoms personnels.

Tableau 5. Pronoms personnels du dan-gouèta

	Singulier				Duel	Pluriel				
	1 pers.	**2 pers.**	**3 pers.**	**Refl.**	**Incl.**	**1 incl**	**1 excl.**	**2 pers.**	**3 pers**	**Refl.**
Non-sujet	*ŋ̄*	*ū ~ ī*	*ȁ*	*ɤ̄*	*kō*	*kwā*	*yī*	*kā*	*ȁ-dhȕn*	*wō*
Possessifs	*bhān*	*ū bhā*	*ȁ bhȁ*	*ɤ̄ bhā*	*kōȍ*	*kwāȁ*	*yīȉ, yāȁ*	*kāȁ*	*ȁ-dhȁan*	*wōȍ*
Possessifs honorifique						*kwēe̋*		*kēe̋*		
Autonome	*bhān*	*bhī*	*yɤ̄*	–	*kō*	*kwā*	*yī*	*kā*	*wō*	–
Restrictif	*bhānŋ ~ bhāan*	*bhīi*	*yɤ̄ɤ*	–	*kōo*	*kwāa*	*yīi*	*kāa*	*wōo*	–
Sélectif	*bhán*	*bhí*	*yɤ́*		*kó*	*kwá*	*yí*	*ká*	*wó*	
Négatif focalisé	*bhāáan*	*bhīáa*	*yɤ̄áa*		*kōáa*	*kwāáa*	*yīyáa*	*kāáa*	*wōáa*	
Coordinatif simple	*yāa ~ yāȁ*	*kāa ~ kāȁ*	*wāa ~ wāȁ*	–	–	*kwāa ~ kwāȁ (... dhȕn)*	*yāa ~ yāȁ ... dhȕn*	*kāa ~ kāȁ ... dhȕn*	*wāa ~ wāȁ ... dhȕn*	–
Coordinatif lié	*yāȁ*	*kāȁ*	*wāȁ*	–	–	*kwāȁ (...dhȕn)*	*yāȁ ... dhȕn*	*kāȁ ... dhȕn*	*wāȁ ... nȕ*	–
Coordinatif portemanteau	*yɛ̄ŋ ~ yɛ̄ŋ̏*	*kɛ̄ŋ ~ kɛ̄ŋ̏*	*wɛ̄ŋ ~ wɛ̄ŋ̏*	–	*kwɛ̄ŋ ~ kwɛ̄ŋ̏*	*kwɛ̄ŋ ~ kwɛ̄ŋ̏ ... dhȕn*	*yɛ̄ŋ̏ dhȕn*	*kɛ̄ŋ ~ kɛ̄ŋ̏ dhȕn*	*wɛ̄ŋ ~ wɛ̄ŋ̏ dhȕn*	–

Comme la fusion de la série possessive est incomplète, on peut la considérer comme marginale.

III. Série possessive honorifique

Cette série est défectueuse, elle ne comprte que deux pronoms : *kwēē̋* 'notre' (inclusif, sans distinction entre le duel et le pluriel) et *kēē̋* 'votre'. On utilise ces pronoms pour exprimer son respect envers l'interlocuteur ou son attitude positive envers l'objet discuté, ex: *kwēē̋ dhʌ́n-dhǜn* 'nos enfants' (dans la situation où on veut dire du bien des enfants).

L'utilisation des pronoms possessifs honorifiques est typique des discours publiques.

IV. Série autonome

Ces pronoms sont utilisés dans les contextes de focalisation (préposé à la marque de focalisation *dhʌ̀n*), de topicalisation (préposé à la marque *zʌ̀*), comme sujet de l'énoncé non-verbal présentatif avec la copule *bhǜn,* en combinaison avec la conjonction distributive *...dhɤ́ ... dhɤ́* 'et ... et', ex. : *Bhī bháa bhǜn.* 'Ce n'est pas toi'.

V. Série restrictive

Ces pronoms apparaissent devant les déterminants *dèbɤ́ɤ* 'soi-même', *dō* 'seul', *dōsēŋ* 'seul' et devant le déterminant interrogatif *dē* 'qui?'

VI. Série sélective

Les pronoms sélectifs apparaissent toujours avec le suffixe sélectif *–sɯ̀* et sont suivis de la particule de topicalisation *zʌ̀,* ex. :

(8)	*Bhán-sɯ̀*	*zʌ̀,*	*ā*	*dhɔ̀*	*kɔ́*	*dɔ̄'.*
	1SG.SLA-SEL	en.tout.cas	2SG.EXI	aller\NEUT	maison	bâtir\INF

'Moi, je bâtirai une maison !'

VII. Série négative focalisée

Cette série provient de la fusion des pronoms autonomes avec l'opérateur négatif *áa.*

(9)	*Yīáa*	*dhʌ̀n*	*yí*	*wʌ́ʌ̀gā*	*bhā*	*kwàan.*
	1EXCL.NEG	FOC	1EXCL.JNT	argent	ART	voler\JNT

'Ce n'est pas nous qui a volé l'argent'.

Séries pronominales coordinatives

Le plus souvent, la coordination en dan de l'Est est exprimée par les pronoms personnels des séries coordinatives. [17] On peut dire que dans ces pronoms, la conjonction est amalgamée avec le pronom (ou les pronoms) désignant un ou plusieurs participants du syntagme coordinatif.

Selon le nombre des participants amalgamés, trois séries se distinguent. Les formes de toutes ces séries sont dérivées des pronoms pluriels, ce qui a une certaine logique : un syntagme coordinatif désigne toujours un groupe d'objets ou des personnes, plutôt qu'un seul objet ou une seule personne. Mais cette technique crée des problèmes quant à la distinction du nombre de participants.

Évidemment, un syntagme coordinatif prototypique décrit une situation avec deux participants X et Y. Chacun de ces participants peut être au singulier et au pluriel. Le fait que le dan de l'Est suit une stratégie incorporative, et fait le choix de bases pronominales plurielles comme point de départ, limite considérablement les possibilités de distinguer entre les différents cas. On utilise la marque du pluriel *–dhȕn* comme un procédé supplémentaire, mais cela ne résoud pas tous les problèmes.

VIII. La série coordinative simple

Chaque pronom de cette série a deux variantes : un ton moyen sur les deux syllabes ou un ton moyen-extra-bas. Ces pronoms peuvent se combiner avec la conjonction coordinative *bhān* (voir 3.11), ce qui apparemment n'a pas d'incidence sur leur sémantisme et leur fonctionnement. Un pronom de cette série désigne le premier participant du syntagme coordinatif (X), le deuxième participant (Y) étant exprimé par un nom :

(10)	*Yāa*	*Gbȁtȍ*	*yá*	*dhūn.*
	1SG.et	Gbato	1PL.EXCL.JNT	venir\JNT

'Moi et Gbato, nous sommes venus.'

Là où on doit indiquer le pluriel de X, on met la marque *dhȕn* après le nom désignant le Y :

(11)	*Kāȁ*	*dhēbʌ̏-dhȕn*	*ká*	*dhūn.*
	2SG.et	femme-PL	2PL.PRF	venir

Cependant, cette phrase est ambiguë :

1) 'Vous et les femmes, vous êtes venus' (la marque du pluriel porte sur chacun des deux participants), ou

2) 'Toi et les femmes, vous êtes venus' (la marque du pluriel porte sur le deuxième participant seulement).

---

[17] Voir 3.11 pour les deux autres façons d'exprimer la coordination : la conjonction *bhān* ~ *bhàn* et la conjonction disjointe *dhɤ́ ... dhɤ́*.

Mais on peut distinguer entre les deux situations par le biais d'une construction avec une conjonction distributive :

(12) *Bhī* *dhɤ́,* *dhēbʌ̏-dhȕn* *dhɤ́,* *ká* *dhūn.*
2SG.AUT être femme-PL être 2PL.PRF venir
'Et toi, et les femmes, vous êtes venus.'

Le pronom inclusif *kwāa/kwāȁ* présente un cas particulier. En l'absence de la marque *–dhȕn* après le participant Y, son sens est ambiguë : la phrase *Kwāȁ Gbȁtȍ kwá dhūn* peut désigner 'Nous deux (toi et moi) et Gbato, nous sommes venus' ou 'Nous (nous et vous, nous et toi, ou moi et vous) et Gbato, nous sommes venus.' Autrement dit, l'opposition entre le duel et le pluriel est neutralisée dans la série coordinative simple. Avec la marque du pluriel *–dhȕn* (*Kwāȁ dhēbʌ̏-dhȕn kwá dhūn* 'Nous et les femmes, nous sommes venus') l'ambiguïté disparaît.

IX. La série coordinative liée

Le pronom de cette série apparaît là où le deuxième participant est représenté par un syntagme déterminant dont la première composante est le pronom non-subjectif de la 3ème pers. du sg. *ȁ.* En fait, les pronoms de la série en question proviennent de la fusion avec ce pronom. Ils ne se distinguent pas, par leurs formes, des variantes à ton final extra-bas des pronoms coordinatifs simples, mais il serait quand même erroné d'amalgamer ces deux séries : d'une part, les pronoms « liés » n'ont pas de variantes à ton moyen-moyen ; d'autre part, le contexte suffit toujours pour établir la présence d'un pronom *ȁ* sous-jacent :

(13) *Kāȁ* *gbɤ̄,* *kā* *dhȍ* *dhó'.*
2SG.et>3SG.NSBJ fils 2PL.EXI aller\NEUT aller\INF
'Toi et son fils, vous allez partir.'

La stratégie de la pluralisation des participants suit le même modèle que celui de la série coordinative simple.

X. La série coordinative portemanteau

Tous les pronoms de cette série, sauf la 1ère personne exclusive, ont des variantes facultatives à ton moyen sur les deux voyelles ou à ton moyen-extra-bas. Tous les pronoms de la série, sauf *kwɛ̄ŋ,* expriment l'idée « X et lui » ; autrement dit, un pronom est l'équivalent de toute une construction coordinative :

(14) *Kɛ̄ŋ̏ ~ kɛ̄ŋ* *kā* *dhȍ* *dhó'.*
2SG.et.3SG 2PL.EXI aller\NEUT aller.INF
'Lui et toi, vous partirez.'

Les formes plurielles rendent l'idée d'un nombre total des participants supérieur à 2, quelle que soit la répartition numérique entre les X et les Y. Par exemple, *yɛ̄ŋ̏-dhȕn* peut signifier 'nous et lui', 'moi et eux', 'nous et eux'.

Le seul pronom qui n'inclut pas des tierces personnes dans le nombre de ses référents est *kwɛ̄ŋ ~ kwɛ̄ŋ̏* 'moi et toi'. En fait, c'est la seule combinaison logiquement possible de personnes qui n'inclut que les participants de la communication.

3.6. Adjectifs

(Pour une étude détaillée des adjectifs, voir (Vydrine 2007).) Considérons d'abord les limites de la classe des adjectifs et les critères selon lesquels un mot est classé parmi les adjectifs. Malgré la prolifération des catégories morphologiques d'adjectif (le nombre, l'intensité et la focalisation), l'irrégularité de ces catégories place le critère syntaxique en position dominante.

3.6.1. Les trois fonctions syntaxiques des adjectifs

1) attributive (A), dans la position post-nominale. L'adjectif constitue un syntagme nominal avec le nom :

(15) *Bhán kɔ́ dhɤ̋ɤdhɤ̏ɤ yɤ̏.*
1SG.PRF maison rond voir
'J'ai vu une maison ronde'.

2) prédicative (P), suivant une MPP de la série existentielle :

(16) *Bhān kɔ́ yɤ̏ dhɤ̋ɤdhɤ̏ɤ.*
1SG.POSS maison 3SG.EXI rond
'Ma maison est ronde.'

À la différence des verbes, les adjectifs :

– ne changent pas leur ton lexical contre un ton extra-bas lorsqu'ils sont construits avec une MPP existentielle, cf. une phrase verbale : *Yɤ̏ dhȕn.* 'Il est venu' (le ton lexical de ce verbe étant moyen, *dhūn*) ;

– peuvent être précédés par un circonstant :

(17) *Dhɛ̄ŋ̏dhɛ̏ yā yɤ̏ gblɛ̀ɛn pɤ̋dhɛ̏ ká.*
hameau.CMM ce 3SG.EXI long village de
'Ce champ est loin du village.'

Cette phrase est l'équivalent de *Dhɛ̄ŋdhɛ̏ yā yɤ̏ pɤ̋dhɛ̏ ká gblɛ̀ɛn.*

Évidemment, il s'agit de la même fonction prédicative lorsque l'adjectif suit les verbes de transformation, surtout *kʌ̄* 'devenir' :

(18)

N̄	*gɛ̏n*	*yȁ*	*kʌ̄*	*gbínŋ̏.*
1SG.NSBJ	pied/jambe	3SG.PRF	devenir	lourd

'Mes jambes se sont alourdies.'

3) La fonction prédicative avec la postposition *ká* (S). D'un point de vue formel, l'adjectif représente un complément d'objet indirect par rapport à la MPP.

(19)

Bhān	*kɔ́*	*yɤ̏*	*dhɤ̋ɤdhɤ̏ɤ*	*ká.*
1SG.POSS	maison	3SG.EXI	rond	par

'Ma maison est ronde.'

Du point de vue sémantique, la valeur de cette construction est quasiment identique à celle de la construction précédente, dans laquelle l'adjectif est en fonction prédicative.

À côté des adjectifs qui peuvent apparaître dans les trois fonctions, il y en a d'autres (surtout des formes dérivées) qui n'assument qu'une ou deux fonctions. Il faut préciser qu'il suffit qu'un lexème puisse apparaître dans une seule des deux premières fonctions (attributive ou prédicative) pour qu'on le range parmi les adjectifs.

3.6.2. Pluriel de l'adjectif

Le pluriel de l'adjectif peut être exprimé de deux façons : par la marque plurielle régulière *–dhȕn* ou par une modification morphologique de la base (cette modification exprime à la fois le pluriel et l'intensité).[18] Ce n'est que dans quelques rares exceptions[19] que *–dhȕn* peut être ajouté (facultativement ou en conditionnement syntaxique) à la modification à valeur intensive et plurielle de la base :

bhȁan zœ̏œndhē 'un oiseau rouge' → *bhȁan zœ̏nzœ̏ndhē* ou *bhȁan zœ̏nzœ̏ndhē-dhȕn* 'des oiseaux très rouges'.

À la différence de la plupart des autres langues mandé, le morphème du pluriel –*dhȕn* peut être placé après le nom (devant l'adjectif) :

bhȁan-dhȕn zœ̏nzœ̏ndhē 'des oiseaux très rouges'

En position finale, *–dhȕn* peut être répété. On peut l'interpréter comme un accord formel de nombre :

bhȁan-dhȕn zœ̏nzœ̏ndhē-dhȕn 'des oiseaux très rouges'

---

[18] La seule exception que nous ayons pu trouver est l'adjectif *sɛ̄ɛ̋ndhʌ́n* 'petit' → *sɛ́ɛndhʌ́n* 'petits', où la pluralisation morphologique n'est pas accompagnée de la valeur d'intensif.

[19] Par exemple, l'adjectif *plʌ̋ʌplʌ̏ʌ* 'facile ; mou ; savoureux' a une forme intensive plurielle *plʌ̋ʌplʌ̋ʌ* 'très savoureux' (les sens 'facile' et 'mou' ne vont pas avec cette forme !) qui ne se combine pas avec la marque *–dhȕn.*

Le changement de position de la marque *–dhǜn* n'entraîne aucune modification de sens. Il y a cependant des restrictions d'ordre syntaxique qui rendent la présence de *–dhǜn* tantôt obligatoire, tantôt impossible.

3.6.3. L'intensité de qualité

On peut avoir en dan-gouèta jusqu'à trois degrés d'intensité : zéro – intensif – superintensif. Comme cela a déjà été mentionné, il y a une très forte tendance au cumul des valeurs intensive et plurielle. Cependant, il est rare d'avoir pour un adjectif à la fois les formes morphologiques du singulier intensif, du singulier superintensif et du pluriel intensif. Je n'ai de plus relevé aucun cas où les quatre formes (les trois énumérées ci-dessus plus le pluriel superintensif) coexisteraient.

Pour un seul adjectif, ces quatre degrés d'intensité ont été relevés :
sʌ̏ 'joli' – Intensif Pluriel : *sɛ̏ŋbʌ̏* 'très jolis' – Super-intensif Pluriel : *sʌ̏sʌ̏* 'très-très jolis' – Extraintensif Pluriel : *bhëbhë* 'extrêmement jolis'.

Il faut dire qu'un nombre important d'adjectifs en dan-gouèta n'a pas de formes intensives dérivées par une modification de la base. Pour de tels adjectifs, l'intensif est exprimée par les adverbes *dɛ̏dɛ̏wō* 'très', *yāawō* 'horriblement, très'.

3.6.4. Modifications de la base adjectivale

Les procédés formels servant à exprimer les valeurs grammaticales (le pluriel et l'intensif) de l'adjectif en dan-gouèta sont les suivants :

1) Le redoublement de la base qui peut être :

– complet : *dɛ̏e* 'nouveau' – Pl. SupInt. *dɛ̏edɛ̏e* 'très-très nouveaux' ; *gbɛ̋ɛ* 'large' – Pl. Int. *gbɛ̋ɛgbɛ̋ɛ* 'très larges' ;

– accompagnée du dédoublement de la voyelle : *tīi* 'noir' – Pl. Int. *tītī* 'très noires' ; *dɛ̏e* 'nouveau' – Pl. Int. *dɛ̏dɛ̏* 'très nouveaux'.

2) Le changement du contour tonal : *bhʌ́ŋ̏bhʌ̏ŋ* 'potelée' – Pl. Int. *bhʌ́ŋ̏bhʌ́ŋ̏* 'très potelées' ; *dhɛ̋ɛndhɛ̏ɛn* 'goûteux, savoureux' – Pl. Int. *dhɛ̋ɛndhɛ̋ɛn* 'très goûteux, très savoureux' ;

3) la transfixation (le transfixe *-k-k-*) : *dhɛ̋ɛndhɛ̏ɛn* 'goûteux, savoureux' – Pl. SupInt. *dhɛ̋nkɛ̋dhɛ̏nkɛ̏* 'très gouteux, très savoureux' ; *gblɤ̋ɤgblɤ̏ɤ* 'sec et dur' – Sg. Int. *gblɤ̋kɤ̋gblɤ̏kɤ̏* 'très sec et dur' ;

4) la suffixation (les suffixes *–sǜ* et, plus rarement, *-dhɛ̏*) : *glɔ̋ɔglɔ̏ɔ* 'émoussé' – Sg. Int. *glɔ̋ɔ̋glɔ̋ɔ̋sǜ* 'très émoussé' ; *dɔ̋ɔndɔ̏ɔn* 'collant' (en parlant d'une personne) – Sg. Int. *dɔ̋ɔndɔ̋ɔnsǜ* 'très collant' ; *yāa* 'mauvais' – *yāayädhɛ̏* 'très mauvais' ;

5) rarement, la supplétion : *sʌ̏* 'joli' – Pl. Extra-Int. *bhëbhë* 'extrêmement jolis'.[20]

[20] Lors de la supplétion les formes grammaticales d'un lexème sont dérivées de bases différentes. La forme *bhëbhë* semble être le seul cas de supplétion en dan gwɛɛtaa.

Les procédés énumérés peuvent se combiner. Par exemple, la forme super-intensive singulière de *tīi* 'noir' est *tīitïdhɛ̀* 'extrêmement noir' ;[21] elle combine à la fois la réduplication, le dédoublement de la voyelle (dans la deuxième partie de la base redoublée), la modification tonale et la suffixation.

Il y a certaines tendances dans la dérivation des formes plurielles et intensives qui permettent de proposer plusieurs modèles de flexion. Cependant, les limites de ces modèles sont assez floues et comportent de nombreuses irrégularités. On ne peut généralement pas prédire, en partant de la forme de base de l'adjectif, s'il existe une forme dérivée particulière et quelle en est la forme. C'est la raison pour laquelle toutes les formes morphologiques plurielles et intensives des adjectifs sont mentionnées dans le présent dictionnaire.

3.6.5. Focalisation

L'adjectif en dan-gouèta admet une marque spéciale de « focalisation sélective actuelle », le suffixe *–sʉ̀*: un des objets d'un ensemble supposé connu des interlocuteurs est sélectionné par référence à la qualité exprimée par l'adjectif, cf. (20b).

(20a) *Gbɛ̂n tīi bhā yà dhūn.*
chien noir ART 3SG.PRF venir
'Le chien noir est venu.'

(20b) *Gbɛ̂n tīi-sʉ̀ bhā yà dhūn.*
chien noir-SLA ART 3SG.PRF venir
'C'est le chien noir (parmi tous les autres chiens) qui est venu.'

La plupart des adjectifs (y compris aux formes plurielles et intensives) peuvent être focalisés de cette façon ; il y a cependant des restrictions qui nous obligent à indiquer dans le dictionnaire, pour chaque forme adjectivale sa possibilité de focalisation.

3.6.6. Dérivation des adjectifs à partir des autres parties de discours

Deux suffixes dérivent des adjectifs à partir des noms.

1) *sʉ̀* (avec une variante facultative *sɪ̀*) produit des adjectifs à valeur « qui contient X », « qui ressemble à X » (X renvoie au nom dont l'adjectif est dérivé) : *wèe* 'sel' → *yí wèesʉ̀* 'eau salée' ; *dhʉ̃́ dhɔ̄ŋ* 'ombre d'un arbre' → *bhɛ̄n dhɔ̄ŋsʉ̀* 'homme calme' ; *pɛ̄ŋ* 'feu' → *pɛ̄ŋsʉ̀* 'chaud' ; *kpʌ́nŋ̀* 'ruse' → *bhɛ̄n kpʌ́nŋ̀sʉ̀* 'personne rusée'. Cette dérivation est d'un rendement limité, elle s'avère impossible dans de très nombreux cas où il semblerait n'y avoir aucun obstacle d'ordre sémantique.

---

[21] Cette forme semble être réservée au dialecte de Gwɛ̃̀ɛ̃tàa, les locuteurs d'autres dialectes dan de l'Est l'ignorent.

Occasionnellement, *sɯ̀* produit des adjectifs à partir des adjectifs, avec une modification du sens : *zīī* 'vieux' → *zīīsɪ̀* 'ancien', comme dans *dhɯ̀tɪ̄ɪ̀ zīīsɪ̀* 'ancien chef du village'.

Il faut mentionner que beaucoup de formes au suffixe dérivatif *sɯ̀* peuvent être redoublées (le plus souvent, il s'agit d'un redoublement complet de la base, sans modifications supplémentaires) pour rendre la valeur de l'intensif singulier : *bhúʌ̀ʌsɯ̀* 'barbu' – *bhúʌ̀ʌbhúʌ̀ʌsɯ̀* 'très barbu' ; *flɛ́ɛsɯ̀* 'pauvre' – *flɛ́ɛflɛ́ɛsɯ̀* 'très pauvre', etc. Ces formes de surcroît sont souvent focalisées : *flɛ́ɛsɯ̀-sɯ̀* 'celui qui est pauvre' (parmi tous les gens).

2) *dhē* dérive des adjectifs dénominaux à valeur ornative (caractérisée par un trait typique, de la forme ou du matériau, ou encore de la destination) : *sʌ́ʌdhɛ̋* 'papier' → *fâàn sʌ́ʌdhɛ̋dhē* 'chapeau en papier' ; *pɪ̀ɤgā* 'fer' → *gbɔ̄ pɪ̀ɤgādhē* 'marmite en fer' ; *dhɯ̋dhʌ́n* 'bâtonnet'→ *bɔ̀ŋbɔ̄ŋ̀ dhɯ̋dhʌ́ndhē* 'sucette', *gɛ̂n* 'pied, jambe' → *gbɔ̄ gɛ̀ndhē* 'marmite à pieds', *sɪ̋* 'scie' → *dhȁa sɪ̋dhē* 'couteau à lame dentelée', etc. Le suffixe *dhē* est peu productif, il se combine avec une petite minorité des radicaux nominaux de la langue.

3.7. Numéraux

Les numéraux sont proches des adjectifs par le fait qu'ils suivent le nom, mais ils s'utilisent aussi dans certains contextes qui ne sont pas typiques des adjectifs. En tant qu'un adverbe le numéral suit le verbe :

(21) *Yȁ* *zlòo* *zʌ̄* *yȁagā.*
3SG.PRF guib tuer trois
'Il a tué des antilopes guib trois fois (dans sa vie).'

3.7.1. Numéraux cardinaux

Les numéraux cardinaux ont les formes suivantes :

1 *dō*	9 *sɯ̋ɛ̀sīɤ*
2 *plɛ̀* ou *pȅedʌ̄*	10 *kœ̀œŋ dō*
3 *yȁagā*	11 *kœ̀œŋ dō ɤ̄ gā dō*
4 *yɪ̏isīɤ*	12 *kœ̀œŋ dō ɤ̄ gā plɛ̀*
5 *sɔ̋ɔdhɯ̋*	13 *kœ̀œŋ dō ɤ̄ gā yȁagā*
6 *sœ̋œ̀dō*	20 *kœ̀œŋ plɛ̀*
7 *sœ̋œ̀plɛ̀*	21 *kœ̀œŋ plɛ̀ ɤ̄ gā dō*
8 *sâàgā*	22 *kœ̀œŋ plɛ̀ ɤ̄ gā plɛ̀* ou *pȅedʌ̄*

30 *kœ̀œŋ yàagā*	1000 *gblṹ dō*
40 *kœ̀œŋ yììsīɤ*	2000 *gblṹ plɛ̀*
90 *kœ̀œŋ sṹɛ̃̀sīɤ*	10 000 *gblṹ kœ̀œŋ dō*
100 *kʌ̄ŋ dō*	100 000 *gblṹ kʌ̄ŋ dō*
200 *kʌ̄ŋ plɛ̀*	1 000 000 *gblṹ bhɛ̄ɛ̀n dō*

NOTES. 1. La forme alternative du numéral 2, *pèedʌ̄,* est moins fréquente que la forme principale, elle ne peut pas être employée dans certains contextes. 2. L'élément *kœ̀œŋ* 'dizaine' a une variante libre *kɔ̀ŋ,* et dans certains contextes *kɔ̀.* Sans doute, il provient du mot *kɔ̀* 'main'. 3. Le sens original du mot *gblṹ* '1000' est 'panier de noix de cola' (cola est une denrée commerciale très prisée des Dan ; un panier *gblṹ* contient 1000 noix de cola). 4. Les numéraux de 6 à 9 proviennent de la composition de *sɔ́ɔdhṹ* '5' avec les numéraux de 1 à 4 et avec, probablement, un élément intermédiaire *tà.*

Le groupe nominal précédant un numéral n'a normalement pas de marque du pluriel. Si pourtant cela arrive, la marque du pluriel exprime alors la valeur d'un défini :

(22) *Pɛ́ŋ̀ dhēbʌ̀-dhùn plɛ̀ ɤ́ wó bhā à kʌ̄*
jumeau femme-PL deux REL 3PL.JNT là 1SG.EXI RETR
kpàn à-dhùn bhà yāandhíɤ...
voir\NEUT 3SG.NSBJ sur hier
'Ces deux jumelles, je les ai rencontrées hier.'

Un numéral peut avoir une marque de pluriel postposition qui exprime soit la valeur du l'exactitude du nombre, soit le caractère approximatif du nombre.

Dans les nombres composés, les nombres désignant les unités sont précédés par *ɤ̄ gā,* lit. 'son unité' :

(23) *tɔ̀ kœ̀œŋ sáàgā ɤ̄ gā sœ́œ̀dō*
poulet 10 8 REFL.SG unité 6
'86 poulets' (lit. « 80 poulets et 6 de ses unités »).

Les parties des nombres composés de 101 à 109 sont reliées par le pronom coordinatif *wāà* ; le nom objet du décompte est répété devant chaque partie du nombre composé : *tɔ̀ kʌ̄ŋ dō wāà tɔ̀ plɛ̀* '102 poulets'.

Les composantes d'un nombre tel 110 peuvent être liées entre elles par un pronom cooordinatif ou par le pronom réfléchi : *tɔ̀ kʌ̄ŋ dō wāà tɔ̀ kœ̀œŋ dō* ou *tɔ̀ kʌ̄ŋ dō ɤ̄ kɔ̀ dō* '110 poulets'.

Les composantes des nombres à trois décimales à partir de 111 peuvent être liées entre elles par des pronoms coordinatifs : *tɔ̀ kʌ̄ŋ dō wāà tɔ̀ kœ̀œŋ dō wāà tɔ̀ dō.* Le pronom coordinatif peut aussi être remplacé par le pronom réfléchi soit devant la dizaine soit devant l'unité : *tɔ̀ kʌ̄ŋ dō* ***ɤ̄ kɔ̀*** *dō wāà tɔ̀ dō* ou *tɔ̀ kʌ̄ŋ dō wāà tɔ̀ kœ̀œŋ dō ɤ̄* ***gā*** *dō* '111 poulets'.

Dans les nombres composés supérieurs à 1000, les noms des unités peuvent être reliés à l'ensemble par la combinaison du pronom coordinatif avec le pronom réfléchi suivi du nom *gā* 'os' : *tɔ̀ gblűű plɛ̀ wāà tɔ̀ kʌ̄ŋ plɛ̀ ɤ̄ kɔ̀ plɛ̀ wāà ɤ̄ gā plɛ̀* '2222 poulets'. Dans le même contexte, on ne peut pas utiliser le pronom réfléchi sans le pronom coordinatif.

3.7.2. Numéraux ordinaux

Les numéraux ordinaux sont dérivés des numéraux cardinaux par le suffixe *-dhàan*. Dans les numéraux composés, le suffixe n'apparaît qu'une seule fois, après le nombre d'unités : *kwɛ̀ gblűű dō wāà kwɛ̀ kʌ̄ŋ sűɛ̀sīɤ ɤ̄ kɔ̀ sœ̋œ̀dō wāà kwɛ̀ yììsīɤ-dhàan* 'l'année 1964'.

Le numéral ordinal « premier » est exprimé par une forme supplétive, *blɛ̀ɛsùì*. Il n'entre pas dans la composition des nombres ordinaux. Dans les contextes où il va de paire avec d'autres nombres ordinaux, il prend le suffixe *-dhàan* :

(24) *Dhūn tɔ̀ kœ̀œŋ dō-dhàan, blɛ̀ɛsùì-dhàan wāà kœ̀œŋ plɛ̀ ɤ̄ gā dō-dhàan ká.*
venir poulet dix un-ORD premier-ORD 3SG.et dix deux REFL unité un-ORD avec
'Amène le dixième, le premier et le vingt-et-unième poulet.'

3.7.3. Noms des fractions

Les fractions sont rendues par une construction descriptive :

(25) *à pɛ̀gúí-sùì pɛ̋ɛn yàagā-dhàan*
3SG.NSBJ diviser-GER partie trois-ORD
'la troisième partie (de cela).'

(26) *à pɛ̀gúí-sùì ɤ́ kœ̀œŋ dō à pɛ̋ɛn yàagā-dhàan*
3SG.NSBJ diviser-GER REL dix un 3SG.NSBJ partie trois-ORD
'3/10 (de cela)'.

3.7.4. Valeur distributive

La valeur distributive est rendue par une répétition du nombre, qui intervient dans la position après le verbe, soit avant le complément d'objet indirect soit après lui :

(27a) *Kà dà kɔ́ɔdhɤ̄ sœ̋œ̀plɛ̀ sœ̋œ̀plɛ̀*
2PL.IMP entrer maison.LOC sept sept
'Entrez à la maison sept par sept'.

On peut dire aussi :

(27b) *Kà̰ dà̰ sœ̋œ̀plɛ̀ sœ̋œ̀plɛ̀ kɔ́ɔdhɤ̄.* (le même sens)

Pour les nombres supérieurs à 10, seule la dernière composante (le nom des unités) se répète dans la construction distributive :

(28) *Kà̰ dà̰ kœ̀œŋ dō ɤ̄ gā plɛ̀ plɛ̀.* 'Entrez par douze.'

Les Dan considèrent les nombres pairs comme « masculins », et les nombres impairs comme « féminins ».

3.8. Verbes

3.8.1. Transitif, intransitif, réfléchi

Les verbes dan peuvent être transitifs ou intransitifs, ce qui n'a aucune incidence sur leurs structures morphologiques. La seule différence est qu'un verbe transitif est obligatoirement précédé d'un complément d'objet direct (qui se trouve donc dans la position entre la marque prédicative et le prédicat verbal), et un verbe intransitif n'admet pas de complément d'objet direct.

Il y a de nombreux verbes **ambivalents**, c.-à-d. des verbes qui peuvent fonctionner comme transitifs ou intransitifs, sans que cette différence d'emploi soit marquée dans la forme verbale :

(29) *Sàagā yà̰ gbà̰n bhḭ̀ʌ gbã̋n gṹ.*
flèche 3SG.PRF enfoncer biche cuisse dans
'La flèche s'est plantée dans la cuisse de la biche royale.'

(30) *Tòkpà̰ yà̰ sàagā gbà̰n bhḭ̀ʌ gbã̋n gṹ.*
Tokpa 3SG.PRF flèche enfoncer biche cuisse dans
'Tokpa a enfoncé la flèche dans la cuisse de la biche royale.'

L'ambivalence des verbes n'est pas prévisible, donc la nature transitive, intransitive ou ambivalent d'un verbe doit être marquée dans le dictionnaire.

Le dan n'a pas de catégorie de voix. La valeur passive peut être exprimée par une transformation syntaxique (qui n'est pas marquée dans la forme verbale) où l'ex-sujet est ramené dans la position du complément d'objet indirect :

(31) *Dhēbʌ̰̀ bhā yà kɔ̰̀ɔ wṹ.*
femme ART 3SG.PRF calebasse casser
'La femme a cassé une calebasse.' →

(32) *Kɔ̰̀ɔ bhā yà̰ wṹ dhēbʌ̰̀dhʌ́n bhā à̰ kɔ̰̀ɔ.*
calebasse ART 3SG.PRF casser femme ART 3SG.NSBJ main.COM
'La calebasse a été cassée par la femme.'

Cette transformation ne s'applique pas à tous les verbes transitifs ; on dirait même qu'elle est plutôt rare. Lorsqu'on a besoin de suppression du sujet, on utilise beaucoup plus souvent la construction avec la marque prédicative de la 3 pers. du pluriel à valeur impersonnelle :

(33) *… wó dhūn ȁ ká Mɑ̋adhɤ̄.*
3SG.PL.JNT venir\JNT 3SG.NSBJ avec Man.LOC
'… on l'a amené à Man.'

Sont considérés comme **réfléchis** les verbes qui peuvent avoir un pronom réfléchi en position de complément d'objet direct (donc, techniquement parlant, les verbes réfléchis sont toujours des transitifs) :

(34) *Yɤ̏ ɤ̄ gĩ̏-sɪ̄ʌ yɔ̋ɔ ká.*
3SG.EXI REFL.SG frotter-DUR kaolin avec
'Il est en train de s'enduire la peau de kaolin.'

3.8.2. « Modes impersonnels »

On peut parler des « modes impersonnels » du verbe avec beaucoup de réserve, parce que le verbe n'a pas de conjugaison selon les personnes ; il peut donc s'agir de l'impossibilité, pour ces formes, d'être employées dans la position verbale avec une marque prédicative pronominale.

3.8.2.1. Infinitif

L'infinitif est dérivé par l'adjonction d'un suffixe tonal extra-bas à la forme verbale de base. Il intervient comme deuxième prédication après des verbes de mouvement (*dhó* 'aller, s'en aller', *dhūn* 'venir') et des auxiliaires (*gūn* 'être dans le passé', *tȕn* 'continuer'), dans les constructions verbales du futur, du présomptif, du subjonctif négatif.

(35) *Dȕdhȅe yà dhūn yí bhūn'.*
cow-female 3SG.PRF come water drink\INF
'Une vache est venue boire de l'eau'.

3.8.2.2. Gérondif

Le gérondif est dérivé par l'adjonction de la marque clitique *–sȕ* (sans doute, provient-elle du verbe *sű* 'attraper'). Il fonctionne :

a) comme un nom verbal (le nom d'un événement ou d'une situation) :

(36) *Zân bhȁ yʌ̄ bhȕn bhɛ̄n dhɔ̄ŋ-sȕ ká.*
Jean POSS travail être homme compter-GER avec
'Le travail de Jean est de compter les gens.'

b) comme un participe ; le nom défini par le gérondif peut correspondre au sujet comme au complément d'objet du verbe :

(37) *Yɤ̀ ɤ̄ kwɛ̀ɛ̀ dhú-sɯ̀ ká.*
3SG.EXI REFL.SG charge charger-GER avec
'Il a déjà attaché son bagage.'

(38) *yí̃ zīɤ-sɯ̀* 'ruisseau' (litt. « eau passant »).

Là où le contexte n'est pas suffisant, les deux interpretations sont possibles : *yí̃ wɛ̀ŋ-sɯ̀* 'l'acte de verser de l'eau' ou 'l'eau versée'.

Le même clitique *–sɯ̀* sert de marque de nominalisation phrastique associé au circonstant, tandis que le verbe prend le ton extra-bas (qui est donc un indicateur supplémentaire de la nominalisation) :

(39) *dɛ̏ kɯ̏n wɔ́n dhí̃ɤ-sɯ̀*
même attraper\NMLZ affaire devant-GER
'la maîtrise de soi'.

3.8.2.3. Le masdar (nom verbal)

Cette forme est marquée par le clitique *dhɛ̏* (provenant du nom *dhɛ̏* 'endroit, lieu'). Certains verbes exigent le masdar comme complément d'objet :

(40) *Yɤ̀ dɔ̏ pʌ̄ kpà-dhɛ̏ ká.*
3SG.EXI savoir\NEUT chose cuire-MSD avec
'Elle sait faire la cuisine.'

3.8.2.4. Le nom verbal nu

Le nom d'action peut être dérivé de tous les verbes sans aucune marque morphologique. Il maintient les valences verbales et s'utilise comme un nom dépendant auprès des noms *dhɔ̏* 'amour, envie', *kɔ̏* 'façon, manière', *wɔ́n* 'affaire' et dans la construction de la « relativisation à gauche » :

(41) *Dhó dhɔ̏ yà n̄ kún.*
aller envie 3SG.PRF 1SG.NSBJ attraper
'Je veux partir.'

(42) *sí̃ɤ yà' ká pʌ̀*
feu mettre-3SG.NSBJ avec chose
'allume-feu'.

3.8.3. Aspect, temps, modalité, polarité

Les catégories grammaticales verbales sont exprimées par des combinaisons de plusieurs procédés formels, à savoir :

– série des marques prédicatives pronominales (MPP). Toute construction verbale doit comporter une MPP (sauf dans les cas où une MPP de la 3ème pers. est omis au niveau superficiel) ;

– modification du ton de la base verbale. Il y existe en dan-gouèta trois modèles de modifications tonales des verbes : a) substitution du ton lexical par un ton extra-bas (dans la construction de l'aspect neutre) ; b) abaissement du ton selon un schéma plus nuancé (dans la construction conjointe) ; c) addition d'un suffixe tonal extra-bas (l'infinitif) ;

– suffixes verbaux ;

– verbes auxiliaires : *dhó* (sens primaire : 'aller, s'en aller'), *gūn* (sens primaire : 'être dans le passé'), *tȕn* (sens primaire : 'continuer') ;

– opérateurs qui occupent la position après les MPP : *kʌ̄* marque du rétrospectif, *dhȕn* marque du présomptif.

Vu la pluralité des éléments, on ne peut décrire le système grammatical du verbe autrement que par les formules de constructions. Les constructions peuvent être subdivisées en constructions de base (formées avec les MPP, les modifications tonales et les suffixes) et en constructions dérivées (bâties avec des verbes auxiliaires). Du point de vue du sémantisme grammatical, on peut parler de constructions à valeurs a) aspecto-temporelles, b) modales. Le sous-système des constructions négatives n'est souvent pas en parallèle avec le sous-système positif, il sera donc examiné séparément.

3.8.3.1. Constructions aspectuelles de base

1) **L'aspect neutre :** MPP existentielle (série I) + le verbe dont le ton lexical est remplacé par un ton extra-bas. Si le ton lexical du verbe est extra-bas, alors aucun changement du ton ne se produit. Dans les verbes à *-dhūn* (comme *dɔ́ɔ̀ndhūn* 's'arrêter'), seulement la dernière syllabe change son ton : → *dɔ́ɔ̀ndhȕn*. Il en va de même pour les autres verbes (très peu nombreux) composés de deux pieds : *gɛ̄nyɛ̄n* → *gɛ̄nyɛ̏n* 'gagner'. Par contre, les verbes redoublés changent les tons des deux pieds : *wūūȕwūūȕ* 'casser en de nombreuses pièces' → *wȕɯɯwȕɯɯ*.

Dans des propositions subordonnées ou des propositions simples avec une question partielle ou une focalisation, la construction de l'aspect neutre est remplacée par une « **construction conjointe** »,[22] avec la MPP de la série II (« Conjointe ») et la modification du ton du verbe selon un modèle plus complèxe.

Le type de modification dépend du ton de base et du type segmental du verbe (nombre de voyelles dans le pied ; le caractère homogène ou hétérogène des voyelles ; la présence de *-ŋ* à la fin du pied et de *–l-* à l'intérieur). Voici à ce propos quelques règles.

a) Verbes à ton lexical extra-haut :

→ moyen (un seul verbe du type CVVV) : *dhʌ̋ʌʌ* → *dhʌ̄ʌʌ* 'écraser en pâte' ;

→ bas (types CVV à voyelles identiques, CVŋ, CVVV) : *bhɤ̋ɤ* → *bhɤ̀ɤ* 'tarir', *bhʌ̋nŋ* → *bhʌ̀nŋ* 'avaler', *dhű ɤɤ* → *dhùɤɤ* 'priver de nourriture';

[22] Il s'agit, en fait, d'une variante syntaxiquement conditionnée de la construction de l'aspect neutre.

→ extra-bas (types CV, ClV et CVV à voyelles hétérogènes, sauf *-ŋ*) : *blʌ̋* → *blʌ̏* 's'user', *gãn* → *gȁn* 'tirer', *sűɤ* → *sȕɤ* 'avoir peur'.

b) Verbes à ton lexical haut :

→ moyen (tous les verbes à ton haut sont du type CV) : *bhúú* → *bhūū* 'briller', *dhó* → *dhō* 'aller', *kʌ́n* → *kʌ̄n* 'se rassasier'.

c) Verbes à ton lexical moyen :

→ moyen (la majorité des verbes des types CVV à voyelles hétérogènes et CV) : *bān* → *bān* 'pleuvoir', *dɔ̄* → *dɔ̄* 'savoir', *zūa* → *zūa* 'percer' ;

→ bas (types CLVV, CVŋ et CVV à voyelles homogènes) : *slʌ̄ʌ* → *slʌ̀ʌ* 'tourner', *dhōŋ* → *dhòŋ* 'compter', *gɔ̄ɔn* → *gɔ̀ɔn* 'faire, accomplir' ;

→ extra-bas (quelques rares verbes des types CVV à voyelles hétérogènes et CV) : *dhī* → *dhȉ* 'plaire', *kʌ̄* → *kʌ̏* 'faire', *wɔ̄* → *wɔ̏* 'se coucher', *zīɤ* → *zȉɤ* 'passer'.

d) Verbes à ton lexical bas :

→ bas (la quasi-totalité de cas) : *bhɔ̀ɔn* → *bhɔ̀ɔn* 'pouvoir', *lòo* → *lòo* 'arriver' ;

→ extra-bas (un seul verbe) : *kɤ̀ɤ* → *kɤ̏ɤ* 'éructer'.

e) Verbes à ton lexical extra-bas ne changent pas leurs tons : *bhȁn* → *bhȁn* 'frapper'.

f) Les verbes à tons modulés (tous des types CVV et ClVV) les remplacent par des tons bas : *gíi-* → *gìi* 'badigeonner', *dhūű* → *dhùu* 'éteindre', *gblāȁ* → *gblàa* 'crier, hurler'.

Les verbes composés d'origine du type de *dɔ̋ɔ̏ndhūn* 's'arrêter' suivent le modèle prédominant des verbes à ton moyen et ne changent pas leur ton : *bháȁndhūn* 'tomber' → *bháȁndhūn*. Les verbes redoublés changent les tons des deux parties : *gblāagblāa* → *gblàagblàa* 'crier fort'.

Ainsi la modification tonale du verbe dans la construction conjointe s'avère prévisible à un très haut degré. Les seuls cas où l'indication du ton modifié dans le dictionnaire est indispensable sont ceux des verbes du type CVVV à ton extra-haut (d'ailleurs, nous n'avons trouvé que deux verbes de ce type), ainsi que trois verbes CV et un verbe CVV dont le ton moyen est remplacé par le ton extra-bas.

La construction de l'aspect neutre en dan de l'Est exprime une rangée très large des valeurs aspectuelles et temporelles, leur réalisation dépend du sémantisme lexicale du verbe et du contexte syntaxique, voir plus en détail (Vydrin 2020a).

Le sens le plus fréquent rendu par la construction de l'aspect neutre est **l'habituel** (l'action qui se produit d'habitude) ; il est attesté pour la quasi-totalité des verbes :

(43) *Yɤ̏ gblʌ̏n yī gúú dhʌ́nbháwō.*
3SG.EXI ronfler\NEUT sommeil dans un.peu
'Il ronfle un peu dans le sommeil' (c'est son habitude).

(44) *Fɛ̂tɤ̏ yī-dhȕn ká, yɤ̏ gœ̏œ n̄ gɔ̏.*
fête jour-PL par 3SG.EXI faire.cadeau\NEUT 1SG.NSBJ à
'Les jours de fêtes, il me fait des cadeaux.'

Un autre emploi très fréquent de l'aspect neutre est **la construction de la condition irréelle** (« contrafactuelle ») avec la particule *dhún* :

(45) *Ā bɤ̏ vȁandhɤ̄ dhún, kɤ̄*
1SG.EXI reveiller\NEUT vite déjà alors
kó dhó.
1DUEL.INCL.SBJV aller
'Si je me réveillais vite, nous partirions.'

Les autres sens de l'aspect neutre se réalisent avec certains verbes seulement (plus précisément, avec les sens de certains verbes).

Le sens **résultatif** (« un état qui résulte d'une action précédente désigné par le verbe en question ») ne se conjugue qu'avec les verbes désignant des événements :

(46) *Yɤ̏ n̄ bɔ̏ ɤ̄ dhòo pɪ́ɤdhɤ̄.*
3SG.EXI 1SG.NSBJ envoyer\NEUT REFL.SG frère.aîné maison.LOC
'Il m'a envoyé chez son frère aîné' (et je suis en route).

Dans certains cas on peut parler plutôt du sens du **parfait** (une action qui est accomplie et dont le résultat reste valable) :

(47) *Yɤ̏ bhɛ̄n dhōŋ kótȁ plɛ̀.*
3SG.EXI homme compter\NEUT fois deux
'Il a compté les gens deux fois' (et nous attendons les résultats de son compte).

(48) *Bhʌ̀n ɤ́ kʌ̀ ɯ́ yʌ̄ kʌ̀ dhɛ̀*
quoi REL.3SG.JNT faire\JNT 2SG.JNT travail faire\JNT comme
pɛ́ɛdhɤ́ ?
mauvais
'Pourquoi as-tu fait le travail d'une si mauvaise façon ?'

Avec de nombreux verbes, la construction de l'aspect neutre exprime la valeur **imperfait** (« l'action se déroule pendant un laps de temps indiqué ») :

(49) *Yɤ̏ sʌ́ʌdhɛ̋ dlȁan kwɛ̏ plɛ̀ ká.*
3SG.EXI papier apprendre année deux avec
'Il a fait ses études pendant deux ans.'

(50) *ɤ́ yī pɪ́ɤ yɤ̄ yʌ̀n…*
3SG.JNT 1PL.EXCL chez ici quelque.part
'(Quand) il est chez nous ici…'

Pour d'autres verbes à l'aspect neutre, l'indication du laps de temps produit un sens **perfectif** « achever l'action en question pendant le laps de temps indiqué » :

(51) *Dhēbʌ̀-dhʉ̀n bhā wɔ̀ bhlʉ̀n bɪ̀ɤɤ dhɛ̋dhɛ̋ plɛ̀ ká.*
femme-PL ART 3SG.EXI riz piler heure deux en
'Les femmes ont pilé le riz en deux heures.'

(52) *Yɤ̀ gblʌ̋ʌ̀dhʉ̀n ɤ̄ dʌ̄ wlɤ̀ɤ gɔ̄nŋdhɤ̄.*
3SG.EXI prosterner REFL.SG père sous paillote.LOC
'Il s'est prosterné devant son père dans la paillote du chef' (une action récente ; au moment de la parole, il ne se prosterne plus).

La construction de l'aspect neutre peut désigner, avec certains verbes terminatifs ou décrivant un événement, une action ponctuelle, à condition que le moment de l'action soit indiqué dans la phrase (par un circonstant ou par une autre prédication) :

(53) *Yɤ̀ dʉ̀a yāandhɪ̋ɤ gbēŋ zìnŋgʉ́.*
3SG.EXI s'évader hier nuit entre
'Il s'est évadé hier à minuit.'

(54) *Yɤ̀ dàn kɤ̄ à kɔ́ɔdhɤ̄.*
3SG.EXI mesurer que 3SG.EXI maison.LOC
'Cela a été mesuré lorsque j'étais à la maison.'

Dans une narration, pour des actions consécutives, la construction conjointe de l'aspect neutre est utilisée :

(55) *Dhɛ̀ kɤ́ bʉ̋kʌ̄bhɛ̀n ɤ́ gō*
que REL brousse-faire-humain\IZF 3SG.JNT s'en.aller\JNT
bʉ̋ bhōo, yɤ́ wɔ̀ɔ-dhʉ̀n wó dhūn.
brousse.LOC sitôt CONS singe-PL 3PL.JNT venir\JNT
'Dès que le chasseur a quitté la forêt, les singes sont revenus'.

2) Parfait

La formule de la construction verbale du parfait est la suivante : MPP de la série du parfait + verbe à ton de base.

Le parfait renvoie à une action dont l'effet a toujours une incidence sur la situation actuelle. Le point de référence de l'action du parfait peut être le moment de la parole, mais aussi un moment de référence dans le passé :

(56) *Ā kʌ̄ dhɔ̀ bhūn á kpàn dhʌ́n*
1SG.EXI RETR aller\NEUT là 1SG.SBJV voir enfant
bhā bhà, kɤ̄ ***yà wáàndhūn…***
ART-3SG.NSBJ sur et 1SG.PRF se.coucher…

‘Je suis allé là-bas, et j’ai trouvé l’enfant couché…’

Le parfait est régulièrement utilisé dans la première partie de la phrase complexe à valeur temporelle pour exprimer le fait que l'action en question précède l'action de la deuxième proposition :

(57) *Bhá dhó bhūn, kíi kɑ̃́n sɔ̀ dō dhūn…*
2SG.PRF aller là que.2SG.JNT morceau étoffe un donner\JNT
‘Lorsque tu y vas, tu donnes une pièce d’étoffe…’

3) Imperfectif négatif

MPP négative imperfective + verbe en forme de base. Le plus souvent, cette construction exprime l’habituel :

(58) *Yáa bhɛ̄n dhɯ̃́ɤɤ bhɤ̀pʌ̀ gṹ.*
3SG.NEG.PRS humain priver manger-chose dans
‘Il ne prive pas les gens de nourriture.’

Avec les verbes à valeur non-terminative, la construction désigne des situations statives (dont le point de référence peut être le présent comme le passé) :

(59) *Yáa à wɔ́n dɔ̄ dhɛ̀ dhʌ́n bhā*
3SG.NEG.PRS 3SG.NSBJ affaire savoir que enfant ART
yà pɤ̀ yí bhàa.
3SG.PRF tomber eau chez
‘Il ne savait pas que l'enfant était tombé dans l'eau.’

A la différence de la construction affirmative de l'aspect neutre, l'imperfectif négatif n’exprime pas d’actions ponctuelles.

4) Perfectif négatif :

Pronom négatif du passé + verbe en forme de base.

Cette construction sert à la négation d’actions ponctuelles à nuances sémantiques différentes, en particulier :

– parfait/résultatif.

(60) *Ɯ̄ bhā dhɛ̄ɛ́kpɔ́ yíi dhī n̄ dhɛ̀.*
2SG.NSBJ POSS question 3SG.NEG.PFV plaire 1SG.NSBJ devant
‘Ta question ne m’a pas plu’.

– ponctuel :

(61) *Kɛ́ɛ wíi wō kɔ̀ yà à bhà.*
mais 3PL.NEG.PVF 3PL.REFL main.CMM mettre 3SG.NSBJ sur
‘Mais ils ne l’ont pas accepté’.

– ponctuel habituel :

(62) *Yà* *yʌ̄* *kʌ̄,* *yɤ̀* *ɤ̄* *bɔ̀* *kɤ̄* *bhìnŋdîì*
3SG.PRF travail faire 3SG.EXI REFL.SG finir SMLT midi
yíi *wɔ̀* *kɤ̀.*
3SG.NEG.PFV apparaître encore
'Quand il travaille, il finit avant midi.'

5) Résultatif

MPP existentielle ou conjointe + gérondif (base verbale à ton de base + suffixe –*sɯ̀*) + postposition comitative *ká.* En fait, cette construction est du même type que la construction avec l'adjectif en fonction prédicative postpositionnelle (cf. 3.6.1.). La construction exprime un sens résultatif (un état résultant de l'action désignée par le verbe) et peut être intransitive comme transitive :

(63) *Bhān* *kɔ́ɔdhɛ̀* *yɤ̀* *gblɤ̀-sɯ̀* *ká.*
1SG.POSS maison.CMM 3SG.EXI balayer-GER avec
'Ma maison est déjà balayée.'

(64) *Wèe* *yɤ̀* *à* *kún-sɯ̀* *ká.*
sel 3SG.EXI 3SG.NSBJ attraper-GER avec
'Il est suffisamment salé' (litt. : « le sel l'a attrapé »).

La négation du résultatif s'exprime par la substitution de la MPP existentielle ou conjointe par la MPP négative imperfective : *Bhān kɔ́ɔdhɛ̀ yáa gblɤ̀-sɯ̀ ká.*'Ma maison n'est pas balayée', *Wèe yáa à kún-sɯ̀ ká.* 'Il n'est pas suffisamment salé.'

6) Duratif :

MPP existentielle ou conjointe + verbe en forme de base + suffixe *–sīʌ.* Sans doute, le suffixe du duratif provient historiquement de la fusion de la marque du gérondif –*sɯ̀* avec la postposition *gú* 'dans'. Autrement dit, c'est une construction d'origine locative. Elle exprime un continu dynamique et statique : *Gbàtɔ̀ yɤ̀ yáàdhūn-sīʌ.* 'Gbato est assis' ou 'Gbato est en train de s'asseoir'.

(65) *Dhʌ́n-dhǜn* *wɔ̀* *tlōo* *kʌ̄-sīʌ* *kpɛ́nŋdhɤ̄.*
enfant-PL 3SG.EXI jeu faire-DUR extérieur.LOC
'Les enfants sont en train de jouer dehors.'

(66) *Ʌ̀* *bhà* *gɔ̄* *yɤ̀* *dɔ̄-sīʌ* *tɔ̀n* *tà.*
3SG.NSBJ POSS voiture 3SG.EXI arrêter-DUR colline sur
'Sa voiture est arrêtée sur la colline.'

Pour exprimer la négation du duratif, le pronom existentiel est remplacé par un pronom négatif imperfectif : *Dhʌ́n-dhǜn wáa tlōo kʌ̄-sīʌ kpɛ́nŋdhɤ̄.* 'Les enfants ne sont pas en train de jouer dehors.'

7) Prospectif

MPP prospective + verbe à ton lexical. La construction exprime une action qui doit s'effectuer dans le futur immédiat et dont les conditions sont réunies (la volonté de l'acteur, etc.) :

(67) *Yɤ́' pɤ̄ yɤ̄ɤ yɔ̀ɔn kɔ́ dhɪ́ bhà,*
3SG.JNT-3SG.NSBJ dire\JNT 3SG.PROS bouger maison porte sur
kɤ̄ bhɛ̄n-dhʉ̀n wà à kún.
SMLT homme-PL 3SG.PRF 3SG.NSBJ attraper
'Elle voulait s'approcher de la porte de la maison, mais les gens l'ont attrapée.'

Le prospectif apparaît régulièrement dans une proposition conditionnelle après la conjonction *kɤ́* 'même si' :

(68) *Kɤ́ zúu yɤ̄ɤ à wɔ́n dɔ̄, à dhɛ̀*
même.si encore 3SG.PROS 3SG.NSBJ affaire savoir 3SG.NSBJ place
yɤ̀ à bhà kɤ̄ yɤ̀ tɔ̀n kún kɤ̀ blɛ̀ɛsʉ̀.
3SG.EXI 3SG.NSBJ sur SMLT 3SG.SBJV colline attraper encore d'abord
'Même s'il savait ça, il devait d'abord gravir la colline.'

8) Négation du prospectif

MPP négative imperfective + MPP prospective + verbe à ton lexical.

(69) *Bhɛ̄n yāayädhɛ̀ ɤ́ yā bháan bhāan*
humain mauvais.INT REL.3SG.JNT ce 1SG.NEG.IPFV 1SG.PROS
tɔ́' gɔ̀.
rester-3SG.NSBJ à
'Je ne vais pas me marier avec cet homme horriblement laid.'

9) Rétrospectif

Le rétrospectif est dérivé des constructions de l'aspect neutre par l'introduction de l'opérateur *kʌ̄* après la MPP. Cet opérateur provient, sans doute, du verbe *kʌ̄* 'faire', mais, à la différence des verbes auxiliaires, son ton ne change pas ; par contre, c'est le verbe notionnel qui change son ton :

(70) *Gɔ̄ yɤ̀ **kʌ̄** **dhʌ̀nŋ** bɤ̄ɤ̀ gúɪ.*
voiture 3SG.EXI RETR coller-NEUT boue dans
'La voiture s'est enlisée dans la boue.'

(71) *Gbàtɔ̀ dhʌ̀n ɤ́ **kʌ̄** dhā n̄ sáàgúɪ.*
Gbato FOC REL.3SG.JNT RETR sauver\JNT 1SG.NSBJ grace.à
'C'est Gbato qui s'est sauvé grace à moi' (une histoire ancienne).

Cela signifie que dans la langue dan-gouèta contemporaine, *kʌ̄* n'est plus un verbe.

Le rétrospectif indique le plus souvent que le résultat de l'action n'est plus actuel, ou qu'il est annulé :

(72) *Gbȁtȍ yɤ̏ kʌ̄ kɔ́ dɔ̏.*
Gbato 3SG.EXI RETR maison bâtir\NEUT
'Gbato bâtit une maison' (sous-entendu que la maison n'existe plus ; ou que Gbato est mort depuis, etc.).

Dans d'autres contextes, *kʌ̄* peut tout simplement rendre une distance temporelle plus considérable (par rapport à la construction de l'aspect neutre) :

(73) *Yɤ̏ kʌ̄ n̄ dhɛ̄ɛ́ kpɔ̏ ɤ̄ bhā*
3SG.EXI RETR 1SG.NSBJ question étaler-NEUT REFL.SG POSS
bhɤ̏pʌ̏ wɔ̏n ká.
nourriture affaire avec
'Il m'a posé la question au sujet de son repas' (la situation est toujours actuelle, mais moins que dans la construction sans *kʌ̄*).

(74) *Yɤ̏ kʌ̄ kʌ̏ dhɤ́ n̄ yʌ̋an.*
3SG.EXI RETR faire-NEUT ainsi 1SG.NSBJ yeux.COM
'Cela s'est passé devant mes yeux' (en ma présence).

On trouve également des cas où les constructions avec la marque rétrospective désignent les situations n'ayant pas encore perdu leur actualité, comme dans le cas suivant :

(75) *Bȉaŋgā yɤ̏ kʌ̄ dɔ̏ yāandhíɤ.*
coureur 3SG.EXI RETR savoir\NEUT hier
'Hier le meilleur coureur a été révélé' (et il reste toujours le meilleur).

10) Passé négatif

MPP négative perfective ou imperfective[23] + *kʌ̄* + verbe à la forme de base. La construction rend la valeur négative ponctuelle dans le passé.

(76) *Bhɛ̄n bhá yíi kʌ̄ ȁ gó dhɛ̏ dɔ̄.*
humain certain 3SG.NEG.PST RETR 3SG.NSBJ quitter place savoir
'Personne ne savait d'où il était venu.'

En fait, la différence sémantique entre le passé négatif et le perfectif négatif est minimale, souvent presque non-existante, on trouve les deux constructions dans des contextes absolument identiques :

---

[23] Apparemment, dans cette construction les deux séries des MPP sont absolument équivalentes et interchangeables.

(77) *Pʌ̄ bhá yíi dhēbʌ̀dhʌ́n bhā à kʌ̄, íin*
chose certain 3SG.NEG.PFV femme ART 3SG.NSBJ faire ou
pʌ̄ bhá yíi kʌ̄ à bhà dhʌ́n kʌ̄.
chose certain 3SG.NEG.PFV RETR 3SG.NSBJ POSS enfant faire
'Rien n'arriva à la femme, et rien n'arriva à l'enfant.'

Malgré la présence de la marque retrospective *kʌ̄* dans la construction, elle peut se référer aux situations qui restent actuelles au moment de la parole :

(78) *Dīì yáa kʌ̄ à kún kɤ̀.*
faim 3SG.NEG.IPFV RETR 3SG.NSBJ attraper encore
'Il n'a pas encore faim.'

11) Futur

La construction de l'aspect neutre du verbe auxiliaire *dhɔ̋*[24] 'aller' + l'infinitif du verbe notionnel (marqué d'un ton extra-bas suffixé). Cette construction exprime des modalités différentes du futur : une prédiction, une promesse, une assertion…

(79) *Kɤ̄ kíi ū kɔ̀ yɤ̄ bhān dhʌ́n*
SMLT SMLT.2SG.SBJV 2SG.NSBJ main.CMM voir 2SG.POSS enfant
bhā' bhà, ā dhɔ̀ ū bhàn'.
ART-3SG.NSBJ sur 1SG.EXI aller-NEUT 2SG.NSBJ frapper-INF
'Si tu touches à mon enfant, je te frapperai.'

Précédeé d'une proposition à l'aspect neutre, la construction du futur, suivi de la particule *dhún*, exprime une valeur d'irréel :

(80) *Yɤ̀ bɔ̀ yɤ̄, ā dhɔ̀ kpàn à bhà*
3SG.EXI passer\NEUT ici 1SG.EXI aller\NEUT voir.INF 3SG.NSBJ sur
dhún.
déjà
'S'il était passé ici, je l'aurais vu.'

Négation du futur : le verbe auxiliaire *dhó* se met au négatif perfectif.

(81) *Kɤ̄ kíi (ū) bhā wʌ̀ʌ̀gā dhɛ̀ŋ, bhíin*
SMLT SMLT.2SG.SBJV 2SG.NSBJ POSS argent perdre 1SG.NEG.PFV
dhó' wɛ̋ɛ dhūn'.
aller-3SG.NSBJ autre donner-INF
'Si tu perds ton argent, je ne t'en donnerai pas d'autre.'

[24] Quand ce verbe apparaît en tant qu'un verbe auxiliairaire, sa voyelle se change souvent en ɤ : *dhɤ̋.*

12) Imparfait

Cette valeur s'exprime par la constuction d'apsect neutre du verbe auxiliaire du verbe *gūn* (« être dans le passé ») suivi du verbe notionnel avec le suffixe *–sīʌ* du duratif. L'imparfait rend une action continue ou répétitive qui se déroule simultanément avec une autre action dans le passé, ou tout simplement, une action continuelle dans le passé :

(82)	*Yī*	*zɪ̋ɤ̀ɤ-dhȕn*	*wɔ̏*	*gȕn*	*gèebʌ̏*
	1PL.EXCL.NSBJ	grand-père-PL	3SG.EXI	être.PST\NEUT	fétiche

bhȁ-yɔ́-sīʌ	*yɔ̋n*	*pűu*	*ká.*
surface-enduire-DUR	huile	blanc	avec

'Nos grands-pères huilaient le fétiche avec de l'huile rouge.'

La **négation de l'imparfait** se produit par le remplacement de la MPP existentielle avec la MPP négative imperfective ; le verbe auxiliaire *gūn* garde son ton lexical : *Yī zɪ̋ɤ̀ɤ-dhȕn wáa gūn gèebʌ̏ bhȁ-yɔ́-sīʌ yɔ̋n pűu ká.* 'Nos grands-pères n'huilaient pas le fétiche avec de l'huile rouge.'

13) Continuatif

La formule : le verbe auxiliaire *tȕn* ('être encore') en construction de l'aspect neutre suivi de l'infinitif du verbe notionnel. Cette construction exprime la continuation de l'action ou l'état :

(83)	*Wɔ̋n*	*zīizïdhȅ*	*ɤ́*	*dhɤ̋*	*bhā,*	*yɤ́*	*ɯ́*
	affaire	vieux.SUPINT	REL.3SG.JNT	ainsi	ART	CONS	2SG.JNT

tȕn	*ȁ*	*dhȉaŋ*	*zʌ̄'*	*n̄*	*tőodhɤ̄*	*bhā*	*ȅe?*
continuer\JNT	3SG.NSBJ	parole-IZF	tuer-INF	1SG.NSBJ	oreille.LOC	ART	Q

'Cette affaire qui est tellement ancienne, tu m'en parles encore ?'

(84)	*Yɤ̏*	*tȕn*	*yáȁdhūn'.*
	3SG.EXI	continuer	être.assis-INF

'Il reste assis' (malgré tout).

Pour la négation du continuatif on utilise la MPP imperfective négative :

(85)	*Dhēbʌ̏-dhȕn*	*wáa*	*tȕn*	*kɤ̀ŋ*	*yɪ́*	*ɓȁ-kʌ̄'.*
	femme-PL	3PL.NEG.IPFV	continuer	encore	eau	surface-faire-INF

'Les femmes ne font plus la pêche'.

14) Ultérieur

La construction de l'ultérieur a deux variantes équivalentes.

a) MPP subjonctive + verbe auxiliaire *gūn* + l'infinitif du verbe notionnel + suffixe *–dhȁan*, ou sa forme abrégée *–ŋ̏*.

b) MPP subjonctive + verbe auxiliaire *gūn* + suffixe *–dhȁan* + l'infinitif du verbe notionnel. Dans ce cas, la forme abrégée *–ŋ̏* du suffixe n'est pas admise.

La construction est toujours attestée dans la proposition subordonnée qui suit la proposition principale. Elle désigne une action ultérieure par rapport à l'action de la proposition principale, qui peut se référer au futur, au passé, à l'habituel, ou être à un mode autre que l'indicatif :

(86) *Ȁ bhȁ pʌ̄bhèe yɤ̏ dhȉʌʌ yɤ́*
3SG.NSBJ POSS nourriture 3SG.EXI refroidir\NEUT alors.3SG.SBJV
gūn-dhȁan ȁ bhɤ̏'.
être.PST-SUBS 3SG.NSBJ manger-INF
'C'est quand sa nourriture se refroidit, qu'il la mange.'

(87) *Gbȁtȍ yɤ̏ dhȍ yáȁdhūn kɤ̄ yɤ̏ gūn*
Gbato 3SG.EXI aller\NEUT s'asseoir SMLT 3SG.SBJV être.PST
dhó-ŋ̏.
aller-INF-SUBS
'Gbato s'asseyera avant de partir.'

(88) *Dhűű bhā ȁ tūűn kɤ̄ ȁ bhɛ̏ yɤ̏ gūn*
arbre ART 3SG.NSBJ sécouer SMLT 3SG.NSBJ fruit 3SG.SBJV être.PST
pɤ̏'-ŋ̏.
tomber-INF-SUBS
'Secoue l'arbre jusqu'à ce que ses fruits tombent.'

La deuxième proposition peut être introduite par la conjonction *yɤ́* qui exprime l'idée de séquence des actions ; dans ce cas, la MPP de la deuxième proposition est celle de la série conjointe :

(89) *Yʌ́nŋ̏ yɤ̏ kʌ̄ bhȕȕ dhɛ̋dhɛ̋ plɛ̀ ká, yɤ́ dhā ɤ́*
soleil 3SG.EXI RETR briller heure deux avec CONS pluie 3SG.JNT
gūn bān'-dhȁan.
être.PST\JNT pleuvoir-INF-SUBS
'Le soleil a brillé pendant deux heures, puis la pluie est tombée.'

Il n'y a pas de construction négative analogue de l'ultérieur.

15) Progressif dépendant

Le progressif dépendant n'apparaît que dans une proposition relative subordonnée. La construction a la structure suivante : MPP conjointe + verbe à ton de base + suffixe

–dhȁan (ou sa variante abrégée *-ŋ̏* ou *-ŋ̏*).[25] Le progressif dépendant désigne une action qui se déroule au moment de la parole :

(90) *Dhʌ́n ɤ́ ɯ́ɯ́' gɤ̋n-dhȁan bhā, bhá dhɔ́'*
enfant REL 2SG.JNT-3SG.NSBJ traîner-PROG ART 2SG.PRH aller\INF
ȁ gbȅ bho' bhȁ.
3SG.NSBJ bras enlever-INF-3SG.NSBJ sur
'L'enfant que tu es en train de tirer, ne lui arrache pas le bras !'

(91) *Pʌ̄ dhɛ́ ɤ́ ɯ́ɯ́ dhó-ŋ̏ ȁ ká bhā,*
chose l'autre REL 2SG.JNT aller-PROG 3SG.NSBJ avec ART
ɯ̄ bhā yáa bhȕn.
2SG.NSBJ possession 3SG.NEG.IPFV être
'L'autre chose que tu es en train d'emporter, n'est pas à toi.'

La marque du progressif dépendant s'utilise avec beaucoup de restrictions ; elle s'emploie de fait avec une minorité des verbes. Ainsi, elle ne se conjugue pas avec les verbes *lɔ̄ɔ* 'descendre', *kpʌ̀ŋ* 'secouer', *bhʌ́nŋ* 'avaler', et bien d'autres.

Il n'y a pas de construction négative analogue du progressif dépendant.

16) Impératif

La formule: MPP impérative + verbe à ton de base.

Exprime un ordre ou un souhait. L'impératif ne se conjugue qu'avec les personnes qui incluent la 2ème pers., donc les deux personnes inclusives ainsi que les 2èmes personnes du singulier et du pluriel :

(92) *Kȁ dɔ̄ n̄ gbȁn gɔ̏ !*
2PL.IMP mettre 1SG.NSBJ appui à
'Soutenez-moi!' (aux élections, etc.)

(93) *Kwȁ ȁ tɔ̏ dhʌ́n gbɤ̋n yɛ́ do.*
1PL.INCL.IMP 3SG.NSBJ poulet enfant cuisse casser finalement
'Cassons finalement les pattes du poulet !' (c.-à-d. : finissons l'affaire !).

A la 2e personne du singulier, la MPP peut ne pas être exprimée (« une MPP zéro »), dans ce cas l'ordre a un caractère plus catégorique.

17) Subjonctif

La formule: MPP subjonctive + verbe à ton de base.

[25] Se pose alors la question suivante : est-ce que c'est le même suffixe que dans la construction à valeur d'ultérieur ? Il se peut qu'historiquement ce soit le même morphème (provenant, sans doute, du nom *dhȁan* 'limite'), mais la distribution et les fonctions tout à fait différentes nous obligent à y voir plutôt deux suffixes homonymiques.

Le plus souvent, cette construction est introduite par la conjonction *kɤ̄* (souvent fusionnée avec la MPP suivante). Elle exprime la valeur du but, du devoir, de l'injonction :

(94) *Dhūn kɤ̄ kwá kwā dhı̋dhı̋ dɔ̋ŋ kɔ̋n.*
venir SMLT 1PL.INCL.SBJV 1PL.INCL.NSBJ salive visqueux couper
'Viens, prenons le petit déjeuner'.

(95) *Dɔ̄ n̄ dhɛ̏ gbéɛ̏ káa n̄ bō.*
mettre 1SG.NSBJ devant très SMLT.1SG.SBJV 1SG.NSBJ finir
'Aide-moi bien, pour que je finisse.'

Là où on doit exprimer deux ordres consécutifs, le premier sera à l'impératif, et le second au subjoncitf :

(96) *Dhūn kɤ̄ kwá kwā dhı̋dhı̋ dɔ̋ŋ*
venir SMLT 1PL.INCL.SBJV 1PL.INCL.NSBJ salive substance.visqueuse
kɔ̋n.
couper
'Viens, prenons le petit-déjeuner.'

De la même façon, tout ordre exprimé par une prédication non-initiale de l'énoncé est au subjonctif :

(97) *Yȁ kʌ̄ dhɛ̀ bhá ȁ dhı̋ʌʌ, kı́i dhūn.*
3SG.PRF faire que 2SG.PRF 3SG.NSBJ écraser SMLT.2SG.SBJV venir
'Quand tu l'auras écrasé, viens.'

Là où le subjonctif exprime un ordre indirect, il n'est pas introduit par la conjonction *kɤ̄* :

(98) *Yɤ̏ yáȁndhūn tɔ̀n.*
3SG.SBJV s'asseoir maintenant
'Qu'il s'asseye maintenant.'

18) Subjonctif négatif

La formule : MPP subjonctive négative + verbe auxiliaire *dhó* + l'infinitif du verbe notionnel.[26]

C'est un analogue négatif de l'impératif et du subjonctif. Le subjonctif négatif exprime une interdiction directe ou indirecte.

(99) *Bhá dhó dhīaŋ zʌ̄ n̄ kèɛ̀ tȁ !*
2SG.PRH aller parole tuer 1SG.NSBJ occiput sur

[26] Dans certains cas, le verbe notionnel est employé dans sa forme de base, sans suffixe tonal.

'Ne parle pas dans mon dos !'

(100) *Kɤ̄ dhēbʌ̀dhʌ́n bhā yá dhó ɤ̄ dɛ̀ zʌ̄'...*
SMLT femme ART 3SG.PRH aller REFL.SG même tuer-INF
'Pour que la femme ne se suicide pas...'

19) Subjonctif ultérieur

La formule : Conjonction *kɤ̄* + subjonctif du verbe *gūn* + l'infinitif du verbe notionnel.

Cette construction exprime un ordre qui suit un autre ordre :

(101) *Kwà pʌ̄ bhɤ̀ bhlɛ̀ɛsɯ̀ kɤ̄ kwá gūn*
1INCL.PL.IMP chose manger premier SMLT 1INCL.PL.SBJV être.PST
wē bhūn'.
vin boire-INF
'Mangeons d'abord, avant de prendre du vin.'

20) Irréel (contrefacuel)

La formule de la deuxième proposition (l'apodose) : MPP existentielle + verbe auxiliaire *gūn* 'être dans le passé' (à ton extra-bas) + MPP prospective + verbe notionnel dans sa forme de base. Dans la première proposition (la protase), la présence de la particule *dhún* est obligatoire.

La construction exprime une action hypothétique qui ne peut plus se réaliser, parce que les conditions nécessaires n'ont pas été réunies, et que le moment approprié est passé.

(102) *Gɔ̄ bhā yɤ̀ dɔ́ɔ̀ndhɯ̀n dhún, yɤ̀ gūn*
voiture ART 3SG.EXI s'arrêter\NEUT déjà 3SG.EXI être.PST\NEUT
yɤ̄ɤ kʌ̄ sʌ̀.
3SG.PROS faire bien
'Si la voiture s'arrêtait, cela serait bien.'

Négation de l'irréel. La protase : MPP négative imperfective + *gūn* en forme de base + MPP prospective + verbe notionnel sous sa forme lexicale. A la fin de l'apodose, la particule *dhún* est obligatoire.

(103) *Yà kʌ̄ dhɛ̀ yɤ̀ kɔ̀n ɤ̄ bhā gīzābhɛ́n*
3SG.PRF devenir que 3SG.EXI rater\NEUT REFL.SG POSS examen
ká dhún, kɤ̄ kwáa gūn kwāa dhó
avec déjà que 1PL.INCL.NEG.IPFV être.PST 1PL.INCL.PROS aller
Dándhándhɤ̄ dhīá̄.
Danané demain
'S'il ratait son examen, nous n'irions pas à Danané demain.'

21. Présomptif

La formule: MPP présomptive + opérateur *dhȕn* + verbe en infinitif. La construction exprime les valeurs évidentielles : présomptive (le locuteur fait le jugement en se basant sur ses connaissances de l'ordre des choses et des prémisses), inférentive (le locuteur fait le jugement en se basant sur des indices indirectes) ou probabilitive (le locuteur considère l'évenement comme hautement probable).

(104) *Gwēe yāȁ dhȕn gā'.*
léopard 3SG.PRSM PRSM mourir\INF
'Sans doute, la panthère est déjà morte'.

Négation du présomptif : MPP négatif du passé + opérateur *dhȕn* + verbe en infinitif.

(105) *Gāadɪ̂ɛ̄n yíi dhȕn kō yɤ̄'.*
gardien 3SG.NEG.PST PRSM 1DU.INCL.NSBJ voir\INF
'Sans doute, le gardien ne nous a pas vus'.

22. Séquence négative

La formule de la construction : MPP de séquence négative + verbe auxiliaire *dhó* ~ *dhɤ́* + verbe notionnel en infinitif. Cette construction apparaît dans l'apodose d'une phrase conditionnelle.

(106) *Kɤ̄ ɯ́ɯ́ n̄ gbā wʌ́ʌ̏ ká, bhí dhɤ́*
SMLT 2SG.SBJV 1SG.NSBJ donner argent avec 2SG.NEG.CNS aller
gā'.
mourir\INF
'Si tu me donnes d'argent, tu ne mourras pas'.

3.8.4. Dérivation et composition verbale

3.8.4.1. Préverbes

Le modèle dérivationnel le plus fréquent est l'adjonction des préverbes. La plupart des préverbes sont liés étymologiquement aux postpositions et/ou aux noms à valeur locative :

gɔ̏ nom : 'tête', postposition : 'à, pour', etc., préverbe : *gɔ̏-dɔ̄* 'achever' ;

dhɪ̋ɤ nom : 'bord, sommet', postposition : 'devant ; jusqu'à' ; préverbe : *dhɪ̋ɤ-gɯ̋n* 'attendre', etc.

Dans la langue moderne, ces correspondances sont irrégulières : certaines postpositions n'ont pas de préverbes correspondants, et vice-versa ; il en va de même des correspondances entre préverbes et noms.

Il y a cependant des préverbes qui proviennent de noms à valeur non-locative : *pʌ̄* 'chose' + *kʌ̄* 'faire' → *pʌ̄-kʌ̄* 'réparer', 'fabriquer' ; *dīn* 'goût' + *gȁ* 'regarder' → *dīn-*

gà 'goûter', etc. Il y existe aussi des préverbes qui n'ont pas de correspondances avec des noms ou avec des postpositions : *dhɛ̄ɛ́* (dans *dhɛ̄ɛ́-kpɔ́* 'demander', 'poser question'), *yēe* (dans *yēe-kʌ̄* 'revenir').

Par défaut le préverbe se place immédiatement devant la base verbale :

(107a)	*Gbàtò*	*yà*	*ɤ̄*	*bhā*	*dhēbʌ̀*	*tà-kún.*
	Gbato	3SG.PRF	REFL.SG	POSS	femme	surface-attraper

'Gbato a aidé sa femme.'

Mais la particularité frappante des préverbes en dan de l'Est est leur capacité à être séparés de leurs bases verbales par les éléments divers (les marques prédicatives pronominales, le focalisateur, la marque du pluriel, l'article, des adjectifs...), ce qui laisse cependant intacte leur liaison sémantique avec les bases. Plus précisement, les déterminants et les adjectifs intercalés entre le préverbe et la base portent sur l'ensemble du verbe composé :

(107b)	*Gbàtò*	*yà*	*ɤ̄*	*bhā*	*dhēbʌ̀*	*tà-dhʊ̀n*	*kún.*
	Gbato	PRF	REFL.SG	POSS	femme	surface-PL	attraper

'Gbato a aidé sa femme plusieurs fois', plutôt que *« Gbato a attrapé plusieurs surfaces de sa femme ».

(107c)	*Gbàtò*	*yà*	*ɤ̄*	*bhā*	*dhēbʌ̀*	*tà*	*sɛ̄ɛ́ndhʌ́n*	*kún.*
	Gbato	PRF	REFL.SG	POSS	femme	surface	petit	attraper

'Gbato a un peu aidé sa femme', plutôt que *« Gbato a attrapé la petite surface de sa femme ».

(107d)	*Gbàtò*	*yà*	*ɤ̄*	*bhā*	*dhēbʌ̀*	*tà*	*bhā*	*kún.*
	Gbato	PRF	REFL.SG	POSS	femme	surface	ART	attraper

'Gbato a aidé sa femme de façon préméditée', 'Gbato a aidé sa femme, comme prévu.'

Ces exemples attestent clairement que la liaison des préverbes avec leurs bases verbales est beaucoup plus forte qu'avec les groupes nominaux du complément d'objet direct, ce qui nous permet de considérer les préverbes comme des parties intégrantes des verbes.

3.8.4.2. Dérivation postverbale

Un autre modèle de la dérivation verbale est l'adjonction d'une postposition à droite du radical verbal. Nous n'avons relevé que deux verbes de ce type : *pɛ́* 'se fendre' → *pɛ́-gʊ́* 'diviser' ; *slʌ̄ʌ* 'tourner (virer)' → *slʌ̄ʌ-gʊ́* 'tourner (pivoter)'. Dans la construction résultative, la postposition *gʊ́* peut être séparée (facultativement) de la base verbale par la postposition *ká* (qui fait partie de la construction résultative) :

(108a) *Tɛ́ɛpʌ̀-dhȕn* *wɔ̏* *pɛ́-sȕ* *ká* *à* *gṹ* *yȉisīɤ.*
créature-PL 3PL.EXI fendre-GER avec 3SG.NSBJ dans quatre
'Les créatures animées se subdivisent en quatre groupes.'

On peut dire également :

(108b) *Tɛ́ɛpʌ̀-dhȕn wɔ̏ pɛ́-gṹ-sȕ ká yȉisīɤ.*

Seule la base verbale (*pɛ́, slʌ̄ʌ*) change son ton en aspect neutre.

3.8.4.3. Dérivation en –dhūn

Un petit groupe de verbes (tous à structure CV) désignant des positions du corps produit des formes dérivées selon le modèle suivant : la voyelle de base est redoublée, parfois modifiée et, plus ou moins facultativement, nasalisée ; le ton de la base modifée devient H-eB ou eH-eB ; un élément *–dhūn* est rajouté à droite. Le verbe dérivé désigne le plus souvent un changement de position :

dɔ̄ 'mettre, se mettre ; rester' → *dɔ́ɔ̏ndhūn* 's'arrêter',

wɔ̄ ~ *wɔ̏* 'se coucher, mettre' → *wáȁndhūn, wáȁdhūn* 'se coucher',

yȁ 'être assis, mettre' → *yáȁndhūn, yáȁdhūn* 's'asseoir'.

Dans certains cas, on ne trouve que les verbes « dérivés » et pas de verbe de base correspondant : *gblʌ́ʌ̏dhūn* 'se prosterner', *dháȁndhūn* 'courber (la tête)'.

Dans la construction de l'aspect neutre, seul le ton de la deuxième composante *dhūn* change : *dɔ́ɔ̏ndhȕn, wáȁndhȕn,* etc. Cela nous fait penser que cette composante a pour origine le verbe *dhūn* 'venir' ou son homonyme *dhūn* 'donner', tandis que la composante initiale a pour origine une forme nominalisée du verbe notionnel.

3.8.4.4. Redoublement

En dan-gouèta il y a trois types de redoublement des verbes.

1) **Le redoublement complet** peut exprimer soit la pluralité d'action (l'action qui se reitère), soit la pluralité d'objets, soit la pluralité des acteurs, soit une combinaison des deux.

(109) *Yɤ̏* *bhlȕn* *bhìɤɤ-bhìɤɤ-dhȁan,* *kɛ́ɛŋ* *yáa* *ȁ*
3SG.EXI riz piler~MLTPL-PROG mais 3SG.NEG.IPFV 3SG.NSBJ

flɤ̋.
blanchir

'Elle pilait le riz (une grande quantité) longuement, mais elle ne l'a pas blanchi'.

(110) *Dhʌ́n-dhȕn* *wȁ* *bȉn-bȉn.*
enfant-PL 3SG.PRF cacher~MLTPL
'Les enfants se sont cachés.

Dans la construction de l'aspect neutre ou conjointe, les deux parties d'un verbe redoublé subissent la modification tonale.

(111) *Yȁ* *gèè* *bāȁ-bāȁ.*
3SG.PRF fétiche décorer~MLTPL
'Il a décoré les fétiches.' →

(112) ... *ɤ̋* *gèè* *bàà-bàà.*
3SG.JNT fétiche décorer~MLTPL\JNT
(le même sens, dans une construction conjointe).

Lorsque le redoublement complet concerne un verbe à préverbe, c'est l'ensemble de la forme qui subit le redoublement.

(113) *Yȁ* *ɤ̄* *kɔ̏* *bhȁ-pā-bhȁ-pā.*
3SG.PRF REFL.SG main.CMM sur-laper-sur-laper
'Il a léché sa main' (chaque doigt).

Moins de la moitié de tous les verbes du dan de l'Est subissent le redoublement complet.

2) Le redoublement vocalique (le rallongement de la voyelle), sans modification tonale, exprime l'idée de l'intensité, complétude ou grande durée de l'action.

Pour les verbes à voyelle simple, il s'agit d'une triplication de la voyelle :
gűn 'tirer' → *gűaan* 'tirer avec une force et pendant longtemps'.

La voyelle double devient triple :
gwʌ̀ʌ 'durer' → *gwʌ̀ʌʌ* 'trop durer'.

Dans les verbes à trois voyelles, les deux dernières sont toujours identiques. Le rallongement produit une voyelle finale triple, ex. :

pīɤ̏ɤ 's'enrouler' → *pīɤ̏ɤɤ* 's'enrouler solidement, à beaucoup de tours'.

Si on verbe se termine en *–ŋ,* le redoublement concerne à la fois le *–ŋ* et la voyelle précédente :

dhʌ̀nŋ 'coller' → *dhʌ̀ʌnŋŋ* 'se coller fortement', *klòŋ* 'courber' → *klòoŋŋ* 'courber avec l'effort'.

Les verbes à préverbes ont, le plus souvent, la voyelle de leur préverbe allongée :
dhɛ̄ɛ́-kpɔ́ 'interroger' → *dhɛ̄ɛ́ɛ-kpɔ́* 'interroger avec l'insistance'.

Plus rarement, l'allongement concerne la voyelle de la base verbale :
gúʉ-blɯ̄ɯ̏ 'fouiller' → *gúʉ-blɯ̄ɯ̏ɯ* 'fouiller longuement'.

Les verbes pour lesquels ce type d'allongement vocalique est possible sont relativement peu nombreux.

3) Le redoublement de voyelle accompagné d'une modification tonale concerne un petit groupe de verbes, presque tous de structure CV, à ton extra-haut, souvent à

sémantisme de destruction ou de démembrement. Un seul verbe de ce groupe a une structure ClV, et en même temps un sens différent, c'est *gblʌ̋* 'crier' (de douleur).

Pour presque tous ces verbes, il s'agit du redoublement à valeur d'intensif (parfois accompagné d'une modification sémantique) ; le ton devient Moyen-Extra-bas :

gblʌ̋ 'crier (de douleur)' → *gblʌ̄ʌ̏* 'crier (contre quelqu'un)',

kwʌ̋n 'éplucher' → *kwʌ̄ʌ̏n* 'gratter',

pɛ̋ 'se fendre' → *pɛ̄ɛ̏* 'se fendre partout'.

3.9. Adverbes

3.9.1. La syntaxe des adverbes

Les adverbes déterminent les verbes et, plus rarement, des adjectifs (*pűu pőpő* 'blanc comme la neige').

Ils se caractérisent par leur position à droite du verbe. Si le verbe a un circonstant exprimé par un groupe nominal avec une postposition ou par un nom locatif, la plupart des adverbes peuvent soit le précéder soit le suivre :

(114)	*Yʌ̏*	*dhūn*	*yī*	*gɔ̏*	*pɤ̏dhɤ̄*	*dȅe.*
	3SG.PRF	venir	1PL.EXCL.NSBJ	POSS.LOC	village.LOC	récemment

'Il est venu dans notre village récemment'.

Cette phrase est l'équivalent de *Yʌ̏ dhūn dȅe yī gɔ̏ pɤ̏dhɤ̄.*

Certains adverbes (plutôt une minorité) peuvent être transposés dans la position au début de l'énoncé :

(115)	*Kpɛ̏kpɛ̏wō*	*yī*	*dhʌ̀n*	*ɤ̋'*	*zʌ̄.*
	constamment	sommeil	FOC	3SG.JNT-3SG.NSBJ	tuer\JNT

'Il dort constamment'.

Cette phrase est l'équivalent de *Yī dhʌ̀n ɤ̋' zʌ̄ kpɛ̏kpɛ̏wō.*

3.9.2. Les types morphologiques d'adverbes

Selon leurs formes morphologiques, les adverbes peuvent être divisés en trois groupes :

a) Plus d'une moitié d'adverbes sont des **adverbes à suffixe -*dhɤ̄*** qui sont surtout des adverbes de manière. Étymologiquement, le suffixe *–dhɤ̄* est proche du suffixe du cas locatif des noms locatifs (cf. 3.3.1). On peut supposer que ce suffixe a pour origine une postposition.

b) **Adverbes à suffixe *–wō* ~ *-bhō*,** dérivés d'adjectifs ou de déterminants : *bhá* 'autre' → *bháwō* 'de nouveau' ; *dȅdȅ* 'véritable' → *dȅdȅwō* 'très, véritablement' ; *yāa* 'mauvais ; incomparable' → *yāawō* 'très'. Pour certais adverbes, l'étymologie est incertaine, ex. : *kpɛ̏ɛwō* ~ *kpɛ̏ɛbhō* ‘toujours’ (probablement, de *kpɛ̏ɛ* ‘le reste’), *dhȕnwō* ‘parfois’ (probablement, de *–dhȕn* marque du pluriel). Sans doute, le suffixe provient des « verbes légers » *wō* ‘faire’ et *bhō* ‘enlever’.

c) Adverbes non-suffixés. Certains d’entre eux sont dérivés d’adjectifs par conversion : *dȅe* ‘nouveau’ → ‘récemment’, *gbɛ́ɛ̏* ‘difficile’ → ‘très (difficile, sévère)’, *sʌ̏* ‘bon’ → ‘bien’, etc. D’autres sont originaux : *pɤ́* ‘aussi’, *sìʌ* ‘parfois’, *tɔ̀n* ‘enfin’, *wɛ́ɛ* ‘vainement’, etc.

d) Restricteurs : ils se distinguent des autres adverbes par leur grande mobilité syntaxique. Ils peuvent déterminer les verbes, les adjectifs, les numéraux, les adverbes.

Les restricteurs sont peu nombreux et chacun possède ses propres particularités. *dōsēŋ* ~ *dōsɛ̄nŋ* ‘seulement’ a une forme intensive *dōsēŋsēŋ* et peut déterminer un groupe nominal, un verbe ou un énoncé entier. Dans cette dernière fonction, il a une grande mobilité. Ainsi, dans la phrase suivante, le restricteur peut être placé après *gɔ̏* ou après *dhūn* sans aucune modification du sens :

(116)

Ā	*à*	*dhɛ̏*	*à*	*gɔ̏*	*dōsēŋ*	*kɤ̄*
1SG.EXI	3SG.NSBJ	demander	3SG.NSBJ	à	seulement	SMLT

yɤ̏	*dhūn.*
3SG.SBJV	venir

‘Je lui ai seulement demandé de venir.’

Cela vaut également pour les restricteurs *zʌ̏wō* ‘quant à’, *zȉaanwō* ‘tout un…’, *zɔ̀ɔ* ‘même si, mais comment…’. Ce dernier va de pair avec la particule *wȁ* toujours placée en fin de l’énoncé :

(117)

Wȍ	*kœ̏œŋ*	*dō*	*zɔ̀ɔ,*	*kɛ́ɛ*	*wáa*	*bhɔ̀ɔn*
3PL.EXI	dix	un	mais.comment	mais	3PL.NEG.IPFV	pouvoir

à	*bhà*	*kɤ̄*	*wȍ*	*yʌ̄*	*bhā’*	*kʌ̄*	*wȁ !*
3SG.NSBJ	sur	SMLT	3SG.SBJV	travail	ART-3SG.NSBJ	faire	exactement

‘Ils sont exactement dix, et ils ne peuvent pas faire ce travail !’

Dans cet énoncé, l’élément *zɔ̀ɔ* peut être mis dans la position après *bhɔ̀ɔn,* après *bhā* ou devant *wȁ.*

e) On trouve en dan-gouèta des adverbes composés provenant de la fustion des noms avec des postpositions, ex. *yʌ́ŋ̏gṹ* ‘dans la journée’, *kwɛ̀ŋzṹ* ‘autrefois’.

3.9.3. Adverbes locatifs deïctiques

Le dan-gouèta a cinq adverbes locatifs (qu'on peut considérer comme des pronoms adverbiaux) : *yɤ̄, yā, bhā, bhūn, tȉ̄dhɤ̏* ~ *tȉ̄dhē.* Ils se distinguent (i) par le degré d’éloignement par rapport aux participants de la communication, (ii) par l’indication d’une localisation exacte ou approximative, et (iii) par quelques autres nuances.

1) *yɤ̄* (le ton devient haut, *yɤ́*, lorsque le mot précédent se termine par un ton moyen) indique un endroit près du locuteur ou équidistant du locuteur et de son interlocuteur, dans tous les cas, permettant la visibilité des communicants : *Dhūn yɤ́ !* 'Viens ici !' *Ūl bhā glɛ̄ɛ́ yà yɤ̄.* 'Mets ton sac ici.' *Gó n̄ gɔ̀ yɤ̄ !* 'Fiche le camp ! (litt. : 'Quitte pour moi ici !')

2) *yā* désigne la même position spatiale que *yɤ̄* par rapport aux communicants, la différence entre les deux adverbes est la suivante :

– *yā* indique une position statique, tandis que *yɤ̄* peut également indiquer la direction de mouvement ;

– *yā* n'apparaît que dans les énoncés comportant une focalisation, ce qui n'est pas obligatoirement le cas de *yɤ̄*.

Yā et *yɤ̄* ont développé une fonction qui les rapproche des pronoms demonstratifs :

(118)	*Dhàa*	*ɤ́*	*yā/yɤ̄*	*à*	*súú.*
	couteau	REL.3SG.JNT	ici/ce	3SG.NSBJ	prendre

'Prends ce couteau.'

En fait, la construction *dhàa ɤ́ yā/yɤ̄* 'ce couteau' a la structure d'une phrase relative, « le couteau qui est ici ». Mais le plus souvent, dans la parole, le relativiseur *ɤ́* est omis : *Dhàa yā/yɤ̄ à súú.*

3) *bhā* (change le ton moyen en ton haut lorsque le mot précédent se termine par un ton moyen) indique un endroit près de la personne à qui l'on parle ; que cet endroit soit visible ou invisible pour le locuteur. Tout comme *yā* et *yɤ̄*, *bhā* peut désigner un endroit éloigné des deux interlocuteurs, mais tout de même visible par les deux. La différence réside dans le fait que *yā* et *yɤ̄* sont employés lorsque l'endroit en question peut être montré de la main ou du doigt ; sinon, on emploie *bhā.*

Tout comme *yā* et *yɤ̄*, *bhā* a développé une fonction de pronom démonstratif :

(119)	*N̄*	*bhànwɔ̀n*	*yɤ̀*	*dhàa*	*bhā'*	*bhà.*
	1SG.NSBJ	besoin	2SG.EXI	couteau	là-3SG.NSBJ	dans

'J'ai besoin de ce couteau-là.'

Une évolution ultérieure a amené *bhā* jusqu'à la fonction de l'article défini (voir la division « Déterminants »).

4) *bhūn* (le ton moyen est remplacé par un ton haut lorsque le mot précédent se termine par un ton moyen) a deux emplois principaux :

– désignation d'un endroit connu des locuteurs, mais hors de leur vision ; un endroit qui peut être décrit, mais pas montré du doigt ;

– *bhūn* exprime un mouvement dont le point de départ se trouve près du locuteur, et dont le point d'arrivée est inconnu :

(120) *Bhɤ̀* *ɯ̄ɯ* *bhɤ́* *yɔ̀ɔn* *bhūn !*
2SG.IMP 2SG.NSBJ même bouger là
'Pousse-toi un peu là-bas !'

5) *tı̄ı̀dhɤ̀ ~ tı̄ı̀dhē* désigne un endroit éloigné, à la limite de la sphère de visibilité ou un peu en dehors de cette limite, dont on connait la direction, mais pas la localisation exacte. L'emploi de cet adverbe s'accompagne obligatoirement d'une indication de la main ou du doigt. Une forme intensive *tı̄ıtı́dhɤ̀* renforce davantage l'idée de l'éloignement.

Il y a deux adverbes de correction locative (conjuguée avec une focalisation) qui se combinent forcement avec d'autres circonstants locatifs : *yʌ̀n* donne une localisation plus approximative, et *dhàà̀n* une indication locative plus exacte :

(121a) *Bhɤ̀ dhūn yɤ́ yʌ̀n !* 'Viens ici!' (un espace large entourant le locuteur est sous-entendu).

(121b) *Bhɤ̀ dhūn yɤ́ dhàà̀n !* 'Viens ici!' (un endroit exact, à côté du locuteur est sous-entendu).

3.9.4. Redoublement des adverbes

Beaucoup d'adverbes peuvent être redoublés, ce qui leur donne une valeur d'intensif : *kpɛ̄ɛnŋdhɤ̄* 'complètement, exactement' → *kpɛ̄nŋkpɛ̄nŋdhɤ̄* 'jusqu'à complète satisfaction', *tı̄ı̀dhɤ̀ ~ tı̄ı̀dhē* 'là-bas' (loin) → *tı̄ıtı́dhɤ̀* 'là-bas' (très loin, à peine vu), *zı̄ı* 'depuis longtemps' → *zı̄ı̄ı* 'depuis très longtemps' (l'intensif) → *zı̄kkı́zı̀kı̀* 'depuis très-très longtemps' (le superintensif), etc. Même certains adverbes composés peuvent être redoublés, ex. :

(122) *Tɔ̀* *gɔ̄n* *yɤ̀* *dhɛ̀ɛdhı́ɤ* *bhò*
poulet mâle 3SG.EXI chant.de.coq enlever-NEUT
yʌ́nŋ̀-gúı-yʌ́nŋ̀-gúı
soleil.CMM-dans-soleil.CMM-dans
'Le coq pousse des cocoricos toute la journée (sans cesse).'

Lors du redoublement, des adverbes en *–dhɤ̄* et en *–wō ~ -bhō*, seule la base est répétée, et non pas le suffixe : *zádhɤ̄* 'brusquement' → *zázádhɤ̄* 'vite', *lɛ́ɛdhɤ̄* 'lentement' → *lɛ́ɛɛdhɤ̄* 'très lentement' (l'intensif) → *lɛ́ɛlɛ́ɛdhɤ̄* 'très-très lentement' (le superintenstif) ; *bháwō* 'de nouveau' → *bhábháwō* 'et encore, de nouveau' (l'intensif).

3.10. Déterminants

Un déterminant suit le groupe nominal ; il ne peut pas s'intercaler entre le nom et l'adjectif ou le numéral. Les déterminants constituent une classe fermée, et pourtant, assez hétérogène quant à leur comportement morphologique.

3.10.1. Déterminants à statut pragmatique

Cette sous-classe inclut les focalisateurs *dhʌ̀n* et *dhūn,* le topicalisateur *zʌ̀,* les articles définis *bhā* et *dhɔ̀ɔ,* les pronoms démonstratifs *yā* et *yɤ̄.* Ces déterminants demandent une reprise pronominale (le groupe nominal avec un déterminant de ce type doit être suivi d'un pronom personnel qui réfère à ce groupe ; cependant, ce pronom est souvent élidé en discours) :

(123)	*… yɤ̏*	*gbő*	*bɔ̄-sīʌ*	*kɔ́*	*ɤ́*	*bhā*	***à̏***	*gúı.*
	3SG.EXI	pleurs	passer-DUR	maison	REL.3SG.JNT	ART	3SG.NSBJ	dans

'… il pleure dans la maison'…

Les constructions avec ces déterminants (sauf probablement *zʌ̀*) ont sans doute pour origine des propositions relatives, et ces déterminants proviennent des adverbes.

Le déterminant pronominal interrogatif *bhɛ̏ɛn* 'quel ? lequel ?' est proche de ce groupe, mais sa reprise pronominale semble être lexicalisée (elle dépend du contexte).

3.10.2. Déterminants quantificateurs[27] et autres

Les autres déterminants n'exigent pas de reprise pronominale. Ils ont chacun des caractéristiques propres, par exemple :

— *bhá* 'un certain' ; 'aucun' (avec la négation) ; 'autre'.[28] À la différence des autres déterminants, *bhá* peut être suivi de la marque du pluriel : *Dhēbʌ̀ bhá-dhʉ̀n wà̏ dhūn.* 'Certaines femmes sont venues.' La position de la marque du pluriel peut varier modifiant le statut pragmatique du groupe nominal : s'il suit le déterminant *bhá,* le groupe nominal est « faiblement déterminé » (le locuteur connaît les femmes, mais il pense que son interlocuteur ne les connaît pas). Si la marque du pluriel se met entre le nom et *bhá,* le statut du groupe nominal est indéterminé : *Dhēbʌ̀-dhʉ̀n bhá wà̏ dhūn.* 'Des femmes / quelques femmes sont venues.'

— *gbàn* 'tous', 'tout, entier', 'chaque'. Ce déterminant fusionne régulièrement avec le pronom 3SG.PRF : *gbàn + yà̏ → gbàan.* Il se combine souvent aussi avec l'adverbe *pɛ̋pɛ̋* pour rendre les sens 'tout' et 'chaque' :

(124)	*Dhɛ̀*	*ɤ́*	*pʌ̄*	*gbàn*	*pɛ̋pɛ̋*	*dhūn*	*dhēbʌ̀dhʌ́n*	*dhɛ̏…*
	que	3SG.JNT	chose	tout	chaque	donner-JNT	femme	devant

'Lorsqu'il a donné toutes les choses à la femme…'

[27] Pour l'analyse détaillé des déterminants quantificateurs, voir (Vydrin 2017).

[28] Il y existe en dan-gouèta un adjectif *wɛ̋ɛ* dont le sens est très proche de *bhá,* mais qui se distingue de *bhá* par son comportement syntaxique. En particulier, *wɛ̋ɛ* peut s'intercaler entre un autre adjectif et un nom, ce qui n'est pas possible pour *bhá.*

Pour rendre le sens « tous », on peut placer la marque du pluriel *-dhȕn* entre le nom et le déterminant *gbàn,* mais cette marque est facultative : *Dhūn tɔ̏-dhȕn gbàn ká* ou *Dhūn tɔ̏ gbàn ká* 'Apporte tous les poulets.'

— *dè* 'même' (« correcteur des attentes de l'adressé »). Le pronom personnel qui va avec ce déterminant apparaît sous sa forme contrastive :

(125) *Bhāŋŋ dè pɤ́, bhán pɛ̀nŋ dhɔ́.*
1SG.CNTR même aussi 1SG.PRF aubergine acheter
'Moi aussi, j'ai acheté des aubergines.'

D'autres déterminants : *bhɤ̋* 'même', *bhɤ̋dhʌ́nbhá* 'un peu', *dèbɤ̋ɤ* 'même ; exactement', *dèe, dɛ̏dɛ̏* 'même', *dō* 'un, certain', *dódó* 'peu nombreux ; rares ; certains ; différents', *dhʌ̀n ~ dhūn* — marqueur de la focalisation contrastive, *dhʌ́nbhá* 'un peu', *dhɛ́* 'l'autre' (d'un paire d'objets), *gbɛ̋ŋ* 'seulement' (avec des numéraux)', *kɛ̋ɛ* 'peu', *sēŋ* 'seulement' (avec des numéraux).

3.11. Postpositions

Les postpositions marquent des relations syntaxiques, le plus souvent entre le verbe et un groupe nominal subordonné ; plus rarement, entre des noms (ou des groupes nominaux).

Les postpositions expriment, avant tout, des localisations spatiales dont leurs autres sens peuvent être dérivés. Les postpositions en dan (à la différence des prépositions françaises) ne distinguent pas la position statique du mouvement en direction ou de la provenance d'un lieu ; ces différences sont normalement exprimées par les verbes :

(126) *Dhűu yȁ yȁ dhāŋ̏ bhȁ.*
nuage 3SG.PRF mettre ciel sur
'Les nuages ont couvert le ciel.'

(127) *Ā bɔ̀bɪ̏ bhɔ̏ gblɔ̀o bhȁ.*
1SG.EXI poussière enlever\NEUT siège sur
'J'essuie la poussière du siège.'

(128) *Gbȁtɔ̀ yɤ̏ dūn-sīʌ bhɪ̄ʌ́ bhȁ.*
Gbato 3SG.EXI suspendre-DUR corde sur
'Gbato est suspendu à une corde.'

La relation étymologique de la plupart des postpositions avec des noms (le plus souvent, des noms des parties du corps) est évidente.

Voici la liste des postpositions dan-gouèta, avec de brèves indications de leurs sens[29] :

[29] Pour leur sémantisme plus détaillé, voir le Dictionnaire. Les équivalents français présentés ici ne le reflètent que très approximativement.

bhà̰ 'sur', *bhàa* 'à' (l'eau)' ; 'chez' ; *dhɛ̰̀* 'devant', 'à' ; *dhɪ̰́ɤ* 'devant, en face de, avant' ; *gɔ̰̀* 'à', 'pour' ; *gṹ* 'dans', *ká* 'avec', 'par', etc. ; *kèŋ̰̀* 'après', *kósɔ̀n* 'à cause de', *kɔ̄ɔ, kœ̄œ* 'par' ; *pɪ̰́ɤ* 'chez', *plɤ̀ɤ* 'chez', *sòòtà̰* 'à califourchon', *sɔ̰́ɔ* 'à côté de', *súgṹ* 'pour', 'au profit de', *tà̰* 'sur' ; *tàa* 'sur' ; *tàabhà̰n* 'derrière, après' ; *wlɤ̀ɤ* 'sous', *zìnŋgṹ* 'entre', *zlɤ̀ɤ* 'derrière', 'au dela', *zṵ̀* 'autour de'.

Cinq postpositions ont des formes redoublées à valeur d'intensif ou de pluralité qui porte sur le verbe ou sur un de ses arguments (une action multiple ; la pluralité des objets ; une intensité de l'action...) : *kèŋ̰̀kèŋ̰̀* 'après', *pɪ̰́ɤpɪ̰́ɤ* 'chez', *sɔ̰́ɔsɔ̰́ɔ* 'près de', *tàaabhà̰* (l'intensif), *tàatá̰bhà̰n* ou *tàaatá̰bhà̰* 'derrière', *zṵ̀zṵ̀* 'autour de'.

3.12. Conjonctions

Les conjonctions marquent des relations syntaxiques entre les propositions, et aussi, la relation de coordination, entre les groupes nominaux.

bhàn ~ bhān 'et' est relativement rare en dan de l'Est, pour exprimer la coordination on utilise beaucoup plus les pronoms coordinatifs, voir 3.5. D'ailleurs, cette conjonction peut se combiner avec les pronoms coordinatifs.

dhɛ̰̀ est une conjonction polyfonctionnelle qui apparaît a la fin de la proposition principale (précédant une proposition subordonnée) et qui introduit une proposition complément, temporelle ou comparative.

dhɪ̰́n 'si' (emprunté aux langues mandingues) introduit une proposition conditionnelle ou explicative.

... dhɤ̰́, ... dhɤ̰́ 'et ... et' lie des groupes nominaux formant une énumération (là où il s'agit d'une liste fermée), avec une nuance distributive :

(129) *Yɔ̰̀ dhɤ̰́, Zân dhɤ̰́, Gbà̰tò̰ dhɤ̰́, wà̰ dhūn.*
Yo et Jean et Gbato et 3PL.PRF venir
'Yo, Jean et Gbato sont venus' (un à un).

L'élément *dhɤ̰́* a sans doute pour origine le verbe d'existence *dhɤ̰́*.

dhɤ̰́dhɤ̰́ 'jusqu'à ce que' introduit une proposition temporelle et exige la construction conjointe.

ɛ̰́ɛ̀n, ɛ́ɛn 'sinon', exprime une hésitation.

ɪ̰́n 'ou' lie des propositions coordonnées mais pas des groupes nominaux.

kɛ̰́ɛ ~ kɛ̰́ɛŋ 'mais', 'bien que' exprime les valeurs adversative ou concessive, parfois il introduit une proposition de précision. Elle peut être attestée avec les conjonctions *yɤ̰́* et *kɤ̰̄*.

kɤ̄ est une conjonction polyvalente (elle peut marquer une relation de subordination ou de coordination) à valeur générale de simultanéité, mais elle peut aussi exprimer d'autres valeurs grammaticales, en particulier, le but. Cette conjonction fusionne facultativement avec les marques prédicatives singuliers de la série subjonctive : *kɤ̄ á* → *káa* 'pour que je...', *kɤ̄ ɯ́* → *kíi* 'pour que tu...', *kɤ̄ ɤ́* → *kɤ́ɤ* 'pour qu'il...'. Elle peut également fusionner avec les MPP prospectives.

kɤ́ 'même si' lorsque le verbe de la proposition est dans la construction prospective ou celle de l'aspect neutre ; 'avant que' lorsque le verbe de la proposition est dans la construction subjonctive ; 'même quand' lorsque le verbe de la proposition est dans la construction du parfait.

kɤ̄dhɤ́ 'pour que ne...', une conjonction négative de but, qui exige la construction conjointe.

kʌ̀dhɤ́kɤ̄ 'pour que' introduit une proposition de but où le verbe est dans la construction subjonctive (affirmative ou négative).

ő̋o lie des groupes nominaux ou leurs composantes en exprimant une valeur universelle : 'quel que soit...', 'tout ...'.

... ōo, ... ōo 'et ... et' lie des groupes nominaux en énumération non-exhaustive :

(130) *Yàobâ-dhɯ̀n wɔ̀ dhɛ̀ gbàn pɛ̋pɛ̋ gɯ́ : Bîyà-dhɛ̀ ōo,*
Yacouba-PL 3SG.EXI place tout chaque dans Abidjan-CMM et
Sɛ̋nŋpedloo-dhɛ̀ ōo, Dɛ̋lő̋a-dhɛ̀ ōo, wɔ̀ bhɯ̄n.
San-Pedro-CMM et Daloa-CMM et 3SG.EXI là
'Il y a des Yacouba partout : à Abidjan, à San-Pedro, à Daloa...'

ɤ́, plus rarement *kɤ́* introduit une proposition relative.

ɤ́ introduit une proposition à valeur temporelle de simultanéité. Dans beaucoup de contextes, cette conjonction est facultative.

pāsɤ́ 'parce que' (un emprunt au français), introduit une proposition subordonnée de cause.

sɛ̋ndhìn 'avant de', 'au lieu de' (emprunté aux langues mandingues).

yɤ́ 'et', 'alors' exprime une idée de séquence, il fusionne facultativement avec les pronoms singuliers de la série conjointe : *yɤ́ á* → *yáa, yɤ́ ɯ́* → *yíi, yɤ́ ɤ́* → *yɤ́ɤ*.

3.13. Particules phrastiques

Les particules se placent à la fin de la proposition et expriment des valeurs modales : *ɛ̀e* une question générale, *wà* un étonnement désagréable ou une affirmation insistante, *dhɛ́* un étonnement positif, *wɛ́* une irritation ou surprise, *āa* 'eh bien' (une impulsion), *sá* 'quand même' (une concession), etc.

3.14. Interjections

Interjections ont une valeur holophrastique étant des mots équivalents des énoncés. Ils se subdivisent en :

a) mots modaux, comme *ìì* 'oui', *ȁbɪ̋n* 'non', *ɯ̋ɯn* 'non' (familier), *áabhōo* 'non' (respectueux), *ȁòo* 'oui!' (réponse à une salutation),

b) interjections propres, comme *ɛ̋kɛ̋* 'hélas!', *yàá* 'tiens!', *yɤ̋* 'mais comment ?!', *kpȁ̋sȁ̋kpōsō* 'oh-là-là!', etc.

3.15. Pronoms non-personnels

Les pronoms non-personnels en dan-gouèta ne constituent pas une partie de discours spécifique. C'est un groupe de mots embrayeurs qui se distribuent sur différentes parties de discours, selon leurs caractéristiques syntaxiques : *dē* 'qui ?' et *bhʌ̀n* 'quoi ?' sont des noms, *kó* 'l'un l'autre' est un nom locatif, *dhɛ̀* 'combien ?' est un numéral, *bhɛ̏ɛn* 'quel ? lequel ?' est un déterminant, *bhɛ́n* 'où ?' est un adverbe. Les noms *bhɛ̄n* 'personne' et *pʌ̄* 'chose' remplissent un rôle proche du rôle des pronoms indéfinis. Il y a deux « pro-verbes », ou verbes postiches, *wō* et *bhō*, qui se substituent au verbe notionnel lors de sa focalisation ou topicalisation.

4. Éléments de syntaxe

Dans cette section, on se limitera à la présentation des constructions nominales et des énoncés simples. L'étude des phrases complexes n'est pas traitée dans cette esquisse grammaticale dont le but est plutôt de donner un aperçu des bases de la grammaire dan de l'Est.

4.1. Types de construction nominales

4.1.1. Construction génitivales sans connecteur

Cette construction est composée de deux noms (le premier pouvant être remplacé par un pronom), en suivant l'ordre déterminant déterminé. La construction a deux variantes : « simple », lorsque la relation entre les deux noms est directe (non-marquée), et « à ton extra-bas » lorsque le ton lexical de la deuxième composante est remplacé par le ton extra-bas. La différence entre les deux variantes n'est pas stricte, elle peut être formulée en termes de tendances :

a) lorsque la relation entre les membres de la construction sont du type « partie – tout », il s'agira plutôt de la construction « simple », et lorsque cette relation désigne l'objet entier, on utilisera la construction à ton extra-bas : *bāa dhɯ̋ɯ̋* <manioc arbre> 'tige de manioc' et *bāa dhɯ̏ɯ̏* (← *dhɯ̋ɯ̋*) 'plante de manioc' ; *bīɤ sɔ̋n* <éléphant dent> 'défense d'éléphant' et *bīɤ wɯ̏ɯ̏* (← *wɯ̄ɯ̄*) <éléphant viande> 'viande d'éléphant, corps d'éléphant' ;

b) les noms de sens plus générique sont plus aptes à porter un ton extra-bas en position de détarminé dans le syntagme génitival, cf. : *tòo pʌ̏* <tô chose>'plat du « tô »' (une pâte malaxée) et *bhlɯ̏ɯn wɛ̋ŋ* <riz gerbe> 'gerbe de riz' ;

c) l'abaissement du ton du déterminé de la construction génitivale peut être en relation avec la position de la construction dans l'énoncé, il s'agit donc des facteurs rythmiques.

4.1.2. Construction génitivale à connecteur

La construction à connecteur (une postposition liant les deux noms) est beaucoup moins fréquente dans les textes que la construction sans connecteur : *bȕu bhȁ tɤ́ŋ* <harmattan sur temps>'le temps de l'harmattan'.

Une **construction possessive** peut être considérée comme une variante de la construction génitivale à connecteur. Par défaut, c'est la postposition *bhȁ* qui sert de connecteur :

(131) *Yɔ̏ bhȁ kɔ́* 'maison de Yo'.

Et si la construction possessive apparaît dans la position du circonstant locatif, le connecteur est le plus souvent *gɔ̏.*

(132)	*Yȁ*	*gbʌ̀gā*	*dɔ̄*	*ɤ̄*	*gɔ̏*	*bhláā.*
	3SG.PRF	ratière	mettre	REFL.SG	POSS.LOC	champ.LOC

'Il a mis une ratière sur son champ.'

4.1.3. Construction attributive

La construction attributive est composée d'un nom (qui n'est que rarement remplacé par un pronom) et d'un adjectif. Un nom peut être déterminé par deux adjectifs (ou plus), dans ce cas, leur position relative est indifférente : *gbɛ̂n tīi wɛ́ɛ* égale *gbɛ̂n wɛ́ɛ tīi* 'autre chien noir'. Par contre, les déterminants sont, eux, toujours postposés à l'adjectif : *gbɛ̂n tīi bhá* 'autre chien noir' (**gbɛ̂n bhá tīi* est impossible).

La marque du pluriel *–dhȕn* peut suivre le nom, l'adjectif ou les deux (cf. 3.2.2).

4.1.4. Construction superlative

La construction superlative se compose de deux noms identiques connectés par une postposition (*tȁ, bhȁ* ou *gúʉ́*) ; le ton lexical du deuxième nom est, le plus souvent, remplacé par l'extra-bas.

Il y a deux types pour cette construction :

– pour les noms à valeur numérique, avec la postposition *tȁ*: *kʌ̄ŋ tȁ kʌ̀ŋ* 'des centaines', *glűʉ̄ tȁ glȕʉ̀* 'des milliers' ;

– pour quelques termes de parenté, l'insertion des postpositions *bhȁ* ou *gúʉ́* sert à spécifier le degré élevé d'éloignement du parent par rapport à Ego : *zláȁ bhȁ zlȁa* 'frère cadet/sœur cadette qui suit Ego par-dessus un', *zláȁ bhȁ zláȁ bhȁ zlȁa* 'frère cadet/sœur cadette qui suit Ego par-dessus deux autres' ; *zíɤ̏ɤ gúʉ́ zíɤ̏ɤ gúʉ́ zȉɤɤ* ou *zíɤ̏ɤ bhȁ zíɤ̏ɤ bhȁ zȉɤɤ* 'trisaïeul, arrière-arrière-grand-père'.

4.1.5. Construction nominale coordinative

Cette construction est formée avec les pronoms personnels coordinatifs (voir 3.5.) et/ou avec la conjonction *bhān* ~ *bhȁn*. Un pronom coordinatif peut relier deux noms ou deux groupes nominaux :

(133)	*Bhán*	*zē*	*tīi*	*wāȁ*	*zē*	*zœ̏œndhē*	*dhɔ́.*
	1SG.PRF	haricot	noir	3SG.et	haricot	rouge	acheter

'J'ai acheté des haricots noirs et rouges.'

Une construction nominale coordonnée peut être séparée par un verbe, de façon à ce que sa deuxième composante, avec le pronom coordinatif, soit reportée à droite du verbe : *Bhán zē tīi dhɔ́ wāȁ zē zœ̏œndhē.* (même sens que l'énoncé précédent).

4.2. Types d'énoncés non-verbaux[30]

4.2.1. Énoncé d'identification

Ce type d'énoncé correspond aux formules suivantes :

a) Sujet + copule *bhȕn* (quand l'objet ou la personne en question est hors de la vue des interlocuteurs) ou bien

(b) Sujet + copule *bhā* (quand elle est visible).

Le sujet peut être exprimé par un groupe nominal (sans reprise pronominale) ou par un pronom personnel de la série autonome : *N̄ dʌ̄ bhȕn.* 'C'est mon père' (qui a fait l'action en question); *Yɤ̄ bhā.* 'C'est lui' (celui dont on a parlé). Dans un énoncé présentatif négatif, le sujet est forcement suivi par une MPP imperfective négative : *Bhɔ̏ɔn yáa bhȕn.* 'Ce n'est pas une souris.' L'équivalent négatif de l'énoncé d'identification à *bhā* est un énoncé verbal : *Yɤ̄ yáa kʌ̄ dhɤ̋.* 'Ce n'est pas lui / Ce n'est pas ça.'

Dans l'énoncé équatif, la copule *bhȕn* est suivie d'un complément d'objet indirect construit avec la postposition *ká* : *Bhlʌ̀ʌgúbhɛ̏n bhȕn Gbȁtȍ ká.* 'Gbato est une personne respectable.'

La valeur équative peut également être exprimée par un énoncé à MPP existentielle avec la postposition *ká,* cf.:

(134)	*Dūī*	*wɔ̏n*	*yɤ̏*	*tǣæ̏n*	*ká.*
	sorcier	affaire\IZF	être	verité	PP

'La sorcellerie est une chose vraie' (le même sens que *Tǣæ̏n bhȕn dūī wɔ̏n ká*).

[30] Les types d'énoncés non-verbaux en dan de l'Est sont analysés en détail dans (Vydrin 2020b).

4.2.2. Énoncé présentatif

L'énoncé présentatif est formé avec la copule *dhɛ̀n* et concerne un objet (ou d'une personne) qui est dans la zone de visibilité des deux interlocuteurs : *Yī̀ dhʌ́n tɔ̀tàabhàn dhɛ̀n* 'Voici notre benjamin.' Le sujet peut être exprimé par un pronom de la série autonome : *Yɤ̄ dhɛ̀n.* 'Le voici.' Ce type d'énoncé n'a pas d'analogue négatif.

4.2.3. Énoncé locatif

L'énoncé locatif répond à la formule (Sujet) MPP Circonstant. La MPP appartient à la série existentielle ou conjointe pour l'affirmatif, et à la série imperfective négative, pour le négatif. Le Circonstant peut être représenté par un adverbe ou un groupe nominal muni d'une postposition ou comportant un nom locatif :

(135) *Ā* *n̄* *flʌ́ʌ̀* *gúú.*
1SG.EXI 1SG.NSBJ santé dans
'Je suis en bonne santé.'

(136) *Bhān* *kɔ́* *yɤ̀* *tī̀dhɤ̀.*
1SG.POSS maison 3SG.EXI là-bas
'Ma maison est là-bas.'

À part les valeurs purement locatives, l'énoncé locatif exprime de nombreux autres sens (possession, état psychophysique, etc.).

4.2.4. Énoncé qualitatif

La formule est : (Sujet) MPP + Adjectif. La MPP est de la série existentielle ou conjointe pour l'affirmatif, et de la série imperfective négative, pour le négatif : *Slʌ̀ʌ yɤ̀ dhɪ́ɤ̀ɤ.* 'Le piment est piquant.' *Yáa klɤ́ɤklɤ̀.* 'Il n'est pas en bonne santé.'

4.3. Énoncé verbal

L'ordre des mots de base est : (Sujet) – MPP – (Complément d'objet direct) – Prédicat verbal – Oblique. Dans le cadre de l'énoncé verbal, les valeurs dynamique et statique peuvent être exprimées, et même la valeur existentielle :

(137) *Dūū-bhɛ̀n-dhʉ̀n* *bhà* *víɔŋ̀* *yɤ̀* *dhɤ̀.*
sorcier-personne\IZF-PL POSS avion 3SG.EXI être
'Il existe un avion des sorciers.'

Références

Green, Christopher R. 2015. The foot domain in Bambara. *Language* 91(1). e1–e26.

Kuznetsova, Natalia. 2007. Le statut fonctionnel du pied phonologique en gouro. *Mandenkan* (43). 13–45.

Leben, William R. 2002. Tonal feet. In Ulrike Gut & Dafydd Gibbon (eds.), *Proceedings, typology of African prosodic systems* (Bielefeld Occasional Papers in Typology 1), 27–40. Bielefeld.

Makeeva, Nadezhda. 2017. Kla-dan jazyk (Кла-дан язык) [Kla-Dan]. In Valentin Vydrin, Yulia Mazurova, Andrej Kibrik & Elena Markus (eds.), *Jazyki mira: Jazyki mande (Языки мира: Языки манде) [Languages of the world: Mande languages]*, 617–679. St. Petersburg: Nestor-Historia.

Vydrin, Valentin. in print. Featural foot in Bambara. Ms.

Vydrin, Valentin. 2001. Jazyki mande i teorija jazykov slogovogo stroja (Языки манде и теория языков слогового строя) [Mande languages and the theory of syllabic languages]. In *VI mezhdunarodnaja konferencija po jazykam Dal'nego Vostoka, Jugo-Vostochnoj Azii i Zapadnoj Afriki (25-27 sent'abr'a 2001). Materialy i tezisy dokladov (VI-я международная конференция по языкам Дальнего Востока, Юго-Восточной Азии и Западной Африки (25-28 сентября 2001 г.): Материалы и тезисы докладов) [VI International conference on languages of Extreme Orient, South-Eastern Asia and Western Africa (September 25-27 2001). Proceedings]*, 45–53. St. Petersburg: Vostochnyj fakultet SPbGU.

Vydrin, Valentin. 2011. Déclinaison nominale en dan-gwèètaa (groupe mandé-sud, Côte-d'Ivoire). *Faits de langues: Les Cahiers* 3. 233–258.

Vydrin, Valentin. 2017. Quantifiers in Dan-Gwɛɛtaa (South Mande). In Denis Paperno & Edward L. Keenan (eds.), *Handbook of quantifiers in natural language* (Studies in Linguistics and Philosophy 97), vol. 2, 203–280. Springer.

Vydrin, Valentin. 2020a. The neutral aspect in Eastern Dan. *Language in Africa* 1(1). 93–108. https://doi.org/10.37892/2686-8946-2020-1-1-83-108.

Vydrin, Valentin. 2020b. Non-verbal predication and copulas in three Mande languages. *Journal of West African Languages* 7(1).

Vydrine, Valentin. 2007. Les adjectifs en dan-gwèètaa. *Mandenkan* 43. 77–103.

Vydrine, Valentin. 2010. Le pied métrique dans les langues mandé. In Franck Floricic (ed.), *Essais de typologie et de linguistique générale. Mélanges offerts à Denis Creissels*, 53–62. Lyon: ENS Éditions. http://halshs.archives-ouvertes.fr/halshs-00715537.

Weidman, Scott & Sharon Rose. 2006. A Foot-Based Reanalysis of Edge-in Tonal Phenomena in Bambara. In Donald Baumer, David Montero & Michael Scanlon (eds.), *Proceedings of the 25th West Coast Conference on Formal Linguistics*, 426–434. Somerville, MA.

Publications sur la langue dan

Bearth, Thomas & Hugot Zemp. 1967. The phonology of Dan (Santa). *Journal of African Languages* 6(1). 9–29.

Bolli, Margrit. 1976. *Etude prosodique du Dan (Blossé)* (Publications conjointes I.L.A.-S.I.L. 1). Abidjan: Institut de linguistique appliquée - Société Internationale de Linguistique.

Bolli, Margrit. 1978. Writing tones with punctuation marks. *Notes on Literacy* 23. 16–18.

Bolli, Margrit. 1980a. Progress in literacy in Yakouba country. *Notes on Literacy* 31. 1–6.

Bolli, Margrit. 1980b. Yacouba literacy report II: March 1977-February 1979. *Notes on Literacy*. 31.

Bolli, Margrit. 1983. The Victor Hugoes in Dan country: Developing a mother-tongue body of literature in a neoliterate society. *Journal of reading* 27(1). 16–21.

Bolli, Margrit. 1991. Orthography difficulties to be overcome by Dan people literate in French. *Notes on literacy* 65. 25–34.

Bolli, Margrit & Eva Flik. 1970. Yakouba dialect survey report. https://www.sil.org/resources/search/language/dnj.

Bolli, Margrit & Eva Flik. 1973. *Phonological statement: Dan (Blossé)*. Abidjan: SIL.

Bolli, Margrit, Eva Flik & John Bendor-Samuel. 1972. Testing the mutual intellegibility of dialects: Yacouba dialect survey. In *10th West African Languages Congress, 21-27 March, 1972*. Accra.

Doneux, Jean. 1968. *Esquisse grammaticale du Dan* (Documents Linguistiques 15). Université de Dakar. Dakar.

Dunah, Menmon-Paul Z. 2001. *Dan gɛ̃gbã kwi. Plema 1 / The Dan primer 1*. Monrovia: Liberian Bible Translation and Literacy Organization.

Erman, Anna. 2002. Субъектные местоимения в дан-блово и модально-аспектно темпоральные значения [Les pronoms subjectifs en dan-blowo et le sémantisme modal, aspectuel et temporel]. In Valentin Vydrin & Alexander Zheltov (eds.), *Южные манде: Лингвистика в африканских ритмах. Материалы петербургской экспедиции в Кот д'Ивуар. К 50-летию Константина Позднякова [The South Mande Languages: Linguistics in African Rhythms. To the 50th anniversary of Konstantin Pozdniakov]*, 154–182. St. Petersburg: European Space Publishers.

Erman, Anna. 2005a. Повелительное наклонение в языке дан-бло [La mode impérative dans la langue dan-blowo]. In Vera I. Podlesskaya (ed.), *Четвёртая Типологическая Школа. Ереван, 21-28 сентября 2005*, 364–368. Moscow: Russian State University for the Humanities.

Erman, Anna. 2005b. Le grammaticalisateur -ga en dan-blo. *Mandenkan* 41. 41–61.

Erman, Anna. 2008. Тональная система языка дан-бло [Le système tonal de la langue dan-blo]. In : *Африканский сборник – 2007 [Collection africaine – 2007]*, 345–354. St. Petersburg: Museum of Anthropology and Ethnography.

Erman, Anna. 2009. Условные конструкции в языке дан-бло [Les constructions conditionnelles en dan-blo]. In Valentin Vydrin (ed.), *Африканский Сборник - 2009 [Collection africaine – 2009]*, 372–390. St. Petersburg: Museum of Anthropology and Ethnography.

Erman, Anna. 2012. Прогрессив в дан-бло [Le progressif en dan-blo]. *Acta Linguistica Petropolitana. Труды института лингвистических исследований* 7(2). 648–661.

Erman, Anna & Japhet Kahoué Loh. 2008. *Dictionnaire Dan–Français (dan de l'Ouest) avec un index français-dan*. St Pétersbourg: Nestor-Istoria.

Flik, Eva. 1977. Tone glides and registers in five Dan dialects. *Linguistics* 201. 5–59.

Flik, Eva. 1978. Dan tense-aspect and discourse. In Joseph E. Grimes (ed.), *Papers on discourse*, 46–62. Dallas, Texas: Summer Institute of Linguistics.

Griffes, Kenneth E. 1959. *A start in Gio*. Hartford, Connecticut.

Griffes, Kenneth E. & William E. Welmers. 1960. *Gio. Structural studies and pedagogical materials*. Hartford, Connecticut.

Grossmann, Rebecca & Samuel Cooper. 2012. Dan Sociolinguistic Survey.

Halaoui, Nazam, Kalilou Téra & Monique Trabi. 1983. *Atlas des langues mandé-sud de Côte-d'Ivoire*. Abidjan: I.L.A.

Latahn, Tii Tonah & Maarten Bedert. n.d. Dan grammar. An elementary introduction to the Karnplay dialect.

Lauber, Edward. 1983. The indigenisation of literacy in Dan (Yacouba). *Notes on Literacy* 37. 16–21.

Makeeva, Nadezhda. 2008a. Фонологическая система кла-дан [Le système phonologique du kla-dan]. In *Африканский сборник – 2007 [Collection africaine – 2007]*, 331–344. St. Petersburg: Nauka.

Makeeva, Nadezhda. 2008b. Morphologie des pronoms personnels en kla-dan. In Valentin Vydrin (ed.), *Mande languages and linguistics. 2nd International Conference, St. Petersburg (Russia), September 15-17, 2008. Abstracts and Papers*, 104–112. St. Petersburg.

Makeeva, Nadezhda. 2009a. Глагольная редупликация в языке кла-дан [Le redoublement verbal en kla-dan]. In Valentin Vydrin (ed.), *Африканский сборник – 2009 [Collection africaine- 2009]*, 332–371. St. Petersburg: Museum of Anthropology and Ethnography.

Makeeva, Nadezhda. 2009b. Модификации в языке кла-дан [Modifications en kla-dan]. In : *Исследования по языкам Африки [Études des langues africaines]*, 196–210. Moscow: Institute of Linguistics.

Makeeva, Nadezhda. 2010a. Pronoms réfléchis en kla-dan. In *Personal pronouns in niger-kongo languages. International workshop. St. Petersburg, September 13-15, 2010. Abstracts and papers working materials*, 70–78. St. Petersburg: St. Petersburg State University.

Makeeva, Nadezhda. 2010b. Сопряжённые конструкции в языке кла-дан [Les constructions conjointes en kla-dan]. In Victor Vinogradov (ed.), *Основы африканского языкознания. Синтаксис именных и глагольных групп [Fondements de la linguistique africaine : La syntaxe des groupes nominal et verbal]*, 401–412. Academia. Moscow.

Makeeva, Nadezhda. 2011a. Актантная деривация и лабильность глагола в кла-дан [La labilité et la dérivation Lability and valency-changing derivation in Kla-Dan]. In Nikolaj Kazanskiy & Valentin Vydrin (eds.), *Mandeica Petropolitana II* ACTA LINGUISTICA PETROPOLITANA. Труды Института лингвистических исследований РАН [ACTA LINGUISTICA PETROPOLITANA. Actes de l'Institut des études linguistiques] VII), vol. 2. St. Petersburg: Nauka.

Makeeva, Nadezhda. 2011b. Отрицательные конструкции в языке кла-дан *(Le monde mandé: К 50-летию В. Ф. Выдрина. Материалы экспедиции в Западную Африку (2001–...)) [*Constructions négatives en kla-dan. In: *Le monde mandé : Papers presented to Valentin Vydrin on the occasion of his 50th birthday. Materials of the field trips to West Africa (2001-...)]*, 122–131. St. Petersburg: Nestor-Istoria.

Makeeva, Nadezhda. 2011c. Превербные глаголы в языке кла-дан [Verbes à préverbes en kla-dan]. *Voprosy filologii* 3 (39). 45–56.

Makeeva, Nadezhda. 2012a. Стратегии релятивизации в языке кла-дан [Stratégies de relativisation en kla-dan]. In Alexander Ju. Zheltov (ed.), *Африканский сборник – 2011 [Collection africaine – 2011]*, 231–252. St. Petersburg: Nauka.

Makeeva, Nadezhda. 2012b. *Грамматический строй языка кла-дан в типологическом контексте родственных языков [Le système grammatical du kla-dan dans le contexte typologique des langues prochement apparentées]*. Moscow: Institut de linguistique. Thèse de doctorat.

Makeeva, Nadezhda. 2013a. Категория числа в языке кла-дан [La catégorie du nobre en kla-dan]. In *Человек и язык в коммуникативном пространстве [L'homme dans l'espace communicatif]*, 361–366. Krasnojarsk: Siberian Federal University.

Makeeva, Nadezhda. 2013b. Коммуникативные стратегии и коррелятивная конструкция в языке кла-дан и других южных манде [Les stratégies communicatives et la construction corrélative en kla-dan et autres langues mandé-sud]. *Voporsy jazykoznanija* (1). 77–94.

Makeeva, Nadezhda. 2013c. Les préverbes en kla-dan. *Mandenkan* 50. 85–102. https://doi.org/doi:10.4000/mandenkan.254.

Makeeva, Nadezhda. 2013d. Система утвердительных глагольных конструкций в языке кла-дан [Les constructions verbales affirmatives en kla-dan]. In *Исследования по языкам Африки*, 126–158. Moscow: Kl'uch-S.

Makeeva, Nadezhda. 2013e. Условные конструкции в языке кла-дан [Constructions conditionnelles en kla-dan]. In Alexander Zheltov (ed.), *Collection africaine - 2013*, 377–395. St. Petersburg: Musée d'Anthropologie et Ethnographie.

Makeeva, Nadezhda. 2014. Таксисные конструкции в языке кла-дан [Les constructions du taxis en kla-dan]. In Valentin Vydrin & Natalia Kuznetsova (eds.), *От Бикина до Бамбалюмы, из варяг в греки. Экспедиционные этюды в честь Елены Всеволодовны Перехвальской*, 161–176. St. Petersburg: Nestor-Istoria.

Makeeva, Nadezhda. 2015. Грамматические заимствования из языков манден в языке кла-дан [Emprunts grammaticaus kla-dan au mandingue]. In Alexander Zheltov (ed.), *Африканский сборник – 2015 [Collection africaine — 2015]*, 465–476. St. Petersburg: Museum of Anthropology and Ethnography.

Makeeva, Nadezhda. 2016. Уступительные конструкции в языке кла-дан [Les constructions concessives en kla-dan]. In Victor Vinogradov, Antonina Koval, Maria Kosogorova & Andrey Shluinsky (eds.), *Исследования по языкам Африки 6 [Études des langues d'Afrique 6]*, 178–194. Moscou: Kliutch-S.

Makeeva, Nadezhda. 2017a. Кла-дан язык [Kla-Dan]. In Valentin Vydrin, Yulia Mazurova, Andrej Kibrik & Elena Markus (eds.), *Языки мира: Языки манде [Langues du monde: les langues mandé]*, 617–679. St. Petersburg: Nestor-Historia.

Makeeva, Nadezhda. 2017b. Conjonctions de taxis en kla-dan. *Mandenkan* 48. 47–67.

Makeeva, Nadezhda. 2018. Marques rétrospectives en kla-dan. *Mandenkan* 60. 123–147.

Piper, Klaus. 1983. Das qualifikative System im Gio (Dan). In Reiner Vossen & Ulrike Claudi (eds.), *Sprache, Geschichte und Kultur in Afrika. Vorträge, gehalten auf dem III. Afrikanistentag, Köln, 14./15. Oktober 1982*, 113–124. Hamburg: Helmut Buske Verlag.

Roberts, David, Dana Basnight-Brown & Valentin Vydrin. 2019. Marking tone with punctuation: Orthography experimentation and reform in Eastern Dan (Côte d'Ivoire). In Yannis Haralambous (ed.), *Graphemics in the 21st Century /gʁafematik/. Brest, June 13–15, 2018. Proceedings*, 315–349. Brest: Fluxus.

Roberts, David, Ginger Boyd, Johannes Merz & Valentin Vydrine. 2020. Quantifying written ambiguities in tone languages: a comparative study of Elip, Mbelime and Eastern Dan. *Language Documentation and Conservation* 14. 108–138.

Sternstein, Martin. 2008. Mathematics and the Dan culture. *The Journal of Mathematics and Culture* 3(1). 1–13.

Van den Avenne, Cécile. 1998. Partage de territoire : coexistence du français et des autres langues locales dans une ville ivoirienne. In A. Queffélec (ed.), *Le français en Afrique francophone - Recueil d'étudesofferts en hommage à Suzanne Lafage*, 311–318. Paris: Didier Erudition.

Vydrin, Valentin. 2005a. Средства выражения прагматических статусов в дан-гуэта (Кот д'Ивуар) [Modes d'expression des statut pragmatiques en dan-gouèta (Côte d'Ivoire)]. In Vera I. Podlesskaya (ed.), *Четвёртая Типологическая Школа. Ереван, 21-28 сентября 2005 [La 4e École typologique. Erevan, Septembre 21-28, 2005]*, 117–125. Erevan.

Vydrin, Valentin. 2005b. Терминология родства и свойства в дан-гуэта (Кот д'Ивуар) [Terminologie de parenté en dan-gouèta (Côte d'Ivoire)]. In Valentin Vydrin, David I. Raskin, Valentina G. Uzunova, Sevir B. Chernetsov & Juruj K. Chistov (eds.), *Ad hominem. Памяти Николая Гиренко [Ad hominem. In memoria Nikolaj Girenko]*, 41–66. St. Petersburg: Muzej antropologii i etnografii RAN (Kunstkamera).

Vydrin, Valentin. 2006. Личные местоимения в южных языках манде [Pronoms personnels dans les langues mandé-sud]. In Nikolaj Kazanskiy (ed.), *Mandeica Petropolitana.* ACTA LINGUISTICA PETROPOLITANA. Труды Института лингвистических исследований РАН [Acta Linguistica Petropolitana. Transaction of the Instiute for linguistic studies] II (2)), 327–413. St. Petersburg: Nauka. https://alp.iling.spb.ru/static/alp_II_2.pdf.

Vydrin, Valentin. 2007. South Mande reconstruction: Initial consonants. In Anna V. Dybo, Vladimir A. Dybo, Oleg A. Mudrak & George S. Starostin (eds.), *Aspects of comparative linguistics* (Orientalia et Classica. Papers of the Institute of Oriental and Classical Studies XI), vol. 2, 409–498. Moscow: Russian State University for the Humanities.

Vydrin, Valentin. 2009a. Negation in South Mande. In Norbert Zyffer & Erwin Ebermann (eds.), *Negation Patterns in West African Languages and Beyond*, 223–260. John Benjamins. http://halshs.archives-ouvertes.fr/halshs-00715534.

Vydrin, Valentin. 2009c. Areal features in South Mande and Kru languages. In Norbert Zyffer & Georg Ziegelmeyer (eds.), *When languages meet: Language contact and change in West Africa*, 91–116. Rüdiger Köppe Verlag. Köln: Norbert Cyffer, Georg Ziegelmeyer.

Vydrin, Valentin. 2009d. Превербы в языке дан-гуэта [Préverbes en dan-gwèètaa]. *Voporsy jazykoznanija* (2). 75–84.

Vydrin, Valentin. 2011a. Déclinaison nominale en dan-gwèètaa (groupe mandé-sud, Côte-d'Ivoire). *Faits de langues: Les Cahiers* 3. 233–258.

Vydrin, Valentin. 2011b. Идиом дан-гуэта [Le Dan-Gouèta]. In Vadim Kasevich (ed.), *Грамматика и семантика восточного текста: Квантитативные характеристики [La grammaire et le sémantisme du texte oriental: Les caractéristiques quantitatives]*, 100–113. St. Petersburg: St. Petersburg State University.

Vydrin, Valentin. 2012. Аспектуальные системы южных манде в диахронической перспективе [Les systèmes aspectuels des langues mandé-sud dans une perspective dyachronique]. In Vladimir Plungian (ed.), *Исследования по теории грамматики. Выпуск 6: Типология аспектуальных систем и категорий [Studies in the theory of grammar. Iss. 6: Typology of aspectual systems and categories]* ACTA LINGUISTICA PETROPOLITANA. Труды Института лингвистических исследований РАН [ACTA LINGUISTICA PETROPOLITANA. Transactions of the Institute for Linguistic Studies] 8 (2)), 566–647. St. Petersburg: Nauka.

Vydrin, Valentin. 2013. Согласование местоименного предикативного показателя с подлежащим в дан-гуэта [L'accord de la marque prédicative avec le sujet en dan-gouèta]. In Alexander Zheltov (ed.), *Африканский Сборник — 2013) [Collection africaine — 2013]*, 263–285. St. Petersburg: Muzej antropologii i etnografii RAN (Kunstkamera).

Vydrin, Valentin. 2016a. Tonal inflection in Mande languages: The cases of Bamana and Dan-Gwɛɛtaa. In Enrique L. Palancar & Jean Léo Léonard (eds.), *Tone and Inflection: New facts and new perspectives* (Trends in Linguistics Studies and Monographs 296), 83–105. De Gruyter — Mouton.

Vydrin, Valentin. 2017a. Дан язык [Dan]. In Valentin Vydrin, Yulia Mazurova, Andrej Kibrik & Elena Markus (eds.), *Языки мира: Языки манде [Langues du monde: Les langues mandé]*, 469–583. St. Petersburg: Nestor-Historia.

Vydrin, Valentin. 2017b. Quantifiers in Dan-Gwɛɛtaa (South Mande). In Denis Paperno & Edward L. Keenan (eds.), *Handbook of quantifiers in natural language* (Studies in Linguistics and Philosophy 97), vol. 2, 203–280. Springer.

Vydrin, Valentin. 2020a. Dan. In Reiner Vossen & Gerrit Dimmendaal (eds.), *The Oxford Handbook of African Languages* (Oxford Handbooks), 451–462. Oxford: OUP.

Vydrin, Valentin. 2020b. The neutral aspect in Eastern Dan. *Language in Africa* 1(1). 93–108. https://doi.org/10.37892/2686-8946-2020-1-1-83-108.

Vydrin, Valentin & David Roberts. 2019. Tonal oral reading errors in the orthography of Eastern Dan (Côte d'Ivoire). *Nordic Journal of African Studies* 28(1). 1–28.

Vydrine, Valentin. 2007. Les adjectifs en dan-gwèètaa. *Mandenkan* 43. 77–103.

Vydrine, Valentin & Mongnan Alphonse Kességbeu. 2008. *Dictionnaire Dan-Français (dan de l'Est) avec une esquisse de grammaire du dan de l'Est et un index français-dan*. St. Petersburg: Nestor-Istoria. http://halshs.archives-ouvertes.fr/halshs-00715560.

Zemp, Hugot. 1971. *Musique dan : La musique dans la pensée et la vie sociale d'une société africaine*. Paris – La Haye: Mouton.

Zhang, Jie. 2001. *The effects of duration and sonority on contour tone distribution - typological survey and formal analysis*. Los Angeles: University of California Ph.D. dissertation.

Introduction au
Dictionnaire dan de l'Est – français

1. Vocabulaire

1.1. Dialectes

Comme le dialecte de Gouèta (Gwɛ̋ɛ̏tàa) (gw) sert de base à la norme standard du dan de l'Est, c'est ce dialecte qui est représenté dans le Dictionnaire. Cependant, des mots provenant des autres dialectes de la zone orientale sont occasionnellement inclus (surtout ceux qui sont connus des habitants du canton de Gouèta). Ces formes sont dotées de marques dialectales :

(l) – dialecte de Logoualé
(m) – dialecte de Man
(t) – dialecte de Biankouma Tɛ̋ɛ̏
(tp) – village de Tokpapleu (Gwɛ̋ɛ̏tàa)

1.2. Morphèmes grammaticaux

Les morphèmes grammaticaux non-autonomes (qu'ils soient collés ou écrits avec un trait d'union en orthographe) figurent dans le Dictionnaire comme des entrées à part :

-sīʌ *mrph suffixe verbal du duratif; exprime les valeurs dynamiques ou statives*
-dhɛ̏ 3 *mrph marque du nom verbal*

2. Structure de l'entrée

2.1. Entrée principale et entrées de référence

Pour les mots ayant des variantes phonologiques en dialecte gouèta, toutes les variantes sont représentées dans le Dictionnaire. Par ex. :

sɯ́ɯ, sí 1 *vt* prendre ; 2 *vt* effectuer…

Les variantes phonologiques de statut secondaire sont également introduites dans l'ordre alphabétique comme des « entrées de renvoi » :

sí → sɯ́ɯ *prendre*

De la même façon, les formes relevant des paradigmes morphologiques (formes intensives et plurielles des adjectifs et des adverbes ; cas obliques des noms locatifs) sont recensées par ordre alphabétique avec renvoi à l'entrée principale.

2.2. Homonymes

Les homonymes sont distingués par des chiffres qui suivent immédiatement la forme principale de l'entrée :

kpȁ 1 *vt* **faire bouillir**
kpȁ 2 *n* **arbuste** *(esp.)*

Les homonymes lexico-grammaticaux (c'est-à-dire les mots appartenant aux parties de discours différentes, liés par des relations de conversion) sont dotés des chiffres suivis d'une parenthèse, p.ex. :

gbɛ́ 1) *adj* **grand ; nombreux**
gbɛ́ 2) *adv* **beaucoup**

2.3. Parties du discours

Chaque lexème est doté d'une désignation indiquant la partie du discours, dont voici la liste :

adj – adjectif
adv – adverbe
conj – conjonction
cop – copule
dtm – déterminant
itj – interjection
loc.n – nom locatif
mpp – marque prédicative pronominale
n – nom
num – numéral
pp – postposition
prev – preverbe
pron – pronom personnel
prt – particule
restr – restricteur
v – verbe

Les lexèmes appartenant aux différentes parties du discours ont leur particularités syntaxiques et/ou morphologiques, leurs modèles d'inflexion (segmentale ou tonale).

Les morphèmes non-autonomes, *mrph,* sont pris en considération au même titre que les parties du discours.

2.3.1. Verbes

2.3.1.1. Tous les verbes sans exception changent leurs tons au registre extra-bas dans la construction de l'aspect neutre ; cette forme n'est pas signalée dans le dictionnaire.

Par contre, les modifications tonales des verbes dans la construction « conjointe » ne sont pas toujours prévisibles, et même là où elles le sont, elles sont conditionnées par des règles assez compliquées. Les formes verbales à ton modifié dans la construction « conjointe » sont systématiquement incluses dans le Dictionnaire et mentionnées en {accolades}, à l'exception des verbes aux tons lexicaux bas et extra-bas, qui ne changent jamais de tons :

kā̏ 1 {kàa} *v* 1.1. 1) *vt* **gratter** *(corps)...*
blȕ̈ *v* 1 *vt* pousser ...

2.3.1.2. Pour chaque sens du verbe, son schéma de valence est indiqué. Il s'agit, avant tout, de présence ou d'absence du complément d'objet direct :

vi – verbe intransitif (sans complément d'objet direct)
vt – verbe transitif (avec un complément d'objet direct)
vr – verbe réfléchi (le complément d'objet direct est représenté par un pronom co-référent au sujet, donc un pronom de 1ère ou 2ème personne par un pronom réfléchi).

Le verbe peut avoir pour chaque sens deux ou trois sous-sens qui ne se distinguent que par leurs valences, par exemple :

dūn *v* **1** 1) *vi* **être suspendu ; se suspendre ;** 2) *vt* **suspendre ;** 3) *vr* **se pendre**

Les autres valences verbales sont également indiquées de la façon la plus claire possible. En règle générale, la postposition dan figure entre parenthèses, accompagnée de la préposition française correspondante :

dhű̍ɤɤ {dhùɤɤ} *vt* **priver qn** *(de – gúɩ́)*
gó {gō} *vt* **vendre** *(à – gɔ̏, pour – bhȁ)*

Si l'équivalent français est construit avec une préposition à laquelle ne correspond pas de postposition dan, cela veut dire que le complément d'objet indirect français correspond au complément d'objet direct en dan. Si, par contre, un complément d'objet direct français correspond à un complément d'objet indirect en dan, celui-là est désigné par *qn* (pour les animés) ou par *qch* (pour les inanimés) :

gbā 1 {gbā} *v* **1** *vt* **donner à** *(qch – ká) ...*
gbɔ̏ɔn *v* **1** *vi* **fatiguer** *(qn – tȁ)*

2.3.1.3. Les verbes à préverbes (préfixes détachables), selon les règles de l'orthographe dan de l'Est (2014), sont écrits avec un trait d'union. Ils apparaissent dans le dictionnaire :

tà̰-kún *vt* **aider**

En même temps, les préverbes sont donnés dans le Dictionnaire comme des entrées à part :

yēe *prev* **retour** *m*

2.3.2. Noms

2.3.2.1. Le pluriel est régulièrement marqué par une marque clitique *–dhȕn.* Il y a très peu de noms en dan gouèta qui ont des formes plurielles irrégulières. Les formes irrégulières sont présentées entre accolades avec une marque {pl. …} :

dhēbʌ̀ *n* {pl. dhēbʌ̀-dhȕn, dhōo-dhȕn, dhōŋ–dhȕn} *la deuxième et la troisième forme du pl. ne sont utilisées que dans quelques expressions figées* **femme** *f*

2.3.2.2. Certains noms changent leur ton lexical à un ton extra-bas en position finale d'une construction génitivale, ce ton sert marqueur du statut syntaxique (« izafet») du nom principal (cf. 4.1.1 de l'Esquisse de grammaire). Il s'agit surtout des noms à sens générique. Pour ces noms, leurs formes à ton modifié sont signalées entre accolades :

tɛ́ɛ 1) {tɛ̏ɛ} *n* **1 vent** *m*…

En dan gouèta quelques rares noms à valeur générique (*bhɛ̄n* 'personne', *pʌ̄* 'chose', *yī* 'jour') changent leur ton lexical moyen en un ton haut losqu'ils sont relativisés. La forme à ton haut est également indiquée dans les accolades, avec une marque « REL » :

bhɛ̄n {bhɛ̏n; bhɛ́n REL} *n* **humain** *m*

(Dans ce cas, la première forme entre les accolade, *bhɛ̏n,* et celle de l'izafet, et la deuxième, *bhɛ́n,* est une forme relativisée.)

3.3.2.3. Dans le dictionnaire, les noms relationnels (cf. « Esquisse de grammaire », 3.2.1) sont dotés d'une désignateur *rn.* Pour les noms libres (aliénables), il n'y aucune marque (sauf quelques cas spéciaux ; dans ces cas, la marque est *fn*).

Si un nom a plusieurs sens, il peut être relationnel dans certains de ses sens, et libre dans d'autres :

gèe *n* **1** *rn* **cadavre** *m* ; **2 masque** *m*

L'opposition des noms relationnels et libres n'est valable en dan que par rapport aux possesseurs humains. Pour cette raison les noms ou les sens des noms utilisés seulement pour les « possesseurs non-humains » ne sont pas marqués *rn.*

2.3.3. Noms locatifs

2.3.3.1. La forme principale (lemma) des noms locatifs est celle du cas commun. Les formes attestées de cas obliques sont mentionnées entre accolades.

kɔ́ɔdhɛ̏ {LOC kɔ́ɔdhɤ̄, LOC INT kɔ́ɔkɔ́ɔ, SUP kœ́œ̏, kɔ́ɔ̏, IN kɔ́ɔ̄} *n.loc* **maison** *f*

En outre, les formes des cas obliques (sauf celles qui ne se distinguent de la forme du cas commun que par le ton) figurent dans le dictionnaire à titre d'entrée de référence :

kɔ́ɔ̏ *SUP de* kɔ́ɔdhɛ̏ *maison*

2.3.3.2. D'habitude, le pluriel se dérive régulièrement des formes du cas commun (par une simple adjonction de la marque clitique *–dhʉ̏n*, comme pour les noms). Par contre, les formes des cas obliques des noms locatifs n'ont que rarement la forme du pluriel, ce qui rend nécessaire leur représentation dans le Dictionnaire :

zīaan {AD zī̏aan, AD pl. zīaantȁdhɛ̏-dhʉ̏n gʉ́ʉ} *n.loc* **route** *f*

2.3.3.3. Les noms locatifs, comme les noms, se subdivisent en relationnels (*rn*) et noms libres :

bhɛ̄ɛ́dhɛ̏, bhǣǣ́dhɛ̏ {LOC bhɛ̄ɛ́dhɤ̄, bhǣǣ́dhɤ̄, IN bhɛ̄ɛ́, bhǣǣ́; SUP bhœ̄œ̏} *loc.n rn* **cou** *m*, **gorge** *f*

bhláȁdhɛ̏ {LOC bhláā} *loc.n* **champ** *f*

2.3.4. Adjectifs

2.3.4.1. Beaucoup des adjectifs ont des formes irrégulières de l'intensif et/ou du pluriel (cf. « Esquisse de grammaire », 3.6). Ces formes sont présentées dans l'entrée principale entre accolades, accompagnées des indications de leur valeur : pl. (pluriel), foc. (forme focalisée), Int (intensif), SupInt (super-intensif), ExtInt (extra-intensif). Les contextes syntaxiques accessibles pour chaque forme sont indiqués comme suit : A (attributif), P (prédicatif), S (prédicatif à postposition *ká*). Par exemple :

pʉ̋u {A P S, pʉ̋u-dhʉ̏n pl. A, pʉ̋u-sʉ̏ foc. A S, pʉ̋u-sʉ̏-dhʉ̏n foc. pl. A; pʉ̋pʉ̋ Int. pl. A P S, pʉ̋pʉ̋-dhʉ̏n Int. pl. A S, pʉ̋pʉ̋-sʉ̏ Int. pl. foc. A S, pʉ̋pʉ̋-sʉ̏-dhʉ̏n Int. pl. Foc. A S; pʉ̋upʉ̋u SupInt pl. A P S, pʉ̋upʉ̋u-dhʉ̏n SupInt pl. A S, pʉ̋uu ExtInt} *adj* **blanc**

Toute forme dérivée (excepté les formes dérivées par des clitiques) figure dans le dictionnaire à sa place alphabétique à titre d'entrée de référence :

pʉ̋pʉ̋ *Int. pl. de* pʉ̋u *blanc*

2.3.4.2. Tous les adjectifs dérivés sont recensés dans le Dictionnaire, y compris ceux dérivés par le moyen des suffixes peu productifs *–dhē* et *–sǜ.*

2.3.5. Pronoms personnels et marques prédicatives pronominales

Toutes les formes pronominales sont recensées dans le Dictionnaire, avec l'indication de leurs caractéristiques grammaticales.

2.4. Polysémie

Un mot peut avoir plusieurs sens. Les sens sont ordonnés selon leur proximité sémantique et séparés par des chiffres arabes :

gblű̋ 1 *n* **1 panier** *m* **pour noix de cola** *(rectangulaire ou rond, pour plus de 100 noix)* **2 mille** *m*

Lorsque les sens sont nombreux, ils sont présentés selon une hiérarchie exprimée par une numérotation décimale :

dȁ *v* **1** 1) *vi* **monter** *(sur – bhȁ)* 2) *vt* **monter 2.1** *vt* **porter** *(vêtement)* **2.2** *vt* **mettre** *(machette sur la manche) ...*

2.5. Présentation du sens

Chacun des sens d'un mot dan de l'Est est représenté, autant que possible, par son équivalent français. Le genre grammatical est indiqué pour les noms français (*f* pour féminin, *m* pour le masculin ; *fpl* et *mpl* pour le pluriel féminin et le pluriel masculin). Là où l'équivalent français n'est pas exact (ce qui est souvent le cas), il est complété par un commentaire en italiques et entre parenthèses précisant le sens du mot dan. Des commentaires servent également à désambiguïser un éventuel équivalent français polysémique :

dȕɛɛ *n* 1 *rn* place *f (surtout par référence à des objets verticaux)*
bhádhɤ̄ *adv* au vol *(attraper)*

Des commentaires culturels sont présentés entre crochets :

bű̋kʌ̄bhȅn, blű̋kʌ̄bhȅn *n* **chasseur** *m [les Dan de Gwɛɛtaa n'ont pas d'associations de chasseurs]*

Les noms des plantes et des animaux, là où l'identification des espèces a été faite, sont accompagnés de leurs noms scientifiques (latins) en gras italique. Pour l'identification, les ouvrages suivants ont été utilisés :

Arbonnier, M. *Arbres, arbustes et lianes des zones sèches d'Afrique de l'Ouest.* Paris-Montpellier : CIRAD–MNHN, 2002 (2ème éd.), 573 p.

Boorman, J. *West African insects.* London : Longman Group, 1981, 88 p.

Cansdale, G.S. *West African snakes.* London : Longman Group, 1961/1978, 74 p.

Chippaux, J.-Ph. *Les serpents d'Afrique occidentale et centrale.* Paris : Édition de l'IRD, 2001, 292 p.

Kingdon, J. *The Kingdon field guide to African mammals.* London-San Diego : Academic Press, 1997, 465 p.

Reed, W. et al. *Fish and fisheries of Northern Nigeria.* Zaria : Gaskiya Corporation, 1967, 226 p.

Reed, W. & Holden, M. *West African freshwater fish.* London : Longman Group, 1972, 68 p.

Reshetnikov Yu. et al. Dictionary of animal names in five languages : Fishes. Moscow : Russky Yazyk Publishers, 1989, 734 p.

Serle, W. & Morle, G.J. *Les oiseaux de l'Ouest africain.* Paris, Delachaux et Niestlé, Neuchâtel, 1979, 331 p.

Villiers, A. *Les serpents de l'Ouest African.* Dakar : INAN, 1963, 187 p.

Je remercie beaucoup le botaniste Alexey Oskolsky qui m'a aidé avec l'identification de certaines plantes.

2.6. Marques stylistiques

Les indications stylistiques ou se référant de façon générale à l'usage sont en italique et en police différente. Lorsqu'une désignation syntaxique porte sur le mot dan, elle se trouve devant l'équivalent français. Au cas où elle caractérise l'équivalent français, elle suit ce dernier :

dhēzőo *rn resp.* **sœur** *f* **aînée** *(dans le sens classificatoire : sœur aînée propre ; fille de frère du père ou de la sœur cadette de mère plus âgée qu'Ego ; sœur cadette du père ; forme d'adresse utilisée par rapport à la sœur aînée initiée)*

(La marque *resp.* indique qu'en dan, le mot *dhēzőo* appartient au régistre respectueux.)

sȉɤ̏ *m* **querelle** *f*, **palabre** *m Iv.*

(La marque *Iv.* indique que *palabre* est un mot de la variante ivoirienne du français.)

Liste des désignations stylistiques, ou se référant aux usages spécialisés

Afr. – français africain
anat. – terme anatomique
arch. – archaïque
badin – mot badin
bot. – mot botanique
chass. – terme des chasseurs
chr. – mot ou expression utilisé(e) dans la pratique et la littérature chrétienne

euph. – terme euphémique
ext. – par extension
fam. – familier
gros. – grossier
hist. – historique
imagé – mot/expression imagé
iron. – ironique
Iv. – français ivoirien
neol. – néologisme
pej. – péjoratif
rare – rare
resp. – mot respectueux
rude – mot rude
rur – mot rural
vulg. – mot vulgaire
!!! – obscène

2.7. Relations sémantiques.

Les relations sémantiques entre les sens des mots dan sont indiquées par des renvois mutuels :

Ant. – antonymes
HPnym – hyponymes
HRnym – hypéronymes
Qsyn. – quasi-synonymes
Syn. – synonymes

Les référents, avec leurs marques respectives, suivent la description du sens (donc l'équivalent ainsi que les commentaires sémantiques et culturels).

bɤ̏ɤ *n* **pâte** *f (d'arachide, de banane plantain) Syn.* kɔ̏n

kāibhân *n* **machette** *f,* **coupe-coupe** *m (à lame étroite et longue, de la fabrication industrielle) HRnym* bâ̋ŋ

2.8. Les tournures phraséologiques et collocations

Les expressions figées sont précédées de la marque ♦. Elles sont introduites à la suite de la description du sens particulier que leur usage évoque. Toutefois, dans les cas où elles n'entretiennent de rapport particulier avec aucun des sens énumérés à propos d'un mot, elles sont introduites à la fin de l'entrée.

Certaines composantes des expressions figées peuvent varier. Dans le Dictionnaire, ces variantes sont séparées par une barre oblique. Ex.:

♦ *yà kwɛ̀ɛ̏ sṹ ɤ̄ gwìnŋ̄/gwìnŋ̄dhɤ̄* elle porte le bagage sur sa tête

Cela veut dire que les expression *yà kwɛ̀ɛ̏ sṹ ɤ̄ gwìnŋ̄* et *yà kwɛ̀ɛ̏ sṹ ɤ̄ gwìnŋ̄dhɤ̄* sont équivalentes.

Il y existe également des expressions dont une composante est facultative. Cette composante est présentée en accolades, ex. :

♦ *zīaan klȍo{gā}* sentier

Cela signifie que les expressions *zīaan klȍogā* et *zīaan klȍo* sont équivalentes.

Par l'économie, des expressions du même type peuvent être présentées de la façon que les parties différentes sont données entre les crochets, ex. :

♦ *ä bhä wūn yɤ̏ lȍo ä bhɔ̄ pɤ̋ [ä gbān tä, ä kpȍŋ dhɤ̋]* ses cheveux lui atteignent le cou [les épaules, le front]

Cela est équivalent à la présentation complète :

♦ *ä bhä wūn yɤ̏ lȍo ä bhɔ̄ pɤ̋* ses cheveux lui atteignent le cou ♦ *ä bhä wūn yɤ̏ lȍo ä gbān tä* ses cheveux lui atteignent les épaules ♦ *ä bhä wūn yɤ̏ lȍo ä kpȍŋ dhɤ̋* ses cheveux lui atteignent le front

2.9. Les exemples illustratifs

Les exemples illustratifs sont présentés immédiatement à la suite de la description du sens particulier ou de l'expression figée dont ils servent à illustrer l'usage. Elles sont précédées de la marque ◊.

A a

ȁ 1 ***prn*** *souvent omis, le ton extra-bas se rattache alors au mot précédent* **1 le, la, son, sa** *pronom non-sujet de la 3e pers. sg.* **2** *précédant le nom : article défini situatif (l'objet n'est pas mentionné directement, mais son statut défini ressort du contexte général) Qsyn. bhā 1, dhɔ̀ɔ* ◊ *dhɛ̀ á lòo bhūn yɤ́ ȁ Zȕzȕgwɛ̏ ɤ́' pɤ̄...* lorsque j'y suis venu, ce Zouzougwè-là a dit...

ȁ 2 → bhȁ 2 *connecteur possessif*

ā ***mpp*** **je** *MPP existentiel de la 1re pers. sg.*

á 1 ***mpp*** **je** *MPP de la 1re pers. sg. de la série conjointe*

á 2 ***mpp*** **je** *MPP de la 1re pers. sg. de la série subjonctive*

a̋ ***intj*** **ah !** *(exclamation traduisant une forte émotion)* ◊ *a̋, bhɛ́n bhā, yɤ̏ kʌ̄ dɤ̄ŋ dhɪ̏ɤ !* ah, cet homme-là, il savait tendre des pièges !

â ***intj*** **1 et voilà 2 comment ? !** *interjection d'étonnement*

ȁa̋ ***intj*** **ce n'est pas grave** *(on cherche à dissiper les doutes de l'interlocuteur, on l'invite à ne pas s'inquiéter)*

āa, **àa** ***prt*** **1 eh bien** *exprime une injonction* ◊ *pʌ̄ yȁagā ɤ́ dhɔ̀ɔ bhá' gbàn pɛ́ɛ dȁ kwʌ́ʌ̏ āa, yɤ́ ɯ́ dhō yíi zā dhī' ká* eh bien, ramasse ces trois choses-là, va et arrange l'affaire avec ça **2 eh bien** *à la fin de l'énoncé; exprime un déplacement de l'attention* ◊ *gɔ̄ dhɪ́ɤ-tá̋-sɯ́-bhɛ̏n dè pɤ́-pɤ́ āa, ȁ bhȁ gɯ́...* quant au chauffeur, selon lui...

áa 1 ***prt*** *introduit une question supposant une réponse affirmative*

áa 2 → yáa *il ne*

áa 3 ***oper*** *marque de négation dans le groupe nominal focalisé; précède la marque de focalisation dhʌ̀n* ◊ *wɯ̄ɯ áa dhʌ̀n ɤ́ Yɔ̏ ɤ́ ȁ kpȁ* ce n'est pas la viande que Yo a préparée

a̋a ***intj*** **comment ?** *exprime l'étonnement*

áabhōo ***intj*** resp. **non** *Syn. ȁbɪ̋n*

āa̋dhìn <Manding àní> ***conj*** **et même**

àaha̋an, **ǹhɯ̋un** ***intj*** **d'accord ! vraiment !**

àan ***intj*** **merci** *réponse à une salutation*

āan, **ȁan** ***intj*** **a-a...** *(interjection de l'hésitation) le ton est extra-bas dans la position initiale et moyen dans les autres contextes*

áaòo ***prt*** **par exemple, disons**

āa̋yɪ̏, **láyɪ̏** <Fr. ail> ***n*** **ail** *[les Dan ne le plantent pas et ne l'utilisent que rarement]*

ȁbɪ̋n ***intj*** **non** *peu courant au Gouèta Syn. áabhōo* ◊ *ȁbɪ̋n, n̄ dʌ̄ bhȁ gbɛ̂n yáa bhɯ̏n* non, ce n'est pas le chien de mon père

ȁ-dhȁan <*ȁ-dhȕn bhȁ> ***prn*** **leur**, **leurs** *pronom de la 3e pers. pl. de la série possessive*

à-dhùn *prn* **les, eux, elles, leurs, leur** *pronom non-sujet de la 3e pers. pl.*

àhâân, **àhāân** *intj* **voilà ! tiens !** *(exclamation traduisant une compréhension, un malin plaisir; signal de faire le bilan)* ◊ *àhâân ! bhá wɔ́n yà ūū dè bhà* tiens ! tu t'es créé un problème !

ālōzóà, **lōzúà** *n* **arrosoir** ◊ *yà yí wɛ̀nŋ tőo tà lōzúà ká* il a arrosé les légumes avec un arrosoir

àòo *intj* **1 oui** *(réponse à une salutation)* **2 d'accord !** *(réponse à un ordre, à une proposition)* Qsyn. ìi

Átāndhān *n* **le Tout Puissant**

Λ ʌ

ʌ̄ʌ *intj* **a-a...** *(interjection de l'hésitation)*

B b

bà *v* **1** *vi* **grossir** *(prendre du poids)* *[la corpulence est bien vue chez les Dan]* Syn. fāan súú ◊ *dhēbʌ̀-dhùn wà dhó kwíplɤ̀ɤ, wò bà* quand les femmes vont en ville, elles grossissent **2** *vt* **dégager**, **nettoyer**, **débroussailler** *(les hautes herbes)*; **se frayer** *(un chemin)* ◊ *bhán bhān bhláàdhè bà* j'ai défriché mon champ ◊ *wà kpìnŋ tà bà gbɛ̋ɛ ká* ils ont défriché la route et l'ont élargie ♦ *bāa dhè bà* nettoyer le terrain pour un champ de manioc

bāa *n* ***Manihot esculenta*** **manioc** Syn. gwɛ̄ɛ́ ♦ *bāa dhè* champ de manioc ♦ *bāa dhɛ́* feuilles de manioc *(utilisées pour la sauce)* ♦ *bāa dhűű* tige de manioc ♦ *bāa kɔ̀n* foutou de manioc Iv. ♦ *bāa kpɛ́ɛ, bāa gā kpɛ́ɛ* manioc séché *(coupé en morceaux; une façon habituelle de préparer le manioc pour le stockage ou pour la vente)* ♦ *bāa sɛ̀ɛ* manioc cru ♦ *bāa kɛ́ɛ bhō à bhà* éplucher le manioc ♦ *bāa tā* planter le manioc ♦ *bāa wò* déterrer le manioc

bāà 1 {bàa} *v* 1) *vt* **parer**, **décorer** ◊ *yà gèebʌ̀ bāà* il a habillé l'idole ♦ *kɔ́ bāà* décorer la maison *(à l'extérieur comme à l'intérieur)* ♦ *gèe bāà* habiller le masque 2) *vr* **s'habiller bien** Syn. zűű ◊ *yà ɤ̄ bāà* elle s'est bien habillée

bāá 2 {bàa} *v* **1** *vi* **préparer**, **apprêter** *(pour pouvoir le présenter; qch – bhà)* ◊ *pʌ̄bhèe bhā bhɤ̀ bāá à bhà sʌ̀ ká* présente bien la nourriture ◊ *fétɤ̀ bhā kwà bāá à bhà* préparons bien la fête 2) *vr* **s'apprêter 2** *vt* **réparer** *(mécanisme, outil)* Syn. pʌ̀ kʌ̄ ◊ *yà bhān gō bāá* il a réparé ma voiture

báà *n* **1 bas-fond** *(terrain marécageux près d'un cours d'eau)* *[on y cultive du riz]* ♦ *báà dhè* champ de bas-fond ◊ *bhíin dhó báà dhè kʌ̄' kwɛ̄ɛ* cette année je ne cultiverai pas le bas-fond ♦ *báà gúú* au bas-fond **2 boue** *(terre)* Syn. bɤ̄ɤ̀

bàandî <Fr. bandit> *n* **bandit**

bā̀ā̀ndhɛ̀ {LOC bāandhɤ̄} *loc.n* **dépression** *(basses terres)*

bāandhɤ̄ *loc.n LOC de* bā̀ā̀ndhɛ̀ *dépression*

bàdhâsǜ <Fr. barrage> *n* **barrage**

bádhíká <Manding bárika> *intj* **merci** Syn. dhūnwɛ̋ɛ

bàdhóŋ̀ <Fr. ballon> *n* **ballon, football** Syn. dhɤ̀ɤkpɤ̄ ♦ *bàdhóŋ̀ zǜɤ* jouer au football ◊ *à gɛ̀n yáa dhɤ́ kɤ̄ yɤ̀ dhǜn tó bàdhóŋ̀ zǜɤ-sǜ bhà* il n'a pas de pieds pour jouer au foot *(se dit de celui qui ne sait pas jouer)*

bádhɤ̄ 1 *adv* **à côté** *(à proximité) dans une expression seulement :* ♦ *dɔ̄ n̄ ká bádhɤ̄* i) attends-moi à côté ii) écarte-toi un peu

bádhɤ̄ 2 *adv* **carrément** *(d'un mouvement brusque et précis)* ◊ *bɛ̋ŋ ɤ́' zǜɤ, yà tɔ̋ kpɤ̄ bhò bhūn wɛ̋ bádhɤ̄* d'un seul coup, la machette lui a carrement coupé l'oreille

bɛ̋kɛ̋ <Manding bága> *n* **bouillie** *(du riz ou du maïze)* ♦ *bɛ̋kɛ̋ yísǜ* bouillie trop liquide ♦ *bɛ̋kɛ̋ kún-sǜ* bouillie épaisse

bān {bān} *v* **1** *vi* **pleuvoir**, **tomber** *(de pluie)* ♦ *dhā yɤ̀ bàn yɤ̄* il pleut ici ♦ *dhā kpɩ̂ɩ̀ yà bān Tòkpà bhà* Tokpa a été pris par la pluie **2** *vi* **tomber en gouttes** ◊ *bhɛ̋ŋ yí yɤ̄ɤ bān kā tà !* la "salive" du parasite bhɛ̋ŋ est sur le point de tomber sur vous !

bɛ̋n *n* **association d'entraide** *(masculin, féminin ou mixte; on se rassemble pour travailler dans les champs des membres, ou, contre une récompense, dans les champs des autres)* Syn. bɛ̋nkpɤ̄ Qsyn. kêkpɤ̄, gwɛ̋ ◊ *dɛ̀ɛ dhʌn bɛ̋n yɤ̄ɤ dhūn' ká n̄ plɤ̀ɤ* c'est aujourd'hui que l'association de travail va travailler chez moi ♦ *Zân bhà bɛ̋n yī dhūn ɤ́ dɛ̀ɛ* le jour de travail dédié à Jean, c'est aujourd'hui *(c'est dans son champ que l'association travaille aujourd'hui)*

bɛ̋nkpɤ̄ <association.de.travail-boule> *n* **association de travail** *(masculine, féminine ou mixte; on se rassemble pour travailler dans les champs de ses membres, ou, contre une récompense, dans les champs des autres)* Syn. bɛ̋n Qsyn. kêkpɤ̄, gwɛ̋ ♦ *bhán dà bɛ̋nkpɤ̄ gúí* j'ai adhéré à l'association de travail

bánŋ̀ → báŋ̀ *banc*

bàŋ *n* **bassine, cuvette** *(pour la lessive) le mot s'emploie dans des contextes restreints*

báŋ̀, **bánŋ̀** <Fr. banc> *n* **banc**

bɛ̋ŋ *n* **machette, coupe-coupe** ♦ *bɛ̋ŋ dhɛ́* lame de machette ♦ *bɛ̋ŋ dhíɤ* le tranchant de la machette ♦ *bɛ̋ŋ gɔ̀* manche de machette ♦ *bɛ̋ŋ kō* dos de lame de machette ♦ *bɛ̋ŋ zɔ̋* bout de la lame de la machette ♦ *bɛ̋ŋ wɛ̄ŋgādhē* machette avec de rainures sur la lame ♦ *bɛ̋ŋ yà gó ɤ̄ gɔ̀ gúí* la lame de la machette s'est détachée du manche ♦ *bhán bɛ̋ŋ dà ɤ̄ gɔ̀ gúí* j'ai remis la lame de la machette dans le manche

bàŋbɛ̋ŋ *n* **balancement** ◊ *dhɯ̋ kwɛ̄ɛ̄-dhǜn wò bàŋbɛ̋ŋ kʌ̄-sīʌ* les branches de l'arbre se balancent ◊ *dhʌ́n dō bhá yɤ̀ dhɯ̋ kwɛ̄ɛ̄-dhǜn bàŋbɛ̋ŋ kʌ̄-sīʌ* un enfant secoue les branches d'un arbre

bàŋdhɤ̀ ***adv*** **en bas** ◊ *yà kɔ́n tɔ̀n ká yɤ̀ slʌ̄ʌ-sīʌ ɤ̄ gú ɤ́ dhō bàŋdhɤ̀* il est tombé sur la montagne et descend en roulant

báŋkɤ̀ < Fr. banque > ***n*** **banque**

bὰyí ***n*** *le plus souvent bὰyí tɤ̋n* **"bayi"** *(danse moderne de réjouissance; les participants chantent des chants avec des proverbes, au son des tambours)* ♦ *wὰ bὰyí tɤ̋n kʌ̄* ils ont dansé "bayi"

bɛ̀ 1 ***n*** **1 ballot, liasse, régime** *Qsyn. bɤ̋ɤ* ♦ *wɔ̋ bɛ̀* fagot, fagot de bois ◊ *yà wɔ̋ bɛ̀ kʌ̄* elle a fait des fagots de bois ♦ *glɔ̄ɔ bɛ̀* régime de bananes **2 rouleau** *(une natte roulée, etc.)* ♦ *sɛ̄ɛ́ bɛ̀* natte en rouleau

bɛ̀ 2 {Int. bɛ̀bɛ̀} ***adv*** **autrefois** ◊ *ā ɯ̄ dɔ̀ bɛ̀* je t'ai connu avant ◊ *ā ɯ̄ dɔ̀ bɛ̀bɛ̀* je te connais depuis très longtemps

bɛ̀bɛ̀ ***adv*** *Int. de* bɛ̀ *autrefois*

bɛ̀-kʌ̄ {bɛ̀-kʌ̀} ***v vt*** **rouler, mettre en rouleau**

Bɛ̀tɛ́ɛ̀ ***n*** **bété** *(groupe ethnique du Centre-Ouest de la Côte-d'Ivoire; la langue bété, appartenant à la famille krou)* ◊ *Bɛ̀tɛ́ɛ̀-dhʉ̀n wɔ̀ dɔ̀ Gbὰgbō gbὰn gɔ̀ kpɛ̄ɛwō* les Bété soutiennent toujours Gbagbo

bɛ̀dhɛ́ < ?-feuille> ***n*** **1 médicament, remède** *(traditionnel ou moderne)* ♦ *bhɛ̄n tīi bɛ̀dhɛ́* médicament traditionnel ♦ *kwí bɛ̀dhɛ́* médicament de la médecine moderne ♦ *bɛ̀dhɛ́ gā* comprimé ♦ *bɛ̀dhɛ́ yāa* i) mauvais médicament ii) poison, magie noire **2 poison; procédé magique** *(nocif)* ♦ *yà bɛ̀dhɛ́ kʌ̄ ɤ̄ gɔ̀n ká* elle a envoûté son mari *(pour le dominer)* ♦ *yὰ bɛ̀dhɛ́ kʌ̄ ɤ̄ bhāŋdhē ká kɤ̋ɤ' zʌ̄* elle a empoisonné sa coépouse pour la tuer

bɛ̀dhɛ́kʌ̄bhɛ̀n <médicine-faire-homme> ***n*** **guérisseur** ♦ *bɛ̀dhɛ́kʌ̄bhɛ̀n yāa* guérisseur puissant

bɛ̀dhɛ́yāakʌ̄bhɛ̀n <médicine-mauvais-faire-homme> ***n*** **sorcier** *(celui qui produit les poisons et les procédés de la magie noire)*

bɛ́ɛ̀ {pl. masc. bɛ́ɛ̀zʌ̀-dhʉ̀n, pl. fem. bɛ́ɛ̀dhōo-dhʉ̀n, bɛ́ɛ̀dhōŋ-dhʉ̀n, bɛ́ɛ̀dhēbʌ̀-dhʉ̀n} ***n*** **1 neveu, nièce** *(enfant de la "sœur aînée classificatoire", donc enfant de la sœur aînée d'ego; enfant de la fille du frère aîné ou cadet du père; enfant de la soeur cadette du père, considéré en même temps comme sibling d'Ego; enfant de la cousine aînée (fille de la soeur cadette du père)) [Le neveu manifeste son attitude de respect vis-à-vis de l'oncle maternel, voir* dhʉ̄ʌ̀ʌ. *Il participe obligatoirement aux sacrifices offerts par l'oncle, c'est lui qui égorge l'animal dont le cou lui revient. Le neveu peut manifester une agression rituelle, surtout s'approprier les vêtements de l'oncle, et ce dernier ne peut pas les lui refuser. À la limite, l'oncle peut les racheter au prix d'une noix de cola. Aux funérailles les neveux lavent le corps de l'oncle et l'accompagnent jusqu'à l'enterrement, ils peuvent plaisanter et pousser les gens à rire, ils prennent les vêtements du défunt et la viande du repas funéraire. Le neveu ne peut pas épouser une fille de son oncle maternel, mais celui-ci doit contribuer aux dépenses de son mariage si nécessaire. Le neveu ne* *doit pas toucher l'oreille de son oncle]* ♦ *bɛ̋ɛ̏ wlɔ̋sɔ̋* petit-neveu, petite-nièce *(descendant de bɛ̋ɛ̏) [manifeste une agressivité rituelle encore plus forte que le neveu]*

bɛ̋ɛ̏zʌ̏-dhʉ̏n *pluriel du* bɛ̋ɛ̏ ***n*** **neveux**

bɛ̏n 1 ***n*** **écriture** *(action)* ♦ *sʌ́ʌdhɛ̋ bɛ̏n zʌ̄* écrire Syn. *pʌ̄ yȁ* ◊ *yà pʌ̄ bɛ̏n zʌ̄ yɛ̋ɛn gʉ́* il a écrit quelque chose sur le sable

bɛ̏n 2 ***n*** **1** *rn ne se conjugue pas avec la marque de pluriel* **lèvre, lèvres** ♦ *bɛ̏n ȁ kȁa* moustache ♦ *bɛ̏n dhɛ́ ɤ̋ dhʉ̋ɤ̋* lèvre supérieure ♦ *bɛ̏n dhɛ́ ɤ̋ sɯ̋ȁ yʌ̀n* lèvre inférieure ♦ *yà ɤ̄ bɛ̏n bhō kwʌ́ʌ̀* il a écarté les lèvres ♦ *bhɛ̄n bɛ̏n bhʉ̄n* embrasser qn sur les lèvres ♦ *yà ɤ̄ bɛ̏n yɔ̀ɔn kwʌ́ʌ̀, yà ɤ̄ bɛ̏n kplɛ̀ɛn bhō* il a fait la moue ♦ *yà ɤ̄ sɔ̋n yɤ̄ ɤ̄ bɛ̏n tȁ* il s'est mordu la lèvre ♦ *ɤ̄ bɛ̏n bhō* jeûner (pour les Chrétiens); (t) refuser de manger (par politesse); (t) refuser ◊ *Zân yȁ ɤ̄ bɛ̏n bhō dɛ̀ɛ* Zan ne mange pas aujourd'hui (il est en jeûne) ♦ *yɤ̏ tɯ̋n bhō-sɪʌ ɤ̄ bɛ̏n pɪ́ɤ* il fredonne tout bas ♦ *ȁ bɛ̏n yɤ̏ kʌ̀ dhɛ̀ bhɔ̏ bɛ̏n dhɤ́* ses lèvres ressemblent à celles d'un cochon *(peu jolies, larges et longues)* **2** *rn* **bec**

bɛ̏nzʌ̏kápʌ̏ <écriture-tuer-avec-chose> ***n*** **crayon, bic, stylo** *(tout instrument d'écriture)*

bɛ̏ŋ → bȉaŋ *course*

bɛ̋ŋ ***n*** **position horisontale** ◊ *yȁ wɔ̏ bɛ̋ŋ ká* il est couché horisontalement ♦ *gbàn bɛ̋ŋ (gw), gblȁȁ bɛ̋ŋ (t)* poutre maitresse

bɛ̏ŋgā → bȉaŋgā *champion en course*

bɛ̀tɛ̀bɛ̋tɛ̋ ***n*** **sorte précauce d'igname** *(à haut rendement, mais de goût médiocre)*

bȉ ***n*** **farine, poudre** ♦ *blʉ́ʉ̀ bȉ* farine de blé ♦ *blɔ̄ɔ̋n bȉ* poudre de fusil ♦ *dhʉ̋ bȉ* sciure de bois ♦ *pȉɤ bȉ* limailles ♦ *sɛ̋ bȉ* poussière *(terre sèche et meuble)* ♦ *tòo bȉ bhō* piler la farine pour le tô

bȉaŋ, bɛ̏ŋ, bǣæŋ ***n*** **1 course** ♦ *bȉaŋ sʉ́ʉ* courir ♦ *bȉaŋ wlɤ̏* (m) courir ◊ *gèe bhā yɤ̏ bȉaŋ sʉ́-sɪʌ ɤ́ dhʉ̄n kā zȉan ká* le masque est en train de courir vers nous ♦ *yȁ dhʉ̄n bɛ̏ŋ ká* il est venu en courant ♦ *ɤ̄ gɛ̏n wɔ̏ bɛ̏ŋ ká* prendre un pas de course ♦ *dɔ̄ bɛ̏ŋ bhȁ* se mettre à courir ♦ *bɛ̏ŋ dɔ̄ ɤ̄ gɔ̏ɔ* se mettre à courir à pleine vitesse **2.1 vitesse 2.2 hâte, précipitation** ◊ *bháan ī bhȁ kʌ̄ bȉaŋ tȁ* je n'agis pas avec précipitation

bȉaŋgā, **bɛ̏ŋgā** <course-os> ***n*** **coureur de classe**, **champion en course** Syn. gɛ̀ngbɛ̋ɛ̏bhɛ̏n ◊ *wōo bȉaŋ sʉ́ kɤ̄ wɔ̏ bɛ̏ŋgā dɔ̄* ils vont courir pour savoir qui d'entre eux est le meilleur coureur ♦ *bȉaŋgā yāa* coureur sans égal

bȉaŋsʉ́bhɛ̏n ***n*** **coureur** *(celui qui court à la course sans masque)* Syn. gbȁngèegɔ̏bhɛ̏n

bȉaŋsʉ́gèe <course-prendre-masque> ***n*** **masque de course, masque-coureur**

bȉdhē ***n*** **"bilé"** *(danse des adultes, surtout des femmes, mais dont le meneur est un homme; accompagnée de tambours et de yɔ̋ŋbhē)*

bȉdhēbhàa ***n*** **tambour** *(à double membrane, caisse cylindrique) [on l'utilisait autrefois pendant des danses de guerre et d'autres danses aujourd'hui obsolètes, et pour accompagner une musique associée à la maison sacrée]* Syn. fɤ̄, yȁgbȁ

bìdhóò <Fr. bureau> ***n*** **bureau**

bĩ̀ĩ <Fr. but> ***n*** **but** *(football)*

bĩ̀n ***v*** 1) *vi* **se cacher** 2) *vt* **cacher** Syn. *gblɛ̃̀n-kpɔ́* ◊ *ā à bĩ̀n-sɯ̀ ká* je l'ai caché ♦ *wɔ́n bĩ̀n-sɯ̀.* secret, affaire secrète 3) *vr* **se cacher** *(de – gɔ̀)*

bĩ́n 1 ***n*** **1 obscurité** *(de nuit)* Qsyn. *gbēŋ* ♦ *bĩ́n yà bhán* la nuit est tombée ♦ *bĩ́n bhān dhɛ̀ kpɶ̀ɶ* jour et nuit, constamment **2** *rn* **ombre** *(d'un objet)* ◊ *bhɛ́n ɤ́ dhɤ́, à bĩ́n yɤ̀ à kɛ̀ŋ* prov. l'ombre suit l'homme *(l'homme porte avec lui son comportement et ses manières)* **3** *rn* **image** *(dessin, mais surtout photo)* Qsyn. *blɛ̃̀n* ◊ *yà pʌ̄ bĩ́n gbɛ́ kʌ̄ kɶ́ɶ̀* il a mis beaucoup d'images sur le mur/les murs ♦ *yà n̄ bĩ́n sɯ́* il m'a pris en photo ♦ *yà n̄ bĩ́n pɛ́* il a déchiré ma photo

bĩ́n 2 ***n*** **fleur** ♦ *dhɯ̃́ yà ɤ̄ bĩ́n yà* l'arbre a fleuri ♦ *bhʌ̃́nŋglőo bĩ́n yà pɤ̀* les fleurs du manguier sont tombées

bĩ̀ngɯ́wɔ̃̀n <cacher-dans-affaire> ***n*** **secret**

bīŋbīŋdhɤ̄ ***adv*** *exprime l'idée de tension physique* ◊ *... à bhìʌʌn yɤ̀ dɔ̀ bīŋbīŋdhɤ̄* ses muscles ont enflé ◊ *wà à lɤ̀ bīŋbīŋdhɤ̄* on l'a attaché bien solidement

bĩ́oodhɤ̄ ***adv*** **très** *(ressemblant)* ◊ *dhēbʌ̀ plɛ̀ yā wò bhɔ̀ wō kwʌ́ʌ̀ bĩ́oodhɤ̄* ces deux femmes se ressemblent beaucoup

bīɔŋdhɤ̄ (m) ***adv*** **en se courbant**

bīɤ {bìɤ} ***n Loxodonta africana*** **éléphant** ◊ *bīɤ yáa zīɤ, flĩ́nŋ yáa dɔ̄* là où l'éléphant passe, il ne reste plus de rosée *(proverbe : après que l'aîné s'est prononcé, les jeunes n'ont plus rien à rajouter)* ◊ *wɯ̄ sūu gbàn yɤ̀ slɔ̀ɔ bīɤ wɯ̀ gɯ́* le corps d'éléphant contient toutes les sortes de viande *(une croyance des Dan)* ♦ *bīɤ dhőŋ* trompe d'éléphant *[la viande la plus recherchée]* ♦ *bīɤ sɔ̃́n* défense{s} d'éléphant ♦ *bīɤ yɤ̀ wɛ̃́-sīʌ* l'éléphant barrit ♦ *yɤ̀ yʌ̄ kʌ̀ dhɛ̀ bīɤ dhɤ́* il travaille comme un éléphant *(il est infatigable)*

bīɤdhɯ̀ <éléphant-arbre> ***n Adansonia digitata*** **baobab** Syn. *gwɛ̄*

bìɤɤ ***v*** **1** *vt* **piler** *(dans le mortier, jusqu'à réduire en petits morceaux qu'on tamise, s'il s'agit de la banane plantain sèche ou du manioc sec, ou qu'on vanne, s'il s'agit de céréales)* ◊ *bhán bhlɯ̀n bìɤɤ* j'ai pilé le riz ♦ *ntòo bìɤɤ* faire de la farine de "tô" **2** *vt* **rosser** ◊ *yɤ́ Yɔ̀ ɤ́ à pɤ̄, yɤ̄ɤ Flɛ̀en bìɤɤ dhɛ̀ bhēn yɤ̀ bhlɯ̀n bìɤɤ* alors Yo a dit qu'elle rosserait Flèen, comme on pile le riz

blʌ̀blʌ̀dhɤ̄ ***adv*** **très** *(chaud)* ♦ *kɔ́ɔdhɛ̀ gbàan kún blʌ̀blʌ̀dhɤ̄* la maison est devenue très chaude

blǣǽ → blɛ̄ɛ́ *saison sèche*

blʌ́ 1) {blʌ̀} ***v*** **1** 1) *vi* **s'user**; **pourrir** Qsyn. *bű* ◊ *pàŋ blʌ́-sɯ̀* pantalon usé ◊ *dhɯ̃́ kpʌ̀ yà blʌ́ pɛ́ɛpɛ́dhɤ̄* le tronc d'arbre a complètement pourri ◊ *kɔ́ yā, à gbà yà blʌ́* le toit de cette maison-ci est usé 2) *vt* **user** ◊ *bhá bhān pàŋ blʌ́* tu as usé mon pantalon **2** *vt* **déchirer en morceaux** ◊ *būu yà dhʌ́n bhā' blʌ́* le coup de fusil a déchiré l'enfant en morceaux

blʌ́ 2) {A S, blʌ́-dhǜn pl. A, blʌ́-sǜ foc. A S, blʌ́-sǜ-dhǜn foc. pl. A S; blʌ́blʌ́ Int. pl. A S, blʌ́blʌ́-dhǜn Int. pl. A S, blʌ́blʌ́-sǜ-dhǜn Int. pl. foc. A S} ***adj*** **pourri** *Syn.* *kɛ́ɛn* *Qsyn.* *zīī* ◊ *dhű́ kpʌ̀ blʌ́ ɤ́ wɔ̄ bhā ā̀ bhō bhū̄n* enlève le tronc d'arbre pourri qui est là

blʌ̄ʌ ***n*** **1 verdure** *(herbes, buissons) [les Dan ont l'habitude de désherber entièrement le village pour empêcher les serpents et les insectes de se cacher dans la verdure]* *Syn.* *kpȁa, kpɔ̀ɔ* ◊ *blʌ̄ʌ dhɔ̀ yáa bhēn dhǜn kʌ̄ kɔ́ zǜ* les gens n'aiment pas la verdure autour de la maison ♦ *blʌ̄ʌ kpɤ̄* buisson **2 brousse** *Syn.* *bű́* ◊ *yà dhó blʌ̄ʌ gú* il est parti en brousse ♦ *bhán dhó dɔ̄' blʌ̄ʌ bhȁ* euph. je vais faire mes besoins **3** *pl. = sg.* **déchets, ordures** *Syn.* *glű́ (m)* ◊ *bhá dhó blʌ̄ʌ bhō' bhá !* ne mets pas la saleté là-bas ! ♦ *bāa blʌ̏ʌ* pelure de manioc **4 Bleu** *(nom souvent donné à un enfant tardif, qu'on veut protéger contre les génies et la magie)*

blʌ́blʌ́ *Int. pl. de* blʌ́ *pourri*

blée ***n*** **bord** *(de la place publique remplie du monde)* ◊ *... yɤ́ zɪ̏ɤ kɤ̀ dhɛ́ɛdhɛ̏ blée pɪ́ɤ* ... il passe au bord de la place publique

blẽ́eblẽ́e ***loc.n*** *LOC.INT de* blẽ́edhɛ̏ *bord du champ*

blẽ́edhɛ̏ {LOC blẽ́edhɤ̄, LOC.PL blẽ́edhɤ̄dhɛ̏-dhǜn gú, LOC.INT blẽ́eblẽ́e} ***loc.n*** *rn* **bord** *(du champ)* ◊ *yɛ̄ŋ yī dhȁan bhǜn blẽ́edhɛ̏ ɤ́ zɪ̏ɤ Mā dhɪ́ɤ bhā ká* la limite entre nos champs passe le long du bord du Ma ◊ *á dhō dhēŋdhɤ̄, ā kʌ̄ zɪ̏ɤ blẽ́eblẽ́e á dɤ̄ŋ-dhǜn gȁ* quand je suis allé au champ, je suis passé par tout le périmètre très minutieusement en examinant les pièges

blẽ́edhɤ̄ ***loc.n*** *LOC de* blẽ́edhɛ̏ *bord du champ*

blɛ̏blɛ̏sǜ ***adj*** *Int. de* blɛ̏ɛsǜ *premier*

blɛ̏ɛ ***n*** **caleçon, culotte**

blɛ̄ɛ́, blǣǣ́ ***n*** **saison sèche** *(octobre/novembre-février) [temps de l'abondance, des fêtes et des cérémonies rituelles]* *Qsyn.* *blɛ̄ɛ́yī, yʌ́nŋ̏bhúútɤ̄ŋ* ◊ *blɛ̄ɛ́ yȁ wɔ̀ kɤ̄ á kɔ́ dɔ̄* quand la saison sèche arrive, je bâtis une maison

blɛ̃́ɛ̏n ***n*** **1.1** *rn* **ombre** *(de l'objet)* *Qsyn.* *dhɔ̄ŋ* ◊ *yī kʌ̄ kpȁn bhēn blɛ̃́ɛ̏n bhá bhȁ* nous avons vu l'ombre de quelqu'un **1.2** *rn* **reflet** *(dans l'eau, dans le miroir)* ◊ *bhàn kpȁn n̄ blɛ̃́ɛ̏n bhȁ dhǜaŋdhɛ̏ gú* j'ai vu mon reflet dans le miroir ◊ *bhán n̄ blɛ̃́ɛ̏n yɤ̄ yí bhàa* j'ai vu mon reflet dans l'eau **1.3** *rn* **empreinte** ◊ *dhēbʌ̏-dhǜn wà bhēnkɔ̏ blɛ̃́ɛ̏n kʌ̄ kɔ́ bhãŋ bhȁ* les femmes ont fait les empreintes des mains sur le mur de la maison *(comme décoration)* **2** *rn* **image** *(dessin, portrait)* *Qsyn.* *bɪ́n* ◊ *ā̀ blɛ̃́ɛ̏n á' pʌ̏ kʌ̏* son portrait que j'ai fait ◊ *yà n̄ blɛ̃́ɛ̏n pɛ́* il a déchiré mon portrait ◊ *sʌ́ʌdhɛ́ bɛ̀ yā, pʌ̄ blɛ̃́ɛ̏n sʌ̏ yȁa gɔ̃́ŋ tȁ* il y a une belle image sur la couverture de ce livre

blɛ̏ɛsǜ 1) {Int. blɛ̏blɛ̏sǜ} < ?-adj.> ***adj*** **premier** *Qsyn.* *blɛ̏ɛsǜdhȁan, dōdhȁan*

blɛ̏ɛsǜ 2) *peut suivre le verbe ou le précéder* ***adv*** **1 d'abord** ◊ *kwȁ pʌ̄ bhɤ̄ blɛ̏ɛsǜ* mangeons d'abord ◊ *... yɤ́ ú' bhō blɛ̏ɛsǜ bhā ...* tu l'as raconté en premier lieu ◊ *yíi'* *blɛ̀ɛsɯ̀ kʌ̄ dō* il ne l'a pas fait même une fois **2 avant** ◊ *yɤ̄ zʌ̀ kɤ̄' gbɛ́ yà kʌ̄ dhɤ̄ blɛ̀ɛsɯ̀* cela s'est déjà produit souvent

blɛ̀ɛsɯ̀dhàan <premier-ord.> ***adj*** **premier** *apparaît dans le contexte de l'énumération, avec d'autres numéraux ordinaux* *Qsyn.* *blɛ̀ɛsɯ̀,* *dōdhàan* ◊ *dhūn tɔ̀ kœ̀œŋ̄ dōdhàan, blɛ̀ɛsɯ̀dhàan wāà kœ̀œŋ̄ plɛ̀ ɤ̄ gā dōdhàan ká* apporte la dixième, la première et la vingt-et-unième poule

blɛ̀ɛsɯ̀wō <premier-adv.> ***adv*** **déjà** ◊ *bhán dlɔ́ɔ dīǹ-gà blɛ̀ɛsɯ̀wō* j'ai déjà goûté à la grenouille

blɛ̄ɛ́yī, blǣǣ́yī <saison sèche-jour> ***n*** **période de saison sèche** *Qsyn.* *blɛ̄ɛ́, yʌ́nŋ̀bhúŧɤ́ŋ* ◊ *wláàn bhā kwàa kʌ̄ blɛ̄ɛ́yī ká* cette grande fête-là, organisons-la en saison sèche

blíbáádhā́n ***n*** **"blibana"** *(masque sonore des femmes, dont la voix est produite par des ustensiles de cuisine utilisés comme sonnailles, par un tambour d'eau, des cris stridents et le chant des femmes)*

blíkɤ̀, blìkīī <Fr. brique> ***n*** **brique** ◊ *yà sɛ́ blíkɤ̀ kʌ̄* il a fabriqué des briques de terre

blɔ̀ɔ ***n*** **1 consolation** ♦ *bhɔ̀ɔ bō bhēn zɔ̀/zūʌ́ bhà* consoler quelqu'un **2 action de convaincre** ♦ *bhɔ̀ɔ bō bhēn zó/zūʌ́ bhà* ramener quelqu'un à la raison

blɔ̄ɔ́n <Fr. plomb> ***n*** **poudre** *(noir, de fabrication locale)* ♦ *blɔ̄ɔ́n bì* poudre de fusil ♦ *blɔ̄ɔ́n tīi* → blɔ̄ɔ́n ♦ *blɔ̄ɔ́n gā* grain de poudre *[on mettait un grain de poudre dans un trou de dent pour arrêter la carie]*

blɔ̄ɔ̀n ***n*** **bêtise** *(acte)*

blɔ̄ɔ̀nblɔ̄ɔ̀nsɯ̀ ***adj*** *Int. de* blɔ̄ɔ̀nsɯ̀ *bête*

blɔ̄ɔ̀nsɯ̀ {A P, blɔ̄ɔ̀nsɯ̀-dhùn pl. A, blɔ̄ɔ̀nsɯ̀-sɯ̀ foc. A, blɔ̄ɔ̀nsɯ̀-sɯ̀-dhùn pl. foc. A; blɔ̄ɔ̀nblɔ̄ɔ̀nsɯ̀ Int. A P, blɔ̄ɔ̀nblɔ̄ɔ̀nsɯ̀-dhùn Int. pl. A, blɔ̄ɔ̀nblɔ̄ɔ̀nsɯ̀-sɯ̀ Int. foc. A, blɔ̄ɔ̀nblɔ̄ɔ̀nsɯ̀-sɯ̀-dhùn Int. pl. foc. A} ***adj*** **bête**

blɤ́ŋblɤ̀ŋ {A P S} ***adj*** **brillant** ◊ *yɤ̀ blɤ́ŋblɤ̀ŋ ká dhè dhùaŋdhɛ̀ dhɤ́* il brille comme un miroir

blúù ***n*** **pain** ♦ *blúù kʌ̄* faire du pain ♦ *blúù bhē* pain baguette ♦ *blúù bhē klɤ̀ɤ̀* pain baguette courte ♦ *blúù bhē gúŋ̀gùŋ* pain court et épais ♦ *blúù dhɤ́ɤdhɤ̀ɤ* pain rond *(300-400 grammes)* ♦ *blúù dhɤ́ɤdhɤ́ɤ{dhʌn}-dhùn* petits pains ronds *(50-100 grammes)*

blɯ̀ ***v*** **1** *vt* **pousser**, **bousculer** *(brusquement, avec force)* *Qsyn.* *yɔ̀ɔn* *2* ◊ *dhʌ́n-dhùn bhā wò wō kó blɯ̀ yā* les enfants se poussent violemment ♦ *yí blɯ̀* faire la pêche au barrage *(les femmes barrent un ruisseau, puis puisent l'eau pour le drainer, et prennent le poisson)* **2** *vt* **repousser** ◊ *zàŋ-dhùn wáa bhɔ̄ɔ̀n' bhà kɤ̄ wò bhēn tɛ̀tɛ̀ blɯ̀* les gendarmes ne peuvent pas repousser la grande foule

blɯ́ɯ́ → bɯ́ɯ́ brousse

blɯ́ɯ́kʌ̄bhɛ̀n → bɯ́ɯ́kʌ̄bhɛ̀n *chasseur*

blű̋ŋ ***n Hystrix cristata*** **porc-épic** *[de nos jours, animal rare; on croit que le porc-épic jette ses piquants, sɛ̋ŋ, sur les ennemis]*

blùŋŋ → blùŋ *miette*

blùŋ, blùŋŋ ***n*** **miette, miettes** ◊ *tɔ̀-dhɯ̀n wà bháa blùŋ bhɤ̀* les poules ont mangé les miettes de riz cuit ♦ *dhɯ̋ blùŋ* sciure ♦ *kàa blùŋ* brins de tige de canne à sucre *(déchets)*

blɯ̋tánbhōbhɛ̀n <brousse-danser-cueillir-homme> ***n*** **griot des chasseurs** *(peut lui-même ne pas être un chasseur)*

blɯ̄ɯ̀ {blɯ̀ɯ} ***v*** *base du verbe* gú-blɯ̄ɯ̀

bö̀ → bɤ̀ se réveiller

bō {bō} ***v*** **1** *vr* **finir** *(qch – ká)* ◊ *bhán ń bō bhān yʌ̄ ká* j'ai terminé mon travail ◊ *yʌ̄ bhā yɤ̀ ɤ̄ bö̀ ȁ kʌ̄-sɯ̀ ká kɤ̄ bhíin dhūn kɤ̀* il avait fini le travail avant que je ne sois venu **2** *vi* **finir** *(maladie)*, **se cicatriser** *(blessure)* Syn. *gā* ◊ *bhān sídâ yāȁ dhɯ̀n bō'* apparemment, mon sida a disparu

bö̀bì ***n*** **poussière** *(qu'elle se répande dans l'air ou recouvre des objets)* ♦ *bö̀bì bhō* enlever la poussière ♦ *bö̀bì dhɯ̋u* nuage de poussière ♦ *bö̀bì dhɯ̋u yà yȁ/dɔ̄* un nuage de poussière s'est levé

bö̀bí ***n Urotriorchis macrourus*** **autour à longue queue**

bö̀ŋ ***n*** *rn* **gros intestin**

bōŋ {A S} ***adj*** **vaste** ◊ *kɔ́ ɤ́ yā ȁ gú yɤ̀ bōŋ* cette maison est spacieuse ♦ *bhɛ̄n dhí dɔ̄ bōŋ ká* stupéfier qn

bōŋdhúȁn <du nom de la ville Bonoua à l'est d'Abidjan> ***n*** **bonoua** *(sorte de manioc à peau rougeâtre, à bon rendement, bon pour l'atiéké)*

bòo (, t) <de bö 'se réveiller'> ***v*** *bhá bòo* salutation adressée à une seule personne *(le matin de 6 à 12 h)* ♦ *ȁòo, bhá bòo bhōo* réponse à cette salutation ♦ *ká bòo* salutation adressée à plusieurs personnes *(le matin de 6 à 12 h)* ♦ *ȁòo, bhá/ká bòo bhōo* réponse à cette salutation

bōo (t,) ***n Scotopelia peli*** **hibou**

bōőbōődhɤ ***adv*** *Int. de* bōődhɤ *soudainement*

bōődhɤ {Int. bōőbōődhɤ} ***adv*** **brusquement et mal à propos** *(manière de parler)*

bōoŋ ***adv*** **clair**, **éclairé**

bɔ̄ {bɔ̄} ***v*** **1.1** *vi* **passer** Syn. *zīɤ* ◊ *bɔ̄ zīaan wɛ̋ɛ tȁ* passe par une autre route ◊ *yɤ̀ bɔ̄ dhɛ̀ bhā ȁ gú dhɤ́ kɤ̄ wö̀ kpȁn ɤ̄ bhȁ* il passe devant les gens de manière qu'on le voie ◊ *kpìnŋgā ɤ́ dhó Zlȁanwö̀plɤ̀ɤ, yɤ̀ bɔ̄ Kpȁnŋgwìnŋ̀* la route à Zlanwopleu passe par Kpangouin **1.2** *vi* **glisser** ◊ *yɤ́ dhʌ́n bhā, yɤ́ bɔ̄ dhʌ́nglɔ̄ɔ́ndhʌ́n bhā ȁ gbān tȁ, yɤ́ bɔ̄ gɔ̄ ɤ́ bhā ȁ yɛ̀ ká yɤ́ pɤ̀ yí bhàa* et l'enfant a glissé par l'épaule du jeune homme, il est passé par un trou dans la grille de la voiture et est tombé dans l'eau **1.3** 1) *vi* **dépasser**

(qch – tȁ) ♦ *yí yɤ̏ bɔ̏ bhɛ̄n tȁ* le niveau de l'eau dépasse la taille d'un homme 2) *vt bɔ̄ ɤ́ tȁ* **soulever au-dessus de la tête 2** *vt* **envoyer, commissionner** *(faire qch – MSD; à – dhɛ̏, chez – gɔ̏)* Syn. *yʌ̄-kʌ̄ (t)* ◊ *bhán sʌ́ʌdhɛ̏ bɔ̄* j'ai envoyé une lettre ◊ *bhɛ̄n bɔ̄* envoyer qn ◊ *wȁ kűnbhắndhắn dȅe dō bɔ̄ kwā dhɛ̏* on nous a nommé un nouveau préfet **3.1** *vi* **échapper** *(d'une liquide)* ◊ *yí yȁ bɔ̄ bàŋ zūū ká yȁ wɛ̀nŋ* l'eau s'est écoulée par le fond de la bassine et s'est répandue **3.2** *vt gbɔ̋ bɔ̄* **pleurer 4.1** *vt* **frayer** *(chemin)* **4.2** *vt* **labourer** *(terre, pour les semailles)* ◊ *bhlȕȕŋ bɔ̄* couvrir le riz (couvrir les semailles avec de la terre) **5** 1) *vt* **abattre** *(un arbre)* Qsyn. *yɛ̋* 2 *vi* **être abattu** *valeur passive* **6** *vt* **tresser** *(cheveux, natte)* **7** *vt* **semer** *(riz : on jette d'abord les grains, puis on remue la terre)* **8** *vi* **voter** *(pour – ká)* **9** *vi* **manger ensemble** *(avec – ká)*

bɔ̋ *n* **accouchement** ♦ *bɔ̋ bhɔ̄* accoucher

bɔ̋n {LOC bɔ̋n} *loc.n* **initiation** Syn. *gbáandhʌ́n* ♦ *yà gó bɔ̋n* il /elle/ a passé l'initiation

bɔ̀nŋbɔ̄nŋ̏ <Fr. bonbon> *n* **bonbon** ♦ *bɔ̀nŋbɔ̄nŋ̏ dhűűdhʌ́ndhē* sucette

bɔ́ŋ̏bɤ̏ <Fr. bombe> *n* **bombe** ◊ *bɔ́ŋ̏bɤ̏ dhʌ̀n ɤ́ pɤ̀ɤ* c'est une bombe qui a éclaté

bɔ̄ɔ *n* **grande grenouille** *[viande très recherchée]* Qsyn. *dlɔ̋ɔ*

bɔ̄ɔ̋ *n* **abri** *(fait hâtivement de branches et de feuilles de palmier, loin du village ou du campement)* Qsyn. *gbâ*

bɤ̏, bȍ *v* 1) *vi* **se réveiller**; **revenir à soi** *(après un évanouissement)* ♦ *n̄ zȍ yíi {kʌ̄} bɤ̏ ȁ tɔ́ ká* je n'arrive pas à me rappeler son nom 2) *vt* **ressusciter** ◊ *zőobhīn yà dhʌ́n bhā' bɤ̏* le magicien a ressuscité l'enfant

bɤ̋ŋdhɤ̄ *onomat imite le découpage d'un seul coup*

bɤ̏ɤ *n* **pâte** *(d'arachide, de banane plantain)* Syn. *kɔ̏n* ♦ *blúȕ bɤ̏ɤ* pâte (de farine)

bɤ̄ɤ̏ *n* **1 boue** *(terre)* Syn. *báȁ* ◊ *dhā yà bān, kpȉnŋ gbāan kʌ̄ bɤ̄ɤ̏ ká* la pluie est tombée, et toute la route est devenue boueuse ◊ *yȁ n̄ zʌ̄ bɤ̄ɤ̏ ká* il a jeté de la boue sur moi **2 boue** *(utilisée dans la construction)*, **banco** Afr. ◊ *ūū bɤ̄ɤ̏ zīɤ-sīʌ kɔ́ bhắŋ bhȁ* tu es en train d'enduire le mur de la maison avec de la boue

bɤ̋ɤ *n* **1 régime** *(de palmier)* Qsyn. *bȅ* **2** *bɤ̋ɤ dō rn mot quantificateur, utilisé avec les numéraux et avec gbàn pour exprimer le sens "entier"* ◊ *Gbȁtȍ yà tɔ̏ bɤ̋ɤ dō gbàn bhɤ̏* Gbato a mangé le poulet entier

bɤ̋ɤkpîì *n* **énorme**

bɤ̋ɤwɛ̋ (m) *adj* **nombreux**; **beaucoup** Syn. *gbɛ́*

bȕ *n rn* **nombril** Syn. *bȕgā, bȕgɔ̏* ♦ *bȕ bhɛ̏n* personne au grand nombril

bű {bȕ} *v vi* **pourrir** *(complètement)* Qsyn. *blʌ́, fín* ◊ *bāa bű-sȕȕ* manioc pourri

bȕaanbȕaandhɤ̄ *adv* péj. **à grands pas** ♦ *yɤ̏ tá sȕȕ bȕaanbȕaandhɤ̄* il marche à grands pas ♦ *ūū gɛ̀n súȕ bȕaanbȕaandhɤ̄ !* marche vite !

būắbūắdhɤ̄ *adv* **indiscrètement** *(comportement de celui qui ne sait pas garder des secrets)*

bűaŋ ***n*** **écuelle d'un kilo** *(de différentes tailles pour différents grains)* ◊ *yɤ̀ kấflée dȁn bűaŋ́ gúű* il mesure le café avec une écuelle d'un kilo

búʌŋ̏bȕʌŋ {A P S, búʌ̏ŋbȕʌŋ-dhȕn A S, búʌ̏ŋbȕʌŋ-sȕ A S, búʌ̏ŋbȕʌŋ-sȕ-dhȕn A; pl. int. bűʌ̏ŋbúʌ̏ŋ A P S, búʌ̏ŋbúʌ̏ŋ-sȕ-dhȕn A} ***adj*** **long et ample** *(habits)* ◊ *sɔ̄ búʌŋ̏bȕʌŋ dȁ dhɔ̏ yɤ̏ bhʌ̄nŋ́-dhȕn kʌ̏* les musulmans aiment les habits longs et amples

bűdhấŋsȕ {A P S, bűdhấŋsȕ-dhȕn pl. A S} <Fr. bleu-ADJ> ***adj*** **bleu**

bűɛ̏ɛdhȅ < ?-femelle> ***n*** **femelle avec ses petits** ♦ *tɔ̏ bűɛ̏ɛdhȅ* poule avec ses poussins

bȕgā <nombril-grain> ***n rn*** **nombril** Syn. *bȕ, bȕgɔ̏* ♦ *bȕgā bhȅn* personne à un grand nombril

bȕgɔ̏ <nombril-tête> ***n rn*** **nombril** Syn. *bȕ, bȕgā*

būn 1 {būn} ***v*** **1.1** *vt* **élever** *(nourrir, éduquer)* Qsyn. *tȕɤ* ◊ *yà ȁ būn kwɛ̏ sɔ̋ɔdhű ká/pɨ́ɤ* il l'élève depuis cinq ans **2.1** *vt* **bercer** ◊ *bhɛ́n bhā yɤ̏ dhʌ́n bȕn sʌ̏* cette personne sait bercer un enfant **2.2** *vt* **accueillir**

būn 2 ***n*** **tombe, tombeau**

būŋgēɛdhɤ̄ (gw), **būŋgēedhɤ̄** (m) ***adv*** **largement** *(s'éparpiller)* ◊ *bhlȕngā yà wɛ̀nŋ, yȁ dɔ̄ būŋgēɛdhɤ̄* le riz s'est éparpillé partout

bútȅdhɨ́ɤ <Fr. bouteille> ***n*** **bouteille** Syn. *sȁŋdhȅ, zȕɛɛbhɛ̄*

bùtígɤ̏ <Fr. boutique> ***n*** **boutique**

būtɔ́nŋ̏ <Fr. bouton> ***n*** **bouton** *(de vêtement)* ♦ *ȁ bhȁ būtɔ́nŋ̏ dhɨ́ɤ yȁ pɔ̋* il a un bouton qui s'est défait

bȕu ***n*** **harmattan** *(vent sec et froid de janvier-février qui amène de la poussière)* ♦ *bȕu bhȁ tɤ̋ŋ* période de l'harmattan ♦ *bȕu dhɛ̋ndhɛ̋n* période froide *(décembre-janvier)*

būu ***n*** **fusil** ♦ *būu gɔ̏* canon de fusil ♦ *būu tā* charger le fusil ♦ *būu dhɨ́ yȁ ȁ bhȁ* pointer le fusil à ♦ *ȁ bhȁ būu yȁ kɔ̏ ȁ gɔ̏* son fusil s'est enrayé

bȕudhấan ***n*** **brouillard d'harmattan** Qsyn. *dhűu*

bȕufȁa <harmattan-brume> ***n*** **janvier** *(début de l'harmattan)*

būugā <fusil-os> ***n*** **1 cartouche** *(de fusil)* Qsyn. *dhűgā* **2 balle** *(de fusil)*, **chevrotin**

bȕukpȉ <harmattan-grand> ***n*** **février**

bȕuyídɔ̏sɛ̄ɛ̋tȁ ***n*** **partie froide de l'harmattan** *(janvier-février)*

bűwấtɨ́ <Fr. boîte> ***n*** **boîte**

bűű 1), blűű {bȕ, blȕ} *la forme blűű est archaïque* ***n*** **1 brousse, étendue sauvage** Syn. *blʌ̄ʌ* ◊ *yà dhó bűű gúű* il est allé en brousse ♦ *bűű tīi* forêt vierge ♦ *bűű zʌ̄* couper la forêt, couper la brousse **2 chasse** *(au gibier)* ♦ *bűű kʌ̄* faire la chasse ♦ *gbȇn bȕȕ* chasse avec un chien

bűű 2), blűű *la deuxième forme est archaïque* {LOC bűű, blűű, LOC.INT bűűbűű} ***loc.n*** **en brousse** ◊ *yà dhó bűű* il est allé en brousse ◊ *yɤ̄ɤ zʌ̏ yɤ̏ bűűbűű dhàȁn kpæ̏æbhō* il est en brousse tout le temps ♦ *yà ɤ̄ bhā dhēbʌ̀ bhō bűű* il a abandonné sa femme, il a divorcé ♦ *yà ʌ̈-dhȕn dʌ̈ bűű* il les a anéantis

bűűbűű *loc.n LOC.INT de* bűű *brousse*

bűűdhɔ̏kʌ̄sȕȕ <brousse-adorer-faire-gérondif> *n* **forêt sacrée**

bűűgȁan <pintade de la brousse> ***n Guttera edouardi*** **pintade huppée**

bűűgúúdhɛ̏ *n* **brousse** ◊ *bűűgúúdhɛ̏ áa dhʌ̀n ɤ́ dhō ʌ̈ bhʌ̈* ce n'est pas en brousse qu'il est allé

bűűkʌ̄bhɛ̏n, **blűűkʌ̄bhɛ̏n** <brousse-faire-homme> *n* **chasseur** *[les Dan du Gouèta n'ont pas d'associations de chasseurs]*

Bh bh

bhʌ̈ 1 1) *prev* **surface**

bhʌ̈ 1 2) *pp* **1 sur** *(une surface plate, horizontale ou verticale)* ◊ *ā bɔ̏bì bhɔ̀ gblɔ̀o bhʌ̈ sìʌsìʌ* j'enlève souvent la poussière des sièges ◊ *gwʌ̀ yà wɔ̀ yɤ̏ slʌ̄ʌ-sīʌ gúú tɔ̏n bhʌ̈* une pierre a bougé et descend la pente de la montagne **2 tous les** *(valeur distributive)* ♦ *kwɛ̏ bhʌ̈* tous les ans **3 selon** ◊ *Zlʌ̀an yɤ̏ bhɛ̄n dhʌ̈ bhɛ̄n kʌ̄ wɔ̏n dhʌ̀n' bhʌ̈* Dieu sauve l'homme selon ses actes ◊ ... *yʌ̈ kʌ̄-sȕȕ ká ʌ̈ kɔ̏ bhʌ̈ dhűɛɛdhɤ̄* il l'a fait exactement de cette façon **4.1 pour** ◊ *tɛ̋ɛ sɛ̏ɛ yáa sʌ̀ dhʌ́n-dhȕn bhʌ̈* l'air humide n'est pas bon pour les enfants **4.2 trop ... pour** ◊ *ī zíɤ̏ yɤ̏ flɛ̋ɛsȕȕ bhlʌ̋a zʌ̄-sȕȕ bhʌ̈ dhɔ̋ɔgɔ̏ gbàn ká* mon beau-père est trop pauvre pour égorger un mouton toutes les semaines

bhʌ̈ 2 1), **ʌ̈** <de bhʌ̈ 'sur'> *pp connecteur du groupe possessif avec les noms non-relationnels; son ton change au registre moyen après un pronom réfléchi singulier, sauf dans les contextes focalisés* ◊ *yɤ̏ ɤ̄ bhā wɔ́n-dhȕn yʌ̋n-bhɔ̄* il arrange ses affaires ◊ *yɤ̏ ɤ̄ bhʌ̈ wɔ́n-dhȕn yʌ̋n-bhɔ̄ ɤ̄ dɛ̏ tʌ̈* ce sont ses propres affaires qu'il arrange seul

bhʌ̈ 2 2) *n rn* **celui-ci** *(remplace un nom dans la position du possédé, pour éviter sa répétition)* ◊ *pʌ̄ dhé ɤ́ úú dhóŋ̏ ʌ̈ ká bhā, ūū bhʌ̈ yáa bhȕn* une des choses que tu es en train d'emporter n'est pas à toi ◊ *ūū bhā dhīaŋ yɤ̏ bhlʌ̀ʌbhlʌ̀ʌsȕȕ ɤ́ zìɤ' ká Gődhőn bhʌ̈ tʌ̈* ta parole est plus importante que celle de Gono ♦ *ʌ̈ bhʌ̈ gúú* à son avis; il lui semble

bhʌ̈ 3 ***n Nyctecius schlieffeni*** **chauve-souris** *[vit dans les fentes des contreforts des grands arbres; on fait la chasse à la chauve-souris en mettant du feu aux contreforts et en y jetant du piment. Viande très appréciée]* ♦ *yà dhó bhʌ̈ bhō'* il est allé à la chasse aux chauves-souris

bhā 1 1) *adv* **là** *(auprès de l'auditeur, que ce soit dans la zone de visibilité du locuteur ou non; à distance des interlocuteurs et dans leur zone de visibilité, quand l'objet n'est pas indiqué avec la main; là où l'auditeur se trouve d'habitude, même s'il n'est pas là au moment où on parle) après le ton moyen, le ton change facultativement en ton haut* ♦ *gó bhā !* va-t-en !

bhā 1 2) ***dtm*** *article défini, suit le groupe nominal déterminé, requiert la reprise pronominale* Syn. dhɔ̀ɔ Qsyn. ä ◊ *fétɤ̀ bhā kwȁ bāȁ ä bhȁ* préparons la fête ◊ ... *dhēbʌ̀dhʌ́n bhā yà' pɤ̄ dhɛ̀* ... ... la femme a dit que ...

bhā 1 3) ***cop*** **être** *copule des énoncés d'identification et d'équation, dans la situation où l'objet en question est visible pour l'interlocuteur* Qsyn. bhȕn ♦ *bhʌ̀n bhā ?* qu'est-ce que c'est ? *(l'objet est hors de la vue du locuteur, mais il est visible pour l'interlocuteur)* ◊ *n̄ dʌ̄ bhā* c'est mon père (il est absent)

bhā 2 {bhā} ***v*** **1** *vi* **fructifier en abondance** *(café, cacao, ananas, piment, mangue, avocat et autres arbres fruitiers)* Qsyn. dhī ◊ *yı̏ bhánŋlōo dhȕ yɤ̏ bhā-sȕ ká kwɛ̄ɛ dɛ̀dɛ̀wō* cette année, notre manguier a bien donné **2** *vi* **apparaître** *(gale, éruption)* ◊ *fʌ́yígā yà bhā ä bhȁ* il a eu une éruption à cause de la chaleur

bhá 1 1) ***dtm*** **1.1 certain** *(l'objet est censé être connu de celui qui parle, mais supposé inconnu de l'auditeur) peut apparaître dans une position argumentale sans déterminé; la marque du pluriel suit le déterminatif* Qsyn. dō ◊ *n̄ dhɛ̄ɛ́bhāŋ dō bhá yɤ̏ gȕn bhūn...* il y avait un de mes frères... ◊ *dhēbʌ̀ bhá-dhȕn wà dhūn* certaines femmes sont venues ♦ *bhá ɤ́ bhūn* un certain *(connu du locuteur qui ne voit pas de nécessité à l'identifier pour l'auditeur)* ◊ *bhēn bhá ɤ́ bhūn yɤ̏ ä pɤ̏ yɤ̄ɤ n̄ dhú sú* un certain veut épouser ma fille **1.2 quelconque** *(indéfini) la marque du pluriel suit le nom et précède le déterminatif* ◊ *dhēbʌ̀-dhȕn bhá wà dhūn* des femmes sont venues **1.3** *dans un énoncé négatif* **aucun** *(d'un groupe déterminé)* ◊ *kɔ́ bhá yíi wúú* aucune maison ne s'est écroulée *(parmi les maisons en question)* ◊ *ɤ́ yő gú-blùɯ, yíi pʌ̄ bhá yɤ* il a fouillé dans le cendre, il n'a rien trouvé **2 autre** Qsyn. wɛ́ɛ 1 ♦ *bhá bhȕn kɤ...* peut-être que... ♦ *bhá bhūn* tantôt ♦ *bhá bhūn dhɤ́ wɛ̀* on ne sait jamais **3** *comme un attribut d'un préverbe* **de nouveau** ◊ *dhʌ́n bhā yà ɤ̄ bhā sɔ̄ dhı̏i bhá kún* l'enfant a encore sali son vêtement

bhá 1 2) ***n*** **1.1** *rn* **beau-frère cadet** *(frère cadet du mari) [terme d'adresse plutôt que de référence]* Qsyn. gɔ̀n, dhı̀nbhɔ́ɔ̀n **1.2** (, tp) *rn* **beau-frère cadet** *(frère cadet de la femme d'ego)* **2** badin, *iron. rn* **cher, chère, chers** *(en s'adressant à une ou plusieurs personnes)*

bhá 2 ***mpp*** **tu** *MPP du parfait de la 2e pers. sg.*

bhá 3 ***mpp*** **pour que tu ne** *(MPP prohibitif de la 2e pers. sg.)*

bhá 4 → bhā 1. 1) *là*

bhàa 1 ***n*** **1 tambour** *(taille variable, peau lacée, tendue aux coins, caisse en forme de mortier ou cylindrique; très répandu en pays dan)* **2 tambour** *(nom générique)* ♦ *bhàa zʌ̄* jouer du tambour

bhàa 2 ***pp*** **1 dans** *(l'eau)*, **de** *(l'eau comme point de départ d'un déplacement)*, **près** *(de l'eau)*, **vers** *(l'eau)* ◊ *yɤ́ pɤ̏ yí bhàa* il est tombé dans l'eau ◊ *ɤ́ dhō yí bhàa* ... elle est allée chercher de l'eau... ◊ *n̄ dɔ̄ yí bhàa* accompagne-moi vers le marigot **2 chez** *(avec les noms locatifs wɛ̀ɛ, yɛ̀ɛ)* ◊ *yɤ́ gɔ̄ sū kɤ̄ ɤ́ ɤ̄ yēe-kʌ̄ ɤ̄ yɛ̀ɛ bhàa Gbȁȁplɤ̀ɤ* alors elle a pris la voiture pour revenir chez elle à Gbapleu ♦ *gó n̄ yɛ̀ɛ bhàa !* ôte-toi d'ici ! (litt. : de ma place)

bhāa 1 ***n*** **venin** ♦ *bhlɛ̀ɛn bhāa* venin de serpent

bhāa 2 ***prt*** **vraiment** *(s'emploie pour signaler un rappel ou un renvoi à ce qui c'est passé; se trouve à la fin de l'énoncé)* Syn. *dhɔ̀ɔ 1*

bhāà ***mpp*** **tu** *MPP présomptif de la 2e pers. sg.*

bháa 1 ***mpp*** **tu ne** *MPP négatif imperfectif de la 2e pers. sg.*

bháa 2 <de *bhá yáa 'certain-3SG.NEG'> ***mpp*** **personne** *forme contractée du déterminatif avec un MPP de la 3e pers. sg. négatif imperfectif* ◊ *bhēn bháa yʌ̄ kʌ̄ dɛ̀ɛ* aujourd'hui personne ne travaille

bha̋a ***n*** **1 bouillie de riz** ◊ *bha̋a pűu yà kʌ̄ plʌ́ʌplʌ̀ʌ sʌ̀* la bouillie de riz est cuite à point ◊ *bha̋a pűu yà kʌ̄ plʌ́ʌplʌ̀ʌ gbɛ̋ɛ* la bouillie de riz est trop cuite **2 riz cuit** ♦ *bāa dhɛ̋ bha̋a* riz mélangé à la pâte de feuilles de manioc

bhāáan, **bhānyáa** ***prn*** **moi** *pronom de la série focalisée négative* ◊ *bhāáan dhʌ̀n, á wʌ́ʌ̀gā yā kwàan* ce n'est pas moi qui ai volé cet argent

bháāan ***mpp*** **je ne** *(forme fusionnée des marqueurs prédicatifs négatif et prospectif)*

bhàabhàasṳ̀ ***adj*** *Int. de* bhàasṳ̀ *banal*

bhàadʌ̄ ***n*** ***Uromanis tetradactyla*** **pangolin arboresque** *[viande très recherchée]*

bhāadhʌ́n <*bhāŋ bhà dhʌn 'enfant-sur-enfant'> ***n*** **1** *rn* **petit-fils, petite-fille** *(au sens classificatoire : enfant de l'enfant de l'ego; enfant de zlàà; enfant de frère aîné ou cadet de la femme; enfant de la sœur cadette du mari; enfant du frère cadet ou de la soeur cadette du mari)* ♦ *bhāadhʌ́n gṳ́ bhāadhʌ́n* arrière-petit-enfant **2** *ext. rn* **arrière-petit-fils**, **arrière-petite-fille**

bhàagṳ́ ***adv*** **bizarrement**; **à la légère** *(d'une façon peu sérieuse)*; **indignement** ◊ *bhɛ́n-dhṳ̀n ɤ́ wó bhā wɔ̀ gà bhàagṳ́* ces gens meurent d'une manière bizarre ◊ *yɤ̀ gà bhàagṳ́* il est mort d'une mort indigne ◊ *bhá ī sṳ́ bhàagṳ́* il m'a traité sans respect ◊ *yà gèe dhɔ̋ɔ-dɔ̄ bhàagṳ́* il a vendu le masque d'une façon très bête *(en cachette et pour une somme indigne)*

bháaīi ***mpp*** **tu ne** *(forme fusionnée des marqueurs prédicatifs négatif et prospectif)*

bhàan 1 ***n*** **oiseau**

bhàan 2 ***prt*** *intensificateur des formules de bénédiction, particule d'une affirmation insistante; particule d'une question insinuante* ◊ *ā à pɤ̀ dhìn bhàan* j'ai dit à faire exactement comme ça ♦ *ṳ́ dhʌ́n gbɛ́ kpɔ́ bhàan* que tu aies beaucoup d'enfants

bhāan 1 ***mpp*** **je** *MPP prospectif de la 1re pers. sg.*

bhāan 2 → bhānŋ *moi*

bhāàn ***mpp*** **je** *MPP présomptive de la 1re pers. sg.*

bháan ***mpp*** **je ne** *MPP négatif imperfectif de la 1re pers. sg.*

bha̋an ***n*** **awalé** *(jeu : les pions sont déplacés et redistribués puis capturés selon certaines règles sur un plateau de bois évidé comportant douze trous)* ♦ *bha̋an gɔ̄ɔn* jouer à l'awalé

bhʌ̀anbhɔ̰̃ɔn *n* **gaffeur, gaffeuse** *(qui fait des actes maladroits, asociaux)*

bhʌ̀anbhɔ̰̃ɔn-dhɛ̀ *n* **bêtise** *(acte bête, asocial)* ♦ *bhʌ̀anbhɔ̰̃ɔn-dhɛ̀ kʌ̄* faire des bêtises ♦ *yɤ̀ dhīaŋ zʌ̀ bhʌ̀anbhɔ̰̃ɔn-dhɛ̀ píɤ* il parle bêtement

bhʌ̃́andhɔ̰̃ɔyī <Man-marché-jour> *n* **vendredi** Syn. *dhɔ̰̃ɔyī*

bháʌ̀ndhūn {bháʌ̀ndhūn, NEUT bháʌ̀ndhùn} *v vi* **tomber**

bhʌ̀an-kʌ̄ {bhʌ̀an-kʌ̀} <oiseau-chasser> *v vt* **surveiller**

bhàanŋzı̰̂ı̰ < Fr. machine > *n* **machine; moteur, engin; bulldozer** ◊ *bhàanŋzı̰̂ı̰ bhā ɤ́ wɛ́-sīʌ, yɤ̀ wɛ̀ gbìgbìgbìdhɤ̄/dùdùdùdhɤ̄* le moteur gronde ♦ *bhàanŋzı̰̂ı̰ wɔ̀* bruit d'une voiture, bruit d'un moteur

bhʌ̀antɛ̃́ɛ <oiseau-rouge> *n* ***Ploceus cucullatus, P. collaris*** **tisserin gendarme** Syn. *dɛ̀bhʌ̀an, bhʌ̀antɛ̃́ɛ, gɔ̀plɤ́ɤ̄, pɤ̂bhʌ̀an*

bhʌ̃́apʌ̀ *n* **plat de riz cuit** Syn. *yʌ̃́pʌ̀*

bhʌ̀asɯ̀ {Int. bhʌ̀abhʌ̀asɯ̀} *adv* **banal, ordinaire**

bhábhʌ̀bhádhɤ̄ *adv* **indistinctement** *(d'une manière inarticulée)* ◊ *yɤ̀ dhīaŋ zʌ̀ bhábhʌ̀bhádhɤ̄* il parle d'une manière inarticulée

bhʌ̀-bhʌ̀-bhʌ̀-sɔ̰̃ɔkpɤ̄dhı̰́! *intj* **merci !** *(se dit lors de la réception d'un cadeau important, par celui qui reçoit le cadeau ou par d'autres gens qui assistent au don)*

bhábháwō *adv* *Int. de* bháwō *encore*

bhʌ̃́dhʌ̃́ < Manding báara > *n* **1 travail** Syn. *yʌ̄* **2 problème, difficulté** ◊ *yà kʌ̄ bhʌ̃́dhʌ̃́ dɛ̀dɛ̀ ká* cela est devenu un vrai problème

bhʌ̀dhɛ̀ *n rn* **surface** ◊ *ʌ̀ gɛ̀n bhʌ̀dhɛ̀* la surface de ses pieds

bhàdhı̰ʌ̀, bhàdhı̰ʌ̀n *n* **demande de nouvelles** ♦ *kʌ̀ bhàdhı̰ʌ̀n dhɛ̀ ʌ̀ gɔ̀* (gw) ♦ *kʌ̀ bhàdhı̰ʌ̀n dʌ̀ ʌ̀ gɔ̀* (m) demandez-lui des nouvelles

bhádhɤ̄ *adv* **au vol** *(attraper)*

bhʌ̀-kʌ̄ <sur-chasser> *v vt* *yı́ bhʌ̀-kʌ̄* **faire la pêche** ◊ *dhēbʌ̀-dhùn wɔ̀ yı́ bhʌ̀ sɛ̃́ɛndhʌ́n kʌ̄-sīʌ* les femmes font une petite pêche

bhʌ̀-kún (t) {bhʌ̀-kūn} *v* **1** *vt* **embêter, gêner** Syn. *gúı-kún* **2** *vt* **convenir à, être digne de** *(pour des raisons sociales)* ◊ *pı̀ɤgāsòò yáa ɯ̄ bhʌ̀-kún* le vélo ne te convient pas (tu es digne d'avoir une voiture)

bhʌ̀n 1 *v* **1.1** 1) *vt* **frapper** ♦ *yɤ́ wó ʌ̀ zʌ̄-dhɛ̀ bhʌ̀n wō* ils l'ont passé à tabac 2) *vi* **se cogner, se heurter** ◊ *pı̀ɤgā-dhùn wɔ̀ bhʌ̀n wō kwʌ́ʌ̀* la ferraille cliquette **1.2** *vt* **dépiquer, battre** *(riz)* **2** *vt* **battre** *(des ailes)* ♦ *bhʌ̀an yà ɤ̄ gbān bhʌ̀n* l'oiseau a battu des ailes **3** *vi* **faire mal** *(à – ká)* ◊ *gblūŋ gā dō ɤ́ n̄ kún dɛ̀ɛ, yɤ̀ kʌ̄ bhʌ̀n n̄ ká* la punaise qui m'a piqué aujourd'hui m'a fait mal

bhʌ̀n 2 *prev* **surface** *(extérieur)*

bhān 1 {bhān} *v* 1) *vi* **cuire** *(nourriture)* Syn. *kpʌ̀ 1* 2) *vt* **cuire** *(en s'agissant du feu)*

bhān 2 {bhān} *v* **1** *vt* **entendre** ♦ *kwá à bhān bhūn ?* quelles sont les nouvelles ? **2** *vt* **comprendre**

bhān 3 ***prn*** **moi** *pronom de la 1re pers. sg. de la série autonome*

bhān 4 ***prn*** **mon**, **ma**, **mes** *pronom de la 1re pers. sg. de la série possessive*

bhān 5, **bhàn** ***conj*** **et** *rarement utilisé, se combine souvent avec les pronoms inclusors* ◊ *bɨ́n bhān dhɛ̏ kpɶ̀ɶ, ȁ bhȁ gɔ̄n yɤ̏ dɔ̀n dhʌ̀n' bhō' ká* son mari la grondait jour et nuit ◊ *klȁŋ̀gɔ̀bhɛ̀n yȁ yāa bhàn n̄ dhē yī dhɛ̏* le maître d'école a invité moi et ma mère ◊ *bhán bhlɯ̀n wāȁ bhàn ȁ bhȁ tőo dhɔ́* j'ai acheté le riz avec sa sauce

bhán 1 {bhān} *v* **1.1** 1) *vi* **apparaître**; **occuper** *(un espace)* ◊ *bhɛ̄n yà bhán dhɔ̋ɔkwʌ̏ʌ̀dhɛ̏ gbàn pɛ̋pɛ̋ gɯ́* au marché, il y a du monde partout ♦ *bhán ɤ̄ gblőo ká* retourner 2) *vt* **mettre** *(dedans)* ◊ *ȁ bhán bhlʌ̋nŋ gɯ́* mets-le dans le sac en plastique ♦ *pʌ̄ bhán yɨ́ bhàa* plonger une chose dans l'eau **1.2** 1) *vi* **envelopper** *(qch – bhȁ)* ◊ *sɨ́ɤ yȁ bhán kɔ́dhēɛ̋ bhā bhȁ* la case a été couverte des flammes 2) *vt* **envelopper avec** *(qch – bhȁ)* ◊ *yȁ dhɛ̋ bhán glɔ̄ɔ bhȁ* il a enveloppé les bananes dans des feuilles **1.3** *vi* **pénétrer** *(froid; qn – gɯ́)* ♦ *dhɛ̋ndhɛ̋n yà bhán n̄ kɔ̏ gɯ́* j'ai les mains gelées **1.4** *vi* **brûler** *(en parlant du soleil, du feu; qch, qn – ká)*, **faire mal** *(à – ká)* ◊ *yʌ́nŋ̏ yɤ̏ bhán-sīʌ n̄ ká* le soleil me brûle ◊ *gbɔ̄ wɔ̄wɔ̄sɯ̀ yȁa kɔ̏ gɤ̋, yɤ̏ bhán-sīʌ ȁ kɔ̏ ká* il s'est brûlé la main avec un pot chaud, et sa main est brûlée **2.1** *vt* **cacher** *(en enfermant)* ◊ *yȁ glɔ̄ɔ bhán ɤ̄ gɔ̏ blɛ̏ɛ gɯ́* il a caché les bananes dans sa culotte **2.2** *vi* **se cacher** ♦ *wɔ́n á' gbɔ̋ bɔ̄ yɤ́ n̄ yɑ̋n gbàn yɤ̏ bhān kɔ́ gɯ́ ȁ tȁ bhā yɤ́ bhā* voici pourquoi j'ai pleuré jusqu'à ce que mes yeux soient enflés (et devenus invisibles) **3** *vi* **tomber** *(de la nuit, du crépuscule)* ♦ *bɨ́n yà bhán* la nuit est tombée ♦ *bɨ́n yɤ̏ bhȁn yī bhȁ zīaȁn / zīaan tȁ* la nuit nous a surpris en route **4.1** *vi* **irriter** *Qsyn.* sɨ̄ɤ **4.2** *vi bhán ȁ bhȁ* **exagérer** *(se conduire d'une manière trop provocante)* **5** *vi* **glisser** *(dans – pɨ́ɤ)* *Syn.* zīɤ ♦ *ȁ gɯ́ yà bhán' bhȁ* il a une constipation **6.1** *vi* **surprendre** *(qn – bhȁ)* **6.2** *vi* **se jeter** *(sur – tȁ)* **7** *vt* **faire** *(le ramadan)* ◊ *bhʌ̄nŋ́-dhɯ̀n wɔ̏ sɯ́ɯ̀ŋ bhȁn kwɛ̏ gbàn tȁ* les musulmans font le ramadan tous les ans

bhán 2 ***mpp*** **je** *MPP du parfait*

bhán 3 ***mpp*** **pour que je ne** *MPP prohibitif de la 1e pers. singulier*

bhán 4 ***prn*** **moi** *(pronom sélectif de la 2re pers. sg., utilisé avec le suffixe -sɯ̀)*

bhánbhɔ̏ɔndhʌ́n ***n*** **masque-pompier** *(pendant la saison sèche, apparaît au village vers midi et éteint les feux des foyers)*

bhȁn-bhūn *v vt* **boire vite et furtivement**, **manger vite et furtivement**

bhȁndhȁn ***n*** **inquiétude maladive**

Bhɑ̋ndhɔ̋n ***n*** **Mano** *(le peuple et la langue)*

bhānklɔ̄ɔdhîn, **bhānklōodhîn** <Fr. macaroni> ***n*** **macaroni** *Syn.* kwɨ́gblʌ̄ʌ́n

bhȁn-kɔ̏ *v vi* **sécher** *(d'une surface; légèrement)* ◊ *yà kʌ̄ dhɛ̀ ȁ bhȁn yà kɔ̏ kɤ̄ kɤ̄ ɯ́ sɔ̄ dȁ ȁ bhȁ* quand la pluie finit et que la cour sèche, tu peux étaler le riz

bhānŋ, **bhāan** ***prn*** **moi** *pronom 1re pers. sg. de la série restrictive*

bhánŋglōo (gw), **bhánŋglóo** (, Sipilou) <Manding mángoro> ***n*** **mangue** ◊ *yɤ̀ bhánŋ̀glōo kpɔ̀ dhʌ̀n à bhɤ̀* la mangue qu'il a mangée n'était pas encore mûre

bhȁn-pā {bhȁn-pā} ***v*** **1** *vt* **lécher** *(une surface)* ◊ *gbên bhā yɤ̀ slʌ̄ʌ-sīʌ ɤ̄ gúú kɤ̄ ɤ́ ɤ̄ wēŋ bhȁn-pā* le chien se tourne pour lécher sa queue ◊ *kɔ̄ŋ̄gā bhȁn-pā sʌ̀ ká !* lèche bien tes doigts ! **2** *vt* **râcler** *(un récipient, avec un doigt courbé)* ◊ *tǽǣ bhȁn-pā !* râcle la cuvette ! *[une obligation des enfants à la fin de repas]*

bhànsɔ́nŋ̀ <Fr. maçon> ***n*** **maçon** ◊ *ūū kʌ̄ bhànsɔ́nŋ̀dhɛ̀ kʌ̀ bhɛ́n ?* où as-tu pratiqué la maçonnerie ?

bhȁnwɔ̀n, **bhȁwɔ̀n** *la forme bhȁwɔ̀n est moins fréquente* ***n*** *rn* **besoin** ◊ *ū bhȁnwɔ̀n yɤ̀ glɔ̄ɔ bɛ̀ plɛ̀ bhȁ* j'ai besoin de deux régimes de bananes ♦ *bhȁnwɔ̀n tó* pardonner ♦ *ȁ bhȁnwɔ̀n yɤ̀ sɪ̀ɤ* il est capricieux

bhānyáa →bhāáan *pas moi*

bhȁn-yɔ́ → bhȁ-yɔ́ *huiler*

bhāŋ 1 ***n*** **1** *rn* **enfant** *(au sens classificatoire : enfant d'ego; enfant de dhòo; pour une femme, enfant de sœur aînée ou de coépouse; pour un homme, femme de frère cadet de femme, enfant de soeur) moins usité que dhʌ́n* Syn. dhʌ́n ♦ *pʌ̄ dō bhāŋ* c'est la même chose **2** *rn, pl. ext.* **membre de la famille** *(définie par rapport au père de famille)*

bhāŋ 2 ***n*** **estrade de briques** *(support d'une jarre d'eau et dépôt d'ustensiles)*

bhāŋ 3 ***n*** **palmier raphia** *(sans doute, une variété qui ne pousse pas au pays dan, mais plus au nord)*

bhȁ̋ŋ ***n*** *rn* **mur** *(en terre battue ou en briques)* ♦ *kɔ́ bhȁ̋ŋ* mur de la case

bhȁŋbhȁ̋ŋ ***n*** **1 clapotement** ♦ *bhȁŋbhȁ̋ŋ kʌ̄* clapoter **2 instabilité** *(de la situation)* ◊ *sɛ̋ yɤ̀ bhȁŋbhȁ̋ŋ kʌ̄-sīʌ* la situation au pays est instable

bhāŋdhē <enfant-femelle> ***n*** *rn* **coépouse cadette** *(la préséance des femmes dépend de la séquence des mariages, plutôt que de l'âge)* Syn. dhēdhʌ́n

bháŋdhɛ̋ ***n*** **époussette de feuille de raphia** *(attribut de danseur)*

bhȁŋglɤ̀ɤ ***n*** **papaye** *(l'arbre, le fruit)* ◊ *bhȁŋglɤ̀ɤ yɤ̀ ɤ̄ dhɯ̀ bhȁ* papayes sont suspendus au papayer ♦ *bhȁŋglɤ̀ɤ bhɛ̄* fruit de papaye ♦ *bhȁŋglɤ̀ɤ gā* grain de la papaye

bháwō {Int. bhábháwō} <autre-faire> ***adv*** **de nouveau**, **encore** Syn. dèewō ◊ *yà ɤ̄ yēe-kʌ̄ bháwō* il est revenu de nouveau ♦ *dhūn ū kèŋ̀ bháwō !* ose encore te montrer chez moi !

bhȁwɔ̀n → bhȁnwɔ̀n *besoin*

bhȁ-yɔ́, **bhȁn-yɔ́** {bhȁ-yɔ̄, bhȁn-yɔ̄} ***v*** *vt* **huiler** *(la surface)* ◊ *kwȁ̋ŋ̀dhɛ̀ dʌ̄ bhɛ̀n yà gèebʌ̀ bhȁ-yɔ̋ pũ̋u ká* le chef de famille a enduit le fétiche d'huile rouge

bhǣǽ 1 → bhɛ̄ɛ́ 1 *prier*

bhǣǽ 2 *IN de* bhɛ̄ɛ́dhɛ̀ *cou*

bhǣǽdhɛ̀ → bhɛ̄ɛ́dhɛ̀ *cou*

bhǣǣ́dhɤ̄ *LOC de* bhɛ̄ɛ́dhɛ̀ *cou*

bhæ̀æn ***n*** **présentation** *(des résultats de travail, etc.)* ♦ *pʌ̄ bhæ̀æn bhō bhɛ̄n bhà* présenter qch à qn

bhǣæn, **bhǣængā** ***n*** **fétiche tueur** *(en peau, décoré avec des cauris, contient de la poudre; est utilisé par le masque chasseur de sorciers; il tue celui sur qui le masque le dirige)*

bhǣængā 1 ***n*** **1** ***Barbus occidentalis*** **barbeau** *(le plus gros poisson du genre Barbus en Afrique Occidentale : jusqu'à 75 cm et 5 kg, corps argenté gris, souvent aux reflets jaunâtres ou rosés; nageoire dorsale grise, avec un liséré rouge doré; nageoire caudale dorée; nombreuses arêtes)* **2** ***Barilius niloticus, Leptocypris niloticus*** **barbeau du Nil**

bhǣængā 2 → bhǣæ *fétiche.tueur*

bhʌ̀n ***n*** **1 quoi ?** ◊ *bhʌ̀n ɤ́ dhʌ́n kūn ?* qu'est-ce qui a mordu l'enfant ? ♦ *bhʌ̀n ɤ́ bhūn ?* qu'est-ce qu'il y a ? ◊ *bhʌ̀n ɤ́ kʌ̀ yɤ́ bhɛ̄n-dhùn wò wɛ̀ dhɤ́ ?* pourquoi les gens crient comme ça ? **2 ce qu'il faut** *dans l'expression :* ♦ *dhɛ̀ bhɛ̄n yɤ̀ bhʌ̀n kʌ̀* comme il faut

bhʌ̄ŋ́ ***n*** **Dioula**, **Manding**

bhʌ̋ŋ 1 {bhʌ̀ŋ} ***v*** **1** *vt* **avaler** *(nourriture solide)* ♦ *yɤ̀ yí bhʌ̋ŋ-sɪ́ʌ* il est en train de se noyer **2** *vi* **disparaître** *(la voix)* ♦ *à wò yà bhʌ̋ŋ* il a perdu la voix ♦ *à wò dhɪ́ɤ gbàn yà bhʌ̋ŋ gbɔ̋ tà* il a perdu la voix à cause des sanglots **3** *vt* **envahir**, **infester**

bhʌ̋ŋ 2, **bhɯ̋ŋ** ***n Parkia biglobosa (gen. Mimosaceae)*** **néré de Gambie**

bhʌ̄ŋgā ***n*** **grêle** ♦ *bhʌ̄ŋgā yà wɛ̀ŋ* la grêle est tombée

bhʌ́ŋ̀bhʌ̀ŋ {A P S, bhʌ́ŋ̀bhʌ̀ŋ-dhùn pl. A S, bhʌ́ŋ̀bhʌ̀ŋ-sɯ̀ foc. A S, bhʌ́ŋ̀bhʌ̀ŋ-sɯ̀-dhùn pl. foc. A; bhʌ́ŋ̀bhʌ́ŋ̀ A P S, bhʌ́ŋ̀bhʌ́ŋ̀-dhùn A S, bhʌ́ŋ̀bhʌ́ŋ̀-sɯ̀ P S, bhʌ́ŋ̀bhʌ́ŋ̀-sɯ̀-dhùn A S} ***adj*** **potelé** *(propriété attribuée à une femme ou à une partie de corps) [est considéré comme une qualité positive]* ♦ *Yɔ̀ zū yɤ̀ bhʌ́ŋ̀bhʌ̀ŋ* Yo a des fesses potelées

bhʌ́ŋ̀bhʌ́ŋ̀ *pl. Int. de* bhʌ́ŋ̀bhʌ̀ŋ *potelé*

bhɛ̋a → bhḯa *craquer*

bhëbhë *ExtInt. pl. de* sʌ̀ *bon*

bhɛ̋ɛ̀ {A, bhɛ̋ɛ̀-dhùn pl. A} ***adj*** **1 vivant** *(de l'être humain, par opposition aux animaux)* *Qsyn.* *bhɛ̋ɛ̀dhɛ̄* **2 suffisant**

bhɛ̋ɛ̀dhɛ̀ {A S, bhɛ̋ɛ̀dhɛ̀-dhùn pl. A S, bhɛ̋ɛ̀dhɛ̀-sɯ̀ foc. A, bhɛ̋ɛ̀dhɛ̀-sɯ̀-dhùn foc. pl.} <vivant-adj.> ***adj*** **vivant** *(de l'être humain – par opposition aux morts, mais aussi par rapport aux animaux et à Dieu)* *Qsyn.* bhɛ̋ɛ̀

bhɛ̄ɛ́dhɤ̄ ***adv*** **en bas** *(enfoncement, enfoncement avec une résistance)* ♦ *dhó ɤ̄ gúí bhɛ̄ɛ́dhɤ̄* s'enfoncer ◊ *gɔ̀dɔ̄tāpʌ̀ gbɛ̋ɛ̀ yáa dhó ɤ̄ gúí bhɛ̄ɛ́dhɤ̄* l'oreiller dur ne s'enfonce pas ◊ *wà kwɛ̀ɛ̀ gbínŋ̀ yà gɔ̄ tà, yà dhó ɤ̄ gúí bhɛ̄ɛ́dhɤ̄* ils ont mis une lourde charge sur le toit de la voiture, et le toit s'est enfoncé

bhɛ̄ŋ̏ ***n*** **1** ***Gymnobucco calvus*** **barbu chauve** *(oiseau moyen, brun, tête noire sans plumes; bruyant et sociable; niche dans les troncs d'arbres morts)* **2** ***Campethera nivota*** **pic** *(oiseau)* ♦ *bhɛ̄ŋ̏ yɛ̏* trou du pic

bhɛ̋ŋ ***n*** **parasite sous-cutané** *(tombe sur l'homme de filets visqueux descendant des arbres et pénètre sous la peau)* ♦ *bhɛ̋ŋ yí* filet visqueux du parasite bhɛ̋ŋ

bhɛ̄ ***n*** **1 fruit** ◊ *glɔ̄ɔ bhɛ̄ yà dūn ɤ́ dhùù bhà* des bananes sont sur le bananier ♦ *dhűű bhɛ̄* fruit **2 chose** *(mot pour compter des objets oblongs)* ♦ *blúù bhɛ̄ dō* un pain

bhɛ̋bhǎ̋n ***n rn*** **ancêtre**

bhɛ̄ɛ̋ 1 1), **bhǣǽ** {bhɛ̀ɛ, bhæ̀æ} ***v vi*** **prier**, **supplier** *(qn – dhɛ̏)*, **demander pardon** *(à qn – dhɛ̏)*, **prier** *(Dieu – dhɛ̏)* Qsyn. dhɛ̏, dhɛ̄ɛ́-kpɔ̏ ◊ *Zân yɤ̏ bhɛ̀ɛ Tòkpà dhɛ̏ dhɛ́dhɛ́ sɔ̋ɔdhű pɯ́ɤ* Zan a supplié Tokpa pendant cinq heures

bhɛ̄ɛ̋ 1 2), **bhǣǽ** ***n*** **prière** ♦ *bhɛ̄ɛ̋ gúu wɔ̏n* sujet de prière

bhɛ̄ɛ̋ 2 ***loc.n*** *IN de* bhɛ̄ɛ̋dhɛ̏ *cou*

bhɛ̋ɛ 1 ***n*** ***Terminalia superba*** **fraquet, franké**, **fraké** *(un arbre à 4 contreforts ailés, dont on fait des planches)*

bhɛ̋ɛ 2 ***n*** **chemise longue** ♦ *bhɛ̋ɛ kɔ̏* manche de chemise ♦ *bhɛ̋ɛ gbān* col de chemise

bhɛ̄ɛ̋dhɛ̏, **bhǣǽdhɛ̏** {LOC bhɛ̄ɛ̋dhɤ̏, bhǣǽdhɤ̏, IN bhɛ̄ɛ̋, bhǣǽ; SUP bhœ̄œ̏} ***loc.n*** *rn* **cou, gorge** Qsyn. bhɔ̄ 1 ◊ *yàa kún à bhɛ̄ɛ̋* il l'a attrapé par la gorge ◊ *yúɤ̏ɤ glɛ́ɛn yà dhʌ̀nŋ à bhɛ̄ɛ̋ / bhɛ̄ɛ̋dhɤ̏* l'arête de poisson l'a fait s'étrangler

bhɛ̄ɛ̋dhɤ̏ ***loc.n*** *LOC de* bhɛ̄ɛ̋dhɛ̏ *cou*

bhɛ̏ɛn ***dtm*** **lequel ?** ◊ *wɔ́n dɔ̋ɔndɔ̏ɔnsùù bhɛ̏ɛn ɤ́ dà à gúu yā ?* quel est le problème très pénible où il est impliqué ?

bhɛ̄ɛn {bhɛ̏ɛn} ***n*** arch. **multitude** *(toujours en combinaison avec glűű)* ♦ *glűű bhɛ̄ɛn* i) des milliers 2) arch. million *suivi d'un nombre* ♦ *glűű bhɛ̄ɛn dō* un million ♦ *glűű bhɛ̄ɛn tà bhɛ̏ɛn* des milliers et des milliers *(un nombre supérieur à glűű tà glùù)*

bhɛ̋ɛ̏n <Fr. maire> ***n*** **maire**

bhɛ́ɛ̄n 1 <forme contractée de bhɛ́n yí yā 'nous qui sommes ici'> ***n*** **nous qui sommes ici**

bhɛ́ɛ̄n 2 <forme contractée de bhɛ́n ɤ́ yā 'celui qui est ici'> ***n*** **celui qui est ici**

bhɛ̋ɛngā ***n*** ***Distichodus brevipinnis*** **poisson** *(esp. : jusqu'à 50 cm et 5 kg, gris, a des taches foncées sur les flancs; se nourrit d'herbes)*

bhɛ̄ɛ̋wɔ̏ <prière-voix> ***n*** **1 prière 2 messe**

bhɛ̄n {bhɛ̏n; REL bhɛ́n} ***n*** **1 humain, personne 2 on**, **quelqu'un** *(fonctionne à l'instar du pronom indéfini)* **3 celui qui** *nom explétif fonctionnant comme tête d'une propostion relative; normalement, à ton haut* ◊ *bhɛ́n ɤ́ wʌ̀ʌ̀gā yáa' gɔ̏, yɤ̏ gó gō gúu* que celui qui n'a pas d'argent descende de la voiture

bhɛ́n, **bhɛ̋n** ***adv*** **où ? d'où ?** *la variante à ton extra-haut exprime une interrogation plus insistante* ◊ *sɔ̄ ɤ́ bhā yɤ̏ bhɛ́n ?* où est le pagne ? ◊ *ūū gɔ̀ bhɛ́n ?* d'où viens-tu ?

bhɛ̄nbhɛ́ɛ̀dhɛ̀ <humain-vivant-adj.> *n* **1 humanité** *(le genre humain, les êtres humaines pris ensemble)* **2 être humain** ◊ *bhɛ̄nbhɛ́ɛ̀dhɛ̀ bhʌ̀n* c'est un être humain

bhɛ̄nbhɛ̄ndhɤ̄ (t) *adv* **immensément, à perte de vue** ◊ *yí yà pá, à tàdhɛ̀ yà wɔ̄ bhɛ̄nbhɛ̄ndhɤ̄* la rivière s'est répandue à perte de vue

bhɛ̄n-dhɛ̀ <humain-abstr> *n* **vie en aisance** *(situation d'un homme ayant acquis une position sociale élevée)* ♦ *yɤ̀ bhɛ̄n-dhɛ̀ kʌ̄-sīʌ* il jouit de respect et d'aisance ♦ *bhɛ̄ndhɛ̀ ɤ́ dhì à gɔ̀* il a réussi dans la vie

bhɛ̄ndhíɤdɔ̄dhɛ̀ <personne-devant-mettre-place> *n* **endroit de danger mortel**

bhɛ̄ngāzʌ̃́ŋ <personne-os-tabac> *n* **squelette** *(humain)*

bhɛ̄ngɔ̀dhíɤbhɛ̀n <personne-tête-devant-personne> *n* **patron, chef, supérieur** *(désigné par les autorités; relations fondées sur la force)*

bhɛ̄ngɔ̀tàbhɛ̀n <personne-tête-sur-personne> *n* arch. **leader, chef** *(position élective ou héréditaire, fondée sur le respect)*

bhɛ̄nkɔ̀kàngúɩ <personne-main-couper-dans> *n* **1 abandon** *(de projet)* ◊ *bhɛ̄nkɔ̀kàngúɩ dhɛ̀ yáa dhɤ́ zúɩ* on ne peut plus abandonner cela (un travail commencé) **2 négligence**

bhɛ̄nkpàdhɛ̀ <homme-préparer-feuille> *n* ***Hoslundia opposita (gen. Lamiaceae)*** **arbrisseau** *(1-5, odeur aromatique; baie globuleuse, 4-5 mm, jaunâtre ou orange, comestible) [les feuilles sont pilées et utilisées pour faire des lavements censés faciliter l'accouchement]*

bhɛ̄ntīi <personne-noir> *n* **Africain, Africaine**

bhɛ́ntlʌ̀ < Fr. mètre > *n* **mètre**

bhɛ̄nzɩ̀i <personne-vieux ?> *n* **fantôme**

bhī *prn* **toi** *pronom de la 2e pers. sg. de la série autonome*

bhí 1 *mpp* **tu** *MPP de la 2e pers. sg. de la conséquence négative*

bhí 2 *prn* **toi** *(pronom sélectif de la 2e pers. sg., utilisé avec le suffixe -sɯ̀)*

bhīʌ̃́, bhīʌ̃a *n* **piège à singes** Qsyn. dɤ̄ŋ, sɔ̃́, zɛ̀tà

bhíʌ, bhɛ̃a {bhìa, bhɛ̀a} *v vi* **craquer** *(du dos)*; **bondir, se détendre** *(du piège)* ♦ *ī kō yà bhíʌ ī bhʌ̀* j'ai eu un craquement dans le dos ◊ *ī kō yà bhíʌ à tà* mon dos a craqué ♦ *bhān dɤ̄ŋ yà bhíʌ* mon piège a sauté

bhīáa, bhīyáa *prn* **toi** *pronom de la 2e pers. sg. de la série focalisée négative*

bhíaaɔ̀ɔnbhíaaɔ̀ɔndhɤ̄ *onomat* **miaou**

bhìʌ *n* ***Neotragus pygmaeus*** **antilope royale**; **biche royale** *lv.*

bhīʌ́, bhīʌ́ʌ *n* **1 corde** *(dans quelques contextes)* Syn. bhīʌ́gā ♦ *wɔ́sɯ̀gúbhīʌ́* corde pour lier le fagot de bois *(en tiges d'herbes)* ◊ *yà bhīʌ́ zɔ̃́ kplɯ̀ kwʌ́ʌ̀* il a attaché les bouts de la corde **2 ascaride, ténia, ver de Guinée** *(tout ver parasite)* ♦ *bhīʌ́ yɯ̀a* ver intestinal *(maladie)* **3 liane** ◊ *bhīʌ́ dhɔ̃́ŋ yà pīɤ́ɤ kɤ̄ŋ gɔ̀ ká* des plantes volubiles se sont enroulés autour des épis de maïs

bhĩ̀ʌʌ <de bhĩ̄ʌ́ 'corde'> ***n*** *rn* **rang** ◊ *tɔ̀n bhĩ̀ʌʌ gblɛ̀ɛn* chaîne montagneuse ◊ *kɔ́-dhũ̀n wó'-dhũ̀n dɔ̄ bhā wɔ̀ bhĩ̀ʌʌ gúú* les maisons qu'on construit là-bas, elles sont en rang ♦ *kà̰ dɔ̄ {kā} bhĩ̀ʌʌ gúú !* mettez-vous en rang

bhīʌʌ ***n*** *rn* **blessure, plaie** ◊ *bhã́ŋ bhīʌʌ* blessure résultant d'un coup de machette ♦ *sɪ́ɤ bhīʌʌ* brûlure ♦ *bhīʌʌ yà gā* la blessure a cicatrisé

bhìʌʌn ***n*** *rn* **veine, artère**

bhīʌ́dhʌ́n <corde-enfant> ***n*** **ver intestinal**

bhĩ̄ʌ́gā <corde-os> ***n*** **1 liane 2 corde; fil** Syn. bhĩ̄ʌ́ ◊ *bhĩ̄ʌ́gā yɤ̀ dɔ̄-sṹ̀ ká bīŋbīŋdhɤ̄* la corde est tendue étroitement

bhīi 1 ***mpp*** **tu** *MPP prospectif de la 2e pers. sg.* Qsyn. yīi 3

bhīi 2 ***prn*** **toi** *pronom de la 2e pers. sg. de la série restrictive*

bhíi ***mpp*** **tu ne** *MPP négatif du passé de la 2e pers. sg.*

bhìiinbhĩ́iin ***prev*** *Int. de* bhĩ́inbhiin *balancement*

bhìin ***n*** **fruit de liane** *(comestible, ressemble à l'igname par son goût)* ♦ *bhìin dhṹ̀* liane ressemblant à l'igname *(les feuilles ressemblent aux feuilles d'igname; on la cultive parfois)*

bhíin ***prn*** **je ne** *MPP de la série négative du passé de la 1re pers. sg.*

bhĩ́in → bhlĩ́in *coussinet de tête*

bhìinbhĩ́in {Int. bhìiinbhĩ́iin} ***prev*** **balancement** *(d'un objet suspendu)*

bhìinbhĩ́in-kʌ̄ {bhìinbhĩ́in-kʌ̀; Int. bhìiinbhĩ́iin-kʌ̄} ***v*** *vt* **balancer** *(pour un objet suspendu)* ◊ *Bhã́anbhin yà bhɔ̀ɔn bhìinbhĩ́in-kʌ̄ Bhɔ̀ɔtî dhɛ̃̀* Maami balance une souris devant Booti

-bhīn ***mrph*** **-eur** *(suffixe de représentant d'un groupe ethnique, habitant d'une localité, ou suffixe de nom d'agent masculin)* ♦ *bhʌ̄nŋ́bhīn* homme dioula ♦ *bhã́anbhīn* habitant de Man, Manois ♦ *zɔ̃́obhīn* chasseur aux sorciers

bhín ***mpp*** **je** *MPP de la 2e pers. sg. de la conséquence négative*

bhīndhānbhìndhànbhīndhāndhɤ̄ ***onomat*** **flip-flap** *(son du clapotement de l'eau)* ◊ *yí yɤ̀ kʌ̄-sīʌ bhīndhānbhìndhànbhīndhāndhɤ̄* l'eau clapote : flip-flap

bhīndhʌ́n (gw,) ***n*** **1** (gw) *toujours au sg.* **homme** *(à partir d'environ 30 ans ou plus)* Qsyn. gɔ̄ndʌ̄dhʌ́n **2** (m) **jeune homme** *(par rapport à celui qui est plus âgé)*

bhīndhīáà < Fr. milliard > ***n*** **milliard**

bhīndhínslɤ̀ < Fr. ministre > ***n*** **ministre**

bhìnŋdĩ̂ < Fr. midi > ***n*** **midi** ♦ *bhìnŋdĩ̂ yíi wɔ̀ kɤ̀* il n'est pas encore midi

bhìnsîkɔ̀ < Manding mìsirí - maison > ***n*** **mosquée** Syn. bhɔ̃́ɔn sʌ́ʌ̀ bhɔ̀ gúú kɔ̀

bhĩ̂ŋ ***n*** **sac en raphia**

bhīyáa → bhīáa *pas toi*

bhlà ***v*** 1) *vi* **se gonfler**, **enfler** ◊ *à gbɛ̀ yà bhlà* son bras a enflé 2) *vt* **enfler** ◊ *gbɔ̃́ bhɔ̄-sṹ̀ yà à yã́n gā bhlà* ses yeux ont enflé à cause des pleurs

bhláà {bhl̀àa} ***n*** **1 champ** *toujours en combinaison* Qsyn. bhláàdhɛ̏ ♦ *bāa bhl̀àa* champ de manioc ◊ *bhán dhó bhān bhl̀ùn bhl̀àa gúú* je vais à mon champ de riz ◊ *zóŋ̏ yɤ̏ n̄ gɔ̏ bhláà* il y a beaucoup d'aubergines dans mon champ **2 campement** *(dans les champs)* Syn. kɑ̋ŋbhɑ̋

bhláā ***loc.n*** *LOC de* bhláàdhɛ̏ *champ*

bhlɑ̋a ***n*** **mouton, brebis** ◊ *Zân yɤ̏ wɛ̏ dhɛ̀ bhlɑ̋a dhɤ́* Jean a bêlé *(en parlant d'un adulte, très péjoratif)*

bhláābhɛ̏n ***n*** **cultivateur** *(personne)* Syn. bhláàkɛ̏kʌ̄bhɛ̏n, kêkʌ̄bhɛ̏n

bhláàdhɛ̏ {LOC bhláā} ***loc.n*** **champ** Qsyn. bhláà ◊ *à bhà bhláàdhɛ̏ yɤ̏ kpɩ̋ɩ* son champ est grand ◊ *bhán kpàn bhàandhʌ́n dō bhà bhān bhláàdhɛ̏ tà dhɯ̋ɤ́* j'ai vu un oiseau au-dessus de mon champ ◊ *yà dhó bhláā* il est allé au champ ◊ *bhán wɔ̀ɔ dō kún n̄ gɔ̏ bhláā* j'ai attrapé un singe dans mon champ de manioc

bhláàkɛ̏kʌ̄bhɛ̏n <champ-cultivation-faire-personne> ***n*** **cultivateur** *(personne)* Syn. bhláābhɛ̏n, kêkʌ̄bhɛ̏n

bhlàànbʌ̏, bhlàànbɔ̏ (m) ***n*** **amant** *(pour un femme non-mariée comme pour une mariée)*

bhlɑ̋nŋ <Manding mána> ***n*** **1 sac en plastique 2 polyéthylène** *(matière dont on fait des sacs en plastique)*

bhlʌ̋ ***n*** **termite** *(volant, comestible; plus grand que d'autres espèces; se mangent crus ou cuits)* ♦ *bhlʌ́ dhà* "pluie des termites" *(une pluie en février suivie par l'apparition massive des termites comestibles volants)* ♦ *bhlʌ́ gā* = bhlʌ́

bhlʌ̀ʌ ***n*** **1** *rn* **respect** ◊ *... kɤ̄ à bhlʌ̀ʌ yɤ̏ kʌ̄ bhɛ̄n wɛ̋ɛ-dhùn yɑ̋n gúú* pour qu'il soit respecté par les autres ♦ *bhlʌ̀ʌ yà yà à bhà kā sáà gúú* il a été honoré grâce à vous ♦ *bhlʌ̀ʌ yà bho' bhà* il a été déshonoré ◊ *yɤ̄ɤ bhlʌ̀ʌ bhō ɤ̄ dɛ̀ bhà* il allait se déshonorer ♦ *bhɛ̄n bhlʌ̀ʌ yà* obéir qn **2** *rn* **utilité** *(pour – bhà)*

bhlʌ̀ʌbhlʌ̀ʌsɯ̀ɯ ***adj*** *Int. de* bhlʌ̀ʌsɯ̀ɯ *important*

bhlʌ̀ʌgúúbhɛ̏n <respect-dans-personne> ***n*** **personne respectable**

bhlʌ̋ʌŋ {Int. bhlʌ̋ŋbhlʌ̋ŋ A} ***adj*** **1 jeune** ◊ *à bhɛ̄n bhlʌ̋ʌŋ-sɯ̀ɯ* la personne la plus jeune **2 aigu** *(voix)* ◊ *à-dhùn wɔ̀ yɤ̏ bhlʌ̋ʌŋ* leurs voix sont aiguës

bhlʌ̀ʌsɯ̀ɯ {A P, bhlʌ̀ʌsɯ̀ɯ-dhùn pl. A, bhlʌ̀ʌsɯ̀ɯ-sɯ̀ɯ foc. A; bhlʌ̀ʌbhlʌ̀ʌsɯ̀ɯ Int. A P, bhlʌ̀ʌbhlʌ̀ʌsɯ̀ɯ-dhùn Int. pl. A} ***adj*** **important** *(affaire, non-humain)* ◊ *wɔ́n bhlʌ̀ʌsɯ̀ɯ dhʌ̀n ɤ́ gūn yí bhā' ká* ce jour-là un événement important s'est produit ◊ *bhá' pɤ̄ bhīi wɔ́n kʌ̄, wɔ́n bhlʌ̀ʌsɯ̀ɯ-sɯ̀ɯ dhʌ̀n à kʌ̄* si tu veux faire quelque chose, fais ce qui est important

bhlʌ̏bhlʌ̏dhɤ̄ ***adv*** **inconsolablement** ◊ *yɤ̏ gbɔ̋ bɔ̄-sīʌ bhlʌ̏bhlʌ̏dhɤ̄* il pleure inconsolablement

bhlʌ̋ŋbhlʌ̋ŋ ***adj*** *Int. de* bhlʌ̋ʌŋ *jeune*

bhlʌ̋tɩ̋ʌʌ ***n*** **champignon** *(petit, à chapeau blanc, comestible, pousse à côté des termitières)*

bhlʌ̋tlɔ̏ <termite- ?> ***n*** **termitière cathédrale** *(grande, rouge)*

bhlɛ̀ɛn ***n rn*** **1 alliance** *(relation entre des groupes de parents ou des groupes ethniques impliquant des plaisanteries et l'interdiction de faire du mal l'un à l'autre, comme p.ex. entre les Dan et les Gouro)* Qsyn. *dhʌ̀ŋŋkwʌ́ʌ̀dhē* **2 amitié** ♦ *kwāà bhlɛ̀ɛn yí yɤ̀ kā̋n-sīʌ* nous nous entendons très bien ♦ *bhlɛ̀ɛn gɛ̀n* lien d'amitié

bhlɛ̀ɛn ***n*** **serpent** ♦ *bhlɛ̀ɛn yà ī kún* le serpent m'a mordu ♦ *bhlɛ̀ɛn yɤ̀ wɛ́-sīʌ* le serpent siffle

bhlɛ̄ɛ̋n {bhlɛ̀ɛn} (m) ***v vt*** **chercher** Syn. *bhɔ̄ɔ̀n (gw)*

Bhlɛ̀ɛnkɛ̂n <Fr. Américain> ***n*** **Américain**

bhlɛ̀ɛntīi <serpent noir> ***n*** **serpent noir** *(esp.; venimeux)*

bhlíín, **bhíín** ***n*** **coussinet de tête** *(pour supporter une charge; le plus souvent, un morceau d'étoffe roulé en rond)* ◊ *yà bhlíín kʌ̄ kɤ̄ yɤ̀ kwɛ̄ɛ̀ yà à gbìŋ̄* elle a fait un coussin pour se mettre la charge sur la tête

bhlíɔ̄n <Fr. million> ***n*** **million**

bhlō ***n*** **boule blanche** *(se forme à l'intérieur du tronc de l'arbre dlīŋ̄ en état de putréfaction, on l'utilise en médecine traditionnelle)*

bhlɔ̀ɔ 1 ***n*** **arbuste** *(4-5 de hauteur)*

bhlɔ̀ɔ 2 ***n*** **réponse à une devinette** ◊ *Zân yà à bhlɔ̀ɔ pɤ̄* Zan a donné la réponse à la devinette

bhlɔ̄ɔ 1 1) ***n rn*** **défi; outrage** ♦ *bhlɔ̄ɔ dhìaŋ̄* paroles outrageuses; défi *(verbal)* ♦ *bhlɔ̄ɔ wɔ̀n* acte outrageux; défi *(acte)* ♦ *bhlɔ̄ɔ wɔ̀n kʌ̄ bhɛ̄n ká* outrager qn ♦ *bhlɔ̄ɔ yà bhán à gúú* il s'est offensé; un défi lui a été lancé ♦ *bhlɔ̄ɔ yíi gó' gúú* il n'était pas satisfait

bhlɔ̄ɔ 1 2) ***prev*** **défi, outrage**

bhlɔ̄ɔ 2 → bhɔ̄ɔ *sac*

bhlɔ̄ɔbhlɔ̄ɔsɯ̀ɯ ***adj*** *Int. de* bhlɔ̄ɔsɯ̀ɯ *défiant*

bhlɔ̄ɔ-bhō {bhlɔ̄ɔ-bhō} ***v vt*** **venger qn** *(sur – gɔ̀, en s'agissant d'une punition physique seulement)* ◊ *bhán ī dhòo bhlɔ̄ɔ dɛ̀dɛ̀ bhō Zân gɔ̀* j'ai vengé sérieusement l'outrage de mon frère aîné sur Jean

bhlɔ̀ɔn ***n Genetta genetta*** **genette commune**

bhlɔ̄ɔsɯ̀ɯ {A P, bhlɔ̄ɔsɯ̀ɯ-dhùn pl. A, bhlɔ̄ɔsɯ̀ɯ-sɯ̀ɯ foc. A; bhlɔ̄ɔbhlɔ̄ɔsɯ̀ɯ Int. A P, bhlɔ̄ɔbhlɔ̄ɔsɯ̀ɯ-dhùn Int. pl. A} ***adj*** **provocateur** ◊ *wɔ́n bhlɔ̄ɔsɯ̀ɯ yà kʌ̄ ī ká* un fâcheux incident m'est arrivé ◊ *yà dhīaŋ bhlɔ̄ɔbhlɔ̄ɔsɯ̀ɯ-dhùn zʌ̄* il a prononcé des paroles très provocatrices

bhlṹkṹbhlùkù ***adj*** *Int. sg. de* bhlṹubhlùu *confus*

bhlùu ***n*** **moelle** *(plante)* ♦ *gbɔ̄ŋ bhlùu* moelle du pétiole de la feuille de raphia

bhlṹu ***n rn*** **foie; poumons** ◊ *à bhlṹu yà bhlà* son foie a enflé

bhlṹubhlùu {Pl. bhlṹubhlṹu; Int. Sg. bhlṹkṹbhlùkù} ***adj*** **confus, qui ne mène nulle part** *(affaire)*

bhlűubhlűu *adj Pl. de* bhlűubhlùu *confus*

bhlùu 1 *n* **paquet enveloppé**

bhlùu 2 → bhɤ̀ɤ *vipère du Gabon*

bhlùun *n* **riz** ♦ *bhlùun wɛ̋ŋ* gerbe de riz ♦ *bhlùun bɔ̄* semer du riz *(on jette d'abord les grains, puis on remue la terre)* ♦ *bhlùun gɔ̀ yɛ̋* couper des épis de riz *(sans les attacher en gerbes; les femmes le font pour préparer le même jour)* ♦ *bhlùun kā̋n* moissonner le riz *(on le coupe avec un morceau de la tige et on l'attache en gerbes pour le stocker dans le grenier)*

bhlűun *n* **pressentiment** *(d'un danger)* ◊ *dhè wó sɔ̋dhā̋-dhùn bhā'-dhùn bhlűn kūn...* quand ils ont senti l'approche des soldats...

bhlűunbhlűunsùu {An P, bhlűnbhlűnsùu-dhùn pl. A, bhlűnbhlűnsùu-sùu foc. A, bhlűnbhlűnsùu-sùu-dhùn pl. foc. A} *adj* **extraordinaire**; **effrayant**

bhlùundhīɤ <riz-tranchant> *n* **1 riz pilé** *(fin) [utilisé pour la bouillie destinée aux bébés]* **2 variole; varicelle; rougeole** *(maladie d'enfants)* ♦ *bhlùundhīɤ yà lòo ā̀ bhā̀* il a la variole / varicelle

bhɔ̀ *n* **cabri, chèvre**

bhō 1 {bhō} *v* **1.1** *vt* **enlever** ◊ *bāa kɛ̋ɛ bhō ā̀ bhā̀* pèle le manioc ◊ *bhá dhó blʌ̄ʌ bhō bhá !* ne fais pas de saletés là-bas ! ◊ *kā̀ ā̀ bhán' gúu, kā̀ ā̀ bhō' gúu* insérez-le, puis retirez-le ◊ *ūu gɔ̀ dhɛ̋ yà kʌ̄ zììsùu, ā̀ bhō* tu as trop de cheveux, coupe-les ♦ *wɔ́n-dhùn bhō kő̋o* i) détacher en pièces composantes ii) expliquer en détail ♦ *dhɛ̀ bhō* défricher le terrain **1.2** *vt bhō dhīɤ* **enlever**, **arracher** **1.3** *vt* **enlever** *(d'un piège – ká)* ◊ *Tòkpā̀ yā̀ dhùn wūu bhō' bhān dhɤ̄ŋ ká* apparemment, c'est Tokpa qui a pris le gibier de mon piège **1.4** 1) *vt* **décharger** *(bagage)* ◊ *kā̀ kwɛ̀ɛ bhō gɔ̄ tā̀ dhűɤ* enlevez le bagage du haut de la voiture 2) *vi* **être déchargé** *(bagage)* ◊ *kwɛ̀ɛ̀ yɤ̀ bhɔ̀ gɔ̄ gúu kɤ̄ yɤ̀ lòo kɔ́ɔdhɤ̄* le bagage est en train d'être enlevé de la voiture pour être apporté à la maison 3) *vt* **décharger** *(une personne, un moyen de transport)* ◊ *yɤ̀ ń bhɔ̀ kɤ̄ á ń tɛ̋ɛ dhʌ́nbhá pā* il est en train de me décharger pour que je me repose un peu **1.5** *vt* **distribuer** ◊ *Yɔ̀ yā̀ tőo bhō klùu ká* Yo a distribué la sauce avec une louche **1.6** *vt* **raconter** ◊ *kwɛ̀zlā̀an á ā̀ bhō-sīʌ ūu dhɛ̀...* l'histoire que je te raconte... **2** *vt* **récolter** ◊ *yɤ̀ kɤ̄ŋ bhō-sīʌ* il récolte le maïs **3** *vt* **extraire** ◊ *Sìagbɛ̋ yɤ̀ pʌ́ bhā ā̀ dhìʌʌ kɤ̄ ɤ́ ā̀ yí bhō dhʌ́n dhɛ̀* Siagbè est en train de broyer cette chose afin d'en extraire le jus pour l'enfant **4** *vt* **avancer** *(ses lèvres)* ♦ *yà ɤ̄ bɛ̀n kplɛ̀ɛn bhō ń gɔ̀* il m'a fait une mine méprisante **5** *vt* **porter** *(vêtement)* Syn. dā̀ 2 ◊ *yɤ̀ blɛ̀ɛ bhɔ̀ ɤ̄ dɛ̀ kɔ̄ɔ !* il sait mettre la culotte ! *(d'un petit enfant)* **6** *vt* **atteindre** *(quantité, dimension)* ◊ *bhɛ́n wó bhɛ̄n pɛ̋ɛn dō bhō wɔ̀ sʌ́ʌdhɛ̋ dɔ̀* à peu près une moitié des gens sont alphabétisés **7** *vt bhō kő̋o* **mettre en ordre** **8** *vt* **distinguer** *(de – pīɤ)* ◊ *ā̀ bhɔ̀ kó pīɤ-dhɛ̀ ɤ́ gūn yɤ̄ bhùn dhɛ̀...* la seule chose qui les distinguait, c'est que... **9** *vt* **faire** *un verbe vide de sens, apparaît lors de la nominalisation du verbe principal* ◊ *gbên yā ā̀ bhā̀n úu ā̀ bhō yāandhīɤ...* hier, lorsque tu a frappé ce chien... Qsyn. wō 1

bhō 2 {bhō} *v vt* **piquer** *(guêpe, abeille)*

bhɔ̋bhɔ̋ *n* **sourd-muet**

bhɔ̋bhɔ̋gɔ̀ <sourd.muet-cola> *n* **noix de cola sans division en lobes** *[de telles noix sont parfois demandées pour les sacrifices; on croit que celui qui les mange aura des enfants sourds-muets]*

bhɔ̀dhɛ̀e *n* **chèvre**

bhɔ̀gɔ̀n *n* **bouc**

bhō-gblɔ̋o, bhō-glɔ̋o {bhō-gblɔ̋o, bhō-glɔ̋o} <déplacer-trace> *v quelques adverbes peuvent être placés entre les deux composants vt* **déplacer** ◊ *dhūn kíi bhā gɔ̄ bhō-gblɔ̋o* viens déplacer ta voiture ♦ *ā dhùn kɤ̄ á ūū bhā pʌ̄-dhʌ́n bhá bhō-gblɔ̋o* resp., euph. je suis venu pour te demander un prêt ♦ *bhɛ̄n kwī bhō-gblɔ̋o* bronzer la peau de qn *(un Blanc)* ◊ *yʌ́nŋ̄ bhɯ́ kɔ̀ yāa yà à kwī bhō-glɔ̋o* le soleil brûlant lui a bronzé la peau

bhɔ̀kɔ̋o <enlever-l'un l'autre> *n rn* **différence** ◊ *Sàó zʌ̀ yáa dùɤ dhɤ́ dù dhɤ́ à-dhùn bhɔ̀kɔ̋o dɔ̄* Sao ne connaît pas la différence entre un boeuf et un buffle

bhɔ̀ŋ *n* **pousse** Qsyn. dìŋ

bhɔ̄ŋ̋bhɔ̀ŋbhɔ̄ŋ̋dhɤ̄ *onomat imitation des gargouillements*

bhōo 1 *intj interjection de désolation* ♦ *kà tɛ̋ yī dhɛ̀ bhōo !* au secours !

bhōo 2 *adv* **sitôt** ◊ *dhὲ kɤ́ ɤ́ wó à dhɛ̀ zɔ̀n bhōo, yɤ́ wó dhō wó klɛ̋e yà à kɔ̀ɔ* sitôt qu'on eut montré où il était, ils vinrent et lui passèrent les menottes

bhōo 3 *prt exprime une sympathie à l'interlocuteur* ◊ *ī dhɛ̋n, bhá bòo bhōo* grand-mère, bon matin !

bhɔ̀ *n* **cochon** ◊ *yɤ̀ bhɔ̀ bhɤ̀* il mange du porc *(le cochon n'est pas son totem; il n'est pas musulman)*

bhɔ̄ 1 *n rn* **cou** *(partie derrière)* Qsyn. bhɛ̄ɛ́dhɛ̀ ♦ *yà à kún bhɔ̄ ká* il l'a attrapé par le cou ♦ *ī bhɔ̄ yà wɛ̋* mon cou a craqué ♦ *à bhɔ̄ yɤ̀ gbɛ̋ɛ ká dhὲ gbàa bhɔ̄ dhɤ́* son cou est aussi large que celui du cobra cracheur ♦ *à bhɔ̄ yɤ̀ gblὲɛn ká dhὲ zlòo bhɔ̄ dhɤ́* son cou est aussi long que celui de l'antilope guib

bhɔ̄ 2 {bhɔ̄} *v* **1.1** *vi* **naître** Syn. kpɔ́ ♦ *à bhɔ̄ kwɛ̀ yɤ̀ dhɛ̀ ?* il est né en quelle année ? **1.2** *vi* **pousser** ◊ *bhlɯ̀n yɤ̀ bhɔ̀ dhā yí bhà yī dhʌ̀n ká* le riz pousse pendant l'hivernage **1.3** *vi* **saillir** ♦ *à gú gbàan bhɔ̄* son ventre a grossi ◊ *à gú yɤ̀ bhɔ̄-sɯ̀ ká dhὲ dhēgbɪ̋ɤ̀ɤdhʌ́n bhà dhɤ́* il est ventru comme une femme enceinte **2** *vt* **fabriquer** Syn. bhà **3.1** *vi* **ressembler** *(à – bhà)* ◊ *yɤ̀ bhɔ̀ ɤ̄ dʌ̄ bhà* il ressemble à son père ◊ *yíi bhɔ̄ ī gɯ́ wɔ́n bhà ?* est-ce que cela ne t'a pas paru bizarre ? ♦ *yɤ̀ bhɔ̀ à bhà dhɛ...* sans doute... Syn. yɤ̀ dhɔ̀ kʌ̄' dhɛ̀, yíi dɔ̄ sʌ̀ ◊ *yɤ̀ bhɔ̀ à bhà dhὲ yɤ̀ dhɔ̀ kʌ̄' zīàan* sans doute, il est en route **3.2** *vi* **être digne** *(de – bhà)*, **être convenable** *(à – bhà)* ◊ *yɤ́' pɤ̄ ɤ̄ dʌ̄ dhɛ̀, yɤ̀ à wɛ̋ɛ kʌ̄, kɛ̋ɛ sɛ́ɛ̀ ɤ́ bhɔ̄ ɤ̄ bhà* alors il a dit à son père qu'il lui fabrique un autre arc qui serait digne de lui **3.3** *vi* **sembler**, **se présenter** *(comme – bhà, à qui – gɯ́)* ◊ *wɔ́n bhā yɤ́ yà bhɔ̄-sɯ̀ bhà gɔ̄ɔ̀n bhā' gɯ́ wɔ́n bhá bhà* cette affaire a commencé à sembler bizarre à l'homme **4.1** *vi* **transmettre ses capacités** *(à – dhɛ̀)* **4.2** *vi* **être donné en cadeau** *(à – dhɛ̀)*

4.3 *vt* **rembourser** *(crédit)* ◊ *bhān wʌ̂ʌ̀gā ɤ́ ȁ gɔ̏ bhā, ȁ gbú dhʌ̀n ɤ́ ȁ pɔ́ bhɔ̄* il a remboursé la moitié de l'argent qu'il me doit **5.1** *vi* **fuir** *(de toit, récipient, etc.)* Qsyn. bhɔ̄ 1 ♦ *Gbȁtɔ̏ dhı́dhı́ bhɔ̄-sı̄ʌ* Gbato est en train de baver ♦ *ȁ yūn yɤ̏ bhɔ̏ gbɛ́* son nez coule beaucoup ♦ *dhā ɤ́ bān-sı̄ʌ, kɔ́ yā yɤ̏ bhɔ̏ tɤ́tɤ̏tɤ́dhɤ̄* lorsqu'il pleut, le toit de cette maison fuit ◊ *gbɔ̋ŋgbɔ̋ yā yɤ̏ bhɔ̏* ce seau-ci fuit **5.2** 1) *vi* **échapper** *(liquide)* ◊ *yı́ gbàn yȁ bhɔ̄* toute l'eau s'est échappée 2) *vt* **faire couler** ◊ *yȁbhȁ yɤ̏ bhēn yȁ́n yı́ bhɔ̏* l'oignon fait couler les larmes **6** *vi* **brûler** *(une substance caustique; qch – gúʉ)* ◊ *sȁȁ yı́ yɤ̏ bhɔ̄-sı̄ʌ bhān bhı̄ʌʌ gúʉ* l'eau savonneuse brûle ma plaie ◊ *slʌ̏ʌ yɤ̏ bhɔ̄-sı̄ʌ n̄ bhɛ̄ɛ̄dhɤ̄* le piment me brûle la gorge **7** *vi* **s'ébattre**; **être agité** ◊ *dhʌ́n yā yɤ̏ bhɔ̏ gbɛ́ɛ̏, ȁ kʌ̄ ȁ gɔ̏ sʌ̏* cet enfant est trop agité, surveillez-le ◊ *kɛ́ɛ kʌ̄ gèe bhā yɤ̏ bhɔ̏ dȅdȅwō* ce masque-agresseur est trop agité ◊ *gȁan yɤ̏ bhɔ̏ kɔ́ kpȁ́n bhā ȁ tȁ* des francolins s'ébattent sur le fondement de la maison ◊ *ká dhɤ́ bhɔ̄' kɔ́ɔdhɤ̄ !* ne vous amusez pas dans la maison ! **8** *vi bhɔ̄ {ɤ̄} tāa, bhɔ̄ zūı ká* **reculer**; **se retirer** ◊ *gblʉ̏gɔ̄ɔnbhȅn-dhʉ̏n wà bhɔ̄ wō tāa* les guerriers se sont reculés ◊ *wà bhɔ̄ wō tāa, yɤ́ wó wlɤ̏* on recule avant de sauter **9** *vi* **être depuis la naissance** *(comme – ká)* ◊ *Zân yɤ̏ bhɔ̏ kwàn ká* Jean est né voleur ♦ *bhɔ̄ ȁ ká dhɤ̏* depuis **10** *vi* **assister** *(dans – bhȁ)* ◊ *ȁ bhȁ gɔ̄n yáa dhūn bhláā kɤ̄ yɤ̄ɤ bhɔ̄ dhʌ́n dhı́ɤ-bhō wɔ̏n dhʌ̀n' bhȁ* son mari ne venait pas au champ pour l'aider à s'occuper de l'enfant

bhɔ̋ *n* **ceinture pour grimper au palmier** Syn. bhɔ̋gā *(avec les nombres seule la forme en -gā est utilisée)*

bhɔ̏bhȁ <naître-sur> *n rn* **image** *(reflet)* ♦ *Zlȁan yɤ̏ kwā dȁ ɤ̄ bhɔ̏bhȁ ká* Dieu nous a créés à son image

bhɔ̄bhȁpʌ̏ <cou-sur-chose> *n* **collier**

bhɔ̄gā <cou-os> *n rn* **vertèbres cervicales**

bhɔ̋gā *n* **ceinture pour grimper au palmier** Syn. bhɔ̋

bhɔ́nbhɔ́n *adv* **très** *(noir)* ◊ *bhān dʉ̏dhēe yɤ̏ tı̄i bhɔ́nbhɔ́n* ma vache est très très noire

bhɔ̋nbhɔ̏nsʉ̏ *adj* **stupide** *(qui fait des bêtises)*

bhɔ̋nkɔ̋nbhɔ̏nkɔ̏n *adj Int. de* bhɔ̋ɔnbhɔ̏ɔn *abruti*

bhɔ̄ŋ́dhɛ̋ *n* ***Canna indica (Cannaceae)*** **balisier, faux sucrier** *(à feuilles larges et fleurs rouges)*

bhɔ̄ŋdhɤ̄ *adv le plus souvent précédé de la particule wɛ̋* **complètement** *(être couvert – de fumée, de brouillard ou d'autres choses qui gênent la vue ou empêchent l'accès)* ◊ *gɔ̄ yȁ zı̄ɤ blɛ̄ɛ̋yı̄ ká, bɔ̏bı̏ dhʉ̋u yɤ̏ dɔ̏ wɛ̋ bhɔ̄ŋdhɤ̄* lorsqu'une voiture passe pendant la saison sèche, la poussière est partout dans l'air ♦ *dhȅ gúʉ yȁ yȁ wɛ̋ bhɔ̄ŋdhɤ̄* il est devenu tout sombre *(avant la pluie)* ◊ *yı́ tȁdhȅ yà wɔ̄ bhɔ̄ŋdhɤ̄* l'eau a tout inondé

bhɔ̄ŋ́tȁbhȁan <Canna.indica-sur-oiseau> *n* ***Merops pusillu, Melittophagus p.*** **guêpier nain** *(oiseau : 15 cm, dos et ailes vert-brillant, cou jaune, ventre châtain; une barre d'un noir profond limite la gorge; bec très court)*

bhɔ́nŋ̀tlʌ̏ <Fr. montre> ***n*** **montre** *(instrument)* ♦ *bhɔ́nŋ̀tlʌ̏ ɤ́ tʌ̋ súu-sīʌ, à vīn yɤ̏ dɔ̏ tɤ́tɤ́tɤ́dhɤ̄* lorsque la montre marche, elle fait tic-tac

bhɔ̄ɔ 1, **bhlɔ̄ɔ** {bhɔ̏ɔ, bhlɔ̏ɔ ~ bhɔ̄ɔ, bhlɔ̄ɔ} ***n*** **sac** *(grand, pour café ou cacao)* ♦ *bhlʌ̋nŋ bhɔ̄ɔ* sac en plastique *(pour café et cacao)* Qsyn. glɛ̄ɛ́

bhɔ̄ɔ 2 → bhœ̄œ *tortue*

bhɔ̄ɔ́ ***n*** **mouches mellifères** *(habitent dans les trous d'arbres; ne piquent pas; le miel, lourd et sucré, est recherché)*

bhɔ̄ɔ̋ ***prev*** *seulement dans le verbe bhɔ̄ɔ̋-bhō*

bhɔ̄ɔ̋-bhō {bhɔ̄ɔ̋-bhō} ***v vr*** **examiner**, **chercher** ◊ *ā kʌ̄ n̄ bhɔ̄ɔ̋ dèdè bhȍ* j'ai cherché soigneusement ◊ *wó wō bhɔ̄ɔ̋-bhō bhūn, kɤ̄ dhʌ́n bhā à gèe yɤ̏ bhūn* ils cherchèrent là, le cadavre de l'enfant était là

bhɔ̄ɔdʌ̄ (t) ***n rn*** **hôte,** *(par rapport à l'étranger)* ♦ *dhɛ̏ŋ bhɔ̄ɔdʌ̄* (gw) hôte

bhɔ̏ɔn ***n*** **souris** *(nom générique)* ♦ *bhɔ̏ɔn-dhùn wɔ̀ wɛ́-sīʌ kwɛ̋ɛkwɛ̀ɛkwɛ̄ɛ́dhɤ̄* les souris sont en train de couiner

bhɔ̀ɔn {bhɔ̀ɔn} ***v*** **1.1** *vi* **pouvoir** *(qch – bhà, faire qch – kɤ̄ ou la construction conjointe)* ◊ *yà kʌ̄ glòo-sùu ká, à kɔ̏ yɤ̏ bhɔ̏ɔn à bhà* si c'est le repos, il sait le faire ◊ *dhùutīì yɤ̄ɤ dèbɤ̋ɤ yáa bhɔ̀ɔn à bhà kɤ̄ yɤ̏ à bhɤ̏* même le chef du village lui-même ne peut pas en manger ◊ *dhœ̀œn yɤ̏ n̄ dhòo gɔ̏, ɤ́ bhɔ̀ɔn' bhà ɤ́ gō dhō* mon frère aîné est riche, il peut acheter une voiture ♦ *yà bhɔ̀ɔn X bhà* il y a environ (temps) X ◊ *à gbɛ̀ ɤ́ bhlà yà bhɔ̀ɔn dhɛ́dhɛ́ plɛ̀ bhà* son bras a enflé il y a environ deux heures **1.2** *vi* **devoir** ◊ *bháa yīi bhɔ̀ɔn à bhà kɤ̄ úu à pɤ̄ Zân dhɛ̏* tu ne peux pas / ne dois pas le dire à Zan **2.1** *vi* **atteindre** *(un nombre – bhà)* ◊ *yɤ̏ bhɔ̏ɔn kœ̀œŋ dō ɤ̄ sœ̋œ̀dō bhà*... leur nombre atteint quinze **2.2** *vi* **atteindre ou dépasser** ◊ *yɤ̏ bhɔ̏ɔn à bhà ɤ́ bhlùn pʌ̏ plɛ̀ bhɤ̏* il mangera au moins deux plats de riz **2.3** *vi* **être de la bonne taille**, **aller** *(à – bhà)*, **convenir** ◊ *fʌ̋ʌ̀n yɤ̏ n̄ kùn kpēnŋkpēnŋdhɤ̄, yáa bhɔ̀ɔn n̄ gɔ̏ bhà* le chapeau est trop petit pour moi, il ne convient pas à ma tête ◊ *sàbhʌ̋ bhā yáa bhɔ̄ɔ̏n ūu gɛ̏n bhà* cette chaussure ne te va pas (en dimension) **3** *vi* **envahir** *(qch – gúu)* ◊ *yí yà bhɔ̀ɔn dhɛ̏ gbàn gúu wɛ́ bhɔ̄nŋdhɤ̄* l'eau a envahi toute la place *(on ne peut plus passer)* **4** *vt* **vaincre**, **prendre le dessus** *(sur – bhà)* ◊ *bhēn kɛ́ɛ kā yā, káa à bhɔ̀ɔn n̄ bhà !* vous, en petit nombre que vous êtes, ne pourrez pas prendre le dessus sur moi ! ◊ *n̄ kɔ̏ yà bhɔ̀ɔn tɔ̏gɔ̄n bhà* j'ai vaincu le coq **5.1** *vi* **tomber d'accord** *(par rapport à – gúu)* **5.2** *vi* **être en bonnes termes** *(avec – gúu, bhà)* ♦ *bhɔ̀ɔn kwʌ̋ʌ* agir ensemble, en bonne entente ◊ *yɤ́ wàà dʌ̄bhāŋ-dhùn wó bhūn bhā, yɤ́ wíi bhɔ̀ɔn' gúu* mais entre lui et ses demi-frères qui étaient là il n'y avait pas d'entente ◊ *Gbàtȍ wāa Yɔ̏, wɔ̀ bhɔ̏ɔn wō kó wɔ̏n bhà* Gbato et Yo s'entendent bien **5.3** *vi bhɔ̀ɔn kwʌ̋ʌ* **agir ensemble**, **agir en bonne entente**

bhɔ̄ɔ̏n {bhɔ̀ɔn} ***v*** **1.1** *vt* **chercher** Syn. bhlɛ̄ɛ̋n (m) ♦ *dhɛ̏ŋ dhí bhɔ̄ɔ̏n* offrir un repas à l'étranger **1.2** *vt après un verbe de mouvement, désigne le but du déplacement* **chercher** ◊ *Zân ɤ́ dhūn yí bhɔ̄ɔ̏n n̄ pɤ́ɤ*... Jean est venu chez moi chercher de l'eau... **1.3** *vt*

chercher à gagner, **gagner** ◊ *wɔ̀ wʌ́ʌ̀gā bhɔ̀ɔn dhɔ́ɔdhíndhɔ́ɔdhín* on gagne de l'argent petit à petit **2** *vi* **être égal** ◊ *bhā́ŋ ɤ́' bhà gblɛ̀ɛndhɛ̀ ɤ́ dhō dhű́ɤ́, wāà bhēn bhɛ́ɛ̀dhɛ̀ wó bhɔ̀ɔn* un mur à hauteur d'homme ◊ *Zân wāà Tòkpà dhàan dhœ̀œn yɤ̀ bhɔ̀ɔn {kwʌ́ʌ}* Jean et Tokpa sont égaux en biens **3** *vt* **essayer** ◊ *bhāan' bhɔ̄ɔ̀n, kɤ̄ á à bɔ̄ à dhɛ̀* je vais faire un effort pour le lui envoyer

bhɔ̄ɔ̀n < Manding móri > ***n*** **musulman**; **marabout** *surtout dans les composés* ♦ *bhɔ̄ɔ̀n sʌ́ʌ̀* prière musulmane ♦ *bhɔ̄ɔ̀n sʌ́ʌ̀ bhɔ̀ gú kɔ̀* mosquée Syn. bhìnsîkɔ̀ ♦ *yà dhó' ká bhɔ̄ɔ̀n pɪ́ɤ* il est allé régler cette affaire chez le marabout *(pour lancer un sort à son ennemi)*

bhɔ̄ɔ̀nbhīn {pl. bhɔ̄ɔ̀nzʌ̀-dhùn} <marabout-homme> ***n*** **imam** ♦ *yà dhó' ká bhɔ̄ɔ̀nbhīn pɪ́ɤ* il est allé consulter l'imam pour ce problème

bhɔ̀ɔnbhɔ̄ɔn ***n*** **acte de mâcher** *(à bouche fermée, se dit des humains)* ♦ *pʌ̄ bhɔ̀ɔnbhɔ̄ɔn kʌ̄* mâcher qch

bhɔ̄ɔnbhɔ̀ɔn {Int. bhɔ̄nkɔ̄nbhɔ̀nkɔ̀n} ***adj*** **abruti**

bhɔ̀ɔngbɤ̄slűŋ <souris-fils- ?> ***n*** ***Malacomys longipes*** **rat à grandes oreilles** *(13-18 cm de longueur, longues pattes, poil court, grandes oreilles, museau conique; dessus gris ou brun, dessous plus clair) [pue, considéré comme non comestible]*

bhɔ̄ɔ̀n-sʌ́ʌ̀-dhɛ̀ɛdhɪ́ɤ-bhō-bhɛ̀n <musulman-prière-appel-sortir-personne> ***n*** **muezzin**

bhɔ̀ɔnsɪ̄ɪ <de Mossi, le groupe ethnique dominant du Burkina Faso parlant une langue gur> ***n*** **Burkinabé**, ♦ *bhɔ̀ɔnsɪ̄ɪ-dhùn gɔ̀ sɛ́* Burkina Faso

bhɔ̄ɔ̀nzʌ̀-dhùn *pluriel du* bhɔ̄ɔ̀nbhīn *musulman*

bhɔ̀tīi <cochon-noir> ***n*** ***Hylochoerus meinertzhageni*** **hylochère** *(cochon sauvage, 100-250 kg, brun foncé à noir, un peu de blanc sur les flancs et la poitrine; les canines inférieures sont longues, dirigées vers l'extérieur, utilisées comme arme)*

bhɔ̀zœ̀œndhē <cochon-rouge> ***n*** ***Potamochoerus porcus*** **potamochère** *(cochon sauvage des forêts humides; corps rouge-brun ou gris, pattes noires; de longues touffes aux oreilles; la canine supérieure de 10 à 16 cm; corps et la tête 1-1,5, pèse 45-120 kg)*

bhɤ̀ 1 ***v*** **1** *vt* **manger** ◊ *... kɤ̄ yēŋ yí pʌ̄ bhɤ̀ yī kwʌ́ʌ̀ ...* pour que nous (lui et moi) mangions ensemble **2** *vt* **gaspiller** *(argent)* **3** *vt* **brûler** *(feu)* ◊ *sɪ́ɤ yà pɤ̄dhɤ̄ gűnŋ bhɤ̀* le feu a brûlé la case sacrée du village

bhɤ̀ 2 ***mpp*** **tu** *MPP impératif du 2e pers. sg.*

bhɤ̋ 1 ***dtm*** **1 même** *s'emploie avec un pronom réfléchi ou personnel* ◊ *yà ɤ̄ bhɤ̋ yɔ̀ɔn bhūn* il s'est un peu éloigné de moi ◊ *ūi bhɤ̋ tɛ́ɛ pā !* va te reposer ! ♦ *à bhɤ̋ yà kʌ̄ sʌ̀* c'est bien fait pour lui ! **2 seul** *dans les constructions avec une proposition relative non-restrictive et la négation* ◊ *bhēn bhɤ̋ ɤ́ yɤ̄ɤ dhó yáa dhɤ́* il n'y a personne qui voudrait partir **3 un peu** Syn. bhɤ̋dhʌ́nbhá, dhʌ́nbhá

bhɤ̋ 2 (gw), **bhɤ̋ɤ** (t) ***n*** **igname sauvage**

bhɤ̋dhʌ́nbhá <un peu-diminutif-certain> ***oper*** **un peu** *peut apparaître devant la base du verbe ou devant le MPP* *Syn.* *bhɤ̋* ◊ *zīaan bhɤ̋dhʌ́nbhá yȁ kʌ̄ sʌ̏* la route est devenue un peu meilleure ◊ *ā dhɤ̏ yʌ̄ bhɤ̋dhʌ́nbhá kʌ̄' n̄ dhòo dhɛ̏* je travaillerai un peu pour mon grand frère

bhɤ̋dhèe <igname sauvage-tubercule> ***n*** **tubercules de la plante bhɤ̋glɛ̋ɛn**

bhɤ̋glɛ̋ɛn <igname sauvage-épine> ***n*** **tubercule sauvage** *(épineux; on le mange pendant la période de disette)*

bhɤ̏ɤ, **bhlɯ̀ɯ** *la seconde forme est considérée comme "villageoise" et archaïque* ***n*** ***Bitis gabonica*** **vipère du Gabon** *[viande très recherchée]*

bhɤ̋ɤ {bhɤ̏ɤ} ***v*** **1** *vi* **tarir** *(de l'eau)* ◊ *tɔ̋oyí yà bhɤ̋ɤ* la sauce s'est évaporée (sur le feu) ◊ *wèe yí yáa bhɤ̋ɤ dhɛ̀ yí wɛ̋ɛ yɤ̏ bhɤ̏ɤ* personne n'échappera à la vengeance pour ses crimes *(proverbe, litt. : l'eau salée ne tarit pas comme l'eau simple)* ♦ *ȁ zūʌ́ {dhíɤ} yɤ̏ bhɤ̏ɤ gbɛ́* elle se fait trop de soucis **2** *vi fig.* **diminuer**, **tendre à disparaître** ◊ *ȁ bhȁ dhœ̀œn yɤ̏ bhɤ̋ɤ-sīʌ* son argent touche à sa fin

bhɤ̏pʌ̏ <manger-chose> ***n*** **nourriture** *Syn.* *kɔ̋ŋ* ♦ *Gbȁtȍ yáa bhɤ̏pʌ̏ zʌ̄ ɤ̄ dhí* Gbato n'est pas difficile en ce qui concerne la nourriture

bhœ̄œ, **bhɔ̄ɔ** ***n*** **tortue** ♦ *sɛ́ bhœ̄œ* tortue terrestre ♦ *yí ȁ bhœ̄œ* tortue aquatique ♦ *yɤ̏ klɤ̏ɤ̏ ká dhè bhœ̄œ dhɤ́* il est de petite taille comme une tortue

bhœ̄œ̏ ***loc.n*** *SUP de* bhɛ̄ɛ́dhɛ̏ *cou*

bhœ̋œŋ̏ ***n*** ***Xerus erythropus*** **rat palmiste**, **écureuil terrestre**

bhrrȕubhrrȕubhrrȕudhɤ̄ ***onomat*** **grondement** *(de voiture)* ◊ *sīapɤ̄bháȁn áa gɔ̄ ɔ̋o gɔ̄ bhȁ, gɔ̄ wɛ̏ bhrrȕubhrrȕubhrrȕudhɤ̄* une voiture qui n'a pas de pot d'échappement pétarade

bhúʌ̏ʌ ***n rn*** **barbe** ♦ *yáa ɤ̄ bhúʌ̏ʌ bhɔ̄* il ne se rase pas ♦ *ȁ bhúʌ̏ʌ yȁ dȁ* sa barbe a poussé ♦ *bhúʌ̏ʌ bhɛ̏n* un barbu, homme barbu ♦ *ȁ bhúʌ̏ʌ yɤ̏ lȍo ȁ tȍŋ tȁ* sa barbe arrive jusqu'à la poitrine *(les Dan n'ont pas de barbes plus longues que ça)*

bhűʌʌ ***n*** **1** ***Khaya ivorensis*** **acajou** **2** **arbre** *(esp., ressemble à l'acajou : la résine sert de glu pour les calebasses et les pots, on le brûle pour l'éclairage)* *Syn.* *kpɛ̄ɛnŋdhɯ̏ɯ*

bhúʌ̏ʌbhúʌ̏ʌsɯ̏ɯ ***adj*** *Int. de* bhúʌ̏ʌsɯ̏ɯ *barbu.INT*

bhúʌ̏ʌsɯ̏ɯ {A P S, bhúʌ̏ʌsɯ̏ɯ-dhȕn pl. A, bhúʌ̏ʌsɯ̏ɯ-sɯ̏ɯ foc. A, bhúʌ̏ʌsɯ̏ɯ-sɯ̏ɯ-dhȕn pl. foc. A; bhúʌ̏ʌbhúʌʌ̏sɯ̏ɯ Int. A P S, bhúʌ̏ʌbhúʌ̏ʌsɯ̏ɯ-dhȕn Int. pl. A, bhúʌ̏ʌbhúʌ̏ʌsɯ̏ɯ-sɯ̏ɯ Int. foc. A, bhúʌ̏ʌbhúʌ̏ʌsɯ̏ɯ-sɯ̏ɯ-dhȕn Int. pl. foc. A} <barbe-adj.> ***adj*** **barbu**

bhȕʌŋ ***n*** **plante herbacée** *(esp.; 2-3 fruits longs et rouges au pied de la tige, jus sucré comestible; pousse en savane) [dans le cadre du cousinage de plaisanterie, les habitants du Gouèta se moquent des habitants de Pleepleu en relevant leur avidité pour les fruits de cette plante]*

bhȕɛɛndhɤ̄ ***adv*** *yɛ̋e tó bhȕɛɛndhɤ̄* **sourire**

bhūn *n* arch. **femelle** Syn. *dhèe* ♦ *gbɛ̂n bhūn* chienne

bhûn *n* **herbe** *(molle) [utilisée pour couvrir le sommet du toit de la case]*

bhūnŋ *n* **ballot** ♦ *yɛ̄ɛ́ bhūnŋ* ballot de coton

bhūɤɤ *n* **champignon** *(brun, à tête pointue, agaricacée, pousse sur les termitières, très nourrissant)* Syn. *gwɛ̄bùŋbúŋ*

bhūtū *n* **panier** *(de bambou, couvert, avec un trou en bas; on l'utilise pour garder les habits etc.) [confectionné par les femmes]* Qsyn. *tɤ̄ɤ*

bhȕu *n wūn bhȕu kún* **coiffer à va-vite**

bhúȕ *n* **champ exploité la deuxième ou troisième année après le défrichage**

bhűu *n* ***Viverra civetta*** **civette**

bhùugwʌ̀ *n* **latérite** ◊ *wáa kê kʌ̄ bhùugwʌ̀ gú* on ne cultive pas sur la latérite

bhú 1 1) {bhū} *v vi* **briller**; **brûler** *(du soleil)* ♦ *yʌ́nŋ̀ yɤ̏ bhȕ gbɛ́ɛ̏ dhɛ̏ yā' gú* le soleil brûle beaucoup à cet endroit ♦ *ȁ yán gú yɤ̏ bhȕ kpɤ́kpɤ́dhɤ̄* ses yeux brillent d'une façon saine

bhú 1 2) *n* **lumière** *(d'un objet brillant)* ♦ *dhàŋbhá bhú pűu* la vive lumière de la lampe ♦ *sɪ́ɤ bhú* lumière ◊ *sɪ́ɤ bhú gbɛ́ɛ̏ yȁ bhú kɔ́ɔ̏dhɤ̄* une lumière vive a éclairé la maison

bhú 2 *n* **faim de viande** *(on l'attribue surtout aux vieux)* ♦ *yɤ̏ bhú kʌ̀* il aime trop la viande

bhúkʌ̄ *n* **passion pour la viande**

bhúkʌ̄bhɛ̏n *n* **celui qui aime manger la viande, amateur de viande**

bhȕn *cop* **être** *(copule d'énoncés d'identification et équatif, lorsque l'objet visé est hors de vue)* Qsyn. *bhā 1 3)* ◊ *bhī bhȕn* c'est toi ◊ *bháa bhȕn* ce n'est pas toi ◊ *Zân bhȁ yʌ̄ bhȕn bhɛ̄n dhōŋ-sȕ ká* le travail de Jean consiste à compter les gens

bhūn 1 {bhūn} *v vt* **boire** ♦ *yɤ̏ yɪ́ bhūn-sɪ̄ʌ* i) il boit de l'eau ii) il est en train de se noyer

bhūn 2 *adv après un ton moyen, le ton passe au registre haut* **1 là-bas** *(hors de la zone accessible à la vue des interlocuteurs)* ◊ *yà ɤ̄ bhā kɔ́ dɔ̄ yɛ́ɛn tȁ tīidhɤ̏, yɤ́ dhō bhún* il a construit sa maison là sur le sable et il est allé (habiter) là-bas ♦ *bhūn yʌ̀n* là-bas, loin d'ici **2 en dehors** *(désigne la trajectoire provenant du centre de repère vers l'extérieur)* ♦ *ūı dhūnwɛ́ɛ yʌ̄ bhȁ bhūn !* merci pour le travail ! que Dieu t'aide ! *(se dit à celui qui est loin)*

bhūndhɛ̀ <là-pourquoi> *adv* **comment ?** ◊ *yɤ̏ ȁ kʌ̀ bhūndhɛ̀ ?* comment a-t-elle fait ça ?

bhűnŋ → bhʌ́nŋ *nèrè de Gambie*

D d

dȁ *v* **1.1** 1) *vi* **monter** *(sur – bhȁ, tȁ, vers – ká)* ◊ *dȁ yɤ̄ !* monte ici ! ◊ *Gbȁtȍ yɤ̏ dȁ sɤ̄ bhȁ* Gbato monte sur les palmiers à huile ◊ *Tȍkpȁ yà dȁ tɔ̏n tȁ* Tokpa est monté une montagne ◊ *yī dȁ tɔ̏n bhā ȁ bhȁ* nous étions en train de gravir la montagne *(sans atteindre le sommet)* ◊ *yī dȁ tɔ̏n bhā gwìnŋ̏* nous avons monté au sommet de la montagne 2) *vt* **lever** ◊ *tɛ́ɛ yà sɪ́ɤ tɛ́ɛ dȁ dhāŋ̄ ká* le vent a levé la fumée vers le ciel **1.2** 1) *vi* **entrer** ◊ *yɤ̏ dȁ gbàúȕ gʊ́ dhɤ́ kɤ̄ yɤ̏ yɪ́ bhʊ̄n* il est en train d'entrer dans la cuisine pour boire de l'eau ◊ *bhán dȁ yɪ́ bhȁ, bhān sàbhá̰ yà tɔ̀ɔ* je suis entré dans l'eau, et ma chaussure s'est mouillée 2) *vt* **mettre** ◊ *wà pɪ̀ɤ wɔ̃́wɔ̃́sʊ̏ dȁ yɪ́ sæ̀æ bhàa* on a trempé le fer très chaud dans l'eau froide ♦ *wʌ́ʌ̏ dȁ wʌ́ʌ̏kɔ̏ gʊ́* déposer l'argent à la banque **1.3** *vi* **faire l'irruption** *(chez – tȁ)* ◊ *yɤ̏ dȁ n̄ tȁ kɔ́ɔdhɤ̄ gbēŋ zɔ̀ɔ wȁ !* la nuit, il a fait l'irruption chez moi à la maison ! **2.1** *vt* **porter** *(vêtement)*, **mettre** *(vêtement; sur – bhȁ)* Syn. bhō, yȁ ◊ *yȁ sɔ̄ sʌ̏ dȁ ɤ̄ bhā dhʌ́n bhȁ* elle a habillé son enfant avec de beaux vêtements ◊ *yɤ̏ sɔ̄ dȁ ɤ́ dhō ɤ̄ dhòo pɪ́ɤ* il s'est habillé et est parti chez son frère aîné **2.2** *vt* **mettre** *(la lame de la machette dans le manche)* ♦ *bhán bá̰ŋ dȁ ɤ̄ gɔ̏ gʊ́* j'ai mis la lame de la machette dans le manche **3.1** *vi* **partir** *(se mettre en route)* ◊ *bhán dȁ ʊ̄ dhɪ́ɤ sɪʌ* je partirai avant toi **3.2** *vi* **commencer à bouillir** ◊ *gwɛ́ɛ yɪ́ yɤ̏ dȁ vá̰andhɤ̄* la sauce d'arachide se met vite à bouillir **4.1** *vi* **adhérer** *(à – gʊ́)* ◊ *yá wɛ́' bhȁ kɤ̄ n̄ tɛ́ɛdō yɤ̏ dȁ bá̰nkpɤ̄ gʊ́* nous avons admis un de mes amis dans l'association de travail **4.2** *vi* **entrer** *(une profession – gʊ́)* ◊ *yɤ́ á dȁ plàŋtɪ̃ɪ̃dhɛ̏ gʊ́ ...* et je suis devenu un apprenti maçon **4.3** *vt dȁ kwʌ́ʌ̏* **rassembler** ◊ *pʌ̄ yȁagā ɤ́ dhɔ̀ɔ bhá' gbàn pɛ́ɛ dȁ kwʌ́ʌ̏ āa...* eh bien, quand ces trois choses seront réunies... **4.4** *vi* **s'impliquer** *(dans – gʊ́)* ◊ *wɔ́n dɔ̃́ɔndɔ̃̏ɔn-sʊ̏ bhɛ̏ɛn ɤ́ dȁ ȁ gʊ́ yā ?* quel est ce problème très pénible dans lequel il s'est impliqué ? **4.5** *vt* **mettre**; **charger** ◊ *dhɛ̀ ɤ́ kwɛ̀ɛ̏ bhā' dhū, yɤ́' dȁ gɔ̄ gʊ́* quand il a eu emballé le bagage, il l'a mis dans la voiture **4.6** *vt dȁ ɤ̄ kèŋ̏* **amener** *(personne)* ◊ *ká dhó'-dhʊ̏n dȁ' kā kèŋ̏* ne les amenez pas **4.7.1** *vi* **faire la cour** *(à – kèŋ̏)* **4.7.2** *vi* **obtenir du succès** *(auprès d'une femme – kèŋ̏)* **4.7.3** *vi dȁ dhēbɔ̏ gɔ̏ gʊ́* **séduire une femme**, **détourner une femme** **4.8** *vi* **commencer une vie ensemble** *(wō kó kèŋ̏)* ◊ *yī zɪ́ɤ̏ɤ-dhʊ̏n bhā, yɤ́ wó wɛ̏' gɔ̏ bhȁ, yɤ́ wēŋ wó dȁ wō kó kèŋ̏* nos ancêtres ont donné leur accord, et ils on commencé leur vie commune **4.9** *vt* **frapper avec qch** *(sur – gʊ́)* ◊ *yɤ̏ bá̰ŋ dȁ' gɔ̏ gʊ́ kɤ̄ wȍ dhēŋdhɤ̄* il lui a fendu la tête avec la machette lorsqu'ils étaient au champ ♦ *gbȉŋgbɤ̄ yà dȁ n̄ gʊ́* l'anguille électrique m'a donné une décharge **5.1** *vt* **créer** Qsyn. kʌ̄ ◊ *Zlȁan dhʊ̄n ɤ́ sɛ́ dȁ* c'est Dieu qui a créé la terre **5.2** *vt* **naître** ◊ *n̄ tɔ́ dȅdȅ ɤ́ kʌ̏ n̄ tɔ́ dȅdȅ ká wó n̄ dȁ ȁ bhȁ...* mon vrai nom, celui qui est devenu mon vrai nom lorsque je suis né **6** *vt* **rajouter** *(à – tȁ)* ◊ *yà ȁ vìtɛ̂sʊ̏ bhá dȁ ȁ tȁ* il a accéléré **7** *vi* **offenser** *(un aîné – dhɪ́ɤ)* **8** (t) *vt* **domestiquer**; **élever** *(bétail)* Qsyn. tʊ̏ɤ **9.1** *vi ɤ̄ dhɪ́ dȁ* **se mettre** *(à – gʊ́)* Syn. yȁ ... bhȁ, zʊ̄n ... bhȁ, yɤ̄ ... bhȁ, zʊ̄-bhō **9.2** *vi* **se mettre** *(à – bhȁ)* ◊ *Zân yɤ̏ dȁ yʌ̄ kʌ̄-sʊ̏ bhȁ, ȁ yī yȁ gwʌ̀ʌ* Zan a commencé à travailler depuis longtemps **9.3** *vi* **apparaître** *(parmi – gʊ́)* ◊ *dhē yà sɔ́, kɤ̄ ȁ fɔ̃́ɔfɔ̀o-dhʊ̏n wà dȁ ȁ-dhʊ̏n gʊ́ prov.* lorsque les femmes deviennent nombreuses, certaines parmi elles deviennent inutiles **9.4** *vi* **tomber**, **descendre** *(soir)*

10 *vt* **nommer** *(d'après qn – dhɛ̏) [normalement, on nomme l'enfant après une consultation avec le devin; on croit que, si le nom "ne plaît pas à l'enfant", il sera souvent malade]* ◊ *yɤ̏ dhʌ́n dȁ ɤ̄ dʌ̄ dhɛ̏* il a donné à l'enfant le nom de son père **11** *vt* **toucher** *(en conversation)* **12** *vt* **fixer** *(la date)* Syn. *kpɔ́* ◊ *Yɔ̏ dɔ̄ yī wó ȁ dȁ, yà lòo* le jour fixé pour l'arrivée de Yo chez le mari est venu **12** *vi* **troubler** *(qn – gɛ̏n gúu)* **13** *vi dȁ bhɛ̄n dhɛ̏ pʌ̄ pɪ́ɤ* **empoisonner qn**; **trahir qn**

dà *n rn* **belle-mère** *(au sens classificatoire : "femme du groupe des donneurs d'épouse", mais aussi "parente aînée de l'époux ou de l'épouse", nommément : belle-mère, soeur aînée de femme; (tp) soeur aînée du mari; femme de zlάȁ; femme du fils; sœur et mère de femme de fils; femme de fils de n'importe quel frère ou sœur; femme de fils de fils)* Qsyn. *dhɯ̋n* ♦ *dà sɛ̋ɛ́ndhʌ́n* femme de petit-fils *(pour un homme : femme de n'importe quel bhāadhʌ́n)*

dȁa *n* **accord** ♦ *ȁ dȁa kʌ̄* accepter qch ◊ *bhán pɤ̄ yɤ̏ dhūn, yáa ȁ dȁa kʌ̄* quand je lui dis de venir, il refuse ◊ *yɤ́ dhɯ̋ndhē-dhʌ́n bhā ɤ́' dȁa kʌ̀' gɔ̏ ɤ́' pɤ́* la vieille a accepté cela, elle a dit...

dȁbɯ̋ɯ́dȕ <monter-brousse-boeuf> *n* **vache désobéissante 2 petit voyou, polisson**

dɑ̋dhɔ̋a <Daloa, nom d'une ville> *n* **daloa** *(sorte de cola blanc; sucré, peu astringent) [jugé inapproprié pour les sacrifices]*

Dàn *n* **Dan** *(peuple et langue)*

dān {dān} *v* **1** 1) *vt* **mesurer** *(avec – gúu)*, **peser** *(sur – tȁ)* 2) *vi* **être mesuré** ◊ *yɤ̏ dȁn kɤ̄ ā kɔ́ɔdhɤ̄* cela a été mesuré lorsque j'étais à la maison **2** 1) *vi dān kwʌ̋ʌ* **se résoudre** 2) *vt dān kwʌ̋ʌ* **résoudre** *(problème)*

dân *n* ***Acacia ataxacantha (gen. Mimosaceae)*** **liane épineuse**

dʌ̄ 1) *n* **1** *rn* **père** *("père classificatoire" : le père, le frère cadet du père; le mari de la sœur cadette de la mère; le mari de la fille du frère aîné de la mère; après la mort du père, le frère aîné est considéré comme père)* ♦ *dʌ̄ kpɪ́ɪ̄* père d'ego *(les frères aînés du père sont des zɪ́ɤ̏ɤ, donc le père est le plus âgé de tous les dʌ̄)* ♦ *dʌ̄-dhȕn* parents, grande famille ◊ *ȁ dʌ̄-sȕ dhʌ̀n wāȁ ɤ̄ dʌ̄-dhȕn wó dhɪ́dhȁan bhān* son père s'est brouillé avec sa grande famille ♦ *dʌ̄ sɛ̋ɛ́ndhʌ́n* mari de la fille du frère cadet de la mère; fils de la fille du frère cadet de la mère ♦ *kɔ́ dʌ̄* chef de famille **2** resp. **père** *(terme d'adresse utilisé vis-à-vis des hommes de la génération des parents, aux supérieurs, parfois même aux plus jeunes)*

-dʌ̄ 2) ***mrph*** *suffixe désignant le propriétaire ou le porteur du nom de possesseur d'un trait* ♦ *wɛ̄ŋgādʌ̄* homme avec une scarification ♦ *yídhɯ̋ndʌ̄* magicien

dʌ́ʌ̏; **dlʌ́ʌ̏** (t) *la deuxième forme est archaïque* ***n*** **"sœur de famille "** lv. *(pour l'homme : femme de son clan, de la génération cadette)*

dʌ́ʌ̏-dhɛ̏ *n* **visite de "sœur de famille"** *(visite chez les parents pour une femme mariée)*

dʌ̄bhāŋ <père-enfant> *n rn* **demi-frère, demi-sœur** *(enfant de la coépouse de la mère) [inusité comme terme d'adresse, marque la distance]*

dʌ̄bhɛ̏n <père-personne> *n* **1** *rn* **maître 2** Christ. **Seigneur**

dʌ̄dhú <père-fille> ***n*** **1** *rn* **demi-sœur** *(fille de la coépouse de la mère) [n'est pas utilisé comme forme d'adresse, met en relief la distance]* **2** *rn* **sœur** *(terme d'adresse utilisé par une femme envers une autre femme de son clan et de sa génération)*

dʌ̄gbɤ̄ <père-fils> ***n*** **1** *rn* **demi-frère** *(fils de la coépouse de la mère) [inusité comme terme d'adresse, marque la distance]* **2** *rn* **"frère"** *(terme d'adresse poli employé par un homme envers celui qui n'est pas son parent, marque la distance)*

dʌ̄zőo <père-magicien> ***n*** *rn* **frère aîné** *(terme d'adresse utilisé envers un frère aîné initié, au sens large)* Qsyn. dhòo

dȅ ***n*** **résine blanche collante** *(de l'arbre klɨ̋ŋ̀gbɔ̄kún, liane dȅklȍo; on en fait des pièges pour les oiseaux)* ◊ *yà sʌ́ʌ̀ kún dȅ ká; à bhà dȅ yà sʌ́ʌ̀ kún* il a attrapé l'épervier avec de la résine

dè; **dȅ** (t) ***dtm*** **même** *(apparaît après les pronoms personnels réfléchis et restrictifs, des noms personnels)* Syn. dȅdȅ 1 Qsyn. dèbɤ̋ɤ ◊ *yáa yī dȅ wȍ gúˑ-bhān* nous ne nous entendons pas nous-mêmes ◊ *bhāŋ dè pɤ́, bhán pɛ̀ŋ dhɔ́* moi aussi, j'ai acheté des aubergines ♦ *dè kún wɔ́n gúˑ* se maîtriser ♦ *ɤ̄ dè súˑ kpɨ̏ˑ* être orgueilleux ♦ *ɤ̄ dè yǎan* exprès *peut suivre le verbe ou le sujet* ◊ *yíi à kʌ̄ dȅ yǎan* il ne l'a pas fait exprès ◊ *yɤ̏ ɤ̄ dè yǎan yī zʌ̀* il prétend dormir

dē ***n*** *fusionne facultativement avec la marque prédicative ɤ́ : dē ɤ́ > dée, dé* **qui ?** ◊ *dē à gbɛ̂n dhɛ̀n ?* à qui est ce chien ? ◊ *dē bhȕn ūˑ ká ?* qui es-tu ? ◊ *bhīi dē {úˑ} bhā ?* qui es-tu ? ◊ *ūˑ bhā dē ɤ́ yɤ̄ ?* celui-ci est qui pour toi ? ◊ *dē ɤ́ Tòkpà dhȅ ?* qui a appelé Tokpa ?

dé → dée *qui ?*

dèbɤ̋ɤ ***dtm*** **1** **même** *précédé d'un pronom de la série restrictive* Syn. dèe, dȅdȅ, zɨ̀aan ◊ *bhāŋ dèbɤ̋ɤ ā kʌ̄ dhȍ bhūn* moi-même, je suis allé là ◊ *bhāŋ dèbɤ̋ɤ, yɤ̏ kʌ̀ yǎan* cela a eu lieu devant mes propres yeux **2** **exactement** *(avec les numéraux)* Syn. kpɛ̄ɛnŋdhɤ̄ ◊ *bhɛ̄n kœ̀œŋ dō gā yɨ̀isīɤ dèbɤ̋ɤ* exactement quatorze personnes

dèbɤ̋ɤwō <même-adv.> ***adv*** **exactement** *(avec les numéraux en fonction adverbiale)* ◊ *Gbàtȍ yà dhūn plɤ́ɤ̄ yàagā dèbɤ̋ɤwō* Gbato est venu au village exactement trois fois

dȅdȅ 1, **dèedhè** (t) ***adj*** *Int. de* dèe *véritable*

dȅdȅ 2 *Int. pl. de* dȅe *nouveau*

dȅdȅwō <véritable-adv.> ***adv*** **1.1** **très, trop** Syn. yāawō, gbɛ̋ɛ **1.2** **en grand nombre** ◊ *Kèsɛ́ yɤ̏ dɤ̄ŋ dhɨ̀ɤ-sȕ ká ɤ̄ gɔ̏ dhɛ̄ŋdhɤ̄ dȅdȅwō* Kessé a beaucoup de pièges tendus dans son champ **1.3** **bien** Syn. kpɛ̄nŋkpɛ̄nŋdhɤ̄ **2.1** **sûrement**, **certainement** Syn. kpákpádhɤ̄ ◊ *ā dhȍ dhūn' dȅdȅwō* il viendra certainement **2.2** **vraiment** ◊ *dȅdȅwō yɤ́ gɔ̄ndʌ̄dhʌ́n bhā ɤ́ à kʌ̀ dhɤ́* vraiment, cet homme-là fit ainsi **3** **complètement** ◊ *bhlɔ̄ɔ yà pā gwǣǣ ká dȅdȅwō* ce sac est rempli de manioc

dȅe 1) {A P S, dȅe-dhȕn pl. A, dȅe-sȕ foc. A; dȅdȅ Int. pl. A P S, dȅdȅ-dhȕn pl. A S, dȅdȅ-sȕ-dhȕn foc. pl. A; dȅedȅe SupInt. pl. A P S, dȅedȅe-dhȕn pl. A, S, dȅedȅe-sȕ-dhȕn foc. pl. A} ***adj*** **1.1**

nouveau 1.2 de nouveau *en position de l'attribut du préverbe* **2 frais, froid** *(eau)*; **calme** *(coeur)* ◊ *yí dȅe* l'eau fraîche ◊ *ɤ̄ zūʌ́ kʌ̄ dȅe* sois patient

dȅe 2) ***adv*** **récemment**

dȅe 3) ***n*** **passé récent** ◊ *yȁ ȁ zū-bhō dȅe gúu* il l'a commencé récemment ♦ *dȅe yā' gúu* tout de suite *(par rapport au passé ou au futur)* ◊ *tőo yā yɤ̏ gȉi dȅe yā' gúu* cette sauce a aigri tout de suite *(après avoir été préparée)*

dèe {dȅdȅ Int. A, dèe-dhȕn pl. A, dèe-sȕu foc. A; dèkédȅkȅ SupInt. A, dèkédȅkȅ-dhȕn SupInt. pl. A, dèkédȅkȅ-sȕu SupInt. foc. A, dèkédȅkȅ-sȕu-dhȕn SupInt. foc. pl. A} ***adj*** **1.1 véritable** Syn. dèedhē ◊ *tææ̀n wɔ̀n dȅdȅ* la pure vérité ◊ *kwípɤ̏ sʌ̏ dȅdȅ bhȕn* c'est une très jolie ville **1.2** *tojours en forme intensive, dȅdȅ* **pur** *(sans addition)* ◊ *sʌ́ŋ dȅdȅ* l'or pur ♦ *sɛ́ dȅdȅ* la laine pur **2 en question** ◊ *bhēn dèkédȅkȅ ɤ́ á wȅ' ká, yɤ̄ dhʌ̀n* c'est exactement la personne dont j'ai parlé **3 même** *(identique) le pronom précédent apparaît à la forme restrictive* ◊ *dhȕutîi yɤ̄ɤ dèe yɤ̏ dhɤ̏ dhūn'* le chef de village lui-même viendra ◊ *bhīi dȅdȅ bháa ȁ wɔ́n bhá dɔ̄* toi-même, tu n'en sais rien **4 principale** *(connu ou utilisé par tout le monde)* ◊ *zīaan dèe* la route principale

dée ***n*** *une forme fusionnée du pronom interrogatif avec la marque prédicative 3SG : dē ɤ́ > dée* **qui ?** ◊ *dé bhēn kpîi-sȕu ká ?* qui est le plus âgé ?

dȅedȅe *SupInt. pl. de* dȅe *nouveau*

dȅedhʌ́n <nouveau-enfant> ***n*** **bébé**

dèedhè (t) → dȅdȅ *véritable.INT*

dèedhē {A S} ***adj*** **vrai, véritable** Syn. dèe ◊ *wɔ́n ɤ́ yáa dèedhē ká* une histoire qui n'est pas vraie

dȅewō <nouveau-adv.> ***adv*** **de nouveau** Syn. *bháwō*

dèkédȅkȅ ***adj*** *Int. de* dȅdȅ 1.2) *véritable*

dȅklȍo <résine-entrelancement> ***n*** **liane** *(esp.; la résine blanche et collante est utilisée pour les pièges contre les oiseaux)*

déŋ̋déŋ̋ ***n*** **morceaux** *(égaux en dimension)* ◊ *dhűu bhā ȁ kplűu-kấn déŋ̋déŋ̋ ká* découpe ce bois en morceaux de dimension égale

dēpāndân <Fr. indépendant> ***n*** **mauvaise herbe** *(haute, fleurs bleu clair; très envahissante, apparue en Côte d'Ivoire au temps de l'Indépendance, d'où le nom)*

dȅslɔ̏ɔ <même-trouver> ***adj*** **1 réussi, prospère** *(personne) toujours accompagné de la marque de focalisation* ◊ *bhēn pɛ́pɛ́ ɤ́ wó tō, kwí gblɤ́gblɤ́ dȅslɔ̏ɔ dhʌ̀n ɤ́ wó' ká* tous les autres, sans exception, devinrent des grands fonctionnaires accomplis **2 même** *de nombreux acteurs* ◊ *bhá wɔ̀ɔ dȅslɔ̏ɔ yɤ̄ dō kɤ̄ wȍ dhȅ-bhō-sīʌ dhɛ̀ kɔ̏ yā' dhɤ́ ȅe ?* as-tu vu des singes en train de défricher comme ça ?

dȅsúukpîi, dèsúukpîi <même-prendre-grand> ***n*** **orgueil** ◊ *Yɔ̏ yɤ̏ dèsȕukpîibhȅn ká* Yo est orgueilleuse

dɛ̀ *n* **divination ♦** *dɛ̀ bɔ̄* dire la bonne aventure

dɛ̀bɔ̄bhɛ̀n *n* **devin** Syn. *dɛ̀bhīn*

dɛ̀bhàan <divination-oiseau> *n* ***Ploceus cucullatus, P. collaris*** **tisserin gendarme** Syn. *bhàantɛ́ɛ, gòplɤ́ɤ̄, pɤ̄bhàan*

dɛ̀bhīn {pl. dɛ̀zʌ̀-dhùn, dɛ̀bhīn-dhùn} *n* **devin** Syn. *dɛ̀bɔ̄bhɛ̀n*

dɛ́dɛ̀, dɛ́dɛ̀dhʌ́n, dɛ́ɛdɛ̀ (t,) *adj* **petit** Syn. *sɛ̄ɛ́ndhʌ́n* ◊ *ī zūʌ́ dhɪ́ɤ tɛ̀ɛ gúi wɔ̀n dɛ́dɛ̀ bhùn* c'est une affaire qui m'inquiète

dɛ́dɛ̀ *adv* **un peu**

dɛ̀ɛ *n* **aujourd'hui** ◊ *ī gɛ̀n ɤ́ yā yɤ̀ bhlà dɛ̀ɛ gbēŋ* cette nuit ma jambe a enflé

dɛ̀ɛ̀n *prev* **cache** *(fait de cacher, de se cacher)*

dɛ̀ɛ̀n-kpɔ́ (gw), **dɪ̀ŋ-kpɔ́** (m) *v* **1** 1) *vt* **cacher** *(de – gɔ̀)* Syn. *bɪ̀n, gblɛ̀ɛn-kpɔ́* 2) *vr* **se cacher** Syn. *gblɛ̀ɛn-kpɔ́* **2** *vr* **dresser une embuscade** Syn. *gblɛ̀ɛn-kpɔ́* ◊ *zīaankʌ̋nbhɛ̀n-dhùn wà wō dɛ̀ɛ̀n-kpɔ́ zīaan pɪ́ɤ* les coupeurs de routes ont dressé une embuscade près de la route

dɛ̀ɛnŋdɛ́ɛnŋ *n* **libellule**

dɛ̂n *n* **chiendent** *[utilisé pour la toiture]*

dɛ̀nŋdɛ̀nŋdhɤ̄ *adv* **bien aiguisé et brillant** *(arme blanche)*

dɛ̂npʌ̀dʌ̄ (m) <chiendent-chose-père> *n* ***Atilas paludinosus*** **mangouste des marais** Syn. *kpɔ̀*

dɛ̋ŋ *n* ***Piliostigma thonningii (gen. Caesalpiniaceae)*** **arbre** *(esp. : feuilles rondes, on extrait une teinture rougeâtre de la racine, on en teint les habits des chasseurs, avec la technique bogolan)*

dɛ̋ŋdɛ̀ŋ {A P S, dɛ̋ŋdɛ̀ŋ-dhùn A, dɛ̋ŋdɛ̀ŋ-sùi A S, dɛ̋ŋdɛ̀ŋ-sùi-dhùn A S} *adj* **plat** *(toit)* ◊ *kɔ́ gbà dɛ̋ŋdɛ̀ŋ {sùi} dhʌ̀n {ɤ́} à dɔ̄* il a bâti une maison à toit plat

dɛ̀zʌ̀-dhùn *n pluriel du* dɛ̀bhīn *devin*

dìʌnŋ *n* **génie nain de brousse** *(ressemble à l'homme, à cheveux longs descendant sur le dos, pousse des cris nocturnes, parfois fait la circoncision des enfants à l'insu des parents; les sorciers et les magiciens savent parler avec lui)*

dìʌnŋtlòo <génie.nain-termitière> *n* **termitière** *(petite, grise, sans chapeau)*

dìbhánŋ̋sùi < Fr. dimanche > *n* **dimanche**

dīdhētʌ́ʌ̀ < Fr. directeur > *n* **directeur** *(d'école)* Syn. *klàŋ̋gɔ̀bhɛ̀n kpɪ̂ɪ̀*

dɪ̂ɪ̀ *n* **poudre médicinale** *(médicament à base de feuilles contre le mal de ventre, le ballonnement de ventre, l'impuissance sexuelle)* ◊ *yà dɪ̂ɪ̀ zɔ̄n* il a pilé des plantes en poudre médicinale

dīinŋdīnŋdhɤ̄ *adv Int. de* dīnŋdhɤ̄ *silencieusement*

dɪ̋ɪŋ *n* ***Pilostigma reticulatum*** **arbre** *(esp.; ses racines sont utilisées pour noircir le tissu)*

dìn *n rn* **découragement** ♦ *n̄ dìn yà yʌ̀n* je suis découragé

dīn *n* **goût** ◊ *bhēn gblṹṹùdhɛ̀ dhʌ̀n bhɤ̀pʌ̀ dīn dhɤ́ dhì à bhà* c'est dans le ventre de l'homme que passe le goût de la nourriture *(on dit cela à celui qui doit avaler un médicament ou une nourriture mauvais au goût)* ♦ *à dīn yɤ̀ dhì* c'est délicieux ♦ *yɤ́ à dīn yɤ̀ tō' tṍo* et il a beaucoup apprécié son goût

dīǹ, dīn *n* **faim** Syn. vâ (m) *suivi d'un ton haut, se réalise avec un ton moyen* ♦ *dīǹ yà n̄ kún; dīǹ yɤ̀ n̄ kʌ̄-sīʌ* j'ai faim ♦ *dīǹ yáa à bhà* il n'a pas faim ♦ *tó dīn ká* rester affamé

dìnbhìn → tìnbhìn *pièce de monnaie coloniale*

dīn-dān <goût-mesurer> *v vt* **goûter** Syn. dīn-gà ◊ *Gbàtò yɤ̀ dhɔ́ndhɔ́n dīn-dàn kɤ̄ yɤ̀ klàŋdhɪ́ɤ* Gbato a goûté le lait lorsqu'il était à l'école

dīn-gà <goût-regarder> *v vt* **goûter** Syn. dīn-dān ◊ *bhãa dīn sɛ̄ɛ́ndhʌ́n gà !* goûte un peu de riz !

dīŋdhɤ̄ {Int. dīiŋdīŋdhɤ̄} *adv* **1 silencieusement** ♦ *dīŋdhɤ̄ yà à kún !* silence ! ♦ *kà dɔ̄ dīŋdhɤ̄ !* calmez-vous ! taisez-vous ! **2 stupéfait** Syn. zītīŋdhɤ̄

dìŋ 1 ***n* *Pycnanthus angolense (gen. Myristicaceae)* plante** *[le jus est utilisé contre la stomatite]*

dìŋ 2 *n* **bourgeon, jeune pousse** *(sur un arbre)* Qsyn. bhòŋ

dīŋdìŋ {P S} *adj* **engourdi** ♦ *n̄ kɔ̀ yà kʌ̄ dīŋdìŋ dhɛ́ndhɛ́n kɔ̄ɔ* le froid a engourdi mes mains

dīŋdhɤ̄ *adv* **1 longuement** *(se taire, ne pas bouger)* ◊ *tɛ́ɛ yà dɔ̄ dīŋdhɤ̄* le vent a longtemps dormi **2 immobile** ◊ *yɤ́ dɔ̄ sɛ́ɛnŋdhɤ̄ tɤ́ŋdhʌ́n bhá ká* il demeura un instant immobile

dìŋ-kpɔ́ (m) → dɛ̀ɛ̀n-kpɔ́ *cacher*

dìɤ *adv* **déjà** ◊ *yɤ̀ yʌ̄ zū-bhò dìɤ* il a déjà commencé le travail

dlã́ *n* **pont de lianes**

dlàaká <Manding dàraka> *n* **petit-déjeuner**

dlāàn 1 {dlàan} *v* **1** *vt* **instruire, enseigner à** *(qch – ká)* ◊ *Zân yɤ̀ Tòkpà dlāàn-sīʌ yí kʌ̄-sǜ ká* Zan est en train d'apprendre Tokpa à nager **2.1** *vt* **apprendre** ◊ *yɤ̀ kʌ̄ pʌ̄ yà-sǜ dlàan vãandhɤ̄* il a vite appris à écrire **2.2** *vt* **étudier** *(chez – kèŋ)* ◊ *yɤ̀ sʌ́ʌdhɛ́ dlàan, kɛ́ɛ yáa gēnyēn* il fait des études, mais il ne réussit pas ◊ *wò sʌ́ʌdhɛ́ dlāàn-sǜ bhà kwɪ́plɤ̀ɤ* ils font leurs études en ville ◊ *yɤ̀ gɔ̄ dlàan n̄ kèŋ* il a appris à conduire la voiture chez moi

dlāàn 2 {dlàan} *v vi* **glisser** ◊ *ā dlàan gwʌ̀ dhʌ̀n' tà yɤ́ á pɤ̀* j'ai glissé sur le caillou et je suis tombé ♦ *bhēn bhā yɤ̀ dlàan dhīaŋ gú* c'est un menteur effronté

dlʌ́ʌ̀ (t) → dʌ́ʌ̀ *"sœur de famille"*

dlɛ́ɛsǜ <Fr. adresse> *n rn* **adresse**

dlīŋ̈ ***n*** **arbre** *(espèce de : grand, à bois mou; on utilise son écorce en médecine traditionnelle)*

dlőo ***n*** **termite** *(esp.; vivent sous la terre, sortent après les premières pluies en février; se mangent crus)* Qsyn. *dɔ̋ɔ̏*

dlɔ̋kɔ̋dlɔ̏kɔ̏ *SupInt. de* dlɔ̋ɔdlɔ̏ɔ *glissant*

dlɔ̏ɔ 1 <Manding dɔ̀lɔ> ***n*** **vin**

dlɔ̏ɔ 2, dʌ̏ʌ (dial.) ***n*** **fourmis rouges** *(font leur nids sur les arbres; la piqûre peut entraîner l'évanouissement sinon la mort)* ♦ *dlɔ̏ɔ kɔ́* nid des foumis rouges

dlɔ̀ɔ ***n*** **jalousie** *(entre co-épouses, voisins, etc.)* ♦ *dlɔ̀ɔ kʌ̄ bhɛ̄n ká* envier qn

dlɔ̋ɔ ***n*** **grenouille** *(de moyenne dimension) [viande très recherchée]* Qsyn. *bɔ̄ɔ*

dlɔ̋ɔdlɔ̏ɔ {A P S, dlɔ̋ɔdlɔ̏ɔ-dhʉ̏n pl. A, dlɔ̋ɔdlɔ̏ɔ-sʉ̏ foc. A S, dlɔ̋ɔdlɔ̏ɔ-sʉ̏-dhʉ̏n pl. foc. A; dlɔ̋ɔdlɔ̋ɔ Int. pl. A S, dlɔ̋ɔdlɔ̋ɔ-dhʉ̏n Int. pl. A S, dlɔ̋ɔdlɔ̋ɔ-sʉ̏-dhʉ̏n Int. foc. pl. A S, dlɔ̋kɔ̋dlɔ̏kɔ̏ SupInt. A P S, dlɔ̋kɔ̋dlɔ̏kɔ̏-dhʉ̏n SupInt. pl. A S, dlɔ̋kɔ̋dlɔ̏kɔ̏-sʉ̏ SupInt. foc. A S, dlɔ̋kɔ̋dlɔ̏kɔ̏-sʉ̏-dhʉ̏n SupInt. foc. pl. A S} *(dlɔ̋ɔdlɔ̏ɔ seulement au sens de "glissant"; dlɔ̋ɔdlɔ̋ɔ Int. pl. seulement au sens de "lisse")* ***adj*** **1 glissant 2 lisse**

dlɔ̋ɔdlɔ̋ɔ *Int. pl. de* dlɔ̋ɔdlɔ̏ɔ *glissant*

dlɔ̏ɔgādhʉ̏ <vin-os-arbre> ***n*** **vigne** *(néologisme dans la traduction du Nouveau Testament)*

dlɤ̏ŋ ***n*** **toupie** *(jouet; on le fait tourner et on frappe)*

dlūuŋ (m) → dūuŋ *tas*

dlʉ̏nŋ, dlʉ̏ŋ *la première des deux formes est plus usitée* ***n*** **escargot** *(nom générique) [totem du clan de Dhoo]* ◊ *yȁ dlʉ̏nŋ wlɤ̏* il a ramassé des escargots

dlʉ̏ŋ → dlʉ̏nŋ *escargot*

dō 1) ***num*** **un** ◊ *yɤ̄ɤ dō bhā yɤ̏ gʉ̏n tɔ̏n plɛ̀ zìnŋgʉ́* il était seul entre les deux montagnes ♦ *ȁ dō kɤ́ yā* cette fois-ci ♦ *yɤ̄ dō ɤ́ bhā* et en plus ◊ *Sȁkpȁ yáa yʌ̄ kʌ̄, yɤ̄ dō ɤ́ bhā, yɤ̏ kwȁan bhɔ̏* Sakpa ne travaille pas, et en plus, il vole ◊ *yɤ̄ ɤ́ dō yáa zʉ̋* et en plus, il ne se lave pas

dō 2) ***dtm*** **certain** *(l'objet est supposé connu du locuteur, mais inconnu de l'auditeur)* Qsyn. *bhá 1* ◊ *yɤ́ bhīndhʌ́n dō bhá yɤ̏ bhʉ̄n ɤ́ dhʉ̄n* il y avait un autre homme qui était venu ♦ *dō bhā* le même

dō 3) ***adv*** **1.1 finalement**, **enfin** *(appel s'adressant à qn qui hésite)* ◊ *kȁ dȁ kɔ̋ɔdhɤ̄ dō !* entrez donc dans la maison ! **1.2 sans détours**, **directement** ◊ *dhʉ̄n dō !* viens ici directement ♦ *pɤ́ dhɤ́ dō* directement, sans arrêt, sans gêne **2 jusqu'à la fin** ◊ *ȁ kpɛ̏ɛ bhɤ̏ dō kɤ̄ ȁ fɛ̏ɛ yɤ̏ gó n̄ bhȁ* mange le reste et cesse de m'embêter avec ton pleurnichage ◊ *kwȁ ȁ tɔ̏ dhʌ́n gbʌ́n yɛ́ dō* cassons définitivement les pattes du poulet *(prov. : menons l'affaire à terme)* ♦ *ȁ zʌ̄ dō* achève-le **3** *dans les énoncées négatifs ou interrogatifs* **jamais**

(du passé) Qsyn. *tōŋtōŋdhɤ̄* ◊ *bhɛ̄n ɤ́ bhíi ȁ bhȁ pʌ̄ bhɤ̏ dō...* si tu n'a jamais mangé la nourriture d'une personne...

dōdō <un-un> ***adv*** **un à un** ◊ *wò dhȕn n̄ kèŋ̏ dōdō* ils sont venus chez moi un à un

dódó 1) ***dtm*** **1.1 peu nombreux**, **rares** *peut apparaître en position de prédicat sans mot déterminé* ◊ *bhɛ̄n dódó dhʌ̀n wó dhɤ̄ kwànbhɛ̏n bhā' dɔ̄* peu nombreux sont ceux qui connaissent le voleur ◊ *gbēŋ bhɛ̄n yʌ̋n yɤ̏ síɤ bhúú dódó yɤ̏ plɤ́ɤ̄* la nuit, on voit de rares feux dans le village **1.2 certains** *(après un nom pluralisé)* ◊ *yɤ̏ bhɛ̄n-dhȕn dódó dɔ̏* il connaît quelques-uns des gens **2 différents** ◊ *búúkʌ̄bhɛ̏n dhɛ̀ ɤ́ dhɤ́ wȁ wūū sūu dódó zʌ̏* chaque chasseur a tué un animal différent

dódó 2) ***adv*** **1 occasionellement**, **de temps en temps** ◊ *ūū gbɤ̄ yɤ̏ yʌ̄ kʌ̏ bhláā sìʌ dódó* ton fils travaille au champ rarement **2 chaque fois** ◊ *bhān dhʌ́n-dhȕn wȁ dhūn dódó, ȁ-dhȕn bhȁn dhʌ̀n úú' bhō* chaque fois que mes enfants viennent, tu les frappes **3.1 rarement**, **avec des intervalles** *(temporel)* ◊ *yɤ̏ sʌ́ʌdhɛ̋ wò pɤ̏ dódó* il lit mot à mot ◊ *yɤ̏ wɛ̏ dódó kɤ̄ síɤ bhúú yȁ kʌ̄ vɛ̄ɛ̄* les signaux sonores deviennent espacés quand le feu vert s'allume ♦ *tó dódó* être rare **3.2 rarement** *(en espace)* ◊ *blúú yā gúú, dhúú-dhȕn wȁ tó dódó* dans cette brousse les arbres sont rares Qsyn. *dɔ̄ɔ̏ndhɤ̄*

dō-dhȁan <un-ORD> ***adj*** **1 premier** *apparaît dans les numéraux ordinaux de l'ordre des dizaines et supérieurs ainsi que dans l'ordre des unités des numéraux composés* Qsyn. *blɛ̏ɛsȕȕ, blɛ̏ɛsȕȕdhȁan* ♦ *kɤ̏ɤœŋ dō-dhȁan* dixième ◊ *kɔ́ kɤ̏ɤœŋ yȁagā ɤ̄ gā dō-dhȁan* la trente et unième maison **2 l'autre** *(parmi deux)* ◊ *bhɛ̄n plɛ̀ ɤ́ ɤ̄ yʌ̋n-tō'-dhȕn gɔ̏, ȁ bhɛ̄n dō-dhȁan yíi dhūn kɤ̏* des deux personnes qu'il attend, la deuxième n'est pas encore venue

dȍŋ ***n*** ***Mansonia altissima*** **bois bété** *(la sève était utilisée comme poison pour les flèches)*

dőŋ ***n*** **fil de substance visqueuse** ♦ *zʌ̋n yí dőŋ* le fil visqueux de la liane "zan" ♦ *yūn yí dőŋ gblɛ̀ɛn* longue morve ♦ *zìnŋtőŋ dőŋ* toile d'araignée; fil de toile d'araignée

dőŋdőŋsȕȕ ***adj*** *Int. de* dőŋsȕȕ *visqueux.INT*

dőŋsȕȕ {A P S, dőŋsȕȕ-dhȕn pl. A, dőŋsȕȕ-sȕȕ foc. A, dőŋsȕȕ-sȕȕ-dhȕn pl. foc. A; dőŋdőŋsȕȕ Int. A P S, dőŋdőŋsȕȕ-dhȕn Int. pl. A, dőŋdőŋsȕȕ-sȕȕ Int. foc.A S, dőŋdőŋsȕȕ-sȕȕ-dhȕn Int. pl. foc. A S} ***adj*** **visqueux** *(salive, sauce)* ◊ *Yɔ̏ bhȁ zʌ̋n yí yɤ̏ dőŋdőŋsȕȕ ká ɤ́ zìɤ' ká Sàayí bhȁ tȁ* la sauce zan de Yo est plus visqueuse que celle de Saï

dōo ***n*** **pistachier** ♦ *dōo flɛ̋ɛ̀* pistaches décortiquées

dōő ***dtm*** **seul** *(suit un pronom réfléchi ou personnel)* ♦ *yɤ̏ kʌ̏ ɤ̄ dōő ká* il vit seul ♦ *yȁ dhó ɤ̄ dōő ká* il est parti vivre seul

dōsēŋ 1), **dōsēnŋ** {Int. dōsēŋsēŋ} ***restr*** **1.1 un seul** ◊ *ī gā yɤ̏ n̄ gɔ̏ dhɤ́ dōsēŋsēŋ* je n'ai que toi **1.2 seulement** **2 une fois** ◊ *n̄ zíɤɤ̏ yɤ̏ dɔ̄n zʌ̏ dōsēŋ* mon grand-père a toussé une fois **3 égal, le même** ◊ *wò gbàn yɤ̏ dōsēŋ* toutes les langues sont égales

dōsēŋ 2), **dōsēnŋ** {Int. dōsēŋsēŋ} <un- ?> ***adv*** **directement**, **tout droit** ◊ *bhá dhūn dōsēŋ...* si tu vas tout droit...

dōsēŋdhàan, **dōsēnŋdhàan** *num* **le tout premier** ◊ *kwɛ̀ɛ̀ dōsēŋdhàan ɤ́' sūū, yɤ̀ kʌ̄ fīʌʌ' bhā̀* le tout premier bagage qu'il avait pris, il a été incapable de le porter ♦ *dōsēŋdhàan ... tàabhàn* le tout dernier ◊ *à̀ dōsēŋdhàan ɤ́ á dhō' súú' tàabhàn, yɤ́ pɤ̀ yí́ bhàa* le tout dernier (poisson) que j'allais prendre est retombé dans l'eau

dōsēŋsēŋ *restr Int. de* dōsēŋ *seulement*

dòzínŋ̀ *n* **sorte de riz de marécage** *(à grand rendement, peu apprécié à cause de son goût fade; consommé surtout pendant l'hivernage qui est la période de disette)*

dɔ̄ 1.1) {dɔ̄} *v* **1** 1) *vi* **se mettre** Syn. gbàn ♦ *dɔ̄ yɤ̄ !* mets-toi ici ! ♦ *dɔ̄ à̀ píɤ* succéder à, suivre ♦ *dɔ̄ bhēn gbàn gɔ̀* soutenir qn *(donner son appui)* 2) *vt* **mettre** ♦ *n̄ gɔ̀bhɛ̀n yɤ̀ kʌ̄ dhùn dɔ̄' n̄ gɔ̀ zīaàn sʌ̀ ká* mon supérieur m'a bien accueilli *(en allant à ma rencontre)* 3) *vr* **être debout** 4) *vt* **aider à mettre la charge sur la tête** ◊ *n̄ dɔ̄* aide-moi à mettre la charge sur ma tête **2** *vi* **s'arrêter** ♦ *à̀ gú yà dɔ̄* il est rassasié **3.1** *vi* **rester** ◊ *bīɤ yáa zīɤ, flīnŋ yáa dɔ̄* là où l'éléphant passe, il ne reste plus de rosée ♦ *dɔ̄ n̄ ká bádhɤ̄* éloigne-toi un peu de moi ♦ *ɤ́ dɔ̄ yā* maintenant **3.2** *vi* **être occupé** *(par – ká)* ◊ *wɔ́n bhlʌ̀ʌbhlʌ̀ʌsǜ dhʌ̀n ɤ́ kwá dɔ̄' ká yā* nous sommes maintenant occupés par une affaire très importante **4** *vt* **bâtir** **5.1** *vi* **attendre** *(debout; qn – gɔ̀)* Syn. dhíɤ-gān, yān-tó ♦ *dɔ̄ n̄ ká bádhɤ̄* attends-moi à l'écart **5.2** *vi* **attraper** *(ne pas laisser passer; qn, qch – gɔ̀)* ♦ *dɔ̄ bhánŋlōo bhɛ̄ gɔ̀ !* attrape les mangues ! *(appel lancé à celui qui est sous le manguier)* ♦ *kà̀ dɔ̄' gɔ̀ !* attrapez-le ! *(le voleur, p.ex.)* **6.1** 1) *vi* **accompagner** *(qn– bhā̀)* ◊ *kà̀ dɔ̄ n̄ bhā̀, kɤ̀ kwá dhó* escortez-moi 2) *vt* **accompagner** ◊ *dhūn kɤ̀ kó dhó n̄ dɔ̄'* viens avec moi **6.2** *vi* **s'agglutiner** *(sur – bhā̀)* ◊ *zlʌ̄ʌndhʌ́n-dhùn wà dɔ̄ sūkā̄dhū̄ bhā' bhā̀* les fourmis noires se sont agglutinées sur le sucre **6.3** *vi* **étouffer** *(un organe des sens – gúú)* ◊ *yʌ́nŋ̀ yà dɔ̄ n̄ yān gúú* le soleil m'éblouit la vue ◊ *bhànŋzīī wɔ̀ yà dɔ̄ n̄ tɔ̄ɔdhɤ̄* le bruit des moteurs remplit mes oreilles **7.1** *vt* **donner** *(surtout temporairement, ou pour une tierce personne; à – gɔ̀)*, **envoyer** *lv.* Qsyn. gbā 1, dhūn 2 **7.2** *vt* **remettre** *(à – gɔ̀)* ◊ *bhán wʌ̄ʌ̀gā dɔ̄ à̀ gɔ̀* je lui ai remis l'argent **8.1** *vi* **faire un effort** *(dans – dhɛ̀)* ◊ *dɔ̄' dhɛ̀ gbɛ̄ɛ̀ kíi zīɤ !* fais un effort pour passer *(l'examen)* **8.2** *vi* **s'efforcer** *(à – gɔ̀)* ◊ *dɔ̄ à̀ gɔ̀ gbɛ̄ɛ̀, kɤ̀ úú lòo à̀ gwìnŋ̄dhɤ̄* fais un effort pour atteindre le sommet **8.3** *vi* **aider** *(qn – dhɛ̀)* ◊ *dɔ̄ n̄ dhɛ̀ gbɛ̄ɛ̀ káa n̄ bhō* aide-moi sérieusement pour que je puisse finir **9.1** *vi dɔ̄ ɤ̄ gúú* **se mettre en colère** ♦ *yà dɔ̄ ɤ̄ gúú vōodhɤ̄ péj.* il a boudé ♦ *yà dɔ̄ ɤ̄ gúú tīt̀īdhɤ̄* il est au point d'éclater de colère **9.2** *vt ... dɔ̄ à̀ gúú* **tendre** ◊ *yà ɤ̄ gbɛ̀ dɔ̄ à̀ gúú* il a tendu le bras **9.3** *vi* **se gonfler** ◊ *à̀ gèe yà dɔ̄ vōodhɤ̄* son cadavre a gonflé **10** *vt à̀ gɛ̀n dɔ̄ bhēn dhɛ̀* **rapporter qch à qn** **11** *vi dɔ̄ bhēn gɔ̀ yâ* **devenir difficile pour qn** ◊ *bɛ̀ŋ bhā yà dɔ̄ ī gɔ̀ yâ dhɛ̀ ɤ́' gúú...* quand la course sera trop dure pour toi... **12** *vi* **dépendre** *(de – wɔ́n bhā̀)*

dɔ̄ 1.2) *n* **construction** *(processus)*

dɔ̄ 2 {dɔ̄} *v* **1.1** 1) *vt* **savoir** ♦ *yíi dɔ̄ sʌ̀* sans doute, probablement Syn. yɤ̀ bhɔ̀ à̀ bhā̀, yɤ̀ dhɔ̀ kʌ̄' dhɛ̄ ◊ *yíi dɔ̄ sʌ̀, kwā dhē yɤ̀ tùn kɤ̀ dhɔ̄ɔ kwʌ́ʌ̀* sans doute, notre mère est encore au marché ♦ *yɤ̀ sʌ́ʌdhɛ́ dɔ̄* il est très instruit 2) *vi* **être connu** **1.2** 1) *vt* **apprendre** *(obtenir une information)* ◊ *wōo bìaŋ súú kɤ̀ wɔ̀ bɛ̀ŋgā dɔ̄* ils vont courir pour savoir qui d'entre eux est le meilleur coureur 2) *vi* **se manifester** ♦ *à vin yɤ̀ dɔ̀ tɤ́tɤ́tɤ́dhɤ̄* il sonne : tic-tac **2** *vt* **savoir faire** *(qch – -dhɛ̀ ká)* ◊ *yáa dɔ̄ pʌ̄ yà-dhɛ̀ ká* il ne sait pas écrire **3** *vt dɔ̄ à ká* **reconnaître** ◊ *kwàa wɔ́n dɔ̄' ká dhɛ̀...* reconnaissons que...

dɔ̀n *n* **réprimande, reproche** ♦ *dɔ̀n bhō bhɛ̄n ká* grogner contre qn

dɔ̄n {dɔ̀n} *n* **toux** ♦ *dɔ̄n zʌ̄* tousser ♦ *dɔ̄n yɤ̀ à bhà* il a la toux

dɔ́ndɔ̀n {A P} *adj* **humide** *(étoffe)* Syn. sæ̀æ ◊ *bhán sɔ̄ bhō yʌ́nŋ̀ dhʌ̀, kɛ̄ɛn yɤ̀ gùn kɤ̀ŋ dɔ́ndɔ̀n* j'ai retiré le linge qui était au soleil, mail il était encore humide

dɔ̋nkɔ̋ndɔ̀nkɔ̀n *SupInt. de* dɔ̋ɔndɔ̀ɔn *collant*

dɔ̀ŋ *n* **jeune pousse de palmier de raphia**

dɔ̄ŋ *n wɔ̋ dɔ̄ŋ* **tronc** *(de bois de cuisine)*

dɔ̀ŋgɔ̄ <perche de raphia- ?> *n* **bourgeon de palme issu d'une jeune pousse de raphia**

dɔ̄ɔ, dœ̄œ *n rn* **marque, signe**

dɔ̋ɔ̀ *n* **termite** *(esp.; sortent en juillet, dans la nuit; sont séchés au soleil et consommés)*

dɔ̋ɔ 1 *n* **causerie** ♦ *dɔ̋ɔ dɔ̄* causer

dɔ̋ɔ 2 *n* **début de la soirée** *(entre 16 et 18 heures)* ♦ *dɔ̋ɔ yà dà* la nuit est tombée ♦ *dɔ̋ɔ ká gbàn ká* tous les soirs ◊ *dɔ̋ɔ ká gbàn ká yɤ̀ bɔ̀ yɤ̄* il passe par ici tous les soirs ◊ *yɤ̀ n̄ dhɛ̋-kʌ̀ dɔ̋ɔ yā à ká* il m'a soigné aujourd'hui au début de la soirée

dɔ́ɔdhín < Manding dɔ́ɔnin > *adv* **un peu**

dɔ́ɔdhíndɔ́ɔdhín < Manding dɔ́ɔnindɔɔnin > *adv* **petit à petit**

dɔ̋ɔ̀n, dœ̋œ̀n *n* **araignée** *(non venimeuse)*

dɔ̋ɔn *n* **problème inattendu** *(et difficile à résoudre)* Syn. *dhʌ̄nŋ* ♦ *yà dɔ̋ɔn sɯ́* il s'est fourré dans une affaire désagréable

dɔ̋ɔndɔ̀ɔn {A P, dɔ̋ɔndɔ̀ɔn-dhùn pl. A, dɔ̋ɔndɔ̀ɔn-sɯ̀ foc. A, dɔ̋ɔndɔ̀ɔn-sɯ̀-dhùn pl. foc. A; dɔ̋ɔndɔ̋ɔnsɯ̀ Int. A, dɔ̋ɔndɔ̋ɔnsɯ̀-dhùn Int. pl. A; dɔ̋nkɔ̋ndɔ̀nkɔ̀n SupInt. A P, dɔ̋nkɔ̋ndɔ̀nkɔ̀n-dhùn SupInt. pl. A, dɔ̋nkɔ̋ndɔ̀nkɔ̀n-sɯ̀ SupInt. foc. A, dɔ̋nkɔ̋ndɔ̀nkɔ̀n-sɯ̀-dhùn SupInt. pl. foc. A} *adj* **1 visqueux** *(substance)* ◊ *bɤ̄ɤ̀ yā yɤ̀ dɔ̋ɔndɔ̀ɔn* cette boue est gluante **2 collant** *(personne, affaire)* Syn. *dɔ̋ɔnsɯ̀*

dɔ̋ɔ̀ndɔ̋ɔ̀ndhɤ̄ *adv Int. de* dɔ̋ɔ̀ndhɤ̄ *un par un*

dɔ̋ɔndɔ̋ɔnsɯ̀ *Int. de* dɔ̋ɔndɔ̀ɔn *collant, ou* dɔ̋ɔnsɯ̀ *collant*

dɔ̋ɔ̀ndhɤ̄ {Int. dɔ̋ɔ̀ndɔ̋ɔ̀ndhɤ̄} <un-adv.> *adv* **un à un, successivement** *(sans arrêts)* Qsyn. *dódó* ◊ *yɤ́ zɪ̀ɤ pɤ̄-dhùn gɯ́ dɔ̋ɔ̀ndhɤ̄* il est passé par les villages en les dépassant un par un (sans arrêts) ◊ *wɔ̀ dɔ̀ wō bhɪ̀ʌʌ gɯ́ dɔ̋ɔ̀ndhɤ̄* ils font une ligne dense (sans intervalles) ◊ *dhʌ́n-dhùn wɔ̀ zɪ̀ɤ wō kó kèŋ̀ dɔ̋ɔ̀ndɔ̋ɔ̀ndhɤ̄ wó dhō* les enfants passent à la file, puis ils s'en vont *(il s'agit d'un grand nombre d'enfants)*

dɔ̋ɔ̀ndhūn {dɔ̋ɔ̀ndhūn, NEUT dɔ̋ɔ̀ndhùn} *v* **1.1** 1) *vi* **s'arrêter** Syn. *gbáàndhūn* ◊ *gɔ̄ bhā yɤ̀ dɔ̋ɔ̀ndhùn dhún, yɤ̀ gùn yɤ̄ɤ kʌ̄ sʌ̀* si la voiture s'arrêtait, ce serait bien 2) *vt* **arrêter** Syn.

gbáàndhūn **1.2** *vi* **cesser** ◊ *à gɔ̀ gúú yà dɔ̃̀ɔndhūn* sa folie s'est calmée **2** *vi* **rester** *(debout)* ◊ *wɔ̀ dɔ̃̀ɔndhùn dhɛ́dhɛ́ plɛ̀ ká, yɤ́ wó dhō* ils sont restés pendant deux heures, puis ils sont repartis **3** *vi* **attendre** *(debout; qn – gɔ̀)* **4** *vi* **tomber enceinte**, **devenir enceinte** Syn. gú súú

dɔ̃́ɔnsṹũ {A P, dɔ̃́ɔnsṹũ-dhùn pl. A} <difficulté-adj> ***adj*** **collant** *(personne, affaire)* Syn. dɔ̃́ɔndɔ̀ɔn ♦ *wɔ́n dɔ̃́ɔnsṹũ dhʌ̀n ɤ́ yà à kɔ̀ tà* il s'est impliqué dans une affaire compliquée

dɤ ***adv*** **là-bas** *(loin, mais plus proche que tììdhɤ̀)*

dɤ̄ŋ ***n*** **1 fibre des palmes du palmier à huile 2 piège** *(nom générique)* ♦ *dɤ̄ŋ kpēɛ́* bâton flexible *(d'un piège)* ♦ *pɪ̀ɤ dɤ̄ŋ* piège en fer Syn. glā́bā́ ♦ *dɤ̄ŋ dhɪ̀ɤ* tends les pièges ♦ *dà dɤ̄ŋ gúú* tomber dans un piège ♦ *dɤ̄ŋ gà* examiner un piège

dɤ́ŋdɤ̀ŋ {A P, foc. A, pl. A, pl. foc. A; dɤ́ŋgɤ́dɤ̀ŋgɤ̀ Int. A P, dɤ́ŋgɤ́dɤ̀ŋgɤ̀-sṹũ Int. foc. A, dɤ́ŋgɤ́dɤ̀ŋgɤ̀-dhùn Int. pl. A, dɤ́ŋgɤ́dɤ̀ŋgɤ̀-sṹũ-dhùn Int. pl. foc. A} ***adj*** **1 collant** ◊ *bɤ̄ɤ̀ ɤ́ zīàan yā yɤ̀ dɤ́ŋdɤ̀ŋ, wɔ̀ bhɔ̀ɔn à bhà wó gbɔ̄ kʌ̀ à ká* la boue sur la route est si collante qu'on peut en faire des pots **2 avare**

dɤ̄ŋgā ***n*** **corde, fil de fer** *(pour les pièges)* ♦ *pɪ̀ɤ dɤ̄ŋgā* fil de fer

dɤ́ŋgɤ́dɤ̀ŋgɤ̀ 2 ***adj*** *Int. de* dɤ́ŋdɤ̀ŋ *avare*

dɤ́ŋgɤ́dɤ̀ŋgɤ̀ 1 {dɤ́ŋgɤ́dɤ́ŋgɤ́ Int.} ***adj*** **collant** *(boue)* Qsyn. tɤ́ŋgɤ́tɤ̀ŋgɤ̀

dɤ́ŋgɤ́dɤ́ŋgɤ́ *Int. de* dɤ́ŋgɤ́dɤ̀ŋgɤ̀ 1 *collant*

dɤ́ɤ̀ ***n*** ***Cordia mixa*** **arbre** *(esp.)*

dœ̄œ → dɔ̄ɔ *marque*

dœ́œ̀n → dɔ́ɔ̀n *araignée*

dœ̄œŋ ***n rn*** **dimension** ◊ *à bhà kɔ́ dœ̄œŋ̄ dhò dhɯ̃́ɤ́-sṹũ yɤ̀ glɛ̀ɛn* sa maison est haute

dù ***n*** **bœuf** ♦ *dù yɤ̀ wɛ̀ n̄bhúù, n̄bhúù* la vache meugle

dùa 1 ***n*** **hache**

dùa 2 ***v*** **1** *vi* **fuir**, **s'enfuir** *(devant – gɔ̀)* ◊ *yà dùa yà dhó ɤ̄ dʌ̄-dhùn pɪ́ɤ* elle a fui pour aller chez ses parents ◊ *yà dùa kàsò gúú* il s'est évadé de prison ◊ *dhʌ́n bhā yɤ̀ dùa gèe gɔ̀* cet enfant s'enfuit à la vue des masques **2** *vt* **enlever**, **ravir** *(à – dhɛ̀)*

dūā́ <Fr. doit> ***n rn*** **devoir, obligation** *demande une proposition subordonnée au subjonctif* ◊ *ɯ̄ dūā́ bhùn kɤ̄ ɯ́ dhó* tu dois partir

dūaŋ, **dūaŋgā** ***n*** **lance pour couper les régimes des grains de palmier** *(avec un bout arrondi)*

dùʌʌ → dlɔ̀ɔ *fourmis rouges*

dūʌŋ ***n*** *yí dūʌŋ* **endroit profond** *(de rivière)*

dűʌŋ ***n*** **gombo coupé et séché** ♦ *dűʌŋ bì* poudre de gombo ♦ *dűʌŋ yí* sauce de poudre de gombo

dùbɔ̀ŋdhē <bœuf-estomac-adj> ***adj*** *zù ká sɔ̀ dùbɔ̀ŋdhē* **serviette éponge**

dűdű ***adj*** **innombrables** ◊ *bhɛ̄n dűdű* des gens innombrables

dǜɛɛ *n* **1** *rn* **place** *(surtout par référence à des objets verticaux)* Qsyn. dhɛ̏ 1 ◊ *kɔ́ dǜɛɛ* emplacement de la maison **2.1** *rn* **position, poste** ♦ *dǜɛɛ tó* outrepasser ses droits **2.2** *neol., ling.* **fonction, position** ♦ *dǜɛɛ dhɯ́wɔ̀yàn gṹ* fonction syntaxique **3** *rn* **part** ◊ *dhūʌ̏ʌ dǜɛɛ* la part de l'oncle maternel (lors du partage de la viande, etc.)

dūn {dūn} *v* **1** 1) *vi* **être suspendu**; **se pendre** ◊ *bhȁŋglɤ̏ɤ bhē yɤ̏ dūn-sīʌ ɤ̄ dhȕ bhȁ* la papaye est suspendue au papayer ♦ *sɔ̄ kʌ́nŋ yȁ dūn* une frange s'est formée sur l'habit 2) *vt* **suspendre** ◊ *bhʌ̄nŋ́dhē yɤ̏ sɔ̄ dȕn bhīʌ́ʌ bhȁ kɤ̄ yɤ̏ gā* une femme dioula a étendu les vêtements sur la corde pour qu'ils sèchent ♦ *wà dhó wō gɔ̏ dūn'* ils sont allés faire un tête-à-tête 3) *vr* **se pendre** ♦ *ɤ̄ dȅ dūn bhīʌ́ʌ bhȁ* se pendre **2.1** *vi* **envahir** *(oiseaux, insectes volants; qch, un lieu – bhȁ),* **se ruer en masse** ◊ *bhȁan-dhȕn wɔ̀ dȕn dhṹ yā' gā bhȁ* les oiseaux envahissent cet arbre pour en manger les fruits ◊ *pʌ̄bhèe bhā, dhʌ́n-nȕ wɔ̀ kʌ̄ dȕn' bhȁ* les enfants se sont rués en masse sur la nourriture **2.2** *vi* **s'accumuler** *(autour de – tȁ)* ◊ *bhēn-dhȕn wɔ̀ dȕn ȁ bhȁ kwɛ̏ɛ tȁ kɤ̄ wó ȁ kʌ̋n* les gens se rassemblent autour de sa marchandise afin de l'acheter en gros **3** *vi* **être à l'approche** *(de – tȁ)* ◊ *kāȁ dhɛ̏ŋ-dhȕn wà dūn kā tȁ* vos visiteurs sont en route

dūnŋ → dūuŋ *tas*

dṹnŋ *n* **tas d'ordures** Syn. tūŋ (t) ♦ *dṹnŋ tàa* au tas d'ordures ◊ *yà blʌ̄ʌ wènŋ dṹnŋ tàa* elle a jeté les déchets sur le tas d'ordures

dȕnŋdhɤ̄ *adv évoque un attroupement provoqué par un événement triste ou dramatique*

dȕɤ *n* **buffle**

dȕɤɤ → dìoo *conseil*

dȕtȁbhȁan <bœuf-sur-oiseau> *n* **grande aigrette, pique-bœuf** *[tabou (mais non pas kɯ́an) pour les Dan de l'est; on croit qu'il est noir à l'intérieur et que celui qui le mange meurt]*

dȕuŋ *onomat imite la chute d'un objet lourd*

dūuŋ, **dūnŋ** (gw), **dlūuŋ** (m) *n* **1 tas** ♦ *bhēn dūnŋ* foule ♦ *dūnŋ dɔ̄ sɯ́āa* se répandre sur le sol et former un tas **2 sédiment** *(matière en suspension dans un liquide)* ♦ *yɯ́ yȁ dūuŋ bhɔ̄* l'eau s'est troublée ♦ *yɯ́ɤ̏ɤ yȁ yɯ́ dūuŋ bhɔ̄* le poisson a troublé l'eau ♦ *Gbȁtɔ̀ yʌ́n gṹ yȁ dūuŋ bhɔ̄* Gbato est en désarroi

dūū *n* **1 fétiche** *(protecteur contre les voleurs)* ◊ *yà dūū dɔ̄ ɤ̄ bhā bhlʌ́ȁdhɛ̏ tȁ* il a mis le gris-gris protecteur sur son champ **2 sorcellerie, magie** ♦ *dūū plɤ̏ɤ* chez les sorciers, parmi les sorciers ♦ *gbēŋ dȕȕ* magie noire ♦ *yʌ́nŋ̏ gṹ dȕȕ* magie blanche *(pour se protéger contre les sorciers)* ♦ *dūū kʌ̄ bhēn ká* jeter un sort sur qn

dû̂ *n* **lance** Syn. dû̂gā

dūūbhɛ̏n *n* **sorcier, sorcière** *[autrefois, une personne accusée de sorcellerie devait subir l'ordalie en buvant de la décoction de l'arbre glṹ; sa mort était vue comme la preuve de son tort, on brûlait le corps, une partie du corps pourrait être mangée par vengeance]*

dȕȕdȕȕdȕȕdhɤ̄ *onomat imitation du grondement du moteur* Syn. gbȉgbȉgbȉdhɤ̄

dû̂gā <lance-grain> *n* **lance** Syn. dû̂

Dh dh

dhā 1 {dhà} *n* **pluie** ♦ *tɛ́ɛ dhà* orage *(pluie avec vent violent)* ♦ *dhā yɤ̀ bɤ̃́n-sīʌ* il pleut ♦ *dhā yí bhà yī* hivernage ♦ *dhā yɤ̀ wɛ̃́-sīʌ* il tonne ♦ *dhā yà {ɤ̄} yɤ̃́n kún* la foudre a brillé ♦ *dhā yáa dhɤ́ dɛ̀ɛ* il n'y a pas de pluie aujourd'hui

dhā 2 {dhā} *v* 1) *vi* **se sauver** *(de – gɔ̀),* **échapper** ♦ *dhā ɤ̄ kāà ká* l'échapper belle; échapper de justesse *lv.* ♦ *bhɛ́n ɤ́ dhā à kɔ̀ bhà...* celui qui a survécu 2) *vt* **sauver** *(de – gɔ̀)* ◊ *ká wɔ́n sʌ̀ kʌ̄, Zlàan dhò kā dhā'* si vous faites du bien, Dieu vous sauvera ♦ *ɤ̄ dè dhā* sauve-toi *(une action active)* ◊ *bhɛ́n ɤ́ dhɤ́, yɤ̀ ɤ̄ dè dhā !* sauve qui peut !

dhàa *n* **1 couteau** ♦ *kwɪ́ bhà dhàa* couteau de fabrication industrielle ♦ *dhàa kō* dos de couteau **2 petit couteau** *(pour couper le riz dans les bas-fonds)*

dhã́ã̀ *n* **van** *(rond; pour le riz, café, maïs, mil etc.)*

dhã́a 1 *n* **1 jupe de raphia** *(habillement de masque)* ♦ *dhã́a yà* mettre la jupe de raphia **2 ceinture de danseuse dhɛ̈ɛdhɪ̃́ɤ** *(avec ourlets ornés de glands)*

dhã́a 2 *n bhɛ̄n dhã́a* arch. **foule immense** *(qui ne se déplace pas)* Qsyn. kpɤ̄, tǜʌŋ ♦ *bhɛ̄n bhɛ̃́ɛ̀ dhã́a yà bhán* une foule s'est rassemblée

dhàagā <couteau-os> *n* **1 lame de couteau 2 virginité** ♦ *yà dhàagā sú* elle s'est avérée être vierge *(au moment de l'initiation)* ♦ *yàa bhà dhàagā yɛ́* il l'a déflorée

dhàan *n* **1** *rn* **limite** *(du champ, du village)* ◊ *yī dhàan* limite entre nos champs ♦ *sɛ̃́ dhàan dhɪ̃́ɤ* frontière du pays **2** *rn* **différence** ♦ *yáa wɔ́n-dhǜn dhàan dɔ̄* il est naïf **3 fissure** ◊ *à bhà kɔ́ dhàan yà dɔ̄* une fissure est apparue sur le mur de sa maison

-dhàan 1 *mrph suffixe de nombre ordinal* ◊ *yàagā-dhàan* troisième ◊ *dhɛ̀-dhàan ?* quantième ? ◊ *yɤ̀ dhò Bhã́andhɤ̄ dhɛ́dhɛ́ plɛ̀-dhàan ká yāandhɪ̃́ɤ* il est parti à Man hier à deux heures

-dhàan 2, **-ŋ̀** *mrph suffixe verbal de l'action ultérieure (par rapport à l'action exprimée par le verbe de la proposition principale); s'ajoute à l'infinitif du verbe notionnel ou au verbe auxiliaire gūn, dans ce dernier cas seule la variante en -dhàan est possible* ◊ *dhṹ yā yɤ̀ kʌ̄ bhà kwɛ̀ yàagā píɤ, yɤ́ gūn gā'-dhàan* cet arbre a donné des fruits pendant trois ans avant de mourir ◊ *dhɛ̀ ɤ́ bhɛ̄n dhòŋ, yɤ́ gūn dhó'-dhàan* quand il avait compté les gens, il est parti

-dhàan 3, **-ŋ̄**, **-ŋ̀** *mrph suffixe du progressif subordonné, s'attache au verbe à la forme de base dans la proposition relative subordonnée; il y a des restrictions considérables à sa combinaison avec des verbes* ◊ *pʌ́ ɤ́ ú' dhɔ́-ŋ̀ bhā, à bhá tó n̄ gɔ̀ kɤ̄ á' dhɔ́* ce que tu es en train d'acheter, laisse-le moi, pour que je l'achète

'-dhàan 4 <-dhün+ bhä> *mrph contraction de la marque du pluriel avec la marque possessive* ◊ *dhʌ́n-dhàan kèedhɤ̄ yüa yáa sʌ̀* les escarres de l'occiput sont dangereuses pour les enfants

dhàà̀n ***adv*** *balise de focalisation circonstantielle et localisation exacte; s'adjoint aux circonstants de lieu* Ant. *yʌ̀n* ◊ *yɤ̀ ɤ̄ dè̀ dùn bhīʌ́ bhà̀ yɤ̄ dhàà̀n* c'est ici même qu'il s'est pendu ◊ *dhūn yɤ́ yʌ̀n dhàà̀n* viens ici, de ce côté ◊ *bhɤ̀ dhó ūū kwàa gúú dhàà̀n* va plutôt à gauche ◊ *dhūn yɤ́ dhàà̀n !* viens ici ! *(pour orienter vers le locuteur qn qui cherche à s'approcher de lui)*

dhāà̀n, **dhàan** ***prt*** *marque de focus contrastif sur le prédicat; se met après le verbe ou à la fin de la proposition. Exprime une affirmation insistante de la situation, contrairement aux attentes; parfois une évaluation négative est impliquée* **rien autre que** ◊ *dhēbʌ̀dhʌ́n bhā yà̀ pɤ̀ wà Tòkpà̀ gìi è̀e ? – áabhōo, yà̀ pɤ̀ yà dhó dhāà̀n yī zʌ̄* 'est-ce que la femme a dit que Tokpa est blessé ? - Non, elle a dit qu'il est allé dormir ◊ *kāà̀ dhùutīī̀ yɤ̀ Yàobâ ká è̀e ? – áabhóo, yɤ̀ bhʌ̄nŋ́ ká dhāà̀n* est-ce que votre chef de village est un Dan ? - non, il est Dioula *(et cela crée des problèmes)*

dhàanbhā ***adv*** **1 quand même**, **malgré tout** *(par rapport à une action future)* ◊ *bhāan yī zʌ̄ dhàanbhā* je vais dormir malgré tout **2 enfin** ◊ *bhāan pʌ̄ bhɤ̀ dhàanbhā* je vais manger, enfin

dhà̀andhà̀an ***n*** **fissures** *(nombreuses)* ◊ *sɛ́ yà̀ dhà̀andhà̀an dɔ̄* la terre s'est fissurée

dhàandháà̀n, **dhàndhân** <Fr. ananas> ***n*** **ananas** Syn. *dhàŋdlàa*

dhā̋andhā̋an (m) ***n*** **plante herbacée** *(des fleurs jaunes, des petits fruits qui se collent aux habits; on en utilise la sève contre les maux de ventre, et les feuilles pour soigner la mycose de pieds)* Syn. *kɔ̋bhɔ̋ (gw)*

dhāandhāansɯ̀ɯ 1 ***n*** **insistance** ◊ *Tòkpà̀ yà wʌ́ʌ̀gā dhè̀ dhāandhāansɯ̀ɯ ká* Tokpa a demandé de l'argent avec insistance

dhāandhāansɯ̀ɯ 2 ***adj*** *Int. de* dhāà̀nsɯ̀ɯ *ennuyeux*

dháà̀ndhūn {dháà̀ndhūn, NEUT dháà̀ndhùn} ***v vt*** **courber** *(la tête)* Syn. *gbà̀n* ◊ *yà̀ ɤ̄ gɔ̀ dháà̀ndhūn* il a courbé la tête ◊ *ūū kō dháà̀ndhūn* courbe ton dos

dhāà̀nsɯ̀ɯ {A; Int. dhāandhāansɯ̀ɯ A} ***adj*** **ennuyeux** *(travail)* ◊ *yʌ̄ dhāà̀nsɯ̀ɯ yà̀ ῑ sʌ̄ʌ bhō* le travail ennuyeux m'a fatigué

dhā̋bhlīīsɯ̀ɯ <Manding dàbari 'moyen magique'-adj> ***adj*** **bizarre** *(inattendu, étonnant et plutôt mauvais)*

dhā̋bhlīīwɔ̀n <Manding dàbari 'moyen magique'-affaire> ***n*** **miracle** *(un événement bizarre, étonnant, plutôt mauvais)* Syn. *dhìdhā̋wɔ̀n*

dhàdīò̀o <Fr. radio> ***n*** **radio**

dhāfīīdhʌ́n <pluie- ?-diminutif> ***n*** **bruine, pluie fine** ♦ *dhāfīīdhʌ́n yɤ̀ bān-sīʌ* il bruine

dhāgā <pluie-os> ***n*** **foudre** *(on croit que la foudre est produite par une pierre taillée qui tombe du ciel)* ◊ *dhāgā yà̀ dà̀ dhűű tà̀* la foudre est tombée sur l'arbre

dhàklɛ̋e, làklɛ̋e <Fr. la clé> ***n*** **clé, clef** *(de serrure)* Syn. klɛ̋e◊ *dhàklɛ̋e dà kó tà yàagā* tourne la clé trois fois dans la serrure ◊ *làklɛ̋e yà dɔ̄ bīŋbīŋdhɤ̄, kwɛ̋ɛ yáa pʉ̋* la serrure est trop raide, la porte ne s'ouvre pas ♦ *dhàklɛ̋e kɔ́* serrure ♦ *dhàklɛ̋e sɔ̋n* panneton

dhākpóŋ̋ <pluie-porte> ***n*** **nuage** ♦ *dhākpóŋ̋ yɤ̀ dhāŋgʉ́dhɤ̄* il y a des nuages dans le ciel ♦ *dhākpóŋ̋ yà kɑ̋n kwʌ́ʌ̀* le ciel s'est dégagé

dhān ***prev*** **approche furtive**

dhɑ̋n {dhɑ̀n} ***n*** **1** *rn* **grand-mère** *("grand-mère classificatoire" : grand-mère maternelle ou paternelle; arrière-grand-mère, arrière-arrière-grand-mère, etc.; soeur de grand-mère; soeur aînée du père ou de la mère; descendante directe de la soeur aînée du père; femme du descendant direct de la soeur aînée du père; femme du frère aîné de la mère d'ego, sa fille, petite-fille, etc.; femme du fils, petit-fils, etc. du frère aîné de la mère; femme du frère cadet de mère, femme de son fils, petit-fils etc.; co-épouse aînée de la mère) [la tendresse usuelle qui caractérise les rapports entre grand-mère et petits-enfants se démarque d'une certaine rigueur qui prévaut dans le modèle éducatif des Dan]* ♦ *dhɑ̋n sɛ̄ɛ̋ndhʌ́n* sœur cadette de la grand-mère maternelle ♦ *dhɑ̋n bhà dhɑ̋n, dhɑ̋n gʉ́ dhɑ̀n la forme dhɑ̋n gʉ́ dhɑ̀n est plus archaïque* arrière-grand-mère ♦ *dhɑ̋n bhà dhɑ̋n bhà dhɑ̋n, dhɑ̋n gʉ́ dhɑ̀n gʉ́ dhɑ̋n la forme dhɑ̋n gʉ́ dhɑ̀n gʉ́ dhɑ̋n est plus archaïque* arrière-arrière-grand-mère ◊ *dhʌ́n dhò ɤ̄ dhɑ̋n kèŋ̋-sʉ̀ yáa sʌ̀ gbɛ́, yà kʌ̄ dhɤ̋ à dhɑ̋n yà yí bhò* il n'est pas très bon qu'un enfant aille chez sa grand-mère, parce qu'elle le gâte **2** *rn* **belle-mère, sœur aînée du mari, femme du frère aîné du mari** Qsyn. dà **3** *rn* **mama** *(une adresse polie à une femme de n'importe quel âge)*

dhàndhân → dhàandháàn *ananas*

dhɑ̋ndhēdhʌ́n <grand-mère-femme-diminutif> ***n*** **vieille**

dhān-kʌ̄ *v vi* **chasser à l'approche, s'approcher furtivement** *(de – bhà)*

dhàŋ ***n*** *rn* **bosse** *(sur le dos)* Syn. kwʌ̄ŋ̋

dhāŋ̋ ***n*** **ciel** ◊ *dhākpóŋ̋ yáa dhāŋ̋ bhà* il n'y a pas de nuages dans le ciel

dháŋ̋ ***n*** **foi, confiance** ♦ *dháŋ̋ bhō bhɛ̄n dhɪ́ɤ* croire à; avoir confiance en qn ◊ *yɤ̀ dháŋ̋ bhò Zlàan dhɪ́ɤ* il croit en Dieu

dhɑ̋ŋ ***n*** **malédiction**

dhàŋbhá <Fr. lampe> ***n*** **lampe tempête**

dháŋ̋bhòdhɪ́ɤ-sʉ̀ ***n*** **confiance** ♦ *yà n̄ bhā dháŋ̋bhòdhɪ́ɤ-sʉ̀ sɛ̄ɛ̀* il a trahi ma confiance

dhàŋdlàa → dhàŋtlàa *ananas africain*

dhāŋ̋gʉ́dhɛ̏, dhāŋgʉ́dhɛ̏ {Loc. dhāŋ̋gʉ́dhɤ̄, dhāaŋgʉ́dhɤ̄} ***loc.n*** **ciel** ◊ *bhàan yà dhó dhāŋ̋gʉ́dhɤ̄ / dhāaŋgʉ́dhɤ̄* l'oiseau s'est envolé au ciel ♦ *dhāŋ̋gʉ́dhɛ̏ yɤ̀ pʉ̋u* le ciel est clair

dhāŋ̋gʉ́dhɤ̄, dhāaŋgʉ́dhɤ̄ ***loc.n*** *Loc. de* dhāŋ̋gʉ́dhɛ̏ *ciel*

dhāŋ̋pɔ̏ <ciel-crapaud> *n* **crapaud** *(gros, couleur ressemblant à celle des feuilles sèches) [les Dan croient que ce crapaud produit l'arc-en-ciel]*

dhàŋtlàa, **dhàŋdlàa** *n* **1 ananas africain** *(petit, très sucré, avec des nombreuses épines sur les feuilles et tige)* **2** arch. **ananas** Syn. *dháandháan (m)*

dhȁŋtlȁadhɛ̋ *n* **champignon** *(esp.; 12 à 15 cm de diamètre, comestible; très rare de nos jours dans le Gouèta)*

dhásí 1 <Fr. soldat> *n* **militaire**

dhásí 2 {pl. dhásí-dhȕn, dhásízʌ̏-dhȕn} *n rn* **partenaire du cousinage à plaisanterie** *(interdit de mariage et de verser le sang mutuellement)* Qsyn. *sànbhűnzʌ̏*

dhásí-dhɛ̏ *n* **cousinage à plaisanterie** *(pour cerains, implique l'interdiction mutuelle de mariage; pour d'autres, peut ne pas impliquer l'interdiction de mariage)* ♦ *yɛ̄ŋ̄-dhȕn yī dhásí-dhɛ̏ gű* nous sommes liés entre nous par le cousinage à plaisanterie ♦ *dhásí-dhɛ̏ yɤ̏ yī zìnŋgű* il y a cousinage à plaisanterie entre nous

dhásízʌ̏-dhȕn *pl. de* dhásí *cousin à plaisanterie*

dhàsóŋ̏, **dhàsô**, **dhàsóɔ̏** <Fr. la chaux> *n* **béton** ◊ *yȁ dlāȁn dhàsóɔ̏ sɛ̏ɛ tȁ, yȁ pɤ̏* elle a glissé sur le sol en béton, et elle est tombée ♦ *dhàsóŋ̏ bɪ̏* ciment

dhǣæ 1 *n* **obligation** ♦ *ȁ dhǣæ ȁ bhȁ* il faut que

dhǣæ 2 *n* **silence** Syn. *dhɛ̏tȁ* ♦ *dhǣæ yȁ gā ȁ tȁ* il s'est tu ♦ *ȁ dhǣæ gā !* calme-le ! (un bébé)

dhǣǽ → dhɛ̄ɛ́ *question*

dhǽæ → dhɛ́ɛ *tas*

dhǣædhɪ́ɤ → dhɛ̏ɛdhɪ́ɤ *chant de coq*

dhǣǽ-kpɔ́ → dhɛ̄ɛ́-kpɔ́ *demander*

dhǣækpɔ̏œ <dhɛ̏ yà kpɔ̏œ 'il a fait jour'> *intj* **bonjour** ♦ *dhǣækpɔ̏œ bhūn* comment ça va chez toi ?

dhǣŋ → dhɛ̏ŋ *étranger*

dhʌ̏ → dhɛ̏ *devant*

dhʌ̏ʌ *n* **1 pâte de riz envoûtée** *(procédé de magie utilisé contre les voleurs : on prépare le dhʌ̄ʌ, puis on prononce des incantations censées faire sortir une pâte blanche des oreilles du voleur qui en meurt)* ♦ *dhʌ̏ʌ yȁ ȁ kún* il (le voleur) a été frappé par l'effet de l'envoûtement à la pâte de riz (et il en est mort) **2 rite d'envoûtement à la pâte de riz**

dhʌ̄ʌ 1 *n* **pâte de riz** *(le riz décortiqué est trempé dans l'eau, pilé, et on y rajoute un peu d'eau et parfois du sucre) [utilisée pour les sacrifices]*

dhʌ̄ʌ 2 *n* **habitude** ♦ *dhʌ̄ʌ bhō ȁ ká (m), dhʌ̄ʌ bhō ȁ bhȁ* s'habituer à qch, se faire à qch ◊ *bhán dhʌ̄ʌ bhō bhlȕn bhɤ̏-sȕ bhȁ* je suis habitué à manger du riz

dhʌ̀n; **dhūn** (gw) *dtm marque de focalisation contrastive* ◊ *tǣǣn dhūn ɤ́ á' pɤ̏* c'est la vérité, ce que je dis

dhʌ́n {dhʌ̀n} ***n*** **1.1 enfant** *(par rapport aux parents, dans le sens classificatoire : enfant d'ego; enfant de dhòo; pour une femme, enfant de la sœur aînée ou de la coépouse; pour un homme, femme du frère cadet de sa femme, enfant de la sœur d'ego)* *Syn.* *bhāŋ 1* **1.2 enfant** *(qui n'est pas adulte)* ♦ *dhʌ́n sɛ̄ɛ́ndhʌ́n* petit enfant (jusqu'à environ 10 ans) **2 personne** *(mot pour compter des personnes)*

-dhʌ́n <de dhʌ́n 'enfant'> ***mrph*** **1** *suffixe diminutif (avec les adjectifs, désigne un degré abaissé de la qualité)* ◊ *bhɤ̏ sɔ̄ sɛ̀edhʌ́n bhā sɯ́, kɤ̄ ɯ́' zīɤ tɛ́blʌ̂ bhȁ, bhá dhɤ́' kʌ̄ sɔ̄pɛ́n sɛ̀ɛ gbɛ́ ká* essuye la table avec un chiffon humide, ne l'essuye pas avec un chiffon mouillé **2** *suffixe du singulier de certains noms* ♦ *dhēbʌ̀dhʌ́n dō* une femme ♦ *gɔ̄ndʌdhʌ́n* homme, garçon *lv.* ♦ *sʌ̄ndhʌ́n* lièvre

dhʌ́nbʌ̋-dhɛ̏ <enfant- ?-abstr.> ***n*** **enfance**

dhʌ́nblʌ̋ ***n*** **nouveau né** *(2 à 4 jours après la naissance)* ♦ *dhʌ́nblʌ̋ pűu* nouveau né (avec le cordon ombilical)

dhʌ́nbhá <enfant-autre> ***dtm*** **un peu** *Syn.* *bhɤ́, bhɤ́dhʌ́nbhá* ◊ *yà yī dhʌ́nbhá zʌ̄* il a dormi un peu *peut apparaître dans une position argumentale sans déterminé*

dhʌ́nbháwō, **dhʌ́nbhábhō** <enfant-autre-faire> ***adv*** **1 un peu 2 quand même** ◊ *ȁ bhȁ pi̋ɤgāsòȍ gɛ̀n-dhȕn wȁ yȁ gɤ́ŋ tȁ, kɛ́ɛ wȍ slʌ̏ʌ zʌ̏ wȍ' gɯ́ dhʌ́nbháwō* les roues de son vélo sont tordues, mais elles tournent quand même **3 au moins** ◊ *ká pɤ̏ kāa dhó bhláā kȁ kʌ̄ dhʌ́nbháwō bhēn kœ̀œŋ̏ dō ɤ̄ gā sɔ́ɔdhű* si vous allez au champ, vous devez être au moins quinze

dhʌ́ndhīʌŋ́ <enfant- ?> ***n*** **1 jeune fille** *(à l'âge de se marier),* **femme non-mariée** *(mariable)* **2** *pej.* **femme non-mariée**

dhʌ́nglɔ̄ɔ́n <enfant- ?> ***n*** **jeune homme**

dhʌ́nglɔ̄ɔ́n-dhʌ́n-gɯ́-tɔ̏ <jeune homme-enfant-dans-nom> ***n rn*** **nom de jeunesse** *(nom qu'on porte pendant sa jeunesse)*

dhʌ́ngɔ̏ɔ̀n <enfant-mâle> ***n*** **garçon, jeune homme**

dhʌ́nkpɔ́dhē <enfant-engendrer-nominalis.> ***n*** **natalité, procréation**

dhʌ̀nŋ 1 ***v*** **1.1** 1) *vi* **coller**, **se coller** *(à – bhȁ)* ◊ *dhɛ́gā plɛ̀ wȁ dhʌ̀nŋ kwʌ́ʌ̀* deux feuilles se sont collées 2) *vt* **coller** *(à – bhȁ)* ♦ *Yɔ̏ ɤ̄ bhā dhʌ̀nŋ wō Gɤ̏ɤ̏ bhȁ* Yo s'est mariée avec Geu (de sa propre initiative) **1.2** *vt* **fixer, accrocher** ◊ *wȁ là dhʌ̀nŋ ȁ tȍŋ /kȕu/ tȁ* on lui a accroché une médaille à la poitrine **1.3** *vi* **s'enliser**; **se coincer** ◊ *gɔ̄ yɤ̏ kʌ̄ dhʌ̀nŋ bɤ̏ɤ̏ gɯ́* la voiture s'est enlisée dans la boue **2.1** 1) *vt* **fermer** *(boucher)* *Qsyn.* *tā* 2) *vi* **être bloqué** *(d'une porte)* **2.2** 1) *vi* **s'appuyer** *(sur qn qui est couché – tȁ, sur qn qui est debout – bhȁ)* ♦ *yȁ dhʌ̀nŋ ȁ tȁ kpēnŋkpēnŋdhɤ̄* il est passé sur lui de tout son poids 2) *vt* **presser** ◊ *yȁ ɤ̄ bhā dhʌ́n dhʌ̀nŋ ɤ̄ tȍŋ bhȁ* il a serré son enfant contre sa poitrine **2.3** *vi* **s'arrêter** *(payer attention; sur – tȁ)* ◊ *yɤ̏ kʌ̄ dhʌ̀nŋ dhēbʌ̀-dhȕn wɔ̏n dhi̋aŋ tȁ* dans son discours il s'est arrêté sur le problème féminin **2.4** *vi* **insister** *(sur – tȁ)* ◊ *Tȍkpȁ yɤ̏ dhʌ̀nŋ dhɛ̄ɛ́ bhā' tȁ* Tokpa a insisté sur cette question **3** *vt* **rajouter** *(à – bhȁ)*

dhʌ̀ŋ 2 1 *rn* **chair; corps** ◊ *būugā yà yɤ̄ bhɛ̄n dhʌ̀ŋ bhà* la balle a frappé le corps de l'homme **2** *rn* **muscle**

dhʌ̄ŋ ***n*** **difficulté inattendue** *(et difficile à résoudre)* Syn. *dɔ̋ɔn*

dhʌ̄ŋ̋gɯ́tɔ̀ <enfant- ?-dans-nom> ***n*** **nom d'enfant** Syn. *sɛ̄ɛ́ndhʌ́ngɯ́tɔ̀*

dhʌ̀ŋkwʌ́ʌ̀ <coller-ensemble> ***n*** **coopération; alliance** *(résultat d'un accord) ainsi dans :* ♦ *dhʌ̀ŋkwʌ́ʌ̀ dɛ̀e [zīi] sʌ́ʌdhɛ̋* Chr. Nouveau [Ancien] Testament

dhʌ̀ŋkwʌ́ʌ̀dhē <coller-ensemble-nominalis.> ***n*** **coopération; alliance** *(résultat d'un accord)*

dhʌ́nwlɯ̄ɯ̋sɯ̀ <enfant-grandir-gérondif> ***n*** **adolescent**

dhʌ̀nwōdō ***adv*** **tout de suite, coûte que coûte, définitivement** ◊ *dhūn dhʌ̀nwōdō !* viens ici directement

dhʌ̋ŋgbō < ?-pot> ***n*** **grande jarre** *(pour garder l'eau dans la case)*

dhɛ̀ ***prt*** **1 sans aucun doute** ◊ *kɤ̄ yɤ̄ɤ pɤ̀ dhɛ̀* il va tomber, sans aucun doute ◊ *ā dhɔ̀ dhūn' dhɛ̀* je viendrai certainement ◊ *bhāan à gú-dān dhɛ̀* j'essayerai, malgré tout *(le médicament, même si je ne connais pas ses effets)* **2 allons !** *(dans les propositions impératives, une invitation polie à une action impliquant que l'action est obligatoire)* ◊ *bhɤ̀ dhó dhɛ̀* vas-y *(à celui qui doit partir et lambine)* **3 sans doute** *(exprime le doute)*

dhē 1 ***n*** **1.1** *rn* **mère** *("mère classificatoire" : mère; sœur cadette de la mère; femme du frère cadet du père; coépouse cadette de la mère)* ♦ *dhē sɛ̄ɛ́ndhʌ́n* 1) cousine croisée *(fille du frère cadet de la mère)* 2) fille de la cousine croisée *(fille de la fille du frère cadet de la mère)* 3) coépouse cadette de la mère **1.2** *rn* **coépouse aînée** *(la préséance des femmes dépend de la séquence des mariages et non de l'âge) [terme d'adresse, plutôt que de référence]* Syn. *yàpɪ́ɤdhē* **2** *rn* resp. **mère** *(terme d'adresse utilisé envers les femmes de la génération des parents)*

dhē {dhɛ̀} **2** ***n*** *dans certains contextes* **1 femme 2 épouse** Syn. *dhēbʌ̀* ◊ *bhán n̄ dhú dō dhūn ɯ̄ dhɛ̀ dhē ká* je te donne une de mes filles pour femme

-dhē 1 ***mrph*** *suffixe improductif de l'adjectif dénominal* Qsyn. *-sɯ̀ 2* ◊ *klɯ̀u dhɯ̋dhē* louche en bois

-dhē 2 <de dhē 'femme'> ***mrph*** **1 -esse** *(suffixe du nom d'agent féminin)* **2** *suffixe du nom de propriétriss*

-dhē 3 ***mrph*** *suffixe du nom verbal ou du nom de résultat d'action*

-dhē 4 ***mrph*** *marque de la focalisation sélective* Qsyn. *sɯ̀* ◊ *slʌ̀ʌ pɯ̋u-dhē dhʌ̀n bhāan à tā* c'est le piment blanc que je vais planter *(parmi toutes les espèces de piment)*

dhēbʌ̀ 1), dhēbɔ̀ (t) {pl. dhēbʌ̀-dhùn, dhōo-dhùn, dhōŋ-dhùn} ***n*** *la deuxième et la troisième forme du pl. ne sont utilisées que dans quelques expressions figées* **1 femme** *(de n'importe quel âge)* Syn. *dhē 2* **2.1 épouse, femme** Syn. *dhē 2* Qsyn. *kɔ́dhɛ̄ɛ́* ♦ *dhēbʌ̀ kpɪ̄ɪ-sɯ̀* épouse aînée *(d'un polygame; la préséance des femmes dépend de la séquence des mariages, et non* *de leur âge)* Syn. *kɔ́dhēe* ♦ *dhēbʌ̏ sɛ̋ɛ́ndhʌ́n-sʌ̏* femme cadette *(d'un polygame)* **2.2 belle-sœur cadette** *(sœur cadette de l'épouse) [terme d'adresse, plutôt que de référence]* Qsyn. *dhìnbhɔ̋ɔ̏n*

dhēbʌ̏ 2) {pl. dhēbʌ̏-dhʌ̏n, dhōo-dhʌ̏n, dhōŋ-dhʌ̏n} *adj* **femelle** ♦ *zlʌ̋ʌ̏ dhēbʌ̏* sœur cadette

dhēbʌ̏dhʌ́n <femme-diminutif> *n* **femme**

dhēbɔ̏ (t) → dhēbʌ̏ *femme*

dhēdhʌ́n <femme-diminutif> *n* **coépouse cadette** *(la préséance des femmes dépend de la séquence des mariages et non de l'âge)* Syn. *bhāŋdhē*

dhɛ̏e *n* **femelle** Syn. *bhūn* ♦ *gbɛ̂n dhɛ̏e* chienne

dhèe *n bot.* **tubercule** ◊ *bāa dhèe gʉ́ŋgʉ̀ŋ* tubercule de manioc court et épais

dhēɛ́ *mrph* **féminin**

dhēɛ́bhāŋ {pl. dhēɛ́bhāŋzʌ̏-dhʌ̏n} <mère- ?-enfant> *n* **1** *rn* **frère, sœur** *(au sens classificatoire : enfant de la "mère classificatoire" d'ego, dhē, parfois dhʌ̋n)* **2** *ext.* **parent; compatriote,**

dhēɛ́bhāŋ-dhɛ̏ *n* **lien de parenté** ♦ *wɔ̏ gūn dhēebhāŋ-dhɛ̏ bhʌ̏ plɛ̏* ils étaient deux frères

dhēɛ́bhāŋzʌ̏-dhʌ̏n *pluriel de* dhēɛ́bhāŋ *n* **frères**

dhègliízʌ̏, dhēglízɤ̏ <Fr. église> *n* **église**

dhēgɔ̀ndʌ̄ <femme-mari-père> *n* **époux** *[s'emploie pour mettre en évidence le lien conjugal]*; **jeune marié** Qsyn. *gɔ̀n*

dhēgbáan <femme-initiation> *n rn* **sœur aînée** *(au sens classificatoire : sœur aînée d'ego; fille du frère du père ou de la sœur cadette de mère plus âgée qu'ego; soeur cadette du père)* Syn. *dhɤ̄ɤ (t)* Qsyn. *dhēzɔ̋o*

dhēgbíɤ̏ɤ, dhēgbíɤ̏ɤdhʌ́n <femme-grossesse(-enfant)> *n* **femme enceinte** *(la forme avec -dhʌ́n est la plus usitée)*

dhɛ̋ŋdhɛ̋ŋkpʌ̏adhɛ̏ (m), **dhɛ̋ŋkpàadhɛ̏** (t) *n* **papillon**

dhɛ̋ŋkpàadhɛ̏ (m) → dhɛ̋ndhɛ̋nkpʌ̏andhɛ̏ *papillon*

dhēzɔ̋o <femme-magicienne> *n rn resp.* **sœur aînée** *(au sens classificatoire : sœur aînée d'ego; fille du frère du père ou de la sœur cadette de la mère plus âgée qu'ego; soeur cadette du père; terme d'adresse utilisé par rapport à la soeur aînée initiée)* Qsyn. *dhēgbáan; dhɤ̄ɤ (t)*

dhɛ̏ 1 *n* **1.1 place, endroit** Qsyn. *dʉ̏ɛ* ◊ *ā wʌ̏ʌ̏gā dhɛ̏ŋ dhɛ̏ yā' gʉ́* j'ai perdu de l'argent à cet endroit ◊ *bhɛ̄n bhá yíi kʌ̄ ʌ̏ dhɛ̏ dɔ̄* personne ne savait d'où il venait ♦ *ʌ̏ yʌ̋n yáa dhɛ̏ yɤ̄ sʌ̏ ká* il voit mal **1.2 moment, situation** ◊ *á' wɔ́n dɔ̄ dhɛ̏ ɤ́' bhʌ̏ dhè dʉ̄ wɔ̏n ɤ́ bhā yɤ̏ tæ̏ɛ̏n ká...* la situation qui m'a fait comprendre que la sorcellerie est réelle... ♦ *ʌ̏ dhɛ̏ yɤ̏ ʌ̏ bhʌ̏...* le moment est venu pour... ♦ *dhɛ̏ ɤ́ ..., yɤ́ ...* comme ... ◊ *dhɛ̏ ɤ́ dhʉ̋ ɤ́ bhɔ̄ sʌ̏ ká, yɤ́ wó ʌ̏ kʌ̏n* comme l'arbre s'est mis à grandir, on l'a coupé ♦ *dhɛ̏ yɤ̄ zʉ́* cette fois-ci **1.3 champ, plantation** ♦ *bāa dhɛ̏* champ de manioc **2 nécessité, obligation** ♦ *à dhɛ̏ yɤ̏ à bhɤ̏ kɤ̄... demande le mode subjonctif* il faut que... **3** *exprime le focus de contraste sur le nom précédent* ◊ *wɔ́n dhɛ̏ ɤ́ yáa sʌ̏ yɤ́ bhà* ce qui n'est pas bon dans cette affaire, c'est ça ◊ *tlōo kʌ̏ ká pʌ̏ dhɛ̏ ɤ́ yā dhʌ̀n ɤ́ à pɪ́ɤ ɤ́ tlōo kʌ̄ à ká* c'est précisement avec ce jouet qu'il veut jouer

dhɛ̏ 2, **dhʌ̏** *pp* **1 devant** ◊ *bhɛ̄n sɛ̄ɛ́ndhʌ́n yáa ɤ̄ kṹu tà bhàn bhɛ̄n kpɪ̂ɪ̀ dhɛ̏* un jeune ne se frappe pas la poitrine devant un aîné ♦ *yʌ́nŋ̏ dhɛ̏* au soleil **2 pour** *(indique le bénéficiaire)* ◊ *wɔ́n dhɪ́asṹù dō yà kʌ̄ n̄ dhɛ̏* un événement agréable m'est arrivé ◊ *Dhɑ̃́ntīi yɤ̏ bhɑ̃́a dhɪ̏ʌʌ ɤ̄ zlɑ̃́à dhɛ̏* Natii est en train de refroidir le riz cuit pour son petit frère **3** *indique le destinataire auquel la parole est adressée* ◊ *yà à pɤ̄ à dhɛ̏* il lui a dit **4** *indique le récipient, avec le verbe dhūn 'donner'*

dhɛ̏ 3 *v* **1.1** *vt* **appeler** *(attirer l'attention)* **1.2** *vt* **appeler** *(dénommer)* ◊ *wó' dhɛ̏ Màdhî* on l'appelait Marie ◊ *yɤ̏ ɤ̄ dʌ̄ dhɛ̏ à tɔ́ ká* il appelle son père par son nom *[considéré comme très impoli]* ♦ *wò ɯ̄ dhɛ̏ dē ?* comment t'appelles-tu ? **2** *vt* **demander** *(qch; à – gɔ̏) s'emploie le plus souvent à l'aspect neutre dans le contexte performatif* Qsyn. bhæ̏æ, dhɛ̄ɛ́ kpɔ̏ ◊ *ā' dhɛ̏ ɯ̄ gɔ̏ kɤ̄ ɯ́ dhūn sʌ́ʌdhɛ́ yā' ká* je te demande d'apporter ce livre ◊ *ā dhɛ̏-sṹù ká kṹnbhɑ̃́ndhɑ̃́n sɛ̄ɛ́ndhʌ́n gɔ̏ kɤ̄ yɤ̏ n̄ tà-kún* j'ai demandé au sous-préfet de m'aider **3** *vt* **inviter** ◊ *dhùutɪ̂ɪ̀ yɤ̏ n̄ dhɛ̏ yāandhɪ́ɤ pʌ̄ bhɤ̏ wɔ̀n gɯ́* hier le chef du village m'a invité à manger *(mais je ne suis pas venu)* ◊ *dhùutɪ̂ɪ̀ yɤ̏ n̄ dhɛ̏ yāandhɪ́ɤ pʌ̄bhèe ká* hier le chef du village m'a invité à manger *(et je suis venu)*

dhɛ̏ 4, **dhɛ̀** *n* **jour** *(toujours avec le verbe kpœ̀œ)* ♦ *dhɛ̏ yà kpœ̀œ* le jour s'est levé ♦ *dhɛ̏ pɯ̃́u ɤ́ kpœ̀œ* chaque jour

-dhɛ̏ 1 <de dhɛ̈ 'endroit'> ***mrph*** *suffixe nominal désignant la qualité ou le statut* ♦ *gɔ̄ɔ̀n-dhɛ̏* état d'homme

-dhɛ̏ 2 <de dhɛ̈ 2 'devant'> ***mrph*** *marque du nom verbal; s'écrit avec un trait d'union* ◊ *bháa dɔ̄ pʌ̄ yà-dhɛ̏ ká* tu ne sais pas écrire

-dhɛ̏ 3 ***mrph*** *suffixe du cas commun*

dhɛ̀ 1 *num* **1 combien ?** ◊ *ɯ̄ dhɛ̄ɛ́bhāŋ-dhɯ̀n wò dhɛ̀ ?* combien de frères et soeurs as-tu ? ◊ *dhʌ́n dhɛ̀ ɤ́ ɯ̄ gɔ̏ ?* combien d'enfants as-tu ? **2 pourquoi ? 3 comment ?** ◊ *... kwā gɯ̀n kwāà à kʌ̄ dhɛ̀ ?* qu'est-ce que nous ferions ? ♦ *yɤ̏ kʌ̏ bhɯ̄n dhɛ̀ ?* qu'est-ce qu'il y a ? ◊ *ɯ̄' pʌ̏-kʌ̏ bhɯ̄n dhɛ̀ ?* comment l'as-tu fabriqué ?

dhɛ̀ 2 *conj* **1 que** *(introduit une proposition complémentaire)* ◊ *yɤ́ dhɛ̏ ɤ́ kʌ̏ dhɛ̀ ā gɯ̀n kāatɪ̂ɛ̀ Dōbhōndhô...* comme je demeurais dans le quartier de Domoro... ◊ *dhēbʌ̏dhʌ́n bhā yɤ̏ kʌ̄ dhɔ̀, kɛ́ɛ pʌ́ bhā dhɛ̀ ɤ́ dhō' ká...* la femme est partie, mais ce qu'elle a amené... **2 quand** *(introduit une subordonnée temporelle; est suivi d'un pronom sujet conjoint; peut être accompagné par la conjonction relative)* ◊ *dhɛ̀ á lòo bhɯ̄n yɤ́ à bhɛ́n bhā ɤ́' pɤ̄...* quand j'y suis arrivé, cet homme a dit... ◊ *yà kʌ̄ dhɛ̀ bhá à dhɪ́ʌʌ, kɪ́i dhūn* quand tu auras écrasé cela, viens ♦ *dhɛ̀ ɤ́..., dhɛ̀ kɤ́...* aussitôt que... ◊ *dhɛ̀ ɤ́ á n̄ yɑ̃́n kpàn à bhà...* lorsque je l'ai vue... ♦ *dhɛ̀ ɤ́ dhɤ́* ainsi donc ♦ *dhɛ̀ ɤ́ kʌ̏ dhɤ́ yɤ́...* et alors...

♦ *dhè pʌ̄ dhɤ́* approximativement; presque ♦ *dhè ɤ́ kʌ̀ dhè* comme, car ♦ *kɛ́ɛ dhè ɤ́ kʌ̀ dhè* comme **3 comme** *(exprime une comparaison)* ◊ *yɤ̀ bhánŋglōo bhɔ̀ dhè kɔ̀ bhā à dhɤ́ kɤ́ɤ à dhɔ̃́ɔ-dɔ̄* il cueille les mangues de façon à pouvoir les vendre ♦ *yɤ̀ yʌ̄ kʌ̀ dhè bīɤ dhɤ́* il travaille comme un éléphant **4** *dhè ɤ́* **comme**

dhé ***dtm*** **1 l'autre** *(membre d'une paire d'objets qui se distingue de l'autre par une qualité bien définie; toujours suivi d'une phrase relative)* Qsyn. wɛ́ɛ 1 ◊ *dhàa plè ɤ́ wó yā à bhɛ̀ɛn ɤ́ bhīi' sú ? à dhé ɤ́ klɤ̄ɤ̀ ká yā ɛ̀e, ı́ın à dhé ɤ́ gblɛ̀ɛn ká yā ɛ̀e ?* lequel de ces deux couteaux prendras-tu, le plus court ou le plus long ? ◊ *bhɛ̄n dhé ɤ́ á wɛ̃́ŋ' ká bhā, à bhà sɔ̄ yã́n yɤ̀ zɔ̃̀ɔnzɔ̃̀ndhē ká* l'autre homme, celui dont je parle, son vêtement est très très rouge ♦ *dhé ɤ́ dhɤ́* chaque **2 celui** ◊ *tàabhàn kɤ̄ wɔ́n dhé ɤ́ bhā kɤ̄ kwà dān kwʌ̃́ʌ* prochainement nous allons résoudre ce problème ♦ *à dhé kɤ́ bhā...* quant à cela...

dhɛ̃́ 1 ***n*** **1 feuillage** ♦ *dhṹ dhɛ̃́{-dhùn}* feuillage **2 page 3 lame** ♦ *bã́ŋ dhɛ̃́* lame de machette **4.1 médicament** ♦ *dhṹ dhɛ̃́{-dhùn}* remède à base de feuilles et d'herbes **4.2 remède** ◊ *zūʌ́ sæ̀æ dhʌ̀n ɤ́ wɔ́n gbàn pɛ́pɛ́ dhɛ̃́ ká* la patience est un remède contre toute chose

dhɛ̃́ 2 ***prt*** **vraiment !** *marqueur du focus de véracité* ◊ *wʌ́ʌ̀-gā yɤ̀ à gɔ̀ dhɛ̃́ !* il a vraiment de l'argent ! ◊ *bhlɛ̀ɛn-dhùn zʌ̀, wáa sʌ̀ dhɛ̃́ !* les serpents, c'est méchant

dhèdhàan ***prn*** **lequel ?** *(en séquence)*, **quantième ?** ◊ *glɔ̄ɔ bhē dhèdhàan ɤ́ ú' bhɤ̀-sīʌ bhā ?* c'est le quantième banane que tu manges ?

dhɛ̃̀dhɛ̃́ (t) ***prev*** **question** Syn. dhɛ̄ɛ́kpɔ́

dhɛ̃́dhɛ̃́ <Fr. l'heure> ***n*** **heure** Syn. yʌ́nŋ̀gɛ̀nsú

dhɛ̃̀dhɛ̃́-dà (t) ***v*** **interroger** Syn. dhɛ̄ɛ́-kpɔ́

dhɛ̃́dhɛ̃́kɔ́ <heure-maison> ***n*** **montre** Syn. yʌ́nŋ̀kɔ́

dhèɛ ***adv*** **très, énormément**; **véritablement** ◊ *Zân yà pʌ̄ bhɤ̀ dhèɛ !* Jean a trop mangé ! ◊ *víɔŋ̀ yā yɤ̀ zīɤ-sīʌ dhṹɤ́ dhèɛ !* cet avion vole très haut ! ◊ *yɤ̀ sʌ̀ dhèɛ !* c'est vraiment joli !

dhɛ̄ɛ̀, dhè ***n*** *zɔ̃́ dhɛ̄ɛ̀* **ruche** *(habitation naturelle des abeilles) [au Goueta, l'apiculture n'existe pas traditionnellement, et les ruches artificielles sont inconnues]* Qsyn. dhɛ̄ɛ̀dhɛ̀ ◊ *dhʌ́n bhā yà gwʌ̀ zùɤ zɔ̃́ dhɛ̄ɛ̀ ká* l'enfant a jeté un caillou sur la ruche ♦ *zɔ̃́ dhɛ̄ɛ̀ gɤ́* enfumer des abeilles

dhɛ̄ɛ́, dhǣǣ́ ***prev*** **question**

dhɛ̃́ɛ, dhǽæ ***n*** **tas de marchandises** ◊ *glɔ̄ɔ dhɛ́ɛ* tas de bananes ♦ *à yà dhǽæ ká* mets-le en tas

dhɛ̄ɛ̀dhɛ̀ {LOC dhɛ̄ɛdhɤ̄} ***loc.n*** *zɔ̃́ dhɛ̄ɛ̀dhɛ̀* **ruche** *(habitation naturelle des abeilles) [en Goueta, l'apiculture n'existe pas traditionnellement, et les ruches artificielles sont inconnues]* Qsyn. dhɛ̄ɛ̀ ◊ *zɔ̃́-dhùn wà dà zɔ̃́ dhɛ̄ɛdhɤ̄* les abeilles sont entrées dans leur ruche ♦ *zɔ̃́ dhɛ̄ɛ̀dhɛ̀ bhɤ̀* ravager une ruche

dhɛ̋ɛdhɛ̏ {LOC dhɛ̋ɛdhɤ̄, dhɛ̋ɛgʉ́dhɤ̄} ***loc.n*** **place du village, place publique** ◊ *dhɛ̋ɛdhɛ̏ ɤ́ Sáŋtàa yáa gbɛ̋ɛ* la place publique à Santa n'est pas grande ◊ *bhēn gbàan dhó dhɛ̋ɛdhɤ̄* tout le monde est allé sur la place publique ♦ *à dhɔ̏ yáa dhɛ̋ɛdhɛ̏ kʌ̄* les gens ne l'aiment pas

dhɛ̏ɛdhí́ɤ 1, dhæ̏ædhí́ɤ ***n*** **1 chant de coq, cocorico** ♦ *tɔ̏ gɔ̄n bhā yà yà dhɛ̏ɛdhí́ɤ bhō-sʉ̀ bhà* le premier coq a chanté **2 appel; proclamation** *(surtout émise par un crieur public)* ♦ *dhæ̏ædhí́ɤ bhō* proclamer une nouvelle ◊ *bhɔ̋ɔ̏n-sʌ́ʌ̏-dhɛ̏ɛdhí́ɤ-bhō-bhɛ̏n yà yà dhɛ̏ɛdhí́ɤ bhō-sʉ̀ bhà* le muezzin a commencé l'appel à la prière ◊ *yɛ̄ɛbhīn yɤ̏ dhɛ̏ɛdhí́ɤ bhɔ̏* le griot a proclamé la nouvelle.

dhɛ̏ɛdhí́ɤ 2 ***n*** **danseuse de dhɛ̏ɛdhí́ɤ tɛ̋n** *(belle fille célibataire, qui danse en costume de dhɛ̋a et kòŋbhó) [depuis le début du XXI siècle cette danse n'a plus été exécutée]* <u>*Syn. sànbhàn*</u>

dhɛ̏ɛdhí́ɤbhōbhɛ̏n <clcorico-sortir-personne> ***n*** **crieur public**, **héraut** ♦ *bhɔ̋ɔ̏n sʌ́ʌ̏ dhɛ̏ɛdhí́ɤbhōbhɛ̏n* muezzin

dhɛ̄ɛdhɤ̄ ***loc.n*** *LOC de* dhɛ̄ɛ̏dhɛ̏ *ruche*

dhɛ̋ɛdhɤ̄ ***loc.n*** *LOC de* dhɛ̋ɛdhɛ̏ *place publique*

dhɛ̋ɛgʉ́dhɤ̄ ***loc.n*** *LOC de* dhɛ̋ɛdhɛ̏ *place publique*

dhɛ̄ɛ̋kpɔ́, dhǣæ̋kpɔ́ <question-étaler> ***n*** **question** <u>*Syn.*</u> <u>*dhɛ̏dhɛ̋ (t)*</u> ◊ *ʉ̄ bhā dhɛ̄ɛ̋kpɔ́ yíi dhī n̄ dhɛ̏* ta question ne m'a pas plu ◊ *yɤ́ wó dhɛ̄ɛ̋kpɔ́ kʌ̏ dhɛ̏ dɛ̏dɛ̏ ɤ́ dhʌ́n bhā ɤ́ pɤ̏ à bhà à wɔ̏n ká* et ils ont demandé où l'enfant était tombé ◊ *yà bhān dhɛ̄ɛ̋kpɔ́ yɔ̏ɔ-dhʉ̏n bɔ̄* il a répondu à mes questions

dhɛ̄ɛ̋-kpɔ́, dhǣæ̋-kpɔ́ {dhɛ̄ɛ̋-kpɔ̄} ***v vt*** **demander** *(au sujet de – wɔ̏n ká)* ◊ *yɤ̏ n̄ dhɛ̄ɛ̋-kpɔ́ ɤ́ bhā bhɤ̏pʌ̏ wɔ̏n ká* il m'a posé une question concernant sa nourriture

dhɛ̏ɛn ***n*** **chenille venimeuse** *(verte ou brune; la morsure donne une forte démangeaison et enfle)* ◊ *dhɛ̏ɛn yà Sàó bhɔ̄* Sao a été piqué par une chenille venimeuse

dhɛ̀ɛn, dhɛ̀ɛngā < Manding nɛ̀gɛ 'fer' > ***n*** **rasoir** *(petit couteau) avec les nombres, les deux formes s'utilisent, avec ou sans -gā*

dhɛ̄ɛ̏n ***n*** **chauve-souris**

dhɛ̋ɛ̏n ***n*** *rn anat.* **langue** <u>*Syn.*</u> <u>*dhɛ̋ɛ̏ngā*</u> ♦ *dhīaŋ zʌ̄ ɤ̄ dhɛ́ɛ̏n dhí́ɤ* bredouiller ♦ *à dhɛ́ɛ̏n yà dhʌ̀nŋ à dhí* sa langue s'est collée dans sa bouche *(il ne peut pas parler, par la peur etc.)* ♦ *à dhɛ́ɛ̏n/dhɛ́ɛ̏ngā yáa à dhí* il n'a pas de langue dans la bouche ♦ *sí́ɤ dhɛ́ɛ̏n* langues de feu ♦ *à sɔ́n yà yɤ̄ à dhɛ́ɛ̏n tà* il s'est mordu la langue *(accidentellement)*

dhɛ̋ɛ̏nbʌ̏-dhʉ̏n ***n*** *arch.* **enfants**

dhɛ̋ɛndhʌ́n ***n*** **vieille femme** *(d'un âge très avancé)*

dhɛ̋ɛndhʌ́n-dhɛ̏ <vieille.femme-abstr.> ***n*** **vieillesse** *(d'une femme)*

dhɛ̋ɛndhɛ̏ɛn {A P S, dhɛ̋ɛndhɛ̏ɛn-dhʉ̏n pl. A S, dhɛ̋ɛndhɛ̏ɛn-sʉ̏ foc. A, dhɛ̋ɛndhɛ̏ɛn-sʉ̏-dhʉ̏n foc. pl. A; dhɛ̋ɛndhɛ́ɛn Int. pl. A S, dhɛ̋ɛndhɛ́ɛn-dhʉ̏n Int. pl. A S, dhɛ̋ɛndhɛ́ɛn-sʉ̏-dhʉ̏n Int. pl. foc.

A; dhɛ̋nkɛ̋dhɛ̏nkɛ̏ SupInt. pl. A P S, dhɛ̋nkɛ̋dhɛ̏nkɛ̏-dhùn SupInt. pl. A S, dhɛ̋nkɛ̋dhɛ̏nkɛ̏-sɯ̏ SupInt. pl. foc. A, dhɛ̋nkɛ̋dhɛ̏nkɛ̏-sɯ̏-dhùn SupInt. foc. pl. A S} *adj* **1 savoureux, goûteux** ♦ *ȁ dhídhɛ̏ yɤ̏ dhɛ̋ɛndhɛ̏ɛn* i) il est bon orateur ii) ses paroles sont flatteuses **2 sucré** ◊ *pʌ̄ dhɛ̋ɛndhɛ̏ɛn gbɛ́ yà bhán n̄ sɔ̋n ká* la consommation excessive des sucreries m'a donné des maux de dents

dhɛ̋ɛndhɛ̋ɛn *Int. pl. de* dhɛ̋ɛndhɛ̏ɛn *savoureux*

dhɛ̏ɛndhɛ̏ɛnsɯ̏ *SupInt. de* dhɛ̏ɛnsɯ̏ *sévère*

dhɛ̀ɛngā → dhɛ̀ɛn *razoir*

dhɛ́ɛ̀ngā <langue-os> *n rn anat.* **langue** Syn. dhɛ́ɛ̀n ♦ *n̄ dhɛ́ɛ̀ngā yà kʌ̄ gbíŋgbɪ̀ŋ n̄ dhí* ma langue est devenue insensible

dhɛ̀ɛngɯ́ < ?-dans> *n* **hivernage** *(mars/avril à septembre; la période de la disette)* ◊ *dīn yɤ̄ɤ Dhùaa kʌ̄ dhɛ̀ɛngɯ́* pendant l'hivernage, Doua souffrira de la faim ♦ *dhɛ̏ɛngɯ́ tɤ̋ŋ* → dhɛ̏ɛngɯ́

dhɛ̏ɛnkɛ́ɛn *intj* **très doux !**

dhɛ̏ɛnsɯ̏ {A P S, dhɛ̏ɛnsɯ̏-dhùn pl. A S, dhɛ̏ɛnsɯ̏-sɯ̏ foc. A, dhɛ̏ɛnsɯ̏-sɯ̏-dhùn pl. foc. A; dhɛ̏ndhɛ̏nsɯ̏ Int. A P S, dhɛ̏ndhɛ̏nsɯ̏-dhùn Int. A S, dhɛ̏ndhɛ̏nsɯ̏-sɯ̏ Int. foc. A S, dhɛ̏ndhɛ̏nsɯ̏-sɯ̏-dhùn Int. pl. foc. A; dhɛ̏ɛndhɛ̏ɛnsɯ̏ SupInt. A P S, dhɛ̏ɛndhɛ̏ɛnsɯ̏-dhùn SupInt. pl. A, dhɛ̏ɛndhɛ̏ɛnsɯ̏-sɯ̏ SupInt. foc. A, dhɛ̏ɛndhɛ̏ɛnsɯ̏-sɯ̏-dhùn SupInt. pl. foc. A} *adj* **1 strict, sévère** *(personne)*, **méchant** *(chien)* ♦ *yɤ̏ dhʌ́n-dhùn bhȁ dhɛ̏ɛnsɯ̏* il est sévère avec les enfants **2 faisant mal** *(d'une partie de corps)* ◊ *n̄ sɛ́ŋ̀dhɛ̏ yɤ̏ dhɛ̏ɛnsɯ̏* mes côtes me font mal ◊ *n̄ kɛ̀ɛ̀dhɛ̏ yà tó dhɛ̏ɛnsɯ̏* j'ai mal à l'occiput ◊ *slʌ̀ʌ fìi yà n̄ bhɛ̄ɛ́dhɛ̏ tó dhɛ̏ɛnsɯ̏* le piment me brûle la gorge

dhɛ̄ɛ́yɔ̏ɔ (m) *n* **réponse** *(à une question)*

dhɛ̏-gȁ *v vt* **examiner, regarder** ◊ *dhɛ̏ yáa gȁ ȁ tȁ* on ne devait pas le regarder

dhɛ̄gā *n* **bouclier** *(les Dan n'ont jamais eu de boucliers, ils les ont vus chez les ennemis)*

dhɛ̋gā <feuille-os> *n* **feuille** *(de plante)*

dhɛ̏gɯ́ *n* **ciel** *(l'éclairage du ciel)* ♦ *dhɛ̏gɯ́ dhɯ̋ɤɤdhɯ̏ɤɤ* un jour sombre, un ciel sombre ♦ *dhɛ̏gɯ́ pɯ̋u* ciel clair

dhɛ̏gɯ́tīi <jour-intérieur-noir> *n* **dernières ombres de la nuit** ◊ *yāandhɪ̋ɤ dhʌ́n bhā yɤ̏ bɤ̏ dhɛ̏gɯ́tīi gɯ́* hier l'enfant s'est réveillé lorsque il faisait encore tout noir

dhɛ̋gbȁ̋ <feuille- ?> *n* **haie de chasse** *(aux passages piégés)* ◊ *sɔ̋nŋdhɛ̋ sɔ̏ dhɛ̋gbȁ̋ bhā pɪ́ɤpɪ́ɤ* insérez des feuilles des palmiers dans la haie de chasse

dhɛ̋-kʌ̄ <feuille-faire> *v vt* **soigner, traiter** *(la maladie, le malade)* ◊ *yà ɤ̄ bhā gɔ̋ŋ dhɛ̋-kʌ̄ bèdhɛ̋ bhā' ká* il a soigné son paludisme avec le médicament en question ◊ *yà ɤ̄ bhāŋdhē dhɛ̋-kʌ̄* elle a soigné sa coépouse

dhɛ̋kpɤ̄ <feuille-balle> *n* **balle de feuilles et chiffons** *(pour les jeux traditionnels)* Syn. pɛ́ŋ̀kpɤ̄ *ce synonyme est beaucoup plus usité que dhɛ̋kpɤ̄*

dhɛ̏kpœ̀œ, dhɛ̏kpœ̏œ <endroit-faire jour> ***n*** **jour** *(en tant qu'opposé à la nuit) n'apparaît pas au pluriel* ◊ *ā kʌ̄ sȉɤ dhɛ̏kpœ̏œ tīi gúú* je me suis levé de bonne heure ♦ *dhɛ̀ ɤ́ dɔ̄ dhɛ̏kpœ̀œ dhɪ́ɤ* à l'aube ♦ *ȁ tȁ dhɛ̏kpœ̀œ tȁ dhīá* le lendemain ♦ *ȁ tȁ dhɛ̏kpœ̏œ tȁ dhīá ȁ pɪ́ɤ* le lendemain de bonne heure

dhɛ̏kpœ̀œyȉ <matin-jour> ***n*** **jour, jour et nuit** *(24 heures)* ◊ *yɤ̏ bhláȁdhɛ̏ bhā ȁ bɔ̏ dhɛ̏kpœ̀œyȉ yȁagā ká* il a labouré le champ pendant trois jours ◊ *wɔ̏ bhɔ̏ kpɪ̂ȉ bhā bhɤ̏ dhɛ̀kpœ̀œyȉ yȁagā ká* ils ont mangé ce gros cochon en trois jours ♦ *dhɛ̏kpœ̀œyȉ dō ká* un jour

dhɛ̀n ***cop*** **voici** *introduit l'énoncé présentatif et remplit en même temps une fonction démonstrative* ◊ *dē ȁ gbɛ̂n dhɛ̀n ?* à qui est ce chien ? ◊ *yɪ̄ȉ dhʌ́n tòtàabhȁn dhɛ̀n* voici notre benjamin ♦ *ȁ dhɛ́dhɛ́ plɛ̀ dhɛ̀n* il y a deux heures ♦ *ȁ dhɛ́dhɛ́ plɛ̀-dhȁan dhɛ̀n* depuis deux heures déjà

dhɛ́ndhɛ́n ***n*** **1 froid** Qsyn. sæ̏æ ♦ *dhɛ́ndhɛ́n yà bhán ī gúú* j'ai gelé ♦ *dhɛ́ndhɛ́n yà dhūn ī tȁ* j'ai froid ◊ *yɛ̄ɛ́npɪ́ɤ yɤ̏ gȕn sɛ̄ɛ ɤ́ dhɛ́ndhɛ́n ɤ́ zɪ̏ɤ* le soir était humide et froid **2 fièvre** ♦ *dhɛ́ndhɛ́n yɤ̏ ī bhȁ dɛ̀ɛ; dhɛ́ndhɛ́n kɔ̏ yɤ̏ ī bhȁ dɛ̀ɛ; dhɛ́ndhɛ́n yɤ̏ ī kʌ̄-sīʌ dɛ̀ɛ* j'ai la fièvre aujourd'hui

dhɛ́ndhɛ́ngā <froid-os> ***n*** **chair de poule** ♦ *dhɛ́ndhɛ́ngā yà lòo ȁ bhȁ* il a la chair de poule

dhɛ̏ndhɛ̏nsȕȕ *Int. de* dhɛ̏ɛnsȕȕ *sévère*

dhɛ́nkɛ́dhɛ̏nkɛ̏ ***adj*** *SupInt. pl. de* dhɛ́ɛndhɛ̏ɛn *savoureux*

dhɛ́nkɛ́ndhɛ̏nkɛ̏ndhɛ̏nkúndhɛ̄ɛ́n ***intj*** **que c'est savoureux !**

dhɛ̏ŋ, dhæ̏ŋ ***n*** **1 étranger** *(p. ex. d'une autre ethnie ou nationalité)* **2 étranger** *Iv.*, **visiteur** ◊ *yɤ̏ kʌ̄ ɤ̄ kɔ̏ yȁ ī dhɛ̏ŋ bhȁ sæ̏æ ká* il m'a accueilli froidement ♦ *ɤ̄ dhæ̏ŋ bhō bhɛ̄n tȁ* rendre visite à qn

dhɛ̀ŋ ***v*** **1** 1) *vi* **se perdre** ◊ *Tȍkpȁ yà dhɛ̀ŋ bűű gúú* Tokpa s'est perdu dans la brousse ♦ *ȁ tɔ́ yà dhɛ̀ŋ ī gɔ̏* j'ai oublié son nom 2) *vt* **perdre** ◊ *yɤ̏ pʌ̄ dhɛ̀ŋ gbɛ́* il perd souvent les choses **2** *vi* **disparaître** **3** *vi* **se cacher** ◊ *bȉaŋsúbhɛ̀n bhā yɤ̏ dhɛ̀ŋ dhɤ́ kɤ̄ gèe yá dhó ɤ̄ kún'* le coureur se cache de façon que le masque ne l'attrape pas

dhɛ̄ŋ̏ ***n*** *premier terme de composé nominal* **champ** Qsyn. dhɛ̄ŋ̏dhɛ̏ ♦ *dhɛ̄ŋ̏ gbȃa* partie du champ laissé non-ensemencée

dhɛ̀ŋbhɛ̏n <perdre-personne> ***n*** **qui se perd facilement dans un endroit inconnu**

dhɛ̏ŋbhɛ̏ndhē ***n*** **hôte, étrangère**

dhɛ̏ŋbhɛ̏ngɔ̄n, dhæ̏ŋbhɛ̏ngɔ̄n ***n*** **hôte, étranger**

dhɛ̏ŋbhɔ̄ɔdʌ̄, dhɛ̏ŋbhɔ̄ɔ <étranger- ?-père> ***n rn*** **hôte**

dhɛ̄ŋ̏dhɛ̏ {LOC dhɛ̄ŋdhɤ̄, LOC pl. dhɛ̄ŋ̏dhɛ̏-dhȕn gúú} ***loc.n*** **hameau, campement de culture** *(maisons aux champs éloignés du village et ces champs) pour la forme du cas locatif, un redoublement à valeur d'intensivité de l'action est possible* Qsyn. bhláā, bhláadhɛ̏ ◊ *yɤ̏ ɤ̄* *bhà̰ tɤ́ŋ gbàn kʌ̀ dhɛ̄ŋdhɤ̄ dhɛ̄ŋdhɤ̄* il passe tout son temps au campement de culture ♦ *ā kʌ̄ dhɛ̄ŋ̀dhɛ̏ kpɔ̏/kʌ̀* j'ai cultivé un champ lointain

dhɛ̄ŋdhɤ̄ *loc.n LOC de* dhɛ̄ŋ̀dhɛ̏ *hameau*

dhɛ̏ŋ-kún *v vt* **accueillir**, **recevoir** *(visiteur)*

dhɛ̋pű̋u *n* **plante herbacée à feuilles larges** *[pousse dans les bas-fonds; les feuilles sont utilisées pour envelopper la cola et la nourriture]*

dhɛ̏tà̰ *n* **silence** Syn. *dhæ̏æ* ♦ *dhɛ̏tà̰ yà̰ gā n̄ tà̰* je me suis tu ♦ *dhɛ̏tà̰ gā-sṵ̀ yà̰ gwʌ̀ʌ* le silence a duré ♦ *dhɛ̏tà̰ yà̰ dɔ̄* la silence s'est établi

dhɛ̏-yɤ̏ *v vt* **remarquer**

dhī 1) {dhì̏} *v* **1** *vi* **donner une bonne récolte** *(de riz, maïs, arachide, tubercules, piment, banane, ananas, café, cacao)* ◊ *yʌ́nŋ̀ yà̰ à̰ kʌ̄ dhɤ̋ bhān glɔ̄ɔ yíi dhī* à cause de la sécheresse mes bananes n'ont pas donné de bonne récolte Qsyn. *bhā* 2 **2.1** *vi* **plaire** *(à – dhɛ̏)*, **satisfaire** *(qn – dhɛ̏)* ◊ *yɤ̏ dhì̏ à̰ dhɛ̏ kɤ̄ kó dhó* il est d'accord que nous partions; il veut que nous nous allions ◊ *tòo yā yɤ̏ dhì̏ n̄ dhɛ̏ kɤ̄ kó à̰ bhɤ̏* ce tô me plaît, je veux que nous le mangions ♦ *dhì̏ bhɛ̄n dhɛ̏ pʌ̀, dhì̏ bhɛ̄n dhɛ̏ wɔ̏n* chose acceptable **2.2** *vi* **ne pas être indespensable** *(pour – dhɛ̏) la construction conjointe dépendante est introduite par la conjonction yɤ́* ◊ *yà dhī n̄ dhɛ̏ yɤ́ á yī zʌ̄* je peux ne pas dormir ◊ *yà̰ dhī n̄ dhɛ̏ yɤ́ á tō yɤ̄* je peux ne pas rester ici **2.3** *vi* **être joli** *(d'un homme ou d'une femme, en s'agissant des vêtements, coiffure, etc.)* ◊ *bhá dhī !* tu es joli(e) ! **3.1** 1) *vi* **être favorable** ◊ *tʌ̋ yɤ̏ dhì̏* la mission aura du succès ♦ *à̰ bhà̰ zā yà̰ dhī* il a été acquitté 2) *vt* **corriger** *(améliorer)* ◊ *... yɤ́ ú dhō yíi zā dhī' ká ...* alors tu iras et régleras l'affaire avec ça **3.2** *vi* **s'occuper** *(de – bhà̰)* **4** *vi* **aller bien** *(vêtement; à – ká)* ◊ *sɔ̄ yɤ̏ dhì̏ à̰ ká* le vêtement lui va ♦ *dɔ̄ yíi dhī n̄ ká* ce n'est pas de chance **5** *vt zā dhī* **s'excuser**, **demander pardon** *(à – gɔ̏)*

dhī 2) *n* **beauté** ♦ *dhī kɔ̏ ɤ́' gɔ̏, yɤ̏ kʌ̀ dhè bhīi pʌ̄ zīɤ' bhà̰ kɤ̄ í' bhɤ̏* elle est si belle qu'on peut mettre de la nourriture sur elle et la manger

dhí̋ {dhì̏; LOC dhí̋} *loc.n* **1** *rn* **bouche** ◊ *slʌ̀ʌ yɤ̏ bhɔ̄-sīʌ n̄ dhí̋* le piment me brûle la bouche ♦ *yà̰ ɤ̄ dhí̋ tā n̄ gɔ̏* il ne me parle plus ♦ *ɤ̄ dhí̋ dà̰ bhɛ̄n tà̰* parler avec qn ♦ *ɤ̄ dhí̋ tā bhɛ̄n gɔ̏* ne pas adresser sa parole à qn ♦ *ɤ̄ dhí̋ bhō wɔ́n/dhīaŋ tà̰* avouer son tort ♦ *à̰ dhí̋ yɤ̏ gbɛ́ɛ ká dhè kòo báà̰ bhɤ̏ dhì̏ dhɤ́* sa bouche est large comme celle de la carpe, mangeuse de vase ♦ *à̰ dhí̋ yɤ̏ fɛ́ɛnfɛ̀ɛn ká dhè drɔ́ɔ dhí̋ dhɤ́* sa bouche est étroite comme celle de la petite grenouille *[signe de beauté]* **2** *rn* **orifice, ouverture** **3** *rn* **repas** ◊ *dhí̋ blɛ̏ɛsṵ̀* le premier repas **4** *rn* **nombre** *(quantité)* ♦ *à̰-dhṵ̀n dhí̋ (yɤ̏) dɔ̄* ils sont du même nombre

dhīa̋ *n* **1 demain** ♦ *yɤ̏ dhɔ̏ sṵ̀ɤ yʌ̄ tà̰ dhīa̋* il commencera le travail demain de bonne heure **2** *dhīa̋ pīɤ* **matin** ♦ *dhīa̋ pīɤ gbàn ká* tous les matins ♦ *dhīa̋ à̰ pīɤ* de bonne heure *(de 5 à 7 heures du matin)* ♦ *kwā dhīa̋ pīɤ* à demain matin ! *(lorsqu'on s'adresse à plusieurs personnes)*

dhīa *n* **1** *rn* **plaisir** **2** *rn* **amour** ♦ *X dhīa yà̰ bhán Y gṵ́* Y a beaucoup aimé X

dhi̋aa ***n*** **lombric, ver de terre** *[les Dan détestent les lombrics et en ont peur; on croit qu'un lombric écrasé crache sur l'homme, ce qui entraîne la lèpre; la vue d'un grand lombric en saison sèche est de mauvais augure]* ◊ *dhi̋aa yà dhídhí wɛ̀nŋ Gbȁtȍ bhȁ, wèe yȁ lòo Gbȁtȍ bhȁ* un lombric a craché sur Gbato, et celui-ci a eu la lèpre ♦ *dhi̋aa bhɛ̄* grand lombric ◊ *wȁ kpȁn dhi̋aa bhɛ̄ bhȁ blɛ̄ɛ́yí ká kɤ̄ wāa wɔ́n yāa bhá bhān* si on voit un grand lombric en saison sèche, on s'attend à un malheur

dhía-dhɛ̏ ***n*** **beauté**

dhíadhíasȕ ***adj*** *Int. de* dhíasȕ *beau.INT*

dhīaŋ {dhi̋aŋ} ***n*** **1.1 parole** ♦ *dhīaŋ zʌ̄* parler; prononcer un discours ◊ *yɤ̏ dhīaŋ zʌ̏ ɤ̄ dȅ pɪ́ɤ* il parle à lui-même ◊ *yà dhīaŋ bhlʌ̀ʌbhlʌ̀ʌsȕ zʌ̄ n̄ dhɛ̏* il a parlé avec moi d'une affaire très importante ◊ *Gbȁtȍ dhʌ̀n ɤ́ dùa, yɤ́ yí' dhi̋aŋ zʌ̄-sɪʌ* c'est Gbato qui s'est évadé, et nous sommes en train d'en parler ◊ *dhīaŋ ɤ́ ká' zʌ̄ bhā, yɤ̏ dhȉ n̄ dhɛ̏* la parole que vous avez prononcée m'a plu ♦ *ȁ zʌ̄ dhi̋aŋ yáa dɔ̄* ses paroles ne sont pas fiables ♦ *dhīaŋ yȁa dhí pā* il est resté bouche bée ♦ *dhīaŋ dȁ bhɛ̄n tȁ* entamer une conversation avec qn **1.2 récit** *(portant sur des événements dont le narrateur fut témoin)* **2 litige; différend, palabre** *lv.* ◊ *yí kpɔ́dhē wɔ̏n yà kʌ̄ dhīaŋ ká* l'affaire de la bénédiction (qui doit faire la bénédiction) est devenu un palabre **3 affaire** ♦ *ȁ dhīaŋ gúú* grâce à cela

dhīaŋdhűsúbhɛ̏n <parole-arbre-prendre-personne> ***n*** *rare* **avocat** Syn. vòokāȁ

dhīaŋkpɤ̏ <parole-boule> ***n*** *neol.* **texte** ♦ *yēe-kʌ̄ dīaŋkpɤ̄ tȁ-sȕ* texte de rattrapage

dhīaŋyɔ̏ɔ (gw) ***n*** **réponse** *(à une question)* Syn. dhɛ̄ɛ́yɔ̏ɔ (m)

dhíasȕ {A, dhíasȕ-dhȕn pl. A; dhíadhíasȕ Int. A, dhíadhíasȕ-dhȕn Int. pl. A} <plaisir-adj.> ***adj*** **1 beau 2 agréable**

dhi̋ʌ ***n*** *hist.* **place à manger** *(traditionnellement, avec des sièges en pierre en cercle; la marmite avec la nourriture dont on mange ensemble est mise au centre)*

dhìʌʌ 1 ***v*** 1) *vi* **se refroidir** *(de la nourriture ou de l'eau atteignant la température requise pour la consommation)* Syn. zɔ̀nŋ Qsyn. sæ̏æ ◊ *ȁ bhȁ pʌ̄bhèe yɤ̏ dhìʌʌ, yɤ́ gūn ȁ bhɤ̏ dhȁan* c'est quand sa nourriture s'est refroidie qu'il la mange 2) *vt* **refroidir** *(surtout en parlant de la nourriture qu'on évente)* ◊ *Yɔ̏ yà bhãa dhìʌʌ* Yo a refroidi le riz

dhi̋ʌ̏ʌ ***n*** **furoncle** ♦ *dhìʌ̏ʌ yà dɔ̄ ȁ kèedhɤ̄* il a eu un furoncle sur l'occiput

dhíʌʌ {dhīʌʌ}, **dhìʌʌ** ***v*** *vt* **écraser** *(en pâte)*, **broyer** ◊ *yɤ̏ kɛ́ŋslʌ̏ʌ dhìʌʌ gwʌ̏ yā' tȁ* elle a broyé le piment rouge sur ce caillou

dhi̋ʌʌn ***n*** *rn* **gencives** *(le devant, ce qu'on voit quant la bouche est ouverte)*

dhìʌʌn ***v*** **1** *vi* **se promener 2** *vi* **être de petite vertu** *(une femme)*

dhi̋ʌnŋkwãnȉŋpíɤ ***n*** **expédition, voyage** ◊ *yɤɤ dhó ɤ̄ bhā dhi̋ʌnŋkwãnȉŋpíɤ gú Gàan sɛ́ gúú* il se préparait à faire une expédition dans le pays de Gaan

dhíʌŋ 1 (gw) ***n*** *rn, fn* **vie** Qsyn. tȍsǽæ̏ ♦ *yɤ̏ kʌ̄ dhíʌŋ kʌ̏ dȅdȅwō* il a vécu longtemps

dhı̋ʌŋ 2 ***n rn*** **palais** anat. ♦ *yȁ ɤ̄ dhı̋ʌŋ sűű ȁ ká* il a fait claquer sa langue (signe de désaccord, désapprobation, mépris)

dhı̀bhɔ̋ɔ̀n → dhı̀nbhɔ̋ɔ̀n *frère cadet du mari*

dhı̏dásűı̏ ***adj*** **miraculeux** *(supernaturel)* ◊ *wɔ́n dhı̏dásűı̏ dō yȁ kʌ̄* un miracle s'est produit

dhı̏dhā ***n*** **disparition** ♦ *dhı̏dhā sűű* disparaître

dhídhȁan ***n*** **discorde; querelle; bagarre** ♦ *dhídhȁan bhán bhɛ̄n ká* se disputer avec qn, faire palabre à qn ♦ *dhídhȁan dȁ* provoquer une querelle

dhídhɛ̏kʌ̄ <bouche-place-faire> ***n*** **stomatite**

dhídhı́ <bouche- ?> ***n rn*** **salive** ♦ *dhídhı́ bhō* cracher ♦ *dhā dhídhı́ gā* goutte de pluie ♦ *dhídhı́ vűu* bave ♦ *ūū dhídhı́ dőŋsűı̏ bhā yɤ́ űű' zı̏ɤ n̄ bhȁ ȅe !* mais tu m'as sali de ta bave ? ! ♦ *dhūn kɤ̄ kwá kwā dhídhı́ dőŋ kűn* arch. viens, prenons le petit-déjeuner ♦ *bhá ūū dhídhı́ bhá bhʌ̋nŋ āan yɤ́ kwá dhō' bhȁ dhȅ* quand tu te réposes un peu (de la causerie), nous continuerons

dhı̏dhı̏sűı̏ ***adj*** *Int. de* dhı̏isűı̏ *sale*

dhı̏i ***n rn*** **saleté** ♦ *dhı̏i kún* se salir ◊ *kwāȁ kɔ́ɔdhɛ̏ yȁ dhı̏i kún* il est devenu sale dans notre maison ♦ *yà yȁ {ɤ̄} dhı̏i ká gblȍo sʌ̏ tȁ* il s'est assis tout sale sur un joli siège

dhı̂ı̂ < Fr. lit > ***n*** **lit** *(de type moderne)*

dhı̏idhı̏isűı̏ *SupInt. de* dhı̏isűı̏ *sale*

dhı̏ifȁa <saleté-chicote> ***n*** **tourteaux de graines de palmier à huile** ◊ *wȍ sı́ɤ yȁ sɤ̄ dhı̏i dhı̏ifȁa ká* on allume le feu avec les tourteaux de graines de palmier à huile

dhı̏i-kún {dhı̏i-kūn, INT dhı̏ii-kún, INT CNJ dhı̏ii-kūn} ***v vt*** **salir**

dhı̀in ***n*** **moisissure; patine verte sur les dents** ◊ *dhı̀in yɤ̏ kpɔ́-sīʌ ūū bhā kœ̋œ̀* il y a de la moisissure sur les murs de ta maison ♦ *ȁ zūʌ́ dhı̀in yȁ dȁ* il est content

dhı̂ı̂n ***n rn*** **âme** Qsyn. zűu ♦ *ȁ dhı̂ı̂n yȁ pɤ̏* il est mort ♦ *ȁ dhı̂ı̂n yɤ̏ gbɛ̋ɛ̀* il est ferme ♦ *yȁ dhı̂ı̂n yāa kʌ̄ bhɛ̄n bhȁ* il a agi méchamment envers l'homme ♦ *dhı̂ı̂n yāȁdhɛ̏* mauvaises intentions ◊ *yȁ flɛ̏ɛn dhı̂ı̂n yāȁdhɛ̏ bhȁ* il l'a pincé avec la méchanceté

dhı̀indȁ ***n*** *zūʌ́ dhı̀indȁ* **satisfaction** ◊ *dhı̀indȁdhē kʌ̄ ūū gɔ̏* tâche d'être heureux !

dhı̏isűı̏ {A P, dhı̏isűı̏-dhȕn pl. A, dhı̏isűı̏-sűı̏ foc. A, dhı̏isűı̏-sűı̏-dhȕn pl. foc. A; dhı̏dhı̏sűı̏ Int. A P, dhı̏dhı̏sűı̏-dhȕn Int. pl. A, dhı̏dhı̏sűı̏-sűı̏ Int. foc. A, dhı̏dhı̏sűı̏-sűı̏-dhȕn Int. pl. foc. A; dhı̏idhı̏isűı̏ SupInt. A P, dhı̏idhı̏isűı̏-dhȕn SupInt. pl. A, dhı̏idhı̏isűı̏-sűı̏ SupInt. foc. A, dhı̏idhı̏isűı̏-sűı̏-dhȕn SupInt. pl. foc. A} <saleté-adj.> ***adj*** **sale** ◊ *sɔ̄ dhı̏isűı̏ yɤ̏ bhɛ̄n kȁa* les habits sales provoquent des démangeaisons ◊ *bhá dhó ūū zű' yı́ dı̏isűı̏ bhȁa* tu ne dois pas te baigner dans l'eau sale

dhı̏kó-dhɛ̏ <réussir-l'un.l'autre-pour> ***n*** **paix** *(accord)*, **amitié**

dhı̀n ***adv*** **comme ça, ainsi** *(semblable à l'échantillon qui se trouve devant le locuteur)* Ant. dhɤ́ ◊ *gbɛ̂n yáa kʌ̄ dhı̀n* ce n'est pas un chien ◊ *ā kʌ̄ pɤ̏ dhı̀n, kɛ́ɛŋ bhı́in' pɤ̄ dhɤ́* j'ai dit (de faire) comme ça (ici), mais je n'ai pas dit (de faire) comme ça (là) ◊ *bhán' pɤ̄'-dhǜn dhɛ̏ kȁ ȁ kʌ̄ dhìn, ȁ kʌ̄ dhʌ̀n wó wɔ̄* lorsque je leur dis : "Faites-le comme ça", ils le font

dhĩ́n <Manding ní> ***conj*** **si** ◊ *yɤ̏ n̄ dhɛ̄ɛ́-kpɔ̏ ū̃ wɔ̏n ká dhĩ́n ú́ yɤ̄* il me demande si tu es ici ◊ *dhĩ́n yà kʌ̄ dhɛ̀ bháa bhīi dhūn, ȁ wɔ́n pɤ̄ n̄ dhɛ̏* s'il arrive que tu ne viennes pas, dis-le moi

dhĩ́nbhlɔ̂n, **dhĩ́nbhlɔ̏ɔ̏n** <Fr. numéro> ***n*** **1 numéro, chiffre, nombre** ♦ *pìɤgā bhȁn dhĩ́bhlɔ̏ɔ̏n* numéro de téléphone **2** *neol., ling.* **nombre** ♦ *dōŋdhē dhínbhlɔ̂n* nombre cardinal ♦ *dǜɛɛ dhínbhlɔ̂n* nombre ordinal

dhìnbhɔ̄ɔ̏n, **dhìbhɔ̄ɔ̏n** {pl. masc. dhìnbhɔ̄ɔ̏nzʌ̏-dhǜn} ***n*** **1** *rn* **frère cadet du mari** *(pour une femme)*, **femme du frère aîné**, **sœur cadette de la femme d'ego** *[n'est pas utilisé comme un terme d'adresse, mais plutôt comme un terme de référence; partenaires potentiels de mariage]* Syn. gɔ̀n Qsyn. bhá 1 **2** *rn* **parent par alliance, parente par alliance** *(pour une femme, mari de la sœur aînée; mari de la fille du frère aîné; mari de sa propre fille et de toute sa famille; mari de la soeur cadette du père; mari de la fille du frère cadet ou aîné du père; mari de la fille de la soeur cadette de mère. Pour l'homme : mari de sa fille et ses parents; mari de la fille du frère aîné; mari de la soeur cadette; mari de la soeur cadette du père; mari de la fille du frère aîné ou cadet du père; mari de la fille de la soeur cadette de la mère) [implique des relations familières]* Ant. zíɤ̏ɤ **3** *rn* **beau-frère** *(frère cadet ou aîné de la femme d'ego; une forme d'adresse, plutôt qu'un terme de référence)* Qsyn. zíɤ̏ɤ

dhìnbhɔ̄ɔ̏n-dhɛ̏ ***n*** **relations de plaisanterie** *(entre les époux potentiels, surtout entre une femme et ses beaux-frères, cadets de son mari, mais aussi entre un homme et les frères et soeurs de sa femme)*

dhìnbhɔ̄ɔ̏nzʌ̏-dhǜn *pluriel masculin de* dhìnbhɔ̄ɔ̏n **beaux-parents cadets** *(hommes)*

dhìoo, **dhǜɤɤ** ***n*** **conseil** Qsyn. glȅŋ ♦ *dhìoo dɔ̄ bhɛ̄n tȁ* donner conseil à qn ◊ *yà dhìoo dɔ̄ n̄ tȁ kɤ̄ bhán dhó dȁ' yí bhȁa* il m'a conseillé de ne pas entrer dans l'eau

dhìoodɔ̄bhɛ̏n <conseille-arrêter-personne> ***n*** **conseiller**

dhìɔɔ ***n*** **appel** ◊ *bhán ȁ dhìɔɔ kʌ̄* je l'ai appelé ◊ *wíi dhūn kwāȁ dhìɔɔ wȍ bhȁ* ils ne se sont pas rendus à notre appel

dhìɔɔnsǜ {A S; P rare; dhìɔɔnsǜ-dhǜn pl. A S; dhìɔɔnsǜ-sǜ foc. A; dhìɔɔnsǜ-sǜ-dhǜn foc. pl. A} ***adj*** **infirme**

dhìɤ 1 *v vi* **gémir** ◊ *bhīʌʌ ɤ́' bhȁ bhā, yɤ̏ dhìɤ ȁ dhɛ̏ gbɛ̄ŋ gbɛ́ ȁ wɔ̏n gú́* il gémit beaucoup la nuit à cause de sa plaie

dhìɤ 2 *v vt* **tendre** *(piège)*

dhíɤ 1) ***n*** **1** *rn* **tranchant 2 sommet** *(de montagne)* ♦ *ȁ-dhǜn gɔ̏ dhíɤ yà dhɛ̀ŋ* elles étaient disparues de la vue **3 bord** *(de fleuve, rivière)* ◊ *Bhān dhíɤ* bord de la rivière de Ma **4 devant** ♦ *dhíɤ sú́ bhɛ̄n ká* guider qn

dhíɤ 2) *pp* **1 devant** ◊ *kɤ̄ kó dhó kō dhíɤ* pour que nous avancions ◊ *yɤ̀ dɔ̀ ȁ dhíɤ* il le précède **2 avant** *(sens temporel)* ◊ *wɔ́n bhā yɤ̀ kʌ̀ dhɤ́ ɯ̄ dhíɤ* cela s'est passé avant toi *(avant que tu ne viennes)* ◊ *gbēŋ yɤ̀ dhȅkpœ̀œ-sɯ̀ dhíɤ* la nuit précède l'aube **3 avant** *(en importance)* ◊ *dhʌ́n kpɔ́-sɯ̀ yáa ȁ dhíɤ, kɛ́ɛ bhá ȁ kpɔ́ ȁ kún gbɛ̋ɛ̏* donner naissance à un enfant n'est pas le plus important; c'est s'en occuper sérieusement qui est important **4 vers** ◊ *dhā ɤ́ gūn bānŋ̏ dhɔ̀ɔ, kɤ̄ ā dhūn-sīʌ zīaan dhíɤ* pendant qu'il pleuvait, je marchais vers la route **5 pour** ◊ *... yɤ́ dhʌ́n dō kpɔ̄ ɤ̄ bhȁ gɔ̄n bhā' dhíɤ ...* et elle a donné naissance à un enfant pour son mari

dhíɤ 3) *adv* **devant** ♦ *dhó dhíɤ !* avance ! ♦ *dȁ dhíɤ* s'accroître

dhíɤ 4) *prev* **bord**

dhíɤ-blɯ̏ *v vt* **désobéir** *(à une demande, une commission)* ◊ *á ȁ pɤ̄ yɤ̀ dhó bhān yí sɯ́', ī wò dhíɤ dhʌ́n ɤ́ ȁ blɯ̏* quand je lui ai dit de m'apporter de l'eau, elle n'a pas tenu compte de mes paroles

dhíɤ-bɔ̄ *v vt* **aiguiser** ◊ *yɤ̀ dhȁa dhíɤ-bɔ̏ gwʌ̀ tȁ* il aiguise (d'habitude) le couteau sur le caillou ◊ *yà gbɔ̋ŋ gā dhíɤ-bɔ̄ ɤ̄ zɔ̋ sɯ̀ ká* il a taillé la canne de bambou en biseau ♦ *dhȁa-dhíɤ-bɔ̄ bhànŋzíí* rouleau aiguiseur

dhíɤ-bhȁn *v vt* **ajuster en frappant** *(étape initiale pour aiguiser, suivie par dhíɤ-bɔ̄)* ◊ *yɤ̀ bãŋ dhíɤ-bhȁn-sīʌ kɔ̀ɔdhíɤ ká* il est en train d'ajuster le tranchant de la machette avec un marteau

dhíɤbhȅn <devant-personne> *n* **leader, dirigeant**

dhíɤ-bhō {dhíɤ-bhō} *v vt* **s'occuper de** *(enfant)*

dhíɤ-dȁ *v vt* **honnir**

dhíɤ-dɔ̄ *v* **1** *vt* **finir, achever** *(amener au bout)* ◊ *yȁ yʌ̄ kʌ̄, yȁ ȁ dhíɤ-dɔ̄* il a fait le travail jusqu'à la fin **2** *vt* **cesser, arrêter** *(interrompre)* ◊ *ȁ dhíɤ-dɔ̄ !* cesse cela !

dhíɤ-dɔ̋ɔ̏ndhūn {dhíɤ-dɔ̋ɔ̏ndhūn, Neut. dhíɤ-dɔ̋ɔ̏ndhȕn} *v vt* **arrêter** *(voiture, par celui qui se trouve dehors)* Syn. dhíɤ-gbáȁndhūn Qsyn. gbáȁndhūn, dɔ̋ɔ̏ndhūn

dhíɤdhíɤsɯ̀ *Int. de* dhíɤsɯ̀ *tranchant*

dhíɤdhɤ̄ *adv* **devant** ◊ *dhó dhíɤdhɤ̄ !* avance ! ◊ *kídhőŋ dō síbhán yɤ̀ dhíɤdhɤ̄* il reste environ un kilomètre devant (nous)

dhíɤ-dhūn *v* **rendre** *(à – dhȅ)*

dhíɤfíʌʌbhȅn *n* **misérable** *(personne indigente qui n'a pas d'avenir)*

dhíɤ-gấn {dhíɤ-gȁn} *v vt* **attendre** *(celui qui doit venir; un fuyard)* Syn. dɔ̄ 1, yấn-tó

dhíɤ-gbā *v vt* **nourrir** *(celui que est enfermé ou caché)*

dhíɤ-gbáȁndhūn {CNJ dhíɤ-gbáȁndhūn, Neut. dhíɤ-gbáȁndhȕn} *v vt* **arrêter** *(voiture)* Syn. dhíɤ-dɔ̋ɔ̏ndhūn Qsyn. gbáȁndhūn, dɔ̋ɔ̏ndhūn

dhíɤ-kʌ̄ *v* 1) *vi* **devenir** *(entrer dans un état)* 2) *vt* **rendre** *(faire entrer dans un état)* ◊ *wē yà ȁ dhíɤ-kʌ̄ bhɔ̋ɔnbhɔ̏ɔn* l'alcool l'a abruti

dhíɤ̋kɤ̋dhìɤkɤ̀ ***adj*** *SupInt. de* dhíɤsɯ̀ *tranchant*

dhíɤ-kpɔ́ {dhíɤ-kpɔ̄} ***v*** *vr* **tourner son regard** *(à – bhà)*

dhíɤ-lòo {dhíɤ-lòo} ***v*** **présenter**, **transmettre** *(paroles; à – bhà)*

dhíɤ̋ɤ → dhíɤsɯ̀ *tranchant*

dhíɤ̋ɤ-dhɛ̀ ***n*** **sévérité**

dhíɤ-pā {dhíɤ-pā} <bord-remplir> ***v*** *vt* **completer**, **terminer**

dhíɤpāwɔ̀ <terminer-voix> ***n*** *neol., ling.* **voyelle** ♦ *dhígúɯ́dhíɤpāwɔ̀* voyelle orale ♦ *yūngɯ̋ɯ́dhíɤpāwɔ̀* voyelle nasale

dhíɤpʌ̀ <devant-chose> ***n*** *neol., ling.* **postposition**

dhíɤpɛ̀ ***n*** *rn* **fente des yeux**

dhíɤ-pɔ̋, **dhíɤ-pɯ̋** {dhíɤ-pɔ̀, dhíɤ-pɯ̀} <bord-ouvrir> ***v*** *vt* **ouvrir** *(une porte ou un couvercle sans gonds)* Syn. *pɔ̋* Qsyn. *dhí-pɔ̋*

dhíɤsɯ̀, **dhíɤ̋ɤ** {A, dhíɤsɯ̀-dhùn pl. A, dhíɤsɯ̀-sɯ̀ foc. A; dhíɤ̋ɤ Int. A P, dhíɤ̋ɤ-dhùn Int. pl. A, dhíɤ̋ɤ-sɯ̀ Int. foc. A, dhíɤ̋ɤ-sɯ̀-dhùn Int. pl. foc. A, dhíɤdhíɤsɯ̀ Int. A S, dhíɤdhíɤsɯ̀-dhùn Int. pl. A, dhíɤdhíɤsɯ̀-sɯ̀ Int. foc. A, dhíɤdhíɤsɯ̀-sɯ̀-dhùn Int. pl. foc. A, dhíɤ̋kɤ̋dhìɤkɤ̀ SupInt A P} <tranchant-adj.> ***adj*** *dhíɤsɯ̀, dhíɤdhíɤsɯ̀ expriment un état temporaire, dhíɤ̋ɤ exprime une qualité permanente* **1** **tranchant** ◊ *n̄ bhànwɔ̀n yɤ̀ dhàa dhíɤsɯ̀-sɯ̀ bhà* j'ai besoin d'un couteau qui est tranchant **2** **brûlant** *(soleil)* **3** *pour certains, seule la forme dhíɤ̋ɤ peut apparaître dans ces sens* **3.1** **piquant** *(nourriture)*, **fort** *(boisson)* ◊ *dhɯ̋ bɪ́n fii yɤ̀ dhíɤ̋ɤ* l'odeur des fleurs est forte **3.2** *pas de superintensif dhíɤ̋kɤ̋dhìɤkɤ̀ pour ce sens* **féroce** *(animal)* ◊ *... yɤ́ wūū dhíɤ̋ɤ bhá dhɤ́ à-dhùn kʌ̀ ...* mais un animale féroce les a chassé **3.3** *pas de superintensif dhíɤ̋kɤ̋dhìɤkɤ̀ pour ce sens* **sévère** *(personne)* **3.4** **perçant** *(voix)*

dhíɤ-sɯ́ {dhíɤ-sɯ̄} ***v*** *vt* **nuire** *(par les moyens magiques)*

dhíɤ-tā {dhíɤ-tā} ***v*** **1.1** *vt* **terminer**, **achever** **1.2** *vi* **finir** ◊ *kɔ̋ɔ̀ ! yɤ́ à wɔ́n ɤ́ yā à dhíɤ yɤ̀ tà dhè kɔ̀ bhā dhɤ́ɤ ?* quoi ? c'est de cette manière que cette affaire s'est terminée ? ! **2** *vt* **fermer** *(à clé)*

dhíɤtásɯ́bhɛ̀n <devant-marcher-prendre-personne.GEN> ***n*** **conducteur** *(de voiture)*, **chauffeur**

dhíɤtó <bord-laisser> ***n*** **fin** ◊ *bhān kɔ́ yɤ̀ kpɪ̀nŋ dhíɤtódhɛ̀ gúɯ* ma maison est au bout de la route

dhíɤ-tó {dhíɤ-tō} ***v*** **1** 1) *vi* **s'arrêter**, **atteindre** ◊ *n̄ zláà gɔ̄ɔ̀n dhíɤ yɤ̀ tò n̄ gbān píɤ* mon jeune frère atteint mon épaule ◊ *n̄ zláà bhà gblɛ̀ɛndhɛ̀ dhíɤ́ yɤ̀ tò n̄ tòŋ gúɯ* mon petit frère m'arrive déjà à la poitrine ◊ *kɯ̋nbhándhán dhɛ́ ɤ́ dhɤ́ à bhà yʌ̄ dhíɤ yɤ̀ tò à bhà kɔ̋bhí dhʌn' gúɯ* les activités de chaque préfet se limitent à sa préfecture 2) *vt* **arrêter**, **cesser** ◊ *yʌ̀ bhā à dhíɤ-tó* arrête ce travail **2** *vt* **achever**

dhíɤ-wlɯ̄ɯ́ɯ́ ***v*** *vt* **soulever** ♦ *bhɛ̄n zɯ̄ʌ́ dhíɤ-wlɯ̀ɯ* révolter qn

dhíɤ-yà *v* **1** *vt* **élever** ♦ *dhʌ́n dhíɤ-yà kɔ̀ yāa* (t) mal élever l'enfant **2** (t) *vt* **gâter** *(l'enfant)* **3** (t) *vt* **finir** *(par – tà)*

dhíɤ-zīɤ {dhíɤ-zìɤ} *v vt* **dépasser** ◊ *yà wɔ́n dhíɤ-zīɤ* il a trop exagéré

dhí-pő, dhí-pű {dhí-pò, dhí-pù} <bouche-ouvrir> *v* **1** *vt* **ouvrir** *(une porte ou un couvercle à gonds)* *Syn.* *pő* *Qsyn.* *dhíɤ-pő* **2.1** *vt* **allumer** *(télévision)* **2.2** *vt* **commencer** *(conversation)* ◊ *yà dhīaŋ dhí-pű* il a rompu le silence

dhíwɔ̀gā <bouche-voix-os> *n neol.* **mot**

dhíwɔ̀yàn <bouche-voix-contenu> *n neol., ling.* **phrase**

dhó, dhɤ́ {dhō} *la forme dhɤ́ n'apparaît que dans la fonction auxiliaire* *v* **1** *vi* **aller** *(quelque part)* ◊ *Bīyàdhɛ̀ dhʌ̀n ɤ́ dhō à bhà* c'est à Abidjan qu'elle est allée ♦ *dhó à ká* emmener, emporter ♦ *dhó à ká bhɛ̄n píɤ* passer la parole à qn *[lors de la discussion des problèmes importants, la parole passe du cadet à l'aîné, donc cette expression signifie en même temps "regarder qn comme un aîné"]* ♦ *dhó gwāàn* se marier *(pour une femme)* ♦ *dhó yí wlɤ̀ɤ* couler *(bâteau)* ◊ *yà à kʌ̄ dhɤ̄ bhān kplắgɔ̄ yà dhó yí wlɤ̀ɤ* il a coulé ma pirogue **1.2** *vi* **faire un mouvement**, **passer** *(avec – ká)* ♦ *yà dhó ɤ̄ kɔ̀ ká* il a fait un mouvement avec sa main, il a cherché avec sa main **2.1** *vi* **aller** *(pour faire qch; suivi d'un verbe à l'infinitif)* ◊ *dhʌ́n-dhùn bhā wà dhó tlōo kʌ̄', wɔ̀ wō kó blǜ kɔ̀ yāa kʌ̀* quand ces enfants vont jouer, il se bousculent dangereusement **2.2** *vi verbe auxiliaire : à l'aspect neutre + infinitif du verbe principal exprimant le futur ou une hypothèse; dans la construction négative, le sujet est exprimé par un pronom négatif perfectif* ♦ *yɤ̀ dhɔ̀ kʌ̄' dhɛ̀* ... sans doute... *Syn.* *yɤ̀ bhɔ̀ à bhà, yíi dɔ̄ sʌ̀* ◊ *yɤ̀ dhɔ̀ kʌ̄' dhɛ̀ yɤ̀ zīàan* sans doute, il est en route **2.3** *vi l'auxiliaire du prohibitif* ◊ *bhá dhó bìaŋ sű'* ne cours pas ! **2.4** *vi auxiliaire introduisant le verbe principal dans une construction à valeur d'irréel* ◊ *yɤ̀ dà kɔ́ɔdhɤ̄ dhún, ā dhɔ̀ à bhàn'* s'il entrait dans la maison, je le frapperais **3** *vi* **atteindre** *(en dimension)* ◊ *yɛ̀gā ɤ́ bhà gblɛ̀ɛndhɛ̀ ɤ́ dhō sīāa wāà bhɛ̄n bhɛ̃̀ɛdhɛ̀ wó bhɔ̀ɔn* un trou grand et profond pouvant contenir un être humain **4** *vi* **entrer** *(dans – gű)* ◊ *yí ɤ́ dhō' bhà sàbhấ gű bhā...* l'eau qui est entrée dans ses chaussures... ◊ *sāà yí yà dhó bhɛ̄n yʌ̃́nŋ* l'eau savonneuse est entrée dans les yeux de l'homme **5** *vi* **continuer** *(qch – bhà)* ♦ *yɤ́ ɤ́ dhɤ̄ bhā* en plus, à part ça

dhòŋ *n* **1** **trou de secours** *(d'un rat, d'une souris)* **2** **trou** *Syn.* *dhòŋgā* *(seule la forme dhòŋgā est utilisé dans le compte)* ♦ *kɔ́ dhòŋ* i) fenêtre *Syn.* *fɤ̀dhéntlʌ̀* ii) trou dans le toit ◊ *dhā dhídhí gā yɤ̀ lɔ̄ɔ-sīʌ kɔ́ dhòŋ ká* les gouttes de pluie tombent en passant par les trous dans le toit

dhōŋ {dhòŋ} *v vt* **compter** ◊ *yɤ̀ bhɛ̄n dhɔ̀ŋ kótà plɛ̀* il a compté les gens deux fois

dhőŋ *n* **1** *rn* **trompe** *[la viande la plus recherchée]* ♦ *bīɤ dhőŋ* = dhőŋ **2** *rn* **hémorroïdes** ♦ *dhőŋ yà wɔ̀/dɔ̄ à bhà* il a des hémorroïdes **3** **corde** *(d'une plante rampante)*

dhőŋbhɛ̃́ɛ *n* **sésame** *[peu cultivé dans les villages]*

dhōŋdhē *n* **compte**

dhōŋ-dhùn *pl. de* dhēbʌ̀ *femme*

dhòŋgā <trou de secours-os> *n* **1** *kɔ́ dhòŋgā* **fenêtre 2 trou dans le mur** *(se fait par affaissement naturel)* Syn. *dhòŋ*

dhòo *n rn* **frère aîné, grand frère** *lv. (au sens classificatoire : frère aîné d'ego; fils du frère du père, de la sœur cadette du père ou de la mère, s'il est plus âgé qu'ego) [en s'adressant à un grand frère initié on utilise dʌ̄zȍo. Pour s'adresser à un grand frère d'ego devienu chef de famille, on utilise le terme "père", dʌ̄]*

dhōȍ *n* ***Triplochiton seleroxylon*** **samba, abachi, wawa, ayous** *(un grand arbre aux contreforts ailés)*

dhőo *n* **1 enclos** *(fermé, à travers lequel on ne voit pas)* ◊ *kwa̋ŋ̏dhɛ̏ yā ȁ dhőo yà blʌ́* la clôture de cette cour est pourrie **2** *également zȕ gúu dhőo* **douchière et toilettes ensemble** *(avec ou sans clôture; on y va pour se laver et pour uriner)* ♦ *gbō bhɔ̏' gúu dhőo* toilettes *(cabinet d'aisances) [rare dans les villages; le plus souvent, on va déféquer derrière le village]*

dhōo-dhùn *pl. de* dhēbʌ̀ *femme*

dhòokô <Fr. ivoirien loko> *n* **aloko** *(banane plantain coupée en morceaux et frite)*

dhɔ̏ *n rn* **amour, envie, désir** ♦ *ȁ dhɔ̏ yɤ̏ bhēn kʌ̀* cela plaît à l'homme; l'homme aime cela ♦ *yí bhūn dhɔ̏ yà n̄ kún* j'ai soif ♦ *ȁ-dhùn dhɔ̏ dhɤ́ kó kʌ̀* ils se sont aimés ◊ *dhɔ̏ Sa̋ŋ̏tàadhɛ̏ dhɔ̏ n̄ bhȁ kpēnŋdhɤ̄* je veux vraiment aller à Santa ◊ *ȁ tàkún dhɔ̏ yɤ̏ dȁ ȁ gúu* il a voulu l'aider

dhɔ́ {dhɔ̄} *v vt* **acheter** *(à qn – gɔ̏, pour le montant de – ká)* ◊ *bhlȕn yɤ̏ dhɔ́-sȕ ká* le riz est acheté ◊ *yɤ̏ dhɛ̏ bhā' dhɔ̏ wʌ́ʌ̀ gblúu plɛ̀ ká* il a acheté cet endroit pour dix mille francs ♦ *dhēbʌ̀ dhɔ́* payer la dot *(pour la future épouse)*

dhɔ̏-kʌ̄ {dhɔ̏-kʌ̀} <amour-chasser> *v* **1** *vt* **honorer qn** *lv. (faire honneur en offrant de la nourriture – ká)* ◊ *yɤ̏ kʌ̄ dhɛ̏ŋ dhɔ̏-kʌ̄ tɔ̏ ká* il a honoré l'étranger en lui offrant un poulet ◊ *yɤ̏ ɤ̄ dʌ̄ ȁ gèe dhɔ̏-kʌ̀ dȕ ká* il a honoré le masque de son père avec un boeuf **2** *vt* **adorer qn** ◊ *wɔ̏ gèe bhā ȁ bȁa dhɤ́ kɤ̄ yɤ̏ yɤ̄ kpéŋ kɤ̄ wȁ dhɔ̏-kʌ̄* ils sont en train d'habiller le masque pour qu'il apparaisse dehors afin qu'on l'adore ♦ *yɤ̏ Zlȁan dhɔ̏-kʌ̄-sīʌ* il est en train d'adorer Dieu

dhɔ̋nbʌ̀, dhɔ̋nbɔ̏ (t) *n* **1 amante; amour** *(femme qu'on aime)* ♦ *bhān dhɔ̋nbʌ̀* mon amour *(terme d'adresse à une femme)* ♦ *ȁ bhȁ dhɔ̋nbʌ̀ dhɔ̄ɔbhàa-sȕ* son amante la plus aimée **2 fiancée** ◊ *wà dhó dhɔ̋nbʌ̀ zȁ-dɔ̄'* ils sont allés faire les fiançailles **3 fille**

dhɔ̋ndhɔ̋n <Manding nɔ́nɔ> *n* **lait** *[surtout lait concentré en boîte]*

dhɔ̄ŋ *n* **1** *rn* **ombre** *(ombrage)* Qsyn. *blɛ̋ɛ̋n* **2 humidité** ◊ *dhɔ̄ŋ yà dɔ̄ bhlȕn bhȁ* le riz est devenu humide

dhɔ̄ŋdhɛ̏ *n* **endroit ombragé** ♦ *dhűu dhɔ̄ŋdhɛ̏* ombre de l'arbre

dhɔ̄ŋsɯ̀ɯ *adj* **ombreux**

dhɔ̀ɔ 1 *dtm l'article défini, suit le groupe nominal déterminé et est à son tour suivi par une reprise pronominale* Syn. bhā 1 Qsyn. ā̰ ◊ *yɤ́' dhú dhɔ̀ɔ yɤ́ wó' zʌ̄* et sa fille-là, ils l'ont tuée

dhɔ̀ɔ 2 *prt* **vraiment** *(s'emploie pour signaler un rappel ou un renvoi à ce qui c'est passé; se trouve à la fin de l'énoncé)* Syn. *bhāa*

dhɔ̄ɔ 1, **dhœ̄œ** *n* **grelot en fer** *(deux plaques de fer réunies à leurs bords par une soudure, le battant accroché soit à une anse à l'intérieur, soit à un trou percé dans la paroi) [le tintement de la cloche fortifie le pouvoir magique guerrier, chasse les sorciers et les mauvaises influences pendant les manifestations de masques]* ♦ *dhɔ̄ɔgā, dhœ̄œgā* grelot

dhɔ̄ɔ 2 *n* **igname** *(une sorte, blanche, à grosses tubercules; bon rendement, savoureux, on la cuit épluchée, très cultivée à Gouèta)* Qsyn. *gblɛ̀ɛ, yā́* ♦ *yɤ̀ klɤ̄ɤ̀ gúŋ̄gùŋ ká dhɛ̀ dhɔ̄ɔ dhèe dhɤ́* il est trapu comme un tubercule d'igname

dhɔ̋ɔ 1 *n* **1 marché** Syn. *dhɔ̋ɔkwʌ́ʌ̀dhɛ̏* ♦ *yà dhó dhɔ̋ɔ gúu* il est allé au marché ♦ *dhɔ̋ɔ zʌ̏ dɔ̄* marchander **2 prix** ♦ *yúɤ̏ɤ dhɔ̋ɔ gùn sʌ̏* le poisson n'était pas cher ♦ *ɯ̄ bhā dhɔ̋ɔ yɤ̏ gbɛ̋ɛ̀* ton prix est exagéré

dhɔ̋ɔ 2, **dhɔ̋ɔgā** *n nom générique de plusieurs espèces de poisson* **1** ***Barilius niloticus*** **poisson** *(esp.) [très bon; objet habituel de la pêche des femmes]* **2** ***Petrocephalus simus*** **3** ***Eutropius niloticus*** **4** ***Mormyrus rume***

dhɔ̄ɔbhàa <désir-dans> *n rn* **désir** *(objet désiré)* ◊ *Zlàan dhɔ̄ɔbhàa dhʌ̀n ɤ́ kʌ̀ bhā* c'est la volonté de Dieu ♦ *ī dhɔ̄ɔbhàa yáa kʌ̄ dhɤ́* ce n'est pas ma préférence ◊ *ɤ́ yíi kʌ̄ bɔ̄ ā̀-dhɯ̀n dhɔ̄ɔbhàa zìan tʌ̏* il n'est pas passé par leur voie préférée ♦ *bhɛ̄n dhɔ̄ɔbhàa* personne préférée ♦ *ī dhɔ̄ɔbhàa* ma chérie (une adresse affective à une femme, pas forcement une amante) ♦ *dhɔ̄ɔbhàapʌ̏* chose préférée

dhɔ̄ɔ̋bhàabhɛ̏n, **dhɔ̄ɔbhàabhɛ̏n** *n* **bien-aimé, bien-aimée** ♦ *bhɛ̄n-dhɯ̀n dhɔ̄ɔ̋bhàabhɛ̏n* le plus aimé parmi les gens

dhɔ̋ɔdɔ̄ <marché-mettre> *n* **vente** ◊ *Zlàangɔ̏ yɤ̏ kàkàô dʌ̀n ā̀ dhɔ̋ɔdɔ̄ wɔ̀n gúu* Zlaango est en train de mesurer le cacao pour la vente

dhɔ̋ɔ-dɔ̄ {dhɔ̋ɔ-dɔ̄} *v vt* **vendre**

dhɔ̋ɔdɔ̄bhàan <marché-mettre-oiseau> *n* ***Charadrius hiaticula*** **grand gravelot** *(oiseau, taille pouvant atteindre 20 cm, pelage brun, blanc et noir)*

dhɔ̋ɔdɔ̄bhɛ̏n *n* **marchand**

dhɔ̋ɔdhóbhɛ̏n <marché-acheter-personne> *n* **acheteur, client**

dhɔ̋ɔgā → dhɔ̋ɔ *poisson*

dhɔ̋ɔgɔ̏ <marché-tête> *n* **semaine**

dhɔ̋ɔkʌ̏dhókwʌ́ʌ̀dhɤ̏ <marché-vous-allez-l'un.l'autre-LOC> *n* **herbe** *(esp.; se rétracte si on la touche)*

dhɔ̋ɔkɔ̏ <marché-bagage> ***n*** **magasin, boutique**

dhɔ̋ɔkwʌ́ʌ̀ ***loc.n*** *SUP de* dhɔ̋ɔkwʌ́ʌ̀dhɛ̏ *marché*

dhɔ̋ɔkwʌ́ʌ̀dhɛ̏ {LOC dhɔ̋ɔkwʌ́ʌ̀dhɤ̏, SUP dhɔ̋ɔkwʌ́ʌ̀} <marché-l'un l'autre-lieu> ***loc.n*** **marché** *Syn.* *dhɔ̋ɔ 1* ◊ *dhɔ̋ɔkwʌ́ʌ̀dhɛ̏ tɛ̋ɛ yȁ yȁ* la puanteur du marché se dégage ◊ *yɤ̏ dhȍ kpɛ̏ɛwō dhɔ̋ɔkwʌ́ʌ̀* il va toujours au marché

dhɔ̋ɔkwʌ́ʌ̀dhɤ̏ ***loc.n*** *LOC de* dhɔ̋ɔkwʌ́ʌ̀dhɛ̏ *marché*

dhɔ̋ɔkwɛ̀ɛ̏ ***n*** **marchandise**

dhɔ̏ɔn ***n*** **poisson** *(esp.; gros et gluant; ressemble au silure, mais moins gros et de teint plus clair, vit en eau douce)*

dhɔ̀ɔn ***restr*** **1 hélas** *(exprime la déception, le découragement)* ◊ *ȁ wɔ́n bhā dhɔ̀ɔn, bhán' lòo n̄ kwɛ̄ɛ̏, bháan ȁ gúu-yɤ̄* cette affaire-là, quand je la prends entre les mains, je ne la comprends pas **2** *(exprime un manque d'assurence)* ◊ *bhá dhūn dhɔ̀ɔn, yɤ́ kó dhō dhɛ̏* eh bien, si tu viens, nous irons

dhɔ̄ɔn → dhœ̄œn *message*

dhɔ̄ɔ̋ndhē ***n*** ***Azadarichta indica*** **nim, neem, margousier** *[les branches et racines sont macérées dans l'eau, feuilles et écorce bouillies et utilisées comme remède du paludisme]* ◊ *dhɔ̄ɔ̋ndhē dīn yɤ̏ glűu* le goût du nim est amer

dhɔ̀ɔndhɛ̏ ***n*** **herbe** *(esp.)*

dhɔ̀ɔndhɔ̋ɔndhē ***n*** **mycose de pieds** *(des petites abcès démangeants entre les orteils et sur les semelles; sans traitement, dure jusqu'à 2 semaines; on le traite avec les feuilles de kɔ̋bhɔ̃)*

dhɔ̋ɔyɛ̄ɛ̋n <marché-soir> ***n*** **jeudi**

dhɔ̋ɔyī <marché-jour> ***n*** **vendredi** *Syn.* *bhȁandhɔ̋ɔyī*

dhɔ̋ɔzīandō <marché-côté-un> ***n*** **samedi**

dhɔ̀tlɔ̋ɔ̏ < Fr. docteur > ***n*** *en combinaisons avec des bases nominales, avec la marque du pluriel* **médecin** ♦ *dhɔ̀trɔ̋ɔ̏-dhȕn* médecins ♦ *dhɔ̀tlɔ̋ɔ̏ dhēbʌ̏* femme médecin ♦ *dhɔ̀tlɔ̋ɔ̏ kɔ̏* hôpital

dhɔ̀tlɔ̋ɔ̏bhīn {pl. dhɔ̀tlɔ̋ɔ̏zʌ̏-dhȕn} <docteur-personne> ***n*** **médecin**

dhɔ̀tlɔ̋ɔ̏plɤ̏ɤ <médecin-village> ***loc.n*** **hôpital, à l'hôpital**

dhɔ̀tlɔ̋ɔ̏zʌ̏-dhȕn ***n*** *pluriel du* dhɔ̀tlɔ̋ɔ̏bhīn *médecin*

-dhɤ̄ 1 ***mrph*** *suffixe adverbial* ♦ *dhűaandhȕaandhɤ̄* lentement

-dhɤ̄ 2 ***mrph*** *suffixe de cas locatif*

dhɤ́ 1 {dhɤ́} ***v*** **1** *vi* **être** *(exister)* ◊ *péŋ̋ glűu yāȁ-dhȕn wȍ dhɤ̄* il y a de mauvais jumeaux ◊ *Zlȁan yáa dhɤ́* Dieu n'existe pas ◊ *dūu yɤ̏ dhɤ̄* la sorcellerie existe ♦ *X ɤ́ dhɤ́* n'importe qui, n'importe quoi ♦ *ɤ́ kɪ̄ dhɤ́ (gw), ɤ́ dhɤ́ bhā (t)* pendant ce temps **2** *MPP de la 3 pers. sg. de la série conjointe* ◊ *bhɛ́n bhā, pɪ̄ zȍnzȍndhē dhʌ̀n ȁ dhȍ dhɤ́' kʌ̏* cet homme, il aime surtout les choses très rouges ◊ *yɤ̏ dhȍ dhɔ̋ɔkwʌ́ʌ̀, yɤ́' bhȁ dhʌ́n dhɤ́* *gbő bɔ̄-sīʌ bhā* elle est allée au marché, et son enfant pleure ◊ *n̄ dʌ̄ dhʌ̀n, à̰ bhà̰ gbên dhɤ́ bhā* en ce qui concerne mon père, voici son chien ♦ *dhɛ̀ ... dhɤ́* comme ◊ *yɤ̰̀ gǜn dhɛ̀ gblǜ dhɤ́* c'était comme à la guerre

dhɤ́ 2 → dhó *aller*

dhɤ̰́ 1 ***prt*** **donc** *marque de politesse dans les propositions comportant la particule de focalisation; obligatoire dans la réponse à une question comportant la même particule dhɤ̰́* ◊ *dē ǘ kpà̰n {à̰} bhà̰ dhɤ̰́ ? – Zân dhʌ̀n á kpà̰n {à̰} bhà̰ dhɤ̰́* qui as-tu vu ? – c'est Jean que j'ai vu ♦ *à̰ kʌ̰̀ dhɤ̰́-sǜ gǘ* si c'est comme ça

dhɤ̰́ 2 ***adv*** **1 ainsi** *(semblable à l'échantillon éloigné en temps ou en espace)* ◊ *à̰ gɔ̀n yáa kʌ̄ dhɤ̰́* ce n'est pas son mari ◊ *à̰ bhà̰ dhʌ́n ɤ́ kwá wɛ̋-sīʌ à̰ bhà̰ sʌ̀dhɛ̰̀ ká dhɤ̰́ bhā...* son enfant dont nous parlions ainsi en évoquant sa beauté... ♦ *yɤ̰̀ kʌ̄ kʌ̰̀ dhɤ̰́ n̄ yǎan* cela c'est passé devant mes yeux (en ma présence) ♦ *yɤ̰̀ dhɤ̰́ tæ̰̀æ̰n ká !* c'est vrai ! ◊ *klàŋ̰gɔ̰̀bhɛ̰̀n ɤ́ dhɤ̰́, Zân yáa bhǜn* ce maître d'école n'est pas Zan (celui qui a frappé l'élève) ♦ *à̰ kʌ̰̀ dhɤ̰́-sǜ bhā à̰ gǘ* ainsi donc, pour cette raison **2** *dhɤ̰́ bhūn* **quand même, malgré tout** *(à propos d'une action passée)* ◊ *yɤ̰̀ kʌ̄ yí bhā tɔ̰̀ dhɤ̰́ bhūn* il a puisé de l'eau là-bas, malgré tout

dhɤ́ ... dhɤ́ <de dhɤ́> ***conj*** **et ..., et ...** *conjonction de coordination servant à énumérer les membres d'un ensemble fermé (groupes nominaux, pronoms non-sujet ou autonomes)* ◊ *à̰ dhɤ́, bhān dhɤ́, yīi pʌ̄ bhɤ̰̀* lui et moi, nous allons manger ◊ *Zân dʌ̄ dhɤ́, à̰ dhē dhɤ́ wā̰à̰ dhēɛ́bhāŋ-dhǜn wà̰ dhūn* le père de Jean, sa mère et ses frères et sœurs sont venus

dhɤ́dō ***adv*** **encore**, **toujours** *(contre toute attente, ce n'est pas fini)* ◊ *ū pʌ̄ bhɤ̰̀-sīʌ dhɤ́dō ? !* es-tu toujours en train de manger ? !

dhɤ̰́dhɤ̰́ <redupl. dhɤ̰́ 'ainsi'> ***conj*** **jusqu'à** ◊ *yɤ̰̀ kʌ̄ yʌ̄ kʌ̰̀ dhɤ̰́dhɤ̰́ ɤ́ bín dhɤ́ bhān* il a travaillé jusqu'à ce que la nuit tombe

dhɤ̰̀ŋ ***v vr*** **porter en balançant sur la tête** *(qch – ká)* ◊ *yà̰ ɤ̄ dhɤ̰̀ŋ kwɛ̄ɛ̰̀ ká* elle a marché en balançant la charge sur sa tête

dhɤ̰̄ŋ̰ ***n*** **agrumes** *(surtout la mandarine, mais aussi les oranges et les citrons)[les agrumes ne sont pas prisés par les Dan qui ne les cultivent que rarement]* Syn. *sɛ̄ɛ́* ♦ *bhɛ̄ntīi à̰ dhɤ̰̄ŋ̰* citron ♦ *kwí à̰ dhɤ̰̄ŋ̰* orange, citron

dhɤ̰́ŋ 1, **dhɤ̰́ŋgā** ***n*** **chenille** *(esp.; rougeâtre, vit sur l'arbre pēn) [on la trouve de juin à janvier; se mange bouillie et séchée au soleil avec du sel et du piment] (dans le compte, c'est la forme avec -gā qui s'utilise)* Syn. *yɤ̰́ɤŋgā*

dhɤ̰́ŋ 2 ***n*** **hauteur** *(ciel, étoiles etc.)* Qsyn. *dhǘɤ̰̀* ◊ *Tòkpà̰ yà bhān glɛ̄ɛ́ yà kɔ́ tà̰ dhɤ̰́ŋ gǘ* Tokpa a mis mon sac sur le toit de maison ◊ *gɔ̄ bhāan yɤ̰̀ zīɤ-sīʌ dhɤ̰́ŋ gǘ* l'avion est en vol

dhɤ̰̀ŋdlɤ̰̀ɤ ***loc.n*** *LOC de* dhɤ̰̀ŋdlɤ̰̀ɤdhɛ̰̀ *sous la ceinture*

dhɤ̰̀ŋdlɤ̰̀ɤdhɛ̰̀ {LOC dhɤ̰̀ŋdlɤ̰̀ɤ} ***loc.n*** **taille** *(la peau recouverte par la ceinture)* ◊ *kɛ̀fá dhídhí yà̰ à̰ dhɤ̰̀ŋdlɤ̰̀ɤdhɛ̰̀ bhō* la peau en-dessous de la ceinture est couverte de morsures de poux ◊ *yà ɤ̄ kɔ̀ dà ɤ̄ dhɤ̀ŋdlɤ̀ɤ, yɤ̀ ɤ̄ kāà-sīʌ* il a mis sa main sous la ceinture et se gratte ◊ *wà dà yí bhàa, yɤ̀ bhɛ̄n kùn bhɛ̄n dhɤ̀ŋdlɤ̀ɤ* si on entre dans l'eau, elle atteint la ceinture

dhɤ́ŋgā → dhɤ́ŋ *chenille (esp.)*

dhɤ́ŋgbɤ́ ***n*** **chenille** *(esp.; rouges; comestibles; se trouvent sur l'arbre yɔ̄ɔndhɯ̋; on les fait bouillir, après on les sèche au soleil)*

dhɤ̀ɤ ***n*** **1 caoutchouc, plastique** *(toute matière organique artificielle)* **2 lance-pierre**

dhɤ̄ɤ (t) ***n*** *rn* **sœur aînée** *(au sens classificatoire : sœur aînée d'ego; fille du frère du père ou de la sœur cadette de la mère plus âgée qu'ego; soeur cadette du père)* Syn. dhēgbáan

dhɤ́ɤdhɤ̀ɤ {A P S, dhɤ́ɤdhɤ̀ɤ-dhùn pl. A S, dhɤ́ɤdhɤ̀ɤ-sɯ̀ foc. A S, dhɤ́ɤdhɤ̀ɤ-sɯ̀-dhùn pl. foc. A; dhɤ́ɤdhɤ́ɤ Int. pl. A P S, dhɤ́ɤdhɤ́ɤ-dhùn A S} ***adj*** **rond** ◊ *kɔ́ dhɤ́ɤdhɤ́ɤ {dhʌ́n}* petites maisons rondes

dhɤ́ɤdhɤ́ɤ ***adj*** *Int. pl. de* dhɤ́ɤdhɤ̀ɤ *rond*

dhɤ̀ɤkpɤ̄ <caoutchouc-balle> ***n*** **ballon** *(surtout de football)* Syn. *bàdhóŋ̀ à Man, on dit dhɤ̀ŋkpɤ̄*

dhœ̄œ → dhɔ̄ɔ *grelot en fer*

dhœ̀œn ***n*** **richesse** ◊ *ɯ́ dhœ̀œn slɔ̀ɔ !* que tu aies de la richesse !

dhœ̄œn, **dhɔ̄ɔn** ***n*** **message** Syn. *sāanwò* ◊ *yɤ̀ bhɛ̄n-dhùn bɔ̄ dhɤ́ kɤ̄ wò à bhà dhœ̄œn dɔ̄ dhɛ̀ gbàn gɯ́* il est en train d'envoyer les gens ainsi pour qu'ils apportent son message partout ♦ *dhœ̄œn bɔ̄ bhɛ̄n dhɛ̀* envoyer un message à qn

dhœ̀œnbhɛ̀n <richesse-personne> ***n*** **personne riche** *(qui manifeste sa richesse)*

dhú 1 {dhū} ***v*** *vt* **attacher** *(bagage)*, **charger**; **emballer**; **lier** *(fagot)* ◊ *yà kwɛ̀ɛ dhú gɔ̄ tà* il a chargé les bagages sur le toit de la voiture ◊ *yɤ̀ wɔ́ bhā à dhù ɤ̄ dhú dhɛ̀* il a attaché le fagot pour sa fille

dhú 2 ***n*** *rn* **fille** *(au sens classificatoire : fille d'ego; fille de dhòo; pour une femme, fille de la sœur aînée ou de la coépouse; pour un homme, fille de la sœur) [utilisé comme un terme d'adresse par rapport à la fille de la sœur aînée de la femme; on s'adresse à sa propre fille par son nom]*

dhùaa ***n Cercopithecus petaurista*** **hocheur blanc-nez** *(un singe : les parties inférieures, la gorge, les oreilles et le nez sont blancs; la partie supérieure kaki; la tête noire)*

dhūàa {dhùaa} ***v*** *vt zūʌ́ dūàa* **consoler** ◊ *Yɔ̀ yà à bhà dhʌ́n zūʌ́ dhūàa* Yo a consolé son enfant

dhűaa ***n*** **poison** *[pour la pêche; de plus en plus remplacé par lɛ̄ŋdâ]* ◊ *dhűaa yà yúʌ̀ kʌ̀ tlűnkpắntlùnkpàn {ká}* le poison a étourdi le poisson

dhűaan ***n*** **fourmi** *(petite, noire, à piqûre douloureuse)*

dhṻaandhȕaan {A P S, dhṻaandhȕaan-dhȕn pl. A S, dhṻaandhȕaan-sȕ foc. A S, dhṻaandhȕaan-sȕ-dhȕn foc. pl. A S} *adj* **lent**; **nonchalant** ♦ *ūū dhṻaandhȕaan ká dhɛ̀ gṻudʌ̄ dhɤ̋* tu es lent comme un caméléon

dhȕaandhȕaandhɤ̄ {Int. dhūaandhȕaandhūaandhɤ̄, SupInt. dhȕaandhȕaandhȕaandhɤ̄} *adv* **lentement** *(d'un trait de caractère d'une personne)* ◊ *yɤ̏ ɤ̄ gɛ̏n wȍ-sīʌ dhȕaandhȕaandhɤ̄* elle marche à pas lents

dhȕaandhȕaandhȕaandhɤ̄ *adv SupInt. de* dhȕaandhȕaandhɤ̄ *lentement*

dhūaandhȕaandhūaandhɤ̄ *adv Int. de* dhȕaandhȕaandhɤ̄ *lentement*

dhȕaŋdhɛ̏ *n* **1 miroir** ♦ *dhȕaŋdhɛ̏ gúú* dans le miroir **2 vitre** *(de fenêtre)*

dhūʌ̏ʌ *n* **1.1** *rn* **oncle maternel cadet**, **oncle** lv. *(frère cadet de la mère, par rapport au neveu, bɛ̋ɛ̏; descendant masculin de l'oncle maternel) [est respecté, mais en même temps est victime d'une "agression rituelle" de la part du fils de la sœur aînée, parce que "l'oncle a mangé la dot de sa mère"; en cas de besoin, l'oncle aide son neveu à payer la dot, dans ce cas le neveu vit avec la famille de son oncle]* **1.2** ext. *rn* **oncle maternel aîné** Syn. zɪ̋ɤ̏ɤ **2** *rn* **membre de la famille d'origine de la mère**; **habitant du village d'origine de la mère**

dhúʌ̏ʌ *n* **bénédiction** ◊ *yà dhúʌ̏ʌ kpɔ́ ɤ̄ gbɤ̄ bhȁ* il a béni son fils

dhṻʌʌdhȕʌʌ {A, P} *adj* **1 blême, faible** *(lumière)* ◊ *sɪ̋ɤ bhúú yɤ̏ dhṻʌʌdhȕʌʌ, bháan dhɛ̏ yɤ̄ kɔ́ɔdhɤ̄ sʌ̏ ká* la lumière est blême, je ne vois pas bien dans la maison **2 faible** *(vue)* ♦ *ȁ yṹn gúú yɤ̏ dhṻʌʌdhȕʌʌ* il a une faible vue

dhȕʌŋ (gw), **dhȕaŋ** (m) *n* **esclave**

dhȕʌŋ-dhɛ̏ *n* **esclavage** ♦ *dhȕʌŋdhɛ̏ zʌ̄* languir en esclavage

dhȕʌŋgɔ̏bhɛ̏n <esclave-tête-personne> *n* **maître d'esclave**

dhūeebhīn {pl. dhūeezʌ̏-dhȕn} *n* **chasseur**

dhūeezʌ̏-dhȕn *n pluriel du* dhūeebhīn *chasseur*

dhūɛ̋ɛn *n* **remerciement** ♦ *ūū dhūɛ̋ɛn gbɛ́ !* grand merci ! ♦ *bhɛ̄n dhūɛ̋ɛn bhō* remercier qn

dhṻɛyídhɤ̄ {Int. dhṻɛyídhṻɛyídhɤ̄} *adv* **sérieusement** ◊ *yɤ̏ wɔ́n kʌ̏ dhṻɛyídhɤ̄* il fait des affaires sérieusement

dhṻɛyídhɤ̄ {A, P} *adj* **sérieux** *(qui ne fait pas de bêtises)*

dhṻɛyídhṻɛyídhɤ̄ *adv Int. de dhṻɛyídhɤ̄ sérieusement*

dhȕn *oper* **1** *marque de présomptif, en combinaison avec la série présomptive des marques prédicatives pronominales et l'infinitif du verbe* ◊ *yíí dɔ̄ sʌ̏, wāȁ dhȕn lòo' Yāa̋bhȕnsóklɔ̄ɔn* sans doute, ils sont déjà arrivés à Yamoussoukro **2** *(dans une construction subjonctive introduite par la conjonction kɤ̄, exprime une valeur hypothétique : l'action est perçue comme improbable ou est raportée au futur éloigné)* ◊ *yáa yàobâ wȍ bhān kɤ̄ yɤ̏ dhȕn gwʌ̋ʌŋ dȁ* il ne comprend pas le dan suffisamment bien pour dire des proverbes ♦ *kɤ̄ yɤ̏ dhȕn tó ... bhȁ* à plus forte raison ◊ *pɤ̋bhɛ̏n zȉaan yáa bṻdhɔ̏kʌ̄sȕ* *zǐan dɔ̄, kɤ̄ yɤ̀ dhǜn tó dhɛ̀ŋ zʌ̀ bhâ* ce n'est pas chaque étranger, et même pas chaque habitant du village qui sait où est l'entrée de la forêt sacrée ◊ *bháan wē bhūn, kɤ̄ yɤ̀ dhǜn tó bhɔ̀ bhɤ̀-sǜ bhâ* je ne bois pas de vin, à plus forte raison je ne mange pas de porc

-dhǜn ***mrph*** *marque du pluriel*

dhūn 1 {dhūn} ***v*** **1** *vi* **venir** ♦ *dhūn bhɛ̄n kèŋ* venir chez qn ♦ *dhɛ́ndhɛ́n yà dhūn n̄ tà* la fièvre m'abat **2** *vi* **apporter**, **amener** *(qn, qch – ká)* ◊ ... *wó dhūn' ká Mɑ̃ádhɤ̄ Blókɔ̄ŋsó* ... et on l'a amené à Man, dans le quartier Blocosse **3** *vi dhūn kwʌ̂ʌ̀dhɤ̄* **se rassembler**

dhūn 2 {dhūn} ***v*** *vt* **donner** *(remettre; à – dhɛ̀)*, **envoyer** lv. Qsyn. dɔ̄ 1, gbā 1

dhún ***prt*** **1 déjà** ◊ *á dhō gó' bɯ̃ gú, kɤ̄ bhān dhʌ́n-dhǜn wà yī zʌ̄ dhún* quand je rentre de la brousse, mes enfants sont déjà endormis ◊ *Yɤ̀ gbɛ̂ɛ̀, yʌ́nŋ̀kɔ̀dān plè, kɤ̄ yà sɤ̄ kún dhún* il est fort, il grimpe au palmier à huile en deux minutes seulement ◊ *yɤ̀ gɛ̀œ n̄ gɔ̀ yāandhɪ́ɤ dhún* il m'a déjà donné un cadeau hier **2** *exprime la valeur de l'irréel* ◊ *yɤ̀ bɔ̀ yɤ̄, ā dhɔ̀ kpʌ̀n' bhà dhún* s'il passait par ici, je le verrais ◊ *Tìa yɤ̀ kɤ̀ŋ dhún, yáa gūn yɤ̄ɤ pɤ̀ yɤ̄* si Tia était habile, il ne tomberait pas ici

dhűnŋ, **dhűun** ***n*** **1 hamac 2 filet de pêche** *(assez grand pour barrer un fleuve)* Qsyn. kplɤ́, sàadhè, tē, zūɛŋ

dhūnwɛ̃ɛ ***intj*** **merci** Syn. bádhíká ♦ *ū dhūnwɛ̃ɛ yʌ̄ bhà !* merci pour le travail ! ♦ *kā dhūnwɛ̃ɛ kwā bhà* merci pour ce que vous faites pour nous

dhǜnwō ***adv*** **parfois** Syn. sìʌ

dhɯ̋ɤ̀ {Int. dhɯ̋ɤɤ} ***adv*** **1 dessus** ♦ *kɔ́ tà dhɯ̋ɤ̀* sur le toit de la maison ◊ *dhɯ̋ bhɛ̄ yɤ̀ dhɯ̋ gú dhɯ̋ɤ̀* il y a des fruits sur l'arbre ◊ *bhàan yɤ̀ zīɤ-sīʌ dhɛ́ɛdhɛ̀ tà dhɯ̋ɤ̀* un oiseau vole au-dessus de la place publique **2 au nord** ◊ *Kɔ́dīvɯ̄à pɛ́ndhɛ̀ ɤ́ dhɯ̋ɤ̀ yʌ̀n* la partie nord de la Côte d'Ivoire

dhɯ̋ɤ̀-dhɯ̋ɤ̀ ***adv*** **tout le temps en haut**

dhūɤɤ ***n*** **1 raphia** ♦ *dhūɤɤ dhɛ́* feuille de raphia *(sur le pétiole de la fronde)* ♦ *dhūɤɤ gɔ̄* pétiole de la fronde de raphia **2 costume en fibres de raphia** *(pour un masque)*

dhűɤɤ 1 {dhùɤɤ} ***v*** *vt* **priver qn** *(de nourriture – bhɤ̀pʌ̀ gú)*, **ne pas partager avec qn** *(la nourriture – bhɤ̀pʌ̀ gú)* ◊ *à gbɤ̄ yɤ̀ n̄ dhùɤɤ pʌ̄bhèe dhʌ̀n à gú* son fils n'a pas partagé la nourriture avec moi

dhűɤɤ 2 ***adv*** *Int. de* dhɯ̋ɤ̀ *dessus*

dhűɤɤdhùɤɤ {A P} ***adj*** **sombre** ♦ *dhàŋbhá bhú dhűɤɤdhùɤɤ* une lueur sombre de lampe ♦ *à yɑ̃́n gú yɤ̀ dhűɤɤdhùɤɤ* sa vue est floue (à cause d'une cataracte)

dhǜtîì <Manding dùutîi, dùgutígi> ***n*** **chef du village**

dhùu ***n*** **ampoule** *(lésion)* ♦ *sɪ́ɤ dhùu, pɛ̄ŋ dhùu* braise ♦ *n̄ kɔ̀ yà dhùu dɔ̄* j'ai une ampoule à la main

dhũ̄ű {dhùu} *v* **1** 1) *vi* **s'éteindre** ♦ *sɯ́ɤ dhùu yíi dhũ̄ű kɤ̀* les braises ne sont pas encore éteintes 2) *vt* **éteindre** ◊ *yɤ̀ sɯ́ɤ dhùu n̄ tà dὲɛ gbēŋ zìnŋgɯ́* il a éteint la lumière chez moi aujourd'hui à minuit **2** *vi* **caler** *(véhicule)* ◊ *bhān pòpòdhîn yɤ̀ dhùu n̄ gɔ̀* ma mobylette a calé

dhűu 1 *n* **1 brouillard** *(pendant la saison des pluies)* Qsyn. bùudhãan ♦ *dhűu yà yà dhὲ yā à gɯ́* le brouillard a couvert les lieux ♦ *dhűu yà gó sɯ́āa* le brouillard s'est dissipé **2 nuages** *(blancs)* ◊ *dhűu yà yà dhāŋ̀ bhà wɛ́ bhɔ̄nŋdhɤ̄* les nuages ont couvert tout le ciel

dhűu 2 *n* **boue ferrugineuse** *[les sculpteurs sur bois l'utilisent pour noircir les masques]*

dhűudàdhɛ̃́ *n* ***Combretum racemosum (gen. Combretaceae)*** **liane** *(à fleurs rouges; les feuilles servent de médicament contre les maux de ventre)*

dhűun → dhűnŋ *hammock*

dhű {dhù} *n* **1.1 arbre** *[seuls les vrais arbres sont considérés comme dhű; les palmiers, le bambou, le bananier ne sont pas classés parmi dhű]* ♦ *bhɤ̀ dhù* arbre fruitier **1.2 plante** *toujours dans les syntagmes; le ton change en extra-bas* ♦ *sɤ̄ dhù* palmier à huile adulte **2 tige** ◊ *bāa dhű* tige de manioc **3 bois** *(matière)* ♦ *dhű bὲ* paquet de bois *(branches et tiges, pour la construction)* ◊ *dhű kɔ̀* maison en bois **4** chr. **croix** Syn. klɔ̄â

dhűdhʌ́n *n* **1 petit arbre 2.1 bâton, massue, gourdin 2 bâtonnet** *(pour jouer d'un instrument de musique)* **3** neol. **apostrophe**

dhűdhē *adj* **en bois** ◊ *klùu dhűdhē* louche en bois

dhűdhɛ̃́ *n* **1 feuille** *(d'arbre)*, **foliole** *(de palme)* Qsyn. sɔ̃́nŋ̀dhɛ̃́ **2 fétiche, amulette** *(un objet magique)*

dhűgā <arbre-os> *n* **1.1 tronc** *(d'un arbre vivant, ou abattu, avant que les branches ne soient coupées)* **1.2 perche, rondin** *(long et mince)* ◊ *yɤ̀ n̄ pɯ́ɤ dhὲ á dhűgā kɔ̀ dɔ̄* je veux bâtir une maison en bois **2.1 fruit 2.2** chass., euph. **cartouche** *(d'une arme)* Qsyn. būugā ♦ *yà dhűgā dà būu gɯ́* il a chargé le fusil **2.3 comprimé**

dhűkãŋ <arbre-mince> *n* **planche** Syn. dhűpɛ́n ♦ *dhűkãŋ gɔ̄* camion à caisse faite de planches

dhūn (gw) → dhʌ̀n *focalisateur*

dhűpɛ̃́n <arbre-tranche> *n* **planche** Syn. dhűkãŋ

dhűzʌ̄kpàŋglɔ̀ɔ <arbre-tuer- ?-banane> *n* ***Lybius (Pogonornis) bidentatus*** **barbican à bec denté** *(oiseau, jusqu'à 23 cm de long, noir dessus et rouge dessous, gros bec clair)*

E e

ὲe 1 *prt particule interrogative générale; le plus souvent, assimilée par la voyelle précédente* ◊ *pàŋ ɤ́' gbàan blʌ́ yɤ́ ɯ́' bhō ὲe ? !* comment peux-tu porter un pantalon tout usé ? ! ◊ *ɯ̄ kʌ̄ yī zʌ̀ yâ ὲe ?* as-tu mal dormi ?

ὲe 2 *intj* **fi** *(interjection de désapprobation)*

ēɛ̀ ***intj*** **hé !** *(interjection pour attirer l'attention)* ◊ *ēɛ̀, Tōkpä, dhūn kíi n̄ tà-kún, bhān gɔ̄ yà sēɛ̀* hé ! Tokpa, viens, aide-moi, ma voiture s'est cassée

ɛ́kɛ̋ ***intj*** **hélas !**

ēkîpʌ̈ <Fr. équipe> ***n*** **équipe** *(sportive)*

ēlíkɔ̄nŋtɛ́ɛ̈ <Fr. hélicoptère> ***n*** **hélicoptère**

Ɛ ɛ

ɛ̀ ***intj*** **eh bien** *interjection d'un accord forcé* ♦ *ɛ̀ ! bhɤ̀ dhūn dhɛ̀* eh bien, viens *(même si cela ne me semble pas nécessaire)*

ɛ̀ɛ ***intj*** **1** *signale le changement du thème de conversation* ♦ *ɛ̀ɛ n̄ dʌ̄, bhá bòo* mon père, bon matin ! **2 d'accord**

ɛ́ɛ̀n, **ɛ̋ɛn** ***conj*** **sinon** *(exprime une hésitation)*

ɛ̋ɛ̀n → ĩin *ou*

ɛ̄nfīdhīntífü <Fr. infinitif> ***n*** *neol., ling.* **infinitif**

F f

fǎa ***n*** **cravache, chicote**

fàadhɤ̄ ***adv*** *exprime l'idée de visibilité limitée* ♦ *dhɛ̀ gú yà yà fàadhɤ̄* ♦ *dhɛ̀ gú yà pű fàadhɤ̄* une brume est tombée ♦ *dhɛ̀ gú yà pű fàadhɤ̄ kɤ̄ kwá zīɤ* quand le ciel commencera à s'éclaircir, nous nous mettrons en route ♦ *à yǎn gú yɤ̀ pɔ̋-sīʌ fàadhɤ̄* il commence à revenir à lui *(après un choc, etc.)*

fǎagā, **fǎàgā** ***n*** **peigne** *(de type traditionnel, en bois, à trois ou quatre dents)* ♦ *dhű̃ fǎagā* peigne en bois ♦ *fǎagā sɔ̋n gbé dhē* peigne *(de type européen, avec un plus grand nombre de dents)* ♦ *fǎàgā ɤ́ sɔ̋n ɤ́ yɤ̄-sǜ ká kwʌ́ʌ̈* peigne fin

fàan ***n*** **zèle** ♦ *yʌ̄ kʌ̄-sǜ fàan yɤ̀ à tà* il travaille avec zèle

fāan, **fɔ̄ɔn** ***n*** *rn* **force** *(physique)* ◊ *yī dà tɔ̀n bhā à bhà yī fāan gbàn ká* nous avons monté la montagne, et cela a pris toutes nos forces ♦ *fāan sæ̀æ* force fraîche ◊ *Gɔ́yídʌ̄ yɤ̀ glɔ̄ɔ bhɤ̀ dhɤ́ kɤ̄ fāan sæ̀æ yɤ̀ dà ɤ̄ gú* Goïdeu mange les bananes pour rafraîchir ses forces ♦ *fāan yà gú* il a de la force ♦ *fāan yà bhà* i) il est puissant ii) il a des moyens ♦ *bhɤ̀ ū fāan sú !* prend courage ! **1 embonpoint** ♦ *yà fāan sú* il a grossi <u>*Syn.* *bà*</u>

fáàn ***n*** **couvre-chef** *(chapeau, couronne, foulard, etc., mais aussi écharpe)* ♦ *yà fáàn klǜ ɤ̄ gɔ̀ɔ* elle a attaché un foulard sur sa tête ♦ *fáàn yà* se couvrir la tête *(mettre un chapeau, un foulard)*

fāanfāansǜ *Int. de* fāansǜ *gros*

fáànkɔ́ (m) ***n*** **chapeau**

fāansɯ̀ {A P S, fāansɯ̀-dhùn pl. A; fāanfāansɯ̀ Int. A P S, fāanfāansɯ̀-dhùn Int. pl. A S, fāanfāansɯ̀-sɯ̀ Int. foc (rare) A} *adj* **gros** *(personne)*

fa̋fa̋ *n* **hangar** *(couvert de feuilles de raphia)*

fâfâ {A P S, fâfâ-dhùn pl. A S, fâfâ-sɯ̀ foc. A} *adj ya̋n fâfâ* **paille**

fa̋ŋkpɛ̋ɛ < ?-sec> *n* ***Tockus fasciatus semifasciatus*** **petit calao** ◊ *fa̋ŋkpɛ̋ɛ bɛ̀n yɤ̀ gblɛ̀ɛn* le petit calao a un bec long

fʌ̄nŋ̋ *n* **liane** *(esp. : à feuilles larges; les tiges sont utilisées pour les filets à pêche des femmes)*

fʌ́yí → fɤ́yí *sueur*

fʌ́yígā <sueur-grain> *n* **éruption** *(à cause de la chaleur, surtout chez les enfants)*

fèe *n* **1 pinson** *(nom générique de plusieurs espèces de petits oiseaux)* **1.1** ***Lagonostica senegala*** **amarante commun** *(petit oiseau à tête, nuque et dessous rouges, ventre, dos et ailes bruns, vit dans les toits en paille; gâte le piment et le riz)* **1.2** ***Nigrita fusconota*** **sénégali brun à ventre blanc**

fèekɔ̄ɔ̄dhɤ̀, **fèekœ̄œ̀dhɤ̀** <oiseau (esp.)-maison.LOC> *n* ***Cisticola cantans*** **cisticole chanteuse** *(12 cm, dessus gris foncé, dessous blanchâtre, ailes brun-roux; habite dans les hautes herbes, fait des nids elliptiques à dôme)*

fèekœ̄œ̀dhɤ̀ → fèekɔ̄ɔ̄dhɤ̀ *cisticole chanteuse*

fɛ̋ŋ *n* ***Tatera gerbit*** **rat** *(esp.)*

fɛ̀ɛ *n rn* **bruit** Syn. vīn ◊ *kāà fɛ̀ɛ yà kʌ̄ gbɛ́* vous faites trop de bruit ♦ *bhá dhó fɛ̀ɛ dɔ̄'/yà'* ne fais pas de bruit !

fɛ̀ɛfɛ̀ɛsɯ̀ *Int. de* fɛ̀ɛsɯ̀ *bruyant*

fɛ̀ɛnfɛ̋ɛn *prev* **entassement**

fɛ̋ɛnfɛ̀ɛn {A P} *adj* **étroit** *(ouverture)* ◊ *kɔ́ bhā à dhí yɤ̀ fɛ̋ɛnfɛ̀ɛn* la porte de la maison est très étroite

fɛ̀ɛnfɛ̋ɛn-kʌ̄ *v vt* **entasser** ◊ *wà bhɛ̄n-dhùn fɛ̀ɛnfɛ̋ɛn-kʌ̄ kɔ́ sɛ̋ɛ́ndhʌ́n gɯ́* ils ont entassé les gens dans la petite chambre

fɛ̀ɛsɯ̀ {A P, fɛ̀ɛsɯ̀-dhùn pl. A, fɛ̀ɛsɯ̀-sɯ̀ foc. A, fɛ̀ɛsɯ̀-sɯ̀-dhùn pl. foc. A; fɛ̀ɛfɛ̀ɛsɯ̀ Int. A P, fɛ̀ɛfɛ̀ɛsɯ̀-dhùn Int. pl. A, fɛ̀ɛfɛ̀ɛsɯ̀-sɯ̀ Int. foc. A, fɛ̀ɛfɛ̀ɛsɯ̀-sɯ̀-dhùn Int. pl. foc. A} <bruit-adj.> *adj* **1 bruyant** ◊ *gɔ̄ yā' tlűu yà kʌ̄ fɛ̀ɛsɯ̀* le klaxon de cette voiture est bruyant ◊ *à dhʌ́n fɛ̀ɛsɯ̀-sɯ̀ yà dhó* c'est l'enfant le plus bruyant qui est parti **2 hargneux**, **querelleur**

fɛ̂tɤ̀ <Fr. fête> *n* **fête**

fia (t) → fiʌʌ *amélioration; mieux*

fía 1 (m) → fíaa (gw) *jachère*

fía 2 (m) → fíasɯ̀ *paresseux*

fíaa (gw), **fía** (m) *n* **jachère** *(espace sans arbre, non-cultivé)*

fíaanfìaan {A, P, pl. fíaanfíaan} ***adj*** **chétif** *(plante)◊ kɤ̄n yà kpǽæ kún, yà kʌ̄ fíaanfìaan* le maïs a séché et est devenu chétif ◊ *kɤ̄ŋ-dhùn fíaanfíaan* les pieds de maïs chétifs

fíaanfíaan ***adj*** *PL de* fíaanfìaan *chétif*

fíabhɛ̀n ***n*** **paresseux, paresseuse**

fíafìa {P} ***adj*** **1 léger** *(qui n'est pas dense)◊ dhīá̰ pɪ́ɤ dhākpóŋ̀ fíafìa yà dhūn kɤ̄ dɔ́ɔ́ ká kɤ̄ yɤ̀ kʌ̀ gbínŋ̀* le matin, des nuages légers sont apparus, et vers le soir ils sont devenus épais **2 de peu d'importance** ◊ *bhá dhɤ́ à yɤ̄' wɔ́n fíafìa ká* il ne faut pas prendre cela pour une affaire insignifiante

fíafíasɯ̀ *Int. de* fíasɯ̀ *paresseux*

fíasɯ̀, fía (m) {A P, fíasɯ̀-dhùn pl. A, fíasɯ̀-sɯ̀ foc. A, fíasɯ̀-sɯ̀-dhùn pl. foc. A; fíafíasɯ̀ Int. A P, fíafíasɯ̀-dhùn Int. pl. A, fíafíasɯ̀-sɯ̀ Int. foc. A, fíafíasɯ̀-sɯ̀-dhùn Int. pl. foc. A; fíɛ̀ɛ SupInt. A P, fíɛ̀ɛ-dhùn SupInt. pl. A, fíɛ̀ɛ-sɯ̀ SupInt. foc. A, fíɛ̀ɛ-sɯ̀-dhùn SupInt. foc. pl. A} ***adj*** **paresseux**

fìʌʌ ***v*** **1** 1) *vi* **s'évanouir** ◊ *bhɛ́n ɤ́ bhā yɤ̀ fìʌʌ dhàà̰n, yɤ́ ɤ́ wɔ̀ bhā* la personne qui reste évanouie, elle est couchée là ◊ *yɤ̀ fìʌʌ dhɛ̃́dhɛ̃́ plɛ̀ ká, yɤ́ gūn bɤ̀-dhàan* il est resté évanoui pendant deux heures, puis il a repris conscience 2) *vt* **faire évanouir** ◊ *dḭ̄ì yà à fìʌʌ* il s'est évanoui de faim **2.1** *vi* **échouer** *(dans – bhà)◊ yɤ̀ fìʌʌ-sɯ̀ ká yʌ̄ bhā' bhà* il ne s'est pas acquitté de son (devoir dans le) travail ♦ *yɤ̀ fìʌʌ wɔ́n gbàn bhà* il n'est capable de rien **2.2** *vi* **négliger** *(qch – wɔ̀n bhà)◊ yɤ̀ fìʌʌ ɤ̄ dè wɔ̀n bhà* il se néglige *(il ne soigne pas son apparence, ne s'occupe pas de sa santé; ne pense pas à sa réussite)*

fìʌʌ 1), fìa (t) ***n*** **1 amélioration** ◊ *kpìnŋgā fìʌʌ yà kʌ̄* la route s'est améliorée **2 échange** ♦ *X fìʌʌ bhō Y bhà* échanger X contre Y; préférer X à Y ◊ *yà tòŋ fìʌʌ bhō zá̰n bhà* il a échangé le pigeon contre du tabac ◊ *bhī dhʌ̀n í ī bhà gɔ̄n fìa bhō n̄ bhà ɛ̀e ?* as-tu préféré ton mari à moi ?

fìʌʌ 2), fìa (t) ***adv*** **mieux** ◊ *Tòkpà bhɤ̌dhʌ́nbhá yà kʌ̄ fìʌʌ* Tokpa va un peu mieux

fíʌʌ {A P S, fíʌʌ-dhùn pl. A, fíʌʌ-sɯ̀ foc. A; fíʌʌfíʌʌ Int. pl. A P S, fíʌʌfíʌʌ-dhùn Int. pl. A, fíʌʌfíʌʌ-sɯ̀ Int. foc. A} ***adj*** **vide** ◊ *tàbɛ̃́dhí tà dhɛ̀ yɤ̀ fíʌʌ* la table est vide ♦ *pʌ̄ fíʌʌ* vaisselle ♦ *kɔ̀ gúí fíʌʌ ká* les mains vides

fíʌʌfíʌʌ 1 ***onomat.*** **"fieufieu"** *(cri de l'oiseau slɛ̀ɛn, considéré comme signe de bon augure)*

fíʌʌfíʌʌ *Int. de* fíʌʌ *vide*

fìʌʌn ***v*** 1) *vi* **se rabougrir** ◊ *bhān bhlɯ̀n yà fìʌʌn* mon riz n'a pas poussé suffisamment 2) *vt* **rabougrir** Qsyn. gbɔ̀ɔn ◊ *yʌ́nŋ̀ yà bhān bhlɯ̀n fìʌʌn* la chaleur du soleil a rabougri mon riz

fìʌʌnsɯ̀ ***adj*** **nain** ♦ *bhɛ̄n fìʌʌnsɯ̀* nain ♦ *bhlɯ̀n fìʌʌnsɯ̀* riz rabougri

fíɛ̀ɛ ***adj*** *SupInt. de* fíasɯ̀ *paresseux*

fìi ***n rn*** **odeur, puanteur** Qsyn. gbḭ́ʌ̰n, tɛ́ɛ ◊ *à fìi yâ* il a une mauvaise odeur ◊ *wū fìi yà yà* l'odeur de la viande pourrie s'est répandue

fĩĩ ***n*** **mycose** *(chez l'homme et chez les animaux : des taches blanches apparaissent et s'élargissent rapidement; la peau se détache)* ◊ *fĩĩ yɤ̀ bhɛ̄n kwī kʌ̀ pűu* la mycose blanchit la peau de l'homme

fiifiisʉ̀ʉ ***adj*** *Int. de* fiisʉ̀ʉ *puant*

fĩĩfĩĩsʉ̀ʉ ***adj*** *Int. de* fĩĩsʉ̀ʉ *galeux*

fiisʉ̀ʉ {A P S, fiisʉ̀ʉ-dhʉ̀n pl. A S, fiisʉ̀ʉsʉ̀ʉ foc. A, fiisʉ̀ʉ-sʉ̀ʉ-dhʉ̀n pl. foc. A; fiifiisʉ̀ʉ Int. A P, fiifiisʉ̀ʉ-dhʉ̀n Int. pl. A, fiifiisʉ̀ʉ-sʉ̀ʉ Int. foc. A, fiifiisʉ̀ʉ-sʉ̀ʉ-dhʉ̀n Int. pl. foc. A} <odeur-adj.> ***adj*** **puant** ◊ *wʉ̄ ɤ́ fiisʉ̀ kā yɤ́ ʉ́ dhʉ̄n' ká ɛ̀ɛ ? !* mais tu a apporté la viande qui pue ? !

fĩĩsʉ̀ʉ {A P S, fĩĩsʉ̀ʉ-dhʉ̀n pl. A, -fĩĩsʉ̀ʉsʉ̀ʉ foc. A, fĩĩsʉ̀ʉ-sʉ̀ʉ-dhʉ̀n pl. foc. A; fĩĩfĩĩsʉ̀ʉ Int. A P S, fĩĩfĩĩsʉ̀ʉ-dhʉ̀n Int. pl. A S, fĩĩfĩĩsʉ̀ʉ-sʉ̀ʉ Int. foc. A, fĩĩfĩĩsʉ̀ʉ-sʉ̀ʉ-dhʉ̀n Int. pl. foc. A} <mycose-adj.} ***adj*** **galeux** *(animal; employé à propos d'une personne, ce mot est une injure)* ◊ *à̰ bhà̰ gbɛ̂n fĩĩfĩĩsʉ̀ bhā yà dhɛ̀ŋ* son chien très galeux s'est perdu

fĩn {fĩn} ***v vi*** **tourner** *(de la viande) [la consommation de viande tournée est admise avec certaines précautions]* **moisir** *(du papier etc.)* ◊ *yà̰ sʌ́ʌdhɛ́ dà̰ sɛ́ɛdhɤ̄kɔ̀gʉ́, à̰ gbàn yà̰ fĩn* il a mis les papiers dans le sous-sol, ils ont tous moisi <u>Qsyn.</u> <u>bű</u>

fĩɔfĩɔ {A P; fĩɔkɔ̃fĩɔkɔ̃ Int., fĩɔɔfĩɔɔ SupInt.} ***adj*** **maladif, fatigué par la maladie**

fĩɔkɔ̃fĩɔkɔ̃ ***adj*** *Int. de* fĩɔfĩɔ *maladif*

fiɔ̃nfiɔ̃nfiɔ̃ndhɤ̄ ***onomat*** **grincement** *(de lit)* ◊ *dhĩĩ yà̰ vīn fiɔ̃nfiɔ̃nfiɔ̃ndhɤ̄* le lit a grincé

fĩɔɔfĩɔɔ ***adj*** *SupInt. de* fĩɔfĩɔ *maladif*

fitlĩ <Ar. fitr> ***n*** **crépuscule du soir** ◊ *tɔ̀ yɤ̀ dhɤ̀ kɔ́ɔdhɤ̄ fitlĩ ká* les poulets vont à la maison au crépuscule ♦ *fitlĩ yà̰ bhán* le crépuscule est venu

flã̋ ***n*** **Peul** *(groupe ethnique d'Afrique de l'Ouest) [on trouve des Peuls dans presque tous les villages des Dan, ils exercent les activités de berger et de commerçant; il existe entre les Peuls et les Dan une relation de plaisanterie]*

flʌ́ʌ̀ ***n rn*** **santé; contentement** ♦ *ā n̄ flʌ́ʌ̀ gʉ́* i) je suis en bonne santé ii) je suis en paix iii) je suis content de moi ♦ *ā n̄ flʌ́ʌ̀ gʉ́ n̄ dè gʉ́* je suis content de moi ♦ *yáa ɤ̄ flʌ́ʌ̀ gʉ́* il n'est pas en bonne santé ♦ *yà ɤ̄ flʌ́ʌ̀ bhō* il a guéri

flʌ́ʌ̀bhōdhē <contentement-sortir-nominalis.> ***n*** **aisance, paix, bonheur**

flɛ̃ɛ̀ ***n*** **noyau** *(de grain, de noix; décortiqué, égrené)* ♦ *wɛ̄n flɛ̃ɛ̀* noyau de grain de palmier à huile ♦ *zē flɛ̃ɛ̀* haricot décortiqué ♦ *yà dōo flɛ̃ɛ̀ bhō* il a décortiqué les pistaches

flèesʉ̀ʉ ***n*** **faux grain**

flēgʉ́dhē ***n*** **riz au gras** *(variété locale : avec des aubergines, sel, huile, sans viande)*

flɛ̃ɛ ***n*** **pauvreté** ♦ *flɛ̃ɛ yà n̄ zʌ̄ tɤ̃ŋ ɤ́ yā à̰ gʉ́* je suis à court d'argent ◊ *flɛ̃ɛ yɤ̀ sɛ́ ɤ́ bhā à̰ gʉ́* c'est un pays pauvre

flɛ̃ɛbhɛ̀n <pauvreté-personne> ***n*** **pauvre**

flɛ̋ɛflɛ̋ɛsɯ̏ *Int. de* flɛ̋ɛsɯ̏ *pauvre*

flɛ̏ɛn ***n*** **pinçage** ♦ *yà n̄ flɛ̏ɛn bhō* il m'a pincé ◊ *ɤ́ yɔ́n bhūn-sīʌ ɤ̄ dhē gɔ̀, yà yɔ́n flɛ̏ɛn bhɔ̀* quand il tète le sein de sa mère, il le pince

flɛ̄ɛn {flɛ̀ɛn} ***v*** **1** *vt* **pincer** *(le sein, en parlant d'un nourrisson)* **2** *vt* **sucer** *(avec un effort)*, **téter** Qsyn. pā ◊ *bhá' flɛ̄ɛn bháwō, yɤ́ ɯ́' yí-dhʌ́n bhá tō' gɯ́ ɯ́' dhūn ɯ̄ zlɑ́ɑ̀ dhɛ̏* lorsque tu suces encore, laisse un peu de jus là-dedans et donne-le à ton jeune frère ◊ *dhʌ́n bhā yà yɔ́n sɛ̋ɛ́ndhʌ́n flɛ̄ɛn, kíi dhūn à ká n̄ dhɛ̏* quand l'enfant tète un peu le sein, amène-le moi

flɛ̋ɛsɯ̏ {A P S, flɛ̋ɛsɯ̏-dhùn pl. A, flɛ̋ɛsɯ̏-sɯ̀ foc. A; flɛ̋ɛflɛ̋ɛsɯ̏ Int. A P S, flɛ̋ɛflɛ̋ɛsɯ̏-dhùn Int. pl. A S} <pauvreté-adj> ***adj*** **pauvre** ♦ *yà kʌ̄ flɛ̋ɛsɯ̏* il s'est appauvri

flɛ̄flɛ̀flɛ̄dhɤ ***adv*** **un par un** *(graduellement, lentement)* ◊ *wò dhò dhɤ́ flɛ̄flɛ̀flɛ̄dhɤ ɤ́'-dhùn gbàn wò dhō gbɛ̄ŋ* ils sont tous partis ainsi, un par un, pendant la nuit

flî, **flîi** (m) ***n*** **demande d'attention** ♦ *flî dà* appeler l'attention ♦ *flîi ká* sans considération

flíŋŋ ***n*** **rosée** *(après une nuit fraîche ou après une pluie) [on n'aime pas la rosée et on évite de la toucher]* ♦ *flíŋŋ yà dɔ̄ blʌ̄ʌ bhà* l'herbe s'est couverte de rosée ◊ *flíŋŋ yà lòo kɤ̄ á dhó* quand la rosée aura séché, je partirai

flő 1 {A S, flő-dhùn pl. A, flő-sɯ̀ foc. A S, flő-sɯ̀-dhùn foc. pl. A} ***adj*** **vide** *(œuf, noix)* ♦ *tɔ̏ yàan flő* œuf de poule vide

flő 2 ***n*** **égratignure** *(sur la peau)* ♦ *yà flő bhō* il s'est égratigné ♦ *wò bhɛ̄n flő bhò* elles égratignent les gens

flőkpòŋdhɛ̀, **flőkpòŋdhò** ***n*** **tourbillon** ◊ *Tòkpà yà zɔ̋ŋ gā sɯ́ flőkpòŋdhò gɯ́ yà à zīɤ kèe gɯ́* Tokpa a pris des cailloux dans le tourbillon et en a frotté ses tendons d'Achille *[une croyance d'enfants : celui qui accompli cet acte sera un bon coureur]*

flɔ̄ ***n*** **cire**

flɔ̋ŋ ***n*** **jachère** *(champ abandonné pendant 2-3 ans, déjà couvert de végétation)*

flɔ̄ɔ́flɔ̀ɔflɔ̄ɔ́dhɤ ***onomat*** **schlarf-schlarf** *(son de pataugement dans la boue)* ◊ *yà tɑ́ sɯ́ bɤ̄ɤ̀ gɯ́ flɔ̄ɔ́flɔ̀ɔflɔ̄ɔ́dhɤ* il a pataugé dans la boue : schlarf-schlarf

flɔ̋tí <Fr. forcé ?> ***n*** **contrainte** ♦ *X Y flɔ̋tí bhō kɤ̄ Y ...* X force Y à faire quelque chose ♦ *X flɔ̋tí wɔ̄ Y tà kɤ̄ Y ...* X force Y à faire quelque chose

flɤ̋ {flɤ̀} ***v*** **1** 1) *vi* **blanchir** ♦ *à gɔ̀ dhɛ́ yà flɤ́* sa tête est devenue toute blanche 2) *vt* **blanchir**, **rendre pâle** *(peau, vêtement)* **2.1** *vt* **piler** *(riz; il s'agit du dernier stade du pilage avant la cuisson)* **2.2** *vt* **frapper** *(longuement, avec un bâton, une verge, un fouet, etc.)* ◊ *bhá wlɑ́ɑ̀ zʌ̄, ā dhò ɯ̄ flɤ́'* si tu fais des bêtises, je te donnerai une bastonnade

flȕu ***n*** **beignet** *(friandise traditionnelle des Dan : boule de farine de maïs mélangée avec des bananes, frite dans l'huile rouge et pimentée)* Syn. flȕuflúȕ ◊ *glɔ̄ɔ yā yɤ̏ bȕ dhɤ́ kɤ̄ à flȕu yɤ̏ kʌ̄* ces bananes ont pourri pour qu'on en fasse des beignets ♦ *flȕu pɛ̋n* beignet

flűudhɤ̄ *adv* **1 très longuement** *(marcher, courir, parler)* ◊ *... yɤ́ dhō dhɤ̋ flűudhɤ̄, yɤ́ lòo pɤ̂ bhā ā gúú* il est allé ainsi longuement, et il est arrivé dans ce village **2 partout**

flùuflúù *n arch.* **beignet** *(boule de la farine de maïs mélangée avec des bananes, avec du piment, frite dans de l'huile rouge; une friandise traditionnelle des Dan)* Syn. *flùu*

flùɯ *n* **escroquerie** ♦ *flùɯ bhɛ̏n* escroc ♦ *yà flùɯ kʌ̄ n̄ gɔ̏* il m'a escroqué

flùɯflùɯsɯ̏ɯ *Int. de* flùɯsɯ̏ɯ *frauduleux*

flùɯsɯ̏ɯ {A P, flùɯsɯ̏ɯ-dhȕn pl. A; flùɯflùɯsɯ̏ɯ Int. A P, flùɯflùɯsɯ̏ɯ-dhȕn Int. pl. A S} <escroquerie-adj.> *adj* **frauduleux** *(personne)* ◊ *dhɛ̏ŋ-dhȕn ɤ́ wó dhūn bhā ā bhɛ̄n flùɯflùɯsɯ̏ɯ-dhȕn ɤ́ wó'-dhȕn gúú, wā ā-dhȕn dà kàsɔ̀ gúú* parmi les étrangers qui étaient venus, on a mis en prison ceux qui ont été les plus grands escrocs

flùɯɯ <Manding fidi, fìri> *v vt* **passer à vapeur** *(le riz, la viande, les termites, etc. – avec du sel, peu de temps, pour la conservation)* ◊ *yɤ̏ bhlȕn yā ā flùɯɯ kɤ̄ yɤ̏ gā vǎandhɤ̄* elle est en train de faire bouillir ce riz pour qu'il sèche vite

főkőfòkò *adj Int. de* főofòo *inutile*

fòo 1 *n* **essoufflement** ♦ *fòo yā ā zʌ̄* **il s'est essoufflé**

fòo 2 *n* **1 bale, balle** *(enveloppe des grains de riz)* **2 grain mal formé** *(de riz; sous l'effet de la sécheresse)*

fòodɔ̏n <essoufflement-toux> *n* **tuberculose**

fòodhíɤ *n* **soupir de soulagement** ♦ *yā ɤ̄ fòodhíɤ lòo* il a poussé un soupir de soulagement

fōodhɤ̄, **fɤ̄ɤdhɤ̄** *adv* **longuement et avec intensité** ◊ *yáa sʌ̏ kɤ̄ kwá yā zōgɔ́ndhē tā fōodhɤ̄* il n'est pas bon que nous nous fassions trop de soucis ◊ *ā zūʌ́ dhíɤ yɤ̏ tɛ́ɛ-sīʌ fōodhɤ̄* il est très inquiet

főofòo {A P S, főofòo-dhȕn pl. A, főofòo-sɯ̏ɯ foc. A, főofòo-sɯ̏ɯ-dhȕn foc. pl. A; főkőfòkò Int. A P S, főkőfòkò-dhȕn Int. pl. A S, főkőfòkò-sɯ̏ɯ Int. foc. A, főkőfòkò-sɯ̏ɯ-dhȕn Int. pl. foc. A} *adj* **1 inutile** *(personne)* **2 inadéquat** *(personne)* **3 ingrat** *(personne)*

főofòo-dhɛ̏ *n* **inutilité** ♦ *yā dà főofòo-dhɛ̏ gúú* c'est une personne gâtée *(se dit surtout d'un enfant)*

fōyí → fɤ̄yí *sueur*

fɔ̏dhɤ̄ *adv* **facilement** *(sans rencontrer de résistance)* ◊ *gèe yā kȕn wɛ́ fɔ̏dhɤ̄* le masque l'a attrapé sans difficulté

fɔ̋kɔ̋fɔ̀kɔ̀ *Int. de* fɔ̋ɔfɔ̀ɔ *faible*

fɔ̋n <Fr. (il) faut> *conj* **1 il faut que** ◊ *fɔ̋n kɤ̄ á' bɔ̄...* il faut que je coupe ça... **2 comme**

fɔ̋ŋ *n* **aluminium**

fɔ̋ŋdhē *adj* **d'aluminum** ◊ *klȕu fɔ̋ŋdhē* louche d'aluminium

fɔ́ŋ̏fɔ̏ŋ {A P S, fɔ́ŋ̏fɔ̏ŋ-dhȕn pl. A, fɔ́ŋ̏fɔ̏ŋ-sɯ̏ɯ foc. A} *adj* **1 léger** *(matériel, objet)* **2 faible** *(personne)* ◊ *ā bhɛ̄n fɔ́ŋ̏fɔ̏ŋ-sɯ̏ɯ-dhȕn wà pʌ̄ bhɤ̏ yɤ̏ kʌ̏ dhɛ̀ pʌ́ ɤ́ yɛ̏ yɤ̄ɤ kǎn ā-dhȕn* *wlɤ̀ɤ dhɤ́* quand ceux qui sont sans force mangent, c'est comme si un trou s'ouvre en dessous d'eux *(l'appétit de ces bons à rien est un trou sans fond)*

fɔ̃ŋfɔ̃ŋ ***n*** **colère** ♦ *fɔ̃ŋfɔ̃ŋ yà dà/bhán à gúú* il s'est mis en colère ♦ *yà fɔ̃ŋfɔ̃ŋ súú bhɛ̄n pɪ́ɤ* il s'est mis en colère contre qn ♦ *à yã́n yà kʌ̄ zɔ̀ɛœndhē fɔ̃ŋfɔ̃ŋ dhɪ́ɤ* ses yeux ont rougi de colère

fɔ̃ɔfɔ̀ɔ {A P S, fɔ̃ɔfɔ̀ɔ-dhùn pl. A S, fɔ̃ɔfɔ̀ɔ-sǜ foc. A, fɔ̃ɔfɔ̀ɔ-sǜ-dhùn foc. pl. A S; fɔ̃kɔ̃fɔ̀kɔ̀ Int. A P S, fɔ̃kɔ̃fɔ̀kɔ̀-dhùn Int. pl. A S, fɔ̃kɔ̃fɔ̀kɔ̀-sǜ Int. foc. A, fɔ̃kɔ̃fɔ̀kɔ̀-sǜ-dhùn Int. foc. pl. A} ***adj*** **faible**, **léger** lv. *(se dit d'une personne incapable de faire quoi que ce soit, privée d'autorité)* Qsyn. *fɤ̃ɤfɤ̀ɤ*

fɔ̄ɔn → fāan *force*

fɤ̀ ***n*** **tambour long** *(esp.; à double membrane, caisse cylindrique) [utilisé autrefois pour animer les danses de guerre et d'autres danses aujourd'hui obsolètes, et pour accompagner une musique associée à la "maison sacrée"; aujourd'hui ce tambour se trouve au village de Kpangwin, dans la case sacrée]* Syn. *yã́gbã́, bhɪ̀dhēbhàa*

fɤdhɛ́ntlʌ̀ <Fr. fenêtre> ***n*** **fenêtre** Syn. *kɔ́ dhòŋ*

fɤ̃kɤ̃fɤ̀kɤ̀ *Int. de* fɤ̃ɤ̀, fɤ̃ɤfɤ̀ɤ *léger*

fɤ́ɤ̀ {P, fɤ́ɤ̀-dhùn pl. A, fɤ́ɤ̀-sǜ foc. A, fɤ́ɤ̀-sǜ-dhùn pl. foc. A; fɤ̃kɤ̃fɤ̀kɤ̀ Int. A P, fɤ̃kɤ̃fɤ̀kɤ̀-dhùn Int. pl. A, fɤ̃kɤ̃fɤ̀kɤ̀-sǜ Int. foc. A, fɤ̃kɤ̃fɤ̀kɤ̀-sǜ-dhùn Int. pl. foc. A} ***adj*** **léger** *(qui n'a pas beaucoup de poids)* ◊ *kɔ̀ɔ fɤ́ɤ̀-dhùn* calebasses légères

fɤɤdhɤ̄ → fōodhɤ̄ *longuement et avec intensité*

fɤ̃ɤfɤ̀ɤ {A P, fɤ̃ɤfɤ̀ɤ-dhùn pl. A, fɤ̃ɤfɤ̀ɤ-sǜ foc. A, fɤ̃ɤfɤ̀ɤ-sǜ-dhùn foc. pl. A; fɤ̃kɤ̃fɤ̀kɤ̀ Int. A P S, fɤ̃kɤ̃fɤ̀kɤ̀-dhùn Int. pl. A, fɤ̃kɤ̃fɤ̀kɤ̀-sǜ Int. foc. A, fɤ̃kɤ̃fɤ̀kɤ̀-sǜ-dhùn Int. pl. foc. A} ***adj*** **1 léger** *(objet)*, **trop léger** *(personne souffrant d'un manque de poids)* **2 faible**, **affaibli** Qsyn. *fɔ̃ɔfɔ̀ɔ* ◊ *bhán kʌ̄ fɤ̃ɤfɤ̀ɤ* je me sens faible *(p.ex. après une maladie)*

fɤyí, **fʌyí**, **fōyí** ***n*** **sueur** ♦ *yʌ́nŋ̀ gbɛ̃́ɛ̀ yɤ̀ fɤyí gā lòo bhɛ̄n bhà* le soleil brûlant fait transpirer l'homme

fǜu ***n*** **éponge** *(fabriquée avec des fibres de liane pour le corps ou la vaisselle)* Qsyn. *sɛ̃́ɛ* ♦ *fǜu pɛ̃́n, fǜu kɔ̄ŋgā* fibre d'éponge ◊ *yà fǜu dà Gísɪ́ tàa* elle a lavé le dos de Guissi avec une éponge ♦ *pɪ̀ɤgā fǜu* éponge en fer

fǜudʌ̄ <éponge-père> ***n*** **serpent** *(esp.; petit, gris-brun, très venimeux, peut avaler une proie plusieurs fois plus grande que lui; non comestible)*

fǜudhɤ̄ ***onomat*** *d'un souffle léger* ◊ *tɛ̃́ɛ yɤ̀ zɪ̀ɤ fǜudhɤ̄* le vent souffle légèrement

G g

gà 1 ***v*** **1** *vt* **regarder** Qsyn. *kpàn* ◊ *bhɤ̀ kɔ́ gà* regarde la maison ◊ *yɤ̀ kʌ̄ n̄ gà yâ* il m'a regardé d'un mauvais oeil ♦ *dhɛ̀ gà* regarder *(dhɛ̀ substitue le nom d'objet d'observation que le locuteur ne veut pas mentionner)* ◊ *yɤ̀ dhɛ̀ gà yâ* il regarde d'un mauvais oeil ◊ ...

úú dhɛ̏ gȁ kpȉnŋ gɔ̏ dhűɤ̏ yʌ̀n... ... et si tu regardes la place au-dessus de la route... ♦ *ȁ gȁ* voici **2** *vt* **penser** *(supposer; que – dhɛ̀)* **3.1** *vt* **prendre** *(considérer d'une certaine façon)* ♦ *yɤ̏ wɔ́n gbàn gȁ bhȁagúú* il prend tout à la légère **3.2** *vt* **prendre** *(pour – dhɛ̀ ... dhɤ́; ká)* ◊ *yɤ̏ ň gȁ dhɛ̀ ɤ̄ dhòo dhɤ́* il me prend pour son frère aîné *(par erreur)* ◊ *yà dȕɤ gȁ dȕ ká* il a pris un buffle pour un boeuf

gȁ 2, **gȁgā** *n* **liane** *(esp.; robuste, ressemble à la pousse du cocotier) [la tige est coupée en longueur et utilisée pour tresser des paniers]* ♦ *gȁ pɛ̋n* bande obtenue avec la tige de liane coupée dans le sens du fil ♦ *gȁ tɤ̄ɤ* panier de liane *(pour garder les vêtements, etc.)*

gā 1 *n* **1** *rn* **os** ♦ *gā gúú yɔ̏n* moelle ♦ *bhɛ̄n gā* tibia *dans certains contextes, comme le suivant :* ◊ *bɤ̄ɤ̏ ɤ́ zīaan tȁ bhā, ȁ bhȁ gblɛ̀ɛndhɛ̏ yɤ̏ lɔ̀o bhɛ̄n gā dhɪ́ɤ* la boue qui est sur la route atteint le tibia **2** **grain** **3** *rn* **tranchant** Qsyn. kpȁ̃a **4.1** **chose** *(mot de compte)* ◊ *ȁ gɛ̏n gā ɤ́' wlɤ̀ɤ yɤ̏ dōsēŋ* il n'a qu'une seule jambe **4.2** **unité** *(mot pour compter les unités des numéraux composés, peut être remplacé par le nom de l'objet qu'il sert à compter)* ◊ *kɔ́ kœ̏œŋ̏ plɛ̀ ɤ̄ gā dɔ̄* vingt et une maisons **5** **représentant éminent** *(des plus forts, des plus grands)* ◊ *gwɛ̄gā* un grand fromager ♦ *bȉaŋgā* coureur de classe **6** *X dɛ̏ gā bhȁ Y construction emphatique possessive; se contracte facultativement en gāȁ* ◊ *ň dɛ̏ gā ȁ bhȁ kɔ́, ň dɛ̏ gāȁ kɔ́* ma propre maison

gā 2 1) {gā} *v* **1** *vi* **mourir** ◊ *yɤ̏ gȁ ɤ̄ gɔ̏ dhɪ̋ɪ̏ tȁ* il est mort dans son lit ♦ *yȁ wɔ̄ gā-yȁn tȁ* il est couché en train de mourir ♦ *gā yɪ́ bhàa* se noyer ♦ *bhán gā ī dhɛ̏* je te supplie (litt. : je suis mort pour toi) **2.1** *vi* **sécher** ♦ *kȁ̃flɛ̋e bhā yɤ̏ gā-sīʌ yʌ́nŋ̏ dhɛ̏* le café sèche au soleil **2.2** *vi* **cicatriser** **3.1** *vi* **s'engourdir** *(devenir insensible)* ♦ *ň kɔ̏ yà gā ň bhȁ* ma main s'est engourdie, ma main ne fonctionne pas *(à cause de la fatigue)* **3.2** *vi* **être paralysé** ◊ *ȁ kɔ̏sʌ̏ gúú pɛ̋ɛn yà gā ȁ bhȁ* il est paralysé du côté droit **4** *vi* **rassurer** *(qn – gúú)* ◊ *yáa gūn gā-sȕȕ ká ň gúú* je n'étais pas très rassuré **5** *vi* **tomber amoureux** *(de – bhȁ)*

gā 2 2) *n* **mort** ♦ *gā tɛ́ɛ yȁ ȁ súú* il est marqué par la mort *(litt. : le vent de la mort l'a pris)* ♦ *fɛ̋ŋ yɤ̏ gā kʌ̄-sīʌ dɤ̄ŋ gúú* le rat pris dans le piège est en train de se débattre contre la mort

gāȁ *une forme contractée de la séquence gā ȁ bhȁ, faisant partie de la construction possessive emphatique* ◊ *ň dɛ̏ gāȁ dhʌ́n* mon propre enfant

gȁ̃a *n* **gale de tête** *(ou une autre maladie de peau sur la tête)* ♦ *gȁ̃a kpȁ̃a* cicatrices laissées par la gale de tête

gāadɪ̋ɛ̏n <Fr. gardien> *n* **gardien**

gȁan *n* **pintade commun**

gābhɛ̏n *n* **mortel, mortelle** ◊ *bhɛ̄n pɛ̋pɛ́ wɔ̀ gābhɛ̏n ká* tout homme est mortel

gādɔ̄ *adj* **unique** ♦ *dhʌ́n gādɔ̄* enfant unique

gādhűű *n* ***Phasmatodea sp.*** **phasme, bacille** ◊ *ɪ̄ɪ kpȁ̃æ ká dhɛ̀ gādhűű dhɤ́* tu es maigre comme un phasme

gȁgā → gȁ 2 *liane*

gāgúɪyȕa ***n*** **arthrite**

gȁ̋n 1 {gȁn} ***v*** **1** *vt* **tirer** ◊ *yɤ̏ dhʌ́n bhā ȁ gȁ̋n-sīʌ* il est en train de tirer l'enfant *(celui-ci se tient debout)* ◊ *bhīʌ̋ gȁ̋n yī́ bhàa* retire la corde de l'eau Qsyn. gbìɤɤ **2** *vi* **s'approcher** *(de – tȁ)* ♦ *bhán gȁ̋n ūū tȁ bhā, yɤ̏ dhȍ kʌ̄' gbɛ́ɛ̏* si je m'approche de toi, ça va chauffer **3** *vt* **sucer** ◊ *gblūūŋ yɤ̏ bhɛ̄n yɔ̀ɔn gȁn* la punaise suce le sang humain

gȁ̋n 2 ***n*** **fardeau** *(obligation pénible)* ♦ *bhán gó gȁ̋n gúɪ* i) je suis libéré du fardeau ii) je suis sauvé

gȁ̋n-gúɪ {gȁn-gúɪ} ***v*** **1** *vt* **tirer sur** *(lance-pierres, etc.)* ◊ *Zân yȁ dhɤ̏ɤ gȁ̋n-gúɪ, kɤ̄ yɤ̄ɤ bhȁan zʌ̄* Zan a tendu le lance-pierres pour tuer un oiseau **2** *vr* **s'étirer** *(caoutchouk; pousse de plante)*

gȁ̋n-sȕɪ ***adj*** **tendu**, **élastique** ◊ *ȁ bhȁ kɔ̄nŋ bhīʌ̋gā yɤ̏ gȁ̋n-sȕɪ ká* les cordes de son harpe-luth sont tendues

gȁŋ ***n*** **arc musical** *(fortement courbé; on le tient de la main gauche, le bras tendu, et on fait passer la corde entre ses lèvres, en la frappant avec une mince baguette. De la main gauche on tient un bâtonnet qu'on appuie rythmiquement sur la corde pour modifier la tension) [on l'utilise dans la magie des chasseurs pour assurer une bonne chasse]*

gàŋ ***n*** **trépied** *(support métallique à pieds courts pour mettre un pot sur le feu, à base circulaire et trois saillies vers l'intérieur)*

gāŋ̏ ***n*** **arbre** *(esp.; ombreux)*

gȁ̋ŋ, **gȁ̋ŋgā** ***n*** **pioche** *(pour creuser la terre dure)*

gȁpʌ̏ ***n*** **objet de contemplation** *(un joli objet; le téléviseur, etc.)* ♦ *bhān gȁpʌ̏* ma chérie (une forme d'adresse très affective)

gȁ̋sȁ̋gɔ̄n ***n*** **gaillard** *(homme fort, vigoureux et travailleur)*

gàsítɛ́ɛ̏, **gȁsúɪbhántɛ́ɛ̏** <Manding gàrisɛgɛ, etymologie populaire : gā sȉ tɛ̋ɛ̋ 'le vent de la prise de mort'> ***n*** **1** **grâce** *(faveur, surtout divine)* ♦ *Zlȁan yà gàsítɛ́ɛ̏ kʌ̄ ȁ dhɛ̏* Dieu lui a fait grâce ♦ *gȁsúɪbhántɛ́ɛ̏ yīi tó Zâan bhȁ* c'est grâce à Zan **2** **avarice** *dans l'expression :* ♦ *bhɛ́n bhā gàsítɛ́ɛ̏ yáa' bhȁ* il est généreux

gàtô <Fr. gâteau> ***n*** **gâteau**

gæ̋æ 1 ***n*** **danse de respect** *(de la part d'une "sœur de famille" ou d'une nièce, par rapport à l'homme qui danse, prononce un discours, etc.)* ♦ *dʌ́ʌ̏ wāȁ bɛ́ɛ̏-dhȕn wȍ gæ̋æ kʌ̄-sīʌ Zân zȕ* les "sœurs de famille" et les nièces dansent la danse de respect à Jean ◊ *wà gæ̋æ kʌ̄ sȁ̋ŋ ká* elles ont dansé le "gèa" avec les cuillers

gæ̋æ 2 → gɛ̋ɛ *herbe non-brûlée*

gæ̏æn ***loc.n*** *SUP de* gɛ̄ŋ̏dhɛ̏ *pieds/jambes*

gæ̏æn → gɛ̏ɛn *veuvage*

gææ̋n ***n*** **scorpion** *[au Gouèta on ne trouve que des scorpions noirs]* ◊ *gææ̋n yà dhʌ́n kún* le scorpion a piqué l'enfant

gææ̋n (Yɛ̋ɛ) ***n*** **crabe** *Syn. kā*

gææ̀ndhɛ̀ → gɛ̀ɛndhɛ̀ *veuve*

gææ̋ngææ̋n ***n Ichneumia albicauda*** **mangouste à queue blanche** *(pattes arrière plus longues que pattes antérieures, duvet dense et jaunâtre, poils raides, tête grise, queue touffue, blanche ou noire, 1,8 à 5 kg; animal nocturne qui se nourrit de petits animaux, d'oiseaux, d'oeufs et de serpents; pour se défendre, il émet un liquide nauséabond de ses glandes anales)*

gææ̋-sűű → gɛ̋ɛ-sűű *faire l'essouchement*

gʌ̄n 1 ***n*** **1** *rn* **corde, bout** *(d'une corde, ceinture etc.) Qsyn. zɔ̋* ♦ *sàbhā̋ gʌ̄n* bout de lanière de sandale ♦ *ī gʌ̄n yɤ̏ ūī bhà̏* je ne vais pas te laisser **2 anse** *(de panier, etc.),* **courroie** *(de sac)* ♦ *glɛ̄ɛ̋ gʌ̄n* courroie de sac de voyage

gʌ̄n 2 ***n*** **courge** *(grosse, rouge, peu nourrissante et à goût déplaisant, on la mange, découpée et cuite dans l'eau, pendant les périodes de disette)*

gʌ̏ŋgʌ̄ŋ̋ (gw), **gʌ̋ŋgʌ̄ŋdhɛ̀** (t) ***n*** **mante religieuse** *(insecte vert aux longue pattes)*

gʌ̄ŋgʌ̄ŋ ***n*** **gong** *(bande de fer qu'on frappe avec un bâtonnet de fer pour signaler le début ou la fin des cours à l'école)* ♦ *gʌ̄ŋgʌ̄ŋ bhàn* sonner le gong

gʌ̏ŋgʌ̄ŋ̋klɔ̀o, gʌ̏ŋgʌ̄ŋ̋klɔ̀odhɛ̀ <mante religieuse-entrelacement> ***n Paullinia pinnata (gen. Sapindaceae)*** **liane** *[utilisée pour faire des cure-dents qu'on vend au marché] Syn. gbɛ̋sɛ̋ɛ̀*

gʌ̄ŋ̋gwʌ̏ ***n*** **cilicium**

gèe 1 {gèe} ***n*** **1** *rn* **cadavre** ils enterrent le cadavre ◊ *pɤ̋dhɤ̄, dhɛ̏kpœ̀œyı̏ yà̏agā pı̋ɤ, yɤ́ bhɛ̄n gèe yɤ̏ bı̏ı̏* au village, dès le troisième jour le mort commence à pourrir *[au village dan, on ensevelit le défunt le plus souvent le deuxième, à la limite le troisième jour après le décès]* ♦ *wūū gèe* cadavre d'un animal ♦ *wʌ̋ŋ gèe* cadavre d'une mouche **2** *rn* **carcasse** *(mot quantificateur, utilisé avec des numéraux et avec gbàn pour exprimer le sens "entier")* ◊ *Gbà̏tɔ̀ yà tɔ̏ gèe gbàn bhɤ̏* Gbato a mangé le poulet entier

gèe 2 ***n*** **masque** *(nom générique pour désigner les masques des hommes) [le masque est considéré comme un être surnaturel]* ♦ *gèe gɔ̏* masque *(la partie en bois qui couvre le visage du porteur du masque)* ♦ *gèe bā̋ā-sı̏ı̏* masque habillé ♦ *gèe kpɛ́ɛ̏* "masque nu" *(masque sonore qui ne se manifeste que par la voix)* ♦ *bhɛ̄n zʌ̄ gèe* masque-assassin ♦ *gèe glɛ̀ɛn* masque à échasses ◊ *yɤ̏ glɛ̀ɛn gbā̋klā̋agbà̏klà̏a ká dhɛ̀ gèe glɛ̀ɛn dhɤ́* il est élancé comme le masque sur des échasses

gèebʌ̏ ***n*** **fétiche** *(nom générique) [chaque chef de famille possède son fétiche qu'il décore]* ◊ *gèebʌ̏ gā plɛ̀ yà gɔ̏* il possède deux fétiches ◊ *kwā̋ŋ̏dhɛ̏ dʌ̄bhɛ̀n yà gèebʌ̏ bhà̏ yɔ́ yɔ̋n pűu ká* le chef de famille a oint le fétiche d'huile rouge

gèebɔ̀ɔ <cadavre- ?> ***n*** **l'au-delà** ♦ *wà dhó gèebɔ̀ɔ* ils sont partis dans l'au-delà

gèebɔ̀ɔbhɛ̀n <au-delà-personne> ***n*** **mort** *(habitant de l'au-delà) [n'apparaît pas aux vivants]*

gèebhàan <masque-oiseau> ***n*** **"masque-oiseau"** *(le masque sur les échasses du village Bongtaa, le plus haut en Gouèta; son propriétaire est mort en années 1990)* ♦ *gèebhàan yɤ̀ tɯ̋n kʌ̄-sīʌ n̄ gblɯ̋dhɤ̄* je crèuve de faim

gèedàbhàdhɯ̀, gèedàadhɯ̀ ***n*** **arbre** *(espèce : le tronc est rouge; on se lave avec la décoction de son écorce contre le mauvais sort)*

gèegā ***n Chrysichthys nigrodigitatus*** **machoiron**

gèeglōő ***n*** **masque "mamba vert"** *[un des "masques dangereux" de Gouèta-Santa, père de masque-cobre, gèegbàa; il protège les garçons pendant l'initiation; il chasse les sorciers, il tue les sorciers et ceux qui ne gardent pas le secret; ne doit pas être vu par les femmes et les enfants]*

gèegɔ̀ <masque-tête> ***n*** **masque** *[un mot secret qu'on ne doit pas prononcer devant les non-initiés]*

gèegbàa ***n*** **masque cobra** *[un des "masques dangereux" de Gwèètaa-Santa, fils de masque-serpent vert, gèeglōő; il protège les garçons pendant l'initiation; il chasse les sorciers, il tue les sorciers et ceux qui ne gardent pas le secret; ne doit pas être vu par les femmes et les enfants]*

gèepűu ***n Chrysichthys nigrodigitatus*** **mâchoiron** *(30 cm de long, museau allongé, dos gris-bleu, ventre blanc; nageoires, queue, lèvres et barbes roses)*

Gɛ̂ ***n*** **Guéré** *(groupe ethnique de l'ouest de la Côte-d'Ivoire, voisins des Dan appartenant à la famille krou; la langue guéré) [les Dan les croient agressifs; il y a une ancienne animosité entre les deux peuples; les Dan les classent parmi les Wobe, wɛ̂]*

gɛ̋ɛ 1, gǽæ ***n*** **biomasse** *(herbe et bois sortis indemne du premier brûlis, lors du défrichage)* ♦ *gɛ̋ɛ kɔ́* tas d'herbes et de bois *(ramassés après le premier brûlis et destinés à être brûlés au second tour)* Qsyn. kɯ̋ŋ

gɛ̋ɛ 2 ***n*** *bɪ̀aŋ gɛ̋ɛ* **échauffement avant la course** *(une partie du rituel de la course des masques : les coureurs manifestent leur hardiesse)* ◊ *wɔ̀ bɪ̀aŋ gɛ̋ɛ sɯ́-sīʌ kɤ̄ wɔ̀ gbàn gèe gɔ̀* ils s'échauffent avant de se dresser devant le masque ♦ *bɪ̀aŋ gɛ̋ɛ sɯ́ bhɛ̀n* précurseur *(le jour des courses des masques, des coureurs vétérans, en jupes de raphia et peints de kaolin, courent à l'intérieur du village dès le matin en animant le public, ils surveillent l'ordre pendant les courses)*

gɛ̋ɛdhɛ̀, gǽædhɛ̀ ***n*** **1 champ défriché** *(les plantes sont coupées et brûlées, mais les restes ne sont pas encore mis en tas)* **2 champ pendant la première année après le défrichage**

gɛ̀ɛgɛ̀ɛ (t) ***n*** **arbre** *(esp.)*

gɛ̀ɛn ***loc.n*** *SUP de* gɛ̄nŋ̀dhɛ̀ *pieds/jambes*

gɛ̀ɛn, gæ̀æn ***n*** **veuvage** ♦ *yà gɛ̀ɛn kɯ̋n* elle est devenue veuve

gɛ̄ɛn ***loc.n*** *COM de* gɛ̄ŋ̄ŋ̏dhɛ̏ *pieds/jambes*

gɛ̀ɛndhɛ̏, **gæ̀ændhɛ̏** <veuvage-femme> ***n*** **veuve** *[après la mort de son mari la veuve passe sept jours enfermée dans sa case; la coutume favorise son remariage avec un jeune frère du défunt]*

gɛ̏ɛŋdhɤ̋ <de gɛ̏n 'pied, jambe'> ***adv*** **fixement**, **avec stupeur** ◊ *bhɛ̄n gbàan dɔ̄ gɛ̏ɛŋdhɤ̋* en sursautant, chacun a été frappé de stupeur

gɛ̋ɛ-sűű, **gæ̋æ-sűű** {gɛ̋ɛ-sūū, gæ̋æ-sūū} ***v vt*** **faire l'essouchement** *(ramasser les herbes et le petit bois restés intactes dans les tas)* ◊ *yɤ̏ ɤ̄ bhā dhɛ̄ŋ̏dhɛ̏ gɛ̋ɛ-sűű-sīʌ* il est en train d'essoucher son champ

gɛ̏n ***n*** **1.1** *rn* **jambe et pied** *(ensemble)* Syn. gbɑ̋n, gbɑ̋ngā Qsyn. gɛ̄ŋ̏dhɛ̏ ♦ *ɑ̏ gɛ̏n yà lòo* ses jambes sont paralysées ♦ *ɑ̏ gɛ̏n yɤ̏ kpɑ̋an ká* il est nu-pieds ♦ *ɑ̏ gɛ̏n yɪ́ yɑ̏ kɑ̋n wɛ̋ɛwɛ̋ɛ* ses jambes ne tiennent plus ♦ *ɑ̏ gɛ̏n yɤ̏ yɑ̏ pʌ̄ bhɑ̏* il est tombé sur qch (il l'a trouvé) **1.2** *rn* **patte de derrière** **1.3** *rn* **jambe** *(d'un objet)* **1.4** **roue** *(d'un véhicule)* **2** *rn* **racine** *(pas des plantes)* ♦ *kɔ́ gɛ̏n* pieu des fondations d'une maison ♦ *sɔ̋n gɛ̏n* racine de dent **3** *rn* **cause, raison** Syn. gɛ̏ngódhɛ̏ ♦ *ɑ̏ gɛ̏n yɤ̏ kʌ̏ dhɛ̀...* ♦ *ɑ̏ gɛ̏n bhȕn dhɛ̀...* sa raison est que... ◊ *ɑ̏ gɛ̏n yɤ̏ gȍ bhūn glɛ̀ɛn* il faut en chercher la cause loin **4** **façon, manière** ♦ *ɑ̏-dhȕn dhɪ́ɤ wɔ̏n gɛ̏n dɔ̄* raconter leur histoire ◊ *yɑ̏ ɑ̏ gɛ̏n dɔ̄* il en a raconté

gɛ̏ndhʌ́ngātɔ̄ɔ <pied-diminutif-os-dernier> ***n rn*** **petit orteil** Syn. gɛ̄nŋgādhʌ́ntɔ̄ɔ

gɛ̏ndhɛ̋ <pied-feuille> ***n rn*** **pied** ♦ *tɑ̋ gɛ̏ndhɛ̋ tɑ̏* marcher pieds nus

gɛ̏ndhɛ̋kwɛ̄ɛ̋dhɛ̏, **gɛ̏ndhɛ̋kwɛ̏ŋ̏dhɛ̏** <pied-feuille-poignet-place > ***n rn*** **plante du pied**

gɛ̏ndhɛ̋wlɤ̏ɤdhɛ̏ <pied-feuille-sous-place > ***n rn*** **plante du pied**

gɛ̏ndhűű, **gɛ̏ngādhűű** <pied-(os)-arbre> ***n rn*** **tibia** ♦ *ɑ̏ gɛ̏ndhűű yɤ̏ glɛ̀nglɛ̀n ká dhɛ̀ zlòo gɛ̏n dhɤ́* ses jambes sont aussi longues que celles de l'antilope guib ♦ *ɑ̏ gɛ̏ndhűű yɤ̏ kʌ̏ dhɛ̀ zɛ̄ŋ́ gɛ̏n dhɤ́* ses jambes sont aussi minces que celles d'un moustique *[insulte]*

gɛ̏ngādhűű → gɛ̏ndhűű *tibia*

gɛ̏ngódhɛ̏ <pied-aller-place> ***n rn*** **cause, raison** Syn. gɛ̏n

gɛ̏ngbɛ̋ɛ̏bhɛ̏n <homme de pied lourd> ***n*** **coureur de classe**, **champion en course** Syn. bɪ̏aŋgā ♦ *gɛ̏ngbɛ̋ɛ̏bhɛ̏n yāa* coureur sans égal

gɛ̏ngbɔ̄ <jambe-pot> ***n rn*** **mollet**

gɛ̏nlòobhɛ̏n <jambe-arriver-personne> ***n*** **paralytique de deux jambes**

gɛ̄ŋ̏dhɛ̏ {LOC gɛ̄nŋdhɤ̋, SUP gɛ̏ɛn, gæ̏æn, COM gɛ̄ɛn, gǣæn} ***loc.n*** **1** *rn* **pieds, jambes** Qsyn. gɛ̏n ◊ *yà gwɑ̋ndhʌ́n zʌ̄ gɛ̄ɛn* il a donné un coup de pied au chat ♦ *yà dɔ̄ ɤ̄ gæ̏æn* i) il s'est levé ii) il est sorti *(réponse à la question : est-ce que X est là ?)* ♦ *yɤ̏ zɪ̏ɤ ɤ̄ gǣæn dɔ̄* il est allé directement **2** *rn* **fondation** *(endroit au pied de)*, **fond**, **partie inférieure** ◊ *yɤ̏ yɑ̏-sȕȕ ká dhűű gɛ̄nŋdhɤ̋* il est assis sous l'arbre ◊ *dhā ɤ́ dhūn-sīʌ bhā, ɑ̏ gɛ̄ŋ̏dhɛ̏* *yà tān gbàngbàndhɤ̄* le fond de la nuée d'orage qui était en train de s'approcher, était rouge vif

gɛ̄ŋŋdhɤ̄ 1 *loc.n LOC de* gɛ̄nŋ̀dhɛ̀ *pieds/jambes*

gɛ̄ŋŋdhɤ̄ 2 *adv* **clong** *(son d'un couteau qui s'enfonce)*

gɛ̄ŋŋgā <pied- ?-os> *changement irrégulier du ton de la première composante d'extra-bas à moyen* ***n*** **1** *rn* **orteil** ♦ *gɛ̄ŋŋgā gɔ̄n* gros orteil ♦ *gɛ̄ŋŋgā gblɛ̀ɛnsɯ̀* quatrième orteil *(entre le gros et le moyen orteils)* ♦ *gɛ̄ŋŋgā zìŋgɯ́sɯ̀* orteil moyen ♦ *gɛ̄ŋŋgā dhʌ́n tɔ̄ɔ* petit orteil **2** *rn* **patte** *(d'un insecte)*

gɛ̄ŋŋgādhʌ́ntɔ̄ɔ <orteil-diminutif-dernier> ***n*** *rn* **petit orteil** *Syn.* *gɛ̀ndhʌ́ngātɔ̄ɔ*

gɛ̄ŋŋgāgɔ̄n <orteil-homme> ***n*** *rn* **gros orteil**

gɛ̀nsɯ́ ***n*** *rn* **pas** *(enjambée)* ♦ *yà gɛ̀nsɯ́ dō kʌ̄* il a fait un pas *Syn.* *gɛ̀nyàn*

gɛ̀nwɛ̄ngā <pied-grain.de.palme-os> ***n*** *rn* **cheville; malléole** ♦ *yí dhɯ́ɤ yɤ̀ tò bhɛ̄n gɛ̀nwɛ̄ngā bhà* l'eau arrive aux chevilles

gɛ̀nyàn ***n*** **1 pas** *(enjambée)* *Syn.* *gɛ̀nsɯ́* **2 fois** ◊ *gɛ̀nyàn kœ̀œŋ dō* dix fois

gɛ̄nyɛ̄n {gɛ̄nyɛ̄n; NEUT gɛ̄nyɛ̀n} <Fr. gagner> ***v*** *vi* **gagner**; **réussir**; **passer un examen**

gì (t) → gìi *blesser*

gí ***n*** **buisson** *(esp)*

gî ***n*** **courbature** ◊ *gî yɤ̀ n̄ kʌ̄-sīʌ* j'ai des courbatures

gía {gìa} ***v*** *vi* **blettir** *(du gombo)* *Qsyn.* *kìan*

gīaatàn ***n*** **1 danse de course de masques** *(compétition au cours de laquelle les masques cherchent à attraper les membres d'une équipe opposante; jeu accompagné de musique et de danses acrobatiques)* ♦ *gīaatàn kʌ̄* exécuter la danse « giaatan » **2 danse pour marquer la sortie du masque gèekɛ̋ɛsɯ̀** *(sur la musique gɔ̄dhʌ́n)*

gìææn ***n*** **champignon** *(esp., apparaît en mars-mai)*

gìʌ ***n*** **chiquenaude, pichenette** ◊ *yà dhʌ́n zʌ̄ gìʌ ká à kpōŋ́dhɤ̄* il a donné à l'enfant une chiquenaude au front

gídhʌ̋n *intj* **super !** *(exclamation à l'adresse de celui qui fait des choses extraordinaires et louables)*

gìi ***n*** **arbre** *(esp.; fréquent aux abords des cours d'eau. Les fruits, très appréciés par les oiseaux et les animaux, servent aussi d'appât pour les poissons)*

gìi, gì 1 *v* 1) *vi* **essuyer une blessure** ◊ *yɤ̀ gìi ɤ̄ gɛ̀n bhà* il est blessé à la jambe 2) *vt* **blesser** *(d'habitude, il s'agit d'une blessure peu profonde)* ♦ *yà n̄ zūʌ́ gìi* il m'a attristé ♦ *sàbhʌ́ yà n̄ gìi* les chaussures m'ont écorché les pieds ◊ *pìɤgāsòò yà n̄ gìi* je me suis blessé en tombant du vélo ◊ *dhàa yà n̄ gìi* je me suis blessé avec un couteau *(involontairement)* **2.1** *vi* **se frotter** ◊ *gbɛ̂n yà gìi n̄ gɛ̀n bhà* le chien s'est frotté contre mes jambes ◊ *dhɯ́ɯ́ kwɛ̄ɛ́ plɛ̀ yɤ̀ gìi-sīʌ kwʌ́ʌ̀ víòovìoovíoodhɤ̄* deux branches d'arbre se frottent l'une sur l'autre avec un grincement **2.2** *vi* **s'égratigner**, **se frôler** ◊ *gɔ̄ plɛ̏ wȁ gìi wō kwʌ́ʌ̀* deux voitures se sont frôlées

gı̋ì {gìi} *v* **1.1** 1) *vt* **badigeonner** ◊ *bhán bhān kɔ́ gı̋ì* j'ai badigeonné ma maison 2) *vr* **se frotter** *(avec – ká)* ◊ *yɤ̏ ɤ̄ gı̋ì-sīʌ yɔ̋n ká* elle est en train de se frotter avec de l'huile **1.2** *vt* **enduire de** *(qch – bhȁ)* ◊ *Yɔ̏ yɤ̏ yɔ̋n gı̋ì-sīʌ ɤ̄ bhȁ* Yo s'enduit d'huile ◊ *wɔ̀ dȕ gbō gìi kɔ́ɔdhɤ̄* on enduit les maisons de bouse de vache **2.1** 1) *vi* **aigrir** *(de la sauce, du vin)* Qsyn. kpœ̀œn ◊ *wē bhā yɤ̏ gı̋ì-sȕı ká* le vin a tourné ◊ *gwɛ̋ɛ yí yɤ̏ gìi vȁandhɤ̄* la sauce d'arachide aigrit vite 2) *vt* **aigrir** *(sauce)* **2.2** *vt* **aigrir** *(la bouche)* ◊ *dhàandháȁn yà n̄ sɔ̋n gı̋ì* l'ananas m'a aigri la bouche

gı̋ì *n* **joug** *(sujétion)* Syn. sāȁn ♦ *yɤ̏ gı̋ì gúı ɤ̄ dȅ gɔ̏* il n'a pas d'égard pour lui-même *(il travaille sans se donner de repos, etc.)*

gīoo *n* arch. **chat** Syn. gwȁndhʌ́n, yūȁndhʌ́n

gísí {A} *adj* **une quantité** *(une connotation négative)* ◊ *yɤ̏ glɔ̄ɔ gísí bhā ȁ bhɤ̏ dhɛ̋dhɛ̋ plɛ̀ ká* en deux heures il a mangé une grande quantité de bananes ◊ *yʌ̄ gísí ɤ́ ȁ kʌ̀ bhā, wíi pʌ̄ bhá dhūn ȁ dhɛ̏* pour le grand travail qu'il a fait on ne lui a rien donné

gīzābhɛ́n <Fr. examen> *n* **examen** Syn. pāsēdhē

glà 1 *n* **1** ***Indigofera spp.*** **indigo** *(plante)* ♦ *glà yí* indigo *(peinture)* **2 indigo** *(peinture)* ◊ *yà sɔ̄ dȁ glà gúı* elle a mis le vêtement dans l'indigo

glà 2 *n* **polyartrite** ♦ *glà kpǽæ* polyarthrite *(sans gonflement des articulations)* ♦ *glà sǣæ* polyarthrite *(avec gonflement des articulations)*

glȁ {glȁ} *v* **1.1** *vi* **grandir** Syn. kpǽǣ ◊ *bhá glȁ gbɛ̋ɛ̏ dhɛ̋ !* mais qu'est-ce que tu as grandi ! **1.2** 1) *vi* **se développer** ◊ *yı̋ì sɛ́ yɤ̏ glȁ-sīʌ vȁandhɤ̄* notre pays se développe vite 2) *vt* **développer 2.1** *vi* **changer** *(en – ká)*, **devenir** ◊ *yà glȁ yà kʌ̄ kwí ká !* il est devenu un citadin ! *(dit avec désapprobation)* ◊ *bhá glȁ bhá kʌ̄ sʌ̀* tu es devenu joli *(grâce aux soins)* **2.2** *vi* **se transformer** *(volontairement; en – gúı)* ◊ *ȁ gbɛ́-dhȅ gúı, dūbhȅn-dhȕn wɔ̀ glȁ gwȁndhʌ́n tīi-dhȕn gúı* le plus souvent les sorciers se transforment en chats noirs ◊ *gbīŋgā yɤ̏ glȁ vūnŋdhē gúı* la chenille se transforme en hanneton

glâ (gw), **gláà** (t) *n* **jeune palmier à huile** ♦ *glâ dhɛ́* palme du jeune palmier à huile ♦ *glâ gɔ̄* pétiole de la palme du jeune palmier à huile

glȁadhíɤ <Fr. gardien> *n glȁadhíɤ bhō* garder

glāȁnglȁanglāȁndhɤ̄ *onomat* **crac-crac** *(craquement de petites branches sous les pieds; grincement du sable)* ◊ *yȁ tȁ súı glāȁnglȁanglāȁndhɤ̄* il marche (dans la forêt), ses pas font crac crac ◊ *n̄ sɔ̋n yɤ̏ gwʌ̀ tȁ glāȁnglȁanglāȁndhɤ̄* le sable grince sous mes dents

glȁawē (m) → glʌ̀ʌwē *vin de palmier à huile*

glȁbȁ *n* **chausse-trappe, chausse-trape** Syn. pı̏ɤ dɤ̄ŋ ◊ *bhán glȁbȁ yȁ wɔ̀ɔ gɔ̏* j'ai mis une chausse-trappe pour les singes

glȁglȁdhɤ̄ *onomat* **cling-cling** *tintement de la vaisselle métallique ou des armes* ◊ *tǽǣ yɤ̏ bhȁn kwʌ́ʌ̀ glȁglȁdhɤ̄* les cuvettes tintent

glàglàglàdhɤ̄ ***onomat*** **cataclop, tagadag-tagadag-tagadag** *(résonnement des sabots d'un cheval)◊ sòò yɤ̀ bìaŋ wlɤ̀-sīʌ glàglàglàdhɤ̄* le cheval court, ses sabots font cataclop

glắglắsȕ {A P S, glắglắsȕ-dhȕn pl. A, glắglắsȕ-sȕ foc. A, glắglắsȕ-sȕ-dhȕn pl. foc. A} ***adj*** **difficile** ♦ *dhɔ̀ glắglắsȕ* amour difficile *(avec des querelles et des conflits)* ♦ *bhɛ̄n glắglắsȕ* i) homme difficile à contrôler *(à cause de sa force physique, habileté, etc.)* ii) homme louche *(qui n'inspire pas confiance)* ♦ *yʌ̄ glắglắsȕ* travail d'homme

glắnglắn ***n*** **crampe, convulsion** ♦ *glắnglắn yà dà n̄ gɛ̀n gúú* j'ai une crampe à la jambe

glắŋglàŋ {pl. glắŋglắŋ} ***adj*** **1 difficile** *(difficilement pratiquable)* ◊ *zīaan glắŋglàŋ* une route difficilement praticable **2 louche** *(personne)*

glắŋglắŋ ***n*** *pl. de* glắŋglàŋ *difficile*

glʌ̄ʌn {glʌ̀ʌn} ***v*** **1** *vi* **se rouler 2** *vt* **rouler 3** *vi* **tourner** Syn. glúú (m)

glʌ̀ʌwē, glàawē (m) ***n*** **vin de palmier à huile**

glɛ̀ŋ ***n*** **1 bon sens** *(comportement adéquat, bon ton, sagesse)* ♦ *glɛ̀ŋ dà bhɛ̄n bhà* donner un conseil à qn ◊ *pɤ̄dʌ̄ yà glɛ̀ŋ sʌ̀ dà n̄ bhà* le notable m'a donné un bon conseil ♦ *à bhà glɛ̀ŋ wɔ̀n gúú yáa dhɤ́* il n'est pas normal ♦ *bhɛ́n ɤ́ bhā glɛ̀ŋ yáa à bhà* cet homme est un inadapté *(il se comporte bêtement, il n'a pas de manières)* **2 ruse** ♦ *glɛ̀ŋ kʌ̄ bhɛ̄n gɔ̀* escroquer qn

glɛ̀ŋglɛ̀ŋsȕ *Int. de* glɛ̀ŋsȕ *intelligent*

glɛ̀ŋsȕ {A P, glɛ̀ŋsȕ-dhȕn pl. A P, glɛ̀ŋsȕ-sȕ foc. A, glɛ̀ŋsȕ-sȕ-dhȕn pl. foc. A; glɛ̀ŋglɛ̀ŋsȕ Int. A P S, glɛ̀ŋglɛ̀ŋsȕ-dhȕn Int. pl. A S, glɛ̀ŋglɛ̀ŋsȕ-sȕ Int. foc. A, glɛ̀ŋglɛ̀ŋsȕ-sȕ-dhȕn Int. pl. foc. A} ***adj*** **intelligent** *(ayant un bon sens naturel et des bonnes manières)* Qsyn. kpœ̀œsȕ

glɛ̄ɛ́ ***n*** **sac de voyage** Qsyn. bhɔ̄ɔ 1 ♦ *wʌ́ʌ̀ glɛ̄ɛ́dhʌ́n* porte-monnaie ◊ *glɛ̄ɛ́ dhȕn wó bīɤ kwī ká, à-dhȕn dhɔ̀ yɤ̀ dhēbʌ̀-dhȕn kʌ̀* les femmes aiment les sacs en peau d'éléphant

glɛ̄ɛ́n (m) ***n*** **sac** Syn. kpɔ̄ɔ́ (gw)

glɛ̋ɛn ***n*** **épine** Qsyn. plűűnŋ ♦ *glɛ̋ɛn gā* une épine ♦ *yúɤ̀ glɛ̋ɛn* arête de poisson

glɛ̋ɛnpűu <épine-blanc> ***n*** ***Canthium venosum (gen. Rubiaceae)*** **liane** *(esp.; avec de longues épines vénéneuses)*

glɛ̋ɛntīi <épine-noire> ***n*** **liane** *(esp.; avec des épines noires vénéneuses)*

glɛ̋ɛnwɔ̀dhɛ̀ <piquant-sortir-feuille> ***n*** ***Euphorbia hirta*** **malnommée vraie** *(mauvaise herbe, pousse à côté des chemins, jusqu'à 40 cm de haut; feuilles rhombiques, petites fleurs verdâtres, jus laiteux. Utilisée contre les maladies vénériennes et les maux de ventre)*

glɛ̀ɛŋdhɤ̄ ***adv*** **espacé** ◊ *n̄ sɔ̋n yɤ̀ dɔ̄-sȕ ká glɛ̀ɛŋdhɤ̄, kɛ́ɛ n̄ dhēgbáan zʌ̀, à sɔ̋n yɤ̀ yɤ̄-sȕ ká kɔ̋ɔ* mes dents sont espacées, et ma soeur aînée a des dents serrées

glɛ̀ŋ ***n*** **clôture légère** *(enclos de bétail fait de perches horizontales)*

glòo 1 ***n*** *gbàn glòo* **poutre du plafond**

glɔ̀ɔ 2 *n* **surmaturité** *(gombo; jeune fille)* ♦ *glɔ̀ɔ kún* blettir (gombo); trop durer sans trouver de mari

glòo 1) *v* **1** *vi* **se reposer** *(longuement)* Qsyn. *kōyíbhō* ◊ *bhāan glòo dɛ̀ɛ* je vais me reposer aujourd'hui **2** *vi* **continuer une journée entière** *(à – bhȁ)* ◊ *dhā yȁ glòo bān-sȕ bhȁ* il a plu toute la journée

glòo 2) *n* **repos** Qsyn. *kōyíbhō, tɛ́ɛpā* ◊ *glòo yī dhʌ̀n dɛ̀ɛ* aujourd'hui est le jour de repos

Glɔ̄ɔ̏ *n* **Gouro** *(groupe ethnique du Centre-Ouest de la Côte-d'Ivoire d'appartenance mandé-sud; membre de ce groupe; la langue gouro) [liés aux Dan par un cousinage plaisanterie, dit sànbhűnzʌ̏dhɛ̏, en dan]*

glɔ̄ɔ̋ *n* ***Dendroaspis viridis*** **mamba vert** *(serpent arboricole, jusqu'à 2, fin, très venimeux; attaque souvent suspendu à une branche)*

glőo → gblőo *trace*

glóodhʌ́nkōŋ < ?-diminutif-harpe-luth> *n* **pluriarc** *(instrument à cordes avec un résonateur fait de calebasse et plusieurs manches, chacun avec une corde) [rare aujourd'hui; on pense qu'il vient des Kono; les joueurs de pluriarc chantent d'habitude en langue kono]*

glɔ̀ɔgā *n* *zīaan glɔ̀ɔgā* **ornière**

glōogȉaan *n* ***Musophaga violacea*** **touraco violet** *(taille : 45 cm, dessus bleu sombre, dessous des ailes cramoisi, bec jaune) [désignation onomatopoétique imitant son cri]*

glɔ̋kɔ̋glɔ̀kɔ̀ *SupInt.* de glɔ̋ɔglɔ̀ɔ *émoussé*

glɔ̀ŋ *n* **1 tambour** *(à une seule membrane lacée, tendue par les coins; caisse en forme de mortier à pieds; autrefois fréquent dans les cases sacrées; rare de nos jours)* **2 "glong"** *(danse des hommes accompagnée par ce tambour)*

glɔ̄ɔ {glɔ̀ɔ} *n* **banane** *(nom générique)* ♦ *glɔ̄ɔ bè* régime de bananes ♦ *glɔ̄ɔ kpȁa* grappe de bananes *(une partie du régime)* ♦ *glɔ̄ɔ gɔ̀* i) jeune pousse de banane (pour le repiquage) ii) sommet de bananier ♦ *glɔ̄ɔ kpū* jeune pousse de banane (pour le repiquage) ♦ *kwí glɔ̄ɔ, kwí ȁ glɔ̄ɔ* banane poyo *(sorte de banane douce, grosse et très sucrée, ressemble par son apparence à la banane plantain; fait partie de glɔ̄ɔ dhɛ̋ɛndhɛ̀ɛn)* ♦ *bhɤ̏ glɔ̀ɔ, glɔ̄ɔ sɛ̀ɛ; glɔ̄ɔ dhɛ̋ɛndhɛ̀ɛn* (m) banane douce

glɔ̄ɔdhɛ̋kpɛ̋ɛ *n* **1 feuilles sèches de bananier** *[très légers; on en fait des coussins de tête pour amortir le poids de la charge à porter]* **2 épilepsie** *[on considère cette maladie comme étant "légère comme les feuilles de bananes" et contagieuse; on évite de toucher l'épileptique]*

glɔ̋ɔglɔ̀ɔ {A P S, glɔ̋ɔglɔ̀ɔ-dhȕn pl. A, glɔ̋ɔglɔ̀ɔ-sȕ foc. A, glɔ̋ɔglɔ̀ɔ-sȕ-dhȕn foc. pl. A; glɔ̄ɔ̋glɔ̄ɔ̋sȕ Int. A P S, glɔ̄ɔ̋glɔ̄ɔ̋sȕ-dhȕn Int. A S; glɔ̋kɔ̋glɔ̀kɔ̀ SupInt A P S, glɔ̋kɔ̋glɔ̀kɔ̀-dhȕn SupInt. pl. A, glɔ̋kɔ̋glɔ̀kɔ̀-sȕ SupInt. foc. A, glɔ̋kɔ̋glɔ̀kɔ̀-sȕ-dhȕn SupInt. pl. foc. A} *adj* **émoussé** ♦ *ȁ zūʌ́ gā yɤ̏ glɔ̋ɔglɔ̀ɔ* il est incrédule ♦ *bhēn zūʌ́gā glɔ̄ɔ̋glɔ̄ɔ̋sȕ* incrédule

glɔ̋ɔglɔ̋ɔ {A P, glɔ̋ɔglɔ̋ɔ-dhʉ̀n A} ***adj*** *exprime l'idée du pluriel* **1 robustes et de grande taille** *(jeunes hommes)* **2 moyens** *(objets inanimés)* ◊ *kɔ̀ɔ glɔ̋ɔglɔ̋ɔ* calebasses moyennes

glɔ̄ɔ̋glɔ̄ɔ̋sʉ̀ *Int. de* glɔ̋ɔglɔ̀ɔ *émoussé*

glɔ̄ɔtīi <banane-noire> ***n*** **banane sauvage** *(à tige de couleur foncée et plutôt rare. Ses fruits rougeâtres, à effet tonique, servent de nourriture pendant la période de disette)*

glɔ̄ɔzɔ̀ngʉ́ʉwlɤ̋ <banane-piler-in-mortier> ***n*** **mortier peu profond** *[servant à la préparation du foutou-banane, utilisé en milieu urbain]*

glɔ̄ɔzɔ̀nkáwɤ̄ŋ <banane-piler-avec-pilon> ***n*** **pilon court** *(avec des élargissements aux deux bouts, réservé à la préparation du foutou dans le mortier peu profond)*

glʉ̄ʉ̀n {glʉ̀un} ***v*** 1) *vi* **se tourner, se rouler** Syn. *glʉ̄ʉɯŋ* ◊ *yɤ̀ gbő bɔ̄-sīʌ yɤ̀ glʉ̄ʉ̀n-sīʌ' ká blʌ̄ʌ dhɛ̋ tà bhʉ̄n* elle pleurait et se roulait dans les feuilles 1) *vt* **rouler** Syn. *glʉ̄ʉɯŋ*

glʉ́ʉ (m) {glʉ̀ʉ} ***v*** *vi* **tourner** Syn. *glʌ̄ʌn (gw)* ♦ *glʉ́ʉ ɤ̄ gɔ̀ zʉ́ʉ* tourner en rond

glʉ̋ʉ ***n*** **arbre** *(esp.; la décoction était utilisée dans les ordalies) [on croit qu'un sorcier qui boit de cette décoction meurt; de nos jours, l'ordalie est interdite. Selon une croyance, si on met du sang dans la décoction, elle devient mortelle pour tout le monde. L'écorce est pilée et mélangée avec du kaolin, on la frotte sur la peau pour se protéger contre la magie noire]* ♦ *wà glʉ̋ʉ dɔ̄ bhēn gɔ̀* on lui a fait passé l'ordalie par la décoction de l'arbre "geu"

glʉ̀ʉglʉ̀ʉdhɤ̄ ***adv*** **à pas lourd**

glʉ̋ʉkɔ̋glʉ̀ʉkɔ̀ ***adj*** **qui agace les dents** *(astringent)* ◊ *bhēntīi sɛ̄ɛ̋ dīn yɤ̀ glʉ̋ʉkɔ̋glʉ̀ʉkɔ̀* le citron est astringent

glʉ̋ʉɯ {A, P, glʉ̋ʉɯ-sʉ̀ foc. A, glʉ̋ʉɯ-sʉ̀-dhʉ̀n pl. foc. A; gʉ̋gʉ̋sʉ̀ Int. A P S, gʉ̋gʉ̋sʉ̀-dhʉ̀n Int. pl. A, gʉ̋gʉ̋sʉ̀-sʉ̀ Int. foc. A} ***adj*** **amer** ◊ *gɔ̂ gʉ̋gʉ̋sʉ̀-sʉ̀* la cola qui est très amère

glʉ̄ʉɯŋ {glʉ̀ʉɯŋ} ***v*** 1) *vi* **rouler** Syn. *glʉ̄ʉ̀n* 2) *vt* **rouler** Syn. *glʉ̄ʉ̀n*

gó 1 {gō} ***v*** **1** *vt* **vendre** *(à – gɔ̀, pour le montant de – bhà)* Syn. *dhɔ̋ɔ dɔ̄ (dhɔ̋ɔ 1)* ♦ *yà pʌ̄ gó* i) il a vendu une chose ii) il a payé l'amende **2** *vt* **troquer**, **échanger** *(contre – bhà)* ◊ *bhán bhān bhɛ̋ɛ gó pòtáblɤ̀ bhà* j'ai troqué ma chemise contre un portable

gó 2 {gō} ***v*** **1.1.1** *vi* **s'en aller**; **se déplacer** ◊ *dhɛ̀ ɤ́ á gō' bhà bhā...* la place que j'ai quittée/d'où je suis venu... ◊ *kɤ̄ sɪ́ɤ ɤ́ yā yɤ̀ kʌ̄ gɔ̀ bhén, kɤ̄ yíi kʌ̄ gó bhɛ̋n ɛ̀e ?* on ne sait pas d'où est venu ce feu ◊ *yɤ̀ gɔ̀ Bíyà* a) il est venu d'Abidjan (et maintenant, il est ici); b) il est originaire d'Abidjan ◊ *gwʌ̀ yɤ̀ gó-sīʌ tɔ̀n bhà* une pierre descend de la montagne ◊ *yʉ̋a yɤ̀ gó ɯ̄ gʉ́ʉ* que les maladies te quittent ◊ *yɤ̀ n̄ gɛ̀n bhlōo kɤ̄ à yí yɤ̀ gó à gʉ́* il presse ma jambe pour évacuer le liquide *(en parlant d'une jambe gonflée)* ♦ *gó n̄ gɔ̀ yɤ̄ !* laisse-moi tranquille ! *(litt. : quitte ma place !)* ♦ *bhá gó bhʉ̄n, ɤ́ gō bhʉ́n* et puis; en plus **1.1.2** *vi* **emmener** *(qn, qch – ká)* ◊ *... yɤ́ wó gō' ká Bʉ̀akɛ̄ɛ* alors on l'a emmené de Bouaké **1.1.3** *vi* **abandonner** *(qn – gɔ̀)*, **divorcer** *(en parlant d'une femme; avec – gɔ̀)* **1.1.4** *vi* **quitter** *(son mari – ɤ̄ gɔ̀n kèŋ̀)* **1.1.5** *vi* **s'écarter** ◊ *dhʉ̋ yā yɤ̀ bɔ̀ kɤ̄ yɤ̀ gó kɔ́ tà* cet arbre a été abattu pour qu'il ne soit plus près de la maison **1.2** *vi* **se détacher**, **tomber** *(d'un objet inanimé)* ♦ *n̄ sɔ́ngā yà gó bhʉ̄n* ma dent est tombée ♦ *bʌ̋ŋ yà gó ɤ̄* *gɔ̃ gúú* la lame de la machette s'est détachée du manche **1.3** *vi* **perdre** *(poste – gúú)* **2** *vi* **sortir**, **couler** *(l'eau du robinet)* **3** *vi* **abandonner**, **renoncer** *(à un mode de vie – gúú)* ◊ *yà gó ɤ̄ sɔ̀ŋ gúú* il a renoncé à son mauvais comportement **4** *vi combiné avec un pronom existentiel et le verbe principal à l'infinitif ou à la forme du masdar, sert à exprimer l'idée de passé immédiat* ◊ *ä bhä̀ dhēbʌ̀ yɤ̋ gɔ̀ tőo kʌ̄-dhɛ̋ gúú* sa femme vient de préparer la sauce ◊ *yɤ̋ gɔ̀ ɤ̄ dhòo tùaa bhō'* il vient de saluer son grand frère

gōgō *n* **boîte** *(en fer blanc ou en plastique; généralement cylindrique et verticale)* ◊ *yà dhɔ̋ndhɔ̋n gōgō dhí-pűű* il a ouvert une boîte de lait

gɔ̀ŋ *n* **creux** ♦ *dhűű gɔ̀ŋ* creux d'arbre

gɔ̋ŋ 1 *n* **paludisme, palu, malaria** Syn. yàkpàyőo ♦ *gɔ̋ŋ slɔ̀ɔ* attraper le palu

gɔ̋ŋ 2 *n* **1** *dhűű gɔ̋ŋ* **surface intérieure de la fissure du tronc d'arbre 2 écorce** *(un grand morceau, on l'utilisait autrefois comme des nattes)* **3 couverture** *(de livre)*

gɔ̀ŋgɔ̋ŋ *n* **tambour, tambourin** *(de types différents; pour la danse tlűu tắn des notables) [cet instrument est joué par les membres des castes inférieures]* **1 tambourin d'aisselle** *(en forme de sablier, il se joue avec un bâtonnet)* **2 tambour** *(se joue avec deux bâtonnets)*

Gɔ̀ɔ {LOC Gɔ̀ɔdhɤ̄} *n* **Goo** *(peuple, langue et zone)*

gōo *n* **1 pente de colline** ♦ *tɔ̀n gōo* pente de colline/ de montagne **2 lit** *(de rivière, surtout dans les montagnes)*, **vallée** Syn. gōogā ◊ *yí yáa gōo tó* l'eau ne laisse pas son lit

gōɔ̀ *n* **cafard, blatte** *(les cafards au pays Dan sont gros, roux, ils piquent)*

gòodhē *n* ***Halcyon chelicuti*** **martin-chasseur strié** *(16 cm de long, poitrine et ventre blancs, ailes et croupion de couleur bleue ternie de grisâtre) [très répandu au Gwèètaa; s'attaque au mil]* ♦ *gòodhē bhä̀an* = gòodhē

Gɔ̀ɔdhɤ̄ *LOC de* Gɔ̀ɔ *Goo*

gōogā <pente-os> *n* **lit** *(de rivière, surtout dans les montagnes)*, **vallée** Syn. gōo

gɔ̀plɤ̀ɤ̄ <quitter-village.LOC> *n* ***Ploceus cucullatus, P. collaris*** **tisserin gendarme** Syn. dɛ̋bhä̀an, bhä̀antɛ̋ɛ, pɤ̂bhä̀an

gòyâ <Fr. goyave> *n* ***Psidium Guajava*** **goyave**

gɔ̃ 1) {LOC gɔ̄ɔdhɤ̄, SUB gɔ̀ɔ, gœ̀œ} ***loc.n*** *le cas locatif ne s'utilise que dans le sens 4.* **1.1** *rn* **tête** Qsyn. gwìnŋ̀dhɛ̋ ♦ *gɔ̃ gúú yɔ̀n* cerveau ♦ *yí yɤ̋ bhɛ̄n gɔ̀ɔ* l'eau arrive à la tête de l'homme ♦ *wà dhó wō gɔ̃ dūn'* ils sont partis pour les délibérations ♦ *yà ä̀ gɔ̃ bhō/kắn ä̀ dhíɤ* il lui a coupé la tête ♦ *tó ɤ̄ gɔ̃ píɤ* rester oisif, rester sans soucis ♦ *bhɛ̄n gɔ̃ bhō yʌ́nŋ̀dhɛ̋* mettre fin à la vie de qn **1.2 sommet** *(de toit)* ◊ *yà gbɔ̄ yà kɔ́dhɛ̄ɛ́ gɔ̀ɔ* il a mis le canari au sommet du toit de la case ronde *[pour protéger la jointure de la paille du toit contre la pluie]* **1.3** *rn* **pensées** *(ce qui remplit la tête)* ◊ *Yɔ̃ gɔ̃ yà tó yắ bhä̀* toutes les pensées de Yo ont été pour l'igname **2** *rn* **manche** *(d'un outil)* **3.1 partie extérieure** *(de plante)*, ext. **plante** *(entière)* ◊ *bāa gɔ̃* plante de manioc **3.2 fronde** *(de palme)* **4 terminaison** ♦ *yʌ̄ gɔ̃* fin de travail **5 préambule**

gɔ̀ 2) ***pp*** **1 à** *(exprime la possession ou la localisation temporaire chez qn)* ◊ *à lòo pɔ̄ŋ tà tɤ́ŋ dèdè bhā kɤ̄ dhʌ́n bhā yɤ̀ dhʌ́nglɔ̄ɔ́ndhʌ́n dō gɔ̀* au moment où ils ont atteint le pont, l'enfant y était avec un jeune homme ♦ *wʌ́ʌ̀gā yɤ̀ à gɔ̀* il a de l'argent *(même si l'argent est physiquement ailleurs)* **2 pour**, **de** *(indique au profit ou au détriment de qui se fait l'action)* ◊ *yà kwɛ́ɛ tā bhò gɔ̀* il a fermé la porte au cabri ◊ *bháa yà ī gɔ̀* réserve-moi du riz ◊ *bòbì yà yà ī gɔ̀* la poussière m'ennuie ◊ *yà wɔ̄ wɔ̀ɔ gɔ̀* il s'est couché par terre en attendant les singes ♦ *yɤ̀ dɔ̀ bhɛ̄n gɔ̀ yâ* ça ne va pas chez la personne **3.1 à cause de** ◊ *ī gɔ̀ gúu yà kʌ̄ gbíŋ̀ dɔ̄n gɔ̀* ma tête est lourde à cause de la toux **3.2 par** *(sens de l'agent)* Syn. kɔ̄ɔ 2 ◊ ... *kɛ́ɛ pʌ̄ bhɤ́ kɤ́ wó' bhɔ̀ɔn-sīʌ wáa' dɔ̄ wō dè gɔ̀ zúu* mais ils ne savent plus ce qu'ils cherchent **4** *marque possessive des noms locatifs non-relationnels au cas locatif, parfois des noms dans le groupe nominal du complément oblique* ◊ *bhán wɔ̀ɔ dō kún ī gɔ̀ bhláā* j'ai attrapé un singe sur mon champ de manioc ◊ *yɤ̀ kʌ̄ gà ɤ̄ gɔ̀ dhîì tà* il mourut dans son lit ◊ *Tòkpà yà wɛ́ Gɤ̀ɤ̀ gɔ̀ dhūn wɔ̀n bhà* Tokpa a accepté que Geu vienne (à la demande de Geu)

gɔ̀ 3) ***prev*** **tête**

gɔ̄ 1 ***n*** **1** ***Cordia platythyrsa Bah.*** **arbre** *(10-27 de hauteur, fleurs blanches en forme d'entonnoir qui forment de larges inflorescences)* **2 tambour à fente** *(grand tambour-xylophone sans membrane; fait de Cordia platythyrsa Bah.)* Qsyn. gɔ̄dhʌ́n ♦ *dhè bhɛ̄n bhɛ̄n yɑ́n pɛ́ɛn dō gɔ̄ zʌ̄* en un clin d'œil

gɔ̄ 2 ***n*** **fronde** *(de palme)*

gɔ̄ 3 {gɔ̀} ***n*** **véhicule; voiture, automobile** ◊ *sòò yɤ̀ gɔ̄ gɑ́n-sīʌ* le cheval est en train de tirer la charrette ♦ *gɔ̄ gɔ̀* cabine de chauffeur ♦ *gɔ̄ kɤ̀ɤkɤ̀ɤ* voitures d'occasion

gɔ̋ ***n*** *rare* **panthère, léopard** Syn. gwɛ̄ɛ

gɔ̂ {gɔ̀} ***n*** ***Cola nitida*** **cola, noix de cola** *[chez les Dan la cola est cultivée pour la vente et pour la consommation; on envoie les colas dans un village pour annoncer un événement aux membres de la famille : deux colas rouges signifient une maladie, trois – la mort, dix – la naissance, l'initiation ou le mariage; le messager est soit le neveu ou la nièce, soit encore un ami de la famille]* ♦ *gɔ̂ bhɛ̄* cabosse de cola ♦ *gɔ̂ bhlùu* paquet de cola *(fait de feuilles, ficelé; contient environ 40 noix; la façon habituelle de garder les colas au village)* ♦ *gɔ̂ gā* noix de cola ♦ *gɔ̂ gblúu* panier de colas *(plus de 200 noix)* ♦ *gɔ̂ wúu* casser les cabosses de cola ♦ *gɔ̂ pűu* (m) cola blanche *[plus cher que la cola rouge; est utilisée pour les sacrifices]* ♦ *gɔ̂ tīi, gɔ̂ zœ̀œndhē* cola rouge *[plus "quotidienne", comparée à la cola blanche; la cola rouge est symbole d'événements importants]* ♦ *bhɔ̋bhɔ̋ gɔ̀* noix de cola à surface lisse, dépourvue de partition *[on croit que celui qui mange cette noix aura des enfants sourds-muets]* ♦ *yɔ̋o súu gɔ̂* colas pour annoncer un heureux événement ♦ *dhʌ́n kpɔ́ yɔ̋o súu gɔ̂* colas pour annoncer la naissance ♦ *gbándhʌ́n kʌ̀' ká gɔ̂, gbándhʌ́n yī dà gɔ̂* colas pour annoncer l'initiation ♦ *dhē súu gɔ̂* colas pour annoncer le mariage ♦ *gā gɔ̂* colas pour annoncer la mort

gɔ̄bhàan <véhicule-oiseau> ***n*** *rare* **avion** Syn. vîɔ̀ŋ

gɔ̋bhȁan ***n*** ***Picathartes symnocephalus, P. oreas*** **picatharte chauve de Guinée** *(un oiseau : longues pattes,longs cou, queue et bec; dessous blanc, dessus gris, tête jaune, se déplace sur le sol par bonds)*

gɔ̏bhɛ̏n <tête-personne> ***n*** **1 chef, patron; maître** *(par rapport au serviteur)* <u>*Ant.*</u> <u>*gwʌ̄ʌ̋*</u> <u>*1*</u> ◊ *gwʌ̄ʌ̋-dhȕn wɔ̏n yɤ̏ gbɛ̋ɛ̏ ȁ-dhȕn gɔ̏bhɛ̏n gɔ̏* les serviteurs sont importants pour leur maître **2 personnalité** *(personne importante)*

gɔ̏bhɛ̏ndʌ̄ <tête-personne-père> ***n*** **chef, leader**

gɔ̏-bhō ***v vt*** **résoudre** ♦ *zā gɔ̏-bhō* juger l'affaire, faire l'arbitrage

gɔ̋dʌ̄ ***n*** **responsable de la case sacrée** ◊ *gűnŋkɔ̏ dhé ɤ́ dhɤ́ ȁ bhȁ gɔ̋dʌ̄ yɤ̏ dhɤ̏* chaque case sacrée a son responsable

gɔ̏-dɔ̄ <tête-arrêter> ***v vt*** **achever**; **régler** ◊ *pɤ̂ bhā' gúu wɔ̀ wɔ́n gbàn gɔ̏-dɔ̏ gɔ̄nŋdhɤ̄* dans ce village, on règle les affaires sous la paillote du chef

gɔ̏dɔ̄gāgɔ̏ <tête-attendre-mort-à> ***n*** *arch.* **poutre maîtresse** <u>*Syn.*</u> <u>*kɔ́gbàngɔ̏dhű*</u>

gɔ̏dɔ̄tȁpʌ̏ <tête-mettre-sur-chose> ***n*** **oreiller**

gɔ̄dhʌ́n ***n*** **tambour à fentes** *(fait d'un tronc d'arbre évidé ou d'un tronc de bambou, avec deux fentes; est joué avec deux bâtonnets; autrefois, le tambour était fabriqué en bois de l'arbre gɔ̄ et pouvait avoir jusqu'à quatre fentes) [instrument des hommes, il appartenait à l'association "gwa" et était joué lors de la danse du même nom; maintenant il est surtout utilisé par les enfants pour chasser les animaux des champs]* <u>*Qsyn.*</u> <u>*gɔ̄*</u> <u>*2*</u> ♦ *gɔ̄dhʌ́n zʌ̏ ká dhű{dhʌ́n}* bâtonnet pour jouer du tambour à fentes

gɔ̏dhɛ̋ <tête-feuille> ***n*** **cheveux, chevelure** ◊ *ā gȕn dhʌ́ndhīʌŋ́ ká, ī gɔ̏dhɛ̋ yɤ̏ gȕn gbɛ́, kɛ̋ɛŋ dɛ̀ɛ ī gɔ̏dhɛ̋ yȁ tó dódó* quand j'étais jeune fille, mes cheveux étaient épais, mais maintenant mes cheveux sont rares

gɔ̂dhɛ̋ <cola-feuille> ***n*** **1 feuille de l'arbre cola 2 feuille pour envelopper le cola** *(de la plante sɛ̋ɛ́dhɛ́)*

gɔ̏dhíɤ <tête-devant> ***v vt*** **régner sur**

gɔ̏dhíɤbhɛ̏n <tête-fin-personne> ***n*** **président, leader** ♦ *sɛ́ gɔ̏dhíɤbhɛ̏n* le président du pays

gɔ̏dhíɤsȕ <tête-adj.> ***adj*** **important**, **essentiel**

gɔ̄dhű 1 <tambour-arbre> ***n*** **baguette de tambour**

gɔ̄dhű 2 ***n*** **grand tambour cylindrique** *(à une seule membrane tendue par des fiches) [se trouve dans la case sacrée; le son de ce tambour annonce le décès d'un des membres de l'association secrète de la case sacrée]*

gɔ̏gúsʌ̏bhɛ̏n <tête-dans-bon-personne> ***n*** **personne intelligente** *(éduquée)*

gɔ̏gúsʌ̏-dhɛ̏ <tête-intérieur-bon-abstr.> ***n*** **intelligence**

gɔ̏gúwú <tête-dans-casser> ***n*** **maux de tête** *(dans la zone du front, facile à soigner; la cause peut en être la chaleur, la fatigue, le paludisme)* <u>*Qsyn.*</u> <u>*gɔ̏kʌ̄*</u>

gɔ̀gbàŋdʌ̄ <tête-aîné-père> ***n*** **grosse tête** *(un terme moqueur pour celui dont la tête est disproportionnellement large)*

gɔ̀kʌ̄ <tête-chasser> ***n*** **maux de tête** *(profonds, forts, récurrents, difficiles à soigner; la cause fréquente est le fait de transporter des charges lourdes sur la tête)* Qsyn. *gɔ̀gúwúí* ♦ *gɔ̀kʌ̄ yɔ̃ɔ̃* kaolin pour soigner les maux de tête

gɔ̀-kʌ̄ {gɔ̀-kʌ̀} *v vt* **battre** *(à un jeu)* ◊ *yá kā gɔ̀ bhá kʌ̄* nous vous avons battus de nouveau

gɔ̀-kpɔ́ {gɔ̀-kpɔ̄} *v vt* **épargner**, **économiser** ◊ *Gbàtò yà wʌ̀ʌ̀gā gbɛ́ gɔ̀-kpɔ́* Gbato a épargné beaucoup d'argent

gɔ̀-lɤ̀ <tête-attacher> *v vt* **tresser les cheveux** *(à qn)* ◊ *yà ɤ̄ dhē gɔ̀-lɤ̀* elle a tressé les cheveux à sa mère

gɔ̀n 1 ***n*** **1 paillote** *(hangar, le plus souvent rond, sans murs)* Qsyn. *gɔ̄ndhɛ̀* ◊ *yʌ̄kʌ̄bhɛ̀n-dhùn wò wō tɛ́ɛ-pā-sīʌ gɔ̀n wlɤ̀ɤ* les travailleurs se reposent sous la paillote **2 tas** ♦ *kɤ̄ŋ gɔ̀n* tas d'épis de maïs

gɔ̀n 2 ***n*** **lutte, bagarre** ♦ *gɔ̀n gɔ̄ɔn* lutter, se bagarrer *(en cherchant à renverser l'adversaire)* ◊ *gɔ̀n gɔ̄ɔn-sɯ̀ yáa sʌ̀* se bagarrer n'est pas bon

gɔ̀n ***n*** **1** *rn* **mari, époux** Qsyn. *dhēgɔ̀ndʌ̄* ♦ *ū gɔ̀n-dhùn* mon mari avec ses petits-frères **2** *rn* **beau-frère cadet** *(frère cadet du mari) [n'est que rarement utilisé comme forme d'adresse; l'emploi abusif serait ressenti comme une provocation sexuelle]* Syn. dhìnbhɔ̄ɔ̀n Qsyn. *bhá 1* **3** *rn badin* **belle-sœur cadette** *(sœur cadette du mari)*

gɔ̄n 1 {A, gɔ̄n-dhùn pl. A, gɔ̄n-sɯ̀ foc. A; gɔ̄ngɔ̄n Int. pl. A, gɔ̄ngɔ̄n-dhùn Int. pl. A, la forme avec -dhùn est préférable} ***adj*** **honorable**

gɔ̄n 2 ***n*** **1 mâle** ♦ *dù gɔ̄n* taureau ♦ *gbɛ̂n gɔ̄n* chien mâle **2 homme** *(mâle)*

gɔ́n {gɔ̄n} ***v*** *base du verbe* zò-gɔ́n *regretter l'absence*

gɔ̄ndʌ̄, **gɔ̄ɔ̀ndʌ̄** <homme-père> ***n*** **homme; monsieur** *(terme d'adresse respectueux utilisé envers l'homme plus âgé ou de même âge)*

gɔ̄ndʌ̄dhʌ́n <male-père-diminutif> ***n*** **homme** *(à partir d'environ 30 ans)*, **garçon** *lv. le plus souvent au sg.; (m) avec une nuance péjorative* Qsyn. *bhīndhʌ́n*

gɔ̄ngɔ̄n *Int. pl. de* gɔ̄n *honorable*

gɔ̄nŋ̀dhɛ̀ {LOC gɔ̄nŋdhɤ̄} ***loc.n*** **paillote** *(hangar rond sans mur, mais construction permanente) [sous les paillotes les forgerons font leurs forges, les chefs accueillent les visiteurs] pour la forme du cas locatif, un redoublement à valeur d'intensité de l'action est possible* Qsyn. *gɔ̀n 1* ◊ *pìɤbhōbhɛ̀n yɤ̀ pìɤ bhò gɔ̄nŋdhɤ̄* le forgeron travaille à la paillote ◊ *Tìa bhà gɔ̄nŋ̀dhɛ̀ yà gɤ̄* la paillote de Tia a brûlé ♦ *wà dhó dhīaŋ ká gɔ̄nŋdhɤ̄* ils sont allés avec le litige devant le chef

gɔ̄nŋdhɤ̄ ***loc.n*** *LOC de* gɔ̄nŋ̀dhɛ̀ *paillote*

gɔ̀ŋ ***n*** **1 arbre** *(esp.) [on en met l'écorce dans le vin de palme pour en accélérer la fermentation]* **2 écorce de cet arbre** ♦ *gɔ̀ŋ wɛ̀* vin de palme que l'écorce du "gong" a servi à faire fermenter ♦ *yà gɔ̀ŋ dȁ wē bhȁ* il a fait fermenter le vin de palme avec l'écorce "gong" **3 chenille consommable** *(esp.; noire, grosse, se trouve sur l'arbre "gong", rare)* Syn. *gɔ̀ŋgā*

gɔ̄ŋdʌ̄ ***n Corvus albus*** **corbeau**

gɔ̀ŋgā ***n*** **chenille consommable** *(esp.; noire, grosse, vit sur l'arbre "gong", rare)* Syn. *gɔ̀ŋ*

gɔ̏ɔ ***loc.n*** *SUP de* gɔ̏ 1) *tête*

gɔ̀ɔ ***n*** **champignon** *(esp.; le plus gros champignon, pousse sur les termitières)*

gɔ̄ɔ 1 <*gɔ̏ gú 'tête-dans'> ***n rn*** **tête** *dans quelques expressions figées* ♦ *ȁ gɔ̄ɔ yɤ̏ gbɛ́ɛ̀/sæ̀æ* il est désobéissant ♦ *ȁ gɔ̄ɔ yɤ̏ tā-sʉ̀ʉ ká* il est enrhumé

gɔ̄ɔ 2 → gœ̄œ *impénétrable*

gɔ̄ɔ́ ***n*** **brisure** *(les parties concassées du riz ou du manioc qui restent quand on pile; on les donne aux poulets)*

gɔ́ɔ̏ → gœ́œ̏ *haricot sauvage*

gɔ̄ɔ-bhō ***v vt*** **divertir** *(de – ká)*

gɔ̏ɔdhɛ̏ {LOC gɔ̄ɔdhɤ} ***loc.n*** **source** *(de fleuve, de rivière)* ◊ *ā dhɔ̏ dȁ' yí ká á dhó ȁ gɔ̄ɔdhɤ* je vais monter à la source du fleuve

gɔ̀ɔdhɛ́ <champignon(esp.)-feuille> ***n*** **champignon** *(brun, agaricacée; se mange cru ou en sauce avec la peau)*

gɔ̄ɔdhɤ *LOC de* gɔ̏ɔdhɛ̏ *source*

gɔ̄ɔgbɛ́ɛ̀bhɛ̀n <tête-difficile-personne> ***n*** **1 voyou, brigand 2 personne têtue**

gɔ̄ɔgbɛ́ɛ̀dhʌ̀n <tête-difficile-enfant> ***n*** **polisson** *(enfant désobéissant)*

gɔ̄ɔgblɛ̀ɛn <tête-long> ***adj*** **long, de longue durée**

gɔ̀ɔn <de *gɔ̀n gɔ̄ɔn ? 'lutte-faire'> ***v vi*** **lutter** *[les lutteurs dan cherchent à renverser l'adversaire pour qu'il touche la terre avec son dos]* ◊ *dhʌ́n glɔ̄ɔ́n plɛ̀ wɔ̀ gɔ̀ɔn-sīʌ* les deux jeunes hommes sont en train de lutter

gɔ̄ɔn 1 {gɔ̄ɔn} ***v*** **1** ***vt*** **faire** *(lutte, bagarre, guerre; à – ká)* ◊ *yɤ̏ gɔ̀n gɔ̄ɔn sʌ̏* il lutte bien ◊ *Zân wāȁ ɤ̄ bhā dhēbʌ̏ wɔ̀ gɔ̀n gɔ̄ɔn-sīʌ* Jean et sa femme se bagarrent **2** ***vt*** **jouer** *(un jeu)* ♦ *klȁatīȉ gɔ̄ɔn* jouer aux cartes

gɔ̄ɔn 2 {gɔ̄ɔn} ***v vi*** **grouiller, être en abondance** ◊ *wèe yȁ gɔ̄ɔn ȁ gɔ̏ gú* il a beaucoup de poux sur la tête

gɔ̄ɔ̏n 1) ***n*** **homme** *(mâle, tous les âges)*, **garçon** *Iv.* ◊ *dhʌ́n sʉ̃́ɛ̀sīɤ ɤ̄ n̄ kwɛ̀ɛ̀ bhā, gɔ̄ɔ̏n-dhʉ̀n wɔ̀ sɔ̃́ɔdhʉ̃́, dhēbʌ̏-dhʉ̀n wɔ̀ yȉisīɤ* des neuf enfants qui sont avec moi, cinq sont des garçons et quatre sont des filles ♦ *yáa gɔ̄ɔ̏n ká* il est impuissant *(sexuellement)*

gɔ̄ɔ̀n 2) ***adj*** **mâle** ◊ *yɤ̀ gɔ̄ɔ̀n-dhùn gbàn pɛ́pɛ́ píɤ dhɛ̀ dhʌ́n gɔ̄ɔ̀n yɤ̀ kʌ̄ wō gɔ̀* tous les hommes veulent avoir un fils ♦ *bɛ́ɛ̀ gɔ̄ɔ̀n* neveu

gɔ̄ɔ̀n-dhɛ̀ <mâle-abstr.> ***n*** **1 virilité** *(état et qualités de l'homme)* ♦ *gɔ̄ɔ̀n-dhɛ̀ yùa* maladie de l'homme *(hernie, blennorragie, impuissance, etc.)* **2** *rn, fn* **sexe de l'homme** Syn. *gɔ̄ɔ̀ndhɛ̀gā, kpāán, kpāángā, kplɤ̀ɤ, kplɤ̀ɤgā* ♦ *gɔ̄ɔ̀n-dhɛ̀ yí* sperme ♦ *à {bhà} gɔ̄ɔ̀n-dhɛ̀ yáa wlūū́ű* il est un impuissant **3 force, puissance**

gɔ̄ɔ̀ndhɛ̀gā <male-place-os> ***n*** *rn euph.* **sexe de l'homme** Syn. *gɔ̄ɔ̀ndhɛ̀, kpāán, kpāángā, kplɤ̀ɤ, kplɤ̀ɤgā*

gɔ̄ɔpʌ̀ → gœ̄œpʌ̀ *cadeau*

gɔ̀tà-dhɔ́ {gɔ̀tà-dhɔ̄} ***v*** *vt* **racheter** *(contre une rançon)*

gɔ̀-yɛ́ {gɔ̀-yɛ̀} ***v*** **1** *vt* **couper les épis 2** *vt* **résoudre 3** *vt* **terminer** ◊ *yà sʌ́ʌdhɛ́ dɔ̄ yà à gɔ̀-yɛ́* il a fini ses études

gɔ̂yíbhɤ̀ɤ <cola-eau-vipère du Gabon> ***n*** ***Causus rhombeatus (?)*** **vipère du Cap, vipère qui saute** *(brun-gris, jusqu'à 90 cm de long, la tête et la queue petites; très venimeuse; agressive, peut sauter en hauteur d'un mètre; considérée comme mangeable)*

gɔ̄zīɤbhɛ̀n <véhicule-passer-personne> ***n*** **chauffeur**

gɤ́ {gɤ̀} ***v*** **1** 1) *vi* **brûler** ♦ *à zūʌ́ yà yà gɤ́-sùù bhà* il a eu du chagrin 2) *vt* **brûler** ♦ *dhɛ̀ gɤ́* brûler le champ *(au cours du défrichage)* **2** *vi* **brûler** *(de la nourriture)* ◊ *bháa gɤ́-sùù bhā dhʌ́n-dhùn wàa bhɤ̀* les enfants ont mangé le riz brûlé ◊ *à bhà sɔ̄ yɤ̀ gɤ̀ kɔ́ɔdhɤ́* son vêtement a été entamé par le feu dans la maison **3** 1) *vi* **se brûler** ◊ *yà gɤ́ ɤ̄ gɛ̀ɛn* il s'est brûlé au pied 2) *vt* **brûler** *(provoquer une brûlure)* ◊ *gbɔ̄ wɔ́wɔ́sùù yàa kɔ̀ gɤ́* il s'est brûlé la main avec un pot chaud ♦ *yà ɤ̄ dè gɤ́* il s'est brûlé

gɤ̀ŋ, gɤ́ŋ̀ *les variantes tonales sont en distribution lexicalisée; par rapport aux animaux, gɤ̀ŋ est normalement utilisé, par rapport aux humains, normalement gɤ́ŋ̀, mais il y a des exceptions* ***n*** *rn* **cuisse** Syn. *gbāń, gbāńbhlʌ́* ◊ *yà n̄ gìì n̄ gɤ́ŋ̀ / gɤ̀ŋ bhà* il m'a blessé à la cuisse *avec les autres personnes, seule la forme gɤ́ŋ̀ est possible* ◊ *ūū bhā wūū bhā, n̄ gbā à gɤ̀ŋ ká kɤ̄ á à dhɔ́* vends-moi le gigot de ton animal que voici

gɤ́ŋ ***n*** **bord** ♦ *yāń gɤ́ŋ* coin de l'oeil ♦ *yí gɤ́ŋ* bord de l'eau ♦ *bɔ̄ kpìnŋ gɤ́ŋ píɤ !* va au bord de la route ! ♦ *à yà gɤ́ŋ tà* mets-le de côté ♦ *à bhà pìɤgāsòò gɛ̀n-dhùn wà yà gɤ́ŋ tà* les roues de son vélo sont de travers ♦ *dɔ̄ gɤ́ŋ ká* pencher (un récipient)

gɤ́ŋgɤ̀ŋ {P S, gɤ́ŋgɤ̀ŋ-dhùn pl. A, gɤ́ŋgɤ̀ŋ-sùù foc. A, gɤ́ŋgɤ̀ŋ-sùù-dhùn foc. pl. A; gɤ́ŋgɤ́ŋ-dhùn Int. pl. A, gɤ́ŋgɤ́ŋ-sùù-dhùn Int. foc. pl. A} *la forme plurielle avec le ton extra-haut à la fin transmet une nuance péjorative* ***adj*** **1 déformé** ◊ *bhān pìɤgāsòò gɛ̀n yà kʌ̄ gɤ́ŋgɤ̀ŋ* la roue de mon vélo s'est déformée **2 bizarre**; **ridicule** ♦ *kɔ́ gɤ́ŋgɤ̀ŋ-dhùn* maisons bizarres ♦ *kɔ́-{dhùn} gɤ́ŋgɤ́ŋ-{dhùn}* pej. maisons ridicules ◊ *Zân kʌ̄ wɔ̀n-dhʌ́n-dhùn wɔ̀ gɤ́ŋgɤ̀ŋ / gɤ́ŋgɤ́ŋ ká* le comportement de Jean est bizarre

gɤ́ŋgɤ́ŋ-dhùn *Int. pl. de* gɤ́ŋgɤ̀ŋ *déformé*

gɤ̄ŋgɤ́ŋklɔ̀ɔ ***n*** **liane** *(espèce)*

gɤ̏ŋklɤ̏ɤ̏bhɛ̏n; **gɤ̏ŋklɤ̄ɤ́bhɛ̏n** *arch.* <cuisse-court-personne> ***n*** **boiteux** *(qui a une jambe plus courte que l'autre)*

gɤ̏ɤ̏, **gɤ̀ɤ** *dans les mots composés, le ton final extra-bas est remplacé par le bas si le mot suivant est à ton bas* ***n*** **1** ***Chlorophora excelsa*** **iroko** *(jusqu'à 50 de haut, bois dur et très recherché)* ♦ *gɤ̏ɤ̏ dhṳ̏* arbre iroko **2 Gueu** *(le nom est donné à l'un des jumeaux)*

gœ̏œ 1 ***n*** **1** ***Cercocebus*** **cercocèbe** *(singe gris, à museau allongé et paupières supérieures blanches, pèse 5 à 10 kg)* **2 Gaa** *(masque-coureur des hommes)*

gœ̏œ 2 ***n*** **fois** Syn. *kótȁ* ◊ *yà dhūn gœ̏œ plɛ̀* il est venu deux fois

gœ̏œ 3 *SUP de* gɔ̏ 1) *tête*

gœ̄œ 1 1), **gɔ̄ɔ** {gœ̀œ} ***v vi*** **faire un cadeau** *(à – gɔ̏, spontanément, au cours d'une fête)* Qsyn. *gbœ̄œ*

gœ̄œ 1 2), **gɔ̄ɔ** ***n*** *dans quelques expressions figées* **cadeau** *(fait aux danseurs ou aux travailleurs ayant labouré un champ)* Syn. *gɔ̄ɔpʌ̏* ♦ *yà gœ̄œ bhō tɤ̋n kʌ̄ dhɛ̏ gɔ̏* il a fait un cadeau à la danseuse

gœ̄œ 2, **gɔ̄ɔ** {A} ***adj*** **vierge, dense** *(forêt)*

gœ́œ̏, **gɔ́ɔ̏** ***n*** ***Piliostigma thonningii*** **"haricot sauvage"** *(buisson dont les cosses à la surface laineuse produisent une poussière qui provoque des démangeaisons très fortes)* Syn. *gbɛ̂ndhʌ́ngœ́œ̏* ♦ *gœ́œ̏ yɛ̋ɛn* duvet et poussière du haricot sauvage

gœ̄œpʌ̏, **gɔ̄ɔpʌ̏** <donner cadeau-chose> ***n*** **cadeau** *(offert en général aux danseurs ou aux travailleurs ayant travaillé au champ)* Syn. *gœ̄œ*

gū ***n*** ***Nandinia binotata*** **nandinie**

gú (gw), **gwɯ́** (t) {gȕ} ***n rn*** **ventre** Qsyn. *glű́*, *glű́dhɛ̏* ♦ *gú sɯ́* devenir enceinte, tomber enceinte Syn. *dɔ̏ɔ̏ndhūn* ◊ *bhlȕn dhɔ̀ɔ yɤ̏ bhɔ̏ kɤ̄ ā Kwɪ́tīi gȕ ká* ce riz a poussé lorsque j'étais enceinte de Kouatii ♦ *kȁa [bhlȕn, kɤ̄ŋ] yà gú sɯ́* la canne à sucre [le riz, le maïs] a fait des épis ♦ *ň gú yà dɔ̄* je suis rassasié *(refus poli d'une offre de nourriture)* ♦ *ȁ gú yà dɔ̄ ȁ dhɪ́ɤ* son ventre est ballonné ♦ *ȁ gú yà bhɔ̄* son ventre a grandi ♦ *ȁ gú yà bhán ȁ bhȁ* il est constipé ♦ *ň gú yà tó dhɛ̏ɛnsɯ̏* j'ai mal au ventre ♦ *yà fȁan sɯ́ ȁ gú gbàan bhɔ̄* il a pris du poids, son ventre a grossi *[contrairement à l'embonpoint général, le gros ventre est mal vu par les Dan]* ♦ *yȁ wɔ̄ ɤ̄ gú tȁ* il s'est couché sur le ventre

gūdlɔ́nŋ̏ <Fr. goudron> ***n*** **asphalt; route asphaltée, goudron** *Iv.*

gūdhʌ́n ***n*** **pointeau** *(de forgeron)*

gű́dhɛ̏ (t) ***n*** **douleurs de l'accouchement** Syn. *glű́kʌ̄ -ya kun* ♦ *gű́dhɛ̏ yȁ' kūn* elle a eu les douleurs de l'accouchement

gūɛ̋ɛndhɤ̄ ***onomat*** *exprime le bond d'un carnassier vers sa proie* ◊ *gwʌ̋ndhʌ́n yȁ sā bhɔ̄ɔ̏n tȁ gūɛ̋ɛndhɤ̄* le chat s'est jeté sur la souris

gūn {gūn} ***v*** **1** *vi* **être** *(au passé)* ◊ *pʌ́ ɤ́ gūn ň gɔ̏, bhán ȁ gbàn dhūn' dhɛ̏* je lui ai donné tout ce que j'avais **2** *verbe auxiliaire servant à reporter l'action au passé* ◊ *Gbȁtȍ yà gūn yà* *yâàdhūn dhún, kɛ́ɛ yɤ́ wlùɯ zúú* Gbato était déjà assis, mais il s'est levé de nouveau **3** *le plus souvent en combinaison avec la conjonction kɤ̄, avec le pronom subjonctif du sujet et l'infinitif du verbe principal, il sert à marquer une action qui doit en suivre une autre* ◊ *kwā̀ pʌ̄ bhɤ̄̀ blɛ̀ɛsɯ̀, kɤ̄ kwá gūn wē bhūn'* mangeons d'abord avant de prendre du vin de palme **4** *suivi du prospectif, exprime une action non-réalisée (qui dépend d'une condition irréelle)* ◊ *yɤ̄̀ kʌ̄ n̄ bhlòo dhún, ā gùn bhāan à gɔ̄̀ bhā̀n* s'il m'avait coincé, je l'aurais giflé **5** *dans une proposition introduite par la conjonction kɤ̄ et suivi de l'adverbe kɤ̀, exprime le sens de continuation d'un état, "encore"* ◊ *ūū dhɔ̀ dhó' kűnbhánhdhán tùaabhō' kɤ̄ ūū bhā pàŋ bhā yɤ̄̀ gùn kɤ̀ŋ pűu* tu dois aller saluer le préfet, tant que ton pantalon est encore propre

gùnŋ (gw) ***n*** **farine fine du riz** *(on l'obtient après le 5ème pilage, à côté des grains décortiqués)* *Syn.* *gbòŋ* ♦ *yà gùnŋ bhō* elle a obtenu de la farine de riz fine

gűnŋ ***n*** **endroit sacré**, **case sacrée** ◊ *pɤ̄̀ bhɛ̀n-dhùn wà gűnŋ dō dɔ̄* les habitants du village ont bâti une case sacrée ♦ *dhīaŋ tɛ́ɛ yà kʌ̄ à-dhùn bhà gbɛ́ɛ̀, wà dhó gűnŋ gúú* *arch.* l'affaire s'étant avérée difficile pour eux, ils sont allés se consulter

gűnŋdhɛ̀ {LOC gűnŋdhɤ̄, LOC pl. gűnŋdhɛ̀-dhùn gúú} ***loc.n*** **case sacrée** *(avec l'espace environnant clôturé) [on y discute des questions importantes concernant tout le village, les décisions prises à la case sacrée sont obligatoires pour tout le village; seuls les notables peuvent y entrer]* *Qsyn.* *gűnŋkɔ̀* ◊ *Zân yà dhó gűnŋdhɤ̄* Jean est allé dans la case sacrée

gűnŋdhɤ̄ ***loc.n*** *LOC de* gűnŋdhɛ̀ *case sacrée*

gűnŋkɔ̀ <endroit sacré-maison> ***n*** **case sacrée** *(ronde, clôturée, une par village, surveillée par un gardien; seuls les hommes initiés peuvent y entrer; on y organise des réunions des notables)* *Qsyn.* *gűnŋ*, *gűnŋdhɛ̀* ◊ *Zân yà dhó gűnŋkɔ̀ gúú* Jean est allé dans la case sacrée ◊ *wɔ̀ gűnŋkɔ̀ dɔ̀ dhɛ̀kpœ̀œyì dōsɛ̄nŋ dhʌ̀n à ká* on bâtit la case sacrée en un seul jour

gűnŋkɔ̀dhíɤbhɛ̀n ***n*** **garant de la case sacrée**

gúŋ̀gùŋ {A P S, gúŋ̀gùŋ-dhùn pl. A, gúŋ̀gùŋ-sɯ̀ foc. A, gúŋ̀gùŋ-sɯ̀-dhùn pl. foc. A, S; gúŋ̀gúŋ̀ Int. pl. A P S, gúŋ̀gúŋ̀-dhùn Int. pl. A S, gúŋ̀gúŋ̀-sɯ̀ Int. pl. foc. A, gúŋ̀gúŋ̀-sɯ̀-dhùn Int. pl. foc. A} ***adj*** **trapu**, **court et gros** *(des gens, des objets allongés)* ♦ *blúù bhɛ̄ gúŋ̀gùŋ* pain court ♦ *glɔ̄ɔ bhɛ̄ gúŋ̀gúŋ̀* banane courte et épaisse ◊ *bhɛ̄n klɤ̄ɤ̀ gúŋ̀gùŋ* homme gros et trapu

gúŋ̀gúŋ̀ ***adj*** *Int. pl. de* gúŋ̀gùŋ *court et gros*

Gűu ***n*** **Gou** *(masque des femmes) [est considéré comme la "petite sœur" du masque Kòŋ; sort lors de l'initiation des femmes, aux baptêmes et aux funérailles des femmes]* ♦ *Gűu tấn* "guutan" *(chant et danse de l'association des femmes durant lesquels les hommes jouent des tambours)*

gűudʌ̄ < ?-père> ***n*** **caméléon**

gùuŋdhɤ̄̀ ***onomat*** **boum** *(un son grondant)* ◊ *yà ɤ̄ gɔ̄̀ bhàn sı́āa gùuŋdhɤ̄̀* il s'est cogné la tête par terre : boum !

gɯ́ɯ 1) *n rn* **intérieur** Qsyn. gɯ́, gblɯ̃ɯ, gblɯ̃ɯdhɛ̏ ◊ *dhɛ̏ gɯ́ yà tlɤ̄ɤ* il fait noir (à l'intérieur) ◊ *dhɛ̏ gɯ́-dhùn wà yà wɛ́ bhɔ̄nŋdhɤ̄* il est devenu sombre tout d'un coup ♦ *à yɑ̃n gɯ́ yɤ̏ sʌ̀* ses rêves sont prophétiques ◊ *kɔ́ yā à gɯ́ dhɛ̏ yɤ̏ sʌ̀* l'intérieur de cette maison est jolie ♦ *à yɑ̃n gɯ́ ɤ́ kàn* il est habile (s'adapte vite; ses mouvements sont rapides et précis)

gɯ́ɯ 2) *pp* **1 dans** ◊ *wà dhɯ̃ɯ tā sɛ́ yā' gɯ́...* si un arbre est planté dans ce sol... **2 sur** *(arbre)* ◊ *Gbàtò yɤ̏ sɤ̄ dhɯ̀ gɯ́* Gbato est sur le palmier **3 dans** *(localisation temporelle)* ◊ *yī dà tɔ̀n bhā à bhà yūʌŋ gɯ́* nous avons grimpé à la montagne il y a un certain temps ◊ *yɤ̏ dhʌ́n bhā à dɔ̀ dɛ̀ɛ dhʌ̀n à gɯ́* c'est aujourd'hui qu'il a connu la nature de cet enfant **4** ... *wɔ̀n gɯ́* **pour qch, à cause de qch** ◊ *yɤ̏ kwā dhɛ̏ pʌ̄bhɤ̏ wɔ̀n gɯ́* elle nous a appelés pour manger ◊ *yɤ̏ yɔ̃n pɯ̃u bhā à dīn-gà à dhɔ́ wɔ̀n gɯ́* il est en train de goûter l'huile rouge pour l'acheter ◊ *à gɯ́ tɑ̃n* une danse à cette occasion **5 à l'avis de** ◊ *yɪ́gā yā yɤ̏ bhɤ̀ɤ n̄ gɯ́ vɑ̃andhɤ̄* à mon avis, cette rivière est en train de tarir vite ◊ ... *kɤ̄ yɤ̏ kʌ̄ klàŋ̀gɔ̀bhɛ̀ndʌ̄ gɯ́ dhɛ̀ yáa ɤ̄ flʌ́ʌ̀ gɯ́...* afin que le professeur pense qu'il ne se sent pas bien

gɯ́ɯ 3) *prev* **intérieur**

gɯ́-bà <dans-grossir> *v vt* **débroussailler** *(avec la machette, quand les mauvaises herbes sont déjà grandes)* Syn. gɯ́-zʌ̄ ♦ *bāa {dhɛ̏} gɯ́-bà* débroussailler le champ de manioc

gɯ́-blɯ̄ɯ̀ {gɯ́-blɯ̀ɯ; Int. gɯ́-blɯ̄ɯ̀-blɯ̄ɯ̀} *v vt* **fouiller dans**

gɯ́-bhān {gɯ́-bhān} *v vt* **comprendre** ◊ *wò wō kó wò gɯ́-bhān* ils se comprennent

gɯ́-bhō {gɯ́-bhō} *v vt* **désherber** *(avec les mains ou la houe, quand les mauvaises herbes ne sont pas encore trop grandes)* ♦ *bāa {dhɛ̏} gɯ́-bhō* désherber le champ de manioc

gɯ́-bhɔ̄ {gɯ́-bhɔ̄} *v vt* **brûler** *(à l'intérieur, intensivement; d'une substance caustique)* ◊ *kwɪ́ dhàan bɛ̀dhɛ́ bhá yɤ̏ bhūn, yɤ̏ bhɪ̄ʌʌ gɯ́-bhɔ̀ wɛ́ɛndhɤ̄* il y a un médicament des Blancs, il brûle la plaie

gɯ́-dān {gɯ́-dān} *v* **1** *vt* **essayer** *(pour l'efficacité)* **2** *vt* **essayer** *(de faire qch)*

gɯ́-dɔ̄ {gɯ́-dɔ̄} <dans-savoir> *v* **1.1** *vt* **s'habituer à** *(personne)* ◊ *kwā kwā kó gɯ́-dɔ̀* nous sommes habitués l'un à l'autre **1.2** *vt* **bien supporter** ◊ *yɤ̏ dhɛ́ndhɛ́n gɯ́-dɔ̀* il supporte bien le froid, il est habitué au froid **2** *vr* *ɤ̄ gɯ́-dɔ̄ gbɛ́ɛ̀* **s'efforcer**, **faire un effort**

gɯ́dhɛ̏ {LOC gɯ́dhɤ̄} *loc.n rn* **intérieur** ◊ *wà dhūn glɔ̄ɔ ká kɔ́ yā à gɯ́dhɤ̄* ils ont apporté les bananes dans cette maison ♦ *n̄ dɛ̀ gɯ́dhɛ̏ wɔ̀n bhɯ̀n* c'est mon affaire à moi

gɯ́-dhìʌʌn *v vi* *à yɑ̃n gɯ́ yɤ̏ dhìʌʌn-sīʌ* **avoir des vertiges**, **avoir la tête qui tourne** Syn. gɯ́-zīɤ ◊ *dīi yɤ̏ n̄ yɑ̃n gɯ́ sɛ̄ɛ́ndhʌ́n dhìʌʌn-sīʌ* j'ai des vertiges légers causées par la faim

gɯ́dhɤ̄ *loc.n LOC de* gɯ́dhɛ̏

gɯ́-gā {gɯ́-gā} *v* **1** 1) *vi* **se fatiguer** *(à – bhà)* ◊ *n̄ gɯ́ yà gā* je suis épuisé ◊ *Sàó gɯ́ yà gā Gɤ̀ɤ̏ tà-kún-sɯ̀ bhà* Sao est fatigué d'aider Geu 2) *vt* **fatiguer**; **embêter** ◊ *dhʌ́n* *yíbhōsɯ̀-dhɯ̀n wò bhɛ̄n wɛ́ɛ-dhɯ̀n gɯ́-gà* les enfants gâtés embêtent les gens **2** 1) *vi* **être déçu** *(de – wɔ̀n ká)* ◊ *n̄ gɯ́ yà gā ɯ̄ wɔ̀n ká* je suis déçu par toi 2) *vt* **décourager**, **décevoir** ◊ *Sàkpà yà n̄ gɯ́-gā* Sakpa m'a déçu

gɯ́-gɑ̋n {gɯ́-gàn} *v* **1** *vt* **masser** *(frictionner)* **2.1** 1) *vt* **remettre en place** *(luxation)* 2) *vr* **s'étirer** **2.2** *vt gɯ́-gɑ̋n kő̄o* **résoudre** *(problème)* **3** *vt gɯ́-gɑ̋n kő̄o* **changer** *(de l'argent)* ◊ *bhān wʌ́ʌ̀ glɯ̋ɯ́ dō yā à gɯ́-gɑ̋n kő̄o n̄ dhɛ̀* fais-moi la monnaie de ce billet de cinq mille francs

gɯ́glà <intérieur-grandir> *n* **miracle**

gɯ̋gɯ̋sɯ̀ *adj Int. de* glɯ̋ɯ *amer*

gɯ́-gbàn <dans-enfoncer> *v vt* **mettre sous la protection du fétiche** *(la maison, en cachant le fétiche sous le sol)* ♦ *yà ɤ̄ bhā kɔ́ gɯ́-gbàn* il a caché le fétiche-protecteur dans sa maison

gɯ́gbɛ́ɛ̀-dhɛ̀ <intérieur-difficile-abstr.> *n* **force** *(physique)*, **capacité**

gɯ́-gblɤ̀ *v vt* **nettoyer** *(la maison)*

gɯ́-gblɯ̀ <dans-diviser> *v vt* **diviser**, **distribuer** *(entre – tà)* ◊ *kɔ̀lòokótà bhā yɤ̀ bhɤ̀pʌ̀ gɯ́-gblɯ̀ bhɛ̄n-dhɯ̀n tà* cette association distribue les produits alimentaires aux gens

gɯ́-klōo {gɯ́-klòo} *v vt* **nettoyer en grattant** *(le fond du récipient)* ◊ *tǽǣ gɯ́-klōo sʌ̀ ká* nettoie bien la cuvette *(avec le doigt)*

gɯ́klɤ̀bhā (m) *adv* **soudain** Syn. *sɩ́àabhā*

gɯ́-kún {gɯ́-kūn} *v* **1** *vt* **insister sur**, **ne pas renoncer à** ◊ *Gbàtò yà wɔ́n bhā gɯ́-kún* Gbato a insisté sur cette affaire, il n'a pas renoncé **2.1** *vt* **embarrasser** ◊ *wɔ́n yà bhɛ̄n gbàn gɯ́-kún* l'affaire a embarrassé tout le monde **2.2** *vt* **embêter**, **gêner** Syn. *bhà-kún (t)* ◊ *à wò yɤ̀ n̄ gɯ́-kún-sīʌ* sa voix me gêne

gɯ́-kpʌ̀ŋ {Int. gɯ́-kpʌ̀ŋ-kpʌ̀ŋ} *vt* **secouer** Syn. *kpʌ̀ŋ*

gɯ́-kplà *v vt* **gêner** *(incommoder, mettre mal à l'aise)* ◊ *Gbàtò bhà dhūn-sɯ̀ yà yī gɯ́-kplà* la venue de Gbato nous a gênés

gɯ́-kplɯ̀ *v* 1) *vi* **s'exténuer** *(une personne)*, **perdre la sensibilité** *(d'une partie du corps)* ◊ *à gɯ́ yà kplɯ̀* il est exténué ◊ *n̄ gɛ̀n gɯ́ yà kplɯ̀* mes jambes sont exténuées ♦ *n̄ gɯ́ yà gɯ́-kplɯ̀* j'ai le torticolis 2) *vt* **exténuer** ◊ *yʌ̄ yà n̄ gɯ́-kplɯ̀* le travail m'a exténué

gɯ́kplɯ̀dhē < intérieur-attacher-nominalis.> *n* **torticolis**

gɯ́kplɯ̀yɔ̋ɔ <intérieur-attacher-kaolin> *n* **kaolin pour soigner le torticolis**

gɯ́-pɩ̀ɤ <dans-souffler> *v vt* **peigner** ◊ *ā n̄ gɔ̀ gɯ́-pɩ̀ɤ kpɛ̀ɛwō fáagā ká* je me peigne toujours avec un peigne

gɯ́-pő, **gɯ́-pɯ̋** *v* **1** 1) *vi* **se dégourdir** ◊ *Tòkpà yɤ̀ dɔ̀ ɤ̄ gɛ̀en kɤ̄ ɤ̄ gɛ̀n gɯ́ yɤ̀ pő* Tokpa s'est levé pour se dégourdir les jambes 2) *vt* **dégourdir** **2** *vt* **expliquer** *(à – dhɛ̀)*

gɯ́-pɤ̄ {gɯ́-pɤ̄} *v vt* **expliquer** *(la parole)*

gɯ́-pɯ̋ → gɯ́-pő *se dégourdir*

gúi-sɛ̄ɛ̀ {gúi-sèe} *v vt* **gaspiller**

gúisɪ̀ɤ *n* **indisposition, malaise** ♦ *gúisɪ̀ɤ yɤ̀ à bhà* il ne se porte pas bien

gúi-sɪ̀ɤ *v* **1** *vi* **être malade** ◊ *à gúi yɤ̀ sɪ̀ɤ* il ne se porte pas bien **2** *vt* **serrer** *(visage)* ♦ *yà ɤ̄ wʌ̄ʌ́ gúi-sɪ̀ɤ* il a eu un visage renfrogné

gúisɪ̀ɤdhē <ventre-fâcher-nominalis.> *n* **maladie**

gúi-sùɤ *v vt* **mâcher**

gúisùi *adj* **dense** ◊ *dhűu gúisùi* brouillard épais ◊ *dhűi dhɛ́ yɤ̀ gúisùi, bháan bhɔ̀ɔn à bhà kɤ̄ á dhɛ̀ yɤ̀ sʌ̀ ká* le feuillage est dense, et je ne peux pas bien voir

gúi-tó {gúi-tó} *v* **1** 1) *vi gúi-tó dhɛ̀ɛnsùi* **se fatiguer** *(une partie de corps)* ◊ *n̄ gɛ̀n gúi yà tó dhɛ̀ɛnsùi* mes jambes sont fatiguées 2) *vt* **fatiguer** ◊ *tá̋ yà n̄ gɛ̀n gúi sɛ̋ɛ́ndhʌ́n tó dhɛ̀ɛnsùi* la marche a un peu fatigué mes pieds **2** *vr* **s'efforcer** ◊ *ūi gúi-tó gbɛ́ɛ̀, kɤ̄ úi lòo à pɪ́ɤ bhūin* fais un effort pour passer chez lui là-bas

gúi-wɛ̋ {gúi-wɛ̀} *v* **1** 1) *vt* **frapper fort** 2) *vi* **ressentir une douleur** *(d'un coup, etc.)* ◊ *ūi zɔ̄n ɤ́ bhāan à wō kɔ̄ɔ ūi gúi yɤ̀ dhɔ̀ wɛ̋'* je vais te frapper, tu vas souffrir **2** *vt* **craquer** *(des doigts)*

gúi-wúi {gúi-wūi} *v vi* **faire mal** *(d'une partie du corps)* ◊ *n̄ gɔ̀ gúi yɤ̀ wúi-sɪ̄ʌ* j'ai mal à la tête

gúi-yɤ̄ {gúi-yɤ̄} *v vt* **comprendre** *(l'essence de qch; voir la solution)*

gúi-zʌ̄ {gúi-zʌ̄} *v* **1** *vt* **désherber** *(avec la machette, quand les mauvaises herbes sont déjà grandes)* Syn. gúi-bà ♦ *bāa {dhɛ̀} gúi-zʌ̄* désherber le champ de manioc **2** *vt* **désinfecter** ◊ *kwɪ́-dhàan bèdhɛ́ bhá yɤ̀ bhūin, yɤ̀ bhɪ̄ʌʌ gúi-zʌ̀* il y a un médicament des Blancs qui désinfecte la plaie **3** *vt* **secouer**, **remuer** ◊ *bhɔ̄ sʌ̀ yɤ̀ zlòo gɔ̀ kɛ́ɛ yáa' dɔ̄ à gúi-zʌ̄-dhɛ̀ ká tɔ̀n* le guib a un joli cou, mais, malheureusement, il ne sait pas le remuer

gúi-zɪ̄ɤ {gúi-zɪ̀ɤ} *v vi à yá̋n gúi yɤ̀ zɪ̄ɤ-sɪ̄ʌ* **avoir des vertiges**, **avoir la tête qui tourne** Syn. gúi-dhɪ̀ʌʌn ◊ *dɪ̄n̄ yɤ̀ n̄ yá̋n gúi sɛ̋ɛ́ndhʌ́n zɪ̄ɤ-sɪ̄ʌ* j'ai des vertiges légers causés par la faim

gúi-zű {gúi-zù} *v vt* **laver** *(tête)*

Gb gb

gbà *n* ***Cephalophus niger*** **céphalophe noir** *(antilope : le mâle comme la femelle ont des cornes; le corps brun foncé à noir, 15-20 kg, habitant les forêts humides) [pratiquement disparu de nos jours]* Syn. súù

gbà *n* **toit** Qsyn. pɪ̄ɤdhɛ́, yɛ́ ♦ *gbɔ̄ŋ gbà* toit à une ou deux pentes ♦ *kɔ́ gbà* toit en pente ♦ *kɔ́dhɛ̄ɛ́ gbà* toit conique ♦ *wà kɔ́ gbà yà* on a mis le toit sur la maison

gbā 1 {gbā} *v* **1** *vt* **donner à** *(qch – ká)*, **envoyer** lv. Qsyn. dɔ̄ 1, dhūn 2 ◊ *wʌ̀ʌ̀gā ɤ́ n̄ gbā' ká, bhán' súi* j'ai pris l'argent qu'il m'a donné ◊ *dhʌ́n ɤ́ Zlàan ɤ́ n̄ gbā' ká...* les enfants que Dieu m'a donné... **2** *vt* **adorer qn/qch** ◊ *wà dhó tɔ̀n gbā'* ils sont allés adorer la montagne

gbā 2 ***n*** **accusation** *(d'une infraction des règles de l'association, etc.)* ♦ *gbā bhō* transgresser l'ordre ♦ *wà gbā yà̰ ȁ bhȁ* ils ont porté une accusation contre lui

gbā 3; gbáȁ (ka) ***n*** ***Paraxerus palliatus*** **écureuil de brousse**

gbá ***n*** **guet-apens** ♦ *gbá kpɔ́ ȁ gɔ̏* se tenir en embuscade contre qn ♦ *ɤ̄ gbá dɔ̄ ȁ bhȁ* dresser une embuscade pour surveiller qch ♦ *gbá kpɔ́ ȁ bhȁ* s'approcher à pas de loup de qn

gbâ 1 ***n*** **hangar** *(à deux pentes, structure improvisée avec des branches et des feuilles de palmier)* *Qsyn.* *bɔ̄ɔ̋* ◊ *yà dhó wáȁndhūn' gbâ wlɤ̀ɤ* il est allé se coucher sous le hangar ♦ *gbâ gbà déŋ̏dȅŋ* hangar à toit plat ♦ *gbâ dɔ̄ wūū bhȁ* dresser une embuscade à un animal

gbâ 2, **gbâgā** ***n*** **chenille** *(grosse, noire, poilue; de juin à janvier, comestible : bouillie et séchée au soleil) dans les calculs, seule la forme gbâgā est utilisée*

gbȁa ***n*** **cobra, serpent cracheur** ♦ *bhlɛ̄ɛn gbȁa* serpent cracheur ◊ *gbȁa yà ɤ̄ dhídhí bhō dhʌ́n yʌ́nŋ* le cobra a craché dans les yeux de l'enfant

gbáȁ ***n*** **sorte de banane plantain** *(la plus longue et la plus grosse de toutes les sortes de bananes)*

gba̋a ***n*** **champ non-ensemencé** *(débroussaillé, mais laissé en jachère par manque de semailles)* ♦ *bhláȁ gba̋a* = gbáȁ ♦ *gba̋a yà tó* un lopin de terre est resté en jachère

gbȁadhʌ́n ***n*** **chaise**

gbàan tout cela, eux tous *forme contractée gbàn "tout" + 3e pers. sg. ou 3e pers. pl. du parfait"* ◊ *kpȉnŋ gbàan kʌ̄ yâ* la route s'est dégradée tout le long du parcours

gbáandhʌ́n ***n*** **initiation** *Syn.* *bɔ̋n* ♦ *yà gbáandhʌ́n kʌ̄* il a organisé une initiation ♦ *yà gó gbáandhʌ́n gúú* il/elle est passé(e) par l'initiation

gbàandhɤ̄ 1 ***loc.n*** *LOC de* gbàn 1 *plafond*

gbàandhɤ̄ 2 ***loc.n*** *LOC de* gbān 1 *épaule*

gbáȁndhɤ̄ {Int. gbáȁngbáȁndhɤ̄} ***adv*** **1 vraiment**, **parfaitement vrai** ◊ *yɤ̏ ɤ̄ bhā dhȅŋgɔ̄ɔ̀n dhȕɤɤ pʌ̄bhèe gú gbáȁndhɤ̄* il ne partageait pas la nourriture avec son visiteur ♦ *yɤ̏ dhɤ̋ gbáȁndhɤ̄* c'est parfaitement vrai **2 exactement**, **entièrement** *(en parlant d'un laps de temps)* ◊ *yɤ̏ kʌ̄ sű dō kʌ̏ yűa gú gbáȁndhɤ̄* il a été malade pendant un mois entier

gbáȁndhūn {gbáȁdhūn; NEUT gbáȁdhȕn} ***v*** **1** 1) *vi* **s'arrêter** *Syn.* *dɔ́ɔ̀ndhūn* 2) *vt* **arrêter** *Syn.* *dɔ́ɔ̀ndhūn* ◊ *gɔ̄ sòfɛ̏ɛ̏ yà gɔ̄ gbáȁndhūn* le chauffeur a arrêté la voiture **2** *vt* **interrompre** ◊ *yà súnŋ̏ gbáȁndhūn* il a interrompu la carême

gbȁȁndhȕȕ ***n*** **échelle** *(nom générique)* ♦ *yà dȁ gbȁȁndhȕȕ bhȁ* il est monté à l'échelle

gbáȁngbáȁndhɤ̄ ***adv*** *Int. de* gbáȁndhɤ̄ *vraiment*

gbādhȅbhȅn <donner-MSD-personne> ***n*** **quémandeur, quémandeuse** *[les Dan sont tolérants envers les quémandeurs]*

gbâgā → gbâ *chenille.noire*

gbȁ̋gèe <danse(esp.)-masque> ***n*** **masque qui danse "gbatan"**

gbâgɔ̏ɔ ***n*** **1** ***Heliosciurus gambianus*** **écureuil** *(petit, demeure sur les autres arbres, plutôt que sur les palmiers; dessus de couleur olive foncé, tacheté en orange ou gris; dessous de couleur orange à gris ou blanc; la queue a 14 cercles foncés)* **2 Heliosciurus rufobrachium héliosciure à jambes rousses** *(250-400 g, dessus rouge, pattes grises; dessous de couleur crème; queue longue, avec des rayures en noir et blanc)*

gbȁgbɤ̄, gbȁgbō <d'après le nom de Laurent Gbagbo, pendant la présidence duquel les gens se sont mis à manger ces champignons> ***n*** **champignon** *(esp. : ressemble à dhȁŋtlȁ̋adhɛ̋, mais est dit moins savoureux)*

gbȁ̋kklȁ̋agbȁkklȁa ***adv*** **très** *(personne : taille grande et corpulente) va généralement avec l'adjectif gblɛ̀ɛn* ◊ *wà bhɛ̄n gblɛ̀ɛn gbȁ̋klȁ̋agbȁklȁa dō kún* ils ont attrapé un géant

gbȁn 1) ***v*** **1** 1) *vi* **s'enfoncer** ◊ *sœ̄œ̀gā yà gbȁn bhīʌ gbȁ̋n gúí* la flèche s'est plantée dans la cuisse de la biche royale 2) *vt* **planter**, **enfoncer** ◊ *yà pɔ̋dhín gbȁn dhűpɛ̋n tȁ* il a enfoncé le clou dans la planche ◊ *yȁ ȁ gȅn gbȁn pɛ̄n ká* il a fabriqué ses pieux en bois de "pèn" **2.1** *vi* **se mettre** Syn. dɔ̄ ◊ *gbȁn yɤ̄ !* mets-toi ici ! ◊ *bȉaŋ gɛ̋ɛ sʊ́-sȕ yíi gwʌ̀ʌ, yɤ̄ wó gbȁn gèe gɔ̏* l'échauffement n'a pas duré, et ils se sont dressés devant le masque ♦ *yà gbȁn bhɛ́ɛndhȅ bhȁ* il a posé sa candidature pour le poste de maire ♦ *ȁ bhȁ gȅn yȁ gbȁn* son pouvoir s'est consolidé **2.2** 1) *vi* **se coincer**, **s'enrayer** ◊ *ȁ bhȁ pȉɤgāsòȍ lɔ̄ɔ̋gā yȁ gbȁn kpɛ̄nŋdhɤ̄* la chaîne de son vélo s'est enrayée 2) *vt* **fixer** *(faire tenir de façon durable)* ◊ *yà kʌ̋ʌ gā gbȁn ɤ̄ gɔ̏ gúí* il a fixé la lame de la houe ◊ *yɤ̄ gblȍo gȅn gbȁn-sīʌ* il est en train de réparer un pied de la chaise ♦ *klȁa gbȁn* mettre une cravate **3** 1) *vi* **se cogner** *(contre – bhȁ)* ◊ *Zân bhȁ gɔ̄ yȁ gbȁn dhűí bhȁ* la voiture de Jean s'est cognée contre l'arbre 2) *vt* **cogner avec** *(qch – bhȁ)* ◊ *yà ɤ̄ bhā gɔ̄ gbȁn dhúí bhȁ* il a cogné l'arbre avec sa voiture *(volontairement)* **4.1** *vt* **courber** *(la tête)* Syn. dhȁ̋ȁndhūn ◊ *ɤ̄ tȁ̋ sʊ́-sīʌ, yɤ̄ ɤ̄ gɔ̏ gbȁn* en marchant il courbe la tête **4.2** *vi* **supplier** *(qn – bhȁ)* ♦ *yà gbȁn ī bhȁ kɤ̄ á dhó* il m'a supplié de partir **5** *vi* **concerner** *(qch – bhȁ)* ◊ *wɔ́n ɤ̄ gbȁn wɔ́n zīi bhȁ...* ce qui concerne les anciennes affaires... **6** *vi ȁ gȅn yɤ̄ gbȁn ȁ gúí, ȁ gȅn yɤ̄ gbȁn ȁ bhȁ* **c'est sa cause** ◊ *ȁ bhȁ dhā-sȕ gȅn gbȁn Gbȁtȍ bhȁ* il doit sa vie à Gbato **7** *vi* **insister** *(sur – tȁ)*

gbȁn 2) ***n*** **appui, support** *(sous le toit)* ◊ *kȁ dhű gbȁn gbȁn gɔ̏* mets le support sous le toit ♦ *dɔ̄ bhɛ̄n gbȁn gɔ̏* soutenir qn

gbàn 1 {LOC gbàandhɤ̄} ***loc.n*** **1 plafond** *(de la case ronde des femmes)*, **grenier** *(partie la plus élevée de la maison)* Syn. gblȁ̋ȁ (t) ♦ *gbàn dȁ ȁ dhű* rondin servant d'escalier au grenier ♦ *gbān bɛ̋ŋ* poutre maîtresse ♦ *gbàn gā* planche de plafond ♦ *yà dȁ gbàn bhȁ* il est monté au grenier ♦ *yà ɤ̄ bhā bhlȕn lòo gbàandhɤ̄* elle a mis le riz au grenier **2 échafaudage** *(installé à côté des gros arbres afin de les couper en haut du tronc, là où ce* *dernier est moins épais)◊ yà gbàn yȁ dhűű bhȁ kɤ̄ ɤ́ ȁ bɔ̄* il a placé l'échafaudage contre l'arbre pour le couper

gbàn 2 ***n*** **pression**

gbàn 3 ***dtm*** *tend à se contracter avec le pronom de la 3e pers. sg. ou 3e pers. pl. du parfait, cf. gbàan* **1 tout 2 tous** *la marque du pluriel, facultative, s'accolle au nom◊ dhūn tɔ̏{-dhȕn} gbàn ká* apporte tous les poulets ♦ *gbàn pɛ́pɛ́* chacun ◊ *yɤ̄ dhūn ɤ́ bhɛ̄n gbàn pɛ́pɛ́ yī kɔ̄nbhānŋdē tɔ̀n* c'est lui qui nous commande tous maintenant *peut apparaître dans une position argumentale sans déterminé* ♦ *ȁ yɤ̄ zʌ̏ gbàn gúú* (gw) ♦ *ȁ yēȅ gbàn gúú* (, t) finalement, à la fin du compte ♦ *yɤ̄ zʌ̏ gbàn gúú* cependant

gbān 1 {LOC gbàandhɤ̄ (gw), gbǣǣ́n (t)} ***loc.n*** **1** *rn* **épaule** *(inclut la partie supérieure du bras, au-dessus du coude)◊ bhán glɛ̄ɛ́ zīɤ n̄ gbān gúú* j'ai chargé le sac sur l'épaule ◊ *yà ɤ̄ kɔ̏ dȁ ɤ̄ gbān wlɤ̏ɤ* il a posé sa main sous son aisselle Syn. *yɔ́nŋ̏dhɤ̄* ♦ *yȁ zɔ̏ dȁ ɤ̄ gbān gúú* il a mis le carquois sur l'épaule ♦ *ūū kɔ̏ bhō n̄ gbàandhɤ̄* enlève ta main de mon épaule ♦ *yíí yɤ̏ bhɛ̄n kȕn bhɛ̄n gbān bhȁ* l'eau arrive aux épaules des gens **2** *rn* **aile** Syn. *gbȅ, gbɛ̄ɛ́n* **3 colle** *(de vêtement)* **4 grand gerbe** *(du riz)◊ bhlȕn wɛ́ŋ sɔ́ɔdhűű dhʌ̀n ɤ́ bhlȕn gbān dō ká* cinq petites gerbes de riz font une grande gerbe

gbān 2 ***n Lycaon pictus*** **cynhyène, lycaon** *(un loup africain, du couleur noire à jaunâtre, avec des zones blanches irrégulières; 18-28 kg; fait la chasse en meute, en poursuivant la proie; prédateur très dangereux)*

gbắn ***n*** **1** *rn* **jambe** *(pied non compris),* **patte** *(en calcul, les deux formes, gbắn et gbắngā, peuvent être utilisées)* Syn. *gȅn, gbắngā* ◊ *wūū bhā ká ȁ zʌ̄ kȁ n̄ gbā ȁ gbắn ká* si vous tuez cet animal, donnez-moi sa patte **2** *rn* **cuisse** Syn. *gɤ̏ŋ, gbắnbhlʌ́*

gbân 1 ***n*** **vacarme** *(d'une foule)* ◊ *bhɛ̄n-dhȕn wȍ gbân dɔ̄-sīʌ* la foule hurle *(en poursuivant le voleur)*

gbân 2 ***n*** **malédiction** *(un type particulier : on la prononce contre un ennemi dans le cadre d'un rituel spécial, collectivement, en piétinant le sol avec le pied gauche)* ♦ *wà gbân yɤ̄ ȁ tȁ* ils ont mis la malédiction sur lui

gbân 3 ***n*** **fourmi** *(esp. : grosse, noire, fait des nids sur la cîme des arbres; cherche à entrer dans les oreilles des gens)* ♦ *gbân kɔ́* fourmilière

gbân 4 ***n Ricinus communis (gen. Euphorbiaceae)*** **arbre** *(deux variétés, avec des feuilles rouges et vertes) [le lavage avec la décoction des feuilles est un médicament contre le paludisme; les graines brûlées sont utilisées contre les éruptions et les abcès : on les brûle, les pile, on y rajoute de l'eau et on met la substance sur l'abcès]*

gbắnbhlʌ́ <jambe-termite.volant> ***n*** *rn* **cuisse** Syn. *gɤ̏ŋ, gbắn* ◊ *Yɔ̏ gbắnbhlʌ́ yɤ̏ glɤ́gblɤ́* Yo a de grosses cuisses ♦ *yíí yɤ̏ bhɛ̄n kȕn bhɛ̄n gbắnbhlʌ́ bhȁ* l'eau arrive aux cuisses

gbàndȁadhȕȕ <*gbàn-dä-ä-bhä-dhűű 'arbre pour monter le grenier'> ***n*** **échelle** *(de grenier)*

gbắngā <jambe-os> ***n*** *rn* **jambe** *(pied non compris),* **patte** Syn. *gȅn, gbắn*

gbàngèegɔ̀bhɛ̀n <se.dresser-masque-devant-homme> ***n*** **coureur** *(celui qui court à la course sans masque)* Syn. *bìaŋsúbhɛ̀n*

gbàngbàn ***adv*** **éclatant, vif** *(rouge)* ◊ *yɤ̀ zɤ̀œndhē gbàngbàn* il est très rouge

gbàngbàndhɤ̄ ***adv*** **éclatant, vif** *(rouge)* ◊ *pɪ̀ɤ yà tān gbàngbàndhɤ̄* le fer est devenu rouge vif

gbānsɛ̃́ɛ ***n*** **enclume**

gbāntàdhɛ̀ ***n*** *rn* **haut du dos**

gbànwō ***adv*** **presque** ◊ *yà wɛ́ à bhà gbànwō* il l'a presque accepté

gbàŋ 1 {A P, gbàŋ-dhùn pl. A, gbàŋ-sù foc. A; gbāŋgbāŋ Int. pl., gbāŋgbāŋ-dhùn Int. pl. A} ***adj*** **1 aîné** Syn. *kpɪ̃́* ◊ *Pɔ̄dhɤ̀ yɤ̀ gbàŋ Yɔ̀ gɔ̀* Paul est plus âgé que Yo ♦ *bhān bhɛ̄n gbàŋ-dhùn, bhān bhɛ̄n {dhùn} gbāŋgbāŋ-dhùn* mes aînés *(parents ou non)* **2 bas** *(voix)*

gbàŋ 2 ***n*** *nom déterminant ou déterminé d'un groupe nominal* **albinos** *[on croyait autrefois à la puissance magique supérieure des albinos, raison pour laquelle ils étaient exclus de la participation aux sacrifices; on considère d'habitude les albinos comme des monstres]* ♦ *gbàŋ bhɛ̀n* albinos ♦ *gbàŋ gōn* albinos homme ♦ *gbàŋ dhɛ̀* femme albinos ♦ *gbàŋ dhʌ́n* enfant albinos ♦ *gbàŋ pú̃u* albinos blanc ♦ *gbàŋ zɤ̀œndhē* albinos roux

gbàŋ 3 ***n*** **contrôle** ♦ *à wɔ́n yà dà ī gɔ̀ gbàŋ tà* cette affaire a échappé à mon contrôle

gbàŋ 1 ***n*** **bruit** *(de foule)*, **tumulte** ♦ *bhɛ̄n kpɤ̄ wò gbàŋ dɔ̄-sɪ̄ʌ* la foule fait du bruit ♦ *ī tó̃ yà dà gbàŋ wò gú* j'ai entendu le bruit de la foule

gbàŋ 2 ***n*** **procession** *(groupe de gens marchant avec un but)*

gbã́ŋ ***n*** **1 séchoir** *(pour sécher le café, le cacao, etc. : plate-forme en bambou dressée en plein air sur une carcasse de bois, couverte d'une natte gbàsàgbã́sã́)* Qsyn. *kplâ* **2 passerelle** *(de bambou)* Syn. *gblāã́* ♦ *wà gbã́ŋ kʌ̄ yí tà* on a fait une passerelle pour traverser le cours d'eau **3 brancard**

gbāŋgbāŋ *Int. pl. de* gbàŋ 1 *aîné*

gbāŋgbāŋdhɤ̄ ***onomat*** **ding** *son de frappes de fer* ◊ *pɪ̀ɤ yɤ̀ bhàn kwʌ́ʌ̀ gbāŋgbāŋdhɤ̄* le fer frappe le fer : ding

gbàŋpɛ̃́ŋ (t) ***n*** **foulard de tête** *(féminin)* Qsyn. *fã́àn (gw)*

gbã́ŋyɛ̃́ ***n*** **serpent** *(esp.; gros reptile, mais plus petit que le python)*

gbāpʌ̀ <adorer-chose> ***n*** **objet d'adoration** *(ne s'applique pas à Dieu)*

gbāpʌ̄ <accusation-chose> ***n*** **amende** *(payée pour une infraction aux règles de l'association)* Qsyn. *tɔ́ŋ̀* ♦ *yà gbāpʌ̄ gó* il a payé une amende

gbàsàgbã́sã́ ***n*** **natte faite de lattes** *(disposée sur le séchoir gbã́ŋ)*

gbã́tã́n ***n*** **"gbatan"** *(danse des jeunes hommes, chacun tient deux bâtons dans les mains, on chante en frappant les bâtons l'un contre l'autre; quelqu'un fait résonner un grelot vanné sɛ̀gbɛ̄)* ◊ *dhʌ́nglɔ̃́ɔ́n-dhùn ɤ́ wó Tòkpàplɤ̀ɤ, gbã́tã́n yɤ̀ à-dhùn gɔ̀* la danse "gbatan" appartient aux jeunes de Tokpapleu

gbàúù <Manding gbàbúgu> ***n*** **cuisine** *(hangar ou bâtiment séparé)* ◊ *n̄ dhē yà dɜ̀ gbàúù gúɯ* ma mère est entrée dans la cuisine

gbāwû ***n*** **boubou** *(grande tenue traditionnelle masculine dan, bleu et blanc)*

gbǽæ̀ → gbɛ́ɛ̀ *petit crocodile*

gbǽ̋æ 1 → gbɛ̋ɛ *endroit secret*

gbǽ̋æ 2 → gbɛ̋ɛ *large*

gbǽ̋ægúɯ → gbɛ̋ɛgúɯ *endroit secret.LOC*

gbǽ̋ægúɯdhɛ̀ → gbɛ̋ɛgúɯdhɛ̀ *endroit secret*

gbǣæ̀n → gbɛ̄ɛ̀n *tenailles*

gbǣǽn (t) ***loc.n*** *LOC de* gbān 1 *épaule*

gbǽ̋ætàzʌ̄bhɛ̀n <large-sur-tuer-personne> ***n*** **raconteur, raconteuse**

gbʌ̀ 1, **gbʌ̀gā** ***n*** **ratière** *(l'animal marche sur le mécanisme de détente, un panneau lourd tombe)* ♦ *gbʌ̀ yà, gbʌ̀ dɔ̄* tendre une ratière

gbʌ̀ 2 ***prev*** *seulement dans le verbe gbʌ̀-kʌ̄*

gbʌ̀ʌ ***n*** **tique** *(de chien)*, **puce** ♦ *gbɛ̂n yɤ̀ ɤ̄ kāà-sīʌ gbʌ̀ʌ gɔ̀* le chien se gratte à cause des tiques et des puces ♦ *gbɛ̂n yɤ̀ gbʌ̀ʌ bhɤ̀-sīʌ* le chien cherche les puces *(avec ses dents)*

gbʌ̀ʌ ***n*** **1 valise** ♦ *gbʌ̀ʌ gʌ̄n* poignée de valise **2 cercueil** ♦ *bhɛ̄n gèe gbʌ̀ʌ* cercueil ♦ *wàa dɜ̀ gbʌ̀ʌ gúɯ* on l'a mis dans le cercueil

gbʌ̋ʌlòo ***n*** **serpent** *(esp.; rouge, long d'un mètre, venimeux, agressif)*

gbʌ̄ʌnŋdhɤ̄ ***onomat*** **crac** *(son de craquement de mur, verre)* ◊ *vɛ̋dhɛ̋ dhàan yà dɔ̄ gbʌ̄ʌnŋdhɤ̄* le verre s'est fêlé : crac !

gbʌ̀gā → gbʌ̀ *ratière*

gbʌ̂gbʌ̀ {A P S, gbʌ̂gbʌ̀-dhùn pl. A S, gbʌ̂gbʌ̀-sɯ̀ foc. A, gbʌ̂gbʌ̀-sɯ̀-dhùn pl. foc. A; gbʌ̂gbʌ̂ Int. pl. A P S, gbʌ̂gbʌ̂-dhùn A S} ***adj*** **bas**, **trapu** *(objets inanimés) devant les suffixes diminutif et pluriel, le ton final est facultativement remplacé par le ton haut : pl. dim. gbʌ̂gbʌ́dhʌ́n-dhùn* ♦ *dhɯ̋dhʌ́n gbʌ̂gbʌ̀* arbuste, petit arbre ♦ *tɔ̀n gbʌ̂gbʌ̀* colline ♦ *tɔ̀n gbʌ́gbʌ́-dhùn, tɔ̀n-dhùn gbʌ́gbʌ́, tɔ̀n-dhùn gbʌ́gbʌ́-dhùn* les collines

gbʌ̂gbʌ̂ *Int. pl. de* gbʌ̂gbʌ̀ *bas*

gbʌ̀kʌ̄ ***n*** **échelle** *(pour monter au raphia)* ♦ *yà dɜ̀ gbʌ̀kʌ̄ bhà* il a monté au raphia *(par l'échelle)*

gbʌ̀-kʌ̄ ***v vt*** **monter par une échelle** *(palmier raphia)*

gbʌ̂n ***n*** **fourmi** *(esp., habitent sur les caféiers)*

gbʌ̄ŋ́ŋ́gā < ?-os> ***n*** **manille** *(bracelet ouvert en cuivre ou bronze, utilisé comme monnaie avant la période coloniale, surtout à l'époque de la traite des esclaves)*

gbʌ́ŋ̀gbʌ̀ŋ {A P S, gbʌ́ŋ̀gbʌ̀ŋ-dhüǹ pl. A, gbʌ́ŋ̀gbʌ̀ŋ-sǜ foc. A, gbʌ́ŋ̀gbʌ̀ŋ-sǜ-dhüǹ foc. pl. A; gbʌ́ŋ̀gbʌ́ŋ̀ Int. pl. A, gbʌ́ŋ̀gbʌ́ŋ̀-dhüǹ Int. pl. A S, gbʌ́ŋ̀gbʌ́ŋ̀-sǜ-dhüǹ Int. pl. foc. A} ***adj*** **long, gros et lourd** ◊ *yà dhṹgā gbʌ́ŋ̀gbʌ̀ŋ wɔ̏ ɤ̄ gwìnŋ̀* il a chargé une grosse perche sur sa tête ♦ *bhɛ̄n gbʌ́ŋ̀gbʌ̀ŋ* personne grande, grosse, molle

gbʌ́ŋ̀gbʌ́ŋ̀ *Int. pl. de* gbʌ́ŋ̀gbʌ̀ŋ *long, gros, lourd*

gbɛ̏ ***n*** **1** *rn* **bras** Syn. gbɛ̀gādhṹ ♦ *n̄ gbɛ̏ yà gā n̄ gɔ̏* je suis découragé ◊ *dhʌ́n ɯ́' gʌ̋n-dhàan bhā, bhá dhó' gbɛ̏ bhō' bhà* n'arrache pas le bras de l'enfant que tu es en train de tirer ! **2** *rn* **épaule** *(de poulet)* Syn. gbān 1, gbɛ̄ɛ́n

gbɛ̋ ***n*** *hist.* **machette courte**, **coupe-coupe court** *(la lame, fabriquée par les forgerons locaux, est recourbée en avant et ne dépasse pas 30 cm)* *[de nos jours, s'utilise pour des petits travaux ou par des gens faibles]*

gbɛ̋ɛ̏ 1) {A P S, gbɛ̋ɛ̏-dhüǹ pl. A, gbɛ̋ɛ̏-sǜ foc. A, gbɛ̋ɛ̏-dhüǹ-sǜ pl. foc. A; gbɛ̋ɛgbɛ̏ɛ Int. A P S, gbɛ̋ɛgbɛ̏ɛ-dhüǹ Int. pl. A, gbɛ̋ɛgbɛ̏ɛ-sǜ Int. foc. A, gbɛ̋ɛgbɛ̏ɛ-sǜ-dhüǹ Int. foc. pl. A; gbɛ́kɛ̋gbɛ̀kɛ̏ SupInt. A P S, gbɛ́kɛ̋gbɛ̀kɛ̏-dhüǹ SupInt. pl. A S, gbɛ́kɛ̋gbɛ̀kɛ̏-sǜ SupInt. foc., gbɛ́kɛ̋gbɛ̀kɛ̏-sǜ-dhüǹ SupInt. foc. pl.} ***adj*** **1.1 difficile** *(temps; travail)* ◊ *blɛ̄ɛ̋yī yà kwɛ̄ɛ yɤ̏ kʌ̄ kʌ̏ n̄ bhà gbɛ̋ɛ̏* cette année la saison sèche a été difficile pour moi ◊ *Dhɔ̀ɔdhɛ̏ yɤ̏ gbɛ̋ɛ̏* dans la famille Doo il y a des sérieux problèmes **1.2 dangereux** ◊ *ȁ bhà yṹa yɤ̏ kʌ̄-sīʌ gbɛ̋ɛ̏* sa maladie s'aggrave **1.3 fort**; **brûlant** *(soleil)*; **vif** *(lumière)* ◊ *tɛ́ɛ̏ yí yā yɤ̏ gbɛ̋ɛ̏* ce thé-ci est fort ◊ *kíi tʌ̋ sɯ́ gūdlɔ́nŋ̀ tȁ yʌ́nŋ̀ gbɛ̋ɛ̏ gɯ́...* si tu marches sur le goudron sous le soleil ardent... **1.4 fort**, **vigoureux** *(personne)* ◊ *Dhɔ̀ɔbhɛ̏n-dhüǹ wò gbɛ̋ɛ̏ dū gɯ́* les gens du clan de Doo sont fort en sorcellerie ◊ *Yɔ̏dhē yà ȁ sɔ̋n yʌ́n kɤ̄ wò ȁ wɔ́n dɔ̄ dhɛ̀ yɤ̏ gbɛ̋ɛ̏* Yodé lui a taillé les dents pour qu'on sache qu'elle est courageuse ♦ *ȁ dhí yɤ̏ gbɛ̋ɛ̏* il est disputeur ardent; il est effronté **2 dur**; **serré**, **raide** ◊ *dhṹ gbɛ̋ɛ̏* arbre à bois dur ◊ *dhı̋ gbɛ̋ɛgbɛ̏ɛ* un lit dur ◊ *būtɔ́nŋ̀ gbɛ̋ɛ̏* bouton serré ◊ *ȁ gbʌ̋nbhlʌ́ yɤ̏ gbɛ̋ɛgbɛ̏ɛ* ses cuisses sont dures **3 important** *(pour – gɔ̏)* ◊ *dhʌ́n wɔ̏n yɤ̏ gbɛ̋ɛ̏* les enfants sont importants

gbɛ̋ɛ̏ 2) ***adv*** *peut précéder le verbe ou le suivre* **très** ◊ *yɤ̏ dhɛ̏ɛnsǜ gbɛ̋ɛ̏ ɤ̄ bhā kɔ́ɔbhɛ̏n-dhüǹ bhà* il est très sévère envers les gens de sa famille ♦ *sı́ɤ / pɛ̄ŋ yɤ̏ dɔ̄-sīʌ gbɛ̋ɛ̏* la chaleur est forte ◊ *ɯ̄ dɛ̏ gbɛ̋ɛ̏ tȁ-bhō kɤ̄ ɯ́ dhūn* fais un effort pour venir ♦ *kɤ̄ bhɤ̏ dɔ̄ gbɛ̋ɛ̏ !* s'il te plaît !

gbɛ̋ɛ̏-dhɛ̏ ***n*** **1.1 force, vigueur** ◊ *wɔ́n ɤ́ ɯ́ ȁ kʌ̄-sīʌ bhā, gbɛ̋ɛ̏-dhɛ̏ yáa kʌ̄ dhɤ̋* ce que tu es en train de faire n'est pas génial **1.2 autorité** ♦ *Tȍkpȁ yà gbɛ̋ɛ̏-dhɛ̏ yɤ̄ Yɔ̏ tȁ* Tokpa a imposé son autorité sur Yo **2 ordre** *(commandement)* ◊ *gbɛ̋ɛ̏-dhɛ̏ bhüǹ* c'est un ordre ! ◊ *Tȍkpȁ yà gbɛ̋ɛ̏-dhɛ̏ yɤ̄ Yɔ̏ tȁ kɤ̄ yɤ̏ yʌ̄ kʌ̄* Tokpa a ordonné à Yo de travailler

gbɛ̋ɛgbɛ̏ɛ ***adj*** *Int. de* gbɛ̋ɛ̏ 1) *difficile*

gbɛ̄ɛ̋gbɛ̏ɛgbɛ̄ɛ̋dhɤ̄ ***adv*** **assourdissant** ◊ *yɤ̏ dhūn-sīʌ wɛ̋ gbɛ̄ɛ̋gbɛ̏ɛgbɛ̄ɛ̋dhɤ̄* il était en train de venir, et le bruit de ses pas était assourdissant

gbɛ̏ɛŋ → gbɛ̏ŋ *écureuil*

gbɛ̀gādhṹ <bras-os-arbre> ***n*** *rn* **bras** Syn. gbɛ̏

gbɛ̋gbɛ̏ ***intj*** **mon Dieu !** *(exclamation d'étonnement desagréable)*

gbɛ̋kɛ̋gbɛ̏kɛ̏ *SupInt. de* gbɛ̋ɛ̏ 1) *difficile*

gbɛ̏kɔ̏ ***n*** **juillet**

gbɛ̏ŋ 1 ***n*** **1 embranchement** ♦ *dhṹ gbɛ̏ŋ* branche *(arbre, plante)* ♦ *yí gbɛ̏ŋ* affluent ♦ *zīaan gbɛ̏ŋ* embranchement de route, bifurcation **2 intervalle** *(entre les branches d'une bifurcation)* ♦ *tɔ̏n gbɛ̏ŋ* vallée entre les montagnes ◊ *kɔ̏dhɛ̋ dō gbɛ̏ŋ gṹ dhɛ̏ yɤ̏ yȉisīɤ* il y a quatre intervalles entre les doigts d'une main

gbɛ̏ŋ 2, **gbɛ̏eŋ** ***n Funisciurus sp.*** **funisciure à pattes rousses** *(écureuil aux pattes et au visage roux, queue et dos gris foncé, dessous blanc ou orange; lance des pépiements stridents)* ◊ *gbɛ̏eŋ yɤ̏ yɛ̋e tó-sīʌ bhɤ̏ɤ bhȁ* l'écureuil rit de la vipère du Gabon *[on croit que l'écureuil se met à crier à la vue d'un serpent]*

gbēŋ 1) ***n*** **nuit** *(de crépuscule à crépuscule; la nuit fait partie du jour précédent)* *Qsyn. bɯ̋n* ◊ *yɤ̏ kʌ̄ gbēŋ kʌ̏ ɤ̄ bhā dhēbʌ̏ pɯ̋ɤ* il a passé la nuit avec sa femme ♦ *gbēŋ kpɤ̄* noir d'encre ♦ *gbēŋ zìnŋgṹ* à minuit ♦ *dhɔ̋ɔzīȁandōká gbēŋ* la nuit de samedi ♦ *gbēŋ dhɛ̏ gṹ tīi gṹ* nuit noire

gbēŋ 2) {gbēŋ-gbēŋ Int.} ***adv*** **la nuit** ◊ *wɔ̏ tɛ̋ sṳ̏ gbēŋ* ils marchent la nuit ◊ *wɔ̏ kʌ̄ gbɛ̋ɛtȁ zʌ̏ gbēŋ* ils causaient pendant la nuit ♦ *gbēŋ ɤ́ dɛ̀ɛ* la nuit à venir ♦ *yà dō gbēŋ...* lorsque la nuit tombe... ♦ *yɤ̏ ɤ̄ bhā wɔ́n-dhṳ̏n yɛ̋n-bhɔ̏ gbēŋ* il est dans des affaires louches *(lit. : il résout ses affaires la nuit)* ◊ *wȁ tɛ̋ sṳ̏ gbēŋ-gbēŋ wà dhūn* ils ont marché toute la nuit et sont venus ◊ *wɔ̏ kʌ̄ tɛ̋n kʌ̏ gbēŋ-gbēŋ ɤ́ dhɛ̏ dhɤ́ kpœ̀ ȁ ká* ils ont dansé toute la nuit jusqu'à l'aube

gbɛ̋ŋ {INT gbɛ̋ŋgbɛ̋ŋ} ***dtm*** **seulement** *(avec les numéraux, sauf dō 'un')* ◊ *gɔ̄ yȁagā gbɛ̋ŋ dhʌ̏n ɤ́ gūn ȁ-dhṳ̏n gɔ̏ pɤ̏dhɤ* il n'y avait que trois voitures dans leur village

gbēŋbhȁan <oiseau de nuit> ***n*** **1 oiseau de nuit** *(toute espèce)* **2** (gw) ***Bubo poensis*** **grand-duc à aigrettes** *(43 cm, roux foncé dessus, dessous plus pâle, couvert de fines rayures brunes; les aigrettes et le disque facial encadrés de noir) [on pense que les sorciers se transforment en hiboux, on les craint]* ♦ *gbēŋbhȁan yɤ̏ wɛ̏ kúkúdhūkúdhû* le grand-duc crie ♦ *gbēŋbhȁan yɤ̏ wɛ̏ ṹṹ-ṳ̀ṳ* le grand-duc ulule

gbēŋ-gbēŋ ***adv*** *Int. de* gbēŋ *la nuit*

gbɛ̋ŋgbɛ̋ŋ ***dtm*** *Int. de* gbɛ̋ŋ *seulement*

gbēŋkpɤ̄ <nuit-boule> ***n*** **place sombre** *(dans la nuit)*

gbɛ́ 1) {A P} ***adj*** **1 nombreux**; **beaucoup** *Syn. bɤ̋ɤwɛ̋ (m)* *peut apparaître dans une position argumentale et dans celle du prédicat sans déterminé* ◊ *bhɛ̄n gbɛ́ wà lòo kó tȁ fɛ̄tɤ̏ kʌ̄yàn gṹ* beaucoup du monde s'est rassemblé à la fête ◊ *sɔ̄ yɛ̋n gbɛ́ dhɔ̏ yɤ̏ bhɔ̏ɔnsî kʌ̏* les Burkinabé aiment les tissus multicolores ♦ *gbɛ́ dɛ̀dɛ̀* trop **2 suffisant** ◊ *yá yʌ̄kʌ̄bhɛ̏n gbɛ́ sú kɤ̄ wɔ̏ bláà dɛ̀e zū-bhō* nous avons embauché suffisamment de travailleurs pour commencer une nouvelle plantation

gbɛ́ 2) ***adv*** **beaucoup**; **souvent** ◊ *dhʌ́n-dhʋ̀n wɔ̀ bhɛ̄n-dhʋ̀n dhɛ̄ɛ́-kpɔ̀ gbɛ́* les enfants posent beaucoup de questions ◊ *Gbàtò dhʌ̀n ɤ́ pʌ̄ dhɛ̀ŋ gbɛ́* c'est Gbato qui perd souvent les choses ♦ *gbɛ́ dɛ̀dɛ̀wɔ̄* très souvent

gbɛ́bhō ***v*** **1** *vi* **se confier** *(à – dhɛ̀)* **2** *vt* **prendre sous sa protection** *(par Dieu; qn – dhɛ̀)*

gbɛ́-dhɛ̀ ***n*** **majorité** *peut apparaître dans une position argumentale sans déterminé* ♦ *à gbɛ́-dhɛ̀ gʋ́* le plus souvent

gbɛ̄ɛ ***n*** **campagne** *(régions rurales)* ♦ *yà dhó gbɛ̄ɛ gʋ́* il est allé à la campagne

gbɛ̄ɛ́, **gbɛ̄ɛ́sɛ́** ***n*** **argile** ◊ *wɔ̀ gbɔ̄ kʌ̀ gbɛ̄ɛ́/gbɛ̄ɛ́sɛ́ ká* on fait des pots en argile

gbɛ́ɛ̀, **gbǽæ̀** ***n*** **petit crocodile** ◊ *gbɛ́ɛ̀ wɛ̄ŋ dhʌn {ɤ́} à fɔ̄ɔn ká* la force du petit crocodile est dans sa queue

gbɛ̋ɛ 1, **gbǽ̋æ** {A P, gbɛ̋ɛ-dhʋ̀n pl. A S, gbɛ̋ɛ-sʋ̀ foc. A, gbɛ̋ɛ-sʋ̀-dhʋ̀n A; gbɛ̋ɛgbɛ̋ɛ, gbǽ̋ægbǽ̋æ Int. pl. A P S, gbɛ̋ɛgbɛ̋ɛ-dhʋ̀n, gbǽ̋ægbǽ̋æ-dhʋ̀n Int. pl. A S} ***adj*** **large, étendu** ◊ *dhɪ́ gbɛ̋ɛ* bouche large ◊ *bhláà {tà} dhɛ̀ gbɛ̋ɛ* grand champ ◊ *kɔ́ dhɪ́ yà pʋ̋ gbɛ̋ɛ ká* la porte est largement ouverte

gbɛ̋ɛ 2, **gbǽ̋æ** ***n*** **endroit sacré** *(où on lave les plaies des nouveaux circoncis; autrefois aussi l'endroit où les hommes faisaient leurs réunions secrètes)* ◊ *yà dhó gbɛ̋ɛ gʋ́* il est allé là où on lave les plaies des nouveaux circoncis

gbɛ̋ɛ-dhɛ̀ ***n*** **largeur** ◊ *yʋ́ɤ̀ɤ ɤ́' bhà gbɛ̋ɛ-dhɛ̀ ɤ́ dhè bhɛ̄n kɔ̀ dhɛ́ dhɤ́* ce poisson est aussi large que la paume d'une main ♦ *à dhó à dhɛ̀ gbǽ̋æ-dhɛ̀ gʋ́* il est parti dans le vaste monde

gbɛ̋ɛgʋ́, **gbǽ̋ægʋ́** ***loc.n*** *LOC de* gbɛ̋ɛgʋ́dhɛ̀ *endroit secret*

gbɛ̋ɛgʋ́dhɛ̀, **gbǽ̋ægʋ́dhɛ̀** {LOC gbɛ̋ɛgʋ́} ***loc.n*** **endroit sacré** <u>*Syn.*</u> <u>*gbɛ̋ɛ*</u> <u>*1*</u> ◊ *wà gbǽ̋ægʋ́dhɛ̀ zʋ̀-klʌʌn* ils ont clôturé l'endroit secret sacré

gbɛ̄ɛ̀n, **gbǣæ̀n** ***n*** **pince, tenaille** *(de forgeron)*

gbɛ̄ɛ́n ***n*** *rn* **aile** <u>*Syn.*</u> <u>*gbān*</u> <u>*1*</u>, <u>*gbɛ̀*</u>

gbɛ̋ɛtà ***n*** **causerie** <u>*Qsyn.*</u> <u>*dhīaŋ*</u> ◊ *yɤ̀ gbɛ̋ɛtà zʌ̀-sīʌ à ká* il cause avec lui ◊ *wɔ̀ kʌ̄ gbɛ̋ɛtà zʌ̀ gbɛ̄ŋ* ils continuèrent la causerie après la tombée de la nuit

gbɛ̂n ***n*** **chien** *[on mange les chiens au cours de certains sacrifices, mais dans la vie quotidienne, il est mal vu de le faire]* ♦ *gbɛ̂n yɤ̀ wɛ̀ wáʋ̀u-wáʋ̀u* le chien aboie : ouah ! ouah ! ♦ *gbɛ̂n yɤ̀ gblʌ̀n-sīʌ bhɛ̄n-dhʋ̀n bhà* le chien gronde contre les gens ♦ *gbɛ̂n yɤ̀ wɛ̀-sīʌ bhɛ̄n-dhʋ̀n bhà* le chien aboie aux gens ◊ *gbɛ̂n bhā à wɛ́ wɔ̀ yà kʌ̄ wʌ̀ʌsʋ̀* le chien a gémi

gbɛ̂ndhʌ́ngɔ́ɛ̀ <chien-enfant-haricot.sauvage> ***n*** ***Piliostigma thonningii*** **"haricot sauvage"** *(buisson ayant des cosses à surface laineuse dont la poussière cause de fortes démangeaisons)* <u>*Syn.*</u> <u>*gɔ́ɛ̀*</u>

gbɛ́sɛ̂ <Manding gbɛ́sɛ́> *n* **cure-dent** *(bâtonnet en bois avec lequel on se frottait autrefois les dents le matin) [pratique tombée en désuétude à force d'être remplacée par l'usage des brosses à dents]*

gbḯa (m) → gbḯaa (gw) *torche de rafia*

Gbı̏ȁa {LOC Gbı̏ȁadhɤ̄} *loc.n* **Toura** *(langue, zone et peuple)*

gbḯaa (gw), **gbḯa** (m) *n arch.* **torche de raphia** *(ou de palmier à huile) Syn. sɔ̋nŋ* ♦ *gbḯaa dɔ̄* allumer la torche ♦ *gbḯaa gɔ̏* tête de flambeau ♦ *gbḯaa zū̄* manche de torche

Gbı̏ȁadhɤ̄ → Gbı̏ȁa *toura*

gbḯʌn *n* **1** *rn* **odeur** *Qsyn. fı̄i* ◊ *gbàúù gbḯʌn yȁ yȁ* l'odeur de la cuisine est apparue ♦ *pɛ̄ŋ/sḯɤ gbḯʌn* fumée **2 puanteur** *Syn. tɛ́ɛ* ◊ *gbō gbḯʌn yȁ yȁ* la puanteur de l'excrément s'est répandue

gbídhō *n* ***Cuculus canorus*** **coucou gris**

gbı̏gbı̏dhɤ̄ *onomat imitation du grondement du moteur Syn. dȕdȕdȕdhɤ̄*

gbìi → gbìŋ *grotte*

gbìigbáȁnbhȁan *n* ***Coracias naevia*** **rollier varié** *(oiseau prédateur, 32 cm, dessus brun, dessous d'un roux vineux marqué de stries blanches serrées; perche longuement guettant une proie sur le sol; se trouve dans les grottes)*

gbı̏iŋ *onomat imite le son d'un coup fort et sourd*

gbı̏iŋdhɤ̄ *adv* **avec un bruit étouffé** ◊ *dhű yà pɤ̏ wɛ́ gbı̏iŋdhɤ̄ Yɔ̏ bhȁ kɔ́ tȁ* l'arbre est tombé sur la maison de Yo avec un bruit étouffé

gbínkígbı̏nkı̏, **gbínkíngbı̏nkı̏n** *adj SupInt de* gbínŋ̏ *lourd*

gbìnŋ̏ → gwìnŋ̏ *SUP sommet*

gbīnŋ → gblūŋ *punaises*

gbínŋ̏ {A P S, gbínŋ̏-dhȕn pl. A, gbínŋ̏-sȕ foc. A S, gbínŋ̏-sȕ-dhȕn A; gbínŋgbı̏nŋ Int. A P S, gbínŋgbı̏nŋ-dhȕn Int. pl. A, gbínŋgbı̏nŋ-sȕ Int. foc. A, gbínŋgbı̏nŋ-sȕ-dhȕn Int. pl. foc. A; gbínŋ̏gbínŋ̏ Int. pl. A P S, gbínŋ̏gbínŋ̏-dhȕn Int. pl. A, gbínŋ̏gbínŋ̏-sȕ Int. pl. foc. A, gbínŋ̏gbínŋ̏-sȕ-dhȕn Int. pl. foc. A S; gbínkíngbı̏nkı̏n, gbínkígbı̏nkı̏ SupInt A P S, gbínkíngbı̏nkı̏n-dhȕn SupInt pl. A S, gbínkíngbı̏nkı̏n-sȕ SupInt foc. A, gbínkíngbı̏nkı̏n-sȕ-dhȕn SupInt pl. foc. A} ***adj*** **1 lourd** ♦ *n̄ gɛ̏n yà kʌ̄ gbínŋ̏* mes jambes sont lourdes *(de fatigue)* ♦ *n̄ yấn yà kʌ̄ gbḯnkḯngbı̏nkı̏n yī kɔ̄ɔ* mes pauières sont lourdes de sommeil ♦ *ȁ wɔ̏ yɤ̏ gbínŋ̏* sa voix pèse *(on écoute ce qu'il dit)* ♦ *dhāŋgúdhɛ̏ yȁ kʌ̄ gbínŋ̏* le ciel est couvert des nuages

gbīnŋgā *n* **asticot** *(larves de hanneton qu'on trouve dans les troncs tombés de raphia et des palmiers à huile) [très appréciés; surtout les asticots de raphia; on les mange dans la sauce, plus rarement crus]* **chenille** *(; demeure dans les troncs pourris des palmiers)* ◊ *dhūɤɤ bhȁ gbīŋgā dīn yɤ̏ sʌ̏, ɤ́ zı̏ɤ ká yɔ̄ bhȁ tȁ* la chenille de raphia est plus savoureuse que celle du palmier à huile

gbínŋgbı̏nŋ *adj Int de* gbínŋ̏ *lourd*

gbínŋ̏gbínŋ̏ ***adj*** *Int. pl. de* gbínŋ̏ *lourd*

gbȉnŋgbɤ̄ → gbȉŋgbɤ̄ *poisson électrique*

gbìŋ, **gbìi** ***n*** *arch.* **grotte** *Syn.* *gwʌ̏yɛ̏* ◊ *kwàbhɛ̏n-dhȕn wà wō gblɛ̏ɛn-kpɔ́ gbìŋ wlɤ̏ɤ* les voleurs se sont cachés dans la grotte ◊ *yà dɔ̄ gbìŋ tȁ dhűɤ̄* il s'est mis debout au bord de la grotte ◊ *yȁ dȁ gbìŋ gú, yà dhó gbìŋ zūū gɔ̏* il est entré au plus profond de la grotte

gbȉŋgbɤ̄, **gbȉnŋgbɤ̄** ***n Chiloglanis niloticus waterloti; Chiloglanis micropogon*** **poisson électrique**, **gymnote, anguille électrique** ◊ *gbȉŋgbɤ̄ yɔ̋n yɤ̏ gbɛ́* le poisson électrique a beaucoup de graisse

gbìɤɤ ***v vt*** **tirer**, **traîner par terre** *Qsyn.* *gʌ̋n* ◊ *yɤ̏ dhʌ́n bhā ȁ gbìɤɤ-sīʌ* il est en train de traîner l'enfant par terre

gbɪ̋ɤ̏ɤ 1) ***n*** **grossesse** ♦ *yɤ̏ gbɪ̋ɤ̏ɤdhɛ̏ ká* elle est enceinte

gbɪ̋ɤ̏ɤ 2) {P} ***adj*** **enceinte**

gblʌ̋ 1) {gblʌ̏; Int. gblʌ̄ʌ̏, SupInt. gblʌ̄ʌ̏gblʌ̄ʌ̏} ***v vi*** **crier** *(de douleur; avec irritation, mécontentement; contre – tȁ)* ♦ *dhā yà gblʌ̋ gblʌ̋ʌ̏ndhɤ̄* la tonnerre a retenti

gblʌ̋ 2) ***n*** *rn gblʌ̋ wɔ̏* **cri** *(de douleur, colère, pour effrayer, etc.)* *Qsyn.* *wɛ̋* ◊ *ȁ gblʌ̋ wɔ̏ yɤ̏ gbɛ̋ɛ̏* son cri est fort ♦ *yɤ̏ gbɔ̋ bɔ̄-sīʌ gblʌ̋-sȕ ká* il hurle *(une personne)*

gblʌ̄ʌ̏ 1 ***n*** **chapeau à rebords** *(fait des fibres de raphia ou de paille, parfois de cuir; pour les hommes)* ♦ *gblʌ̄ʌ̏ tɔ̋* rebord de chapeau

gblʌ̄ʌ̏ 2 {gblʌ̀a} <intensif de gblʌ̋ 'crier'> ***v vi*** **crier**, **gronder** *(contre – tȁ)* ◊ *yà gblʌ̄ʌ̏, yà sʌ̄ʌ bhɔ̄* il a crié jusqu'à épuisement

gblʌ̄ʌ̋ (t) ***n*** **plafond** *(de la case ronde des femmes)*, **grenier** *(partie la plus élevée de la maison)* *Syn.* *gbàn (gw)*

gblʌ̄ʌ̏gblʌ̄ʌ̏ {gblʌ̀agblʌ̀a} <intensif de gblʌ̄ʌ̏ 'crier'> ***v vi*** **crier** *(excessivement; contre – tȁ)*

gblʌ̋agblʌ̏a (m) ***n*** *pluriel inusité* **homme fort** *(utilisé surtout comme terme d'adresse envers qn dont le nom est inconnu du locuteur)* *Syn.* *gʌ̋sʌ̋* ♦ *gblʌ̋agblʌ̏a, dhɛ̏ yà kpɔ̀œœ !* homme fort, bonjour !

gblʌ̄agblʌ̀gblʌ̄adhɤ̄ ***onomat*** **cliquetis** ◊ *pɪ̀ɤgā-dhȕn wɔ̏ bhʌ̏n wō kwʌ́ʌ̏ wɔ̏ vīn dɔ̏ gblʌ̄agblʌ̀gblʌ̄adhɤ̄* la ferraille cliquette (dans une brouette)

gblʌ̋ʌ̏ndhɤ̄ → gblʌ̋anŋ̏dhɤ̄ *crac*

gblʌ̋anŋ̏dhɤ̄, **gblʌ̋ʌ̏ndhɤ̄** ***onomat*** **craac** *(imitation du coup de tonnerre)* ◊ *dhā yȁ gblʌ̋ gblʌ̋anŋ̏dhɤ̄* le tonnerre a grondé : craac

gblʌ̋ʌ̏nsȕ ***adj*** **rauque** ♦ *ȁ wɔ̏ yȁ kʌ̄ gblʌ̋ʌ̏nsȕ* sa voix est rauque

gblʌ̏dhɤ̄ ***onomat*** **baoum** *(son d'une chute de haut par terre)* ◊ *yȁ gó dhűű gú yȁ pɤ̏ gblʌ̏dhɤ̄* il est tombé de l'arbre : baoum !

gblʌ̏n ***v*** **1** *vi* **rugir** *(animal)*, **ronronner** *(chat)* ◊ *gbɛ̂n yɤ̏ gblʌ̏n-sīʌ kwànbhɛ̏n bhȁ* le chien hurle après le voleur ◊ *dȕ gɔ̄n yɤ̏ gblʌ̏n-sīʌ* le taureau beugle *(en rage)* **2** *vt* **ronfler** ◊ *bhɛ́n bhā yɤ̏ gblʌ̏n yī gú* cet homme ronfle ♦ *yī gblʌ̏n* ronfler

gblɤ̋n ***n*** **ocre** *(peinture)* Amer. ♦ *gblɤ̋n sɔ̄* habit de couleur ocre

gblɤ̋ngblɤ̋n ***n*** arch. **engourdissement** Qsyn. *tlʉ́ʉ̄nŋ* *seulement dans l'expression :* ♦ *gblɤ̋ngblɤ̋n yà dɤ̀ ɲ̄ gɛ̀n gʉ́* j'ai les jambes engourdies *(à cause d'une position inconfortable)*

gblɤ̋nsɔ̄ ***n*** **boubou magique** *(brun à dessins foncés; est porté par les chefs et les hommes versés en magie; un atribut de certains masques)*

gblɤ̋ŋ ***n*** **roublard**

gblàzœ̀œ ***n*** ***Sylvicapra grimmia*** **céphalophe couronné** *(de 11 à 25 kg; taille environ 1 mètre, cornes droites chez les mâles seulement)*

gblæ̀ægbɤ̋n → gblɛ̀ɛgbɤ̋n *sorte de manioc*

gblʌ́ʌ̀ ***n rn*** **devant du corps** *(humain ou animal)* ◊ *yà wɔ̄ ɤ̄ gblʌ́ʌ̀ tà* il s'est tourné sur le ventre

gblʌ̋ʌ̀ ***n*** **1 vautour** *[le plus gros oiseau connu des Dan; l'image du vautour est positive; le fait qu'il se nourrisse de charogne n'est pas pris en considération; sa viande est très appréciée]* **2 Gbleu** *(nom masculin)*

gblʌ́ʌ̀dhɛ̀ {LOC gblʌ́ʌ̀dhɤ̀} ***loc.n*** *rn* **devant du corps** *(humain ou animal)* ◊ *yà ɲ̄ zʌ̄ bàdhóŋ̄ ká ɲ̄ gblʌ́ʌ̀dhɤ̀* il m'a frappé avec un ballon sur le devant ◊ *wɔ̀ ʉ̄ tàadhɛ̀ zʉ̋-sīʌ, yɤ́ bhīi dè bhɤ́ zʌ̀ yɤ́ ʉ́ ʉ̄ gblʌ́ʌ̀dhɛ̀ zʉ̀* si on te lave le dos, lave-toi le devant

gblʌ́ʌ̀dhɤ̀ ***loc.n*** *LOC de* gblʌ́ʌ̀dhɛ̀ *devant*

gblʌ̋ʌ̀dhūn {gblʌ̋ʌ̀dhūn, NEUT gblʌ̋ʌ̀dhʉ̀n} ***v*** 1) *vi* **se mettre à plat ventre**, **tomber en avant** *(d'une personne)* ♦ *gblʌ̋ʌ̀dhūn ɤ̄ gú tà* se coucher face contre terre ♦ *gblʌ̋ʌ̀dhūn ɲ̄ dhɛ̀ !* devant moi ! 2) *vt* **renverser** *(faire tomber)* ◊ *yà bàŋ gblʌ̋ʌ̀dhūn* il a renversé la bassine

gblʌ̄ʌ̀n ***n rn*** **intestin grêle** ♦ *gblʌ̄ʌ̀n gā* boyau ◊ *wʉ̄ gblʌ̄ʌ̀n dīn yɤ̀ sʌ̀* les boyaux d'animaux sont bons à manger

gblèe ***n*** **plante** *(esp., on sèche les feuilles pour la sauce d'une couleur très verte)* ♦ *gblèe yí* sauce des feuilles séchées et pilées de la plante gblèe *(couleur vert vif)*

gblèeyídhē ***n*** **couleur verte** ◊ *yà ɤ̄ bhā gɔ̄ yɤ̋n kʌ̄ gblèeyídhē ká* il a peint sa voiture en vert

gblɛ̀ɛ ***n*** **sorte d'igname** *(à larges feuilles, sans épines; le tubercule est jaune à violet à l'intérieur; peu sucré, mais savoureux; tardif) [auparavant, cette sorte prédominait; de nos jours, elle est remplacée par yɤ̋; on ne la cultive que pour sa propre consommation, plutôt que pour la vente; on la cuit non-épluchée]* Qsyn. dhɔ̄ɔ 2, yɤ̋ ◊ *gblɛ̀ɛ dīn yɤ̀ sʌ̀ ɤ́ zìɤ ká dhɔ̄ɔ tà* l'igname "gblèè" est plus savoureux que l'igname "doo"

gblɛ̀ɛgbɤ̋n, **gblæ̀ægbɤ̋n** ***n*** **manioc local** *(à bon rendement, bon pour le foutou et le tô; se mange cuit ou cru)*

gblɛ̀ɛn, **gbɛ̀n** ***prev*** *seulement dans le verbe gblɛ̀ɛn-kpɔ́*

gblɛ̀ɛn 1) {A P S, pl. gblɛ̀ɛn-dhǜn pl., gblɛ̀ɛn-sǜ foc. A; gblɛ̀ngblɛ̀n Int. pl. A P S, gblɛ̀ngblɛ̀n-dhǜn Int. pl. A, gblɛ̀ngblɛ̀n-sǜ Int. pl. foc. A S, gblɛ̀ngblɛ̀n-sǜ-dhǜn Int. pl. foc. A S; gblɛ̀ɛngblɛ̋ndhɛ̏, gblɛ̀nkɛ̋ngblɛ̏nkɛ̏n SupInt. A, gblɛ̀ɛngblɛ̋ndhɛ̏-sǜ, gblɛ̀nkɛ̋ngblɛ̏nkɛ̏n-sǜ SupInt. foc. A} *adj* **1 long**, **profond** *(récipient, trou)*, **grand**, **haut** ◊ *zīaan gblɛ̀ɛngblɛ̋ndhɛ̏ bhā yɤ́, bhāny dō bhāan ȁ sṹ ȅe ?* dois-je m'engager tout seul sur ce chemin si long ? ♦ *bhɛ̄n gblɛ̀ɛn* personne de grande taille **2 éloigné** *(espace ou temps)* ◊ *Bīyȁ dhɛ̏ yɤ̏ gblɛ̀ɛn* Abidjan est loin ◊ *ɯ̄ n̄ ká gblɛ̀ɛn* tu es loin de moi ◊ *ȁ tɛ́ɛ-dhɛ̏ yáa gblɛ̀ɛn zɯ́* elle (l'eau) va bouillir bientôt **3 longue** *(temps)* ◊ *ā dhǜn kɤ̄ á tɤ̋ŋ gblɛ̀ɛn kʌ̄ yɤ́* je suis venu ici pour longtemps

gblɛ̀ɛn 2) *adv* **loin** ◊ *yīȉ gbǽæ yáa dhɛ̏ yā ká gblɛ̀ɛn* notre endroit secret n'est pas loin d'ici

gblɛ̄ɛ̋n (m) *n* **jalousie**

gblɛ̄ɛ̋nbhōdhɛ̏ *n* **femme jalouse**

gblɛ̀ɛn-dhɛ̏ *n* **longueur, hauteur, profondeur** ◊ *yɛ̏gā ɤ́ bhȁ gblɛ̀ɛn-dhɛ̏ ɤ́ bhɛ́ntlʌ̏ dō* un trou d'un mètre de profondeur

gblɛ̀ɛngblɛ̋ndhɛ̏ *adj SupInt. de* gblɛ̀ɛn *long*

gblɛ̏ɛn-kpɔ́ (gw) {gblɛ̏ɛn-kpɔ̄} *v* **1** 1) *vt* **cacher** *(de – gɔ̏)* Syn. bȉn, dɛ̀ɛ̏n-kpɔ́ 2) *vr* **se cacher** Syn. dɛ̀ɛ̏n-kpɔ́ ◊ *yà tó ɤ̄ gblɛ̏ɛn-kpɔ́-dhɛ̏ gɯ́, yī yà ȁ kɯ́n* il est resté assis caché et s'est endormi **2** *vr* **dresser une embuscade** Syn. dɛ̀ɛ̏n-kpɔ́

gblɛ̄ɛ̋nsǜ *adj* **jaloux** ♦ *gɔ̄n gblɛ̄ɛ̋nsǜ* homme jaloux

Gblɛ̏ɛsé *n* **Kpellé**, **Guerzé** *(un groupe ethnique en Guinée Forestière et au Liberia et sa langue appartenant au groupe mandé sud-ouest)*

gblɛ̀ngblɛ̀n 1 *adv* **éloignés et nombreux** ◊ *wȍ gȍ bhɯ̄n gblɛ̀ngblɛ̀n wó dhɯ̄n* ils sont venus d'endroits lointains (et différents)

gblɛ̀ngblɛ̀n 2 *adj Int. pl. de* gblɛ̀ɛn *long*

gblɛ̀nkɛ̋ngblɛ̏nkɛ̏n *adj SupInt. de* gblɛ̀ɛn *long*

gblɔ̀ŋ *n rn* **molaires** ◊ *ȁ gblɔ̀ŋ yáa ȁ dhí* il n'a pas de molaires dans la bouche ◊ *yɛ̏gā yȁ' gblɔ̀ŋ gɯ́* il a des trous dans sa molaires ♦ *gblɔ̀ŋ gā* molaire *(gā est obligatoire dans le compte)* ◊ *yɛ̏gā yȁ' gblɔ̀ŋ gā gɯ́* il a un trou dans son molaire

gblȍo, **glȍo** *n* **tabouret, chaise, divan** *(tout meuble pour s'asseoir)* Syn. yȁtȁglȍo ♦ *tòo kpȁtȁ gblȍo* petit tabouret de cuisine ♦ *gɔ̋ gblȍȍ* chaise dans la case sacrée, couverte d'une peau de léopard

gblóȍ *n Hibiscus esculentus* **gombo** ♦ *gblóȍ gā* cosse de gombo

gblőo, **glőo** *n* **1** *rn* **trace** Syn. pínŋ̏ ◊ *būugā gblőo yɤ̏ kɔ́ bhȁ* il y a une trace de balle sur la maison ◊ *gbɛ̂n yà zīɤ wɯ̄ gblőo kèŋ̏* le chien a suivi la trace de l'animal ◊ *yɤ̏ tɑ̋ sɯ́ blɯ̋n glőo tȁ* il suit la trace d'un porc-épic ◊ *kȍ dhó n̄ dʌ̄-dhǜn pīɤ yʌ̀n āan kō gblőo ká āa, kíi yȁ bhɯ̄n* allons retourner chez mes parents, et tu t'y installeras ♦ *gbɛ̂n sɔ̋n* *gblɔ̋o* morsure de chien *(blessure)* ♦ *kɔ̀ gblɔ̋o* écriture *(manière d'écrire)* ♦ *bhá dhó gó' ūū gblɔ̋o !* ne bouge pas ! **2** *rn* **résultat** Syn. *pínŋ̀* ♦ *ɤ̄ gblɔ̋o yɤ̄* avoir des bons résultats **3** *rn gblɔ̋o gúú* **au lieu de, à la place de** **4** **lit** *(d'une rivière)* ◊ *yí yɤ̀ zīɤ-sīʌ ɤ̄ glɔ̋o tà* la rivière coule dans son lit

gblɔ̀okōtàŋgúúdhē <tabouret-dos-appuyer-dans-nominalis.> *n* **chaise** *(avec le dos)*, **fauteuil**

gblɔ̀ *n* **lièvre** *(dans le dialecte de Gwèètaa, ce mot est emprunté au dialecte Téé)* Syn. *sʌ̄ndhʌ́n*

gblɔ̀dhɛ̀e < ?-féminin> *n* **mai**

gblɔ̀gɔ̄n < ?-masculin> *n* **avril**

gblɔ̄ŋ́ *n* ***Upupa epops*** **huppe** *(28 cm, corps et tête brun cannelle, queue et ailes noires à larges rayures blanches, huppe érectile à frange noire, long bec fin et recourbé)*

gblɔ̄ŋ́gblɔ̀ŋgblɔ̄ŋ́dhɤ̄ *adv* **en titubant** ♦ *wò tà /tá sùù/ gblɔ̄ŋ́gblɔ̀ŋgblɔ̄ŋ́dhɤ̄* ils marchent en titubant

gblɤ̀ *v vt* **balayer** Syn. *wlɤ̀* ◊ *yà dhɛ̀ gblɤ̀ kɔ́ɔdhɤ̄* elle a balayé la maison ◊ *dhēbʌ̀dhʌ́n bhā yà dhɛ̀ gblɤ̀ kwáŋ̄dhɤ̄* la femme a balayé la cour ♦ *dhɛ̀ gblɤ̀-sùù* balayage ♦ *yà kɔ́ɔdhɛ̀ gblɤ̀* elle a balayé la maison

gblɤ̀ (t) *n* **arbre** *(espèce de)*

gblɤ́gblɤ́ {pl. A P S, gblɤ́gblɤ́-dhùn pl. A S, gblɤ́gblɤ́-sùù foc. A S, gblɤ́gblɤ́-sùù-dhùn foc. pl. A S} *adj pluralia tantum, mais peut aller avec un pronom singulier s'il s'agit d'un déterminé collectif* **1.1 grands** Qsyn. *kpíì* ♦ *kwɛ̀ɛ̀ gblɤ́gblɤ́* bagages volumineux ◊ *bhʌ̄nŋgā ɤ́ wɛ̀nŋ dɛ̀ɛ yɤ̀ gùn gblɤ́gblɤ́ ká* il y a eu une énorme chute de grêle aujourd'hui **1.2 gros** *(jambe; signe de beauté féminine)* ◊ *dhēbʌ̀ gɛ̀ngbɔ̄ gblɤ́gblɤ́ dhʌ̀n ɤ́ sʌ̀* les femmes aux gros mollets sont jolies **2 important** ♦ *dhīaŋ gblɤ́gblɤ́ zʌ̄ dhɔ̀ yà kʌ̀* i) il aime les grands mots ii) il aime régler les grands litiges **3 aîné** Qsyn. *kpíì* ♦ *à bhà bhēn gblɤ́gblɤ́ yáa dhɤ́* il n'a pas d'aînés *(il ne respecte personne)*

gblɤ́kɤ́gblɤ̀kɤ̀ *Int. de* gblɤ́ɤgblɤ̀ɤ *sec et dur*

gblɤ́kɤ́gblɤ̀kɤ̀gblɤ̀kɤ́gblɤ̀ɤ̀ *intj* **que c'est sec et dur !** *(de la nourriture)*

gblɤ̀ɤdhɛ̀ <ventre- ?-femme> *n* **femme stérile**

gblɤ́ɤ̀dhɛ̀ → gblúúdhɛ̀ *ventre*

gblɤ́ɤgblɤ̀ɤ {A P S, gblɤ́ɤgblɤ̀ɤ-dhùn pl. A S, gblɤ́ɤgblɤ̀ɤ-sùù foc. A, gblɤ́ɤgblɤ̀ɤ-sùù-dhùn foc. pl. A S; gblɤ́kɤ́gblɤ̀kɤ̀ Int. A P S, gblɤ́kɤ́gblɤ̀kɤ̀-dhùn Int. pl. A, gblɤ́kɤ́gblɤ̀kɤ̀-sùù Int. foc. A, gblɤ́kɤ́gblɤ̀kɤ̀-sùù-dhùn Int. foc. pl. A} *adj* **dur et sec** Ant. *plʌ́ʌplʌ̀ʌ* ♦ *blúù gblɤ́ɤgblɤ̀ɤ* pain dur

gblű (m) *n* **déchets, ordures** Syn. *blʌ̄ʌ*

gblúgblùgblúdhɤ̄ *onomat* bruit de bouillonnement ◊ *gbɔ̄ yɤ̀ tɛ̀ɛ gblúgblùgblúdhɤ̄* la marmite bout

gblūǘdhɤ̄ *onomat* **soudain et fort**

gblǜuuu *onomat* **pan !** *(coup de feu)*

gblɯ̀ 1 *n* **1 guerre** ◊ *yī gùn yī kó kèŋ gblɯ̀ bhà* nous avons fait la guerre ensemble ♦ *yí sæ̀æ gblɯ̀* guerre languissante, guerre froide ♦ *gblɯ̀ yāa* une sale guerre (sans respect des conventions) ♦ *gblɯ̀ gɔ̄ɔn bhēn ká* faire la guerre à qn ♦ *gblɯ̀ yà ȁ kún* i) il est tombé dans une embuscade ii) il s'est trouvé dans une situation très difficile ◊ *gblɯ̀ yà n̄ kún, kȁ tá̋ n̄ dhɛ̏* au secours ! ◊ *ā dhò gblɯ̀ bhȁ* je vais à la guerre **2 troupe, armée** ♦ *gblɯ̀ sɯ́* rassembler la troupe; aller à la guerre **3 malheur**

gblɯ̀ 2 *v vt* **diviser**, **partager**

gblɯ̀ 3 *v vt* **couvrir avec** *(qch – tȁ)* ◊ *bhán kɔ̏ gblɯ̀ wʌ́ʌ̀gā tȁ* j'ai couvert la pièce de monnaie avec ma main

gblɯ̀ 4 → gblɯ̀ *trou*

gblɯ̀, **gblɯ̀** *n* **trou** *(cavité)* *Qsyn.* *gblɯ̀gā (avec les numéros, les deux formes s'utilisent, gblɯ̀gā et gblɯ̀)* ◊ *bhān yí tɔ̏ ká bhīʌ́gā yà pɤ̏ klòŋ gblɯ̀ gɯ́* ma corde pour puiser de l'eau est tombée dans le puits

gblɯ́ 1 {gblɯ̀} *n* **1** *gɔ̂ gblɯ́* **panier pour les noix de cola** *(rectangulaire ou rond, pour plus de 100 noix)* **2 mille** ♦ *gblɯ́ dō* mille, un millier ♦ *gblɯ́ tȁ gblɯ̀* milliers ◊ *bhēn gblɯ́ tȁ gblɯ̀ wɔ̏ sɛ́ ɤ́ yā ȁ gɯ́* il y a des milliers de gens dans cette région

gblɯ́ 2 *n rn* **ventre** *Qsyn.* *gú, gɯ́, gblɯ́dhɛ̏* ♦ *ȁ gblɯ́ yɤ̏ zīɤ-sīʌ* il a la diarrhée ♦ *ȁ gblɯ́ yɤ̏ yâ* il est méchant ♦ *yɤ̏ gblɯ́ yāȁ kʌ̄-sīʌ* il est en train de manger sans partager sa nourriture avec les autres

gblɯ̀dʌ̄ <guerre-père> *n* **chef, leader; roi**

gblɯ̀dhānkʌ̄bhɛ̏n <guerre-approche furtive-faire-personne> *n* **éclaireur** *(soldat envoyé en reconnaissance)*

gblɯ̀dhɛ̏ {LOC gblɯ̄ɯdhɤ̄} *loc.n* **trou** *(en sol)* *Qsyn.* *gblɯ̀* ◊ *yȁ pɤ̏ gblɯ̄ɯdhɤ̄* il est tombé dans le trou ◊ *bhān bhīʌ́gā yɤ̏ pɤ̏ klɔ̏ŋ ɤ́ gɯ́ bhā, ȁ gblɯ̀dhɛ̏ yɤ̏ gbɛ́ɛ* le puits dans lequel ma corde est tombée, son intérieur est large

gblɯ́dhɛ̏, **gblɯ́ɯ̀dhɛ̏**, **gblɤ̋ɤ̀dhɛ̏** {LOC gblɯ́dhɤ̄, SUP gblɯ́ɯ́} *loc.n les formes gblɯ́dhɛ̏ et gblɯ́ɯ̀dhɛ̏ sont en alternance libre dans certains contextes et pas dans d'autres* **1** *rn* **ventre** *Qsyn.* *gú, gɯ́, gblɯ́* ♦ *ȁ gblɯ́dhɛ̏ yà pīɤ̏ɤ-sīʌ* il a des maux de ventre ♦ *ȁ gblɯ́dhɛ̏ yà tó dhɛ̏ɛnsɯ̏* il a des maux de ventre ♦ *n̄ gblɯ́dhɛ̏ yɤ̏ wɛ́-sīʌ bhōŋ́bhòŋbhōŋ́dhɤ̄* j'ai des gargouillements *(après un repas abondant)* ♦ *gèebhȁan yɤ̏ tá̋n kʌ̄-sīʌ n̄ gblɯ́dhɤ̄/gblɯ́ɯ́* je crève de faim *(lit. : un masque-oiseau danse dans mon ventre)* **2** *rn* **intérieur** *(d'une personne)* *Qsyn.* *gɯ́* ◊ *bhēn bháa ȁ gbɯ́ɯ́ wɔ̀n dɔ̄* personne ne connait ses pensées ♦ *ȁ gblɯ́dhɛ̏ yɤ̏ gblèɛn* il est rancunier ♦ *ȁ gblɯ́dhɛ̏ yɤ̏ pɯ́u* il est bienveillant ♦ *ȁ gblɯ́dhɛ̏ yɤ̏ tīī* il est malveillant; c'est un sorcier

gblɯ́dhɤ̄ *loc.n LOC de* gblɯ́dhɛ̏ *ventre*

gblɯ̀gā *n* **trou profond**, **gouffre** *(plutôt rond)* *Qsyn.* *yègā, gblɯ̀*

gblʉ̀ʉ̀gɔ̄ɔnbhɛ̀n <guerre-faire-personne> ***n*** **guerrier, militaire** ♦ *gblʉ̀ʉ̀gɔ̄ɔnbhɛ̀n-dhʉ̀n gɔ̀bhɛ̀n* chef de guerre

gblʉ̋ʉ̋kʌ̄ ***n*** **douleurs de l'accouchement** Syn. *gʉ̋dhɛ̀ (t)*

gblʉ̀ʉ̀kplʌ́ʌnŋ ***n*** **héros** *(de guerre)*

gblʉ̀ʉ̀ŋ ***n Python sebae*** **python** *(serpent africain le plus grand, jusqu'à 7,5 de longueur; il frappe la victime avec sa tête, la mord, l'écrase avec ses cercles, et l'avale)* ◊ *wà gblʉ̀ʉ̀ŋ gbìɤɤ yɤ̀ ɤ̄ yɔ̋n kʌ̀* lorsqu'on traîne le python, il en engraisse *[selon une croyance des Dan]* ♦ *gblʉ̀ʉ̀ŋ kplʉ̋ zìŋŋgʉ́* corps de python *(tête et queue non comprises)*

gblʉ̄ʉ̄ŋ, **gbīnŋ** ***n*** **punaises** ◊ *gbīnŋ yɤ̀ sǣǣ́ yā' gʉ́* il y a des punaises dans cette natte

gblʉ̋ʉ̋ʉ́ ***loc.n*** *SUP de* gblʉ̋dhɛ̀ *ventre*

gblʉ̄ɯɯdhɤ̄ ***loc.n*** *LOC de* gbʉ̀dhɛ̀ *trou*

gblʉ̄ɯɯsɔ̀ <trou-piège> ***n*** **trappe** *(une piège constitué d'un trou peu profond avec une verge élastique, une corde et une fiche)* ◊ *bhān gblʉ̄ɯɯsɔ̀ yā yɤ̀ bhìa ɤ̄ dè kɔ̄ɔ* ma trappe s'est déclenchée toute seule

gblʉ̋ʉ̋yāà <ventre-mauvais ?> ***n*** **pingrerie** *(refus de partager de la nourriture ou des biens)* ♦ *gblʉ̋yāà kʌ̄* faire le pingre ◊ *Zân yà gblʉ̋yāà kʌ̄ ɴ̄ ká* Jean a été avare à mon égard

gblʉ̋ʉ̋zīɤ <estomac-passer> ***n*** **diarrhée** ♦ *gblʉ̋zīɤ zǣǣndhē* diarrhée cholériforme ♦ *gblʉ̋zīɤ gbɛ̋ɛ̀ yà bhà* il a une diarrhée grave

gbō {gbò} ***n*** **1** *rn* **excrément, merde** gros. *(sans autre précision il s'agit d'excréments humains)* ◊ *bhán gbō-dhʉ̀n yɤ̄* j'ai vu des tas d'excréments ♦ *gbō pɛ̋n* crotte ♦ *gbō yí* excrément liquide ♦ *à gbō yɤ̀ tò sīāa bhʉ̄n* il a chié dans son froc ♦ *à gbō yà zūa à bhà* il a chié dans ses culottes **2.1 dépôt** *(du liquide)*, **résidu** Qsyn. *kɛ̋ɛ 1* ◊ *kāflɛ̋ɛ̀ gbō yà tó vɛ̋dhɛ̋ gʉ́* le marc du café est resté dans le verre ◊ *wà bhlʉ̀ʉ̀n pìɤ yɤ́ wó à gbò wɛ̀nŋ* quand on vanne le riz, on jette sa balle ♦ *dhʉ̋ gbò* sciure de bois ♦ *pìɤ gbō* limaille de fer ♦ *ʉ̄ fɔ̋ofòo ká dhɛ̀ bhlʉ̀ʉ̀n gbò dhɤ́* tu es inutile comme le son de riz **3** *rn* **sécrétion solide** ♦ *tɔ̋ gbō* cérumen ♦ *yɑ̋n gbō* chassie

gbő {gbò} ***n*** **pleurs; gémissement** *(chien)* ◊ *yɤ́' dhē yɤ̀ dà' dhɛ̀ gbő gʉ́* et sa mère s'est mise à le pleurer ♦ *gbő bɔ̄* pleurer; gémir *(chien)* ♦ *dhʌ́n bhā yɤ̀ dīì gbò bɔ̄-sīʌ* l'enfant pleure de faim ◊ *gbő gbɛ́ bɔ̄-sʉ̀ʉ yáa sʌ̀* il n'est pas bon de beaucoup pleurer ♦ *gɔ̄ɔ̀n yɤ̀ gbő bɔ̀ ɤ̄ zʉ̄ʌ́ pɩ́ɤ* l'homme pleure en silence ♦ *gbő kpɤ̄sìan yàa kún* il sanglote *(d'un enfant épuisé par ses pleurs)*

gbô ***n*** **arbre** *(espèce : grande, avec une sève blanche; autrefois son écorce était battue et transformée en tissu libérien)* ♦ *gbô kɤ̀ sɔ̄, gbô sɔ̄* tissu libérien *[on l'obtenait par battage de l'écorce de gbô, ce qui était un travail des hommes; dans les anciens temps cette écorce était rare, seuls les riches l'avaient; avec l'apparition de l'étoffe tissé, on l'a déclassée comme habit des pauvres, puis on a abandonné sa fabrication]* ◊ *yà gbô kɛ́ɛ bhàn kɤ̄ yɤ̀ à kʌ̄ sɔ̄ ká* il a battu l'écorce de gbô pour obtenir du tissu libérien

gbɔ̋gbɔ̋kɔ̋ < ?-maison> ***n*** **cadenas**

gbōkȁa <excrément-gale> ***n*** **mycose** *(cause des démangeaisons, la peau parte en lambeaux)* ♦ *gbōkȁa yà lòo ȁ bhȁ* il a une mycose

gbōkȕngbōkȕndhɤ̄ ***adv*** **à tout prix** *Syn. gbōŋgbōŋdhɤ̄*

gbòŋ (m) ***n*** *bhlȕn gbòŋ* **farine fine du riz** *(reste après un pilage prolongé) [on la donne d'habitude aux enfants, c'est un délice du village; le mot est utilisé surtout à Man] Syn. gùnŋ*

gbɔ̋ŋgbɔ̋ ***n*** **seau** *(en plastique ou en fer)* ♦ *gbɔ̋ŋgbɔ̋ gʌ̄n* anse de seau ♦ *pɪ̏ɤɤgā gbɔ̋ŋgbɔ̋* seau en fer

gbōŋgbōŋdhɤ̄ ***adv*** **à tout prix** *Syn. gbōkūngbōkūndhɤ̄* ◊ *ā dhɔ̀ dhūn' gbōŋgbōŋdhɤ̄* je ferai tout pour venir

gbōo {gbòo} <*gbō bhō excrément-sortir> ***v vr*** **déféquer, faire caca, chier** gros. ♦ *bhīi ū gbōo bhān dhʌ̀n n̄ bhȁ ȅe ?* c'est avec moi que tu vas faire tes bêtises ?

gbɔ̋ɔ̀ ***n*** **vieillard décrépit, vieille décrépite** ♦ *yà kʌ̄ gbɔ̋ɔ̀ ká, yà gbɔ̋ɔ̀ kún, yà gbɔ̋ɔ̀ kȁn* il a beaucoup vieilli

gbōobhȅn <déféquer-personne> ***n*** **chieur** *(celui qui défèque)* ♦ *gbōobhȅn yȁ ɤ̄ yȅɛ kún, yɤ́ kὲfá sɯ́ prov.* c'est après s'être assis confortablement qu'un chieur se met à attraper les poux *(il faut d'abord acquérir une position dans la société pour obtenir le droit de faire ce qu'on veut)*

gbɔ̋ɔ̀-dhȅ ***n*** **décrépitude** *(de l'humain)* ♦ *gbɔ̋ɔ̀dhȅ yáa sʌ̀* la vieillesse n'est pas bonne

gbōokɔ̀ <déféquer-maison> ***n*** **toilettes** *(là où on peut déféquer)*

gbɔ̄ {gbɔ̀} ***n*** **marmite, pot, canari** lv. *(générique; par défaut, en métal)* ♦ *gbɔ̄ gʌ̄n* anse de marmite ♦ *gbɔ̄ tɔ́* bord de marmite ♦ *fɔ̋ŋ gbɔ̄* casserole en aluminium, casserole en acier inoxydable ♦ *pɪ̏ɤ gā gbɔ̄* marmite en fer ♦ *yɪ́tȁgbɔ̀* jarre pour l'eau ♦ *sɛ́ gbɔ̄* pot d'argile ♦ *dù gbɔ̀* canari contenant de la viande de bœuf ◊ *yɛɛdhē-dhȕn dhʌn ɤ̄ wó sɛ́ gbɔ̄ kʌ̀* ce sont les griottes qui font les canaris

gbɔ̄dȉʌʌ ***n*** ***Chrysococcyx caprius, Lampromorpha caprius*** **coucou didric** *(19 cm, dos vert brillant à reflets cuivrés, ventre blanc; parasite des nids des autres oiseaux)*

gbɔ̄dɔ̄dhȅ <pot-construire-femme> ***n*** **potière** *[chez les Dan, les pots sont fabriqués par les femmes de la caste des griots, yɛ̄ɛdhē]*

gbɔ̂n (, t) ***n*** ***Carapa procera (gen. Meliaceae)*** **carapa** *(arbre, esp.; normalement environ 15 de haut, parfois jusqu'à 60, 2 de diamètre; tronc droit, avec des contreforts; bois dur, fruits rouges-bruns à enveloppe dure et rugueuse, à goût amer; les petits porc-épics apprécient les grains de carapa)* ♦ *gbɔ̂n yɔ̋n* huile de carapa

gbɔ̀ŋ ***n*** **guêpe, guêpes** *(nom générique)*, **frelon** ♦ *gbɔ̀ŋ gā* guêpe ◊ *gbɔ̀ŋ yɤ̀ n̄ bhɔ̀ yāandhɪ́ɤ* les guêpes m'ont piqué hier ♦ *gbɔ̀ŋ kɔ́* nid de guêpes

gbɔ̄ŋ, gbœ̄œŋ ***n*** **case rectangulaire** *(case d'homme) Syn. kɔ́dhʌ́n*

gbɔ́ŋ {A} ***adj*** **grand** *(pierre)* ♦ *gwʌ̀ gbɔ́ŋ* rocher, grande pierre

gbɔ̋ŋ 1 ***n*** **pétioles des palmes de raphia** *(beaucoup utilisées dans différents travaux)* ♦ *gbɔ̋ŋ gā* un pétiole de palme de raphia

gbɔ̋ŋ 2 {A, pl. gbɔ̋ŋgbɔ̋ŋ A, gbɔ̋ŋgbɔ̋ŋ-dhȉn A} ***adj*** *la forme gbɔ̋ŋgbɔ̋ŋ-dhȉn est utilisée pour les humains, gbɔ̋ŋgbɔ̋ŋ pour les non-humains* **1 jeune** *(un humain de 17-25 ans; un animal)* **2 de moyenne taille, petit** ◊ *tɔ̀n gbɔ̋ŋ* petite montagne

gbɔ̋ŋgbɔ̋ŋ ***adj*** *Pl. de* gbɔ̋ŋ *jeune*

gbɔ̀ɔ ***n*** **dépôt**

gbɔ̄ɔ̋ <*gbɔ̄-dhʌ́n ?> ***n*** **pot magique** *(pour des drogues traditionnelles)* ♦ *n̄ dhē à gbɔ̄ɔ̋* le pot magique de ma mère *(une formule d'invitation à la lutte; en la prononçant, on tend un poing avec du sable; en acceptant le défi, l'adressé frappe le poing en cherchant à éparpiller le sable)*

gbɔ̋ɔ̀, gbœ̋œ̀ ***n*** **fronde** *(tressée en fibres de raphia, utilisée par les gardiens des champs pour chasser les oiseaux)* ♦ *gbɔ̋ɔ̀ kɔ́* poche de fronde ♦ *gbɔ̋ɔ̀ gʌ̄n* lanière de fronde ♦ *gbɔ̋ɔ̀ zȕɤ à ká* lancer une pierre à qn/qch avec la fronde ♦ *wūn gbɔ̋ɔ̀ bɔ̄* faire des tresses longues *(le plus souvent, avec des mèches artificielles)*

gbɔ̄ɔ́dȕʉ <*gbɔ̄dhʌn gʉ́ dȕ pot-diminutif-dans-sorcellerie> ***n*** **sorcellerie** *(pratiquée avec un canari, pour manger les âmes)*

gbɔ̀ɔn, gbœ̀œn ***v*** **1** *vi* **fatiguer, embêter** *(faire souffrir; qn – tà)* ◊ *klàŋ̀ yà gbɔ̀ɔn n̄ tà* je suis fatigué par les études ♦ *dīŋ̀ yà gbɔ̀ɔn n̄ tà* je suis fatigué par la faim **2** *vi* **rabougrir** *(qch – tà)* Qsyn. fiʌʌn ♦ *yʌ́nŋ̀ yà gbɔ̀ɔn bhlȕn tà* la chaleur du soleil a rabougri le riz **3** *vi* **être trop exigeant** *(par rapport à – tà)* ♦ *yà gbɔ̀ɔn wɔ́n bhā à tà* il est trop exigeant dans cette affaire *(p.ex., en exigeant une amende trop élevée)*

gbɔ̄ɔŋ ***n*** **chauve-souris** *(grande, mange les fruits)*

gbɤ̄ ***n*** **1** *rn* **fils** *(dans le sens classificatoire : propre fils; fils de dhòo; pour une femme, fils de la sœur aînée ou de la coépouse; pour un homme, fils de la sœur) [utilisé comme terme d'adresse par rapport au fils de la sœur aînée de la femme; on s'adresse à son propre fils par son nom ou, si son nom est le même que le nom de son grand-père, son parent dit n̄ dʌ̄]* **2** *rn* **beau-frère, beau-fils** *(par rapport à une femme : mari de sa sœur cadette; mari de la fille ou de la petite-fille de sa sœur cadette)* **3** *rn* **fils** *(terme d'adresse à un homme de plus jeune génération, sans lien de parenté)*

gbɤ̋ŋ ***n*** **grelots du plomb** *(instrument musical des femmes, en forme de sonnailles; on en met de 40 à 50 sur la corde qu'on attache à la cheville du pied; pendant la danse kòŋ tʌ̋n, ils se portent aussi au bras)* ♦ *gbɤ̋ŋ gā* un grelot ◊ *Kòŋ yà gbɤ̋ŋ yà* le masque féminin Kong porte des grelots

gbɤ̋ŋgā ***n*** **balle** *(pour une arme)*

gbœ̀œ 1 {gbœ̀œ} ***v*** *vt* **faire cadeau de qch** *(à – gɔ̀, dans la situation où on s'attend le cadeau)* Qsyn. gœ̄œ ◊ *yà wūɪ gbœ̀œ n̄ gɔ̀* il m'a fait cadeau de viande

gbœ̀œ 2 ***n*** ***Myrianthus arboreus (gen. Cecropiaceae)*** **arbre** *(à feuilles larges)*

gbœ̄œ ***n*** **bambou, bambou de Chine** *Iv.* ♦ *gbœ̄œgā* tige de bambou

gbœ̋œ̀ → gbɔ̋ɔ̀ *fronde*

gbœ̄œdhē ***n*** **1 cadeau** Qsyn. tāa, sāan ◊ *yà gbœ̄œdhē kʌ̄ n̄ gɔ̀ dù ká* il m'a fait cadeau d'un bœuf **2 aumône**

gbœ̀œdhɛ̋ ***n*** **1 feuille de l'arbre Myrianthus arboreus** *(on les mâche ou on en mange une sauce contre les vertiges)* **2.1 vertige** ♦ *gbœ̀œdhɛ̋ yà dà à gúí* il a eu le vertige **2.2 rotation** *(un élément de danse : sans se déplacer, on tourne avec une grande intensité) [l'aptitude de tourner longuement et d'une manière intense est un signe du grand pouvoir magique d'un masque]* ♦ *yɤ̀ gbœ̀œdhɛ̋ kʌ̄-sīʌ* il tourne sur place ◊ *kɔ̀bhán yà gbœ̀œdhɛ̋ súí* le masque Koma a exécuté une rotation

gbœ̀œn → gbɔ̀ɔn *fatiguer*

gbœ̄œŋ → gbɔ̄ŋ *case rectangulaire*

gbœ̄œpʌ̀ <donner cadeau-chose> ***n*** **cadeau** ♦ *bhān gbœ̄œpʌ̀ dhɛ̀n* voici mon cadeau

gbú ***n*** **moitié** ◊ *dhɛ̋dhɛ̋ gbú ká* en une demi-heure ◊ *wē gbú dhʌ̀n úí n̄ gbā à ká zɔ̀ɔ wà* c'est un demi-verre de vin que tu m'as donné

gbúgbúdhɤ̄ ***onomat*** **glougloutant, gargouillant** ◊ *yí yɤ̀ bhɔ̄-sīʌ gbúgbúdhɤ̄* l'eau fait glouglou (en sortant d'une bouteille) ◊ *yí yɤ̀ zīɤ-sīʌ gbúgbúdhɤ̄* l'eau sort à la surface en faisant glouglou (d'une source d'eau)

gbūŋgbùŋgbūŋdhɤ̄ ***onomat*** **pop** *(bruit de pas sur le toit en tôle)* ◊ *yà tá súí kɔ́ tà gbūŋgbùŋgbūŋdhɤ̄* il a marché sur le toit

gbūuŋdhɤ̄ ***onomat*** **baoum** *(son d'un coup sourd)* ◊ *yà pɤ̀ sí̃āa gbūuŋdhɤ̄* il est tombé par terre : baoum !

gbūuŋgbūŋdhɤ̄ ***onomat*** **boum-boum** *(son de tambour)*

gbúùu ***intj*** **boum !** *(détonation)*

Gw gw

gwɑ̋ ***n*** **1 "gwa"** *(groupe de danse à Santa, formé par les hommes de la même classe d'âge, le plus souvent membres du même clan) [avec l'introduction de l'éducation scolaire, ce groupe ne fonctionne presque plus]* Qsyn. bɑ̋nkpɤ̄, kêkpɤ̄ ♦ *gwɑ̋ gɔ̀bhɛ̀n* chef du groupe "gwa" ♦ *gwɑ̋ gɔ̀bhɛ̀n kɔ̀ wlɤ̀ɤ bhɛ̀n* chef adjoint du groupe "gwa" ♦ *gwɑ̋ dhʌ́n* arch. membre de "gwa" *(qui peut participer à la danse)* ♦ *gwɑ̋ tɑ̋n* la danse du groupe "gwa" *(accompagnée de la musique du tambour gɔ̄dhʌ́n)* ♦ *gwɑ̋'-dhàan kê kpɤ̄* la brigade de travail champêtre du groupe "gwa" ♦ *yɤ̀ gwɑ̋ kpɤ̄ gúí* il est membre de l'association "gwa" **2 Gwa** *(groupe masculin de danse) [les membres de ce groupe dansent avec des bâtons et un masque sur la tête]* ♦ *gwɑ̋ gèe* le masque du groupe Gwa

gwàa ***n*** **rocher plat** *en quelques combinaisons* Qsyn. gwàadhɛ̀

gwàa̋dhɛ̏ {LOC gwàadhɤ̄, LOC pl. gwàadhɛ̏-dhùn gúɯ} ***loc.n*** **rocher plat**; **plateau rocheux** *[près du village, on y organise des réunions; auprès des cours d'eau, on y fait sécher les habits]* Qsyn. gwàa ◊ *gwàa̋dhɛ̏ dō yɤ̄ n̄ gɔ̏ bhláā* il y a un large rocher plat dans mon champ ◊ *bhȁan dō yà pɤ̏ gwàadhɤ̄* un oiseau est tombé sur le rocher plat ◊ *yà sɔ̄ kpɔ́ gwàa̋dhɛ̏-dhùn gúɯ* elle a étalé les vêtements sur les rochers plats

gwàadhɤ̄ ***loc.n*** *LOC de* gwàadhɛ̏ *rocher plat*

gwāa̋gbɛ̂n <rocher-sur-chien> ***n*** ***Procavia ruficeps*** **daman de rocher** *(herbivore ongulé nocturne, ressemble à un lapin, mais à la différence de ce dernier, ses oreilles sont courtes et arrondies; son dessus varie de rouge-brun à gris-jaune; le cou, les épaules et le ventre sont plus clairs; ses excréments ressemblent à ceux des caprins)*

gwàan ***n*** **fleuve**

gwāa̋n *SUP de* gwān *mariage*

gwāandhɤ̄ ***loc.n*** *LOC de* gwān *mariage*

gwāa̋nkpɔ́yɔ̋ɔ ***n*** *rn* **co-épouse**

gwàawɯ̏ <rocher-animal> ***n*** ***Procavia ruficeps*** **daman de rocher** Syn. gwāa̋gbɛ̂n

gwàn 1 ***n*** **sang** *(coulant du nez)* ♦ *gwàn yȁ kɯ̋n ȁ yūn gúɯ* il a saigné du nez

gwàn 2 ***n*** **Gwan** *(rivière entre le village de Santa et celui de Tokpapleu)*

gwān {LOC gwāandhɤ̄, SUP gwāa̋n} ***loc.n*** **mariage** *(du point de vue de la femme)* ♦ *gwān bhȁ dhɛ̏* femme mariée ◊ *gwān wɔ̏n yà kʌ̄ Yɔ̏ bhȁ gbɛ́ɛ̄* il est difficile pour Yo de se trouver un mari ♦ *gwān kpɔ́ bhɛ̄n gɔ̏* se marier avec qn *(en parlant d'une femme)* ♦ *dhó gwān bhȁ* se marier *(d'une femme)* ♦ *yà dhó gwāa̋n/gwāandhɤ̄* elle s'est mariée ♦ *Yɔ̏ yà gwān kɯ̋n Zân gɔ̏* Yo a divorcé de Jean ♦ *gwāa̋n ɤ́ sɪ̏ɤ ȁ bhȁ* elle est une femme mal-aimée ♦ *ī gwàa̋n bhȁ ȅe ?* es-tu mariée ?

gwɯ̋n, **gwɯ̋ndhʌ́n** ***n*** **chat** *[beaucoup de Dan mangent le chat]* Syn. yūnbhȁandhʌ́n ♦ *gwɯ̋ndhʌ́n sɛ̄ɛ̋ndhʌ́n* chaton Syn. gīoo, yūa̋ndhʌ́n ♦ *gwɯ̋n dhȅe* chatte *(femelle de chat)* ♦ *gwɯ̋n gɔ̄n* chat *(mâle)* ♦ *gwɯ̋ndhʌ́n yɤ̏ wȅ bhíaaɔ̏ɔnbhíaaɔ̏ɔndhɤ̄* le chat miaule ♦ *gwɯ̋ndhʌ́n yɤ̏ gblȁn-sɪ̄ʌ* le chat ronronne

gwāndȅegúɯslāa̋ <mariage-nouveau-dans-folie> ***n*** *iron., badin* **grande cuvette** *(pour la lessive)*

gwàngā <rivière-os> ***n*** **1 fleuve 2 Sassandra** *(nom de fleuve)*

gwāngɔ̏dhɛ̏ <mariage-tête-femme> ***n*** **femme mariée**

gwǣǣ → gwɛ̄ɛ́ *manioc*

gwǣȅgèe <*gwɛ̄ bhȁ gèe 'fromager-sur-masque'> ***n*** **écureuil** *(esp. : petit, demeure sur le fromager, pousse des cris qui ressemblent aux cris d'un masque dan)*

gwʌ̏ ***n*** **pierre, caillou** ♦ *gwʌ̏dhʌ́n* caillou *(2-3 cm)* ◊ *yɤ̏ ɤ̄ tɛ́ɛdō blɯ̏ dhʌ̀n ȁ wō gwʌ̏ gúɯ* ce qu'il a fait, c'est de pousser son ami sur les cailloux ♦ *gwʌ̏ kpɤ̄* pierre ♦ *gwʌ̏ gɔ̄n* rocher *(aussi gros qu'une maison)* ♦ *gwʌ̏ gbɔ́ŋ̄* rocher

gwʌ̀ʌ *v* **1.1** 1) *vi* **durer** *(longuement)* ◊ *yíi gwʌ̀ʌ gbɛ́* il n'a pas vécu longtemps ◊ *ʉ́ gwʌ̀ʌ pīnpīndhɤ̄ !* longue vie à toi ! ♦ *à yī yà gwʌ̀ʌ* depuis ça; depuis longtemps 2) *vt* **prolonger** *(vie)* ◊ *Zlàan yíi kʌ̄' sìi gwʌ̀ʌ gbɛ́* Dieu ne lui a pas donné une très longue vie **1.2** *vt* **prolonger la vie à** ♦ *tɔ̀sǽǽ kʌ̄ kɔ̀ sʌ̀ yɤ̀ bhɛ̄n gwʌ̀ʌ* une bonne existence prolonge la vie humaine **2** 1) *vi* **trop durer** ◊ *yɤ̀ kʌ̄ gwʌ̀ʌ n̄ píɤ* il a trop duré chez moi *(de visiteur, etc.)* 2) *vt* **retarder**

gwʌ̄ʌ́ 1 *n* **1 factotum** *(homme ou femme de confiance)* Syn. gwʌ̄ʌ́bhīn Ant. gɔ̀bhɛ̀n, **2 disciple** *(d'un chasseur, marabout, griot, etc.)*

gwʌ̄ʌ́ 2 *n* **crocodile de Nil** Syn. yíàgwʌ̄ʌ́ ◊ *ʉ̄ dhí yɤ̀ kʌ̀ dhɛ̀ gwʌ̄ʌ́ dhí dhɤ́* ta bouche est comme la gueule d'un crocodile

gwʌ̀ʌbhɛ̀n <durer-personne> *n* **personne d'une grande longévité**

gwʌ̄ʌ́bhīn {pl. gwʌ̄ʌ́bhīn-dhʉ̀n, gwʌ̄ʌ́zʌ̀-dhʉ̀n} <factotum-personne> *n* **1 factotum** *(homme de confiance)* Syn. gwʌ̄ʌ́ Ant. gɔ̀bhɛ̀n **2 disciple** *(d'un chasseur, marabout, griot, etc.)*

gwʌ̄ʌ́dhē {pl. gwʌ̄ʌ́dhōo-dhʉ̀n, gwʌ̄ʌ́dhōŋ-dhʉ̀n, gwʌ̄ʌ́dhēbhʌ̀-dhʉ̀n} *n* **servante, bonne**

gwʌ̄ʌ́zʌ̀-dhʉ̀n *pluriel du* gwʌ̄ʌ́bhīn *factotum*

gwʌ̀dhʌ́n *n* **ponce, pierre ponce** *[on garde un pierre ponce dans la toilette pour enlever la peau dure des talons]*

gwʌ̀gā <pierre-os> *n* **caillou** *(petit)*

gwʌ́nŋ *n* **proverbe** ◊ *bhɛ̄n sɛ̄ɛ́ndhʌ́n yáa gwʌ́nŋ dà bhɛ̄n kpíì dhɛ̀* une jeune personne ne dit pas de proverbes à une personne âgée

gwʌ̀yɛ̀ <pierre-trou> *n* **grotte** Syn. gbìŋ

gwēe *n* **panthère, léopard** Syn. gɔ̋

gwēè *n* **médicament contre les maux de ventre** *(ingurgité sous forme de sauce compacte, noire et verte, pimentée et salée)* ♦ *yà gwēè bhɤ̀* il a pris le médicament contre les maux de ventre

gwēéyɔ̃n *n* **huile des fruits de carapa** *(cf. gbɔ̂n) [utilisée comme médicament pour soigner les maux d'estomac]*

gwɛ̄ *n* **1** ***Ceiba pentandra, Bombax pentandrum, B. guineense, Eriodendron guineense, E. anfractuosum, E. orientale*** **fromager** *(le plus grand arbre de l'Afrique de l'Ouest, jusqu'à 65 d'hauteur et 10 de circonférence; tronc cylindrique, racines aériennes; se trouve souvent près des habitats humains; son bois est blanc, très mou et léger, se casse facilement; les gousses, dont la taille est de 10-14 cm, voire jusqu'à 37 cm, sont remplies de duvet gris ou blanc dont on obtient le kapok; les grains contiennent une huile comparable à l'huile d'arachide) [est considéré par les Dan comme "le roi des végétaux"]* ♦ *gwɛ̄ kpʌ̀* tronc du fromager *(jusqu'à la hauteur des branches)* ◊ *Sítà gɛ̀n yɤ̀ dhɛ̀ gwɛ̄ gɛ̀n dhɤ́* les jambes de Sita sont grosses comme le tronc de fromager *[les jambes grosses et poilues sont appréciées comme un signe de beauté féminine]* **2** ***Adansonia digitata*** **baobab** Syn. bīɤdhʉ̀

gwɛ̄bʉ̀ŋbʉ̄ŋ́ <fromager- ?> *n* **champignon** *(blanc, à chapeau pointu, agaricacée, pousse sur les vieux troncs de fromagers, très nourrissant; apparaît en mai)* Syn. *bhūɤɤ*

gwɛ̄ɛ́, **gwǣǽ** *n* arch., rare ***Manihot esculenta*** **manioc** Syn. *bāa* ♦ *gwɛ̄ɛ́ kɔ̏n* foutou de manioc

gwɛ̋ɛ *n* **arachide** ♦ *gwɛ̋ɛ bɤ̏ɤ, gwɛ̋ɛ kɔ̏n* pâte d'arachide ♦ *gwɛ̋ɛ gā* noix d'arachide *(avec la coquille)* ♦ *gwɛ̋ɛ flɛ̋ɛ̏* grain d'arachide ♦ *gwɛ̋ɛ yí* sauce d'arachide

gwɛ̋ɛdhūɤɤ <arachide-raphia> *n* **serpent vert** *(esp.; venimeux)*

gwɛ̄kpʌ̀bhʌ̀tíʌʌ <fromager-tronc-sur-champignon> *n* **champignon** *(esp.; pousse sur les troncs du fromager, apparaît en août)*

gwɛ̋nŋ *n rn vulg.* **vulve, con** *vulg.* Syn. *pʌ̄ʌ, slōo* ♦ *gwɛ̋nŋ gúu dhɛ̏* vagin

gwìnŋ̏, **gbìnŋ̏** *loc.n SUP de* gwìnŋ̏dhɛ̏ *sommet*

gwìnŋ̏dhɛ̏ {LOC gwìnŋ̏dhɤ̄, gwìnŋ̄dhɤ̄, LOC pl. gwìnŋ̏dhɛ̏-dhʉ̀n gúu; SUP gwìnŋ̏, gbìnŋ̏} *loc.n rn* **sinciput, vertex; sommet** Qsyn. *gɔ̏* ◊ *ūu gwìnŋ̏dhɛ̏ yà kʌ̄ yâ* tu as des saletés sur la tête ◊ *tɔ̏n ɤ́ yā à gwìnŋ̏dhɛ̏ yɤ̏ gblɛ̀ɛn* le sommet de cette montagne est étendu ◊ *yà kwɛ̀ɛ̏ yà ā gwìnŋ̏* il m'a posé la charge sur la tête ◊ *yà kwɛ̀ɛ̏ yà ɤ̄ gwìnŋ̏* il a posé la charge sur sa (propre) tête ◊ *yà kwɛ̀ɛ̏ súu ɤ̄ gwìnŋ̏/gwìnŋ̄dhɤ̄* elle porte le bagage sur sa tête ◊ *à bhà kwɛ̀ɛ̏ yà gó à gbìnŋ̏ yà wɛ̀nŋ* son bagage est tombé de sa tête ◊ *bhàan bhā yɤ̏ yà-sʉ̀ kā dhʉ̋ gwìnŋ̏* l'oiseau est assis au sommet de l'arbre ♦ *wɔ́n zīzī-dhʉ̀n wáa dhó ā gwìnŋ̏ /gwìnŋ̄dhɤ̄* je ne m'intéresse pas aux affaires très anciennes

gwìnŋdhɤ̄ *n* **inflammation du vertex** *(maladie infantile : le vertex prend une couleur sombre, l'enfant a des syncopes et peut succomber)* ◊ *gwìnŋdhɤ̄ yɤ̏ Zân bhà dhʌ́n kʌ̄-sīʌ* l'enfant de Jean souffre d'une inflammation du vertex

gwìnŋ̄dhɤ̄, **gwìnŋ̏dhɤ̄** *loc.n LOC de* gwìnŋ̏dhɛ̏ *vertex*

gwʉ́ʉ (t) → gú (gw) *ventre*

H h

hāá *intj* **ouf !** *(exclamation traduisant un soulagement, p.ex. en réaction à une bonne nouvelle qu'on n'attendait plus)* ♦ *hāá ! bhá dhūn* ouf ! tu es venu

I i

ī 1, 2 → ʉ̄ 1, 2 *te*

í 1, 2 → ʉ́ 1, 2 *te*

ìi *intj* **oui** *réponse à une question affirmative ou négative* Syn. *ʉ̀n* Qsyn. *ʌ̀òo* ◊ *ʉ̄ kʌ̄ yī zʌ̀ yâ ʌ̏e ? – ìi* as-tu mal dormi ? – oui (j'ai mal dormi) ◊ *bhíi kʌ̄ yī zʌ̄ sʌ̀ ʌ̏e ? – ìi* n'as-tu pas bien dormi ? – oui (je n'ai pas bien dormi)

ìiyà *intj* **aïe !** *interjection de l'étonnement désagréable*

ĩĩn, **ɛ̃ɛ̃n** ***conj*** **ou** *lie des groupes nominaux, des verbes ou des phrases conjointes* ◊ *dhȁa plɛ̀ ɤ́ wó yā ȁ bhɛ̏ɛn ɤ́ bhīi' sɯ́ ? ȁ dhɛ́ ɤ́ klɤ̄ɤ̏ ká yā ȅe, ĩĩn ȁ dhɛ́ ɤ́ gblɛ̏ɛn ká yā ȅe ?* lequel de ces deux couteaux prendras-tu, le court ou le long ?

K k

kȁ ***mpp*** **vous** *MPP impératif 2e pers. du pluriel*

kā 1; **kāȁ** (t) ***n*** **crabe** *Syn. gɛ̃æn* ♦ *kā kɤ̏* carapace de crabe ♦ *kā sɔ̃n* pince de crabe ♦ *kā yà n̄ kún* le crabe m'a pincé

kā 2 ***mpp*** **vous** *MPP existentiel 2e pers. du pluriel*

kā 3 ***prn*** **vous** *pronom 2e pers. du pluriel de la série autonome*

kā 4 ***prn*** **vous** *pronom non-sujet 2e pers. du pluriel*

ká 1 ***pp*** **1.1 avec** *(comitatif)* **1.2** *indique une action secondaire accompagnant l'action principale* ◊ *yɤ̏ ɤ̄ dʌ̄ dhɛ̏-sīʌ gbɔ̋ ká* il appelle son père en pleurant **2.1** *exprime l'idée de l'instrument* ◊ *wɔ̀ sɤ̄ dhìi bhlòo wō kɔ̏ plɛ̀ ká* elles pressent les tourteaux de graines de palme avec les deux mains **2.2 grâce à** ◊ *yɤ̏ dhȁ sìʌ ɤ̄ bhā dhēbʌ̏ dhʌ̀n' ká* parfois il se sauve grâce à sa femme **3.1 sur**, **par**, **de** *(localisation approximative de l'action par rapport à l'objet)* ◊ *yà sɯ́ɤ dȁ kɔ́ ká* il a mis le feu à la maison ◊ *tæ̋æ̏ bhā wà yí lòo ȁ gɯ́, yɤ̏ bɔ̏ ȁ yɛ̏gā ká yɤ́ ɤ́ wɛ̀nŋ* lorsqu'on remplit cette bassine d'eau, l'eau s'échappe par le trou et se répand ◊ *pʌ́ bhā yí yɤ̏ bɔ̏' ká* l'eau s'en échappe ◊ *dhūn pɛ̋ɛn yā' ká* viens de ce côté **3.2 dans** *(localisation abstraite de l'action par rapport à son domaine)* ◊ *yíi kʌ̄ dhó klàŋ̀ ká gblɛ̏ɛn* il n'est pas allé loin dans les études **4.1 à** *(sens temporel)* ◊ *Zân wāȁ ɤ̄ bhā dhēbʌ̏ wà kɯ̋n kwɛ̏ ɤ́ zìɤ yā ȁ ká* Jean et sa femme ont divorcé l'année passée ◊ *bhān klɔ̀ŋ yɤ̏ bhɤ̄ɤ blɛ̄ɛ́yī ká* en saison sèche mon puits tarit ◊ *yāandhíɤ áa dhʌ̀n ɤ́ dhō ȁ ká* ce n'est pas hier qu'il est parti **4.2 pendant**, **en** *Syn. píɤ* ◊ *yɤ̏ ɤ̄ bhā bhláȁdhɛ̏ bȁ dhɛ̏kpœ̀œyì plɛ̀ ká* il a défriché son champ en deux jours ◊ *Zân yɤ̏ glȁ dhœ̏œnbhɛ̏n gɯ́ kwɛ̏ plɛ̀ ká* Jean est devenu riche pour une période de deux ans **5** *exprime l'équivalence* ◊ *dūː wɔ̏n ɤ́ bhā yɤ̏ tæ̏æ̏n ká* la sorcellerie est réelle ◊ *yɤ̄ dhūūn ɤ́ gūn zɔ̋obhīn ká* c'est lui qui était le chasseur des sorciers **6 à** *(au sens de bénéficiaire ou maléficiaire)* ◊ *wɔ́n bhlɔ̄ɔsɯ̏ yà kʌ̄ n̄ ká* il m'est arrivé un fâcheux incident **7 au sujet de** *(thème de parole, de réflexion)* ◊ *bhɛ̄n gɛ̀n kpáansɯ̏ dhʌ̀n á wɛ̏ ȁ ká* c'est l'homme nu-pieds dont je parle **8 sauf**, **seulement** ◊ *bhȁandhʌ́n yā, bhɛ̄n yɯ́n yáa kpȁn ȁ bhȁ plɛ̀-plɛ̀, kɤ̄ yíi kʌ̄ Dádhándhɛ̏ ká* c'est un rare oiseau, il ne se trouve qu'à Danané

ká 2 ***mpp*** **vous** *MPP du parfait, 2e pers. du pluriel*

ká 3 ***mpp*** **vous** *MPP conjoint, 2e pers. du pluriel*

ká 4 ***mpp*** **vous** *MPP subjonctif, 2e pers. du pluriel*

ká 5 ***mpp*** **pour que vous ne** *MPP prohibitif de la 2e pers. du pluriel*

ká 6 ***prn*** **vous** *pronom sélectif, utilisé avec le suffixe -sɯ̏*

kȁa ***n* 1** ***Cymbopogon citratus*** **roseau** *(plante sauvage, pousse près de l'eau) [utilisé pour les clôtures autour des champs et les douchières]* ◊ *yȁ ɤ̄ bhā bhláȁdhɛ̏ zȕ-klʌ̏ʌn kȁa dhúɯ́ ká* il a clôturé son champ avec des tiges de roseau ◊ *kê kʌ̄-sȕ ɤ́ kȁa gúɯ́ yɤ̏ gbɛ́ɛ̏* le défrichement d'un terrain couvert de roseaux est difficile **2 canne à sucre** *[chez les Dan on la mange crue, on n'en fait aucun usage dans la préparartion de boissons ou d'aliment]* ♦ *bhɤ̏ kȁa* canne à sucre ◊ *bhɤ̏ kȁa yȁ ɤ̄ bɯ́n yȁ, kɤ̄ gā yɤ̄ɤ bhɔ̄ ȁ tā bhɛ̏n bhȁ* quand la canne à sucre fleurit, la mort apparaît chez celui qui l'a plantée *[selon les croyances, les sorciers font mourir un des membres de la famille dans une cour où fleurit la canne à sucre ou dans laquelle fructifie un arbre; pour cette raison, jusqu'à tout récemment, on ne plantait pas la canne à sucre au village, ou on la coupait avant la fleuraison]* ♦ *kȁa kpɤ̄* morceau de tige de canne à sucre ♦ *sʌ́nŋ kȁa* "canne de l'or" *(sorte rare de canne à sucre, très sucrée, à tige mince)* ◊ *ɯ̄ gɛ̏ndhɯ̋ kɑ̋ŋkɑ̋ŋ ká dhɛ̀ sʌ́nŋ kȁa dhɤ́* tes jambes sont minces comme la "canne de sucre de l'or"

kāa 1 ***mpp*** **vous** *MPP prospectif 2e pers. du pluriel*

kāa 2 ***prn*** **vous** *pronom 2e pers. du pluriel de la série restrictive*

kāȁ 1 {kȁa} ***v*** **1.1** 1) *vt* **gratter** *(corps)* 2) *vr* **se gratter 1.2** *vt* **caresser**, **flatter** ◊ *gwɑ̋ndhʌ́n kāȁ dhɔ̏ yáa Tȍkpȁ kʌ̏* Tokpa n'aime pas flatter les chats **2.1** *vt* **démanger qn** *(partie du corps)* ◊ *ɯ̄ bhǣǣ́dhɛ̏ yɤ̏ ɯ̄ kāȁ-sɪʌ* le devant du cou me démange **2.2** *vt* **démanger qn, provoquer des démangeaisons** *(par qch)* ◊ *gbɛ̂ndhʌ́ngɔ̋ɔ̏ yɤ̏ bhɛ̄n kȁa dɛ̏dɛ̏wɔ̄* le "haricot sauvage" provoque de fortes démangeaisons

kāȁ 2 {kȁa} ***n*** **1** *rn* **poil** *(animal ou humain) [le poil sur le corps de la femme est pour les Dan un signe de beauté]* ♦ *bɛ̏n ȁ kȁa* moustache ◊ *dhēbʌ̏ ɤ̂ kāȁ dhɤ́ gbɛ́, ȁ dhɔ̏ yɤ̏ bhɛ̄n gbɛ́ {dhɛ̏} kʌ̏* la plupart des gens aiment les femmes qui ont beaucoup de poils sur le corps **2** *rn* **plume** ♦ *bhȁan kāȁ gā dɔ̄* une plume d'oiseau ♦ *bhȁan gbān bhȁ kȁa* plume de l'aile d'un oiseau **3** *rn* **aile** *(d'insecte)*

kāȁ 3 ***prn*** **votre, vos** *pronom de la série possessive*

kāȁ 4, **kāa** ***prn*** **toi et...** *pronom coordinatif* ♦ *kāȁ ... -dhȕn* vous et... ◊ *kāȁ dhēbʌ̏-dhȕn* vous et une femme; toi et des femmes; vous et des femmes

kāȁ 5 ***prn*** **toi et son..., toi et sa...** *pronom coordinatif fusionné avec le pronom non-sujet de la 3e pers. sg. suivant* ◊ *kāȁ gbɤ̄* toi et son fils

kāȁ 6 ***mpp*** **vous** *MPP du 2e pers. pl. de la série présomptive*

káa 1 ***mpp*** **vous** *MPP négatif imperfectif 2e pers. du pluriel*

káa 2 <de *kɤ̄ á> ***mpp*** **pour que je** *forme fusionnée : conjonction kɤ̄ + MPP de la 1re pers. sg. de la série conjointe*

kɑ̋a ***n*** **gale, éruption** *(toute dermatose)* ♦ *kɑ̋a gā sɛ̋ɛ́ndhʌ́n* éruption à petit grain ♦ *kɑ̋a yȁ bhā ȁ bhȁ* il a eu une éruption; il a la gale

kāáa, **kāyáa** ***prn*** **vous** *pronom de la série focalisée négative*

káāa ***mpp*** **vous ne** *(forme fusionnée des marqueurs prédicatifs négatif et prospectif)*

kȁabȕŋ *n Setaria barbuta, S. barbata (gen. Poaceae)* **herbe bambou, herbe bassine** *(feuilles de 15-35 cm de long, une mauvaise herbe très répandue)*

kȁ̋a-bhō *v* **gémir, se lamenter**

kȁagȁ <*kä ä gä 'regardez'> *prt* **voici** *(une parenthèse)* ♦ *kȁagȁ, dhȅkpœ̏œyȉ do ká...* voici un jour...

kāȁn {kàan} {intensif de kȁ̋n} *v vt* **couper en petits morceaux** ♦ *kāȁn kwʌ̋ʌ* pétrir ◊ *bɤ̏ɤ kāȁn kwʌ̋ʌ* pétrir la pâte

kāȁ̋n 1 *n* **arbre** *(esp.)*

kāȁ̋n 2 {kàan} *v* **1** *vt kāȁ̋n kwʌ̋ʌ* **mélanger 2** *vt kāȁ̋n kwʌ̋ʌ* **confondre** ◊ *Gbȁtȍ yȁ wɔ́n gbàn kāȁ̋n kwʌ́ʌ̀* Gbato a tout mélangé

kȁanbhō *v vi* **préoccuper sérieusement** *(qn – dhȅ)* ◊ *wɔ́n bhā' yɤ̏ kȁanbhō-sȕ ká n̄ dhȅ* cette affaire me concerne sérieusement

kāȁnkāȁn {kàankàan} <intensif de kȁ̋n 'couper'> *v vt* **couper en plusieurs morceaux**

kāarɔ̂ <Fr. carreaux> *n* **carreau** *(sol)* ◊ *bhá dhɤ́ tȁ̋ kāarɔ̂ tɔ̀ɔ-sȕ tȁ* ne marche pas sur le sol mouillé !

kāatȋȅ <Fr. quartier> *n* **quartier** *(de ville)*

kȁ̋bhȁ̋kȍ̋ 1 <Manding kábako> *intj* **c'est un miracle !** *(exprime l'étonnement pour une action extraordinaire)*

kȁ̋bhȁ̋kȍ̋ 2 <Manding kábakulu> *n* **boule de savon** *(blanc, très caustique)*

kàbhɔ̋n <Manding kàramɔ̀ɔ> *n* **maître** *(par rapport à un apprenti)* ◊ *kàbhɔ̋n dhɛ́ ɤ́ dhɤ̋ ȁ bhȁ kāyéȅdhʌ́n yɤ̏ dhɤ̏* chaque maître a des apprentis

kȁdō <2pluriel.impératif-attendre> *n* ***Rana catesbeiana*** **ouaouarou, grenouille-taureau** *seulement dans le proverbe :* ♦ *dlɔ̋ɔ yȁ wɛ́, yɤ́ kȁdō yɤ̏ wȅ* lorsque les grenouilles se prononcent, la parole passe à ouaouarou *(le dernier mot appartient au plus aîné, au chef)*

kȁ̋fȅe → kȁ̋flȅe *café*

kȁ̋flȅe, kȁ̋fȅe <Fr. café> *n* **café** ♦ *kȁ̋flȅe bȉ* café moulu ♦ *kȁ̋flȅe dhȅ, kȁ̋flȅe bhlȁa* plantation de café ♦ *kȁ̋flȅe dhȕ* caféier ♦ *kȁ̋flȅe gā* grain de café ♦ *kȁ̋flȅe gbō* marc de café ♦ *kȁ̋flȅe yȋ* café *(boisson)[dans les villages dan, les femmes boivent rarement du café]* ♦ *kȁ̋flȅe bhō* cueillir le café

kāibhân <Fr. caïman, à cause de l'image du crocodile sur la lame, la marque de fabrique> *n* **machette, coupe-coupe** *(à lame étroite et longue, de fabrication industrielle)*

kàkàô <Fr. cacao> *n* **cacao**

kȁ̋n 1) {kȁn} *v* **1.1** *vt* **couper**; **scier** *Qsyn. kplȕ̋, yɛ̋ 1* ◊ *Gbȁtȍ yȁ gɤ̏ɤ zīi kȁ̋n* Gbato a découpé un vieil iroko (déjà abattu) ♦ *yȁ ɤ̄ dȅ kȁ̋n dhȁa ká* il s'est coupé avec le couteau ♦ *dhȕ̋ kplȕ̋ kȁ̋n sȋ̋ ká* scier un morceau de bois ♦ *yȁa kplȕ̋ kȁ̋n bɤ̋ŋdhɤ̄* il en a coupé un morceau d'un seul coup **1.2** *vt* **moissonner 1.3** *vt* **couper** *(fabriquer en coupant)* ◊ *yɤ́* *kœ̀œ kɑ̀n, yɤ́' yà dân gɔ̀* il a coupé des bâtons fourchés et a soulevé avec les lianes épineuses **2** 1) *vi* **cesser** ◊ *yī ɤ́ dhɤ́ bhā kɤ̄ gblɯ̀ yà kɑ̋n* ce jour-là la guerre s'est terminée 2) *vt* **couper** *(interrompre une activité ou une prestation)* ♦ *wà sɪ́ɤ kɑ̋n yī tà* on nous a coupé le courant ♦ *gwān kɑ̋n* divorcer **3** *vt* **tracer** *(ligne)* ♦ *yà kɔ́ kplɔ̋ŋ kɑ̋n* il a tracé le plan de la maison *(avant de commencer la construction)* ♦ *à dhí yɤ̀ kɑ̀n dhīaŋ bhà* il parle clairement (sa prononciation est claire; il exprime clairement ses propos) **4** *vt* **attacher** *(pagne)* Syn. *kplɯ̀* ♦ *yà sɔ̄ kɑ̋n dhʌ́n tà* elle a attaché le bébé sur le dos avec un pagne *[c'est la façon habituelle de porter les enfants en Afrique]* **5** *vt* **traverser** *(fleuve, pont)* **6.1** 1) *vi kɑ̋n wō kwʌ́ʌ̀* **se séparer**, **se disperser** ◊ *bhɛ̄n gbàan kɑ̋n wō kwʌ́ʌ̀* tout le monde s'est dispersé 2) *vt kɑ̋n kwʌ́ʌ̀* **séparer** *(amis)* **6.2** *vi* **divorcer** **6.3** *vt ɤ̄ kɔ̀ kɑ̋n à gɯ́* **se débarasser de** **7.1** *vi* **surprendre** *(qn – gɯ́)*, **tomber** *(sur – gɯ́)* ◊ *wà kɑ̋n kwànbhɛ̀n gɯ́* ils ont surpris un voleur ◊ *ɤ́ kɑ̀n ɤ̄ bhā yʌ̄kʌ̄bhɛ̀n-dhɯ̀n gɯ́ kɤ̄ wɔ̀ yī zʌ̄-sɪ̄ʌ* il a surpris ses travailleurs en train de dormir **7.2** *vi kɑ̋n ɤ̄ tà* **être surpris**, **sursauter de surprise**, **tressaillir de surprise** ◊ *bhɛ̄n-dhɯ̀n wó dhō kɑ̋n' wō tà dōsɛ̄ŋ kɤ̄ kɔ́dhɛ̄ɛ́ bhā yɤ̀ gɤ́-sɪ̄ʌ* les gens se sont soudainement rendu compte que la case brûlait **7.3** *vi yà kɑ̋n à dhɪ́ɤ yà bhɑ́ɑ̀ndhūn* **ses jambes l'ont laché, et il est tombé** **7.4** *vi kɑ̋n ɤ̄ tà* **se gêner**; **se rendre compte** *(soudainement)* **8** *vi à yí yà kɑ̋n* **c'est agréable** ◊ *wɔ́n bhā à yí yà kɑ̋n n̄ dhɛ̀* cela m'a réjoui ◊ *tɔ̀ yí yɤ̀ kɑ̀n* le poulet est très bon ◊ *tőo yí yà kɑ̋n* la sauce est délicieuse **9** *vt wɔ́n kɑ̋n à dhɛ̀* **déclarer son amour à qn** **10** 1) *vi sɯ̋ɤ yà kɑ̋n à gɯ́* **il a pris peur** 2) *vt sɯ̋ɤ kɑ̋n bhɛ̄n gɯ́* **effrayer qn** **11** *vt* **acheter en gros**

kɑ̋n 2) *n* **pièce** *(d'étoffe)* ◊ *kɑ̋n sɔ̀ dɛ̀e yà' gɔ̀* elle a un pagne neuf

kɑ̀nbhɛ̄ngɯ́wɔ̀n *n* **surprise** ◊ *yíi kʌ̄ kɑ̀nbhɛ̄ngɯ́wɔ̀n ká...* ce n'est pas un hasard...

kɑ̀nkwʌ́ʌ̀-sɯ̀ *n* **désaccord** *(manque d'entente)* ◊ *kɑ̀nkwʌ́ʌ̀-sɯ̀ yáa sʌ̀* le manque d'accord n'est pas bon

kɑ̋nŋbhɑ̋ <Fr. campement ?> *n* **1 campement** *(dans les champs)* Syn. *bhlɑ́ɑ̄* **2 hameau** *(campement rural aménagé en lieu d'habitation permanente* Syn. *kɔ́ídhɛ̀*

kɑ̋nsɔ̀ <couper-étoffe> *n* **pagne** *(traditionnel, tissé sur le métier)* Syn. *wāŋdhʌ́n*

kɑ̄ŋ́ *n* **petite pierre** *(2-3 cm)*

kɑ̋ŋ 1 *n* **1.1 tiges d'herbes non-brûlées** *(après le feu de brousse)* ♦ *kɑ̋ŋ dà bhɛ̄n gɛ̀n gɯ́* couper l'herbe sous les pieds de qn **1.2 brousse aux alentours de village** ◊ *yà dhó kɑ̋ŋ gɯ́* il est allé en brousse à côté du village **2 tas d'herbes et de bois** *(destiné à être brûlé)* Qsyn. *gɛ́ɛ kɔ́, klɑ́a 2* ♦ *kɑ̋ŋ kpɤ̄* = kɑ̋ŋ

kɑ̋ŋ 2 {kɑ̋ŋkɑ̋ŋ, kʌ̋ŋkʌ̋ŋ pl. A P S, kɑ̋ŋkɑ̋ŋ-dhɯ̀n pl. A S, kɑ̋ŋkɑ̋ŋ-sɯ̀ foc. pl. Int. A S, kɑ̋ŋkɑ̋ŋ-sɯ̀-dhɯ̀n foc. pl. Int. A S} *adj* **mince** *(surtout un objet de bois)* ♦ *wɔ̋ kɑ̋ŋ* branche sèche ◊ *wɔ̋ kɑ̋ŋkɑ̋ŋ-dhɯ̀n dhʌ̀n ɤ́ à-dhɯ̀n yɛ̀ n̄ dhɛ̀* ce sont les brindilles qu'il a cassées pour moi ♦ *bhɛ̄n gbɑ̋ngā kɑ̋ŋkɑ̋ŋ* personne à jambes minces

kɑ̋ŋ 3 *n* **croc-en-jambe** ◊ *Gbɑ̀tò yà kɑ̋ŋ dà dɯ̀ gɔ̀* Gbato a donné un croc-en-jambe au boeuf

kʌ̋ŋkʌ̋ŋ *adj pl. de* kʌ̋ŋ 2

kʌ́ŋ̀kʌ́ŋ̀dhɤ̄ ***onomat*** *son de craquement des doights* ◊ *yɤ̏ kɔ̄ŋgā gúɯ wɛ̏ kʌ́ŋ̀kʌ́ŋ̀dhɤ̄* il se fait craquer les doigts

kāŋtɔ̂n <Fr. canton> ***n*** **canton**

kàsɪ́ʌ̂ʌtīi, kàsɪ́ʌ̂ʌtīidhʌ́n ***n*** ***Lagonosticta senegala*** **amarante commun** *(oiseau de la taille d'un moineau; couleurs rouge et brun-gris (mâle) ou olive-brune (femelle); très lié à l'homme) la forme avec -dhʌ́n est la plus usitée*

kʌ̋slɔ̋ <Fr. casserole> ***n*** **casserole**

kʌ̏sɔ̏ <Fr. cachot> ***n*** **prison, cachot** ♦ *wʌ̏ kwànbhɛ̏n bhā ʌ̏ dʌ̏ kʌ̏sɔ̏ gúɯ* ils ont mis le voleur en prison ♦ *wʌ̏ ʌ̏ bhō kʌ̏sɔ̏ gúɯ* on l'a libéré de prison

kʌ̏sɔ̏gɔ̏dhɪ́ɤbhɛ̏n <prison-tête-sur-personne> ***n*** **geôlier**

kʌ̏sɔ̏gúɯbhɛ̏n <prison-dans-personne> ***n*** **prisonnier**

kāyáa → kāáa *pas vous*

kāyéɛ̀dhʌ́n ***n*** **élève,, apprenti, apprentie**

kāyéɛ̀-dhɛ̏, kāyéɛ̀-dhʌ́n-dhɛ̏ ***n*** **apprentissage** ◊ *ā bhān kāyéɛ̀-dhʌ́n-dhɛ̏ kʌ̏ ʌ̏ kɛ̀ŋ̀* j'ai fait mon apprentissage chez lui

kæ̋æ 1 → kɛ̋ɛ *plusieurs*

kæ̋æ 2 → kɛ̋ɛ 1 *écorce*

kæ̋æ 3 → kɛ̋ɛ 3 *geste menaçant*

kæ̋ægā, **kɛ̋ɛga** ***n*** **bracelet de coureur** *(porté sur le biceps; procédé magique permettant au coureur de distancer ses concurrents)*

kæ̋æn → kɛ̋ɛn *usé*

kæ̋ænkæ̋æn *Int. pl. de* kɛ̋ɛn *usé*

kʌ̄ 1 {kʌ̏} ***v*** **I 1.1** 1) *vt* **faire** ♦ *bhēnkɔ̏ blɛ̋ɛn kʌ̄ ... bhʌ̏* laisser les empreintes des mains sur qch ♦ *kʌ̄-sɯ̏ɯ kāʌ̏nkwʌ́ʌ̏-sɯ̏ɯ* neol., ling. verbe composé 2) *vi* **avoir lieu** ◊ *... kɤ̄ bhān klɔ̏ŋ ɤ́ bhɤ̏ɤ yà kʌ̄ dhɛ̏kpœ̀œyɪ̏ yʌ̏agā ...* mais mon puits avait tari trois jours auparavant ◊ *kɤ̄ dhīaŋ ɤ́ dèbhīn ɤ́ ʌ̏ zʌ̄ ʌ̏ dhɛ̏ ʌ̏ gúɯ wɔ̏n yɤ̏ kʌ̄ ...* pour que la parole que le devin lui a dit s'accomplisse **1.2** *vi* **être** *(qch – ká)* ◊ *... ɤ́ dhō dhɔ̋ɔ gúɯ kwɪ́pɤ̏ ɤ́ kʌ̏ Gbīaangwìnŋ̀dhɛ̏ ká* elle est allée au marché de la ville à savoir à Biankouma **1.3** *vi* **vivre**, **demeurer** ◊ *bhʌ̏-dhɯ̏n wɔ̏ kʌ̏ dhɯ̋ yɛ̏ gúɯ* les chauves-souris vivent dans les cavités des arbres **1.4** *vt* **passer** *(temps)* ◊ *kʌ̋flée bhā, dhɛ́dhɛ́ plɛ̏ dhʌ̀n ɤ́' kʌ̏ yʌ́nŋ̀ dhɛ̏ yɤ́ gā* le café a séché au soleil pendant deux heures **1.5** *vt* **causer**, **faire** *(à qn – ká)* ◊ *pʌ́ ɤ́ Gbʌ̏tɔ̏ ɤ́ ʌ̏ kʌ̏ ɯ̄ ká bhā...* ce que Gbato t'a fait... **1.6** *vt* **agir avec** ◊ *wó Tɔ̀kpʌ̏plɤ̏ɤdhɛ̏ kʌ̏ dhìn* ils ont agi avec Tokpapleu de cette manière-ci **2** *vt* **cultiver** *(terre, champ)* **3** *vt* **fabriquer** Qsyn. dʌ̏ 2 ◊ *Zlʌ̏an dhɯ̄n ɤ́ sɛ́ kʌ̄* c'est Dieu qui a créé la terre ♦ *sʌ́ʌdhɛ́ kʌ̄ ... dhɛ̏* écrire une lettre à qn **4.1** *vi* **se transformer** *(en – ká)* ◊ *kpɪ̏nŋ gbʌ̀an kʌ̏ bɤ̏ɤ̏ ká* toute la route s'est transformée en cloaque **4.2** *vi* **devenir** ◊ *gbɛ̂n bhā ʌ̏ wɛ́ wɔ̏ yà kʌ̄* *wʌ̀ʌsṻ̀* le chien a gémi *(litt. : la voix du chien est devenue triste)* **5** *vt* **appeler**, **nommer** *(le nom est mis dans la position du complément d'objet direct, précédé du pronom correspondant à la personne en question)* ◊ *n̄ dhìnbhɔ̋ɔ̀n bhā̀ dhʌ́n wó' Màdhî kʌ̀* l'enfant de mon beau-parent qu'on appelait Marie **6.1** *vt* **chasser**, **poursuivre** ♦ *ā̀ dhɔ̄̀ yɤ̄̀ bhēn kʌ̀* cela plait à l'homme, l'homme aime cela **6.2** *vt* **chasser** *(éloigner)* **7.1** *vt* **faire mal** *(partie du corps; douleur aiguë)* ◊ *n̄ sɛ́n̄ŋ̀dhɛ̄̀ yɤ̄̀ n̄ kʌ̄-sīʌ* j'ai mal aux côtes **7.2** *vt* **nuire à**, **faire du mal à** ◊ *pʌ̄ bhá yíi dhēbʌ̀dhʌ́n bhā ā̀ kʌ̄* rien de mal n'est arrivé à la femme **8** *vt* **verser** ♦ *slʌ̀ʌ kʌ̄ tőo bhā̀* mettre du piment dans la sauce **IIA** *dans la construction de l'aspect neutre, rapporte la situation dans le plan du passé inactuel* **était** ◊ *ā kʌ̀ n̄ flʌ́ʌ̀ gṹ* j'ai été en bonne santé *(mais je ne le suis plus)* **IIB 1.1** *yɤ̄̀ kʌ̀ X gṹ dhɛ̀* **il semble à X que**, **X pense que 1.2** *yɤ̄̀ kʌ̀ dhɛ̀...* **probablement** *(une supposition spéculative)* ◊ *yɤ̄̀ kʌ̀ dhɛ̀ bhān sídâ yà bō* probablement, mon sida est parti **2** *vi yà kʌ̄ dhɛ̀ ...* **si 3** *vi yɤ́ ɤ́ kʌ̀* **c'est pourquoi**

kʌ̄ 2 <de kʌ̄ 'faire'> ***oper*** *marque du rétrospectif; se met après le sujet dans une construction de l'aspect neutre*

kʌ̀ʌ ***n*** **moucheron piqueur** *(habite dans les fruits du jeune arbre iroko)*

kʌ̋ʌ 1 ***n*** *rn* **vésicule biliaire** ♦ *kʌ̋ʌ yí* bile ◊ *ā̀ kʌ̄ sʌ̀ kɤ̄ tɔ̀ bhā ā̀ kʌ̋ʌ yá dhó wṹ' bhā̀* il ne faut pas faire crever la vésicule biliaire du poulet

kʌ̋ʌ 2 ***n*** **houe** <u>*Qsyn.*</u> <u>*kʌ̋atɔ̋*</u> ♦ *bɤ̄ɤ̀ slʌ̀ʌ gṹ kʌ̋ʌ* houe pour tourner la terre dans le bas-fond ♦ *bhlṻ̀n bō kʌ̋ʌ* houe pour cultiver le champ de riz

kʌ̀ʌdhṻ̀ <moucheron-arbre> ***n*** **jeune arbre iroko** *(ses petits fruits sont constamment entourés de moucherons qui piquent)*

kʌ̀dhɤ̋kɤ̄ ***conj*** **pour que**, **afin que** *(introduit une proposition de but dont le verbe est en construction subjonctive)* ◊ *yɤ̄̀ dhʌ́n kplṻ̀, kʌ̀dhɤ̋kɤ̄ yɤ̄̀ tó* il a attaché l'enfant pour qu'il reste ◊ *yā̀ n̄ gbā wʌ́ʌ̀gā ká kʌ̀dhɤ̋ kɤ̄ bhán dhó dùa'* il m'a donné de l'argent pour que je ne m'enfuie pas

kʌ̄kɔ̄̀ <faire-façon> ***n*** *neol.* **adverbe**

kʌ́n {kʌ̄n} ***v*** *vi* **se rassasier** ♦ *bhán kʌ́n* je suis rassasié *[forme considérée comme étant plutôt directe]*

kʌ̋nŋ ***n*** **frange** *(à la bordure de l'étoffe effilochée)* <u>*Qsyn.*</u> <u>*sǽæ*</u> ♦ *sɔ̄ kʌ̋nŋ gā, sɔ̄ kʌ̋nŋ* un fil de frange ♦ *ā̀ bhā̀ sɔ̄ kʌ̋nŋ gā yà kʌ̄ gbɛ́* son habit s'est effiloché jusqu'à créer une frange

kʌ̋nŋ̀ ***n*** **mascara** *[les Dan l'achètent aux Dioula]*

kʌ̋nŋkʌ̀nŋ ***adj*** **1 cahoteux** ♦ *zīaan kʌ̋nŋkʌ̀nŋ* route cahoteuse **2 douteux** ◊ *ṻ̄ kʌ̄kɔ̄̀dhʌ́n-dhṻ̀n wɔ̀ kʌ̋nŋkʌ̀nŋ* tes petites façons sont douteuses

kʌ̄ŋ {kʌ̀ŋ} ***n*** **cent** ♦ *kʌ̄ŋ tā̀ kʌ̀ŋ* des centaines

kʌ̄ŋ̋ ***n*** *arch.* **gravier** <u>*Syn.*</u> <u>*zɔ̋ŋ*</u>

kʌ̋ŋkʌ̋ŋ ***adj*** *pl. de* kʌ̋ŋ 2 *mince.PL*

kʌ̄yɔ̃ɔ <faire-pareil> ***n rn*** **concitoyen**

kê {kȅ} ***n*** **1 champ** *(surtout de riz)* ◊ *ā kʌ̄ kê kʌ̏* j'ai cultivé un champ de riz ◊ *ȁ bhȁ kê yɤ̏ kʌ̄ dhɪ̏ dȅdȅwō kwɛ̄ɛ* cette année son champ a eu un très bon rendement ♦ *glɔ̄ɔ kȅ* plantation de banane ♦ *bāa kȅ* champ de manioc **2 travail agricole**

kêdhɪ́ <champ-bouche> ***n*** **tour de rôle** *(dans le travail champêtre)* ♦ *Zân bhȁ kêdhɪ́ yī dhūn ɤ́ dɛ̀ɛ* c'est le tour de Jean aujourd'hui *(c'est dans son champ que travaillera l'association d'entraide dont il est membre)*

kȅe ***n*** **1** ***rn*** **tendon d'Achille** ◊ *bhɛ̄n yíi tá̰ sɯ́ vá̰andhɤ̄, ā dhȍ tá̰ sɯ́' ȁ bhɛ̄n kȅe gɯ́* celui qui ne marche pas vite, je marcherai sur ses talons ♦ *sȍȍ kȅe* creux du paturon *(au-dessus du talon de cheval)* ♦ *Zân yȁ Tȍkpȁ kȅe ká̰n ɤ̄ plɤ̏ɤ* Zan a interdit à Tokpa de venir chez lui ♦ *ɤ̄ bhȍ kȅe bhȁ* bouger, quitter sa place **2** ***rn*** **partie arrière** ◊ *kɤ̄ ȁ zláȁ dȅ pɤ́ yɤ̏ yȅ pɔ́n-sīʌ kɔ́ kèȅ tȁ dhȅ bhá gɯ́ bhūn*... et son petit frère était en train de creuser le trou quelque part derrière la maison

kèe *devant un ton extra-bas – kèȅ* ***n rn*** **occiput** ♦ *yȁ pɤ̏ ɤ̄ kèe ká, yȁ pɤ̏ ɤ̄ kèȅ tȁ* il est tombé à la renverse ♦ *yȁ wɔ̄ ɤ̄ kèe ká* il s'est couché à la renverse ♦ *bhá dhó dhīaŋ zʌ̄' n̄ kèȅ tȁ !* ne parle pas dans mon dos !

kēɛ́ ***prn*** **votre** *(pronom possessif honorifique)* ◊ *kēɛ́ kwá̰ŋ̏dhɤ̄* dans votre cour (resp.)

kèȅdhȅ {LOC kèedhɤ̄} ***loc.n rn*** **occiput** ◊ *yȁ ɤ̄ gɔ̏ bhō yȁ ɤ̄ kèȅdhȅ tó dhɤ̄* il s'est rasé le crâne en épargnant l'occiput ◊ *dhɪ̏ʌʌ yȁ dɔ̄ ȁ kèedhɤ̄* il a eu un furoncle sur l'occiput ♦ *kèedhɤ̄ yȕa* maladie de l'occiput

kèedhɤ̄ ***loc.n*** *LOC de* kèȅdhȅ *occiput*

kèȅsȍo <occiput- ?> ***n*** *tɔ̏ kèȅsȍo* **ergot de coq**

kêkʌ̄bhȅn <cultivation-faire-personne> ***n*** **cultivateur** *(personne)* Syn. bhláàkȅkʌ̄bhȅn

kêkpɤ̄ <travail champêtre-groupe> ***n*** **association de travail** *(cultive les champs de ses membres à tour de rôle)* Qsyn. bá̰nkpɤ̄, gwá̰ ◊ *gɔ̄ɔ̄n-dhȕn dhȁan kêkpɤ̄* association de travail masculine ◊ *dhēbʌ̏-dhȕn dhȁan kêkpɤ̄* association de travail féminine

kȅŋ {kȅŋkȅŋ Int.} ***pp*** **1 après** ♦ *dhūn n̄ kȅŋ* viens chez moi ♦ *zīɤ n̄ kȅŋ* suis-moi ! ♦ *gó bhɛ̄n kȅŋ* quitter qn; laisser qn en paix **2 pour** *(but d'action)* ♦ *wà dhūn ɯ̄ kȅŋ* il y a des gens qui sont venus te voir **3** *kó kȅŋ* **ensemble** Qsyn. kó pɪ́ɤ̄ ◊ *wȍ wō kó kȅŋ* ils sont ensemble *(au moment donné)* ◊ *ā kʌ̄ kpȁn Zân dhɤ́, Pɪ́ɛ̀ɛ dhɤ́, ... ȁ-dhȕn bhȁ kó kȅŋ* j'ai rencontré Jean, Pierre ... ensemble

kɛ̄́ŋ ***n*** **prétention** ♦ *kɛ̄́ŋ ká̰n* faire le malin

kɛ̄́ŋ ***n Holarrhena floribunda, H. africana, H. wulfsbergii*** **hollarhène du Sénégal** *(petit arbre des forêts et savanes, bois blanc et mou, fleurs blanches odorantes en grappes, produit du latex de qualité inférieure)*

kɛ̄́ŋgbá̰ ***n*** **sécrétion sèche** ♦ *yūn kɛ̄́ŋgbá̰* morve sèche ♦ *dhɪ́ kɛ̄́ŋgbá̰* trace de salive sur la joue

kèŋkèŋ *Int. de* kèŋ *après*

kɛ̋ŋslʌ̀ʌ < ?-piment> ***n*** **piment** *(plante de 1,5 de hauteur; capsules avec des grains rouges qu'on pile pour en obtenir du piment rouge très fort; désigne aussi ce piment même, variété la plus répandue chez les Dan)* ♦ *wà̰ kɛ̋ŋslʌ̀ʌ bhán' bhà̰* on l'a lavé avec de l'eau pimentée *(punition sévère appliquée aux enfants)*

kɛ̋sɔ̋ <Fr. caisse> ***n*** **caisse, tiroir**

kɛ̏ɛ, kɛ̏ ***prt*** **1 quand même** *(constatation d'une vérité généralement admise)* **2 vraiment** ◊ *tæ̏æn wɔ̏n bhȕn kɛ̏* c'est la vérité

kɛ̄ɛ ***n*** **arbre** *(espèce)*

kɛ̋ɛ 1, kæ̋æ ***n*** **1 glume** *(de riz)*, **coquille** *(de noix, d'œuf)*, **peau** *(de fruit, de tubercule)*, **épluchures** Qsyn. gbɔ̀ ♦ *bāa kɛ̋ɛ bhō à̰ bhà̰* éplucher le manioc **2** (gw) **écorce** *(en petits morceaux utilisés dans la médecine traditionnelle)* Syn. kɤ̏

kɛ̋ɛ 2, kɛ̋ɛŋ ***conj*** **1 mais** ◊ *ɯ̄ bhā gbɛ̂n-dhȕn wɔ̀ fiisȕ-dhȕn ká, kɛ̋ɛ wɔ̀ bṹ kʌ̀* tes chiens puent, mais ils font la chasse ◊ *yɤ̀ kwànbhɛ̏n dhɪ̋ɤ-gàn dhɛ̋dhɛ̋ plè ká, kɛ̋ɛ yɤ̋ yíi dhūn* il a attendu le voleur pendant deux heures, mais celui-ci n'est pas venu **2 bien que** ◊ *yɤ̀ dhɔ̀ gó' yɤ̄ kɤ̄ yɤ̀ dhó kɤ̄ yɤ̀ lòo Gɤ̀ɤwlɤ̀ɤ, kɛ̋ɛ kɤ̄ gɔ̄ yáa dhɤ́ èe ?* comment ira-t-elle à Guélémou, puisqu'il n'y a pas de voiture ? **3 c'est-à-dire** *(introduit une précision)* **4 et** *(introduit la proposition principale lors de la topicalisation de la proposition se référant au sujet de celle-ci)* ◊ *yà dhó dhʌ̀n wō, kɛ̋ɛŋ yíi dhī n̄ dhɛ̀* il est parti, cela ne m'a pas plu

kɛ̋ɛ 3, kæ̋æ ***n*** **gestes menaçants** ◊ *gwēe dhèe yɤ̀ kɛ̋ɛ kʌ̄-sɪʌ búkʌ̄bhɛ̏n bhà ɤ̄ bhā dhʌ́n-dhȕn tà* la femelle du léopard fait des gestes menaçants envers le chasseur pour protéger ses petits

kɛ̋ɛ 4, kæ̋æ ***dtm*** **peu** *(par rapport aux attentes)* ◊ *bhán yúɤ̏ɤ kæ̋æ gā dhʌ́nbhá sú* j'ai attrapé peu de poissons *peut apparaître dans une position argumentale et celle du prédicat sans déterminé* ◊ *Gbàtò yà dhūn plɤ̋ɤ̄ kɛ̋ɛ ká* Gbato est venu au village quelques rares fois

kɛ̋ɛgā → kæ̋ægā *bracelet de coureur*

kɛ̋ɛkʌ̄gèe <menacer-masque> ***n*** **masque-agresseur** *(peut sortir le jour ou la nuit; pourchasse les gens et les fouette, protège le village contre les malfaiteurs)*

kɛ̋ɛn, kæ̋æn {A S, kɛ̋ɛn-dhȕn pl. A S kɛ̋ɛn-sȕ foc. A S, kɛ̋ɛn-sȕ-dhȕn foc. pl. A S; kɛ̋ɛnkɛ̋ɛn, kæ̋ænkæ̋æn Int. pl. A S, kɛ̋ɛnkɛ̋ɛn-dhȕn, kæ̋ænkæ̋æn-dhȕn Int. pl. A, kɛ̋ɛnkɛ̋ɛn-sȕ, kæ̋ænkæ̋æn-sȕ Int. pl. foc. A S, kɛ̋ɛnkɛ̋ɛn-sȕ-dhȕn, kæ̋ænkæ̋æn-sȕ-dhȕn Int. pl. foc. A S} ***adj*** **usé** *(objets tressés devenus inutilisables)* Qsyn. blʌ́ 2), zīi ◊ *sæ̋æ̋ [tɤ̄ɤ, yɔ̄ɔ̀n] kɛ̋ɛn* natte [panier, séchoir] usée

kɛ̋ɛnkɛ̋ɛn *Int. pl. de* kɛ̋ɛn *usé*

kɛ̋ɛŋ → kɛ̋ɛ *mais*

kɛ̀fá ***n*** *toujours au singulier* **pou de corps, poux de corps** *[on les trouve chez les hommes seulement; pour s'en débarrasser, on fait bouillir les vêtements, et on se lave au savon noir]*

Qsyn. wèe 1 ♦ *kɛ̀fã́ dhídhí* trace de piqûre de pou ♦ *kɛ̀fã́ yà n̄ kún* un pou m'a piqué ♦ *bhán kɛ̀fã́ súː* j'ai saisi un pou/des poux ♦ *yà kʌ̄ wlɛ́ɛwlɛ̀ ká dhɛ̀ dhēdhʌ́n gúː kɛ̀fã́ dhɤ́* elle était joyeuse comme un pou sur le corps d'une jeune fille

kɛ̀fádʌ̄bhɛ̀n <pou-père-personne> ***n*** *iron.* **homme infecté de poux**

kɛ̀gbœ́œ ***n*** **célibataire**

kɛ̀gbœ́œ-dhɛ̀ ***n*** **célibat**

kɛ̂n ***n*** *rn* **héritage** *[chez les Dan l'héritage est réparti parmi les enfants par ordre d'âge (la part de l'aîné est la plus importante); on ne fait pas de testament; exceptionnellement, on peut distribuer la propriété aux héritiers même avant la mort, pour éviter d'éventuels conflits. On hérite des femmes, des champs de café et de cacao; l'argent ne fait pas nécessairement partie de l'héritage]* ◊ *Yàobâ-dhùn wɔ̄kɔ̀ gúː dhʌ́ngɔ̄ɔ̀n dhūn ɤ̄ dʌ̄ kɛ̂n sūː* chez les Yacouba, c'est le fils qui hérite de son père ◊ *n̄ dʌ̄ yà n̄ gbā kã́flɛ́ɛdhɛ̀ dō ká kɛ̂n pʌ̄ ká* mon père m'a laissé un champ de café en héritage ♦ *kɛ̂n pʌ̄* héritage ◊ *yà ɤ̄ bhà kɛ̂n pʌ̄ slɔ̀ɔ* il a reçu sa part de l'héritage *(on n'est jamais l'unique héritier)* ♦ *kɛ̂n pʌ̄-dhùn wɔ̀n* règles d'héritage

kɛ̀nŋ, **kɛ̀nŋgā** ***n*** *(avec les nombres, les deux formes s'utilisent, avec ou sans -gā)* **écrevisse, crevette** *[est classée par les Dan parmi les poissons]* ♦ *kɛ̀nŋ kɔ̄ŋgā* pince d'écrevisse ♦ *kɛ̀nŋ yí* sauce à l'écrevisse *[mode préféré de consommation, très recherché]* ◊ *kɛ̀nŋgā yã́n yáa dhɤ́* l'écrevisse n'a pas d'yeux

kɛ́nŋzúù ***n*** **rhum de canne** *[supérieur à koutoukou et plus cher, importé du Libéria]*

kɛ̄ŋ̀, **kɛ̄ŋ** ***prn*** **lui et toi**, **elle et toi** *pronom coordinatif incorporant*

kɛ̄ŋ̀-dhùn, **kɛ̄ŋ-dhùn** ***prn*** **vous et lui**, **vous et elle**, **vous et eux**, **vous et elles**, **toi et eux**, **toi et elles** *pronom coordinatif*

kɛ̀sēɛ́ ***n*** **citron vert**

kí ***mpp*** **vous** *MPP de la conséquence négative*

kíaan ***n*** **maladie de nez** *(plaies dans le nez qui saignent de temps en temps; à un stade avancé, le nez s'affaisse) [on la soigne avec le charbon des piquants de porc-épic, sɛ́ŋ]*

kìan ***v*** *vi* **se former** *(gombo, manioc, mangue, avocat, maïs, etc.)* Qsyn. *gĩ́a*

kĩ́an, **tĩ́an** ***n*** *rn* **totem** *(animal ou plante considéré comme le sauveteur de l'ancêtre du clan, promu en conséquence en interdit alimentaire du lignage qu'on doit honorer)* Syn. *zʌ̀nŋ* ◊ *bhén ɤ́ kɛ̄ŋ kā kĩ́an dhɤ́ dō kɤ̄ kā dhēɛ́bhāŋ-zʌ̀-dhùn ká* celui avec qui tu as le même totem, vous êtes des frères ◊ *yɤ̀ sʌ̀ kɤ̄ bhén ɤ́ dhɤ́ yɤ̀ ɤ̄ kĩ́an dhɔ̀ kʌ̄* il est bien qu'on adore son totem

kīã́nkìankīã́ndhɤ *onomat* **grincement** *(de chaussures)* ◊ *sàbhã́ yɤ̀ vìn kīã́nkìankīã́ndhɤ* les chaussures grincent

kìankìansùː ***adj*** *l'intensif du gérondif du verbe kìan* **très bien formé** *(fruit)*

kìansùː ***adj*** *le gérondif du verbe kìan* **dense** *(forêt)*

kìaŋ ***n*** **serre-tendeur** *(pour serrer un fagot)* ♦ *kìaŋ dȁ wɔ̋ bhȁ* serrer un fagot avec un tendeur

kı̋atő ***n*** **pic** *(esp.; sert à casser le sol dur; plus étroit et plus long que kʌ̋ʌ; est fabriqué par les forgerons)* Qsyn. *kʌ̋ʌ*

kı̋ʌʌ ***n*** **messager; représentant** ♦ *Zlȁan bhȁ kı̋ʌʌ* ange ♦ *gèe bhȁ kı̋ʌʌ* accompagnateur de masque *(un membre de l'équipe du masque qui le suit à distance pour contrôler l'observation de la procédure)* ♦ *yɔ̏ kı̋ʌʌ* marieur, entremetteur

kı̋ʌʌdhɛ̋ <messager-feuille ?> ***n*** **champignon** *(esp.)*

kīʌŋ 1, **tīʌŋ** ***n*** **fuseau**

kīʌŋ 2 ***n*** **grill pour fumer** *(poisson, viande, bananes, etc.)*

kīʌŋgbō <fuseau-canari> ***n*** **fuseau avec support**

kı̋dhőŋ <Fr. kilo> ***n*** **1 kilo, kilogramme 2 balance** ◊ *bhʌ̄nŋ́bhīn yɤ̏ bhān gɔ̂ dȁn kı̋dhőŋ tȁ yāandhı̋ɤ* hier un Dioula a pesé mes colas sur la balance **3 kilomètre**

kı̋ɛɛsȕ {A, Int. kı̋ɛkı̋ɛsȕ A> ***adj*** **féroce** *(animal, masque)* Syn. *dhı̋ɤ̏ɤ*

kı̋ɛkı̋ɛsȕ ***adj*** *INT de* kı̋ɛɛsȕ *féroce*

kíi 1 ***mpp*** **vous ne** *MPP négatif du passé du 2e pers. pl.*

kíi 2, **kúɯ** <de *kɤ̄ ɯ́ 'que tu...'> ***mpp*** **pour que tu** *forme fusionnée : conjonction + MPP de la 2e pers. sg. de la série conjointe*

kíi 3 <de *kɤ̄ ɯ́ ɯ̄ 'que tu ton...'> ***mpp*** **pour que tu ton...** *forme fusionnée : conjonction + MPP de la 2e pers. sg. de la série subjonctive + pronom 2e pers. sg. en fonction de complément d'objet direct* ◊ *kɤ̏ kíi bhā wʌ̋ʌ̀gā dhèŋ, bhı́in dhó' wɛ̋ɛ dhūn'* si tu perds ton argent, je ne t'en donnerai pas d'autre

kı̋oodhɤ̄ ***adv*** **avec grincement** ◊ *kwɛ̋ɛ ɤ́ yā wȁ ȁ pɔ̋ ȁ vīn yɤ̏ dɔ̏ kı̋oodhɤ̄* quand on ouvre cette porte, elle grince

kìɔɔn ***n*** **champignon** *(blanchâtre, pousse en mai sur les termitières) [très apprecié]*

klȁa ***n*** **1 verge** *(pour fouetter)*, **badine, fouet** Qsyn. *klàŋgā* ♦ *klȁa kpūdhē* nœud de fouet ♦ *klȁa yȁn dō bhō' gúɯ* donne-lui un coup de badine **2 cravate** Syn. *klāvātɤ̏* ♦ *klȁa gbȁn* nouer la cravate ♦ *klȁa pɔ̋* dénouer la cravate

klāā̋ 1 ***n*** **lime** *(instrument)* ◊ *yī bɑ̋ŋ dhı̋ɤ-bɔ̏ klāā̋ dhʌ̀n ȁ ká* nous aiguisons les machettes avec une lime ♦ *bɑ̋ŋ dhı̋ɤ-bɔ̏ ȁ ká klāā̋* pierre à aiguiser *(installée dans la cour)* ♦ *klāā̋ dhɯ̋ɯ* billot pour aiguiser la machette

Klāā̋ 2 {LOC Klāā̋dhɤ̄} ***loc.n*** **Kla** *(un groupe de Dan à l'ouest de la préfecture de Touba, leur pays et langue)*

klɑ̋a 1 ***n*** *kɔ́ klɑ̋a* **ossature de la maison** ♦ *yȁ kɔ́ klɑ̋a bhō* il a fabriqué l'ossature de la maison

klɑ̃a 2 ***n*** **tas d'herbe semi-brûlée** *(ramassée dans la savane après le passage du feu)* Qsyn. *gɛ̃ɛ, kɑ̃ŋ* ◊ *klɑ̃a sú-sǜ fɪ̃ʌ̀ʌ yɤ̀ dhɤ̀ ɤ́ zɪ̀ɤ ɑ̀ ká gɛ̃ɛ sú-sǜ tɑ̀* il est plus facile de ramasser des herbes brûlées {en savane} que des souches {en brousse}

klāadʌ̄ ***n*** **fougère** *(pousse au bord de l'eau, sur les troncs de palmiers)*

Klāɑ̃dhɤ̄ ***loc.n*** *LOC de* Klāɑ̃ *Kla*

klɑ̀ɑ̀n ***n*** **étincelle, flammèche** ◊ *yɤ̀ sɪ́ɤ dhǜu dhɤ́ kɤ̄ tɛ́ɛ yá dhó dhó' ɑ̀ klɑ̀ɑ̀n-dhǜn ká* il est en train d'éteindre le feu pour que le vent ne disperse pas les étincelles

klɑ̀atɪ̃ɪ̀ <Fr. cartes> ***n*** **cartes** *(à jouer)* ♦ *klɑ̀atɪ̃ɪ̀ dhɛ́* carte *(à jouer)* ♦ *klɑ̀atɪ̃ɪ̀ dhɛ́ bɛ̀* jeu de cartes ♦ *klɑ̀atɪ̃ɪ̀ dhɛ́ wlɤ̀ɤ dhɛ̀* face de carte ♦ *klɑ̀atɪ̃ɪ̀ dhɛ́ tɑ̀ dhʊ̃́ɤ dhɛ̀* dos de carte ♦ *klɑ̀atɪ̃ɪ̀ gɔ̄ɔn* jouer aux cartes

klɑ̀atɪ̃ɪ̀gɔ̄ɔnbhɛ̀n <cartes-jouer-personne> ***n*** **joueur de cartes**

klɑ̃bhɪ́ <Manding kàrafe> ***n*** **mors** ◊ *yɑ̀ klɑ̃bhɪ́ dɑ̀ sòò dhɪ́* il a mis le mors dans la bouche du cheval

klɑ̀klɑ̀dhɤ̄ ***onomat*** *crépitement des feuilles ou du bois au feu* ◊ *dhɛ́ yɤ̀ pɤ̀ɤ sɪ́ɤ gú klɑ̀klɑ̀dhɤ̄* les feuilles crépitent dans le feu

klɑ̃klɑ̃dhɤ̄ ***onomat*** *bruit de craquement des doigts* ◊ *yɤ̀ kɔ̄ŋgā gú wɛ̀ klɑ̃klɑ̃dhɤ̄* il fait craquer ses doigts

klɑ̀ŋ̀, klɑ̀ŋ {klɑ̀ŋ} <Manding kàran> ***n*** **1 études, formation** ♦ *klɑ̀ŋ̀-dhǜn* écoliers **2 école** Qsyn. *klɑ̀ŋdhɪ́ɤ* ♦ *kwɪ́ klɑ̀ŋ̀, kwɪ́ klɑ̀ŋ* école française *(modèle européen)* ♦ *bhɔ̃́ɔn klɑ̀ŋ, bhɔ̃́ɔn klɑ̀ŋ̀, bhʌ̄nŋ́ klɑ̀ŋ, bhʌ̄nŋ́ klɑ̀ŋ̀* école coranique

klɑ̃ŋ̀ ***n*** ***Cercopithecus nictitans*** **hocheur, pain à cacheter** *Iv. (singe) [devient rare au Gouèta; prisé en tant que gibier]* ♦ *klɑ̃ŋ̀ yɪ́* la sauce de singe

klɑ̀ŋdhɪ́ɤ, klɑ̀ŋ̀dhɪ́ɤ {LOC klɑ̀ŋ̀dhɪ́ɤ} <école-avant> ***loc.n*** **école** Qsyn. *klɑ̀ŋ̀* ♦ *yɤ̀ klɑ̀ŋ̀dhɪ́ɤ* il fait des études ◊ *ɑ̀ bhɑ̀ dhʌ́n-dhǜn bhá yíi dhó klɑ̀ŋ̀dhɪ́ɤ* parmi ses enfants, aucun n'est allé à l'école ♦ *klɑ̀ŋdhɪ́ɤ kɔ́* classe Syn. *kɔ́dhɪ́* ♦ *yɑ̀ ɤ̄ bhā klɑ̀ŋ̀dhɪ́ɤ tā* il a terminé ses études

klɑ̀ŋ̀dhɪ́ɤdhʌ́n <école-enfant> ***n*** **étudiant**

klɑ̀ŋgā < ?-os> ***n*** **fouet, chicotte** *Iv.*, **matraque** Qsyn. *klɑ̀a*

klɑ̀ŋ̀gɔ̀bhɛ̀n, klɑ̀ŋ̀gɔ̀bhɛ̀ndʌ̄ <école-tête-personne> ***n*** **enseignant, instituteur, professeur** *(de lycée)* ♦ *klɑ̀ŋ̀gɔ̀bhɛ̀n dhēbʌ̀* maîtresse d'école, institutrice ♦ *klɑ̀ŋ̀gɔ̀bhɛ̀n kpɪ̃ɪ́* directeur d'école Syn. *dīdhɛ̄tʌ́ʌ̀*

klɑ̀ŋ̀wɔ̀ <étude-voix> ***n*** *neol.* **leçon**

klāvɑ̃tɤ̀ <Fr. cravate> ***n*** **cravate** Syn. *klɑ̀a* ◊ *klāvɑ̃tɤ̀ yɑ̀ bhɔ̄ kǜn kpɛ̄nŋkpɛ̄nŋdhɤ̄* la cravate serre son cou fortement

klʌ̀ʌn 1 ***v*** **1** *vi* **entourer** *(qch – zǜ)* ◊ *tɑ̃nbhōbhɛ̀n-dhǜn wɑ̀ dhūn plɤ́ɤ̄, dhʌ́n-dhǜn wɔ̀ klʌ̀ʌn ɑ̀-dhǜn zǜ* quand les musiciens viennent au village, les enfants se ressemblent autour d'eux **2** *vt* **entourer avec** ◊ *wà̰ sáan klʌ̀ʌn pɤ̄ zṵ̀ṵ* le village a été entouré par un rempart

klʌ̀ʌn 2 *n* **cage**

klʌ́ʌn *n* **mil, petit mil** *[rarement cultivé chez les Dan, considéré comme étant une culture dioula]*

klʌ̀nklʌ̀ndhɤ̄ *onomat* *imite le son de crépitement de la tôle*

klɛ̰́ɛ <Fr. clé> *n rare* **clé, clef** *(de serrure)* <u>Syn.</u> <u>dhàklɛ̰́ɛ</u> ♦ *klɛ̰́ɛ dà̰* fermer la porte à clé ♦ *klɛ̰́ɛ yà bhɛ̄n kɔ̰̀ɔ* passer les menottes à qn ♦ *klɛ̰́ɛ bhō bhɛ̄n kɔ̰̀ɔ* enlever les menottes de qn

klɛ̰̀klɛ̰̀dhɤ̄ *adv* **avec éclat** *(briller)* ◊ *sṵ́dhʌ́n gbàn yá̰n bhɔ̰̀ klɛ̰̀klɛ̰̀dhɤ̄* toutes les étoiles brillent avec éclat

klɛ̄yɔ̂n, **klīyɔ̂n** <Fr. crayon> *n* *la forme klīyɔ̂n est utilisée surtout par des analphabètes, et klɛ̄yɔ̂n, par ceux qui ont fait l'école* **crayon** ♦ *klīyɔ̂n ga* crayon

klḭ́ŋ̰ *n* **arbre** *(nom générique pour deux espèces qui se ressemblent et produisent un latex)*

klḭ́ŋ̰bhɛ̄ɛn *n* **arbre** *(esp.; un caoutchoutifère, le bois est bon pour tailler les masques)*

klḭ́ŋ̰gbɔ̄kún *n* **arbre** *(esp.; de sa résine blanche collante, dɛ̀, on fait des pièges pour les oiseaux; le bois est fragile)*

klḭ̀ŋklḭ̄ŋ̰ *n* **stupéfaction** *(de peur, d'étonnement)* ♦ *klḭ̀ŋklḭ̄ŋ̰ yà yɤ̄ ñ tà̰* je suis stupéfié

klīyɔ̂n → klɛ̄yɔ̂n *crayon*

klɔ̰́ *n* **éducation** ♦ *dhʌ́n klɔ̰́ bhō* éduquer un enfant

klōâ <Fr. croix> *n* **croix** <u>Syn.</u> <u>dhṵ́ṵ</u>

klòŋ (gw), **klɔ̀ŋ** (m) *v* **1** 1) *vt* **courber** ◊ *ṵ̄ kɔ̄ŋgā klòŋ kɤ̄ ṵ́' zīɤ tǽǽ̀ gṵ́* courbe le doigt et essuie l'écuelle 2) *vi* **se courber** *(d'un objet inanimé)* ◊ *bhān kʌ́ʌ zɔ̰́ yà klòŋ* la lame de ma houe s'est courbée 3) *vr* **se courber** *(d'un être animé)* ♦ *yɤ̰̀ ɤ̄ klòŋ ɤ́ tá̰ sṵ̄* il marche courbé **2** *vi* **tourner** ◊ *yà klòŋ yà dhó ɤ̄ kwàa gṵ́* il a tourné à gauche

klòŋdhɛ̰̀ <courber-place> *n* **coude, courbure** ◊ *yí yā dhṵ̄n ɤ́' klòŋdhɛ̰̀ dhɤ́ gbé* cette rivière est très sinueuse

klɔ̰̀o *n* **entrelacement, enchevetrêment** ♦ *bhīʌ́ʌ klɔ̰̀o* liane entrelacée ♦ *zīaan klɔ̰̀o{gā}* *arch.* sentier

klōo {klòo} *v vt* **égrener**, **égrainer** *(riz)*

klɔ́ɔ̰̀ *n* ***Corythaeola cristata*** **touraco géant** *(76 cm; tête, cou, dos, ailes de couleur bleue; ventre jaune, cuisses châtain, queue longue à bout noir, huppe noire)*

klɔ̰́o *n rn* **caractère** *(tempérament)* ◊ *à̰ klɔ̰́o yɤ̰̀ sʌ̰̀/yâ* il est bon, gentil/mauvais, méchant

klɔ̰́sʌ̰̀bhɛ̰̀n <éducation-bon-personne> *n* **généreux, généreuse** ♦ *klɔ̰́sʌ̰̀bhɛ̰̀n yáa gwʌ̀ʌ* un homme généreux ne vit pas longtemps

klɔ̀ŋ 1 ***n*** **puits** *[toujours à l'intérieur de la cour; innovation d'origine maninka]* ♦ *klɔ̀ŋ tő* rebord de puits

klɔ̀ŋ 2 → klòŋ *courber*

klɔ̄ɔ̀ ***n*** **malheur** *[arrive à celui qu'on n'a pas prévenu à temps, parfois aussi suite à un mauvais présage, tel qu'une humiliation publique sans raison]* ♦ *klɔ̄ɔ̀ yȁ dɔ̄ n̄ bhȁ* j'ai eu un mauvais présage

klɔ̄ɔ̀ ***n*** **sens, signification** ◊ *dhīaŋ klɔ̄ɔ̀* le sens de la parole

klɤ́-kʌ̄ {klɤ́-kʌ̄} ***v*** **1** *vt* **enrouler** *(autour – bhȁ)* **2.1** *vt* **rouler** *(faire un cercle)* ◊ *yà bhīʌ́gā klɤ́-kʌ̄* il a enroulé la corde **2.2** *vr* **se louver** ◊ *bhlɛ̀ɛn yà ɤ̄ klɤ́-kʌ̄* le serpent s'est lové

klɤklɤ, klɤklɤ̀ɤ (m) *Int. pl. de* klɤ̄ɤ̀ *court*

klɤklɤ̄dhɤ {Int. klɤ́klɤ̀klɤ́dhɤ} ***adv*** *évoque douleur légère, picotement* ♦ *yɤ̀ n̄ kún-sīʌ klɤklɤ̄dhɤ* ça me pique *(blessure)* ♦ *n̄ yǟn gā yɤ̀ n̄ kún-sīʌ klɤklɤ̄dhɤ* j'ai un tic nerveux de l'oeil ◊ *n̄ kwī yɤ̀ n̄ kún-sīʌ klɤ́klɤ̀klɤ́dhɤ* j'ai des picotements partout

klɤ́klɤ́dhɤ ***adv*** *SupInt. de* klɤ̄ɤ́dhɤ *près*

klɤ́klɤ̀klɤ́dhɤ ***adv*** *Int. de* klɤklɤ̄dhɤ *picotement*

klɤ́kɤ́klɤ̀kɤ̀ ***adj*** *Int. de* klɤ́ɤklɤ̀ *bien portant*

klɤ̀ɤ ***n*** **1** ***Pilocolobus badius*** **colobe bai d'Afrique Occidentale** *(singe à partie supérieure noire ou gris foncé et à partie inférieure et pattes rousses ou oranges; 5,5 à 10 kg)* ♦ *ȁ sɔ̋n ká dhɛ̀ klɤ̀ɤ sɔ̋n dhɤ́* ses dents ressemblent à celles du colobe *(vilaines, tordues)* **2** (m) **singe** <u>*Syn.*</u> <u>*wɔ̀ɔ (gw)*</u>

klɤ̄ɤ̀ {A P S, klɤ̄ɤ̀-dhȕn pl. A S, klɤ̄ɤ̀-sȕ foc. A S, klɤ̄ɤ̀-sȕ-dhȕn A S; klɤ̄ɤ́ Int. A P S, klɤ̄ɤ́-dhȕn Int. pl. A, klɤ̄ɤ́-sȕ Int. foc. A; klɤ̄ɤ́klɤ̄ɤ́, klɤklɤ, klɤklɤ̀ɤ (m) Int. pl. A P S, klɤ̄ɤ́klɤ̄ɤ́-dhȕn, klɤklɤ-dhȕn Int. pl. A S, klɤklɤ-sȕ Int. pl. foc. A S, klɤklɤ-sȕ-dhȕn Int. pl. foc. A S} ***adj*** **1.1 court** *(taille)* ◊ *gbên-dhȕn klɤ̄ɤ́klɤ̄ɤ́-dhȕn* très petits chiens **1.2 bref** ♦ *gúː klɤ̄ɤ̀ bhȁ* tout de suite **1.3 proche** ◊ *ȁ bhȁ bhláȁdhɛ̏ yɤ̀ pɤ̄dhɛ̏/pɤ̀ ká klɤ̄ɤ̀* son champ est près du village **2** *rare, arch.* **petit** *(homme, arbre, chemin, voiture)*, **peu profond** *(eau)*

klɤ̄ɤ́ 1) ***adj*** *Int. de* klɤ̄ɤ̀ *court*

klɤ̄ɤ́ 2) ***adv*** **à proximité**

klɤ̄ɤ̀-dhɛ̏ ***n*** **petitesse** *(de taille, en parlant d'un homme ou d'un objet)*

klɤ̄ɤ́dhɤ {Int. klɤ́ɤ̄ɤ̀dhɤ, SupInt. klɤ́klɤ́dhɤ} ***adv*** **près** <u>*Qsyn.*</u> <u>*klɤ̄ɤ̀*</u> ♦ *yɤ̀ dɔ̄ n̄ ká klɤ̄ɤ́dhɤ* il est mon proche parent ♦ *bhá dɔ̄ n̄ ká klɤ̄ɤ́dhɤ* tu es trop proche de moi *(une invitation adressée à l'autre de s'éloigner)*

klɤ́ɤdhɤ {Int. krrɤ́ɤɤdhɤ} ***adv*** **vite et bref** *(idée d'un mouvement rapide et court, évoque le mode de déplacement des crabes, punaises, poux et tiques; la forme intensive exprime un mouvement rapide et plus longue)* ♦ *kā [gblūūŋgā] yɤ̀ tȁ/zīɤ/tá sȕ klɤ́ɤdhɤ* le crabe [la punaise] rampe

klɤ́ɤklɤ̀, klɤ́ɤklɤ̀ɤ {P S; klɤ̀kɤ́klɤ̀kɤ̀ Int. P, S} *la fonction S est rare* ***adj*** **en bonne santé, bien portant** *(d'un être humain* ◊ *yɤ̀ klɤ́ɤklɤ̀ dèdèwō* il est en très bonne santé

klɤ̄ɤ́klɤ̄ɤ́ *Int. pl. de* klɤ̄ɤ̀ *court*

klɤ́ɤklɤ̀ɤ ***adv*** **en bonne santé** *dans l'expression :* ♦ *kʌ̀ klɤ́ɤklɤ̀ɤ-sṳ̀ yɤ̀ kʌ̄ ɯ̄ gɔ̀* porte-toi bien ! ◊ *bhán kʌ̄ klɤ́ɤklɤ̀ɤ* j'ai guéri

klɤ̄ɤ́klɤ̀ɤklɤ̄ɤ́dhɤ̄ ***onomat*** *imite le grincement des dents [le grincement des dents n'est pas considéré comme exprimant des émotions]*

klɤ́ɤɤ̀dhɤ̄ ***adv*** *Int. de* klɤ̄ɤ́dhɤ̄ *près*

klúgā <Fr. écrou> ***n*** **écrou** ◊ *bhán klúgā slʌ̄ʌ' gúṹ* j'ai tourné l'écrou

klṵ̀u ***n*** **louche** *(traditionnellement faite d'une moitié de calebasse; aujourd'hui souvent en laiton)* ◊ *Yɔ̀ yà tő̃o bhō klṵ̀u ká* Yo a servi la sauce avec une louche ♦ *klṵ̀u gɔ̀* creux de louche ♦ *klṵ̀u wēŋ* manche de louche

klɯ̄ɯ, klɯ̄ɯgā ***n*** **gris-gris** *(contre les balles) seule la forme en -gā s'utilise avec les nombres*

klɯ̄ɯgā → klɯ̄ɯ̄ *gris-gris*

klɯ̄ɯgādʌ̄ <gris-gris-père> ***n*** *euph.* **rebelle** *(pendant la guerre civile du 2002-2011)*

kɔ̀ ***mpp*** **nous** *MPP impératif, inclusif 1re pers. duel : "moi et toi"*

kō 1 ***n*** **1.1** *rn* **reins** *(partie inférieure du dos)* *Qsyn.* *tàa 1), tàadhɛ̀* ◊ *ī kō yɤ̀ bhìa à tà* mon dos a craqué ♦ *gó ɤ̄ kō tà* faire une pause pendant le travail ♦ *ī kō yí yà kấn* j'ai des douleurs dans le dos ♦ *ɤ̄ kō yí bhō* se reposer **1.2** *rn* **dos** *(d'un animal)* **2 dos** *(de lame, instrument)* ♦ *bấŋ kō* dos de lame de machette ♦ *klṵ̀u kō* dos de louche

kō 2 ***mpp*** **nous** *MPP existentiel inclusif 1re pers. duel : "moi et toi"*

kō 3 ***prn*** **nous** *pronom inclusif 1re pers. duel : "moi et toi" de la série autonome*

kō 4 ***prn*** **nous** *pronom non-sujet inclusif 1re pers. duel : "moi et toi"*

kó 1 {LOC kwʌ́ʌ̀dhɤ̄, IN kő̃o, COM kwʌ́ʌ, SUP kwʌ́ʌ̀} ***loc.n*** *rn* **l'un l'autre** *(pronom réciproque)* ◊ *wɔ̀ kó zʌ̄-sīʌ* ils se battent ◊ *wɔ̀ yʌ̄ kʌ̀ wō kwʌ́ʌ̀* ils travaillent ensemble (d'habitude) ◊ *wà yʌ̄ kʌ̀ wō kwʌ́ʌ* ils ont travaillé ensemble ♦ *kó kèŋ̀ / pɯ́ɤ* ensemble ♦ *zīɤ kő̃o* s'entrelacer ♦ *ī gɤ́ŋ̀ yà zīɤ kő̃o* j'ai eu une luxation à la cuisse

kó 2 ***mpp*** **nous** *MPP du parfait, inclusif 1re pers. duel : "moi et toi"*

kó 3 ***mpp*** **nous** *MPP conjointe inclusif inclusif 1re pers. duel : "moi et toi"*

kó 4 ***mpp*** **nous** *MPP subjonctif inclusif inclusif 1re pers. duel : "moi et toi"*

kó 5 ***mpp*** **pour que nous ne** *MPP prohibitif inclusif 1re pers. duel. : "moi et toi"*

kó 6 ***prn*** **nous** *(pronom sélectif 1re pers. inclusif duel, utilisé avec le suffixe -sṳ̀)*

kó 7 ***n*** **bagarre** ♦ *kó zʌ̄ à tà* se bagarrer, se quereller à cause de qn ♦ *Zân yà kó yà Yɔ̀ bhà* Zan s'est bagarré avec Yo

kōáa, **kōyáa** ***prn*** **nous** *pronom exclusif 1re pers. duel, "nous sans vous", de la série focalisée négative*

kő̄bhí̋ <Manding kóbi 'bâtiment administratif'> ***n*** **1 commune 2 préfecture**

kōgā <dos-os> ***n rn*** **échine, colonne vertebrale** *(hors vertèbres cervicales)*

kōkʌ̄yȕa ***n*** **rhumatisme**

kòŋ 1 ***n*** **cercle, cerceau** ♦ *pȉɤgāsòȍ kòŋ* roue de vélo; pneu de vélo; jante de roue de bicyclette ◊ *gɔ̄ kòŋ* pneu de voiture, roue de voiture, disque de roue

kòŋ 2 ***n*** **1 Kong** *(masque des femmes)[est considérée comme la "grande sœur" du masque Gű̋u; sort lors de l'initiation des femmes, aux baptêmes et aux funérailles des femmes; ne doit pas être vu par les hommes, à l'exception de ző̋o]* ♦ *wȁ dhʌ́n Kòŋ kʌ̄* ils ont fait le baptême *[lit. : "on a chassé le masque de femmes"; le baptême est une fête de reconnaissance aux femmes qui ont assisté à l'accouchement; si le nouveau-né est un garçon, le baptême est organisé le 4e jour, si c'est une fille, au 3e jour]* **2 danse du masque "kong"** *(danse des femmes adultes que les hommes ne doivent pas voir : les danseuses produisent des mouvements aisés en tournant le torse et en écartant les bras; on peut tenir un bâton ou un sabre dans la main; se produit dans les maisons, lors des baptêmes, des funérailles des vieilles ou lors de l'initiation des filles)* ◊ *yī dhē yà dhó kòŋ tȁ* notre mère est allée à la danse "kong"

kōŋ ***n*** **1 fourche** ♦ *dhű̋ kōŋ* fourche d'un arbre **2 joug** *(fait d'une fourche d'arbre)* ◊ *wȁ dhű̋ kōŋ dȁ dȕ bhɔ̄ gúu* on a mis le joug sur le cou du boeuf

kòŋbhó ***n*** **coiffure de la danseuse dhɛ̏ɛdhı̋ɤ** *(tortillon d'étoffe avec des bandes de tissu)*

kòŋ-kʌ̄ {kòŋ-kʌ̏} ***v vt*** **rouler en cercle**

kòŋtá̋n <masque Kong-danse> ***n*** **"kongtan"** *(le chant et la danse de l'association des femmes adultes possédant le masque; se fait à l'occasion des événements importants, accompagnés du tintement des sonnailles gbɤ̋ŋ; la présence des hommes est permise)*

kòo ***n Tilapia sp.*** **tilapia** ◊ *kòo glɛ̋ɛn yɤ̏ gbɛ́* le tilapia a trop d'arêtes ◊ *Zân dhí yɤ̏ kʌ̏ dhɛ̀ kòo báȁ bhɤ̏ dhȉ dhɤ́* la bouche de Zan est comme celle du tilapia-mangeur-de-boue

kōo 1 ***mpp*** **nous** *MPP prospectif inclusif 1re pers. duel. : "moi et toi"*

kōo 2 ***prn*** **nous** *pronom inclusif 1re pers. duel. : "moi et toi" de la série restrictive*

kōo 3 ***prn*** **moi et...** *pronom coordinatif*

kōȍ 1 ***prn*** **notre, nos** *pronom inclusif du 1re pers. duel de la série possessive*

kōȍ 2 ***mpp*** **nous** *MPP inclusif du 1re pers. duel de la série présomptive*

kóo 1 ***mpp*** **nous** *MPP négatif imperfectif inclusif 1re pers. duel. : "moi et toi"*

kóo 2 ***mpp*** **nous** *MPP négatif inclusif 1re pers. duel du passé : "moi et toi"*

kő̋o ***loc.n*** *IN de* kó 1 *l'un l'autre*

kő̋ȍ ***intj*** **hou la !** *exclamation de surprise; se place au début de la phrase)*

kōɔ̋kɔ̀o (m) ***n Colocasia esculenta* taro** *(tubercule comestible)* Syn. *plʌ̋ʌ̀*

kɔ́ōo ***mpp*** **nous (du.) ne** *(forme fusionnée des marqueurs prédicatifs négatif et prospectif de la 1e personne duel)*

kòopűu <carpe-blanc> ***n Lates niloticus*** **capitaine** *(le plus gros des poissons des eaux douces de l'Afrique de l'Ouest : jusqu'à 2, 80 kg; flancs argentés ou argentés blancs; dos bronzé, olive ou gris foncé; ventre blanchâtre ou jaunâtre; des nageoires très tranchantes; se nourrit de petits poissons, vit dans les marigots et rivières; chair très savoureuse)* Syn. *kpɔ̀n*

kòotīi <carpe-noir> ***n Lutjanus sp.*** **vivaneau** *(poisson)*

kőoudhɤ̄ ***onomat*** **paf** *(son d'une chiquenaude)* ◊ *yà̰ à zʌ̄ gʌ̀ʌ ká kőoudhɤ̄* il lui a donné une chiquenaude : paf

kɔ̀sɔ̀ < Manding kòso > ***n*** **couverture en laine**

kósɔ̀n < Manding kósɔ̀n > ***pp*** **à cause de**

kósúdhē <l'un l'autre-prendre-nominalis.> ***n*** **noce, mariage** ◊ *kósúdhē ɤ́ tɤ̋ŋ yā' yáa dɔ̄ dhœ̀œn wɔ̀n bhà̰* de nos jours, la fête de mariage ne dépend pas de la richesse (une fête opulente n'est pas obligatoire)

kósúfɛ̄tɤ̀ <l'un l'autre-prendre-fête> ***n*** **fête de mariage**

kósú-sṵ̀ <l'un l'autre-prendre-gérondif> ***n*** **fête de mariage** ◊ *à̰-dhàan kósú-sṵ̀ yɤ̀ kʌ̄ kʌ̀ sʌ̀* leur fête de mariage a été réussie

kósútlɔ̀o <l'un l'autre-prendre-jeu> ***n*** **fête de mariage** ◊ *kósútlɔ̀o yɤ̀ kʌ̄ kʌ̀ dhɛ̀kpœ̀œyì yà̰agā* la fête de mariage a duré pendant trois jours

kótà̰ <l'un l'autre-sur> ***n*** **fois** Syn. *gœ̀œ 2* ◊ *yà dhūn kótà̰ plɛ̀* il est venu deux fois

kówɔ̀gúbhān-sṵ̀ <l'un l'autre-voix-intérieur-entendre-gérondif> ***n*** **entente**

kōyáa → kōáa *pas nous (duel)*

kɔ̀ 1 {AD kɔ̀ɔ, SUP kwɛ̀ŋ, kwɛ̀ɛ̄, SUP.INT kwɛ̀ŋkwɛ̀ŋ, COM kɔ̄ɔ} ***loc.n*** **1.1** *rn* **main** *(avant-bras et main)* ◊ *dhēbʌ̀-dhùn wà bhēn kɔ̀ blɛ̋ɛn kʌ̄ kɔ́ bhã̋ŋ bhà̰* les femmes ont laissé des empreintes de leurs mains sur le mur de la maison *(comme décoration)* ◊ *wà bhēn zɔ̄n kɔ̄ɔ à tàa...* lorsqu'on frappe une personne sur le dos avec la main... ♦ *kɔ̀ gblőo* écriture *(manière)* ♦ *à kɔ̀ yɤ̀ fɤ̋ɤfɤ̀ɤ* i) il frappe facilement ii) il est généreux ♦ *yà ɤ̄ kɔ̀ dūn ɤ̄ ká* i) il a arrêté de donner des cadeaux i) il a fait une pause dans la réception des visiteurs ♦ *à kɔ̀ yɤ̀ gbĩ́nŋ̀ à bhà̰* il fait cela difficilement ♦ *à kɔ̀ yɤ̀ fɤ̋ɤfɤ̀ɤ à bhà̰* il fait cela facilement ♦ *ɤ̄ kɔ̀ dà̰ à gú* saisir qch/qn ♦ *à kɔ̀ yáa wɔ̀* il est très avare ♦ *à kɔ̀ yáa dhɤ́* il ne sait pas quoi faire ♦ *bhī dhʌ̀n ū kɔ̀ ɤ́' bhà̰* cela est manigancé par toi ♦ *yíi kʌ̄ n̄ kwɛ̀ŋ wɔ̀n ká* ce n'est pas de ma faute ◊ *wɔ́n ɤ́ bhā yíi kʌ̄ kʌ̄ ū kwɛ̀ŋ wɔ̀n ká* cela n'est pas de ta faute ♦ *tó ɤ̄ kɔ̀ bhà̰* rester les mains vides ♦ *kɔ̀ bhō wɔ́n gú* abandonner l'affaire ♦ *yà ɤ̄ kɔ̀ bhō ɤ̄ bhā dhēbʌ̀ gú* il a divorcé de sa femme ♦ *ɤ̄ kɔ̀ yà̰ à bhà̰* i) accepter qch *(un don, une rançon)* ii) embaucher qn, admettre (dans un établissement d'éducation) iii) aider à monter ♦ *ɤ̄ kɔ̀ yɤ̄ à bhà̰* i) accepter qch *(don, rançon)* ii) toucher à *(faire du mal)* ◊ *kɤ̄ kíi ū kɔ̀ yɤ̄ bhān dhʌ́n bhā' bhà̰, ā dhɔ̀ ū bhà̰n'* si tu touches à mon enfant, je vais te frapper ♦ *bhɛ̄n-dhʉ̀n kɔ̏ yà kwʌ́ʌ̀* inciter les gens à la querelle ♦ *ū kɔ̏ dȁ ȁ kwɛ̏ɛ̏* serre-lui la main ♦ *bhlʉ̀n yɤ̏ dhȉ ȁ kɔ̏ bhȁ* le riz donne bien chez lui ♦ *ȁ kɔ̏ tȁ* à cause de lui ♦ *dhʌ́n sʉ̋ɛ̀sīɤ dhʌ̀n ɲ̄ kwɛ̏ɛ̏* j'ai neuf enfants ♦ *ȁ kɔ̏ yáa' kwɛ̀ɛ̏ wɔ̏n ká* incomparablement **1.2** *rn* **patte de devant 1.3 manche** *(d'un vêtement)* **2 manière** Qsyn. *kǽæn* ◊ *ȁ bhȁ yʌ̄kʌ̄ kɔ̏ yɤ̏ sʌ̀* sa manière de travailler est bonne ◊ *dhó dhɔ̏ yà ɲ̄ kún, kɛ̋ɛ kɔ̏ bhɤ̋ ɤ́ bhāan ȁ kʌ̄ ȁ bhȁ kɤ̄ á dhó bháan' yɤ̄* j'ai envie de partir, mais je ne vois pas comment je peux partir ♦ *yɤ̄ɤ kʌ̄ kɔ̏ őo kɔ̏ ɤ́' bhȁ...* quoi qu'il en soit... **3** *mot qui sert à compter les dizaines dans la formation des nombres complexes* Qsyn. *kɔ̏ŋ* **4 branche** Syn. *kwɛ̄ɛ̋*

kɔ̏ 2 *v* **1** *vi* **refuser** *(à – dhɛ̏, qch – bhȁ, à faire qch – -sʉ̏ ká)* ◊ *yà wʌ́ʌ̀ dhɛ̏ ɲ̄ gɔ̏, ā kɔ̏ ȁ dhɛ̏ kpǣ̀æwō* chaque fois qu'il me demande de l'argent, je refuse ◊ *Gbàtò yà kɔ̏ dhò fɛ̄tɤ̏ tȁ wɔ̏n ká, kɤ̄ ɤ́ tó kwáŋ̏dhɤ̄* Gbato a refusé d'aller à la fête pour rester à la maison ◊ *yà kɔ̏ dhó-sʉ̏ ká* il a refusé de s'en aller ◊ *yà kɔ̏ ɲ̄ tȁ-kún-sʉ̏ bhȁ* il a refusé de m'aider **2** *vi* **ne pas obéir** *(à – gɔ̏)*, **rater** *(fusil)*, **caler** *(engin)* ◊ *yà kɔ̏ ɲ̄ gɔ̏, yà pɤ̏ yáa yɤ̄ɤ dhó* il ne m'a pas obéi, il n'a pas voulu partir ◊ *ȁ bhȁ gɔ̄ yà kɔ̏ ȁ gɔ̏* sa voiture a calé ♦ *yà kɔ̏ ɲ̄ gɔ̏* elle n'a pas accepté ma déclaration d'amour

kɔ̏ 3 *adv* **véritablement** ◊ *ā yʌ̄ dɔ̏ kɔ̏* il connaît vraiment le travail

kɔ̏ 4 *v vi* **sécher** *(d'un objet humide)* ◊ *yà kʌ̄ dhɛ̀ kɔ́ɔdhɛ̏ yà kɔ̏, kɤ̄ ú sǣ̀ǣ kpɔ́* quand (le sol de) la maison sèche (après le lavage), tu peux étaler la natte

kɔ́ {kɔ̏} *n* **1 maison, case, bâtiment** Qsyn. *kɔ́ɔdhɛ̏* ◊ *kɔ́ yā yɤ̏ sʌ̀* cette maison est jolie *(extérieurement)* ♦ *kɔ́ gɔ̏* faîte *(du toit)* ♦ *kɔ́ gɛ̀n* pieu des fondations d'une maison ♦ *kɔ́ dhʉ̋* les poteaux de l'ossature de la maison ♦ *yà kɔ́ dhʉ̋ gbȁn* il a fabriqué la structure de la maison ♦ *dhɔ̋ɔ kɔ̏* boutique ♦ *klàŋ kɔ̏* école ♦ *sʌ́ʌ̀ bhȍ gú kɔ̏* mosquée ♦ *Zlȁan kɔ̏* église ♦ *kɔ́ dɔ̄ ɲ̄ tȁ* donne ta fille en mariage à mon fils ! (litt. : construis une maison sur moi !) **2 habitat, nid** ♦ *bhȁan kɔ́* nid d'oiseau ♦ *dɔ̋ɔn kɔ́* nid d'araignée

kɔ̀bhán *n* **Koma** *(un masque, chasseur de sorciers)*

kɔ̋bhɔ̋ (gw) *n* **plante herbacée** *(des fleurs jaunes, des petites fruits qui se collent aux habits; on utilise sa sève contre les maux de ventre, et ses feuilles pour soigner la mycose des pieds)* Syn. *dhãandhãan (m)*

kɔ̏dā *n* **poignée** ♦ *kɔ̏dā dō dȁ ȁ gú !* prends au moins une poignée !

kɔ̄dhānklīi <du nom de la capitale de la Guinée Conakry> *n* **conakry** *(sorte de banane douce : petite, très sucrée et recherchée)*

kɔ́dhʌ́n <maison-enfant> *n* **maison carrée** *(pour les hommes; sans grenier, on n'y allume pas de feu)* Syn. *gbɔ̄ŋ* Ant. *kɔ́dhɛ̄ɛ̋*

kɔ́dhɛ̄ɛ̋ 1 <maison-féminin> *n* **case ronde** *[case de femme, avec un grenier; des hommes âgés y habitent parfois également]*

kɔ́dhɛ̄ɛ̋ 2 <maison-féminin ?> *n* **épouse** Qsyn. *dhɛ̄bʌ̀*

kɔ̏dhɛ̋ <main-feuille> *n* **main**

kɔ̏dhɛ̋tȁ <main-feuille-surface> *n rn* **dos de la main**

kɔ̏dhɛ̋wlɤ̏ɤdhɛ̏ <main-feuille-sous-place> *n rn* **paume**

kɔ́dhí <maison-porte> *n* **1 porte de la maison 2 famille, concession** ♦ *kɔ́dhí dʌ̄* père de la famille ♦ *kɔ́dhí gúɯ́ bhɛ̄n-dhȕn* membres de famille **3 appartement; chambre 4 classe** *(école)* Syn. klàŋdhíɤ kɔ̏ ◊ *yɤ̏ kɔ́dhí yȁagā-dhȁan gúɯ́* il est en troisième année {d'école}

kɔ́dhígúɯ́bhɛ̏n *n* **personne de la famille**

kɔ̏dhíɤ {kɔ̏dhíɤ-kɔ̏dhíɤ Int.} <main-devant> *adv* **entre les mains** ◊ *ȁ bhȁ glɛ̄ɛ́ yɤ̏ ȁ kɔ̏dhíɤ-kɔ̏dhíɤ* son sac est constamment entre ses mains

Kɔ̏dhɔ̏n *n* **Kono** *(peuple de la sous-préfecture de Lola en Guinée dont la langue est proche du kpellé)*

kɔ́gúɯ́dhɛ̏ → kɔ́ɔdhɛ̏ *maison*

kɔ́gbȁngɔ̏dhɯ̋ɯ <maison-toit-tête-arbre> *n arch.* **poutre maîtresse** Syn. gɔ̏dɔ̄gāgɔ̏

kɔ̏kèetȁwɔ̏n *n* **bagatelle** *(affaire peu importante, inutile)*

kɔ̄kɔ̄ *onomat* **toc toc** *(frapper à la porte)* ◊ *yɤ̏ kwɛ̄ɛ bhȁn-sīʌ kɔ̄kɔ̄* il frappe à la porte : toc-toc

kɔ̀kɔ̀kpāȁdhɛ̏, **kɔ̀kpȁpāȁdhɛ̏** *n* **chrysalide**

kɔ̏kɔ̏ŋkɔ́ɔ̏ *onomat* **cocorico** *(chant de coq)*

kɔ̏kúndhɛ̏ <main-attraper-place> *n* **1 manche 2 approche** *(façon d'aborder)*, **contrôle n** ♦ *bhɛ́n yā, kɔ̏kúndhɛ̏ yáa ȁ bhȁ* cette personne est intenable, ingouvernable ♦ *dhīaŋ bhā, kɔ̏kúndhɛ̏ yáa ȁ bhȁ* on ne sait pas comment aborder ce problème

kɔ̏kpɤ̄ <main-boule> *n rn* **poing** ◊ *yà ȁ zʌ̄ kɔ̏kpɤ̄ ká' wʌ̄ʌ́dhɤ̄* il l'a frappé au visage avec le poing

kɔ̏lȍokótȁ <main-arriver-réciproque-sur> *n* **association**

kɔ̏n *n* **1 pâte** Syn. bɤ̏ɤ ♦ *bāa dhɛ́ kɔ̏n* pâte de feuilles de manioc *(les feuilles sont cuites dans l'eau, puis pilées; parfois on les pile sans les faire cuire)* ♦ *gwɛ̄ɛ kɔ̏n* pâte d'arachide **2 foutou** *Iv. (pâte épaisse et élastique de manioc ou de banane plantain; les tubercules ou les bananes sont pelés, cuits et ensuite pilés)* ◊ *bhān dhēbʌ̏ yà bāa kɔ̏n zɔ̄n* ma femme a pilé le foutou de manioc

kɔ́n {kɔ̄n} *v* **1** *vt* **étonner** *(négativement)* ◊ *bhá n̄ kɔ́n* tu m'as étonné ! (négativement) **2.1** *vi* **rater** *(qch – ká)* ◊ *bhá ȁ kʌ̄ dhɤ́ bhán kɔ́n bhȁandhʌ́n bhā' ká* à cause de toi j'ai manqué l'oiseau ♦ *kɔ́n kwʌ́ʌ̏* diverger, être en contradiction ◊ *yà kɔ́n ȁ-dhȕn gɔ̏ kwʌ́ʌ̏* ils ont eu un malentendu **2.2** *vi* **tomber** *(par malchance; de – ká)* ◊ *yà kɔ́n pɔ̄ŋ ká, yà pɤ̏ yí bhàa* il a fait un faux pas sur le pont et est tombé dans l'eau ◊ *yà kɔ́n dhɯ̋ɯ ká yà pɤ̏ bàŋdhɤ̄* il est tombé de l'arbre

kɔ̄nbhānŋdē {kɔ̄nbhānŋdē, NEUT kɔ̄nbhānŋdɛ̏} <Fr. commander> *v vt* **commander**

kɔ̄nŋ ***n*** **harpe-luth** *(résonateur en calebasse ou en bois) [en Gouèta, un instrument des chasseurs, utilisé pour accompagner des chansons et des narrations]* ♦ *kɔ̄nŋ gā* la corde de harpe-luth ♦ *kɔ̄nŋ gbɔ̄* résonateur de harpe-luth ♦ *kɔ̄nŋ dhűű* manche de harpe-luth ♦ *kɔ̄nŋ sɛ̋ɛ* tête de harpe-luth ♦ *kɔ̄nŋ zʌ̄* jouer de la harpe-luth

kɔ̏nŋkɔ̏nŋdhɤ̄ ***adv*** **sur la pointe des pieds** ♦ *zīɤ kɔ̏nŋkɔ̏nŋdhɤ̄* marcher sur la pointe des pieds

kɔ̀nŋsóɔ̀dhɯ̏ ***n*** **paon** *[très rare chez les Dan]* ♦ *yà bhlʌ̏ ɤ̄ gɯ́ dhɛ̀ kɔ̀nŋsóɔ̀dhɯ̏ dhɤ́* il s'est mis en colère, comme un paon

kɔ̄nŋtʌ̋n <harpe-luth-danse> ***n*** **chant et danse des chasseurs** *(accompagné du harpe-luth)*

kɔ̏ŋ, **kœ̏œŋ** <main- ?> ***n*** **dizaine** *unité de comptage se rapportant aux dizaines dans les numéraux complexes* *Qsyn.* *kɔ̏ 1* ♦ *kɔ̏ŋ dō-dhʌ̏an* dixième

kɔ̄ŋ ***n rn*** **doigt** *dans quelques expressions* *Qsyn.* *kœ̄œŋgā* ♦ *kɔ̄ŋ gbɛ̏ŋ gɯ́* intervalle entre les doigts

kɔ̋ŋ {kɔ̀ŋ} ***n*** **repas, nourriture, nourriture de base** *Syn.* *bhɤ̏pʌ̏* *le mot n'est pas beaucoup utilisé à Gouèta, mais connu* ♦ *bhɛ̄n kɔ̏ŋ* une foule dense ♦ *bɤ̄ɤ̏ kɔ̏ŋ* motte de boue

kɔ̄ŋgā, **kœ̄œŋgā** <main- ?-os> ***n rn*** **doigt** *Qsyn.* *kɔ̄ŋ* ♦ *kœ̄œŋgā gɔ̄n* pouce ♦ *wèe pʌ̏ ká kœ̄œŋgā* index *(doigt)* ♦ *kœ̄œŋgā dhʌ́n glɔ̄ɔ́n* majeur, médius ♦ *kœ̄œŋgā zìnŋgɯ́ sɯ̏* majeur, médius ♦ *kœ̄œŋgā dhʌ́n tɔ̄ɔ* petit doigt ♦ *kœ̄œŋgā kpɤ̄* articulation du doigt ♦ *kœ̄œŋgā wɛ́* faire craquer les doigts; faire claquer ses doigts *[on claque les doigts pour attirer l'attention; ce geste est vu comme convenable]* ◊ *ɤ́ dhīaŋ zʌ̄-sīʌ kɤ̄ yɤ̏ ɤ̄ kɔ̄ŋgā wɛ́-sīʌ* lorsqu'il parle, il fait claquer ses doigts ◊ *dɔ̄ kɤ̄ á ɯ̄ kɔ̄ŋgā wɛ́* attends, je vais faire craquer tes doigts *[un jeu d'enfants : on presse les doigts du partenaire; si aucun doigt ne craque, on dit : "tu es un sorcier !"]*

kɔ̄ŋgāʌ̏pʌ̏ <doigt-sur-chose> ***n*** **bague**

kɔ̏ŋkɔ̏ŋ, **kɔ̏ŋkɔ̏ŋdhɤ̄** ***adv*** **à pas de loup** *(un humain)* ◊ *wɔ̀ tʌ̏ kɔ̏ŋkɔ̏ŋ, wó wɯ̄ zʌ̄, wá dhűű kʌ̋ŋ yɛ̋, wáa wɯ̄ zʌ̄* si on marche à pas de loup, on tue l'animal; si on casse un branche, on ne tue pas l'animal (un chant) ◊ *yɤ̏ dhɔ̏ kɔ̏ŋkɔ̏ŋdhɤ̄ bhɛ́n ?* où va-t-il à pas de loup ?

kɔ̄ŋ́kɔ̄ŋ́ {A, kɔ̄ŋ́kɔ̄ŋ́-dhùn pl. A, kɔ̄ŋ́kɔ̄ŋ́-sɯ̏ foc. A} ***adj*** **clopinant avec une canne** ◊ *kwɛ̏ɛdhʌ́n kɔ̄ŋ́kɔ̄ŋ́ dō yà dhūn* un vieillard cacochyme est venu en clopinant avec une canne

kɔ̄ŋsɛ̋ɛdhɯ̏ <doigt-terre-arbre> ***n*** ***Cassia alata, Senna alata*** **dartrier**, **quatre épingles**, **épis d'or**, **fleurs de Saint-Christophe** *(arbuste ornemental s'ouvrant le matin et se fermant le soir; feuilles composées-pennées, fleurs grandes, en longs épis jaunes-orangés; les petites graines brunes foncées ont une forme triangulaire et un hile proéminent) [les* *feuilles sont utilisées comme médicament contre les maux de ventre; on les sèche, les pile et on en met la poudre dans l'eau]*

kɔ̏ɔ 1 ***n*** **calebasse** *(récipient fait d'une moitié de fruit; on l'utilise surtout par stocker le grain)* ◊ *yȁ kɔ̏ɔ pɛ̋-dhɛ̏ wɔ̏* il a cousu la fente de la calebasse ◊ *wȍ kɔ̏ɔdhʌ́n kȕn ȁ wēŋ dhūn' bhȁ* on prend une petite calebasse par son cou ♦ *tòo bhō' ká kɔ̏ɔ* louche de calebasse ♦ *bhɑ̋a yɪ́ bhȕn' ká kɔ̏ɔ* cuillère de calebasse pour la bouillie de riz ♦ *kɔ̏ɔ zʌ̄* jouer du tambour d'eau

kɔ̏ɔ 2 *AD de* kɔ̏ 1 *main*

kɔ̀ɔ, **kœ̀œ** ***n*** **crochet, fourche** *(de types différents)* ◊ *bhān glɛ̋ɛ́ yɤ̏ dūn-sīʌ kœ̀œ bhȁ* mon sac est accroché à un crochet ♦ *dɤ̄ŋ dhȉɤ ká kɔ̀ɔ* fourche pour monter les pièges *(munie d'un manche de 20-30 cm)* ♦ *dhɛ̏ bȁ ká kɔ̀ɔ* bâton recourbé dont on se sert pour désherber la brousse *(pour soulever l'herbe avant de la couper)* ♦ *kɑ̋flɛ̋e bhȍ ká kœ̀œ* bâton recourbé pour abaisser les branches du caféier ♦ *kɔ́ dɔ̏ ȁ ká kɔ̀ɔ* support fourchu *(à la maison)* ♦ *pʌ̄ bhȍ ȁ ká kɔ̀ɔ* perche pour la cueillette des fruits *(à bout courbé)*

kɔ̄ɔ 1, **kœ̄œ** ***n*** ***Cussonia arborea*** **chou palmiste poulpe** *(jusqu'à 13; les fruits contiennent des grains bruns qu'on sèche, pile et utilise pour une sauce; les femmes les collectent au temps de disette)* ♦ *kɔ̄ɔ yɪ́* sauce des grains de "koo" *(ressemble à la sauce d'arachide; sa préparation demande beaucoup de travail)*

kɔ̄ɔ 2, **kœ̄œ** <*kɔ̏ ká 'avec la main'> ***pp*** **par** *(sens de l'agent, cause)* *Syn.* *gɔ̏ 2)* ◊ *kɔ̄ɔ yà wʊ́ʊ �n̄ kɔ̄ɔ* la calebasse a été cassée par moi ♦ *�n̄ yɑ̋n yà kʌ̄ gbínkígbȉnkȉ yī kɔ̄ɔ* j'ai les paupières lourdes {de sommeil}

kɔ̄ɔ 3 ***loc.n*** *COM de* kɔ̏ 1 *main*

kɔ́ɔ̏ ***loc.n*** *SUP de* kɔ́ɔdhɛ̏ *maison*

kɔ́ɔ̄ ***loc.n*** *IN de* kɔ́ɔdhɛ̏ *maison*

kɔ̋ɔ, **kœ̋œ** ***n*** **rouille** ♦ *kɔ̋ɔ yȁ ȁ kún* il a rouillé

kɔ̏ɔdhē ***adj*** **fait de calebasse** ◊ *klȕu kɔ̏ɔdhē* louche en calebasse

kɔ́ɔdhɛ̏, **kɔ́gʊ́ʊdhɛ̏** {LOC kɔ́ɔdhɤ̄, LOC INT kɔ́ɔkɔ́ɔ, SUP kœ́œ̏, kɔ́ɔ̏, IN kɔ́ɔ̄} ***loc.n*** *la forme IN kɔ́ɔ̄ est archaïque et recherchée* **maison** *(l'intérieur)* *Qsyn.* *kɔ́* ◊ *yà kɔ́gʊ́ʊdhɛ̏ / kɔ́ɔdhɛ̏ bɑ̄ɑ̏* elle a décoré l'intérieur de la maison ◊ *kɔ́ɔdhɛ̏ yȁ dhȉi kún, kwȁ ȁ zʊ̋* c'est devenu sale dans la maison, lavons-la ◊ *bhá dhó bhɔ̏ zʌ̄' kɔ́ɔdhɤ̄* ne tue pas le cochon dans la maison ◊ *yɔ̋ɔ pʊ̋u yɤ̏ kɔ́ɔ̏* la maison a été badigeonnée à la chaux ◊ *Sȉɑ̋o zʌ̏ yɤ̏ kɔ́ɔkɔ́ɔ tɤ̋ŋ gbàn gʊ́* Siao est à la maison tout le temps

kɔ̀ɔdhɪ́ɤ, **kœ̀œdhɪ́ɤ** <crochet-point> ***n*** **marteau** *(traditionnel, et éventuellement moderne)* *Syn.* *yɤ̋ŋ, yɤ̋ŋgā*

kɔ́ɔdhɤ̄ ***loc.n*** *LOC de* kɔ́ɔdhɛ̏ *maison*

kɔ̀ɔdhȕ, **kœ̀œdhȕ** <crochet-arbre> ***n*** **croc** *(un bâton avec un croc à la fin, pour faire pencher les branches)*

kɔ́ɔkɔ́ɔ ***loc.n*** *LOC.INT de* kɔ́ɔdhɛ̏ *maison*

kɔ̀ɔnbhɛ̏n ***n*** *rn* **protecteur, défenseur** ♦ *pɤ̂ kɔ̀ɔnbhɛ̏n* chef de village ♦ *sɛ́ kɔ̀ɔnbhɛ̏n* président (du pays); gouverneur

kɔ̋ɔsɯ̏ɯ, **kœ̋œsɯ̏ɯ** ***adj*** **rouillé**

kɔ̏ɔtȁ <calebasse-sur> ***n*** **1 sanza sur calebasse** *(une table en bois sur laquelle sont attachées cinq à sept lamelles en fer forgé - aujourd'hui remplacées par des morceaux de baleines de parapluie - d'une calebasse hémisphérique fixée par ses bords au-dessous de la table) [fabriquée par le musicien lui-même qui conserve aussi l'instrument - souvent au campement de brousse où il en joue le soir après les travaux des champs; le musicien peut chanter en même temps]* **2 tambour d'eau** *(on met une calebasse renversée sur l'eau, puis on tape dessus avec la main)[est considéré comme un instriment dioula]* Syn. *yíkɔ̏ɔ*

kɔ̏ɔyí <Manding kɔ̀gɔ̀jí, kɔ̀ɔ̀jí> ***n*** **mer, océan** Qsyn. *wèeyȉ*

kɔ̏pā <main-remplir> ***n*** **poignée** ◊ *bhlɯ̏n kɔ̏pā sɔ́ɔdhű dhʌ̀n ɤ́ bhlɯ̏n wɛ̋ŋ dō ká* cinq poignées de riz font une petite gerbe

kɔ̏-pá {kɔ̏-pā} <main-toucher> ***v*** *vr* **toucher**, **palper** *(qch – ká)* ♦ *ɯ̄ kɔ̏ sɛ̄ɛ́ndhʌ́n pá ȁ ká* touche-le légèrement

kɔ̏sʌ̏ <main-bon> ***n*** *rn* **main droite**, **côté droit** Ant. *kwàa* ♦ *kɔ̏sʌ̏ gɯ́ pǽæn* côté droit ◊ *yȁ tàabhȁn, gōzīɤbhɛ̏n kɔ̏sʌ̏ gɯ́ pɛ̋ɛn ká* assis-toi à la siège arrière du côté droit ◊ *Tòkpȁ yà ɤ̄ slʌ̄ʌ gɯ́ yà dhó ɤ̄ kɔ̏sʌ̏ gɯ́* Tokpa a tourné à droite ♦ *wɔ̄ ɯ̄ kɔ̏sʌ̏ tȁ !* bonne nuit !

kɔ̏tíiŋ ***n*** **claquement des doigts** ◊ *yɤ̏ ɤ̄ kɔ̏tíiŋ zʌ̄-sīʌ* il fait claquer ses doigts

kɔ̏wlɤ̀ɤ ***n*** **1 subalterne**; **assistant** ♦ *kɔ̏wlɤ̀ɤ bhɛ̏n* subalterne **2 objet sous la main**

kɔ̏yān <main-mesure> ***n*** **poignée**

kɔ́yídhɛ̏ {Loc. kɔ́yídhɤ̄, pl. LOC kɔ́yídhɛ̏-dhɯ̏n gɯ́} ***loc.n*** **1 campement** *(au champ)* ◊ *Tòkpȁ yà dhó ɤ̄ gɔ̏ kɔ́yídhɤ̄* Tokpa est allé à son campement **2 hameau** *(campement rural aménagé en lieu d'habitation permanente)* Syn. *kɑ̋nŋbhɑ̋* ◊ *gɔ̄ɔgbɛ́ɛ̀bhɛ̏n-dhɯ̏n wȁ kɔ́yídhɛ̏ gɤ́* les brigands ont brûlé le hameau ◊ *ān Gɔ̋dhɔ̋n tɔ̀ kɔ́yídhɤ̄ yɤ́ á dhō bhláā* j'ai laissé Gono au hameau et suis parti au champ

kɔ́yídhɤ̄ ***loc.n*** *Loc. de* kɔ́yídhɛ̏ *campement*

kɔ́záȁ (gw) ***n*** **1 hangar** *(où on passe le temps en causerie)* Syn. *záa* (m) **2 structure** *(d'une maison, pas encore couverte)*

kɤ̏ ***n*** **1 copeau** Syn. *kɤ̏kɤ̏* ♦ *dhű kɤ̏-dhɯ̏n* copeaux de bois **2 écorce** *(petits morceaux utilisés dans la médecine traditionnelle)* Syn. *kɛ̋ɛ*

kɤ̀, **kɤ̀ŋ** ***adv*** **1.1 encore** ◊ *ȁ dhɛ̏ yȁ bhȁ kɤ̄ yɤ̏ tɔ̏n kún kɤ̀ blɛ̏ɛsɯ̏* il fallait encore qu'il montât d'abord la pente ◊ *Zân yɤ̏ tɯ̏n kɤ̀ŋ yʌ̄ kʌ̄'* Zan travaille encore (continue de travailler) **1.2 encore** *(avec la négation)* ◊ *dhɛ̏ yíi kpɔ̏œ kɤ̀* le jour ne s'est pas encore levé ◊ *dhē yáa' gɔ̏ kɤ̀* il n'a pas encore pris de femme **2 plus** *(pas)* ◊ *dhēbʌ̏-dhɯ̏n wáa tɯ̏n* *kɤ̀ŋ yí bhà-kʌ̄'* les femmes ne font plus la pêche **3 pour le moment** ◊ *yà ɤ̄ kwāà kɤ̀ŋ kā̋flē̋e tā-sù̀ zù̀* il a arrêté la plantation du café ◊ *ū̄ tɛ́ɛ bhá pā kɤ̀ŋ* va te reposer un peu pour le moment

kɤ̄ ***conj*** *fusionne avec les pronoms singuliers conjoints, cf. káa, kíi, kɤ́ɤ et avec le pronom non-sujet à, cf. kɤ̂* **1 que**, **pour que** *doit être suivi d'une construction subjonctive ou du prohibitif* ◊ *yà būu tā kɤ̄ ɤ́ dhó bű̃* il a chargé le fusil pour aller en brousse ◊ *ā wʌ́ʌ̀ bɔ̀ ū̄ dhɛ̀ kɤ̄ dīì yá dhɤ́ ū̄ zʌ̄'* je t'envoie de l'argent pour que tu ne meures pas de faim ◊ *n̄ zíɤ̀ yɤ̀ flɛ̋ɛsù̀ kɤ̄ yɤ̀ bhlā̋a zʌ̄ dhɔ̋ɔgɔ̀ gbàn ká* mon beau-père est trop pauvre pour égorger un mouton toutes les semaines **2 alors** *(dans une proposition conditionnelle ou temporelle)* ◊ *yà ɤ̄ kên gú-gblù̀ kɤ̄ yɤ̀ tùn ɤ̄ yā̋an* il a partagé son héritage de son vivant **3 mais** *devant une proposition négative* **4 alors** *introduit une proposition à valeur performative ou une assertion concernant une action à venir* ◊ *kɤ̄ bhán ū̄ gbā dhīaŋ ká* alors, je te donne la parole ◊ *kɤ̄ yɤ̄ɤ pɤ̀ dhɛ̀* il va tomber *(sans doute)* **5 si** *(dans la préposition dépendante; la proposition principale comporte une construction consécutive négative)* ◊ *kɤ̄ ú blʌ̄ʌ bhō dɛ̀ɛ, bhí dhɤ́ yʌ̄ kʌ̄' dhīā̋* si tu enlèves les herbes aujourd'hui, tu ne travailleras pas demain

kɤ́ 1 ***conj*** **même si** *requiert une construction prospective ou de l'aspect neutre; souvent en combinaison avec la particule zú* ◊ *kɤ́ zú yɤ̄ɤ dhūn /yɤ̀ dhùn/ wɛ̀, bháan bhāan' gbā bhɤ̀pʌ̀ ká* même s'il vient, je ne lui donne pas de nourriture

kɤ́ 2, **kɤ̄** ***conj*** **que** *conjonction introduisant l'article défini, les pronoms démonstratifs, une proposition relative accompagnée d'un article défini* Qsyn. *ɤ́ 1* ◊ *yɤ̄ dhūn kɤ̄ zœ̀œ* c'est lui qui nie (sa culpabilité)

kɤ̂ <de *kɤ̄ à 'que son...'> ***prn*** **pour que son** *forme fusionnée : conjonction + pronom de la 3e pers. sg. de la série non-sujet* ◊ *à sű̃ɤ yɤ̀ Tòkpà kʌ̄-sīʌ kɤ̂ zíɤ̀ yɤ̀ dhūn dɛ̀ɛ* Tokpa a peur que son beau-père ne vienne aujourd'hui

kɤ́bhūndhē ***n*** *kɤ́bhūndhē ká* **par hasard**

kɤ̋dhìngbɤ̄tá ***intj*** **sois maudit** *(une malédiction de la mère ou du père)* ♦ *kɤ̋dhìngbɤ̄tá, bhíin kʌ̄ ū̄ kpɔ́* sois maudit, ce n'est pas moi qui t'ai mis au monde ! (formule de la malédiction maternelle)

kɤ̄dhɤ́ ***conj*** **pour ne pas** *(introduit une construction conjointe)* ◊ *yà ɤ̄ dè kplù̀, kɤ̄dhɤ́ ɤ́ pɤ̀* il s'est attaché pour ne pas tomber ◊ *kwà pʌ̄ bhɤ̀, kɤ̄dhɤ́ kwá dhɤ́ wē bhūn'* mangeons, mais ne buvons pas

kɤ̄dhɤ̄ŋkɤ̄dhɤ̄ŋdhɤ̄ ***onomat*** **ding-ding** *(tintement d'un grelot)* ◊ *kpɤ̋dhàa yɤ̀ wɛ́-sīʌ kɤ̄dhɤ̄ŋkɤ̄dhɤ̄ŋdhɤ̄* le grelot tinte

kɤ̄kkɤ̄dhɤ̄ ***adv*** **fortement** *(se coller)* ◊ *klúugā yà kɤ̄kkɤ̄dhɤ̄* un écrou s'est collé très fort

kɤ̀kɤ̀ <la forme redoublée de kɤ̀ 'copeau'> ***n*** **copeau** Syn. kɤ̀ *la forme redoublée est la plus courante* ♦ *bāa kɤ̀kɤ̀-dhùn wà tó sīā̋a* les copeaux de manioc sont restés par terre

kɤ̀ŋ *n* **1** *rn* **poitrine** *(thorax, intérieur de la poitrine; humain, animal, oiseau)* Qsyn. *tɔ̀ŋ 1*, *kùu* ♦ *ɤ̄ kɤ̀ŋ tà bhàn* se frapper la poitrine **2** *rn* **sternum**

kɤ̀ŋ 1 *v vi* **être habile** *(lutte, jeux sportifs etc.)*, **savoir bien garder son équilibre** *(au sens physique)* ♦ *Zân yɤ̀ kɤ̀ŋ dhè gwấndhʌ́n dhɤ́* Jean sait garder son équilibre comme un chat

kɤ̀ŋ 2 → kɤ̀ *encore*

kɤ̄ŋ *n* **maïs** ◊ *wáa kɤ̄ŋ sæ̀æ bhɤ̀* on ne mange pas le maïs cru ◊ *wáa kɤ̄ŋ kpæ̋æ kpà, à sæ̀æ dhūn ɤ́ wó' kpà* on ne fait pas bouillir le maïs séché, on le fait bouillir frais ♦ *kɤ̄ŋ bì* poudre sucrée de maïs *(une friandise : les grains de maïs sont séchés, grillés, pilés longuement, vannés, la poudre est mélangée avec du sucre)* ♦ *kɤ̄ŋ bhɛ̄* épi de maïs ♦ *kɤ̄ŋ dhɛ̋* feuilles de maïs *(sur la tige)* ♦ *kɤ̄ŋ dhíɤ bhấa* bouillie de maïs *(préparée avec des grains séchés et brisés, souvent mélangés avec des feuilles de manioc) [très nourrissante, mais peu appréciée, on la mange surtout en période de disette lorsque la réserve de riz est épuisée]* ♦ *kɤ̄ŋ flɛ̋ɛ̀* grains décortiqués de maïs ♦ *kɤ̄ŋ gā* grain de maïs *(extrait de l'épi)* ♦ *kɤ̄ŋ gɔ̀* i) fleur de maïs ii) partie supérieure de l'épi de maïs *[appartient à celui qui est le plus âgé]* ♦ *kɤ̄ŋ gbɔ́ŋ̀* maïs avant l'éclosion des épis ♦ *kɤ̄ŋ kɛ̋ɛ* feuilles qui enveloppent l'épi de maïs ♦ *kɤ̄ŋ sɛ̋ɛ* fibres au sommet de l'épi de maïs ♦ *kɤ̄ŋ pűu* maïs blanc *(espèce tardive, plus productive que la variété rouge)* ♦ *kɤ̄ŋ sœ̄œ* maïs rassis *(épluché et ayant passé une nuit au grenier)* ♦ *kɤ̄ŋ sœ́œ̀* "maïs-arc" *(sorte à tige haute dont l'épi peut atteindre 30 cm, à rendement élevé et goût agréable; sa maturation dure jusqu'à quatre mois, il est rarement cultivé au Gouèta)* ♦ *kɤ̄ŋ sɔ̋n* grain de maïs *(dans l'épi)* ♦ *kɤ̄ŋ sű plèdhē, kwí bhà kɤ̄ŋ* maïs de deux mois *(espèce précoce, à épis petits, peu cultivé au Gouèta)* ♦ *kɤ̄ŋ zœ̀œndhē* maïs rouge *(espèce tardive et peu productive, qui exige trois mois de maturation)* ♦ *kɤ̄ŋ bhō* récolter le maïs *(on coupe la tige au ras du sol avec une machette)* ♦ *kɤ̄ŋ bhō ɤ̄ dhùu bhà* détacher l'épi de maïs de la tige ♦ *kɤ̄ŋ tā* planter du maïs

kɤ̀ŋgbɤ̄ *adv* **d'abord**, **pour le moment** ◊ *kwà dɔ̄ kɤ̀ŋgbɤ̄* arrêtons-nous pour le moment ◊ *dhūn kɤ̀ŋgbɤ̄ !* viens d'abord ! (en attendant, on trouvera une solution)

kɤ̋ŋkɤ̋ŋdhɤ̄ *onomat* *imitation du son de cliquetement*

kɤ̀ɤ 1 (gw), **klùu** (m) {A S, kɤ̀ɤ-dhùn pl. A S, kɤ̀ɤ-sùu foc. A S, kɤ̀ɤ-sùu-dhùn foc. pl. A; kɤ̀ɤkɤ̀ɤ Int. pl. A S, kɤ̀ɤkɤ̀ɤ-dhùn Int. pl. A S, kɤ̀ɤkɤ̀ɤ-sùu Int. pl. foc. A S, kɤ̀ɤkɤ̀ɤ-sùu-dhùn Int. pl. foc. A S} *adj* **1 cassé** *(ustensile, récipient, mécanisme, maison)*, **usé** *(chaussure, hors usage)* ◊ *yɤ̀ bhān sàbhấ kɤ̀ɤkɤ̀ɤ dhʌn à-dhùn zùɤ dűnŋ tàa* il a jeté mes chaussures (plusieurs paires) à la décharge ♦ *bhɛ̄n dhí kɤ̀ɤ* personne à la bouche édentée **2 usé** *(toujours utilisable)* ◊ *sɛ̄tí kɤ̀ɤkɤ̀ɤ dhūn ɤ́ dhūn' ká n̄ dhɛ̀* ce sont des assiettes usées qu'il m'a apportées

kɤ̀ɤ 2 *v vi* **roter, éructer** ◊ *ū kɤ̀ɤ dhɤ́ dhè ?* pourquoi as-tu roté ? *[éructer devant les aînés est impoli]*

kɤ̀ɤ 3 *n* **souricière** *(fait d'une baguette flexible et d'une feuille d'arbre; ces pièges sont mis par les enfants en forêt)* ♦ *yà kɤ̀ɤ yà bhɔ̀ɔn gɔ̀* il a dressé un piège à souris

kɤ̀ɤ 4 ***n*** **tessons, débris** ◊ *vɛ̋dhɛ̋ ɤ́ ʊ́' wʊ̄ bhā, ȁ kɤ̀ɤ wlɤ̏* ramasse les tessons du verre que tu as cassé

kɤ́ɤ 1 <de *kɤ̄ ɤ̋ 'qu'il...'> ***mpp*** **pour qu'il, pour qu'elle** *forme fusionnée : conjonction + MPP de la 3e pers. sg. de la série subjonctive* ◊ *yɤ̏ dhò kɤ́ɤ dhʊ̄n* il s'en va pour revenir

kɤ́ɤ 2 <de *kɤ́ yɤ̄ɤ> ***mpp*** **même s'il, même si 'elle** *forme fusionnée : conjonction + MPP de la 3e pers. sg. de la série prospective*

kɤ́ɤ̏ ***intj*** **hé** *(exclamation pour attirer l'attention)* ◊ *kɤ́ɤ̏ ! yɤ́ bháa' wɔ́n dɔ̄ dhè bhán sʌ̄ʌ bhō ȅe ?* hé ! est-ce que tu ne sais pas que je suis fatigué ?

kɤ̀ɤkɤ̀ɤ ***adj*** *Int. pl. de* kɤ̀ɤ *cassé*

kɤ̋ɤkɤ̋ɤkɤ̋ɤdhɤ̄ ***onomat*** **gla gla** *(son de claquement des dents, à cause du froid etc.)* ◊ *ȁ sɔ̋n yɤ̏ bhȁn kwʌ́ʌ̀ kɤ̋ɤkɤ̋ɤkɤ̋ɤdhɤ̄* il claque des dents : gla gla (sensation de froid)

kɤ̄ɤtɛ̏ɛn, kɤ̄ɤtɛ̏ɛndhʌ́n < ?-rouge> ***n Macrosphenus concolor*** **fauvette nasique grise** *(un oiseau, 11 cm, gris-vert, long bec droit)*

kœ̀œ → kɔ̀ɔ *crochet*

kœ̄œ 1 ***n Francolinus bicalcaratus*** **francolin commun, perdrix** lv. *(35 cm, bande noire sur le front, dessous fortement marqué de lames noires sur fond crème; dessus : finement vermiculé avec stries de couleur crème; les vieux mâles ont deux ergots) [sa viande est très recherchée]*

kœ̄œ 2 → kɔ̄ɔ 2 *par*

kœ̄œ 3 → kɔ̄ɔ 1 *arbre (esp.)*

kœ́œ̏ ***loc.n*** *SUP de* kɔ́ɔdhɛ̏ *maison*

kœ̋œ → kɔ̋ɔ *rouille*

kœ̀œdhɪ́ɤ → kɔ̀ɔdhɪ́ɤ *marteau*

kœ̀œdhʊ̏ʊ → kɔ̀ɔdhʊ̏ʊ *croc*

kœ̏œŋ → kɔ̏ŋ *composant des noms de dizaines*

kœ̄œŋgā → kɔ̄ŋgā *doigt*

kœ̄œŋ̏pʌ̏ <main-sur-chose> ***n*** **bague** *[d'habitude on met la bague sur l'annulaire ou le médius de la main gauche; portée ailleurs, elle sert d'objet de protection magique]* *Syn. yȁkɔ̏dhʌ́ngābhȁpʌ̏, yȁkɔ̄ŋgāapʌ̏* ◊ *bhá kœ̄œŋ̏pʌ̏ yȁ ʊ̄ kɔ̏ sʌ̏ bhȁ bhá' dȁ bhɛ̄n-dhʊ̏n pɪ́ɤ tőo gʊ́ʊ, yɤ̏ dhɔ̏ ȁ-dhʊ̏n pɛ̏'* si tu mets un anneau à la main droite et qu'ensuite tu mets cette main dans la sauce chez certaines gens, cela les fera vomir

kœ̄œŋ̏pʌ̏pɛ́ɛpɛ̏ɛ <bague- ?> ***n*** **anneau à cachet** ◊ *kœ̄œŋ̏pʌ̏pɛ́ɛpɛ̏ɛ yɤ̏ ȁ kɔ̏ɔ* il porte à sa main un anneau à cachet

kœ̋œsʊ̏ʊ → kɔ̋ɔsʊ̏ʊ *rouillé*

krrɔ̏ɔdhɤ̄ ***onomat*** *craquement des os quand on s'étire* ◊ *yȁ ɤ̄ gʊ́ʊ-gɑ̋n, ȁ gā yɤ̏ wɛ̏ krrɔ̏ɔdhɤ̄* il s'est étiré, et ses os ont craqué

krrɤ́ɤdhɤ̄ *onomat* **croc-croc-croc** *(son de rongement)* ◊ *bhɔ̀ɔn-dhȕn yɤ̀ pʌ̄ bhɤ̀-sīʌ krrɤ́ɤdhɤ̄* les souris sont en train de ronger quelque chose : croc-croc-croc

krrɤ̋ɤɤdhɤ̄ *adv Int. de* klɤ̋ɤdhɤ̄ *vite.bref*

kūdhân, kūlánŋ̀ <Fr. courant> *n* **courant** *(électrique)*, **électricité**

kūdhândhű̃ <électricité-arbre> *n* **réverbère** *(électrique)*

kúkúdhūkúdhû *onomat* **cri** *(d'un oiseau rapace)*

kūlánŋ̀ → kūdhân *électricité*

kún {kūn} *v* **1.1** *vt* **attraper** ♦ *yűa yà ȁ kún* il est tombé malade **1.2** *vt* **piquer** *(insecte, chien; parfois des gens; aussi kún sɔ̋ɔn)* ◊ *yȁ ɤ̄ tɛ́ɛdō kún sɔ̋ɔn* il a mordu son camarade ◊ *zēnŋ́ yȁa kún ȁ bhɔ̄ bhȁ* le moustique l'a piqué au cou ◊ *lāa yà n̄ kún n̄ gɛ̏n bhȁ* le lion m'a mordu à la jambe; le lion m'a attrapé par la jambe **1.3** *vt* **atteindre** ◊ *yɤ̀ gwʌ̏ zȕɤ ɤ̄ zlȁȁ dhʌ̀n ȁ ká, kɛ́ɛ yíi ȁ kún* il a jeté le caillou sur son petit frère, mais il ne l'a pas atteint **1.4** *vt* **prendre**, **percevoir** *(de – gɔ̏)* ◊ *ȁ kún !* tiens ! (on passe qch de main en main, il ne s'agit pas forcément du changement de propriétaire) ◊ *yà wʌ́ʌ̏ kún yī gɔ̏* il a récolté l'argent auprès de nous **2.1** *vt* **traiter** ◊ *wȍ kʌ̄ dhɛ̏ŋ gɔ̄ɔ̏n bhā ȁ kȕn sʌ̏* ils ont bien accueilli ce visiteur ♦ *wȍ wō kó kȕn sʌ̏* ils s'entendent bien ♦ *yɤ̀ kȕn sʌ̏ gúu* on s'occupe bien de lui ♦ *ɤ̄ dȅ kún sʌ̏* se surveiller (sa santé, ses habits...) **2.2** *vi* **se mettre** *(commencer; à – bhȁ)* **2.3** *vr* **prendre garde**, **faire attention** *(à qch – bhȁ)* ♦ *ɤ̄ dȅ kún ȁ bhȁ !* fais attention à cela ! **2.4** *vr* **se méfier** *(de – gɔ̏)* ◊ *bhɛ́n ɤ́ dɔ̄ bhā, gblɑ̋ŋ bhȕn, ūu dȅ kún ȁ gɔ̏* l'homme debout là-bas est un escroc, méfie-toi de lui **3** *vt* **retenir** *(émotions)* ♦ *ȁ kún ɤ̄ bhȁ* sois patient ◊ *dȅ kȕn wɔ́n dhɪ́ɤ-sȕ dhūn ɤ́ sʌ̏* c'est la maîtrise de soi qui est bonne **4** *vt* **sentir** *(odorat)* **5** *vt* **enivrer** **6.1** *vt* **monter**, **grimper** *(à l'arbre)* ◊ *yɤ̀ sɤ̄ kȕn yʌ́nŋ̀kɔ̀dān plɛ̀ ká* il grimpe sur un palmier en deux minutes **6.2** *vt* **atteindre** ◊ *yí yɤ̀ bhēn kȕn dhɤ̀ŋdlɤ̀ɤ* l'eau atteint la ceinture **6.3** *vt* **suffire** ◊ *wèe yɤ̀ ȁ kún-sȕ ká* c'est suffisamment salé **6.4** *vi* **bouillir** *(huile)* **6.5** *vi* **se chauffer** ♦ *ȁ kwī yà kún* il a la fièvre ◊ *tőo yȁ kún* la sauce a réchauffé ♦ *pȉɤ yȁ kún gbȁngbȁndhɤ̄* le fer a chauffé au rouge **6.6** *vi* **s'épaissir** *(sauce)* ◊ *tőo yí kún-sȕ dhʌ̀n dhɔ̏ ɤ́ ūu kʌ̏ ȅe, ɛ̋ɛn tőo yí wlɑ̋awlȁa ?* aimes-tu une sauce épaisse ou une sauce claire ? **7** *vi* **être supportable** *(pour – gúu)* ♦ *wɔ́n yɤ̀ kún bhɔ̀ n̄ gúu* je peux supporter la chose **8** *vt* **devenir trop serré pour** ◊ *Gbȁtɔ̀ yȁ ɤ̄ fāan súu, ȁ bhȁ pàŋ yȁ ȁ kún kpēnŋkpēnŋdhɤ̄* Gbato a grossi, et son pantalon est devenu trop serré pour lui **9** *vt* **ourler** ◊ *yȁ sɔ̄ dhɪ́ɤ kún* il a ourlé le tissu

kű̃nbhɑ̋ndhɑ̋n <Fr. commandant> *n* **préfet** ♦ *kű̃nbhɑ̋ndhɑ̋n sɛ̋ɛndhʌ́n* sous-préfet

kún-sȕ *adj* **épais**, **dense**

kűŋ *n* **réservoir de soufflet en argile** *(de forge, avec la manivelle)*

kȕu (Blapleu, Klapleu, Gwele, Gbèné) *n rn* **poitrine** *(la surface; humain, animal, oiseau)* <u>Syn. tȍŋ 1</u> <u>Qsyn. kɤ̀ŋ</u> ◊ *būugā yȁa kȕu zūa* la balle lui a troué la poitrine ♦ *kȕu dhɪ́ɤ* devant qn

kʉ̃ʉ̀ ***n*** **igname** *[en Gouèta, une culture plutôt secondaire; l'igname est pelé, découpé et cuit à l'eau, on le mange avec du sel et du piment]* ♦ *kʉ̃ʉ̀ kplʉ̀* igname bouillie

kʉ̄kkʉ̄dhɤ̄ {Int. kʉ̄kʉ̄kʉ̄dhɤ̄} ***adv*** **à ras bord, jusqu'au bord, à déborder** ♦ *yà dɔ̄ ɤ̄ gʉ́ kʉ̄kkʉ̄dhɤ̄* il s'est arrêté bloqué *(d'un bègue qui s'efforce de prononcer quelque chose)* ◊ *bhlɔ̄ɔ yà pā kʉ̄kkʉ̄dhɤ̄* le sac est rempli à ras bord ◊ *n̄ kɔ̄ŋgā yà dɔ̄ kʉ̄kʉ̄kʉ̄dhɤ̄* mon doigt a horriblement gonflé

kʉ̄kʉ̄kʉ̄dhɤ̄ ***adv*** *Int. de* kʉ̄kkʉ̄dhɤ̄ *à ras bord*

kʉ́ʉ → kíi *pour que tu*

Kp kp

kpà 1 ***v*** **1** *vt* **cuire, faire bouillir** *(nourriture)* *Qsyn.* bhān 1 ◊ *kɤ̄ŋ kpà-sʉ̀ dīn yɤ̀ sʌ̀* le maïs bouilli a bon goût ♦ *pʌ̄ kpà* préparer le repas ◊ *yɤ̀ dɔ̀ pʌ̄ kpà-dhɛ̀ ká* elle sait faire la cuisine ♦ *tòo kpà* faire cuire le "to" **2** *vt* **empoisonner** *(arme)* ◊ *... yɤ́ wó à-dhʉ̀n bhàn glɛ̃ɛn kpà-sʉ̀ ká yɤ́ wó à-dhʉ̀n zʌ̄ ...* ils les frappaient avec des épines empoisonnées et les tuaient

kpà 2 ***n*** **liane** *(esp., épineuse) [est utilisée pour faire des ceintures pour grimper aux palmiers]*

kpā {kpā} ***v*** **1** *vt* **couvrir** ◊ *wà blʌ̄ʌ kpā wō tà* ils se sont couverts de verdure **2** *vi* **se répandre** *dans l'expression :* ♦ *dhɛ̃ndhɛ̃n sæ̀æ yà kpā n̄ tà* j'ai eu un frisson *(la peur)* **3.1** *vi* **pourchasser** *(qn – kèŋ)* **3.2** *vi* **être sur le point de rattraper** *(un fugitif – tà)* **4** *vi kpā bhɛ̄n zɔ̀ tà* **consoler qn**

kpá ***adv*** **autrefois, jadis** *dans l'expression :* ♦ *ɤ́ gūn kpá* autrefois

kpã́ ***n*** **"colis sans timbre"** lv. *(plat de bananes et de maïs; on mélange la pâte de bananes avec du maïs et du piment pilés, on pile ce mélange et on en met dans la feuille qu'on utilise pour emballer la cola, puis on l'attache et le fait cuire dans une marmite) [un paquet coûte de 10 à 25 francs CFA]*

kpàa ***n*** **sauterelle** *(mais aussi d'autres insectes sautant : puce, criquet, etc.)* ♦ *gbɛ̂n bhà kpàa* puce de chien

kpàa ***n*** **arbre** *(espèce : le bois est noir et très dur; l'écorce est claire; les cosses rouges contiennent 3-4 grains sucrés) [les Dan n'utilisent pas le bois, trop dur pour le travail]*

kpã̀à ***n*** **gazon** *(terre couverte d'herbes)* *Qsyn.* kpɔ̀ɔ, blʌ̄ʌ ♦ *yà kpã̀à zʌ̄* il a dégagé le sol de l'herbe *(avec la houe) [chez les Dan, l'herbe est considérée comme de la saleté; un bon propriétaire doit éliminer l'herbe autour de sa maison]*

kpã́a 1 ***n*** *rn* **cicatrice** ♦ *kpã́a kã́n* se cicatriser

kpã́a 2, kplã́a {A S, kpã́a-sʉ̀ foc. A S, kpã́a-sʉ̀-dhʉ̀n foc. pl. A S; kpã́akpã́asʉ̀ Int. A P, kpã́akpã́asʉ̀-dhʉ̀n Int. pl. A S, kpã́akpã́asʉ̀-sʉ̀ Int. foc. A S} ***adj*** **chauve, rasé** *(tête)* ♦ *yà ɤ̄ gɔ̀ kpã́a bhō* il s'est fait raser la tête

kpa̋akpa̋asʉ̏ *Int. de* kpa̋a *chauve*

kpāa̋n *n* rn vulg. **pénis** Syn. *g̲ɔ̄ɔ̏ndhɛ̏, g̲ɔ̄ɔ̏ndhɛ̏gā, k̲pāa̋ngā, k̲plɤ̏ɤ, k̲plɤ̏ɤgā*

kpa̋an 1) {A S, kpa̋an-sʉ̏ foc. A} *adj* **nu** *(pied, personne)* ◊ *a̋ ga̋ ɤ̄ dɔ̄ ɤ̄ kpa̋an ká yā* le voici arrêté nu

kpa̋an 2) *adv* **1 sans raison, juste comme ça** ◊ *wɔ́n yà dà n̄ gɛ̀n gʉ́ kpa̋an* cela m'a troublé sans raison **2 seulement** *(avec les nombres)* ◊ *ā yī zʌ̀ dhɛ̀kpœ̀œyì plɛ̀ kpa̋an* je ne me suis couché que deux fois

kpáànbhɔ̏ɔn *n Arvicanthis* **rat rossard** *(rat diurne, brun ou gris)*

kpa̋àndhɛ̏ {LOC kpa̋àndhɤ̄} *loc.n* **ruines**

kpa̋àndhɤ̄ *loc.n LOC de* kpa̋àndhɛ̏ *ruines*

kpāa̋ngā <pénis-os> *n* rn vulg. **pénis** Syn. *g̲ɔ̄ɔ̏ndhɛ̏, g̲ɔ̄ɔ̏ndhɛ̏gā, k̲pāa̋n, k̲plɤ̏ɤ, k̲plɤ̏ɤgā*

kpàantīi *n* **liane épineuse** *(vénéneuse; si on se pique, le sang qui sort est noir)*

kpàasʉ̏ (m) *adj* **intelligent, sage**

kpàdhɛ̋ɛ̏ *n Scotopelia peli* **chouette pêcheuse** *(60 cm, grosse tête ronde sans aigrettes; fauve ponctuée de brun; oiseau nocturne)*

kpàdhʉ̋ʉ̏ (gw) <cuire-arbre> *n* **mouvette** *(un bâtonnet se terminant en croix servant à mélanger la sauce; on la tourne en la serrant entre les paumes des mains qui vont dans les sens opposés)* Syn. *k̲pœ̄œdhʉ̋ʉ̏*

kpágwʌ̀ *n* **aimant naturel** *[a été utilisé traditionnellement comme minerai de fer]*

kpa̋kɔ̏ *n* **coco**

kpákpá <redoubl. kpá 'autrefois'> *n rn* **temps de jeunesse** *(pour un vieux)* ♦ *yà kʌ̄ n̄ kpákpá ká...* quand j'étais tout jeune...

kpákpádhɤ̄ *adv* **1 parfaitement** ◊ *yɤ̀ kwɪ́ wɔ̀ bhàn kpákpádhɤ̄* il sait parler français parfaitement ◊ *yà yʌ̄ kʌ̄ kpákpádhɤ̄* il a bien travaillé **2 distinctement** *(d'une façon claire; parler)*

kpákpákpádhɤ̄ *onomat* **scrontch** *le bruit de celui qui mange bruyamment* ◊ *yɤ̀ ɤ̄ dhɪ́ bhàn-sɪ̄ʌ kpákpákpádhɤ̄* il fait du bruit en mangeant : scrontch

kpàn *v* **1.1** 1) *vi* **voir** *(qch – bhà)* Syn. *g̲a̋* 2) *vt* *ɤ̄ ya̋n kpàn a̋ bhà* **voir qch de ses propres yeux 1.2** *vi* **regarder** *(qch, qn – bhà)* ◊ *... ā kʌ̄ dhɔ̀ bhʉ̄n á kpàn dhʌ́n bhā' bhà* j'y suis allé pour regarder cet enfant **2** *vi* **rencontrer** *(qn – bhà)* **3** *vi* **trouver** *(qch – bhà)* ◊ *wà kpàn būu yàagā bhà a̋ gɔ̀ kɔ́ɔdhɤ̄* on a trouvé trois fusils dans sa maison

kpa̋n *n* **fondation** *(d'une maison, avec une petite rampe)* ◊ *yà yáàndhūn kɔ́ kpa̋n tà* il s'est assis sur la rampe du fondement de la maison ♦ *kɔ́ kpa̋n yà (gw), kɔ́ kpa̋n ka̋n (t)* poser/jeter les fondements d'une maison ♦ *kpa̋n dhɪ́ɤ* devant la porte d'entrée (à l'intérieur et à l'extérieur de la maison)

kpa̋ndhɪ́ɤ <fondation-devant> *n* **entrée** *(espace à l'intérieur de la maison devant la porte d'entrée, non séparée)*

kpâ̋sâ̋ ***n*** *hist.* **caleçon traditionnel** *(étroit, en tissu de coton; autrefois la principale pièce vestimentaire, aujourd'hui inusité)* ◊ *Bhàŋbhà yɤ̀ kpâ̋sâ̋ bhò dhɤ̋ kɤ̄ ɤ́ dhó gɔ̀n gɔ̄ɔn' bhɛ̄n-dhùn ká* Bamba a mis le pantalon traditionnel pour aller faire la lutte avec les gens

kpâ̋sâ̋kpōsō ***intj*** **oh là là !** *(interjection traduisant la perplexité)*

kpầtầ <*kpä ä tä 'mets sur lui'> ***n*** **couverture**

kpæ̀æ → kpɛ̀ɛ *reste*

kpǣæ̀ {kpæ̀æ} ***v vi*** **grandir** Syn. *glâ̋*

kpæ̋æ → kpɛ̋ɛ *sec*

kpæ̀æbhō → kpɛ̀ɛwō *toujours*

kpæ̋ækpæ̋æ *Int. pl. de* kpɛ̋ɛ *sec*

kpǣæn → kpɛ̄ɛn *arbre (esp.)*

kpæ̋æsùı ***adj*** **paddy**

kpæ̀æwō → kpɛ̀ɛwō *toujours*

kpæ̀kpæ̀wō ***adv*** *Int. de* kpɛ̀ɛwō *toujours*

kpʌ̏ ***n*** **plante** *(esp. : succulente, avec une tige grise et dure dont on obtient des fibres très dures)*

kpʌ̀ ***n*** **1 tronc** *(d'arbre)* Qsyn. *dɔ̄ŋ* **2 rondin, bille**

kpʌ̄ ***n*** **1** ***Anomalurus beecrofti*** **écureuil volant de Beecroft** *(650 g, corps jaune-orange, membranes entre les pattes) [considéré comme un oiseau; on en fait la chasse avec le fusil]* **2 brute** *(celui qui se comporte asocialement; une insulte)*

kpʌ̄ʌ (m) → kpɤ̄ɤ *apparence*

kpʌ̄ʌ̋, kpɤ̄ɤ̋ ***n*** **1 liane** *(terme générique)* **2 corde pour les pièges** *(en calcul, les deux formes, kpʌ̄ʌ̋ et kpʌ̄ʌ̋gā, peuvent être utilisées)*

kpʌ̄ʌ̋gā <liane-os> ***n*** **corde pour les pièges**

kpʌ̋ʌkpʌ̀ʌ {A P, kpʌ̋ʌkpʌ̀ʌ -sùı A; kpʌ̋kʌ̋kpʌ̀kʌ̀ Int. P} ***adj*** **engourdi** *(insensible)* ♦ *ī kɔ̀ yà kʌ̄ kpʌ̋ʌkpʌ̀ʌ* ma main s'est engourdie

kpʌ́dhɤ̄ {S, Int. S kpʌ̋kpʌ̋dhɤ̄ rare} ***adj*** **sérieux** *(personne)*

kpʌ̏gā <plante-os> ***n*** **corde fabriquée avec les fibres de la plante kpʌ̏** *(très dure; utilisée pour le tressage)*

kpʌ̋kʌ̋kpʌ̀kʌ̀ ***adj*** *Int. de* kpʌ̋ʌkpʌ̀ʌ *engourdi*

kpʌ̋kpʌ̋dhɤ̄ ***adj*** *Int. de* kpʌ́dhɤ̄ *sérieux*

kpʌ̄nŋ 1 ***n*** **mille-pattes, millepatte** *[normalement, les Dan ne mangent pas les mille-pattes, mais les Mano et les Kono les mangent; si un millepatte croise le chemin de quelqu'un, c'est un mauvais signe pour lui]* ♦ *kpʌ̄nŋ bhɛ̄* = kpʌ̄nŋ ◊ *ɯ́ dhó-sīʌ dhɛ̀ bhá gɯ́, bhá kpʌ̀n kpʌ̄nŋ bhɛ̄ bhà, bɔ̄' wʌ̄ʌ́dhɤ̄, yɤ̀ bhɔ̀ à bhà dhɛ̀, yà kʌ̄ dhɤ̋, tâ̋ yɤ̀ dhì* si tu vas quelque part et que tu rencontres un mille-pattes, passe devant lui; si tu fais ça, sans doute, tu auras de la chance

kpʌ̄nŋ 2 {kpʌ̄nŋ} *v vr* **trembler** *(de colère)*

kpʌ̋nŋ̏ *n* **ruse** ♦ *kpʌ̋nŋ̏ kʌ̄* user de ruse ♦ *kpʌ̋nŋ̏ kʌ̄ bhɛ̄n gɔ̏* duper qn

kpʌ̋nŋ̏kpʌ̋nŋ̏sɯ̏ *Int. de* kpʌ̋nŋ̏sɯ̏ *rusé*

kpʌ̋nŋ̏sɯ̏ {A P S, kpʌ̋nŋ̏sɯ̏-dhʉ̏n pl. A, kpʌ̋nŋ̏sɯ̏-sɯ̏ foc. A, kpʌ̋nŋ̏sɯ̏-sɯ̏-dhʉ̏n foc. pl. A S; kpʌ̋nŋ̏kpʌ̋nŋ̏sɯ̏ Int. A P S, kpʌ̋nŋkpʌ̋nŋsɯ̏-dhʉ̏n Int. pl. A S, kpʌ̋nŋ̏kpʌ̋nŋ̏sɯ̏-sɯ̏ Int. foc. A, kpʌ̋nŋ̏kpʌ̋nŋ̏sɯ̏-sɯ̏-dhʉ̏n Int. pl. foc. A} *adj* **rusé**

kpʌ̀ŋ *v* **1** *vt* **secouer** <u>*Syn.*</u> <u>*gʉ́-kpʌ̀ŋ*</u> **2** *vt* **pulvériser**

kpȅe *n* **fourreau**

kpēe, kpēedhʌ́n *n* **écuelle en bois** *(la forme kpēe est moins usitée)*

kpēē̋, kpēŋ̋ (t) *n dɤ̄ŋ kpēē̋* **bâton flexible** *(d'un piège)*

kpéȅ *n* **nudité, corps nu**

kpēeŋdhɤ̄ *adv* **directement** *(dire)*

kpȅkʉ̏ *n rn* **coude** ◊ *wȁa kún ȁ kpȅkʉ̏ bhȁ* on lui a saisi le coude

kpēŋkpēŋdhɤ̄ *adv* **distinctement et à haute voix** *(appeler)*

kpɛ̏ɛ, kpæ̏æ *n* **reste** ♦ *ȁ kpɛ̏ɛ bhɤ̏ dō* mange jusqu'à la fin ◊ *yɤ́ Wʌ̀nŋ ɤ́ dhō bhʉ̄n, yɤ́' tȁ kpæ̏æ dɔ̄* et alors Lézard est allé l'achever

kpɛ̋ɛ 1), kpæ̋æ {A P S, kpɛ̋ɛ-dhʉ̏n pl. A S, kpɛ̋ɛ-sɯ̏ foc. A S, kpɛ̋ɛ-sɯ̏-dhʉ̏n foc. pl. A S; kpɛ̋ɛkpɛ̋ɛ, kpæ̋ækpæ̋æ Int. pl. A P S, kpɛ̋ɛkpɛ̋ɛ-dhʉ̏n, kpæ̋ækpæ̋æ-dhʉ̏n Int. pl. A S, kpɛ̋ɛkpɛ̋ɛ-sɯ̏, kpæ̋ækpæ̋æ-sɯ̏ Int. foc pl. A S, kpɛ̋ɛkpɛ̋ɛ-sɯ̏-dhʉ̏n, kpæ̋ækpæ̋æ-sɯ̏-dhʉ̏n Int. foc. pl. A S} *adj* **1 sec** ◊ *yɤ̏ kàkàô kpɛ̋ɛ kpɔ̏ gbʌ̋ŋ tȁ* il fait sécher le cacao sur le séchoir ◊ *n̄ bɛ̏n yȁ kʌ̄ kpæ̋æ* mes lèvres se sont fendues (à cause du froid) **2 mince** *(homme, animal)* ◊ *yɤ̏ kpɛ̋ɛ dhɛ̀ sɛ̀dhá dhɤ́* il est mince comme une aiguille **3 strident** *(voix)*

kpɛ̋ɛ 2), kpæ̋æ *n* **sécheresse** ◊ *n̄ bhǣæ̋dhɛ̏ yȁ kpæ̋æ kpɔ́* j'ai la gorge sèche ♦ *ȁ bhɛ̄ɛ̋dhɛ̏ yà kpæ̋æ kún* il a eu la gorge sèche ♦ *bhān bhlʉ̏n yà kpæ̋æ kún* mon riz a séché *(au champ)* ♦ *kpæ̋æ kpɔ́* sécher (surtout au soleil, au feu)

kpɛ̋ɛkpɛ̋ɛ *Int. pl. de* kpɛ̋ɛ *sec*

kpéɛn, kpǽæn *n* ***Lecaniodiscus cupanioides (Sapindaceae)*** **arbre** *(6-12, bois très dur, drupes ovoïdes jusqu'à 1 cm, couvertes de poils roux) [est utilisé pour faire des pièges]*

kpɛ̄ɛnŋ *n* **résine de l'arbre kpɛ̄ɛnŋdhʉ̏** *(devient collant si réchauffé; sert de glu pour les calebasses et les pots, on le brûle pour l'éclairage)*

kpɛ̄ɛnŋdhɤ̄ 1, kpʌ́dhɤ̄ {A, kpɛ̄ɛnŋdhɤ̄-dhʉ̏n pl. A, kpɛ̄ɛnŋdhɤ̄-sɯ̏ foc. A, kpɛ̄ɛnŋdhɤ̄-sɯ̏-dhʉ̏n foc. pl. A; kpɛ̄nŋkpɛ̄nŋdhɤ̄ Int. A, kpɛ̄nŋkpɛ̄nŋdhɤ̄-dhʉ̏n Int. pl. A} *adj* **1 véritable, vrai** ◊ *kwā dhȅŋbhɔ̄ɔ kpɛ̄ɛnŋdhɤ̄ dhʌ̀n Gbāan gbɤ̄* notre vrai-vrai logeur était le fils de Gbaan **2** *dhʌ́n kpɛ̄nŋdhɤ̄* **fils raisonnable, fille raisonnable** *(respectueux, sérieux, travailleur, etc.)* **3 juste** ♦ *bháa kpɛ̄ɛnŋdhɤ̄* tu es injuste

kpɛ̄ɛnŋdhɤ̄ 2 {Int. kpɛ̄nŋkpɛ̄nŋdhɤ̄} ***adv*** **1 complètement** ◊ *yà bhɯ̃a bhɤ̀ kpɛ̄nŋkpɛ̄nŋdhɤ̄* il a mangé du riz cuit jusqu'à être complètement repu **2 exactement** *(avec les numéraux)* Syn. dèbɤ̃ɤ

kpɛ̄ɛnŋdhɯ̀ɯ ***n*** **arbre résineux** *(esp)* Syn. bhɯ̃ʌʌ

kpɛ̀ɛwō, kpæ̀æwō, kpæ̀æbhō {Int. kpɛ̀kpɛ̀wō, kpæ̀kpæ̀wo} ***adv*** **toujours** *(chaque fois; en permanence),* **souvent** ◊ *yɤ̀ n̄ tùaa bhɔ̀ kpɛ̀ɛwō* il me salue toujours ◊ *pʌ̄ dhʌ̀n à bhɤ̀ kpɛ̀ɛwō* il ne fait que manger tout le temps ◊ *Tòkpà yɤ̀ pʌ̄ dhɔ̀ bùtígɤ̀ gú kpæ̀æwō* Tokpa achète souvent des choses à la boutique

kpɛ̀kpɛ̀wō ***adv*** *Int. de* kpɛ̀ɛwō *toujours*

kpɛ̀nŋ ***v vt*** **serrer** ◊ *bhá n̄ kpɛ̀nŋ gbɛ̃ɛ* tu m'as trop serré

kpɛ́nŋ̀ (m) → kpɛ́ŋ̀ (gw) *petit escargot*

kpɛ̃nŋ ***loc.n*** *IN de* kpɛ̃nŋdhɛ̀ *extérieur*

kpɛ̃nŋdhɛ̀ {IN kpɛ̃nŋ, LOC kpɛ̃nŋdhɤ̄} <dehors-endroit> ***loc.n*** **partie extérieure** ◊ *fɛ̃ŋ bhá yíi yɤ̄ kpɛ̃nŋ / kpɛ̃nŋdhɤ̄* aucun rat n'est sorti ♦ *dhó kpɛ̃nŋdhɤ̄ / kpɛ̃nŋ !* va dehors ! ♦ *kɔ́ kpɛ̃nŋdhɛ̀ bāà* décorer la maison à l'extérieur ♦ *kpɛ̃nŋ dhʌ̀n* enfant adultérin *(pour un homme : tout enfant qui n'est pas né de son épouse; pour une femme : enfant né avant le mariage; le terme n'est pas appliqué à un enfant né d'un amant pendant que la femme est mariée)*

kpɛ̃nŋdhɤ̄ ***loc.n*** *LOC de* kpɛ̃nŋdhɛ̀ *extérieur*

kpɛ̄nŋkpɛ̄nŋdhɤ̄ 1 ***adv*** **1 certainement** *(sans aucun doute)* **2 solidement** Syn. dɛ̀dɛ̀wō ◊ *yàa lɤ̀ kpɛ̄nŋkpɛ̄nŋdhɤ̄* il l'a attaché solidement

kpɛ̄nŋkpɛ̄nŋdhɤ̄ 2 ***adj*** *Int. de* kpɛ̄nŋdhɤ̄ *véritable*

kpɛ̄nŋkpɛ̄nŋdhɤ̄ 3 ***adv*** *Int. de* kpɛ̄ɛnŋ̄dhɤ̄ 2 *complètement*

kpɛ́ŋ̀ (gw), **kpɛ́nŋ̀** (m) ***n*** **escargot** *(petit, à coquille pas trop dure; on le mange)* ◊ *yà kpɛ́ŋ̀ kún blʌ̄ʌ tà* il a cueilli des petits escargots dans les herbes ♦ *kpɛ́ŋ̀ dhɯ̀* l'arbre où les petits escargots habitent *(des feuilles larges, le bois mou)*

kpɛ́ŋgā ***n*** (Yorodougou, Sipilou) ***Barilius senegalensis (Raiamus senegalensis), Barilius loati*** **vairon** *(poisson de 10-12 cm, parfois jusqu'à 20 cm, avec des raies verticales bleu noirs sur les flancs)*

kpɛ̄ŋkpɛ̄ŋdhɤ̄ ***adv*** **hermétiquement**, **fortement** *(fermer, museler)*

kpı̃annŋkpı̃annŋdhɤ̄ ***adv*** **en boitant** *(décrit la démarche d'un boiteux)* ♦ *gɤ̀ŋklɤ̄ɤ̀bhɛ̀n yɤ̀ tà kpı̃annŋkpı̃annŋdhɤ̄* le boiteux marche en boitant

kpı̃anŋ → kpı̃ʌŋ *joue*

kpìʌʌ ***n*** **chimpanzé** *[il existe, chez les Dan, une croyance selon laquelle les chimpanzés sont des gens de la forêt. Et en même temps, on les mange; la chair de la paume de la main est particulièrement appréciée]* ◊ *kpìʌʌ yɤ̀ yâ* le chimpanzé est vilain

kpìʌʌkāàgúı <chimpanzé-poil-dans> ***n*** **varicelle**

kpīʌ̋ŋ *n kpīʌ̋ŋ zœ̀œndhē* ***Hibiscus sabdariffa*** **oseille de Guinée**

kpíʌŋ, **kpíaŋ** (t) *n rn* **joue** ♦ *kpíʌŋ dhṹɤ̌* mâchoire inférieure ♦ *kpíʌŋ sı́ʌ̄ʌ* mâchoire supérieure ♦ *kpíʌŋ bhȁ kȁa* favoris ♦ *yà ɤ̄ kpíʌŋ kpū dɔ̄* il a gonflé ses joues

kpíʌŋsōȁ <joue- ?> *n rn* **menton**

kpı̂ı̂ {A P S, kpı̂ı̂-dhȕn pl. A, kpı̂ı̂-sɯ̏ foc. A, kpı̂ı̂-sɯ̏-dhȕn foc. pl.; kpíkpı̏ Int. A P S, kpíkpı̏-dhȕn Int. pl. A, kpíkpı̏-sɯ̏ Int. foc. A, kpíkpı̏-sɯ̏-dhȕn Int. foc. pl. A; kpíkíkpı̏kı̏ SupInt. A P S, kpíkíkpı̏kı̏-dhȕn SupInt. pl. A S, kpíkíkpı̏kı̏-sɯ̏ SupInt. foc. A, kpíkíkpı̏kı̏-sɯ̏-dhȕn SupInt. foc. pl. A} *adj* **1 grand**, **gros** *(taille; importance)* *Qsyn.* *gblɤ̋gblɤ̋* ◊ *gbìŋ bhā yɤ̏ gbɛ̋ɛ kpíkíkpı̏kı̏* la grotte est très large et spacieuse ◊ *yúɤ̏ɤ bhā yɤ̏ kpı̂ı̂ ká dhè n̄ gbȁnbhlʌ̋ dhɤ̌* le poisson est grand comme ma cuisse ♦ *kwı́ kpı̂ı̂* grand fonctionnaire **2** *Int. ne s'utilise pas* **aîné** *Syn.* *gbȁŋ 1* *Qsyn.* *gblɤ̋gblɤ̋*

kpı̂ı̂-dhȅ *n* **grande majorité** ♦ *kpı̂ı̂dhȅ gbàn* presque tous

kpíkíkpı̏kı̏ *SupInt. de* kpı̂ı̂ *grand*

kpíkpı̏ *Int. de* kpı̂ı̂ *grand*

kpı̂n *n* **rhume, grippe**

kpı̏nŋ, **kpìnŋ** *n* **1 route carrossable** *Syn.* *kpı̏nŋgā* *Qsyn.* *zīaan* ♦ *kpı̏nŋ bɔ̄* frayer le chemin ♦ *kpı̏nŋ gɤ̋ŋ pɤ́ɤ* au bord de la route **2 lit en terre battue** *(fait de briques couvertes de terre damée sur laquelle l'aîné s'installe avec une natte, tandis que les enfants dorment par terre, à côté du lit; devenu rarissime de nos jours)* ◊ *yà wɔ̄ kpı̏nŋ tàa* il s'est couché sur le lit en terre

kpı̏nŋgā, **kpìnŋgā** *n* **route, rue** *Syn.* *kpı̏nŋ*

kpı̏nŋtàa <lit-dos> *n* **lit en terre battue** *(fait de briques couvertes de terre damée sur laquelle l'aîné s'installe avec une natte, tandis que les enfants dorment par terre, à côté du lit; devenu rarissime de nos jours)*

kpīɤ̏ɤ *n rn* **genou** *Syn.* *kpīɤ̏ɤgɔ̏* ♦ *yà yȁ ɤ̄ kpīɤ̏ɤ gúı* il s'est agenouillé

kpīɤ̏ɤgɔ̏ *n rn* **genou** *Syn.* *kpīɤ̏ɤ* ♦ *yı́ yɤ̏ bhēn kùn bhēn kpīɤ̏ɤgɔ̏ bhȁ* l'eau arrive aux genoux ◊ *yȁ yɤ̄ ɤ̄ kpīɤ̏ɤgɔ̏ gúı* il s'est agenouillé

kplȁ 1 *v* **1** *vi* **céder** *(à – gɔ̏)* ◊ *ā gùn bhāan ȁ bhȁn kɛ̋ɛ bhán kplȁ ȁ dʌ̄ gɔ̏* j'allais le frapper, mais j'ai renoncé à cause de son père **2** *vi* **être empêché** *(par – ká)*

kplȁ 2 *n* **besoin** ♦ *sɔ̄ kplȁ yà n̄ kún, sɔ̄ kplȁ yɤ̏ n̄ bhȁ* j'ai besoin d'habits

kplȁ́ 1 *n* **navette** *(accessoire du métier à tisser)*

kplȁ́ 2 *n* **1** *rn* **gésier** *[la partie la plus recherchée de la chair d'une poule etc.; revient aux aînés]* ♦ *dhṹ kplȁ́* bâton, bout de bois **2** *rn* **pomme d'Adam** ◊ *ɯ̄ kplȁ́ ká dhè tɔ̏ kplȁ́ dhɤ̌* ta pomme d'Adam est comme le gésier d'un poulet

kplâ *n* **mirador-séchoir** *(pour la vaisselle et les aliments, sur quatre poutres, pas très grand)* *Qsyn.* *gbȁ́ŋ*

kplàa ***n*** **1** *rn* **jambes** *(du genou au pied)*, **tibias** *(les deux tibias d'une personne)* **2** *rn* **pattes** *(les quatre pattes d'un animal)*

kplàagā ***n*** **1** *rn* **jambe** *(du genou au pied)* Qsyn. kplàa ♦ *à kplàagā yɤ̀ gbɛ̃́ɛ̀ / gbɛ̃́ɛgbɛ̀ɛ* ses jambes sont fortes *(un footballeur qui traumatise les autres joueurs; un coureur champion)* **2 patte** Qsyn. kplàa

kplɑ̃́gɔ̄ ***n*** **pirogue** *(fabriquée d'habitude du bois de yɤ̀ŋ)* ♦ *yɤ̀ kplɑ̃́gɔ̄ zīɤ-sīʌ* il est en train de conduire la pirogue

kplāŋkplāŋdɤ̀ (m) → kplɛ̄ŋkplɛ̄ŋdhɤ̀ *droit*

kplātɑ̃́n ***n*** **"kplatan"** *(danse et chant des chanteurs de chasse; se joue au clair de lune, accompagné de hochets-sonnailles et de battements sur des carapaces de tortue)*

kplɑ̃́tɔ̃́ ***n*** **calvitie** ♦ *kplɑ̃́tɔ̃́ yà bhɑ̀ à gɔ̀* il est devenu chauve

kplǣǣ̀, kplǣǣ́ → kplɛ̄ɛ̀ *maigrir*

kplʌ̀ʌ ***n*** **incirconcis, inexcisée** *(qui n'est pas passé par l'initiation)*

kplʌ̄ʌ́ ***n*** **épi décortiqué** *(de maïs)*

kplʌ̃́ʌ, kplʌ̃́ʌbhīn ***n*** **preux, chef de guerre** ♦ *gblʉ̀ʉ kplʌ̃́ʌ* → kplʌ̃́ʌ ◊ *kɔ̀ yà zīɤ gblʉ̀ʉ kplʌ̃́ʌ gɔ̀ kɤ̄ yà kʌ̄ gblʉ̀ʉgɔ̄ɔnbhɛ̀n-dhʉ̀n kpǣ̀æ bhà gbɛ̃́ɛ̀* quand le preux est capturé, la situation des autres guerriers devient difficile

kplʌ̀ʌkpɑ̃́ɑ̀ ***n*** **herbe** *(esp. : des petits graines se détachent facilement et se collent aux vêtements)* ◊ *kplʌ̀ʌkpɑ̃́ɑ̀ yɤ̀ à gɛ̀ɛn* il n'a pas encoré lavé la poussière de la route (litt. : il a encore des grains de kplʌ̀ʌkpɑ̃́ɑ̀ sur les pieds) *(une expression péjorative concernant des nouveaux venus)*

kplʌ́ʌnŋ ***n*** *rn* **champion** *(qui excelle; le plus souvent, guerrier, mais pas seulement) l'indication de l'activité ou de l'aire géographique est nécessaire* ◊ *Sɑ́ŋ̄tàa kplʌ́ʌnŋ-dhʉ̀n* héros de Santa

kplʌ́ʌnŋbhīn {pl. kplʌ́ʌnŋzʌ̀-dhʉ̀n} ***n*** **champion** *(qui excelle)* ◊ *wà kplʌ́ʌnŋzʌ̀-dhʉ̀n gbàn zʌ̄* ils ont tué tous les héros

kplʌ́ʌnŋzʌ̀-dhʉ̀n ***n*** *pluriel du* kplʌ́ʌnŋ *champion*

kplʌ̃́nŋ (s), **kwlʌ̃́nŋ** (t,) ***n*** **1 rapport, compte-rendu** *(de voyage)* ♦ *kplʌ̃́nŋ bhō, kplʌ̃́nŋ dɑ̀* informer du but de la visite; donner le rapport d'un voyage **2 cadeau** *(à une fête, aux funérailles)* ♦ *kplʌ̃́nŋ bhō* faire une déclaration de don **3** *rn* **le fait de confier** *(un enfant pour l'éduction; des soucis)*, **surveillance** *(d'un objet)* ◊ *Sàkpà yà ɤ̄ bhā dhʌ́n kplʌ̃́nŋ bhō n̄ bhɑ̀* Sakpa m'a confié l'éducation de son enfant ◊ *Zân yà ɤ̄ gɔ̀ wɔ̀n kplʌ̃́nŋ bhō n̄ bhɑ̀* Zan m'a confié son souci

kplɛ̄ɛ̀, kplɛ̄ɛ́, kplǣǣ́, kplǣǣ̀ {kplɛ̀ɛ, kplæ̀æ} ***v*** **1** *vi* **maigrir** *[toujours considéré comme un changement négatif]* ◊ *yɤ̀ kʌ̀ kplɛ̄ɛ̀-sʉ̀ kɑ́ dhʉ́n, à gɔ̀n yɤ̀ gʉ̀n yɤ̄ɤ à bhō bʉ̃́* si elle maigrissait, son mari la chasserait **2** *vt* *ɤ̄ kɔ̀ kplɛ̄ɛ̀* **faire une geste menaçant** *(un movement tournant avec les doigts des deux mains; à – dhɛ̀)*

kplɛ̄ɛ̀dhɛ̀ ***n* *Turtur tympanistria, Tympanistria tympanistria*** **tourterelle tambourette** *(21 cm; la femelle : blanc teinté de gris; le mâle : dessus brun avec une barre noirâtre sur le croupion)*

kplɛ̀ɛn ***n*** *bɛ̀n kplɛ̀ɛn* **moue méprisante** *(les lèvres avancées, souvent accompagnée du son ressemblant au bruit de pet)* Qsyn. *sùɛɛ* ♦ *yà ɤ̄ bɛ̀n kplɛ̀ɛn bhō n̄ ká* il m'a fait une moue méprisante

kplɛ̂kplɛ̀, **kplɛ̂kplɛ̂** {A P S, kplɛ̂kplɛ̀-dhʉ̀n pl. A S, kplɛ̂kplɛ̀-sʉ̀ foc. A S, kplɛ̂kplɛ̀-sʉ̀-dhʉ̀n foc. pl. A S} ***adj*** **1 bas, court, de petite taille** *(animal domestique ou volaille)* **2** *iron.* **aplati** *(nez)*

kplɛ̄ŋkplɛ̄ŋdhɤ̄ (gw), **kplāŋkplāŋdɤ̄** (m) ***adv*** **droit** ♦ *yà wɔ̀ kplɛ̄ŋkplɛ̄ŋdhɤ̄* il est couché tout droit par terre ♦ *yà dō kplɛ̄ŋkplɛ̄ŋdhɤ̄* il se tient droit

kplĭĭ ***n*** **goitre** ♦ *kplĭĭ yà yà̰ à̰ bhǣǣ* il a un goitre

kplőŋ ***n*** **plan n** *(tracé à la main dans le sable)* ♦ *yà kɔ́ kplőŋ kɑ̋n* il a tracé le plan de la maison *(pour la construction)*

kplɔ̄ɔ̋ ***n*** **épinard**

kplɤ̋ ***n*** **filet de pêche** *(pour hommes)* Qsyn. *dhűun, sàadhè, tèe, zūeŋ*

kplɤ̀ɤ ***n*** *rn vulg.* **pénis** Syn. *gɔ̄ɔ̀ndhɛ̀, gɔ̄ɔ̀ndhɛ̀gā, kpāɑ̋n, kpāɑ̋ngā, kplɤ̀ɤgā*

kplɤ̀ɤgā ***n*** *rn vulg.* **pénis** Syn. *gɔ̄ɔ̀ndhɛ̀, gɔ̄ɔ̀ndhɛ̀gā, kpāɑ̋n, kpāɑ̋ngā, kplɤ̀ɤ*

kplʉ̀ʉ ***v*** **1** 1) *vi* **s'attacher** 2) *vt* **attacher** Qsyn. *lɤ̀* Ant. *pɔ́* ◊ *yà n̄ kplʉ̀ʉ kɤdhɤ̋ á pɤ̀* il m'a attaché pour que je ne tombe pas ♦ *kplʉ̀ʉ kwʌ́ʌ̀* lier {ensemble} ♦ *kplʉ̀ʉ à̰ bhà̰* attacher à qch **2** *vt* **attacher** *(pagne, foulard, ceinture)* Qsyn. *kɑ̋n* ◊ *ʉ̄ bhā sɔ̄ kplʉ̀ʉ sʌ̀ ká* attache bien ton pagne

kplʉ̀ʉ ***n*** **1 tubercule bouilli** ◊ *bāa kplʉ̀ʉ* manioc bouilli **2 caillot** *(de sang)* ♦ *à̰ yɔ̀ɔn yà̰ kplʉ̀ʉ kún* son sang s'est coagulé

kplʉ̋ʉ 1) ***n*** **morceau** *(coupé contre le sens du fil)* Qsyn. *kpɤ̄, pɛ̋n* ♦ *à̰ kɔ̀ yɤ̀ kplʉ̋ʉ ká* il a la main coupée ◊ *Sàó yà̰ Zân kɔ̀ kplʉ̋ʉ bhō / kɑ̋n* Sao a coupé la main de Zan ◊ *Sàó yà̰ sɔ̄ kplʉ̋ʉ-kplʉ̋ʉ bhō / kɑ̋n* Sao a coupé le tissu en petits morceaux

kplʉ̋ʉ 2) ***prev*** **morceau**

kplʉ̋ʉ-kɑ̋n {kplʉ̋ʉ-kɑ̀n} ***v vt*** **couper** ◊ *yà gbɔ̋ŋ gā bhā' kplʉ̋ʉ-kɑ̋n bɤ̋ŋdhɤ̄* il a coupé le pétiole de raphia d'un seul coup

kplʉ̀ʉtlɛ̄ɛgā <attacher-trait-os> ***n*** *neol.* **trait d'union**

kpɔ̀ 1 ***n* *Atilas paludinosus*** **mangouste des marais** Syn. *dɛ̂npʌ̀dʌ̄ (m)*

kpɔ̀ 2 ***adj*** **pas mûr** *(vert)* ◊ *bhán bhánŋglóo kpɔ̀ bhō* j'ai cueilli une mangue verte ◊ *ʉ̄ bhā bhánŋglōo yɤ̀ kpɔ̀* ta mangue n'est pas mûre

kpɔ̀ 3 ***v vi*** **partir** *(coureur)* Syn. *zīɤ gèe ká* ♦ *yà̰ à̰ pɤ̄ yɤ̄ɤ kpɔ̀, yáa kpɔ̀* il a fait semblant de partir, mais il n'est pas parti *(une stratégie du coureur pour tromper le masque)*

kpȍdhēŋ̄bhō, kpȍdhēŋbhō, kpȍdhēŋ̄ ***n*** **devinette** ♦ *kpȍdhēŋ̄bhō yɔ̏ɔbɔ̄* trouver la réponse à une devinette

kpȍkpȍsɯ̏ ***adj*** *Int. de* kpȍsɯ̏ *non mûr*

kpȍŋ ***n*** *rn* **front** ◊ *yȁ yɔ̋ɔ zīɤ ɤ̄ kpȍŋ dhɯ́ɤ* il a enduit son front de kaolin

kpóŋ̏ ***n*** arch. **battant de la porte** *(en bois, en écorce)* Qsyn. kwɛ̋ɛ

kpőŋ ***n*** **rive, bord** ♦ *yɯ́ kpőŋ dhɯ́ɤ* rive, côté **2 berge, pente**

kpōŋ̋dhɛ̏, kpȍŋgúdhɛ̏ {LOC kpōŋ̋dhɤ̄} ***loc.n*** *rn* **front** ◊ *yȁ ɤ̄ kɔ̏ pá dhʌ́n kpōŋ̋dhɛ̏ ká* il a touché le front de l'enfant avec sa main ◊ *yȁ yɔ̋ɔ zīɤ ɤ̄ kpōnŋ̋dhɤ̄* il a enduit son front de kaolin

kpōŋ̋dhɤ̄ ***loc.n*** *LOC de* kpȍŋgúdhɛ̏ *front*

kpőŋtàa <rive-dos> ***n*** **monde** Syn. kpőŋtàadhɛ̏

kpőŋtàabhɛ̏n-dhɯ̏n <rive-dos-personne> ***n*** **gens d'ici-bas, humains vivants** ♦ *kpőŋtàabhɛ̏n-dhɯ̏n wāȁ gèebɔ̀ɔbhɛ̄n wáa dō* les gens d'ici-bas et les habitants de l'au-delà ne sont pas semblables

kpőŋtàadhɛ̏ <rive-dos-endroit> ***n*** **1 monde** Syn. kpőŋtàa ◊ *Zlȁan yɤ̏ kpőŋtàadhɛ̏ dȁ dhɛ̏kpœ̀œ sœ̋œ̀plɛ̀ ká* Dieu a créé le monde en sept jours **2 vie** ♦ *kpőŋtàadhɛ̏ yà kʌ̄ gbɛ̋ɛ̏* la vie est devenue difficile

kpőŋtàapʌ̏-dhɯ̏n ***n*** **tout ce qui existe dans le monde** *(à part les humains)*

kpōo ***n*** *bhān kpōo kún* rude **je m'en fiche** *(refus d'obéir, impoli)*

kpȍsɯ̏ {A P S; kpȍkpȍsɯ̏ Int.} ***adj*** **non mûr**

kpɔ́ {kpɔ̄} ***v*** **1.1** *vt* **étaler** Syn. sā ◊ *Tìa bhā dhēbʌ̏ yà sɔ̄ kpɔ́ gɔ̏n tȁ* la femme de Tia a étalé les vêtements sur la paillotte ♦ *yɯ́ kpɔ́* verser de l'eau *(lors de la bénédiction, on verse de l'eau par terre)* ♦ *slʌ̏ʌ kpɔ́ bhɛ̄n gɔ̏* jeter du piment dans les yeux de qn ♦ *ɤ̄ wɔ̏ kpɔ́ ȁ bhȁ* donner des consignes à qn **1.2** *vt* **tendre, étendre** *(vêtement, natte)* **1.3** *vt* **étendre** *(linge)* ◊ *wà sɔ̄ yɯ́sɯ̏ kpɔ́ bhɪ̄ʌ́ bhȁ* ils ont étendu les habits trempés sur la corde **1.4** 1) *vi* **apparaître** *(couche de substance)* ◊ *dhìin yà kpɔ́ ȁ sɔ̋n bhȁ* une patine verte est apparue sur ses dents 2) *vt* **enduire** *(de qch; une surface – bhȁ)* ◊ *yà yɔ̋ɔ kpɔ́ ɤ̄ bhœ̄œ̀* il s'est enduit la gorge de kaolin *(un traitement médical traditionnel)* **2** 1) *vt* **mettre au monde, accoucher de**; **procréer** ◊ *... ȁ bhȁ dhēbʌ̏ ɤ́ dhʌ́n gɔ̄ɔ̏n dō kpɔ̄* sa femme a accouché d'un garçon ◊ *yɤ́ n̄ dʌ̄ ɤ́ n̄ kpɔ̄ ...* et mon père qui m'a procréé... ♦ *ȁ kpɔ́ pɤ̏* son village natal 2) *vr* **accoucher** ♦ *tɯ̏ʌʌ ɤ́ yáa ɤ̄ kpɔ́* une femelle stérile 3) *vi* **naître** ♦ *dhʌ́n yáa kpɔ́* il n'est pas facile de donner naissance à un enfant **3** *vt* **défricher** *(un nouveau champ)* **4** *vt* **fixer** *(la date)* Syn. dȁ ◊ *wà Yɔ̏ dɔ̄ yī kpɔ́* on a fixé la date de l'arrivée de Yo chez son futur mari **5** *vi* **éviter** *(qch – ká)*

kpɔ́bhɛ̏n-dhɯ̏n <donner.naissance-personne-PL> ***n*** **parents** ◊ *yɤ̏ kʌ̄ ɤ̄ kpɔ́bhɛ̏n-dhɯ̏n dhɔ̏-kʌ̏* il a honoré ses parents en leur offrant un repas

kpɔ̏n ***v*** *vi* **s'aigrir** ◊ *wē yȁ kpɔ̏n* le vin s'est aigri

kpɔ̄n ***n*** **poisson** *(esp. : ressemble à l'anguille, mais a des écailles et n'est pas électrique)*

kpɔ̀nsɯ̀ ***adj*** **aigre**

kpɔ̀ŋ ***n*** **troupeau**

kpɔ́ŋ̀kpɔ̏ŋ {A P} ***adj*** **tiède** *(eau, repas)* ◊ *ȁ gbɛ́-dhɛ̏ gṹ kwɪ́plɤ̀ɤbhɛ̏n-dhɯ̀n dhɯ̄n ɤ́ yɪ́ kpɔ́ŋ̀kpɔ̏ŋ dhɔ̏ dhɤ́'-dhɯ̀n kʌ̀* ce sont les citadins qui aiment le plus souvent l'eau tiède (pour se laver) ***adj***

kpɔ̏ŋkpɔ̏ŋ-dhɯ̀n ***adj*** *pl. de* kpɔ̀ɔŋ̀ *jeune*

kpɔ̏ɔ ***n*** **mauvaises herbes**, **maquis**, **broussaille** *(buissons ou hautes herbes, sur le champ ou dans la brousse)* Syn. *vɔ̃ɔ (t)* Qsyn. *kpáȁ* ◊ *kpɔ̏ɔ kpɤ̄* touffe de mauvaises herbes ♦ *kpɔ̏ɔ yȁ dȁ kɑ̃́flɛ́ɛ gṹ* la plantation de café est envahie par des broussailles

kpɔ̄ɔ, **kpœ̄œ** ***n*** **1 moquerie** *(humiliante)* ♦ *kpœ̄œ dɔ̄/pɛ́ bhɛ̄n bhȁ* se moquer de qn ♦ *kpœ̄œ pɛ́ ȁ ká bhɛ̄n bhȁ* honnir qn **2 désagrément** *(précurseur d'un malheur)* ◊ *gā kpœ̄œ yȁ dɔ̄ n̄ bhȁ* il m'est arrivé un désagrément *(qui s'est avéré un précurseur de la mort d'un proche)*

kpɔ̃́ɔ, **kpœ̃́œ** (gw) ***n*** **sac de voyage** *(de types différents)* Syn. *glɛ̄ɛ̃n (m)*

kpɔ̀ɔŋ̀ {A, pl. kpɔ̏ŋkpɔ̏ŋ-dhɯ̀n, kpɔ̀ɔŋ̀-dhɯ̀n} ***adj*** **jeune** *(humain)* ♦ *bhɛ̄n kpɔ̀ɔŋ̀ arch.* jeune personne (jusqu'à 20 ans environ) ♦ *dhʌ́n kpɔ̀ɔŋ̀ dɛ̀ɛ* enfant nouveau-né (jusqu'à 1 mois)

kpɤ̄ ***n*** **1 boule 2 morceau** Qsyn. *kplɯ̃́, pɛ̃́n* **3 groupe**, **foule** Qsyn. *dhɑ̃́a, tʌ̀ʌŋ* ♦ *yɯ́ɤ̏ kpɤ̄* banc de poissons ♦ *bhȁan kpɤ̄* volée d'oiseaux ♦ *gbɛ̂n kpɤ̄* harde de chiens ♦ *lāa kpɤ̄* troupe de lions **4 noeud** ♦ *kpɤ̄ tā* faire un noeud ♦ *kpɤ̄ pɯ̃́* délier un noeud ◊ *yȁa kpɤ̄ tȁ gbɛ̃́ɛ ká, bhɪ́in bhɔ̀ɔn ȁ bhȁ kɤ̄ á kpɤ̄ pɯ̃́* il a serré fort le noeud, je n'ai pas pu le délier **5 chose** *(des objets ronds)* ◊ *kwɛ̀ɛ̏ kpɤ̄ tīi* un colis noir

kpɤ́dhȁa ***n*** **clochette en bronze** *[amulette des guerriers et des coureurs de la course des masques]*

kpɤ́kkpɤ́dhɤ̄ ***adv*** **à ras bord** ◊ *yà pʌ̄ bhɤ̏ kpɤ́kkpɤ́dhɤ̄* il est repu ◊ *yɤ̏ sákɤ̏ pȁ kpɤ́kkpɤ́dhɤ̄* il a rempli le sac à ras bord

kpɤ́kpɤ́dhɤ̄ ***adv*** **à l'excès** ◊ *yʌ́nŋ̀ yɤ̏ bhɯ̀ kpɤ́kpɤ́dhɤ̄* le soleil brille impitoyablement

kpɤ̀ŋ ***n*** **arc-en-ciel** *[on croit que l'arc-en-ciel est produit par le crapaud dhāŋ̀pö, et qu'il fait cesser la pluie]* ♦ *dhā kpɤ̀ŋ* arc-en-ciel

kpɤ̄ŋ, **kpɤ̄ŋgā** ***n*** **fourmi noire** *(petite, piquante, fait des trous dans les maisons) se combine avec le marqueur du pluriel*

kpɤ̄ɤ (gw), **kpʌ̄ʌ** (m), **kpʌ̄ʌ́** (t) ***n rn*** **apparence** ◊ *ȁ kpɤ̄ɤ yɤ̏ sʌ̀* il est joli ♦ *ȁ kpʌ̄ʌ yɤ̏ yāa* il est vilain ♦ *ȁ kpʌ̄ʌ dhī* sa beauté

kpɤ́ɤ̏dhɤ̄ 1) ***adv*** **directement**, **sans hésitation** ◊ *yȁ ȁ pɤ̄ kpɤ́ɤ̏dhɤ̄* il l'a dit directement, sans hésitation

kpɤ̋ɤ̏dhɤ 2) ***intj*** **exactement**

kpɤ̄sl̀an ***n*** **hoquet** *[certains Dan disent que le malade qui a le hoquet a peu de chances de survivre; quand un enfant a le hoquet, on dit que l'enfant va grandir]* ◊ *kpɤ̄sl̀an yà̰ dà̰ yṵ̋a gú, kɤ̄ yṵ̋a bō-dhɛ̏ yà̰ sɪ̏ɤ* si le hoquet se combine avec la maladie, la fin de la maladie s'avère difficile ♦ *kpɤ̄sl̀an yà̰ à̰ kún* il a le hoquet

kpœ̏œ ***n*** **commission** *(mission)* ♦ *kpœ̏œ dɔ̄* ordonner ♦ *kpœ̏œ bɔ̄ bhɛ̄n dhɛ̏* envoyer un ordre à qn

kpœ̀œ ***v vi*** **se lever** *(du jour)* ♦ *dhɛ̏ yà kpœ̀œ dódó, dhɛ̏ yà kpœ̀œ dō* chaque jour ♦ *dhɛ̏ yíi kpœ̀œ kɤ̀* le jour ne s'est pas encore levé ♦ *dhɛ̀ ɤ́' tà̰ dhɛ̏ yɤ̏ kpœ̀œ* le lendemain ♦ *dhɛ̏ yɤ̏ kʌ̄ kpœ̏œ à̰-dhȕn bhà̰ zīà̰an* le jour les a surpris sur la route

kpœ̄œ → kpɔ̄ɔ *moquerie*

kpœ̋œ → kpɔ̋ɔ *sac de voyage*

kpœ̀œ-dhɛ̏ (m) ***n*** **sagesse, intelligence** ◊ *yɤ̏ yʌ̄ kʌ̏ kpœ̀œ-dhɛ̏ ká* il travaille avec intelligence

kpœ̄œdhṵ̋ (m) ***n*** **mouvette** *(un bâtonnet se terminant en croix servant à mélanger la sauce; on le tourne en serrant entre les paumes des mains qui vont en sens opposé)* Syn. *kpàdhṵ̋*

kpœ̀œkpœ̀œsṵ̏, **kpœ̋œkpœ̀œsṵ̏** arch. ***adj*** *Int. pl. de* kpœ̀œsṵ̏ *sage*

kpœ̀œn ***v vi*** **tourner** *(sauce; pemier stade, quand la sauce est encore mangeable)* Qsyn. *gɪ̰̏*

kpœ̀œsṵ̏ {A P S, kpœ̀œsṵ̏-dhȕn pl. A S, kpœ̀œsṵ̏-sṵ̏ foc. A, kpœ̀œsṵ̏-sṵ̏-dhȕn pl. foc. A; kpœ̀œkpœ̀œsṵ̏, Int. A P S, kpœ̋œkpœ̀œsṵ̏ (arch.) Int. A, kpœ̀œkpœ̀œsṵ̏-dhȕn Int. pl. A S, kpœ̀œkpœ̀œsṵ̏-sṵ̏ Int. foc. A, kpœ̀œkpœ̀œsṵ̏-sṵ̏-dhȕn Int. pl. foc. A} ***adj*** **sage** *(surtout d'un enfant)* Qsyn. *glɛ̀ŋsṵ̏*

kpœ̀œsṵ̏-dhɛ̏ (gw) ***n*** **sagesse**

kpū ***n*** **1 chicot** ◊ *kà̰a kpū bhà̰ bhɛ̄n gìi-dhɛ̏ yáa gbɛ̋ɛ* les chicots de roseau blessent facilement **2 ballonnement** ◊ *à̰ kpɪ́ʌŋ kpū yɤ̏ vīn-sīʌ* ses joues bien remplies (de nourriture) bougent **3 bosse** ◊ *kpū yɤ̏ à̰ gɔ̏ bhà̰* il a une bosse sur la tête ◊ *kpū yɤ̏ à̰ tàa* il a une bosse sur le dos

kpūŋ́ ***n*** **souche** *(d'un arbre)*

kpūú ***n*** **moignon, bout** ♦ *dhṵ̋ kpūú* souche ♦ *kɔ́ kpūú* base d'une maison *(détruite)* ♦ *pɛ̄ŋ kpūú, sűɤ kpūú* tison ◊ *sɪ́ɤ kpūú zīi yɤ̏ kwʌ́ʌ̏-dhɛ̏ yáa gbɛ̋ɛ* l'amour reprend vite (litt. : des vieux tisons se mettent ensemble facilement)

kpṵ̋ ***n*** **serment de l'accusé en sorcellerie** *(prononcé avant de boire une boisson empoisonnée pour prouver son innocence)* ♦ *kpṵ̋ dɔ̄* faire un serment de sorcier

kpúdhɤ̄ ***adv*** **d'un coup** *(prendre)* ♦ *yáa dɔ̄ kpúdhɤ̄ gɛ̀n tà̰* il ne peut pas se mettre debout comme il faut *(à cause d'une maladie)*

Kw kw

kwȁ ***mpp*** **nous** *MPP impératif inclusif 1e pers. pl. : "nous et vous", "moi et vous", "nous et toi"*

kwā 1 ***mpp*** **nous** *MPP existentiel inclusif 1e pers. pl. : "nous et vous", "moi et vous", "nous et toi"*

kwā 2 ***prn*** **nous** *pronom inclusif 1e pers. pl. : "nous et vous", "moi et vous", "nous et toi" de la série autonome*

kwā 3 ***prn*** **nous** *pronom non-sujet inclusif 1e pers. pl. : "nous et vous", "moi et vous", "nous et toi"*

kwá 1 ***mpp*** **nous** *MPP du parfait, inclusif 1e pers. pl. : "nous et vous", "moi et vous", "nous et toi"*

kwá 2 ***mpp*** **nous** *MPP conjointe inclusif 1e pers. pl. : "nous et vous", "moi et vous", "nous et toi"*

kwá 3 ***mpp*** **nous** *MPP subjonctif inclusif 1e pers. pl. : "nous et vous", "moi et vous", "nous et toi"*

kwá 4 ***mpp*** **pour que nous ne** *MPP prohibitif inclusif 1e pers. pl. : "nous et vous", "moi et vous", "nous et toi"*

kwá 5 ***prn*** **nous** *(pronom sélectif 1re pers. inclusif pluriel, utilisé avec le suffixe -sɯ̏)*

kwàa, **kwàȁ** <de *kɔ̏ yāa ? 'mauvaise main'> *le ton final devient extra-bas devant un autre ton extra-bas* ***n rn*** **côté gauche** <u>*Ant.*</u> <u>*kɔ̏sʌ̏*</u> ◊ *yɤ̏ gɯ̀n wɔ̏-sɪʌ ɤ̄ kwàȁ tȁ* il était couché sur le côté gauche ♦ *kwàa gɯ́* à gauche

kwāa 1 ***mpp*** **nous** *MPP prospectif inclusif 1e pers. pl. : "nous et vous", "moi et vous", "nous et toi"*

kwāa 2 ***prn*** **nous** *pronom inclusif 1e pers. pl. : "nous et vous", "moi et vous", "nous et toi" de la série restrictive*

kwāȁ 1 {kwàa} ***v*** **1** *vi* **permettre** *(à – zɯ̏)* **2** *vr* **renoncer** *(à – gérondif + ká, zɯ̏)* ◊ *wà wō kwāȁ dhān-kʌ̄-sɯ̀ ká pɤ̂ bhȁ* ils ont renoncé à leur tentative de s'approcher du village en cachette

kwāȁ 2 ***prn*** **notre**, **nos** *pronom inclusif de la 1e pers. pl. de la série possessive*

kwāȁ 3, **kwāa** ***prn*** *kwāȁ ... -dhɯ̀n* **nous et...** *pronom coordinatif inclusif de 1e pers. duel ou pl.* ◊ *kwāȁ dhēbʌ̏-dhɯ̀n* nous et une femme; nous et des femmes

kwāȁ 4 ***mpp*** **nous** *MPP inclusif du 1re pers. pl. de la série présomptive*

kwáa ***mpp*** **nous ne** *MPP négatif imperfectif inclusif 1e pers. pl. : "nous et vous", "moi et vous", "nous et toi"*

kwāáa, **kwākwáa**, **kwāyáa** ***prn*** **nous** *pronom inclusif 1re pers. pl., "nous et vous", de la série focalisée négative (la forme kwāyáa est peu usitée)*

kwáāa ***mpp*** **nous (et vous) ne** *(forme fusionnée des marqueurs prédicatifs négatif et prospectif de la 1 pers. inclusive, pluriel)*

kwàan *v vt* **voler** *(dérober)*

kwāȁn {kwàan} <Intensif de kwa̋n 'gratter'> *v vt* **gratter** *(pour enlever)* ◊ *gbɔ̄ ɤ́ yā bhán' bhȁ-kwāȁn* cette marmite-ci, j'en ai gratté le fond ♦ *n̄ gblűűdhɛ̏ yɤ̏ n̄ kwāȁn-sīʌ* j'ai des gargouillements *(de faim)*

kwāȁnkwāȁn {kwàankwàan} *v vt* **gratter** *(très fort, pour enlever tout)*

kwākwáa → kwāáa *pas nous (incl.)*

kwàn ***n*** **vol** *(appropriation par la force ou la fraude)*

kwa̋n {kwȁn} *v vt* **éplucher**

kwànbhɛ̏n <vol-personne> ***n*** **voleur**

kwa̋nŋ̏, **kwǽænŋ̏**, **kwɛ̋nŋ̏** ***n*** *dans les mots composés* **concession** *Iv. (cour dont les habitants partagent le même totem)* ♦ *kwa̋nŋ̏ gɔ̏ dhíɤ bhɛ̏n, kwa̋nŋ̏ dʌ̄* chef de concession, chef de famille ♦ *kwa̋nŋ̏ dhē* mère de famille ♦ *kwa̋nŋ̏ dō gúu bhɛ̏n-dhȕn* membres d'un clan ♦ *dhó kwa̋nŋ̏ píɤ* aller se promener

kwa̋nŋ̏dhɛ̏, **kwǽænŋ̏dhɛ̏**, **kwɛ̋nŋ̏dhɛ̏** {LOC kwa̋nŋ̏dhɤ̄, kwǽænŋ̏dhɤ̄, kwɛ̋nŋ̏dhɤ̄; kwɛ̋ɛ (t)} ***loc.n*** **concession** *Iv.*, **cour** *pour la forme du cas locatif, un redoublement à valeur d'intensivité de l'action est possible* ◊ *yɤ̏ dhīaŋ bhā' gɔ̏-dɔ̏ ɤ̄ gɔ̏ kwa̋nŋ̏dhɤ̄* il a terminé son discours dans sa cour *[il est approprié de régler les affaires importantes à la maison, plutôt qu'au bureau]* ◊ *bhān gbɛ̂ndhʌ́n yɤ̏ kwɛ̋nŋ̏dhɤ̄-kwɛ̋nŋ̏dhɤ̄, yáa dhó dhɛ̏ bhá gúu* mon chien est toujours dans la cour, il ne va nulle part ♦ *kwa̋nŋ̏dhɛ̏ dʌ̄ bhɛ̏n* chef de concession, chef de famille

kwa̋nŋ̏dhɤ̄, **kwǽænŋ̏dhɤ̄**, **kwɛ̋nŋ̏dhɤ̄**, **kwɛ̋ɛ** (t) ***loc.n*** *LOC de* kwa̋nŋ̏dhɛ̏ *concession*

kwāyáa → kwāáa *pas nous (incl.)*

kwǽænŋ̏, kwǽænŋ̏dhɛ̏, kwǽænŋ̏dhɤ̄ → kwa̋nŋ̏dhɛ̏, kwa̋nŋ̏dhɤ̄ *concession*

kwʌ́ʌ̏ ***loc.n*** *SUP de* kó 1 *l'un l'autre*

kwʌ̋ʌ ***loc.n*** *COM de* kó 1 *l'un l'autre*

kwʌ́ʌ̏dhɤ̄ ***loc.n*** *LOC de* kó 1 *l'un l'autre*

kwʌ̄ŋ̋ ***n*** *rn* **bosse** *(sur le dos)* Syn. dhàŋ

kwēɛ̋ ***prn*** **notre** *(pronom inclusif possessif honorifique)* ◊ *kwēɛ̋ kwa̋nŋ̏dhɤ̄* dans notre cour (resp.)

kwēɛ̋bhɛ̏n-dhȕn <1 pluriel.inclusif.respectueux-personne-pluriel> ***n*** **chers parents** *(terme affectif utilisé envers parents et voisins)* ◊ *yɤ́' pɤ̄ kwēɛ̋bhɛ̏n-dhȕn dhɛ̏ bhāa, kȁ wlūűű kwá dhó Sáŋ̏tàa* il a dit à ses proches : "Levez-vous, allons à Santa"

kwēedhʌ́n ***n*** **bouteille de calebasse** ♦ *kwēedhʌ́n bhɔ̄* le goulot de la bouteille

kwɛ̋ekwɛ̏ekwēɛ̋dhɤ̄ ***onomat*** *imitation du cri de nombreuses souris*

kwɛ̀ŋbhìʌ ***n*** **il y a longtemps**

kwɛ̏ ***n*** **1 an, année** ◊ *Zân yɤ̏ zɔ́ bhö kwɛ̏ bhà̈* Jean extrait le miel tous les ans ◊ *yɤ̏ dhö klàŋ dhíɤ kɤ̄' kwɛ̏ yɤ̏ sɶ̋ɶ̏plɛ̀* il est allé à l'école quand il avait sept ans ♦ *kwɛ̏ ɤ́ zìɤ à̈ ká* l'année dernière ♦ *à̈ bhɔ̄ kwɛ̏ yɤ̏ dhɛ̀ ?* quelle est l'année de sa naissance **2** *rn* **âge** ♦ *à̈ kwɛ̏ yɤ̏ dhɛ̀ ?* quel âge a-t-il ?

kwɛ̋dhɛ̋n ***n*** **calcul** ♦ *kwɛ̋dhɛ̋n kʌ̄* calculer

kwɛ̏ɛ ***n*** **1 vieillard** Syn. kwɛ̏ɛdhʌ́n ◊ *Zân yà̈ kʌ̄ kwɛ̏ɛ ká* Zan est devenu vieillard **2 ancêtre** *[on croit que les ancêtres ne meurent pas, mais continuent leur vie dans la case sacrée, gűnŋkɔ̈]*

kwɛ̏ɛ̏ 1 *le ton change facultativement à ton bas devant le ton moyen* ***n rn*** **fardeau, charge, bagage** /v. ◊ *kwɛ̀ɛ sūu ɤ́ á' sū yāandhíɤ, yɤ̏ gùn zìizʌ̀* le fardeau dont je m'étais chargé hier était énorme ◊ *yɤ̏ ɤ̄ kwɛ̏ɛ̏ dhú-sīʌ* il est en train d'attacher son bagage

kwɛ̏ɛ̏ 2 ***loc.n*** *SUP de* kɔ̈ 1 *main*

kwɛ̄ɛ 1 <de *kwɛ̏ yā à̈ ká> ***adv*** **cette année** ◊ *bhíin dhó bá̈à̈ dhɛ̏ kʌ̄' kwɛ̄ɛ* je ne vais pas faire de champ au bas-fond cette année

kwɛ̄ɛ 2 ***n*** **remisse, lice** *(du métier à tisser)*

kwɛ̄ɛ̋ <de *kɔ̈ dhɛ̋ ? 'main-feuille'> ***loc.n*** **1.1** *rn* **bras** *(du coude à la main)* Syn. gbɛ̀, kɔ̈ ◊ *yà̈ à̈ kún kwɛ̄ɛ̋* il l'a pris par la main ♦ *n̄ kwɛ̄ɛ̋ yɤ̏ sʌ̀ gbɔ̋ɔ̏ zùɤ-sù bhà̈* je sais bien lancer les projectiles avec la fronde ♦ *ɤ̄ kwɛ̄ɛ̋ kún à̈ bhà̈* applaudir qn/qch ♦ *à̈ kwɛ̄ɛ̋ yà̈ sìɤ* sa cuisine n'a pas réussi **1.2** *rn* **patte de devant, pattes de devant** *(d'un animal)* Syn. kɔ̈ **2** *dhű kwɛ̄ɛ̋* **branche** *(petite)*

kwɛ̋ɛ ***n*** **porte** *(en bois, bambou)* Qsyn. kpóŋ̏ ◊ *yɛ̋n ɤ́' bɔ̄ kwɛ̋ɛ píɤ ɤ́ dhō dhɛ̏ gà̈'*il a regardé à travers les fentes de la porte et il a vu... ♦ *kwɛ̋ɛ tɛ̀* porte non-attachée (sans gondes ni pentures) faite de pétioles de raphia ♦ *dhàklɛ́e dà̈ kwɛ̋ɛ gú* mets la clé dans la serrure ♦ *kwɛ̋ɛ pìɤgā* gond

kwɛ̏ɛdhʌ́n <ancêtre-diminutif> ***n*** **vieillard** Syn. kwɛ̏ɛ ◊ *yà kʌ̄ kwɛ̏ɛdhʌ́n kɔ̄ŋ̋kɔ̄ŋ̋ ká* il est très vieux

kwɛ̄ɛdhʌ́n 1 ***n*** **métier à tisser**

kwɛ̏ɛdhʌ́n-dhɛ̏ <vieillard-abstr.> ***n*** **vieillesse** *(d'un homme)*

kwɛ̄ɛ̋dhɛ̏ {LOC kwɛ̄ɛ̋dhɤ̏} <de *kɔ̈-gú-dhɛ̏ 'main-dans-lieu'> ***loc.n*** *rn* **poignet** ◊ *yà̈a kún à̈ kwɛ̄ɛ̋dhɤ̏* il l'a attrapé par le poignet

kwɛ̋ɛdhɛ̏ {LOC kwɛ̋ɛdhɤ̏} <porte-endroit> ***loc.n*** **espace près du mur** *(sous le bord de la toiture)* ◊ *yɤ̏ dɔ̄-sīʌ kwɛ̋ɛdhɤ̏* il est debout sous le bord de la toiture ♦ *gwān kwɛ̋ɛdhɛ̏* vie conjugale *(d'une femme)* ♦ *gwān kwɛ̋ɛdhɛ̏ yà kʌ̄ Yɔ̏ bhà̈ gbɛ̋ɛ̏* la vie conjugale de Yo est devenue difficile

kwɛ̄ɛ̋dhɤ̏ *LOC de* kwɛ̄ɛ̋dhɛ̏ *poignet*

kwɛ̀ɛgbɤ̄ <vieux-fils> ***n*** **sage; papa** *lv. (forme d'adresse d'un homme à un homme considérablement plus âgé) [dans la bouche d'une femme cela sonne ironique]*

kwɛ̄ɛ̋ndhɤ̄ ***onomat*** **fracas** *(bois cassé)* ◊ *dhű̋ yà̰ yɛ́ kwɛ̄ɛ̋ndhɤ̄* l'arbre s'est cassé avec fracas

kwɛ̀ɛnkwɛ̋ɛn ***n*** **froissement** ♦ *kwɛ̀ɛnkwɛ̋ɛn kʌ̄* froisser ◊ *sʌ́ʌdhɛ́ yà kwɛ̀ɛnkwɛ̋ɛn kʌ̄* le papier est tout froissé

kwɛ̋nŋ̏ ***n*** → kwa̋nŋ̏ *concession*

kwɛ̋nŋ̏dhɛ̏ ***loc.n*** → kwa̋nŋ̏dhɛ̏ *concession*

kwɛ̋nŋ̏dhɤ̄ ***loc.n*** *LOC de* kwa̋nŋ̏dhɛ̏ *concession*

kwɛ̀ŋ̏ ***loc.n*** *SUP de* kɔ̏ 1 *main*

kwɛ̄ŋ̏, **kwɛ̄ŋ** ***prn*** **toi et moi** *pronom coordinatif incorporant*

kwɛ̄ŋ̏-dhȕn, **kwɛ̄ŋ-dhȕn** ***prn*** **nous (incl.) et lui**, **nous (incl.) et elle**, **nous (incl.) et eux**, **nous (incl.) et elles** *pronom coordinatif incorporant*

kwɛ̀ŋ̏kwɛ̀ŋ̏ ***loc.n*** *SUP.INT de* kɔ̏ 1 *main*

kwɛ̀ŋzű <an- ?-encore> ***adv*** *arch.* **autrefois**

kwɛ̏yɤ̏kódhɪ́ɤ <an-voir-l'un l'autre-devant> ***n*** **anniversaire**

kwɛ̏zlȁan <an-Dieu> ***n*** **histoire, conte** *(récit portant sur des événements dont le conteur n'a pas été témoin)* ♦ *kwɛ̏zlȁan bhō* raconter une histoire

kwī {kwȉ} ***n*** **1** *rn* **peau** ♦ *à̰ kwī yà kún* il a de la fièvre **2** *rn* **corps**

kwí ***mpp*** **nous**, **moi et toi** *MPP 2e pers. inclusive de la la série de conséquence négative*

kwɪ́ ***n*** **1 homme blanc** *(de race blanche ou mongoloïde; les Arabes n'y sont pas compris)* ♦ *kwɪ́ pű̋u* homme blanc, un Blanc ♦ *kwɪ́ sɛ́* pays des Blancs **2.1 citadin** *(représentant de la civilisation urbaine)* ♦ *kwɪ́ sɛ́* ville (en opposition au village) **2.2 fonctionnaire** *(celui qui a un travail intellectuel)* ◊ *à̰ gbàn wɔ̀ kwɪ́ gblɤ́gblɤ́ ká* ils sont tous des grands fonctionnaires ♦ *kwɪ́ yʌ̀* travail de bureau, travail qualifié

kwɪ́gblʌ̄ʌ̀n <homme blanc-intestin> ***n*** *iron.* **macaroni** *(mot du langage villageois)* <u>*Syn.* *bhānklɔ̄ɔdhîn*</u> ♦ *kwɪ́gblʌ̄ʌ̀n gā* un macaroni

kwíi ***mpp*** **nous ne** *MPP négatif inclusif 1re pers. pl. du passé : "nous et vous", "moi et vous", "nous et toi"*

kwīkúnyȕa <peau-attraper-maladie> ***n*** **fièvre**

kwɪ́plɤ̀ɤ ***loc.n*** *LOC de* kwɪ́plɤ̀ɤdhɛ̏ *ville*

kwɪ́plɤ̀ɤdhɛ̏ {LOC kwɪ́plɤ̀ɤ} <Blanc-chez-place> ***loc.n*** **ville** *(pour un villageois, n'importe quelle ville; pour un citadin, une ville dans le pays des Blancs)* <u>*Syn.*</u> <u>*kwɪ́pɤ̂*</u> ◊ *kwɪ́plɤ̀ɤdhɛ̏ yà kʌ̄ yâ* la vie en ville est devenue dangereuse

kwĩpɤ̏ <homme.blanc-village> ***n*** **ville** *(pour un villageois, n'importe quelle ville; pour un citadin, une ville dans le pays des Blancs)* Syn. *kwĩplɤ̏ɤdhɛ̏* ◊ *kwĩpɤ̏ yā yà kʌ̄ kpĩĩ* cette ville est devenue grande

kwīzʌ̄gā <peau-tuer-os ?> ***n*** **cola rose** *[plus chère que la cola rouge; utilisée pour les sacrifices]* Syn. *vɔ̏ɔ*

kwlǽætǽn ***n*** **chant et danse des chanteurs de chasse**

kwlʌ̋nŋ → kplʌ̋nŋ *compte-rendu*

L 1

là ***n*** **1 foulard** *(de cou, de tête)* ♦ *yà là yȁ* elle a mis un foulard sur sa tête **2 épaulette** *(grade)* ♦ *wȁ là dhʌ̀nŋ ȁ gbān tȁ* i) on lui a octroyé un grade (militaire) ii) il a été élevé en grade ♦ *wȁ ȁ bhȁ là tāa kʌ̄* il a été élevé en grade ♦ *wȁ ȁ bhȁ là dȁ dhĩɤ* il a été élevé en grade (militaire) ♦ *wȁ ȁ bhȁ là lɔ̄ɔ* il a été dégradé **3 médaille** ♦ *wȁ là dhʌ̀nŋ ȁ tȍŋ tȁ* on l'a décoré ♦ *ȁ là yɤ̏ ȁ gɔ̏* il est spécialiste dans ça

lāa ***n*** **lion** ♦ *lāa yɤ̏ gblȁn* le lion rugit

làagā ***n*** **poisson** *(esp. : jusqu'à 20-25 cm, le corps est allongé et brillant)* ♦ *làagā bhɛ̄* gros poisson "laaga"

làklɛ̋e → dhàklɛ̋e *clé*

lánklʌ̏ <Fr. encre> ***n*** **encre**

láyì → āǻyì *ail*

lʌ̋ʌlʌ̏ʌ {P} ***adj*** **lent** *(comme un escargot ou une tortue)* ◊ *dlȕnŋ yɤ̏ lʌ̋ʌlʌ̏ʌ* l'escargot est lent

lʌ̏ʌn ***n*** ***Scodra griseipes, Stromatopelma calceata*** **mygale** *(araignée venimeuse)*

lēbēlɤ̏ <Fr. rebelle> ***n*** **rebelle,** *(surtout pendant la guerre civile 2003-2011)*

lɛ̋ɛdhɤ̄ {Int. lɛ̋ɛɛdhɤ̄, SupInt. lɛ̋ɛlɛ̋ɛdhɤ̄} ***adv*** **1 lentement** *(plus lentement que la normale)* ◊ *yɤ̏ bȅŋ sȕ lɛ̋ɛdhɤ̄* il court lentement **2 légèrement**, **doucement** ◊ *kɛ̋ɛ yɤ́ yɛ̋e tō lɛ̋ɛdhɤ̄* mais il rit doucement

lɛ̋ɛɛdhɤ̄ ***adv*** *Int. de* lɛ̋ɛdhɤ̄ *lentement*

lɛ̋ɛlɛ̋ɛdhɤ̄ ***adv*** *SupInt. de* lɛ̋ɛdhɤ̄ *lentement*

lɛ̄ŋdâ ***n*** **poison** *(de fabrication industrielle; utilisé à la pêche et contre les aulacodes)*

lōbīdhɛ̂n, **wlōbīdhɛ̂n** <Fr. robinet> ***n*** **robinet** ◊ *yĩ yɤ̏ gó-sīʌ lōbīdhɛ̂n gṹ* l'eau est en train de couler du robinet

lòo ***v*** **1.1** 1) *vi* **arriver** Qsyn. *dhūn* ◊ *... kɤ̄ bhán lòo tɔ̏n gbȅŋ gṹ ...* lorsque je suis arrivé au vallon ♦ *lòo kó tȁ* se rassembler, se réunir 2) *vt* *lòo kó tȁ* **rassembler** ◊ *Tòkpȁ yà bhɛ̄n gbɛ́ lòo kó tȁ fɛ̄tɤ̏ kʌ̄-yàn gṹ* Tokpa a rassemblé beaucoup de gens à la fête **1.2** *vi* **atteindre** ◊ *ȁ bhȁ wūn yɤ̏ lȍo ȁ bhɔ̄ pĩɤ [ȁ gbān tȁ, ȁ kpȍŋ dhĩɤ]* ses cheveux lui atteignent le cou [les épaules, le front] ◊ *sɔ̄ búʌ̏ŋbȕʌŋ̏ ɤ́ lòo bhɛ̄n gȅn pĩɤ* vêtement long qui arrive jusqu'aux pieds ◊ *dɔ̄ ȁ gɔ̏ gbɛ́ɛ̏, kɤ̄ ɯ́ lòo ȁ gwìnŋ̄dhɤ̄* fais un effort pour atteindre le sommet **1.3** *vi* **visiter**, **passez** *(chez – pɯ́ɤ)* **2.1** *vt* **mettre**, **verser** *(dans un récipient)* ◊ *yà sáŋ̏sɯ̏ lòo pòpòdhîn gɯ́* il a mis du carburant dans la mobylette **2.2** *vi* **se jeter** *(sur – tȁ)* **2.3** *vi* **embrasser** *(serrer dans ses bras; qn – bhȁ)* ♦ *lòo wō kwʌ́ʌ̏* s'embrasser, s'étreindre **2.4** *vt pʌ̄ lòo ɤ̄ kwɛ̄ɛ̏* **prendre qch entre les mains** **3** *vi* **apparaître** *(dermatose)* ◊ *bhlɯ̏ndhɯ́ɤ yà lòo ȁ bhȁ* il a attrapé la variole / varicelle **4** *vi* **s'effeuiller**, **tomber** *(feuilles)* ♦ *ȁ bɯ́n yà lòo* ses fleurs sont tombées **5** 1) *vi* **devenir paralysé** *(partie du corps)* ◊ *ȁ gɛ̏n yà lòo* il est paralysé des jambes 2) *vt* **bloquer**, **immobiliser** ◊ *kwȁ kwā tó lòo kɤ̄ kwá dhó dhīaŋ bhā ȁ bhān'* bouchons-nous les oreilles pour ne pas entendre ces paroles **6** *vi lòo kóo* **se confondre** ♦ *lòo bhɛ̄n gɔ̏ kóo* se confondre dans la tête de qn **7** *vi lòo ȁ gɯ́* **se mettre** *(à – ká)* ◊ *yà lòo' gɯ́ gbɔ̋ ká* il s'est mit à pleurer **8.1** *vi* **s'adresser** *(à – bhȁ)* **8.2** *vt* **communiquer** *(à – bhȁ)*, **informer de** *(qn – bhȁ)*

lōzɯ́ȁ → ālōzóȁ *arrosoir*

lɔ̄ɔ 1 {lɔ̀ɔ} ***v*** 1) *vi* **descendre** ♦ *yà lɔ̄ɔ dhɯ́ɯ́ [bhīʌ́ʌgā] bhȁ* il est descendu par un arbre [par une corde] ◊ *dhāyɪ́ yɤ̏ lɔ̄ɔ-sīʌ tɔ̏n bhȁ* l'eau de la pluie est en train de descendre de la montagne 2) *vt* **descendre de** ◊ *yɤ́ wó tɔ̏n lɔ̀ɔ...* et ils sont descendus de la montagne ◊ *dhīaŋ pɛ̄pɛ́ ɤ́ wó gūn' zʌ̄-sīʌ' dhɛ̏ bhā, yɤ̏ kʌ̄' zūʌ́ lɔ̀ɔ* tout ce qu'on lui disait ravivait sa douleur *(litt. : faisait descendre son cœur)*

lɔ̄ɔ 2 ***n*** **herbe** *(esp. : jusqu'à 2, des feuilles larges utilisées pour envelopper l'attiéké; la pellicule de la tige sert comme lien pour faire des pièges, pour lier des gerbes de riz)* ♦ *lɔ̄ɔ tīi* = lɔ̄ɔ

lɔ̄ɔ̋gā ***n*** **chaîne**

lɤ̏ ***v vt*** **attacher**, **ligoter** Qsyn. kplɯ̏ Ant. pɔ̋

lɤ́ɤ̏ ***n*** **serpent** *(esp.; noir, long, ni venimeux ni agressif, vit dans l'eau) [comestible]*

M m

mōtô <Fr. moto> ***n*** **motocycle, moto**

N n

n̄ ***prn*** **me**, **mon**, **ma** *pronom non-sujet de la 1re pers. sg.*

Ŋ ŋ

-ŋ̏ 1 → -dhȁan 2 *suffixe de l'ultérieur*

-ŋ̏ 2 → -dhȁan 3 *suffixe du progressif subordonné*

-ŋ̄ (m) ***mrph*** *suffixe du nom verbal, s'attache au verbe à sa forme de base dans la construction durative*

ŋ̄bhɛ́ɛ̏ɛ̏ ***onomat*** **bêe** *son de bêlement du mouton* ♦ *bhlɑ̃́a yɤ̏ wɛ̏ n̄bhɛ́ɛɛ̏* le mouton a bêlé

ŋ̄bhúȕu ***onomat*** **meuh** *(cri de la vache)*

Ŋdhōɛdhɤ̏ <Fr. Noël> ***n*** **Noël**

ŋ̏hű̃un → àahɑ̃́an *d'accord*

ŋ̏ŋ̋ ***intj*** **oui** *réponse à une question affirmative ou négative* <u>*Syn.*</u> <u>*ìi*</u>

O o

ȍo ***prt*** *marque d'empathie*

őo ***conj*** **n'importe quel**, **quel que soit** *joint deux noms identiques ou deux marqueurs dhɛ́ ... dhɛ́ pour former un syntagme distributif :* ◊ *yɤ̏ dɔ̏ tőo őo tőo ɤ́ dhɤ́ à kʌ̄dhɛ̏ ká /yɤ̏ dɔ̏ tőo dhɛ́ őo dhɛ́ ɤ́ dhɤ́ à kʌ̄dhɛ̏ ká* elle sait préparer n'importe quelle sauce

ōo, ... ōo ***conj*** **et ..., et** *marqueur de coordination des groupes nominaux en énumération non exhaustive*

Ɔ ɔ

ɔ̄ɔ́ ***intj*** **ah** *(exclamation pour rassurer l'interlocuteur)*

Ɤ ɤ

ɤ̄ 1 ***mpp*** **il**, **elle** *MPP existentiel logophorique sg.*

ɤ̄ 2 ***prn*** **1 se**, **son**, **sa**, **soi** *pronom réfléchi singulier* **2** *formatif marquant la jonction entre dizaines et unités dans la constitution des numéraux composés* ◊ *tɔ̏ kœ̏œŋ̏ sɑ̃́ɑ̏gā ɤ̄ gā sœ̃́œ̏dō* quatre-vingt six poules

ɤ́ 1 ***conj*** *conjonction introduisant une proposition relative, l'article défini, les pronoms démonstratifs* <u>*Qsyn.*</u> <u>*kɤ́*</u> <u>*2*</u>

ɤ́ 2, **yɤ́** ***mpp*** **il**, **elle** *MPP de la 3e pers. sg. de la série conjointe, peut être omis facultativement*

ɤ́ 3 ***mpp*** **il**, **elle** *MPP logophorique sg. de la série conjointe*

ɤ́ 4 ***conj*** **1 quand** *(apparaît au début d'une proposition à marque prédicative de la série conjointe, marque la simultanéité d'une action au passé avec l'action d'une autre proposition; facultatif dans la majorité des contextes;)* ◊ *ɤ́ Yɔ̏ ɤ́ à tà-kún-sīʌ, kɤ̄ ā' tà-kún-sīʌ* quand Yo l'aidait, je l'aidais aussi **2 si** ◊ *ɤ́ dīn ɤ́ ɯ̄ bhȁ, bhá dhɤ́ yʌ̄ kʌ̄'* si tu as faim, ne travaille pas **3** *(souvent en combinaison avec la conjonction dhɛ̀)* **comme**, **puisque** *(valeur de cause)* ◊ *dhɛ̀ ɤ́ dīn ɤ́ ɯ̄ bhȁ, bhá dhɤ́ yʌ̄ kʌ̄'* comme tu as faim, ne travaille pas ◊ *ɤ́ Gɤ̀ɤ̏ yáa yʌ̄ kʌ̄...* puisque Geu ne travaille pas... ◊ *kɤ̄ dhā yɤ̏ à tɔ̀ɔ, yɤ́ ɤ́ Gɤ̀ɤ̏ ɤ́ dȁ dhā gɯ́* c'est pour se mouiller que Geu est entré sous la pluie

ɤ́ 5 *forme fusionnée : conjonction relative + marque prédicative 3e pers. sg. de la série conjointe*

ɤ́ 6 → yɤ́ 1 *conjonction consécutive*

ɤ́ 7 ***conj*** *forme fusionnée : conjonction relative + marque prédicative 3e pers. sg. de la série conjointe*

ɤ̋ ***mpp*** **il, elle** *MPP logophorique sg. de la série subjonctive*

ɤ̄ɤ, ɤ́ɤ, yɤ́ɤ, ɤ̄ɤ̏ ***intj*** **eh bien** *(marque le passage à l'essentiel)*

ɤ́ɤ que, pour que *doit être suivi d'une MPP de la série subjonctive* Syn. *kɤ̄* ◊ *kɛ́ɛ wɔ́n dhɛ́ ɤ́ kʌ̀ dhɛ̀ ūū' dɔ̏ ɤ́ɤ úú' pɤ̄...* mais l'autre affaire qui est ici, ce que tu en connais, raconte-le...

ɤ̄ɤdʌ̄ ***n*** **lézard** *(noir-vert, ressemble à un varan; au début de la saison sèche, lance des cris stridents : "ɤ̄-ɤ̄-ɤ̄") [son cri est interprété comme le signe que la fin de la récolte est arrivée; non comestible]*

P p

pā 1 {pā} ***v*** **1** 1) *vi* **se remplir** ◊ *kɔ̏ɔ yà pā yí ká* la calebasse s'est remplie d'eau 2) *vt* **remplir** ◊ *yí yȁ bàŋ pā* la bassine est remplie d'eau ◊ *dhʌ́n-dhȕn fɛ̏ɛsȕ-dhȕn wà kɔ́ pā tīi̋dhɤ̏* des enfants bruyants ont rempli la maison là-bas **2** *vi* **déborder** *(d'un cours d'eau)* ◊ *yí yȁ pā Gɤ̏ɤ̏ bhȁ* l'eau a innondé la maison de Geu

pā 2 {pā} ***v*** **1** *vt* **laper, lécher** ◊ *tőo pā !* lèche la sauce ! **2** *vt* **sucer** Qsyn. *flɛ̄ɛn*

pá {pā} ***v*** **1** *vt* **toucher** *(avec qch; qch, qnn. – ká) le complément d'objet direct à valeur d'instrument s'incorpore au verbe, son attribut porte sur le groupe verbal entier* ◊ *bhán ñ kɔ̏ pá ñ sɔ́n ká* j'ai touché mes dents ◊ *bhɤ̏ dhű sɛ̄ɛ́ndhʌ́n pá à ká* touche-le légèrement avec un bâton **2** *vi* **réveiller** *(qn – bhȁ)* ◊ *wɔ́n ɤ́ yà kʌ̄ zīkízìkì dhún bhā yɤ́ yà pá' bhȁ dɛ̀ɛ* il a aujourd'hui remis sur le tapis cette très très vieille affaire **3** *vi pá ɤ̄ dȅ ká* **bouger**

pȁa ***n*** **rameau de palmier** ♦ *pȁa dhíɤ* (t) sommet d'un arbre

pa̋a ***n*** **arbre** *(esp.; utilisé comme bois à brûler)*

pa̋an ***n*** **sangsue** ◊ *pa̋an yà dhʌ̀nŋ à gȅn bhȁ* une sangsue s'est collée à son pied

pāanpāandhɤ̄ ***onomat*** **tuut** *(klaxon de voiture)* ◊ *gɔ̄ yɤ̏ wɛ́-sīʌ pāanpāandhɤ̄* le véhicule klaxonne

pādhīféŋ̏ <Fr. parfum> ***n*** **parfum** *(substance)* ◊ *pādhīféŋ̏ fìi yȁ yȁ sʌ̀* la fragrance du parfum se répand

pàŋ <Fr. pantalon> ***n*** **pantalon**

pápádhɤ̄ {Int. páppádhɤ̄} ***adv*** **1 très** *(blanc)* **2** *toujours à la forme intensive* **clairement, de façon compréhensible** ◊ *tæ̏æ̀nwɔ̏n pűu páppádhɤ̄ bhȕn* c'est la pure vérité

pa̋pő *n* **papot, papo** *(panneau de feuilles de raphia, de palmier à huile ou de cocotier, entrelacées, sert à couvrir les toits ou à faire des cloisons)* ♦ *pa̋pő dhɛ̋* panneau de papot ♦ *pa̋pő bɛ̏* pile de papot

páppádhɤ̄ *Int. de* pápádhɤ̄ *très blanc*

pāsē {pāsē; NEUT pāsè} <Fr. passer> *v vt* **passer** *(examen)*

pa̋sɛ̋ *n* **repassage** ♦ *sɔ̄ pa̋sɛ̋ bhɔ̄* repasser des habits

pāsēdhē <Fr. passer> *n* **examen** Syn. gīzābhɛ̂n

pāsɤ́ <Fr. parce que> *conj* **parce que**

pæ̋æn → pɛ̋ɛn *partie*

pʌ̄ {pʌ̀; pʌ́ REL} *n* **1.1 chose** ◊ *síasíabhā yɤ́ pʌ́-dhùn bhā ɤ́'-dhùn gbàn pɛ́pɛ́ ɤ́ slɔ̀ɔ* toutes ces choses qui ont été trouvées immédiatement... ♦ *pʌ̄ pɪ́ɤ pʌ̀* nourriture secondaire **1.2 ce qui** *nom explétif fonctionnant comme tête d'une proposition relative, à ton haut* **1.3 quelque chose** *(fonctionne à l'instar d'un pronom indéfini)* ◊ *bhá dhó pʌ̄ sɯ́' ɯ̄ kɔ̏ kpʌ́ʌkpʌ̀ʌ bhā' ká* ne prends rien avec la main engourdie **2 portion** ♦ *tòo pʌ̀* portion de tô **3 fois** ♦ *dhɛ̀ pʌ̄ dhɤ́ kœ̀œŋ* environ dix fois **4 monstre, génie** *(créature surnaturelle)*

pʌ̄ʌ *n rn vulg.* **vulve, con** ! ! ! Syn. gwɛ̋nŋ, slōo

pʌ́ʌ *n* **la chose qui** *seulement dans l'expression :* ♦ *pʌ́ʌ kʌ̀ ... yɤ́ bhā* c'est pourquoi ◊ *pʌ́ʌ kʌ̀ tɔ̏n bhā wó' dhɛ̏ Gbádhīʌʌ plɤ̀ɤ bhā yɤ́ bhā* c'est pourquoi la montagne est nommée Gbadieupleu

pʌ̄bɪ̋n <chose-ombre> *n* **image, dessin, photographie, photo**

pʌ̄bhèe *n* **nourriture** ◊ *dhūn kɤ̄ kwá pʌ̄bhèe bhɤ̏* viens, mangeons ◊ *pʌ̄bhèe yɤ̏ kpɔ́ɔŋ̏kpɔ̏ɔŋ* le repas est tiède

pʌ̄bhɛ̏n *n* **personne aisée** *(qui peut ne pas manifester sa richesse)*

pʌ̀-kʌ̄ <chose-faire> *v* **1** *vt* **fabriquer**, **faire**, **créer** ◊ *yà bɛ̀dhɛ̋ yāa pʌ̀-kʌ̄* il a fabriqué le poison / le procédé de magie noire **2** (m) *vi* **mûrir** Syn. tān **3.1** *vt* **réparer** Syn. bāa̋ ◊ *yáa kʌ̄ bhān gɔ̄ pʌ̀-kʌ̄* il n'a pas réparé ma voiture **3.2** *vt* **réparer**, **rapiécer** ◊ *yà pàŋ pʌ̀ dhʌ̀n' kʌ̄* c'est le pantalon qu'elle a raccommodé

pʌ̄kúnpʌ̀ <chose-attraper-chose> *n arch.* **carnassier** Syn. wūkúnwɯ̏

pʌ̄-yà <chose-mettre> *v* **écrire** Syn. pʌ̄ bɛ̏n (bɛ̏n 1) ◊ *yɤ̀ kʌ̄ pʌ̄-yà-sɯ̏ dlàan va̋andhɤ̄* il a vite appris à écrire

pɛ̏ 1) *v* 1) *vi* **vomir** *(de – ká)* 2) *vt* **faire vomir**

pɛ̏ 2) *n* **nausée** ♦ *pɛ̏ dhɔ̏ yà' kʌ̄-sɪʌ* il a mal au coeur ♦ *pɛ̏ yɤ̏ dà-sɪʌ' ká* il a mal au coeur

pēdáyɤ̏ <Fr. pédale> *n* **pédale** ◊ *ä bhà pɪ̀ɤgāsòò pēdáyɤ̏ yà dɔ̄ bīŋbīŋdhɤ̄, ä slʌ̀ʌ gú-dhɛ̏ yà kʌ̄ gbɛ́ɛ̏* les pédales de sa bicyclette sont raides, il est difficile de pédaler

pȅe ***n*** **entonnoir** *(pour verser un médicament liquide, pour transvaser le vin de palme)* ♦ *yà dhɛ̋ pȅe kɤ̄* il a fait un entonnoir avec une feuille ♦ *yȁ pȅe yɤ̄ ɤ̄ yʌ̋nŋ* il a mis le médicament dans son oeil avec un entonnoir

péē <de *pɤ̂ yā gɯ́ 'village ce dans'> ***loc.n*** **dans ce village** ◊ *vàkánŋ̏sɯ̏ gbàn ká klàŋ̏-dhɯ̏n wȍ gȍ Bíyȁ wó dhūn péē* à chaque vacance les écoliers quittent Abidjan et viennent au village ici

pȅdʌ̄ ***num*** **deux** *variante moins usitée, par rapport à plɛ̀, pour se référer à la valeur numérique '2'; n'est pas utilisée pour compter, ni dans les numéraux 12, 102 etc.* *Syn.* *plɛ̀*

pȅegā ***n*** **herminette**

péŋ̏ ***n*** **jumeau**, **jumeaux** *[intelligents et rusés, mais difficiles à éduquer, selon une croyance locale]* ◊ *péŋ̏ dhēbʌ̏-dhɯ̏n plɛ̀* deux jumelles

péŋ̏kpɤ̄ <jumeau ?-balle> ***n*** **balle de feuilles et chiffons** *(pour les jeux traditionnels)* *Syn.* *dhɛ̋kpɤ̄* ◊ *Sáŋ̏tàa dhʌ́n-dhɯ̏n wȍ péŋ̏kpɤ̄ zɯ̏ɤ sɯ̋ bhɯ́ ká sìʌ* à Santa les enfants jouent souvent à la balle de feuilles au clair de lune

péŋ̏pȅŋ, **péŋ̏pȅŋdhʌ́n** ***n*** ***Vanellus spinosus, Hoplopterus s.*** **vanneau armé** *(26 cm, dos et ailes brun terre, côtés du cou et joues blanc pur; un noir sur la poitrine, une calotte noire; queue blanche et large à extrémité noire, pattes noires; proteste bruyamment contre celui qui pénètre son territoire et l'escorte en criant)*

pɛ̋pɛ̋ ***adv*** **complètement** *(blanc)*

pētíkōládhɯ̏ <Fr. petit cola> ***n*** ***Garcinia kola*** **petite cola**

pɛ̋tő <Fr. pelle ?> ***n*** **pelle**

pɛ̋ {pɛ̀} ***v*** **1** 1) *vi* **se fendre** ◊ *n̄ bȅn yà pɛ̋* j'ai les lèvres gercées ♦ *yɤ́ pɛ̀ ȁ-dhɯ̏n zìnŋgɯ́ zœ̄œdhē ká* ils se sont mis à discuter à ce propos ◊ *sɛ́ yȁ pɛ̋ gbʌ̄ʌnŋdhɤ̄* la terre s'est fendue 2) *vt* **fendre**, **casser**, **découper** ♦ *yà ɤ̄ bhā sɔ̄ pɛ̋ dhȁa ká vîȍodhɤ̄* il a taillé son étoffe avec le couteau d'un seul mouvement brusque ♦ *yȁa pɛ̋ bȁŋ ká wʌ̋nŋdhɤ̄* il l'a cassé d'un coup de machette **2** *vt* **déchirer** ♦ *yà n̄ bǐn pɛ̋* il a déchiré ma photo **3** *vi* **tomber en désaccord** ◊ *kɔ́dhí yà pɛ̋, yɤ́ gōo dhɤ́ ɤ̄ wɛ̏ɛ slɔ̀ɔ* si une famille tombe en discorde, la blatte y trouve son compte **4** *vi pɛ̋ yɛ̋ɛ bhȁ* **éclater de rire**

pɛ̋dhē <fendre-nominalis.> ***n*** **1** **division** *(action de diviser)* **2** **désaccord**

pɛ̄ɛ̏ {pɛ̀ɛ} <Intensif de pɛ̋ 'fendre'> ***v*** 1) *vi* **se fendre partout** 2) *vt* **faire fendre partout**

pɛ̋ɛ = pɛ̋pɛ̋ *tout*

pɛ́ɛdhɤ́, **pɛ́ɛ̏dhɤ́** <*pʌ́ ɤ́ yā ȁ dhɤ́ 'cette chose, son existence'> ***intj*** **comme ça** *est introduit par la conjonction dhɛ̀* ◊ *bhʌ̏n ɤ́ kʌ̏ ɯ́ yʌ̄ kʌ̏ dhɛ̀ pɛ́ɛdhɤ́ ?* pourquoi as-tu fait le travail si mal ? ◊ *yʌ̄ yā ȁ kʌ̄ sʌ̏ ká dhɛ̀ pɛ́ɛdhɤ́* fais ce travail bien, comme ceci

pɛ̋ɛ̏dhɯ̏ <Fr. père> ***n*** **prêtre** *(catholique)*, **missionnaire,** *(protestant) [les prêtres et les missionnaires sont vus comme des "Blancs pauvres", on leur attribue l'avarice]* ♦ *bhá pɛ̋ɛ̏dhɯ̏ kȁn !* tu es devenu chiche !

pɛ̋ɛn, pǽæn *n* **1 partie** ♦ *pɛ̋ɛn dō* la moitié ♦ *à pɛ̀-gúː-sùː pɛ̋ɛn yàagā-dhàan* un tiers de qch ♦ *pɛ̋ɛn kpíː* majorité, la majeure partie ♦ *pɛ̋ɛn sɛ̋ɛ̋ndhʌ́n* minorité **2 côté** ◊ *kɔ́ pɛ̋ɛn dō yà wɛ̀nŋ* un mur de la maison s'est écroulé ♦ *sɪ́ɤ pɛ̋ɛn* côté du feu *(dans la case)* ♦ *à pɛ̋ɛn tà* vers cela **3 moitié 4 pays** *(lieu d'habitation)* ◊ *klàŋ̀ ɤ́ bhān zùglù bhà kwāà pɛ̋ɛn tà bhā...* l'école qui est perturbée dans notre pays... **5 parti**

pɛ̋ɛpɛ̋ *dtm Int. de* pɛ̋pɛ̋ *chaque*

pɛ̋ɛpɛ̋dhɤ̄ *adv* **1 très** ◊ *bhá dhī pɛ̋ɛpɛ̋dhɤ̄* tu es très bien habillé Qsyn. dèdèwō **2 complètement, sans laisser le reste** ◊ *Zân yà à gbàn bhɤ̀ pɛ̋ɛpɛ̋dhɤ̄* Zan a tout mangé ◊ *Yɔ̀ yɑ̋n yà zɪ̄ɤ Sàó gúː pɛ̋ɛpɛ̋dhɤ̄* Yo ne respecte pas Sao du tout

pɛ̄ɛ̀pɛ̄ɛ̀ {pɛ̀ɛpɛ̀ɛ, NEUT pɛ̀ɛpɛ̀ɛ} <superintensif de pɛ̋ 'fendre'> *v* 1) *vi* **se fendre partout** 2) *vt* **faire se fendre partout** ◊ *bùu yà à bɛ̀n pɛ̄ɛ̀pɛ̄ɛ̀* à cause de l'harmattan ses lèvres se sont douloureusement gercées

pɛ̋ɛpɛ̋ɛ *n* ***Hirundo senegalensis*** **hirondelle**

pɛ̋-gúː {pɛ̀-gúː} <fendre-dans> *v* 1) *vt* **diviser** 2) *vr* **se diviser** ◊ *wà wō pɛ̋-gúː yàagā* il se sont divisés en trois groupes

pɛ̀n 1 *v vi* **se disperser** ◊ *dhā yà à kʌ̄ dhɤ̋ bhɛ̄n gbàan pɛ̀n* la pluie a dispersé les gens

pɛ̀n 2 *n* **1 ver de cola** ◊ *pɛ̀n yà à bhà gɔ̂ bhɤ̀* le ver a rongé sa cola **2 percebois** *(un insecte volant qui met des larves dans l'écorce, ses vers rongent le bois)*

pɛ̄n *n* **arbre** *(esp.; haut, le bois est très dur; les feuilles tombées rougissent vite)* ◊ *pɛ̀n yáa pɛ̄n bhɤ̀* le percebois ne ronge pas l'arbre "pèn" *(il n'est si bon cheval qui ne bronche)*

pɛ̋n *n* **tranche** *(coupée dans le fil)*, **quartier** *(de fruit, détaché)*, **bande** *(d'étoffe)* Qsyn. kplűː, kpɤ̄ ♦ *pɛ̋n bhō* trancher *(dans le sens du fil)* ♦ *sō pɛ̋n* ruban, bande d'étoffe

pɛ̋ndhɛ̀ *n* **partie** *(de territoire)* ◊ *Kɔ́dīvúà pɛ̋ndhɛ̀ ɤ́ dhűɤ́ yʌ̀n* la partie nord de la Côte d'Ivoire

pɛ̀nŋ (gw), **plɛ̀e, plɛ̀ŋ** (m) *n* **aubergine** Syn. zóŋ̀gā

Pɛ̄ŋ́dhē *n* **Pengdé-Unijambiste** *(un génie de brousse : unijambiste, yeux brillants, couvert de poil très urticant; méchant, tue des gens)*

pɛ̄ŋ *n* **feu** Syn. sɪ́ɤ ◊ *pʌ̄bhèe yɤ̀ pɛ̄ŋ tà* la nourriture est sur le feu ♦ *pɛ̄ŋ dhɛ̋ɛ̀n* langue de feu (petit) ♦ *pɛ̄ŋ dà blűː/yɛ́ ká* mettre feu à la brousse ♦ *pɛ̄ŋ yà* allumer le feu ◊ *pɛ̄ŋ ɤ́' yà bhā dhʌ̀n, à pɛ̄ŋ dà bhā* l'incendie s'est produit à cause du feu qu'il a allumé

pɛ̄ŋgɔ̄n <feu-mâle> *n* **flamme** *(grande)*

pɛ̄ŋkɔ́ <feu-maison> *n* **boîte d'allumettes** Syn. sɪ́ɤkɔ́, tákláa kɔ́

pɛ̄ŋtɛ́ɛ <feu-vent> *n* **fumée** Syn. sɪ́ɤtɛ́ɛ

pɛ̋pɛ̋, pɛ̋ɛ {Int. pɛ̋ɛpɛ̋} *dtm* **tout, chaque** ♦ *gbàn pɛ̋pɛ̋* tous sans exception ◊ *wà zɪ̄ɤ dhɛ̀ gbàn pɛ̋pɛ̋ gúː* ils sont passés partout

pìa *n* **balai** *(de maison; fait de feuilles de raphia)* Qsyn. sɛ̀nŋ

pìa (m) → pìaa *griller*

pīą̋, pīą̋a ***n*** **1** *rn* **chance** *seulement dans les expressions suivantes :* ♦ *ȁ pīą̋ yɤ̏ sʌ̏* il a la chance ♦ *ȁ pīą̋ yɤ̏ yâ* il n'a pas de chance **2 Pia** *(nom masculin, rare)*

pìaa (gw), **pìa** (m) ***v*** *vt* **griller, braiser** *lv. (sur le feu ouvert)* ♦ *kɤ̄ŋ pìaa* braiser du maïs

pìaaglɔ̏ɔ <griller-banane> ***n*** **banane plantain**

pȉāasòȍ → pȉɤgāsòȍ *bicyclette*

pȉan ***n*** **1 conte** *(ce sont souvent les femmes qui disent les contes, accompagnés de refrains, d'une voix chantante)* **2 proverbe** ♦ *pȉan ką̋n* dire un proverbe **3 devinette** ◊ *yȁ pȉan dȁ, ȁ bhlɔ̏ɔ yáa dhɤ́* il a posé une devinette qui n'a pas de réponse

pīą̋sʌ̏bhȅn <chance-bon-personne> ***n*** **homme chanceux**

pīą̋yāȁbhȅn <chance-mauvais-personne> ***n*** **malchanceux** ♦ *pīą̋yāȁbhȅn yáa ȁ pɤ̄ "kō zīaan tȁ plɛ̏" prov.* le malchanceux ne dit pas : "nous sommes deux à faire route ensemble" *(ce qui est une réussite pour l'un, peut être un échec pour l'autre)*

pīʌ̏ʌ ***n*** **son propre village** *dans les mots composés* ♦ *pīʌ̏ʌdhē, pīʌ̏ʌdhēbʌ̏* femme du village ♦ *pīʌ̏ʌdhʌ́n* enfant du village

pīʌ̏ʌbhȅn → pīʌ̏ʌbhīn *personne du même village*

pīʌ̏ʌbhīn, pīʌ̏ʌbhȅn {pl. pīʌ̏ʌbhȅn-dhȕn} ***n*** **personne du même village** ♦ *pīʌ̏ʌbhīn bhȕn kɛ̏* c'est quand même quelqu'un de notre village

pīʌ̏ʌdhɛ̏ {LOC pīʌ̏ʌdhɤ̄} ***loc.n*** **son propre village** ◊ *ā pīʌ̏ʌdhɤ̄, bháan dhɛ̏ŋ plɤ̏ɤ* je suis chez moi, je ne suis pas dans le village d'autrui ♦ *pīʌ̏ʌdhɛ̏ yɤ̏ gbɛ́ɛ̏* le fait d'être du même village, c'est dur *(dans la situation où on est offensé par quelqu'un de son village et où on veut se venger)*

pīʌ̏ʌdhɤ̄ ***loc.n*** *LOC de* pīʌ̏ʌdhɛ̏ *son propre village*

pīʌ̏ʌdhɤ̄kȍ, pīʌ̏ʌkȍ ***n*** **différend, palabre** *lv. (entre les habitants d'un village)* ♦ *pīʌ̏ʌ{dhɤ̄}kȍ yà wlūű* un différend s'est noué au village

pīʌ̏ʌkȍ → pīʌ̏ʌdhɤ̄kȍ *différend*

píʌʌnpȉʌʌn 1) {P S} ***adj*** **mou et rare** *(poils, surtout chez les enfants malades)* ◊ *Tòkpȁ bhȁ wūn dhɛ́ yɤ̏ píʌʌnpȉʌʌn* les cheveux de Tokpa sont mous et rares

píʌʌnpȉʌʌn 2 ***n*** **barbes** *(de plume)* ♦ *tɔ̏ kāȁ {gā} píʌʌnpȉʌʌn* barbes de plumes de poule

pīkéȅdhű <Fr. piquet-arbre> ***n*** **piquet**

pínŋ̏ ***n*** **1.1** *rn* **trace** *Syn. gblőo* ◊ *bhlɛ̀ɛn zīɤ pínŋ̏ dhɛ̀n* voici une trace de serpent ◊ *ȁ bhȁ pàŋ yɤ̏ ȁ kȕn kpēnŋkpēnŋdhɤ̄, ȁ pínŋ̏ yȁ tó' bhȁ* son pantalon le serre fort, il laisse une trace sur son corps **1.2** *rn* **trace** *(résultat d'une activité : une ligne, une inscription, etc.)* ♦ *ȁ pínŋ̏ yɤ̏ sʌ̏* il fait un bon travail *(le champ qu'il a labouré se présente bien)* ♦ *ȁ kɔ̏ pínŋ̏ yɤ̏ sʌ̏* il a une belle main **2 piqûre** *(d'insecte)* ◊ *zēnŋ́ pínŋ̏ yɤ̏ bhēn kȁa* la piqûre de moustique démange **3** *rn* **résultat** *Syn. gblőo* ◊ *ñ pínŋ̏ dhɛ̀n* voici les résultats de mon travail

pīŋŋdhɤ̄ {Int. pīŋŋpīŋŋdhɤ̄, pīnpīndhɤ̄, SupInt pı̏ŋŋkúnpı̏ŋŋkúndhɤ̄, pı̏ŋŋkɔ́pı̏ŋŋkɔ́dhɤ̄} ***adv*** **longtemps** ◊ *yűa yɤ̏ kʌ̄ ȁ kʌ̄ pīŋŋpīŋŋdhɤ̄* la maladie l'a tourmenté longtemps

pīŋŋgāpīŋŋgādhɤ̄ ***adv*** **à maintes reprises**

pı̏ŋŋkɔ́pı̏ŋŋkɔ́dhɤ̄ ***adv*** *SupInt. de* pīŋŋdhɤ̄ *longuement*

pı̏ŋŋkúnpı̏ŋŋkúndhɤ̄ ***adv*** *SupInt. de* pīŋŋdhɤ̄ *longuement*

pīŋŋpīŋŋdhɤ̄, **pīnpīndhɤ̄** ***adv*** *Int. de* pīŋŋdhɤ̄ *longuement*

pīőodhɤ̄ ***adv*** **lentement** *(se calmer)* ◊ *bhȁandhʌ́n-dhȕn wȁ dɔ̄ tűuŋ pīőodhɤ̄* les oiseaux se sont tus petit à petit

pı̏ɔɔndhɤ̄ ***adv*** **à perte de vue** *(pour un espace vide, inhabité)*

pı̏ɤ 1 ***n*** **fer** *Syn.* *pı̏ɤgā* ♦ *pı̏ɤ bı̏* limailles ♦ *pı̏ɤ pűu* fer blanc ♦ *pı̏ɤ tı̄i* fer noir *(lourd et solide)* ♦ *pı̏ɤ bhɔ̄* forger le fer ♦ *pı̏ɤ bhɔ̏ ȁ tȁ pʌ̏* enclume ♦ *Yɔ̏ yɤ̏ pı̏ɤ bhȁn-sīʌ kwʌ́ʌ̏ kɤ̋ŋkɤ̋ŋdhɤ̄* Yo fait cliqueter le fer ♦ *yȁ pı̏ɤ zȕɤ bhɛ̄n bhȁ* il a blessé qn *(avec une machette)*

pı̏ɤ 2 ***v*** **1** ***vi*** **souffler** ♦ *tlűu pı̏ɤ* jouer de la trompe **2** ***vt*** **vanner**

pīɤ̋ ***n*** **ligne de pêche** *Syn.* *pīɤ̋gā* ◊ *yà yúɤ̏ɤ gā dhʌ́n dō súi pīɤ̋ ká* il a attrapé un poisson avec la ligne de pêche ♦ *pīɤ̋ dȁ* pêcher à la ligne ♦ *yúɤ̏ɤ yɤ̏ pīɤ̋ zʌ̄-sīʌ* le poisson mord à l'hameçon ♦ *pīɤ̋ gɑ̋n* tirer la ligne ♦ *yȁ pīɤ̋ dhɤ̋ɤ pʌ̏* amorce *(à la pêche)*

pīɤ̋ (m) ***adv*** **tôt**, **vite**

pɤ́ɤ 1) {Int. pɤ́ɤpɤ́ɤ} ***pp*** **1 chez** ♦ *wà dhūn ūi pɤ́ɤ* il y a des gens qui sont venus te voir ◊ *yɤ̏ kʌ̄ gbēŋ kʌ̏ ɤ̄ bhā dhēbʌ̏ pɤ́ɤ* il a passé la nuit chez sa femme **2.1 dans** *(à l'intérieur)* ◊ *kȁ yɔ̋n bhán ȁ pɤ́ɤ* mettez-y de l'huile **2.2 à** *(localisation générale par rapport à un événement)* ◊ *tɑ̋n pɤ́ɤ* au dancing ♦ *zīaan pɤ́ɤ* sur la route, près de la route **3** *dans une construction locative, exprime le sens "aimer; vouloir"; ce qu'on désire peut être exprimé par une construction verbale subjonctive (l'action dont on cherche la réalisation) ou par un groupe nominal (l'objet désiré)* ◊ *tőo yí kún-sȕi dhʌ̀n úi ȁ pɤ́ɤ ȅe, ɛ̋ɛn ȁ yísȕi ?* aimes-tu une sauce épaisse ou liquide ? **4 pendant**, **en** *Syn.* *ká 1* ◊ *Yɔ̏ yȁ bȁ sű plɛ̀ pɤ́ɤ* Yo a grossi en deux mois ◊ *yɤ̏ ī bȕn kwɛ̏ sɔ̋ɔdhű pɤ́ɤ* il m'a élevé pendant cinq ans **5** *kó pɤ́ɤ* **ensemble** *Qsyn.* *kó kèŋ̏* ◊ *wɔ̏ wō kó pɤ́ɤ* ils vivent au même endroit *(dans la même maison ou dans la même ville)*

pɤ́ɤ 2) ***prev*** **chez**

pɤ́ɤ-bȁ ***v vt*** **élargir** *(un espace défriché)* ◊ *wà kpìŋŋ pɤ́ɤ-bȁ* ils ont élargi la route

pɤ́ɤbhɛ̏n <chez-human> ***n rn*** **membre de famille**

pı̏ɤbhōbhɛ̏n <fer-sortir-personne> ***n*** **forgeron**

pı̏ɤdhɛ̋ <fer-feuille> ***n*** **tôle** ♦ *pı̏ɤdhɛ̋ kɔ̏* maison en tôle ♦ *yʌ́ŋŋ̏ ɤ́ bhúi-sīʌ yāawō, pı̏ɤdhɛ̋ vīn yɤ̏ dɔ̏ klʌ̏nklʌ̏ndhɤ̄* lorsque le soleil brûle, la tôle crépite

píɤdhɛ̏ {LOC píɤdhɤ̏} ***loc.n*** *rn* **maison, cour** *(chez soi)* <u>*Qsyn.*</u> <u>*plɤ̏ɤdhɛ̏*</u> ◊ *á dhō n̄ dhòo píɤdhɤ̏* je vais chez mon frère aîné ◊ *ȁ píɤdhɛ̏ yà kʌ̄ yāayädhɛ̏* son lieu d'habitation est devenu désagréable

píɤdhɤ̏ *LOC de* píɤdhɛ̏

pɤ̏ɤgā <fer-os> ***n*** **1 fer** *(le matériau)* <u>*Syn.*</u> <u>*pɤ̏ɤ*</u> ♦ *pɤ̏ɤgā bhȁn bhɛ̄n dhɛ̏* téléphonner à qn, appeller qn **2 pièce en fer**

pɤ̄ɤ́gā < ?fer-os> ***n*** **1 hameçon 2 ligne de pêche** <u>*Syn.*</u> <u>*pɤ̄ɤ́*</u>

pɤ̏ɤgāsòȍ, **pɤ̏āasòȍ** <fer-os-cheval> ***n*** **vélo, bicyclette** ♦ *pɤ̏āasòȍ gɔ̏* guidon de vélo ♦ *pɤ̏ɤgāsòȍ lɔ̄ɔ́gā* chaîne de vélo

pɤ̄ɤ́gbɔ̄ɔ́ŋ <ligne.de.pèche-pétiole.de.raphia> ***n*** **bouchon** *(de ligne de pêche)*

pɤ̄ɤ̏ɤ 1), pɤ̄ɤ́ɤ {pɤ̀ɤɤ} ***v*** **1.1** 1) *vi* **s'enrouler** *(autour – ká)* ◊ *bhɪ̄ʌ́gā yà pɤ̄ɤ̏ɤ dhűű ká* une liane s'est enroulée autour d'un arbre ◊ *gɔ̄ yɤ̏ pɤ̏ɤɤ tɔ̏n bhā dhʌ̀n ȁ ká* la voiture monte la montagne en virages 2) *vt* **enrouler** *(autour de – ká)* ◊ *yà fâȁn pɤ̄ɤ̏ɤ ɤ̄ bhɔ̄ ká* il a enroulé l'écharpe autour de son cou **1.2** *vt pɤ̄ɤ̏ɤ ȁ tȁ* **tordre** *(la main)* ♦ *yȁ ȁ kɔ̏ pɤ̄ɤ̏ɤ ȁ tȁ* il lui a tourné le bras par derrière **2** *vt* **faire mal à** *(ventre)* ◊ *Zân gblúúdhɛ̏ yȁ pɤ̄ɤ̏ɤ-sɪ̄ʌ* Jean a des maux de ventre

pɤ̄ɤ̏ɤ 2) ***n*** *rn* **douleur**

pɤ̄ɤɤdhɤ̏ {Int. pɤ̄ɤpɤ̄ɤdhɤ̏} ***adv*** **1 à perte de vue** ◊ *yí yȁ wɔ̄ pɤ̄ɤpɤ̄ɤdhɤ̏.* l'eau s'étend à perte de vue **2** *pas d'intensif avec ce sens* **constamment** *(de l'angoisse, etc.)*

píɤpíɤ ***pp*** *Int. de* píɤ

pɤ̄ɤpɤ̄ɤdhɤ̏ ***adv*** *Int. de* pɤ̄ɤɤdhɤ̏ *constamment*

plákɤ̏ <Fr. plaque> ***n*** **plaque** ♦ *gɔ̄ plákɤ̏* plaque d'immatriculation

plàŋtíȉ <Fr. apprentis> ***n*** **apprenti**

plʌ̏ʌ̏ ***adj*** **nombreux**; **abondant** ◊ *yɤ̏ dhɪ̄aŋ plʌ̏ʌ̏ zʌ̏* il parle beaucoup

plʌ̏́ʌ̏ ***n*** ***Colocasia esculenta*** **taro** *(tubercule comestible)* <u>*Syn.*</u> <u>*kōőkȍo*</u>

plʌ́ʌplʌ̀ʌ {A P S, plʌ́ʌplʌ̀ʌ-dhȕn pl. A, plʌ́ʌplʌ̀ʌ-sȕȕ foc. A, plʌ́ʌplʌ̀ʌ-sȕȕ-dhȕn foc. pl. A; plʌ́ʌplʌ́ʌ Int. pl. A; plʌ́kʌ́plʌ̀kʌ̀ SupInt. A P S, plʌ́kʌ́plʌ̀kʌ̀-dhȕn SupInt. pl. A, plʌ́kʌ́plʌ̀kʌ̀-sȕȕ SupInt. foc. A, plʌ́kʌ́plʌ̀kʌ̀-sȕȕ-dhȕn SupInt. pl. foc. A} *plʌ́ʌplʌ̀ʌ-sȕȕ foc. seulement dans les sens de "facile; mou"; plʌ́ʌplʌ́ʌ Int. pl. seulement dans le sens de "savoureux"* ***adj*** **1 facile 2 mou** *(terre)* <u>*Ant.*</u> <u>*gblɤ̏ɤgblɤ̏ɤ*</u> **3 savoureux 4 faible** *(voix)*

plʌ́ʌplʌ́ʌ *Int. pl. de* plʌ́ʌplʌ̀ʌ *savoureux*

plʌ́kʌ́plʌ̀kʌ̀ *SupInt. de* plʌ́ʌplʌ̀ʌ *facile*

plɛ̏e → pɛ̀nŋ (gw) *aubergine*

plēe ***n*** **gale** <u>*Qsyn.*</u> <u>*kȁa,*</u> <u>*sīakādhâ*</u> ♦ *plēe yà lòo ȁ bhȁ* il a attrapé la gale

pléе ***n*** **criquet** *(petit) [apparaît pendant la période de récolte, parasite des champs redoutable; on ne le mange pas]*

plèŋ (m) → pènŋ (gw) *aubergine*

plɛ̀ ***num*** **deux** *[considéré comme nombre masculin]* *Syn.* *pɛ̀ɛdʌ̄* ♦ *bhɛ̄n gā plɛ̀* une poignée de gens

plɛ̀ɛ <de plɛ̀ 'deux'> *seulement dans l'expression :* ♦ *yī plɛ̀ɛ bhȁ* très prochainement ♦ *kwā yī plɛ̀ɛ bhȁ* au revoir ! *(en s'agissant d'une séparation relativement longue)*

plɛ̋ɛ ***n*** **juin**

plɛ̄ɛplɛ̄ ***num*** **par deux** *une forme facultative, coexistant avec la forme régulière plɛ̀-plɛ̀)*

plɛ̄gbȁan ***n*** ***Clamator glandarius*** **coucou geai** *(41 cm, huppe, dessus brun taché de blanc, longue queue bordée de blanc, dessous blanc crème, parasite des autres oiseaux)*

plɛ̄ŋgbȁan ***n Macrodipteryx longipennis, syn. Caprimulgus longipennis*** **engoulevent à balanciers** *(oiseau de nuit, gris foncé et noir; une aile mesure de 16 à 19 cm, mais le plumage nuptial du mâle fait agrandir la 9e plume de l'aile jusqu'à 50 cm, avec un vexille à la fin)*

plɛ̀-plɛ̀ <deux-deux> ***adv*** **1 deux par deux** *Syn.* *plɛ̄ɛplɛ̄* **2** *avec la négation* **pas souvent, rarement** ◊ *yáa gbɔ̋ bɔ̄ plɛ̀-plɛ̀* il ne pleure pas facilement ♦ *wáa kpȁn ȁ bhȁ plɛ̀-plɛ̀* c'est rare ◊ *sɛ̄ɛ̋dhɛ̋ yā, bhɛ̄n ya̋n yáa kpȁn ȁ bhȁ plɛ̀-plɛ̀* c'est un livre rare

plō̋ŋplȍŋplō̋ŋdhɤ̄ ***onomat*** **plouf-plouf** *(clapotement de l'eau)* ◊ *wȍ wō zṹ-sīʌ plō̋ŋplȍŋplō̋ŋdhɤ̄ yí bhàa* ils se baignent dans l'eau : plouf-plouf

plɔ̏ɔgā ***n*** hist. **centime** *(pièce de monnaie de la période coloniale)* ♦ *plɔ̏ɔgā bhá yáa n̄ gɔ̏* je suis sans le sou

plɤ̀ɤ <village- ?> ***pp*** **chez** *(dans le village de qn)* ◊ *yà dhó ɤ̄ plɤ̀ɤ* il est allé chez lui

plɤ́ɤ̄ ***loc.n*** *LOC de* pɤ̀dhɛ̏ *village*

plɤ̀ɤdhɛ̏ ***n*** *rn* **maison, village, campement** *(de qn)* *Qsyn.* *pɤ̋ɤdhɛ̏* ◊ *Da̋an plɤ̀ɤdhɛ̏ yà kʌ̄ yâ* le lieu de résidence de Daan est devenu désagréable

plɯ̋ɯnŋ 1 ***n*** **promesse** ◊ *bhán plɯ̋ɯnŋ bhō ɯ̄ dhɛ̏ dhɛ̀ ā dhɔ̀ ɯ̄ gbā bhān gɔ̏ ká* je te promets que je te donnerai ma voiture

plɯ̋ɯnŋ 2 ***n*** **piquant** *(de porc-épic)* *Syn.* *sɛ̋ŋ* *Qsyn.* *glɛ̋ɛn*

pő → pű *ouvrir*

póȅe <pɤ̀-ȅȅ 'aussi-question'> ***prt*** *particule d'une question rhétorique conjuguée avec un reproche* ◊ *ɯ̄ dhēbʌ̏ ká póȅe ?* toi aussi, es-tu femme ? *(un reproche adressé à un homme)*

pōlísɤ̄, pōlīsíyɛ̀ <Fr. police> ***n*** **policier**

pōlītíkʌ̀ <Fr. politique> ***n*** **politique**

póŋbhɯ̏ <Fr. pomme> ***n*** **pomme**

pōŋpōŋdhɤ̄ {Int. pōoŋpōŋdhɤ̄} ***adv*** **de loin** ♦ *yà zīɤ ȁ tȁ pōŋpōŋdhɤ̄* il l'a dépassé de loin

pōo {pȍo} ***n*** **crapaud** *[non consommé par les Dan]*

pōoŋpōŋdhɤ̄ ***adv*** *Int. de* pōŋpōŋdhɤ̄ *de loin*

pṍpṍ, **pṹpṹ** ***adv*** **comme la neige** *(blanc)* ♦ *pṹu pṍpṍ* blanc comme la neige ◊ *ȁ bhȁ wūndhɛ̋ gbàan kʌ̄ pṍpṍ wlɛ̋n kɔ̄ɔ* ses cheveux sont devenus tout blancs

pòpòdhîn <Manding póponin> ***n*** **mobylette** ♦ *pòpòdhîn kúndhɛ̏* guidon de mobylette

pṍpṍdhɤ̄ {Int. pópȍpódhɤ̄} ***adv*** **en petits jets** *(du vent, de l'eau)* ◊ *tɛ̋ɛ yà wȍ pṍpṍdhɤ̄* il sort de petits jets d'air ◊ *yı̋ wȍ-sīʌ kplɛ̋gɔ̄ gúu pópȍpódhɤ̄* le bateau fait eau en nombreux petits jets

pópȍpódhɤ̄ ***adv*** *Int. de* pṍpṍdhɤ̄ *en.petits.jets*

pȍtāasȕu <ouvrir- ?-gérondif> ***n*** **liberté** ◊ *bhāan ūu gbā pȍtāasȕu ká kɤ̄ úu dhó* je te permets de partir

pɔ̋ ***n rn*** **prêt, emprunt** ◊ *ȁ bhȁ sʌ̋nŋ gā pɔ̋ gȕn Gblʌ̏ʌ̏ bhȁ* Gbleu lui devais un lingot d'or ◊ *bhán ȁ bhȁ pɔ̋ bhā bhō* je lui ai remboursé la dette ♦ *pɔ̋ dɔ̄ bhɛ̄n bhȁ, pɔ̋ dhūn bhɛ̄n dhɛ̏* accorder un prêt à qn ♦ *pʌ̄ dhɔ́ pɔ̋ ká* acheter qch à crédit ♦ *pɔ̋ kʌ̄ bhɛ̄n ká* réclamer une dette ♦ *dhȕn pɔ̋ tȁ* venir encaisser une dette

pɔ̄bhándɤ̏ <Fr. pommade> ***n*** **pommade**

pɔ̋dhı̋n <Fr. pointe> ***n*** **clou, pointe**

pɔ́n {pɔ̄n} ***v*** **1** *vt* **creuser** **2** *vt* **forer** *(trou)* ◊ *dhā yà glȕgā pɔ́n* la pluie a creusé un trou **3** *vt* **déterrer** *(tubercules)* Syn. wȍ 2 **4** *vt* **terrasser** *(jeter à terre)*

pɔ̄ŋ <Fr. pont>. ***n*** **pont**

pɔ̋ɔ ***n*** **humidité** ◊ *pɔ̋ɔ yȁ dɔ̄ sɔ̄ bhȁ* les habits sont devenues humides

pɔ̏ɔn ***n*** **hernie**

pɔ̋ɔn ***n*** ***Ceratogymna atrata*** **grand calao à casque noir** *(90 cm, mâle : casque cylindrique noir, plumage noir sauf l'extrémité blanche de la queue; femelle : tête et cou roux; vol lent, bruyant et lourd)* ♦ *gèe pɔ̋ɔn* masque calao

pɔ̄táblʌ̏ <Fr. portable> ***n*** **portable** *(téléphone)*

pɤ̏ ***v*** **1** 1) *vi* **tomber** ♦ *sɤ̄ bɤ̋ɤ yà gó ɤ̄ dhȕ gúu yà pɤ̏, ȁ vīn yɤ̏ dɔ̏ dȕuŋ* lorsqu'une grappe de noix de palmier à huile tombe, cela produit un bruit "doung" 2) *vt* **faire tomber** **2** *vi* **attaquer** *(qn – tȁ)* **3** *vi* **se ruiner** *(perdre ses biens)*

pɤ̄ {pɤ̄} ***v*** **1** *vt* **dire, parler** Qsyn. dhīaŋ zʌ̄ ◊ *yɤ̏ ȁ pɤ̄ dhìn* il l'a dit de cette manière; il a dit de le faire comme ça ♦ *sʌ́ʌdhɛ̋ wȍ pɤ̄* lire **2** *vt* **avoir l'intention** *(de – proposition au prospectif ou au subjonctif)* ◊ *wȁ ȁ pɤ̄ wōo bhɛ̄n gɔ̏ tȁ-dhɔ́, bhʌ̏n ɤ́ wó' dhūn ?* quand on veut racheter une personne, qu'est-ce qu'on donne ? ◊ *gɔ̄ yȁ ȁ pɤ̄ yɤ̄ɤ tɔ̏n kún...* quand une voiture s'apprête à gravir une pente... ◊ *bhá dhó ȁ pɤ̄' úu bɔ̄ zīaan dèe bhā' tȁ* n'emprunte pas la route principale **3** *vt* **s'appeler** *(par un nom)* ◊ *kɛ̋ɛ pʌ́ ɤ́ kʌ̏ ɤ́ á Dȁȁn tɔ̏ pɤ̄...* mais la raison, pour laquelle on m'appelle Daan... **4** *vt* **lire** *(dans une langue)* ◊ *kwȁ dɔ̄ ȁ yȁdhɛ̏ wāȁ pɤ̄dhɛ̏ ká* apprenons à écrire et à lire **5** *vi* **presque accomplir** *(toujours* *au parfait; le verbe sémantique est sous la forme infinitive nu ou du masdar, introduit par la postposition bhà)* ◊ *Zân yà pɤ̄ bɤ̀-dhɛ̀ bhà* Jean s'est presque réveillé ◊ *Zân yà pɤ̄ ɤ̄ bō dhűű kǎn-sǜ ká* Jean a presque fini de couper l'arbre

pɤ́ ***adv*** **aussi** ◊ *yɤ́ zàŋ-dhǜn wó klɛ̋ɛ yà à kɔ̀ɔ, yɤ́ wó à yà dhʌ́nglɔ̄ɔ́ndhʌ́n bhā à kɔ̀ɔ pɤ́* les policiers lui ont passé les menottes, et ils les ont aussi passées au jeune homme

pɤ̂ {pɤ̀} ***n*** **village** Qsyn. *pɤ̂dhɛ̀* ♦ *pɤ̂ gúú bhɛ̀n* villageois ♦ *pɤ̂ kǎn* fonder un village

pɤ̂bhàan <village-oiseau> ***n*** **1** ***Melichneutes robustus*** **indicateur à lyre** *(23 cm; rectrices noires, externes blanches, en forme de lyre; décrit des arabesques aériennes au-dessus de la forêt, au cours des piqués produit un bruit de sirène nasillarde par la vibration des rectrices)* **2** ***Ploceus cucullatus, P. collaris*** **tisserin gendarme** *(17 cm, mâle : tête, bavette et nuque noires, dessous jaune doré, bec noir et œil rouge; femelle : tête vert olive, dos gris olivâtre, dessous jaune pâle; vit en colonies) [totem du clan Dhoo]* Syn. *dɛ̀bhàan, bhàantɛ̋ɛ, gɔ̀plɤ́ɤ̄*

pɤ̂dʌ̄ <village-père> ***n*** **1 père de village** *("maître de terre" : son accord est nécessaire au chef du village pour la prise des décisions; il bénit le village; auparavant, il représentait le chef supérieur)* **2 notable**

pɤ̂dɔ̄bhɛ̄nká <village-bâtir-homme-avec> ***n Sylvia communis*** **fauvette grisette** *(14 cm, gorge blanche, couvertures claires marron, rectrices externes blanches)*

pɤ̂dhɛ̀ {LOC pɤ̂dhɤ̄, plɤ́ɤ̄} ***loc.n*** **village** Syn. *pɤ̂* ◊ *gó plɤ́ɤ̀ kïi dhó bhlàà* quitte le village et va au champ ◊ *yà dhó ɤ̄ gɔ̀ pɤ̂dhɤ̄* il est allé à son village

pɤ̂dhɤ̄ ***loc.n*** *LOC de* pɤ̂dhɛ̀ *village*

pɤ̋ŋpɤ̀ŋpɤ̋ŋdhɤ̄ ***onomat*** *imite le crépitement des feuilles vertes dans le feu*

pɤ̋ɤ {pɤ̀ɤ} ***v*** **1** *vi* **grésiller** *(huile)*, **pétiller** *(maïs en train d'être braisé)* ♦ *wà dhɛ̋ sɛ̀ɛ gbɛ́ lòo sɤ́ɤ kpïì gúú, wɔ̀ pɤ̀ɤ pɤ̋ŋpɤ̀ŋpɤ̋ŋdhɤ̄* lorsqu'on met des feuilles vertes dans un grand feu, elles crépitent **2** *vi* **exploser** ◊ *sɤ́ɤwɛ̀nŋtɔ̀n yà pɤ̋ɤ* le volcan a eu une éruption

pɤ̋ɤŋ̋pɤ̋ɤŋ̋dhɤ̄ ***onomat*** *imite le crépitement de l'huile chaude*

pɤ́pɤ́ ***adv*** **encore**, **de nouveau** *(qch indésirable)* ◊ *bhá dhūn pɤ́pɤ́ !* tu es encore venu ! (et cela est indésirable)

pú {pū} ***v*** 1) *vi* **s'allumer** ◊ *sɤ́ɤ bhúú dhűʌʌdhǜʌʌ yà pú* une faible lumière est apparue 2) *vt* **allumer** *(feu, torche électrique)*

pű (gw,), **pɔ̋** (m) {pò, pù; (m) pò, pù} ***v*** **1** 1) *vt* **ouvrir** Syn. *dhí-pɔ̋* 2) *vi* **s'ouvrir** ◊ *kwɛ̋ɛ yà pɔ̋* i) la porte s'est ouverte ii) la porte est ouverte ◊ *dhɛ̀gúú yɤ̀ pɔ̋-sīʌ* il commence à faire jour **2** 1) *vi* **se délier** Ant. *klǜù, lɤ̀* 2) *vt* **délier, détacher** ◊ *yà n̄ pű kɤ̄ á pɤ̀* il m'a détaché pour que je tombe

pūpê <Fr. poupée> ***n*** **poupée**

pűpű ***adj*** *Int. pl. de* pűu *blanc*

pùpūŋ̄dhɛ̋ *n* ***Cardiospermum grandiflorum (gen. Sapinaceae)*** **liane** *(à fruits en boules) [on la pile avec du kaolin, on chauffe le tout et on le met sur les entorses]*

pūű {pùu} *n* **gourde pour le vin de palme** *(pour le stockage et le transport; grande, à petit orifice)* ♦ *wē pùu* = pūű ♦ *pūű bhɛ̄* i) fruit de calebassier *(pas encore travaillé)* ii) = pūű ♦ *yɔ̋n pùu* *hist.* calebasse pour l'huile de palme

pűu 1) {A P S, pűu-dhùn pl. A, pűu-sùu foc. A S, pűu-sùu-dhùn foc. pl. A; pűpű Int. pl. A P S, pűpű-dhùn Int. pl. A S, pűpű-sùu Int. pl. foc. A S, pűpű-sùu-dhùn Int. pl. Foc. A S; pűupűu SupInt pl. A P S, pűupűu-dhùn SupInt pl. A S, pűuu ExtInt} *adj* **1 blanc** ◊ *à gɔ̀ dhɛ́ yà kʌ̄ pűuu* ses cheveux sont devenus tout blancs **2 clair 3 propre** *(mains; ciel; feuille),* **clair** *(ciel)* ♦ *à zūʌ́ yɤ̀ pűu* il n'a pas de rancune

pűu 2) *n* **vérité** *dans l'espression :* ♦ *yà pűu pɤ* il a dit la vérité

pűupűu *SupInt. pl. de* pűu 1) *blanc*

pűuu *adj ExtInt. pl. de* pűu 1) *blanc*

S s

sā {sā} *v* **1** *vt* **répandre régulièrement** *(matières sèches)* Qsyn. *kpɔ́* **2** *vi* **se jeter** *(pour attraper; qn – tà)*

sá *prt* **1 quand même** *particule de concession* ◊ *... kɛ̋ɛ kɤ sá sʌ́ʌdhɛ́ dhɔ̀ dèdè yɤ̀ kwāà dhʌ́n-dhùn bhà* mais quand même, nos enfants ont vraiment envie à étudier ◊ *ā à pɤ̀ dhʌ́n-dhùn wá dhɤ́ bhɔ̄' kɔ́ɔdhɤ, kɛ̋ɛŋ wà bhɔ̄ sá* j'ai dit aux enfants de ne pas s'ébattre dans la maison, mais ils l'ont fait quand même **2 et en plus** ◊ *tɔ̀gɔ̄n bhā yáa bhɔ̀ɔn' bhà kɤ yɤ̀ gó' gúu, sá yà wɛ́, à wò yáa dhó gblɛ̀ɛn* le coq ne pouvait pas sortir, et en plus, quand il criait, sa voix n'allait pas loin

sàa {A P} (m) *adj* **paresseux**

sàa 1 *n* **1 latte** *(de pétiole de palme de raphia)* **2 flèche** *(sans fer) (pour compter, on utilise la forme sàagā)* Syn. sàagā ♦ *sàa kpà-sùu* flèche empoisonnée ♦ *sàa zùɤ* lancer une flèche **3 attelle, éclisse** *(faite de 5-6 lattes de raphia)* ◊ *bhán Zân gbè dà sàa gúu* j'ai mis des attelles au bras de Zan

sàa 2 *n rn* **salaire** ◊ *bhíin ī sàa slɔ̀ɔ* je n'ai pas touché mon salaire ♦ *sàa bhɔ̄* payer le salaire ◊ *yʌ̄ ɤ́ yā bhʌ̄nŋ̄bhīn yà à sàa bhɔ̄ ī gɔ̀ wʌ́ʌ̀ kʌ̄ŋ dɔ̄* le Dioula m'a payé 500 francs pour ce travail

sāà *n* **savon** ♦ *bhɛ̄ntīi sāà* savon noir ♦ *sāà yí* eau savonneuse ♦ *sāà kpɤ yàagā* trois savons, trois morceaux de savon, trois boules de savon ♦ *sāà gā* bout de savon

sáà 1 *n* **charme** ◊ *à bhà sáà yà bhɛ̄n gbàn kún* il a charmé tout le monde ♦ *sáàbhɛ̀n* personne charmante ♦ *sáà yɤ̀ à tà* il a du charme

sáà 2 *n gwʌ̀ sáà* **étendue** *(d'un rocher)*

sáà 3 ***n*** *sáà gúú* **grâce à** ◊ *yɤ̀ dhà bhān dhʌ̀n ī sáà dɛ̀dɛ̀ gúú* il a été sauvé uniquement grâce à moi

sáà <Arab. ṣadaqa via Manding sádaka, sáraka> ***n*** **sacrifice** ♦ *sáà bhō* faire un sacrifice ♦ *sáà pʌ̄* victime immolée ◊ *à gbɛ̂n tīītīdhɛ̀-sɯ̀ dhʌ̀n ɤ́ wó kʌ̄ à kʌ̀ sáà pʌ̄ ká* c'est le chien extrêmement noir qu'ils ont immolé

sáàa = sáàgā *huit*

sàadhē ***n*** **nasse** Syn. zɔ̄ɔ (t)

sàa-dhɛ̀ (m) ***n*** **paresse**

sàagā ***n*** **flèche** *(sans fer)* Syn. sàa

sáàgā, **sáàa** ***num*** **huit** *[considéré comme nombre masculin]*

sāan ***n*** *rn* **cadeau, cadeaux** *(qu'on envoie par qn ou qu'on ramène d'un voyage)* Syn. sāanpʌ̄ Qsyn. gbœ̄œdhē, tāa ♦ *yà ī sāan bɔ̄* il m'a envoyé des cadeaux ♦ *yà dhūn yī sāan ká* il nous a apporté des cadeaux

sāán 1 1) {sàan} ***v*** **souffrir**

sāán 1 2) ***n*** **1 souffrance 2 joug** *(sujétion)* Syn. gĩ̂ ♦ *yɤ̀ sāán gúú ɤ̄ bhā dhēbʌ̀ gɔ̀* il est sous le joug de sa femme

sāán 2 ***n*** **champignon** *(petit, blanc, comestible, pousse en groupes au mois de mai sur les anciennes termitières)* Syn. tíʌʌpṹu

sáan ***n*** **rempart**

sáandhíɤ ***n*** **entrée du village**

sāanpʌ̄ <cadeau-chose> ***n*** *rn* **cadeau, cadeaux** *(qu'on envoie par qn ou qu'on rapporte d'un voyage)* Syn. sāan ◊ *dhɛ́ɛ̀nbʌ̀-dhɯ̀n wà sāanpʌ̄ bhá-dhɯ̀n bɔ̄ yī bhá-dhɯ̀n ká* les enfants m'envoient parfois des cadeaux

sāanwɔ̀ <cadeau-mot> ***n*** **message** Syn. dhœ̄œn

sàbhá <Arab. sabbaaṭ ou Port. sapata, via Manding sànbada ou sàbara> ***n*** **chaussure** ◊ *ɤ́ tá sú-sīʌ, à bhà sàbhá yɤ̀ wɛ̀ vɛ̄ɛ́nvɛ̀ɛnvɛ̄ɛ́ndhɤ̄/wɛ̄ɛ́nwɛ̀ɛnwɛ̄ɛ́ndhɤ̄* lorsqu'il marche, ses chaussures grincent ♦ *dhɯ́ɯ sàbhá* sandales de bois *(les semelles ont été faites en bois de klɪ́nŋ̄)* ♦ *yà ɤ̄ bhā sàbhá bhō ɤ̄ gɛ̀ɛn* il s'est déchaussé

sàbhlìigā < ?-os> ***n*** **fouet** *(tressé de trois cordes, parfois en cuir)* ◊ *gèekɛ́ɛsɯ̀ yà sàbhlìigā yàn dō bhō' gúú* le masque-agresseur lui a donné un coup de fouet

sàfá ***n*** *rn* **tendon**

sákɤ̀ <Fr. sac> ***n*** **sac**

sákpádʌ̄ ***n*** ***Herpestes sanguinea*** **mangouste rouge**, **mangouste de Dybowsky** *(26-34 cm, 350-800 g, corps allongé, pattes courtes, arboricole, couleur variable)* Syn. wɛ̀nŋ

sàn ***n*** **1** *rn* **dégoût** ♦ *à sàn yà yɤ̄ ī gúú* je le déteste, ça me dégoûte ♦ *à sàn yɤ̀ ī kʌ̀* ça me dégoûte **2** *rn* **haine** ♦ *à sàn yɤ̀ ī zʌ̀* je ne l'aime pas, je le hais

sànbhàn *n* arch. **danseuse de dhɛ̏ɛdhı̋ɤ tı̋n** *(fille non-mariée, très belle, danse en costume de dhı̋a et kòŋbhó)* *[depuis le début du XXI siècle cette danse n'a plus été exécutée]* *Syn.* *dhɛ̏ɛdhı̋ɤ*

sȁnbhɛ̄nzʌ̏ {Indep. sȁnbhɛ̄nzʌ̏} *la forme à ton final moyen, sȁnbhɛ̄nzʌ̄, apparaît si celui qui haït est indiqué; sinon, on utilise la forme à ton final extra-bas, sȁnbhɛ̄nzʌ̏* ***n*** **haine** ◊ *Gbȁtȍ bhȁ sȁnbhɛ̄nzʌ̄ ɤ́ Zân bhȁ* la haine de Gbato envers Zan ♦ *sȁnbhɛ̄nzʌ̏ yāa* haine mortelle

sȁnbhɛ̄nzʌ̄-dhɛ̏ ***n*** **haine** *(comme émotion abstraite)*

sànbhűnzʌ̏, **sànbhɔ̋nzʌ̏** ***n*** *rn* **partenaires du cousinage à plaisanterie** *(sans interdiction de mariage)* *Qsyn.* *dhı̋sű* ♦ *sànbhűnzʌ̏ bhȕn yɛ̄ŋ yī ká* nous sommes des cousins à plaisanterie

sànbhűnzʌ̏-dhɛ̏ sànbhɔ̋nzʌ̏-dhɛ̏ ***n*** **cousinage à plaisanterie** *(sans interdiction de mariage)* ◊ *sànbhűnzʌ̏-dhɛ̏ dhʌn ɤ́ Yàkùbâ wāȁ Glōȍ-dhȕn zìnŋgú* entre les Dan et les Gouro, il existe un cousinage à plaisanterie

sȁndhɛ̏ → sȁnŋdhɛ̏ *bouteille*

sı̋ndhìn <Manding sánì, sánni> ***conj*** *le verbe de la phrase introduit par cette conjonction est au subjonctif* **1 avant de** ◊ *sı̋ndhìn yɤ̏ pʌ̄ bhɤ̏, kɤ̄ yȁ ɤ̄ kɔ̏ zű* avant de manger, il s'est lavé les mains **2 au lieu de**

sánkɛ̄ɛŋ̏dʌ̄ ***n*** *gblɔ̏ sánkɛ̄ɛŋ̏dʌ̄* **"bossu"** *(un épithète pour le lièvre utilisé dans les contes)*

sȁnŋdhɛ̏, **sȁndhɛ̏** ***n*** **bouteille** *(de verre)* *Syn.* *bútɛ̀dhı̋ɤ, zȕɛɛbhɛ̄*

sánŋ̏sȕ <Fr. essence> ***n*** **essence** *(carburant)*

sı̋ŋ ***n*** **cuiller, cuillère** *[on danse gœ̋œ avec des cuillers]*

sāyɛ̂n ***n*** **gond**

sæ̏æ, **sɛ̏ɛ**; **sȁa** (m) {A P S, sæ̏æ-dhȕn pl. A S, sæ̏æ-sȕ foc. A, sæ̏æ-sȕ-dhȕn foc. pl. A} ***adj*** **1 frais** ◊ *dhɛ̋ndhɛ̋n yà n̄ kwī kʌ̄ sæ̏æ* le froid a refroidi ma peau ◊ *dhɛ̏ sæ̏æ dhɔ̏ yáa n̄ kʌ̄* je n'aime pas le froid ◊ *tɛ́ɛ sæ̏æ dhɔ̏ yáa n̄ kʌ̄* je n'aime pas le vent froid ♦ *ū zūʌ́ kʌ̄ sɛ̏ɛ* sois patient ♦ *tɛ́ɛ yɤ̏ sɛ̏ɛ dhɛ̋ndhɛ̋n kœ̄œ* l'air est froid (comme en Europe en hiver) **2 cru** *(qui n'est pas cuit)* **3 humide** *(et frais)* *Syn.* *dɔ́ndɔ̏n* ◊ *bhán sɔ̄ bhō yʌ́nŋ̏ dhʌ̏, kɛ́ɛn yɤ̏ gȕn kɤ̀ŋ sɛ̏ɛ* j'ai retiré le linge du soleil, mail il était encore humide ◊ *tȁ gɛ̀ndhɛ́ tȁ-sȕ dhɔ̏ yáa n̄ kʌ̄ blʌ̄ʌ dhɛ́ sɛ̏ɛ tȁ* je n'aime pas marcher pieds nus sur l'herbe humide **4 frais**; **vert** *(feuille)* **5 calme**

sǣæ̋ → sɛ̄ɛ̋ *natte*

sæ̋æ 3 → sɛ̋ɛ *frange*

sæ̋æ̏ → sɛ̋ɛ̏ *témoin*

sæ̏æ-dhɛ̏ ***n*** **froid** ♦ *yí sæ̏æ-dhɛ̏ yɤ̏ bhȁn bhɛ̄n kɔ̏ gú* l'eau froide refroidit les mains

sæ̋æ̏dhɛ̏ ***n*** **marque**

sæ̋ŋ ***n*** **touffe de queue de porc-épic**

sʌ̀ 1) {A P S, sʌ̀-dhʉ̀n pl. A S, sʌ̀-sʉ̀ foc. A, sʌ̀-sʉ̀-dhʉ̀n foc. pl. A S; sʌ̀ʌdhʌ́n Int. A P; sɛ̀ŋbʌ̀ Int. pl. A P S, sɛ̀ŋbʌ̀-dhʉ̀n Int. pl. A S, sɛ̀ŋbʌ̀-sʉ̀-dhun Int. pl. foc. A S; sʌ̀sʌ̀ SupInt. pl. A P S, sʌ̀sʌ̀-dhʉ̀n SupInt. pl. A S, sʌ̀sʌ̀-sʉ̀-dhʉ̀n SupInt. foc. pl. A; bhëbhë ExtInt. pl. A P S, bhëbhë-dhʉ̀n ExtInt. pl. A S, bhëbhë-sʉ̀ ExtInt. pl. foc. A S, bhëbhë-sʉ̀-dhʉ̀n ExtInt. pl. foc. A S} ***adj* 1 bon**, **plaisant** ◊ *ȁ dīn yɤ̏ sʌ̀* c'est bon à manger ♦ *ȁ sʌ̀ kʌ̄-sʉ̀ ká* il est content ♦ *dhɛ̀ ɤ́ ... sʌ̀ ká, yɤ́ ...* à peine (qch s'est mis en bonne voie), et... ◊ *dhɛ̀ ɤ́ yʌ̄ kʌ̀ sʌ̀ ká, yɤ́ wó dhūn ȁ dhɛ̏* il est à peine entré dans le rythme de travail, on est venu l'appeler ♦ *ȁ wɔ̏n yɤ̏ kʌ̀ bhēn gʉ́ sʌ̀* l'homme s'y est intéressé ♦ *sʌ̀ ká dans certains contextes* un peu ◊ *dhɛ̀ ɤ́ yɛ̀ bhā' pɔ̄n sʌ̀ ká...* quand il a un peu creusé ce trou... **2 beau**, **joli** Qsyn. dhī ◊ *dhʌ́n ɤ́ bhā yɤ́ gūn sʌ̀ dɛ̀dɛ̀wɔ̄* c'était un enfant très beau **3** *avec une négation* **terrible** *(remarquable)* ◊ *yʌ̄ kɤ́ yí' kʌ̀ bhʉ̄n, ȁ kʌ̀ gbɛ́ kɔ̀ yáa sʌ̀* le travail que nous avons fait là, c'était terrible **4 rapide**, **vite** ◊ *pʌ̄bhèe ɤ́ yā, ȁ sɛ̄ɛ̀-dhɛ̏ yɤ̏ sʌ̀* cette nourriture se gâte vite

sʌ̀ 2) ***adv* bien** ◊ *yɤ̏ dhʌ́n-dhʉ̀n klɔ̋ bhɔ̀ sʌ̀* il éduque bien les enfants

sʌ̀ʌ ***n* fétiche protecteur** *(pour tout une famille ou un village; on le met dans un cube en argile qu'on met au centre de la place publique ou dans la cour, parfois on met une paillotte au-dessus; on l'adore régulièrement)* ♦ *wà sʌ̀ʌ yȁ /dɔ̄ pɤ̏ tȁ* ils ont installé le fétiche protecteur dans le village

sʌ̄ʌ ***n* fatigue** *dans la locution* ♦ *sʌ̄ʌ bhɔ̄* se fatiguer; fatiguer; tourmenter ◊ *yʉ̋a yɤ̏ kʌ̄' sʌ̄ʌ bhɔ̀ sʉ́ plɛ̀ ká yɤ́ ɤ́ gūn gā-dhȁan* la maladie le fatiguait pendant deux mois, avant qu'il meure

sʌ́ʌ̀ 1 ***n*** *nom générique pour plusieurs espèces d'oiseaux prédateurs :* **1 *Circaetus gallicus* circaète jean-le-blanc** *(65 cm, grande tête, yeux orange, dessous blanc, dessus brun avec bordures blanches)* **2 *Accipiter spp.* épervier** Syn. slɤ̋ɤŋ

sʌ́ʌ̀ 2 <Manding séli> ***n* prière** *(avant tout musulmane, mais peut désigner une prière chrétienne aussi)*

sʌ̄ʌbhōdhē <fatigue-sortir-nominalis.> ***n* fatigue** ◊ *sʌ̄ʌbhōdhē yà n̄ dhɪ́ɤ-kʌ̄ zʉ̋aanzʉ̀aan ká* la fatigue m'a rendu apathique

sʌ̀ʌdhʌ́n ***adj*** *Int. de* sʌ̀ *bon*

sʌ́ʌdhɛ̋ <Manding sɛ́bɛ́ 'papier'-feuille> ***n* 1 papier; lettre** *(message)* ♦ *sʌ́ʌdhɛ̋ bɛ̀n zʌ̄* écrire ♦ *sʌ́ʌdhɛ̋ kʌ̄ ... dhɛ̏* écrire une lettre à qn ♦ *sʌ́ʌdhɛ̋ wɔ̀ pɤ̄* lire **2 savoir moderne**; **éducation formelle** ◊ *yɤ̏ ɤ̄ dʌ̄ ȁ gèe dhɔ̏-kʌ̀ kɤ̄ ȁ bhȁ dhʌ́n-dhʉ̀n wɔ̀ sʌ́ʌdhɛ̋ dɔ̄ klȁŋdhɪ̋ɤ* il est en train d'honorer le masque de son père pour que ses enfants réussissent à l'école ♦ *sʌ́ʌdhɛ̋ dlāàn* études *(à l'école, à l'université)* ♦ *yɤ̏ sʌ́ʌdhɛ̋ bhȁ* il fait des progrès dans ses études **3 document**, **papier** *(carte d'identité, etc.)* ◊ *ʉ̄ tɔ́ ɤ́ sʌ́ʌdhɛ̋ gʉ́ ?* et ton nom qui est dans les papiers ?

sʌ́ʌdhɛ̋bɛ̀ <papier-régime> ***n* livre** ♦ *klȁŋkȁgʉ́ sʌ́ʌdhɛ̋bɛ̀ neol.* syllabaire

sʌ́ʌdhɛ̋bɛ̀nzʌ̄bhɛ̀n <papier-écrire-battre-personne> ***n* secrétaire** *(qui s'occupe de la documentation)*

sʌ́ʌdhɛ̋dɔ̄bhɛ̏n <papier-connaître-personne> ***n*** **personne éduquée**

sʌ́ʌdhɛ̋dhē ***adj*** **en papier** ◊ *fa̋àn sʌ́ʌdhɛ̋dhē* chapeau en papier

sʌ́ʌdhɛ̋gā ***n*** **feuille de papier** ♦ *sʌ́ʌdhɛ̋gā pűu ɤ́ pʌ̄ bháa à tà* feuille vierge

sʌ́ʌdhɛ̋yȁngā <papier-oeil-os> ***n*** *neol.* **lettre, caractère** ♦ *sʌ́ʌdhɛ̋yȁngāplɛ̀* digraphe

sʌ́ʌdhɛ̋yȁngākpɤ̄ <lettre-boule> ***n*** *neol.* **alphabet**

sʌ́ʌ̏gwʌ̏ ***n*** **meule à aiguiser** *(blanchâtre, avec un mélange de noir)*

sʌ̏bhɛ̏n ***n*** *rn* **bien-aimé, bien-aimée** ♦ *n̄ sʌ̏bhɛ̏n* ma belle (une forme d'adresse très affective)

sʌ̏-dhɛ̏ <joli-abstr.> ***n*** **beauté**

sʌ̏n ***n*** **fruit non-mûr** *(mangue, avocat, banane, papaye, manioc; épi de maïs dont les grains sont trop petits et mous)*

sʌ̄n, **sʌ̄ndhʌ́n** ***n*** **lièvre** *(la forme sʌ̄n est moins usitée que sʌ̄ndhʌ́n)* *Syn. gblɔ̏*

sʌ́n {sʌ̄n} ***v*** *vt* **attraper au vol** *Syn. yà ... bhà* ♦ *yūn sʌ́n* éternuer

sʌ̄ndhʌ́n → sʌ̄n *lièvre*

sʌ̄nŋ ***n*** ***Aframomum alboriolaceum (gen. Zingiberaceae)*** **arbre** *(esp.) [pilées avec le citron et le kaolin, les feuilles servent de remède contre la varicelle]*

sʌ́nŋ̏ ***n*** **plante herbacée** *(esp. : fruits rouges allongés en bas de la tige, à jus sucré qu'on consomme; pousse près de l'eau) [dans le cadre du cousinage à plaisanterie, les habitants de Pleepleu se moquent des habitants du Gouèta en leur attribuant une avidité pour les fruits de cette plante]*

sʌ̋nŋ ***n*** **or** ♦ *sʌ̋nŋ gā* lingot d'or ♦ *sʌ̋nŋ kɔ̄ŋgāàpʌ̏* bague en or ♦ *sʌ̋nŋ yí* or liquide ♦ *bhān sʌ̋nŋ* ma chérie (adresse affective à une femme)

sʌ̋nŋpɪ̏ɤbhɛ̏n <or-fer-personne> ***n*** **bijoutier**

sʌ́nsʌ́n ***adv*** **très** *(noir)*

sʌ̋ŋ ***n*** *rn* **salutation** ◊ *tɔ̋ŋ̏dʌ̄zʌ̏-dhȕn plɛ̀ wó wō kó sʌ̋ŋ bhō-sɪʌ, wɔ̏ wō kó kɔ̄ŋgā wɛ̏* lorsque deux amis se saluent, ils s'accrochent des doigts et les claquent *[si le claquement ne se produit pas, on répète la salutation; sinon, on croit qu'un désaccord se produirait]*

sʌ̏sʌ̏ *SupInt. pl. de* sʌ̏ *bon*

sē ***n*** *rn vulg.* **poil pubien** *[chez les Dan, d'habitude, les hommes comme les femmes se rasent le pubis]* ♦ *à sē yà kʌ̄ gbɛ́, à sē yà dà* il a le poil pubien dense

sɛ̋ 1 ***n*** **1 laine** ◊ *sɔ̄ ɤ́ yā yɤ̏ kʌ̄-sȕ ká sɛ̋ dɛ̀dɛ̀ dhɛ̀n à ká* cet habit est fait en pure laine **2 ceinture en lainage, ceinture en laine** *(des filles initiées)*

sɛ̋ 2 ***n*** **choix** *seulement dans l'expression suivant :* ♦ *à sɛ̋ yáa X dhɛ̏ ...* le X est obligé... ◊ *à sɛ̋ yáa n̄ dhɛ̏ ā dhō yʌ̄ bhā dhʌ̀n ɤ́ à kʌ̄'* je suis obligé de faire ce travail

sēɛ̏, **sīɤ** (m) {sèe} ***v*** 1) *vi* **se détériorer, se gâter** ◊ *bhɤ̏ dhāa sēɛ̏-sȕ zȕɤ* jette le couteau abîmé ♦ *à wɔ̏n yà sēɛ̏* il est mort 2) *vt* **abîmer, gâter** ◊ *Gbàtò yɤ̏ gɔ̄ dhɔ̏ tɛ̄nŋyī ká, yɤ́'* *sèe dhɔ̃ɔyī ká* Gbato a acheté une voiture le lundi et l'a cassée le vendredi ♦ *dhʌ́n sɛ̄ɛ̀* gâter l'enfant

sɛ̄ɛ́ (, t) ***n*** **agrumes** *(mandarine, orange, citron) [les agrumes ne sont généralement pas prisés chez les Dan, qui ne les cultivent que rarement]* *Syn.* *dhɤ̄ŋ̀* ♦ *bhɛ̄ntīi à̰ sɛ̄ɛ́, bhɛ̄ntīi sɛ̄ɛ́* citron

sékùtūlē <du nom de Sékou Touré, premier président de la Guinée> ***n*** **1 arbuste épineux** *(petits fruits amers, les Ghanéens en font une sauce)* **2 arbuste** *(les feuilles donnent des démangeaisons; envahit les champs; on croit que cet arbuste a été apporté par les Guinéens dans les années 1960)*

sēŋ {INT sēŋsēŋ} ***dtm*** **seulement** *(avec les nombres qui se terminent en dō : 1, 11, 21 etc.; certains acceptent de les combiner également avec sɔ̃ɔdhṹ 'cinq', sœ̃œ̀dō 'six' et kœ̀œŋ dō 'dix')*

séŋ̀, séŋ̀gā ***n*** **charbon de bois** ♦ *séŋ̀ kʌ̄* fabriquer du charbon

sēŋsēŋ ***dtm*** *Int. de* gbéŋ̀ *seulement*

sɛ́ {IZF sɛ̀; LOC sɛ́ɛ, sɛ́ɛdhɤ, LOC.INT sɛ́ɛsɛ́ɛ, sɛ́ɛdhɤsɛ́ɛdhɤ, SUP sı̃́ãa, SUP.INT sı̃́ãası̃́ãa} ***loc.n*** **1 terre** ◊ *dhṹgā kɔ̀ dhṹ gbʌ̀n dhʌn ɤ́ wó à̰ bhō sɛ́ɛdhɤ* les perches avec lesquelles on bâtit une maison en bois sont plantées dans le sol ◊ *à̰ tā sɛ́ sɛ̀ɛ gúu* plante-le dans le sol humide ◊ *bhɤ̀ n̄ blɛ̃́ɛ̀n gà̰ sı̃́ãa* regarde mon ombre (qui se dessine) sur le sol ◊ *bhɛ́n bhā yáa zīɤ dō, yɤ̀ sı̃́ãası̃́ãa* cette personne ne se promène pas du tout, elle passe tout le temps couchée ◊ *kɤ̄ŋ tā-sùu bhà̰, wò kɤ̄ŋ gā dà̰ sɛ́ɛsɛ́ɛ* lorsqu'on plante le maïs, on met des grains de maïs dans la terre partout ♦ *sɛ́ bı̀* poussière *(sur le sol)* ♦ *sɛ́ kpɤ̄ (gw), sɛ́ kpɔ̄ (t)* lot de terrain ♦ *sɛ́ kpǣæ tà̰* terre ferme ♦ *yɤ́ ɤ̄ bhā dà̰ wō sɛ́ pı́ɤ* il est parti à l'aventure **2 argile** ◊ *yà̰ sɛ́ bhlíkɤ̀ kʌ̄* il a fait des briques en argile **3.1 pays; département; canton** ◊ *sɛ́ bhā' gúu* dans ce pays ♦ *dà̰ sɛ́ pı́ɤ* aller à l'aventure **3.2 village** *dans certains contextes, par exemple :* ◊ *Gwɛ̃́ɛ̀tàa sɛ́ sɔ̃ɔdhṹ ɤ́ yɤ̄ bhā, à̰ kpı̃ı̀sùu dhʌ̀n ɤ́ Tòkpàplɤ̀ɤ* parmi les cinq villages du canton de Gouèta, le plus important est celui de Tokpapleu **4.1 partie inférieure** ♦ *yɤ́ ɤ́ dhō sı̃́ãa, ɤ́ yáàndhūn* puis il est entré et s'est assis **4.2 sud** ◊ *Kɔ́dīvṹà̰ pɛ́ndhɛ̀ ɤ́ sı̃́ãa yʌ̀n* la partie sud de la Côte d'Ivoire

sɛ́dʌ̄ <terre-père> ***n*** **chef de terre, chef de canton, roi, président**

sèdhá, sèdhágā <Manding sèyilán-bone> ***n*** **1 aiguille** *(à coudre) (dans le calcul, les deux formes sont utilisables)* ◊ *bhɛ́n-dhùn wó yā wò wō bɛ̀n pɛ̀ sèdhágā ká* ces gens-là se percent les lèvres avec des aiguilles ♦ *yɤ̀ kpɛ̃́ɛ ká dhè sèdhá(gā) dhɤ́* il est maigre comme une aiguille **2 aiguille** *(de montre)*

sɛ̀ɛ → sǣæ *froid*

sɛ̀ɛ̀ **terme de salutation** *(composante de formules de salutation utilisées pendant la deuxième moitié de la journée)* ♦ *ū sɛ̀ɛ̀* salut ! *(salutation s'adressant à une personne)* ♦ *kā sɛ̀ɛ̀* salut ! *(salutation s'adressant à plusieurs personnes)*

sɛ̄ɛ́, sǣǽ ***n*** **natte** ♦ *sɛ̄ɛ́ bɔ̄* tresser une natte

sɛ̋ɛ 1 ***n*** **éponge pour laver la vaisselle** Qsyn. *fȕu*

sɛ̋ɛ 2, sæ̋æ ***n*** **1 frange** Qsyn. *kʌ̋ŋ* ♦ *sɔ̄ sɛ̋ɛ* frange d'habit ♦ *kɔ́ sɛ̋ɛ* avant-toit **2 résonateur de tambour** *(en fer-blanc, avec des sonnailles sur le pourtour)*

sɛ̋ɛ 2 *LOC de* sɛ̋ *terre*

sɛ̏ɛ̀, sæ̏æ̀ ***n*** *rn* **témoin** *(de qn)* ◊ *ī sɛ̏ɛ̀ bhȕn Zân ká* Jean est mon témoin Syn. *sɛ̏ɛ̀dhɛ̏kʌ̄bhɛ̏n*

sɛ̄ɛ̄ ***n*** **ce village** ◊ *dhɤ̋ŋ yáa yī gɔ̏ sɛ̄ɛ̄ gɯ́* dans notre zone il n'y a pas de chenille "deung"

sɛ̄ɛ̋dhɛ̋ <natte-feuille> ***n*** **herbe** *(les tiges sont utilisées pour tresser les nattes; on enveloppe les colas dans ses feuilles, gɔ̂dhɛ̋)*

sɛ̏ɛ̀dhɛ̏kʌ̄bhɛ̏n <témoin-abstr.-faire-personne> ***n*** **témoin** Syn. *sɛ̏ɛ̀*

sɛ̋ɛdhɤ̄ ***loc.n*** *LOC de* sɛ̋ *terre*

sɛ̋ɛdhɤ̄kɔ̏gɯ́ {Loc. sɛ̋ɛdhɤ̄kɔ̏gɯ́} ***loc.n*** **sous-sol** ◊ *bhān sɛ̋ɛdhɤ̄kɔ̏gɯ́ yɤ̏ sɛ̏ɛ* mon sous-sol est humide et froid

sɛ̄ɛ̋ɛ̏ɛndhʌ́n ***adj*** *int. de* sɛ̄ɛ̋ndhʌ́n *petit*

sɛ̄ɛ̋ndhʌ́n 1) {A P S, sɛ̄ɛ̋ndhʌ́n-sȕ foc. A, sɛ́ɛndhʌ́n pl. A P S, sɛ́ɛndhʌ́n-dhȕn pl. A S, sɛ́ɛndhʌ́n-sȕ-dhȕn foc. pl. A; sɛ̄ɛ̋ɛ̏ɛndhʌ́n Int. A P S, sɛ̄ɛ̋ɛ̏ɛndhʌ́n-sȕ Int. foc. A; sɛ́nsɛ́ndhʌ́n Int. pl. A P S, sɛ́nsɛ́ndhʌ́n-dhȕn Int. pl. A S, sɛ́nsɛ́ndhʌ́n-sȕ-dhȕn Int. pl. foc. A} ***adj*** **1 petit** Syn. *dɛ́dɛ̏ (t)* ◊ *yɤ̏ dhʌ́n sɛ́ɛndhʌ́n-dhȕn flɛ̏ɛn bhɔ̏ gbɛ̋ɛ̀* il pince souvent les petits enfants **2 peu** *surtout là où il y a une opposition de nombre peut apparaître dans une position argumentale et dans celle du prédicat sans déterminé* ♦ *sɛ̄ɛ̋ndhʌ́n bhá* plusieurs *(moins qu'attendu)*

sɛ̄ɛ̋ndhʌ́n 2) ***adv*** **un peu** ◊ *â ! ā̀ wɔ̏n yɤ̏ tɔ̏ sɛ̄ɛ̋ndhʌ́n !* ah, je l'ai raté de justesse !

sɛ́ɛndhʌ́n ***adj*** *pl. de* sɛ̄ɛ̋ndhʌ́n *petit*

sɛ̄ɛ̋ndhʌ́ngɯ́tɔ̏ <petit-in-nom> ***n*** **nom d'enfant** Syn. *dhʌ̄ŋ̏gɯ́tɔ̏*

sɛ̋ɛnŋdhɤ̄ ***adv*** **1 calmement** *(rester sur place)* **2 attentivement**

sɛ̋ɛnŋsɛ̋ɛnŋdhɤ̄ ***adv*** **doucement** *(lentement et sans bruit)* ◊ *bɯ̋kʌ̄bhɛ̏n yɤ̏ tɛ̋ sȕ sɛ̋ɛnŋsɛ̋ɛnŋdhɤ̄ kɤ̄ yɤ̏ yɔ̀ɔn wū sɔ̋ɔ* le chasseur s'approche à pas de loup vers le gibier

sɛ̏ɛsɛ̈dhɛ̏ <Intensif de sɛ̄ɛ̋ndhʌ́n 'petit' ?> ***adj*** *apparaît dans l'expression : sɛ̏ɛsɛ̈dhɛ̏ ká dhɛ̀ pʌ̄ dhɤ́ bhɛ́n !* je l'ai raté de justesse !

sɛ̋ɛsɛ̋ɛ ***loc.n*** *LOC.INT* sɛ̋ *terre*

sɛ̏ɛ̀sɛ̏ɛ̀sȕ ***adj*** *Int. de* sɛ̏ɛ̀sȕ *ridé*

sɛ̋ɛslʌ̏ʌ <terre-piment> ***n*** **gingembre** *(dissous dans une boisson sucrée, sert de remède contre la toux)*

sɛ̏ɛ̀sȕ {S; sɛ̏ɛ̀sɛ̏ɛ̀sȕ Int. S} ***adj*** **ridé, enfilé** *(la partie devant du cou) [cela est considéré comme un signe de beauté]* ♦ *ā̀ bhɔ̄ yɤ̏ sɛ̏ɛ̀sȕ ká* son cou est ridé

sɛ̋ɛsȕ ***adj*** **de terre** ♦ *yɑ̋ sɛ̋ɛsȕ* igname

sɛ̋gàbhɛ̏n <terre-regarder-personne> ***n*** **explorateur** *(celui qu'on envoie examiner l'emplacement d'un futur village ou champ)*

sɛ̋gɔ̏ <terre-tête> ***n*** **État**

sɛ̏gbɛ̏ ***n*** **hochet en vannerie** *(instrument d'animation de danse, de taille variable; tenus verticalement, un dans chaque main, ils sont agités à tour de rôle)*

sɛ̋kɔ̏pɛ̋n <terre-main-tranche> ***n*** **pays, région**

sɛ̏kpɛ̏ ***n*** **castagnettes**

sɛ̋n, **sɛ̋ngā** ***n n*** *rn* **côte** *(anatomique) dans le calcul, seule la forme sɛ̋ngā est utilisée*

sɛ̋ngā → sɛ̋n *côte*

sɛ̏nŋ ***n*** **1 balai** *(de cour; est fait des nervures des feuilles du palmier à huile)* ♦ *sɛ̏nŋgā* i) un verge de balai ii) ***Sida acuta*** arbre dont les branches sont utilisées pour la fabrication des balais Syn. *zűɯ*

sɛ̋nŋ̏dhɛ̏ {LOC sɛ̋nŋ̏dhɤ̄} <côte-sur-endroit> ***loc.n*** *rn* **flanc** *(partie latérale du corps)* ◊ *yà n̄ zɔ̄n kɔ̀kpɤ̄ ká n̄ sɛ̋nŋ̏dhɤ̄* il m'a donné un coup de poing sur le flanc ◊ *n̄ sɛ̋nŋ̏dhɛ̏ yà tó dhɛ̏ɛnsɯ̏* mon flanc me fait mal ♦ *yí yɤ̏ bhɛ̄n kȕn bhɛ̄n sɛ̋nŋ̏dhɤ̄* l'eau arrive aux côtes

sɛ̋nŋ̏dhɤ̄ ***loc.n*** *LOC de* sɛ̋nŋ̏dhɛ̏ *flanc*

sɛ̏nŋpűu <balai-blanc> ***n*** ***Sida corymbosa (gen. Malvaceae)*** **plante herbacée** *(esp.) [utilisée pour fabriquer des balais]* Syn. *zɤ̋ɤpűu*

sénséndhʌn *Int. pl. de* sɛ̄ɛ̋ndhʌn *petit*

sɛ̋ŋ̏ ***n*** **herbe** *(espèce de, utilisée pour couvrir les toits)*

sɛ̋ŋ ***n*** **piquant de porc-épic** Syn. *plűnŋ* ◊ *kíaan ɤ́ bhɛ̄n yūn bhɤ̏ bhā, wà dhɛ́-kʌ̏ blűn sɛ̋ŋ zía ká* la maladie qui ronge le nez de l'homme est soignée avec des piquants carbonisés de porc-épic

sɛ̏ŋbʌ̏ *Int. pl. de* sʌ̏ *bon*

sɛ̋ŋdhɤ̄ {Int. sɛ̋ŋsɛ̋ŋdhɤ̄} ***adv*** **sans bruit** *(marcher)* ◊ *Tȍkpà yɤ̏ tɤ̋ sú-sīʌ sɛ̋ŋdhɤ̄* Tokpa marche sans bruit, doucement

sɛ̋ŋsɛ̋ŋdhɤ̄ ***adv*** *Int. de* sɛ̋ŋdhɤ̄ *sans bruit*

sɛ̋tà ***n*** **silence de mort** ♦ *sɛ̋tà yà dɔ̄* un silence de mort s'est imposé

sɛ̋tí <Fr. assiette> ***n*** **assiette**

sí ***n*** **injure** ♦ *sí bhō bhɛ̄n gɔ̏* insulter qn

sīāa ***loc.n*** *SUP de* sɛ̋ *terre*

sīàabhā {Int. sīàsīàbhā} ***adv*** **1 tout de suite** ◊ *sīàsīàbhā yɤ́ wó dhō zàŋ-dhȕn dhɛ̏* ils sont tout de suite allés chercher les gendarmes ◊ *ā dhūn-sīʌ sīàsīàbhā* je viens tout de suite ! **2** (gw) **soudain** Syn. *gúklɤ̄bhā (m)*

sĩãadhɛ̏ <par terre-place> *n* **terre, surface du sol** ◊ *yíi ɤ̄ tɤ́ŋ wɛ́ɛ bhá kʌ̄ sĩãadhɛ̏ wɔ̏n gúú* il ne fit pas attention au sol

sĩãasĩãa *loc.n SUP.INT* sɛ̃ *terre*

sīakādhâ <Fr. chocolat> *n* **gale** *(esp., provoque des démangeaisons douloureuses)* Qsyn. plēe

sĩakwɛ̃dhɛ̃n *n* **machette à lame large** *(servant à couper les petits arbres)*

sȉandhɛ̃ < ?-feuille> *n Solanum nigrum (gen. Solanaceae)* **crève-chien, morelle noire** *(plante herbacée annuelle, 70 cm et plus, la tige rameuse, droite, les feuilles paires, ovales; les fruits : baies noires, consommables losqu'ils sont mûrs, vénéneux non-mûrs) [on la mange à la place du sel]*

sȉaŋ, **sȉaŋgā** *n* **sabre**

sīapɤ̏bháàn <Fr. échappement> *n* **pot d'échappement**, **tuyau d'échappement**

sĩàsĩàbhā *adv Int. de* sĩàabhā *tout de suite*

sĩatő *n* **rivelaine** *(pic à lame étroite à deux pointes, l'une plus large que l'autre)*

sȉʌ 1, **sȉɤ** {Int. sȉʌsȉʌ, sȉɤsȉɤ} *adv* **parfois**; **souvent** Syn. dhȕnwō ◊ *yɤ̏ n̄ bɔ̏ sȉʌ pɤ̏dhɤ̄* il m'envoie parfois au village ♦ *yà kʌ̄ sȉʌ* souvent

sȉʌ 2 *prt* **bien** *(marque de respect, rend la phrase moins catégorique)* ◊ *bhán dȁ ū dhíɤ sȉʌ* (si tu es d'accord), je te devance

-sīʌ <de *-sȕ gúú 'gérondif-dans'> *mrph suffixe verbal du duratif; exprime une valeur dynamique ou stative*

sĩʌ̀ʌ *n* **prétention; affectation** ◊ *ȁ bhȁ sĩʌ̀ʌ yɤ̏ gbɛ́* il est très prétentieux ♦ *yɤ̏ sĩʌ̀ʌ kȕn gbɛ́* il fait trop le malin *lv. (il se prend pour qn d'important, il se met trop en scène)* ◊ *yɤ̏ yée tȍ sĩʌ̀ʌ ká* il rit avec affectation

sĩʌ̏ŋ *n* **emprunt** ♦ *pʌ̄ sĩʌ̏ŋ dɔ̄ bhēn bhȁ* prêter qch à qn

sȉʌsȉʌ *Int. de* sȉʌ *souvent*

síbhɑ̃n 2 → sȕbhɑ̃n *grand*

síbhɑ̃n 1 *n rn* **semblable** *(notions abstraites ou situations)* ◊ *ȁ síbhɑ̃n kʌ̀ dhɛ̀ pʌ́ ɤ́ ā Flánŋ̏sɤ̏ dhɤ́* c'est comme si j'étais en France Syn. tɛ̀ɛdhɩ̃n

sȉbhȉʌŋ *n* **1 balançoire** *(suspendue en hauteur, faite d'une liane, sans barre ni planchette en bas)* ♦ *sȉbhȉʌŋ blȕȕ* se balancer au bout d'une balançoire *[un amusement des jeunes gens]* **2 barre fixe** ◊ *Tȍkpȁ yɤ̏ sȉbhȉʌŋ blȕȕ-sīʌ ɤ́ slʌ̀ʌ ȁ ká ɤ̄ gúú* Tokpa tourne à la barre fixe

sĩdâ <Fr. SIDA> *n* **SIDA, syndrome immunodéficitaire acquis**

sȉɛtĩȉ, **sĩȅɛtĩȉ** <Fr. cigarette> *n* **cigarette** ♦ *sȉɛtĩȉ tɛ́ɛ* fumée de cigarette ♦ *sȉɛtĩȉ bhūn* fumer une cigarette

sȉi *n rn* **vie** *(durée)* ◊ *ȁ sȉi yíi kʌ̄ gblɛ̏ɛn* il n'a pas eu une longue vie ◊ *ȁ gɔ̏ bhȕn sȉi ká !* la vie, c'est le plus important ! (la dernière bénédiction de la série) ◊ *sȉi ɤ́ kʌ̄ bhēn* *dhɛ̀, ɤ́ bhɛ̄n ɤ́ gwʌ̀ʌ, yɤ̀ kɯ̄ ɯ̄ dhɛ̀ bhàan* la vie que l'homme a et qui fait durer l'homme, qu'elle soit pour toi (bénédiction finale)

sı̋ı 1 ***n Aquila wahlbergi*** **aigle de Wahleberg** *(58-63 cm, brun foncé, huppe courte)*

sı̋ı 2 <Fr. scie> ***n*** **scie** ◊ *n̄ bhā sı̋ı sɔ̋n yɤ̀ yɤ̄-sɯ̀ ká kőo, kɛ̋ɛŋ Tòkpà à sı̋ı sɔ̋n yɤ̀ dɔ̄-sɯ̀ ká glɛ̀ɛŋdhɤ̄* les dents de ma scie sont serrées, et celles de Tokpa sont espacées ♦ *sı̋ı bāŋ* machette sans rainures sur la lame

síkā̋ <Arab. šaqq, via Manding síka> ***n*** **doute** ◊ *à síkā̋ yɤ̀ n̄ gɯ́* j'ai des doutes à ce propos

sínbhā̋n → sűbhān *grand*

sínbhā̋nwō <beaucoup-adv.> ***adv*** **trop**

sīɔ́kɔ̀sīɔ́kɔ̀dhɤ̄ ***onomat*** **schling** *(son d'aiguisage d'une machette)*

sı̀ɤ 1 ***v*** **1.1** *vi* **énerver**, **irriter**, **fâcher** *(qn – dhɛ̀)* Qsyn. bhàn ◊ *wɔ́n yà sı̀ɤ à dhɛ̀ dɛ̀dɛ̀wō* cela l'a beaucoup énervé ◊ *... kɤ̄ wɔ́n yɤ̀ tɯ̀n sı̀ɤ-sɯ̀ ká n̄ dhɛ̀...* parce que j'étais encore mécontent ♦ *à gɯ́ yɤ̀ sı̀ɤ-sɯ̀ ká* il est malade **1.2** *vt* *bhɛ̄n sı̀ɤ̀ kó dhɛ̀* **brouiller les gens** **2** *vt* **endommager** *(réputation)* ◊ *Tòkpà yà ɤ̄ dɛ̀ bhlʌ̀ʌ sı̀ɤ* Tokpa s'est déshonoré ◊ *Yɔ̄ yà Tòkpà bhlʌ̀ʌ sı̀ɤ* Yo a désobéi à Tokpa

sı̀ɤ 2 ***n*** **querelle, palabre** *lv.*

sı̀ɤ → sı̀ʌ *souvent*

síɤ {IN ? síɤɤ} ***loc.n*** **1.1 feu** Syn. pɛ̄ŋ ◊ *síɤ bhā yɤ̀ dhūű-sɯ̀ ká* le feu s'est éteint ◊ *síɤ ɤ́ dà à bhà kɔ́dhēɛ̋ ká* sa case ronde a pris feu ◊ *yà síɤ dà kɔ́ gbà ká* il a mis le feu au toit ♦ *síɤ dhɛ̋ɛn* des flammes ♦ *ā yà-sīʌ síɤ bhà* je suis assis près du feu **1.2 lumière** ♦ *síɤ yà dɔ̄ n̄ yā̋n gɯ́* la lumière m'éblouit **2 courant** *(électrique)* ♦ *wà síɤ kā̋n yī tà* on nous a coupé le courant **3 impatience; hâte** ◊ *dhò Bíyà-sɯ̀ síɤ yɤ̀ à tà* il est impatient de partir pour Abidjan ◊ *kɤ̄ klàŋ̀ wɔ̀n bhā, síɤ yɤ̀ yà à gɯ́* pour que ce problème de l'école soit résolu urgemment

síɤdɔ̄-sɯ̀ <feu-mettre-gérondif> ***n*** **chaleur** ◊ *yɤ̀ síɤdɔ̄-sɯ̀ gɯ́-dɔ̀* il supporte la chaleur

sı̀ɤ-dhɛ̀ ***n*** **mécontentement** ◊ *yà n̄ sı̀ɤ-dhɛ̀ wɔ̀n kɯ̄* il m'a mis en colère

síɤkɔ́ <feu-maison> ***n*** *arch.* **boîte d'allumettes** Syn. pɛ̄ŋkɔ́, tā̋klā̋a kɔ́

sı̀ɤ̀ɤ {P} ***adj*** **batailleur**, **belliqueux** ◊ *yɤ̀ sı̀ɤɤ̀ dɛ̀dɛ̀wō* il est très belliqueux

síɤɤ ***loc.n*** *IN de* síɤ *feu*

sı̀ɤsı̀ɤ *Int. de* sı̀ʌ *souvent*

síɤtɛ̋ɛ <feu-vent> ***n*** **fumée** Syn. pɛ̄ŋtɛ̋ɛ ♦ *síɤtɛ̋ɛ yà yà n̄ gɔ̀* la fumée me gene ◊ *síɤ tɛ̋ɛ yɤ̀ gɯ́sɯ̀* la fumée est dense ◊ *síɤ tɛ̋ɛ fı̋afı̋a* une fumée légère

sı̄ɯ̀ < Fr. chou > ***n*** **chou**

slā̋ā; **sō** (t, kaa) ***n*** **folie** ♦ *slā̋ā yà dà à gɯ́* il est devenu fou

slā̋ābhɛ̀n ***n*** **fou** ◊ *bhā sɔ̄ yà dhı̀i-kún dhɛ̀ slā̋ābhɛ̀n dhɤ́* ton habit est sale comme celui d'un fou ♦ *ɯ̄ slā̋ābhɛ̀n ká póɛ̀e ?* es-tu fou ?

slàan *n* **1** ***Accipiter toussenelii*** **autour tachiro** *(oiseau de 40 cm, dessus gris, dessous entre le roux uni et le roux barré de blanc, queue noirâtre)* **2** ***Malierax gabar, Micronisus g.*** **autour gabar** *(30-36 cm, gris clair avec croupion blanc, pattes rouge terne)*

slàan *n* **brûlé; gratin** *lv.* ◊ *gbɔ̄ ɤ́ bhā à kwāàn kɤ̄ slàan yɤ̀ gó' bhà* gratte la marmite et enlève le brûlé

slʌ́ *n* **1 astuce, ruse 2 technique**

slʌ̀ʌ *n* **piment** *(nom générique)* ♦ *slʌ̀ʌ pűu* piment blanc *(esp., avec de longues cosses; on le met dans la sauce)* ♦ *yà slʌ̀ʌ kʌ̄ tőo bhà* elle a mis du piment dans la sauce ♦ *yà slʌ̀ʌ zīɤ tőo gɔ̀* elle a trop pimenté la sauce ♦ *slʌ̀ʌ yà yà n̄ zūʌ́ bhà* le piment m'a coupé le souffle

slʌ̄ʌ {slʌ̀ʌ} *v* **1.1** *vi* **tourner** *(le coin de qch – ká)* ◊ *yà slʌ̄ʌ kɔ́ ká* il a contourné la maison **1.2** *vi* **contourner** *(qch – ká)* ◊ *Tòkpà yà slʌ̄ʌ kɔ́ ká yà dhó* Tokpa a contourné la maison et continué sa route **1.3** *slʌ̄ʌ ká vi* **faire le tour** *(de – zǜ)* ◊ *kɔ̄nŋtʌ́n bhɛ̄n-dhǜn wò tʌ́n kʌ̄-sīʌ wó slʌ̀ʌ à ká síɤ zǜ* les gens qui font la danse des chasseurs passent autour du feu **1.4** *vi* **se réfugier** *(derrière qn – ká)* Qsyn. gblɛ̀ɛn-kpɔ́ ◊ *yà slʌ̄ʌ ɤ̄ zíɤ̀ɤ ká kɤ̄ wá dhó' ɤ̄ bhàn'* il s'est réfugié derrière son grand-père pour qu'on ne le frappe pas **2** *vt* **tourner** *(vers – píɤ)* ◊ *kwà kwā wʌ̄ slʌ̄ʌ kwā dè wò píɤ* tournons-nous vers notre langue **3.1** i) *vi slʌ̄ʌ ɤ̄ gú le pronom réfléchi est le plus souvent omis* **tourner** *(autour de son axe)*; **circuler** ◊ *ēlíkɔ̄nŋtɛ́ɛ̀ bhà tɛ́ɛkʌ̄bǜbǜ yɤ̀ slʌ̄ʌ-sīʌ gú* l'hélice de l'hélicoptère tourne ◊ *à yɔ̀ɔn yáa slʌ̄ʌ gú* son sang ne circule pas ◊ *dhɛ́-dhǜn wò slʌ̄ʌ-sīʌ gú wó pɤ̀* les feuilles tournoient en tombant 2) *vt slʌ̄ʌ à gú le pronom est le plus souvent omis* **tourner**; **retourner** ◊ *wà gwʌ̀ yà gbœ́œ̀ gú, yɤ́ wó' slʌ̀ʌ gú...* quand on met le caillou dans la fronde, on la fait tourner... ◊ *Tòkpà yà tó yà ɤ̄ gɔ̀ slʌ̄ʌ gú* Tokpa a tourné sa tête vers l'arrière ◊ *yà yī wlōbīdhên slʌ̄ʌ gú* il a tourné le robinet ◊ *sòfɛ́ɛ̀bhīn yà gɔ̄ slʌ̄ʌ gú ɤ̄ kwàa gú* le chauffeur a tourné à gauche ♦ *ɤ̄ wʌ̄ʌ́dhɛ̀ slʌ̄ʌ gú* se détourner 3) *vr* **tourner** *(sur soi-même, une personne)*; **se retourner, faire demi-tour** ◊ *yɤ̀ ɤ̄ slʌ̄ʌ-sīʌ gú ɤ̄ bhà glɛ̄ɛ́ ká* il tourne sur lui-même avec son sac ♦ *slʌ̄ʌ ɤ̄ gú ɤ̄ zǜ* tourner (autour d'un axe) ◊ *kwɛ́ɛ sāyên dhʌ̀n à sáà gú yɤ́ kwɛ́ɛ dhɤ́ slʌ̀ʌ gú ɤ̄ zǜ* c'est grâce aux gonds que la porte tourne **3.2** *vi* **rouler, se rouler** ◊ *dhídhàan bhán bhɛ̀n-dhǜn plɛ̀ bhā wà wō kó pɤ̀ wò slʌ̄ʌ-sīʌ wō gú bòbì gú* les deux bagarreurs se sont fait tomber et se roulent dans la poussière **3.3** *vr* **se tourner** *(personne couchée)* ◊ *yɤ̀ tò ɤ̄ slʌ̀ʌ gú-sǜ bhà gbēŋgbēŋ* il se tournait et se retournait toute la nuit **3.4** 1) *vi* **changer, se transformer** ◊ *á dhē sū̀, yɤ́ bhān tòsǽǽ ɤ́ slʌ̀ʌ gú* je me suis marié, et ma vie a changé 2) *vt* **changer** *(transformer)* **4** *vt* **égrener, égrainer**

slʌ̀ʌʌslʌ̀dhɤ̄ *adv Int. de* slʌ̀slʌ̀dhɤ̄ *lentement (le mouvement est pratiquement invisible)*

slʌ́ʌnslʌ̀ʌn {A P S, slʌ́ʌnslʌ̀ʌn-dhǜn pl. A, slʌ́ʌnslʌ̀ʌn-sǜ foc. A, slʌ́ʌnslʌ̀ʌn-sǜ-dhǜn foc. pl. A; slʌ́nkʌ́nslʌ̀nkʌ̀n Int. A P S, slʌ́nkʌ́nslʌ̀nkʌ̀n-dhǜn Int. pl. A, slʌ́nkʌ́nslʌ̀nkʌ̀n-sǜ Int. foc. A, slʌ́nkʌ́nslʌ̀nkʌ̀n-sǜ-dhǜn Int. pl. foc. A; slʌ́ʌnslʌ́ʌn Int. pl. A P, slʌ́ʌnslʌ́ʌn-dhǜn Int. pl. A S} *adj* **sucré** ◊ *kàa slʌ́ʌnslʌ̀ʌn* canne à sucre très sucrée

slʌ́ʌnslʌ́ʌn *Int. pl. de* slʌ́ʌnslʌ̀ʌn *sucré*

slʌ̀ʌvóò̀dhē <piment-gonflé-nominalis.> ***n*** **piment** *(cosses courtes et vertes)*

slʌ̀ʌwɛ̄ngā <piment-noyau.de.noix.de.palme-os> ***n Phyllastrephus icterinus*** **bulbul ictérin** *(petit oiseau vert olive dessus, jaune dessous, queue brun-roux, remuant et agile)*

slʌ́nkʌ́nslʌ̀nkʌ̀n *Int. de* slʌ́ʌnslʌ̀ʌn *sucré*

slʌ̀slʌ̀dhɤ̄ {Int. slʌ̀ʌʌslʌ̀dhɤ̄} ***adv*** **lentement** *(avec les verbes de mouvement)*

slʌ́slʌ̀slʌ́dhɤ̄ ***adv*** **à pas de loup** *(avancer latéralement, sans bruit)*

slɛ̀ɛn ***n*** **1 oiseau** *(esp.) [quand il crie slɛ̀ɛn, c'est de bon augure; quand il crie fíʌʌfíʌʌ, c'est de mauvais augure]* **2** *le cri de l'oiseau qui sert de bon augure*

slòo ***v*** **1.1** *vi* **suffire 1.2** *vi* **se valoir** *sujet au pluriel* ◊ *yāà n̄ zláà yī slòo* mon jeune frère et moi avons la même taille **2** *vi* **être en accord** *sujet au pluriel*

slōo ***n*** *rn vulg.* **vulve, con** *vulg.* Syn. gwɛ́nŋ, pʌ̄ʌ

slɔ̄ŋgā <vulve-os> ***n*** *vulg. rn* **clitoris** Syn. sōŋgā

slɔ̀ɔ ***v*** **1** 1) *vi* **se trouver** ◊ *wūū sūu gbàn yɤ̀ slɔ̀ɔ bīɤ wùù gúú* la viande d'éléphant (dit-on) comporte toutes les sortes de viande 2) *vt* **trouver, obtenir** ◊ *bhá wʌ́ʌ̀gā slɔ̀ɔ dhāàn ɛ̀e ?* as-tu vraiment gagné d'argent ? ♦ *ɤ̄ dɛ̀ slɔ̀ɔ* réussir dans la vie **2** *vt* **accoucher** Syn. kpɔ́ **3** *vt* **recevoir** *(de la part de – gɔ̀)* ◊ *bṹṹ ɤ́ yí' slɔ̀ɔ Tōkpàplɤ̀ɤ bhɛ̀n-dhùn gɔ̀ yā...* la brousse que nous avons reçue de la part des gens de Tokpapleu...

slɔ̀ɔdhɤ̄ ***onomat*** **sans relâche** *(parler)* ◊ *Yɔ̀ yɤ̀ dhīaŋ zʌ̀ slɔ̀ɔdhɤ̄* Yo jacasse sans relâche

slɔ̀ɔpʌ̀ <trouver-chose> ***n rn*** **propriété** ◊ *à slɔ̀ɔpʌ̀ yɤ̀ gbɛ́* il a beaucoup de biens

slɔ̃́ɔslɔ̃̀ɔ {P S} ***adj*** **apathique, nonchalant** ♦ *yà kʌ̄ slɔ̃́ɔslɔ̃̀ɔ dīn̄ kɔ̄ɔ* la faim l'a rendu apathique

slɤ̄ɤ, slɤ̄ɤdhʌ́n ***n*** **cigale, grillon** *(la forme avec -dhʌ́n est la plus usitée)* ♦ *slɤ̄ɤ wɔ̀ yɤ̀ fɛ̀ɛsùù* les cigales font de bruit

slɤ̄ɤdhʌ́n 1 ***n Napoleonaea vogelii (Napoleonaeaceae)*** **arbre** *(petit, à bois dur) [les feuilles séchées et pilées sont utilisées comme condiment pour le vin de palme; les jeunes branches dans la construction de pièges]*

slɤ̄ɤdhʌ́n 2 → slɤ̄ɤ *cigale*

slɤ́ɤdhɤ̄ ***onomat*** *son du murmure de l'eau* ◊ *yí yɤ̀ zīɤ slɤ́ɤdhɤ̄* l'eau chante

slɤ́ɤŋ ***n Accipiter spp.*** **épervier** Syn. sʌ́ʌ̀

slɤ́ɤslɤ̀ ***adj*** **1 propre** *(habits, aire, vaisselle, maison, etc.),* **pur** ◊ *kɔ̀ɔ slɤ́ɤslɤ̀* une calebasse propre **2** *Christ.* **saint**

slṹkṹ ***n*** **hyène** *(chez les Dan, un animal des contes, très féroce, plus fort que le le lion)*

slṹngā ***n*** **flèche à pointe de fer**

sō (t, kaa) → slāá *folie*

sōfá <Manding sòfá 'guerrier'> ***n*** **Sofa** *(groupe social le plus bas chez les Dan) [descendants des guerriers de Samory, dans la société Dan ont le statut d'esclaves; ne sont pas intouchables, les Dan se marient avec leurs femmes, mais ne leur donnent pas leurs propres femmes en mariage]*

sòfɛ̀ɛ̀, sòfɛ̀ɛ̀bhīn <Fr. chauffeur> ***n*** **chauffeur** ♦ *gɔ̄ sòfɛ̀ɛ̀* chauffeur d'une voiture

sóŋ̀ 1 ***n*** *gbàŋ sóŋ̀* **suie**

sóŋ̀ 2 ***n*** **arbre** *(espèce; le jus et l'écorce sont utilisés comme peinture jaune)*

sōŋgā < ?-os> ***n*** *rn vulg.* **clitoris** Syn. slɔ̄ŋgā

sóŋ̀yídhē <arbre sp.-eau-adj.> ***adj*** **jaune** ◊ *Yɔ̀ yà sɔ̄ yɑ̋n sóŋ̀yídhē dhɔ́* Yo a acheté un tissu jaune

sòo (t) → sūʌ́ *ongle*

sòò, sòo ***n*** *la variante sòo apparaît devant un ton bas* **cheval**

sòòfʌ̄ŋ <Manding sòfali> ***n*** **âne, mulet** ♦ *sòòfʌ̄ŋ yɤ̀ wɛ́-sīʌ* l'âne brait ◊ *yà yà sòòfʌ̄ŋ tà* il s'est assis sur l'âne

sòòtà <cheval-sur> ***pp*** **à califourchon** ◊ *yà yà dù sòòtà* il est monté sur le boeuf

sɔ̀ ***v*** **1** 1) *vi* **pénétrer** ◊ *ɤ́ sɔ̀ kɔ́ ɤ́ bhā à gúù...* dès qu'elle avait pénétré dans la maison... 2) *vt* **insérer, faire entrer** ◊ *sɔ́nŋ sɔ̀ zɔ̋ dhɛ̄ɛ̀ ká !* mets la torche dans la ruche ! **2** *vt* **reprendre** *(recommencer; qch – bhà (gw), ká (t))* ◊ *yà à sɔ̀ bɛ̀ŋ súù-sùù bhà* il a repris sa course

sɔ̄ {sɔ̀} ***n*** **1 tissu** *(étoffe)* ♦ *sɔ̄ bhūnŋ* ballot de tissu ♦ *sɔ̄ bɔ̄* tisser ♦ *sɔ̄ gú* une bande de tissu, fabriqué sur un métier traditionnel **2 pagne 3 vêtement** *(fait d'étoffe)* ◊ *yà sɔ̄ sʌ̀ dà ɤ̄ bhā dhʌ́n bhà* elle a mis de jolis vêtements à son enfant

sɔ́ {sɔ̄} ***v*** *vi* **se répandre**; **devenir très nombreux** ◊ *sɔ̄ dà kɔ̀ yāa yà sɔ́* une mauvaise mode d'habillement s'est répandue partout ◊ *yɤ́ blʌ̄ʌ ɤ́ sɔ̄ à bhà bhlùn tà* et les mauvaises herbes ont envahi son riz

sɔ̋ {sɔ̀} ***n*** **1** *arch.* **piège** *(pour gros gibier)* Qsyn. dɤ̄ŋ, bhīá̋, zèà, vá (t) ♦ *bhɔ̀ɔn bhà pīɤ́ sɔ̋* souricière *(pour les souris à la maison)* ◊ *sɔ̋ yɤ̀ bhìa, ɤ́ dhō ɤ̄ tàabhàn* quand le piège se déclenche, il se referme vers l'arrière ◊ *yà bhűu bhō sɔ̋ ká* il a pris une civette au piège **2** *hist.* **corde de raphia**

sɔ̄blʌ̋ <étoffe-pourri> ***n*** **1 loques, haillon 2 teigne** *(sous la ceinture)* ♦ *sɔ̄blʌ̋ yùa* teigne ♦ *sɔ̄blʌ̋ yà lòo à bhà* il a eu la teigne sous la ceinture

sɔ̀bhɛ́ɛ̀ <Manding sɔ̀bé> ***n*** *rn* **sérieux** ◊ *dhʌ́n bhā yɤ̀ dhìɤ dɛ̀ɛ gbēŋ sɔ̀bhɛ́ɛ̀ ká yűa bhā à gɔ̀* l'enfant a beaucoup gémi cette nuit à cause de cette maladie ♦ *ɪ̄ɪ sɔ̀bhɛ́ɛ̀ súù yʌ̄ ɤ́ yā à pīɤ* prends ce travail au sérieux

sɔ̄dùnbhàbhīʌ́ʌ <habit-suspendre-sur-corde> ***n*** **corde à linge**

sɔ̄dùnbhàdhùù <habit-suspendre-sur-arbre> ***n*** **portemanteau horizontal** *(traditionnel : tronc de bambou ou une perche suspendu horizontalement dans la maison)*

sɔ̋dhã̋ <Fr. soldat> ***n*** **soldat, militaire**

sɔ̄gā <tissu-os> ***n*** **vêtement recherché**

sɔ̋n {COM sɔ̋ɔn} ***loc.n*** *rn* **dent, dents** ◊ *Yɔ̋dhē yà ȁ sɔ̋n yʌ́n kɤ̄ yɤ̏ kʌ̄ sʌ̏* Yodé lui a taillé les dents pour qu'elle soit belle ♦ *bīɤ sɔ̋n* défense{s} d'éléphant ♦ *yȁ ȁ kún sɔ̋ɔn* il l'a mordu ♦ *ȁ sɔ̋n yà yɤ̄ ȁ dhɛ́ɛ̀n tȁ* il s'est mordu la langue *(accidentellement)* ♦ *gbɛ̂n sɔ̋n glőo yɤ̏ ñ kʌ̄-sīʌ* la morsure de chien me fait mal ♦ *yɤ̏ ɤ̄ sɔ̋n bhɤ̏ yī gǘ klɤ̄ɤ̋klɤ̏ɤklɤ̄ɤ̋dhɤ̄* il grince les dents en dormant ♦ *ǖ sɔ̋n ká dhɛ̀ fɛ̋ŋ sɔ̋n dhɤ́* tes dents ressemblent à celles d'un rat *(espacées, ou deux dents plus longues que les autres)* ♦ *ȁ sɔ̋n yɤ̏ kʌ̏ dhɛ̀ bāa kɔ̏n yɤ̏ pɤ̏ zɔ̋ŋ gǘ* ses dents sont comme le foutou de manioc tombé sur le gravier *(c'est-à-dire qu'elles sont très espacées)*

sɔ̄nŋ ***n*** **prix**

sɔ̋nŋ ***n*** **torche** *(de raphia)* *Syn.* *gbíaa* ♦ *sɔ̋nŋ gā* brin de torche de raphia ♦ *sɔ̋nŋ dɔ̄* allumer un flambeau

sɔ̋nŋdɔ̄gèètȁ <torche-allumer-masque-sur> ***n*** ***Apaloderma vittatum*** **couroucou à queue barrée** *(oiseau : 25 cm, richement coloré; queue noire et blanche barrée)*

sɔ̋nŋdhɛ̋ <torche-feuille> ***n*** **palme du palmier** *(à huile ou raphia)*

sɔ̋npíɤ {Int. sɔ̋npíɤ-sɔ̋npíɤ} <dent-chez> ***adv*** **par les dents** ◊ *dhí zű ká gbɛ́sɛ̂ ɤ́ bhā, wȁ zīɤ bhēn sɔ̋n píɤ sɔ̋n píɤ* cure-dent dont on se nettoie la bouche, on le passe à de nombreuses reprises sur les dents

sɔ̋npíɤdhɛ̏ <dent-chez-place> ***n*** **gencive**

sɔ̀ŋ ***n*** *rn* **comportement, caractère** ♦ *bhēn sɔ̀ŋ yíi kún bhō kó gǘ* s'ils ne se supportent pas l'un l'autre...

sɔ̋ɔ 1 ***n*** ***Thryonomys swinderianus*** **aulacode, agouti** *Iv. (gros rongeur nocturne, 4-8 kg, viande très prisée)*

sɔ̋ɔ 2 {sɔ̋ɔsɔ̋ɔ Int.} ***pp*** **près de, auprès de** ◊ *dɔ̄ ñ sɔ̋ɔ* reste à côté de moi ◊ *yɔ̀ɔn ñ sɔ̋ɔ* approche-toi de moi ◊ *yɤ̏ dhūn-sīʌ pɤ̂ sɔ̋ɔ* il arrive aux abords du village

sɔ̋ɔdhű ***num*** **cinq** *[considéré comme nombre féminin]*

sɔ̏ɔn, **sœ̏œn** ***n*** **coquille** *(d'escargot)*

sɔ̋ɔn ***loc.n*** *COM de* sɔ̋n *dent*

sɔ̋ɔsɔ̏ɔ {A P S, sɔ̋ɔsɔ̏ɔ-dhǜn pl. A S, sɔ̋ɔsɔ̏ɔ-sǜ foc. A S, sɔ̋ɔsɔ̏ɔ-sǜ-dhǜn foc. pl. A S} ***adj*** **étroit**

sɔ̋ɔsɔ̋ɔ *Int. de* sɔ̋ɔ *près de*

sɔ̄pɛ̋ <tissu-fendre> ***n*** **bande de tissu, bandage**

sɔ̄pɛ̋n <tissu-tranche> ***n*** **mouchoir; chiffon** *(pour essuyer la poussière, etc.)*

sɤ̏ 1 ***n*** **corne** *Syn.* *sɤ̏dhʌ́n*

sɤ̏ 2 ***n*** **1 fétiche** *(sous forme d'onguent, de poudre, de bague; pour protéger les champs ou contre l'adultère; pouvant provoquer la mort ou des paroxysmes de rire chez celui qui en* *est la cible)* Qsyn. dū ♦ *yà sɤ̀ yà à tà* il a dressé un gris-gris contre lui **2 serment** ♦ *sɤ̀ bhɤ̀* jurer ◊ *bhán à sɤ̀ bhɤ̀ dhɛ̀ bhíin dhó dhó'* je jure que je ne partirai pas

sɤ̄ *n* **grain de palmier à huile** ♦ *sɤ̄ dhɪ̀ɪ̀* tourteau des graines de palme ♦ *sɤ̄ dhɛ́* palme du palmier à huile adulte

sɤ̀dhʌ́n <corne-diminutif> *n* **petit sifflet** *(fabriqué avec du bambou de Chine ou avec une espèce d'herbe)* *[moyen de diriger un groupe de travailleurs]*

sɤ̄dhɪ̀ɪ̀fáa <grain.de.palmier-saleté-déchet> *n* ***Marisens alternifolis (gen. Cyperaceae)*** **plante herbacée**

sɤ̀ŋ *v* 1) *vi* **se dissoudre**; **se fondre** ◊ *sṹkā̋dhṹ yà sɤ̀ŋ yí bhàa* le sucre s'est dissous dans l'eau ◊ *yɔ̋n yɤ̀ sɤ̀ŋ-sīʌ yʌ́nŋ̀ dhɛ̀* l'huile fond au soleil 2) *vt* **dissoudre**; **fondre** ◊ *sɪ́ɤ [yʌ́nŋ̀, Yɔ̀] yà yɔ̋n sɤ̀ŋ* le feu / le soleil / Yo a fait fondre l'huile

sɤ̋ŋgɤ̋sɤ̀ŋgɤ̀ *adj Int. de* sɤ̋ɤŋsɤ̀ɤŋ *transparent*

sɤ̋ɤŋsɤ̀ɤŋ {A; Int. sɤ̋ŋgɤ̋sɤ̀ŋgɤ̀ A, P} *adj* **1 propre**, **transparent**, **claire**, **limpide** *(eau)*, **pure** *(vérité)* ◊ *à bhà tǣǣ̀nwɔ̀ yɤ̀ sɤ̋ɤŋsɤ̀ɤŋ* ce qu'il dit, c'est la pure vérité ◊ *wē sɤ̋ɤŋsɤ̀ɤŋ* vin de palme transparent **2 léger** *(boisson)* ◊ *kā̋fēe yí tīi dhʌ̀n ɯ́ à pɪ́ɤ ɛ̀e, ɛ̋ɛn kā̋fēe yí sɤ̋ɤŋsɤ̀ɤŋ ?* aimes-tu le café fort ou faible ?

sɤ̄yí <grain du palmier-eau> *n* **sauce graine** *(sauce à graines de palmier à huile)*

sǣœ 1) {A S, sǣœ-dhʉ̀n pl. A S, sǣœ-sʉ̀ɪ foc. A, sǣœ-sʉ̀ɪ-dhʉ̀n foc. pl. A} *adj* **rassis**, **"couché"** *lv. (nourriture de la veille)* ◊ *kɤ̄ŋ sǣœ dīn yáa sʌ̀* le maïs rassis n'a pas bon goût *(maïs épluché la veille et braisé le lendemain)*

sǣœ 2) *n* **manque de fraîcheur** *(se dit d'un aliment qui n'est plus frais)* *sǣœ kā̋n* rassir

sœ́œ̀ *n* **arc** *(arme)* ♦ *sœ́œ̀ yɤ̀ à kwɛ̀ɛ̄* c'est chaud ! *(nourriture, boisson, eau pour se laver)* ♦ *sœ́œ̀ yɤ̀ zūn' gɔ̀ zīaan bhʉ́n* il a péri en voyage *(litt. : l'arc lui a barré la route)*

sœ́œ̀bhīn <arc-humain> *n* **archer; guerrier**

sœ̋œ̀dō *num* **six** *[considéré comme nombre masculin]*

sœ̀œn → sɔ̀ɔn *coquille d'escargot*

sœ̋œ̀plɛ̀ *num* **sept** *[considéré comme nombre féminin]*

sœ́œ̀zʌ̀-dhʉ̀n *n pluriel du* sœ́œ̀bhīn *archer*

sṹ < Wobe cú > *n* **1 lune** ◊ *sṹ dɛ̀e yà wɔ̀* la nouvelle lune est apparue ♦ *sṹ dhɛ̀gɯ́ tīi* nuit sans lune **2 mois** ♦ *sṹ yà gā* à la fin du mois {lunaire} ◊ *wà sɛ́ lòo dhɛ́ tà yɤ̀ bʉ̀ sṹ dhɛ̀ pɪ́ɤ ?* si on recouvre les feuilles de terre, elles pourrissent en combien de mois ? ◊ *bhlʉ̀n dhɔ̀ɔ yɤ̀ bhɔ̀ sṹ ɤ́ zɪ̀ɤ à ká* ce riz a poussé le mois dernier

sūà, **sūà̀**, **sùa** *n* **mensonge** ♦ *sūà bhɛ̄̀n* menteur, menteuse ♦ *sūà kʌ̄ bhɛ̄n bhà* mentir à propos de qn ♦ *sūà bhʉ̀n* c'est faux

súà̀n *n* **attention** ♦ *wɔ́n súà̀n bhō* être attentif, être observateur

súà̀n-bhō *v vt* **épier**, **guetter**

sūàsʉ̀ *adj* **menteur**

súä̀ɛ *n* ***Francolinus squamatus*** **francolin écailleux** *(32 cm, brun et chamois, pattes rouge orangé; cri retentissant au lever et au coucher du soleil)*

sūʌ́ 1 (gw), **sòo** (t) *n* **1** *rn* **ongle** ◊ *kɔ̄ŋgā sūʌ́* ongle *(du doigt de la main)* **2** *rn* **griffe**

sūʌ́ 2 *n* **sifflement** ♦ *sūʌ́ pȉɤ* siffler *(homme)*

sūʌ́ʌ *n* **orgelet** ◊ *bhɛ̄n ɤ́ bhíi ä̀ bhä̀ pʌ̄ bhɤ̏ dō, bhá' bhɤ̏, sūʌ́ʌ yɤ̏ ɗɔ̏ ūi yä̂ä̀n* si tu n'a jamais mangé la nourriture d'une personne, et si tu la manges, tu auras un orgelet *(une croyance des Dan)*

sű̋ʌʌ < ?-grain> *n* ***Xylopia aethiopica (gen. Annonaceae)*** **poivre noir** *[grains utilisés contre les perturbations des règles; les grains pilés et mélangés avec de l'huile sont frottés au corps d'un défunt pour le préserver jusqu'aux funérailles] (utilisé toujours dans les combinaisons)* ♦ *sű̋ʌʌ dhȕ, sű̋ʌʌ gā dhȕ* plante Xylopia aethiopica ♦ *sű̋ʌʌ gā* grains de la plante Xylopia aethiopica

sȕʌŋsȕʌŋ *n* ***Scopus umbretta*** **ombrette** *(60 cm, brun terne, tête prolongée en arrière par une huppe qui lui donne une forme d'enclume) [le nom imite le cri de cet oiseau]*

sűbhā̋n, **sűnbhā̋n**, **sībhā̋n**, **sīnbhā̋n** {A; sűnbhā̋nsȕnbhȁn, sĩnbhā̋nsȉnbhȁn Int. pl. A} *adj* **1 nombreux** ◊ *bhɛ̄n dūŋ sűbhā̋n ɤ́ bhān yā...* la grande foule qui s'est rassemblée ici... **2 grand**, **fort** ◊ *ūi n̄ bhȁn síbhā̋n bhō dhɤ́ dhɛ̀ ? !* pourquoi m'as-tu frappé si fort ? ! **3 pareil**, **égal** ♦ *ä̀ síbhā̋n yáa dhɤ́* il n'a pas son pareil ♦ *ä̀ sűbhā̋n yáa gūn* il n'y avait pas son pareil **4 environ** *(après un numéral)* ◊ *bhlȕ kīdhő̋ŋ sɔ̋ɔdhű sībhā̋n yɤ̏ n̄ gɔ̏* j'ai environ 5 kilos de riz

sűbhōwɛ̏ɛbhä̀ <mois-enlever-place-sur> *n* **serpent** *(esp.; peut rester immobile pendant un mois)*

sűȅe *Int. de* sűɤ-sȕ *peureux*

sűȅsīɤ *num* **neuf** *[considéré comme nombre féminin]*

sȕɛɛ *n* **moue méprisante** *(les lèvres avancées; signe d'un refus catégorique et insultant)* Qsyn. kplɛ̏ɛn ♦ *yà sȕɛɛ bhō n̄ ká, yà sȕɛɛ kā̋n n̄ ká* il m'a fait une moue méprisante

sūȅɛ *n* ***Coturnix delegorguei*** **caille**

sűkā̋dhű <Fr. sucre> *n* **sucre**

sűnbhā̋n → sűbhā̋n *grand*

sűnbhā̋ndhā̋n <Manding súnbala, súnbara> *n* **1 soumbala** *(condiment des grains fermentés de néré)* ♦ *sűnbhā̋ndhā̋n kpɤ̄* boule de soumbala **2 arôme maggi** ♦ *sűnbhā̋ndhā̋n gā* cube d'arôme maggi

sűnbhā̋nsȕnbhȁn *Int. pl. de* sűbhā̋n *grand*

súnȉ̏ŋ → súȉ̏ŋ *ramadan*

súȉ̏ŋ, **súuȉ̏ŋ**, **súnȉ̏ŋ** <Ar. ṣawm, via Manding sún> *n* **ramadan** ♦ *súȉ̏ŋ bhán* faire le ramadan ♦ *ɤ̄ bhä̀ súȉ̏ŋ kā̋n bhɤ̏pʌ̏ dō ká* rompre le jeûne avec une nourriture *(après la descente du soleil)*

sȕɤ ***v*** **1** *vi* **être matinal** ◊ *ā kʌ̄ sȕɤ dhīā́ pī́ɤ* je me suis levé de bonne heure **2** *vi* **faire tôt le matin** *(qch – tȁ)* ◊ *yà sȕɤ yʌ̄ tȁ* il a commencé le travail de bonne heure ◊ *yɤ̏ kʌ̄ sȕɤ yāa gṹ yāa bhō/wō* il s'est réveillé de très bonne heure

sű̃ɤ 1) {sȕɤ} ***v*** *vi* **avoir peur** *(de – gɔ̏)* ♦ *sű̃ɤ-sȕ* peureux Syn. sű̃èe

sű̃ɤ 2) ***n*** **peur** ◊ *sű̃ɤ yɤ̏ Gɤ̏ɤ̏ gṹ kɤ̄ Gbȁtȍ yɤ̏ Yɔ̏ bhȁn* Geu a peur que Gbato ne frappe Yo ♦ *sű̃ɤ bhɛ̄n* personne peureuse ♦ *sű̃ɤ dȁ bhɛ̄n gṹ* faire peur à qn ♦ *sű̃ɤ kȁ́n bhɛ̄n gṹ* effrayer qn ♦ *sű̃ɤ yȁ kȁ́n ȁ gṹ* il a pris peur ◊ *sű̃ɤ dȅdȅ n̄ kʌ̄-sɪʌ* j'ai vraiment peur

sű̃ɤsű̃ɤsȕ ***adj*** *SupInt. de* sű̃ɤ-sȕ *peureux*

sű̃ɤsȕ {A P, sű̃ɤsȕ-dhȕn pl. A, sű̃ɤsȕ-sȕ foc. A; sű̃èe Int. A P S, sű̃ɤsȕ-dhȕn Int. pl. A; sű̃ɤsű̃ɤsȕ SupInt. A P, sű̃ɤsű̃ɤsȕ-dhȕn SupInt. pl. A, sű̃ɤsű̃ɤsȕ-sȕ SupInt. foc. A} <avoir.peur-gérondif> ***adj*** *sű̃ɤsȕ et sű̃ɤsű̃ɤsȕ expriment un état temporaire marqué par la peur; sű̃èe exprime une qualité permanente, "poltron"* **peureux** ◊ *pʌ́ bhā, ȁ dhūn ȁ bhɛ̄n sű̃ɤsű̃ɤsȕ-sȕ dhɛ̏* donne cette chose au plus craintif d'entre eux

sȕɤyī́ <être.matinal-eau> ***n*** *rn* **bouillie matinale** *(que les musulmans mangent pour rompre le jeûne)* ◊ *dhʌ́n yā yɤ̏ bɤ̏ kɤ̄ yɤ̏ sȕɤyī́ bhūn* cet enfant s'est réveillé pour boire la bouillie matinale ♦ *ɤ̄ sȕɤyī́ kȁ́n* manger sa bouillie matinale

sű̃sʌ̄ŋ́ <lune-étoile> ***n*** **étoile**

sȕu ***n*** **sou** *(pièce d'argent de la période coloniale)* Syn. sȕugā ♦ *sȕu yáa n̄ gɔ̏* je suis sans le sou

sūu ***n*** **1** *rn* **sorte** ◊ *gbɛ̂n sūu yɤ̏ gbɛ́* il y a beaucoup de races de chiens **2** *rn* **façon 3** *rn* **clan** ◊ *kā sūu bhȕn dē ká ?* vous êtes de quel clan ? **4** *neol.* **adjectif**

sű̃ȕ ***n Cephalophus niger*** **céphalophe noir** *(80-100 cm, 16-24 kg, robuste, tête allongée, narines gonflées, jambes courtes)* Syn. gbȁ

sūu-dhɛ̏ ***n*** **qualité, état** ◊ *yɛ̄ɛ sūu-dhɛ̏* état de griot

sūű̃dhí ***n*** **suudhi** *(danse des jeunes, pendant laquelle on joue des tam-tams et fait résonner les grelots en fer)*

sȕugā ***n*** **sou** *(pièce d'argent de la période coloniale)* Syn. sȕu

súuŋ̏ → súŋ̏ *ramadan*

sű̃wȅe <lune-mue> ***n*** **mica** Syn. yʌ́nŋ̏wȅe

-sȕ 1 <de sṹ 'prendre'> ***mrph*** *marque de gérondif, adjointe à la base verbale ou au circonstant; dans ce dernier cas, la base verbale prend le ton extra-bas* ◊ *yī́ wȅŋ-sȕ* i) le fait de verser de l'eau ii) eau versée

-sȕ 2 ***mrph*** *suffixe peu productif de l'adjectif dénominal* Qsyn. dhē 1

-sȕ 3 ***mrph*** **1** *clitique de focalisation adjoint aux adjectifs; précède la marque du pluriel -dhȕn* **2** *clitique du sélectif actuel, (le groupe nominal étant déplacé en tête de l'énoncé et*

relativisé) Qsyn. dhē 2 ◊ *bāa-sȕ dhʌ̀n ɤ́ bhāan ȁ bhɤ̏* c'est le manioc (et aucun autre parmi les mets offerts) que je vais manger

sɯ́, sí {sɯ̄, sī} *v* **1.1** *vt* **prendre** *(pour posséder)* ◊ *ȁ sɯ́ !* tiens ! (c'est à toi) ♦ *wà wō kó sɯ́* ils se sont mariés ♦ *ɤ́ sɯ̄ ȁ bhȁ, ..., ɤ́ dèɛ ɤ́ lòo* depuis cela et jusqu'à nos jours **1.2** *vt* **atteindre** ◊ *pɛ̄ŋ yà kɔ́ dhí sɯ́* le feu a englouti la porte de la maison **1.3** *vt* **porter** ◊ *dhʌ́ngɔ̄ɔ̀n-dhȕn plɛ̀ dhʌ̀n ɤ́ wó dhɯ́ dɔ̄ŋ sɯ́-sīʌ* deux jeunes hommes portent un rondin **1.4** *vt* **occuper** *(temps)* ◊ *dhɛ́dhɛ́ plɛ̀ dhʌ̀n ɤ́ ȁ sɯ̄ yɤ́ ɤ̄ dɛ̀ zɔ̀n ȁ ká n̄ dhɛ̏* il s'est présenté à moi pendant deux heures **1.5** *vt* **voler** *(dérober)* ◊ *bhɛ̄n dódó dhʌ̀n wó pʌ̄ ɤ́ kwànbhɛ̏n ɤ́' sɯ̄ wó' dɔ̄* peu sont ceux qui savent ce que le voleur a volé **2** *vt* **effectuer** *(dans quelques expressions figées)* ♦ *bȉaŋ sɯ́* courir **3** *vi* **dépendre** *(de – bhȁ)* **4** *vi ɤ́ sɯ̄ ... bhȁ* **depuis** ◊ *ɤ́ sɯ̄ tɤ́ŋ bhā' bhȁ, tɔ́ŋ yȁ gó ɤ̄ glőo ȅe ?* depuis cette époque, la consigne a changé ?

sɯ́gɯ́ <prendra-dans> *pp* **pour, au profit de**

sȕkplɛ̋edhē *n* ***Amblyospiza albifrons*** **gros-bec à front blanc** *(18 cm, trapu, à grosse tête et à bec massif; pour le mâle : tête, manteau et gorge marron, poitrine et ventre gris; pour la femelle : dessus brun foncé, dessous blanc crème strié de brun)*

T t

tȁ 1) *n rn* **surface** ◊ *bhá ɯ̄ bō pʌ̄ bhɤ̏-sȕ ká, yɤ́ ɯ́ dɔ̄ yɤ́ ɯ̄ gú tȁ dhɤ́ lɔ̀ɔ sʌ̏ ká* quand tu finis de manger, attends le moment où la partie supérieure de ton ventre descend bien *(quand la digestion se termine)* ♦ *ȁ tȁ dhɛ̏ ɤ́ kpœ̀œ* le lendemain ♦ *n̄ tȁ yáa sʌ̏* je ne me sens pas bien ♦ *yɤ̏ dhɔ̀ ȁ tȁ gɯ́* elle est allée à un rendez-vous avec lui

tȁ 2) *pp* **1 sur** ◊ *ȁ bhȁ gɔ̄ yɤ̏ dɔ̄-sīʌ tɔ̀n tȁ* sa voiture est arrêtée sur la colline ◊ *yɤ̏ bhȁan-dhȕn zȕɤ gwʌ̏ ká kɤ̄ wɔ̀ gó bhlȕn tȁ* il jette des pierres aux oiseaux pour qu'ils quittent le riz **2 au-dessus de** ◊ *yɤ́ yígā kpȉ dō ɤ́ gūn bhūn, kɛ̄ɛ yɤ́ pɔ̄ŋ ɤ́ gūn ȁ tȁ...* ... il y avait un grand fleuve, mais le pont qui le traversait...

tȁ 3) *prev* **surface**

tā {tā} *v* **1** 1) *vt* **fermer**; **boucher** ◊ *ȁ dhí yɤ̏ tā-sȕ ká* il a la bouche fermée ◊ *yà kwɛ̋ɛ tā bhɔ̏ tȁ* il a enfermé le cabri 2) *vi* **se fermer** ◊ *kwɛ̋ɛ yà tā* la porte s'est fermée 3) *vi valeur passive* **être bloqué** Qsyn. dhʌ̀nŋ ◊ *zīaan yà tā* la route est bloquée **2** *vt* **planter** *(dans les trous)* ♦ *kɤ̄ŋ tā* planter le maïs ♦ *pʌ̄ tā* planter (des plantes) **3** *vt tā ɤ̄ bhȁ* **s'entourer de** ◊ *yī dō ká, yɤ́ Wɔ̀ɔgblȁȁbhȁan yɤ̏ ɤ̄ bhȁ gwʌ̄ʌ́zʌ̏-dhȕn tā ɤ̄ bhȁ...* un jour, le Calao s'est entouré de ses serviteurs... **4** *vt* **faire** *(noeud)* **5** *vi tā ɤ̄ gɯ́* **être gonflé de colère**

tʌ̋ 1) {tȁ} *n* **1 marche, déplacement** *(se dit des humains et des animaux, mais aussi des serpents, des grenouilles, des escargots etc.)* ♦ *tʌ̋ sɯ́* marcher, se déplacer, avancer **2 voyage** ♦ *dhó tʌ̋ gɯ́* aller en voyage

tā̃ 2) {tã̀} *v* **1.1** *vi* **marcher** *(avoir capacité)* ♦ *yɤ̀ tã̀ kpĩanŋ̃kpĩanŋ̃dhɤ̄* il boite **1.2** *vt ɤ̄ yā̃n tā̃ bhɛ̄n ká* **toiser qn des pieds à tête 2** *vi* **piétiner, marcher** *(sur – tã̀)* Syn. tāã̀ ♦ *yà tā̃ n̄ gɛ̀n tã̀* il m'a marché sur le pied (ou : les pieds) **3** *vi* **venir au secours** *(de – dhɛ̀)*

tàa 1) *n rn* **dos** Qsyn. tàadhɛ̀ ◊ *yɤ̀ gùn wɔ̄-sɪʌ ɤ̄ tàa ká* il était couché sur le dos ♦ *dhó ɤ̄ tàa ká* marcher à reculons

tàa 2) *pp* **sur** ♦ *dṹnŋ tàa* sur le tas d'ordures

tàa 3) *loc.n LOC de* tàadhɛ̀ *dos*

tāa 1 *n rn* **cadeau** *(ce qui est donné à l'acheteur en guise de supplément lors d'une transaction commerciale) [on le donne au client qui achète beaucoup, ou, de temps en temps, au client régulier]* Qsyn. gbœ̄œdhē, sāan ◊ *yà n̄ tāa kʌ̄ glɔ̄ɔ kpàa dō ká* il m'a offert une grappe de bananes

tāa 2 *loc.n COM de* tàadhɛ̀ *dos*

tāà {tàa} *v vi* **piétiner, marcher** *(sur – tã̀)* Syn. tā̃ ♦ *yà tāã̀ n̄ gɛ̀n tã̀* il m'a marché sur le pied (ou : sur les pieds)

tā̃à *n* **tabac** *(à fumer) [inconnu des Dan avant la colonisation; les femmes dan ne fument pas]* ♦ *tā̃à bhũ̄n* fumer (le tabac)

tàaabhà *pp Int. de* tàabhàn *derrière*

tàaatā̃bhà *adv SupInt. de* tàabhàn *derrière*

tā̃àblʌ̀ʌ, tā̃àblʌ̀, tàbɛ̃́dhĩ́ < Fr. table > *la forme tàbɛ̃́dhĩ́ est vue comme moins autentique, probablement empruntée via le dioula* *n* **table**

tàabhà → tàabhàn *derrière*

tàabhàdhɛ̀ <dos-sur-place> *n rn* **partie arrière du corps humain**

tàabhàn 1), tàabhà {tàaabhà HU Int.; tàatā̃bhàn AS, tàaatā̃bhà HU SupInt.} <dos- ?> *pp* **derrière** ♦ *bhán dhó kɔ́ tàabhàn* euph. je vais faire mes besoins ◊ *bhɛ́n ɤ́ tō bhɛ̄n gbàn tàatā̃bhàn, ...* celui qui a été le tout dernier parmi tous... ◊ *yà ɤ̄ dɛ̀ɛ̀n-kpɔ́ dhṹ tàabhà* il s'est caché derrière l'arbre

tàabhàn 2), tàabhà *adv* **1 derrière, après 2 après, prochainement** ♦ *kō tàabhàn !* au revoir ! ♦ *dhó tàabhan* revenir ♦ *tó tàabhàn* rester le dernier; marcher derrière ♦ *tàabhàn sʉ̀ yā' gʉ́* à partir de maintenant

tā̃àbhũ̄nbhɛ̀n <tabac-boire-personne> *n* **fumeur, fumeuse**

tàadhɛ̀, tāàdhɛ̀ {LOC tàadhɤ̄, tàa, LOC.INT tàatàa, COM tāa} *loc.n rn* **dos** *(surface de)* Qsyn. kō 1, tàa 1) ◊ *ʉ̄ tāàdhɛ̀ yà kʌ̄ dhìisʉ̀* ton dos est sale ◊ *yà dhʌ́n bhā yà ɤ̄ tàadhɤ̄/tàa* elle a pris l'enfant sur son dos ◊ *Sɤ́ŋgā dhú dhʌ́n zʌ̀ yɤ̀ à tàatàa, yáa yɤ̄ sĩ́āa* la fille de Seunga est toujours à son dos, elle ne descend pas par terre ◊ *à bhà wūn yɤ̀ lòo à tāa/tàadhɤ̄* ses cheveux lui arrivent jusqu'au dos ◊ *n̄ kā̃à n̄ tàa* gratte-moi le dos

tàadhɤ̄ *loc.n LOC de* tàadhɛ̀ *dos*

tȁadhȕȕ < ?-arbre> ***n*** **canne** *(pour marcher) [symbole de l'âge et de la sagesse de masques]* ♦ *yà tȁadhȕȕ gbȁn ɤ̄ gɔ̄* il s'est appuyé sur sa canne

táȁgbɔ̄ <tabac-pot> ***n*** **pipe**

tàaklȁan <dos- ?> ***n rn*** **garrot** ♦ *lāa tàaklȁan* garrot de lion

táȁsȕȕkɔ̏ ***n*** **maison à étages**

tàatàa ***loc.n*** *LOC.INT de* tàadhȅ *dos*

tàatȁ̋bhȁn, tàaatȁ̋bhȁ 1) ***pp*** *SupInt. de* tàabhȁn *derrière*

tàatȁ̋bhȁn 2) ***adj*** *Int. de* tȍtàabhȁn *dernier*

tàbɛ̋dhí – > táȁblʌ̀ʌ *table*

tȁ-bɤ̏ ***v vt*** **exploiter, abuser; escroquer**

tàbȗ <du nom de la ville de Tabou au sud-ouest de RCI> ***n*** **tabou** *(sorte de manioc à peau blanche, précoce, à bon rendement, bon pour l'atiéké)*

tȁbhan ***adj*** **bête**

tàbhàntȉȉ <Fr. tomate> ***n*** **tomate, tomates**

tȁ-bhō {tȁ-bhō} ***v*** **1** *vt* *bhēn gbɛ̋ɛ̏ tȁ-bhō* **obliger qn** ◊ *ā dhȍ n̄ gbɛ̋ɛ̏ tȁ-bhō, kɤ̄ á dhó dhēŋdhɤ̄* je serai obligé d'aller au champ **2** *vr* **s'efforcer** ◊ *ūū dȅ gbɛ̋ɛ̏ tȁ-bhō kɤ̄ úú dhūn* fais un effort pour venir

tȁ̋bhōo ***n*** **appel au secours** *(situation de danger)* ♦ *tȁ̋bhōo dȁ* crier au secours

tȁ-dɔ̄ {tȁ-dɔ̄} ***v*** **1** *vt* **aider qn à se charger** ◊ *bhán Yɔ̏ tȁ-dɔ̄ yí ká* j'ai aidé Yo à mettre le récipient rempli d'eau sur sa tête **2** *vt* **achever** *(personne, animal, au sens de tuer)* ◊ *yà kwànbhɛ̏n ɤ̄ wó' bhȁn bhā' tȁ-dɔ̄* il a achevé le voleur qu'on avait frappé

tȁdhȅkpɶ̀ɶ <surface-jour-se.lever> ***n*** **lendemain** *dans les expressions :* ♦ *ȁ tȁdhȅkpɶ̀ɶ tȁ* le lendemain ♦ *ȁ tȁdhȅkpɶ̀ɶ yɛ̋ɛ́npíɤ* le lendemain matin

tȁ-gā {tȁ-gā} ***v*** **1** *vt* **calmer, ramener au silence 2** *vi* **se calmer** ♦ *dhȅ tȁ yɤ̏ gā !* silence !

tȁgútȁpʌ̏ <surface-ventre-sur-chose> ***n*** **reptile**

tȁ-kȁ̋n {tȁ-kȁn} ***v vt*** **arrêter, interrompre** *(une danse pour faire des cadeaux)*

tȁ-kʌ̄ {tȁ-kʌ̄} ***v vt*** **couvrir** *(une maison)* ◊ *ɤ̄ gūn kpá pȁ̋pɔ̋ ɛ̋en yɛ̋ dhūn ó wó gūn kɔ́-dhȕn tȁ-kʌ̄-sīʌ' ká* auparavant, on couvrait les maisons avec des papots ou avec de la paille

tȁ̋klȁ̋a <Manding tákala> ***n*** **allumettes** ♦ *tȁ̋klȁ̋a kɔ́* boîte d'allumettes Syn. *síɤkɔ́, pēŋkɔ́* ♦ *tȁ̋klȁ̋a gā* allumette ♦ *tȁ̋klȁ̋a pú* craquer une allumette

tȁ-kó-zʌ̄ {tȁ-kó-zʌ̄} ***v vt*** **rivaliser pour** ◊ *Tȍkpȁ wāa Zân wȁ Yɔ̏ tȁ-kó-zʌ̄* Tokpa et Zan rivalisent pour Yo

tà-kɔ̄ɔ̄ {tà-kɔ̀ɔ} *v* **1** *vt* **protéger** *(contre – gɔ̀)* ◊ *Zân yà ɤ̄ dè tà-kɔ̄ɔ̄ Tökpà gɔ̀* Zan s'est défendu contre l'attaque de Tokpa **2** *vt* **se ruer vers** *(pour rafler)*, **se battre pour sa part** ◊ *tɔ̀-dhǜn wà kɤ̄ŋgā tà-kɔ̄ɔ̄* les poulets se sont rués sur les grains de maïs

tà-kún {tà-kūn} *v* **1** *vt* **aider 2.1** *vr* **se préparer 2.2** *vr* **se parer**

tākű̋ŋ <fermer-soufflet> *n* **réservoir de soufflet en argile** *(forge)*

tà-kpā {tà-kpā; Int. tà-kpā-tà-kpā} *v* **1** *vt* **coller** ◊ *yà bhīʌʌ tà-kpā* il a collé la plaie **2** *vt* **couvrir** *(justifier)* ♦ *yà ɤ̄ dè tà-kpā* il feint d'innocence ◊ *kà n̄ tà-kpā* couvrez-moi

tān 1, **tán** {tān} *v vi* **s'appuyer** *(sur - bhà, gúɪ)*

tān 2 (tān} *v* **1** 1) *vi* **rougir** 2) *vt* **rendre rouge** *(yeux)* **2** *vi* **rouer de coups** *(qn – tà)*

tű̋n *n* **1 danse; chant** *(dansable)* ◊ *kɔ̄nŋ tű̋n yɤ̀ sʌ̀* la musique de la harpe-luth est bonne ♦ *tű̋n bhō* chanter *(en solo)* ♦ *tű̋n kʌ̄* danser ♦ *tű̋n wɔ̋sǜ* musique / danse rapide ♦ *tű̋n kű̋n* interrompre la danse **2 balancement** *(branche)* ◊ *dhű̋ kwɛ̄ɛ̋-dhǜn wɔ̀ tű̋n kʌ̄-sīʌ* les branches de l'arbre se balancent

tű̋nbhōbhɛ̏n <chant-sortir-personne> *n* **1 chanteur** *(soliste)* **2 musicien**

tű̋nkʌ̄bhɛ̏n <danse-faire-personne> *n* **danseur, danseuse**

tű̋nsàŋgbáà <chant- ?> *n* **chef de la danse** *(celui qui dirige la danse, reçoit et annonce les donations)* ♦ *tű̋nsàŋgbáà dhʌ̀n yɤ̄ ɤ́ tű̋n dhɛ̏ dhɪ́ɤ* le chef de la danse est celui qui la dirige

tántándhɤ̄ *adv* **fortement** *(se coller)* ◊ *klūugā dō yà dhʌ̀nŋ tántándhɤ̄* un écrou s'est collé très fort

tāŋ̏ *n* **tambour d'aisselle** *(en bois de kɔ̄ɔ ou yɔ̋ŋ; avec deux membranes faites de peau de singe ou de rat, caisse en forme de sablier, cordes en coton tendues entre les membranes; placé sous l'aisselle gauche, on le frappe avec une baguette recourbée, parfois aussi avec la main nue; la pression sur les cordes modifie la hauteur du son) [instrument particulier à la caste de griots qui l'utilise pour des performances à un ou deux tambours]*

tàŋgà < Manding táma 'un franc' > *n* **sou** *dans quelques expressions figées pour insister sur un fait négatif :* ♦ *wʌ̀ʌ̀gā tàŋgà zìaan yáa n̄ gɔ̀* je n'ai pas un sou ♦ *à kɔ̀ tàŋgà yáa gūn* il n'y avait aucune possibilité de faire cela

tà-pő {tà-pò} *v* **1** *vt* **éclairer 2** *vt* **enchanter**, **rendre joyeux**

tà-sēɛ̀ *v* 1) *vi à zūʌ́ tà yɤ̀ sēɛ̀-sīʌ* **avoir des nausées** 2) *vt bhēn zūʌ́ tà-sēɛ̀* **donner des nausées à qn** ◊ *bhɤ̀pʌ̀ bhā yà' zūʌ́ tà sɛ̄ɛ̋ndhʌ́n sēɛ̀-sīʌ* cette nourriture lui donne un peu la nausée

tāsî < Fr. taxi > *n* **taxi** ♦ *tāsî zīɤ bhɛ̏n* chauffeur taxi, taximan

tāslʌ̏ʌ < ?-piment> *n* **piment** *(esp.)*

tű̋súbhɛ̏n <marche-prendre-personne> *n* **messager** *(poste permanent)*

tű̋tű̋tű̋tű̋dhɤ̄ → tɤ̋tɤ̋tɤ̋dhɤ̄ *tic-tac*

tű̋yɔ̋ɔ <marcher-pareil> *n rn* **compagnon de voyage**

tǣ̀æ {tǣ̀æ} *n* **cuvette** ♦ *pʌ̄ bhɤ̀ gúú tǣ̀æ* cuvette pour le riz ou la bouillie ♦ *tő̋o yɤ̀ gúú tǣ̀æ* cuvette pour la sauce, soupière

tǣ̋æbʌ̀ → tɛ̋ɛbʌ̀ *camarades*

tǣ̋æbhɔ̀ (m) → tɛ̋ɛbʌ̀ *camarades*

tǣ̋ædō → tɛ̋ɛdō *ami*

tǣ̄æ̀n *n* **vérité** ◊ *yáa bhɔ̀ɔ̀n bhà kɤ̄ yɤ̀ tǣ̄æ̀n wɔ̀n pɤ̄* il ne peut pas dire la vérité ♦ *tǣ̄æ̀nwɔ̀* vérité, parole véridique ◊ *tǣ̄æ̀nwɔ̀ sɤ̋ŋgɤ̋sɤ̀ŋgɤ̀ bhǜn* c'est la pure vérité

tǣ̄æ̀n-dhɛ̀ *n* **véracité**

tʌ̀ *n* ***Calamus gen.*** **rotin** *(liane, 7 cm d'épaisseur, pouvant atteindre 250 en longueur, feuilles jointes à la tige, sans branches; écorce très dure, intérieur plus mou, duramen particulièrement dur)*

tʌ̄ʌ *n* **revendication, prétention** *(n'apparaît que dans quelques expressions figées)* ♦ *tʌ̄ʌ dɔ̄ bhɛ̄n bhà* reprocher qn ◊ *yɤ̀ tʌ̄ʌ dɔ̀ gbɛ̋ɛ̋* il est trop susceptible, il est toujours mécontent ♦ *yáa tʌ̄ʌ dɔ̄* il n'est pas difficile ♦ *tʌ̄ʌ dɔ̄ bhɛ̀n* ronchon, personne plaintive, qui se plaint tout le temps ♦ *yà tʌ̄ʌ bhō n̄ gúú* il a perdu confiance en moi

tʌ́ʌtʌ̀ʌ {A P, tʌ́ʌtʌ̀ʌ-dhǜn pl., tʌ́kʌ́tʌ̀kʌ̀ Int.} *adj* **faible** *(personne)*

tʌ̀ʌtʌ̋ʌtʌ̀ʌdhɤ̄ *adv* **sans force** *(marcher)*

tʌ́kʌ́tʌ̀kʌ̀ *adj Int. de* tʌ́ʌtʌ̀ʌ *faible*

tʌ̀ŋ *n rn* **cervelle**

tʌ̀ŋ {tʌ̀ŋ) *v* **1.1** *vi* **s'approcher** *(dans l'espace; de – tà)* ◊ *yà tʌ̀ŋ kwǣ̋æ̀ndhɛ̀ tà dɛ̀dɛ̀wō* il était déjà tout près de la maison **1.2** *vi* **s'approcher** *(en qualité; de – bhà)* ◊ *tɛ̋n ɤ́' bhō bhā, yɤ́' wɔ̀ tʌ̀ŋ gɔ̄ɔ̀n bhā' wɔ̀ bhà* la chanson qu'il chantait, elle sonnait presque comme la voix de cet homme **1.3** *vi* **être presque à point** ◊ *kɔ́ yɤ̀ tʌ̀ŋ-sǜ ká* la maison est sur le point de s'écrouler ◊ *pʌ̄bhèe yà tʌ̀ŋ* le repas est presque prêt **2** *vr* *ɤ̄ bhɤ̋ tʌ̀ŋ* **s'installer** *(pour une petit moment, pour se reposer) seulement dans l'expression :* ♦ *bhāan n̄ bhɤ̋ tʌ̀ŋ ūū sɔ̋ɔ* resp. puis-je m'installer à côté de vous ?

tʌ̋ŋ̄ *n* **air** *(espace entre ciel et terre)*

tʌ̋ŋ̄tʌ̀ŋ *n* **sans serrer** *(attacher) toujours avec une postposition instrumentale* ◊ *à lɤ̀ tʌ̋ŋ̄tʌ̀ŋ ká* attache-le sans serrer ♦ *yà kʌ̄ tʌ̋ŋ̄tʌ̀ŋ ká ɤ̄ bhā dhēbʌ̀ gɔ̀* il est entièrement sous la coupe de sa femme

tɛ̀ 1, **tɛ̀dhʌ́n** *n* **orphelin, orpheline** *(de père et de mère) (la forme tɛ̀dhʌ́n est plus usitée)*

tɛ̀ 2 *n* **couvercle** ◊ *tɤ̄ɤ tɛ̀* couvercle d'un panier

tɛ̋ *n* ***Atherurus africanus*** **athérure africain, porc-épic, hérisson** lv. *(36-60 cm, 1.5-4 kg)*

tɛ̋bhʌ̋n, **tɛ̋ɛbhʌ̋n** {pl. tɛ́bhʌ̋n-dhǜn, tɛ́bhʌ̋nzʌ̀-dhǜn} *n rn* **camarade de classe d'âge**

tɛ̀dhʌ́n → tɛ̀ *orphelin*

tɛ̀-dhɛ̀ *n* **orphelinage** ◊ *tɛ̀-dhɛ̀ yɤ̀ yâ* être orphelin n'est pas bon

tèdhḯɤ <couvercle-bord> *n* **couvercle** ♦ *tǽǣ̀ [gbɔ̄] tèdhḯɤ* couvercle de cuvette [de pot]

tēe *n* **filet de pêche** *(pour les femmes; le plus petit)* Qsyn. kplɤ̋, dhűun, sàadhè, zūeŋ

téɛ̀ <Fr. thé> *n* **thé** *(surtout en sachets)* ♦ *téɛ̀ bɪ̀* thé en poudre ♦ *téɛ̀ dɔ̄* un sachet de thé ♦ *téɛ̀ gʌ̄n* ficelle de sachet de thé ◊ *bhá sűkǻdhű dà/kʌ̄ téɛ̀ bhàa ɛ̀e ?* as-tu mis du sucre dans le thé ?

tée̋kpȁadhɛ̀ → tétékpȁadhɛ̀ *papillon de nuit*

tée̋ŋtlɤ̄ *n* **grillon**

tée̋tée̋ *adj Int. Sg. de* tété *petit*

tée̋kpédhē *n* **arc-en-terre** *(instrument de musique; trou creusé dans le sol, d'un diamètre d'environ 25 cm de diamètre et de 15 cm de profondeur recouvert de feuilles de bananier superposées et retenues par un cerceau de lianes, soutenu à son tour par des pieux fourchus. Une corde en raphia ou en rotin est fixée au centre des feuilles en les traversant, l'autre bout de la corde est attaché un mètre plus haut à un bâton flexible. Le joueur pince la corde avec l'index de la main droite, les doigts de la main gauche saisissent la corde en son milieu)*

tēlê <Fr. télé> *n* **télévision, téléviseur, télé** ♦ *tēlê gbɔ̄* téléviseur ♦ *tēlê dhūű* éteindre la télé

tēlēfɔ̂n <Fr. téléphone> *n* **téléphone** Syn. tīootīoo

tēŋ *n* ***Piliostigma thonningii, Bauhimia th.*** **arbre** *(6-8 de haut, cime étalée et plus ou moins dense, feuilles à deux lobes; fleurs blanc crème; grandes gousses ligneuses, plates) [racine utilisée pour colorer le bois en rouge]*

tɛ̋ŋ *n rn* **respiration** ♦ *à tɛ̋ŋ yà sɯ́* il suffoque; il est essoufflé ♦ *à tɛ̋ŋ yáa yɤ̄ sīāa* il ne peut pas respirer profondement

tɛ̋ŋsíyȕa <respiration-prendre-maladie> *n* **asthme**

tété {A P; Int. Sg. tée̋tée̋} *adj le mot est plutôt rare en dialecte gouèta* **1** *en fonction prédicative seulement; dans ce sens, n'a pas d'intensif* **petit** *(de taille)* ◊ *ɯ̄ tété !* tu est petit ! ♦ *pʌ́ ɯ́ dhūn n̄ dhɛ̀ yā, yɤ̀ tété* ce que tu m'as donné, c'est peu ! **2** *en fonction épithète seulement* **jeune** ◊ *Zân yɤ̀ dhʌ́n tété ká* Zan est le plus jeune (parmi les enfants) ◊ *dhʌ́n tée̋tée̋ ɤ́ yā, yɤ̀ sí bhɔ̀ bhīn kpîi gɔ̀ ɛ̀e !* cet enfant, tout jeune, a insulté un adulte !

tétékpȁadhɛ̀, **tée̋kpȁadhɛ̀** *n* **papillon de nuit** *(esp.) [les Dan croient qu'il n'a pas d'yeux mais qu'il voit tout]*

tɛ̋ɛ 1) {tɛ̀ɛ} *n* **1.1 vent** ♦ *yí tɛ̋ɛ* courant d'eau ♦ *tɛ̋ɛ yà dɔ̄ n̄ tó gɯ́* j'ai les oreilles prises ♦ *tɛ̋ɛ yɤ̀ zīɤ-sīʌ* le vent souffle **1.2** *rn* **respiration** ♦ *tɛ̋ɛ pā* se reposer ♦ *bhíin n̄ tɛ̋ɛ bhɛ̋ɛ̀ pā* je ne me suis pas reposé suffisamment ♦ *à tɛ̋ɛ yáa à gɯ́* il n'a pas de force ♦ *ɤ̄ tɛ̋ɛ yɤ̄ sīāa* se calmer, respirer calmement **1.3 air** ◊ *tɛ̋ɛ ɤ́ pɤ̂ gblɤ̋gblɤ̋ gɯ́ yɤ̀ dhȉisȕ; tɛ̋ɛ ɤ́ tɔ̀n gɯ́ yɤ̀ slɤ̋ɤslɤ̀* l'air dans les grandes villes est sale, et dans les montagnes, l'air est pur **2** *rn* **puanteur** Syn. gbḯʌn Qsyn. fīi ◊ *gbō tɛ̋ɛ yà yà* la puanteur des excréments se répand

tɛ̋ɛ 2) {tɛ̀ɛ} ***v*** **1** *vi* **bouillir ♦** *à zūʌ̋ dhɯ̋ɤ yɤ̏ tɛ̋ɛ-sīʌ* il est inquiet ◊ *bhān yí dɔ̄ sɯ̋ɤɤ kɤ̄ yɤ̏ tɛ̋ɛ* fais bouillir mon eau **2** *vi* **respirer**

tɛ̋ɛbʌ̏-dhȕn, **tǽæbʌ̏-dhȕn**, **tǽæbhɔ̏-dhȕn** (m) ***n*** *pl. de* tɛ̋ɛdō *camarade*

tɛ̋ɛbhʌ̄ŋ́dhē <vent-Manding-femme> ***n*** **guêpe-maçonne**

tɛ̋ɛdō, **tǽædō** {pl. tɛ̋ɛbʌ̏-dhȕn, tǽæbʌ̏-dhȕn, tǽæbɔ̏-dhȕn} ***n*** *rn* **ami, amie, collègue** *Syn. tǽœŋ̏dʌ̄* ◊ *yɤ̏ kʌ̄ ɤ̄ dhɤ̏ŋ gbɛ́ ɤ́ zɪ̏ɤ' ká ɤ̄ tɛ̋ɛbʌ̏-dhȕn tà* mieux que ses amies elle savait porter les bagages sur la tête ♦ *tǽædō ɤ́ dhūn à dɔ̄ tá̋ gúú* compagnon de route

tɛ̀ɛdhɯ̋n ***n*** *rn* **semblable** *(un objet concret) Syn. síbhɑ̋n* ◊ *à tɛ̀ɛdhɯ̋n kʌ̏ dhɛ̀ bhȁan dhɤ́, à tɛ̀ɛdhɯ̋n kʌ̏ dhɛ̀ fɛ̋ŋ dhɤ́* il est comme un oiseau, il est comme un rat (écureuil volant)

tɛ̋ɛkʌ̄bȕbȕ <vent-faire-onomat.> ***n*** **1 éventail 2 ventilateur 3 hélice** *(d'un hélicoptère, etc.)*

tɛ̋ɛn ***adj*** **rouge** *Syn. zœ̏œndhē surtout dans l'expression* ♦ *tɛ̋ɛn yʌ̋ʌnyʌ̏ʌn* multicolore avec une dominance de rouge

tɛ̋ɛpā <laper le vent> ***n*** **repos** *Qsyn. glòo, kōyíbhō*

tɛ̋ɛpʌ̏ <vent-chose> ***n*** **créature** *(vivante)*

tɛ̋ɛtɛ̀ɛ {A P S, tɛ̋ɛtɛ̀ɛ-dhȕn pl. A, tɛ̋ɛtɛ̀ɛ-sȕ foc. A, tɛ̋ɛtɛ̀ɛ-sȕ-dhȕn foc. pl. A; tɛ́kɛ̋tɛ̀kɛ̏ Int. pl. A P S, tɛ́kɛ̋tɛ̀kɛ̏-dhȕn Int. pl. A S, tɛ́kɛ̋tɛ̀kɛ̏-sȕ Int. pl. foc. A, tɛ́kɛ̋tɛ̀kɛ̏-sȕ-dhȕn Int. pl. foc. A S} ***adj*** **exténué**

tɛ́kɛ̋tɛ̀kɛ̏ *Int. de* tɛ̋ɛtɛ̀ɛ *exténué*

tɛ̀kpɛ̏tɛ̀kpɛ̏dhɤ̄ ***adv*** **1 très** *(joyeux)* ◊ *à dhìin gbàan dà tɛ̀kpɛ̏tɛ̀kpɛ̏dhɤ̄* elle était énormément contente **2** (t) **en grand nombre** *(venir) Syn. tɛ̀ttɛ̀dhɤ̄ (gw)*

tɛ̀nbhɛ̏n <Manding tɛ̀mɛ> ***n*** **tamis ♦** *tɛ̀nbhɛ̏n yɑ̋n sɛ̋ɛ́ndhʌ́n* tamis serré ♦ *tɛ̀nbhɛ̏n yɑ̋n gblɤ̋gblɤ̋* tamis lâche

tēnŋyāandō → tēnŋzīaandō *Mardi*

tēnŋyɛ̄ɛ̋n ***n*** **dimanche**

tēnŋyī, **tēŋyī** ***n*** **lundi**

tēnŋzīaandō, **tēnŋyāandō** ***n*** **mardi**

tēnŋzīaanplɛ̀ ***n*** **mercredi**

tēŋyī → tēnŋyī *lundi*

tɛ̀tɛ̏, **tɛ̀ttɛ̏** *peut être vu comme une forme intensive de gbɛ́* ***adj*** **nombreux** *(des humains ou des animaux, constituant un groupe)* ◊ *bhēn tɛ̀tɛ̏ ɤ́ ká yā !* vous, les (très) nombreuses personnes qui êtes ici ! ◊ *pʌ̄bhèe tɛ̀tɛ̏, wó dhūn à ká* ils ont apporté une grande quantité de nourriture

tɛ̀tɛ̀dhɤ̄, **tɛ̀ttɛ̀dhɤ̄** (gw) ***adv*** **en masse**, **en grand nombre** *(venir; les humains ou les animaux) Syn. tɛ̀kpɛ̏tɛ̀kpɛ̏dhɤ̄ (t)* ◊ *bhɔ̏ yà dhūn tɛ̀tɛ̀dhɤ̄* les cochons sont venus nombreux

tı̏aandhē 1) {A P S, tı̏aandhē-dhȕn pl. A S, tı̏aandhē-sȕ foc. A, tı̏aandhē-sȕ-dhȕn foc. pl. A; tı̏antı̏andhē Int. A P S, tı̏antı̏andhē-dhȕn Int. pl. A, tı̏antı̏andhē-sȕ Int. foc. A, tı̏antı̏andhē-sȕ-dhȕn Int. foc. pl. A} ***adj*** **1 bon 2 respectable**

tı̏aandhɤ̄ 2) ***adv*** **bien**

tı̋an → kı̋an *totem*

tı̏antı̏andhē ***adj*** *Int. de* tı̏aandhē *bon*

tı̋ʌʌ, **tı̋ʌʌdhɛ̋** ***n*** **champignon** *(nom générique)*

tı̋ʌʌdhɛ̋ → tı̋ʌʌ *champignon*

tı̋ʌʌpűu ***n*** **champignon** *(petit, blanc, comestible, pousse en groupes au mois de mai sur les anciennes termitières)* *Syn.* *sāa̋n 2*

tı̋ʌʌtīi <champignon-noir> ***n*** **champignon** *(esp.; poussent au mois d'août sur l'arbre iroko et sur les vieux fromagers)*

tīʌŋ → kīʌŋ 1 *fuseau*

tīi {A P S, tīi-dhȕn pl. A, tīi-sȕ foc. A S, tīi-sȕ-dhȕn foc. pl. A S; tītī Int. pl. A P S, tītī-dhȕn Int. pl. A S, tītī-sȕ Int. pl. foc. A S, tītī-sȕ-dhȕn Int. pl. foc. A S; tīitı̏dhɛ̏ SupInt A S, tīitı̏dhɛ̏-sȕ SupInt. foc. A S; tīitīi SupInt. pl. A P S, tīitīi-dhȕn SupInt. pl. A S, tīitīi-sȕ SupInt. pl. foc. A S, tīitīi-sȕ-dhȕn SupInt. pl. foc. A S} ***adj*** *la forme tīitı̏dhɛ̏ est rare, peu utilisée* **1.1 noir 1.2 fort** *(café)* **2 obscur** ◊ *dhɛ̏ tīi* endroit obscur

tīí ***n*** *rn* **surprise** *(surtout agréable) dans l'expression :* ♦ *(bhɛ̄n) tīí ká* inattendu (pour qn), à la surprise (de qn) ◊ *yɤ̏ kʌ̏ n̄ tīí ká wɔ̏n ká* cela devient une surprise pour moi

tīíbhūn, **tīibhún** (gw), **tīnŋ́bhūn** (m) {Int. tīitíbhūn} ***adv*** **quelque part par là** *(une localisation vague; ne s'accompagne pas d'une indication avec la main; la forme intensive désigne un degré d'éloignement encore plus élevé de l'objet)*

tīidhʌ̄ngbɤ̄ ***n*** **chenille** *(noire; apparaît d'août jusqu'à octobre; comestible : on les grille, on les sèche au soleil et on les met dans la sauce)*

tīı̏dhē → tīı̏dhɤ̏ *là-bas*

tīı̏dhɤ̏, **tīı̏dhē** {Int. tīití́dhɤ̏} ***adv*** **là-bas** *(situe un objet éloigné dans le champ de visibilité des interlocuteurs ou en dehors de ces limites, mais dans une direction connue d'eux; s'accompagne d'une indication avec la main ou du doigt; la forme intensive désigne un degré d'éloignement encore plus élevé de l'objet)* ◊ *yà dhūn sʌ́ʌdhɛ̋ bhā à ká tīı̏dhɤ̏* il a emmené la lettre là-bas ◊ *kɛ̋ɛ ūı bhā bűı kpɤ̄ dhʌ́n ɤ́ tīı̏dhɤ̏ yā, à dhɔ̏ yī kʌ̏* mais nous voulons un petit morceau de ta forêt qui est là-bas

tı̏intı̏ndhɤ̏ ***adv*** *Int. de* tı̏tı̏dhɤ̏ *sur le point d'éclater*

tīínbhūn ***adv*** **très loin** *(à la limite de vision, plus loin que tīı̏dhɤ̏)*

tīitı̏dhɛ̏ ***adj*** *SupInt. de* tīi *noir*

tīitíːdhɤ̏ ***adv*** *Int. de* tīı̏dhɤ̏ *là-bas*

tīitīi *SupInt. pl. de* tīi *noir*

tı̀nbhı̀n; **ɗı̀nbhı̀n** (m) ***n*** **pièce d'argent de la période coloniale** *(50 centimes ?)*

tinŋ́bhūn (m) → tīíbhūn *là*

tı̀ntı̀ndhɤ̄ → tı̄tı̄dhɤ̄ *sur le point d'éclater*

tı̀ŋ ***n*** *rn* **rumeur, nouvelle** *dans quelques expressions figées :* ◊ *ä tı̀ŋ yä̀ dä̀* la nouvelle le concernant s'est répandue partout

tı́ŋ ***n*** *rn* *gẽ̀n tı́ŋ* **talon** *(de pied)* ♦ *sòò gẽ̀n tı́ŋ* sabot de cheval

tīŋtīŋdhɤ̄ ***adv*** **fortement** *(évoque un gonflement)*

tīootīoo ***n*** rare **téléphone** Syn. tēlēfɔ̃n

tìsı́ɤ̄ɤ ***n*** **éternuement** ♦ *tìsı́ɤ̄ɤ bhō* éternuer

tītī *Int. pl. de* tīi *noir*

tītībhɔ́nbhɔ́n ***n*** **croque-mitaine** *(personnage imaginaire dont on effraie les enfants dans l'obscurité)*

tı̄tı̄dhɤ̄, **tı̀ntı̀ndhɤ̄** {Int. tı̄iintı̀ndhɤ̄} ***adv*** **sur le point d'éclater** ◊ *wɔ́n yä̀ sı̀ɤ Yɔ̈ dhɛ̈, yà dɔ̄ ɤ̄ gúı tı̄iintı̀ndhɤ̄* Yo est fâchée, elle est sur le point d'éclater de colère ♦ *dhā yà dhūn tı̄tı̄dhɤ̄* la pluie est au point d'éclater ◊ *dhā yà dhūn tı̄iintı̀ndhɤ̄* la pluie va tomber dans quelques secondes

tı́ukɤ̄ ***n*** **turque**

tlʌ̀nkʌ́ntlʌ̀nkʌ́ndhɤ̄ ***adv*** *Int. de* tlʌ̄ntlʌ̄ndhɤ̄ *totalement écraser*

tlʌ̄ntlʌ̄ndhɤ̄ {Int. tlʌ̀nkʌ́ntlʌ̀nkʌ́ndhɤ̄} ***adv*** **totalement** *(écraser)* **en poudre** *(piler)* ◊ *Zân gẽ̀n yä̀ yɛ̃́ tlʌ̄ntlʌndhɤ̄* le pied de Zan a été brisé définitivement

tlɛ̄ɛ <Fr. trait> ***n*** **trait, trait d'union** Syn. kplüìtlɛ̄ɛgā

tlēn <Fr. train> ***n*** **train**

tlōo, **tlōő** {tlȍo} ***n*** **1 jeu, amusement** ♦ *tlōo kʌ̄* jouer ◊ *yɤ̈ bhláädhɛ̈ bä̀ dhɛ̀, bhēn yɤ̈ tlōo kʌ̈* il défriche le champ comme si c'était un jeu ◊ *pʌ́ ɤ́ gó-sīʌ ä gblűdhɤ̄ dhɛ̀ yɔ̀ɔn dhɤ́ tlōo yáa ä bhä̀* il a un saignement abdominal terrible **2 amusement 3 fête**

tlōȍ ***n*** **caille arlequin**

tlőo {tlȍo}, **tlőokpāa** (t) ***n*** **termitière cathédrale** *(rouge et haute, un demeure des termites bhlʌ̈)* ♦ *bhlʌ̈ tlȍo le même que tlőő* ♦ *tlőo yā yà gó* cette termitière a perdu sa productivité *(les termites sont toujours là, mais elle ne produit plus d'éphemères comestibles)*

tlɔ̈ɔ ***n*** **oiseau** *(esp.; petit, chante beaucoup le matin)*

tlɔ̈ɔdhɤ̄ <oiseau(esp.)-adv.> ***adv*** **prodigieusement** *(bavardage)* ♦ *yɤ̈ dhīaŋ zʌ̈ tlɔ̈ɔdhɤ̄* il est bavard

tlɔ̀ɔn ***n*** *rn* **bénéfice** *(gain financier)*

tlɤ̄ɤ {tlɤ̈ɤ} ***v*** **1 1)** *vi* **s'assombrir**, **noircir** ◊ *dhɛ̈ gúı yà tlɤ̄ɤ* il fait noir *(à l'intérieur)* Qsyn. kʌ̄ tīi ◊ *dhēbʌ̈ yā yä̀ tlɤ̄ɤ zúı èe ?* la peau cette femme est redevenue foncée ?

(sans doute, elle n'utilise plus des produits pour le blanchissement) ♦ *yà tlɤ̄ɤ̄ dhı̀ı̀ ká* il est tout sale ♦ *dhɛ̀ tlɤ̄ɤ-sı̀ı̀* endroit très sombre (où on ne voit vraiment rien) ♦ *bhɛ̄n tlɤ̄ɤ-sı̀ı̀* la personne à peau très noire ♦ *à tà yà tlɤ̄ɤ* il est confus **2)** *vt* **noircir**, **rendre sombre** ◊ *ā dhùn kɤ̄ ú n̄ bhā sɔ̄ tlɤ̄ɤ* je suis venu pour que tu teignes mon tissu en noir ♦ *dhı̀ı̀ yà à tlɤ̄ɤ* il est tout sale **2** *vt* **aveugler**, **éblouir** ◊ *yʌ́nŋ̀ dhʌ̀n {ɤ́} n̄ yʌ́nŋ tlɤ̀ɤ* c'est le soleil qui m'a aveuglé

tlùkpɛ̀tlùkpɛ̀dhɤ̄ *adv* **en petits morceaux** *(casser)*, **en poudre** *(écraser)*

tlùu *n rn* **inconvenance** *dans l'expression figée :* ♦ *dhīaŋ zʌ̄ ɤ̄ tlùu gwìnŋ̀* parler sans égards

tlűu *n* **trompe traversière** *(en corne de bœuf)* ♦ *tlűu tɛ̋n* "trou-tan" *(danse des notables, exécutée lors d'événements publics importants : visite d'un haut fonctionnaire; funérailles d'un chef etc.)* ♦ *gɔ̄ tlűu* klaxon ♦ *tlűu wɛ̋, tlűu pı̀ɤ* jouer de la trompe

tlűnŋ 2 *n* **épaisseur**

tlűnŋ 1, **tlűŋ** *n* **paralysie; engourdissement** Syn. gblɛ̋ngblɛ̋n ♦ *tlűnŋ yūa yà bhà* il est paralysé ♦ *tlűnŋ yà dà n̄ gɛ̀n gúí* j'ai les jambes engourdies *(à cause d'une pose inconfortable)*

tlűnŋgúsı̀ı̀ {A S} <épaisseur-dans-adj.> *adj* **épais** ◊ *Yɔ̀ bhà wūngā-dhùn, wò tlűnŋgúsı̀ı̀ ká dhè bhɛ̄n kɔ̄ŋgā dhɤ́* les tresses de Yo ont l'épaisseur d'un doigt ◊ *dhű pɛ̋n tlűnŋgúsı̀ı̀-dhùn dhʌ̀n ɤ́'-dhùn sűı* ce sont des planches épaisses qu'il prend

tó {tō} *v* **1** 1) *vi* **rester** ◊ *yɛ̄ŋ̀ -dhùn dhʌ̀n yá tó kwɛ̋nŋ̀dhɛ̀ yā' bhɛ̀n ká* moi et elle, nous sommes restés des gens de cette famille ♦ *à gɔ̀ yà tó yɛ̋ bhà* il a été entraîné à la consommation d'igname ♦ *ɤ́ tō à ká dhɤ́* jusqu'à ici 2) *vt* **laisser** ◊ *yɤ̀ ɤ̄ bhɤ̋ tó kɤ̀ŋ bhūn* qu'il reste là-bas pour le moment ♦ *ɤ̄ tő tó ... bhà* écouter qch ♦ *{gbàn} tó dhɤ́* entier ◊ *dhūn tɔ̀ tò dhɤ́-sı̀ı̀ ká* apporte le poulet tout entier ♦ *tlɛ̄ŋ̀ [gɔ̄, vɪ̀ɔŋ] yà n̄ tó* j'ai raté mon train [bus, avion] **2** *vi* **se marier** *(d'une femme; avec – gɔ̀)* Syn. dhó gwān bhà, gwān kpɔ́ bhɛ̄n gɔ̀ ◊ *bhɛ̄n yāayädhɛ̀ ɤ́ yā, bháan bhāan tó' gɔ̀* je ne me marierai pas avec cet homme horriblement laid **3** *vi* **faire sans arrêt** *(qch – bhà)* **4** *vt* **pendant que ...** *(exprime la simultanéité d'un événement avec un autre)* ◊ *yɤ́ wó' tō zīāan, yɤ́' dhú dhɔ̀ɔ, yɤ́ wó' zʌ̄* et pendant qu'elle était en route, ils ont tué sa fille **5** *vi avec la négation, suivi d'une proposition négative* **ne pas agir avec précipitation** ◊ *wáa n̄ dhɛ̀, bháan tó bháan dhó* lorsqu'on m'appelle, je ne me précipite pas pour y aller ♦ *bháan tó bháan yà n̄ bhà kʌ̄-sı̀ı̀ bhà* je ne réagis pas tout de suite **6** *vi tó à bhà* **avoir lieu** ◊ *tlōo yɤ̀ kʌ̄ tó à bhà* la fête a eu lieu ◊ *yɤ̄ɤ kʌ̄ kɔ̀ ɔ̋o kɔ̀ ɤ́' bhà, gā wɔ̀n dhʌ̀n tō' bhà* quoi qu'il en soit, la mort viendra quand même **7** *vi tó à gbɛ̋ɛ̀ ká* **remporter une victoire**, **vaincre** *(guerre, bagarre, courses de masques; qn – tà)*

tő {LOC tőodhɤ̄} *loc.n* **1.1** *rn* **oreille** ◊ *n̄ tő yà dà gbàŋ dɔ̄ wò gúí* j'ai entendu le bruit de la foule ♦ *yí yɤ̀ bhɛ̄n kùn bhɛ̄n tő dhɛ́ bhà* l'eau atteint les oreilles ♦ *wɔ́n dhīaŋ zʌ̄ bhɛ̄n tőodhɤ̄* rabâcher qch à qn ♦ *ɤ̄ tő tó ... bhà* écouter qch/qn ♦ *à tő yɤ̀ tā-sı̀ı̀ ká* il est sourd *(complètement)* ♦ *à tő {gúí} yɤ̀ gbínŋ̀* il est dur d'oreille ♦ *à tő yɤ̀ wúí-sı̀ı̀ ká* il n'entend pas bien ♦ *à tő gúu yɤ̀ gbínŋ̀ {wɔ̀ wɛ̋ɛ dlāàn-sɯ̀ bhà}* il a du mal à apprendre des langues étrangères ♦ *bhànŋzīì wɔ̀ yà n̄ tó pā* le bruit des moteurs m'embête **1.2** *rn* **ouïes** *(partie extérieure)* **2 bord** *(de récipient)* ◊ *bàŋ tő* bord de bassine

tö *n* **arbre** *(esp.; grand, à bois très mou; écorce utilisée comme aphrodisiaque, fruits de la dimension d'un poing, non comestibles)*

tődhɛ̋ <oreille-feuille> *n rn* **oreille externe** Syn. tőkpɤ̄ ♦ *à tődhɛ̋ yɤ̀ kʌ̀ dhɛ̀ dhàŋtrāadhɛ̋ dhɤ́* ses oreilles sont comme le champignon "dhangtraadhè" ♦ *à tődhɛ̋ yɤ̀ kʌ̀ dhɛ̀ bīɤ tő dhɛ̋ dhɤ́* il a des oreilles grandes comme celles d'un éléphant

tődhɛ̋gā <oreille-feuille-os> *n rn* **oreille, pavillon d'oreille** ◊ *yɤ́ ɤ̄ tődhɛ̋gā plɛ̀ ɤ́' gɔ̀ bhà bhā' gbàn bhō bhūūn, yɤ́' dà ɤ̄ dhí ɤ́' bhɤ̀* il a arraché ses deux oreilles sur le champ, les a mis dans sa bouche et les a mangées

tòdhɤ̋ <rester-ainsi> *n* **éternité** ◊ *pʌ́ dhɤ̄ tó tòdhɤ̋ ká, yɤ̄ dhʌ̀n yíi' bɛ̀n-zʌ̄* nous écrivons des choses éternelles

tòdhɤ́sɯ̀ <rester-ainsi-gérondif> *adj* **restant** ◊ *sűsʌ̄nŋ́gā tòdhɤ́-sɯ̀* les autres étoiles; toutes les étoiles

tőglɔ̀ɔ <oreille-banane> *n* **banane douce** *(esp.; très sucré)*

tőgúudhɛ̀, **tőodhɛ̀** <oreille-intérieur-place> *n* **oreille moyenne** ♦ *n̄ tőgúudhɛ̀ yɤ̀ n̄ kʌ̄-sīʌ* j'ai des élancements à l'oreille

tőgúupʌ̀, **tőopʌ̀** <oreill-dans-chose> *n* **boucle d'oreille**

tőkpɤ̄ <oreille-boule> *n rn* **oreille externe** Syn. tődhɛ̋

tòŋ 1 *n rn* **poitrine** *(extérieur; humains, animaux, oiseaux)* Syn. kùu Qsyn. kɤ̀ŋ

tòŋ 2 *n* **pigeon** *(sauvage)*

tőŋ (t) → tűuŋ *silencieusement*

tòŋpűu *n* **criquet** *(une espèce large)* *[comestible]*

tōŋtōŋdhɤ̄ {Int. tōooŋtōŋdhɤ̄} *adv* **1 jamais** Qsyn. dō ◊ *bhíin dhɔ̋ndhɔ̋n dīn-gà tōŋtōŋdhɤ̄* je n'ai jamais goûté de lait ◊ *bhíin dhó kpàn' à bhà zúu tōŋtōŋdhɤ̄ dhàan bhā* je ne le verrai plus jamais **2 aucunement, en aucun cas** ◊ *bháan bhāan dhūn tōŋtōŋdhɤ̄* je ne viendrai en aucun cas

tōŋtōŋgīà <imitation du cri> *n* ***Nycticorax nycticorax*** **héron bihoreau** *(taille : 50 cm; gris clair, calotte et dos noirs)*

tòo *n* **tô** *(bouillie gluante de mil, plantain ou manioc : le manioc est pelé, découpé en morceaux, séché pendant quelques jours, pilé et cuit dans l'eau pendant une heure)* ♦ *tòo bì* farine de tô *(à base de banane plantain ou de manioc)* ♦ *tòo pʌ̀* portion de tô ♦ *tòo kʌ̄, tòo kpà* cuire le tô ♦ *tòo bìɤɤ* faire la pâte de tô ♦ *tòo bì bhō* piler la farine de tô ♦ *tòo gblɤ̋ɤgblɤ̀ɤ* tô sec et épais ♦ *tòo plʌ́ʌplʌ̀ʌ* tô mou

tóò (t) *n* **visite** ♦ *dhó bhēn bhà tóò gúu* aller rendre visite à qn

tɔ̋ɔ ***n*** **sauce** *(nom générique)* ♦ *sɤ̄yí tɔ̋ɔ* sauce graine ♦ *bāa dhɛ̋ tɔ̋ɔ* sauce de feuilles de manioc *(on coupe les feuilles avant de les faire bouillir)*

tɔ̋ɔdhɛ̏ 1 <sauce-endroit> ***n*** **potager**

tɔ̋ɔdhɛ̏ 2 ***n*** → tɔ̋gúdhɛ̏ *oreille moyenne*

tɔ̋ɔdhɛ̋ <sauce-feuille> ***n*** **légume vert** *(feuilles pour la sauce)*

tɔ̋ɔdhɤ̄ ***loc.n*** *LOC de* tɔ̋ *oreille*

tòogā <tô-os> ***n*** **tô demi-produit** *(morceaux de manioc ou d'aloko, séchés et prêts à être pilés)* ◊ *tòogā bhā yɤ̏ gā-sɯ̏ ká, kȁ ȁ zɔ̄n* le tô est sec, pilez-le

tɔ̋ɔŋ ***n*** **désert** ♦ *tɔ̋ɔŋ tȁ* dans le désert

tɔ̄ɔɔŋtɔ̄ŋdhɤ̄ ***adv*** *Int. de* tɔ̄ŋtɔ̄ŋdhɤ̄ *jamais*

tɔ̋ɔpʌ̏ → tɔ̋gúpʌ̏ *boucle d'oreille*

tóȍtȁdhʌ̏n ***n*** *pej.* **bâtard**

tɔ̋ɔzɔ̄ngúwlɤ̋ <sauce-piler-dans-mortier> ***n*** **mortier à piler les condiments pour la sauce**

tɔ̋pɪ́ɤdhɛ̏ <oreille-chez-place> ***n*** *rn* **tempe**

tȍsǣǣ <de *tö-sɛ̈-tä 'rester sur terre'> ***n*** *rn, fn* **vie** Q*syn.* dhɪ́ʌŋ ◊ *bhá ȁ bhȁ tȍsǣǣ dhā* tu lui as sauvé la vie

tȍtàabhȁn {A S, tȍtàabhȁnsɯ̏ foc. A; tàatā́bhȁn Int. A, tàatā́bhȁn-sɯ̏ Int. foc. A} <rester-derrière> ***adj*** **dernier** ◊ *dhʌ́n tȍtàabhȁn* benjamin ◊ *bhɛ́n ɤ́ tā ȁ-dhɯ̏n tàatā́bhȁn-sɯ̏ ká, yɤ̄ bhɯ̏n Gɔ̋dhɔ̋n ká* celui qui a été le tout dernier parmi eux, c'est Gono

tɔ̋wlɯ̀bhɛ̏n <oreille- ?-personne> ***n*** **sourd**

tɔ̏ ***n*** **poulet** ♦ *tɔ̏ gɔ̄n* coq ♦ *tɔ̏ gbɔ̋ŋ* poulette *(qui n'a pas encore pondu)* ♦ *plɤ́ɤ̏ tɔ̏* poulet de village *[dont la viande est préférée à celle du poulet de ville]* ♦ *kwɪ́ bhȁ tɔ̏* poulet de ville ♦ *kwɪ́ tɔ̏* canard ♦ *tɔ̏ kɔ̏* poulailler

tɔ́ 1 {tɔ̄} ***n*** **1** *rn* **nom, prénom** *[le vrai nom d'une personne est peu utilisé comme forme d'adresse, sa mention par des gens plus jeunes est considérée comme impolie]* ◊ *yɤ́ dhūn yī zɪ́ɤ̏ɤ-dhɯ̏n bhā ȁ-dhɯ̏n tɔ́ bhȁ* alors il est venu au nom de nos ancêtres en question ♦ *yɤ̏ tɔ́* c'est parce que Syn. pāsɤ́ ♦ *bhɛ̄n kwɪ́ dhɛ̏ tɔ̏* nom européen de la personne *[coexiste avec le vrai nom, parfois on le met dans les documents officiels; on l'utilise librement comme forme d'adresse]* ♦ *ȁ tɔ́ yȁ bhɔ̄ sɛ́ yā tȁ* il a régné sur ce pays ♦ *tɔ́ yȁ pɤ́ bhȁ* baptiser le village ♦ *ȁ tɔ́ dhɤ́ dȁ* il est devenu célèbre ♦ *yà dhūn Gbȁtȍ tɔ́ bhȁ* il est venu chercher Gbato, il est venu saluer Gbato *(parce qu'il a entendu le nom de Gbato);* il est venu chercher ceux qui sont liés avec Gbato **2** *neol., ling* **nom**

tɔ́ 2 {tɔ̄} ***v vt*** **puiser** ◊ *yȁ yí tɔ́ klɔ̏ŋ gɯ́* elle a puisé de l'eau au puits

tɔ̏bhȁnwɛ̏e <poulet-sur-lèpre> ***n*** **puces de poule**

tɔ́bhɔ̄bhɛ̏n <nom-apparaître-personne> ***n*** **célébrité** *(personne connue)*

tɔ́bhɔ̄dhē <nom-apparaître-nominalis.> ***n*** **gloire** ◊ *Tɔ̀kpä bhä̀ tɔ́bhɔ̄dhē yä̀ sɛ̋ gbàn bhɔ̄* la gloire de Tokpa s'est répandue partout dans le pays

tɔ́gblɔ̋ɔgúpʌ̀ <nom-trace-dans-chose> ***n*** *neol., ling.* **pronom**

tɔ̀n ***n*** **1 montagne; colline** ◊ *tɔ̀n gbʌ́gbʌ̀* colline basse ◊ *yä̀ tɔ̀n kún, yä̀ tɔ̀n lɔ̄ɔ* il a escaladé une montagne, puis il est descendu de la montagne ♦ *tɔ̀n gɛ̄nŋdhɤ̄* au pied d'une montagne **2 pente** ◊ *yɤ́ dhō dhɤ́ yɤ́ tɔ̀n kūn yɤ́ gɔ̄ dɔ̋ɔ̀ndhūn* ainsi, il a roulé, gravi la pente et arrêté la voiture

tɔ̀n ***adv*** **1.1 maintenant 1.2 enfin**; **déjà** ◊ *yà n̄ dhæ̋æ̋ bhā kpɔ́ tɔ̀n* il m'a enfin posé la question **2 malheureusement**

tɔ̂n ***n*** **pet** ♦ *tɔ̂n bhɔ̄* lâcher un pet

tɔ̏ŋ ***n*** **nouvelles feuilles** *(d'arbre)*

tɔ́ŋ̀, tœ́œ̀ŋ ***n*** **1 loi 2 interdit 3 amende** *(imposée par les autorités)* Qsyn. gbāpʌ̄, tɔ́ŋ̀pʌ̄ ♦ *tɔ́ŋ̀ bhɔ̄* écoper une amende ♦ *ɯ̄ dhɤ̀ tɔ́ŋ̀ kʌ̄'* tu payeras une amende, tu dois payer une amende

tɔ̋ŋ ***n*** **arbre** *(espèce)*

tɔ̋ŋ̀ → tœ̋œŋ̀ *homonyme*

tɔ̋ŋ̀dʌ̄ → tœ̋œŋ̀dʌ̄ *ami*

tɔ́ŋ̀dɔ̄bhɛ̏n <loi-mettre-personne> ***n*** **législateur**

tɔ̋ŋ̀dhēɛ́-dhɛ̏, tœ̋œŋ̀dhē-dhɛ̏ <homonyme-mère-abstr.> ***n*** **1.1 amitié** *(entre les femmes)* **1.2 sympathie, amour** *(de la part de l'homme envers une femme)* **2 fiançailles, accordailles** *(l'annonce par un homme de son intention d'épouser une femme; s'accompagne d'un petit cadeau)* ♦ *tœ̋œŋ̀dhē-dhɛ̏ kún ä̀ bhä̀* se fiancer *(à une femme)* ◊ *wä̀ Zân bhä̀ tɔ̋ŋ̀dhēɛ̋dhɛ̏ kún Yɔ̏ bhä̀* on a engagé Yo à Zan

tɔ́ŋ̀gɔ̄bhɛ̏n <loi-tête-personne> ***n*** **chef législateur**

tɔ́ŋ̀pʌ̄ <amende-chose> ***n*** **amende** *(imposée par les autorités)* Qsyn. gbāpʌ̄, tɔ́ŋ̀ ♦ *tɔ́ŋ̀pʌ̄ gó* payer l'amende

tɔ̀ɔ 1 ***v*** 1) *vi* **s'imbiber, devenir mouillé, devenir moite** ◊ *dhā yɤ̀ gù̈n bān-sīʌ dɛ̀dɛ̀wō tɛ́ɛ ká, ā kʌ̄ tɔ̀ɔ pɛ́ɛpɛ́dhɤ̄* il y avait une pluie avec du vent, j'ai été complètement mouillé ◊ *Tɔ̀kpä yä̀ dhūn kwa̋ŋ̀dhɤ̄ ɤ̄ tɔ̀ɔ-sǜ ká* Tokpa est venu à la maison mouillé ◊ *wɔ́n yä̀ sɪ̀ɤ n̄ dhɛ̏, n̄ kɔ̀dhɛ́ yɤ̀ tɔ̀ɔ* quand quelque chose m'irrite, mes mains deviennent moites 2) *vt* **mouiller**; **imbiber** ◊ *fʌ́yí yä̀a' bhä̀ sɔ̄ tɔ̀ɔ* son vêtement est imbibé de sueur ◊ *Gɤ̀ɤ̀ yä̀ dä̀ dhā gú, kɤ̄ dhā yɤ̀ ä̀ tɔ̀ɔ* Geu est entré sous la pluie pour que la pluie le mouille

tɔ̀ɔ 2 ***n*** *rn* **potin**

tɔ̄ɔ {A, tɔ̄ɔ-dhù̈n pl. A, tɔ̄ɔ-sǜ foc. A, tɔ̄ɔsǜ-dhù̈n foc. pl. A} ***adj*** **cadet**

tɔ́ɔ̀sǜ < Fr. torche > ***n*** **torche électrique** ♦ *bhán tɔ́ɔ̀sǜ pű [dhūű]* j'ai allumé [éteint] la torche électrique

tɔ́tɔ̀tɔ́dhɤ̄ ***adv*** **se dandinant** *(de la démarche du coq ou de poule)*

tɤ́ŋ ***n*** **1 temps** ◊ *tɤ́ŋ gbàn gúu yɤ̏ gblȁa bhɛ̄n-dhȕn tȁ* il crie constamment sur les gens ♦ *dhɛ̀ tɤ́ŋdhʌ́n bhá ɤ́ zȉɤ...* un peu plus tard... ♦ *ȁ tɤ́ŋ ɤ́ bhā ȁ gúu kɤ̄...* en ce temps-là... ♦ *... yɤ̏ tɤ́ŋ súu-sīʌ* cela prend du temps ♦ *tɤ́ŋ yɤ̄ gúu bhā* maintenant, ce temps-ci **2 adresse, habileté** ◊ *ȁ kɔ̏ yáŋ tɤ́ŋ yɤ̏ dɔ̏* il est adroit de ses mains ♦ *ȁ tɤ́ŋ yɤ̏ n̄ gúu* i) il compte sur moi ii) je le surveille **3.1 direction** ◊ *yȁ dhūn kɔ́ tɤ́ŋ ká* il a marché vers la maison ♦ *tɤ́ŋ kʌ̄ ȁ gúu* gérer qch **3.2 niveau** ◊ *gbàndȁadhȕu yɤ̏ dhíɤ-tȍ fɤ̄dhɛ́ntlʌ̏ tɤ́ŋ bhȁ* l'échelle atteint la fenêtre **4** *tɤ́ŋ gúu* **insuffisamment**; **un peu** *(dans les contextes négatifs seulement)* ◊ *dhā yíi bān tɤ́ŋ gúu* la pluie n'a pas été suffisante **5** *rn* **image, pensée** ◊ *n̄ tɤ́ŋ yáa ȁ gúu dhɛ̀ yɤ̏ dhɤ̏ dhūn'* je ne pense pas qu'il viendra ♦ *tɤ́ŋ kʌ̄ pʌ̄ gúu* s'imaginer qch, penser à qch, surveiller qch **6 attention** ♦ *tɤ́ŋ kʌ̄ ȁ gúu* prêter attention à, protéger **7 temps** *(état de l'atmosphère)* ◊ *tɤ́ŋ yȁ kʌ̄ sɛ̏ɛ, dhā yɤ̏ bȁn yī gbàn ká* il fait humide, il pleut tous les jours

tɤ́ŋbhȁsȕu ***n*** **multitude, grande quantité** *n'apparait que dans les propositions négatives* ◊ *báŋ tɤ́ŋbhȁsȕu yáa ȁ gɔ̏* il n'a que quelques machettes ◊ *yíi yí tɤ́ŋbhȁsȕu bhūn* il n'a pas bu beaucoup d'eau *peut apparaître dans une position argumentale et dans celle du prédicat sans déterminé* ◊ *bhíin kʌ̄ tɤ́ŋbhȁsȕu dhɔ́* je n'en ai pas acheté beaucoup

tɤ́ŋbhō-dhɛ̏ <temps-enlever-abstr.> ***n*** **précision; intelligence** ◊ *Zân yɤ̏ yʌ̄ kʌ̏ tɤ́ŋbhō-dhɛ̏ ká* Zan travaille avec précision, intilligence

tɤ́ŋgɤ́tɤ̏ŋgɤ̏ ***adj*** **collant** *(boue)* Qsyn. dɤ́ŋgɤ́dɤ̏ŋgɤ̏ 1

tɤ́ŋgbàn {Int. tɤ́ŋgbàntɤ̏ŋgbàn} <temps-tout> ***n*** **permanence** ♦ *tɤ́ŋgbàn gúu* sans cesse ◊ *dhā yɤ̏ bȁn yɤ̄ tɤ́ŋgbàntɤ̏ŋgbàn gúu* il pleut ici constamment ♦ *tɤ́ŋgbàn ká* tout le temps (des intervalles sont possibles)

tɤ́ŋgbàntɤ̏ŋgbàn ***n*** *Int. de* tɤ́ŋgbàn *permanence*

tɤ́ŋ-kʌ̄ {tɤ́ŋ-kʌ̏} ***v*** **1** *vr* **surveiller** *(qch – gúu)* ◊ *ūu tɤ́ŋ-kʌ̄ ūu bhā kɔ́ gúu* surveille ta maison **2** *vr* **imaginer** *(qch – gúu)*

tɤ̏ɤ {tɤ̏ɤ} ***n*** **panier** ♦ *Yɔ̏ yȁ Sàó tɤ̏ɤ̏ súu* 1) Sao est très attaché à Yo 2) Sao ne pardonnera pas cela à Yo

tɤ́tɤ́tɤ́dhɤ̄ 1, **tɤ́tɤ̏tɤ́dhɤ̄** ***onomat*** *imitation du son des gouttes*

tɤ́tɤ́tɤ́dhɤ̄ 2, **tȁtȁtȁtȁdhɤ̄** ***onomat*** **tic-tac** ◊ *ȁ bhȁ bhɔ́nŋ̏tlʌ̏ yɤ̏ wɛ̏ tȁtȁtȁtȁdhɤ̄* sa montre fait tic-tac

tɤ̋ɯ̋tɤ̋ɯ̋dhɤ̄ ***adv*** *évoque le goutte-à-goutte* ♦ *yí yɤ̏ wɛ̀nŋ-sīʌ tɤ̋ɯ̋tɤ̋ɯ̋dhɤ̄* l'eau tombe goutte à goutte

tœ̏œŋ ***n*** **1** *rn* **nouvelle** ◊ *yī ȁ tœ̏œŋ-dhȕn bhȁn* nous avons entendu beaucoup de nouvelles à ce sujet ◊ *ȁ tœ̏œŋ sʌ̏ yɤ̏ dhūn-sīʌ* il y a des bonnes nouvelles de sa part **2** *rn* **renommé**, **réputation**

tœ̄œŋ ***n*** **garantie, gage**

tœ́œŋ̏ → tɔ́ŋ̏ *loi*

tœ̋œŋ̋, tɔ̋ŋ̋ ***n*** *rn* **homonyme** *(personne de même nom) [celui dont le nom est donné à l'enfant se voit de ce fait attribuer un rôle comparable à celui du parrain]*

tœ̋œŋ̋dʌ̄, tɔ̋ŋ̋dʌ̄ {pl. tœ̋œŋ̋dʌ̄zʌ̀-dhʉ̀n, tɔ̋ŋ̋dʌ̄zʌ̀-dhʉ̀n} <homonyme-père> ***n*** *rn* **ami** *(intime)* Qsyn. *tǣædō*

tœ̋œŋ̋dʌ̄-dhɛ̏ <homonyme-père-abstr.> ***n*** **amitié** *(entre les hommes; son établissement est annoncé publiquement et s'accompagne des cadeaux symboliques; normalement, on peut avoir un seul tœ̋œŋ̋dʌ̄)*

tœ̋œŋ̋dhē-dhɛ̏ → tɔ̋ŋ̋dhēé-dhɛ̏ *amour*

tû ***n Sterculia tragacantha (gen. Sterculiaceae)*** **arbre** *(esp.; à feuilles caduques, feuilles en grappes, gousses 5-6 cm)*

tùaa ***n*** **5 salutation** *(paroles)* ♦ *bhɛ̄n tùaa bhō* saluer qn

tūa̋a ***n*** *rn* **soulagement, consolation** *(de qn qui pleure de douleur)* ♦ *bhɛ̄n tūa̋a bhō* calmer qn ♦ *kā tūa̋a* consolez-vous ! *(exhortation adressée à des personnes qui souffrent d'une douleur physique ou morale)*

tùaabhō ***n*** **1** *rn* **salutation** *(l'action)* **2 visite** ◊ *ī dha̋n bhà̀ tùaabhō yà̀ tó dódó* les visites de ma grande-mère sont rares

tʉ̀ʌ → tʉ̀ɤ 1, 2 *bétail; élever*

tʉ̀ʌʌ → tʉ̀ɤ 1, 2 *bétail; élever*

tʉ̀ʌʌbhà̀ankʌ̄bhɛ̏n <bétail- ?-faire-personne> ***n*** **berger**

tʉ̀ʌʌgla̋adhíɤbhōbhɛ̏n <bétail-gardien-faire-personne> ***n*** **berger de nuit**

tūbhûn < Manding tùmu 'chenille' > ***n*** **nid de chique** *(sous la peau humaine)* ♦ *tūbhûn kpà̀a* ***Sarcopsylla penetrans*** chique, puce pénétrant la peau

tʉ̀n; **tʉ̀n** (t,) ***v*** **1** *vi* **être encore** *dans une proposition introduite par la conjonction kɤ̄* ◊ *à̀ bhà̀ dhʌ́n bhā yɤ̏ bhɔ̏ kɤ̄ yɤ̏ tʉ̀n Klà̀aplɤ̀ɤ* cet enfant à lui est né lorsqu'il était encore à Klaapleu ◊ *kɤ̄ zīaan yɤ̏ tʉ̀n sʌ̏* et que la route était encore bonne **2** *vi* **continuer**; **encore** ◊ *yʌ̄ dhíɤ-tó-dhɛ̏ yɤ̏ tʉ̀n {kɤ̀} gblɛ̀ɛn* le travail est encore loin d'être fini ◊ *dhā yáa tʉ̀n kɤ̀ŋ bān'* il ne pleut plus **3** *vi verbe auxiliaire : dans une construction d'aspect neutre avec l'infinitif du verbe principal exprime la continuation de la situation* ◊ *yɤ̏ tʉ̀n yáà̀dhūn'* il reste assis

tʉ̋nŋ → tʉ̋uŋ *silencieusement*

tʉ̄ŋ ***n*** **tas d'ordures** Syn. *dʉ̋nŋ*

tʉ̋ŋtʉ̋ŋ ***adv*** *Pl. de* tʉ̋uŋ *silencieusement*

tʉ̀ɤ 1, **tʉ̀ɤɤ**, **tʉ̀ʌ**, **tʉ̀ʌʌ** ***v*** *vt* **élever** *(l'enfant d'autrui; un animal, même sauvage, en le gardant chez soi)* Qsyn. *dà̀* ◊ *yɤ̏ dhʌ́n tʉ̀ɤ sʌ̏* il élève des enfants correctement

tʉ̀ɤ 2, **tʉ̀ɤɤ**, **tʉ̀ʌ**, **tʉ̀ʌʌ** ***n*** **1 bétail** ♦ *yɤ̏ tʉ̀ɤ dà̀* il élève le bétail ◊ *Tòkpà̀ yɤ̏ tʉ̀ʌ-dhʉ̀n yā à̀-dhʉ̀n dà̀ ī dhɛ̏* Tokpa élève ce bétail pour moi **2 troupeau** *(bœufs, moutons, caprins)* Qsyn. *kpɤ̄*

tǜɤɤ → tǜɤ 1, 2 *bétail; élever*

tǜɤɤpʌ̏ <élever-chose> ***n*** **animal domestique** *(y compris le gros et le petit bétail, la volaille, les chats et les chiens)*

tǜtǘ {A} ***adj*** **innombrable** *(très nombreux)*

tǜun *v vi ā tǜun !* **tu es le bienvenu !**

tūǘn; **tūń** {tùn, tùun} ***v vt*** **secouer**

tùuntǘun ***n*** **balancement** ◊ *yȁ ȁ tùuntǘun kʌ̄* elle l'a balancé ◊ *yȁ sʌ́ʌdhɛ́ tùuntǘun kʌ̄ bhɛ̄n-dhǜn yɑ̋n dhíɤ* il a balancé un papier devant les gens

tǘuŋ, **tǘnŋ**, **tɔ̋ŋ** (t) {Pl. tǘŋtǘŋ} ***adv*** *la forme tǘŋtǘŋ désigne la pluralité des participants* **silencieusement** *le plus souvent (mais pas exclusivement), dans un énoncé non-verbal :* ♦ *ī dhí tǘuŋ, ī tǘuŋ* je me tais ◊ *wȍ dhǜn wō dhí tǘuŋ* ils sont venus sans dire un mot ◊ *yáa yȁ ɤ̄ dhí tɔ̋ŋ* il ne restait pas silencieux ♦ *dɔ̄ ɤ̄ dhí tǘnŋ, dɔ̄ ɤ̄ tǘnŋ* se taire

tūǘtūǘ ***n Centropus leucogaster*** **coucal à ventre blanc** *(oiseau; taille : 50 cm; queue longue et large; tête, gorge, poitrine supérieure et dessus noirs, dos et ailes châtains; poitrine inférieure et ventre blancs) [son cri en pleine journée, surtout lorsque le coucou est sur un arbre sec, porte un malheur à celui qui l'entend]* ♦ *tūǘtūǘ yɤ̏ wȅ tūǘtūǘdhɤ̄* le coucal chante

tūǘtūǘdhɤ̄ ***onomat*** **coucou**

U u

ȕun ***intj*** **d'accord**

ǘȕ-ȕu ***onomat*** **hululement** *(d'un hibou)*

ū 1, **ī** ***mpp*** **tu** *MPP existentiel de la 2e pers. sg.*

ū 2, **ī** ***prn*** **te**, **ton**, **ta** *pronom non-sujet de la 2 pers. sg.*

ú 1, **í** ***mpp*** **te** *MPP de la 2e pers. sg. de la série conjointe*

ú 2, **í** ***mpp*** **te** *MPP de la 2e pers. sg. de la série subjonctive*

V v

vá (t) ***n*** **piège** *(pour les oiseaux)* Syn. *dɤ̄ŋ, sɔ́*

vâ (m) ***n*** **faim** Syn. *dȉn*

vȁa ***n*** **jouet en raphia**

vɑ̋aandhɤ̄ ***adj*** *Int. de* vɑ̋andhɤ̄ *vite*

vɑ̋andhɤ̄ {Int. vɑ̋aandhɤ̄, SupInt. vɑ̋nvɑ̋ndhɤ̄} ***adv*** **1.1 vite** Syn. *plɛ̀plɛ̀* ◊ *yɤ̏ bɛ̏ŋ sǜ vɑ̋andhɤ̄* il court vite **1.2 facilement** *(sans difficulté)* ◊ *bhɛ́n bhā yɤ̏ fīʌʌ vɑ̋andhɤ̄* cette personne s'évanouit facilement **2 de bonne heure** *pas de formes intensives dans ce sens* ◊ *Gbȁtȍ yɤ̏ bɤ̏ vɑ̋andhɤ̄* Gbato se réveille de bonne heure

vȁangɔ̄n ***n*** **champion, personne remarquable; guerrier éminent**

vàkánŋ̏sṵ̏ < Fr. vacances > ***n*** **vacances**

vàláŋ̏ < Fr. volant > ***n*** **volant** *(de voiture)* *Syn. vòdháŋ̏*

vân ***n*** **arbre** *(esp. : de petite taille, avec les épines sur le tronc, à bois mou)*

vȁnvȁndhɤ̄ ***adj*** *SupInt. de* vȁandhɤ̄ *vite*

vʌ̏ ***n*** ***Cephalophus leucogaster*** **céphalophe à ventre blanc**

vɛ̋ ***n*** **poisson** *(une petite espèce)*

vɛ̋bhɤ̏bhȁandhʌ́n, **vɛ̋bhɤ̏bhȁan** <petit.poisson-manger-oiseau-diminutif> ***n*** *la forme vɛ̋bhɤ̏bhȁan est utilisée plus rarement* ***Alcedo cristata, Corythornis cristata*** **petit martin-pêcheur huppé** *(taille : 12 cm, dos bleu, huppe érectile; mange des petits poissons)*

véɛ̏ ***n*** *rn* **avertissement** *(mise en garde impliquant une menace) dans les expressions figées :* ♦ *ɯ̄ / kā véɛ̏ !* gare à toi ! / gare à vous ! *(ne saurait être adressée aux aînés)* ◊ *bhɛ́n ɤ́ ɯ́ pʌ̄ sèe yā, kɤ̄ ɯ̄ véɛ̏, ɯ́' bhá kʌ̄ dhɤ̋ tàabhān* toi qui as gâté la chose ici, gare à toi, ne fais plus ça ♦ *véɛ̏ zīɤ bhɛ̄n gɔ̏* mettre qn en garde

vɛ̄ ***n*** ***Cercopithecus patas, C. sabaeus*** **singe rouge** *(nom générique de plusieurs espèces de singes : singe rouge, singe noir)*

vɛ̄bɤ̂ < Fr. verbe > ***n*** **verbe**

vɛ̋dhɛ̋ < Fr. verre > ***n*** **verre** *(récipient)* ♦ *sɔ̄ vɛ̋dhɛ̋ bhō* repasser les habits

vɛ̄ɛ̋dhɛ̏ {LOC vɛ̄ɛ̋dhɤ̄} ***loc.n*** *rn* **bas-ventre**

vɛ̄ɛdhɤ̄ {Int. vɛ̄ɛvɛ̄dhɤ̄} ***adv*** **directement**, **tout droit** ◊ *Yɔ̏ yà tǣæ̏n wɔ̏n pɤ̄ Gɤ̏ɤ̏ dhɛ̏ vɛ̄ɛvɛ̄dhɤ̄* Yo a dit la vérité à Geu sans ambages

vɛ̄ɛ̋dhɤ̄ ***loc.n*** *LOC de* vɛ̄ɛ̋dhɛ̏ *bas-ventre*

vɛ̄ɛ̋nvɛ̏ɛnvɛ̋ɛndhɤ̄ ***onomat*** *imitation du grincement des chaussures* *Syn. wɛ̄ɛ̋nwɛ̏ɛnwɛ̋ɛndhɤ̄*

vɛ̄ɛvɛ̄dhɤ̄ ***adv*** *Int. de* vɛ̄ɛdhɤ̄ *directement*

vɯ̋aandhɤ̄ {Int. vɯ̋anvɯ̋andhɤ̄} ***adv*** **d'un seul coup**, **d'une seule bouchée** *(boire, manger; la forme intensive exprime une action itérative)* ◊ *Gɤ̏ɤ̏ yȁ wē bhūn vɯ̋anvɯ̋andhɤ̄* Geu a bu le vin de palme à plusieurs reprises cul sec

vɯ̋adhɤ̄ ***adv*** **rapidement** ◊ *Gɤ̏ɤ̏ yȁ dhūn yī tùaa bhō kɛ̋ɛ yȁ zīɤ vɯ̋adhɤ̄* Geu est venu nous saluer, mais il est reparti tout de suite

vɯ̋anvɯ̋andhɤ̄ ***adv*** *Int. de* vɯ̋aandhɤ̄ *d'un seul coup*

vɯ̋anvɯ̋anvɯ̋andhɤ̄ ***onomat*** **snif** *(bruit de reniflement d'un nez enrhumé)* ◊ *yɤ̏ ɤ̄ yūn gȁn vɯ̋anvɯ̋anvɯ̋andhɤ̄* il renifle (enrhumé)

vɯ̋avɯ̋adhɤ̄ <Intensif de vɯ̋adhɤ̄ 'vite'> ***adv*** **impétueusement** *(un écoulement)* ◊ *yɯ́ yȁ pā yɤ̏ zīɤ vɯ̋avɯ̋adhɤ̄* la rivière a gonflé, l'écoulement est devenu rapide

víʌʌ (gw), **vűʌ** (t) *n* **1.1 fibre** ♦ *yēɛ̋ víʌʌ* fibre de coton *(non-filé)* **1.2 cheveux** *(coupés)* **2 mousse** *(du savon, de la bière)* ◊ *sāà víʌʌ yà dà* le savon a moussé

vīdhɛ̂nglɤ̀ <Fr. vinaigre> *n* **vinaigre**

vìi, vìiga *n* **ride verticale au centre du front** *(caractéristique de nombreux masques)*

vīn 1) {vīn, vìn HU} *v* **1** 1) *vi* **bouger** 2) *vt* **remuer** ◊ *yɤ̀ ɤ̄ kpíʌnŋ vīn-sīʌ* il remue les joues **2** *vi* **toucher** *(à – bhà)* ◊ *wà vīn gbɔ̀ŋ kɔ́ bhà, yɤ̀ bhɛ̄n bhɔ̀* quand on touche à un guêpier, on est piqué par les guêpes ♦ *bhɤ̀ vīn �n̄ bhà, kɤ̄ á gó �n̄ kō tà* sers-moi, car ma calebasse est vide *(adressé à l'échanson, litt. : "Touche-moi, pour que j'aille détendre le dos")* **3** *vi* **faire du bruit, bruire** ◊ *kpò yà dà tɔ̀ kɔ́ɔdhɤ̄, tɔ̀-dhùn wɔ̀ vìn* quand une mangouste entre au poulailler, les poules font du bruit ♦ *�n̄ tő gúɯ yɤ̀ vīn-sīʌ* i) j'entends un bruit lointain ii) les oreilles me bourdonnent

vīn 2) {vìn} *n* **bruit** Syn. fɛ̀ɛ ♦ *à vīn yɤ̀ dɔ̀ tɤ́tɤ́tɤ́dhɤ̄* il sonne : tic-tac

víòodhɤ̄ *onomat* *imitation du bruit de la taille d'une étoffe ou d'une natte d'un seul mouvement brusque*

víòovìoovíoodhɤ̄ *onomat* *imitation du grincement du bois*

víɔ̀ŋ <Fr. avion> *n* **avion** Syn. gɔ̄bhàan ◊ *yɤ̀ kʌ̄ dhò víɔ̀ŋ gúɯ* elle est partie en avion ♦ *dūbhɛ̀n-dhùn bhà víɔ̀ŋ* avion des sorciers *(on croit que les sorciers savent se déplacer dans un avion magique en utilisant du sang humain comme carburant)*

víɔ̀ŋsó <Fr. avion, Manding só 'maison'> *n* **aéroport**

vìtêsɯ̀ <Fr. vitesse> *n* **vitesse**

vlàanvlàan {A P S} *adj* **malpropre**, **négligé**

vlàanvlàan *adj* **inutiles** *Pluralia tantum, intensif* ◊ *kpɔ̀ɔ-dhʌ́n-dhùn vlàanvlàan bhá-dhùn wɔ̀ bṹ gúɯ, wɔ̀ bhɛ̄n flő bhò* il y a des herbes inutiles en brousse, elles égratignent les gens

vlàvlàdhɤ̄ *onomat* *imitation du bruit de défrichage avec une machette*

vlúɯdhɤ̄ [Int. vlúɯvlɯ̀ɯvlúɯdhɤ̄] *adv* **précipitamment et sans hésiter** ◊ *yà zīɤ vlúɯdhɤ̄* il est parti subitement (d'une façon impolie) ◊ *Yɔ̀ yɤ̀ yʌ̄ kʌ̀ vlúɯvlɯ̀ɯvlúɯdhɤ̄* Yo arrive à faire beaucoup de travaux vite et sans fatigue

vlɯ̀ɯndhɤ̄ *adv* **autour** ◊ *yɤ̀ zīɤ-sīʌ kɔ́ zɯ̀ wɛ̋ vlɯ̀ɯndhɤ̄* il tournait autour de la maison

vlɯ̀ɯvlɯ̋ɯ *n rn ɤ̄ vlɯ̀ɯvlɯ̋ɯ kʌ̄ à gɔ̀* **s'échapper des mains de qn** *(en se débattant)* ◊ *yà ɤ̄ vlɯ̀ɯvlɯ̋ɯ kʌ̄ bhɛ́n-dhùn bhā à-dhùn gɔ̀ yà sɔ̀ kɔ́ ɤ̄ bhā à gúɯ* elle a pu leur échapper et entrer dans la maison

vlúɯvlɯ̀ɯ *adj* **dynamique** *(travailleur, entrepreneur)*

vlúɯvlɯ̀ɯvlúɯdhɤ̄ *adv Int. de* vlúɯdhɤ̄ *précipitamment*

vòdháŋ̀ <Fr. volant> *n* **volant** *(de voiture)* Syn. vàláŋ̀

vòkāà <Fr. avocat> *n* **avocat** *(fruit)*

vōodhē ***adj*** **gonflé** *(piment)*

vōodhɤ̄ ***adv*** **fortement** *(se gonfler, se fâcher)*

vòokāà <Fr. avocat> ***n*** **avocat** *(juriste)* Syn. *dhīaŋdhűsúbhɛ̏n*

vòtéȅ <Fr. voter> ***n*** **élections** ◊ *yɤ̏ kʌ̄ dɔ̄ n̄ gbȁn gɔ̏ vòtéȅ yī kʌ́* il m'a soutenu le jour des élections

vɔ̏ŋ ***n Pelomys spp.*** **rat** *(taille : 10-16 cm; 50-100 g, museau court, châtain, longueur égale du corps et de la queue)*

vɔ̏ɔ ***n*** **1 cola, rose** *[plus cher que le cola rouge; utilisé pour les sacrifices]* Syn. *kwīzʌ̄gā* ♦ *vɔ̏ɔ tīi* cola rose foncé ♦ *vɔ̏ɔ pűu* cola rose clair **2 cola blanc**, **cola blanche**

vɔ̋ɔ (t) ***n*** **mauvaises herbes, maquis, broussaille** *(buisson ou hautes herbes, sur le champ ou dans la brousse)* Syn. *kpɔ̏ɔ*

vɔ̄ɔ̋dhɤ̄ ***onomat*** *imite une piqûre rapide* ◊ *yà ɤ̄ zlāà zūa dhȁa kʌ́ vɔ̄ɔ̋dhɤ̄* il a flanqué un coup de couteau à son jeune frère *(et retiré le couteau)*

vɤ̋ ***n*** **lérot, loir** *(rongeur qui vit dans les bananiers tombés)*

vɤ̋dhʌ́n <lérot-diminutif> ***n Mastomys natalensis*** **rat** *(taille : 6-16 cm, 12-70 g; poils mous et courts, dessus brun ou jaune, dessous gris; queue velue, plus courte que le corps; très fécond; vecteur du virus Lassa)*

vɤ̂dhɤ̄ ***adv*** **brusquement** *(d'un coup sec sur le corps)*

vɤ̄ɤ̄ ***n Anomalurus erythronotus*** **anomalure à dos rouge** *(esp. d'écureuil volant)*

vɤ̋ɤ ***n*** **famine** ◊ *vɤ̋ɤ yà dʌ̏* la famine s'est installée

vɤ̋ɤ̏dhɤ̄ ***adv*** **brusquement** *(se lever)* **subitement** *(mourir)*

vűʌ (t) → vɪ́ʌʌ *fibre*

vūnŋdhē ***n*** **hanneton** *[selon les Dan, le hanneton représente l'avant-dernier stade de transformation du papillon]* ◊ *dhʌ́n-dhȕn wà bhīʌ́gā kplȕ vūnŋdhē gɛ̄nŋgā bhȁ, wȁ bɛ̏ŋ súʼ ká, yɤ̏ yà wɛ́-sȕ bhȁ* les enfants attachent un fil à la patte du hanneton, ils courent, et il vrombit ♦ *vūnŋdhē yɤ̏ wȅ vūuun* le hanneton vrombit

vűu ***n*** **écume** ◊ *yɪ́ vűu yà yȁ* l'eau a moussé

vȕúbhȕn-vȕubhȕn-vȕúbhȕn ***onomat.*** *(imitation du vrombissement d'un moteur)*

vūuun ***onomat*** **vrooo** *(imitation du vrombissement du hanneton, de la guêpe)* ◊ *gbɔ̏ŋ gā yɤ̏ wɛ́-sɪʌ vūuun* la guêpe vrombit : vrooo

vȕuvűu ***n*** **agitation** *(de l'eau)* ◊ *yɪ́ yɤ̏ vȕuvűu kʌ̄-sɪʌ* le fleuve est agité

vūúvūú ***onomat*** **wouuuh** *(hurlement de vent)* ◊ *tɛ́ɛ yɤ̏ vūúvūú kʌ̄-sɪʌ, tɛ́ɛ yɤ̏ zīɤ-sɪʌ vūúvūú* le vent hurle : wouuuh

vūŋ ***n*** **hibou** *(esp.)*

W w

wȁ 1 ***prt*** **1 aïe !** *particule connotant une surprise désagréable ◊ Gbȁtȍ ȁ kɔ́ yà gɤ̋ wȁ !* aïe ! la maison de Gbato a brûlé ! **2** *particule d'insistance ou de mise en garde* **3** *particule de politesse*

wȁ 2 <de *wö ä> ***mpp*** **ils le, ils la, elles le, elles la** *forme contractée : MPP existentiel de la 3e pers. pl. + pronom non-sujet de la 3e pers. sg.*

wà, **wȁ** ***mpp*** **1 ils, elles** *MPP du parfait de la 3e pers. pl.* **2 on** *MPP perfectif à référent générique ou indéterminé*

wā, **wlā** *la forme wlā est archaïque* ***n Alchornea cordifolia*** **arbre** *(esp.; avec de petites baies) [les animaux sauvages aiment ses fruits; les chasseurs se mettent souvent en embuscades près de cet arbre; le bois est apprécié pour les fagots]*

wá 1 ***mpp*** **ils**, **elles** *MPP du parfait, logophorique pluriel*

wá 2 ***mpp*** **1 pour qu'ils ne, pour qu'elles ne** *MPP pl. prohibitif de la 3e pers.* **2 on** *MPP prohibitif à référent générique ou indéterminé*

wȁa ***n*** **herbe** *(à feuilles larges; un bon fourrage)* ♦ *wȁa dhɛ̋* = wȁa

wàȁ ***n*** **fourmi** *(esp.)*

wāȁ 1, **wāa** ***prn*** **lui et..., elle et...** *(pronom coordinatif de la 3e pers. sg.) la forme wāȁ est plus usitée* ♦ *wāȁ ... -dhȕn* eux et..., elles et... ◊ *wāȁ dhēbʌ̏-dhȕn* eux et une femme; lui et des femmes; eux et des femmes

wāȁ 2 ***prn*** **lui et son..., lui et sa..., elle et son..., elle et sa...** *pronom de la 3e pers. sg. coordinatif fusionné avec le pronom non-sujet 3e pers. sg. suivant ◊ wāȁ gbɤ̄* lui et son fils ◊ *bhán zē tīi wāȁ zœ̏œndhē dhɔ́* j'ai acheté des haricots noirs et rouges

wāȁ 3 ***mpp*** **ils**, **elles** *MPP présomptif de la 3e pers. pl.*

wáa ***mpp*** **1 ils**, **elles** *MPP négatif imperfectif de la 3e pers. pl.* **2 on** *MPP négatif imperfectif à référent générique ou indéterminé*

wɛ̋a ***n*** **bâillement** ♦ *wɛ̋a bhō* bâiller

wȁadhɤ̄ ***adv*** *évoque le bruit de la pluie*

wáadhūn → wáȁndhūn *se coucher*

wāɛ̋n ***onomat*** *(son d'une peau arrachée)*

wáȁndhūn, **wáȁdhūn** {wáȁndhūn, wáȁdhūn; Neut. wáȁndhȕn, wáȁdhȕn} ***v*** 1) *vi* **se coucher** *Syn. wɔ̄* ♦ *wȁ wáȁndhūn wō kó pɪ̋ɤ* euph. ils ont couché ensemble *(homme et femme)* ♦ *yà wáȁndhūn ɤ̄ gú tȁ* il s'est couché à plat ventre 2) *vt* **coucher**

wáaōo ***mpp*** **ils ne** *(forme fusionnée des marqueurs prédicatifs négatif et prospectif)*

wɛ̄lɛ̋ < Maninka wáadɛ > ***n*** **parapluie**

wāntīi < ?-noir> ***n*** **pagne** *(traditionnel, rayé bleu et blanc ou uni) [vêtement de femme, en même temps, fait partie du costume des masques; était autrefois une composante nécessaire de la dot]*

wāŋ {A, pl. wāŋ-dhʉ̀n, wāŋwāŋ-dhʉ̀n A} ***adj*** **large** ◊ *kɔ̀ɔ wāŋwāŋ-dhʉ̀n* calebasses larges

wāŋdhʌ́n ***n*** *arch.* **pagne** *(traditionnel, tissé sur le métier)* *Syn.* *kɤ̋nsɔ̀*

wáŋ̋wàŋ {A P S, wáŋ̋wàŋ-dhʉ̀n pl. A, wáŋ̋wàŋ-sʉ̀ foc. A S, wáŋ̋wàŋ-sʉ̀-dhʉ̀n pl. foc. A; wáŋ̋wáŋ̋ Int. pl. A P S, wáŋ̋wáŋ̋-dhʉ̀n Int. pl. A S, wáŋ̋wáŋ̋-sʉ̀ Int. pl. foc. A S, wáŋ̋wáŋ̋-sʉ̀-dhʉ̀n Int. pl. foc. A S} ***adj*** **large** *plus large que wāŋ*

wáŋ̋wáŋ̋ *Int. pl. de* wáŋ̋wàŋ *large*

wāŋwāŋ-dhʉ̀n *Pl. de* wāŋ *large*

wàpɤ̏ ***n*** **rumeur** *(nouvelle non confirmée)* ◊ *ɯ̄ bhā wàpɤ̏ yɤ̏ gbɛ́* tu colportes trop de rumeurs

wáʉ̏u-wáʉ̏u ***onomat*** **ouah ! ouah !** *(aboiement du chien)*

wáwádhɤ̄ ***onomat*** **sans soucis** *(divulger des secrets)* ◊ *Yɔ̄ yɤ̏ dhīaŋ zʌ̀ wáwádhɤ̄* Yo divulgue des secrets

wʌ̄, wɔ̄ ***n rn*** **visage** *Qsyn.* *wʌ̄ʌ́dhɛ̏* ◊ *à wʌ̄ yà bhlà yī kɔ̄ɔ* son visage est enflé par le sommeil ◊ *bhɛ̄n gbàn wɔ̀ wɔ̄ wʌ̄ yà kwʌ́ʌ̀* tout le monde est face à face ♦ *ɤ̄ wʌ̄ dɔ̄* se diriger

wʌ̀ʌ ***n*** **1** *rn* **pitié** ◊ *à wʌ̀ʌ yɤ̏ n̄ kʌ̄-sīʌ* j'ai pitié de lui **2 malheur**

wʌ̄ʌ́ ***n*** *rn dans quelques expressions figées* **visage** ♦ *yà ɤ̄ wʌ̄ʌ́ gʉ́-sīɤ* il a eu un visage serré

wʌ́ʌ̀ ***n*** **1 argent** *(métal)* **2.1 argent** *(monnaie)* *Syn.* *wʌ́ʌ̀gā* ♦ *yɤ̏ wʌ́ʌ̀ gʉ́-sèe* il gaspille l'argent **2.2 cinq francs** *(dans le compte d'argent, l'emploi de la forme wʌ́ʌ̀gā peut faire penser que le montant est plus petit que prévu, et wʌ́ʌ̀, que le montant est plus élevé que prévu)* ◊ *wʌ́ʌ̀ gblʉ̋ʉ̋ dɔ̄* 5000 francs CFA *(et c'est beaucoup)* ◊ *wʌ́ʌ̀ kāŋ dɔ̄* cinq cent francs ◊ *wʌ́ʌ̀ gblʉ̋ʉ̋ yȉisīɤ* vingt mille francs

wʌ̀ʌbhɛ̏n <pitié-personne> ***n*** **miséreux**

wʌ̀ʌ-dhɛ̏ <pitié-endroit> ***n*** **tristesse** ♦ *bhɛ̄n wʌ̀ʌdhɛ̏ bhɔ̄* maltraiter qn

wʌ̄ʌ́dhɛ̏ {LOC wʌ̄ʌ́dhɤ̄} ***loc.n*** **1** *rn* **visage** *Qsyn.* *wʌ̄* ◊ *à-dhʉ̀n wʌ̄ʌ́dhɛ̏ yɤ̏ bhɔ̀ kwʌ́ʌ̀* leurs visages se ressemblent ◊ *Yɔ̀ dhʌ̀n ɤ́ à bhàn à wʌ̄ʌ́dhɤ̄* Yo l'a frappé au visage **2** *rn* **devant** ◊ *bɔ̄' wʌ̄ʌ́dhɤ̄* passe devant elle

wʌ̄ʌ́dhɤ̄ ***loc.n*** *LOC de* wʌ̄ʌ́dhɛ̏ *visage*

wʌ́ʌ̀gā <argent-os> *dans la parole rapide souvent prononcé comme wáàā* ***n*** **1 argent** *(monnaie)* *Syn.* *wʌ́ʌ̀* ♦ *wʌ́ʌ̀gā dhȉisʉ̀* argent sale, argent mal acquis **2 cinq francs** *Syn.* *wʌ́ʌ̀* *(dans le compte d'argent, l'emploi de la forme wʌ́ʌ̀gā peut faire penser que le montant est plus petit que prévu, et wʌ́ʌ̀, que le montant est plus élevé que prévu)* ◊ *wʌ́ʌ̀gā gblʉ̋ʉ̋ dɔ̄* 5000 francs CFA *(et c'est peu)*

wʌ́ʌ̀kɔ̀ <argent-maison> ***n*** **banque** ◊ *yɤ̏ wʌ́ʌ̀ dà wʌ́ʌ̀kɔ̀ gʉ́ sʉ́ bhà* il dépose l'argent à la banque tous les mois

wʌ́ʌ̀kɔ̏bhàpʌ̄ <argent-main-sur-chose> ***n*** **anneau d'argent**

wʌ́ʌ̀kúnbhɛ̏n ***n*** **percepteur, collecteur d'impôts**

wʌ̀ʌsʉ̏ {P; Int. wʌ̀ʌwʌ̀ʌsʉ̏} ***adj*** **1 triste** ◊ *yɤ̏ gʉ̀n gbɛ́ɛ̏, yɤ̏ gʉ̀n wʌ̀ʌsʉ̏* c'était difficile, c'était triste **2 malheureux**

wʌ̀ʌsʉ̏-dhɛ̏ ***n*** **misère**

wʌ́ʌ̀yɛ̏ɛbhōbhɛ̏n <argent-enterrer-personne> ***n*** **trésorier**

wʌ̄ʌ́zi̋aan <visage-route> ***n*** **devant, partie avant** *(de l'homme)*

wʌ̀nŋ ***n*** **lézard** *(nom générique)*

wʌ̋nŋ ***n*** **mouche, mouches** Qsyn. wőo ◊ *wʌ̋nŋ yɤ̏ dʉ̀n bhīʌʌ bhȁ* les mouches s'agglutinent sur la plaie ♦ *wʌ̋nŋ-dhʉ̀n wȍ wɛ́-sīʌ yūudhɤ̄* les mouches bourdonnent

wʌ̋nŋdhɤ̄ ***onomat*** *imitation d'un coup cassant*

wʌ̋nŋkʌ̄zʉ̄bhȁ <mouche-chasser-fond-on> ***n*** *hist.* **slip à queue** *(pour les hommes; n'est plus usité)*

wē ***n*** **1 vin de palme 2 bière**

wɛ̋ 1) ***n*** **son** *(bruit)* ◊ *būu wɛ́ wȍ yɤ̏ sʉ̋ɤ dȁ bhɛ̄n gʉ́* le bruit des fusillades fait peur aux gens

wɛ̋ 2) {wɛ̀} ***v*** **1** *vi* **parler** ♦ *wɛ́ ȁ ká* parler de qn/qch ♦ *wɛ́ ȁ bhȁ* chanter en réponse ♦ *wɛ́ bhɛ̄n píɤ / tȁ* chanter les louanges de qn ♦ *wɛ́ bhɛ̄n wȍ wlɤ̏ɤ* contredire qn **2.1** *vi* **émettre des bruits** *(animal, oiseau, insecte)* ◊ *bhɔ̏ yɤ̏ wɛ̀* le cochon grogne **2.2** *vi* **pleurer** *(être humain)* **3** 1) *vi* **résonner** *(instrument de musique, tonnerre, appareil avertisseur)* ◊ *yɤ̏ wɛ̀ kwʌ̋ʌ klɤ̄klɤ̄...* les signaux sonores devient brefs... 2) *vt* **jouer** *(d'un instrument de musique à vent)* **4.1** *vi* **accepter** *(qch – bhȁ)* ◊ *yá wɛ́' bhȁ kɤ̄ n̄ tɛ́ɛdō yɤ̏ dȁ bʌ̋nkpɤ̄ gʉ́* nous avons admis un de mes amis dans l'association de travail ◊ *wíi kʌ̄ wɛ́ ȁ bhȁ kɤ̄ wȍ dhìʌʌn bʉ̋ gʉ́* ils n'ont pas voulu s'aventurer en brousse ◊ *Zân yɤ̏ bhɛ̏ɛ Tòkpȁ dhɛ̏ dhɛ́dhɛ́ sɔ́ɔdhʉ́ píɤ, kɛ́ɛ yíi wɛ́' bhȁ* Jean a supplié Tokpa pendant cinq heures, mais celui-ci n'a pas accepté ses excuses **4.2** *vi* **excuser** *(qch – bhȁ)* ◊ *yɤ̏ bhɛ̏ɛ n̄ dhɛ̏ yāandhɪ́ɤ, kɛ́ɛ bhíin wɛ́ ȁ bhȁ* il m'a demandé pardon hier, mais je ne lui ai pas pardonné **5** *vi* **répondre** *(à – gɔ̏)*

wēbhʉ̄ndʉ̀dʉ̀ ***n*** **alcoolique** *(qui s'est déjà mis en dehors des relations sociales)*

wɛ́dhɛ̏ <son-place> ***n*** **moteur**

wɛ̀e ***n*** **peau qui se détache** *(de l'humain)*, **mue** *(de serpent)* ♦ *bhɛ̄n gɔ̏ wɛ̀e* pellicules ♦ *bhɛ̄n wɛ̀e* pellicules; peau qui se détache ♦ *bhɛ̄n kwī wɛ̀e* peau qui se détache ♦ *bhlɛ̄ɛn wɛ̀e* mue de serpent

wèe 2 ***n*** **1 sel** ♦ *wèe bɪ̏* sel (en grains) ♦ *yɪ́ wèesʉ̏* eau salée **2 lèpre**

wèe 1 ***n*** **pou de tête** Qsyn. kɛ̀fʌ́

wēɛ́ ***n*** *rn* **urine** ♦ *wēɛ́ kɔ́* vessie ♦ *ɤ̄ wēɛ́ bhō* uriner

wèebhɛ̏n ***n*** **homme lépreux**

wēɛ́bhōyʉ̀a <urine-sortir-maladie> ***n*** **gonorrhée, blennorragie, chaude-pisse** *lv.*

wèesʉ̀ ***adj*** **salé**

wèeyì <sel-eau> ***n*** **1 eau salée 2 mer**

wēgā <vin-os> ***n*** **ivrogne** *(qui continue pourtant une vie plus ou moins normale)*

wēŋ ***n*** **queue**

wēŋdhē ***n*** ***Colius striatus*** **coliou barré** *(taille : 30 cm, huppé; ailes courtes et queue très longue; couleur brunâtre, face noire, pattes rouge corail)*

wḗpʌ̀ <son-chose> ***n*** **instrument de musique** *(nom générique)*

wḗsḗ < Mandening wíse, wúse > ***n*** **patate douce**

wɛ̀ ***prt*** **1** *particule qui reporte l'attention sur un nouvel objet* ◊ *yɤ́ bhī zʌ̀ wɛ̀, ...* et toi, tu... **2** *apparaît dans les phrases conditionnelles présomptives* ◊ *gwɛ̄e yíi dhʉ̀n gā' wɛ̀ ?* et si la panthère n'est pas encore morte ?

wɛ̄, **wɛ̄gwʌ̀** ***n*** **granit, basalte** ◊ *wɛ̄gwʌ̀ dhʌ̀n wó gūn kʌ̄-sīʌ būugā ká* on fasait des chevrotines de basalte

wɛ́ ***prt*** **1 tout à coup** ◊ *á dhō dhɛ̀ gā' wɛ́, kɤ̄ yɤ̄ dhūn ɤ́ dɔ̄ n̄ sɔ́ɔ yā* à peine l'ai-je regardé, et le voici tout d'un coup à côté de moi **2** *exprime une émotion forte : irritation, satisfaction...*

Wɛ̂ ***n*** **Wobé**, **Guéré** *(langues de la famille krou, groupes ethniques et représentants de ces groupes)*

wɛ̀ɛ <de *wɔ̄ dhɛ̀ 'se.coucher-place'> ***n rn*** **endroit pour se coucher** ♦ *kwā wɛ̀ɛ bhʉ̀n* asseyez-vous ! il y a de la place ! *lv.* ♦ *ā dhò dó' n̄ wɛ̀ɛ bhàa* j'irai chez moi ♦ *gó n̄ wɛ̀ɛ bhàa !* ôte-toi de ma place (à coucher) ! pousse-toi un peu ! ♦ *wɛ̀ɛ bhō* enterrer

wɛ̀ɛ ***n*** **moquerie** ♦ *wɛ̀ɛ dɔ̄ bhɛ̄n bhà* se moquer de qn

wɛ́ɛ {A, wɛ́ɛ-dhʉ̀n pl. A, wɛ́ɛ-sʉ̀ foc. A, wɛ́ɛ-sʉ̀-dhʉ̀n pl. foc. A} ***adj*** **autre** Syn. *wɛ́ɛwɛ́ 1* Qsyn. *bhá 1, dhɛ́* ◊ *yɤ́ á kpàn à bhɛ̄n wɛ́ɛ dō bhá bhà dɔ́ɔ ká ...* et j'ai rencontré l'autre le soir ◊ *à bhà dhīaŋ yà dhīaŋ wɛ́ɛ dhɪ́ɤ wlʉ̄ʉ́* son discours en a engendré un autre

wɛ́ɛ̀ɛgʉ́ ***adv*** *Int. de* wɛ́ɛ̀gʉ́ *ces jours*

wɛ́ɛ̀gʉ́ [Int. wɛ́ɛ̀ɛgʉ́] < ?-dans> ***adv*** **ces jours-ci** *(la forme intensive est rarement utilisée, elle exprime une insistance)* ♦ *dhūn wɛ́ɛ̀ɛgʉ́ !* viens ces jours-ci précisément

wɛ́ɛn ***n*** ***Bixa orellano*** **roucou** *(une arbuste dont les fruits produisent la peinture rouge)*

wɛ̀ɛndhɤ̄ {Int. wɛ̀nwɛ̀ndhɤ̄} ***adv*** **douloureusement** *(exprime l'intensité de la sensation de brûlure)* ◊ *sɪ́ɤ bhīʌʌ yɤ̀ bhàn bhɛ̄n ká wɛ̀nwɛ̀ndhɤ̄* la brûlure fait très mal

wɛ̄ɛ́ndhɤ̄ ***onomat*** **crac** *son d'une branche cassée* ◊ *dhʉ̄ʉ́ kwɛ̄ɛ́ yà yɛ́ wɛ̄ɛ́ndhɤ̄* la branche d'arbre s'est cassée : crac

wɛ̄ɛ́nwɛ̀ɛnwɛ̄ɛndhɤ̄ ***onomat*** *imitation du grincement des chaussures* Syn. *vɛ̄ɛ́nvɛ̀ɛnvɛ̄ɛndhɤ̄*

wɛ́ɛŋ → wɛ́ŋ *gerbe*

wɛ̃ɛwɛ̃ 1 {A P, wɛ̃ɛwɛ̃-dhùn pl. A} ***adj*** **autre** *Syn.* *wɛ̃ɛ 1*

wɛ̃ɛwɛ̃ 2 1) {A P S, wɛ̃ɛwɛ̃-dhùn pl. A S; wɛ̃kɛ̃wɛ̃kɛ̃ Int. A P S, wɛ̃kɛ̃wɛ̃kɛ̃-dhùn Int. pl. A S} ***adj*** **1 vide 2 guéri** ♦ *yà kʌ̄ wɛ̃ɛwɛ̃* il a guéri

wɛ̃ɛwɛ̃ 2 2) <vide-affaire> ***n*** **rien de tout** *(affaire peu importante)* ◊ *à zūʌ́ yɤ̀ bhɤ̀ɤ wɛ̃ɛwɛ̃ wɔ̀n gúí* il se fait des soucis pour rien de tout

wɛ̃ɛwɛ̃ 2 3) ***adv*** **1 vainement, sans raison** ◊ *yɤ̀ sí bhɔ̀ ī gɔ̀ wɛ̃ɛwɛ̃* il m'a insulté gratuitement **2 à vide** ◊ *gɔ̄ gɛ̀n dhʌ̀n ɤ́ slʌ̀ʌ gúí wɛ̃ɛwɛ̃* les roues de la voiture tournent à vide

wɛ̃ɛyí ***n*** **saison des grandes pluies** *(juillet-août)*

wɛ̃ídhē ***n*** **wèidé** *(danse en rond, avec accompagnement de tam-tams et crécelle yɔ̃ŋbhē; les participants dansent à tour de rôle)*

wɛ̃inŋdhɤ ***onomat*** **paf** *(son d'un coup sur la tête)* ◊ *yà à tɔ̃ bhàn wɛ̃inŋdhɤ* il l'a frappé sur la tête : paf !

wɛ̃kɛ̃wɛ̃kɛ̃ *Int. de* wɛ̃ɛwɛ̃ *vide*

wɛ̄n ***n*** **grain de palmier à huile** *(noyau de noix de palme; utilisé pour faire l'huile noire)* ♦ *wɛ̄n flɛ̃ɛ* noyau de grain de palmier à huile ♦ *wɛ̄n yɔ̃n* huile noire

wɛ̄ngā (gw), **wɛ̄ngādhɤ** (m) <grain de palmier-os> ***adv*** **enfin** ◊ *yɤ̀ zīaan slɔ̀ɔ wɛ̄ngādhɤ* il a découvert enfin une route

wɛ̀nŋ ***v*** **1.1** 1) *vi* **se répandre**, **couler** ◊ *yí yà bɔ̄ bàŋ zūū ká yà wɛ̀nŋ* l'eau s'est échappée par le fond de la bassine et s'est répandue ◊ *bhɑ̃́nŋglɔ̃o bɪ̃́n yà wɛ̀nŋ* les fleurs du manguier sont tombées *(en masse)* 2) *vt* **verser**, **répandre** ◊ *bhá dhó bhɑ̃a blùŋ wɛ̀nŋ' tɑ́ɑ̀blʌ̀ʌ tà* ne laisse pas tomber les miettes de riz cuit sur la table **1.2** *vt* **arroser** **1.3** *vi* **éjaculer** ◊ *yà wɛ̀nŋ plɛ̀* il a éjaculé deux fois **2.1** *vi* **se répandre** *(un liquide, une matière sèche)* ◊ *Yɔ̀ yà yí bhá bhō à tà kɤ yá dhó wɛ̀nŋ'* Yo a versé un peu de l'eau (de la calebasse) afin qu'elle ne se répande pas ◊ *bhān wʌ́ʌ̀ sɛ̃ɛ́dhʌ́n yà wɛ̀nŋ* ma monnaie s'est répandue **2.2** *vt* **renverser** *(par inadvertance)* ◊ *Gbàtò yà wē dhʌ́nbhá wɛ̀nŋ ɤ bhā sɔ̄ bhà* Gbato a renversé un peu de vin de palme sur son vêtement **3.1** *vt* **verser**, **jeter** *(pour libérer le récipient)* **3.2** *vt* **jeter** *(se débarrasser)* ♦ *blʌ̄ʌ wɛ̀nŋ* jeter les ordures **4** *vi* **tomber** *(feuilles)* **5.1** *vi* **piquer en masse** *(smb. – tà)* ◊ *gbɔ̀ŋ yɤ̀ wɛ̀nŋ Kùapṹ tà yāandhíɤ* hier les guêpes ont piqué Kouapou en masse **5.2** *vi* **se jeter** *(sur – gúí)* **6** *vi* **s'écrouler** *(en s'écrasant)*

wɛ̀nwɛ̀ndhɤ ***adv*** *Int. de* wɛ̀ɛndhɤ *douloureusement*

wɛ̄ŋ 1 ***n*** **scarification** *[chez les Dan orientaux, on faisait régulièrement des scarifications dans la région de Sipilou et dans le clan Sɑ̃nŋgwìnŋ̀; en outre, les femmes le faisaient parfois pour l'esthétique]* *Qsyn.* *wɛ̄ŋgā* ♦ *yà wɛ̄ŋ zʌ̄* il a fait la scarification ♦ *yà wɛ̄ŋ zʌ̄ bhún* il a bien rossé les gens de là-bas

wɛ̄ŋ 2, **wɛ̄ŋ̀** ***prn*** **lui et lui**, **elle et lui**, **elle et elle** *pronom coordinatif* ◊ *wɛ̄ŋ dhʌ́n ɤ́ wó kʌ̄ dhō* elle est partie avec cet enfant

wɛ̄ŋ 3 *n Herpestes sanguines* **mangouste rouge, mangouste de Dybowsky** *(26-34 cm, 350-800 g, corps allongé, pattes courtes, arboricole, couleur variable) Syn. sɑ̋kpɑ̋dʌ̄*

wɛ̋ŋ, wɛ̋ɛŋ *n* **petite gerbe** *(de riz) Qsyn. gbān, kɔ̏pā*

wɛ̄ŋ̏-dhʉ̏n, wɛ̄ŋ-dhʉ̏n *prn* **eux et lui, eux et elle, elles et lui, elles et elle, lui et eux, elle et eux, lui et elles, elle et elles, eux et eux, eux et elles, elles et eux, elles et elles** *pronom coordinatif incorporant*

wɛ̄ŋgā <scarification-os> *n* **balafre** *(élément de scarification au visage) Qsyn. wɛ̄ŋ* ♦ *wɛ̄ŋgādʌ̄* homme ayant des scarifications ♦ *wɛ̄ŋgādhɛ̄* femme ayant des scarifications ♦ *wɛ̄ŋgā yáa à wʌ̄ʌ́dhɤ̄* il n'a pas de scarifications sur le visage

wɛ̄ŋsɑ̋kpádʌ̄ <balafre-mangouste> *n* ***Atilax paludinosus*** **mangouste des marais** *(taille : 46-64 cm, 2,2-5 kg; brun foncé, avec du poil épais sur le corps, le cou et la queue; doigts flexibles; museau retroussé)*

wí *mpp* **ils, elle** *MPP de la 3 personne sg. de la conséquence négative*

wȉaadhɤ̄ *adv* **1 en traînant** ◊ *yí yɤ̏ kpɔ̏ɔ gȁn wȉaadhɤ̄* l'eau entraîne les herbes et les broussailles avec de la force et du bruit **2 en masse, en groupe** *(des humains, des animaux, des poissons qui viennent pour se rassembler)* ◊ *wȁ dhūn wȉaadhɤ̄* ils se sont rassemblés en venant de partout

wȉaawȉaadhɤ̄ <Intensif de wȉaadhɤ̄ 'en traînant'> *adv* **bruyamment** *(traîner, balayer)* ◊ *Yɔ̏ yɤ̏ dhɛ̏ gȁn/gblɤ̏ wȉaawȉaadhɤ̄* Yo balaye avec du bruit

wīaawȉaawīaadhɤ̄ *onomat* **frou-frou** *(son de pas sur les feuilles sèches)* ◊ *vʌ̏-dhʉ̏n wɔ̏ tɑ̋ sú-sīʌ wīaawȉaawīaadhɤ̄* les céphalophes marchent en faisant bruisser des feuilles sèches

wȉawȉadhɤ̄ *adv* **vite** *(balayer, nettoyer)*

wíi *mpp* **1 ils, elles** *MPP négatif perfectif de la 3e pers. pl.* **2 on** *MPP négatif du passé à référent générique ou indéterminé*

wlā → wā *arbre (esp.)*

wlɑ̋ȁ *n* **bêtise** *(manque d'intelligence)* ♦ *wlɑ̋ȁwɔ̏n* i) bêtise *(qu'on commet)* ii) une affaire peu signifiante ♦ *wlɑ̋ȁ zʌ̄* faire des bêtises

wláȁn *n* **grande fête** *(non-chrétienne; de village, de clan ou de concession; on égorge un bovin)* ♦ *wláȁn kʌ̄* organiser une grande fête ◊ *wáa dhūn wláȁn tȁ wō kɔ̏ gúː fīʌʌ ká* on ne vient pas à une grande fête les mains vides *(c'est mal vu de venir sans un cadeau pour les organisateurs de la fête)*

wlɑ̋ȁsʉ̏ {A P S, wlɑ̋ȁsʉ̏-dhʉ̏n pl. A S, wlɑ̋ȁsʉ̏-sʉ̏ foc. A, wlɑ̋ȁsʉ̏-sʉ̏-dhʉ̏n pl. foc. A; wlɑ̋ȁwlɑ̋ȁsʉ̏ Int. A P S, wlɑ̋ȁwlɑ̋ȁsʉ̏-dhʉ̏n Int. pl. A S, wlɑ̋ȁwlɑ̋ȁsʉ̏-sʉ̏ Int. foc. A, wlɑ̋ȁwlɑ̋ȁsʉ̏-sʉ̏-dhʉ̏n Int. foc. pl. A} <bêtise-adj.> *adj* **inutile**

wlɑ̋awlȁa *adj* **clair** *(sauce)*

wlɑ̋ȁwlɑ̋ȁsʉ̏ *adj Int. de* wlɑ̋ȁsʉ̏ *inutile*

wlɤ̃n ***n*** **cheveux blancs** ♦ *wlɤ̃n yà dà à gɔ̀ gúí* il a grisonné

wlɤ̃ŋ ***n*** **écartement** *(des bras; signe de regret ou d'étonnement désagréable; avant d'écarter les bras on peut frapper des mains)* ♦ *yɤ̀ ɤ̄ kɔ̀ wlɤ̃ŋ bhɔ̄-sīʌ* il écarte les bras (signe d'étonnement ou de regret; il reste pantois)

wlɛ̄ɛ <Manding wɛ̀rɛ> ***n*** **enclos** ◊ *dù wlɛ̄ɛ yɤ̀ gùn' gɔ̀* il avait un enclos de boeufs

wlɛ̋ɛnŋwlɛ̀ɛnŋwlɛ̋ɛnŋdhɤ̄ ***onomat*** *imitation de tintement des bracelets*

wlɛ̄ɛ̋nwlɛ̀ɛnwlɛ̄ɛ̋ndhɤ̄ ***onomat*** *imitation du bruissement des feuilles sous les pieds*

wlɛ̋ɛwlɛ̀ {A, S} ***adj*** **joyeux**

wlɛ̋ŋ ***n Terminalia glaucesens, T. togoensis*** **arbre** *(esp.; 8-10, parfois jusqu'à 20 de hauteur, cime arrondie, écorce grise fortement fissurée)*

wlōbīdhɛ̂n → lōbīdhɛ̂n *robinet*

wlōőwlòowlōídhɤ̄ ***onomat*** **flicflac** *imitation du bruit de succion*

wlőowlòowlőodhɤ̄ ***onomat*** *imitation du murmure d'eau* ♦ *yí-dhʌ́n bhā yɤ̀ wɛ̀ wlōőwlòowlōődhɤ̄* le ruisseau murmure

wlɔ̄kɔ̄wlɔ̄kɔ̄dhɤ̄ ***onomat*** *son de vibration bruyante* ◊ *gɔ̄ kwɛ̋ɛ yɤ̀ vīn-sīʌ wlɔ̄kɔ̄wlɔ̄kɔ̄dhɤ̄* la porte de la voiture est en train de vibrer

wlɔ̀ŋ ***n gen. Trema (?)*** **arbre** *(esp.; haut, utilisé comme bois de chauffe)*

wlɔ̋ɔ̀ ***n*** **discernement**, **sagesse** ♦ *wlɔ̋ɔ̀ dhʌ́n* personne sage

wlɤ̀ 1 ***v*** **1** *vi* **voler** *(d'oiseau)* **2** *vi* **sauter** *(par-dessus – tà)* ♦ *à yɤ̃n yɤ̀ wlɤ̀ à tà* il l'a négligé

wlɤ̀ 2 ***v*** **1** *vt* **balayer** <u>*Syn.*</u> *gblɤ̀* **2** *vt* **ramasser**

wlɤ́ ***n*** **mortier** *(à piler; nom générique)*

wlɤ̀ɤ ***pp*** **sous** ◊ *dhɛ̋ kpǣæ yɤ̀ wɛ̀ bhɛ̄n wlɤ̀ɤ wlɛ̄ɛ̋nwlɛ̀ɛnwlɛ̄ɛ̋ndhɤ̄* les feuilles sèches font un bruissement sous les pieds

wlɤ̀ɤdhɛ̀ ***n rn*** **en-bas** ◊ *Tìa bhà dhēbʌ̀ yà gɔ̀n wlɤ̀ɤdhɛ̀ wlɤ̀* la femme de Tia a balayé sous la paillotte ♦ *gbɤ̃n wlɤ̀ɤdhɛ̀* partie inférieure de la cuisse

wlűubhōdhɛ̀ ***n Lybius hirsutus, Tricholaema hirsutum, T. flavipunctata*** **barbu hérissé** *(un oisea, taille : 17 cm, dessus sombre moucheté de jaune, dessous jaunâtre rayé et taché de brun)*

wlűnkűnwlùnkùn *Int. de* wlűuunwlùuun *fragile*

wlūūű {wlùu} ***v*** **1** *vi* **se lever** **2** *vi* **quitter** *(la place – LOC)* ◊ *yɤ́ dhēbʌ̀dhʌ́n bhā ɤ́ wlùu Gbàǎplɤ̀ɤ ɤ́ dhō dhɔ̋ɔ gú kwíplɤ̀ɤ* alors la femme a quitté Gbapleu pour aller au marché dans la ville **3** *vi* **avoir une érection** ◊ *Zân yà wlūūű* Jean a une érection **4** *vi* **grandir** ♦ *dhʌ́n-dhùn wó wlùu tɤ́ŋ yā à gúí* les enfants de nos jours

wlűuunwlùuun {A P S, Int wlűnkűnwlùnkùn} ***adj*** **fragile**

wɔ̀ 1 ***n*** **1** *rn* **voix; son** ♦ *wɔ̀ sɛ̋ɛ̋ndhʌ́n* voix aiguë ♦ *wɔ̀ kpɪ̏ɪ̏* voix grave, basse ♦ *ä̀ wɔ̀ yɤ̏ plʌ̋ʌplʌ̏ʌ* sa voix est faible ♦ *wɔ̀ wlɤ̏ɤ* en voix basse ♦ *sʌ́ʌdhɛ̋ wɔ̀ pɤ̄* lire ♦ *ɤ̄ wɔ̀ dä̀ bhɛ̄n dhɛ̏* prendre congé de ♦ *bhɛ̄n wɔ̀ sɯ́* enregistrer quelqu'un au magnétophone ♦ *yɤ́ ä̀-dhɯ̏n wɔ̀ ɤ́ kʌ̏ dō* et ils se sont mis d'accord **2 parole** ♦ *tó ɤ̄ wɔ̀ tä̀* tenir sa parole ♦ *bhɛ̄n gbàn wɔ̀ yä̀ tó ä̀ bhä̀ dō* tout le monde a été unanime à ce sujet ♦ *wɔ̀ kpɔ́ X bhä̀ Y gɔ̏* se lamenter sur Y devant X **3 langue** *(au sens linguistique)*

wɔ̀ 2 ***v*** **1** *vi* **apparaître**; **surgir** ◊ *bhɔ̏ɔn bhā yä̀ wɔ̀ yɤ̄* la souris est apparue ici ◊ *wɔ̀ wɔ̀ wō kwʌ̋ʌ* ils apparaissent ensemble *(des éphémères)* ◊ *yɪ́ yä̀ yä̀ wɔ̀-sɯ̏ bhä̀* l'eau s'est mise à couler ◊ *yɤ́ glɔ̄ɔ kpʌ̀ bhā ɤ́ wɔ̀ dhɛ̏ bhá gɯ́ sɪ́ãa yʌ̀n* et le tronc du bananier surgit quelque part en bas **2.1** *vt* **déterrer** *(tubercules)* Syn. pɔ́n ◊ *bāa wɔ̀* déterrer le manioc **2.2** *vt* **arracher** *(détacher vivement)* **3** *vi* **arriver** **4** *vi* **venir** *(temps)* ◊ *bhlɯ̏n kʌ̋n tɤ̋ŋ yà wɔ̀* le temps de la moisson du riz est venu **5** *vi* **rendre visite** *(à – bhä̀)* ◊ *dhɛ̀ yä̀ kpœ̀œ dō, yɤ̏ dhɯ̏n wɔ̀' ɤ̄ dhē bhä̀* chaque jour il vient rendre visite à sa mère

wɔ̀ 3 ***mpp*** **1 ils**, **elles** *MPP existentiel de la 3e pers. pl.* **2 on** *MPP existentiel à référent générique ou indéterminé*

wɔ̀ 4 ***mpp*** **1 ils**, **elles** *MPP subjonctif de la 3e pers. pl.* **2 on** *MPP subjonctif à référent générique ou indéterminé*

wō 1 {wō} ***v*** *vt* **faire** *verbe substitutif, apparaît lors de la nominalisation du verbe principal; ne s'emploie pas à l'aspect neutre* Qsyn. bhō 1 ◊ *dhó ɤ́ wó gūn ä̀ wō-sɪʌ bhā...* le voyage qu'ils étaient en train de faire...

wō 2 ***mpp*** **ils**, **elles** *MPP existentiel logophorique pluriel*

wō 3 ***prn*** **eux**, **elles** *pronom de la 3e pers. pl. de la série autonome*

wō 4 ***prn*** **se**, **son**, **sa**, **soi** *pronom réfléchi pluriel*

-wō <de wō 'faire'> ***mrph*** *suffixe dérivatif adverbial déadjectival* ♦ *dèewō* de nouveau

wó 1 ***mpp*** **1 ils**, **elles** *MPP conjoint de la 3e pers. pl.* **2 on** *MPP conjoint à référent générique ou indéterminé*

wó 2 ***mpp*** **ils**, **elles** *MPP conjoint logophorique pluriel*

wó 3 ***prn*** **ils**, **elles** *(pronom sélectif de la 3 personne pl., utilisé avec le suffixe -sɯ̏)*

wő ***mpp*** **ils**, **elles** *MPP subjonctif logophorique pluriel*

wōáa ***prn*** **eux**, **elles** *pronom de la 3 personne pl. de la série focalisée négative*

wɔ̀dhɪ́ɤlòobhɛ̏n <voix-devant-arriver-personne> ***n*** **interprète**

wɔ̀dhɪ́ɤlòodhē <voix-devant-arriver-nominalis.> ***n*** **interprétation** *(traduction orale)*

wɔ̀dhɔ̀dhɯ̋ɤ̋gbɛ̏ɛ̏-sɯ̏ <voix-aller-dessus-très-gérondif> ***n*** *neol., ling.* **ton extra-haut**

wɔ̀dhɔ̀dhɯ̋ɤ̋-sɯ̏ <voix-aller-dessus-gérondif> ***n*** *neol., ling.* **ton haut**

wɔ̀dhókɔ̏ <voix-aller-façon> ***n*** *neol., ling.* **ton** ♦ *wɔ̀dhókɔ̏ ɤ́ lɔ̄ɔ-sɯ̏ ká* ton descendant, ton tombant ♦ *wɔ̀dhókɔ̏ ɤ́ dūn-sɯ̏ ká* ton flottant ♦ *wɔ̀dhókɔ̏ dä̀kópɪ́ɤ-sɯ̏-dhɯ̏n* ton modulé

wɔ̀dhɔ̀síaagbɛ́ɛ̀-sɯ̀ɯ <voix-aller-par terre-très-gérondif> *n neol., ling.* **ton extra-bas**

wɔ̀dhɔ̀síaa-sɯ̀ɯ <voix-aller-par terre-gérondif> *n neol., ling.* **ton bas**

wɔ̀dhɔ̀zìnŋgɯ́-sɯ̀ <voix-aller-entre-gérondif> *n neol., ling.* **ton moyen**

wɔ̀gā <voix-os> *n neol., ling.* **syllabe; pied** *(methrique)*

wɔ̀kplɯ̀ɯbhàdhíɤ <voix-attacher-sur-devant> *n neol., ling.* **préverbe**

wɔ̀kplɯ̀ɯbhàtàabhà <voix-attacher-sur-derrière> *n neol., ling.* **suffixe**

wɔ̄o 1 *mpp* **1 ils, elles** *MPP prospectif de la 3e pers. pl.* **2 on** *MPP prospectif à référent générique ou indéterminé*

wɔ̄o 2 *prn* **ils, elles** *pronom de la 3e pers. pl. de la série restrictive*

wɔ̄ɔ̀ *prn* **son, ses** *pronom réfléchi du pluriel de la série possessive*

wɔ̋o *n* **taon**

wɔ̀plʌ̄ʌ̀ <voix-abondant> *n* **causerie** ◊ *yà wɔ̀plʌ̄ʌ̀ kʌ̄ n̄ píɤ* il a causé avec moi

wɔ̀plʌ̄ʌ̀kʌ̄bhɛ̀n <voix-abondant-faire-personne> *n* **farceur, humoriste**

wɔ̀tlóɔ̀ <Fr. voiture> *n* **brouette** ♦ *yɤ̀ ɯ̄ bhā kwɛ̄ɛ̀ blɯ̀-sīʌ wɔ̀tlóɔ̀ gɯ́* il charrie son bagage dans une brouette

wɔ̀ *v vt* **coudre** ◊ *bhɛ́n bhā yɤ̀ sɔ̄ wɔ̀* cet homme est couturier ◊ *yà ɤ̄ bhā sɔ̄ pɛ́-dhɛ̀ wɔ̀* il a recousu son vêtement déchiré

wɔ̄ 1, wɔ̀ {wɔ̀} *v* **1** 1) *vi* **se coucher, être couché** ◊ *gbɛ̂n ɤ́ wɔ̀ bhā yɤ̀ gā-sɯ̀ kà* le chien qui est couché là, est mort *Syn.* *wáàndhūn* ♦ *yà wɔ̀ à píɤ, yà wɔ̀ à ká* gros. il a couché avec elle *Syn.* *zɔ̄n* 2) *vt* **mettre, poser** *(horizontalement)* ♦ *būu wɔ̄ ɤ̄ tàa* mettre le fusil en bandoulière **2** *vi* **se trouver** ◊ *bādhāsɯ̄ Làbia dhɛ̀ ɤ́ wɔ̀ Ābūasô dhɛ̀ tàabhàn bhā* le barrage de Labia se trouve derrière Abousso **3** *vi* **passer la nuit** ◊ *Sítà yà wɔ̄ Yɔ̀ gɔ̀ plɤ̀ɤ plɛ̀* Sita a passé deux nuits au village de Yo **4** *vt* **rajouter** *(à – tà)*

wɔ̄ 2 → wʌ̄ *visage*

wɔ̋ *n* **bois à brûler, fagot** *lv.* ◊ *wɔ̋ yɤ̀ sɛ̀ɛ, yáa bhɔ̀ɔn à bhà kɤ̄ yɤ̀ gɤ́ sʌ̀ ká* le bois est humide, il ne peut pas brûler bien ♦ *wɔ̋ sɯ̀ gɯ́ bhīʌ́ʌ* tortillon pour lier le fagot ♦ *wɔ̋ bɛ̀* fagot, fagot de bois

wɔ̀bɯ̋ɯ <coucher-brousse> *n* **habitude aux séjours prolongés au campement** ♦ *wɔ̀bɯ̋ɯ kʌ̄ bhɛ̀n* celui qui vit longtemps dans le campement

wɔ̀gɯ́kɔ̀ <coucher-dans-maison> *n* **chambre, pièce**

wɔ̄kɔ̀ <se.coucher-main> *n rn, fn* **coutume, règle** ◊ *à-dhɯ̀n bhà wɔ̄kɔ̀* leurs coutumes ◊ *Gbìaabhɛ̀n-dhɯ̀n wāà Yàobâ-dhɯ̀n wɔ̄kɔ̀ yáa dō* les Toura et les Dan n'ont pas les mêmes coutumes

wɔ́n {wɔ̀n} *n* **1 affaire** ◊ *à-dhɯ̀n bhà dhʌ́nkpɔ́dhē wɔ̀n yɤ̀ gbɛ́ɛ̀* le problème de natalité les préoccupe beaucoup ♦ *à wɔ́n gɯ́* concernant qch ♦ *wɔ́n bhá* affaire bizarre **2 problème, difficulté** ♦ *wɔ́n gbɛ́ɛ̀* affaire grave, obstacle ♦ *wɔ́n bhō bhɛ̄n gɯ́* punir qn ♦ *wɔ́n wɔ̄ bhɛ̄n tà* punir qn ◊ *yɤ́ bhɛ̄n bɔ̄ Tɔ̀kpàplɤ̀ɤ bhɯ̄n ɤ̄ bhā sʌ́nŋ gā wɔ̀n gɯ́* alors il a envoyé quelqu'un à Tokpapleu pour l'affaire de son lingot d'or ♦ *wɔ́n bhȁ bhɛ̄n yɤ̄-sṻ gʉ́ yáa gblɛ̀ɛn* on peut facilement avoir des problèmes

wɔ̏nbhɛ̄nkɔ̏n <affaire-personne-étonner> ***n*** **étonnement** ♦ *wɔ̏nbhɛ̄nkɔ̏nwɔ̏n bhṻn* c'est une affaire bizarre (dont on préfère ne pas parler)

wɔ́ngɔ̏tābhɛ̏n <affaire-tête-fermer-homme> ***n*** **autorité morale** *(celui qui a le dernier mot dans une assemblée)*

wɔ́ngʉ́bhānbhɛ̏n <affaire-comprendre-homme> ***n*** **personne compréhensive** *(qui comprend vite et écoute les conseils)*

wɔ́ngʉ́bhān-sṻ ***n*** **entente, compréhension** *(mutuelle)*

wɔ̏ngbɛ́ɛ̀sṻ {A P S, wɔ̀ngbɛ́ɛ̀sṻ-dhṻn pl. A S, wɔ̀ngbɛ́ɛ̀sṻ-sṻ foc. A} <affaire-important-selectif> ***adj*** **préféré, le plus important** *(s'agissant de personnes)*

wɔ̋nkɔ̋nwɔ̏nkɔ̏n *Int. de* wɔ̋ɔnwɔ̏ɔn *nonchalant*

wɔ́nwɔ̏kódhíɤbhɛ̏n <affaire-cocher-l'un l'autre-devant-personne> ***n*** **personne organisée** *(celui qui met tout en ordre)*

wɔ́nyɤ̏bhȁ <affaire-voir-sur> ***n*** **responsable** ◊ *ȁ-dhṻn bhȁ wɔ́nyɤ̏bhȁ bhṻn Tòkpȁ ká* Tokpa est le responsable de cela

wɔ́nzɔ̏nká <affaire-montrer-avec> ***n*** **exemple** ◊ *yȁ wɔ́nzɔ̏nká dō pɤ̄* il a donné un exemple

wɔ̀ɔ ***n*** **singe** *(nom générique, en exceptant le chimpanzés)*

wɔ̀ɔdhʌ́nbhȁbhʌ́nŋ, wɔ̀ɔdhʌ́ȁnbhʌ́nŋ <singe-diminutif-sur-néré> ***n*** **"néré des singes"** *[écorce utilisée comme médicament; fruits prisés des singes]*

wɔ̀ɔgblʌ́ʌ̀bhȁan, wɔ̀ɔgbláȁbhȁan (t) <singe-devant-oiseau> ***n*** ***Tropicranus albocristatus*** **calao à huppe blanche** *(taille : 75 cm; très longue queue étagée; noir avec une huppe blanche)*

wɔ̀ɔ-kɔ̏-bhō-dhʉ̋-bhȁ <singe-main-enlever-arbre-sur> ***n*** **chenille vénémeuse** *(une des espèces de dhɛ̏en; sa piqûere est particulièrement forte)*

wɔ̋ɔnwɔ̏ɔn {A P S, wɔ̋ɔnwɔ̏ɔn-dhṻn pl. A, wɔ̋ɔnwɔ̏ɔn-sṻ foc. A, wɔ̋ɔnwɔ̏ɔn-sṻ-dhṻn foc. pl. A; wɔ̋nkɔ̋nwɔ̏nkɔ̏n Int. A P S, wɔ̋nkɔ̋nwɔ̏nkɔ̏n-dhṻn Int. pl. A S, wɔ̋nkɔ̋nwɔ̏nkɔ̏n-sṻ Int. foc. A, wɔ̋nkɔ̋nwɔ̏nkɔ̏n-sṻ-dhṻn Int. foc. pl. A} ***adj*** **nonchalant, apathique**

wɔ̋ɔwɔ̏ɔ 1, wœ̋œwœ̏œ ***adj*** **faible** *(physiquement; personne)*

wɔ̋ɔ̏wɔ̏ɔ 2, wœ̋œ̏wœ̏œ {A P S, wɔ̋ɔ̏wɔ̏ɔ-dhṻn pl. A S, wɔ̋ɔ̏wɔ̏ɔ-sṻ foc. A S, wɔ̋ɔ̏wɔ̏ɔ-sṻ-dhṻn pl. foc. A} ***adj*** **fade, insipide** ♦ *kȁa wɔ̋ɔ̏wɔ̏ɔ* canne à sucre fade ♦ *wē wɔ̋ɔ̏wɔ̏ɔ* vin fade ♦ *yí wɔ̋ɔ̏wɔ̏ɔ* eau tiède

wɔ̋sṻ {A P S, wɔ̋sṻ-dhṻn pl. A S, wɔ̋sṻ-sṻ foc. A, wɔ̋sṻ-sṻ-dhṻn pl. foc. A; wɔ̋wɔ̋sṻ Int. A P S, wɔ̋wɔ̋sṻ-dhṻn Int. pl. A S, wɔ̋wɔ̋sṻ-sṻ Int. foc. A} ***adj*** **chaud** ◊ *yí wɔ̋sṻ yȁ n̄ kɔ̏ gɤ̋* je me suis brûlé la main avec de l'eau chaude ◊ *bȁyí tɑ̋n ɤ́ gūn dɛ̀ɛ yɤ̏ gṻn wɔ̋wɔ̋sṻ* la danse bayi a été très vive aujourd'hui

wɔ̃wɔ̃sɯ̀ *adj Int. de* wɔ̃sɯ̀ *chaud*

wɔ̃yí <bois à brûler-eau> *n* **pétrole lampant**, **pétrole** *Iv.*

wɤ̄ŋ *n* **pilon**

wœ̄œdhɤ̄ *adv* **à perte de vue** *(d'un espace sans limite : l'eau, la forêt, le désert...)* ◊ *yí tà yà wɔ̄ wœ̄œdhɤ̄* l'eau s'est étendue à perte de vue

wœ́œ̀wœ̀œ → wɔ́ɔ̀wɔ̀ɔ *fade*

wœ́œwœ̀œ → wɔ́ɔwɔ̀ɔ *faible*

wūn *n* **chevelure** ◊ *wà-dhùn bhà wūn bhò à-dhùn kèedhɤ̄* on leur rase la nuque ◊ *bhān wūn bhùu kún, bhán tɤ́ŋ slɔ̀ɔ, kíi' bɔ̄* coiffe-moi à la va-vite; quand j'aurai le temps, tu vas me tresser (comme il faut) ♦ *wūn gā* (un) cheveu <u>Syn.</u> <u>wūndhɛ́</u> ♦ *wàa bhà wūn {gbɛ́ɛ̀} bɔ̄* on lui a tressé les cheveux *(avec des mèches artificielles)* ♦ *wà à bhà wūn lɤ̀* on lui a tressé les cheveux *(sa propre chevelure)*

wūndhɛ́ <chevelure-feuille> *n* **cheveu** ◊ *bhán ī wūndhɛ́ sɔ́ɔdhű wò* je me suis arraché cinq cheveux

wūngā <chevelure-os> *n* **tresse** *(faite avec des mèches artificielles)*

wűnŋ *n* **murmure** *(la conversation dont on ne peut pas distinguer les mots)* ♦ *wűnŋ zʌ̄ bhɛ̄n ká* grommeler contre qn

wūnsʌ́nbhǣændhē *n* **salamandre** *(un petit lézard à corps transparant) [on croit qu'il mange les cheveux des enfants pendant la nuit]*

wɯ̄ {wɯ̀} *n* **1 animal 2** *rn* **viande**

wɯ́ {wɯ̄} *v* **1** 1) *vi* **se casser** ♦ *kɔ́ bhá yíi wɯ́* aucune maison ne s'est écroulée 2) *vt* **casser**, **ruiner** ◊ *yɤ̄ɤ gàan yàan wɯ́ !* tu vas casser les oeufs de pintade ! **2** *vi* **devenir aveugle** *(yeux)* ◊ *à yán yà wɯ́ bhīʌʌ yà bhà-sɯ̀ zīaan gɯ́* il devint aveugle à la suite de sa blessure

wɯ̄kúnwɯ̀ <viande-attraper-viande> *n* **carnassier** <u>Syn.</u> <u>pʌ̄kúnpʌ̀</u>

wɯ̄ɯ̀wɯ̄ɯ̀ {wɯ̀ɯwɯ̀ɯ} <Intensif de wɯ́ 'casser'> *v vt* **briser**

Y y

yà 1 *v* **1.1** 1) *vi* **être assis**, **s'asseoir** ♦ *wɔ́n dɔ̃ɔndɔ̀ɔn yɤ̀ yà à kɔ̀ tà gbɛ́* il a toujours des problèmes pénibles ♦ *bhán yà sʌ̀; ā yà-sɯ̀ ká sʌ̀* merci, je suis rassasié 2) *vt* **mettre** *(s'agissant d'objets à extension horizontale)* **1.2** *vi* **attendre** *(étant dans position assise; qn – gɔ̀)* <u>Qsyn.</u> <u>dɔ̄</u> **2** 1) *vi* **se mettre**, **commencer** *(à – bhà)* <u>Syn.</u> <u>ɤ̄ dhí dà ... gɯ́, zūn ... bhà, yɤ̄ ... bhà, zɯ̄-bhɔ̄</u> ◊ *yɤ́ bhɛ̄n gbàn wó yà gbɔ̃ bɔ̄-sɯ̀ bhà* alors tout le monde s'est mis à pleurer **3.1** 1) *vi* **agir contre** *(qn – bhà)* 2) *vt* **mettre** *(contre – bhà)* ◊ *à bhɛ̄n glɑ́glɑ́sɯ̀-sɯ̀ dhʌ̀n ɤ́ wó' yà ī bhà* ils ont mis contre moi l'homme difficile à manier **3.2** *vt* **faire subir** *(à qn – bhà)* ♦ *gbɛ̂n yà bhɛ̄n bhà* dresser un chien contre qn ♦ *wɔ́n yà bhɛ̄n bhà* accuser qn de qch ◊ *wà sūà wɔ̀n yà à bhà* ils l'ont accusé de mensonge **3.3** *vi* **réprimander**, **grogner**

(qn – bhɛ̄n yɑ̃́n gúɯ; pour – gúɯ)◊ Tòkpà̰ yà̰ yà̰ Zân yɑ̃́n gúɯ wlɑ̃́ɑ̃̀wɔ̃̀n gúɯ Tokpa a grondé Zan pour une affaire peu importante **3.4** *vi* **se heurter** *(contre – bhà̰)* **3.5** *vi* **ennuyer** *(fumée, odeur; qn – gɔ̃̀)◊ yà̰bhà̰ fìi yà yà̰ n̄ gɔ̃̀* l'odeur de l'oignon me gêne **4** *vi* **s'installer** *(pour vivre)◊ wɔ̃̀ yà̰ kwɪ́ sɛ́-dhɯ̀n gúɯ, wó n̄ sāan-dhɯ̀n bɔ̄* ils se sont installés dans les villes, ils m'envoyent des cadeaux **5** *vt* **mettre** *(chapeau, chaussures)* Syn. dà̰◊ *bhán sàbhɑ̃́ tɔ̃̀ɔ-sɯ̀ yà̰* j'ai mis une chaussure mouillée **6** *vt* **faire** *(le feu)* **7** *vt* **former**, **fonder** ♦ *dhɯ̃́ yà ɤ̄ bɪ́n yà̰* l'arbre a fleuri **8** *vi* **saisir** *(en vol; qch – bhà̰)* Syn. sʌ́n◊ *bhɑ̃́nŋglōo bhɛ̄ ɤ́' zɯ̀ɤ bhā, ā yà̰ à̰ bhà̰ wɛ́ bádhɤ̄* j'ai carrément saisi la mangue qu'il a jetée **9** *vt* **élire** *(au poste de – ká)◊ wà̰ ɯ̄ yà̰ bhɛ̃́ɛ̃̀n ká* on t'a élu maire

yà̰ 2 <de *yɤ̈ ä> ***mpp* **il le, il la, elle le, elle la** *forme contractée : MPP existentiel 3 sg. + pronom non-sujet 3 sg.*

yà, **yà̰** *mpp* **il**, **elle** *MPP du parfait de la 3e pers. sg.*

yā 1) *adv* **ici**, **là** *(présentatif situant l'objet soit à proximité du locuteur, soit à une certaine distance du locuteur et de l'auditeur, mais dans leur champ de visibilité, dans le dernier cas accompagné d'un geste ostentatoire de la main) le nom de l'objet désigné comporte une marque de focalisation obligatoire* Qsyn. yɤ̄◊ *yɤ̄ dhɯ̄n ɤ́ yā !* le voici !

yā 2) *dtm* **ce** *suit le mot déterminé; reprise pronominale obligatoire* Qsyn. yɤ̄

yá 1 *mpp* **il**, **elle** *MPP sg. logophorique du parfait*

yá 2 *mpp* **pour qu'il ne**, **pour qu'elle ne** *MPP du parfait de la 3e pers. sg.*

yá 3 *mpp* **nous** *MPP de la 1re pers. exclusif du pl., "nous sans vous", du parfait*

yá 4 *mpp* **pour que nous ne** *MPP prohibitif exclusif 1re pers. pl., "nous sans vous"*

yɑ̃́ *n* **1 igname** *(espèce épineuse) [d'origine baoulé; chez les Dan, cette sorte est apparue récemment; on la cuit non-épluchée]* Qsyn. dhɔ̄ɔ 2, gblɛ̀ɛ ♦ *yɑ̃́ gɔ̃̀* i) fane d'igname ii) bouture d'igname ♦ *yɑ̃́ sɛ́* butte d'igname ♦ *yɑ̃́ sɛ́ɛsɯ̀* igname *(on dit cela pour éviter l'ambiguïté avec le riz)* **2** arch. **riz cuit**

yâ 1) {P; yâyâ Int. pl. P S, yâyâ-dhɯ̀n Int. pl. A S} *adj* **1 mauvais** Syn. yāa **2 fort**

yâ 2) *adv* **mal** ◊ *ā kʌ̄ yī zʌ̀ yâ* j'ai mal dormi ♦ *dɔ̄ bhɛ̄n gɔ̃̀ yâ* barrer la route de qn; déranger qn

yāa *intj* **bien** *(exprime la satisfaction)*

yāá *intj* **tiens !** *(interjection exprimant une grande surprise)*

yāa 1 {A S, yāa-dhɯ̀n pl. A, yāa-sɯ̀ foc. A, yāa-sɯ̀-dhun pl. foc. A; yāayädhɛ̀ Int. A S, yāayädhɛ̀-dhɯ̀n Int. pl., yāayädhɛ̀-sɯ̀ Int. foc. A, yāayädhɛ̀-sɯ̀-dhɯ̀n Int. foc. pl. A S; yáyâ Int. pl. A P S, yāyā-dhɯ̀n Int. pl. A S, yāyā-sɯ̀-dhɯ̀n Int. pl. foc. A S} *adj* **1 mauvais** ◊ *wɔ̃̀ wɔ̄ kó blɯ̀ yāa ká* ils se poussent d'une mauvaise façon ♦ *yāa gúɯ yāa* extraordinaire, terrible ♦ *yà ɤ̄ dɛ̀ kʌ̄ dɛ̀dɛ̀wɔ̄ yāa* il a montré sa stupidité **2 laid 3 incomparable** ♦ *bɛ̀dhɛ́kʌ̄bhɛ̀n yāa* guérisseur sans pareil ◊ *bɪ̀aŋgā yāa bhɯ̀n Gɔ̃́dhɔ̃́n ká* Gono est un coureur sans pareil

yāa 2 *prt* *exprime le respect envers l'interlocuteur, se trouve en fin de proposition*

yāà 1, **yāa** ***prn*** **moi et...** *pronom coordinatif* ♦ *yāà ... -dhùn* nous et... ◊ *yāà dhēbʌ̀-dhùn* nous et une femme; moi et des femmes; nous et des femmes

yāà 2 ***prn*** **moi et son..., moi et sa...** *pronom coordinatif fusionné avec un pronom non-sujet 3e pers. sg. suivant* ◊ *yāà gbɤ̄* moi et son fils

yāà 3 ***mpp*** **il, elle** *MPP présomptif de la 3e pers. sg.*

yāà 4 ***mpp*** **nous** *MPP présomptif exclusif de la 1re pers. pl.*

yāà 5 → yīì *notre*

yāá ***conj*** **tandis que, alors que**

yáa 1, **áa** *la forme áa est typique de la parole rapide* ***mpp*** **il ne, elle ne** *MPP de la 1re pers. sg. négatif imperfectif*

yáa 2 ***mpp*** **nous ne** *MPP négatif imperfectif exclusif de la 1re pers. pl., "nous sans vous"*

yáa 3 <de *yɤ́ á> ***mpp*** **pour que je** *forme fusionnée : la conjonction + le MPP de la 1re pers. sg. de la série conjointe*

yáa ***intj*** **oh !** *(exclamation de surprise)*

yáàdhūn, **yáàndhūn** {yáàdhūn, yáàndhūn; NEUT yáàdhùn, yáàndhùn} ***v*** **1** 1) *vi* **s'asseoir** 2) *vt* **faire asseoir 2.1** *vt* **poser, mettre 2.2** *vt* **réserver, préserver 3** *vi* **s'installer** ◊ *yɤ́ á gūn yáàndhūn* c'est ainsi que je me suis installé définitivement

yàagā ***num*** **trois** *[considéré comme nombre féminin]*

yàan ***n rn*** **œuf** *(d'oiseau)* ♦ *tɔ̀ yàan gɔ̀ zɔ́* bout pointu d'un œuf de poule ♦ *tɔ̀ ɤ́ ɤ̄ yàan tà* une poule sur ses œufs

yāàn ***n*** **surface dénudée** <u>Qsyn.</u> <u>*yāàndhɛ̀*</u> *dans quelques combinaisons* ♦ *yà dhó sɪ́ɤ yāàn tà kʌ̄'* il est allé chercher du gibier après le feu de brousse *(vaste incendie volontaire servant principalement à faciliter la chasse)* ♦ *à gɔ̀ yāàn yɤ̀ sʌ̀* il a la tête bien rasée

yāán (gw), **yāan** ***n*** **ruse** ♦ *yāán bhō* faire le malin

yáan ***loc.n*** *COM de* yán *yeux*

yáàn ***loc.n*** *SUP de* yán *yeux*

yáandhɛ̀ ***adj*** **vivant** ◊ *yɤ́ wó gɔ̄ɔ̀n bhā' sūū yáandhɛ̀ ká wó' dā glùù gúú wó sɛ́ kpā' tà* ils ont pris cet homme vivant, l'ont mis dans le trou et l'ont recouvert de terre

yāàndhɛ̀ ***n*** **surface dénudée** <u>Qsyn.</u> <u>*yāàn*</u> ♦ *gɔ̀ yāàndhɛ̀* tête rasée ♦ *sɪ́ɤ yāàndhɛ̀* brousse brûlée

yāandhɪ́ɤ ***adv*** **1 hier** ♦ *yāandhɪ́ɤ tàabhàn* avant-hier **2 la veille**

yàandhɤ̄ ***adv*** **doucement** *(une chute)*

yáàndhūn → yáàdhūn *s'asseoir*

yáangākʌ̄, **yánkʌ̄** <oeil-chasser> ***n*** **maladie des yeux** *(de toutes sortes)*

yāánpɪ́ɤ → yɛ̄ɛ́npɪ́ɤ *soir*

yȁanyȁan {A, P; Int. yȁnkȁnyȁnkȁn A, P} ***adj*** **transparent**, **à claire-voie** *(étoffe, barrière)* ◊ *Yɔ̏ yȁ sɔ̄ yȁanyȁan dȁ* Yo a mis des habits transparents ◊ *kwɛ̋ɛ tȅ yȁanyȁan yɤ̏ yʌ́nŋ̏ bhɔ̏ kwànbhȅn bhȁ* la porte de raphia laisse passer le soleil sur le voleur (proverbe : un voleur se trahit par son comportement)

yȁáō-yȁáȍo-yȁáōo ***onomat.*** *imitation du son de sanglots*

yáaɤ̄ɤ ***mpp*** **il ne** *(forme fusionnée des marqueurs prédicatifs négatif et prospectif)*

yȁatɛ̋ɛn ***n*** **yaatèèn** *(dialecte dan dans le canton Yii)*

yȁatīi ***n*** **yaatii** *(dialecte dan dans le canton Yii)*

yāawō <mauvais-faire> ***adv*** **très** Syn. *dȅdȅwo*

yāayädhȅ ***adj*** *Int. sg. de* yāa *mauvais*

yáayīi ***mpp*** **nous (excl.) ne** *(forme fusionnée des marqueurs prédicatifs négatif et prospectif)*

yȁbhȁ ***n*** **oignon**

yȁdhȕn <de *yɤ̏ änü '3SG.EXI 3PL> ***mpp*** **il les**, **elle les** *forme contractée : MPP existentiel de la 3e pers. sg. + pronom non-subjectif de la 3e pers. pl.*

yȁgɔ̏ <igname-tête> ***n*** **bouture de l'igname**

yȁgbȁ ***n*** **tambour** *(à double membrane et à caisse cylindrique) [utilisé autrefois pour animer les danses de guerre et d'autres danses aujourd'hui obsolètes, ainsi que pour accompagner les célébrations musicales de la "maison sacrée"; aujourd'hui est considéré comme un tambour dioula]* Syn. *fɤ̏*, *bhȉdhēbhàa*

yȁkȁyȁkȁdhɤ̄ ***adv*** **d'un effort commun** *(en parlant du montage du toit)* ◊ *wȁ kɔ́ gbȁ súı yȁkȁyȁkȁdhɤ̄* ils ont soulevé le toit d'un effort commun

yȁkȅ ***n*** *arch.* **affaire** ◊ *yȁkȅ kó kʌ̄' pɤ̄ yāandhɤ́ɤ bhāa...* l'affaire dont nous avons parlé hier...

yȁkɔ̏dhʌngābhȁpʌ̏, **yȁkɔ̄ŋgāapʌ̏**, **yȁkœ̏œŋ̏gābhȁpʌ̏** <mettre-main-diminutif-os-sur-chose> ***n*** *rare* **bague** Syn. *kœ̏œŋpʌ̏*

yȁkɔ̄ŋgāapʌ̏ → yȁkɔ̏dhʌngābhȁpʌ̏ *bague*

yȁkɔ̏ɔpʌ̏ <asseoir-main.sur-chose> ***n*** **bracelet** ♦ *ȁ bhȁ yȁkɔ̏ɔpʌ̏-dhȕn wɔ̏ wȅ wlɛ̋ɛnŋ̋wlȅɛnŋ̏wlɛ̋ɛnŋ̋dhɤ̄* ses bracelets tintent

yȁkœ̏œŋ̏gābhȁpʌ̏ → yȁkɔ̏dhʌngābhȁpʌ̏ *bague*

yȁkpȁyɔ̋o < Baoulé jɛ̀kwàjó > ***n*** **paludisme, palu, malaria** Syn. *gɔ̋ŋ*

yȁkpȁyɔ̋odhȕ <paludisme-arbre> ***n*** ***Azadirachta indica*** **neem**, **nim**, **margousier** *(arbre de 20, originaire de l'Inde)*

yȁkwʌ̏ʌ̏ <asseoir-réciproque> ***n*** **réunion** ♦ *yȁkwʌ́ʌ̏ kʌ̄* avoir une réunion, organiser une réunion

yà-kwʌ̀ʌ̀-kʌ̀-à-gṹ-gɔ̀ <asseoir-réciproque-faire-3SG-dans-voiture> ***n*** *rur.* **bâchée** *(camionnette recouverte d'une bâche amovible où les passagers sont assis face à face sur des bancs)*

-yàn ***mrph*** *suffixe de supin* ◊ *bhēn gbɛ́ wà lòo kó tà fɛ̄tɤ̀ kʌ̄-yàn gṹ* beaucoup de monde s'est rassemblé à la fête

yã́n 1), yɛ̃́ɛn (t) {IZF yàn; IN yʌ́nŋ, COM yãan, SUP yã̂àn} ***loc.n*** **1.1** *rn* **œil, paire des yeux** ♦ *yã́n gā* œil ◊ *à yã́n gā yà bhlà* ses yeux ont enflé ♦ *ā yã́n gā yɤ̀ ā kún-sīʌ klɤ̄klɤ̄dhɤ̄* j'ai un tic nerveux de l'oeil ♦ *yã́n kɔ́* orbite ◊ *gbɔ̀ŋ yɤ̀ Yɔ̀ bhò yāandhɪ́ɤ à yã́n kɔ́ bhà* hier la guêpe a piqué Yo sur l'orbite ◊ *yɤ̀ zùn kpɛ̃́nŋdhɤ̄ ā yãan {ká}* il est sorti en ma présence ♦ *à wɔ̀n yɤ̀ ā yãan* je suis au courant de cette affaire ♦ *à yã́n yɤ̀ gbɛ̃́ɛ̀* il est éhonté, effronté ♦ *yɤ̀ dɔ̀ bhēn yã́n gṹ* il n'est pas modeste, il est vantard ♦ *yáa dà bhēn yã́n gṹ* il est modeste ♦ *à yã́n gṹ yɤ̀ sʌ̀* ses rêves sont prophétiques ♦ *à yã́n gṹ yɤ̀ yâ* il est coureur de jupons; elle s'intéresse trop aux hommes ♦ *à yʌ́nŋ yɤ̀ dɔ̀* (t) il est coureur de jupons; elle s'intéresse trop aux hommes ♦ *à yã́n yɤ̀ dhò zīɤ' ū gṹ* il ne te respectera pas ♦ *ā yã́n yà kʌ̄ gbínkígbìnkì* j'ai les paupières lourdes ♦ *à yãan* i) veillant ii) vivant ◊ *yà ɤ̄ kɛ̂n gṹ-gblṹ kɤ̄ yɤ̀ tùn ɤ̄ yãan* il a partagé son héritage de son vivant ◊ *ā gbēŋ kʌ̀ ā yãan* j'ai passé une nuit blanche ♦ *yáa X yãan dhɛ̀...* le X ne pense pas que ...; le X doute que... ♦ *yã́n pɛ̃́ɛn dō* un œil ◊ *wà à yã́n pɛ̃́ɛn dō wṹ* on lui a crevé un œil ♦ *à yã́n gā yɤ̀ gblɤ́gblɤ́ ká dhɛ̀ gæ̃́æn yã́n dhɤ́* il a des yeux bombés comme un scorpion ♦ *sūʌ́ʌ yà dɔ̄' yã̂àn* il a eu un orgelet ♦ *yà bhēn yã́n gṹ* faire chut à qn ♦ *ā yã́n yɤ̀ ū gɔ̀* je t'attendrai **1.2** *rn* **coup d'oeil** ♦ *yã́n zṹɤ ɤ̄ pɛ̃́n pɪ́ɤ* jeter un coup d'oeil à côté **2** *rn* **couleur** ♦ *à yã́n yà gā* il a déteint **3** *yãan kʌ̄ avec un verbe nominalisé à gauche* **passer une nuit blanche** ◊ *ā kʌ̄ wɔ̀ yãan kʌ̀* j'ai passé une nuit blanche ◊ *gbēŋ ɤ́ dɛ̀ɛ, dhā yɤ̄ɤ tò yãan kʌ̄* il va pleuvoir pendant toute la nuit à venir **4** **contenu** *(un nom de compte utilisé facultativement avec les noms des récipients)* ◊ *yí kɔ̀ɔ yã́n yàagā* trois calebasses de l'eau

yã́n 2) ***prev*** **œil**

yànbhán ***n*** **malheur**

yã́nbhlṹu (m) ***n*** **légèreté; manque de respect** ◊ *yɤ̀ dhīaŋ zʌ̀ ā dhɛ̀ yã́nbhlṹu ká* il parle avec moi n'importe comment, sans respect

yã́n-bhɔ̄ {yã́n-bhɔ̄} ***v*** 1) *vt* **régler, résoudre** 2) *vi* **se régler, se résoudre** ◊ *kɤ̄ kwāà klàŋ̀ wɔ́n yã́n yíi kʌ̄ bhɔ̄ vãandhɤ̄...* et si l'affaire de notre école ne s'arrange pas vite...

yã́ngā <oeil-os> ***n*** *sɛ́ yã́ngā* **ambassadeur**

yã́ngṹpɛ̃́bhɛ̀n <oeil-intérieur-fendre-personne> ***n*** **clairvoyant**

yã́ngṹtīibhɛ̀n <œil-dedans-noir-homme> ***n*** **sorcier**

yã́ngṹyāabhɛ̀n <œil-dedans-mauvais-homme> ***n*** **1 personne brutale 2 personne turbulente** *(celui qui ne reste pas tranquille)* **3 coureur de jupons, dragueur** *fam.*

yã́nkã́nyànkàn ***adj*** *Int. from* yãanyàan *transparent*

yā̋nkʌ̄ → yā̋angākʌ̄ *maladie des yeux*

yā̋nkpìnŋtʌ̀ {pl. yā̋nkpìnŋtʌ̀dhédhūn} <œil-route-surface> ***n rn*** **sourcils** ♦ *yā̋nkpìnŋtʌ̀ kʌ̀a* poil de sourcil

yā̋nsɛ̄́ɛ <œil-résonateur de tambour> ***n rn*** **cils** ♦ *yā̋nsɛ̄́ɛ gā* cil ◊ *yā̋nsɛ̄́ɛ gblɛ̀ngblɛ̀n yáa sʌ̀* les cils longs, ce n'est pas bon *[chez les hommes]* ◊ *ʌ̀ bhʌ̀ dhēbɔ̀ bhā yà kplɛ̄́ɛ́ yà tó dhɛ̀ bhēn yā̋nsɛ̄́ɛ dhɤ́* sa femme a maigri et est devenue maigre comme un cil

yā̋n-tó {yā̋n-tō} ***v vr*** **attendre** *(qch – gɔ̀) Syn. dɔ̄ 1, dhɪ́ɤ-gā̋n*

yā̋nyí <oeil-eau> ***n rn*** **larmes** ◊ *ʌ̀ yā̋nyí yɤ̀ wɛ̀nŋ-sīʌ ʌ̀ kpɪ́ʌŋ tʌ̀* des larmes coulent sur ses joues

yā̋nzìɤgúú <oeil-passer-dans> ***n*** **1 légèreté; affaire futile** ◊ *yā̋nzìɤgúú bhùn ɛ̀e ?* est-ce une chose futile ? **2 défi** ♦ *yā̋nzìɤgúú dɔ̄ bhēn bhʌ̀* lancer un défi à qn

yāŋ ***n rn*** **plainte** *(contre qn)* ♦ *yà bhēn yāŋ kʌ̄ dhùutī̀ dhɛ̀* porter plainte contre qn auprès du chef du village

yāŋ̋dhē ***n Hybomys univittatus*** **rat à bande dorsale noire** *(taille et poids : 10-16 cm, 40-80 g, petite souris brune)*

yʌ̀ŋgā̋dhɪ́ɤ ***n*** *arch.* **bassine métallique** *(pour la lessive)*

yàobâ ***n*** **Yacouba**, **Dan** *(désignation fréquente des Dan de Côte d'Ivoire, à l'exception des ceux de la préfecture de Touba)* ♦ *Yízlɤ̀ɤ yàobâ* les Dan du Libéria

yā̋pʌ̀ <riz-chose> ***n*** **plat de riz cuit** *Syn. bhā̋apʌ̀*

yʌ̀pɪ́ɤdhē <asseoir-à côté-femme> ***n*** **coépouse aînée** *(la préséance des femmes dépend de la séquence des mariages, et non de l'âge) Syn. dhē*

yʌ̀tʌ̀glɔ̀o <asseoir-sur-tabouret> ***n*** **tabouret** *Syn. gblɔ̀o*

yáyâ *Int. pl. de* yāa *mauvais*

yâyâ *Int. de* yâ *vilain*

yāyā-dhùn *Int. pl. de* yāa *mauvais*

yʌ̀yɔ̄́ɔ <asseoir-pareil> ***n rn*** **voisin, voisine**

yæ̀æ (t) → yɛ̀ɛ *siège*

yǣ́æ, **yɛ̄́ɛ** ***n*** **remède pour la voix** *(adoucit la voix des chanteurs, on le fait à partir de l'écorce d'iroko ou de certains autres arbres, de certaines racines, parfois en ajoutant du piment et du cola)* ◊ *yʌ̀ yɛ̄́ɛ bhɤ̀ kɤ̄ ʌ̀ wɔ̀ dhī* elle a pris du remède "yèè" pour que sa voix s'adoucisse

yǣ́æ̀ ***loc.n*** *SUP de* yʌnŋ̄ *soleil*

yǣ́æn → yɛ̄́ɛn 2 *arbre (esp.)*

yǣŋ̋, **yɛ̄ŋ̋** ***n*** **1 accusation** ◊ *pɤ̀ tɔ̀ dhɤ́-sùù yʌ̀ Zân yǣŋ̋ bhō* tout le village a accusé Jean **2** *rn* **amende** *(selon la coutume)* ◊ *yúa tʌ̀ gèe yʌ̀ ʌ̀ yǣŋ̋ bhō* le "masque de maladie" lui a infligé une amende

yʌ̄ {yʌ̀} *n* **travail** Syn. *bhʌ̋dhʌ̋* ♦ *yʌ̄ kʌ̄* i) travailler ii) (t) envoyer

yʌ̀ʌ, yìʌ (t) *n* **hébergement**

yʌ̄ʌ *n* **1 don** *dans quelques expressions figées* ♦ *yʌ̄ʌ yà bhɔ̄ n̄ dhɛ̀* on m'a honoré **2 bonheur**

yʌ̋ʌ̀ {IN yʌ̋ʌ́} *loc.n la forme contractée de l'inessif, yʌ̋ʌ́, est typique pour la parole rapide; la forme non-contractée, yʌ̋ʌ̀ gú, est vue comme préférable* **poche**

yʌ̋ʌ́ *loc.n IN de* yʌ̋ʌ̀ *poche*

yʌ̋ʌ̀bīɤ <eau-sur-éléphant> *n* **hippopotame**

yʌ̀ʌ-bhɔ̄ {yʌ̀ʌ-bhɔ̄} *v vt* **héberger**

yʌ̄ʌgɔ̀ <don-cola> *n* **cola porte-bonheur** *(à 3 lobes)*

yʌ̋ʌnyʌ̀ʌn → yʌ̋nŋyʌ̀nŋ *bariolé*

yʌ̋ʌnyʌ̋ʌn *adj Pl. de* yʌ̋nŋyʌ̀nŋ *multicolore*

yʌ̄-kʌ̄ (t) {yʌ̄-kʌ̀} *v vt* **envoyer**, **commissionner** *(faire qch – MSD; à – dhɛ̀, chez – gɔ̀)* Syn. *bɔ̄*

yʌ̄kʌ̄bhɛ̀n <travail-faire-personne> *n* **travailleur, ouvrier**

yʌ̀n *adv* **quelque part** *balise de focalisation circonstancielle en combinaison avec la localisation approximative et la définitude* Ant. *dhààn* ◊ *Zân yɤ̀ kpìnŋ gɔ̀ dhɯ̋ɤ yʌ̀n, yɤ́' zláà ɤ́ kpìnŋ gɔ̀ síāa yʌ̀n* Jean habite en haut de la route, et son petit frère quelque part en bas de la route ◊ *ɤ́ kā kpɤ̄ gú bhūn yʌ̀n...* là-bas, dans votre groupe... ◊ *ɤ́ yī pɪ́ɤ yɤ̄ yʌ̀n* chez nous ici ◊ *dhūn yɤ́ yʌ̀n* viens ici ! *(plutôt que de rester là où tu te comportes mal)*

yʌ̄n {yʌ̄n} *v vi* **s'achever**, **se terminer** ◊ *gblɯ̀ ɤ́ yà yʌ̄n zīkízīkī* une guerre qui s'était terminée il y a très longtemps

yʌ́n {yʌ̄n} *v vt* **tailler** ♦ *ɤ̄ sɔ̋n yʌ́n* se tailler les dents *(pour être belle)*

yʌ̋nklʌ̋ʌn *n* **herbe** *(mauvaise herbe très répandue; feuilles longues et étroites; pousse en touffes)*

yʌ̀nŋ *n* **répugnance** ♦ *yʌ̀nŋ kʌ̄ à gɔ̀* dégoûter qn

yʌ́nŋ̀ {SUP yɛ̋ɛ̀, yɛ̋æ̀} *loc.n* **1 soleil** ♦ *yʌ́nŋ̀ tɛ́ɛ yà wɔ̀* le soleil s'est levé ♦ *yʌ́nŋ̀ tɛ́ɛ gbɛ̋ɛ̀ tà* quand le soleil commence à brûler (vers 10 heures) ♦ *yʌ́nŋ̀ yà bhán n̄ gɔ̀ ká* le soleil m'a brûlé la tête ♦ *yʌ́nŋ̀ yɤ̀ dhɤ̀ dɛ̀ɛ* il fait très chaud aujourd'hui ♦ *yà wɔ̀ yɛ̋ɛ̀* il est réapparu ♦ *Kɔ́dīvɯ̋à pɛ́ndhɛ̀ ɤ́ yʌ́nŋ̀ ɤ́ wɔ̀ à ká* la partie est de la Côte d'Ivoire ◊ *Kɔ́dīvɯ̋à pɛ́ndhɛ̀ ɤ́ yʌ́nŋ̀ ɤ́ pɤ̀ à ká* la partie ouest de la Côte d'Ivoire **2 lumière** ♦ *yʌ́nŋ̀ bhɔ̄ bhɛ̄n bhà* mettre la fin aux jours de qn ♦ *yʌ́nŋ̀ bhɔ̄ bhɛ̄n bhà yʌ̄ bhà* retarder le travail de qn

yʌ̋nŋ *loc.n IN de* yʌ̋n *yeux*

yʌ́nŋ̀bhɯ́tɤ̋ŋ <soleil-briller-temps> *n* **saison sèche** *(octobre/novembre – mars/avril; terme à connotations négatives : période de chaleur et des incendies)* Qsyn. *blɛ̄ɛ́, blɛ̄ɛ́yī*

yʌ́ŋ̀dhɛ̀ {Int. yʌ́ŋ̀dhɛ̀-yʌ́ŋ̀dhɛ̀} *adv* **au soleil** ◊ *kâflée yɤ̀ gà yʌ́ŋ̀ dhɛ̀ sʌ̀* le café sèche bien au soleil ◊ *bɛ̀dhɛ́gā dhɔ́ɔdɔ̄bhɛ̀n-dhùn wò zìɤ à ká yʌ́ŋ̀dhɛ̀-yʌ́ŋ̀dhɛ̀* les vendeurs de médicaments passent tout le temps au soleil

yʌ̋ŋdhű *n* ***Santaloides afzelii, Rourea afzelii*** **arbuste** *(2, lianescent sarmenteux jusqu'à 20; fruit à pulpe jaunâtre, sucré et comestible, au goût de cerise)*

yʌ́ŋ̀gɛ̀nsú <soleil-pied-prendre> *n* **heure** Syn. dhɛ́dhɛ́ ◊ *dhēbʌ̀-dhùn bhā wò bhlùn bìɤɤ yʌ́ŋ̀gɛ̀nsú plɛ̀ ká* les femmes ont pilé le riz en deux heures

yʌ́ŋ̀gú *adv* **dans la journée** *le redoublement est possible pour exprimer l'intensité de l'action :* ◊ *tɔ̀ gɔ̄n yɤ̀ dhɛ̀ɛdhíɤ bhò yʌ́ŋ̀gú-yʌ́ŋ̀gú* le coq pousse des cocoricos toute la journée

yʌ́ŋ̀gúdʌ̄ <soleil-dans-possesseur> *n* ***Lemniscomys spp.*** **souris rayée**, **rat rayé** *(taille et poids : 9-14 cm, 18-70 g, raies dorsales longitudinales)*

yʌ́ŋ̀kɔ́ <soleil-maison> *n* **montre** Syn. dhɛ́dhɛ́kɔ́ ♦ *yʌ́ŋ̀kɔ́ bhà sɛ̀dhágā* aiguille de la montre

yʌ́ŋ̀kɔ̀dān <jour-main-tester> *n neol.* **minute**

yʌ̀ŋsǜ {Int. yʌ̀ŋyʌ̀ŋsǜ} *adj* **dégoutant**, **crasseux**

yʌ́ŋ̀wɛ̀e <soleil-mue> *n* **mica** Syn. sűwɛ̀e ♦ *yʌ́ŋ̀wɛ̀e bhō kwʌ́ʌ̀* lameller le mica

yʌ̋ŋyʌ̀ŋ, **yʌ̋ʌnyʌ̀ʌn** {A P S, yʌ̋ŋyʌ̀ŋ-dhùn pl. A S, yʌ̋ŋyʌ̀ŋ-sǜ foc. A S, yʌ̋ŋyʌ̀ŋ-sǜ-dhùn foc. pl. A; yʌ̋ŋyʌ̋ŋ, yʌ̋ʌnyʌ̋ʌn Pl. A P, yʌ̋ŋyʌ̋ŋ-dhùn Int. pl. A S} *adj* **multicolore** *(à 2-3 couleurs)* **bariolé tacheté** ◊ *gwēe kwī yɤ̀ yʌ̋ŋyʌ̀ŋ* la peau du léopard est tachetée ◊ *bhēn-dhùn wà sɔ̄ yʌ̋ŋyʌ̋ŋ dà* les gens ont mis des habits multicolores ♦ *gbɛ̂n yʌ̋n yʌ̋ŋyʌ̀ŋ* chien à pelage multicolore

yʌ̋ŋyʌ̋ŋ *adj Pl. de* yʌ̋ŋyʌ̀ŋ *multicolore*

yʌ̀ŋyʌ̀ŋsǜ *adj INT de* yʌ̀ŋsǜ

yʌ̋ŋ *n* **arbre** *(espèce)*

yʌ́ŋ̀yʌ̀ŋ {A P S, yʌ́ŋ̀yʌ̀ŋ-sǜ foc. P; yʌ́ŋ̀yʌ́ŋ̀ Int. pl. P, yʌ́ŋ̀yʌ́ŋ̀-sǜ Int. pl. foc. P, yʌ́ŋ̀yʌ́ŋ̀-sǜ-dhùn Int. pl. foc. P} *adj* **desserré**, **branlant** ◊ *bhīʌ́gā yà kʌ̄ yʌ́ŋ̀yʌ̀ŋ kwɛ̀ɛ̀ bhà* la corde sur la charge s'est relâchée ◊ *dhűkʌ̋ŋ gɔ̄ yɤ̀ yʌ́ŋ̀yʌ̀ŋ* un camion dont l'arrière est en planches n'est pas solide

yʌ́ŋ̀yʌ́ŋ̀ *adj Int. Pl. de* yʌ́ŋ̀yʌ̀ŋ *branlant*

yʌ̄ŋ̋yʌ̀ŋyʌ̄ŋ̋dhɤ̀ *onomat représente le balancement de qch desserré* ◊ *gɔ̄ yʌ́ŋ̀yʌ̀ŋ ɤ́ zīɤ-sīʌ, yɤ̀ kʌ̀ yʌ̄ŋ̋yʌ̀ŋyʌ̄ŋ̋dhɤ̀* lorsque un camion mal boulonné roule, il se balance d'un côté et de l'autre

yʌ̄ŋzlʌ̄ʌdhű *n* **serpent** *(esp.; petit, non venimeux, peut se déplacer dans les deux directions, on ne le mange pas)*

yēe *prev rn* **retour** ◊ *yēe wó' kʌ̀ wó dhūn yā, yɤ́ kplʌ̋ŋ yɤ̄ wó' bhɔ̄* après leur retour ici, ils ont raconté leur voyage

yɛ̄ɛ̏ (, t) **lui en tout cas**

yɛ̄ɛ́ *n* **1 coton** ◊ *bhīndhʌ́n bhā ȁ gɔ̏dhɛ́ yɤ̏ flɤ̏ dhɛ̀ yɛ̄ɛ́ vı́ʌʌ dhɤ́* les cheveux de l'homme ont blanchi comme la fibre du coton ♦ *yɛ̄ɛ́ bhūnŋ* ballot de coton ♦ *yɛ̄ɛ́ dhȕ* ***Gossypium barbadense*** cotonnier **2 étoffe**

yɛ́e *n* **rire** ♦ *yɛ́e tó bhɛ̄n bhȁ* rire à ♦ *yɛ́e tó bhȕɛɛndhɤ̄* sourire ◊ *Zân yȁ yɛ́e zȁ yɛ́* Zan a éclaté de rire ♦ *yɤ̏ yɛ́e tȍ dhí gbǣ́ædhɛ̏ bhȁ* il éclate de rire

yēe-kʌ̄ *v* **1** *vr* **retourner**, **revenir** ◊ *yà ɤ̄ yēe dȅe kʌ̄, yà ɤ̄ yēe bhá kʌ̄* il est encore retourné ◊ *yɤ́ wó wō yēe-kʌ̏ wó dhūn* et ils se sont retournés **2** *vt ɤ̄ dhíɤ yēe-kʌ̄* **revenir** *(vers – pı́ɤ)*

yɛ́etȍbhȁbhɛ̏n <rire-rester-sur-personne> *n* **personne ridicule**

yɛ̏ 1 *v vt* **griller**

yɛ̏ 2 *n* **1 orifice** Qsyn. yɛ̏gā ♦ *yɛ̏ yà kʌ́n ȁ-dhȕn wlɤ̏ɤ* la terre s'est ouverte sous leurs pieds **2 trou** *(p. ex. de souris)*

yɛ́ 1 {yɛ̏} *v* **1.1** *vt* **casser** Syn. wű **1.2** *vi* **se casser 2** *vt* **couper**, **casser** *(fagot; avec une machette, une hache)* Qsyn. kʌ́n **3** *vt* **plier 4** *vi yɛ́ ɤ̄ gű* **revenir 5** *vt ɤ̄ kɔ̏ yɛ́ ȁ bhȁ* **toucher** *(pour signaler son choix)* ◊ *gèe yà ɤ̄ kɔ̏ yɛ́ bhɛ́n ɤ́ yɤ̄ɤ ȁ kʌ̄ ȁ bhȁ...* celui que le masque a touché, qu'il le poursuivrait... ◊ *Zân yȁ ɤ̄ kɔ̏ yɛ́ Yɔ̏ bhȁ* Zan a choisi Yo **6** *vi* **choquer**, **affliger** *(qn – bhȁ)*

yɛ́ 2 *n* **1 herbe** *(esp.) [utilisée pour la toiture]* ♦ *yɛ́ kɔ̏* maison à toit de paille **2 savane** Syn. yɛ́gā ◊ *yȁ yɛ́ gɤ́* il a brûlé la savane

yɛ́dhē *n* **action d'esquiver** *(le masque)* ♦ *yɤ̏ dɔ̏ yɛ́dhē kʌ̄-dhɛ̏ ká gèe gɔ̏* il sait esquiver le masque

yɛ̏ɛ, **yæ̏æ** (t) <de *yȁ dhɛ̏ 'être assis-place'> *n* **1.1** *rn* **siège** *(la place où on est assis)* ♦ *yɛ̏ɛ bhō* cacher ♦ *kwā yæ̏æ kɔ́ɔdhɤ̄* il y a de la place à la maison (tu es le bienvenu !) **1.2** *rn* **lieu d'habitation** ◊ *ī dʌ̄, bhɤ̏ yī gbā yɛ̏ɛ ká* père, donne-nous une place où nous pourrons nous installer **2** *rn* **chez qn** ♦ *bháan ī yɛ̏ɛ bhàa* je ne suis pas chez moi

yɛ̄ɛ < Manding jèli > *n* **griot** *(une caste inférieure chez les Dan, d'origine manding) [font les louanges, nettoient la place du marché, les femmes sont des potières; les mariages avec les Dan sont interdits; des intouchables, celui qui touche un griot, ne peut plus entrer la case sacrée]*

yɛ́ɛ → yǣ́æ *remède pour la voix*

yɛ̄ɛ̏ *loc.n SUP de* yʌ́nŋ̏ *soleil*

yɛ̄ɛbhīn {pl. yɛ̄ɛzʌ̏-dhȕn, yɛ̄ɛgɔ̄n-dhȕn} *n* **griot** ◊ *yɛ̄ɛzʌ̄-dhȕn wà dhɛ́ɛdhɛ̏ gblɤ̏ sʌ̏ ká* les griots on bien balayé la place publique

yɛ̄ɛdhē <griot-femme> *n* **griotte**

yɛ́ɛdhɤ̄ 1 *intj* **splendide !** *(encouragement pendant la danse)*

yɛ́ɛdhɤ̄ 2 *adv* **lentement**, **doucement**

yɛ̄ɛ́n ***n*** **soir**

yɛ́ɛ̀n ***n*** **moment, instant** *seulement dans les expressions :* ♦ *yɛ́ɛ̀n gúú, yɛ́ɛ̀n gúú yā, yɛ́ɛ̀n yā' gúú* tout de suite ♦ *dɔ̄ ɤ́' wō yɛ́ɛ̀n gúú* présentement, maintenant

yɛ̋ɛn 1 ***n*** **sable** ◊ *yà pʌ̄ bɛ̀n zʌ̄ yɛ̋ɛn gúú* il a écrit quelque chose sur le sable

yɛ̋ɛn 2, **yǽǽn** ***n*** ***Ficus asperifolia, ou Ficus exasperata*** **arbre** *(esp. dont les feuilles provoquent des démangeaisons)*

yɛ̋ɛn 3 ***n*** *rn, fn* **rêve** *(de dormeur)* ◊ *ɯ̄ yɛ̋ɛn sʌ̀ bhɔ̄* fais de beaux rêves ! dors bien !

yɛ̋ɛn 4 (t) → yǎ̋n *oeil*

yɛ̄ɛ́npíɤ, **yāánpíɤ** (m) <soir-chez> ***n*** **soir** *(dès le coucher de soleil)* ◊ *yɛ̄ɛ́npíɤ yɤ̀ gǜn wɔ́sǜ, yɤ̀ gǜn tɔ̀ɔ-sǜ ká* la soirée était chaude et humide

yɛ́ɛ̀wɔ̀ɔ ***n Erythrocebus pathas*** **singe rouge**, **singe pleureur**, **patas**

yɛ̄ɛ̀yɛ̄ɛ̀ <intensif de yɛ̋ 'casser'> ***v*** *vi* **se casser** *(pluralité d'objects)* ♦ *à sɔ́n-dhǜn wà yɛ̄ɛ̀yɛ̄ɛ̀ kó zʌ̄-sǜ tà* il s'est cassé les dents dans la bagarre

yɛ̄ɛzʌ̀-dhǜn ***n*** *pluriel de* yɛ̄ɛbhīn *griot*

yɛ̀gā <orifice-os> ***n*** **1 orifice, trou** *(petit)* <u>*Syn.*</u> <u>*yɛ̀*</u> <u>*2*</u> <u>*Qsyn.*</u> <u>*gblʉ̀*</u> ♦ *dhúú yɛ̀gā* creux d'arbre **2 vulve, sexe féminin**

yɛ́gā <herbe-os> ***n*** *également au pluriel* **savane** <u>*Syn.*</u> <u>*yɛ́*</u> ◊ *blɛ̄ɛ́yī ká bhɛ̄n-dhǜn wɔ̀ yɛ́gā{-dhǜn} gɤ̀ gbé* pendant la saison sèche les gens brûlent souvent la savane

yɛ̀ŋ ***n*** *glɔ̄ɔ yɛ̀ŋ* **bouillie de banane** *(plat de banane plantain non-mûre : on l'épluche, la découpe, la cuit, la pile, y rajoute du piment, du sel, de l'huile, puis on la met dans un canari sur le feu pendant deux ou trois minutes; un repas de disette)*

yɛ̄ŋ̀, **yɛ̄ŋ** ***prn*** **lui et moi, elle et moi** *pronom coordinatif*

yɛ̄ŋ́ → yǣŋ́ *accusation*

yɛ̄ŋ̀-dhǜn ***prn*** **nous (excl.) et lui**, **nous (excl.) et elle**, **nous (excl.) et eux**, **nous (excl.) et elles**, **moi et eux**, **moi et elles** *pronom coordinatif*

yɛ́plɤ́ŋ ***n*** **chaume** *(le reste des tiges des céréales après la moisson)* ◊ *yɛ́plɤ́ŋ yɤ̀ bhɛ̄n zǜa* les chaumes blessent l'homme

yī 1 {yì; yí REL} ***n*** **1 jour** ♦ *yī gbàn ká* tous les jours ♦ *yī bhá-dhǜn ká* parfois ♦ *yī kpɔ́ (gw), yī dà (m)* fixer la date **2 temps** *(période)* ◊ *gɔ̄ndʌ̄dhʌ́n zīi dō bhá yɤ̀ gǜn, yɤ́ yī dō ká* autrefois, il y avait un vieux

yī 2 ***n*** **sommeil** ◊ *yɤ̀ kɔ́ dhí-pǜ kɤ̄ ā tǜn yī gúú* il a ouvert la porte lorsque j'étais endormi ♦ *yī zʌ̄* dormir ♦ *yà yī zʌ̄, yɤ̀ ɤ̄ bɛ̀n bhàn' ká sǣǽ wlɤ̀ɤ* il dort toujours à poings fermés ♦ *yà gó yī gúú* il s'est réveillé

yī 3 ***mpp*** **nous** *MPP existentiel exclusif 1re pers. pl., "nous sans vous"*

yī 4 ***prn*** **nous** *pronom exclusif de la 1re pers. pl., "nous sans vous" de la série autonome*

yī 5 ***prn*** **nous** *pronom non-sujet exclusif 1re pers. pl., "nous sans vous"*

yí 1 ***mpp*** **nous** *MPP conjoint exclusif 1re pers. pl., "nous sans vous"*

yí 2 ***mpp*** **nous** *MPP subjonctif exclusif 1re pers. pl., "nous sans vous"*

yí 3 ***mpp*** **il, elle** *MPP de 3SG de la conséquence négative*

yí 4 ***mpp*** **nous** *MPP 1re pers. exclusive de la la série de conséquence négative*

yí 5 ***prn*** **nous** *(pronom sélectif 1re pers. exclusif pluriel, utilisé avec le suffixe -sʉ̀)*

yí ***n*** **1.1 eau** ♦ *yí gɔ̃̀* source d'eau ♦ *yí gbâ* barrage ♦ *yí gblʉ̀, yí gblʉ̀gā* i) eau profonde *(où l'eau ne coule pas)* i) flaque d'eau ♦ *yí tɛ̃́ɛ* courant d'eau ♦ *yí yà ā̀ zʌ̄* il s'est noyé ♦ *yà ā̀ kʌ̄ dhɤ̃́ yí yà dhʌ́n bhā' zʌ̄* il a noyé l'enfant ♦ *yí yɤ̄ɤ dā̀ yí gúi* prov. l'eau va se mêler avec l'eau *(un étranger va se mêler de notre conversation)* ♦ *ā̀ gɛ̀n yí yā̀ kā̃n* ses pieds refusent de marcher (par la fatigue) ♦ *yí yáa zūn ā̀ wɔ̃̀n bhā̀* il est intouchable **1.2 rivière** ♦ *yā̀ yí kā̃n* il a traversé une rivière **2 sauce** *(comme élément d'expressions complexes)* Syn. tő̃o

yíā̀gwʌ̄ʌ̃́ <eau-dans-crocodile> ***n*** **crocodile du Nil** *[on en prélève le pancréas, qui est un poison puissant, avec beaucoup de précaution. De nos jours, il n'y a presque plus de crocodiles au Gouèta]* Syn. gwʌ̄ʌ̃́ 2

yìʌ (t) → yʌ̀ʌ *hébergement*

yīʌ́kɔ̃̀ɔ <eau-dans- ?> ***n*** **loutre**

yībhā̃́ ***n*** **avenir** ◊ *yɤ̃̀ dhɤ̃̀ kʌ̄' dhœ̀œnbhɛ̀n ká yībhā̃́ ká* il sera riche à l'avenir

yí-bhō {yí-bhō} <cueillir l'eau> ***v*** **1** *vt* **mouiller** ◊ *bhá dhɤ́ pɔ̄bhándɤ̃̀ zīɤ ūi gɔ̃̀dhɛ̃́ ɤ́ yí-bhō-sʉ̀ ká gbɛ́ ɤ́ ā̀ tā̀* ne mets pas de la pommade sur tes cheveux très mouillés **2** *vt ɤ̄ kō yí-bhō* **se reposer** *(brièvement)* Qsyn. glòo, tɛ̃́ɛpā

yíbhōsʉ̀ ***adj*** **gâté** *(enfant)*

yíbhūndhɔ̃̀ <eau-boir-désir> ***n*** **soif**

yídhā̃n < Arab. jinn, via Manding jína > ***n*** **démon** *(habite la brousse ou l'eau; inspire la crainte)* ♦ *yídhā̃n yāa yɤ̃̀ ā̀ gúi* chr. il est possédé par un mauvais esprit

yídhā̃ndʌ̄ <démon-père> ***n*** **magicien** *(homme maîtrisant des procédés de magie reçus des génies)*

yídhā̃ndhē <démon-femme> ***n*** **magicienne** *(femme maîtrisant des procédés de magie reçus des génies; elle-même est souvent réputée possédée des génies)*

yígā <eau-os> ***n*** **1 fleuve, rivière, marigot 2** *dhā yígā* **goutte de pluie**

yígāā̀dhɛ̀ {LOC yígāadhɤ̄} ***loc.n*** **fleuve, rivière, marigot** ◊ *Yɔ̃̀ yā̀ dhó yígāadhɤ̄* Yo est allée au marigot ◊ *yígāā̀dhɛ̀ dhʌ̀n úi dhō ā̀ bhā̀ ēe ?* est-ce que c'est au marigot que tu vas ?

yígāadhɤ̄ ***loc.n*** *LOC de* yígāā̀dhɛ̀ *fleuve*

yígōo <eau-pente> ***n*** **lit de cours d'eau**

yígɔ̃̀gódhɛ̀ <eau-tête-place> ***n*** **source** *(d'eau)*

yĩgblṵ̀ṵ̀ <eau-trou> ***n*** **lac, mare, trou d'eau** ♦ *sɛ̄ɛ́ kpɔ́' bhɛ̄n gɔ̀ yĩgblṵ̀ṵ̀ tà* jouer un vilain tour à qn

yīi 1 ***mpp*** **nous** *MPP prospectif exclusif de la 1re personne pl., "nous sans vous"*

yīi 2 ***prn*** **nous** *pronom exclusif de la 1re personne pl., "nous sans vous" de la série restrictive*

yīi 3 ***mpp*** **tu** *MPP prospectif de la 2e pers. sg., utilisé dans les constructions négatives seulement* Qsyn. bhīi ◊ *bháa yīi tã́n bhō* tu ne vas pas chanter

yīì, **yāà** ***mpp*** **notre**, **nos** *pronom exclusif de la 1re pers. pl. de la série possessive (la forme yāà est typique de la partie ouest du Gouèta et du dialecte tèè)*

yíi 1 ***mpp*** **il ne**, **elle ne** *MPP négatif du passé de la 3e pers. sg.*

yíi 2 ***mpp*** **nous ne** *MPP négatif du passé 1re pers. pl. exclusif, "nous sans vous"*

yíi 3, **yɯ́ɯ** <de *yɤ́ ɯ́> ***mpp*** **pour que tu** *forme fusionnée : conjonction + MPP de la 2e pers. sg. de la série conjointe*

yìisīɤ ***num*** **quatre** *[considéré comme nombre masculin]*

yí-kʌ̄ ***v*** **nager**

yíkʌ̀gblɛ̀ɛndhɛ̀ <eau-chasser-profond-endroit> ***n*** **partie profonde d'une rivière**

yíkɔ̀ɔ <eau-calebasse> ***n*** **tambour d'eau** *(calebasse renversée sur l'eau qu'on frappe avec une louche-calebasse) [instrument de percussion des femmes]* Qsyn. kɔ̀ɔtà

yíkpɔ́dhē <eau-répandre-nominalis.> ***n*** **bénédiction** *(est accompli par l'homme le plus âgé qui prononce les formules en versant petit à petit l'eau d'une calebasse par terre)*

yíɤ̀ɤ, **yɤ́ɤ̀** ***n*** **honte** ◊ *yíɤ̀ɤ yɤ̀ n̄ kʌ̄-sīʌ* j'ai honte ♦ *yíɤ̀ɤ dō bhɛ̄n bhà* faire honte à qn *(pour ses actions maladroites)*

yípíɤbhàan <eau-près-oiseau> ***n*** ***Ardea goliath, Typhon goliath*** **héron goliath** *(taille : 95 cm, gris, calotte noire, gorge blanche; dessous des ailes blanc)*

yípíɤdhɔ̀ŋdhɔ̀ŋ <eau-près-Manding dòndon 'coq'> ***n*** ***Egretta gularis, Demigretta gularis*** **aigrette dimorphe** *(taille : 56 cm, gris ardoisé, partie supérieure de la gorge blancs)*

yísíwò < Manding kílisi-voix > ***n*** **incantation** ♦ *yísíwò blṵ̀* proférer des incantations

yísṵ̀ {A, P, S} <eau-adj> ***adj*** **1 liquide** ◊ *tṍo yí kún-sṵ̀ dhʌ̀n ɯ́ à píɤ èe, ɛ̃́ɛn à yísṵ̀ ?* aimes-tu la sauce épaisse ou liquide ? **2 trempé**, **très mouillé**

yítàgɔ̀ <eau-sur-véhicule> ***n*** **bateau**

yítúɛ̀ɛ <eau- ?> ***n*** **source d'eau** *(où on vient pour puiser)*

yíwɔ̃́sṵ̀ <eau-chaude> ***n*** **pertes blanches**, **leucorrhée**

yīyáa ***prn*** **nous** *pronom exclusif de la 1re personne pl. exclusive, "nous sans vous", de la série focalisée négative*

ylṵ̀ ***n*** **décembre**

yōaabhōdhɛ̀ < ?-enlever-femme> ***n*** **sage-femme**, **matrone** *(traditionnelle)*

yōŋ ***n*** **1 Yong** *(un personnage de conte, joli, avec une épaisse chevelure)* **2** *adresse affective à une femme qui a une épaisse chevelure*

yōŋgɔ̏dhē <Yong-tête-femme> ***n*** **femme à chevelure abondante** *(un trait apprécié)*

yő̃o ***n*** **1 cendre** ♦ *yő̃o bȉ*→ yő̃o **2 allégresse** ◊ *n̄ dʌ̄-dhȕn, kwāȁ yő̃o bhȕn* mes pères, réjouissons-nous ! ♦ *yő̃o sűú* féliciter

yɔ̏ ***n*** **1** *rn* **dot** *lv.* *(biens apportés par la famille du jeune marié aux parents de la jeune mariée)* ♦ *Zân yà ɤ̄ bhā dhēbʌ̏ Sítȁ yɔ̏ kʌ̄* Jean a payé (en partie) la dot de sa femme Sita *[le paiement de la dot est un long processus; les parents de la femme viennent régulièrement chez leur beau-fils, et celui-ci doit leur donner des cadeaux, ce qui est considéré comme une partie de la dot]* ◊ *yȁ' pɤ̏ Gɤ̏ɤ̏ yáa yɔ̏ kʌ̄ ɤ̄ bhȁ zɔ̋yɔ̋n ká* elle a dit que Geu n'a pas mis de miel dans son dot ♦ *dhū yɔ̏ tȁ* venir dans la famille du mari de sa fille pour chercher la dot **2 Yo** *(prénom féminin et masculin)* **3** *fam.* **beau-père, belle-mère**

yɔ̄ ***n*** **palmier à huile**, **palmier** *lv.* ♦ *yɔ̄ gɔ̄* i) fronde du palmier ii) fronde de raphia ♦ *yɔ̄ yí* vin de palme *(raphia ou palmier à huile)* ♦ *yɔ̄ zū̄* souche d'un palmier abattu

yɔ́ {yɔ̄} *v vt* **enduire** *(de – ká)* Syn. zīɤ, kpɔ́

yɔ̀bhīn {pl. yɔ̀zʌ̏-dhȕn} <Yo (nom de personne)-homme> ***n*** **1.1** *fam.* **beau-père** *(père de la mère; inusité comme appellatif)* Qsyn. zíɤ̏ɤ **1.2** *fam.* **beau-frère** *(frère de la femme; peut être utilisé comme appellatif)* Qsyn. zíɤ̏ɤ **2 fils** *(qui a le même prénom que son grand-père du côté maternel)*

yɔ̀dhē <Yo (nom de personne)-femme> ***n*** **1 Yodé** *(prénom féminin)* **2.1** *fam.* **belle-mère** *(mère de l'épouse; inusité comme appellatif)* Qsyn. dà, dhɛ̋n **2.2** *fam.* **belle-sœur** *(sœur de la femme; peut être utilisé comme appellatif)* Qsyn. dà, dhɛ̋n

yɔ̄dhɛ̋gúbhȁan <palmier.à.huile-feuille-dans-oiseau> ***n*** ***Phoeniculus purpureus, Ph. erythrorhynchus, Ph. senegalensis*** **moqueur** *(taille : 40 cm; très longue queue étagée bordée de noir; bec de rouge à noir)*

yɔ̄dhɔ̂n ***n*** ***Milletia zechiana (gen. Papilonaceae)*** **arbre** *(esp.)*

yɔ̏gɔ̏ ***n*** **1 liane épineuse** *[utilisée dans la fabrication des pièges et des vans]* **2 corde** *(fait de la liane du même nom)* ♦ *yɔ̏gɔ̏ gā* = yɔ̏gɔ̏

yɔ́n ***n*** *rn* **sein, seins** ♦ *yɔ́n gā* sein

yɔ̋n ***n*** **1 huile** ♦ *yɔ̋n pű̃u, yɔ̋n zœ̏œndhē* huile rouge *(extraite de la pulpe des graines du palmier à huile)* ♦ *yɔ̋n ɤ́ yà kún, yí yȁ pɤ̏ ȁ gú, ȁ vīn yɤ̏ dɔ̏ pɤ̋ɤ̋ŋ́pɤ̋ɤ̋ŋ́dhɤ̄* lorsque l'huile bout, si l'eau tombe dedans, ça crépite **2** *zɔ̋ yɔ̋n* **miel** **3** *rn* **graisse** ♦ *ɤ̄ yɔ̋n kʌ̄* s'engraisser ◊ *wū̄ ɤ́ ȁ yɔ̋n dhɤ́ gbɛ́, ȁ dhɔ̏ yɤ̏ bhɛ̄n bhá-dhȕn kʌ̏* certaines personnes aiment la viande avec beaucoup de graisse

yɔ̋nbhȁan <huile-oiseau> ***n*** ***Treron waalia, Vinago waalia*** **pigeon à épaulettes violettes** *(taille : 29 cm, tête et jabot gris-verts, ventre jaune citron, épaulettes violettes, queue grise, bec lilas)*

yɔ́nŋ̀ *LOC de* yɔ́nŋ̀dhɛ̀ *aisselle*

yɔ́nŋ̀dhɛ̀, yɔ́nŋ̀dhɤ̀dhɛ̀ {LOC yɔ́nŋ̀dhɤ̄, yɔ́nŋ̀} ***loc.n*** *rn* **aisselle, aisselles** ◊ *yáa ɤ̄ yɔ́nŋ̀ / yɔ́nŋ̀dhɤ̄ kȁa bhō* il ne se rase pas les aisselles ◊ *yà ɤ̄ kɔ̏ dȁ ɤ̄ yɔ́nŋ̀dhɤ̄* il a mis sa main sous son aisselle ♦ *yí yɤ̏ bhɛ̄n kȕn bhɛ̄n yɔ́nŋ̀dhɤ̄* l'eau arrive aux aisselles

yɔ́nŋ̀dhɤ̄ ***loc.n*** *LOC de* yɔ́nŋ̀dhɛ̀ *aisselle*

yɔ́nŋ̀dhɤ̀dhɛ̀ ***loc.n*** → yɔ́nŋ̀dhɤ̀dhɛ̀ *aisselle*

yɔ̋ŋ ***n*** **1 calebasse** *(en forme de sablier, utilisée pour conserver des liquides)* ◊ *yɔ̋ŋ gúɯ yí* calebasse avec de l'eau **2 hochet-sonnaille** *(calebasse entourée d'un filet formé de vertèbres de la vipère du Gabon) [accompagne les tambours tö̀kpä, bhàa, gɔ̄dhʌ́n]* *Syn.* *yɔ̋ŋbhɛ̄* ♦ *yɔ̋ŋ gā* vertèbre de serpent formant une des articulations du hochet-sonnaille ♦ *yɔ̋ŋ zʌ̄* jouer du hochet

yɔ̋ŋbhɛ̄ <calebasse-fruit> ***n*** **hochet** *(calebasse entourée d'un filet fait de vertèbres de serpent)* *Syn.* *yɔ̋ŋ*

yɔ̏ɔ ***n*** **réponse** *(verbale) toujours dans les combinaisons* ♦ *dhīaŋ yɔ̏ɔ* réponse ♦ *Tìa yíi kʌ̄ dhīaŋ yɔ̏ɔ sʌ̀ bhá bɔ̄* Tia n'a pas donné de bonne réponse ♦ *yɔ̏ɔ bhɔ̄* répondre ◊ *yà bhān dhɛ̄ɛ́kpɔ́ yɔ̏ɔ bhɔ̄ gwʌ̋nŋ gúɯ* il a répondu à ma question avec un proverbe

yɔ̀ɔ ***v*** **1** *vi* **salir** *(qch – bhȁ)* ◊ *ȁ yɔ̀ɔn yȁ yɔ̀ɔ dhʌ́n bhȁ* son sang a sali l'enfant **2** *vi* **sous-estimer** *(qn – bhȁ)* ◊ *wáa yɔ̀ɔ wō kwʌ́ʌ̀* il ne faut pas sous-estimer son proche

yɔ̋ɔ 1 ***n*** **kaolin** *(argile blanche) [sert à badigeonner le corps à l'occasion de certains rituels et aussi comme remède contre de nombreuses maladies]* ♦ *yɔ̋ɔ pűu yí* lait de chaux ♦ *gɔ̏kʌ̄ yɔ̋ɔ* kaolin pour traiter les maux de tête

yɔ̋ɔ 2 ***prev*** **vengeance**

yɔ̋ɔ 3 ***n*** *rn* **pareil** ◊ *bhíin kpȁn ȁ yɔ̋ɔ bhȁ* je n'ai pas vu son pareil

yɔ̋ɔ-bhō {yɔ̋ɔ-bhō} ***v*** *vt* **se venger de qch** *(par – ká)* ◊ *wáa wɔ́n yāa yɔ̋ɔ-bhō wɔ́n yāa ká* on ne rend pas le mal pour le mal ♦ *ɤ̄ bhȁ yɔ̋ɔ-bhō bhɛ̄n gɔ̏* se venger de qn

yɔ̋ɔgúɯ <pareil-dans> ***n*** *rn* **remplaçant, équivalent**

yɔ̀ɔn 1 ***n*** *rn* **sang** ♦ *ȁ yɔ̀ɔn yɤ̏ bhɔ̄-sīʌ* le sang suinte, la plaie saigne ♦ *ȁ yɔ̀ɔn yɤ̏ bhɔ̄-sīʌ gbúgbúdhɤ̄* son sang jaillit (de la veine) ♦ *bhɛ̄n yɔ̀ɔn yɤ̏ wɛ̀nŋ gbɛ́* le sang (de l'homme) est en train de jaillir ♦ *ȁ dʌ̄ yɔ̀ɔn yɤ̏ ȁ gúɯ* c'est son père tout craché ♦ *ȁ yɔ̀ɔn yāa yɤ̏ zīɤ-sīʌ ȁ gúɯ* il a des mauvaises idées (litt. : du mauvais sang coule dans ses veines)

yɔ̀ɔn 2 ***v*** **1.1** 1) *vi* **s'approcher** *(de – bhȁ)* ◊ *yɤ́' pɤ̄ yɤ̄ɤ yɔ̀ɔn kɔ́ dhí bhȁ* elle voulait s'approcher de la porte ♦ *yɔ̀ɔn ñ bhȁ !* ose encore t'approcher de moi ! ◊ *wɔ́n yāa yá dhó yɔ̀ɔn' ɯ̄ ká klɤ̄ɤ̀* que des mauvaises choses ne s'approchent pas de toi ♦ *wȍ yɔ̀ɔn kőo-sɯ̏* neol., ling. contraction 2) *vt* **avancer**, **approcher** *(à – bhȁ)* *Qsyn.* *blɯ̏* ◊ *sʌ́ʌdhɛ̋ bhā ȁ yɔ̀ɔn ñ bhȁ yɤ̄* rapproche ce livre de moi ◊ *ɯ̄ gú yɔ̀ɔn táàblʌ̀ʌ bhā ȁ bhȁ kɤ̄ yɤ̏ yɔ̀ɔn ñ sɔ̋ɔ* pousse la table avec ton ventre, pour qu'elle s'approche de moi **1.2** 1) *vi* **s'approcher** *(de – sɔ̋ɔ)* ◊ *yà yɔ̀ɔn ȁ sɔ̋ɔ* il s'est approché d'elle 2) *vr* **s'approcher** *(de –*

sɔ̃ɔ) ♦ *yà ɤ̄ bhɤ́ yɔ̀ɔn à sɔ̃ɔ* il s'est approché un peu d'elle **1.3** *vi* **s'écarter** *(de – gɔ̀)* ♦ *yɔ̀ɔn n̄ gɔ̀* s'il te plaît, cède-moi un peu de ta place **1.4** 1) *vt yɔ̀ɔn bhūn* **écarter** ◊ *kwɛ́ɛ dhɔ̀ɔ à yɔ̀ɔn bhūn* pousse la porte *(pour la rabattre)* 2) *vi yà yɔ̀ɔn bhūn* **ensuite** 3) *vr ɤ̄ bhɤ́ yɔ̀ɔn bhūn* **s'écarter** ♦ *{bhɤ̀} ū bhɤ́ yɔ̀ɔn bhūn* bouge un peu ! *(pour libérer un peu d'espace)* **1.5** *vt* **enfoncer** *(à – tà)* ◊ *yà fáàn yɔ̀ɔn ɤ̄ yán tà* il a enfoncé son chapeau **1.6** *vi yɔ̀ɔn dhíɤ* **avancer** *(en se déplaçant)* ◊ *dhè ɤ́ wó dhō wó yɔ̀ɔn dhíɤ dhè bhá gúí bhūn...* lorsqu'ils s'étaient avancés jusqu'à un certain endroit... **2.1** *vt* **réunir** *(ensemble – kwʌ́ʌ̀)* ◊ *yɤ̀ pɤ́ bhèn-dhùn yɔ̀ɔn-sīʌ kwʌ́ʌ̀* il réunit les villageois ♦ *yà ɤ̄ bèn yɔ̀ɔn kwʌ́ʌ̀* il a fait la moue *(en avançant les lèvres pour exprimer son mécontentement et son mépris)* ♦ *sɔ̄ {pɛ́dhè} yɔ̀ɔn kwʌ́ʌ̀* raccommoder un vêtement **2.2** *vt yɔ̀ɔn kwʌ́ʌ̀* **collectionner** **3** *vi* **grandir** ◊ *yɤ́ á yɔ̀ɔn bhūn tɤ́ŋ bhá gúí ...* et pendant le temps où je grandissais là-bas... **4** *vi* **insister** *(sur – tà)*

yɔ̃̀ɔn *n* **séchoir** *(plate-forme tressée étendue sous le plafond au-dessus du foyer pour faire sécher les aliments et pour les préserver contre les animaux)* ♦ *yà yɔ̃̀ɔn dūn gbàn bhà* il a installé le séchoir sous le plafond

yɔ̃́ɔyɔ̃̀ɔ {A, P; Pl. yɔ̃́ɔyɔ̃́ɔ A, P} *adj* **troublant**, **confus**, **louche** *(affaire)* ◊ *bhá dhɤ́ dà' wɔ́n yɔ̃́ɔyɔ̃̀ɔ gúí* ne te fourre pas dans des affaires louches ◊ *ū bhā wɔ́n-dhùn yɔ̃́ɔyɔ̃́ɔ* tes affaires sont louches

yɔ̃́ɔyɔ̃́ɔ *adj Pl. de* yɔ̃́ɔyɔ̃̀ɔ *troublant*

yɔ̄ɔyɔ̃́ɔ-kʌ̄ {yɔ̄ɔyɔ̃́ɔ-kʌ̀} *v vt* **faire hâtivement**, **faire négligemment** ◊ *yà ɤ̄ bhā bhláàdhè yɔ̄ɔyɔ̃́ɔ-kʌ̄* il a labouré son champ hâtivement

yɔ̀zʌ̀-dhùn *n pluriel du* yɔ̀bhīn *beau-père*

yɤ̀ 1, **yɤ̀** *mpp* **il**, **elle** *MPP de la 3e pers. sg. existentiel*

yɤ̀ 2 *mpp* **il**, **elle** *MPP de la 3e pers. sg. de la série subjonctive, facultativement omise*

yɤ̄ 1 {yɤ̄} *v* **1.1** *vt* **voir** ♦ *à yán yɤ̀ dhè yɤ̀ sʌ̀* il voit bien, il a une bonne vue ♦ *dhè yɤ̄* trouver des défauts ◊ *bhēn ő̃o bhēn ɤ́ dhō' wɔ̀n gúí, yà dhè dhʌ̀n' yɤ̄' bhà* elle trouvait des défauts dans chacun de ceux qui venait la chercher en mariage **1.2** 1) *vt* **considérer** *(comme – ká)* ◊ *wɔ́n bhā ā kʌ̄ à yɤ̀ wɔ́n dhíasùì ká* cette affaire m'avait semblé agréable 2) *vi* **être considéré** *(comme – ká)* ♦ *yáa yɤ̄ zʌ̀ à ká...* à part ça... **2.1** 1) *vi* **se trouver** ◊ *dhā yígā dódó yɤ̀ gùn yɤ̄-sīʌ síaa* de rares gouttes de pluie tombaient par terre ♦ *yà yɤ̄ kpɛ́nŋ* il est sorti ♦ *yɤ̄ à ká kpɛ́nŋ* porter qch dehors ♦ *pèe yà yɤ̄ n̄ yʌ́nŋ* l'entonnoir a permis au médicament d'entrer dans mon oeil ♦ *wɔ́n yà yɤ̄ bhēn gɔ̀ kó dhíɤ* l'homme a réussi dans l'affaire 2) *vt* **présenter**, **produire** **2.2** *vi* **se manifester** *(sur – tà)* ♦ *klīŋklīŋ yà yɤ̄ n̄ tà* je suis stupéfié **2.3** 1) *vt* **placer** ♦ *... yɤ̄ kpɛ́nŋ* faire sortir qn; extraire ◊ *zɔ̃́ yɔ̃́n yɤ̄ kpɛ́nŋ* extrais le miel ♦ *yɤ̄ kó dhíɤ* joindre les deux bouts ♦ *ɤ̄ kɔ̀ yɤ̄ à tà* appuyer sa main sur ♦ *yà ɤ̄ sɔ̃́n yɤ̄ ɤ̄ bèn tà* il s'est mordu la lèvre *(accidentellement)* 2) *vi yɤ̄ kő̃o* **être dense** ◊ *kɔ́ yɤ̀ yɤ̄-sùì ká kő̃o = kɔ́ yɤ̀ yɤ̀ kő̃o-sùì ká* les maisons sont tout près les uns des autres **2.4** *vt* **trouver** **2.5** *vt* **pouvoir** *(trouver la possibilité)* ◊ *wáa yī zʌ̄-dhè yɤ̄ à vīn gɔ̀* on ne peut pas dormir à cause de ce bruit ◊ *à bhǽǽdhè yà tó dhèensùì, yáa dhīaŋ* *zʌ̄-dhɛ̏ yɤ̄* il a mal à la gorge, il ne peut pas parler ♦ *bháan n̄ kʌ̄-dhɛ̏ yɤ̄* je ne sais pas quoi faire **3** *vi* **commencer** *(qch – bhȁ)*, **se mettre** *(à – bhȁ)* Syn. *ɤ̄ dhí dȁ ... gúɯ́, yȁ ... bhȁ, zūn ... bhȁ, zūɯ-bhɔ̄* **4.1** *vi* **atteindre** *(qch – bhȁ)* ◊ *Gbȁtɔ̏ dhʌ̀n ɤ́ sʌ́ʌdhɛ́ dlàan kwɛ̏ plɛ̀ ká, kɛ̋ɛ yɤ́ yíi yɤ̄ pʌ̄ bhá bhȁ bhá bhȁ* quant à Gbato, il a fait des études pendant deux ans, mais il n'a rien obtenu ◊ *bhɛ̄n bhā ȁ bhȁ gblɛ̀ɛndhɛ̏ yɤ̏ yɤ̏ dhāŋ̏ bhȁ* cet homme est si grand qu'il atteint le ciel **4.2** *vi* **entraîner** *(qch – bhȁ)* ◊ *yí kpɔ́dhē wɔ̏n yà yɤ̄ dhīaŋ bhȁ* l'affaire de la bénédiction (le choix de celui qui doit faire la bénédiction) est devenu un palabre

yɤ̄ 2 ***prn*** **lui**, **elle** *pronom de la 3e pers. sg. de la série autonome*

yɤ̄ 3 ***adv*** *après le ton moyen, le ton change au registre haut* **ici**, **là** *(localisation d'un objet soit à proximité du locuteur soit à une certaine distance du locuteur et de l'auditeur, mais dans leur champ de visibilité; dans ce dernier cas, accompagné d'un geste ostentatoire de la main)* Qsyn. *yā* ◊ *dhūn yɤ́ !* viens ici ! ◊ *ɯ̄ bhā glɛ̄ɛ́ yȁ yɤ̄* mets ton sac ici ! ♦ *bhɛ́n ká yɤ̄...* vous savez...

yɤ̄ 4 *le ton change en haut devant un autre ton moyen, yɤ́* ***dtm*** **celui-ci** *suit le mot déterminé* Qsyn. *yā* ♦ *yɤ́ bhā* c'est ça

yɤ́ 1, **ɤ́** ***conj*** *fusionne avec les pronoms singuliers conjoints, cf. yáa, yíi, yɤ́ɤ, introduit des propositions désignant une action consécutive ou liée par un rapport logique à l'action de la précédente; obligatoirement suivi par une MPP de la série conjointe* ◊ *gɔ̄-dhȕn wɔ̏ dɔ̋ɔ̏ndhȕn bhān kwáŋ̏dhɤ̄ yɤ́ wó bhɛ̄n sū̏* des voitures s'arrêtent dans ma cour et prennent les passagers

yɤ́ 2 ***prn*** **lui**, **elle** *(pronom sélectif de la 3e personne sg., s'utilise avec le suffixe -sȕ)*

yɤ́ 3 → *ɤ́ 2 MPP 3SG de la série conjointe*

yɤ̋ ***intj*** **mais comment ? !** *exclamation traduisant un grand étonnement et mécontentement*

yɤ̄áa ***prn*** **lui**, **elle** *pronom de la 3 personne sg. de la série focalisée négative*

yɤ̏dhíɤpʌ̏ <voir-devant-chose> ***n*** **bondon**

yɤ́gíɯ ***n Onychognathus morio*** **étourneau roupenne d'Alexander** *(taille : 30 cm, robuste, longue queue étagée; mâle bleu foncé à reflets pourprés, large tache marron sur l'aile; femelle : tête et gorge grisâtres)*

yɤ̏kőosȕ <mettre-l'un dans l'autre-gérondif> ***adj*** **dense** *(près les uns des autres)* ◊ *Gɤ̏ɤ̏ yȁ Yɔ̏ bhȁ wūn yɤ̏kőosȕ wɔ̏* Geu a arraché les épais cheveux épais de Yo

yɤ̋ŋ, **yɤ̋ŋgā** ***n*** **marteau traditionnel** *(pour aplatir le fer) [objet sacré des forgerons, on lui fait des sacrifices]* Syn. *kɶ̀ɶdhíɤ*

yɤ̄ɤ 1 ***mpp*** **il**, **elle** *MPP de la 3e pers. sg. de la série prospective*

yɤ̄ɤ 2 ***prn*** **lui**, **elle** *pronom de la 3e pers. sg. de la série restrictive*

yɤ́ɤ 1, **yɤ́** <de *yɤ̀ ɤ́> ***mpp*** **pour qu'il, pour qu'elle** *forme fusionnée : conjonction + MPP de la 3e pers. sg. de la série conjointe*

yɤ́ɤ 2 → ɤ̄ɤ *eh bien*

yɤ́ɤ̀ → yíɤ̀ɤ *honte*

yɤ̋ɤ {yɤ̀ɤ} ***v vt*** **malaxer** *(la pâte de noix de palme pour en éliminer les grumeaux)*

yɤ̋ɤŋgā ***n*** **chenille** *(esp.; rougeâtre, vit sur l'arbre pɛ̄n)[on la trouve de juin à janvier; se mange bouillie et séchée au soleil avec du sel et du piment]* Syn. *dhɤ̋ŋ*

yœ́œ̀, **yúù** ***n*** **1** *rn* **ennemi 2 adversaire** *(dans une compétition)◊ dhɤ̀ɤ kpɤ̄ ɤ́ bhɛ́n bhā ɤ́ à bhàn yɤ̀ yà slʌ̀ʌ gú-sùù bhà dhɤ́dhɤ́ ɤ́ dhō ɤ́ sɔ̀ à yœ́œ̀-dhùn gɔ̀ bîi gú* le ballon frappé par le joueur a roulé et est entré le but de l'adversaire

yűa 1 {yùa} ***n*** **maladie** *(nom générique)◊ yűa yíi ī bhā bhɛ̄n bhá kʌ̄* personne parmi mes gens n'est tombé malade ◊ *yűa yáa' zūʌ́{gā} bhà* son cœur ne présente aucune anomalie ♦ *tő kʌ̄ yùa* otite

yűa 2 {yùa} ***v vi*** **irriter** *(qn – bhà)*, **faire mal** *(à – bhà)*

yūándhʌ́n ***n*** *arch.* **chaton** Syn. *gwấndhʌ́n sɛ̄ɛ́ndhʌ́n* Qsyn. *gīoo*

yūaŋ (t) → yūʌŋ (gw) *il y a quelque temps*

yűatàgèe <maladie-surface-masque> ***n*** **"masque de la maladie "** *(s'enferme avec un vieux ou un notable gravement malade jusqu'au décès de ce dernier; quand le masque sort la nuit, il est interdit de faire du bruit sous peine d'amende)* ♦ *yűatàgèe yà dhó Zân bhà yűa dhɛ̀ gú, yűatàgèe yà dhó Zân yűa tà* "le masque de la maladie" est allé là où Jean se trouve avec sa maladie *(en parlant ainsi, on sait que Jean a succombé, mais son décès n'est pas encore officiellement annoncé)*

yūʌŋ (gw), **yūaŋ** (t) ***n*** *yūʌŋ gú* **il y a quelque temps** *(il y a 2-3 mois, maximum un an)* ◊ *yɤ̀ dhɛ̀ bà ī gɔ̀ dhēŋdhɤ̄ yūʌŋ gú* il a débrousaillé un endroit dans mon champ il y a quelque temps *(les herbes ont repoussé depuis)*

yūn 1 ***n*** *rn* **nez** ♦ *yūn yí* morve ♦ *yūn gú kàa* poils du nez *[sont considérés comme répugnants]* ♦ *yūn dhí* narine ♦ *à yūn gú yà tā* il est enrhumé; son nez est pris ♦ *à yūn yɤ̀ bhɔ̀* son nez coule ♦ *ɤ̄ yūn pìɤ (gw), ɤ̄ yūn bhō (t)* se moucher, moucher son nez ♦ *ɤ̄ yūn gấn* renifler ♦ *à yūn kpɤ̄ yɤ̀ gblɛ̀ɛn* il a le nez long ♦ *à yūn kpɤ̄ yɤ̀ kʌ̀ dhɛ̀ táàgbɔ̄ dhɤ́* son nez est long comme une pipe ♦ *à yūn yɤ̀ dhʌ̀ŋ síāa-sùù ká* il a un nez aplati ♦ *ūū kɔ̀ zīɤ à yūn dhíɤ* essuie-lui le nez

yūn 2 ***n*** **racine** *(d'une plante)*

yūnbhàandhʌ́n ***n*** *arch.* **chat** *[comestible pour bon nombre de Dan]* Syn. *gwấndhʌ́n* ♦ *yūnbhàandhʌ́n dhèe* chatte *(femelle de chat)* ♦ *yūnbhàandhʌ́n gɔ̄n* chat *(mâle)*

yūnkpɤ̄ <nez-boule> ***n*** *rn* **nez** *(partie extérieure)* ♦ *yūnkpɤ̄ zɔ̋dhíɤ* bout de nez

yúɤ̀ɤ ***n*** **poisson** ♦ *yúɤ̀ɤ gā dhʌ́n* un poisson ♦ *yúɤ̀ɤ bhɛ̄* un (gros) poisson

yúɤ̀ɤtīi, **yúɤ̀tīi** <poisson noir> ***n*** **silure** *[très apprécié]*

yûù → yœ̂œ̀ *ennemi*

yūudhɤ̄ {Int. yūuudhɤ̄} ***adv*** **brouhaha** *(d'une volée d'oiseaux, d'une foule; d'une meute des chiens; d'un essaim des mouches, etc., surtout en distance)* ♦ *bhɛ̄n kpɤ̄ yɤ̀ wɛ́-sɪ̄ʌ yūudhɤ̄* la clameur de la foule monte ◊ *bhɛ́n ɤ́ ká wɛ̋ yūuudhɤ̄ bhā, kà dɔ̄ !* vous, qui criez fort là, arrêtez-vous !

yùun ***n*** **asticot**

yūúndhɛ̏ {LOC yūúndhɤ̄, Int. LOC yūúndhɤ̄-yūúndhɤ̄} ***loc.n*** **nez** ♦ *yɤ̀ wɛ̀ ɤ̄ yūúndhɤ̄, yɤ̀ wɛ̀ ɤ̄ yūn gúí* il nasille *pour la forme du cas locatif, un redoublement lexicalisé est possible :* ♦ *yɤ̄ɤ zʌ̀ yɤ̀ wɛ̀ ɤ̄ yūúndhɤ̄-yūúndhɤ̄* il grogne toujours

yūúndhɤ̄ ***loc.n*** → yūúndhɛ̏ *nez*

yūuudhɤ̄ ***adv*** *Int. de* yūudhɤ̄ *brouhaha*

yűnklűuun ***n*** **plante herbacée** *(ressemble au roseau)* ◊ *yűnklűuun yà gā, yɤ̀ ɤ̄ bhā dhʌ́n tó kàa gɔ̀* la plante yűŋklűuun est morte, elle a laissé son enfant au roseau *(un proverbe : les enfants du défunt restent avec celui qui le ressemble, c.-à-d. ses parents. cette plante meurt à la saison sèche, tandis que le roseau reste vivant)*

yúɯ → yíi *pour que tu*

Z z

zā 1 {zā} ***n*** **1 litige** ♦ *zā gɔ̀-yɛ̋* résoudre un problème ♦ *zā wɔ̄ bhɛ̄n tà* condamner qn ◊ *Gbàtò bhà zā yà wɔ̄ Yɔ̀ tà* Gbato a eu raison contre Yo ♦ *zāgɔ̀bhōbhɛ̀n yà Gbàtò zʌ̄ zā ká* le juge a jugé Gbato coupable ♦ *wà zā dɛ̀dɛ̀ dhī* ils ont résolu le litige d'une façon correcte *(ils se sont excusés comme il faut)* ♦ *zā yà bhɛ̄n bhà* faire un scandale à qn ♦ *pʌ̄ zà kɑ̋n bhɛ̄n dhɛ̀* réclamer qch à qn ♦ *zā kún bhɛ̄n gɔ̀* prendre sa défense devant qn ♦ *à bhà zā gɛ̀n yáa gbàn-sɯ̀ ká* ses arguments ne sont pas forts **2 procès** ♦ *zā dɔ̄* juger une affaire **3 accusation** ♦ *bhɛ̄n zʌ̄ zā' ká* juger qn coupable **4 fiançailles 5 excuse** ♦ *zā dhī bhɛ̄n gɔ̀* s'excuser auprès de qn

zā 2 ***n*** **oiseau** *(esp.)*

zā 3 ***adj*** **vierge** *(forêt)* ♦ *bú zā* forêt vierge

zāà ***n*** ***Albizia adianthifolia (gen. Mimosaceae)*** **arbre** *(esp.) [le lavement avec la décoction de l'écorce sert de médicament contre la gale]*

záa (gw) ***n*** **gerçure** *(sur la semelle du pied)* ◊ *záa yɤ̀ à gɛ̀n bhà* il a une gerçure sur la semelle

záà (m) ***n*** **hangar** <u>*Syn.* *kɔ́záa* *(gw)*</u>

zàan ***n*** **gros coq rouge**

zāàn ***n*** **porte de perches de raphia**

zɑ̋andhɛ̋yí < ?-feuille-sauce> ***n*** **sauce de feuilles de gombo**

zàazúù̀ ***n*** **maladie des poules** *(les poules deviennent apathiques et meurent en deux ou trois jours)* ♦ *yà kʌ̄ wɔ̃́ɔnwɔ̃̀ɔn ká dhɛ̀ zàazúù̀ tɔ̀ dhɤ́* il est devenu indolent comme une poule malade

zà̰-dɔ̄ {zà̰-dɔ̄} *v vt* **se fiancer avec** ♦ *dhē zà̰-dɔ̄* rechercher une femme en mariage

zādɔ̄bhɛ̀n <litige-mettre-personne> ***n*** **juge instructeur, magistrat instructeur** Syn. *zāgɔ̀yɛ́bhɛ̀n, zāgɔ̀bhōbhɛ̀n*

zādɔ̄dhɛ̀ <litige-mettre-place> ***n*** **cour, tribunal**

zādhīsʉ̀ <litige-réussir-gérondif> ***n*** **excuse** *(plus sérieuse que bhɛ̄ɛ́ : celu qui s'excuse veut modifer son coumportement, faire quelque chose pour corriger la situation)*

zádhɤ̄ {Int. zázádhɤ̄} ***adv*** **brusquement** *(la forme intensive signifie "rapidement")* ◊ *yɤ̀ wɔ́n kʌ̄ zázádhɤ̄* il arrange les affaires vite

zāgɔ̀bhōbhɛ̀n <litige-tête-enlever-personne> ***n*** **juge** Syn. *zāgɔ̀yɛ́bhɛ̀n* ◊ *ɤ́ bɛ̀, dhùtīï dhʌ̀n ɤ́ zā gɔ̀bhōbhɛ̀n ká* autrefois, c'est le chef de village qui était le juge

zāgɔ̀yɛ́bhɛ̀n <affaire-casser-tête-personne> ***n*** **juge** Syn. *zāgɔ̀bhōbhɛ̀n*

zã́n ***n*** **1 liane** *(esp.) [utilisée pour préparer une sauce gluante à partir des tiges pilées et macérées]* ♦ *zã́n yí* sauce de liane "zan" ◊ *zã́n yí dɔ̃́ŋdɔ̃́ŋsʉ̀-dhʉ̀n* des récipients remplis de sauce de liane "zan" ◊ *zã́n yí yɤ̀ dɔ̃́ŋsʉ̀* la sauce de "zan" est gluante **2 sève de liane "zan"**

zānvíɛ̀ <Fr. janvier> ***n*** **janvier**

zà̰nwɛ̃́ɛ < ?-autre> ***n*** **novembre**

zà̰nyísʉ̀ < ?-eau-prendre> ***n*** **octobre**

zàŋ 1 ***n*** **1 plante parasite du cola 2 mauvaise récolte** *(d'arachide ou de cola; plus rarement, d'igname) [on croit que la cause en est un état atmosphérique défavorable entre la saison sèche et l'hivernage, imperceptible pour l'homme]* ♦ *zàŋ yà yà yã́ [gwɛ̃́ɛ] tà* il y a eu une mauvaise récolte d'ignames [d'arachides] ◊ *ʉ́ gwɛ̃́ɛ tā-sīʌ kɤ̄ ʉ́' bhɤ̀, à dhɛ́ ɤ́ yɤ̄ɤ bɔ̄ bhā, zàŋ yɤ̀ yɤ̀ à tà* si tu plantes l'arachide et la manges en même temps, ce qui sera planté ne donnera pas une bonne récolte

zàŋ 2 <Fr. agent> ***n*** **agent de police, policier** ♦ *zàŋ plɤ̀ɤ* poste de police

zã́ŋ ***n*** **tabac à chiquer** *[les Dan, les hommes comme les femmes, chiquaient le tabac même avant la colonisation]* ♦ *zã́ŋ kún* chiquer

zāŋtà ***adv*** **ouvertement** *(seulement dans l'expression :)* ♦ *wɔ̀ zāntà* révéler

zàŋzã́ŋ ***n*** **cahotage** ◊ *à gɔ̄ yɤ̀ zàŋzã́ŋ kʌ̄-sīʌ* la voiture cahotait

zã́ŋzà̰ŋ {P S, zã́ŋzà̰ŋ-dhʉ̀n pl. S, zã́ŋzà̰ŋ-sʉ̀ foc. A S, zã́ŋzà̰ŋ-sʉ̀-dhʉ̀n foc. pl. A S; zã́ŋzã́ŋ Int. pl. A P S, zã́ŋzã́ŋ-dhʉ̀n Int. pl. A S, zã́ŋzã́ŋ-sʉ̀-dhʉ̀n pl. foc. AS} ***adj*** **haut et élancé** *(chien, mouton; personne)*

zã́ŋzã́ŋ *Int. pl. de* zã́ŋzà̰ŋ *haut et élancé*

zázádhɤ̄ ***adv*** *Int. de* zádhɤ̄ *brusquement*

zǽǣzǽǣdʌ̄ ***n*** ***Malimbus scutatus*** **malimbe à queue rouge** *(un oiseau; taille : 18 cm, noir mais tête, cou, jabot et sous-caudales rouges)*

zʌ̀ ***dtm*** **en tout cas** *marque de topicalisation contrastive, s'adjoint à un pronom personnel autonome ou à un groupe nominal◊ bhī zʌ̀ ɯ̄ dɔ̀ sʌ́ʌdhɛ́ wɔ̀ pɤ̄-dhɛ̀ ká* toi en tout cas, tu sais lire

-zʌ̀ ***mrph*** *marque de collectif désignant un ensemble de personnes (surtout mâles) pratiquant le même métier, appartenant à la même classe d'âge ou liées par un lien de parenté descendante (parents cadets); se substitue à la marque d'agent -bhīn ♦ gwʌ̄ʌ́zʌ̀-dhùn* serviteurs *(mâles)* ♦ *tɛ́ɛbhɑ̃́nzʌ̀-dhùn* gens du même âge

zʌ̄ {zʌ̄} ***v*** **1** *vt* **tuer** ♦ *ɤ̄ dɛ̀ zʌ̄* se suicider **2** *vt* **jeter sur** *(qch – ká)◊ yà ɪ̄ zʌ̄ bɤ̄ɤ̀ ká* il m'a jeté de la boue ♦ *dhʌ́n zʌ̄ yɪ́ ká* jeter de l'eau au visage de l'enfant *[pratique traditionnelle des Dan : la mère le fait, surtout quand il fait chaud, pour que le bébé ne pleure pas et s'endorme vite]* **3.1** *vt* **frapper** ♦ *wɔ̀ kó zʌ̄-sīʌ* ils se bagarrent **3.2** *vt* **jouer** *(d'un instrument à percussion ou à cordes; pour – tà)* **4** *vt sʌ́ʌdhɛ́ bɛ̀n zʌ̄* **écrire** **5.1** *vi* **induire en erreur** *(qn – gɔ̀),* **échapper** *(à – gɔ̀)◊ wɔ́n yà zʌ̄ Zân gɔ̀* Zan s'est trompé dans cette affaire◊ *à dān á' wō bhā yɤ̀ zʌ̄ ɪ̄ gɔ̀* je me trompe sur sa taille **5.2** *vt* **embarrasser** ◊ *zā ɤ́ kʌ̄ ɪ̄ zʌ̄...* l'affaire qui m'a piégé... **6** *vt* **couper** *(des feuilles)◊ yà dhɛ́ zʌ̄ yà dhʌ́n bhā' wɔ̄' tà* elle a coupé des feuilles et a mis l'enfant dessus

zʌ̀gɯ́ <frapper-dans ?> ***prev*** *seulement dans le verbe zʌ̀gɯ́-kʌ̄* **tri**

zʌ̀gɯ́-kʌ̄ {zʌ̀gɯ́-kʌ̀; Int. zʌ̀gɯ́-zʌ̀gɯ́-kʌ̄} ***v*** *vt* **trier**; **distinguer** ◊ *bháan bhɛ̄n bhá zʌ̀gɯ́-kʌ̄* je ne distingue pas entre les gens ◊ *bhánŋ̄lōo-dhùn ɤ́ ạ́'-dhùn zʌ̀gɯ́-zʌ̀gɯ́-kʌ̀, wō dhɛ̀n* voici les mangues que j'ai triées à plusieurs reprises

zʌ̀ká-dhɛ̀ ***n*** **défaut**

zʌ̄n ***n*** **laiton, airain, bronze** *(métal lourd de couleur claire)* ♦ *zʌ̄n pɯ̃́u* argent (métal)

zʌ̀nŋ ***n*** *rn* **totem** *(animal ou plante considéré(e) comme le sauveteur de l'ancêtre du clan, promu en conséquence interdit alimentaire du lignage qu'on doit honorer)* Syn. kɪ́an

zʌ̀wō <en tout cas-adv.> ***adv*** **1 aussi** ◊ *ɯ̄ dhɤ̀ dhūn' zʌ̀wō* tu viendra aussi **2** *(marque de topicalisation)◊ Kɛ́ɛ kɤ̄ bhíi' kplɯ̀ zʌ̀wō, yɤ̀ dhɤ̀ dhó' dhɛ̀ ɤ́ dhì à dhɛ̀ à gɯ́ yɤ́ kʌ̀ dhɛ̀ŋpʌ̀ ká* Mais si tu ne l'attaches pas, il ira n'importe où, et il se perdra…

zʌ́zʌ̀zʌ́, **zʌ́zʌ́** ***n*** *arch.* **doute**

zē ***n*** **haricot**

zēgā <haricot-os> ***n*** **1 grain de haricot 2** *rn* **rein**

zēlɔ̄ndífù <Fr. gérondif> ***n*** *neol., ling.* **gérondif**

zɛ̀ ***n*** **termite maçon**

zɛ́ ***n*** **août** ◊ *zɛ́ ɤ́ kwɛ̄ɛ yɤ̀ sɛ̀ɛ* cette année, le mois d'août a été pluvieux

zɛ̀dhɛ̀kpàa → zɛ̀ɛkpàa *criquet*

zɛ̀ɛkpàa, **zɛ̀dhɛ̀kpàa** ***n*** **criquet** *[non consommé]*

zɛ̀kpi̋nŋdʌ̄ <termite-chemin-père> ***n*** **termitière** *(sous forme de champignon)*

zɛ̄ŋ́ŋ́ ***n*** **moustique, phalène, moucheron** *(nom générique)◊ zɛ̄ŋ́ŋ́ yà n̄ kún dɛ̀ɛ gbɛ́ɛ̀* aujourd'hui les moustiques m'ont piqué beaucoup ♦ *zɛ̄ŋ́ŋ́ gā* moustque *(une)*

zɛ̀tȁ <termite-sur> ***n*** **piège d'oiseaux** *(fait d'une corde, avec des termites comme amorce)* ♦ *yȁ zɛ̀tȁ yȁ* il a dressé un piège pour les oiseaux

zi̋a ***n*** **poudre de charbon** ◊ *gèe bi̋aŋsúbhɛ̏n yȁ zi̋a zīɤ ɤ̄ bhȁ kɤ̄ yɤ̏ dhā gèe gɔ̏* le coureur s'est enduit de poudre de charbon pour échapper au masque

zi̋aan ***dtm*** **même** *(pour rencherir)◊ yi̋i bhān dhɛ̄ɛ̋kpɔ́ sɛ̄ɛ̋ndhʌ́n zi̋aan yɔ̏ɔ bɔ̄* il n'a pas répondu même à ma petite question

zīaan {AD zīȁan, AD pl. zīaantȁdhɛ̏-dhȕn gúˊ} ***loc.n*** **chemin, sentier** Qsyn. kpi̋nŋ ♦ *bi̋n yɤ̏ bhȁn yī bhȁ zīȁan / zīaan tȁ* la nuit nous a surpris en chemin ♦ *ȁ zīaan gúˊ* en son absence; en plus; après cela ◊ *yi̋i wɔ́n bhá pɤ̄ ȁ zīaan gúˊ* il n'a plus rien dit ♦ *zīaan gā* piste ♦ *zīaan yà kʌ̋n* la route est devenue impratiquable

zīȁan ***loc.n*** *AD de* zīaan *chemin*

zīaangblȍogā <route-trace-os> ***n*** **sentier**

zīaankʌ̋nbhɛ̏n <route-couper-person> ***n*** **bandit de grand chemin, coupeur de routes** *lv.*

zīaanpi̋ɤ {Int. zīaanpi̋ɤ-zīaanpi̋ɤ} ***adv*** **près de la route** ◊ *zīaankʌ̋nbhɛ̏n-dhȕn wà wō dɛ̏ɛn-kpɔ́ zīaanpi̋ɤ-zīaanpi̋ɤ* les coupeurs de routes ont dressé des embuscades au long de la route

zīaanpi̋ɤgwɛ̋ɛ <chemin-auprès-arachide> ***n Desmodium adscendens, Desmodium procumbens*** **plante rampante** *(herbe vivace, 20-100 cm de haut; tiges grimpantes ou en touffes)*

zi̋aanwō <même-adv.> ***restr*** **toute une ..., tout un...**

zi̋an 1 ***prev*** **tromperie** *dans le verbe composé ♦ zi̋an-kʌ̄*

zi̋an 2 ***n*** **1 sentier**; **voie** ◊ *bɔ̄ zi̋an dhɛ̀n !* voici la voie ! ♦ *bűˊ zi̋an, bűˊ gúˊ zi̋an* sentier de brousse **2** ***rn*** **direction** ◊ *gwʌ̏ bhā yɤ̏ glūŋ-sīʌ kā zi̋an ká* le caillou roule dans votre direction

zīan ***n*** **côté** ♦ *zīan gbàn ká* partout

zi̋an-kʌ̄ {zi̋an-kʌ̏} ***v*** **1** ***vt*** **tromper** *(en promettant qch d'extraordinaire)* **2** ***vt*** **effrayer** *(en parlant de qch surnaturel)*

zi̋ʌʌ ***n*** **parasitisme** *(mode de vie d'un pique-assiette)* ♦ *zi̋ʌʌ dɔ̄, zi̋ʌʌ kʌ̄* mener une vie de pique-assiette

zi̋ʌʌdɔ̄bhɛ̏n <parasitisme-mettre-personne> ***n*** **pique-assiette,** *[mal vu par les Dan, à plus fort raison s'il s'agit d' un jeune]*

zȉgȁ *n* **transe chamanique** *(se produit spontanément; la personne se met à trembler et, envahie par un génie, se met à proférer des paroles divinatoires)* ♦ *zȉgȁ yȁ dȁ ȁ gúʉ́; yȁ zȉgȁ sʉ́ʉ́* il est devenu chaman

zȉi *n rn* **revenant, spectre** ◊ *Gbɔ̀ŋgé yȁ gā kɛ́ɛŋ ȁ zȉi yɤ̏ bhēn-dhȕn zȉan-kʌ̏* Gbongué est mort, mais son revenant effraie les gens

zȉi *v* 1) *vi* **trembler** *(de peur, de froid)* ◊ *ȁ kɔ̏ yɤ̏ zȉi-sīʌ* ses mains tremblent *[on pense que celui qui prend beaucoup de café, aura un tremblement de mains à l'âge avancé]* ♦ *sʉ̋ɤ ɤ́ dȁ ȁ gúʉ́, ȁ gȅn ɤ́ yȁ zȉi-sʉ̏ bhȁ ȁ wlɤ̏ɤ* il a pris peur, et ses jambes se sont mises à trembler 2) *vt* **faire trembler**

zīi 1) {A P S, zīi-dhȕn pl. A S, zīi-sʉ̏ foc. A S, zīi-sʉ̏-dhȕn foc. pl. A; zīiii Int. sg.; zīzī Int. pl. P, zīzī-dhȕn Int. pl. A S, zīzī-sʉ̏-dhȕn Int. pl. foc. A; zīizīdhȅ SupInt A; zīizīi SupInt. pl. P, zīizīi-dhȕn SupInt. pl. A, zīizīi-sʉ̏-dhȕn SupInt. pl. foc. A} *adj* **vieux**, **ancien** ♦ *gɔ̄ɔ̄n zīi* vieillard *Qsyn.* *blʌ́*, *kɛ́ɛn*

zīi 2) {zīii Int., zīkkízȉkȉ SupInt.} *adv* **depuis longtemps** ◊ *yá dhūn yɤ́ zīkkízȉkȉ* nous sommes venus ici il y a très longtemps

zīi-dhȅ <vieux-nominalis.> *n* **vieillesse** ◊ *zīi-dhȅ yɤ̏ dhȕn slʌ̏slʌ̏dhɤ̄* la vieillesse vient lentement ♦ *ň zīi-dhȅ kɔ̏ !* *badin* oh, mon vieux dos !

zīii 1) *adj Int. Sg. de* zīi 1) *vieux*

zīii 2) *adv Int. de* zīi 2) *depuis longtemps*

zīisȉ <vieux-adj.> *adj* **ancien** ◊ *dhȕutíȉ zīisȉ* ancien chef de village

zȉisʉ̏ 1), zȉizʌ̏, zȉisȉ {A P S, zȉisʉ̏-dhȕn pl. A S, zȉisʉ̏-sʉ̏ foc. A, zȉisʉ̏-sʉ̏-dhȕn pl. foc. A; zȉizȉisʉ̏, zȉzȉsʉ̏ Int. A P S, zȉizȉisʉ̏-dhȕn, zȉzȉsʉ̏-dhȕn Int. pl. A S, zȉizȉisʉ̏-sʉ̏, zȉzȉsʉ̏-sʉ̏ Int. foc. A, zȉizȉisʉ̏-sʉ̏-dhȕn, zȉzȉsʉ̏-sʉ̏-dhȕn Int. pl. foc. A} *adj* **1 horrible** ◊ *kwȅzlȁan zȉizȉisʉ̏-sʉ̏* une histoire terrible **2 énorme 3 grave**, **horrible** *(avec des conséquences très négatives)* ◊ *Gɤ̏ɤ̏ yȁ pɤ̏ zȉisʉ̏ wō* Geu est tombé horriblement

zȉizʌ̏ 1), 2) → zȉisʉ̏ 1), 2) *horrible*

zīizīdhȅ *adj SupInt. de* zīi *vieux*

zīizīi *Int. pl. de* zīi *vieux*

zȉizȉisʉ̏ *adj Int. de* zȉisʉ̏ *horrible*

zīkkízȉkȉ *adv SupInt. de* zīi 2) *depuis longtemps*

zìnŋ 1) *n* **1 intervalle, distance 2 différence** ◊ *zìnŋ bhá yíi tó' zìnŋgúʉ́* il n'y avait pas de différence entre eux

zìnŋ 2) *prev* **entre**

zìnŋ-dɔ̄ {zìnŋ-dɔ̄} *v vt* **distinguer** ◊ *Zân yáa bāa wāȁ yʌ̋ zìnŋ-dɔ̄* Zan ne sait pas distinguer entre la manioc et l'igname

zìnŋgúʉ́ *pp* **1 entre** *le redoublement est possible pour exprimer la nature compositionnelle des participants :* ◊ *dhídhȁan ȁ-dhȕn zìnŋgúʉ́-zìnŋgúʉ́* il y a des palabres entre eux (entre ces groupes) **2 au milieu** ◊ *yɤ̏ dȕa yāandhɯ́ɤ gbēŋ zìnŋgúɯ́* elle s'est évadée hier à minuit **3 pendant**

zìnŋgúɯ́sɯ̏ <entre-adj.> ***adj*** **moyen**

zìnŋtőŋ → zìŋtőŋ *araignée*

zìnŋtőo → zìŋtőŋ *araignée*

zìŋtőŋ, **zìnŋtőŋ**, **zìŋtőo**, **zìnŋtőo** ***n*** **araignée** *(nom générique)* ♦ *zìŋtőŋ dőŋ* toile d'araignée; fil de toile d'araignée ♦ *zìŋtőŋ kɔ́* toile d'araignée

zìŋtőo → zìŋtőŋ *araignée*

zīɤ {zı̏ɤ} ***v*** **1.1** 1) *vi* **passer** *(qch – tȁ)* *Syn.* bɔ̄ ♦ *zīɤ dhɔ̏ yà dȁ ȁ gúɯ́* il est pressé (de partir) **1.2** *vi* **pénétrer**, **passer** *(à travers – gúɯ́)* ◊ *bhēn yǘn zı̏ɤ dhǘ dódó yā gúɯ́ ɤ́ dhɛ̏ yɤ̄ plɤ́ɤ̄* on voit le village à travers les rares arbres **1.3** *zīɤ ȁ ká vi* **faire le tour** *(de – zɯ̏)* ◊ *Gbȁtò yà bı̏aŋ súɯ́ yɤ́ yȁ zīʌ ȁ ká sɯ́ɤ zɯ̏* Gbato est passé autour du feu en courant *(plusieurs fois)* **1.4** *vi* **tourner** *(autour de)*, **tourner en cercle** *(au-dessus – zɯ̏* ◊ *sʌ́ʌ̏ yɤ̄ɤ tɔ̏dhʌ́n kún, yɤ́ ɤ́ zı̏ɤ ȁ zɯ̏zɯ̏* l'épervier veut attraper le poussin, il tourne en rond au-dessus de lui ◊ *gbɛ̂n yɤ̏ zīɤ-sīʌ ɤ̄ dʌ̄bhɛ̏n zɯ̏* le chien tourne autour de son maître **1.5** *vi* **se promener** ◊ *yɤ̏ kʌ̄ tɔ̏ zīɤ-sɯ̏ ká yʌ́ŋ̏dhɛ̏ dhɤ́, ɤ́ bı̋n dhɤ́ bhān* il a continué de se promener au soleil jusqu'à l'obscurité **2** 1) *vi* **rouler** *(un moyen de transport)* 2) *vt* **rouler à** *(vélo, mobylette)* ◊ *bhān pòpòdhîn yā, bhán' zīɤ gbɛ́, yɤ̏ dhȕu* ma mobylette que voici, quand je roule beaucoup avec, elle cale **3** *vi zīɤ ȁ ká* **dépasser** *(qch – tȁ)* **4.1** *vt* **enduire de** *(qch – bhȁ)* ◊ *ɯ̄ bɤ̏ɤ̏ zīɤ-sīʌ kɔ́ bhǘŋ bhȁ* tu es en train de badigeonner avec de la boue le mur de la maison ◊ *Tȍkpȁ yà yɔ̋ɔ pǘu zīɤ gwàadhɤ̄* Tokpa a enduit le rocher plat avec du kaolin **4.2** *vt* **essuyer avec qch** ◊ *yà pʌ̄ zīɤ tàbɛ̋dhı́ tȁ* elle a essuyé la table ◊ *ɯ̄ kɔ̏ zīɤ ȁ yǘn gēnŋdhɤ̄* essuie sous ses yeux ◊ *Yɔ̏ yȁ ɤ̄ kɔ̏ tɔ̏ɔ-sɯ̏ zīɤ ɤ̄ bhā sɔ̄ bhȁ* Yo a essuyé ses mains mouillées avec le pagne **4.3** *vt* **traiter** *(agir d'une certaine manière; avec – ká)* ◊ *ɯ̄ kwī yǘn ká dhɛ̀ kènŋ ɤ́ wȁa zīɤ yı́ wɔ̋sɯ̏ ká dhɤ́* la couleur de ta peau est rouge comme celle d'une écrevisse passée à l'eau chaude **5** *vi* **couler** *(eau, sang)* ◊ *yı́ yɤ̏ zīɤ-sīʌ ɤ̄ glőo tȁ* la rivière coule dans son lit **6** *vi* **glisser** *(sur une surface induite de graisse)* *Syn.* bhán *1* **7.1** *vt* **mettre**, **insérer** ◊ *yà glɛ̄ɛ́ zīɤ ɤ̄ bhɔ̄ gúɯ́* il a mis le sac à son cou **7.2** *vi zīɤ kőo* **souffrir une luxation** ◊ *ȁ gȅn yà zīɤ kőo* il s'est luxé la jambe **7.3** *vt ɤ̄ gȅn zīɤ kőo* **croiser les jambes** ◊ *yáȁdhūn kı́i ɯ̄ gȅn zīɤ kőo* assis-toi et croise les jambes *[une pause des jeunes garçons manifestant la résignation devant les aînés]* **8** *vi* **expliquer**, **exposer** *(qch – gúɯ́, à – dhɛ̏)* ◊ *yɤ́ wó zı̏ɤ wɔ́n ɤ́ kʌ̏ bhā ȁ gúɯ́ gɔ̄ndʌ̄dhʌ́n bhā ȁ dhɛ̏* et ils ont expliqué ce qui était arivé à cet homme ◊ *... yɤ́ wɔ̀ɔ ɤ́ zı̏ɤ ɤ̄ wɔ̏ gúɯ́* alors le singe a raconté ce qui avait eu lieu **9** *vi zīɤ gèe ká* **prendre le départ** *(lit. "faire démarrer le masque", dans les courses de masques)* ◊ *bhén ɤ́ gbȁn bhā, yȁ dhı̄ ȁ dhɛ̏, yɤ́ zı̏ɤ kɤ̏ dhɛ̋ɛdhɛ̏ blɛ̋e pɯ́ɤ, yɤ́ gūn zīɤ-dhȁan gèe ká* l'homme qui se dresse (devant le masque), si ça lui plaît, il passe au bord de la place publique avant de faire démarrer le masque **10** *vi* **ne pas respecter** *(qn – gɔ̏)* **11** *vi* **répéter** *(paroles – gúɯ́)*

zı́ɤ̏ → zı́ɤ̏ɤ *grand-père*

zìɤgúɯ <passer-dans> ***n*** **transformation** *(magique)*

zíɤ̀ɤ, zíɤ̀ {zìɤ, zìɤɤ} ***n*** *la forme avec la voyelle longue, zíɤ̀ɤ, s'utilise surtout dans l'adresse* **1** *rn* **grand-père** *("grand-père classificatoire" : grand-père, arrière-grand-père, arrière-arrière-grand-père, etc.; frère aîné du grand-père; frère cadet du grand-père maternel; grand frère du père ou de la mère)* Qsyn. dhūʌ̄ŋ̀ ♦ *zíɤ̀ɤ kpíì* frère aîné du grand-père ♦ *zíɤ̀ɤ gúɯ zíɤ̀ɤ* arch. ♦, *zíɤ̀ɤ bhà zíɤ̀ɤ* arrière-grand-père ♦ *zíɤ̀ɤ gúɯ zìɤɤ gúɯ zíɤ̀ɤ* arch. ♦, *zíɤ̀ɤ bhà zíɤ̀ɤ bhà zíɤ̀ɤ* arrière-arrière-grand-père **2** *rn* **beau-père, beau** *lv.* *(homme, représentant du groupe des "donneurs d'épouses", à qui on doit du respect et des cadeaux : père ou frère aîné de la femme ou du mari; mari de la soeur aînée de la femme ou du mari; père ou frère de la femme du fils; mari de la fille de la fille, et pour un homme, de la fille du fils; mari de la soeur aînée du père ou de la mère; mari de la fille de la soeur cadette du père; mari de la fille de la tante aînée paternelle) [par rapport au frère de la femme, n'est pas utilisé comme une forme d'adresse, cf. dhìnbhɔ́ɔ̀n]* Qsyn. yɔ̀bhīn Ant. dhìnbhɔ́ɔ̀n ♦ *zíɤ̀ɤ sɛ́ɛ́ndhʌ́n* mari de la fille de la fille de la tante paternelle aînée; mari de la fille de la sœur aînée; mari de la fille du frère cadet; mari de la soeur cadette de la femme ou du mari; par rapport à l'homme, mari de la fille de la soeur cadette **3** *rn* *parent masculin de la coépouse*

zītīŋdhɤ̄ ***adv*** arch. **stupéfait** Syn. dīŋdhɤ̄

zīzī ***adj*** *Int. pl. de* zīi *vieux*

zìzìsɯ̀ *Int. de* zìisɯ̀ *horrible*

zláà {zlàa} ***n rn*** **petit frère, petite sœur** *(dans le sens classificatoire : propre frère cadet ou sœur cadette; enfant du frère du père ou de la sœur de la mère, moins âgé qu'ego)* ♦ *zláà bhà zlàa* petit frère / petite soeur, troisième enfant après ego ♦ *zláà bhà zláà bhà zlàa* petit frère / petite soeur d'ego, quatrième après ego dans la séquence des naissances

zláàbɔ̀ (t) ***n rn*** **petit frère, petite sœur**

zlàan ***n*** **Dieu** *(chrétien, animiste, musulman) [les animistes ont une idée de Dieu suprême auquel on s'adresse par l'intermédiaire des idoles]* ◊ *wɔ̀ bhɛ̀ɛ Zlàan dhɛ̀ dhèglííʌ̀ gúɯ* ils prient Dieu à l'église ◊ *Zlàan (yɤ̀) bhūn* Dieu existe ♦ *Zlàan yɤ̀ à gɔ̀* Dieu est avec lui

zlàanwɔ̀pɤbhɛ̀n <Dieu-mot-dire-personne> ***n*** **missionnaire,**

zlʌ̀ʌdhɤ̄ (gw), **zlʌ̄ʌdhɤ̄** (t) ***adv*** **peu après** ♦ *à dhɛ̀ kʌ̀ zlʌ̄ʌdhɤ̄* peu de temps après cela

zlʌ̀ʌn (m) ***pp*** **entre** Syn. zìŋgúɯ

zlʌ̄ʌndhʌ́n, **zlʌ̄ʌn** ***n*** **petite fourmi noire** *(habite dans les maisons) la forme zlʌ̄ʌn est moins usitée*

zlɔ̀ ***n*** **septembre**

zlɔ̋ ***n*** **mars**

zlòo ***n*** ***Tragelaphus scriptus*** **antilope guib** *(mâle : cornes enroulées en spirale, crinière; couleur variée; dessin sur le dos; poids : 40-80 kg mâle, 25-60 kg femelle)*

zlōo {zlòo} *v* **1** 1) *vi* **se ratatiner**, **flétrir** ◊ *gɔ̂ yà zlōo* la noix de cola s'est ratatinée ◊ *ä kwī yà zlōo* sa peau s'est ridée 2) *vt* **faner**; **rider** ◊ *yʌ́nŋ̈ yä ä bhä gɔ̂ zlōo* le soleil a fané son cola *(en le rendant immangeable)* **2** *vt* **filer** *(coton, en l'embobinant sur – bhä)*

zlɔ̀ɔ → zlœ̀œ *se ralentir*

zlɤ̀ɤ *pp* **derrière**, **au-delà** *(du côté opposé, par rapport à un grand objet naturel ou artificiel, comme un fleuve, une forêt, un chemin, un village, etc.)* ◊ *ä bhä kɔ́ yɤ̈ kpìnŋ zlɤ̀ɤ* sa maison est derrière la route

zlœ̀œ, **zlɔ̀ɔ** *v vr* **ralentir**

zlūu *n ne se conjugue pas avec la marque du pluriel* ***Dorylinae*** **fourmis magnan** ◊ *zlūu dhʌ̀n ɤ́ sɔ̄ kwʌ̋nŋ̈dhɤ̄, yɤ́ á yőo wɛ̀nŋ ä-dhùn tä* les fourmis magnan ont envahi la maison, et j'ai versé de la cendre sur elles *[un procédé traditionnel contre les fourmis]* ♦ *zlūu bhʌ̀ʌ* angine ♦ *zlūu gɔ̈ dùɛɛ* demeure des fourmis magnan

zö *prev rn* **cœur** *(comme siège des émotions)* Qsyn. zūʌ́ ♦ *kʌ̄ ɤ̄ zö ká* prendre garde ♦ *X zö yɤ̈ bhɔ̈ Y-dhɛ̈ ká* X a oublié comment faire Y ♦ *bhɛ̄n zö kún* plaire à qn, satisfaire qn ◊ *Tìa bhä dhīaŋ yɔ̈ɔ yíi n̄ zö kún* la réponse de Tio ne m'a pas plu ♦ *ɤ̄ zö lòo* soupirer de soulagement ♦ *ɤ̄ zö tʌ̋* réfléchir

zō *n* ***Agama agama*** **margouillat** *(esp. de lézard : pour le mâle, taille atteignant 30 cm, couleur du corps noir indigo, tête jaune orange souvent hérissée d'une crête; pour la femelle, plus petite, grise foncée, elle demeure souvent immobile sur les surfaces verticales)*

zö-bɤ̈ <cœur-reveiller> *v* 1) *vi* **se souvenir**, **se rappeler** *(qch – ká, tä)* ◊ *n̄ zö yíi bɤ̈ ä tɔ́ ká* je ne me suis pas rappelé son nom 2) *vt* **rappeler**

zódhɤ̄ {Int. zózódhɤ̄} *adv* **brusquement** *(parler; la forme intensive signifie "continuellement et de façon brusque")* ◊ *Zân yɤ̈ dhīaŋ zʌ̈ zózódhɤ̄* Zan parle très vite

zö-gɔ́n {zö-gɔ̄n} <cœur- ?> *v* **1** *vr* **regretter l'absence** *(de qn – wɔ̈n ká, wɔ̈n tä)* ◊ *ā n̄ zö-gɔ́n-sīʌ bhān dhēbʌ̈ wɔ̈n tä* ma femme me manque **2** *vr* **réfléchir** ◊ *bhɤ̈ ū zö-gɔ́n kɤ̄ ú gūn'-dhäan dhīaŋ zʌ̄'* réfléchis avant de parler ♦ *ā n̄ zö sʌ̈ gɔ̈n ū ká* j'ai de bonnes intentions envers toi

zögɔ̈ngúwɔ̈n <réfléchir-dans-affaire> *n* **pensée**, **idée** *(affaire sérieuse, sujet de réflexion)* Syn. zötägúwɔ̈n

zö-gbän <cœur-planter> *v* **1** *vt* **réconforter**, **rassurer** **2** *vr* **se remonter**, **prendre du courage** ♦ *ū zö-gbän !* courage !

zōgbên <margouillat-chien> *n* ***Hydrocynus brevis*** **poisson-chien** *(taille : jusqu'à 1, poids : 10 kg; carnassier)*

zö-kún {zö-kūn} *v vt* **satisfaire**

zőŋ̈ 1 *n rn* **position accroupie** ◊ *yà yä ɤ̄ zőŋ̈ gú* il s'est accroupi

zőŋ̈ 2 *n rare* **aubergine** Syn. pènŋ ♦ *zőŋ̈ gā* fruit d'aubergine

zɔ̀o 1 ***n*** **chenille mangeable** *(esp.; poils roux; vit sur l'arbre samba; sort en mai-juillet, cueillie à l'aube. Grillée et séchée au soleil, elle fournit un supplément fort apprécié à la sauce; vendue au marché comme friandise)*◊ *Yɔ̀dhē yɤ̀ zɔ̀o kún-sīʌ* Yodé est en train de ramasser les chenilles zoo

zɔ̀o 2 ***prev*** **coeur**

zɔ̀o 3 ***n*** **bouderie, rejet** ◊ *yà zɔ̀o kʌ̄ wʌ́ʌ̀gā bhà* il a rejeté l'argent ◊ *yà zɔ̀o kʌ̄ ñ bhà* il m'a boudé

zɔ̋o ***n*** **chasseur de sorciers** *(guérisseur et chasseurs de sorciers)* <u>*Syn.*</u> <u>*zɔ̋obhīn*</u> ♦ *zɔ̋o gèe* masque-chasseur de sorciers

zɔ̋obhīn {pl. zɔ̋o-dhùn, zɔ̋obhīn-dhùn, zɔ̋ozʌ̀-dhùn} ***n*** **chasseur de sorciers** *(guérisseur et chasseurs de sorciers)* <u>*Syn.*</u> <u>*zɔ̋o*</u>

zɔ̀o-bhō {zɔ̀o-bhō} ***v vt*** **venger qn** *(de, sur – gɔ̀)*◊ *yà ñ zɔ̀o-bhō ñ yúù gɔ̀* il m'a vengé de mon ennemi

zɔ̀okúnsű <chenille-attraper-mois> ***n*** **saison de la cueillette des chenilles** *(septembre-octobre)*

zɔ̀osæ̀ædhɯ̀ɯ <chenille-frais-arbre> ***n*** ***Jatrofa curcas (gen. Euphorbiaceae)*** **pourguère** *(taille : jusqu'à 6, couronne dense, écorce bronze-verdâtre; est planté comme enclos, protégeant les aires de culture contre l'invasion des serpents et des termites. Fruits oviformes dont on extrait l'huile, purgatif, le jus produit une teinture noire, l'écorce une teinture bleue; feuilles utilisées comme médicament contre l'irritation de la peau, les boutons, la gale)*

zɔ̋ozʌ̀-dhùn *pl. de* zɔ̋obhīn

zɔ̀-tã̋ (m) {zɔ̀-tà} ***v vr*** **réfléchir**

zɔ̀tã̋dhē <réfléchir-nominalis.> ***n*** **pensée, réflexion**

zɔ̀tàgúɯwɔ̀n <réfléchir-dans-affaire> ***n*** **1 opinion 2 idée, pensée** ◊ *bhán zɔ̀tàgúɯwɔ̀n bhā slɔ̀ɔ* j'ai eu une idée <u>*Syn.*</u> <u>*zɔ̀gɔ̀ngúɯwɔ̀n*</u>

zɔ̀yɤ̀kó-dhɛ̀ <coeur-mettre-l'un l'autre-nominalis.> ***n*** **entente, confiance** *(mutuelle)*

zɔ̀zɔ̀dhà ***n*** ***Hypergerus atriceps*** **timalie à tête noire** *(oiseau, taille : 20 cm, queue longue, bec fin et noir; tête, gorge et haut de la poitrine noirs; dessus jaune-vert vif; dessous jaune vif)*

zózódhɤ̄ ***adv*** *Int. de* zódhɤ̄ *brusquement*

zɔ̀ ***n*** **carquois** *(fait d'un segment de gros tronc de bambou, couvert de cuir)*♦ *yà sàa dà zɔ̀ gúɯ* il a mis des flèches dans le carquois

zɔ̄ ***n*** **1 pangolin géant 2 bulldozer, niveleuse** *(dans ce sens, en dan oriental, surtout dans le dialecte yèa)*

zɔ̋ 1 ***n*** **1 abeille** *(à miel très sucré)*♦ *zɔ̋ bhō* cueillir le miel ◊ *zɔ̋-dhùn wɔ̀ zīɤ-sīʌ dhűű bĩ́n yā à zùzù* les abeilles tournent autour de cette fleure **2 essaim, nid d'abeilles, ruche** ◊ *zɔ̋ zīi* vieuk essaim

zɔ́ 2 ***n*** **1** *rn* **bout, point** *(d'un objet métallique)* ♦ *kʌ́ʌ zɔ́* lame de houe **2** *rn* **bord** *(de vêtement)*, **biseau** *(p. ex. d'une canne)* **3 bout, queue** *(d'une corde, ceinture etc.)* Qsyn. gʌ̄n

zɔ́dhɤ́ɤ <bout-tranchant> ***n*** **sommet, bout** ♦ *dhɯ̋ɯ zɔ́dhɤ́ɤ* sommet d'un arbre ♦ *tɔ̏n zɔ́dhɤ́ɤ* sommet d'une montagne

zɔ̏n ***v*** **1** 1) *vt* **montrer** *(à – dhɛ̏, qch – ká)* ♦ *à zɔ̏n' ká yáa dhɤ́* il n'y avait pas son semblable 2) *vr* **se présenter** ◊ *bhán n̄ dɛ̏ zɔ̏n* je me présente **2** *vt* **enseigner** *(qn – dhɛ̏)* Syn. dlāān ◊ *yɤ̏ sʌ́ʌdhɛ́ bhā à zɔ̏n n̄ dhɛ̏* il m'a enseigné la lecture **3** *vt zɔ̏n kwʌ́ʌ* **comparer**

zɔ̄n {zɔ̄n} ***v*** **1** 1) *vt* **piler** ♦ *bāa kɔ̏n zɔ̄n* préparer du foutou de manioc 2) *vr* **se remuer** *(en dansant : un danse statique, avec des menus mouvements du corps) [le style de danse prédominant chez les Dan]* ◊ *yɤ̏ ɤ̄ zɔ̏n n̄ gúu sʌ̏* à mon avis, elle se remue bien **2** *vt* **frapper** *(avec un objet, brusquement)* ◊ *wà à zɔ̄n dhɯ̋ɯ ká à kèedhɤ̄* on l'a frappé sur l'occiput avec un bâton ♦ *wà bhɛ̄n zɔ̄n kɔ̄ɔ à tàa, à vīn yɤ̏ dɔ̏ gbȉiŋ* lorsqu'on frappe une personne au dos avec la main, ça produit le bruit "gbiing !" **3** *vt imagé* **fouiller au fond 4** *vt imagé* **tringler** *(faire l'amour avec; péjoratif par rapport à la femme)* Syn. wɔ̄ à pɤ́ɤ, wɔ̄ à ká

zɔ̀nŋ ***v*** **1** *vi* **se refroidir** Syn. dhìʌʌ **2** *vi* **se calmer** ♦ *zɔ̀nŋ-sɯ̀ ká* calmement

zɔ́ŋ 1 ***n*** **arbre** *(esp.) [extraction de teinture noire à partir des feuilles]* ♦ *zɔ́ŋ yí* teinture noire

zɔ́ŋ 2 ***n*** **gravier** Syn. kʌ̄ŋ́ ♦ *zɔ́ŋ gā yà dhó n̄ yʌ́nŋ* j'ai reçu un grain de sable dans l'œil

zɔ̀ɔ 1 ***v*** *vi* **bégayer** ◊ *bhɛ́n bhā yà zɔ̀ɔ, yɤ̏ kʌ̏ gbɛ̏ɛ* celui-ci, il bégaye fortement ♦ *à bhà pʌ̄ bhɯ̏n zɔ̀ɔ-sɯ̀ ká* son bégaiement est horrible

zɔ̀ɔ 2 ***v*** **1** *vi* **s'amollir** *(dans l'eau)* ◊ *kɤ̄ŋ yà zɔ̀ɔ* le maïs s'est ramolli (après qu'on l'a fait bouillir) ♦ *bhɔ̏ yɤ̏ à pɤ̏ : bhɛ̄n yáa gwʌ̏ zɔ̀ɔ yì dɔ̄* tente ta chance ! (litt. : le cabri dit : l'homme ne peut pas attendre le jour où la pierre se ramollit) **2** *vt* **digérer 3** *vi* **devenir facile** ♦ *à zūʌ́ yà zɔ̀ɔ* il s'est consolé ♦ *à gɔ̏ gúu yà zɔ̀ɔ* il est devenu calme

zɔ̀ɔ 3 ***restr*** *le plus souvent, requiert la particule wà en fin d'énoncé* **1 mais comment, aïe** *(exprime une surprise désagréable)* ◊ *ā kpàn à bhɛ́n-dhɯ̀n ɤ́ wó bhā zɔ̀ɔ, à bhɛ̄n dō bhà zīaàn wà !* aïe, c'est précisément une des ces (mauvaises) personnes-là que j'ai rencontrée sur la route ! **2 même si** ◊ *kɤ́ zúu yɤ̄ɤ à wɔ́n dō zɔ̀ɔ wɛ̀, à dhɛ̏ yà bhà kɤ̄ yɤ̏ tɔ̏n kún kɤ̏ blɛ̏ɛsɯ̀* même s'il le savait, il fallait d'abord qu'il remonte la pente

zɔ̀ɔ 4 ***prt*** **donc** *(marque de l'insistance)* ◊ *dhó zɔ̀ɔ sīāa kíi yáàndhūn* viens donc t'asseoir

zɔ̄ɔ ***n*** **nasse** Syn. sàadhē

zɔ̄ɔ̏ ***n*** **arbre** *(espèce, avec des feuilles longues et larges)*

zɔ̄ɔ̏n → zūʌ̀n *foyer*

zɔ̀ɔnŋ {zɔ̀ɔnŋ} ***v*** **1** *vt* **adoucir** *(moeurs)* ◊ *Yɔ̏ yà Tɔ̀kpà zɔ̀ɔnŋ* la présence de Yo a adouci Tokpa **2** *vr* **être modéré** *(en – bhà)* ◊ *ɯ̄ zɔ̀ɔnŋ wē bhūn-sɯ̀ bhà* sois modéré en buvant du vin

zɔ̏ɔnzɔ̋ndhē → zœ̏œnzö̋ndhē *rouge, SupInt*

zɔ̀ɔsɯ̏ɯ {A, S} {A P S} ***adj*** **1 calme, peu pressé** ◊ *Zân yɤ̏ yʌ̄ kʌ̏ zɔ̀ɔsɯ̏ɯ ká* Zan travaille doucement **2 ramolli** *(riz)* le riz est bien cuit

zɔ̏ɔzɔ̏ɔdhɤ̄ {Int. zɔ̏zɔ̏zɔ̏dhɤ̄} ***adv*** **à torrent** *(pluie)* ♦ *dhā yɤ̏ bān-sīʌ zɔ̏ɔzɔ̏ɔdhɤ̄* il pleut à torrent ◊ *dhā yɤ̏ bān-sīʌ zɔ̏zɔ̏zɔ̏dhɤ̄* il pleut à torrent et longuement

zɔ̄ɔzɔ̄ɔdhɤ̄ ***adv*** **de temps en temps** ◊ *ā dhūn wɔ̏ ȁ bhȁ zɔ̄ɔzɔ̄ɔdhɤ̄* je lui rends visite de temps en temps

zɔ̋yɔ̋n <abeille-huile> ***n*** **miel**

zɔ̏zɔ̏zɔ̏dhɤ̄ ***adv*** *Int. de* zɔ̏ɔzɔ̏ɔdhɤ̄ *à torrent*

zɤ̏ŋ ***n Orycteropus afer*** **oryctérope**

zɤ̄ŋ 1 ***n*** *se combine avec le marqueur du pluriel* **fourmi** *(petite, rouge ou noire, habite dans la maison, ne pique pas)*

zɤ̄ŋ 2 ***n*** **mange-mil** *[escroc des contes populaires]*

zɤ̄ŋkɔ́dɔ̏bhȁdhɯ̏ɯ <mange-mil-maison-bâtir-sur-arbre> ***n*** **arbre** *(esp., jusqu'à 7 de hauteur; on le plante près des cases sacrées; on pile ses feuilles et on en fait une décoction, avec laquelle on se lave 7 fois pour se protéger contre la magie noire)*

zɤ̋ɤpű̋u < ?-blanc> ***n Sida corymbosa, S. collina*** **plante herbacée** *(esp.)* Syn. *sɛ̏ɛnpű̋u*

zœ̏nzœ̏ndhē ***adj*** *Int. pl. de* zœ̏œndhē *rouge*

zœ̏œ ***n Bycanistes subcylindricus*** **calao à joues grises** *(75 cm)*

zœ̄œ {zœ̏œ} ***v vt*** **rejeter les accusations** *(en ayant tort)* ♦ *wáa wɔ́n dhɤ̏ zœ̄œ* on ne sait jamais

zœ̄œdhē ***n*** **rejet** *(d'une accusation justifiée)* ♦ *zœ̄œdhē dȁ wɔ́n bhȁ* rejeter les accusations en qch ♦ *yȁ pɛ́ ȁ-dhȕn zìnŋgúɯ zœ̄œdhē ká* la dissension a éclaté entre eux

zœ̏œndhē {A P S, zœ̏œndhē-dhȕn pl. A S, zœ̏œndhē-sɯ̏ɯ foc. A S, zœ̏œndhē-sɯ̏ɯ-dhȕn foc. pl. A S; zœ̏nzœ̏ndhē, zœ̏œndhēzœ̏œndhē Int. pl. A P S, zœ̏nzœ̏ndhē-dhȕn, zœ̏œndhēzœ̏œndhē-dhȕn Int. pl. A S, zœ̏nzœ̏ndhē-sɯ̏ɯ, zœ̏œndhēzœ̏œndhē-sɯ̏ɯ Int. pl. foc. A S, zœ̏nzœ̏ndhē-sɯ̏ɯ-dhȕn, zœ̏œndhēzœ̏œndhē-sɯ̏ɯ-dhȕn Int. pl. foc. A S, SupInt zœ̏œnzö̋ndhē, zɔ̏ɔnzɔ̋ndhē A S} ***adj*** *la forme zœ̏œnzœ̈ndhē est rare* **rouge** ◊ *bhán sɪ̏ʌ̏ʌ yɐ̋n zœ̏œnzœ̈ndhē dhɔ́* j'ai acheté un piment extrêmement rouge ♦ *pʌ̄ zœ̏œndhē* rouge à lèvres ◊ *yȁ pʌ̄ zœ̏œndhē gbɛ́ zīɤ ɤ̄ bȅn bhȁ* elle s'est mis beaucoup de rouge aux lèvres

zœ̏œndhēzœ̏œndhē *Int. pl. de* zœ̏œndhē *rouge*

zœ̏œnzœ̈ndhē, **zɔ̏ɔnzɔ̋ndhē** ***adj*** *SupInt. de* zœ̏œndhē *rouge*

zœ́œ̏tɛ́ɛtɛ̏ɛ ***n Aegypius tracheliotus, Torgos tracheliotus*** **oricou** *(un oiseau, taille : 115 cm, envergure des ailes 2,7, poids : 11 kg; gros plis de peau nue de l'oreille jusqu'au cou; longues plumes brunes sur le duvet blanc du ventre, queue noire cunéiforme)*

zű {zǜ} *v* **1** 1) *vt* **laver** 2) *vr* **se laver, se baigner** ♦ *ɤ̄ zű bhɛ̄n-dhǜn ká* se dissimuler parmi les gens *(un truc de sorcier, en utilisant les procédés magiques, à l'approche du masque chasse-sorciers)* **2** *vr* **bien s'habiller, se parer** Syn. bāà

zūa {zūa} *v* **1.1** *vt* **percer** ◊ *yɤ̀ ɤ̄ bhā dhʌ́n tő gú zǜa kɤ̄ yɤ̀ yī gú* elle a percé les oreilles de sa fille lorsque celle-ci dormait ♦ *yà kɔ́ bháŋ̋ bhā' zūa gblūűdhɤ̄* il a percé le mur de la maison d'un coup sec **1.2** *vt* **piquer** ◊ *sɛ̀dhágā yà n̄ zūa* une aiguille m'a piqué **2** *vt* **faire une piqûre à qn**; **faire injection dans** *(une partie du corps)* ◊ *dhɔ̀tlɔ̋ɔ̄bhīn yàa zūa à gɤ́ŋ bhà* le médecin lui a fait une piqûre à la cuisse ◊ *wà Gɤ́ɤ̀ zūı zūa, yűa yáa bhō* on a fait à Geu une piqûre à la fesse, la maladie n'a pas fini **3** *vi* **se déchirer** *(un sac, etc.)* ◊ *à bhà bhɔ̄ɔ yà zūa, yàbhà yà wɛ̀nŋ* son sac s'est déchiré, et les oignons se sont renversés **4.1** *vi* **se jeter, se précipiter** ♦ *à gbō yà zūa à bhà* il a chié dans sa culotte **4.2** *vi* **faire une irruption** *(en entrant chez – tà)* ◊ *yɤ̀ zǜa n̄ tà kɔ́ɔdhɤ̄* il a fait irruption dans ma maison

zǜaadhɛ̀ < ?-femelle> *n* **prostituée, pute** *rude* ♦ *zǜaadhɛ̀ kʌ̄ŋ́ bhō kɔ̋ɔ̀* prostituée de grand chemin *("qu'on baise en l'appuyant contre le mur d'une maison, jusqu'à arracher des graviers du mur")*

zűaanzǜaan {P S} *adj* **exténué** *(le matin, suite à un travail pénible de la veille)* ◊ *n̄ dhɪ́ɤ yà kʌ̄ dhɔ̀ɔn zűaanzǜaan ká dhìn* je me sens tout à fait exténué

zūàglűı *n* **arbre** *(espèce)*

zǜan *v vi* **approcher du stade de mûrissement** ◊ *glɔ̄ɔ bhā yɤ̀ zǜan tɤ̄ɤ gú Dhɛ̀ɛnbháàn gɔ̀ kɔ́ɔdhɤ̄* les bananes ont presque atteint la maturité dans le panier dans la maison de Neema

zǜansǜı {A S; zǜanzǜansǜı Int. A S} *adj* **au point d'atteindre le stade de mûrissement**

zǜanzǜansǜı *Int. de* zǜansǜı *au point d'atteindre le stade de mûrissement*

zūʌ́ *n rn* **cœur** Qsyn. zɔ̀ ♦ *à zūʌ́ yɤ̀ gbínŋ̀* il sait se maîtriser *(il se retient, il est résistant à la douleur, aux souffrances)* ♦ *zūʌ́ dhìin dà* joie ♦ *zūʌ́ sæ̀æ* patience ♦ *n̄ zūʌ́ dhɪ́ɤ yɤ̀ bhɤ́ɤ-sīʌ à wɔ̀n gú* je m'inquiète à ce sujet ♦ *à zūʌ́ dhɪ́ɤ yà tɛ́ɛ* il souffre ♦ *à zūʌ́ yà pā* il s'est calmé ♦ *à zūʌ́ yɤ̀ à kʌ̀* il souffre d'un ulcère à l'estomac ♦ *à zūʌ́ tà yɤ̀ sēè-sīʌ* il a la nausée ♦ *à zūʌ́ yɤ̀ wáàdhūn-sǜı ká* il est heureux ♦ *bhēn zūʌ́ tó tàabhàn* i) donner des soucis à qn ii) rendre qn nostalgique ◊ *Gbàtò wɔ̀n, yɤ̀ bhēnzūʌ́tòtàabhàwɔ̀n ká* l'affaire de Gbato donne des soucis aux gens ♦ *à zūʌ́ yɤ̀ dɔ̀* il est gourmand

zūʌ́dɔ̄ <coeur-mettre> *n* **gourmandise, envie de nourriture**

zūʌ́dhɪ́ɤtɛ̀ɛ <cœur-devant-vent> *n* **souci**

zūʌ́gā *n rn* **coeur** *(comme organe physique)* ◊ *yűa yáa à zūʌ́gā bhà* il n'a pas de maladie de coeur

zūʌ́gìiwɔ̀n <coeur-blesser-affaire> *n* **malheur, trouble**

zūʌ́kʌ̄bhɛ̀n <cœur-chasser-personne> *n* **ulcéreux** *(personne souffrant d'ulcères)* ◊ *zūʌ́kʌ̄bhɛ̀n yáa slʌ̀ʌ bhɤ̀* une personne qui a des ulcères ne doit pas manger de piment

zūʌ̋kʌ̀dō-sʉ̀ʉ <coeur-faire-un-gérondif> ***n*** **entente, compréhension mutuelle**

zūʌ̀n, **zɔ̄ɔ̀n** ***n*** **foyer** *(fait de trois pierres)◊ sɯ́ɤ dhūű gèe yɤ̀ sɯ́ɤ dhùu Sàatɯ̄ɯ̀dhʌ́n gɔ̀ zūʌ̀n dhʌ̀n gúɯ́* le masque-pompier a éteint le feu dans le foyer de Saatinin

zūʌ̀n ***n*** **tort, responsabilité** *seulement dans l'expression :* ♦ *wɔ́n bhá zūʌ̀n yáa n̄ bhà* je n'ai rien à me reprocher

zūʌ̋sæ̀æ-dhɛ̀ <cœur-frais-abstr.> ***n*** **patience**

zūʌ̋sɛ̀ɛbhɛ̀n <coeur-frais-personne> ***n*** **homme patient**

zùee ***n*** **chenille** *(nom générique)*

zūeŋ ***n*** **nasse** *(jusqu'à 4-5 de longueur, faite de rotin)* Qsyn. sàadhē

zūɛ̀ɛ ***n*** **varan** *(esp.) [viande très recherchée]*

zùɛɛbhē (m) ***n*** **bouteille** *(en verre)* Syn. *bútɛ̀dhɯ́ɤ, sànŋdhɛ̀*

zùglù ***n*** **confusion** ♦ *wɔ́n yā zùglù yà bhán à bhà, wɔ́n yā yà bhán zùglù bhà* cette affaire est entrée dans une grande confusion

zʉ́kkʉ̋zʉ̀kʉ̀ ***adj*** *Int.Sg. de* zʉ̋uzʉ̀u *louche*

zūn → zūn *atteindre*

zʉ̀ndhɯ́ɤbhlɔ̀ɔ → zʉ̀ndhɯ́ɤbhlɔ̀ɔ *avenir*

zʉ̀ɤ 1) ***v*** **1.1** *vt* **jeter**, **lancer** *(à – ká)◊ yɤ̀ dhʉ̋ dhʌ̀n à zʉ̀ɤ n̄ ká, zɔ̀ɔ wà !* mais comment, il a jeté un bâton sur moi ! ◊ *yɤ́ wó à zʉ̀ɤ dhɛ̀ dɛ̀dɛ̀ ɤ́ dhʌ́n bhā ɤ́ pɤ̀ à bhà bhā à gúɯ́* et ils l'ont jeté vers l'endroit où l'enfant était tombé **1.2** *vt* **jeter à**, **lancer à** *(qch – ká)◊ yɤ̀ bhàan-dhʉ̀n zʉ̀ɤ gwʌ̀ ká dhɛ́dhɛ́ plɛ̀ ká* ils jetaient des pierres aux oiseaux pendant deux heures **1.3** *vt* **jeter** *(se débarrasser, en parlant d'objets, mais non pas des liquides et des substances)◊ yà kʌ̄ dhɛ̀ yɤ̀ bʉ̀ dhún, kɤ̄ kwā dhɔ̀ à zʉ̀ɤ'* s'il venait à pourrir, nous le jetterions **2** *vt* **frapper brusquement avec** *(un instrument)◊ bɑ̋ŋ ɤ́' zʉ̀ɤ, yà tő kpɤ̄ bhɔ̀ bhūn wɛ́ bádhɤ̄* d'un coup de machette il lui a carrément coupé une oreille ! ◊ *bhlɑ̋a yà bhɔ̄ ɤ̄ zū ká, kɤ̄ yɤ̄ɤ ɤ̄ gɔ̀ zʉ̀ɤ* si in bélier recule, c'est pour frapper avec la tête **3** *vt* **servir à qn** *(vin) seulement dans l'expression suivante :* ♦ *bhá bhēn zʉ̀ɤ, yɤ́ ɯ́ ɯ̄ dɛ̀ zʉ̀ɤ pɤ́* quand tu sers les gens, sers-toi aussi **4** *vi* **faire du bruit** ◊ *yɯ́ yà pā yɤ́ zʉ̀ɤ* quand l'eau déborde, elle fait du bruit ◊ *kā zʉ̀ɤ kɔ́ɔdhɤ̄ yūudhɤ̄ dhɛ̀ ?* pourquoi faites-vous du bruit dans la maison ?

zʉ̀ɤ 2) ***n*** **coup** ◊ *yɯ́gā bhā à zʉ̀ɤ vɯ̀n yɤ̀ fɛ̀ɛsʉ̀* la chute d'eau fait un bruit étourdissant

zʉ̀tɑ̀kwɛ̀ɛ <laver-sur-bagage> ***n*** *rn, fn* **maquillage** *(produits)◊ yà ɤ̄ zʉ̀tɑ̀kwɛ̀ɛ gbɛ́ dhɔ́* elle s'est acheté beaucoup de produits de maquillage ◊ *à bhà zʉ̀tɑ̀kwɛ̀ɛ wɔ̀n yɤ̀ gbɛ̋ɛ̀* elle fait un usage excessif du maquillage

zʉ̀u ***n*** **esprit** *(méchant ou bon)* ♦ *zʉ̀u yāa yɤ̀ Zân tà* Zan est possédé par un esprit maléfique

zʉ̄ʉ̀ ***n*** ***Otus scops, O. senegalensis, O. kucopsis*** **petit-duc africain** *(taille : 18 cm; le plus petit des hiboux; ouïe fortement développée; brun, dessous marqué de longues stries noires)*

zūudhɤ̄ {Int. zūuudhɤ̄} *adv* **pensivement** ◊ *Sàó yɤ̈ yȁ-sīʌ zūudhɤ̄* Sao est assis pensivement

zūuudhɤ̄ *adv Int. de* zūudhɤ̄ *pensivement*

zúȕzȕ {A P S} *adj* **malpropre, peu soigneux** ◊ *sɔ̄ zúȕzȕ* habits fripés ◊ *ȁ bhȁ kɔ́ yɤ̈ zúȕzȕ ká* il est malpropre chez lui

zúȕzúdhɛ̏ *n* **1 malpropreté 2 injustice** ◊ *zúȕzúdhɛ̏ yáa sʌ̏* il n'est pas bon d'être injuste

zȕuzűu *n* **acte de secouer**; **cahotement** ◊ *dhűi bhā ȁ zȕuzűu kʌ̄* secoue cet arbre ◊ *gɔ̄ zȕuzűu ɤ́ kʌ̄-sīʌ bhā dhʌ̀n ȁ wɔ̏n gúi yɤ́ bhēn-dhȕn wó wɛ̋-sīʌ bhā* c'est le cahotement de la voiture qui a fait tant crier les gens

zűuzȕu {Int. Sg. zűkkűzȕkȕ, Int. Pl. zűuzűu} *adj* **louche** *(équivoque)* ◊ *bhēn zűuzűu yáa dȁ ī gɔ̏ kɔ́ɔdhɤ̄* que des gens louches n'entrent pas dans ma maison

zűuzűu *adj Int.Pl. de* zűuzȕu *louche*

zūűzūűdhɤ̄ {Int. zúzȕzúdhɤ̄} *adv* **d'une façon agitée**, **pêle-mêle** ◊ *Yɔ̏ yɤ̈ wɔ́n kʌ̏ zūűzūűdhɤ̄* Yo fait les affaires pêle-mêle ♦ *kʌ̄ zúzȕzúdhɤ̄* s'agiter

zȕzȕ *n* **termite** *(esp.; plus petites que les autres espèces; vivent dans le sous-sol; sortent en juillet, après le coucher du soleil; on les fait cuire et on les sèche au soleil pour enlever les ailes)*

zȕzȕgwɛ̏ *n* **monstre** *(féroce, d'une apparence horrible)*

zúzȕzúdhɤ̄ *adv Int. de* zūűzūűdhɤ̄ *pêle-mêle*

zȕi 1) {zȕizȕi Int.} *pp* **autour** ◊ *yí yȁ bàŋ pā yà wɛ̀nŋ' zȕi* l'eau a rempli la bassine en débordant de tous les côtés ◊ *wʌ́nŋ yɤ̈ zīɤ-sīʌ pʌ̄bhèe zȕizȕi* la mouche tourne en rond au-dessus de la nourriture

zȕi 2) *prev* **autour**

zūi 1) *n* **1** *rn* **bas, fond** *(partie inférieure)* ♦ *bàŋ zūi* fond de cuvette **2** *rn* **fesses** *(postérieur)* Syn. zūikpɤ̄, zūiúdhɛ̏ ♦ *bhɔ̄ zūi ká* reculer

zūi 2) *prev* **bas**

zúi {INT zúizúi} *adv* **1 encore** ◊ *ȁ bhá dhūn zúi* donne encore, donne l'autre ♦ *íin zúi* ... ou encore... **2** *avec la négation* **plus** ◊ *Zân yáa yʌ̄ kʌ̄ zúi* Zan ne travaille plus ◊ *yʌ́nŋ̏ yȁ bhēn gɔ̏ zìnŋgúi-dhɛ̏ yáa gblɛ̀ɛn zúi* il est bientôt midi **3 quand même** *(avec une négation)* ◊ *Zân yíi dhó zúi yʌ̄ kʌ̄'* Zan n'est pas allé au travail quand même

zūi-bhō {zūi-bhō} *v* **1.1** 1) *vi* **reprendre**, **recommencer** *(par, à cause de – tȁ)* ◊ *yʌ̄ zūi yà bhō* le travail a recommencé 2) *vt* **reprendre** *(par – tȁ)* ◊ *kêkʌ̄bhɛ̏n yà yʌ̄ zūi-bhō* l'agriculteur a recommencé le travail ◊ *ȁ zūi ɤ́ bhāan' bhō bhā, ā dhȍ zūi-bhō' sɛ́ wɔ̏n tȁ* en reprenant la parole, c'est par l'affaire concernant la terre que je commencerai **1.2** (t) 1) *vi* **commencer** *(par, à cause de – tȁ)* 2) *vt* **commencer** *(par – tȁ)* ◊ *yɤ́ ɤ̄ kwɛ̀ɛ dhú-sȕi zūi-bhō* et il a commencé à faire ses bagages **2** *vt* **répéter** *(parole, action)*

zūbhō-dhɛ̏ ***n*** **début**

zūbhōwɔ̏ <commencer-voix> ***n*** *neol.* **voyelle**

zū̄-dān {zū̄-dān} ***v vt*** **faire apprendre à s'asseoir** *(petit enfant)*

zūdhí <bas-bouche> ***n rn*** **anus**

zūgbȁngɯ́ <bas-enfoncer-dans> ***n*** **source de puissance**

zȕ-klʌ̏ʌn ***v vt*** **clôturer**

zūkpɤ̄ <bas-boule> ***n rn*** **fesses** *(postérieur)* *Syn.* zū ♦ *ȁ zūkpɤ̄ yɤ̏ gbɛ́ɛ ká dhɛ̀ dháȁ dhɤ́* son derrière est large comme un van *[signe de beauté chez les Dan]* ♦ *ȁ zūkpɤ̄ yɤ̏ sɛ̄ɛ́ndhʌ́n ká dhɛ̀ sɛ̀dhágā dhɤ́* son derrière est étroit comme une aiguille

zū̄n, **zūn** {zū̄n, zūn} ***v*** **1.1** *vi* **parvenir** ♦ *zūn kpɛ́nŋ, zūn kpɛ́nŋdhɤ́* sortir dehors ◊ *fɛ́ŋ yíi zūn kpɛ́nŋ* aucun rat ne s'est montré dehors ♦ *zū̄n kó dhɤ́* finaliser ♦ *wɔ́n bhā yà zūn kó dhɤ́* cette affaire est réglée ◊ *Gbȁtȍ yȁ ɤ̄ bhā dɤ̄ŋ-dhȕn gȁ yȁ' zū̄n kó dhɤ́* Zan a examiné ses pièges, il a fait le tour ◊ *dhó kɤ̄ ɯ́ zūn bhū̄n kɯ́ɯ dhū̄n* va jusque là et reviens **1.2** *vi* **venir chez** *(qn – bhȁ)* ◊ *Tìa yɤ̏ zȕn ɤ̄ dhòo tɛ́ɛdō bhȁ kɤ̄ yɤ̏ ɤ̄ gbā yʌ̄ ká* Tia est venu chez un ami de son frère aîné, pour qu'il lui donne du travail **2** *vi* **rendre visite** *(à – dhɛ̏)* **3** *vi* **toucher** *(qch – bhȁ)* **4** *vi* **se mettre** *(à – bhȁ)* *Syn.* ɤ̄ dhí dȁ ... gɯ́, yȁ ... bhȁ, yɤ̄ ... bhȁ, zū̄-bhō **5** *vi* **retenir**, **bloquer** *(empêcher de partir, de passer; qn – dhɤ́)* ♦ *sɛ́ yà zūn ȁ dhɤ́* il est parti à l'aventure et n'est pas revenu (mais il est en vie) **6** *vi* **s'emparer** *(de – tȁ)*

zȕndhɤ́bhlɔ̏ɔ, **zȕndhɤ́bhlɔ̏ɔ** <atteindre-devant-réponse à devinette> ***n rn*** **avenir** *(de qn, comme raison d'être)* ◊ *ȁ zȕndhɤ́bhlɔ̏ɔ yáa dhɤ́* il n'a pas d'avenir

zɯ́ɯ ***n*** ***Sida acuta*** **arbre** *(esp.; les branches sont utilisées pour les balais)* *Syn.* sɛ̏nŋgā (sɛ̏nŋ)

zūɯ́dhɛ̏ {LOC zūɯ́dhɤ̄} ***loc.n rn*** **fesses** *(postérieur)*

zūɯ́dhɤ̄ ***loc.n*** *Loc. de* zūɯ́dhɛ̏ *fesses*

zȕzȕ *Int. de* zȕ *autour*

zɯ́zɯ́ ***adv*** *Int. de* zɯ́ *encore*

Index français-dan de l'Est

L'Index est un outil supplémentaire, il ne peut pas du tout être considéré comme un vrai dictionnaire français-dan. Pour avoir l'information sur le sémantisme et l'utilisation du mot dan (mais aussi du mot français), il est fortement recommandé de consulter le dictionnaire dan-français.

Seuls les variantes phonétiques principaux des lexèmes dan sont données.

Les sens des lexèmes français sont parfois désambiguïsés, mais cela n'est pas systématique.

Les pronoms personnels et les marques prédicatives sont exclus de l'Index.

Les noms français sont suivis des marques de leur genre grammatical : *m* pour le masculin, *f* pour le féminin, *mpl* pour le masculin pluriel et *fpl* pour le féminin pluriel.

A a

à **gɔ̀, ká, pɯ́ɤ**
abachi **dhɔ̄ɔ̀**
abandon *m* **bhɛ̄nkɔ̀kàngɯ́ɯ**
abandonner **gó**
abandonner l'affaire **kɔ̀ bhō wɔ́n gɯ́ɯ,** il a abandonné sa femme **yà ɤ̄ bhā dhēbʌ̀ bhō bɯ̋ɯ**
abattre, être abattu **bɔ̄,** la fièvre m'abat **dhɛ̋ndhɛ̋n yà dhūn n̄ tà**
abeille *f* **zɔ̋**
abîmer **sɛ̄ɛ̀**
abondant **plʌ̄ʌ̀**
abonder : être en abondance **gɔ̄ɔn**
aborder : on ne sait pas comment aborder ce problème **dhīaŋ bhā, kɔ̀kúndhɛ̀ yáa à bhà**
aboyer : le chien aboie aux gens **gbên yɤ̀ wɛ̀-sɪʌ bhɛ̄n-dhùn bhà**
abri *m* **bɔ̄ɔ̋**
abruti **bhɔ̋ɔnbhɔ̀ɔn**
abuser **tà-bɤ̀**
acajou *m* **bhɯ̋ʌʌ**
accepter qch **à ɗàa kʌ̄, ɤ̄ kɔ̀ yà à bhà, wɛ̋ … bhà**
accompagnateur de masque **gèe bhà kɪ́ʌʌ**
accompagner **dɔ̄**
accord *m* **ɗàa,** et ils se sont mis d'accord **yɤ́ ɤ̀-dhùn wɔ̀ ɤ́ kʌ̀ dō,** être en accord **slòo,** tomber d'accord **bhɔ̀ɔn**
accordailles *fpl* **tɔ̋ŋ̄dhēɛ̋dhɛ̀**
accouchement **bɔ̋**
accoucher **bɔ̋ bhɔ̄, kpɔ́, slɔ̀ɔ**
accrocher **dhʌnŋ**
accroître : s'accroître **ɗà dhɪ́ɤ**
accueillir **būn, dhɛ̀ŋ-kún**
accumuler : s'accumuler **ɗūn**
accusation *f* **gbā, yǽŋ́, zā**
accuser qn de qch **wɔ́n yà bhɛ̄n bhà**
acheter **dhɔ́,** acheter en gros **kɛ̋n**
acheteur *m* **dhɔ̋ɔdhɔ́bhɛ̀n**
achever **dhɪ́ɤ-dɔ̄, dhɪ́ɤ-tā, dhɪ́ɤ-tó, gɔ̀-dɔ̄, tà-dɔ̄,** achève-le **à zʌ̄ dō,** s'achever **yʌ̄n**
acquitter : il a été acquitté **à bhà zā yà dhī**
adhérer **ɗà,** j'ai adhéré à l'association de travail **bhán ɗà bɛ̋nkpɤ̀ gɯ́ɯ**
adjectif *m* **sūu**
admettre *(dans un établissement d'éducation)* **ɤ̄ kɔ̀ yà à bhà**
adolescent *m* **dhʌ́nwlɯ̄ɯ̋sɯ̀**
adoration : objet *m* d'adoration **gbāpʌ̀**
adorer **dhɔ̀-kʌ̄, gbā**
adoucir **zɔ̀ɔnŋ**

adresse *f* **dléɛsɯ̀,** *(habileté)* **tɤ́ŋ**
adresser : s'adresser **lòo**
adverbe *m* **kʌ̄kɔ̀**
adversaire *m* **yœ́œ̀**
aéroport *m* **víɔ̀ŋsó**
affaibli **fɤ́ɤfɤ̀ɤ**
affaire *f* **dhīaŋ, wɔ́n, yàkɛ̀,** affaire futile **yʌ́nzìɤgɯ́**
affamé : rester affamé **tó dīn ká**
affectation *f* **sɪ́ʌ̀ʌ**
affliger **yɛ́**
affluent *m* **yí gbɛ̀ŋ**
afin que **kʌ̀dhɤ́kɤ̀**
Africain *m*, Africaine *f* **bhēntīi**
agacer : qui agace les dents **glɯ́ɯ́kɔ́glɯ̀ɯ̀kɔ̀**
âge *m* **kwɛ̀,** gens du même âge **tɛ́ebhʌ́nzʌ̀-dhɯ̀n,** quel âge a-t-il? **à kwɛ̀ yɤ̀ dhɛ̀?**
agenouiller : il s'est agenouillé **yà yà ɤ̄ kpīɤ̀ɤ gɯ́**
agent *m* de police *f* **zàŋ**
agglutiner : s'agglutiner **dɔ̄**
agir: agir avec **kʌ̄,** agir contre **yà,** agir en bonne entente, agir ensemble **bhɔ̀ɔn**
agitation *f* **vùuvɯ́u**
agité : être agité **bhɔ̄,** d'une façon agitée **zūúzūúdhɤ̄,** s'agiter **kʌ̄ zúzùzúdhɤ̄**
agouti *m* **sɔ́ɔ**
agréable **dhíasɯ̀**
agrumes *mpl* **dhɤ̄ŋ̀, sɛ̄ɛ́**
ah **ɔ̄ɔ́, ʌ̄́**
aider **dɔ̄, tà-kún,** aider à monter **ɤ̄ kɔ̀ yà à bhà,** aider à mettre la charge sur la tête **dɔ̄, tà-dɔ̄**
aïe **zɔ̀ɔ, ììyà, wà**
aigle *m* de Wahleberg **sīì**
aigre **kpɔ̀nsɯ̀**
aigrette *f* dimorphe **yípíɤdhɔ̀ŋdhɔ̀ŋ**
aigrir **gīì,** s'aigrir **kpɔ̀n**
aigu **bhlʌ́ʌŋ**
aiguille *f* **sèdhá,** aiguille de la montre **yʌ́nŋ̀kó bhà sèdhágā,** il est maigre comme une aiguille **yɤ̀ kpɛ̄́ɛ ká dhè sèdhá(ga̋) dhɤ**
aiguisé : bien aiguisé et brillant **dɛ̀nŋdɛ̀nŋdhɤ̄**
aiguiser **dhíɤ-bɔ̄**
ail *m* **āáyì**
aile *f* **gbān, gbɛ̄ɛ́n,** aile *f* d'insecte **kāà**
aimant *m* naturel **kpágwʌ̀**
aimé : le plus aimé parmi les gens **bhēn-dhɯ̀n dhɔ̄ɔ́bhàabhɛ̀n**
aimer : l'homme aime cela **à dhɔ̀ yɤ̀ bhēn kʌ̀,** Y a beaucoup aimé X **X dhía yà bhán Y gɯ́,** ils se sont aimés **à-dhɯ̀n dhɔ̀ dhɤ kó kʌ̀**
aîné **gbàŋ, gblɤ́gblɤ́, kpīì**
ainsi **dhìn, dhɤ́,** ainsi donc **dhè ɤ́ dhɤ́,** ainsi donc, pour cette raison **à kʌ̀ dhɤ́-sɯ̀ bhā à gɯ́**
air *m* **tʌ́ŋ̀, tɛ́ɛ,** l'air est froid (comme en Europe en hiver) **tɛ́ɛ yɤ̀ sɛ̀ɛ dhɛ́ndhɛ́n kœ̄œ**
airain *m* **zʌ̄n**
aisance *f* **flʌ́ʌ̀bhōdhē,** il jouit de respect et d'aisance **yɤ̀ bhēn-dhɛ̀ kʌ̄-sɪʌ**
aisé : personne aisée **pʌ̄bhɛ̀n**
aisselle *f* **yɔ́nŋ̀dhɛ̀**
ajuster en frappant **dhíɤ-bhàn**
albinos *m* **gbàŋ, gbàŋ bhɛ̀n,** albinos blanc **gbàŋ pɯ́u,** albinos homme **gbàŋ gɔ̄n,** albinos roux **gbàŋ zœ̀œndhē**
alcoolique *m* **wēbhɯ̄ndùdù**
allégresse *f* **yɔ̋o**
aller **dhó,** aller bien **dhī,** s'en aller **gó,** aller à la guerre **glɯ̀ sɯ́,** aller *(être de la bonne taille)* **bhɔ̀ɔn,** allons ! *(une invitation polie à l'action)* **dhɛ̀,** va-t-en! **gó bhā!**
alliance *f* **dhʌ̀nŋkwʌ́ʌ̀, dhʌ̀nŋkwʌ́ʌ̀dhē,** *(entre des groups des parents)* **bhlɛ̀ɛn**
allumer **pú, dhí-pɔ̋,** s'allumer **pú,** allumer le feu **pɛ̄ŋ yà,** allumer la torche, le flambeau **gbíaa dɔ̄, sɔ̋nŋ dɔ̄**

allumette *f* **táklāa gā,** allumettes **táklāa**
aloko *m* **dhòokô**
alors **kɤ̄,** alors que **yāá**
alphabet *m* **sʌ́ʌdhɛ̄yāngākpɤ̄**
aluminium *m* **fɔ̄ŋ**
amant *m* **bhlàànbʌ̀**
amante *f* **dhɔ̄nbʌ̀,** son amante la plus aimée **à bhà dhɔ̄nbʌ̀ dhɔ̄ɔbhàa-sɯ̀**
amarante *m* commun **fèe, kàsʌ̄ʌtīi**
amateur de viande **bhúkʌ̄bhɛ̀n**
ambassadeur *m* **yāngā**
âme *m* **dhīìn**
amélioration **fīʌʌ**
amende *f* **gbāpʌ̄, tɔ́ŋ, tɔ́ŋpʌ̄, yǣŋ,** payer l'amende **tɔ́ŋpʌ̄ gó, gbāpʌ̄ gó,** tu dois payer une amende **ɯ̄ dhɤ̀ tɔ́ŋ kʌ̄',** il a payé l'amende **yà pʌ̄ gó**
amener **dà ɤ̄ kèŋ, dhūn … ká**
amer **glɯ̄ɯ**
Américain **Bhlɛ̀ɛnkên**
ami *m* **tɛ̄ɛdō, tœ̄œŋdʌ̄**
amie *f* **tɛ̄ɛdō**
amitié *f* **dhìkó-dhɛ̀, bhlɛ̀ɛn, tœ̄œŋdʌ̄-dhɛ̀, tœ̄œŋdhē-dhɛ̀**
amollir : s'amollir **zɔ̀ɔ**
amorce *f* **yà pīɤ̀ dhīɤ pʌ̀**
amour *m* **dhɔ̀, dhía, tœ̄œŋdhē-dhɛ̀**
ampoule *f* **dhùu,** j'ai une ampoule à la main **ñ kɔ̀ yà dhùu dɔ̄**
amulette *f* **dhɯ̄dhɛ̄**
amusement *m* **tlōo**
an *m* **kwɛ̀**
ananas *m* **dhàandháàn, dhàŋtlàa**
ancêtre *m* **bhɛ̄bhán, kwɛ̀ɛ**
ancien **zīi, zīisì**
âne *m* **sòòfʌ̄ŋ**
anéantir : il les a anéantis **yà à-dhùn dà bɯ̄**
ange *m* **Zlàan bhà kíʌʌ**
angine *f* **zlūu bhìʌʌ**
anguille *f* électrique **gbìŋgbɤ̄**
animal *m* **wɯ̄ɓ** animal domestique **tɯ̀ɤɤpʌ̀**
anneau *m* à cachet **kœ̄œŋpʌ̀pɛ̄ɛpɛ̀ɛ**
anneau *m* d'argent **wʌ́ʌ̀kɔ̀bhàpʌ̄**
année *f* **kwɛ̀,** cette année **kwɛ̄ɛ,** l'année dernière **kwɛ̀ ɤ́ zìɤ à ká**
anniversaire *m* **kwɛ̀yɤ̀kódhíɤ**
anomalure à dos rouge **vɤ̄ɤ̄**
anse *f* **gʌ̄n,** anse de marmite **gbɔ̄ gʌ̄n,** anse *f* de seau **gbɔ̄ŋgbɔ̄ gʌ̄n**
antilope *f* guib **zlòo**
antilope *m* royale **bhìʌ**
anus *m* **zūdhí**
août *m* **zɛ̄**
apathique **slɔ̄ɔslɔ̀ɔ, wɔ̄ɔnwɔ̀ɔn**
aplati **kplɛ̂kplɛ̀,** il a un nez aplati **à yūn yɤ̀ dhʌ̀nŋ sīāa-sɯ̀ ká**
apostrophe *f* **dhɯ̄dhʌ́n**
apparaître **bhán, dà, kpɔ́, wɔ̀,** *(gale, éruption)* **bhā, lòo,** il est réapparu **yà wɔ̀ yɛ̄ɛ̀**
apparence *f* **kpɤ̄ɤ**
appartement *m* **kódhí**
appauvrir : il s'est appauvri **yà kʌ̄ flɛ̄ɛsɯ̀**
appel au secours **tábhōo**
appel *m* **dhɛ̀ɛdhíɤ, dhìɔɔ**
appeler **dhɛ̀,** *(nommer)* **kʌ̄,** *(au téléphone)* **pìɤgā bhàn bhɛ̄n dhɛ̀,** s'appeler **pɤ̄**
applaudir qn/qch **ɤ̄ kwɛ̄ɛ̄ kún à bhà**
apporter **dhūn … ká**
apprendre **dlāàn, dɔ̄**
apprenti *m*, *f* **kāyɛ́ɛ̀dhʌ́n, plàŋtīì**
apprentissage *m* **kāyɛ́ɛ̀-dhɛ̀**
apprêter, s'apprêter **bāá**
approche *f* **kɔ̀kúndhɛ̀,** approche furtive **dhān**
approcher **yɔ̀ɔn,** être à l'approche **dūn,** s'approcher **gán, tʌ̀ŋ, yɔ̀ɔn,** s'approcher furtivement **dhān-kʌ̄**
approximativement **dhɛ̀ pʌ̄ dhɤ́**
appui *m* **gbàn**

appuyer : s'appuyer **dhʌnŋ, tān,** il s'est appuyé sur sa canne **yà tàadhɯ̀ɯ gbàn ɤ̄ gɔ̀,** appuyer sa main sur **ɤ̄ kɔ̀ yɤ̄ à tà**

après **kèŋ̀, tàabhàn,** après cela **à zīaan gɯ́ɯ,** peu de temps après cela **à dhɛ̀ kʌ̀ zlʌ̄ʌdhɤ̄**

arachide *f* **gwɛ̃ɛ**

araignée *f* **dɔ́ɔ̀n, zìŋtɔ̃ŋ**

arbitrage *m* : faire l'arbitrage **zā gɔ̀-bhō**

arbre *m* **dhɯ̃ɯ,** arbre fruitier **bhɤ̀ dhɯ̀ɯ,** arbre iroko **gɤ̀ɤ̀ dhɯ̀ɯ,** arbre *m* résineux **kpēɛnŋdhɯ̀ɯ**

arbres, espèces : **dɛ́ŋ, dĩiŋ, dlīŋ̀, dɤ́ɤ̀, gèeɗàbhàdhɯ̀ɯ, gɛ̀ɛgɛ̀ɛ, glɯ̃ɯ, gɔ̀ŋ, kāãn, kɛ̄ɛ, klĩnŋ̀, klĩnŋ̀bhēɛn, klĩnŋ̀gbōkún, kpɛ́ŋ̀ dhɯ̀ɯ, sóŋ̀, tö, tɔ̃ŋ, tû, vân, yʌ̃ŋ, yōdhɔ̂n, zɔ́ɔ̀, zɤ̄ŋkɔ́dɔ̀bhàdhɯ̀ɯ, zūàglɯ̃ɯ, bhɯ̃ʌʌ, gbô, kpàa, pēn, gāŋ̀, gīi, gō, gbân, glɤ̀, gbœ̀œ, kpɛ́ɛn, pāa, sʌ̄nŋ, slɤ̄ɤdhʌ́n, tēŋ, wā, wlɛ̃ŋ, wlɔ̀ŋ, yɛ̃ɛn, zāà, zɔ̃ŋ, zɯ̃ɯ**

arbrisseau *m* **bhēnkpàdhɛ̀**

arbuste *f* **dhɯ̃ɯdhʌ́n gbʌ̂gbʌ̀**

arbustes, espèces : **sékùtūlē, bhlɔ̀ɔ, yʌ̃nŋdhɯ̃ɯ**

arc *m* **sœ́œ̀,** arc *m* musical **gàŋ**

arc-en-ciel *m* **dhā kpɤ̀ŋ, kpɤ̀ŋ**

arc-en-terre **tɛ́kpɛ̃dhē**

archer *m* **sœ́œ̀bhīn**

arête *f* de poisson *m* **yúɤ̀ glɛ̃ɛn**

argent *m* **wʌ́ʌ̀, wʌ́ʌ̀gā,** argent *m (métal)* **zʌ̄n pɯ̃u,** argent sale, argent mal acquis **wʌ́ʌ̀gā dhìisɯ̀ɯ**

argile *f* **gbɛ̄ɛ̃, sɛ̃**

armée *f* **glɯ̀ɯ**

arôme maggi **sɯ̃nbhãndhãn**

arracher **bhō, wɔ̀**

arrêter **dɔ́ɔ̀ndhūn, dhíɤ-dō, dhíɤ-dɔ́ɔ̀ndhūn, dhíɤ-gbáàndhūn, dhíɤ-tó, gbáàndhūn, tà-kãn,** s'arrêter **dō, dɔ́ɔ̀ndhūn, dhʌnŋ, dhíɤ-tó, gbáàndhūn**

arrière-arrière-grand-père *m* **zíɤ̀ɤ gɯ́ɯ zìɤɤ gɯ́ɯ zíɤ̀ɤ**

arrière-grand-père *m* **zíɤ̀ɤ gɯ́ɯ zíɤ̀ɤ**

arrière-petite-fille **bhāadhʌ́n**

arrière-petit-enfant *m* **bhāadhʌ́n gɯ́ɯ bhāadhʌ́n**

arrière-petit-fils **bhāadhʌ́n**

arriver **lòo, wɔ̀,** l'eau arrive à la tête de l'homme **yí yɤ̀ bhēn gɔ̀ɔ,** l'eau arrive aux aisselles **yí yɤ̀ bhēn kùn bhēn yɔ́nŋ̀dhɤ̄,** l'eau arrive aux chevilles **yí dhíɤ yɤ̀ tò bhēn gɛ̀nwēngā bhà,** l'eau arrive aux côtes **yí yɤ̀ bhēn kùn bhēn sɛ̃nŋ̀dhɤ̄,** l'eau arrive aux cuisses **yí yɤ̀ bhēn kùn bhēn gbãnbhlʌ̃ bhà,** l'eau arrive aux épaules des gens **yí yɤ̀ bhēn kùn bhēn gbān bhà,** l'eau arrive aux genoux **yí yɤ̀ bhēn kùn bhēn kpīɤ̀ɤgɔ̀ bhà,** sa barbe arrive jusqu'à la poitrine **à bhúʌ̀ʌ yɤ̀ lòo à tòŋ tà**

arroser **wènŋ**

arrosoir **ālōzóà**

artère *f* **bhìʌʌn**

arthrite *f* **gāgúɯyùa**

articulation *f* du doigt **kœ̄œŋgā kpɤ̄**

ascaride *m* **bhīʌ̃**

asphalt *m* **gūdlɔ́nŋ̀**

asseoir : s'asseoir **yà, yáàdhūn,** être assis **yà,** asseyez-vous! **kwā wɛ̀ɛ bhɯ̀n,** faire apprendre à s'asseoir **zɯ̄ɯ-dān,** faire asseoir **yáàdhūn**

asseoir : il y a de la place! **kwā wɛ̀ɛ bhɯ̀n**

assiette *f* **sɛ̃tí**

assistant **kɔ̀wlɤ̀ɤ**

assister **bhō**

association *f* **kɔ̀lòokótà,** association *f* de travail *m* **bãn, bãnkpɤ̄, kêkpɤ̄**

assombrir : s'assombrir **tlɤ̀ɤ**

assourdissant **gbēēgbēegbēēdhɤ̄**
asthme *m* **tɛ̃ŋsíyɯ̀a**
asticot *m* **gbīnŋgā, yùun**
astuce *f* **slʌ̃**
athérure *m* africain **tɛ̃**
attacher **dhú, kɛ̃n, kplɯ̀, lɤ̀,** attacher : s'attacher **kplɯ̀,** Sao est très attaché à Yo **Yɔ̀ yà Sàó tɤ̀ɤ̀ sɯ́**
attaquer **pɤ̀**
atteindre **bhō, bhɔ̀ɔn, dhíɤ-tó, dhó, kún, lòo, sɯ́, yɤ̄,** l'eau atteint les oreilles **yí yɤ̀ bhēn kɯ̀n bhēn tɔ̃ dhɛ̃ bhà**
attelle *f* **sàa**
attendre **dō, dɔ́ɔ̀ndhūn, dhíɤ-gɛ̃n, yà, yɛ̃n-tó,** je t'attendrai **n̄ yɛ̃n yɤ̀ ɯ̄ gɔ̀**
attentif : être attentif **wɔ́n súàn bhō**
attention *f* **súàn,** *f* **tɤ̃ŋ,** appeler l'attention **flî dà,** demande d'attention **flî,** faire attention **kún,** fais attention à cela! **ɤ̄ dè kún à bhà!** prêter attention à **tɤ̃ŋ kʌ̄ à gɯ́**
attentivement **sɛ̃ɛnŋdhɤ̄**
attraper **dō, kún,** attraper au vol **sʌ́n,** attraper le palu **gɔ̃ŋ slɔ̀ɔ,** attrapez-le! **kà dō' gɔ̀!**
attrister : il m'a attristé **yà n̄ zūʌ̃ gìi**
au lieu de **gblɔ̃o, sɛ̃ndhìn**
au moins **dhʌ́nbháwō**
au revoir! **kwā yī plèɛ bhà ! kō tàabhàn !**
aube : à l'aube **dhè ɤ́ dō dhèkpœ̀œ dhíɤ**
aubergine *f* **pènŋ, zóŋ̀**
aucun **bhá**
aucunement **tōŋtōŋdhɤ̄**
au-delà **zlɤ̀ɤ**
au-dessus de **tà**
aujourd'hui **dèɛ**
aulacode *m* **sɔ̃ɔ**
aumône *f* **gbœ̄œdhē**
auprès de **sɔ̃ɔ**
aussi **pɤ́, zʌ̀wō**
aussitôt que... **dhè ɤ́..., dhè kɤ́...**
automobile *f* **gō**
autorité *f* **gbɛ̃è-dhɛ̀,** autorité *f* morale **wɔ́ngɔ̀tābhɛ̀n**
autour *m* à longue queue **bɔ̀bí**
autour *m* gabar, autour *m* tachiro **slàan**
autour de **vlɯ̀ɯndhɤ̄, zɯ̀**
autre **bhá, wɛ̃ɛ, wɛ̃ɛwɛ̃,** l'autre **dōdhàan, dhɛ́**
autrefois **bè, kpá, kwèŋzɯ́, ɤ́ gūn kpá**
avaler **bhʌ̃nŋ**
avancer **bhō, yɔ̀ɔn, tɛ̃ sɯ́,** avance! **dhó dhíɤ!**
avant **blɛ̀ɛsɯ̀, dhíɤ**
avant de **sɛ̃ndhìn**
avant-hier **yāandhíɤ tàabhàn**
avant-toit **kɔ́ sɛ̃ɛ**
avare **dɤ̃ŋdɤ̀ŋ,** il est très avare **à kɔ̀ yáa wɔ̀**
avarice *f* **gàsítɛ́ɛ̀**
avec **ká**
avenir *m* **yībhɛ̃, zɯ̀ndhíɤbhlɔ̀ɔ**
aventure : il est parti à l'aventure **yɤ́ ɤ̄ bhā dà wō sɛ̃ píɤ,** il est parti à l'aventure et n'est pas revenu (mais il est en vie) **sɛ̃ yà zūn à dhíɤ**
avertissement *m* **véè**
aveugle : devenir aveugle **wɯ́**
aveugler **tlɤ̄ɤ**
avion *m* **gōbhàan, víɔŋ̀**
avis : à son avis **à bhà gɯ́**
avocat *m (juriste)* **dhīaŋdhɯ̃sɯ́bhɛ̀n, vòokāà**
avocat *m (fruit)* **vòkāà**
avoir lieu **kʌ̄, tó**
avril *m* **gblɔ̀gōn**
awalé *m (un jeu)* **bhāan**
ayous *(un grand arbre)* **dhōò**

B b

bâchée *f* **yà-kwʌ́ʌ̀-kʌ̀-à-gɯ́-gɔ̀**
bacille *m (insecte)* **gādhɯ̃**
badigeonner **gīì**

badine *f* **klȁa**
bagage *m* **kwɛ̏ɛ̏**
bagarre *f* **dhı́dhȁan, gɔ̏n, kó**
bagarrer (se) **gɔ̏n gɔ̄ɔn,** Zan s'est bagarré avec Yo **Zân yȁ kó yȁ Yɔ̏ bhȁ,** ils se bagarrent **wɔ̏ kó zʌ̄-sɪʌ,** se bagarrer à cause de qn **kó zʌ̄ ȁ tȁ**
bagatelle *f* **kɔ̏kèetȁwɔ̏n**
bague *f* **kɔ̄ŋgāȁpʌ̏, kœ̄œŋ̏pʌ̏, yȁkɔ̏dhʌ́ngābhȁpʌ̏**
baguette de tambour *m* **gɔ̄dhűű**
baigner : se baigner **zű**
bâillement *m* **wa̋a**
bâiller **wa̋a bhō**
balafre *f* **wɛ̄ŋgā**
balai *m* **pȉa, sɛ̏nŋ**
balance *f* **kı́dhɔ̋ŋ**
balancement *m* **bàŋba̋ŋ, bhìinbhı̋ın, ta̋n, tùuntűun**
balancer **bhìinbhı̋ın-kʌ̄**
balançoire *f* **sı̀bhı̀ʌŋ**
balayage *m* **dhɛ̏ gblɤ̏-sȕı**
balayer **gblɤ̏, wlɤ̏**
bale *f* **fòo**
balisier *m* **bhɔ̄ŋ̋dhɛ̋**
balle de feuilles et chiffons **dhɛ̋kpɤ̄, péŋ̏kpɤ̄**
balle *f (de fusil)* **būugā, gbɤ̋ŋgā**
balle *f (enveloppe des grains de riz)* **fòo**
ballon *m* **bàdhóŋ̏, dhɤ̏ɤkpɤ̄**
ballonnement *m* **kpū**
ballonner : son ventre est ballonné **ȁ gú yà dɔ̄ ȁ dhı́ɤ**
ballot *m* **bɛ̏, bhūnŋ**
bambou *m (de Chine)* **gbœ̄œ**
banal **bhȁasȕı**
banane *f* **glɔ̄ɔ,** banane douce **tɔ̋glɔ̏ɔ,** banane *f* poyo **kwı́ glɔ̄ɔ, kwı́ ȁ glɔ̄ɔ,** banane plantain **pìaaglɔ̏ɔ,** banane sauvage **glɔ̄ɔtii,** sorte de banane plantain **gbáȁ**
banc *m* **báŋ̏**
banc *m* de poissons **yúɤ̏ kpɤ̄**
banco *m* **bɤ̏ɤ̏**
bandage *m* **sɔ̄pɛ̋**
bande : une bande de tissu, fabriqué sur un métier traditionnel **sɔ̄ gú,** bande *f* de tissu *m* **pɛ̋n, sɔ̄pɛ̋,** bande *f* d'étoffe **sɔ̄ pɛ̋n,** bande obtenue avec la tige de liane coupée dans le sens du fil **gȁ pɛ̋n**
bandit *m* **bàandı̂,** bandit *m* de grand chemin **zīaanka̋nbhɛ̏n**
bandoulière : mettre le fusil en bandoulière **būu wɔ̄ ɤ̄ tàa**
banque *f* **báŋkɤ̏, wʌ̋ʌ̏kɔ̏**
baobab *m* **bīɤdhȕı, gwɛ̄**
baoum **gblȁdhɤ̄, gbūuŋdhɤ̄**
baptiser le village **tɔ́ yȁ pɤ̏ bhȁ**
barbe *f* **bhúʌ̏ʌ,** barbes de plume **pı́ʌʌnpı̏ʌʌn**
barbeau *m* **bhæ̋æŋgā**
barbican *m* à bec denté **dhűűzʌ̄kpȁŋglɔ̏ɔ**
barbu *m* **bhúʌ̏ʌ bhɛ̏n, bhúʌ̏ʌsȕı**
barbu *m* chauve *(un oiseau)* **bhɛ̄ŋ̏**
barbu *m* hérissé *(un oiseau)* **wlűubhōdhɛ̏**
bariolé **yʌ̋nŋyʌ̏nŋ**
barrage *m* **bàdhâsȕı, yı́ gbâ**
barre *f* fixe **sı̀bhı̀ʌŋ**
barrer la route de qn **dɔ̄ bhɛ̄n gɔ̏ yâ**
barrir : l'éléphant barrit **bīɤ yɤ̏ wɛ̋-sɪʌ**
bas *(voix)* **gbȁŋ**
bas **gbʌ̂gbʌ̏, kplɛ̂kplɛ̏**
bas *m (partie basse)* **zȕū**
bas : en bas **bàŋdhɤ̄, bhɛ̄ɛ̋dhɤ̄**
bas *m* : en-bas **wlɤ̏ɤdhɛ̏**
basalte *m* **wɛ̄**
base d'une maison **kɔ́ kpūú**
bas-fond *m* **báȁ**
bassine *f* **bàŋ,** bassine *f* métallique **yȁŋga̋dhı́ɤ**
bas-ventre *m* **vɛ̄ɛ̋dhɛ̏**
batailleur **sı̀ɤ̏ɤ**
bâtard *m* **tóȍtȁdhʌ̏n**

bateau *m* **yítàgɔ̀**
bâtiment *m* **kɔ́**
bâtir **dɔ̄**
bâton *m* **dhɯ̋ɯ kplá̋, dhɯ̋ɯdhʌ́n,** bâton *m* flexible **kpē̋ɛ̋,** bâton *m* flexible *(d'un piège)* **dɤ̄ŋ kpē̋ɛ̋**
bâtonnet *m* **dhɯ̋ɯdhʌ́n**
battant de la porte **kpóŋ̀**
battre **bhàn, gɔ̀-kʌ̄,** se battre pour sa part **tà-kɔ̄ɔ̀**
bavard : il est bavard **yɤ̀ dhīaŋ zʌ̀ tlɔ̀ɔdhɤ̄**
bave *f* **dhídhí vɯ̋u**
baver : Gbato est en train de baver **Gbàtò dhídhí bhɔ̄-sīʌ**
beau **dhíasɯ̀, sʌ̀**
beau *m (parent par alliance)* **zíɤ̀ɤ**
beaucoup **bɤ̋ɤwɛ̋, gbɛ́**
beau-fils *m* **gbɤ̄**
beau-frère *m* **dhìnbhɔ̋ɔ̀n, gbɤ̄, yɔ̀bhīn,** beau-frère *m* cadet **bhá, gɔ̀n**
beau-père *m* **yɔ̀, yɔ̀bhīn, zíɤ̀ɤ**
beauté *f* **dhī, dhía-dhɛ̀, sʌ̀-dhɛ̀,** sa beauté **à kpʌ̄ʌ dhī**
beaux-parents *mpl* cadets **dhìnbhɔ̋ɔ̀nzʌ̀-dhɯ̀n**
bébé *m* **dɛ̀edhʌ́n**
bec *m* **bɛ̀n**
bêe **ŋ̄bhɛ́ɛɛ̀**
bégaiement : son bégaiement est horrible **à bhà pʌ̄ bhɯ̀n zɔ̀ɔ-sɯ̀ ká**
bégayer **zɔ̀ɔ,** bégayer : il s'est arrêté bloqué **yà dɔ̄ ɤ̄ gúɯ kūkkūdhɤ̄**
beignet *m* **flùu pɛ̋n, flùu, flùuflúù**
bêler : le mouton a bêlé **bhlá̋a yɤ̀ wɛ̀ n̄bhɛ́ɛɛ̀**
belle-mère *f* **dà, dhá̋n, yɔ̀, yɔ̀dhē**
belle-sœur *f* **yɔ̀dhē,** belle-sœur *f* cadette **dhēbʌ̀,** sœur aînée du mari **dhá̋n,** sœur *f* cadette de la femme *f* **dhìnbhɔ̋ɔ̀n**
belliqueux **sìɤ̀ɤ**
bénédiction *f* **dhúʌ̀ʌ, yíkpɔ́dhē**
bénéfice *m* **tlɔ̀ɔn**
bercer **būn**
berge *f* **kpɔ̋ŋ**
berger *m* **tɯ̀ʌʌbhàankʌ̄bhɛ̀n,** berger *m* de nuit **tɯ̀ʌʌglá̋adhíɤbhōbhɛ̀n**
besoin *m* **bhànwɔ̀n, kplà,** j'ai besoin d'habits **sɔ̄ kplà yà n̄ kún, sɔ̄ kplà yɤ̀ n̄ bhà**
bétail *m* **tɯ̀ɤ**
bête **blɔ̋ɔ̀nsɯ̀, tàbhan**
bété *m* **Bètéɛ̀**
bêtement : il parle bêtement **yɤ̀ dhīaŋ zʌ̀ bhàanbhɔ̋ɔn-dhɛ̀ píɤ**
bêtise *f* **blɔ̋ɔn, bhàanbhɔ̋ɔn-dhɛ̀, wlá̋à, wlá̋àwɔ̀n,** faire des bêtises **wlá̋à zʌ̄**
béton *m* **dhàsóŋ̀**
bic *m* **bɛ̀nzʌ̀kápʌ̀**
biche *f* royale **bhìʌ**
bicyclette *f* **pìɤgāsòò**
bien **dɛ̀dɛ̀wō, sʌ̀, tìaandhɤ̄,** c'est bien fait pour lui! **à bhɤ̄ yà kʌ̄ sʌ̀**
bien portant **klɤ̋ɤklɤ̀**
bien que **kɛ̋ɛ**
bien-aimé *m*, bien-aimée *f* **sʌ̀bhɛ̀n, dhɔ̄ɔ́bhàabhɛ̀n**
bienveillant : il est bienveillant **à gblɯ̋ɯdhɛ̀ yɤ̀ pɯ̋u**
bienvenu : il y a de la place à la maison (tu es le bienvenu!) **kwā yæ̀æ kɔ́ɔdhɤ̄,** tu es le bienvenu! **ā tɯ̀un!**
bière *f* **wē**
bijoutier *m* **sʌ́nŋpìɤbhɛ̀n**
bile *f* **kʌ̋ʌ yí**
bille *f* **kpʌ̀**
billot pour aiguiser la machette **klá̋á dhɯ̋ɯ**
biomasse *f* **gɛ̋ɛ**
biseau *m* **zɔ̋**
bizarre **dhá̋bhlɯ̋ɯsɯ̀, gɤ̋ŋgɤ̀ŋ,** affaire bizarre **wɔ́n bhá,** c'est une affaire

bizarre *(dont on préfère ne pas parler)* **wɔ̀nbhɛ̄nkɔ̀nwɔ̀n bhɯ̀n**
bizarrement **bhàagɯ́ɯ**
blanc **pʉ̋u**, blanc comme la neige **pʉ̋u pɔ̋pɔ̋**, sa tête est devenue toute blanche **à gɔ̀ dhɛ̋ yà flɤ̋**
Blanc : homme *m* blanc **kwɪ́, kwɪ́ pʉ̋u**
blanchir **flɤ̋**
blatte *f* **gɔ̄ɔ̀**
blême **dhʉ̋ʌʌdhʉ̀ʌʌ**
blennorragie *f* **wɛ̄ɛ̋bhōyʉ̀a**
blesser **gɪ̀i**, il a blessé qn **yà pɪ̀ɤ zʉ̀ɤ bhɛ̄n bhà**
blessure *f* **bhɪ̄ʌʌ**, essuyer une blessure **gɪ̀i**
blettir **gɪ́a**, blettir (gombo) **glɔ̀o kún**
bleu **bʉ̋dhã̋ŋsɯ̀ɯ**
bloquer **lɔ̀o, zɯ̄n**, être bloqué **dhʌ̀nŋ, tā**
bœuf *m* **dʉ̀**
boire **bhɯ̄n**, boire vite et furtivement **bhʌ̀n-bhɯ̄n**
bois bété **dɔ̀ŋ**
bois *m* **dhʉ̋ɯ**, bois *m* à brûler **wɔ̋**, en bois **dhʉ̋ɯdhē**
boîte *f* **bʉ̋wã̋tɪ́, gōgō**, boîte *f* d'allumettes **sɪ́ɤkɔ́, pɛ̄ŋkɔ́, tã̋klã̋a kɔ́**
boiter : en boitant **kpɪ́anŋkpɪ́anŋdhɤ̄**, il boite **yɤ̀ tà kpɪ́anŋ̋kpɪ́anŋ̋dhɤ̄**
boiteux **gɤ̋ŋklɤ̄ɤ̀bhɛ̀n**
bombe *f* **bɔ́ŋ̀bɤ̄**
bon sens *m* **glɛ̀ŋ**
bon **sʌ̀, tɪ̀aandhēɛ̄** bonne nuit! **wɔ̄ ɯ̄ kɔ̀sʌ̀ tà!** j'ai de bonnes intentions envers toi **ā n̄ zɔ̀ sʌ̀ gɔ̀n ɯ̄ ká**
bonbon *m* **bɔ̀nŋbɔ̄ŋ̀**
bondir **bhɪ́a**
bondon *m* **yɤ̀dhɪ́ɤpʌ̀**
bonheur *m* **flʌ́ʌ̀bhōdhē, yʌ̄ʌ**
bonjour **dhæ̀ækpœ̀œ**
bonne aventure : dire la bonne aventure **dɛ̀ bɔ̄**
bonne *f* **gwʌ̄ʌ́dhē**
bonoua **bɔ̄ŋdhʉ́ʌ̀n**
bord *m* **blɛ̋e, blɛ̋edhɛ̀, dhɪ́ɤ, gɤ̋ŋ, kpɔ̋ŋ, tɔ̋, zɔ̋**, bord *m* de marmite **gbɔ̄ tɔ̋**, au bord de la route **kpɪ̀nŋ gɤ̋ŋ pɪ́ɤ**
bosse *f* **dhàŋ, kpū, kwʌ̄ŋ̋**
boubou *m* **gbāwû**, boubou magique **gblã̋nsɔ̄**
bouc *m* **bhɔ̀gɔ̀n**
bouche *f* **dhɪ́**, il est resté bouche bée **dhɪ̄aŋ yàa dhɪ́ pā**, d'une seule bouchée **vɪ́aandhɤ̄**
boucher **tā**
bouchon *m* **pɪ̄ɤ̋gbɔ̋ŋ**
boucle *f* d'oreille **tɔ̋gɯ́ɯpʌ̀**
bouclier *m* **dhɛ̄gā**
bouderie *f* **zɔ̀o**
boue *f* **báà, bɤ̄ɤ̀**, boue *f* ferrugineuse **dhʉ̋u**
bouger **ɤ̄ bhɔ̀ kèe bhà, pá, vɪ̄n**, ne bouge pas! **bhá dhó gó' ɯ̄ gblɔ̋o!**
bouillie *f* : bouillie de banane *m* **yɛ̀ŋ**, bouillie de riz *m* **bhã̋a**, bouillie matinale **sʉ̀ɤyɪ́**, bouillie épaisse **bã̋kã̋ kún-sɯ̀ɯ**, bouillie trop liquide **bã̋kã̋ yɪ́sɯ̀ɯ**
bouillir **kún, tɛ̋ɛ**, faire bouillir **kpà**
boule *f* **kpɤ̄**, boule blanche *(à l'intérieur du tronc de l'arbre dlɪ̄ŋ̀)* **bhlō**, boule de savon **kã̋bhã̋kɔ̋**
boum ! **gʉ̀uŋdhɤ̀, gbúʉ̀u**
boum-boum **gbʉ̄uŋgbʉ̄ŋdhɤ̄**
bourdonner : les mouches bourdonnent **wʌ̋nŋ-dhʉ̀n wɔ̀ wɛ̋-sɪʌ yʉ̄udhɤ̄**, les oreilles me bourdonnent **n̄ tɔ̋ gɯ́ɯ yɤ̀ vɪ̄n-sɪʌ**
bourgeon *m* **dɪ̀ŋ**, bourgeon de palme issu d'une jeune pousse de raphia **dɔ̀ŋgɔ̄**
bousculer **blʉ̀ɯ**
bout *m* **gʌ̄n, kpʉ̄ú, zɔ̋, zɔ̋dhɪ́ɤ**, bout de bois **dhʉ̋ɯ klã̋**, bout de la lame de la machette **bã̋ŋ zɔ̋**, bout de lanière de sandale **sàbhã̋ gʌ̄n**, bout de nez

yūnkpɤ̄ zɔ̋dhíɤ, bout de savon **sāà gā,** bout pointu d'un œuf de poule **tɔ̀ yàan gɔ̀ zɔ̋**
bouteille *f* **bútèdhíɤ, sàŋŋdhè, zùɛɛbhē,** bouteille de calebasse *f* **kwēedhʌ́n**
boutique *f* **dhɔ̋ɔkɔ̀, bùtígɤ̀**
bouton *m* **būtɔ́ŋ̀**
bouture *f* d'igname **yá̋ gɔ̀**
boyau *m* **gblʌ̄ʌ̀n gā**
bracelet *m* **yàkɔ̀ɔpʌ̀,** bracelet *m* de coureur **kǽǽgā**
braire : l'âne brait **sòòfʌ̄ŋ yɤ̀ wɛ́-sīʌ**
braise *f* **síɤ dhùu, pēŋ dhùu**
braiser **pìaa**
brancard *m* **gbá̋ŋ**
branche *f* **kɔ̀, kwɛ̄ɛ́, dhű gbɛ̀ŋ,** branche sèche **wɔ̋ ká̋ŋ**
branlant **yʌ́ŋ̀yʌ̀ŋ**
bras *m* **gbè, gbègādhű, kwɛ̄ɛ́**
brebis *f* **bhlá̋a**
bredouiller **dhīaŋ zʌ̄ ɤ̀ dhɛ́ɛ̀n dhíɤ**
bref **klɤ̄ɤ̀**
brigade de travail champêtre du groupe "gwa" **gwá̋'-dhàan kê kpɤ̄**
brigand **gɔ̄ɔgbɛ́ɛ̀bhɛ̀n**
brillant **blɤ́ŋblɤ̀ŋ**
briller **bhű,** ses yeux brillent d'une façon saine **à yán gű yɤ̀ bhù̀ kpɤ́kpɤ́dhɤ̄**
brin de torche de raphia **sɔ̋nŋ gā**
brins de tige de canne à sucre **kàa blùŋ**
brique *f* **blíkɤ̀**
briser **wūù̀wūù̀**
brisure *f* **gɔ̄ɔ̋**
bronze *m* **zʌ̄n**
bronzer la peau de qn **bhēn kwī bhō-gblő̋o**
brouette *f* **wòtlóɔ̀**
brouhaha **yūudhɤ̄**
brouillard **dhűu,** brouillard d'harmattan **bùudhá̋an**
brouiller les gens **sìɤ**
broussaille *f* **kpɔ̀ɔ, vɔ̋ɔ**
brousse *f* **blʌ̄ʌ, bű, bűgűdhè,** brousse *f* aux alentours de village **ká̋ŋ,** brousse brûlée **síɤ yāàndhè**
broyer **dhíʌʌ**
bruine *f* **dhāfīidhʌ́n**
bruiner : il bruine **dhāfīidhʌ́n yɤ̀ bān-sīʌ**
bruire **vīn**
bruit *m* **fɛ̀ɛ, gbàŋ, vīn,** bruit d'une voiture, d'un moteur **bhàanŋzīì wɔ̀,** j'ai entendu le bruit de la foule **ū tő yà dà gbàŋ wɔ̀ gű,** émettre des bruits **wɛ́,** faire du bruit **vīn, zùɤ,** sans bruit **sɛ́ŋdhɤ̄**
brûlant **dhíɤsù,** *(soleil)* **gbɛ́ɛ̀**
brûlé *m* **slàan**
brûler **bhán, bhɔ̄, bhɤ̀, bhű, gɤ́, gű-bhɔ̄,** se brûler **gɤ́,** le soleil brûle beaucoup à cet endroit **yʌ́ŋ̀ yɤ̀ bhù̀ gbɛ́ɛ̀ dhè yā' gű,** le soleil m'a brûlé la tête **yʌ́ŋ̀ yà bhán ū gɔ̀ ká**
brûlure **síɤ bhīʌʌ**
brusquement **vɤ̂dhɤ̄, vɤ́ɤ̀dhɤ̄, zádhɤ̄, zódhɤ̄,** brusquement et mal à propos **bɔ̄ɔ̋dhɤ̄**
brutal : personne brutale **yá̋ngűyāabhɛ̀n**
brute *f* **kpʌ̄**
bruyamment **wìaawìaadhɤ̄**
bruyant **fɛ̀ɛsù**
buffle *m* **dùɤ**
buisson *m* **gí, blʌ̄ʌ kpɤ̄**
bulbul *m* ictérin **slʌ̀ʌwɛ̄ngā**
bulldozer *m* **bhàanŋzīì, zɔ̄**
bureau *m* **bìdhóɔ̀**
Burkina Faso **bhɔ̀ɔnsīì-dhùn gɔ̀ sɛ́**
Burkinabé *m, f* **bhɔ̀ɔnsīì**
but *m* **bīì**
butte d'igname **yá̋ sɛ́**

C c

cabine de chauffeur **gɔ̄ gɔ̀**
cabosse *f* de cola **gô bhē**

cabri *m* **bhɔ̀**
caca : faire caca **gbōo**
cacao *m* **kàkàô**
cache *f* **dɛ̀ɛ̀n**
cacher **bı̏n, bhán, dɛ̀ɛ̀n-kpɔ́, gblɛ̀ɛn-kpɔ́, yɛ̀ɛ bhō,** se cacher **bı̏n, dɛ̀ɛ̀n-kpɔ́, dhɛ̀ŋ, gblɛ̀ɛn-kpɔ́**
cachot *m* **kàsɔ̀**
cadavre *m* **gèe**
cadeau *m* **gœ̄œ, gœ̄œpʌ̀, gbœ̄œdhē, kplʌ̋nŋ, sāan, sāanpʌ̄, tāa,** il m'a envoyé des cadeaux **yà n̄ sāan bɔ̄,** faire un cadeau **gœ̄œ**
cadenas *m* **gbɔ̋gbɔ̋kɔ̋**
cadet **tɔ̄ɔ**
cafard *m* **gōɔ̀**
café *m* **kɑ̋flḛ̏e,** café moulu **kɑ̋flḛ̏e bı̀**
caféier *m* **kɑ̋flḛ̏e dhı̏ı**
cage *f* **klʌ̀ʌn**
cahotage *m* **zàŋzɑ̋ŋ**
cahotement *m* **zùuzű̋u**
cahoteux **kʌ̋nŋkʌ̀nŋ**
caille *f* arlequin **tlōɔ̀**
caille **sūɛ̀ɛ**
caillot *m* **kplı̀ı**
caillou *m* **gwʌ̀, gwʌ̀gā, gwʌ̀dhʌ́n**
caisse *f* **kɛ̋sɔ̋**
calao *m* : calao à huppe blanche **wɔ̀ɔgblʌ́ʌ̀bhàan,** calao *m* à joues grises **zœ̀œ,** grand calao à casque noir **pɔ̋ɔn,** petit calao **fɑ̋ŋ̀kpɛ̋ɛ**
calcul *m* **kwɛ̋dhɛ̋n**
calculer **kwɛ̋dhɛ̋n kʌ̄**
calebasse *f* **kɔ̀ɔ, yɔ̋ŋ**
caleçon *m* **blɛ̀ɛ,** caleçon *m* traditionnel **kpɑ̋sɑ̋**
caler **dhūű, kɔ̀**
califourchon : à califourchon **sòòtà**
calme **dèe, sæ̀æ, zɔ̀ɔsı̀ı,** il est devenu calme **à gɔ̀ gı́ı yà zɔ̀ɔ**
calmement **sɛ̋ɛnŋdhɤ̄, zɔ̀nŋ-sı̀ı ká**
calmer **tà-gā,** calme-le! *(un bébé)* **à dhæ̀æ gā!,** il s'est calmé **à zūʌ́ yà pā,** se calmer **tà-gā, zɔ̀nŋ, ɤ̄ tɛ́ɛ yɤ̄ sı́ı̄a,** calmez-vous! **kà dɔ̄ dīnŋdhɤ̄!**
calvitie *f* **kplɑ̋tɔ̋**
camarade de classe d'âge **tɛ̋bhɑ̋n**
caméléon *m* **gű̋udʌ̄,** tu es lent comme un caméléon **ı̄ı dhű̋aandhùaan ká dhè gű̋udʌ̄ dhɤ́**
camion à caisse faite de planches **dhű̋ıkɑ̋ŋ gɔ̄**
campagne *f* **gbɛ̄ɛ,** il est allé à la campagne **yà dhó gbɛ̄ɛ gı́ı**
campement *m* **bhláà, kɑ̋nŋbhɑ̋, kɔ́yı́dhɛ̀, plɤ̀ɤdhɛ̀,** campement de culture **dhɛ̄ŋ̀dhɛ̀**
canard *m* **kwı́ tɔ̀**
canari *m* **gbɔ̄**
canne *f* **tàadhı̀ı,** canne *f* à sucre *m* **bhɤ̀ kàa, kàa**
canon *m* de fusil **būu gɔ̀**
canton *m* **kāŋtôn, sɛ̋**
caoutchouc *m* **dhɤ̀ɤ**
capacité **gı́ıgbɛ̋ɛ̀-dhɛ̀**
capitaine *m (poisson)* **kòopű̋u**
capricieux : il est capricieux **à bhànwɔ̀n yɤ̀ sı̀ɤ**
car **dhè ɤ́ kʌ̀ dhè**
caractère *m* **klɔ̋o, sʌ́ʌdhɛ̋yɑ̋ngā, sɔ̀ŋ**
carapa **gbɔ̂n**
carapace *f* de crabe **kā kɤ̀**
carcasse *f* **gèe**
caresser **kāà**
carnassier *m* **pʌ̄kúnpʌ̀, wūkúnwı̀ı**
carquois *m* **zɔ̀**
carreau *m* **kāarɔ̂**
carrément **bádhɤ̄**
carte *f (à jouer)* **klàatı̄ı̀ dhɛ̋,** cartes *fpl* **klàatı̄ı̀**
cartouche *f* **būugā, dhű̋gā**

case *f* **kɔ́,** case *f* rectangulaire **gbɔ̄ŋ,** case *f* ronde **kɔ́dhɛ̄ɛ́,** case *f* sacrée **gɯ̋nŋ, gɯ̋nŋdhɛ̀, gɯ̋nŋkɔ̀**
cassé **kɤ̀ɤ**
casser **pɛ̋, wɯ́ɯ, yɛ̋,** se casser **wɯ́ɯ, yɛ̋, yɛ̄ɛ̀yɛ̄ɛ̀**
casserole *f* **kɑ̋slɔ̋,** casserole en aluminium *m* **fɔ̋ŋ gbɔ̄**
castagnettes *f* **sɛ̀kpɛ̀**
cataclop **glàglàglàdhɤ̄**
cause *f* **gɛ̀n, gɛ̀ngódhɛ̀,** à cause de **gɔ̀, kósɔ̀n, gɯ́,** à cause de lui **à kɔ̀ tà,** c'est sa cause **à gɛ̀n yɤ̀ gbàn à gɯ́, à gɛ̀n yɤ̀ gbàn à bhà**
causer **dɔ̋ɔ dɔ̄, kʌ̄**
causerie *f* **dɔ̋ɔ, gbɛ̋ɛtà, wɔ̀plʌ̄ʌ̀**
ce temps-ci **tɤ̋ŋ yɤ̄ gɯ́ bhā**
ce **yā**
céder **kplà**
ceinture *f* : ceinture de danseuse **dhɛ̀ɛdhɪ̋ɤ dhɑ̋a,** ceinture en laine *f* **sɛ̋,** ceinture *f* pour grimper au palmier *m* **bhɔ̋, bhɔ̋gā**
célèbre : il est devenu célèbre **à tó dhɤ́ dà**
célébrité *f* **tóbhɔ̄bhɛ̀n**
célibat *m* **kɛ̀gbœ̋œ-dhɛ̀**
célibataire *m* **kɛ̀gbœ̋œ**
celui-ci **bhà, yɤ̄**
cendre *m* **yɔ̋o**
cent **kʌ̄ŋ**
centaine : des centaines **kʌ̄ŋ tà kʌ̀ŋ**
centime *m* **plɔ̀ɔgā**
cependant **yɤ̄ zʌ̀ gbàn gɯ́**
céphalophe *m* : céphalophe à ventre blanc **vʌ̀,** céphalophe *m* couronné **glàzœ̀œ,** céphalophe *m* noir **gbà, sɯ́ɯ̀**
cerceau *m* **kòŋ**
cercle *m* **kòŋ**
cercocèbe *m* **gœ̀œ**
cercueil *m* **gbʌ̀ʌ, bhɛ̄n gèe gbʌ̀ʌ**
certain **bhá, dɔ̄,** certains **dódó**
certainement **dɛ̀dɛ̀wɔ̄, kpɛ̄nŋkpɛ̄nŋdhɤ̄**
cérumen **tɔ̋ gbɔ̄**
cerveau *m* **gɔ̀ gɯ́ yɔ̀n**
cervelle *f* **tʌ̀ŋ**
ces jours-ci **wɛ̋ɛ̀gɯ́**
cesser **dɔ̋ɔ̀ndhūn, dhɪ̋ɤ-dɔ̄, dhɪ̋ɤ-tó, kɑ̋n,** sans cesse **tɤ̋ŋgbàn gɯ́**
c'est ça **yɤ́ bhā**
c'est pourquoi **yɤ́ ɤ́ kʌ̀**
c'est-à-dire **kɛ̋ɛ**
cette fois-ci **à dɔ̄ kɤ́ yā, dhɛ̀ yɤ̄ zɯ́**
chacun **gbàn pɛ̋pɛ̋**
chagrin : il a eu du chagrin **à zūʌ̋ yà yà gɤ̋-sɯ̀ bhà**
chaîne *f* **lɔ̄ɔ̋gā,** chaîne de vélo **pɪ̀ɤgāsòò lɔ̄ɔ̋gā**
chair *f* **dhʌ̀nŋ,** chair de poule **dhɛ̋ndhɛ̋ngā,** il a la chair de poule **dhɛ̋ndhɛ̋ngā yà lòo à bhà**
chaise *f* **gbàadhʌ́n, glɔ̀o, glɔ̀okōtàngɯ́dhē,** chaise dans la case sacrée couverte d'une peau de léopard **tòo kpàtà glɔ̀o gɔ̋ glɔ̀ɔ̀**
chaleur *f* **sɪ̋ɤdɔ̄-sɯ̀,** la chaleur est forte **sɪ̋ɤ yɤ̀ dɔ̄-sɪʌ gbɛ̋ɛ̀, pɛ̄ŋ yɤ̀ dɔ̄-sɪʌ gbɛ̋ɛ̀**
chaman : il est devenu chaman **zìgà yà dà à gɯ́; yà zìgà sɯ́**
chambre *f* **kɔ́dhí, wɔ̀gɯ́kɔ̀**
champ *m* **bhláà, bhláàdhɛ̀, dhɛ̀, kê,** champ *m* défriché **gɛ̋ɛdhɛ̀,** champ *m* non-ensemencé **gbɑ̋a,** champ de bas-fond **bɑ́à dhɛ̀,** champ de manioc **bāa dhɛ̀, bāa bhlàa, bāa kɛ̀,** champ exploité la deuxième ou troisième année après le défrichage **bhɯ́ɯ̀**
champignon *m* **tɪ̋ʌʌ**
champignons, espèces: **bhlʌ̋tɪ̋ʌʌ, bhūɤɤ, dhàŋtlɑ̋adhɛ̋, gbàgbɤ̄, gɔ̀ɔ, gɔ̀ɔdhɛ̋, gìææn, gwɛ̄bùŋbūŋ́, gwɛ̄kpʌbhàtɪ̋ʌʌ, kìɔɔn, kɪ̋ʌʌdhɛ̋, sɑ̄ɑ̋n, tɪ̋ʌʌpɯ̋u, tɪ̋ʌʌtīi**

champion *m* **kplʌ́ʌnŋ, kplʌ́ʌnŋbhīn, vʌ̋angɔ̄n,** champion en course **bɪ̀aŋgā, gɛ̀ngbɛ́ɛ̀bhɛ̀n**
chance *f* **pīʌ́,** ce n'est pas de chance **dɔ̄ yíi dhī n̄ ká,** il a la chance **à pīʌ́ yɤ̀ sʌ̄,** il n'a pas de chance **à pīʌ́ yɤ̀ yâ**
changer **glʌ́, gɯ́-gʌ̋n, slʌ̄ʌ**
chant *m* **tʌ̋n,** chant et danse des chanteurs de chasse **kwlǽætʌ̋n,** chant et danse des chasseurs **kɔ̄nŋtʌ̋n,** chant *m* de coq *m* **dhɛ̀ɛdhɪ́ɤ**
chanter **tʌ̋n bhō,** chanter en réponse **wɛ́ à bhà,** le coucal chante **tūʊ́tūʊ́ yɤ̀ wɛ̀ tūʊ́tūʊ́dhɤ̄**
chanteur *m* **tʌ̋nbhōbhɛ̀n**
chapeau *m* **fʌ́ʌ̀nkɔ́,** chapeau à rebords **gblāà**
chaque **dhɛ́ ɤ́ dhɤ́, pɛ́pɛ́,** chaque fois **dódó,** chaque jour **dhɛ̀ pʊ́u ɤ́ kpœ̀œ, dhɛ̀ yà kpœ̀œ dódó, dhɛ̀ yà kpœ̀œ dɔ̄**
charbon *m* de bois *m* **sɛ́ŋ̀**
charge *f* **kwɛ̀ɛ̀**
charger **dʌ̀, dhú,** charger le fusil **būu tā,** il a chargé le fusil **yà dhʊ̋gā dʌ̀ būu gɯ́**
charme *m* **sáà,** il a du charme **sáà yɤ̀ à tʌ̀**
charrier : il charrie son bagage dans une brouette **yɤ̀ ɯ̄ bhā kwɛ̄ɛ̀ blɯ̀-sīʌ wòtlóò gɯ́**
chasse *f* **bʊ́ʊ́,** chasse avec un chien **gbên bʊ̀ʊ̀,** chasser à l'approche **dhān-kʌ̄**
chasser **kʌ̄**
chasseur *m* **bʊ́ʊ́kʌ̄bhɛ̀n, dhūeebhīn**
chasseur *m* de sorciers, chasseur aux sorciers **zɔ̋o, zɔ̋obhīn, zɔ̋obhīn**
chassie *f* **yʌ̋n gbō**
chat *m* **gīoo, gwʌ̋n, yūnbhʌ̀andhʌ́n,** chat *m (mâle)* **gwʌ̋n gɔ̄n, yūnbhʌ̀andhʌ́n gɔ̄n**
chaton *m* **yūʌ̋ndhʌ́n, gwʌ̋ndhʌ́n sɛ̄ɛ́ndhʌ́n**
chatte *f (femelle de chat)* **gwʌ̋n dhɛ̀e, yūnbhʌ̀andhʌ́n dhɛ̀e**
chaud **wɔ̋sɯ̀,** c'est chaud! **sœ́œ̀ yɤ̀ à kwɛ̀ɛ̀,** il fait très chaud aujourd'hui **yʌ́nŋ̀ yɤ̀ dhɤ̀ dɛ̀ɛ,** la maison est devenue très chaude **kɔ́ɔdhɛ̀ gbàan kún blʌ̀blʌ̀dhɤ̄**
chaude-pisse **wɛ̄ɛ́bhōyʊ̀a**
chauffer : se chauffer **kún,** le fer a chauffé au rouge **pɪ̀ɤ yʌ̀ kún gbʌ̀ngbʌ̀ndhɤ̄**
chauffeur *m* **dhɪ́ɤtʌ̋sɯ́bhɛ̀n, gɔ̄zīɤbhɛ̀n, sòfɛ́ɛ̀,** chauffeur d'une voiture **gɔ̄ sòfɛ́ɛ̀,** chauffeur taxi **tāsî zīɤ bhɛ̀n**
chaume *m* **yɛ̋plɤ̋ŋ**
chausse-trape *f* **glʌ̋bʌ̋**
chaussure *f* **sàbhʌ̋**
chauve **kpʌ̋a**
chauve-souris *f* **dhɛ̄ɛ̀n**
chauve-souris, espèces : **bhʌ̀, gbɔ̄ɔŋ**
chef *m* **bhɛ̄ngɔ̀dhɪ́ɤbhɛ̀n, bhɛ̄ngɔ̀tʌ̀bhɛ̀n, gɔ̀bhɛ̀n, gɔ̀bhɛ̀ndʌ̄, gblɯ̀ɯ̀dʌ̄,** chef de concession **kwʌ̋nŋ̀ gɔ̀ dhɪ́ɤ bhɛ̀n, kwʌ̋nŋ̀ dʌ̄, kwʌ̋nŋ̀dhɛ̀ dʌ̄ bhɛ̀n,** chef de famille **kwʌ̋nŋ̀ gɔ̀ dhɪ́ɤ bhɛ̀n, kwʌ̋nŋ̀ dʌ̄, kwʌ̋nŋ̀dhɛ̀ dʌ̄ bhɛ̀n, kɔ́ dʌ̄,** chef de village **pɤ̀ kɔ̀ɔnbhɛ̀n, dhʊ̀tɪ́ɪ̀,** chef de canton *m* **sɛ̋dʌ̄,** chef de guerre *f* **kplʌ̋ʌ, gblɯ̀gɔ̄ɔnbhɛ̀n-dhʊ̀n gɔ̀bhɛ̀n,** chef de la danse **tʌ̋nsàŋgbáà,** chef *m* de terre *f* **sɛ̋dʌ̄**
chef *m* législateur *m* **tɔ́ŋ̀gɔ̀bhɛ̀n**
chemin *m* **zīaan**
chemise *f* longue **bhɛ̋ɛ**
chenille *f* **zʊ̀ee**
chenilles consommables, espèces : **gɔ̀ŋ, gɔ̀ŋgā, zɔ̀o**
chenilles vénémeuses, espèces : **wɔ̀ɔ-kɔ̀-bhō-dhʊ́ʊ́-bhʌ̀, dhɛ̀ɛn**
chenilles, espèces : **dhɤ̋ŋ, dhɤ̋ŋgbɤ̋, gbâ, gbīnŋgā, tīidhʌ̄ngbɤ̄, yɤ̋ɤŋgā**

cher, chère *(forme d'adresse)* **bhá,** le poisson n'était pas cher **yúɤ̀ɤ dhɔ̃́ɔ gɯ̀n sʌ̀**
chercher **bhlɛ̃́n, bhɔ̄ɔ̃́-bhō, bhɔ̄ɔ̃̀n,** chercher à gagner **bhɔ̄ɔ̃̀n,** il a cherché avec sa main **yà̃ dhó ɤ̄ kɔ̃̀ ká**
chérie *f* : ma chérie *(adresse affective à une femme)* **bhān sʌ̃́nŋ, n̄ dhɔ̄ɔbhàa,** ma chérie *(une forme d'adresse très affective)* **bhān gàpʌ̃̀**
chers parents **kwɛ̄ɛ̃́bhɛ̃̀n-dhɯ̀n**
chétif **fíaanfìaan**
cheval *m* **sòɔ̀**
chevelure *f* **gɔ̃̀dhɛ̃́, wūn**
cheveu *m* **wūndhɛ̃́,** un cheveu **wūn gā,** cheveux *(coupés)* **víʌʌ,** cheveux blancs **wlʌ̃́n**
cheville *f* **gɛ̃̀nwɛ̄ngā**
chèvre **bhɔ̃̀dhɛ̀e**
chevrotin *m* **būugā**
chez **bhàa, píɤ, plɤ̀ɤ, yɛ̃̀ɛ**
chiche : tu es devenu chiche! **bhá pɛ̃̀ɛdhɯ̃̀ kʌ̃́n!**
chicot *m* **kpū**
chicote *f*, chicotte *f* **fáa, klàŋgā**
chien *m* **gbɛ̂n,** chien mâle **gbɛ̂n gɔ̄n**
chiendent *m* **dɛ̂n**
chienne *f* **gbɛ̂n bhūn, gbɛ̂n dhɛ̀e**
chier **gbōo,** il a chié dans sa culotte **ʌ̀ gbō yà zūa ʌ̀ bhʌ̀,** il a chié dans son froc **ʌ̀ gbō yɤ̀ tɔ̀ síāa bhūn**
chieur *m* **gbōobhɛ̃̀n**
chiffon *m* **sɔ̄pɛ̃́n**
chiffre *m* **dhɪ́nbhlɔ̂n**
chimpanzé *m* **kpìʌʌ**
chiquenaude *f* **gìʌ**
chiquer **zʌ̃́ŋ kún**
choix **sɛ̃́**
choquer **yɛ̃́**
chose *f* **pʌ̄**
chou *m* **sīɯ̀**
chou palmiste poulpe **kɔ̄ɔ**
chouette *f* pêcheuse **kpàdhɛ̃́ɛ**
chrysalide *f* **kɔ̀kɔ̀kpāàdhɛ̀**
chut : faire chut à qn **yà̃ bhɛ̄n yʌ̃́n gɯ́**
cicatrice *f* **kpʌ̃́a**
cicatriser **gā,** la blessure a cicatrisé **bhīʌʌ yà gā,** se cicatriser **bō, kpʌ̃́a kʌ̃́n**
ciel *m* **dhāŋ̀, dhāŋgɯ́dhɛ̀, dhɛ̀gɯ́**
cigale *f* **slɤ̄ɤ**
cigarette *f* **sìɛtīì**
cil *m* **yʌ̃́nsɛ̃́ɛ gā,** cils **yʌ̃́nsɛ̃́ɛ**
cilicium *m* **gʌ̄nŋ́gwʌ̀**
ciment *m* **dhàsóŋ̀ bī̀**
cinq **sɔ̃́ɔdhɯ̃́,** cinq francs **wʌ́ʌ̀, wʌ́ʌ̀gā**
circaète jean-le-blanc **sʌ́ʌ̀**
circuler **slʌ̄ʌ**
cire *f* **flɔ̃́**
cisticole *f* chanteuse **fɛ̀ekɔ̃̀ɔdhɤ̄**
citadin **kwɪ́**
citron *m* **bhɛ̄ntīi ʌ̀ dhɤ̄ŋ̀, bhɛ̄ntīi ʌ̀ sɛ̄ɛ́, bhɛ̄ntīi sɛ̄ɛ́, kwɪ́ ʌ̀ dhɤ̄ŋ̀,** citron vert **kɛ̃̀sɛ̄ɛ́**
civette *f* **bhɯ̃́u**
clair **bōoŋ, pɯ̃́u, wlʌ̃́awlʌ̀a, sɤ̃́ɤŋsɤ̃̀ɤŋ**
clairement **pápádhɤ̄,** il parle clairement *(sa prononciation est claire; il exprime clairement ses propos)* **ʌ̀ dhí yɤ̀ kàn dhīaŋ bhʌ̀**
claire-voie : à claire-voie **yʌ̃́anyʌ̀an**
clairvoyant *m* **yʌ̃́ngɯ́pɛ̃́bhɛ̃̀n**
clameur *f* : la clameur de la foule monte **bhɛ̄n kpɤ̄ yɤ̀ wɛ̃́-sīʌ yūudhɤ̄**
clan *m* **sūu,** membres d'un clan **kwʌ̃́nŋ̀ dō gɯ́ bhɛ̃̀n-dhɯ̀n**
clapotement *m* **bhàŋbhʌ̃́ŋ**
clapoter **bhàŋbhʌ̃́ŋ kʌ̄**
claquement des doigts **kɔ̃̀tɪ̄ɪ̃ŋ̀**
claquer : il a fait claquer sa langue *(signe de désaccord, désapprobation, mépris)* **yà ɤ̄ dhɪ́ʌŋ sɯ́ ʌ̀ ká**
classe *f (à l'école)* **kɔ́dhɪ́, klàŋdhɪ́ɤ kɔ́**
clé *f*, clef *f* **dhàklɛ̃́e, klɛ̃́e**

client *m* **dhɔ̃ɔdhɔ́bhɛ̃n**
clin d'œil : en un clin d'œil **dhɛ̀ bhɛ̄n bhɛ̄n yɑ̃n pɛ̃ɛn dō gɔ̄ zʌ̄**
cling-cling **glɑ̃glɑ̃dhɤ̄**
cliquetis **gblāagblàgblāadhɤ̄**
clitoris *m* **slɔ̄ŋgā, sɔ̄ŋgā**
clochette *f* en bronze **kpɤ̃dhàa**
clong **gɛ̄nŋdhɤ̄**
clopinant avec une canne **kɔ̄ŋ́kɔ̄ŋ́**
clôture *f* légère **glɛ̀ŋ**
clôturer **zɯ̀-klʌ̀ʌn**
clou *m* **pɔ̃dhĩn**
coaguler (se) : son sang s'est coagulé **à yɔ̀ɔn yà kplɯ̀ kún**
cobra *m* **gbàa**
cochon *m* **bhɔ̀**
coco *m* **kpɑ̃kɔ̀**
cocorico **kɔ̀kɔ̀ŋkɔ́ɔ̀, dhɛ̀ɛdhĩɤ**
co-épouse *f* **gwāànkpɔ́yɔ̃ɔ,** coépouse aînée **dhē, yàpĩɤdhē,** coépouse cadette **bhāŋdhē, dhēdhʌ́n,** coépouse cadette de la mère **dhē sɛ̃ɛ̃ndhʌ́n**
cœur *m* **zɔ̀, zɔ̀o, zūʌ̃, zūʌ̃gā,** il a mal au cœur **pɛ̀ dhɔ̀ yà' kʌ̄-sɪʌ, pɛ̀ yɤ̀ dà-sɪʌ' ká**
cogner avec **gbàn,** se cogner **bhàn, gbàn**
coiffer à va-vite **bhɯ̀u**
coiffure *f* de la danseuse dhɛ̀ɛdhĩɤ **kòŋbhó**
coin de l'oeil **yɑ̃n gɤ̃ŋ**
coincer : se coincer **dhʌnŋ, gbàn**
col *f* de chemise **bhɛ̃ɛ gbān**
cola *m*, *f* **gô,** cola *f* blanche, cola *m* blanc **vɔ̀ɔ,** cola *m*, *f* rose **kwīzʌ̄gā, vɔ̀ɔ,** cola rose clair **vɔ̀ɔ pũu,** cola rose foncé **vɔ̀ɔ tīi,** cola porte-bonheur **yʌ̄ʌgɔ̀,** colas pour annoncer la mort **gā gô,** colas pour annoncer la naissance **dhʌ́n kpɔ́ yõo sɯ́ gô.** colas pour annoncer le mariage **dhē sɯ́ gô,** colas pour annoncer l'initiation **gbándhʌ́n kʌ̀' ká gô, gbándhʌ́n yī dà gô,** colas pour annoncer un heureux événement **yõo sɯ́ gô**
colère *f* **fɔ̃ŋfɔ̃ŋ,** être gonflé de colère **tā ɤ̄ gɯ́,** il est au point d'éclater de colère **yà dō ɤ̄ gɯ́ tĩtĩdhɤ̄,** se mettre en colère **dō ɤ̄ gɯ́,** il s'est mis en colère **fɔ̃ŋfɔ̃ŋ yà dà à gɯ́, fɔ̃ŋfɔ̃ŋ yà bhán à gɯ́,** il s'est mis en colère contre qn **yà fɔ̃ŋfɔ̃ŋ sɯ́ bhɛ̄n pĩɤ,** il s'est mis en colère, comme un paon **yà bhlà ɤ̄ gɯ́ dhɛ̀ kɔ̀nŋsóɔ̀dhɯ̀ dhɤ́**
coliou *m* barré **wɛ̄ŋdhē**
collant **dɔ̃ɔndɔ̀ɔn, dɔ̃ɔnsɯ̀, dɤ̃ŋdɤ̀ŋ, dɤ̃ŋgɤ̃dɤ̀ŋgɤ̀, tɤ̃ŋgɤ̃tɤ̀ŋgɤ̀**
colle *f* **gbān**
collecteur d'impôts **wʌ̃ʌ̃kúnbhɛ̃n**
collectionner **yɔ̀ɔn**
collègue *m* **tɛ̃ɛdō**
coller **dhʌ̀nŋ, tà-kpā,** se coller **dhʌ̀nŋ**
collier *m* **bhōbhàpʌ̀**
colline *f* **tɔ̀n, tɔ̀n gbʌ̂gbʌ̀**
colobe *m* bai d'Afrique Occidentale **klɤ̀ɤ**
colonne *f* vertebrale **kōgā**
combien? **dhɛ̀**
commander **kōnbhānŋdē**
comme ça **dhìn, pɛ́ɛdhɤ́**
comme **dhɛ̀ ɤ́ kʌ̀ dhɛ̀, dhɛ̀, fɔ̃n, kɛ̃ɛ dhɛ̀ ɤ́ kʌ̀ dhɛ̀, dhɛ̀ ... dhɤ́,** comme il faut **dhɛ̀ bhɛ̄n yɤ̀ bhʌ̀n kʌ̀**
commencer **dhĩ-pɔ̃, yà ... bhà, yɤ̄ ... bhà, zū-bhō,** commencer à bouillir **dà**
comment? **bhūndhɛ̀, dhɛ̀,** comment ça va chez toi? **dhæ̀ækpœ̀œ bhūn**
commission *f* **kpœ̀œ**
commissionner **bō, yʌ̄-kʌ̄**
commune *f* **kõbhĩ**
communiquer **lòo**
compagnon *m* : compagnon *m* de voyage *m* **tɑ̃yɔ̃ɔ,** compagnon de route **tæ̃ædō ɤ́ dhūn à dō tɑ̃ gɯ́**
comparer **zɔ̀n**

compatriote *f, m* **dhēébhāŋ**
complètement **d̀ɛd̀ɛwō, kpɛ̄ɛnŋdhɤ̄, pɛ́ɛpɛ́dhɤ̄,** compètement *(blanc)* **pɛ́pɛ́,** complètement *(couvert – de fumée, de brouillard)* **bhɔ̄nŋdhɤ̄**
completer **dhɪ́ɤ-pā**
comportement *m* **sɔ̀ŋ**
comprehensible : de façon compréhensible **pápádhɤ̄**
compréhensif : personne compréhensive **wɔ́ngʉ́bhānbhɛ̀n**
compréhension *f* **wɔ́ngʉ́bhān-sʉ̀,** compréhension mutuelle **zūʌ́kʌ̀dō-sʉ̀**
comprendre **bhān, gʉ́-bhān, gʉ́-yɤ̄**
comprimé *m* **dhʉ̋gā, bèdhɛ́ gā**
compte *m* **dhōŋdhē,** se rendre compte **kʌ̋n**
compter **dhōŋ,** il compte sur moi **à tɤ̋ŋ yɤ̀ n̄ gʉ́**
compte-rendu *m* **kplʌ́nŋ**
con *m* **gwɛ́nŋ, pʌ̄ʌ, slōo**
conakry *m (sorte de banane douce)* **kɔ̄dhānklīi**
concerner **gbʌ̀n,** concernant qch **à wɔ́n gʉ́**
concession *f (cour, grande famille)* **kɔ́dhí, kwʌ̋nŋ̀, kwʌ̋nŋ̀dhɛ̀**
concitoyen *m* **kʌ̄yɔ̋ɔ**
condamner qn **zā wō bhēn tà**
conducteur *m* **dhɪ́ɤtʌ̋sʉ́bhɛ̀n**
conduire : il est en train de conduire la pirogue **yɤ̀ kplʌ̋gō zīɤ-sīʌ**
confiance *f* **dhʌ́ŋ̀, dhʌ́ŋ̀bhɔ̀dhɪ́ɤ-sʉ̀, zɔ̀yɤ̀kó-dhɛ̀,** avoir confiance en **dhʌ́ŋ̀ bhō bhēn dhɪ́ɤ,** il a perdu confiance en moi **yà tʌ̄ʌ bhō n̄ gʉ́,** il a trahi ma confiance **yà n̄ bhā dhʌ́ŋ̀bhɔ̀dhɪ́ɤ-sʉ̀ sēɛ̀**
confier : le fait de confier **kplʌ́nŋ,** se confier **gbɛ́bhō**
confondre **kāʌ̋n,** se confondre **lòo,** se confondre dans la tête de qn **lòo bhēn gɔ̀ kóo**
confus **bhlʉ̋ubhlʉ̀u, yɔ̋ɔyɔ̀ɔ,** il est confus **à tà yà tlɤ̀ɤ**
confusion *f* **zʉ̀glʉ̀**
congé *f* : prendre congé de **ɤ̄ wɔ̀ dà bhēn dhɛ̀**
connaître : **dɔ̄**
conseil *m* **dhɪ̀oo,** donner conseil à qn **dhɪ̀oo dɔ̄ bhēn tà, glɛ̀ŋ dà bhēn bhà**
conseiller *m* **dhɪ̀oodɔ̄bhɛ̀n**
considération *f* : sans considération **fɪ̀ɪ ká**
considérer **yɤ̄,** être considéré **yɤ̄**
consigne : donner des consignes à qn **ɤ̄ wɔ̀ kpɔ́ à bhà**
consolation *f* **blɔ̀ɔ, tūʌ̋a**
consoler **dhūʌ̀a, kpā, bhɔ̀ɔ bɔ̄ bhēn zɔ̀/zūʌ́ bhà,** il s'est consolé **à zūʌ́ yà zɔ̀ɔ**
consolider (se) : son pouvoir s'est consolidé **à bhà gɛ̀n yà gbʌ̀n**
consonne *f* **zʉ̄bhōwɔ̀**
constamment **bɪ̋n bhān dhɛ̀ kpœ̀œ, pīɤɤdhɤ̄**
constipation : il a une constipation **à gú yà bhán' bhà**
constiper : il est constipé **à gú yà bhán à bhà**
construction *f* **dɔ̄**
conte *m* **kwɛ̀zlʌ̀an, pɪ̀an**
contemplation : objet *m* de contemplation *f* **gʌ̀pʌ̄**
content : il est content **à zūʌ́ dhɪ̀in yà dà,** je suis content de moi **ā n̄ flʌ́ʌ̀ gʉ́**
contentement *m* **flʌ́ʌ̀**
contenu *m* **yʌ̋n**
continuer **dhó, tʉ̀n,** continuer une journée entière **glòo**
contourner **slʌ̄ʌ**
contrainte *f* **flɔ̋tí**

contredire qn **wɛ̃ bhɛ̄n wɔ̀ wlɤ̀ɤ**
contrôle *m* **gbàŋ, kɔ̀kúndhɛ̀**
convaincre : action de convaincre **blɔ̀ɔ**
convenir **bhɔ̀ɔn, bhà-kún,** être convenable **bhɔ̄**
convulsion *f* **glánglán**
coopération *f* **dhʌ̀nŋkwʌ́ʌ̀, dhʌ̀nŋkwʌ́ʌ̀dhē**
copeau *m* **kɤ̀, kɤ̀kɤ̀,** copeaux de bois **dhɯ́ɯ kɤ̀-dhùn**
coq *m* **tɔ̀ gɔ̄n,** gros coq rouge **zàan,** le premier coq a chanté **tɔ̀ gɔ̄n bhā yà yà dhɛ̀ɛdhɪ́ɤ bhō-sɯ̀ɯ bhà**
coquille *f* **kɛ́ɛ, sɔ̀ɔn**
corbeau *m* **gɔ̄ŋdʌ̄**
corde *f* **bhīʌ́, bhīʌ́gā, dɤ̄ŋgā, dhɔ̃ŋ, yɔ̀gɔ̀,** corde de raphia **sɔ̃,** corde *f* à linge **sɔ̄dùnbhàbhīʌ́ʌ,** corde *f* fabriquée avec les fibres de la plante kpʌ̀ **kpʌ̀gā,** corde *f* pour les pièges **kpʌ̄ʌ́, kpʌ̄ʌ́gā,** corde *f* : la corde de harpe-luth **kɔ̄nŋ gā,** corde pour lier le fagot de bois **wɔ́sɯ̀gɯ́bhīʌ́ bhīʌ́ yùa**
corne *f* **sɤ̀**
corps *m* **dhʌnŋ, kwī, kpɛ́ɛ̀,** corps de python **gblùŋ kplɯ́ zìnŋgɯ́**
corriger **dhī**
cosse *f* de gombo **gblóɔ̀ gā**
costume en fibres de raphia **dhūɤɤ**
côte *f* **sɛ̃n**
côté *m* **pɛ̃ɛn, zīan,** côté *m (de rivière)* **yí kpɔ̃ŋ dhɪ́ɤ,** côté droit **kɔ̀sʌ̀ gɯ́ pǽæn, kɔ̀sʌ̀,** côté *f* gauche **kwàa,** côté du feu *(dans la case)* **sɪ́ɤ pɛ̃ɛn,** mets-le de côté **à yà gɤ̃ŋ tà,** à côté **bádhɤ̄**
coton *m* **yɛ̄ɛ́**
cou *m* **bhɔ̄, bhɛ̄ɛ́dhɛ̀**
coucal à ventre blanc **tūɯ́tūɯ́**
coucher **wáàndhūn,** se coucher **wáàndhūn, wɔ̄,** endroit pour se coucher **wɛ̀ɛ,** il s'est couché à plat ventre **yà wáàndhūn ɤ̄ gú tà,** il s'est couché sur le ventre **yà wɔ̄ ɤ̄ gú tà**
coucou **tūɯ́tūɯ́dhɤ̄**
coucou *m* didric **gbɔ̄dìʌʌ**
coucou *m* geai **plɛ̄gbàan**
coucou *m* gris **gbídhō**
coude *m* **klòŋdhɛ̀, kpɛ̀kù**
coudre **wɔ̀**
couiner : les souris sont en train de couiner **bhɔ̀ɔn-dhùn wɔ̀ wɛ̃-sɪʌ kwɛ̃ɛkwɛ̀ɛkwɛ̄ɛ́dhɤ̄**
couler **gó, wɛ̀nŋ, zīɤ,** couler *(bâteau)* **dhó yí wlɤ̀ɤ,** son nez coule **à yūn yɤ̀ bhɔ̀**
couleur *f* **yɛ̃n**
coup d'œil **yɛ̃n,** jeter un coup d'œil à côté **yɛ̃n zɯ̀ɤ ɤ̄ pɛ̃n pɪ́ɤ**
coup *m* **zɯ̀ɤ**
coupe : il est entièrement sous la coupe de sa femme **yà kʌ̄ tʌ́ŋ̀tʌ̀ŋ ká ɤ̄ bhā dhēbʌ̀ gɔ̀**
coupe-coupe *m* **bɛ̃ŋ, kāibhân,** coupe-coupe court **gbɛ̃**
couper **kɛ̃n, kplɯ́-kɛ̃n, yɛ̃, zʌ̄,** couper en petits morceaux **kāàn,** couper en plusieurs morceaux **kāànkāàn,** couper la forêt, couper la brousse **bɯ́ zʌ̄,** couper les épis **gɔ̀-yɛ̃,** couper l'herbe sous les pieds de qn **kɛ̃ŋ dà bhɛ̄n gɛ̀n gɯ́,** il a la main coupée **à kɔ̀ yɤ̀ kplɯ́ ká,** il en a coupé un morceau d'un seul coup **yàa kplɯ́ kɛ̃n bɤ̃ŋdhɤ̄,** il lui a coupé la tête **yà à gɔ̀ kɛ̃n à dhɪ́ɤ, yà à gɔ̀ kɛ̃n à dhɪ́ɤ**
coupeur *m* de routes **zīaankɛ̃nbhɛ̀n**
cour *f (de maison)* **kwɛ̃ŋ̀dhɛ̀, pɪ́ɤdhɛ̀**
cour *f (de justice)* **zādɔ̄dhɛ̀**
cour *f* : faire la cour **dà**
courage : prend courage! **bhɤ̀ ɯ fāan sɯ́! ɯ zɔ̀-gbàn!**

courant *m (électrique)* **kūdhân, síɤɓ** on nous a coupé le courant **wȁ síɤ kắn yī tȁ**

courant *m* d'eau **yí tɛ̋ɛ**

courant : je suis au courant de cette affaire **ȁ wɔ̏n yɤ̏ n̄ yấan**

courbature *f* **gî**

courber **dháȁndhūn, gbȁn, klòŋ,** se courber **klòŋ,** en se courbant **bīɔŋdhɤ̄**

courbure *f* **klòŋdhȅ**

coureur *m* **bȉaŋsúɯbhȅn, gbȁngèegɔ̏bhȅn,** coureur de classe **bȉaŋgā, gȅngbɛ̋ɛ̏bhȅn,** coureur sans égal **bȉaŋgā yāa, gȅngbɛ̋ɛ̏bhȅn yāa,** coureur de jupons **yấngúɯyāabhȅn**

courge *f* **gʌ̄n**

courir **bȉaŋ sɯ̋ɯ,** il est venu en courant **yȁ dhūn bȅŋ ká,** , se mettre à courir **dɔ̄ bȅŋ bhȁ,** se mettre à courir à pleine vitesse **bȅŋ dɔ̄ ɤ̄ gɔ̏ɔ**

couroucou à queue barrée **sɔ̋nŋdɔ̄gèetȁ**

courroie *f* **gʌ̄n,** courroie de sac de voyage **glɛ̄ɛ́ gʌ̄n**

course *f* **bȉaŋ, bȅŋ,** prendre un pas de course **ɤ̄ gȅn wɔ̏ bȅŋ ká**

court **klɤ̄ɤ̏, kplɛ̂kplȅ,** je suis à court d'argent **flɛ̋ɛ yà n̄ zʌ̄ tɤ̋ŋ ɤ́ yā ȁ gúɯ,** court et gros **gúŋ̏gȕŋ**

cousinage *m* à plaisanterie *f* **dhấsí-dhȅ, sànbhűnzʌ̏-dhȅ,** il y a cousinage à plaisanterie entre nous **dhấsí-dhȅ yɤ̏ yī zìnŋgúɯ**

cousine *f* croisée **dhē sɛ̄ɛ̋ndhʌ́n**

coussinet *m* de tête **bhlííin**

coûte que coûte **dhʌnwɔ̄dɔ̄**

couteau *m* **dhȁa,** couteau de fabrication industrielle **kwí bhȁ dhȁa**

coutume *f* **wɔ̄kɔ̏**

couvercle *m* **tȅ, tȅdhíɤ**

couverture *f* **gɔ̋ŋ, kpȁtȁ,** couverture en laine **kȍsȍ**

couvre-chef **fấȁn**

couvrir **kpā, tȁ-kʌ̄, tȁ-kpā, glȕɯ,** le brouillard a couvert les lieux **dhűu yȁ yȁ dhȅ yā ȁ gúɯ,** se couvrir la tête **fấȁn yȁ**

craac **glấanŋ̏dhɤ̄**

crabe *m* **gǽæn, kā**

crac **gbʌ̄ʌnŋdhɤ̄, wɛ̄ɛ̋ndhɤ̄**

crac-crac **glāấnglȁanglāấndhɤ̄**

cracher **dhídhí bhō,** c'est son père tout craché **ȁ dʌ̄ yɔ̏ɔn yɤ̏ ȁ gúɯ**

crampe *f* **glấnglấn,** j'ai une crampe à la jambe **glấnglấn yà dȁ n̄ gȅn gúɯ**

crapaud *m* **dhāŋ̏pȍ, pōo**

craquement *m* : j'ai eu un craquement dans le dos **n̄ kō yà bhía n̄ bhȁ**

craquer **bhía, gúɯ-wɛ̋,** craquer une allumette **tấklấa pú**

crasseux **yʌ̏nŋsȕɯ**

cravache *f* **fấa**

cravate *f* **klȁa,** *f* **klāvấtɤ̏**

crayon *m* **bȅnzʌ̏kápʌ̏, klɛ̄yɔ̂n, klīyɔ̂n ga**

créature *f* **tɛ̋ɛpʌ̏**

credit : acheter qch à crédit **pʌ̄ dhɔ́ pɔ̋ ká**

créer **dȁ, pʌ̏-kʌ̄**

crépuscule *m* du soir *m* **fītlî**

creuser **pɔ́n**

creux *m* **gȍŋ,** creux d'arbre **dhűɯ gȍŋ, dhűɯ yȅgā,** creux de louche **klȕu gɔ̏ klȕu wēŋ,** creux du paturon **sɔ̏ɔ̏ kȅe**

crève-chien *f* **sȉandhɛ̋**

crevette *f* **kȅnŋ**

cri *m* **glấ**

cri *m* d'in oiseau rapace **kúkúdhūkúdhû**

crier **glấ, glāȁ, glāȁglāȁ,** crier au secours **tấbhōo dȁ,** le grand-duc crie **gbēŋbhȁan yɤ̏ wȅ kúkúdhūkúdhû**

crieur *m* public **dhȅɛdhíɤbhōbhȅn**

criquet *m* **plɛ́e, tȍŋpűu, zȅɛkpàa**

croc *m* **kɔ̏ɔdhȕɯ**

croc-croc-croc **krrɤ́ɤdhɤ̄**

croc-en-jambe *m* **kấŋ**

crochet *m* **kɔ̀ɔ**
crocodile *m* : crocodile de Nil **gwʌ̄ʌ́, yĩ̂agwʌ̄ʌ́,** petit crocodile **gbɛ́ɛ̀**
croire à **dhã́ŋ̀ bhō bhɛ̄n dhĩ́ɤ**
croiser les jambes **zīɤ**
croix *f* **dhṹɯ, klōâ**
croque-mitaine *m* **tītībhɔ́nbhɔ́n**
crotte *f* **gbō pɛ̃́n**
cru **sæ̀æ**
cube d'arôme maggi **sṹnbhã́ndhã́n gā**
cueillir : cueillir le café **kã́flẽ́e bhō,** cueillir le miel **zɔ̃́ bhō**
cuillère *f* **sã́ŋ,** cuillère de calebasse pour la bouillie de riz **bhã́a yĩ́ bhɯ̃̀n' ká kɔ̀ɔ**
cuire **bhān, kpà̃,** cuire le tô **tòo kʌ̄, tòo kpà̃**
cuisine *f* **gbàúɯ̀**
cuisse *f* **gɤ̃̀ŋ, gbã́n, gbã́nbhlʌ́,:** partie inférieure de la cuisse **gbã́n wlɤ̀ɤdhɛ̀**
culotte *f* **blɛ̀ɛ**
cultivateur *m* **bhláābhɛ̀n, bhláàkɛ̀kʌ̄bhɛ̀n, kɛ̂kʌ̄bhɛ̀n**
cultiver **kʌ̄**
cure-dent *m* **gbɛ́sɛ̂**
cuvette *f* **bàŋ, tǽæ̀,** cuvette pour la sauce **tɔ̃́o yɤ̀ gúɯ tæ̀æ,** grande cuvette *f* **gwāndɛ̀egúɯslāā́**
cynhyène *m* **gbān**

D d

d'abord **blɛ̀ɛsɯ̃̀, kɤ̀ŋgbɤ̄**
d'accord **ɛ̀ɛ, ɯ̀un, àahã́an, ã̀òo**
daloa *(sorte de cola blanc)* **dã́dhɔ̃́a**
daman *m* de rocher **gwã̄ã̀gbɛ̂n, gwàawɯ̃̀**
Dan **yàobâ, Dàn,** Dan du Libéria **Yĩ́zlɤ̀ɤ yàobâ**
dandiner : se dandinant **tɔ́tɔ̀tɔ́dhɤ̄**
danger : endroit de danger mortel **bhɛ̄ndhĩ́ɤdɔ̄dhɛ̀**
dangereux **gbɛ́ɛ̀**
dans **bhàa, gúɯ, ká, pĩ́ɤ**
danse *f* **tã́n,** danse de respect **gǽæ,** danse du masque "kong" **kɔ̀ŋ,** danse *f* de course *f* de masques **gīaatà̃n,** danse *f* rapide **tã́n wɔ̃́sɯ̃̀,** danse pour marquer la sortie du masque gèekɛ̃́ɛsɯ̃̀ **gīaatà̃n,** suudhi *(danse des jeunes)* **sūṹdhí**
danser **tã́n kʌ̄**
danseur *m*, danseuse *f* **tã́nkʌ̄bhɛ̀n,** danseuse de dhɛ̀ɛdhĩ́ɤ tã́n **dhɛ̀ɛdhĩ́ɤ, sànbhàn**
dartrier **kɔ̄ŋsɛ̃́ɛdhɯ̃̀**
de bonne heure **vã́andhɤ̄, dhīã́ à̃ pĩ́ɤ,** il commencera le travail demain de bonne heure **yɤ̀ dhɔ̀ sɯ̀ɤ yʌ tà̃ dhīã́**
de **gɔ̀**
de longue durée **gɔ̄ɔgblɛ̀ɛn**
de nouveau **dèewō**
de petite taille **kplɛ̂kplɛ̀**
de temps en temps **dódó, zɔ̄ɔzɔ̄ɔdhɤ̄**
débarasser : se débarasser de **kã́n**
débattre (se) : le rat pris dans le piège est en train de se débattre contre la mort **fɛ̃́ŋ yɤ̀ gā kʌ̄-sīʌ dɤ̃ŋ gúɯ**
déborder **pā,** à déborder **kūɯkkūɯdhɤ̄**
debout : être debout **dɔ̄**
débris *m* **kɤ̀ɤ**
débroussailler **bà̃, gúɯ-bà̃**
début *m* **zūɯbhō-dhɛ̀**
décembre *m* **ylɯ̃̀**
décevoir, être déçu **gúɯ-gā**
décharge : l'anguille électrique m'a donné une décharge **gbĩ̀ŋgbɤ̄ yà dà̃ n̄ gúɯ**
décharger, être déchargé **bhō**
déchausser : il s'est déchaussé **yà̃ ɤ̄ bhā sàbhã́ bhō ɤ̄ gɛ̀ɛn**
déchets *m* **blʌ̄ʌ, gblṹ**
déchirer **pɛ̃́,** se déchirer **zūa,** déchirer en morceaux **blʌ̃́**

déclaration d'amour : elle n'a pas accepté ma déclaration d'amour **yà̰ kɔ̀ n̄ gɔ̀**
déclarer son amour **kɛ̋n**
décorer **bā̰à̰**, on l'a décoré **wà̰ là dhʌ̀nŋ à̰ tò̰ŋ tà̰**
découper **pɛ̋**
découragement *m* **dìn**
décourager **gúɯ-gā**, je suis découragé **n̄ dìn yà yʌ̀n, n̄ gbɛ̀ yà̰ gā n̄ gɔ̀**
décrépitude *f* **gbɔ̋ɔ̀-dhɛ̀**
défaire : il a un bouton qui s'est défait **à̰ bhà̰ būtɔ́nŋ̀ dhɪ́ɤ yà̰ pő**
défaut *m* **zʌ̀ká-dhɛ̀**, trouver des défauts **dhɛ̀ yɤ̄**
défense *f* d'éléphant **bīɤ sɔ̋n**
défense *f* : prendre sa défense devant qn **zā kún bhɛ̄n gɔ̀**
défenseur *m* **kɔ̀ɔnbhɛ̀n**
déféquer **gbōo**
défi *m* **bhlɔ̄ɔ, bhlɔ̄ɔ dhɪ̀aŋ̀, yɛ̋nzɪ̀ɤgúɯ**, un défi lui a été lancé **bhlɔ̄ɔ yà bhán à̰ gúɯ**
définitivement **dhʌ̀nwōdō**
déflorer : il l'a déflorée **yà̰a bhà̰ dhà̰agā yɛ̋**
déformé **gɤ̋ŋgɤ̀ŋ**
défricher **kpɔ́**, défricher le terrain **dhɛ̀ bhō**
dégager **bà̰**, le ciel s'est dégagé **dhākpɔ́ŋ̀ yà̰ kɛ̋n kwʌ́ʌ̀**
dégourdir, se dégourdir **gúɯ-pő**
dégoût *m* **sà̰n**
dégoutant **yʌ̀nŋsɯ̀ɯ**
dégoûter qn **yʌ̀nŋ kʌ̄ à̰ gɔ̀**, ça me dégoûte **à̰ sà̰n yà̰ yɤ̄ n̄ gúɯ**
dégrader : il a été dégradé **wà̰ à̰ bhà̰ là lɔ̄ɔ**
déjà **blɛ̀ɛsɯ̀ɯwō, dìɤ, dhún, tɔ̀n**
délibérations : ils sont partis pour les délibérations **wà dhó wō gɔ̀ dūn'**
délicieux : c'est délicieux **à̰ dīn yɤ̀ dhì**
délier, se délier **pű**, délier un noeud **kpɤ̄ pű**
demain **dhīā̰**
demande de nouvelles **bhàdhīà̰**
demander **dhɛ̀, dhɛ̄ɛ̋-kpɔ́**, demander pardon **bhɛ̄ɛ̋, dhī**
démangeaison : provoquer des démangeaisons *f* **kā̰à̰**
démanger **kā̰à̰**
demeure des fourmis magnan **zlūu gɔ̀ dùɛɛ**
demeurer **kʌ̄**
demi-frère *m* **dʌ̄bhāŋ, dʌ̄gbɤ̄**
demi-sœur *f* **dʌ̄bhāŋ, dʌ̄dhú**
démon *m* **yɪ́dhɛ̋n**
dénouer la cravate **klà̰a pő**
dense **gœ̄œ, gúɯsɯ̀ɯ, kḭ̀ansɯ̀ɯ, kún-sɯ̀ɯ, yɤ̀kőosɯ̀ɯ**, être dense **yɤ̄ kőo**
dent *m* **sɔ̋n**, par les dents **sɔ̋npɪ́ɤ**
dénudé : surface *f* dénudée **yā̰à̰n, yā̰à̰ndhɛ̀**
département *m* **sɛ̋**
dépasser **bō, dhɪ́ɤ-zīɤ, zīɤ**, il l'a dépassé de loin **yà zīɤ à̰ tà̰ pōŋpōŋdhɤ̄**, le niveau de l'eau dépasse la taille d'un homme **yí yɤ̀ bɔ̀ bhɛ̄n tà̰**
dépendre **dō, súɯ**
dépiquer **bhà̰n**
déplacement *m* **tɛ̋**
déplacer **bhō-gblőo**, se déplacer **tɛ̋ súɯ, gó**
déposer l'argent à la banque **wʌ́ʌ̀ dà̰ wʌ́ʌ̀kɔ̀ gúɯ**
dépôt *m* **gbō, gbɔ̀ɔ**
dépression *f* **bā̰à̰ndhɛ̀**
depuis **bhɔ̄ à̰ ká dhɤ̋**, depuis ça **à̰ yī yà̰ gwʌ̀ʌ**, depuis cela et jusqu'à nos jours **ɤ́ sṵ̄ à̰ bhà̰, ..., ɤ́ dɛ̀ɛ ɤ́ lòo** ; depuis longtemps **zīi, à̰ yī yà̰ gwʌ̀ʌ**
déranger qn **dō bhɛ̄n gɔ̀ yâ**

dernier **tòtàabhàn,** le tout dernier **dōsēŋdhàan ... tàabhàn,** rester le dernier **tó tàabhàn**
derrière **tàabhàn, zlɤ̀ɤ,** marcher derrière **tó tàabhàn**
derrière *m* : son derrière est étroit comme une aiguille **à zūkpɤ̄ yɤ̀ gbɛ́ɛ ká dhè dháà dhɤ́**
désaccord *m* **kànkwʌ́ʌ̀-sɯ̀, pɛ́dhē,** tomber en désaccord **pɛ́**
désagrément *m* **kpɔ̄ɔ**
désarroi : Gbato est en désarroi **Gbàtò yán gɯ́ yà dūuŋ bhō**
descendre **dà, lɔ̄ɔ**
désert *m* **tőoŋ,** dans le désert **tőoŋ tà**
désherber **gɯ́-bhō, gɯ́-zʌ̄**
désinfecter **gɯ́-zʌ̄**
désir *m* **dhɔ̀, dhɔ̄ɔbhàa**
désobéir **dhɪ́ɤ-blɯ̀**
désobéissant : il est désobéissant **à gɔ̄ɔ yɤ̀ gbɛ́ɛ̀, à gɔ̄ɔ yɤ̀ sǽæ**
desserré **yʌ́ŋ̀yʌ̀ŋ**
dessin *m* **pʌ̄bín**
dessus **dhɯ́ɤ̀**
dessus *m* : prendre le dessus **bhɔ̀ɔn**
détacher **pű,** se détacher **gó,** détacher en pièces composantes **wɔ́n-dhùn bhō kőo,** détacher l'épi de maïs de la tige **kɤ̄ŋ bhō ɤ̄ dhɯ̀ bhà**
déteindre : il a déteint **à yán yà gā**
détendre : se détendre **bhía**
détériorer : se détériorer **sēè**
déterrer **pɔ́n, wò,** déterrer le manioc **bāa wò**
détester : je le déteste **à sàn yà yɤ̄ n̄ gɯ́**
détourner : se détourner **ɤ̄ wʌ̄ʌdhɛ̀ slʌ̄ʌ gɯ́,** détourner une femme **dà**
dette *f* : venir encaisser une dette **dhùn pɔ̃ tà**
deux **pèedʌ̄, plɛ̀,** par deux **plɛ̄ɛplɛ̄,** deux par deux **plɛ̀-plɛ̀**
devant **dhɛ̀, dhɪ́ɤ, dhɪ́ɤdhɤ̄, wʌ̄ʌdhɛ̀, wʌ̄ʌzìaan,** devant qn **kùu dhɪ́ɤ,** devant la porte d'entrée *(à l'intérieur et à l'extérieur de la maison)* **kpán dhɪ́ɤ,** devant moi! **gblʌ́ʌ̀dhūn n̄ dhɛ̀!**
devant *m* du corps **gblʌ́ʌ̀, gblʌ́ʌdhɛ̀**
développer, se développer **glá**
devenir **dhɪ́ɤ-kʌ̄, glá, kʌ̄**
devin *m* **dɛ̀bɔ̄bhɛ̀n, dɛ̀bhīn**
devinette *f* **kpɔ̀dhēŋ̀bhō, pìan,** trouver la réponse à une devinette **kpɔ̀dhēŋ̀bhō yɔ̀ɔbɔ̄**
devoir **bhɔ̀ɔn**
devoir *m* **dūá**
diarrhée *f* **gblɯ́zīɤ,** il a la diarrhée **à gblɯ́ yɤ̀ zīɤ-sīʌ,** diarrhée cholériforme **gblɯ́zīɤ zǽ̀ændhē**
Dieu *m* **zlàan,** mon Dieu! **gbɛ́gbɛ̀**
différence *f* **bhɔ̀kőo, dhàan, zìnŋ**
différend *m* **dhīaŋ, pɪ́ʌ̀ʌdhɤ̀kò**
différents **dódó**
difficile **gláglásɯ̀, gláŋglàŋ, gbɛ́ɛ̀,** devenir difficile **dō bhēn gɔ̀ yâ,** Gbato n'est pas difficile en ce qui concerne la nourriture **Gbàtò yáa bhɤ̀pʌ̀ zʌ̄ ɤ̄ dhí,** il n'est pas difficile **yáa tʌ̄ʌ dō,** la vie est devenue difficile **kpɔ́ŋtàadhɛ̀ yà kʌ̄ gbɛ́ɛ̀**
difficilement : il fait cela difficilement **à kɔ̀ yɤ̀ gbínŋ̀ à bhà**
difficulté *f* **bhádhá, wɔ́n,** difficulté inattendue **dhʌ̄nŋ**
digérer **zɔ̀ɔ**
digne : être digne **bhɔ̄ ... bhà, bhà-kún**
digraphe **sʌ́ʌdhɛ́yángāplɛ̀**
dimanche *m* **dìbhánŋ̀sɯ̀, tēnŋyɛ̄ɛ́n**
dimension *f* **dœ̄œŋ**
diminuer **bhɤ́ɤ**
ding **gbāŋgbāŋdhɤ̄**
ding-ding **kɤ̄dhɤ̄ŋkɤ̄dhɤ̄ŋdhɤ̄**
Dioula **bhʌ̄nŋ́**
dire **pɤ̄**

directement **dō, dōsēŋ, kpēeŋdhɤ̄, kpɤ̋ɤ̏dhɤ̄, vɛ̄ɛdhɤ̄,** *(sans arrêt, sans gêne)* **pɤ́ dhɤ́ dō,** il est allé directement **yɤ̏ zìɤ ɤ̄ gǣæn dō**
directeur *m* **dīdhɛ̄tʌ́ʌ̀,** directeur d'école **klàŋ̏gɔ̏bhɛ̏n kpîì**
direction *f* **tɤ̋ŋ, zìan**
dirigeant *m* **dhɪ́ɤbhɛ̏n**
diriger : se diriger **ɤ̄ wʌ̄ dɔ̄**
discernement **wlɔ́ɔ̏**
disciple *m* **gwʌ̄ʌ́, gwʌ̄ʌ́bhīn**
discorde *f* **dhɪ́dhàan**
discuter : ils se sont mis à discuter à ce propos **yɤ́ pɛ̏ à-dhùn zìnŋgɯ́ zœ̄œdhē ká**
disparaître **bhʌ́nŋ, dhèŋ, dhìdhā sɯ́,** tendre à disparaître **bhɤ̋ɤ**
disparition **dhìdhā**
disperser : se disperser **kʌ̋n, pɛ̏n**
disputer : se disputer avec qn **dhɪ́dhàan bhán bhɛ̄n ká**
disputeur : il est disputeur ardent **à dhɪ́ yɤ̏ gbɛ́ɛ̏**
dissension : la dissension a éclaté entre eux **yà pɛ́ à-dhùn zìnŋgɯ́ zœ̄œdhē ká**
dissimuler : se dissimuler parmi les gens **ɤ̄ zɯ́ bhɛ̄n-dhùn ká**
dissoudre, se dissoudre **sɤ̏ŋ**
disspier (se) : le brouillard s'est dissipé **dhɯ̋u yà gó síāa**
distance *f* **zìnŋ**
distinctement **kpákpádhɤ̄,** distinctement et à haute voix **kpēŋkpēŋdhɤ̄**
distinguer **bhō, zʌ̀gɯ́-kʌ̄, zìnŋ-dɔ̄**
distribuer **bhō, gɯ́-gblɯ̀ɯ**
divan *m* **gblòo**
diverger, être en contradiction **kɔ́n kwʌ́ʌ̀**
divertir **gɔ̄ɔ-bhō**
divination *f* **dɛ̏**
diviser **gɯ́-gblɯ̀ɯ, gblɯ̀ɯ, pɛ́-gɯ́,** se diviser **pɛ́-gɯ́**
division *f* **pɛ́dhē**
divorcer **gó, kʌ̋n, gwān kʌ̋n,** il a divorcé **yà ɤ̄ bhā dhēbʌ̀ bhō bɯ̋ɯ,** il a divorcé de sa femme **yà ɤ̄ kɔ̏ bhō ɤ̄ bhā dhēbʌ̀ gɯ́ɯ,** Yo a divorcé de Jean **Yɔ̏ yà gwān kʌ̋n Zân gɔ̏**
dixième **kɔ̏ŋ dō-dhàan, kœ̀œŋ dō-dhàan**
dizaine **kɔ̏ŋ**
document *m* **sʌ́ʌdhɛ́**
doigt *m* **kōŋ, kōŋgā**
domestiquer **dà**
don *m* **yʌ̄ʌ**
donc **dhɤ́, zɔ̀ɔ**
donner **dɔ̄, dhūn, gbā**
dormir **yī zʌ̄**
dos *m* **kō, tàa, tàadhɛ̏,** dos de couteau **dhàa kō,** dos de lame de machette **bʌ̋ŋ kō,** dos de louche **klùu kō,** dos de la main **kɔ̏dhɛ́tà,** dos de carte **klàatîì dhɛ́ tà dhɯ̋ɤ dhɛ̏,** haut *m* du dos **gbāntàdhɛ̏,** ne parle pas dans mon dos! **bhá dhó dhīaŋ zʌ̄' n̄ kèɛ̏ tà!**
dot *f* **yɔ̏,** payer la dot **dhēbʌ̀ dhɔ́,** venir dans la famille du mari de sa fille pour chercher la dot **dhū yɔ̏ tà**
d'où? **bhɛ́n**
doucement **lɛ̋ɛdhɤ̄, sɛ̋ɛnŋsɛ̋ɛnŋdhɤ̄, yàandhɤ̄, yɛ̋ɛdhɤ̄**
douchière *f (et toilettes ensemble)* **dhɔ̋o**
douleur *f* **pīɤ̄ɤ,** j'ai des douleurs dans le dos **n̄ kō yɪ́ yà kʌ̋n,** douleurs de l'accouchement **gɯ̋dhɛ̏, gblɯ̋ɯkʌ̄**
douloureusement **wɛ̏ɛndhɤ̄**
doute *m* **zʌ́zʌ̀zʌ́, síkʌ́,** sans doute **dhɛ̏, yíi dɔ̄ sʌ̀, yɤ̏ bhɔ̏ à bhà dhɛ̀..., yɤ̏ dhɔ̏ kʌ̄' dhɛ̀ ...,** sans aucun doute **dhɛ̏**
douter : le X ne pense pas que ...; le X doute que... **yáa X yʌ̋an dhɛ̀...**
douteux **kʌ̋nŋkʌ̀nŋ**
dragueur *m* **yʌ̋ngɯ́yāabhɛ̏n**
dresser un chien contre qn **gbɛ̂n yà bhɛ̄n bhà**

dresser une embuscade pour surveiller qn/qch ɤ̄ **gbá dō à bhà**
droit **kplēŋkplēŋdhɤ̄**
d'un coup **kpɯ́dhɤ̄**
d'un seul coup **vĩaandhɤ̄**
duper qn **kpʌ̃́nŋ̀ kʌ̄ bhēn gɔ̀**
dur **gbɛ̃́ɛ̀,** dur et sec **gblɤ̃́ɤgblɤ̃ɤ**
durer **gwʌ̀ʌ,** trop durer **gwʌ̀ʌ,** le silence a duré **dhɛ̃̀tà gā-sɯ̀ yà gwʌ̀ʌ,** trop durer sans trouver de mari **glɔ̀o kún**
dynamique **vlɯ́vlɯ̀**

E e

eau *f* **yĩ́,** eau salée **wèeyĩ̀, yĩ́ wèesɯ̀,** eau profonde **yĩ́ gblɯ̀, yĩ́ gblɯ̀gā,** eau savonneuse **sāà yĩ́**
ébattre : s'ébattre **bhō**
éblouir **tlɤ̄ɤ,** la lumière m'éblouit **sĩ́ɤ yà dō n̄ yã́n gɯ́**
écartement **wlã́ŋ**
écarter **yɔ̀ɔn,** s'écarter **gó, yɔ̀ɔn, ɤ̄ bhɤ̃́ yɔ̀ɔn bhūn,** il écarte les bras **yɤ̀ ɤ̄ kɔ̀ wlã́ŋ bhō-sīʌ,** écarte-toi un peu **dō n̄ ká bádhɤ̄**
échafaudage *m* **gbàn**
échange *m* **fĩʌʌ**
échanger **gó,** échanger X contre Y, préférer X à Y **X fĩʌʌ bhō Y bhà**
échapper **dhā, zʌ̄,** échapper de justesse, l'échapper belle **dhā ɤ̄ kāà ká,** *(fuire, de l'eau)* **bō, bhō,** cette affaire a échappé à mon contrôle **à wɔ́n yà dà n̄ gɔ̀ gbàŋ tà,** s'échapper des mains de qn **vlɯ̀ɯvlɯ̃́ɯ**
échauffement *m* avant la course **gɛ̃́ɛ**
échelle *f* **gbààndhɯ̀, gbàndàadhɯ̀, gbʌ̀kʌ̄**
échine *f* **kōgā**
échouer **fĩʌʌ**
éclairé **bōoŋ**
éclairer **tà-pő**
éclaireur *m* **glɯ̀dhānkʌ̄bhɛ̀n**
éclat : avec éclat **klɛ̀klɛ̀dhɤ̄**
éclatant **gbàngbàn, gbàngbàndhɤ̄**
éclater : il éclate de rire **yɛ̃́e yɤ̀ yɛ̃́e tò dhĩ́ gbǣ́ædhɛ̀ bhà**
éclater : sur le point d'éclater **tĩ̀tĩ̀dhɤ̄**
éclisse *f* **sàa**
école *f* **klàŋ̀, klàŋdhĩ́ɤ, klàŋ kɔ̀,** école *f* coranique **bhɔ̃́ɔn klàŋ̀, bhʌ̄nŋ́ klàŋ̀,** école *f* française **kwĩ́ klàŋ̀**
écoliers **klàŋ̀-dhùn**
économiser **gɔ̀-kpɔ́**
écoper une amende **tɔ́ŋ̀ bhō**
écorce *f* **gőŋ, kɛ̃́ɛ, kɤ̀,** écorce, espèce de **gɔ̀ŋ**
écorcher : les chaussures m'ont écorché les pieds **sàbhã́ yà n̄ gìi**
écouter qch ɤ̄ **tő tó ... bhà**
écraser **dhĩ́ʌʌ**
écrevisse *f* **kènŋ**
écrire **pʌ̄-yà, sʌ́ʌdhɛ̃́ bɛ̀n zʌ̄,** écrire une lettre à qn **sʌ́ʌdhɛ̃́ kʌ̄ ... dhɛ̀**
écriture *f* **bɛ̀n,** écriture *(manière)* **kɔ̀ gblőo**
écrou *m* **klúgā**
écrouler : s'écrouler **wɛ̀nŋ**
écuelle d'un kilo **bṹaŋ**
écuelle *f* en bois **kpēe**
écume *f* **vṹu**
écureuil *m* : *Heliosciurus gambianus* **gbâgɔ̀ɔ,** *(espèce)* **gwǣæ̀gèe,** écureuil de brousse **gbā,** écureuil volant de Beecroft **kpʌ̄,** écureuil terrestre **bhɶ́œŋ̀**
éducation *f* **klő,** éducation formelle **sʌ́ʌdhɛ̃́**
éduqué : personne *f* éduquée **sʌ́ʌdhɛ̃́dōbhɛ̀n**
éduquer un enfant **dhʌ́n klő bhō**
effectuer **sɯ́**
effeuiller : s'effeuiller **lòo**

effilocher : son habit s'est effiloché jusqu'à créer une frange **à bhà sō kʌ̋ŋ gā yà kʌ̄ gbɛ́**
efforcer : s'efforcer **ɤ̄ gɯ́-dɔ̄ gbɛ̋ɛ̀, gɯ́-tó, tà-bhō,** s'efforcer à **dɔ̄ ... gɔ̀**
effort *m* : d'un effort commun **yàkàyàkàdhɤ̄,** faire un effort **dɔ̄, gɯ́-dɔ̄**
effrayant **bhlɯ̋nbhlɯ̋nsɯ̀**
effrayer **zìan-kʌ̄, kʌ̋n,** effrayer qn **sɯ̋ɤ kʌ̋n bhēn gɯ́**
effronté : il est effronté **à dhí yɤ̀ gbɛ̋ɛ̀, à yʌ̋n yɤ̀ gbɛ̋ɛ̀,** c'est un menteur effronté **bhēn bhā yɤ̀ dlàan dhīaŋ gɯ́**
égal **dōsēŋ, sɯ́bhʌ̋n,** être égal **bhɔ̄ɔ̀n**
égard : il n'a pas d'égard pour lui-même **yɤ̀ gîì gɯ́ ɤ̄ dè gɔ̀,** parler sans égards **dhīaŋ zʌ̄ ɤ̄ tlùu gwìnŋ̀**
église *f* **dhèglîìzʌ̀, Zlàan kɔ̀**
égrainer, égrener **klōo, slʌ̄ʌ**
égratigner : elles égratignent les gens **wɔ̀ bhēn flɔ̋ bhɔ̀,** il s'est égratigné **yà flɔ̋ bhō**
égratignure *f* **flɔ̋**
eh bien **āa, ɛ̀, ɤ̄ɤ**
éhonté : il est éhonté **à yʌ̋n yɤ̀ gbɛ̋ɛ̀**
éjaculer **wɛ̀nŋ**
élancement *m* : j'ai des élancements à l'oreille **n̄ tɔ̋gɯ́dhè yɤ̀ n̄ kʌ̄-sīʌ**
élargir **píɤ-bà**
élastique **gʌ̋n-sɯ̀**
élections *fpl* **vòtɛ́ɛ̀**
électricité **kūdhân**
éléphant *m* **bīɤ**
élève *m, f* **kāyéèdhʌ́n**
élever **būn, dà, dhíɤ-yà, tɯ̀ɤ,** il élève le bétail **yɤ̀ tɯ̀ɤ dà**
élire *(nommer)* **yà**
éloigné **gblɛ̀ɛn,** éloignés et nombreux **gblɛ̀ngblɛ̀n**
éloigner : éloigne-toi un peu de moi **dɔ̄ n̄ ká bádhɤ̄**
emballer **dhú**
embarrasser **gɯ́-kún, zʌ̄**
embaucher qn **ɤ̄ kɔ̀ yà à bhà**
embêter **bhà-kún, gɯ́-gā, gɯ́-kún, gbɔ̀ɔn,** le bruit des moteurs m'embête **bhànŋzîì wɔ̀ yà n̄ tó pā**
embonpoint **fāan**
embranchement *m* **gbɛ̀ŋ**
embrasser **lòo,** s'embrasser **lòo wō kwʌ̀ʌ̀,** embrasser qn sur les lèvres **bhēn bɛ̀n bhɯ̄n**
embuscade : dresser une embuscade **dɛ̀ɛn-kpɔ́, gblɛ̀ɛn-kpɔ́,** se tenir en embuscade contre qn **gbá kpɔ́ à gɔ̀,** il est tombé dans une embuscade **gblɯ̀ yà à kún**
emmener **dhó à ká, gó à ká**
émoussé **glɔ̋ɔglɔ̀ɔ**
emparer : s'emparer **zɯ̄n**
empêcher : être empêché **kplà**
empoisonner **kpà, dà**
emporter **dhó à ká**
empreinte *f* **blɛ̋ɛ̀n,** laisser les empreintes des mains sur qch **bhēnkɔ̀ blɛ̋ɛn kʌ̄ ... bhà**
emprunt *m* **pɔ̋, sīʌŋ̀**
en aucun cas **tōŋtōŋdhɤ̄**
en **ká, píɤ**
en plus **yɤ́ ɤ́ dhɤ̄ bhā, à zīaan gɯ́, bhá gó bhɯ̄n, ɤ́ gō bhɯ́n**
en question **dèe**
en son absence **à zīaan gɯ́**
en tout cas **zʌ̀**
enceinte **gbíɤ̀ɤ,** devenir enceinte, tomber enceinte **dɔ̋ɔ̀ndhūn, gú sɯ́,** elle est enceinte **yɤ̀ gbíɤ̀ɤdhè ká**
enchanter **tà-pɔ̋**
enchevetrêment *m* **klɔ̀o**
enclos *m* **dhɔ̋o, wlɛɛ**
enclume *f* **gbānsɛ́ɛ, pìɤ bhɔ̀ à tà pʌ̀**
encore **bháwō, dhɤ́dō, kɤ̀, pɤ́pɤ́, tɯ̀n, zɯ́**

encre *f* **lánklʌ̀**
endommager **sì̀ɤ**
endroit *m* **dhɛ̀**
enduire **kpɔ́, yɔ́, gì̀, zīɤ**
énerver **sì̀ɤ**
enfance *f* **dhʌ́nbʌ́-dhɛ̀**
enfant *m* **bhāŋ, dhʌ́n,** enfants **dhɛ́ɛ̀nbʌ̀-dhùn,** enfant nouveau-né *(jusqu'à 1 mois)* **dhʌ́n kpɔ̀ɔŋ̀ dɛ̀e,** enfant unique **dhʌ́n gādō,** enfant du village **pī̀ʌʌdhʌ́n**
enfilé **sɛ̀ɛ̀sɯ̀**
enfin **dō, dhàanbhā, tɔ̀n, wɛ̄ngā**
enfler **bhlà**
enfoncer **gbàn, yɔ̀ɔn,** s'enfoncer **gbàn, dhó ɤ̄ gɯ́ bhɛ̄ɛ́dhɤ̄**
enfuir : s'enfuir **dùa**
enfumer des abeilles **zɔ̋ dhɛ̄ɛ̀ gɤ̋**
engin *m* **bhàanŋzì̀**
engoulevent *m* à balanciers *m* **plɛ̄ŋgbàan**
engourdi **dı̋ŋdìŋ, kpʌ́ʌkpʌ̀ʌ,** s'engourdir **gā,** j'ai les jambes engourdies **gblā̋ngblā̋n yà dà n̄ gɛ̀n gɯ́, tlɯ̋nŋ yà dà n̄ gɛ̀n gɯ́,** ma main s'est engourdie **n̄ kɔ̀ yà kʌ̄ kpʌ́ʌkpʌ̀ʌ, n̄ kɔ̀ yà gā n̄ bhà,** le froid a engourdi mes mains **n̄ kɔ̀ yà kʌ̄ dı̋ŋdìŋ dhɛ́ndhɛ́n kɔ̄ɔ**
engourdissement *m* **gblā̋ngblā̋n, tlɯ̋nŋ**
engraisser : s'engraisser **ɤ̄ yɔ̋n kʌ̄**
enivrer **kún**
enlever **bhō, dùa**
enliser : s'enliser **dhʌ̀nŋ**
ennemi *m* **yœ́œ̀**
ennuyer qn **yà … gɔ̀**
ennuyeux **dhā̀ānsɯ̀**
énorme **bɤ̋ɤkpì̀, zı̀isɯ̀**
énormément **dhɛ̀ɛ**
enrayer : s'enrayer **gbàn,** son fusil s'est enrayé **à bhà būu yà kɔ̀ à gɔ̀**
enregistrer quelqu'un au magnétophone **bhɛ̄n wɔ̀ sɯ́**
enrhumer : il est enrhumé **à gɔ̄ɔ yɤ̀ tā-sɯ̀ ká, à yūn gɯ́ yà tā**
enrouler **klɤ̋-kʌ̄, pīɤ̀ɤ,** s'enrouler **pīɤ̀ɤ**
enseignant *m* **klàŋ̀gɔ̀bhɛ̀n**
enseigner **zɔ̀n, dlā̀ān**
ensemble **kó kɛ̀ŋ, kó pı́ɤ,** agir ensemble, en bonne entente **bhɔ̀ɔn kwʌ̋ʌ**
ensuite **yà yɔ̀ɔn bhūn**
entamer une conversation avec qn **dhīaŋ dà bhɛ̄n tà**
entasser **fɛ̀ɛnfɛ̋ɛn-kʌ̄**
entendre **bhān,** il n'entend pas bien **à tɔ̋ yɤ̀ wɯ́-sɯ̀ ká,** ils s'entendent bien **wɔ̀ wō kó kùn sʌ̀,** nous nous entendons très bien **kwā̀ā bhlɛ̀ɛn yı́ yɤ̀ kā̋n-sīʌ**
entente *f* **kówɔ̀gɯ́bhān-sɯ̀, wɔ́ngɯ́bhān-sɯ̀, zɔ̀yɤ̀kó-dhɛ̀, zūʌ́kʌ̀dō-sɯ̀**
enterrer **wɛ̀ɛ bhō**
entier **tó dhɤ̋, gbàn tó dhɤ̋**
entièrement **gbáàndhɤ̄**
entonnoir *m* **pèe,** il a mis le médicament dans son oeil avec un entonnoir **yà pèe yɤ̄ ɤ̄ yʌ́nŋ**
entourer **klʌ̀ʌn,** s'entourer de **tā ɤ̄ bhà**
entraîner **yɤ̄**
entre **zìnŋgɯ́, zlʌ̀ʌn**
entrée *f* **kpā̋ndhīɤ,** entrée du village **sā̋andhīɤ**
entrelacement *m* **klɔ̀o**
entrelacer : s'entrelacer **zīɤ kɔ̋o**
entremetteur *m* **yɔ̀ kīʌʌ**
entrer **dà,** faire entrer **sɔ̀**
entronnoir : il a fait un entonnoir avec une feuille **yà dhɛ̋ pèe kɤ̄**
envahir **bhʌ̋nŋ, bhɔ̀ɔn, dūn,** la plantation de café est envahie par des broussailles **kpɔ̀ɔ yà dà kā̋flɛ̋e gɯ́**
envelopper **bhán**
envie *f* **dhɔ̀,** envie de nourriture **zūʌ́dɔ̄**
envier qn **dlɔ̀ɔ kʌ̄ bhɛ̄n ká**

environ **súbhấn,** environ dix fois **dhè pʌ̄ dhɤ́ kɛ̀œŋ**
envoûter : elle a envoûté son mari **yà bɛ̀dhɛ̋ kʌ̄ ɤ̄ gɔ̀n ká**
envoyer *(donner)* **dhūn, gbā,** envoyer *(expédier, faire déplacer)* **bɔ̄, dɔ̄, yʌ̄-kʌ̄**
épais **kún-sɯ̏, tlɯ̋nŋgɯ́sɯ̏**
épaisseur **tlɯ̋nŋ**
épaissir : s'épaissir **kún**
épargner **gɔ̏-kpɔ́**
épaule *f* **gbān, gbɛ̏**
épaulette *f* **là**
épervier *m* **sʌ́ʌ̀, slɤ̋ɤŋ**
épi *m* décortiqué **kplʌ̄ʌ́,** épi de maïs **kɤ̄ŋ bhē,** la canne à sucre [le riz, le maïs] a fait des épis **kȁa [bhlɯ̏n, kɤ̄ŋ] yȁ gú sɯ́**
épier **súȁn-bhō**
épilepsie *f* **glɔ̄ɔdhɛ̋kpɛ̋ɛ**
épinard **kplɔ̄ɔ̋**
épine *f* **glɛ̋ɛn**
épis d'or (Cassia alata) **kɔ̄ŋsɛ̋ɛdhɯ̏**
éplucher **kwɛ̋n,** éplucher le manioc **bāa kɛ̋ɛ bhō ȁ bhȁ**
épluchures *fpl* **kɛ̋ɛ**
éponge *f* **fȕu,** éponge en fer **pȉɤgā fȕu,** éponge *f* pour laver la vaisselle **sɛ̋ɛ**
épouse *f* **dhē, dhēbʌ̏, kɔ́dhēɛ̋,** épouse aînée **dhēbʌ̏ kpȋi-sɯ̏,** épouse cadette **dhēbʌ̏ sɛ̄ɛ̋ndhʌ́n-sɯ̏**
époussette *f* de feuille de raphia **bháŋdhɛ̋**
époux *m* **dhēgɔ̀ndʌ̄, gɔ̀n**
équilibre : savoir bien garder son équilibre **kɤ̀ŋ**
équipe *f* **ēkîpʌ̏**
équivalent *m* **yɔ̋ɔgɯ́**
érection : avoir une érection **wlɯ̄ɯ̋**
ergot *m* de coq **kèȅsȍo**
éructer **kɤ̀ɤ**
éruption *f (sur la peau)* **fʌ́yígā, kȁa,** éruption à petit grain **kȁa gā sɛ̄ɛ̋ndhʌ́n**
escalier *m* : rondin *m* servant d'escalier au grenier **gbàn dȁ ȁ dhɯ̋**
escargot *m* **dlɯ̏nŋ,** petit escargot **kpɛ́ŋ̏**
esclavage *m* **dhùʌŋ-dhɛ̏**
esclave *m* **dhùʌŋ**
escroc *m* **flɯ̀ bhɛ̏n**
escroquer qn **glɛ̀ŋ kʌ̄ bhēn gɔ̏, tȁ-bɤ̏**
escroquerie *f* **flɯ̀**
espace près du mur **kwɛ̋ɛdhɛ̏**
espacé **glɛ̏ɛŋdhɤ̄**
esprit *m* **zȕu**
esquiver : action d'esquiver **yɛ̋dhē,** il sait esquiver le masque **yɤ̄ dɔ̏ yɛ̋dhē kʌ̄-dhɛ̏ ká gèe gɔ̏**
essaim *m* **zɔ̋**
essayer **bhɔ̄ɔ̏n, gɯ́-dān**
essence *f* **sánŋ̏sɯ̏**
essentiel **gɔ̏dhíɤsɯ̏**
essouchement : faire l'essouchement **gɛ̋ɛ-sɯ́**
essoufflement *m* **fȍo**
essouffler : il s'est essoufflé **fȍo**
essouflé : il est essoufflé **ȁ tɛ́ŋ yȁ sɯ́**
essuyer **zīɤ,** essuie-lui le nez **ɯ̄ kɔ̏ zīɤ ȁ yūn dhíɤ**
est : la partie est de la Côte d'Ivoire **Kɔ́dīvúȁ pɛ́ndhɛ̏ ɤ́ yʌ́nŋ̏ ɤ́ wȍ ȁ ká**
estrade *f* de briques **bhāŋ**
et **bhān,** et ..., et **ōo, ... ōo, dhɤ́ ... dhɤ́,** et alors... **dhè ɤ́ kʌ̏ dhɤ̋ yɤ́...,** et en plus **yɤ̄ dō ɤ́ bhā,** et puis **bhá gó bhūn, ɤ́ gō bhún**
étaler **kpɔ́**
état *m* **sūu-dhɛ̏**
État *m* **sɛ̋gɔ̏**
état d'homme **gɔ̄ɔ̏n-dhɛ̏**
éteindre, s'éteindre **dhūű,** éteindre la télé **tēlê dhūű,** les braises ne sont pas encore éteintes **síɤ dhùu yíi dhūű kɤ̀**

étendre **kpɔ́**
étendu **gbɛ̃́ɛ**
étendue *f* **sáà**, étendue sauvage **bɯ̃́**
éternité *f* **tɔ̀dhɤ̃́**
éternuement *m* **tìsíɤ̀ɤ**
éternuer **tìsíɤ̀ɤ bhō, yūn sʌ́n**
étincelle *f* **klààn**
étirer : s'étirer **gā̃n-gɯ́, gɯ́-gā̃n**
étoffe *f* **yɛ̄ɛ́**
étoile *f* **sɯ̃́sʌ̄nŋ́**
étonnement *m* **wɔ̀nbhɛ̄nkɔ̀n**
étonner **kɔ́n**
étouffé : avec un bruit étouffé **gbìiŋdhɤ̄**
étouffer **dɔ̄**
étourneau *m* roupenne d'Alexander **yɤ́gíɯ**
étranger *m* **dhɛ̀ŋ, dhɛ̀ŋbhɛ̀ngɔ̄n**
étrangère *f* **dhɛ̀ŋbhɛ̀ndhɛ̄**
être **bhɯ̀n, dhɤ́, gūn, kʌ̄**
être *m* humain **bhɛ̄nbhɛ̃́ɛ̀dhɛ̀**
étreindre : s'étreindre **lòo wō kwʌ́ʌ̀**
étroit **fɛ̃́ɛnfɛ̀ɛn, sɔ̃́ɔsɔ̀ɔ**
études *fpl* **klàŋ̀, sʌ́ʌdhɛ́ dlāān**, il a terminé ses études **yà ɤ bhā klàŋ̀dhíɤ tā**, il fait des études **yɤ̀ klàŋ̀dhíɤ**, il fait des progrès dans ses études **yɤ̀ sʌ́ʌdhɛ́ bhà**
étudiant *m* **klàŋ̀dhíɤdhʌ́n**
étudier **dlāàn**
évanouir : s'évanouir, faire évanouir **fìʌʌ**
éventail *m* **tɛ̃́ɛkʌ̄bùbù**
éviter **kpɔ́**
exactement **dèbɤ̃́ɤ, dèbɤ̃́ɤwō, gbáàndhɤ̄, kpɛ̄ɛnŋdhɤ̄, kpɤ̃́ɤ̀dhɤ̄**
exagéré : ton prix est exagéré **ɯ̄ bhā dhɔ̃́ɔ yɤ̀ gbɛ́ɛ̀**
exagérer **bhán**
examen *m* **gīzābhén, pāsēdhē**
examiner **bhɔ̄ɔ́-bhō, dhɛ̀-gà**, examiner un piège **dɤ̄ŋ gà**
excès : à l'excès **kpɤ́kpɤ́dhɤ̄**
excrément *m* **gbō**, excrément liquide **gbō yí**
excroquer : il m'a escroqué **yà flɯ̀ kʌ̄ n̄ gɔ̀**
excuse *f* **zā, zādhīsɯ̀**
excuser **wɛ́**, s'excuser auprès de qn **zā dhī bhɛ̄n gɔ̀**
exemple *m* **wɔ́nzɔ̀nká**
exigeant : être trop exigeant **gbɔ̀ɔn**
expédition *f* **dhìʌnŋkwā̃nŋ̀píɤ**
expliquer **gɯ́-pɔ̃́, gɯ́-pɤ̄, zīɤ**, expliquer en détail **wɔ́n-dhɯ̀n bhō kɔ̃́o**
exploiter **tà-bɤ̀**
explorateur *m* **sɛ́gàbhɛ̀n**
exploser **pɤ̃́ɤ**
exposer **zīɤ**
exprès **ɤ̄ dè yā̃an**
exténué **tɛ̃́ɛtɛ̀ɛ, zɯ̃́aanzɯ̀aan**
exténuer, s'exténuer **gɯ́-kplɯ̀**
extraire **bhō, yɤ̄ kpɛ̃́nŋ**
extraordinaire **bhlɯ̃́nbhlɯ̃́nsɯ̀, yāa gɯ́ yāa**

F f

fabriquer **bhɔ̄, kʌ̄, pʌ̀-kʌ̄**
face *f* de carte **klàatíì dhɛ́ wlɤ̀ɤ dhɛ̀**
fâcher **sīɤ**
facile **plʌ́ʌplʌ̀ʌ**, devenir facile **zɔ̀ɔ**
facilement **fɔ̀dhɤ̄, vā̃andhɤ̄**, il fait cela facilement **à kɔ̀ yɤ̀ fɤ̃́ɤfɤ̀ɤ à bhà**, il frappe facilement **à kɔ̀ yɤ̀ fɤ̃́ɤfɤ̀ɤ**
façon *f* **gɛ̀n, sūu**
factotum *m* **gwʌ̄ʌ́, gwʌ̄ʌ́bhīn**
fade **wɔ̃́ɔ̀wɔ̀ɔ**
fagot *m* **wɔ̃́**, fagot de bois *m* **wɔ̃́ bɛ̀**
faible **dhɯ̃́ʌʌdhɯ̀ʌʌ, fɔ̃́ŋ̀fɔ̀ŋ, fɔ̃́ɔfɔ̀ɔ, fɤ̃́ɤfɤ̀ɤ, plʌ́ʌplʌ̀ʌ, tʌ́ʌtʌ̀ʌ, wɔ̃́ɔwɔ̀ɔ**, sa voix est faible **à wɔ̀ yɤ̀ plʌ́ʌplʌ̀ʌ**
faim *f* **dīn̄, vâ**, j'ai faim **dīn̄ yà n̄ kún; dīn̄ yɤ̀ n̄ kʌ̄-sīʌ**, je crèuve de faim **gèebhàan yɤ̀ tā̃n kʌ̄-sīʌ n̄ glɯ̃́dhɤ̄**, faim de viande **bhɯ́ɯ**

faire **bhán, bhō, gɔ̄ɔn, kʌ̄, pʌ̀-kʌ̄, wō,** se faire à qch **dhʌ̄ʌ bhō à ká (m), dhʌ̄ʌ bhō à bhà**
faîte *m (du toit)* **kɔ́ gɔ̀**
falloir : il faut que **à dhæ̀æ à bhà; fɔ̄n**
famille *f* **kɔ́dhí,** membres de famille **kɔ́dhí gúu bhēn-dhùn**
famine *f* **vɤ̄ɤ**
fane d'igname **yā gɔ̀**
faner **zlōo**
fantôme *m* **bhēnzìi**
farceur *m* **wòplʌ̄ʌ̀kʌ̄bhèn**
fardeau *m* **gā̃n, kwɛ̀ɛ̀**
farine *f* **bì,** farine *f* fine du riz **gbòŋ, gùnŋ**
fatigue *f* **sʌ̄ʌ, sʌ̄ʌbhōdhē**
fatigué par la maladie **fíɔfìɔ**
fatiguer **gúu-gā, gúu-tó, gbɔ̀ɔn, sʌ̄ʌ bhō,** se fatiguer **gúu-gā, gúu-tó, sʌ̄ʌ bhō,** je suis fatigué par la faim **dīn̄ yà gbɔ̀ɔn n̄ tà,**
faute : ce n'est pas de ma faute **yíi kʌ̄ n̄ kwɛ̀ŋ̀ wɔ̀n ká**
fauteuil *m* **gblòokōtàngúudhē**
fauvette *f* grisette *f* **pɤ̂dɔ̄bhēnká**
fauvette *f* nasique grise **kɤ̄ɤtɛ̀ɛn**
faux : c'est faux **sūà bhùn**
faux grain **flèesùu**
faux sucrier **bhɔ̄nŋ̄dhɛ́**
favorable : être favorable **dhī**
favoris *mpl* **kpíʌŋ bhà kàa**
feindre innoncence : il feint d'innocence **yà ɤ̄ dè tà-kpā**
féliciter **yɔ̄o súu**
femelle *f* **dhēbʌ̀, bhūn, dhèe,** femelle avec ses petits **būɛ̀ɛdhè**
féminin **dhēɛ́**
femme *f* **dhē, dhēbʌ̀, dhēbʌ̀dhʌ́n,** femme à chevelure abondante **yōŋgɔ̀dhē,** femme albinos **gbàŋ dhè.** femme de petit-fils **dà sɛ̄ɛ́ndhʌ́n,** femme du frère aîné **dhìnbhɔ́ɔ̀n,** femme du frère aîné du mari **dhā̃n,** femme du village **píʌʌdhē, píʌʌdhēbʌ̀,** femme enceinte **dhēgbíɤɤ,** femme *f* mariée **gwāngɔ̀dhè, gwān bhà dhè,** femme *f* stérile **gblɤ̀ɤdhè,** femme non-mariée **dhʌ́ndhīʌŋ́,** femme jalouse **gblɛ̄ɛ́nbhōdhè,** elle est une femme mal-aimée **gwāàn ɤ́ sìɤ à bhà**
fendreб se fendre **pɛ́,** faire fendre partout **pɛ̄ɛ̀,** se fendre partout **pɛ̄ɛ̀, pɛ̄ɛ̀pɛ̄ɛ̀**
fenêtre *f* **dhòŋgā, fɤdhéntlʌ̀, kɔ́ dhòŋ**
fente des yeux **dhíɤpɛ̀**
fer *m* **pìɤ, pìɤgā**
ferme : il est ferme **à dhìin yɤ̀ gbɛ́ɛ̀**
fermenter : il a fait fermenter le vin de palme avec l'écorce "gong" **yà gɔ̀ŋ dà wē bhà**
fermer **dhʌ̀nŋ, dhíɤ-tā, tā,** se fermer **tā,** fermer la porte à clé **klɛ̄ɛ dà**
féroce **dhíɤsùu, kíɛɛsùu**
fesses *fpl* **zūu, zūukpɤ, zūuúdhè,** Yo a des fesses potelées **Yɔ̀ zūu yɤ̀ bhʌ́ŋ̀bhʌ̀ŋ**
fête *f* **fɛ̄tɤ, tlōo,** grande fête *f* **wlāàn,** fête de mariage **kósúufɛ̄tɤ, kósúutlòo, kósúu-sùu**
fétiche **dūu, dhūudhɛ́, gèebʌ̀, sɤ̀,** fétiche protecteur **sʌ̀ʌ,** fétiche tueur **bhǣæn,** mettre sous la protection du fétiche **gúu-gbàn**
feu *m* **pɛ̄ŋ, síɤ,** il est allé chercher du gibier après le feu de brousse **yà dhó síɤ yāàn tà kʌ̄'**
feuillage *m* **dhɛ́**
feuille *f* **dhɛ̄gā, dhūudhɛ́,** feuille de l'arbre cola *m* **gôdhɛ́,** feuille pour envelopper le cola **gôdhɛ́,** feuille de l'arbre Myrianthus arboreus **gbœ̀œdhɛ́,** feuille de papier *m* **sʌ́ʌdhɛ̄gā,** feuille *f* vierge **sʌ́ʌdhɛ̄gā pūu ɤ́ pʌ̄ bháa à tà,** feuille de raphia *(sur le pétiole de la fronde)* **dhūɤɤ**

dhɛ̋, feuilles qui enveloppent l'épi de maïs **kɤ̋ŋ kɛ̋ɛ**, feuilles sèches de bananier **glɔ̄ɔdhɛ̋kpɛ̋ɛ**
février **bȕukpȉi**
fi **ȅe**
fiable : ses paroles ne sont pas fiables **ȁ zʌ̄ dhȉaŋ yáa dō**
fiançailles *fpl* **tɔ̋ŋ̏dhēɛ̋-dhȅ, tœ̋œŋ̏dhē-dhȅ, zā**
fiancée *f* **dhɔ̋nbʌ̏**
fiancer : se fiancer avec **zȁ-dɔ̄**, se fiancer **tœ̋œŋ̏dhē-dhȅ kún ȁ bhȁ**
fibre *m* **vɪ̋ʌʌ**, fibre de coton **yēɛ̋ vɪ̋ʌʌ**, fibre d'éponge **fȕu pɛ̋n, fȕu kɔ̄ŋgā**, fibre des palmes du palmier à huile **dɤ̄ŋ**, fibres au sommet de l'épi de maïs **kɤ̋ŋ sɛ̋ɛ**
ficelle *f* de sachet de thé **tɛ́ȅ gʌ̄n**
ficher : je m'en fiche **kpōo**
fièvre *f* **dhɛ̋ndhɛ̋n, kwīkúnyȕa**, il a de la fièvre **ȁ kwī yà kún**
fil *m* **bhīʌ̋gā**, fil de fer **dɤ̄ŋgā, pȉɤ dɤ̄ŋgā**, fil de substance visqueuse **dɔ̋ŋ**, fil de toile d'araignée **zȉnŋtɔ̋ŋ dɔ̋ŋ**
filer **zlōo**
filet *m* de pêche *f* **dhɯ̋nŋ, kplɤ̋, tēe**
filet visqueux du parasite bhɛ̋ŋ **bhɛ̋ŋ yɪ́**
fille *f* **dhɔ̋nbʌ̏, dhú**, fille de la cousine croisée **dhē sēɛ̋ndhʌ́n**, fille raisonnable **kpēɛnŋdhɤ̄**
fils *m* **gbɤ̄, yɔ̀bhīn**, fils de la fille du frère cadet de la mère **dʌ̄ sēɛ̋ndhʌ́n**, fils raisonnable **kpēɛnŋdhɤ̄**
fin *f* **dhɪ́ɤtó**, fin de travail **yʌ̄ gɔ̏**
finalement **dō**
finaliser **zɯ̄n kó dhɪ́ɤ**
finir **bō, dhɪ́ɤ-dɔ̄, dhɪ́ɤ-tā, dhɪ́ɤ-yȁ**
fissure *f* **dhȁan**, fissures **dhȁandhȁan**
fixement **gȅɛŋdhɤ̄**
fixer **dȁ, dhʌ̀nŋ, gbȁn, kpɔ́**, fixer la date **yī kpɔ́ (gw), yī dȁ (m)**
flamme *f* **pēŋgɔ̄n**, des flammes **sɪ́ɤ dhɛ̋ȅn**
flammèche *f* **klȁȁn**
flanc *m* **sɛ̋nŋ̏dhȅ**
flaque *f* d'eau **yɪ́ glɯ̏, yɪ́ glɯ̏gā**
flatter **kāȁ**
flatteur : ses paroles sont flatteuses **ȁ dhɪ́dhȅ yɤ̏ dhɛ̋ɛndhȅɛn**
flèche *f* **sàa, sàagā**, flèche à pointe de fer **slɯ̋ngā**, flèche empoisonnée **sàa kpȁ-sɯ̏**
flétrir **zlōo**
fleur *f* **bɪ́n**, fleur de maïs **kɤ̋ŋ gɔ̏**
fleurir : l'arbre a fleuri **dhɯ̋ yà ɤ̄ bɪ́n yȁ**
fleurs de Saint-Christophe **kɔ̄ŋsɛ̋ɛdhɯ̏**
fleuve *m* **gwàan, gwàngā, yɪ́gā, yɪ́gāȁdhȅ**
flicflac **wlɔ̄ɔ̋wlɔ̀owlɔ̄ɪ́dhɤ̄**
flip-flap **bhīndhānbhìndhànbhīndhāndhɤ̄**
flou : sa vue est floue (à cause d'une cataracte) **ȁ yʌ̋n gɯ́ yɤ̏ dhɯ̋ɤɤdhȕɤɤ**
foi *f* **dháŋ̏**
foie *m* **bhlɯ̋u**
fois *f* **pʌ̄, gœ̏œ, kótȁ, gȅnyȁn**, une fois **dōsēŋ**
folie *f* **slāá**
foliole *f* **dhɯ̋dhɛ̋**
fonction *f* **dȕɛɛ**, fonction syntaxique **dȕɛɛ dhɪ́wɔ̀yȁn gɯ́**
fonctionnaire *m* **kwɪ́**
fonctionner : ma main ne fonctionne pas **n̄ kɔ̏ yà gā n̄ bhȁ**
fond *m* **gēnŋ̏dhȅ, zɯ̄**
fondation *f* **gēnŋ̏dhȅ, kpʌ̋n**
fondements *fpl* : poser/jeter les fondements d'une maison **kɔ́ kpʌ̋n yȁ (gw), kɔ́ kpʌ̋n kʌ̋n (t) kpʌ̋n dhɪ́ɤ**
fonder **yȁ**, fonder un village **pɤ̂ kʌ̋n**
fondre, se fondre **sɤ̏ŋ**
football *m* **bàdhóŋ̏**
force *f* **fāan, gɔ̄ɔ̏n-dhȅ, gɯ́gbēȅ-dhȅ, gbɛ̋ȅ-dhȅ**, force fraîche **fāan sæ̏æ**, il a de la force **fāan yȁ gɯ́**, il n'a pas de

force **à tɛ́ɛ yáa à gúu**, sans force **tʌ̀ʌtʌ́ʌtʌ̀ʌdhɤ̄**
forcer : X force Y à faire quelque chose **X Y flɔ̄tí bhō kɤ̄ Y ..., X flɔ̄tí wɔ̄ Y tà kɤ̄ Y ...**
forer **pɔ́n**
forêt *f* sacrée **bṹudhɔ̀kʌ̄sṵ̀**
forêt *f* vierge **bṹu tīi, búu zā**
forger le fer **pı̀ɤ bhō**
forgeron *m* **pı̀ɤbhōbhɛ̀n**
formation *f* **klàŋ̀**
former **yà**, se former **kı̀an**
fort **dhı́ɤsṵ̀, gbɛ́ɛ̀, súbhán, yâ,** *(café)* **tīi**
fortement : *fermer* **kpɛ̄ŋkpɛ̄ŋdhɤ̄,** *gonfler* **tīŋtīŋdhɤ̄, vōodhɤ̄,** *se coller* **kɤ̄kkɤ̄dhɤ̄, tántándhɤ̄**
fou *m* **slāábhɛ̀n**, il est devenu fou **slāá yà dà à gúu**
foudre *f* **dhāgā**, la foudre a brillé **dhā yà {ɤ̄} yán kún**
fouet *m* **klàa, klàŋgā, sàbhlı̀igā**
fougère *f* **klāadʌ̄**
fouiller **gúu-blūṵ̀**, fouiller au fond **zɔ̄n**
foulard *m* **là**, foulard de tête **gbàŋpɛ́ŋ**
foule *f* **bhɛ̄n dūnŋ, kpɤ̄**, foule immense **dháa**, une foule dense **bhɛ̄n kɔ̀ŋ**, une foule s'est rassemblée **bhɛ̄n bhɛ́ɛ̀ dháa yà bhán**
fourche *f* **kōŋ, kɔ̀ɔ**, fourche d'un arbre **dhṹu kōŋ**
fourmi *f* : fourmi noire **kpɤ̄ŋ**, petite fourmi noire **zlʌ̄ʌndhʌ́n**, fourmis magnan **zlūu**, fourmis rouges **dlɔ̀ɔ**
fourmi *f*, espèces : **dhṹaan, gbân, gbʌ̂n, wàà, zɤ̄ŋ**
fourmilière *f* **gbân kɔ́**
fourreau *m* **kpɛ̀e**
foutou *m* **kɔ̀n**, foutou de manioc **gwɛ̄ɛ́ kɔ̀n, bāa kɔ̀n**
foyer *m* **zūʌ̀n**
fracas **kwɛ̄ɛ́ndhɤ̄**
fragile **wlṹunwlṵ̀un**
frais **dɛ̀e, sæ̀æ**
fraké, franké, fraquet *m* *(l'arbre Terminalia superba)* **bhɛ́ɛ**
francolin *m* commun **kœ̄œ**
francolin *m* écailleux **súæ̀**
frange *f* **sɛ́ɛ, kʌ́nŋ**, frange d'habit **sɔ̄ sɛ́ɛ,** une frange s'est formée sur l'habit **sɔ̄ kʌ́nŋ yà dūn**
frapper **bhàn, flɤ́, zʌ̄, zɔ̄n**, frapper brusquement **zṳ̀ɤ**, frapper fort **gúu-wɛ́**
frauduleux **flṳ̀sṳ̀**
frayer **bɔ̄**, frayer le chemin **kpı̀nŋ bɔ̄**, se frayer *(un chemin)* **bà**
fredonner : il fredonne tout bas **yɤ̀ tán bhō-sīʌ ɤ̄ bɛ̀n pı́ɤ**
frelon *m* **gbɔ̀ŋ**
frère *m* **dhēébhāŋ**, frères **dhēébhāŋzʌ̀-dhṳ̀n**, frère aîné **dʌ̄zőo, dhòo,** frère aîné du grand-père **zı́ɤ̀ɤ kpı̂i**, frère cadet du mari **dhı̀nbhɔ́ɔ̀n**
frisson *m* : j'ai eu un frisson **dhɛ́ndhɛ́n sæ̀æ yà kpā n̄ tà**
froid *m* **dɛ̀e, dhɛ́ndhɛ́n, sæ̀æ-dhɛ̀,** j'ai froid **dhɛ́ndhɛ́n yà dhūn n̄ tà**
froissement *m* **kwɛ̀ɛnkwɛ́ɛn**
froisser **kwɛ̀ɛnkwɛ́ɛn kʌ̄**
frôler : se frôler **gı̀i**
fromager *m* **gwɛ̄**
fronde *f* *(feuille de palme)* **gɔ̀, gɔ̄,** fronde de raphia ou de palmier à huile **yɔ̄ gɔ̄**
fronde *f* *(arme de jet)* **gbɔ́ɔ̀**
front *m* **kpɔ̀ŋ, kpɔ̄ŋ́dhɛ̀**
frontière du pays **sɛ́ dhàan dhı́ɤ**
frotter : se frotter **gı̀i**
frou-frou **wīaawı̀aawīaadhɤ̄**
fructifier en abondance **bhā**
fruit *m* **bhɛ̄, dhṹgā, dhṹu bhɛ̄,** fruit d'aubergine **zɔ́ŋ̀ gā**, fruit d'une liane **bhı̀in**, fruit *m* non-mûr **sʌ̀n**
fuir **bhɔ̄, dùa**
fumée *f* **pɛ̄ŋtɛ́ɛ, sı́ɤtɛ́ɛ, pɛ̄ŋ gbı́ʌn, sı́ɤ gbı́ʌn**, fumée de cigarette **sı̀etı̂i tɛ́ɛ**

fumer *(le tabac)* **táȁ bhɯ̄n,** fumer une cigarette **sìɛtíȉ bhɯ̄n**

fumeur *m*, fumeuse *f* **táȁbhɯ̄nbhɛ̏n**

funisciure à pattes rousses *m* **gbɛ̏ŋ**

furoncle *m* **dhìʌ̏ʌ,** il a eu un furoncle sur l'occiput **dhìʌ̏ʌ yà dɔ̄ ȁ kèedhɤ̄**

fuseau *m* **kīʌŋ,** fuseau avec support **kīʌŋgbɔ̄**

fusil *m* **būu**

G g

Gaa *m (masque-coureur)* **gœ̏œ**

gaffeur *m*, gaffeuse *f* **bhȁanbhɔ̋ɔn**

gage *m* **tœ̄œŋ**

gagner **bhɔ̄ɔ̏n, gɛ̄nyɛ̄n**

gaillard *m* **gȁ̋sȁ̋gɔ̄n**

gale *f* **kȁ̋a, plēe, sīakādhâ,** gale de tête **gȁ̋a,** il a attrapé la gale **plēe yà lòo ȁ bhȁ**

galeux **fíisɯ̏**

garant *m* de la case sacrée **gɯ̋nŋkɔ̏dhíɤbhɛ̏n**

garantie *f* **tœ̄œŋ**

garçon *m (enfant)* **dhʌ́ngɔ̄ɔ̏n,** *(homme)* **gɔ̄ndʌ̄dhʌ́n, gɔ̄ɔ̏n**

garde *f* : mettre qn en garde **véȅ zīɤ bhɛ̄n gɔ̏,** prendre garde **kʌ̄ ɤ̄ zȍ ká,** prendre garde à **kún … bhȁ**

gardien *m* **gāadíȅn**

gare à toi! / gare à vous! **ɯ̄ɯ / kā véȅ!**

gargouillant **gbúgbúdhɤ̄**

gargouillement *m* : j'ai des gargouillements **n̄ gblɯ̋ɯ́dhɛ̏ yɤ̏ wɛ́-sīʌ bhōŋ̋bhòŋbhōŋ̋dhɤ̄, n̄ gblɯ̋ɯ́dhɛ̏ yɤ̏ n̄ kwāȁn-sīʌ**

garrot *m* **tàaklȁan**

gaspiller **bhɤ̏, gɯ́-sēɛ̏,** il gaspille l'argent **yɤ̏ wʌ́ʌ̏ gɯ́-sèe**

gâté **yíbhōsɯ̏,** c'est une personne gâtée **yȁ dȁ főofòo-dhɛ̏ gɯ́**

gâteau *m* **gàtô**

gâter **dhíɤ-yȁ, sēɛ̏,** se gâter **sēɛ̏,** gâter l'enfant **dhʌ́n sēɛ̏**

gazon *m* **kpáȁ**

geler : j'ai gelé **dhɛ̋ndhɛ̋n yà bhán n̄ gɯ́**

gémir **dhȉɤ, kȁ̋a-bhō, gbő bɔ̄**

gémissement *m* **gbő**

gencive *f* **sɔ̋npíɤdhɛ̏,** gencives **dhȉʌʌn**

gêner **bhȁ-kún, gɯ́-kún, gɯ́-kplȁ,** se gêner **kȁ̋n,** la fumée me gêne **síɤtɛ̋ɛ yà yȁ n̄ gɔ̏**

généreux *m*, généreuse *f* **klősʌ̏bhɛ̏n,** il est généreux **bhɛ́n bhā gàsítɛ́ɛ̏ yáa' bhȁ, ȁ kɔ̏ yɤ̏ fɤ̋ɤfɤ̏ɤ**

genette *f* commune **bhlɔ̀ɔn**

génie *m* **pʌ̄,** génie nain de brousse **dìʌnŋ**

genou *m* **kpīɤ̏ɤ, kpīɤ̏ɤgɔ̏**

gens d'ici-bas **kpőŋtàabhɛ̏n-dhȕn**

geôlier *m* **kȁsȍgɔ̏dhíɤbhɛ̏n**

gerbe *f* de riz **bhlɯ̏n wɛ̋ŋ,** petite gerbe **wɛ̋ŋ**

gerçure *f* **záa**

gérer qch **tɤ̋ŋ kʌ̄ ȁ gɯ́**

gérondif *m* **zēlɔ̄ndífȕ**

gésier *m* **kplȁ̋**

gestes menaçants **kɛ̋ɛ**

gingembre *m* **sɛ̋ɛslʌ̏ʌ**

gla gla *(son de claquement des dents)* **kɤ̋ɤkɤ̋ɤkɤ̋ɤdhɤ̄**

glissant **dlɔ̋ɔdlɔ̏ɔ**

glisser **bɔ̄, bhán, dlāȁn, zīɤ**

gloire *f* **tɔ́bhɔ̄dhē**

glougloutant **gbúgbúdhɤ̄**

glume *f* **kɛ̋ɛ**

goitre *m* **kplíi,** il a un goitre **kplíi yà yȁ ȁ bhǣǣ̋**

gombo *m* **gblóȍ,** gombo coupé et séché **dɯ̋ʌŋ**

gond *m* **kwɛ̋ɛ pȉɤgā, sāyɛ̂n**

gonflé **vōodhē**

gonfler : se gonfler **bhlȁ, dɔ̄,** il a gonflé ses joues **yà ɤ̄ kpíʌŋ kpū dɔ̄**

gong *m* **gʌ̄nŋgʌ̄nŋ**

gonorrhée *f* **wēɛ̄bhōyȕa**
Goo *(people et langue)* **Gȍo**
gorge *f* **bhɛ̄ɛ́dhɛ̏**
Gou *(masque de femmes)* **Gű̄u**
goudron *m* **gūdlɔ́nŋ̏**
gouffre *m* **gblɯ̏gā**
goulot de la bouteille **kwēedhʌ́n bhɔ̄**
gourde *f* pour le vin de palme **pūű**
gourdin *m* **dhűdhʌ́n**
gourmand : il est gourmand **ȁ zūʌ̋ yɤ̏ ɗɔ̏**
gourmandise *f* **zūʌ̋dɔ̄**
Gouro *(people et lange)* **Glōȍ**
goût *m* **dīn**
goûter **dīn-dān, dīn-gȁ**
goûteux **dhɛ̋ɛndhɛ̏ɛn**
goutte *f* de pluie *f* **yígā,** goutte de pluie **dhā dhídhí gā,** l'eau tombe goutte à goutte **yí yɤ̏ wènŋ-sɪʌ tɤűtɤűdhɤ**
gouverneur *m* **sɛ̋ kɔ̀ɔnbhɛ̏n**
goyave *f* **gòyâ**
grâce *f* **gàsítɛ́ɛ̏,** grâce à **ká, sáȁ,** grâce à cela **ȁ dhīaŋ gɯ́,** c'est grâce à Zan **gȁsɯ́bhántɛ́ɛ̏ yíi tó Zâan bhȁ**
grade : il a été élevé en grade **wȁ là dhʌ̀nŋ ȁ gbān tȁ, wȁ ȁ bhȁ là tāa kʌ̄, wȁ ȁ bhȁ là ɗȁ dhíɤ**
grain *m* **gā,** grain d'arachide **gwɛ̋ɛ flɛ́ɛ̀,** grain de café **kȁflɛ́ɛ gā,** grain de maïs **kɤ̄ŋ gā,** grain de maïs *(dans l'épi)* **kɤ̄ŋ sɔ̋n,** grains décortiqués de maïs **kɤ̄ŋ flɛ́ɛ̀,** grain de palmier à huile **sɤ̄, wēn,** grain de haricot **zēgā,** grain mal formé **fȍo**
graisse *f* **yɔ̋n**
grand **gblɛ̀ɛn, gbɔ́ŋ, kpîì, sűbhán,** grands, pl. **gblɤ̋gblɤ̋**
grand gravelot *m* **dhɔ̋ɔdɔ̄bhȁan**
grand-duc *m* à aigrettes **gbēŋbhȁan**
grande aigrette *f* **dȕtȁbhȁan**
grande quantité **tɤ̋ŋbhȁsɯ̏**
grandir **glá̋, kpǣǣ̀, wlūɯ́, yɔ̀ɔn,** son ventre a grandi **ȁ gú yà bhɔ̄**
grand-mère *f* **dhán**
grand-père *m* **zíɤ̏ɤ**
grands pas : à grands pas **bȕaanbȕaandhɤ̄**
granit *m* **wɛ̄**
grappe de bananes **glɔ̄ɔ kpȁa**
gratin *m* **slàan**
gratter **kāȁ, kwāȁn, kwāȁnkwāȁn.** se gratter **kāȁ**
grave **zȉisɯ̏**
gravier *m* **kʌ̄ŋ́, zɔ̋ŋ**
grebe : grand gerbe **gbān**
grêle *f* **bhʌ̄nŋgā**
grelot *m* **dhɔ̄ɔgā,** grelot en fer **dhɔ̄ɔ,** grelots du plomb **gbɤ̋ŋ**
grenier *m* **gbàn, gblāá̋,** elle a mis le riz au grenier **yà ɤ̄ bhā bhlɯ̏n lòo gbàandhɤ̄**
grenouille *f* **dlɔ̋ɔ,** *(espèce)* **bɔ̄ɔ,** grenouille-taureau **kȁdɔ̄**
grésiller **pɤ̋ɤ**
griffe **sūʌ̋**
grill *m* pour fumer **kīʌŋ**
griller **pìaa, yɛ̏**
grillon *m* **slɤ̄ɤ, tɛ̋eŋtlɤ̄**
grimper **kún**
grincement **fīɔ̋nfīɔ̋nfīɔ̋ndhɤ̄, kīá̋nkȉankīá̋ndhɤ̄,** avec grincement **kíoodhɤ̄**
grincer : il grince les dents en dormant **yɤ̏ ɤ̄ sɔ̋n bhɤ̏ yī gɯ́ klɤ̄ɤ̋klɤ̄ɤklɤ̄ɤ̋dhɤ̄**
griot *m* **yɛ̄ɛ, yɛ̄ɛbhīn,** griot des chasseurs **blűtá̋nbhōbhɛ̏n**
griotte **yɛ̄edhē**
grippe *f* **kpîn**
gris-gris *m* **klɯ̄ɯ,** il a dressé un gris-gris contre lui **yȁ sɤ̏ yȁ ȁ tȁ**
grogner **yȁ bhēn yá̋n gɯ́,** grogner contre qn **ɗɔ̏n bhɔ̄ bhēn ká,** il grogne toujours **yɤ̄ɤ zʌ̏ yɤ̏ wɛ̏ ɤ̄ yūúndhɤ̄-yūúndhɤ̄**

grommeler contre qn **wű̃nŋ zʌ̄ bhēn ká**
grondement **bhrrùubhrrùubhrrùudhɤ̀**
gronder **gblāà**, le chien gronde contre les gens **gbȇn yɤ̀ gblàn-sīʌ bhēn-dhùn bhà**
gros **fāansùɯ, gblɤ́gblɤ́, kpîì**
gros-bec à front blanc **sùɯkplḗedhē**
grosse tête *f* **gɔ̀gbàŋdʌ̄**
grossesse *f* **gbɪ́ɤ̀ɤ**
grossir **bà**, il a grossi **yà fāan sɯ́ɯ**, son ventre a grossi **à gú gbàan bhɔ̄**
grotte *f* **gbìŋ, gwʌ̀yɛ̀**
grouiller **gɔ̄ɔn**
groupe **kpɤ̀**, en groupe **wìaadhɤ̀**
guêpe *f* **gbɔ̀ŋ**, guêpe-maçonne *f* **tɛ̃́ɛbhʌ̄ŋ́dhē**
guêpier *m* nain **bhɔ̄ŋ́ŋ́tàbhàan**
Guéré *(peuple, langue)* **Gɛ̂, Wɛ̂**
guéri **wɛ̃́ɛwɛ̃́**
guérir : il a guéri **yà ɤ̀ flʌ́ʌ̀ bhɔ̄, yà kʌ̄ wɛ̃́ɛwɛ̃́**
guérisseur *m* **bèdhɛ̃́kʌ̄bhɛ̀n**
guerre *f* **gblɯ̀ɯ**, guerre froide, guerre languissante **yí sæ̀æ gblɯ̀ɯ**, une sale guerre (sans respect des conventions) **gblɯ̀ɯ yāa**, faire la guerre à qn **gblɯ̀ɯ gɔ̄ɔn bhēn ká**
guerrier *m* **gblɯ̀ɯgɔ̄ɔnbhɛ̀n, sœ́œ̀bhīn**, guerrier éminent **vāangɔ̄n**
Guerzé *(peuple, langue)* **Gblɛ̀ɛsɛ́**
guet-apens *m* **gbá**
guetter **súàn-bhɔ̄**
guider qn **dhɪ́ɤ sɯ́ɯ bhēn ká**
guidon *m* : guidon de vélo **pìāasɔ̀ɔ̀ gɔ̀**, guidon de mobylette *f* **pòpòdhîn kúndhɛ̀**
Gwa *(groupe masculin de danse)* **gwā̃**
gymnote *m (poisson électrique)* **gbìŋgbɤ̀**

H h

habile : être habile **kɤ̀ŋ**, il est habile **à yā̃n gúɯ ɤ́ kàn**
habileté *f* **tɤ̃́ŋ**
habiller : bien s'habiller **zɯ́ɯ, bāà**
habitat *m* **kɔ́**
habitation : lieu *m* d'habitation **yɛ̀ɛ**
habitude *f* **dhʌ̄ʌ**
habituer : s'habituer **gɯ́ɯ-dɔ̄**, s'habituer à **dhʌ̄ʌ bhɔ̄ à ká** (m), **dhʌ̄ʌ bhɔ̄ à bhà**
hache *f* **dùa**
haie *f* de chasse **dhɛ̃́gbā̃**
haillon *m* **sɔ̄blʌ́**
haine *f* **sàn, sànbhēnzʌ̀, sànbhēnzʌ̄-dhɛ̀**
haïr : je le hais **à sàn yɤ̀ n̄ zʌ̀**
hamac *m* **dhű̃nŋ**
hameau *m* **dhēŋ̀dhɛ̀, kā̃nŋbhā̃, kɔ́yɪ́dhɛ̀**
hameçon *m* **pīɤ́gā**
hangar *m* **fā̃fā̃, gbâ, kɔ́zāà, zāà**
hanneton *m* **vūnŋdhē**
harde *f* de chiens **gbȇn kpɤ̀**
hargneux **fɛ̀ɛsɯ̀ɯ**
haricot *m* **zē**, haricot décortiqué **zē flɛ̃́ɛ̀**
"haricot sauvage *(Piliostigma thonningii)* : **gœ́œ̀, gbȇndhʌ́ngœ́œ̀**, duvet et poussière du haricot sauvage **gœ́œ̀ yɛ̃́ɛn**
harmattan *m* **bùu**, partie froide de l'harmattan **bùuyɪ́dɔ̀sɛ̄ɛ̃́tà**
harpe-luth *m* **kɔ̄nŋ**, jouer de la harpe-luth **kɔ̄nŋ zʌ̄**
hâte *f* **bìaŋ, sɪ́ɤ**, faire hâtivement **yɔ̄ɔyɔ̃́ɔ-kʌ̄**
haut **gblèɛn**, haut et élancé **zāŋ̀zàŋ**
haut : tout le temps en haut **dhű̃ɤdhű̃ɤ**
hauteur *f* **dhɤ̃́ŋ, gblèɛn-dhɛ̀**
hazard : par hasard **kɤ́bhūndhē**
hé **kɤ́ɤ̀**
hé! **ēè**
hébergement *m* **yʌ̀ʌ**
héberger **yʌ̀ʌ-bhɔ̄**
hélas **dhɔ̀ɔn, ɛ́kɛ̃́**
hélice *f* **tɛ̃́ɛkʌ̄bùbù**
hélicoptère *m* **ēlɪ́kɔ̄nŋtɛ́ɛ̀**
héliosciure *f* à jambes rousses **gbâgɔ̀ɔ**

hémorroïdes *fpl* **dhɔ̋ŋ,** il a des hémorroïdes **bīɤ dhɔ̋ŋ dhɔ̋ŋ yà wɔ̀/dɔ̄ à bhà**
héraut *m* **dhɛ̀ɛdhíɤbhōbhɛ̀n**
herbe *f* bambou *m* **kàabùŋ**
herbe *f* bassine *f* **kàabùŋ**
herbe, espèces : **bhùʌŋ, bhûn, dhấandhấan, dhɔ̃ɔkàdhókwʌ́ʌ̀dhɤ̄, dhɔ̀ɔndhɛ̀, kɔ̃bhɔ̃, klʌ̀ʌkpấà, lɔ̄ɔ, sʌ́nŋ̀, sɛ̄ɛ́dhɛ́, sɛ̀nŋpűu, sɛ́ŋ̀, sɤ̄dhììfấa, wàa, yʌ́nklʌ̃ʌn, yűnklűɯn, yɛ́, zɤ̃ɤpűu**
hérisson *m* **tɛ̃**
héritage *m* **kên, kên pʌ̄,** règles d'héritage **kên pʌ̄-dhùn wɔ̀n**
hermétiquement **kpɛ̄ŋkpɛ̄ŋdhɤ̄**
herminette *f* **pɛ̀egā**
hernie *f* **pɔ̀ɔn**
héron *m* bihoreau **tōŋtōŋgîà**
héron *m* goliath **yípíɤbhàan**
héros *m* **gblɯ̀ɯkplʌ́ʌnŋ**
heure *f* **dhɛ́dhɛ́, yʌ́nŋ̀gɛ̀nsɯ́ɯ**
heureux : il est heureux **à zūʌ́ yɤ̀ wấàdhūn-sɯ̀ɯ ká**
heurter : se heurter **bhàn, yà**
hibou *m* **bōo, vūŋ**
hier **yāandhíɤ**
hippopotame *m* **yʌ̃ʌ̀bīɤ**
hirondelle *f* **pɛ̃ɛpɛ̃ɛ**
histoire *f* **kwɛ̀zlàan**
hivernage *m* **dhɛ̀engɯ́ɯ, dhā yí bhà yī**
hochet *m* **yɔ̃ŋbhɛ̄,** hochet en vannerie **sɛ̀gbɛ̀,** jouer du hochet **yɔ̃ŋ zʌ̄,** hochet-sonnaille *f* **yɔ̃ŋ**
hocheur *m* **klấŋ̀,** hocheur *m* blanc-nez **dhùaa**
hollarhène du Sénégal **kɛ́ŋ̀**
homme *m* **gɔ̄n, gɔ̄ndʌ̄, gɔ̄ndʌ̄dhʌ́n, gɔ̄ɔ̀n,** *(30 ans ou plus)* **bhīndhʌ́n,** homme chanceux **pīấsʌ̀bhɛ̀n,** homme fort **gblấagblàa,** homme patient **zūʌ́sɛ̀ɛbhɛ̀n**

homonyme *m* **tœ̃œŋ̀**
honnir **dhíɤ-dà, kpœ̄œ pɛ́ à ká bhɛ̄n bhà**
honorable **gɔ̄n**
honorer qn **dhɔ̀-kʌ̄,** on m'a honoré **yʌ̄ʌ yà bhɔ̄ n̄ dhɛ̀**
honte *f* **yíɤ̀ɤ,** faire honte à qn **yíɤ̀ɤ dɔ̄ bhɛ̄n bhà**
hôpital *m* **dhɔ̀tlɔ́ɔ̀plɤ̀ɤ, dhɔ̀tlɔ́ɔ̀ kɔ̀,** à l'hôpital **dhɔ̀tlɔ́ɔ̀plɤ̀ɤ**
hoquet *m* **kpɤ̄sìan,** il a le hoquet **kpɤ̄sìan yà à kún**
horrible **zììsɯ̀ɯ**
hôte *f* **dhɛ̀ŋbhɛ̀ndhē**
hôte *m* **bhɔ̄ɔdʌ̄, dhɛ̀ŋbhɛ̀ngɔ̄n, dhɛ̀ŋbhɔ̄ɔdʌ̄**
hou la! **kɔ̃ɔ̀**
houe *f* **kʌ̃ʌ**
huile *f* **yɔ̃n,** huile des fruits de carapa **gwɛ̄ɛ̃yɔ̃n,** huile de carapa **gbɔ̂n yɔ̃n,** huile rouge **yɔ̃n pűu, yɔ̃n zœ̀œndhē,** huile noire **wɛ̄n yɔ̃n**
huiler **bhà-yɔ́**
huit *m* **sấàgā**
hululement **űù-ùu**
humain *m* **bhɛ̄n,** humains vivants **kpɔ̃ŋtàabhɛ̀n-dhùn**
humanité *f* **bhɛ̄nbhɛ̃ɛ̀dhɛ̀**
humide **dɔ́ndɔ̀n, sæ̀æ**
humidité *f* **dhɔ̄ŋ, pɔ̃ɔ**
humoriste *m* **wɔ̀plʌ̀ʌ̀kʌ̄bhɛ̀n**
huppe *f* **gblɔ̄ŋ́**
hurler : il hurle **yɤ̀ gbɔ̃ bɔ̄-sīʌ gblấ-sɯ̀ɯ ká**
hyène *f* **slűkű**
hylochère *m* **bhɔ̀tīi**

I i

ici **yā, yɤ̀**
idée **zɔ̀gɔ̀ngɯ́ɯwɔ̀n, zɔ̀tàgɯ́ɯwɔ̀n**
igname *f* **dhɔ̄ɔ, kűù, yấ, yấ sɛ̃ɛsɯ̀ɯ,** igname bouillie **kűù kplɯ̀ɯ,** igname sauvage **bhɤ̃**

igname, sortes : **gblɛ̀ɛ,** *(précauce)* **bɛ̀tɛ̀bɛ́tɛ́**
il y a : il y a deux heures **à dhɛ́dhɛ́ plɛ̀ dhɛ̀n,** il y a environ *(temps)* X **yà bhɔ̀ɔn X bhà**
image *f* **bín, blɛ́ɛ̀n, bhɔ̄bhà, pʌ̄bín, tɤ́ŋ**
imaginer **tɤ́ŋ-kʌ̄,** s'imaginer qch **tɤ́ŋ kʌ̄ pʌ̄ gɯ́**
imam *m* **bhɔ́ɔ̀nbhīn**
imbiber, s'imbiber **tɔ̀ɔ**
immensément **bhɛ̄nbhɛ̄ndhɤ̄**
immobile **dīŋdhɤ̄**
immobiliser **lòo**
impatience *f* **síɤ**
impétueusement **víavíadhɤ̄**
impliquer : s'impliquer **dà,** il s'est impliqué dans une affaire compliquée **wɔ́n dɔ́ɔnsɯ̀ dhʌ̀n ɤ́ yà à kɔ̀ tà**
importance : de peu d'importance **fíafìa**
important **bhlʌ̀ʌsɯ̀, gɔ̀dhíɤsɯ̀, gbɛ́ɛ̀, gblɤ́gblɤ́,** le plus important **wɔ̀ngbɛ́ɛ̀sɯ̀**
imposer : Tokpa a imposé son autorité sur Yo **Tòkpà yà gbɛ́ɛ̀-dhɛ̀ yɤ Yɔ̀ tà**
impratiquable : la route est devenue impratiquable **zīaan yà kʌ̄n**
impuissant : il est impuissant **yáa gɔ̄ɔ̀n ká,** il est un impuissant, impotent **à bhà gɔ̄ɔ̀n-dhɛ̀ yáa wlɯ̄ɯ́, à gɔ̄ɔ̀n-dhɛ̀ yáa wlɯ̄ɯ́**
inadapté : cet homme est un inadapté **bhɛ́n ɤ́ bhā glɛ̀ŋ yáa à bhà**
inadéquat **fɔ̋ofɔ̀o**
inattendu (pour qn), à la surprise (de qn) **(bhɛ̄n) tīí ká**
incantation *f* **yísíwɔ̀**
incapable : il n'est capable de rien **yɤ̀ fīʌʌ wɔ́n gbàn bhà**
incirconcis *m* **kplʌ̀ʌ**
inciter les gens à la querelle **bhɛ̄n-dhùn kɔ̀ yà kwʌ́ʌ̀**
incomparable **yāa**
incomparablement **à kɔ̀ yáa' kwɛ̀ɛ̀ wɔ̀n ká**
inconsolablement **bhlʌ̀bhlʌ̀dhɤ̄**
inconvenance *f* **tlùu**
incrédule *m* **bhɛ̄n zūʌ́gā glɔ̄ɔ́glɔ̄ɔ́sɯ̀,** il est incrédule **à zūʌ́ gā yɤ̀ glɔ́ɔglɔ̀ɔ**
index *m* **wèe pà ká kœ̄œŋgā**
indicateur *m* à lyre *f* **pɤ̂bhàan**
indignement **bhàagɯ́**
indigo *m* **glà, glà yí**
indiscrètement **būábūádhɤ̄**
indisposition *f* **gɯ́sìɤ**
indistinctement **bhábhàbhádhɤ̄**
indolent : il est devenu indolent comme une poule malade **yà kʌ̄ wɔ́ɔnwɔ̀ɔn ká dhɛ̀ zàazɯ́ɯ̀ tɔ̀ dhɤ́**
induire en erreur **zʌ̄**
inexcisée *f* **kplʌ̀ʌ**
infester **bhʌ́nŋ**
infinitif *m* **ɛ̄nfīdhīntífù**
infirme **dhìɔɔnsɯ̀**
inflammation du vertex **gwìnŋdhɤ̄**
informer de **lòo**
ingrat **fɔ̋ofɔ̀o**
initiation *f* **bɔ́n, gbáandhʌ́n,** il /elle/ a passé l'initiation **yà gó bɔ́n**
injection : faire injection dans **zūa**
injure *f* **sí**
injuste : tu es injuste **bháa kpɛ̄ɛnŋdhɤ̄**
injustice *f* **zúùzúdhɛ̀**
innombrable **tɯ̀tɯ́, dɯ́dɯ́**
inquiet : il est inquiet **à zūʌ́ dhíɤ yɤ̀ tɛ́ɛ-sīʌ**
inquiéter : je m'inquiète à ce sujet **ñ zūʌ́ dhíɤ yɤ̀ bhɤ́ɤ-sīʌ à wɔ̀n gɯ́**
inquiétude *f* maladive **bhàndhàn**
insensible : ma langue est devenue insensible **ñ dhɛ́ɛ̀ngā yà kʌ̄ gbíŋŋgbìŋŋ ñ dhí**
insérer **sɔ̀, zīɤ**
insipide **wɔ́ɔ̀wɔ̀ɔ**
insistance *f* **dhāandhāansɯ̀**

insister **dhʌ̀nŋ, gʉ́-kʉ́n, gbɛ̀n, yɔ̀ɔn**
instabilité **bhɛ̀ŋbhɛ̋ŋ**
installer : s'installer **ɤ bhɤ̋ tʌ̀ŋ, yà, yáàdhūn**
instant *m* **yɛ́ɛ̀n**
instituteur *m* **klàŋ̀gɔ̀bhɛ̀n**
institutrice *f* **klàŋ̀gɔ̀bhɛ̀n dhēbʌ̀**
instruire **dlāàn,** il est très instruit **yɤ̀ sʌ́ʌdhɛ̋ dɔ̀**
instrument de musique **wɛ̋pʌ̀**
insuffisamment **tɤ̋ŋ gʉ́**
insulter qn **sí bhō bhɛ̄n gɔ̀**
intelligence *f* **gɔ̀gʉ́sʌ̀-dhɛ̀, kpœ̀œ-dhɛ̀, tɤ̋ŋbhō-dhɛ̀**
intelligent **glɛ̀ŋsʉ̀, kpàasʉ̀,** personne intelligente **gɔ̀gʉ́sʌ̀bhɛ̀n**
intenable : cette personne est intenable **bhɛ́n yā, kɔ̀kʉ́ndhɛ̀ yáa à bhà**
intention : avoir l'intention **pɤ̀**
interdit *m* **tɔ́ŋ̀**
intéresser (s') : l'homme s'y est intéressé **à wɔ̀n yɤ̀ kʌ̀ bhɛ̄n gʉ́ sʌ̀,** je ne m'intéresse pas aux affaires très anciennes **wɔ́n zīzī-dhʉ̀n wáa dhó ī gwìnŋ̀ /gwìnŋ̄dhɤ**
intérieur *m* **gʉ́, gʉ́dhɛ̀**
interprétation *f* **wɔ̀dhɪ́ɤlòodhē**
interprète *m* **wɔ̀dhɪ́ɤlòobhɛ̀n**
interroger **dhɛ̀dhɛ́-dà**
interrompre **gbáàndhūn, tà-kʌ̋n,** interrompre la danse **tʌ̋n kʌ̋n**
intervalle *m* **gbɛ̀ŋ, zìnŋ,** intervalle entre les doigts **kōŋ gbɛ̀ŋ gʉ́,** avec des intervalles **dódó**
intestin *m* : intestin grêle **gblʌ̀ʌ̀n,** gros intestin *m* **bɔ̀ŋ**
intouchable : il est intouchable **yí yáa zūn à wɔ̀n bhà**
inutile **fɔ̋ofɔ̀o, wlʌ̋ʌ̀sʉ̀, vlʌ̋anvlʌ̋an**
inutilité *f* **fɔ̋ofɔ̀o-dhɛ̀**
inviter **dhɛ̀**
iroko **gɤ̀ɤ̀,** jeune arbre iroko **kʌ̀ʌdhʉ̀**
irriter **bhán, sìɤ, yʉ̋a**
irruption : faire une irruption **zūa**
iterdire : Zan a interdit à Tokpa de venir chez lui **Zân yà Tɔ̀kpà kɛ̀e kʌ̋n ɤ plɤ̀ɤ**
ivrogne *m* **wēgā**

J j

jachère *f* **fɪ́aa, flɔ́ŋ̀,** un lopin de terre est resté en jachère **gbʌ̋a yà tó**
jadis **kpá**
jaillir : le sang (de l'homme) est en train de jaillir **bhɛ̄n yɔ̀ɔn yɤ̀ wɛ̀nŋ gbɛ́,** son sang jaillit *(de la veine)* **à yɔ̀ɔn yɤ̀ bhɔ̄-sɪʌ gbúgbúdhɤ**
jalousie *f* **dlɔ̀ɔ, gblɛ̄ɛ́n**
jaloux **gblɛ̄ɛ́nsʉ̀**
jamais **dō, tōŋtōŋdhɤ**
jambe *f* **gɛ̀n, gɛ̄nŋ̀dhɛ̀, gbʌ̋n, gbʌ̋ngā, kplàa, kplàagā,** jambe et pied **gɛ̀n**
jante *f* de roue de bicyclette **pìɤgāsɔ̀ɔ̀ kòŋ**
janvier **zānvíɛ̀, bʉ̀ufàa**
jarre *f* pour l'eau **yɪ́tàgbɔ̀**
jarred : grande jarre *f* **dhʌ̋ŋgbɔ̄**
jaune **sɔ́ŋ̀yídhē**
jet : en petits jets **pɔ̋pɔ̋dhɤ**
jeter **wɛ̀nŋ, zʉ̀ɤ, zʌ̄,** se jeter **bhán, lòo, sā, wɛ̀nŋ, zūa**
jeu *m* **tlōo,** jeu de cartes **klàatīī dhɛ́ bɛ̀**
jeudi *m* **dhɔ̋ɔyɛ̄ɛ́n**
jeune **bhlʌ̋ʌŋ, gbɔ̋ŋ, kpɔ̀ɔŋ̀, tɛ́tɛ́,** jeune fille **dhʌ́ndhīʌŋ́,** jeune homme **bhīndhʌ́n, dhʌ́nglɔ̄ɔ́n, dhʌ́ngɔ̄ɔ̀n,** jeune marié **dhēgɔ̀ndʌ̄**
jeûner (pour les Chrétiens) **ɤ bɛ̀n bhō**
jeunesse : temps *m* de jeunesse **kpákpá**
joie *f* **zūʌ́ dhìin dà**
joindre les deux bouts **yɤ kó dhɪ́ɤ**
joli **sʌ̀,** être joli **dhī**
joue *f* **kpɪ́ʌŋ**

jouer **gɔ̄ɔn, wɛ̃́, zʌ̄, tlōo kʌ̄,** jouer à l'awalé **bhɑ̃́an gɔ̄ɔn,** jouer au football **bàdhóŋ̀ zȕɤ,** jouer aux cartes **klȁatíì gɔ̄ɔn**

jouet en raphia **vȁa**

joueur *m* de cartes **klȁatíìgɔ̄ɔnbhɛ̏n**

joug *m (fait d'une fourche d'arbre)* **kōŋ,** *(sujétion)* **gíì, sɑ̄ɑ̃́n,** il est sous le joug de sa femme **yɤ̏ sɑ̄ɑ̃́n gúɯ ɤ̄ bhā dhēbʌ̏ gɔ̏**

jour *m* **dhɛ̏, dhɛ̏kpœ̀œ, dhɛ̏kpœ̀œyì, yī,** jour et nuit **dhɛ̏kpœ̀œyì, bɪ́n bhān dhɛ̏ kpœ̀œ**

journée : dans la journée **yʌ́nŋ̏gúɯ**

joyeux **wlɛ̃́ɛwlɛ̏,** rendre joyeux **tȁ-pɔ̃́**

juge *m* **zāgɔ̏bhōbhɛ̏n, zāgɔ̏yɛ́bhɛ̏n,** juge instructeur **zādɔ̄bhɛ̏n**

juger : juger qn coupable **bhɛ̄n zʌ̄ zā' ká,** juger l'affaire **zā gɔ̏-bhō, zā dɔ̄**

juillet *m* **gbɛ̏kɔ̏**

juin *m* **plɛ̃́ɛ**

jumeau **péŋ̏**

jupe *f* de raphia *m* **dhɑ̃́a**

jupon : il est coureur de jupons **ȁ yɑ̃́n gúɯ yɤ̏ yâ**

jurer **sɤ̏ bhɤ̏**

jusqu'à **dhɤ̃́dhɤ́,** jusqu'à ici **ɤ́ tō ȁ ká dhɤ́,** jusqu'à la fin **dō,** jusqu'au bord **kūkkūdhɤ̄**

juste **kpɛ̄ɛnŋdhɤ̄,** juste comme ça **kpɑ̃́an**

K k

kaolin *m* **yɔ̃́ɔ,** kaolin pour soigner le torticolis **gúɯkplȕɯyɔ̃́ɔ**

kilogramme *m*, kilo *m* **kɪ́dhɔ̃́ŋ**

kilomètre *m* **kɪ́dhɔ̃́ŋ**

Kla *(peuple et langue)* **Klāɑ̃́**

klaxon *m* **gɔ̄ tlṹu**

Koma *m (un masque)* **kɔ̀bhán**

Kong *(masque des femmes)* **kòŋ**

Kono *(un peuple et sa langue en Guinée Forestière)* **Kɔ̀dhɔ̀n**

Kpellé *(un peuple et sa langue en Guinée Forestière)* **Gblɛ̏ɛsɛ́**

L l

là **bhā, yā, yɤ̄**

là-bas **bhūn, dɤ̄, tíìdhɤ̏,** là-bas, loin d'ici **bhūn yʌ̀n**

labourer **bɔ̄**

lac *m* **yɪ́gblùɯ**

lâcher un pet **tɔ̂n bhō**

laid **yāa**

laine *f* **sɛ̃́**

laisser **tó,** je ne vais pas te laisser **ā gʌ̄n yɤ̏ ūɯ bhȁ,** laisse-moi tranquille! **gó ā gɔ̏ yɤ̄!** laisser qn en paix **gó bhɛ̄n kèŋ̏**

lait *m* **dhɔ̃́ndhɔ̃́n,** lait de chaux **yɔ̃́ɔ pṹu yɪ́**

laiton *m* **zʌ̄n**

lame *f* **dhɛ̃́,** lame de couteau *m* **dhȁagā,** lame de houe **kʌ̃́ʌ zɔ̃́,** lame de machette **bɑ̃́ŋ dhɛ̃́**

lameller le mica **yʌ́nŋ̏wȅe bhō kwʌ́ʌ̏**

lamenter : se lamenter **kɑ̃́a-bhō,** se lamenter sur Y devant X **wɔ̏ kpɔ́ X bhȁ Y gɔ̏**

lampe *f* tempête **dhàŋbhá**

lance *f* **dûɯ, dûɯgā,** lance pour couper les régimes des grains de palmier **dūaŋ**

lance-pierre *m* **dhɤ̏ɤ**

lancer **zȕɤ,** lancer une flèche **sàa zȕɤ,** lancer une pierre à qn/qch avec la fronde **gbɔ̃́ɔ̏ zȕɤ ȁ ká,** lancer un défi à qn **yɑ̃́nzɪ̏ɤgúɯ dɔ̄ bhɛ̄n bhȁ**

langue *f (anatomique)* **dhɛ́ɛ̏n, dhɛ́ɛ̏ngā,** langue *f (parole)* **wɔ̏,** langue de feu **pɛ̄ŋ dhɛ́ɛ̏n, sɪ́ɤ dhɛ́ɛ̏n,** sa langue s'est collée dans sa bouche **ȁ dhɛ́ɛ̏n yà dhʌnŋ ȁ dhɪ́**

languir en esclavage **dhùʌŋdhɛ̏ zʌ̄**

lanière de fronde **gbɔ̃́ɔ̏ gʌ̄n**

laper **pā**

large **gbɛ̃́ɛ, wāŋ, wáŋ̏wȁŋ**

largement **būŋgɛ̄ɛdhɤ̄**
largeur *f* **gbɛ̋ɛ-dhɛ̏**
larmes *fpl* **yȁnyḯ**
latérite *f* **bhùugwʌ̏**
latte *f* **sàa**
l'au-delà *m* **gèebɔ̀ɔ**
laver **gúɯ-zɯ̋, zɯ̋**, se laver **zɯ̋**
leader *m* **bhēngɔ̏tàbhɛ̏n, dhíɤbhɛ̏n, gɔ̏bhɛ̏ndʌ̄, gɔ̏dhíɤbhɛ̏n, gblɯ̏ɯdʌ̄**
lécher **bhȁn-pā, pā**
leçon *f* **klàŋ̏wɔ̏**
léger **fìafìa, fɔ̋ŋ̏fɔ̏ŋ, fɔ̋ɔfɔ̏ɔ, fɤ́ɤ̏, fɤ̋ɤfɤ̏ɤ, sɤ̋ɤŋsɤ̏ɤŋ**, trop léger **fɤ̋ɤfɤ̏ɤ**, à la légère **bhȁagúɯ**
légèrement **lɛ̋ɛdhɤ̄**
légèreté *f* **yȁnbhlɯ̋u, yȁnzɪ̏ɤgúɯ**
législateur *m* **tɔ́ŋ̏dɔ̄bhɛ̏n**
légume vert **tɔ̋odhɛ̋**
lendemain *m* **tȁdhɛ̏kpɔ̀ɛɔ̀ɛ**, le lendemain **ȁ tȁ dhɛ̏kpɔ̀ɛɔ̀ɛ tȁ dhīá, dhè ɤ́' tȁ dhɛ̏ yɤ̏ kpɔ̀ɛɔ̀ɛ, ȁ tȁ dhɛ̏ ɤ́ kpɔ̀ɛɔ̀ɛ**, le lendemain de bonne heure **ȁ tȁ dhɛ̏kpɔ̀ɛɔ̀ɛ tȁ dhīá ȁ píɤ**, le lendemain matin **ȁ tȁdhɛ̏kpɔ̀ɛɔ̀ɛ yɛ̄ɛ́npíɤ**
lent **dhɯ̋aandhɯ̏aan, lʌ́ʌlʌ̏ʌ**
lentement **dhɔ́ɔdhíndhɔ́ɔdhín, dhɯ̏aandhɯ̏aandhɤ̄, lɛ̋ɛdhɤ̄, pīɔ̋odhɤ̄, slʌ̏slʌ̏dhɤ̄, yɛ̋ɛdhɤ̄**
léopard *m* **gɔ̋, gwēe**
lèpre *f* **wèe**
lépreux **wèebhɛ̏n**
lequel? **bhɛ̏ɛn,** *(numérotation)* **dhèdhȁan**
lérot *m* **vɤ̋**
lettre *f (message)* **sʌ́ʌdhɛ̋**
lettre *f (caractère)* **sʌ́ʌdhɛ̋yȁngā**
leucorrhée *f* **yḯwɔ̋sɯ̏**
lever **dȁ**, se lever **wlɯ̄ɯ̋**, il s'est levé **yà dɔ̄ ɤ̄ gæ̀æn**, se lever *(jour)* **kpɔ̀ɛɔ̀ɛ**, le jour s'est levé **dhɛ̏ yà kpɔ̀ɛɔ̀ɛ**, le soleil s'est levé **yʌ́ŋ̏ tɛ́ɛ yà wɔ̏**
lèvre *f* **bɛ̏n**, lèvre inférieure **bɛ̏n dhé ɤ́ sīá yʌ̀n**, lèvre supérieure **bɛ̏n dhé ɤ́ dhɯ̋ɤ́**
lézard *m* **wʌ̀nŋ**, lézard *m (espèce)* **ɤ̄ɤdʌ̄**
liaison : il est venu chercher ceux qui sont liés avec Gbato **yà dhūn Gbȁtɔ̏ tɔ́ bhȁ**
liane *f* **bhīʌ́, bhīʌ́gā, kpʌ̄ʌ́**, liane épineuse **dân, yɔ̏gɔ̏, kpȁantīi**, liane entrelacée **bhīʌ́ʌ klɔ̏o**, liane ressemblant à l'igname **bhìin dhɯ̏**
liane *f*, espèces : **dɛ̏klɔ̏o, dhɯ̋udȁdhɛ̋, fʌ̄nŋ́, gȁ, gʌ̏nŋgʌ̄nŋ́klɔ̏o, glɛ̋ɛnpɯ̋u, glɛ̋ɛntīi, gɤ̄ŋgɤ̋ŋklɔ̏ɔ, kpȁ, pùpūŋ́dhɛ̋, zȁn**
liasse *m* **bɛ̏**
libellule *f* **dɛ̏ɛnŋdɛ̋ɛnŋ**
libérer : on l'a libéré de prison **wȁ ȁ bhō kȁsɔ̏ gúɯ**, je suis libéré du fardeau **bhán gó gȁn gúɯ**
liberté *f* **pɔ̏tāasɯ̏**
lice *f* **kwɛ̄ɛ**
lien *m* : lien d'amitié **bhlɛ̏ɛn gɛ̏n**, lien de parenté **dhēɛ́bhāŋ-dhɛ̏**
lier **dhú**
lièvre *m* **gblɔ̏, sʌ̄n, sánkɛ̄ɛŋ̏dʌ̄**
ligne *f* de pêche *f* **pīɤ̋, pīɤ̋gā**
ligoter **lɤ̏**
limaille *f* de fer **pɪ̏ɤ gbō, pɪ̏ɤ bɪ̏**
lime *f* **klāá**
limite *f* **dhȁan**
limpide **sɤ̋ɤŋsɤ̏ɤŋ**
lingot d'or **sʌ̋nŋ gā**
lion *m* **lāa**
liquide **yḯsɯ̏**
lire **pɤ̄, sʌ́ʌdhɛ̋ wɔ̏ pɤ̄**
lisse **dlɔ̋ɔdlɔ̏ɔ**
lit *m* **dhīɪ̏**, lit en terre battue **kpɪ̏nŋ, kpɪ̏nŋtàa,** *(de rivière)* **gōo, gōogā, gblɔ̋o, yḯgōo**

litige *m* **dhīaŋ, zā,** il aime régler les grands litiges **dhīaŋ gblɤ̋gblɤ̋ zʌ̄ dhɔ̏ yȁ kʌ̏**
livre *m* **sʌ́ʌdhɛ́bɛ̏**
loi *f* **tɔ́ŋ̏**
loin **glɛ̀ɛn,** de loin **pōŋpōŋdhɤ̄**
loir *m* **vɤ̋**
lombric *m* **dhìaa**
long **gōɔgblɛ̀ɛn, glɛ̀ɛn,** long et ample **búʌŋ̏bȕʌŋ,** long, gros et lourd **gbʌ́ŋ̏gbʌ̏ŋ**
longtemps **pīnŋdhɤ̄,** il y a longtemps **kwɛ̀ŋ̏bhìʌ**
longuement **dīŋdhɤ̄,** longuement et avec intensité **fōodhɤ̄**
longueur *f* **glɛ̀ɛn-dhɛ̏**
loques *fpl* **sɔ̄blʌ̋**
lot de terrain **sɛ̋ kpɤ̄ (gw), sɛ̋ kpɔ̄ (t)**
louange : chanter les louanges de qn **wɛ̋ bhɛ̄n píɤ, wɛ̋ bhɛ̄n tȁ**
louche *(douteux)* **glʌ̋ŋglʌ̀ŋ, yɔ̋ɔyɔ̏ɔ, zűuzȕu,** homme louche **bhɛ̄n glʌ̋glʌ́sɯ̏,** il est dans des affaires louches **yɤ̏ ɤ̄ bhā wɔ́n-dhȕn yʌ́n-bhɔ̏ gbēŋ**
louche *(ustensile) f* : *(pour la sauce)* **klȕu,** louche de calebasse **tòo bhō' ká kɔ̏ɔ**
loup : à pas de loup **kɔ̏ŋkɔ̏ŋ, slʌ́slʌ̏slʌ́dhɤ̄**
lourd **gbínŋ̏,** à pas lourd **glɯ̏glɯ̏dhɤ̄**
loutre *m* **yīʌ́kɔ̏ɔ**
louver : se louver **klɤ̋-kʌ̄**
lueur : une lueur sombre de lampe **dhàŋbhá bhúɯ dhűɤɤdhȕɤɤ**
lumière *f* **síɤ, yʌ́nŋ̏, bhúɯ, síɤ bhúɯ,** la vive lumière de la lampe **dhàŋbhá bhúɯ pűu**
l'un l'autre **kó**
lundi *m* **tēnŋyī**
lune *f* **sű**
lutte *f* **gɔ̏n**
lutter **gɔ̀ɔn, gɔ̏n gɔ̄ɔn**
luxation *f* : j'ai eu une luxation à la cuisse **n̄ gɤ́ŋ̏ yà zīɤ kőo**
lycaon *m* **gbān**

M m

macaroni *m* **bhānklɔ̄ɔdhîn, kwíglʌ̏ʌ̏n**
mâcher **gúɯ-sɯ̏ɤ,** acte de mâcher **bhɔ̀ɔnbhɔ̋ɔn**
machette *f* **bʌ̋ŋ, kāibhân,** machette à lame large **síakwɛ̋dhɛ̋n,** machette courte **gbɛ̋,** machette avec de rainures sur la lame **bʌ̋ŋ wɛ̄ŋgādhē,** machette sans rainures sur la lame **sīi bʌ̋ŋ**
machine *f* **bhàannŋzīi**
mâchoire *f* : mâchoire inférieure **kpíʌŋ dhűɤ,** mâchoire *f* supérieure **kpíʌŋ síʌ̄ʌ**
machoiron, mâchoiron *m* **gèegā, gèepűu**
maçon *m* **bhànsɔ́nŋ̏**
magasin **dhɔ̋ɔkɔ̏**
magicien *m* **yídhʌ́ndʌ̄**
magicienne *f* **yídhʌ́ndhē**
magie *f* **dɯ̄ɯ,** magie blanche **yʌ́nŋ̏ gúɯ dɯ̏ɯ,** magie noire **gbēŋ dɯ̏ɯ, bɛ̀dhɛ̋ yāa**
magistrat *m* instructeur **zādɔ̄bhɛ̏n**
mai *m* **gblɔ̏dhèe**
maigrir **kplɛ̄ɛ̏**
main *f* **kɔ̏, kɔ̏dhɛ̋,** main droite **kɔ̏sʌ̏,** entre les mains **kɔ̏dhíɤ,** il a une belle main **ȁ kɔ̏ pínŋ̏ yɤ̏ sʌ̏,** rester les mains vides **tó ɤ̄ kɔ̏ bhȁ**
mainte : à maintes reprises **pīnŋgāpīnŋgādhɤ̄**
maintenant **tɔ̀n, dɔ̄ ɤ́' wō yɛ̄ɛn gúɯ, ɤ́ dɔ̄ yā, tɤ̋ŋ yɤ̄ gúɯ bhā,** à partir de maintenant **tàabhȁn sɯ̏ yā' gúɯ**
maire *m* **bhɛ̋ɛ̏n**
mais **kɛ̋ɛ,** mais comment ?! **zɔ̀ɔ, yɤ̋**
maïs *m* **kɤ̄ŋ,** maïs avant l'éclosion des épis **kɤ̄ŋ gbɔ́ŋ̏,** maïs de deux mois **kɤ̄ŋ sű plèdhē, kwí bhȁ kɤ̄ŋ**

maison *f* **kɔ́, kɔ́ɔdhɛ̀, pɪ́ɤdhɛ̀, plɤ̀ɤdhɛ̀,** maison à étages **táàsṳ̀kɔ̀,** maison à toit de paille **yɛ̋ kɔ̀,** maison *f* carrée **kɔ́dhʌ́n,** maison en tôle **pɪ̀ɤdhɛ̋ kɔ̀**
maître *m* **dʌ̄bhɛ̀n, gɔ̀bhɛ̀n, kàbhɔ̋n,** maître d'esclave **dhùʌŋgɔ̀bhɛ̀n**
maîtresse *f* d'école **klàŋgɔ̀bhɛ̀n dhēbʌ̀**
maîtriser : se maîtriser **dè kún wɔ́n gɯ́,** il sait se maîtriser **à̰ zūʌ́ yɤ̀ gbínŋ̀**
majeur *m (doigt)* **kœ̄œŋgā dhʌ́n glɔ̄ɔ́n, kœ̄œŋgā zìnŋgɯ́ sɯ̀**
majeure partie *f* **pɛ̋ɛn kpîì**
majorité *f* **gbɛ́-dhɛ̀, pɛ̋ɛn kpîì,** grande majorité **kpîì-dhɛ̀**
mal *m* : j'ai mal au ventre **n̄ gú yà tó dhɛ̀ɛnsɯ̀,** il a des maux de ventre **à̰ gblɯ̋dhɛ̀ yà pɪ̀ɤ̀ɤ-sɪʌ, à̰ gblɯ̋dhɛ̀ yà tó dhɛ̀ɛnsɯ̀,** maux de tête **gɔ̀gɯ́wɯ́, gɔ̀kʌ̄**
mal **yâ,** faire mal **bhàn, bhán, gɯ́-wɯ́, kʌ̄, yɯ̋a, pɪ̀ɤ̀ɤ,** mal aller : ça ne va pas chez la personne **yɤ̀ dɔ̀ bhēn gɔ̀ yâ**
malade : être malade **gɯ́-sɪ̀ɤ,** il est malade **à̰ gɯ́ yɤ̀ sɪ̀ɤ-sɯ̀ ká,** il est tombé malade **yɯ̋a yà à̰ kún**
maladie *f* **gɯ́sɪ̀ɤdhē, yɯ̋a,** maladie de nez **kíaan,** maladie des yeux **yɑ̋angākʌ̄,** maladie des poules **zàazúù**
maladif **fɪ́ɔfɪ̀ɔ**
malaise *m* **gɯ́sɪ̀ɤ**
malaria *f* **gɔ̋ŋ, yàkpàyɔ̋o**
malaxer **yɤ̋ɤ**
malchanceux *m* **pīáyāàbhɛ̀n**
mâle *m* **gɔ̄n, gɔ̄ɔ̀n**
malédiction *f* **dhɑ̋ŋ, gbân**
malgré tout **dhàanbhā, dhɤ̋ bhūn**
malheur *m* **gblɯ̀, klɔ̄ɔ̀, wʌ̀ʌ, yànbhán, zūʌ́gìiwɔ̀n**
malheureusement **tɔ̀n**
malheureux **wʌ̀ʌsɯ̀**
malimbe à queue rouge **zǽæ̀zǽæ̀dʌ̄**
malin : faire le malin **kɛ̋ŋ kɑ̋n, yɑ̄ɑ̋n bhō,** il fait trop le malin **yɤ̀ sɪ̄ʌ̀ʌ kùn gbɛ́**
malléole *f* **gɛ̀nwēngā**
malnommée *f* vraie **glɛ̋ɛnwɔ̀dhɛ̀**
malpropre **vlɑ̋anvlàan, zúùzù**
malpropreté *f* **zúùzúdhɛ̀**
maltraiter qn **bhēn wʌ̀ʌdhɛ̀ bhō**
malveillant : il est malveillant **à̰ gblɯ̋dhɛ̀ yɤ̀ tīi**
mama *f* **dhɑ̋n**
mamba *m* vert **glō ɔ̋**
manche *f* **kɔ̀, kɔ̀kúndhɛ̀,** manche de harpe-luth **kɔ̄nŋ dhɯ̋,** manche de louche **klùu wēŋ,** manche de machette **bɑ̋ŋ gɔ̀,** manche de torche **gbɪ́aa zū,** manche de chemise **bhɛ̋ɛ kɔ̀,** manche d'un util **gɔ̀**
Manding **bhʌ̄nŋ́**
mange-mil *m* **zɤ̄ŋ**
manger **bhɤ̀,** manger ensemble **bɔ̄,** manger sa bouillie matinale **ɤ̄ sɯ̀ɤyɪ́ kɑ̋n,** il est en train de manger sans partager sa nourriture avec les autres **yɤ̀ gblɯ̋ yāà kʌ̄-sɪʌ,** manger vite et furtivement **bhàn-bhūn**
mangouste de Dybowsky **sɑ̋kpɑ̋dʌ̄, wēŋ**
mangouste *f* : mangouste à queue blanche **gǽængǽæn,** mangouste *f* des marais **dênpʌ̀dʌ̄, kpɔ̀, wēŋsɑ̋kpádʌ̄,** mangouste rouge **sɑ̋kpɑ̋dʌ̄, wēŋ**
mangue *f* **bhánŋglōo**
manière *f* **gɛ̀n, kɔ̀**
manifester : se manifester **dɔ̄, yɤ̄**
manigancer : cela est manigancé par toi **bhī dhʌ̀n ɯ̄ kɔ̀ ɤ́' bhà**
manille *f* **gbʌ̄nŋ̋gā**
manioc *m* **bāa, gwɛ̄ɛ́,** manioc local **gblɛ̀ɛgbɑ̋n,** manioc cru **bāa sɛ̀ɛ,** manioc séché **bāa kpɛ̋ɛ, bāa gā kpɛ̋ɛ**
Mano *(peuple et langue)* **Bhɑ̋ndhɔ̋n**
Manois **bhɑ̋anbhīn**

manque *m* de respect **yánbhlṹu**
manque *m* de fraîcheur **sœ̄œ**
mante *f* religieuse **gʌ̀nŋgʌ̄nŋ́**
maquillage *m* **zṳ̀tàkwɛ̀ɛ**
maquis *m* **kpɔ̀ɔ, vɔ̋ɔ**
marabout *m* **bhɔ̋ɔ̀n**
marc *m* de café **káflḗe gbō**
marchand *m* **dhɔ̋ɔdɔ̄bhɛ̀n**
marchander **dhɔ̋ɔ zà dō**
marchandise *f* **dhɔ̋ɔkwɛ̀ɛ̀**
marche *f* **tá̋**
marché *m* **dhɔ̋ɔ, dhɔ̋ɔkwʌ́ʌ̀dhɛ̀**
marcher **tá̋ sɯ́ɯ, tá̋, tāà,** marche vite! **ɯ̄ɯ gɛ̀n sɯ́ɯ bṳ̀aanbṳ̀aandhɤ̄ !** marcher sur la pointe des pieds **zīɤ kɔ̀nŋkɔ̀nŋdhɤ̄**
mardi *m* **tɛ̄nŋzīaandō**
mare *f* **yígblɯ̀ɯ**
margouillat *m* **zō**
margousier *m* **dhɔ̄ɔ̋ndhē, yàkpàyő odhɯ̀ɯ**
mari *m* **gɔ̀n,** mari de la fille du frère cadet de la mère **dʌ̄ sɛ̄ɛ́ndhʌ́n**
mariage *m* **gwān, kósɯ́ɯdhē**
marier : se marier avec **tó … gɔ̀,** se marier *(en parlant d'une femme)* **dhó gwāàn, dhó gwān bhà, gwān kpɔ́ bhɛ̄n gɔ̀,** elle s'est mariée **yà dhó gwāàn, yà dhó gwāandhɤ̄,** ils se sont mariés **wà wō kó sɯ́ɯ,** Yo s'est mariée avec Geu *(de sa propre initiative)* **Yɔ̀ ɤ bhā dhʌnŋ wō Gɤ̀ɤ̀ bhà**
marieur *m* **yɔ̀ kʌ́ʌʌ**
marigot *m* **yígā, yígāàdhɛ̀**
marmite *f* **gbō**
marque *f* **dɔ̄ɔ, sǽǣdhɛ̀**
mars *m* **zlő**
marteau *m* **kɔ̀ɔdhíɤ,** marteau traditionnel **yɤ̋ŋ**
martin-chasseur strié **gòodhē**
mascara *m* **kʌ̋nŋ̀**
masque *m* **gèe,** *(la partie en bois qui couvre le visage du porteur du masque)* **gèegɔ̀,** masque "mamba vert" **gèeglɔ̄ɔ̋,** masque cobra **gèegbàa,** masque du groupe Gwa **gwá̋ gèe,** masque de course *f* **bì aŋsɯ́ɯgèe,** masque qui danse "gbatan" **gbá̋gèe,** masque à échasses **gèe glɛ̀ɛn,** masque calao **gèe pɔ̋ɔn,** masque habillé **gèe bāá̋-sɯ̀ɯ,** masque-agresseur *m* **kɛ̋ɛkʌ̄gèe,** masque-assassin *m* **bhɛ̄n zʌ̄ gèe,** masque-chasseur de sorciers **zőo gèe,** masque-pompier *m* **bhánbhɔ̀ɔndhʌ́n**
masse : en masse **tɛ̀tɛ̀dhɤ, wì aadhɤ**
masser **gɯ́ɯ-gá̋n**
massue *f* **dhɯ̋ɯdhʌ́n**
matin *m* **dhīá̋**
matinal : être matinal **sṳ̀ɤ**
matraque *f* **klàŋgā**
matrone *f* **yōaabhōdhɛ̀**
maudire : sois maudit **kɤ́dhìngbɤ̄tá**
mauvais **yâ, yāa,** mauvaise herbe *(espèce)* **dēpāndân,** mauvaise récolte **zàŋ,** il y a eu une mauvaise récolte d'ignames [d'arachides] **zàŋ yà yà yá̋ [gwɛ̋ɛ] tà,** mauvaises herbes **kpɔ̀ɔ, vɔ̋ɔ,** mauvaises intentions *fpl* **dhı̋ı̀n yāàdhɛ̀**
méchant **dhɛ̀ɛnsɯ̀ɯ,** il est méchant **à glɯ̋ɯ yɤ̀ yâ**
mécontentement *m* **sı̀ɤ-dhɛ̀**
médaille *f* **là**
médecin *m* **dhɔ̀tlɔ́ɔ̀, dhɔ̀tlɔ́ɔ̀bhīn**
médicament *m* **bɛ̀dhɛ́, dhɛ́,** médicament contre les maux de ventre **gwɛ̄ɛ̀,** médicament de la médecine moderne **kwí̋ bɛ̀dhɛ́,** médicament traditionnel **bhɛ̄n tīi bɛ̀dhɛ́**
médius *m* **kœ̄œŋgā dhʌ́n glɔ̄ɔ́n, kœ̄œŋgā zìnŋgɯ́ɯ sɯ̀ɯ**
méfier : se méfier **kɯ́n**
mélanger **kāá̋n**
membre de famille **píɤbhɛ̀n, bhāŋ**

même **bhɤ́, dè, dèbɤ́ɤ, dèe, ɗɛ̀slɔ̀ɔ, zì̀aan,** le même **dō bhā, dōsēŋ,** même si **kɤ́, zɔ̀ɔ,** c'est la même chose **pʌ̄ dō bhāŋ**
menace : faire une geste menaçant **kplɛ̄ɛ̀**
menottes *fpl* : passer les menottes à qn **klɛ́e yà bhēn kɔ̀ɔ**
mensonge *f* **sūà**
menteur *m*, menteuse *f* **sūà bhɛ̀n**
menteur **sūàsɯ̀**
mentir à propos de qn **sūà kʌ̄ bhēn bhà**
menton *m* **kpɪ́ʌŋsōā́**
mer *f* **kɔ̀ɔyí, wèeyì**
merci **bádhíká, dhūnwɛ́ɛ, bhà-bhà-bhà-sɔ́ɔkpɤdhí,** *(réponse à une salutation)* **àan,** merci pour ce que vous faites pour nous **kā dhūnwɛ́ɛ kwā bhà,** merci pour le travail! **ɯ̄ dhūnwɛ́ɛ yʌ̄ bhà! ɯ̄ dhūnwɛ́ɛ yʌ̄ bhà bhɯ̄n!** grand merci! **ɯ̄ dhūɛ́ɛn gbɛ́!** merci, je suis rassasié **bhán yà sʌ̀; ā yà-sɯ̀ ká sʌ̀**
mercredi *m* **tēnŋzīaanplè**
merde *f* **gbō**
mère *f* **dhē,** mère de famille **kwā́ŋ̀ dhē**
message *m* **dhœ̄œn, sāanwɔ̀**
messager *m* **kɪ́ʌʌ, tā́sɯ́bhɛ̀n**
messe *f* **bhɛ̄ɛ́wɔ̀**
mesurer **dān**
métier *m* à tisser **kwɛ̄ɛdhʌ́n**
mètre *m* **bhɛ́ntlʌ̀**
mettre **bhán, ɗà, dɔ̄, lòo, wɔ̄, yà, yáàdhūn, zīɤ,** se mettre **dɔ̄, gbàn,** se mettre à **ɤ dhí ɗà … gɯ́, ɗà ... bhà, kún ... bhà, lòo … ká, yà … bhà, yɤ … bhà, zɯ̄n ... bhà,** mettre au monde **kpɔ́,** il ne peut pas se mettre debout comme il faut **yáa dɔ̄ kpɯ́dhɤ gɛ̀n tà,** mettre du piment dans la sauce **slʌ̀ʌ kʌ̄ tɔ́o bhà,** mettre en ordre **bhō,** ils ont mis le voleur en prison **wà kwànbhɛ̀n bhā à ɗà kàsɔ̀ gɯ́,** mettre feu à la brousse **pɛ̄ŋ ɗà blɯ́ɯ ká,** mettre fin à la vie de qn **bhɛ̄n gɔ̀ bhō yʌ́ŋ̀dhɛ̀, yʌ́ŋ̀ bhɔ̄ bhɛ̄n bhà,** mettre la jupe de raphia **dhā́a yà,** mettre une cravate **klà̀a gbàn,** on a mis le toit sur la maison **wà kɔ́ gbà yà**
meugler : la vache meugle **ɗù yɤ̀ wɛ̀ n̄bhúùu, n̄bhúùu**
meuh **ŋ̄bhúùu**
meule à aiguiser **sʌ́ʌ̀gwʌ̀**
miaou **bhíaaɔ̀ɔnbhíaaɔ̀ɔndhɤ**
miauler : le chat miaule **gwā́ndhʌ́n yɤ̀ wɛ̀ bhíaaɔ̀ɔnbhíaaɔ̀ɔndhɤ**
mica *m* **sɯ́wɛ̀e, yʌ́ŋ̀wɛ̀e**
midi *m* **bhìnŋdîì**
miel *m* **yɔ̃́n, zɔ̃́yɔ̃́n**
miette *f* **blɯ̀ŋ**
mieux **fīʌʌ**
mil *m* **klʌ́ʌn**
milieu : au milieu **zìnŋgɯ́**
militaire *m* **dhā́sí, gblɯ̀gɔ̄ɔnbhɛ̀n, sɔ́dhā́**
mille *m* **gblɯ́ɯ**
millepatte *m*, mille-pattes **kpʌ̄nŋ**
milliard *m* **bhīndhīā̀**
millier *m* **gblɯ́ɯ dō,** des milliers **gblɯ́ɯ bhɛ̄ɛn,** milliers **gblɯ́ɯ tà gblɯ̀ɯ,** des milliers et des milliers **gblɯ́ɯ bhɛ̄ɛn tà bhɛ̀ɛn**
million **bhlɪ́ɔn,** un million **gblɯ́ɯ bhɛ̄ɛn dō**
mince **kā́ŋ, kpɛ́ɛ**
mine *f* méprisante : il m'a fait une mine méprisante **yà ɤ bɛ̀n kplɛ̀en bhō n̄ gɔ̀**
ministre *m* **bhīndhínslɤ̀**
minorité *f* **pɛ́en sɛ̄ɛ́ndhʌ́n**
minuit : à minuit **gbēŋ zìnŋgɯ́**
minute *f* **yʌ́ŋ̀kɔ̀dān**
miracle *m* **dhā́bhlɪ́iwɔ̀n, gɯ́glà,** c'est un miracle! **kā́bhā́kɔ̃́ !**
miraculeux **dhìdásɯ̀**
mirador-séchoir *m* **kplâ**
miroir *m* **dhūaŋdhɛ̀**

misérable **dhíɤfíʌʌbhȅn**
misère *f* **wʌ̏ʌsȕ-dhȅ**
miséreux *m* **wʌ̏ʌbhȅn**
missionnaire *m, f* **pɛ̋ɛ̏dhȕ, zla̋anwɔ̏pɤ̄bhȅn**
mobylette *f* **pòpòdhîn**
modéré : être modéré **zɔ̀ɔnŋ**
modeste : il est modeste **yáa dȁ bhēn yʌ̋n gúɯ,** il n'est pas modeste **yɤ̏ dɔ̏ bhēn yʌ̋n gúɯ**
mœlle *f (de l'os)* **gā gúɯ yɔ̏n,** *(d'une plante)* **bhlȕu**
moignon *m* **kpūú**
mois *m* **sű**
moisir **fín**
moisissure *f* **dhìin**
moissonner **kʌ̋n,** moissonner le riz **bhlȕn kʌ̋n**
moite : devenir moite **tɔ̀ɔ**
moitié *f* **gbú, pɛ̋ɛn, pɛ̋ɛn dō**
molaire *m* **gblòŋ gā,** molaires **gblòŋ**
mollet *m* **gȅngbɔ̄**
moment *m* **dhȅ, yɛ̋ɛ̏n,** le moment est venu pour... **ȁ dhȅ yɤ̏ ȁ bhȁ...**
monde *m* **kpɔ̋ŋtàa, kpɔ̋ŋtàadhȅ,** il est parti dans le vaste monde **ȁ dhó ȁ dhȅ gbǽǣ-dhȅ gúɯ**
monsieur *m* **gɔ̄ndʌ̄**
monstre *m* **pʌ̄, zȕzȕgwȅ**
montagne *f* **tɔ̏n**
monter **dȁ, kún,** monter par une échelle **gbʌ̏-kʌ̄**
montre *f* **bhɔ́nŋ̏tlʌ̏, dhɛ̋dhɛ̋kɔ́, yʌ́nŋ̏kɔ́**
montrer **zɔ̏n**
moquer : se moquer de qn **kpœ̄œ dɔ̄ bhēn bhȁ, kpœ̄œ pɛ̋ bhēn bhȁ, wɛ̀ɛ dɔ̄ bhēn bhȁ**
moquerie *f* **kpɔ̄ɔ, wɛ̀ɛ**
moqueur *m* **yɔ̄dhɛ̋gúɯbhȁan**
morceau *m* **kplúɯ, kpɤ̄,** morceaux *(égaux en dimension)* **déŋ̏déŋ̏,** morceau de tige de canne à sucre **kȁa kpɤ̄,** en petits morceaux **tlȕkpȅtlȕkpȅdhɤ̄**
mordre : il l'a mordu **yȁ ȁ kún sɔ̋ɔn,** il s'est mordu la langue **ȁ sɔ̋n yà yɤ̄ ȁ dhɛ̋ɛn tȁ,** il s'est mordu la lèvre **yà ɤ̄ sɔ̋n yɤ̄ ɤ̄ bȅn tȁ,** le poisson mord à l'hameçon **yúɤ̏ɤ yɤ̏ pīɤ̋ zʌ̄-sīʌ,** le serpent m'a mordu **bhlɛ̀ɛn yà n̄ kún**
morelle *f* noire **sȉandhɛ̋**
mors *m* **klʌ̋bhí**
morsure *f* de chien **gbên sɔ̋n gblɔ̋o,** la morsure de chien me fait mal **gbên sɔ̋n glɔ̋o yɤ̏ n̄ kʌ̄-sīʌ**
mort *f* **gā,** il est marqué par la mort **gā tɛ̋ɛ yȁ ȁ súɯ**
mort *m* **gèebɔ̀ɔbhȅn**
mortel *m,* mortelle *f* **gābhȅn**
mortier *m* **wlɤ̋,** mortier à piler les condiments pour la sauce **tɔ̋ozɔ̄ngúɯwlɤ̋,** mortier peu profond **glɔ̄ɔzɔ̏ngúɯwlɤ̋**
morve *f* **yūn yí,** morve sèche **yūn kɛ̋ŋgbʌ̋,** longue morve **yūn yí dɔ̋ŋ gblɛ̀ɛn**
mosquée *f* **bhìnsîkɔ̏, bhɔ̋ɔ̏n sʌ́ʌ̏ bhɔ̏ gúɯ kɔ̏, sʌ́ʌ̏ bhɔ̏ gúɯ kɔ̏**
mot *m* **dhíwɔ̏gā**
moteur *m* **bhàanŋzíȉ, wɛ̋dhȅ**
moto *m,* motocycle *m* **mɔ̄tô**
motte *f* de boue **bɤ̄ɤ̏ kɔ̏ŋ**
mou **plʌ́ʌplʌ̏ʌ,** mou et rare **píʌʌnpȉʌʌn**
mouche *f* **wʌ́nŋ,** mouches mellifères **bhɔ̄ɔ́**
moucher son nez, se moucher **ɤ̄ yūn pȉɤ (gw), ɤ̄ yūn bhō (t)**
moucheron *m* **zɛ̄nŋ́,** moucheron piqueur **kʌ̏ʌ**
mouchoir *m* **sōpɛ̋n**
moue *f* : il a fait la moue **yà ɤ̄ bȅn yɔ̀ɔn kwʌ́ʌ̏, yà ɤ̄ bȅn kplɛ̏ɛn bhō,** moue méprisante **kplɛ̏ɛn, sȕɛɛ,** il m'a fait une moue méprisante **yà ɤ̄ bȅn kplɛ̏ɛn**

bhō n̄ ká, yà sʋ̀ɛɛ bhō n̄ ká, yà sʋ̀ɛɛ kǻn n̄ ká
mouillé : devenir mouillé **tɔ̀ɔ**
mouiller **tɔ̀ɔ, yí-bhō**
mourir **gā,** il est couché en train de mourir **yà wɔ̄ gā-yàn tà,** il est mort **à dhı̂ı̀n yà pɤ̀, à wɔ̀n yà sēè**
mousse *f* **vı́ʌʌ**
moustache *f* **bèn à kàa**
moustique *m* **zɛ̄nŋ́, zɛ̄nŋ́ gā**
mouton *m* **bhlǻa**
mouvement : il a fait un mouvement avec sa main, il a cherché avec sa main **yà dhó ɤ̄ kɔ̀ ká**
mouvette *f* **kpàdhʉ́ʉ, kpœ̄œdhʉ́ʉ**
moyen **zìnŋgúsʋ̀,** de moyenne taille **gbɔ̋ŋ**
moyens *(objets inanimés)* **glɔ̋ɔglɔ̋ɔ**
moyens : il a des moyens **fāan yà bhà**
mue *f* **wèe,** mue de serpent **bhlɛ̄ɛn wèe**
muezzin *m* **bhɔ̋ɔ̀n-sʌ́ʌ̀-dhɛ̀ɛdhíɤ-bhō-bhèn**
muezzin *m* **bhɔ̋ɔ̀n sʌ́ʌ̀ dhɛ̀ɛdhíɤbhōbhèn**
mulet *m* **sòòfʌ̄ŋ**
multicolore **yʌ̋nŋyʌ̀nŋ,** multicolore avec une dominance de rouge **tɛ̋ɛn yʌ̋nyʌ̀n**
multitude *f* **bhēɛn, tɤ́ŋbhàsʋ̀**
mur *m* **bhǻŋ,** mur de la case **kɔ́ bhǻŋ**
mûr : non mûr **kpɔ̀, kpɔ̀sʋ̀**
mûrir **pʌ̀-kʌ̄**
mûrissement : approcher du stade de mûrissement **zʋ̀an,** au point d'atteindre le stade de mûrissement **zʋ̀ansʋ̀**
murmure *m* **wʉ̋nŋ**
murmurer : le ruisseau murmure **yí-dhʌ́n bhā yɤ̀ wè wlɔ̄ɔ̋wlɔ̀owlɔ̄ɔ̋dhɤ**
muscle *m* **dhʌ̀nŋ**
musicien *m* **tǻnbhōbhèn**
musique *f* rapide **tǻn wɔ̋sʋ̀**
musulman **bhɔ̋ɔ̀n**
mycose *f* **fı̋ı, gbōkǻa,** mycose de pieds **dhɔ̀ɔndhɔ̋ɔndhē**
mygale *f* **lʌ̀ʌn**

N n

nager **yí-kʌ̄**
naïf : il est naïf **yáa wɔ́n-dhʋ̀n dhàan dɔ̄**
nain **fìʌʌnsʋ̀**
nain *m* **bhēn fìʌʌnsʋ̀**
naissance *f* : quelle est l'année de sa naissance ? **à bhɔ̄ kwɛ̀ yɤ̀ dhè?**
naître **bhɔ̄, ɗà, kpɔ́,** il n'est pas facile de donner naissance à un enfant **dhʌ́n yáa kpɔ́**
nandinie *f* **gū**
narine *f* **yūn dhı́**
nasiller : il nasille **yɤ̀ wè ɤ̄ yūúndhɤ, yɤ̀ wè ɤ̄ yūn gʉ́ʉ**
nasse *f* **sàadhē, zɔ̄ɔ, zūeŋ**
natal : son village natal **à kpɔ́ pɤ̀**
natalité *f* **dhʌ́nkpɔ́dhē**
natte *f* **sɛ̄ɛ́,** natte faite de lattes **gbàsàgbǻsǻ,** natte en rouleau **sɛ̄ɛ́ bè**
nausée *f* **pè,** avoir des nausées **tà-sēè,** donner des nausées à qn **tà-sēè,** il a la nausée **à zūʌ́ tà yɤ̀ sēè-sīʌ**
navette *f* **kplǻ**
nécessité *f* **dhɛ̀**
neem *m* **yàkpàyɔ̋odhʋ̀, dhɔ̄ɔ̋ndhē**
négligé **vlǻanvlàan**
négligence *f* **bhēnkɔ̀kàngʉ́ʉ,** faire négligemment **yɔ̄ɔyɔ̋ɔ-kʌ̄**
négliger **fìʌʌ,** il l'a négligé **à yǻn yɤ̀ wlɤ̀ à tà**
néré de Gambie **bhʌ̋nŋ**
néré des singes *(une plante)* **wɔ̀ɔdhʌ́nbhàbhʌ̋nŋ**
nettoyer **bà, gʉ́ʉ-gblɤ̀,** nettoyer en grattant **gʉ́ʉ-klōo,** nettoyer le terrain pour un champ de manioc **bāa dhɛ̀ bà**
neuf **sʉ́ɛ̀sīɤ**
neveu *m* **bɛ́ɛ̀, bɛ́ɛ̀ gɔ̄ɔ̀n**

nez *m* **yūn, yūnkpɤ̄, yūúndhɛ̀,** son nez est pris **à yūn gúɯ yà tā**
nid *m* **kɔ́,** nid de chique **tūbhûn,** nid d'abeilles **zɔ̄,** nid d'araignée **dɔ́ɔ̀n kɔ́,** nid des foumis rouges **dlɔ̀ɔ kɔ́,** nid d'oiseau **bhàan kɔ́,** nid de guêpes **gbɔ̀ŋ kɔ́**
nièce *f* **bɛ́ɛ̀**
nim *m* **yàkpàyőodhɯ̀ɯ, dhɔ̄ɔ́ndhē**
n'importe quel **őo,** n'importe qui, n'importe quoi **X ɤ́ dhɤ́**
niveau *m* **tɤ̋ŋ**
niveleuse *f* **zɔ̄**
noce *f* **kɔ́sɯ́dhē**
Noël **Ŋdhōɛdhɤ̀**
nœud *m* **kpɤ̄,** nœud de fouet **klàa kpūdhē,** faire un nœud **kpɤ̄ tā**
noir **tii,** noir d'encre **gbēŋ kpɤ̄**
noircir **tlɤ̄ɤ**
noix *f* de cola *m* **gô, gô gā,** noix de cola sans division en lobes **bhőbhőgɔ̀**
noix *f* d'arachide **gwɛ̋ɛ gā**
nom *m* **tɔ́,** nom de jeunesse **dhʌ́nglɔ̄ɔ́n-dhʌ́n-gúɯ-tɔ̀,** nom d'enfant **dhʌ̄nŋ̀gɯ́tɔ̀, sɛ̋ɛ́ndhʌ́ngɯ́tɔ̀**
nombre *m* **dhí, dhínbhlɔ̂n,** nombre cardinal **dōŋdhē dhínbhlɔ̂n,** nombre ordinal **dùɛɛ dhínbhlɔ̂n,** ils sont du même nombre **à-dhùn dhí (yɤ̀) dō,** en grand nombre **dɛ̀dɛ̀wō, tɛ̀kpɛ̀tɛ̀kpɛ̀dhɤ̄, tɛ̀tɛ̀dhɤ̄**
nombreux **bɤ̋ɤwɛ̋, gbɛ́, plʌ̄ʌ̀, sűbhʌ̋n, tɛ̀tɛ̀,** devenir très nombreux **sɔ́**
nombril *m* **bù, bùgā, bùgɔ̀**
nommer **dà, kʌ̄**
non **áabhōo, àbín**
nonchalant **dhűaandhùaan, slɔ̄ɔslɔ̀ɔ, wɔ̄ɔnwɔ̀ɔn**
nord : au nord **dhűɤ**
normal : il n'est pas normal **à bhà glèŋ wɔ̀n gúɯ yáa dhɤ́**
nostalgie *f* : rendre qn nostalgique **bhēn zūʌ̋ tó tàabhàn**
notable *m* **pɤ̂dʌ̄**
nouer la cravate **klàa gbàn**
nourrir **dhíɤ-gbā**
nourriture *f* **bhɤ̀pʌ̀, kɔ̋ŋ, pʌ̄bhèe,** nourriture de base **kɔ̋ŋ,** nourriture secondaire **pʌ̄ píɤ pʌ̀**
nouveau **dèe,** nouveau né **dhʌ́nblʌ̋,** nouveau né *(avec le cordon ombilical)* **dhʌ́nblʌ̋ pűu,** de nouveau **bhá, bháwō, dèe, dèewō, pɤ́pɤ́,** nouvelles feuilles **tɔ̀ŋ**
nouvelle *f* **tìŋ, tɯ̀œŋ,** quelles sont les nouvelles? **kwá à bhān bhūn?**
novembre *m* **zànwɛ̋ɛ**
noyau *m* **flɛ̋ɛ̀,** noyau de grain de palmier à huile **wēn flɛ̋ɛ̀**
noyer : se noyer **gā yí bhàa,** il s'est noyé **yí yà à zʌ̄,** il a noyé l'enfant **yà à kʌ̄ dhɤ́ yí yà dhʌ́n bhā' zʌ̄,** il est en train de se noyer **yɤ̀ yí bhʌ̋nŋ-sīʌ**
nu **kpáan**
nuage *m* **dhākpóŋ̀, nuages dhűu,** nuage de poussière **bɔ̀bì dhűu,** le ciel est couvert des nuages **dhāŋgɯ́dhɛ̀ yà kʌ̄ gbíŋ̀**
nudité *f* **kpéè**
nuire **dhíɤ-sɯ́, kʌ̄**
nuit *f* **gbēŋ,** nuit noire **gbēŋ dhɛ̀ gúɯ tīi gúɯ,** nuit sans lune **sű dhɛ̀gɯ́ tii**
numéro *m* **dhínbhlɔ̂n,** numéro de téléphone **pìɤgā bhàn dhíbhlɔ́ɔ̀n**
nu-pieds : il est nu-pieds **à gèn yɤ̀ kpáan ká**

O o

obéir qn **bhēn bhlʌ̀ʌ yà**
obligation *f* **dūʌ̋, dhæ̀æ, dhɛ̀**
obliger **tà-bhō,** le X est obligé... **à sɛ̋ yáa X dhɛ̀ ...**
obscur **tii**

obscurité *f* **bĩ́n**
observateur *m* : être observateur **wɔ́n sṹàn bhō**
obstacle **wɔ́n gbɛ̋ɛ̀**
obtenir **slɔ̀ɔ,** obtenir du succès *(auprès d'une femme)* **dȁ … kèŋ̏**
occasionellement **dódó**
occiput *m* **kèe, kèȅdhɛ̏**
occuper **bhán, sɯ́ɯ,** s'occuper **dhī, dhĩ́ɤ-bhō,** être occupé **dɔ̄ … ká**
océan *m* **kɔ̏ɔyĩ́**
ocre *m* **gblȁn**
octobre *m* **zȁnyĩ́sɯ̏**
octroyer : on lui a octroyé un grade (militaire) **wȁ là dhʌ̀nŋ ȁ gbān tȁ**
odeur *f* **fìi, gbĩ́ʌn**
œil *m* **yȁn,** un œil **yȁn pɛ̋ɛn dō**
œuf *m* **yȁan**
offenser : il s'est offensé **bhlɔ̄ɔ yà bhán ȁ gɯ́ɯ,** offenser *(un aîné)* **dȁ … dhĩ́ɤ**
offrir un repas à l'étranger **dhȅŋ dhĩ́ bhɔ̄ɔ̀n**
oh là là! **kpȁsákpōsō**
oh! **yȁa**
oignon *m* **yȁbhȁ**
oiseau *m* **bhȁan,** oiseau de nuit **gbēŋbhȁan**
oiseau *m*, espèces : **slɛ̏ɛn, tlɔ̏ɔ, zā**
oisif : rester oisif **tó ɤ̄ gɔ̏ pĩ́ɤ**
ombre *f* **bĩ́n, blɛ̋ɛ̀n, dhɔ̄ŋ,** dernières ombres de la nuit **dhȅgɯ́tīi,** ombre de l'arbre **dhűű dhɔ̄ŋdhɛ̏,** endroit ombragé **dhɔ̄ŋdhɛ̏**
ombrette *f* **sṹʌŋsṹʌŋ**
ombreux **dhɔ̄ŋsɯ̏**
oncle *m*, oncle maternel **dhūʌ̏ʌ**
ongle *m* **sūʌ̋**
opinion *f* **zɔ̏tȁgɯ́wɔ̏n**
or *m* **sʌ̋nŋ,** or liquide **sʌ̋nŋ yĩ́**
orage *m* **tɛ̋ɛ dhȁ**
orange *m* **kwĩ́ ȁ dhɤ̄ŋ̏**

orateur : il est bon orateur **ȁ dhĩ́dhɛ̏ yɤ̏ dhɛ̋ɛndhɛ̏ɛn**
orbite *f (anat.)* **yȁn kɔ́**
ordalie : on lui a fait passé l'ordalie par la décoction de l'arbre "geu" **wȁ glűű dɔ̄ bhēn gɔ̏**
ordinaire **bhȁasɯ̏**
ordonner **kpœ̏œ dɔ̄**
ordre *m* **gbɛ̋ɛ̀-dhɛ̏**
ordures *f* **blʌ̄ʌ, gblű**
oreille *f* **tő, tődhɛ́gā,** oreille externe **tődhɛ́, tőkpɤ̄,** oreille *f* moyenne **tőgɯ́dhɛ̏,** il est dur d'oreille **ȁ tő yɤ̏ gbĩ́nŋ̏, ȁ tő gɯ́ yɤ̏ gbĩ́nŋ̏**
oreiller *m* **gɔ̏dɔ̄tȁpʌ̏**
organisé : personne organisée **wɔ́nwɔ̏kódhĩ́ɤbhȅn**
organiser une grande fête **wlȁȁn kʌ̄**
orgelet *m* **sūʌ̋ʌ,** il a eu un orgelet **sūʌ̋ʌ yà dɔ̄' yȁȁn**
orgueil *m* **dȅsɯ́kpĩ̂**
orgueilleux : être orgueilleux **ɤ̄ dè sɯ́ kpĩ̂**
oricou **zœ̏œ̏tɛ̋ɛtɛ̏ɛ**
orifice *f* **dhĩ́, yɛ̏, yɛ̏gā**
ornière *f* **glȍogā**
orphelin *m*, orpheline *f* **tȅ**
orphelinage *m* **tȅ-dhɛ̏**
orteil *m* **gēnŋgā,** orteil moyen **gēnŋgā zìŋgɯ́sɯ̏,** gros orteil **gēnŋgāgɔ̄n**
oryctérope *m* **zɤ̏ŋ**
os *m* **gā**
oser : ose encore t'approcher de moi! **yɔ̀ɔn ñ bhȁ!**
oseille *f* de Guinée **kpīʌŋ̏**
ossature *f* de la maison **klȁa,** il a fabriqué l'ossature de la maison **yȁ kɔ́ klȁa bhō**
ôter : ôte-toi d'ici ! (litt.: de ma place) **gó ñ yɛ̏ɛ bhàa!** ôte-toi de ma place (à coucher)! **gó ñ wɛ̏ɛ bhàa!**
otite *f* **tő kʌ̄ yṹa**

ou **ĩĩn,** ou encore... **ĩĩn zúɯ ...**
où? **bhɛ́n**
ouah! ouah! **wáɯ̏u-wáɯ̏u,** le chien aboie: ouah! ouah! **gbɛ̂n yɤ̏ wɛ̏ wáɯ̏u-wáɯ̏u**
ouaouarou **kȁdō**
oublier : j'ai oublié son nom **ȁ tɔ́ yà dhɛ̀ŋ n̄ gɔ̏,** X a oublié comment faire Y **X zɔ̏ yɤ̏ bhɔ̏ Y-dhɛ̏ ká**
ouf! **hāá**
oui **ȁòo, ìi, ŋ̏ŋ̏**
ouïes *fpl* **tɔ̋**
ourler **kún**
outrage *m* **bhlɔ̄ɔ**
outrager qn **bhlɔ̄ɔ wɔ̏n kʌ̄ bhɛ̄n ká**
outrepasser ses droits **dɯ̏ɛɛ tó**
ouvertement **zāŋtȁ**
ouverture *f* **dhí**
ouvrier *m* **yʌ̄kʌ̄bhɛ̏n**
ouvrir **dhíɤ-pɔ̋, dhí-pɔ̋, pɯ̋,** s'ouvrir **pɯ̋,** la terre s'est ouverte sous leurs pieds **yɛ̏ yà kɛ̋n ȁ-dhɯ̏n wlɤ̏ɤ**

P p

paddy **kpǽæsɯ̏ɯ**
paf **kőoudhɤ, wɛ̋inŋdhɤ**
page *f* **dhɛ̋**
pagne *m* **kɛ̋nsɔ̏, sɔ̄, wāntīi, wāŋdhʌ́n**
paille **fâfâ**
paillote *f* **gɔ̏n, gɔ̄nŋ̏dhɛ̏**
pain *m* **blúɯ̏,** un pain **blúɯ̏ bhɛ̄ dō,** pain dur **blúɯ̏ gblɤ̋ɤgblɤ̏ɤ,** pain baguette **blúɯ̏ bhɛ̄,** pain baguette courte **blúɯ̏ bhɛ̄ klɤ̏ɤ̏,** pain court **blúɯ̏ bhɛ̄ gúŋ̏gɯ̏ŋ,** pain rond **blúɯ̏ dhɤ̋ɤdhɤ̏ɤ,** pain à cacheter *(singe Cercopithecus nictitans)* **klɛ̋ŋ̏**
paire *f* des yeux **yɛ̋n**
paix *f* **dhɪ̏kó-dhɛ̏, flʌ́ʌ̏bhōdhē,** je suis en paix **ā n̄ flʌ́ʌ̏ gúɯ**
palabre *m* **dhīaŋ, pɪ̂ʌ̏ʌdhɤkɔ̏, sɪ̏ɤ,** faire palabre à qn **dhídhȁan bhán bhɛ̄n ká**
palais *m (anat.)* **dhíʌŋ**
pale : rendre pâle **flɤ̋**
palme *f* du palmier **sɔ̋nŋdhɛ̋,** palme du jeune palmier à huile **glâ dhɛ̋,** palme du palmier à huile adulte **sɤ̄ dhɛ̋**
palmier *m* à huile **yɔ̄,** palmier à huile adulte **sɤ̄ dhɯ̏ɯ,** jeune palmier à huile **glâ,** palmier raphia **bhāŋ,** jeune pousse de palmier de raphia **dɔ̀ŋ**
palper **kɔ̏-pá**
paludisme *m*, palu *m* **gɔ̋ŋ, yȁkpȁyɔ̋o**
pan! **gblɯ̏uuu**
pangolin *m* arboresque **bhȁadʌ̄**
pangolin *m* géant **zɔ̄**
panier *m* **tɤ̏ɤ,** panier pour garder les vêtements **bhɯ̋tɯ̋,** panier pour les noix de cola **gblɯ̋ɪ,** panier de colas **gɔ̂ gblɯ̋ɪ,** panier de liane **gȁ tɤ̏ɤ**
panneau *m* de papot **pɛ̋pɔ̋ dhɛ̋**
panneton *m* **dhàklɛ̋e sɔ̋n**
pantalon *m* **pàŋ**
panthère *f* **gɔ̋, gwēe**
paon *m* **kɔ̀nŋsóɔ̏dhɯ̏ɯ**
papa *m* **kwɛ̏ɛgbɤ̄**
papaye *f* **bhȁŋglɤ̏ɤ**
papier *m* **sʌ́ʌdhɛ̋**
papillon *m* **dhɛ̋ŋdhɛ̋ŋkpȁadhɛ̏,** papillon de nuit *f* **tɛ̋tɛ́kpȁadhɛ̏**
papo, papot *m* **pɛ̋pɔ̋**
paquet *m* enveloppé **bhlɯ̀ɪ,** paquet de bois *(branches et tiges, pour la construction)* **dhɯ̋ɪ bɛ̏,** paquet de cola **gɔ̂ bhlɯ̀ɪ**
par **gɔ̏, ká, kɔ̄ɔ,** il est couché tout droit par terre **yà wɔ̏ kplɛ̄ŋkplɛ̄ŋdhɤ**
paralysé : être paralysé **gā,** devenir paralysé **lòo,** ses jambes sont paralysées **ȁ gɛ̏n yà lòo,** il est paralysé **tlɯ̋nŋ yūa yȁ bhȁ**
paralysie *f* **tlɯ̋nŋ**
paralytique *m* de deux jambes **gɛ̏nlòobhɛ̀n**
parapluie *f* **wɛ̄lɛ̋**

parasite *m* sous-cutané **bhɛ̋ŋ**
parasitisme *m* **zȉʌʌ**
parce que **pāsɤ́,** c'est parce que **yɤ̏ tɔ́**
pardonner **bhȁnwɔ̏n tó,** Sao ne pardonnera pas cela à Yo **Yɔ̏ yȁ Sàó tɤ̏ɤ̏ sɯ́**
pareil **sɯ̋bhɑ̋n,** il n'a pas son pareil **yɔ̋ɔ ȁ sɯ́bhɑ̋n yáa dhɤ́**
parent *m* **dhɛ̄ɛ́bhāŋ,** parents **kpɔ́bhɛ̏n-dhȕn,** parents, grande famille **dʌ̄-dhȕn,** parent par alliance **dhìnbhɔ́ɔ̏n**
parer **bāȁ,** se parer **tȁ-kún, zɯ̋**
paresse *f* **sȁa-dhɛ̏**
paresseux **fíasɯ̏, sȁa**
paresseux *m*, paresseuse *f* **fíabhɛ̏n**
parfaitement **kpákpádhɤ̄,** parfaitement vrai **gbáȁndhɤ̄**
parfois **dhȕnwō, sìʌ, yī bhá-dhȕn ká**
parfum *m* **pādhīféŋ̏**
parler **dhīaŋ zʌ̄, pɤ̄, wɛ̋,** parler avec qn **ɤ̄ dhí dȁ bhɛ̄n tȁ,** parler de qn/qch **wɛ̋ ȁ ká,** il ne me parle plus **yà ɤ̄ dhí tā n̄ gɔ̏**
parole *f* **dhīaŋ, wɔ̏,** ne pas adresser sa parole à qn **ɤ̄ dhí tā bhɛ̄n gɔ̏,** paroles outrageuses **bhlɔ̄ɔ dhȉaŋ̏**
part *f* **dȕɛɛ,** à part ça... **yáa yɤ̄ zʌ̏ ȁ ká...,** **yɤ́ ɤ́ dhɤ̄ bhā**
partager **gblɯ̏**
partenaires du cousinage à plaisanterie **dhɑ́sí, sànbhɯ̋nzʌ̏**
parti *m (politique)* **pɛ̋ɛn**
partie *f* **pɛ̋ɛn, pɛ̋ndhɛ̏,** partie avant **wʌ̄ʌ́zȉaan,** partie arrière **kȅe,** partie arrière du corps humain **tàabhȁdhɛ̏,** partie extérieure **kpɛ̋nŋdhɛ̏,** partie extérieure *(de plante)* **gɔ̏,** partie inférieure **gɛ̄nŋ̏dhɛ̏, sɛ̋**
partir **dȁ, kpɔ̏**
partout **flɯ̋udhɤ̄, zīan gbàn ká**
parvenir **zūn**
pas *m* **gȅnsɯ́, gȅnyȁn,** s'approcher à pas de loup de qn **gbá kpɔ́ ȁ bhȁ**
passé *m* récent **dȅe**
passer **bɔ̄, dhó, pāsē, zīɤ,** passer chez qn **lòo … píɤ,** passer *(temps)* **kʌ̄,** passer à vapeur **flɯ̀ɯ,** ils l'ont passé à tabac **yɤ́ wó ȁ zʌ-dhɛ̏ bhȁn wō,** passer la nuit **wɔ̄,** passer un examen **gɛ̄nyɛ̄n,** passer une nuit blanche **yɑ̋n**
passerelle *f* **gbɑ̋ŋ**
passion *f* pour la viande **bhɯ́ɯkʌ̄**
patas *(singe)* **yɛ̋ɛ̏wɔ̏ɔ**
patate *f* douce **wɛ̋sɛ̋**
pâte *f* **bɤ̏ɤ, kɔ̏n,** pâte de riz **dhʌ̄ʌ,** pâte de riz envoûtée **dhʌ̏ʌ,** pâte de farine **blɯ́ɯ̏ bɤ̏ɤ,** pâte d'arachide **gwɛ̋ɛ bɤ̏ɤ, gwɛ̋ɛ kɔ̏n,** pâte de feuilles de manioc **bāa dhɛ̋ kɔ̏n**
patience *f* **zūʌ̋ sæ̏æ, zūʌ̋sæ̏æ-dhɛ̏**
patient : sois patient **ȁ kún ɤ̄ bhȁ, ɯ̄ zūʌ̋ kʌ̄ sɛ̏ɛ**
patine *f* verte sur les dents **dhȉin**
patron *m* **bhɛ̄ngɔ̏dhíɤbhɛ̏n, gɔ̏bhɛ̏n**
patte *f*, pattes **gɛ̄nŋgā, gbɑ̋n, gbɑ̋ngā, kplàa, kplàagā,** patte de derrière **gȅn,** patte de devant **kɔ̏, kwɛ̄ɛ̋**
paume *f* **kɔ̏dhɛ̋wlɤ̏ɤdhɛ̏**
paupière *f* : j'ai les paupières lourdes **n̄ yɑ̋n yà kʌ̄ gbínkígbȉnkȉ**
pause : faire une pause pendant le travail **gó ɤ̄ kō tȁ,** il a fait une pause dans la réception des visiteurs **yà ɤ̄ kɔ̏ dūn ɤ̄ ká**
pauvre **flɛ̋ɛsɯ̏**
pauvre *m* **flɛ̋ɛbhɛ̏n**
pauvreté *f* **flɛ̋ɛ**
pavillon d'oreille **tɔ̋dhɛ̋gā**
payer le salaire **sàa bhō**
pays *m* **pɛ̋ɛn, sɛ̋, sɛ̋kɔ̏pɛ̋n.** pays des Blancs **kwí sɛ̋**
peau *f* **kɛ̋ɛ, kwī,** peau qui se détache **wȅe, bhɛ̄n kwī wȅe, bhɛ̄n wȅe**

pêche : faire la pêche *f* **bhȁ-kʌ̄,** faire la pêche au barrage **yi̋ blɯ̏**

pêcher à la ligne **pīɤ̋ dȁ**

pédale *f* **pēdáyɤ̏**

peigne *m* **fa̋agā,** peigne en bois **dhɯ̋ fa̋agā,** peigne fin **fa̋ȁgā ɤ̋ sɔ̋n ɤ́ yɤ̄-sɯ̏ ká kwʌ́ʌ̏,** peigne de type européen **fa̋agā sɔ̋n gbɛ́ dhē**

peigner **gɯ́-pȉɤ**

peine : à peine (qch s'est mis en bonne voie), et... **dhɛ̀ ɤ́ ... sʌ̏ ká, yɤ́ ...**

pêle-mêle **zūűzūűdhɤ̄**

pelle *f* **pe̋tő**

pellicules *fpl* **bhɛ̄n gɔ̏ wȅe, bhɛ̄n wȅe**

pelure *f* de manioc *m* **bāa blʌ̏ʌ**

pencher (un récipient) **dɔ̄ gɤ̋ŋ ká**

pendant **ká, pı̋ɤ, zìnŋgɯ́,** pendant que ... **tó,** pendant ce temps **ɤ́ kʌ̄ dhɤ́ (gw), ɤ́ dhɤ́ bhā (t)**

pendre : se pendre **dūn, ɤ̄ dȅ dūn bhīʌ̋ʌ bhȁ**

pénétrer **bhán, sɔ̏, zīɤ**

Pengdé-Unijambiste *(un génie de brousse)* **Pɛ̄nŋ̋dhē**

pénis *m* **kpāa̋n, kpāa̋ngā, kplɤ̏ɤ, kplɤ̏ɤgā**

pensée *f* **tɤ̋ŋ, zȍgɔ̏ngɯ́wɔ̏n, zȍta̋dhē, zȍtȁgɯ́wɔ̏n,** pensées *(ce qui remplit la tête)* **gɔ̏**

penser : penser à qch **tɤ̋ŋ kʌ̄ pʌ̄ gɯ́,** penser que **gȁ … dhɛ̀**

pensivement **zūudhɤ̄**

pente *f* **kpɔ̋ŋ, tɔ̏n,** pente de colline *f* **gōo**

perçant **dhı̋ɤsɯ̏**

percebois *m* **pɛ̏n**

percepteur *m* **wʌ́ʌ̏kúnbhɛ̏n**

percer **zūa**

perche *f* **dhɯ̋gā**

perdre **dhɛ̀ŋ, gó,** se perdre **dhɛ̀ŋ,** perdre la sensibilité **gɯ́-kplɯ̏**

perdrix *m* **kœ̄œ**

père *m* **dʌ̄,** père de village **pɤ̂dʌ̄**

période *f* froide *(décembre-janvier)* **bȕu dhɛ̋ndhɛ̋n**

périr : il a péri en voyage **sœ́œ̏ yɤ̏ zūn' gɔ̏ zīaan bhɯ́n**

permanence *f* **tɤ̋ŋgbàn**

permettre **kwāȁ**

personnalité *f* **gɔ̏bhɛ̏n**

personne *(aucune)* **bháa**

personne *f* **bhɛ̄n,** personne charmante **sáȁbhɛ̏n,** personne sage **wlɔ́ɔ̏ dhʌ́n**

perte de vue : à perte de vue **bhɛ̄nbhɛ̄ndhɤ̄, pȉɔɔndhɤ̄, pīɤɤdhɤ̄, wœ̄œdhɤ̄**

pertes blanches **yı̋wɔ̋sɯ̏**

peser **dān**

pet *m* **tɔ̂n**

pétiller **pɤ̋ɤ**

pétiole *m* de la fronde de raphia **dhūɤɤ gɔ̄,** pétiole de la palme du jeune palmier à huile **glâ gɔ̄,** pétioles des palmes de raphia **gbɔ̋ŋ**

petit **dɛ́dɛ̏, gbɔ̋ŋ, klɤ̄ɤ̏, sɛ̄ɛ̋ndhʌ́n, tɛ̋tɛ̋,** petit à petit **dɔ́ɔdhíndɔ́ɔdhín,** petit frère **zláȁ, zláȁbɔ̏,** petite sœur *f* **zláȁ, zláȁbɔ̏,** petit frère / petite soeur d'ego, quatrième après ego dans la séquence des naissances **zláȁ bhȁ zláȁ bhȁ zlȁa,** petit frère / petite soeur, troisième enfant après ego **zláȁ bhȁ zlȁa**

petit doigt *m* **kœ̄œŋgā dhʌ́n tɔ̄ɔ**

petit martin-pêcheur *m* huppé **vɛ̋bhɤ̏bhȁandhʌ́n**

petit mil **klʌ̋ʌn**

petit orteil *m* **gɛ̏ndhʌ́ngātɔ̄ɔ, gɛ̄nŋgādhʌ́ntɔ̄ɔ**

petit-déjeuner *m* **dlȁaká**

petit-duc *m* africain **zūȕ**

petite cola **pētíkōládhɯ̏**

petite-fille *f* **bhāadhʌ́n**

petitesse *f* **klɤ̄ɤ̏-dhɛ̏**

petit-fils *m* **bhāadhʌ́n**

pétrir **kāȁn kwʌ̋ʌ**

pétrole *m* **wɔ̃yı́**
peu **kɛ̃ɛ, sɛ̄ɛ̃ndhʌ́n,** peu après **zlʌ̀ʌdhɤ̄,** peu nombreux **dódó,** peu profond **klɤ̄ɤ̀,** un peu **bhɤ̃,** **bhɤ̃dhʌ́nbhá, dɛ́dɛ̀, dɔ́ɔdhín, dhʌ́nbhá, dhʌ́nbháwō, sɛ̄ɛ̃ndhʌ́n, tɤ̃ŋ,** un peu plus tard... **dhɛ̀ tɤ̃ŋdhʌ́n bhá ɤ́ zı̀ɤ...**
Peul *(groupe ethnique et langue)* **flʌ̃**
peur **sṹɤ,** avoir peur **sṹɤ,** faire peur à qn **sṹɤ dʌ̀ bhɛ̄n gúı,** il a pris peur **sṹɤ yʌ̀ kʌ̃n ʌ̀ gúı, sṹɤ ɤ́ dʌ̀ ʌ̀ gúı**
peureux **sṹɤ-sṳ̀ı**
peut-être que... **bhá bhṳ̀ın kɤ̄...**
phalène *f* **zɛ̄nŋ̃**
phasme *m* **gādhṹı**
photo *f* **pʌ̄bı̃n,** il m'a pris en photo **yà n̄ bı̃n súı**
photographie *f* **pʌ̄bı̃n**
phrase *f* **dhı̃wɔ̀yʌ̀n**
pic *m (oiseau)* **bhɛ̄ŋ̃**
pic *m (instrument)* **kı̃atɔ̃**
picatharte *m* chauve de Guinée **gɔ̃bhʌ̀an**
pichenette *f* **gı̀ʌ**
pièce *f (chambre)* **wɔ̀gúıkɔ̀,** pièce *(d'étoffe)* **kʌ̃n,** pièce d'argent de la période coloniale **tı̀nbhı̀n,** pièce en fer **pı̀ɤgā**
pied *m* **gɛ̀ndhɛ̃, gɛ̄nŋ̃dhɛ̀,** pied *(linguistique)* **wɔ̀gā,** marcher pieds nus **tʌ̃ gɛ̀ndhɛ̃ tʌ̀**
piège *m* **dɤ̄ŋ, sɔ̃, vá,** piège à singes **bhīʌ̃,** piège d'oiseaux **zɛ̀tʌ̀,** piège en fer **pı̀ɤ dɤ̄ŋ,** il a dressé un piège à souris **yà kɤ̀ɤ yʌ̀ bhɔ̀ɔn gɔ̀,** il a dressé un piège pour les oiseaux **yʌ̀ zɛ̀tʌ̀ yʌ̀**
pierre *f* **gwʌ̀, gwʌ̀ kpɤ̄,** pierre ponce *f* **gwʌ̀dhʌ́n,** pierre à aiguiser **bʌ̃ŋ dhı̃ɤ-bɔ̀ ʌ̀ ká klāʌ̃,** petite pierre **kāŋ̃**
piétiner **tʌ̃, tāʌ̀**
pieu *m* des fondations d'une maison **kɔ́ gɛ̀n**
pigeon *m* **tɔ̀ŋ,** pigeon à épaulettes violettes **yɔ̃nbhʌ̀an**
piler **bı̀ɤɤ, flɤ̃, zɔ̄n,** piler la farine de tô **tòo bı̀ bhō**
pilon *m* **wɤ̄ŋ,** pilon court **glɔ̄ɔzɔ̀nkáwɤ̄ŋ**
piment *m* **slʌ̀ʌ,** piment blanc **slʌ̀ʌ pṹu,** espèces de piment : **kɛ̃ŋslʌ̀ʌ, slʌ̀ʌvóɔ̀dhē, tāslʌ̀ʌ,** on l'a lavé avec de l'eau pimentée **wʌ̀ kɛ̃ŋslʌ̀ʌ bhán' bhʌ̀**
pimenter : elle a trop pimenté la sauce **yʌ̀ slʌ̀ʌ zīɤ tɔ̃o gɔ̀**
pinçage *m* **flɛ̀ɛn**
pince *f* **gbɛ̄ɛ̀n,** pince de crabe **kā sɔ̃n,** pince d'écrevisse **kɛ̀nŋ kɔ̄ŋgā**
pincer **flɛ̄ɛn,** il m'a pincé **yà n̄ flɛ̀ɛn bhō,** le crabe m'a pincé **kā yà n̄ kún**
pingre : faire le pingre **gblṹıyāʌ̀ kʌ̄**
pingrerie *f* **gblṹıyāʌ̀**
pinson *m (oiseau)* **fèe**
pintade *f* huppée **bṹıgʌ̀an**
pintade *m* commun **gʌ̀an**
pioche *f* **gʌ̃ŋ**
pipe *f* **táʌ̀gbō**
piquant *(nourriture)* **dhı̃ɤsṳ̀ı**
piquant *m* de porc-épic **plṹınŋ, sɛ̃ŋ**
pique-assiette *m, f* **zı̀ʌʌdɔ̄bhɛ̀n**
pique-bœuf *m* **dṳ̀tʌ̀bhʌ̀an**
piquer **bhō, kún, zūa,** piquer en masse *(insects)* **wɛ̀nŋ,** ça me pique **yɤ̀ n̄ kún-sīʌ klɤ̄klɤ̄dhɤ̄,** un pou m'a piqué **kɛ̀fá yà n̄ kún**
piquet *m* **pīkéɛ̀dhṹı**
piqûre *f* **pínŋ̀,** faire une piqûre **zūa,** trace de piqûre de pou **kɛ̀fá dhı̃dhı̃**
pirogue *f* **kplʌ̃gɔ̄**
pistaches *f* décortiquées **dōo flɛ̃ɛ̀**
pistachier *m* **dōo**
piste *f* **zīaan gā**
pitié *f* **wʌ̀ʌ**

place *f* **dȕɛɛ, dhɛ̏,** place à manger **dhȉʌ,** place publique **dhɛ̋ɛdhɛ̏,** place sombre **gbēŋkpɤ̄,** à la place de **gblőo**
placer **yɤ̏**
plafond *m* **gbàn, gblāã**
plaie *f* **bhīʌʌ**
plainte *f* **yāŋ,** porter plainte contre qn auprès du chef du village **yà bhēn yāŋ kʌ̄ dhùutȋȉ dhɛ̏**
plaire **dhī,** plaire à qn **bhēn zɔ̏ kún,** cela plait à l'homme **ȁ dhɔ̏ yɤ̏ bhēn kʌ̏,** s'il te plaît! **kɤ̄ bhɤ̏ dɔ̄ gbɛ̋ɛ̏!**
plaisant **sʌ̏**
plaisir **dhía**
plan *m* **kplőŋ,** il a tracé le plan de la maison **yà kɔ́ kplőŋ kā̋n**
planche *f* **dhűukā̋ŋ, dhűupɛ̋n,** planche de plafond **gbàn gā**
plantation *f* **dhɛ̏,** plantation de banane **glɔ̄ɔ kɛ̀,** plantation de café **kā̋flɛ̋e dhɛ̏, kā̋flɛ̋e bhlȁa**
plante *f* **dhűu,** espèces de plantes : **glɛ̀e, kpʌ̏,** plante rampante **zīaanpȋɤgwɛ̋ɛ,** plante herbacée à feuilles larges **dhɛ̋pűu,** plante parasite du cola **zàŋ,** plante Pycnanthus angolense **dȉŋ**
plante *f* du pied **gɛ̏ndhɛ̋kwɛ̄ɛ̋dhɛ̏, gɛ̏ndhɛ̋wlɤ̏ɤdhɛ̏**
planter (des plantes) **tā, pʌ̄ tā,** planter *(enfoncer)* **gbȁn**
plaque *f* **plákɤ̏,** plaque d'immatriculation **gɔ̄ plákɤ̏**
plastique *m* **dhɤ̏ɤ**
plat **dɛ́ŋ̏dɛ̏ŋ,** plat de riz cuit **bhā̋apʌ̏, yā̋pʌ̏,** plat « colis sans timbre » **kpā̋**
plat ventre : se mettre à plat ventre **gblʌ̋ʌ̏dhūn**
plateau *m* rocheux **gwȁȁdhɛ̏**
pleurer **gbő bɔ̄, wɛ̋,** l'enfant pleure de faim **dhʌ́n bhā yɤ̏ dȉȉ gbɔ̏ bɔ̄-sīʌ**
pleurs *mpl* **gbő**
pleuvoir **bān,** il pleut **dhā yɤ̏ bā̋n-sīʌ,** il pleut à torrent **dhā yɤ̏ bān-sīʌ zɔ̏ɔzɔ̏ɔdhɤ̄**
plier **yɛ̋**
plonger une chose dans l'eau **pʌ̄ bhán yȋ bhàa**
plouf-plouf **plōŋ̋plɔ̏ŋplōŋ̋dhɤ̄**
pluie *f* **dhā,** pluie fine **dhāfȉidhʌ́n,** il n'y a pas de pluie aujourd'hui **dhā yáa dhɤ́ dɛ̀ɛ**
plume *f* **kāȁ,** une plume d'oiseau **bhȁan kāȁ gā dō,** plume de l'aile d'un oiseau **bhȁan gbān bhȁ kȁa**
pluriarc *m* **glóodhʌ́nkōŋ**
plus *(avec la négation)* **kɤ̏, zúu**
plusieurs **sɛ̄ɛ̋ndhʌ́n bhá**
pneu *m* de vélo **pȉɤgāsɔ̀ɔ̏ kɔ̀ŋ**
poche *f* **yʌ̋ʌ̏,** poche de fronde **gbɔ̋ɔ̏ kɔ́**
poids : il est passé sur lui de tout son poids **yà dhʌ̀nŋ ȁ tȁ kpēnŋkpēnŋdhɤ̄**
poignée *f* **kɔ̏dā, kɔ̏pā, kɔ̏yān,** poignée de valise *f* **gbʌ̀ʌ gʌ̄n,** une poignée de gens **bhēn gā plɛ̀**
poignet *m* **kwɛ̄ɛ̋dhɛ̏**
poil *m* **kāȁ,** poil pubien **sē,** poil de sourcil **yā̋nkpȉnŋtȁ kȁa**
poing *m* **kɔ̏kpɤ̄,** il dort toujours à poings fermés **yà yī zʌ̄, yɤ̏ ɤ̄ bɛ̏n bhȁn' ká sæ̏æ̋ wlɤ̏ɤ**
point *m* **zɔ̋**
pointe *f* **pɔ̋dhȋn,** sur la pointe des pieds **kɔ̏nŋkɔ̏nŋdhɤ̄**
pointeau *m* **gūdhʌ́n**
pointer le fusil à **būu dhȋ yȁ ȁ bhȁ**
poison *m* **bɛ̀dhɛ̋, bɛ̀dhɛ̋ yāa,** poison pour le poisson **dhűaa, lɛ̄ŋdâ**
poisson *m* **yúɤ̏ɤ,** poisson électrique **gbȉŋgbɤ̄,** espèces de poisson : **bhɛ̋ɛngā, dhɔ̋ɔ, dhɔ̏ɔn, kpɔ̄n, làagā, vɛ̋,** un poisson **yúɤ̏ɤ gā dhʌ́n,** un (gros) poisson **yúɤ̏ɤ bhē**
poisson-chien *m* **zōgbên**

poitrine *f* **kʏ̀ŋ, kùu, tòŋ**
poivre *m* noir **sṹʌʌ**
policier *m* **pōlísʏ̀, zàŋ**
polisson *m* **ɗàbṹdù, gɔ̄ɔgbɛ́ɛ̀dhʌ̀n**
politique *f* **pōlītíkʌ̀**
polyarthrite *f* **glà, glà kpǽæ**
polyéthylène *m* **bhlʌ̃́nŋ**
pommade *f* **pɔ̄bhándʏ̀**
pomme *f* **póŋbhù̀, pomme d'Adam **kplʌ̃́**
ponce *f* **gwʌ̀dhʌ́n**
pont *m* **pɔ̄ŋ,** pont de lianes **dlʌ̃́**
pop **gbūŋgbùŋgbūŋdhʏ̄**
porc-épic *m* **blṹn, tɛ̃́**
portable *m* **pɔ̄táblʌ̀**
porte *f* **kwɛ̃́ɛ,** porte de la maison *f* **kɔ́dhĩ́,** porte de perches de raphia **zā̀n,** porte non-attachée (sans gondes ni pentures) faite de pétioles de raphia **kwɛ̃́ɛ tɛ̀**
portemanteau horizontal **sɔ̄dù̀nbhàdhù̀**
porte-monnaie *m* **wʌ́ʌ̀ glɛ̄ɛ́dhʌ́n**
porter **sṹ,** porter *(vêtement)* **bhō, dà,** porter dehors **yʏ̀ à ká kpɛ̃́nŋ,** porter en balançant sur la tête **dhʏ̀ŋ,** ils ont porté une accusation contre lui **wà gbā yà à bhà,** porte-toi bien! **kʌ̀ klʏ̃́ʏklʏ̀ʏ-sù̀ yʏ̀ kʌ̄ ū gɔ̀**
portion *f* **pʌ̄,** portion de tô **tòo pʌ̀**
poser **wɔ̄, yáàdhūn**
position *f* **dùɛɛ,** position accroupie **zóŋ̀,** position horisontale **bɛ̃́ŋ**
possédé : Zan est possédé par un esprit maléfique **zùu yāa yʏ̀ Zân tà**
possibilité : il n'y avait aucune possibilité de faire cela **à kɔ̀ tàŋgà yáa gūn**
poste *m* **dùɛɛ,** poste de police **zàŋ plʏ̀ʏ**
postposition *f (ling.)* **dhíʏpʌ̀**
postuler : il a posé sa candidature pour le poste de maire **yà gbàn bhɛ́ɛndhɛ̀ bhà**
pot *m* **gbɔ̄,** pot d'échappement **sīapʏ̀bháàn,** pot magique **gbɔ̄ɔ́,** pot d'argile **sɛ̃́ gbɔ̄**
potager *m* **tṍodhɛ̀**
potamochère *m* **bhɔ̀zœ̀œndhē**
poteau : les poteaux de l'ossature de la maison **kɔ́ dhṹ**
potelé **bhʌ́ŋ̀bhʌ̀ŋ**
potière *f* **gbɔ̄dɔ̄dhɛ̀**
potin *m* **tɔ̀ɔ**
pou *m* : pou de corps **kɛ̀fá,** pou de tête **wèe**
pouce *m* **kœ̄œŋgā gɔ̄n**
poudre *f* : poudre *(farine)* **bì̃,** poudre de fusil **blɔ̄ɔ́n, blɔ̄ɔ́n bì̃,** poudre de charbon **zĩ́a,** poudre de gombo **dṹʌŋ bì̃,** poudre sucrée de maïs **kʏ̄ŋ bì̃,** poudre médicinale **dì̃ì,** en poudre **tlʌ̄ntlʌ̄ndhʏ̄, tlùkpɛ̀tlùkpɛ̀dhʏ̄**
poulailler *m* **tɔ̀ kɔ̀**
poule *f* : poule avec ses poussins **tɔ̀ bṹɛ̀ɛdhɛ̀,** une poule sur ses œufs **tɔ̀ ʏ́ ʏ̄ yàan tà**
poulet *m* **tɔ̀**
poulette *f* **tɔ̀ gbɔ̃́ŋ**
poumons *mpl* **bhlṹu**
poupée *f* **pūpê**
pour **bhà, dhɛ̀, dhíʏ, gɔ̀, kèŋ̀, súgú,** pour le moment **kʏ̀, kʏ̀ŋgbʏ̄,** pour ne pas **kʏ̄dhʏ́,** pour que **kʌ̀dhʏ́kʏ̄, kʏ̄, ʏ́ʏ**
pourchasser **kpā**
pourguère *m* **zɔ̀osæ̀ædhù̀**
pourquoi? **dhɛ̀,** c'est pourquoi **pʌ́ʌ kʌ̀ ... yʏ́ bhā**
pourri **blʌ̃́**
pourrir **blʌ̃́, bṹ**
poursuivre **kʌ̄**
pousse *f* **bhɔ̀ŋ,** jeune pousse **dìŋ,** jeune pousse de banane (pour le repiquage) **glɔ̄ɔ gɔ̀, glɔ̄ɔ kpū**

pousser **blṹ̀ɯ,** *(plante)* **bhɔ̄,** sa barbe a poussé **à bhúʌ̀ʌ yà dà,** pousse-toi un peu! **gó n̄ wɛ̀ɛ bhàa!**
poussière *f* **bɔ̀bì, sɛ́ bì**
poutre *f* : poutre du plafond **glɔ̀o,** poutre maîtresse **gɔ̀dɔ̄gāgɔ̀, kɔ́gbàngɔ̀dhɯ̋,** **gbàn bɛ̋ŋ (gw), gblāā bɛ̋ŋ (t)**
pouvoir **bhɔ̀ɔn, yɤ̀**
poux *mpl* de corps **kɛ̀fá**
préambule **gɔ̀**
précipitamment et sans hésiter **vlɯ́ɯdhɤ̄**
précipitation *f* **bìaŋ,** ne pas agir avec précipitation **tó**
précipiter : se précipiter **zūa**
précision *f* **tɤ̋ŋbhō-dhɛ̀**
préfecture *f* **kɔ̋bhí**
préféré **wɔ̀ngbɛ̋ɛ̀sɯ̀,** chose préférée **dhɔ̄ɔbhàapʌ̀**
préfet *m* **kɯ̋nbhɤ̋ndhɤ̋n**
premier **blɛ̀ɛsɯ̀, blɛ̀ɛsɯ̀dhàan, dōdhàan,** le tout premier **dōsēŋdhàan**
prendre **kún, sɯ́,** prendre entre les mains **lòo,** prendre pour, comme **gà … ká, gà dhɛ̀ … dhɤ́**
prénom *m* **tɔ́**
préoccuper sérieusement **kàanbhō**
préparer **bāá,** se préparer **tà-kún,** préparer du foutou de manioc **bāa kɔ̀n zɔ̄n**
près **bhàa, klɤ̄ɤ́dhɤ̄, sɔ̋ɔ,** près de la route **zīaanpíɤ**
présage *m* : j'ai eu un mauvais présage **klɔ̄ɔ̀ yà dɔ̄ n̄ bhà**
présentation *f* **bhæ̀æn**
présentement **dɔ̄ ɤ́' wō yɛ́ɛ̀n gɯ́**
présenter **dhíɤ-lòo, yɤ̄,** présenter qch à qn **pʌ̄ bhæ̀æn bhō bhɛ̄n bhà,** se présenter **bhɔ̄, zɔ̀n**
préserver **yáàdhūn**
président *m* **gɔ̀dhíɤbhɛ̀n, sɛ́dʌ̄,** président du pays **sɛ́ kɔ̀ɔnbhɛ̀n, sɛ́ gɔ̀dhíɤbhɛ̀n**
presque **gbànwō, dhɛ̀ pʌ̄ dhɤ́,** presque tous **kpíìdhɛ̀ gbàn**
pressé : il est pressé (de partir) **zīɤ dhɔ̀ yà dà à gɯ́**
pressentiment *m* **bhlɯ̋n**
presser **dhʌ̀nŋ**
pression *f* **gbàn**
prêt *m* **pɔ̋,** accorder un prêt à qn **pɔ̋ dɔ̄ bhɛ̄n bhà, pɔ̋ dhūn bhɛ̄n dhɛ̀**
prétention *f* **kɛ̋ŋ, sɪ́ʌ̀ʌ, tʌ̄ʌ**
prêter qch à qn **pʌ̄ sɪ́ʌŋ̀ dɔ̄ bhɛ̄n bhà**
prêtre *m* **pɛ́ɛ̀dhɯ̀**
preux *m* **kplʌ̋ʌ**
préverbe *m* *(ling.)* **wɔ̀kplɯ̀bhàdhíɤ**
prier **bhɛ̄ɛ́**
prière *f* **bhɛ̄ɛ́, bhɛ̄ɛ́wɔ̀, sʌ́ʌ̀**
principale **dèe**
pris : j'ai les oreilles prises **tɛ̋ɛ yà dɔ̄ n̄ tó gɯ́**
prison *f* **kàsɔ̀**
prisonnier *m* **kàsɔ̀gɯ́bhɛ̀n**
priver qn **dhɯ̋ɤɤ**
prix *m* **dhɔ̋ɔ, sɔ̄nŋ,** à tout prix **gbōkùngbōkùndhɤ, gbōŋgbōŋdhɤ̄**
probablement **yɤ̀ kʌ̀ dhɛ̀..., yíi dɔ̄ sʌ̀, yɤ̀ bhɔ̀ à bhà dhɛ̀...**
problème *m* **bhɤ̋dhɤ́, wɔ́n,** problème inattendu **dɔ̋ɔn**
procédé magique *m* **bɛ̀dhɛ́**
procès *m* **zā**
procession *f* **gbàŋ**
prochainement **tàabhàn,** très prochainement **yī plɛ̀ɛ bhà**
proche **klɤ̄ɤ̀,** il est mon proche parent **yɤ̀ dɔ̀ n̄ ká klɤ̄ɤ́dhɤ̄**
proclamation *f* **dhɛ̀ɛdhíɤ**
proclamer une nouvelle **dhæ̀ædhíɤ bhō**
procréation *f* **dhʌ́nkpɔ́dhē**
procréer **kpɔ́**
prodigieusement **tlɔ̀ɔdhɤ̄**
produire **yɤ̄**
proférer des incantations **yɪ́sɪ́wɔ̀ blṹ̀ɯ**

professeur *m* **klàŋ̀gɔ̀bhɛ̀n**
profit : au profit de **súgúɯ**
profond **gblɛ̀ɛn,** endroit profond **dūʌŋ,** partie profonde d'une rivière **yíkʌ̀gblɛ̀ɛndhɛ̀**
profondeur *f* **gblɛ̀ɛn-dhɛ̀**
prolonger **gwʌ̀ʌ,** une bonne existence prolonge la vie humaine **tɔ̀sǽæ̀ kʌ̄ kɔ̀ sʌ̀ yɤ̀ bhɛ̄n gwʌ̀ʌ**
promener : se promener **dhìʌʌn, zīɤ,** aller se promener **dhó kwáanŋ̀ píɤ**
promesse *f* **plúunŋ**
pronom *m* **tɔ́gblɔ́ogúɯpʌ̀**
prononcer un discours **dhīaŋ zʌ̄**
propre **púu, slɤ́ɤslɤ̀, sɤ́ɤŋsɤ̀ɤŋ**
propriété *f* **slɔ̀ɔpʌ̀**
prospère **dɛ̀slɔ̀ɔ**
prostituée *f* **zṹaadhɛ̀,** prostituée de grand chemin **zṹaadhɛ̀ kʌ̄ŋ́ bhō kɔ́ɔ̀**
protecteur *m* **kɔ̀ɔnbhɛ̀n**
protection : prendre sous sa protection **gbɛ́bhō**
protéger **tʌ̀-kɔ́ɔ̀, tɤ́ŋ kʌ̄ à gúɯ**
proverbe *m* **gwʌ́nŋ, pìan,** dire un proverbe **pìan káan**
provocateur **bhlɔ̄ɔsɯ̀ɯ**
provoquer une querelle **dhídhàan dʌ̀**
proximité : à proximité **klɤ̄ɤ́**
puant **fiisɯ̀ɯ**
puanteur *f* **fii, gbíʌn, tɛ́ɛ**
puce *f* **gbʌ̀ʌ,** puce de chien **gbên bhʌ̀ kpàa,** puces de poule **tɔ̀bhʌ̀nwɛ̀e**
puiser **tɔ́**
puisque **ɤ́**
puissance *f* **gɔ́ɔ̀n-dhɛ̀**
puissant : il est puissant **fāan yʌ̀ bhʌ̀**
puits *m* **klɔ̀ŋ**
pulvériser **kpʌ̀ŋ**
punaises *fpl* **gblūɯŋ**
punir qn **wɔ́n wɔ̄ bhɛ̄n tʌ̀, wɔ́n bhō bhɛ̄n gúɯ**
pur **dèe, slɤ́ɤslɤ̀, sɤ́ɤŋsɤ̀ɤŋ,** la laine pur **sɛ́ dɛ̀dɛ̀**
pute *f* **zṹaadhɛ̀**
python *m* **gblūɯŋ**

Q q

qualité *f* **sūu-dhɛ̀**
quand **dhɛ̀, ɤ́,** quand même **dhàanbhā, dhʌ́nbháwō, dhɤ́, kɛ̀ɛ, sá, zúɯ**
quant à cela... **à dhɛ́ kɤ́ bhā...**
quantième? **dhɛ̀dhàan**
quantité : une quantité **gísí**
quartier *m* **kāatíɛ̂, pɛ́n**
quatre **yììsīɤ**
quatre épingles *(plante Cassia alata)* **kɔ̄ŋsɛ́ɛdhɯ̀ɯ**
quatrième orteil **gēnŋgā gblɛ̀ɛnsɯ̀ɯ**
que **dhɛ̀, kɤ̄, kɤ́, ɤ́ɤ**
quel que soit **ɔ́o**
quelconque **bhá**
quelque : quelque chose **pʌ̄,** quelque part **yʌ̀n,** quelque part par là **tīíbhūn,** quelqu'un **bhɛ̄n**
quémandeur *m*, quémandeuse *f* **gbādhɛ̀bhɛ̀n**
querelle *f* **dhídhàan, sìɤ**
quereller : se quereller à cause de qn **kó zʌ̄ à tʌ̀**
querelleur **fɛ̀ɛsɯ̀ɯ**
qu'est-ce que c'est? **bhʌ̀n bhā?**
qu'est-ce qu'il y a? **bhʌ̀n ɤ́ bhūn? yɤ̀ kʌ̀ bhūn dhɛ̀?**
question *f* **dhɛ̄ɛ́, dhɛ̄ɛ́kpɔ́**
queue *f* **wēŋ, zɔ́**
qui? **dē, dée**
quitter **gó, wlūɯ́ɯ,** quitter qn **gó bhɛ̄n kɛ̀ŋ́,** quitter sa place **ɤ̄ bhɔ̀ kɛ̀e bhʌ̀**
quoi? **bhʌ̀n,** quoi qu'il en soit... **yɤ̄ɤ kʌ̄ kɔ̀ ɔ́o kɔ̀ ɤ́' bhʌ̀...**

R r

rabâcher qch à qn **wɔ́n dhi̋aŋ zʌ̄ bhēn tőodhɤ̄**
rabougrir **fi̋ʌʌn, gbɔ̀ɔn,** se rabougrir **fi̋ʌʌn**
raccommoder un vêtement **sɔ̄ yɔ̀ɔn kwʌ́ʌ̀, sɔ̄ pɛ́dhɛ̀ yɔ̀ɔn kwʌ́ʌ̀**
racheter **gɔ̏tà-dhɔ́**
racine *f* **gɛ̏n, yūn,** racine de dent **sɔ̋n gɛ̏n**
râcler **bhʌ̏n-pā**
raconter **bhō,** raconter une histoire **kwɛ̏zlȁan bhō,** raconter leur histoire **ȁ-dhȕn dhɪ́ɤ wɔ̏n gɛ̏n dɔ̄**
raconteur *m*, raconteuse *f* **gbǽætàzʌ̄bhɛ̏n**
radio *f* **dhàdíɔ̀o**
raide **gbɛ́ɛ̀**
raison *f* **gɛ̏n, gɛ̏ngódhɛ̀,** sa raison est que... **ȁ gɛ̏n bhȕn dhɛ̀...,** à plus forte raison **kɤ̄ yɤ̏ dhȕn tó ... bhȁ,** sans raison **kpȁan, wɛ̋ɛwɛ̋**
rajouter **dȁ, dhʌ̀nŋ, wɔ̄**
ralentir **zlœ̀œ**
ramadan *m* **súŋ̏,** faire le ramadan **súŋ̏ bhán**
ramasser **wlɤ̏**
rameau *f* de palmier **pȁa**
ramener : ramener au silence **tȁ-gā,** ramener quelqu'un à la raison **bhɔ̏ɔ bɔ̄ bhēn zó/zūʌ́ bhȁ**
ramolli **zɔ̀ɔsȕ**
ramper : le crabe [la punaise] rampe **kā [gblūŋgā] yɤ̏ tȁ/zi̋ɤ/tá̋ sȕ klɤ̋ɤdhɤ̄**
rancune : il n'a pas de rancune **ȁ zūʌ́ yɤ̏ pű̋u**
rancunier : il est rancunier **ȁ gblű̋dhɛ̀ yɤ̏ glɛ̀ɛn**
rang **bhi̋ʌʌ,** mettez-vous en rang **kȁ dɔ̄ {kā} bhi̋ʌʌ gú!**
raphia *m* **dhūɤɤ**
rapide **sʌ̏**
rapidement **vɪ́adhɤ̄**
rapiécer **pʌ̏-kʌ̄**
rappeler, se rappeler **zɔ̏-bɤ̏,** je n'arrive pas à me rappeler son nom **n̄ zɔ̏ yíi {kʌ̄} bɤ̏ ȁ tó ká**
rapport *m* **kplʌ́nŋ,** informer du but de la visite; donner le rapport d'un voyage **kplʌ́nŋ bhō, kplʌ́nŋ dȁ**
rapporter **dɔ̄**
rare : être rare **tó dódó,** rares **dódó**
rarement **dódó, plɛ̀-plɛ̀**
ras bord : à ras bord **kūȕkkūȕdhɤ̄, kpɤ́kkpɤ́dhɤ̄**
rasé **kpȁa,** tête rasée **gɔ̏ yȁȁndhɛ̏,** il a la tête bien rasée **ȁ gɔ̏ yȁȁn yɤ̏ sʌ̏**
raser : il ne se rase pas **yáa ɤ̄ bhúʌ̏ʌ bhō,** il s'est fait raser la tête **yà ɤ̄ gɔ̏ kpȁa bhō**
rasoir *m* **dhɛ̀ɛn**
rassasier : se rassasier **kʌ́n,** il est rassasié **ȁ gú yà dɔ̄**
rassembler **dȁ, lòo,** se rassembler **dhūn, lòo kó tȁ,** rassembler la troupe **glȕ sú**
rassis **sœ̄œ**
rassurer **gā, zɔ̏-gbȁn**
rat *m*, espèces : **fɛ̋ŋ, vɔ̏ŋ, vɤ̋dhʌ́n,** rat à bande dorsale noire **yȁŋ̋dhē,** rat à grandes oreilles **bhɔ̏ɔngbɤ̄slű̋ŋ,** rat palmiste **bhœ̋œŋ̏,** rat rayé **yʌ́nŋ̏gúdʌ̄,** rat rossard **kpȁȁnbhɔ̏ɔn,**
ratatiner : se ratatiner **zlōo**
rater **kɔ̏, kɔ́n,** j'ai raté mon train [bus, avion] **tlɛ̄ŋ̏ [gɔ̄, vɪ̏ɔ̏ŋ] yà n̄ tó**
ratière *f* **gbʌ̏**
rattrapage : texte de rattrapage **yēe-kʌ̄ dīaŋkpɤ̄ tȁ-sȕ**
rauque **gblȁȁnsȕ**
ravager une ruche **zɔ̋ dhɛ̄ɛ̀dhɛ̏ bhɤ̏**
ravir **dùa**
rebelle *m* **klūɯɯgādʌ̄, lēbēlɤ̏**
rebord *m* **tő,** rebord de chapeau **glāȁ tő,** rebord de puits **klɔ̏ŋ tő**
récemment **dȅe**

recevoir **dhɛ̀ŋ-kún, slɔ̀ɔ**
rechercher une femme en mariage **dhē zʌ̀-dɔ̄**
récit *m* **dhīaŋ**
réclamer : réclamer qch à qn **pʌ̄ zʌ̀ kʌ̋n bhēn dhɛ̀,** réclamer une dette **pɔ̋ kʌ̄ bhēn ká**
récolte : donner une bonne récolte **dhī**
récolter **bhō,** récolter le maïs **kɤ̄ŋ bhō**
recommencer **zɯ̄-bhō**
réconforter **zɔ̀-gbʌ̀n**
reconnaître **dɔ̄**
reculer **bhɔ̄ zɯ̄ ká, bhɔ̄ ɤ̄ tāa, bhɔ̄ tāa**
reculons : marcher à reculons **dhó ɤ̄ tàa ká**
réfléchir **ɤ̄ zɔ̀ tʌ̋, zɔ̀-gɔ́n**
reflet *m* **blɛ̋ɛ̀n**
réflexion *f* **zɔ̀tʌ̋dhē**
refroidir **dhìʌʌ,** se refroidir **dhìʌʌ, zɔ̀nŋ,** l'eau froide refroidit les mains **yɪ́ sæ̀æ-dhɛ̀ yɤ̀ bhʌ̀n bhēn kɔ̀ gɯ́**
réfugier : se réfugier **slʌ̄ʌ**
refuser **kɔ̀,** ses pieds refusent de marcher (par la fatigue) **ʌ̀ gɛ̀n yɪ́ yʌ̀ kʌ̋n,** refuser de manger *(par politesse)* (t) **ɤ̄ bɛ̀n bhō**
regarder **dhɛ̀-gʌ̀, gʌ̀, kpʌ̀n**
régime *m* **bɛ̀, bɤ̋ɤ,** régime de bananes **glɔ̄ɔ bè**
région **sɛ̋kɔ̀pɛ̋n**
règle *f* **wɔ̄kɔ̀**
régler **gɔ̀-dɔ̄, yʌ̋n-bhɔ̄,** se régler **yʌ̋n-bhɔ̄,** cette affaire est réglée **wɔ́n bhā yà zūn kó dhɪ́ɤ**
régner sur **gɔ̀dhɪ́ɤ,** il a régné sur ce pays **ʌ̀ tó yʌ̀ bhɔ̄ sɛ̋ yā tʌ̀**
regretter l'absence **zɔ̀-gɔ́n**
rein *m* **zēgā**
reins *m* **kō**
rejet *m* **zɔ̀o, zœ̀œdhē**
rejeter les accusations en qch **zœ̀œdhē dʌ̀ wɔ́n bhʌ̀**
relâche : sans relâche *(parler)* **slɔ̀ɔdhɤ̄**
relations de plaisanterie *f* **dhìnbhɔ̋ɔ̀n-dhɛ̀**
remarquable : personne *f* remarquable **vʌ̋angɔ̄n**
remarquer **dhɛ̀-yɤ̄**
rembourser **bhɔ̄**
remède *m* **bɛ̀dhɛ̋, dhɛ̋,** remède pour la voix **yæ̋æ,** remède à base de feuilles et d'herbes **dhɯ̋ dhɛ̋**
remerciement *m* **dhūɛ̋ɛn**
remercier qn **bhēn dhūɛ̋ɛn bhō**
remettre **dɔ̄,** remettre en place **gɯ́-gʌ̋n**
remisse *f* **kwɛ̄ɛ**
remonter : se remonter **zɔ̀-gbʌ̀n**
rempart *m* **sʌ̋an**
remplaçant *m* **yɔ̋ɔgɯ́**
remplir, se remplir **pā**
remporter une victoire **tó**
remuer **gɯ́-zʌ̄, vīn,** se remuer **zɔ̄n**
rencontrer **kpʌ̀n**
rendre **dhɪ́ɤ-dhūn, dhɪ́ɤ-kʌ̄**
renfrogné : il a eu un visage renfrogné **yʌ̀ ɤ̄ wʌ̄ʌ̋ gɯ́-sɪ̀ɤ**
renifler **ɤ̄ yūn gʌ̋n**
renommé **tœ̀œŋ**
renoncer **gó, kwʌ̄ʌ̀,** ne pas renoncer à **gɯ́-kún**
renverse : il est tombé à la renverse **yʌ̀ pɤ̀ ɤ̄ kèe ká, yʌ̀ pɤ̀ ɤ̄ kɛ̀ɛ̀ tʌ̀,** il s'est couché à la renverse **yʌ̀ wɔ̄ ɤ̄ kèe ká**
renverser **gblʌ̋ʌ̀dhūn, wɛ̀nŋ**
répandre **wɛ̀nŋ,** se répandre **kpā, só, wɛ̀nŋ,** répandre régulièrement **sā,** se répandre sur le sol et former un tas **dūnŋ dɔ̄ síāa**
réparer **bʌ̄ʌ̋, pʌ̀-kʌ̄**
repas *m* **dhɪ́, kɔ̋ŋ**
repassage **pʌ̋sɛ̋**
repasser des habits **sɔ̄ pʌ̋sɛ̋ bhō, sɔ̄ vɛ̋dhɛ̋ bhō**
répéter **zīɤ, zɯ̄-bhō**
répondre **yɔ̀ɔ bhō,** répondre à **wɛ̋ … gɔ̀**

réponse *f* **dhɛ̄ɛ̃yɔ̀ɔ, dhīaŋyɔ̀ɔ, yɔ̀ɔ,** réponse à une devinette **bhlɔ̀ɔ**
repos *m* **glòo, tɛ́ɛpā**
reposer : se reposer **glòo, yí-bhō, ɤ kō yí bhō, tɛ́ɛ pā,** je ne me suis pas reposé suffisamment **bhíin n̄ tɛ́ɛ bhɛ̃ɛ̀ pā**
repousser **blɯ̀ɯ**
reprendre **sɔ̀, zɯ̄-bhō**
représentant *m* **kɪ́ʌʌ,** représentant éminent **gā**
réprimande *f* **dɔ̀n**
réprimander **yà**
reproche *f* **dɔ̀n**
reprocher qn **tʌ̄ʌ dɔ̄ bhɛ̄n bhà,** je n'ai rien à me reprocher **wɔ́n bhá zūʌ̀n yáa n̄ bhà**
reptile *m* **tàgútàpʌ̀**
répugnance *f* **yʌ̀nŋ**
réputation **tœ̀œŋ**
réserver **yáàdhūn**
réservoir de soufflet *m* en argile **kɯ̃ŋ, tākɯ̃ŋ**
résidu *m* **gbō**
résine *f* : résine blanche collante **dè,** résine de l'arbre kpɛ̄ɛnŋdhɯ̀ **kpɛ̄ɛnŋ**
résonateur *m* de tambour **sɛ́ɛ**
résonateur *m* de harpe-luth **kɔ̄nŋ gbɔ̄**
résonner **wɛ̃**
résoudre **dān kwʌ̃ʌ, gɔ̀-bhō, gɔ̀-yɛ̃, gɯ́-gʌ̃n kɔ̃o, yʌ̃n-bhɔ̄,** se résoudre **dān kwʌ̃ʌ, yʌ̃n-bhɔ̄,** résoudre un problème **zā gɔ̀-yɛ̃,** ils ont résolu le litige d'une façon correcte **wà zā dèdè dhī**
respect *m* **bhlʌ̀ʌ**
respectable **tìaandhē,** personne *f* respectable **bhlʌ̀ʌgɯ́bhɛ̀n**
respecter : ne pas respecter **zīɤ,** il ne te respectera pas **à yʌ̃n yɤ̀ dhɔ̀ zīɤ' ɯ̄ gɯ́**
respiration *f* **tɛ̃ŋ, tɛ́ɛ**
respirer **tɛ́ɛ,** respirer calmement **ɤ̄ tɛ́ɛ yɤ̄ sɪ́āa,** il ne peut pas respirer profondement **à tɛ́ŋ yáa yɤ̄ sɪ́āa**
responsabilité *f* **zūʌ̀n**
responsable *m* **wɔ́nyɤ̀bhà,** responsable de la case sacrée **gɔ̃dʌ̄**
ressembler **bhɔ̄**
ressentir une douleur **gɯ́-wɛ̃**
ressusciter **bɤ̀**
reste *m* **kpɛ̀ɛ**
rester **dɔ̄, tó,** restant **tòdhɤ́sɯ̀**
résultat *m* **gblɔ̃o, pínŋ̀,** avoir des bons résultats **ɤ̄ gblɔ̃o yɤ̄**
retarder **gwʌ̀ʌ,** retarder le travail de qn **yʌ́nŋ̀ bhɔ̄ bhɛ̄n bhà yʌ̄ bhà**
retenir **kún, zɯ̄n**
retentir : la tonnerre a retenti **dhā yà glʌ̃ glʌ̃àndhɤ**
retirer : se retirer **bhɔ̄**
retour *m* **yēe**
retourner **bhán ɤ̄ gblɔ̃o ká, slʌ̄ʌ, yēe-kʌ̄,** se retourner **slʌ̄ʌ**
réunion *f* **yàkwʌ́ʌ̀**
réunir **yɔ̀ɔn,** se réunir **lòo kó tà**
réussi **dèslɔ̀ɔ**
réussir **gēnyēn,** réussir dans la vie **ɤ̄ dè slɔ̀ɔ,** il a réussi dans la vie **bhēndhè ɤ́ dhì à gɔ̀,** l'homme a réussi dans l'affaire **wɔ́n yà yɤ̄ bhɛ̄n gɔ̀ kó dhɪ́ɤ,** sa cuisine n'a pas réussi **à kwɛ̄ɛ̃ yà sìɤ**
rêve *m* **yɛ̃ɛn,** ses rêves sont prophétiques **à yʌ̃n gɯ́ yɤ̀ sʌ̀**
réveiller qn **pá ... bhà,** se réveiller **bɤ̀,** il s'est réveillé **yà gó yī gɯ́**
révéler **wɔ̀ zāntà**
revenant *m* **zìi**
revendication *f* **tʌ̄ʌ**
revenir **dhó tàabhan, yēe-kʌ̄, yɛ̃,** revenir à soi **bɤ̀**
réverbère *m* **kūdhândhɯ̃**
révolter qn **bhēn zūʌ̃ dhɪ́ɤ-wlɯ̀ɯ**

rhum *m* de canne *f* **kénŋzúù**
rhumatisme *m* **kōkʌ̄yùa**
rhume *f* **kpîn**
riche : personne *f* riche **dhœ̀œnbhɛ̀n**
richesse *f* **dhœ̀œn**
ride verticale au centre du front **vɪ̀i**
ridé **sɛ̀ɛ̀sɯ̀**
rider **zlōo**
ridicule **gɤ̋ŋgɤ̏ŋ,** personne ridicule **yɛ̋ɛtɔ̀bhàbhɛ̀n**
rien : rien autre que **dhāàn,** rien de tout **wɛ̋ɛwɛ̋**
rire *m* **yɛ̋e,** rire à **yɛ̋e tó bhēn bhà,** éclater de rire **pɛ̋**
rivaliser pour **tà-kó-zʌ̄**
rive *f* **kpɔ̋ŋ, yí kpɔ̋ŋ dhíɤ**
rivelaine *f* **síatɔ̋**
rivière *f* **yí, yígā, yígāàdhɛ̀**
riz *m* **bhlɯ̀ɯn,** riz au gras **flēgɯ́dhē,** riz cuit **bháa, yá,** riz pilé **bhlɯ̀ndhíɤ,** sorte de riz de marécage **dòzíŋ̀**
robinet *m* **lōbīdhên**
robustes et de grande taille **glɔ̋ɔglɔ̋ɔ**
rocher *m* **gwʌ̏ gbɔ́ŋ̀,** rocher plat **gwàa, gwàà̀dhɛ̀,** rocher *(aussi gros qu'une maison)* **gwʌ̏ gōn**
roi *m* **glɯ̀ɯdʌ, sɛ́dʌ**
rollier *m* varié **gbììgbáànbhàan**
rompre le jeûne avec une nourriture **súŋ̀ bhán ɤ̄ bhà súŋ̀ kán bhɤ̏pʌ̏ dō ká**
ronchon *m (personne plaintive)* **tʌ̄ʌ dō bhɛ̀n**
rond **dhɤ̋ɤdhɤ̏ɤ**
rondin *m* **dhɯ̋gā, kpʌ̀**
ronfler **gblàn, yī gblàn**
ronronner **gblàn,** le chat ronronne **gwáandhʌ́n yɤ̏ gblàn-sīʌ**
roseau *m* **kàa**
rosée *f* **flíŋ̀ŋ**
rosser **bìɤɤ,** il a bien rossé les gens de là-bas **yà wēŋ zʌ̄ bhɯ́n**
rotation *f* **gbœ̀œdhɛ̋**
roter **kɤ̀ɤ**
rotin *m* **tʌ̏**
roublard *m* **gblʌ̋ŋ**
roucou **wɛ̋ɛn**
roue *f* **gɛ̀n,** roue de vélo **pìɤgāsɔ̀ɔ̀ kòŋ**
rouer de coups **tān**
rouge **tɛ̋ɛn, zœ̀œndhē**
rouge *m* à lèvres **pʌ̄ zœ̀œndhē**
rougeole *f* **bhlɯ̀ɯndhíɤ**
rougir **tān**
rouille *f* **kɔ̋ɔ**
rouillé **kɔ̋ɔsɯ̀,** il a rouillé **kɔ̋ɔ yà à kún**
rouleau *m* **bɛ̀,** rouleau aiguiseur **dhàa-dhíɤ-bō bhànŋzíì,** mettre en rouleau **bɛ̀-kʌ̄**
rouler **bɛ̀-kʌ̄, glʌ̄ʌn, glūùn, glɯ̄ɯŋ, klɤ́-kʌ̄, slʌ̄ʌ, zīɤ,** se rouler **glʌ̄ʌn, glūùn, slʌ̄ʌ,** rouler en cercle **kòŋ-kʌ̄**
route *f* **kpìnŋgā,** route asphaltée **gūdlɔ́ŋ̀,** route carrossable **kpìnŋ**
ruban *m* **sō pɛ̋n**
ruche *f* **dhɛ̄ɛ̀, dhɛ̄ɛ̀dhɛ̀, zɔ̋**
rue *f* **kpìnŋgā**
ruer : se ruer vers **tà-kɔ̄ɔ̀**
rugir **gblàn,** le lion rugit **lāa yɤ̏ gblàn**
ruiner **wɯ́ɪ,** se ruiner **pɤ̏**
ruines **kpáàndhɛ̀**
rumeur *f* **tìŋ, wàpɤ̏**
ruse *f* **glɛ̀ŋ, kpʌ́ŋ̀, slʌ́, yāán,** user de ruse **kpʌ́ŋ̀ kʌ̄**
rusé **kpʌ́ŋ̀sɯ̀**

S s

sable *m* **yɛ̋ɛn**
sabot *m* de cheval **sɔ̀ɔ̀ gɛ̀n tíŋ**
sabre *m* **sìaŋ**
sac *m* **bhɔ̄ɔ, glɛ̄ɛ́n, sákɤ̏,** sac de voyage **glɛ̄ɛ́, kpɔ̄ɔ,** sac en plastique **bhlánŋ, bhlánŋ bhɔ̄ɔ,** sac en raphia **bhíŋ̀**
sachet *m* un sachet de thé **téɛ̀ dō**
sacré : endroit *m* sacré **gɯ́nŋ, gbɛ̋ɛ, gbɛ̋ɛgɯ́dhɛ̀**

sacrifice *f* **sầà**, faire un sacrifice **sầà bhō**
satisfaire **zɔ̀-kún**
sage **kpầasɯ̀, kpœ̀œsɯ̀,**
sage *m* **kwɛ̀ɛgbɤ̂**
sage-femme **yōaabhōdhɛ̀**
sagesse *f* **kpœ̀œ-dhɛ̀, kpœ̀œsɯ̀-dhɛ̀, wlɔ̂ɔ̀**
saigner : il a saigné du nez **gwàn yà̀ kɑ̂n à̀ yūn gɯ́ɯ**, la plaie saigne **à̀ yɔ̀ɔn yɤ̂ bhō-sīʌ**
saillir **bhō**
saint **slɤ̂ɤslɤ̂**
saisir **yà̀**, saisir qch/qn **ɤ̄ kɔ̀ dà̀ à̀ gɯ́ɯ**
saison *f* : saison sèche **blɛ̄ɛ̂yī, blɛ̄ɛ̂, yʌ́ŋ̀bhúɯ́tɤ̂ŋ**, saison des grandes pluies **wɛ̀ɛyí**
salaire *f* **sàa**
salamandre *f* **wūnsʌ́nbhǣændhē**
sale **dhɯ̀isɯ̀**, il est tout sale **yà̀ tlɤ̄ɤ̄ dhɯ̀i ká, dhɯ̀i yà̀ à̀ tlɤ̄ɤ**
salé **wèesɯ̀**
saleté *f* **dhɯ̀i**
salir **dhɯ̀i-kún, yɔ̀ɔ**, se salir **dhɯ̀i kún**
salive *f* **dhídhí**, trace de salive sur la joue **dhí kɛ̂ŋgbɑ̂**
saluer qn **bhɛ̄n tùaa bhō**, il est venu saluer Gbato **yà dhūn Gbà̀tɔ̀ tɔ́ bhà̀**
salut! **ɯ̄ sɛ̀ɛ̀, kā sɛ̀ɛ̀**
salutation *f* **sʌ̂ŋ, tùaa, tùaabhō, sɛ̀ɛ̀**
samba *(arbre Triplochiton seleroxylon)* **dhōɔ̀**
samedi *m* **dhɔ̂ɔzīandō**
sandales *f* de bois **dhɯ̂ɯ sàbhɑ̂**
sang *m* **gwàn, yɔ̀ɔn**
sangloter : il sanglote **gbɔ̂ kpɤ̄sìan yàa kún**
sangsue *f* **pɑ̂an**
santé *f* **flʌ̂ʌ̀**, en bonne santé **klɤ̂ɤklɤ̂, klɤ̂ɤklɤ̂ɤ**, je suis en bonne santé **ā n̄ flʌ̂ʌ̀ gɯ́ɯ**, il n'est pas en bonne santé **yáa ɤ̄ flʌ̂ʌ̀ gɯ́ɯ**
sanza *f* sur calebasse **kɔ̀ɔtà̀**

Sassandra **gwàngā**
satisfaction *f* **dhìindà̀**
satisfaire **dhī**, satisfaire qn **bhɛ̄n zɔ̀ kún**
satisfait : il n'était pas satisfait **bhlɔ̄ɔ yíi gó' gɯ́ɯ**
sauce *f* **tɔ̂o, yí**, sauce de feuilles de gombo **zɑ̂andhɛ̂yí**, sauce graine **sɤ̄yí, sɤ̄yí tɔ̂o**, sauce d'arachide **gwɛ̂ɛ yí**, sauce de feuilles de manioc **bāa dhɛ̂ tɔ̂o**, sauce de liane "zan" **zɑ̂n yí**, sauce des feuilles séchées et pilées de la plante gblɛ̀e **gblɛ̀e yí**, sauce des grains de "koo" **kɔ̄ɔ yí**, sauce de poudre de gombo **dɯ̂ʌŋ yí**
sauf **ká**
sauter **wlɤ̂**
sauterelle *f* **kpà̀a**
sauver, se sauver **dhā**
savane *f* **yɛ̂, yɛ̂gā**
savoir **dō**, savoir faire **dō**, il ne sait pas quoi faire **à̀ kɔ̀ yáa dhɤ́**, je ne sais pas quoi faire **bháan n̄ kʌ̄-dhɛ̀ yɤ̄**, je sais bien lancer les projectiles avec la fronde **n̄ kwɛ̄ɛ̂ yɤ̂ sʌ̀ gbɔ̂ɔ̀ zɯ̀ɤ-sɯ̀ bhà̀**, on ne sait jamais **bhá bhūn dhɤ̂ wɛ̀, wáa wɔ́n dhɤ̂ zœ̂œ**
savoir *m* moderne **sʌ́ʌdhɛ̂**
savon *m* **sầà**, savon noir **bhɛ̄ntīi sầà**
savoureux **dhɛ̂ɛndhɛ̀ɛn, plʌ̂ʌplʌ̀ʌ**, que c'est savoureux! **dhɛ̂nkɛ̂ndhɛ̀nkɛ̀ndhɛ̀nkúndhɛ̄ɛ̂n**
scandale : faire un scandale à qn **zā yà̀ bhɛ̄n bhà̀**
scarification *f* **wɛ̄ŋ**, il a fait la scarification **yà wɛ̄ŋ zʌ̄**
schlarf-schlarf **flɔ̄ɔ́flɔ̀ɔflɔ̄ɔ́dhɤ**
schling **sīɔ́kɔ̀sīɔ́kɔ̀dhɤ**
scie *f* **sīi**
scier **kɑ̂n**, scier un morceau de bois **dhɯ̂ɯ kplɯ̂ɯ kɑ̂n sīi ká**
sciure *f* de bois *m* **dhɯ̂ɯ blɯ̀ɯŋ, dhɯ̂ɯ gbɔ̀, dhɯ̂ɯ bì**

scorpion *m* **gǣǣ́n**
scrontch **kpákpákpádhɤ̄**
seau *m* **gbɔ̋ŋgbɔ̋**
sec **kpɛ̋ɛ**, il a eu la gorge sèche **à bhɛ̄ɛ́dhɛ̏ yà kpǣ́æ kún,** que c'est sec et dur! **gblɤ́kɤ́gblɤ̏kɤ̏gblɤ̏kɤ́gblɤ̄ɤ́**
sécher **bhɤ̏n-kɔ̏, gā, kɔ̏,** *(surtout au soleil, au feu)* **kpǣ́æ kpɔ́**
sécheresse **kpɛ̋ɛ**
séchoir *m* **gbɤ̋ŋ, yɔ̄ɔ̏n**
secouer **gúɯ-kpʌ̀ŋ, gúɯ-zʌ̄, kpʌ̀ŋ, tūűn,** acte de secouer **zùuzűu**
secours : au secours! **kà tɤ̋ yī dhɛ̏ bhōo!**
secret *m*, affaire *f* secrète **bɪ̀ngúɯwɔ̏n, wɔ́n bɪ̏n-sɯ̏ɯ.**
secrétaire *m* **sʌ́ʌdhɛ́bɛ̀nzʌ̄bhɛ̏n**
sécrétion *f* sèche **kɛ̋ŋgbɤ̋**
sécrétion *f* solide **gbō**
sédiment *m* **dūuŋ**
séduire une femme **dɤ̏ dhēbɔ̏ gɔ̏ gúɯ**
s'égratigner **gìi**
Seigneur **dʌ̄bhɛ̏n**
sein *m* **yɔ́n, yɔ́n gā**
sel *m* **wèe,** *(en grains)* **wèe bɪ̏**
selon **bhɤ̏**
semaine *f* **dhɔ̋ɔgɔ̏**
semblable **síbhɤ̋n, tɛ̀ɛdhɪ́n,** il n'y avait pas son semblable **à zɔ̏n' ká yáa dhɤ́**
sembler **bhɔ̄**
semer **bɔ̄,** semer du riz **bhlɯ̏n bɔ̄**
sénégali brun à ventre blanc **fɛ̀e**
sens **klɔ̋ɔ̏**
sentier *m* **zɪ̏an, zīaan, zīaangblɔ̀ogā**
sentir **kún,** je ne me sens pas bien **n̄ tɤ̏ yáa sʌ̏**
séparer **kɤ̋n kwʌ́ʌ̏,** se séparer **kɤ̋n wō kwʌ́ʌ̏**
sept **sɛ́ɛ̀plɛ̀**
septembre *m* **zlɔ̏**
sérieusement **dhűɛyídhɤ̄**
sérieux **dhűɛyídhɤ̄, kpʌ́dhɤ̄**
sérieux *m* **sɔ̀bhɛ́ɛ̏,** prends ce travail au sérieux **ɯ̄ɪ sɔ̀bhɛ́ɛ̏ sɯ́ɪ yʌ̄ ɤ́ yā à pɪ́ɤ**
serment *m* **sɤ̏,** serment de l'accusé en sorcellerie **kpɯ̋ɪ,** faire un serment de sorcier **kpɯ̋ɪ dɔ̄**
serpent *m* **bhlɛ̀ɛn,** serpent cracheur **gbɤ̏a, bhlɛ̄ɛn gbɤ̏a,** serpent vert **gwɛ̋ɛdhūɤɤ,** serpent noir **bhlɛ̀ɛntīi,** espèces de serpents : **fɯ̏udʌ̄, gbɤ̋ŋyɛ́, gbʌ́ʌlɔ̀o, lɤ́ɤ̏, sűbhōwɛ̏ɛbhɤ̏, yʌ̄ŋzlʌ̄ʌdhɯ̋ɪ**
serré **gbɛ́ɛ̏,** devenir trop serré **kún,** il a eu un visage serré **yà ɤ̄ wʌ̄ʌ́ gúɯ-sɪ̏ɤ**
serrer **gúɯ-sɪ̏ɤ,** serrer *(visage)* **kpɛ̀nŋ,** serre-lui la main **ɯ̄ɪ kɔ̏ dɤ̏ à kwɛ̀ɛ̏,** sans serrer *(attacher)* **tʌ́ŋ̏tʌ̏ŋ,** serrer un fagot avec un tendeur **kìaŋ dɤ̏ wɔ̋ bhɤ̏**
serre-tendeur *m* **kìaŋ**
serrure *f* **dhàklɛ́e kɔ́,** mets la clé dans la serrure **dhàklɛ́e dɤ̏ kwɛ̋ɛ gúɯ**
servante *f* **gwʌ̄ʌ́dhē**
serviette *f* éponge **dɯ̀bɔ̀ŋdhē**
servir à qn **zɯ̏ɤ,** sers-moi, car ma calebasse est vide **bhɤ̏ vīn n̄ bhɤ̏, kɤ̄ á gó n̄ kō tɤ̏ n̄ tɔ̋ gúɯ yɤ̏ vīn-sīʌ**
sésame *m* **dhɔ̋ŋbhɛ́ɛ**
seul **bhɤ́, dɔ̄ɔ̋,** il est parti vivre seul **yà dhó ɤ̄ dɔ̄ɔ̋ ká**
seulement **dōsēŋ, gbɛ̋ŋ, kpɤ̋an, sēŋ**
sévère **dhɛ̏ɛnsɯ̏ɪ, dhɪ́ɤsɯ̏ɪ,** il est sévère avec les enfants **yɤ̏ dhʌ́n-dhɯ̏n bhɤ̏ dhɛ̏ɛnsɯ̏ɪ**
sévérité *f* **dhɪ́ɤ̏ɤ-dhɛ̏**
sexe *m* de l'homme **gɔ̄ɔ̏ndhɛ̏gā, gɔ̄ɔ̏n-dhɛ̏**
sexe *m* féminin **yɛ̏gā**
si **dhɪ́n, yà kʌ̄ dhɛ̀, kɤ̄, ɤ́,** si c'est comme ça **à kʌ̏ dhɤ́-sɯ̏ɪ gúɯ**
SIDA *m* **sídâ**
siège **yɛ̏ɛ**
sifflement *m* **sūʌ́**
siffler **sūʌ́ pɪ̏ɤ,** le serpent siffle **bhlɛ̀ɛn yɤ̏ wɛ́-sīʌ**

signe *m* **dɔ̄ɔ**
signifiant : une affaire peu signifiante **wla̋ȁwɔ̏n**
signification **klɔ́ɔ̏**
silence *m#* **dhæ̏æ, dhɛ̏tȁ,** silence de mort **sɛ̋tȁ,** l'homme pleure en silence **gɔ̄ɔ̏n yɤ̏ gbő bɔ̏ ɤ̄ zūʌ̋ píɤ,** silence! **dīnŋdhɤ̄ yȁ ȁ kún! dhɛ̏ tȁ yɤ̏ gā!**
silencieusement **dīnŋdhɤ̄, tűuŋ**
silure *m* **yúɤ̏ɤtīi**
sinciput *m* **gwìnŋ̏dhɛ̏**
singe *m* **klɤ̏ɤ, wɔ̀ɔ,** singe pleureur **yɛ̋ɛ̏wɔ̏ɔ,** singe rouge **vɛ̄, yɛ̋ɛ̏wɔ̏ɔ,** la sauce de singe **kla̋ŋ̏ yí**
sinon **ɛ́ɛ̏n**
sitôt **bhōo**
situation *f* **dhɛ̏,** il s'est trouvé dans une situation très difficile **gblɯ̏ yà ȁ kún**
six **sœ̋œ̏dō**
slip *m* à queue *f* **wʌ̋nŋkʌ̄zɯ̄bhȁ**
snif **vı̋anvı̋anvı̋andhɤ̄**
sœur *f* **dʌ̄dhú, dhēébhāŋ,** sœur aînée **dhēgbáan, dhēzőo, dhɤ̄ɤ,** sœur cadette **zláȁ dhēbʌ̏,** sœur cadette de la grand-mère maternelle **dha̋n sɛ̄ɛ̋ndhʌ́n,** sœur de famille **dʌ́ʌ̏**
soif *m* **yíbhɯ̄ndhɔ̏,** j'ai soif **yí bhɯ̄n dhɔ̏ yà n̄ kún**
soigner **dhɛ̋-kʌ̄**
soir *m* **yɛ̄ɛ̋n, yɛ̄ɛ̋npı̋ɤ,** début de la soirée **dɔ̋ɔ**
soldat *m* **sɔ̋dha̋**
soleil *m* **yʌ́nŋ̏,** quand le soleil commence à brûler (vers 10 heures) **yʌ́nŋ̏ tɛ̋ɛ gbɛ̋ɛ̏ tȁ,** au soleil **yʌ́nŋ̏dhɛ̏**
solidement **kpɛ̄nŋkpɛ̄nŋdhɤ̄**
sombre **dhűɤɤdhɯ̏ɤɤ,** il est devenu tout sombre **dhɛ̏ gɯ́ yȁ yȁ wɛ̋ bhɔ̄nŋdhɤ̄,** rendre sombre **tlɤ̄ɤ**
sommeil *m* **yī**
sommet *m* **dhı̋ɤ, gɔ̏, gwìnŋ̏dhɛ̏, zɔ̋dhı̋ɤ**
son *m (bruit)* **wɛ̋**
son *m* de riz : tu es inutile comme le son de riz **ɯ̄ főofȍo ká dhɛ̀ bhlɯ̏n gbȍ dhɤ́**
sonner : il sonne: tic-tac **ȁ vīn yɤ̏ dɔ̏ tɤ́tɤ́tɤ́dhɤ̄,** sonner le gong **gʌ̄nŋgʌ̄nŋ bhȁn**
sorcellerie *f* **dɯ̄ɯ, gbɔ̄ɔ́dɯ̏**
sorcier *m* **bɛ̀dhɛ̋yāakʌ̄bhɛ̏n, dɯ̄bhɛ̏n, ya̋ngɯ́tīibhɛ̏n,** sorcier : c'est un sorcier **ȁ gblɯ̋dhɛ̏ yɤ̏ tīi**
sort *m* : jeter un sort sur qn **dɯ̄ kʌ̄ bhɛ̄n ká**
sorte *f* **sūu**
sortir **gó,** faire sortir qn **yɤ̄ kpɛ̋nŋ,** il est sorti **yà dɔ̄ ɤ̄ gæ̏æn, yà yɤ̄ kpɛ̋nŋ,** sortir dehors **zūn kpɛ́nŋ, zūn kpɛ̋nŋdhɤ̄**
sou *m* **sȕu, sȕugā, tȁŋgȁ,** je n'ai pas un sou **wʌ́ʌ̏gā tȁŋgȁ zı̏aan yáa n̄ gɔ̏**
souche *f* **kpūŋ́, dhɯ̋ kpūú,** souche d'un palmier abattu **yɔ̄ zɯ̄**
souci *m* **zūʌ̋dhı̋ɤtɛ̏ɛ,** sans soucis **wáwádhɤ̄,** rester sans soucis **tó ɤ̄ gɔ̏ pı̋ɤ,** donner des soucis à qn **bhɛ̄n zūʌ̋ tó tàabhȁn,** elle se fait trop de soucis **ȁ zūʌ̋ {dhı̋ɤ} yɤ̏ bhɤ̏ɤ gbɛ́**
soudain **gɯ́klɤ̄bhā, sı̋ȁabhā,** soudain et fort **gblūűdhɤ̄**
souffle : le piment m'a coupé le souffle **slʌ̏ʌ yȁ yȁ n̄ zūʌ̋ bhȁ**
souffler **pı̏ɤ,** le vent souffle **tɛ̋ɛ yɤ̏ zīɤ-sīʌ**
souffrance *f* **sāa̋n**
souffrir **sāa̋n,** il souffre **ȁ zūʌ̋ dhı̋ɤ yȁ tɛ̋ɛ**
soulagement *m* **tūa̋a**
soulever **dhı̋ɤ-wlɯ̄ɯ̋,** soulever au-dessus de la tête **bɔ̄**
soumbala *(assaisonnement)* **sűnbha̋ndha̋n**
soupière **tőo yɤ̏ gɯ́ tæ̏æ**

soupir *m* : soupir de soulagement **fȍodhíɤ**, il a poussé un soupir de soulagement **yà ɤ̄ fȍodhíɤ lòo**
soupirer de soulagement **ɤ̄ zȍ lòo**
source *f* : source d'eau **yí gɔ̏, yítúɛ̏ɛ, yígɔ̏gódhɛ̏,** source de rivière **gɔ̏ɔdhɛ̏,** source de puissance **zɯ̄gbȁngɯ́**
sourcils *m* **yấnkpȉnŋtȁ**
sourd *m* **tőwlɯ̀bhɛ̏n**
sourd : il est sourd *(complètement)* **ȁ tő yɤ̏ tā-sɯ̏ ká**
sourd-muet **bhőbhő**
souricière *f* **kɤ̀ɤ, bhɔ̏ɔn bhȁ pīɤ́ sɔ̋**
sourire **bhȕɛɛndhɤ̄, yɛ̋e tó bhȕɛɛndhɤ̄**
souris *f* **bhɔ̏ɔn,** souris rayée **yʌ́nŋ̏gɯ́dʌ̄**
sous **wlɤ̀ɤ**
sous-estimer **yɔ̀ɔ**
sous-préfet **kɯ̋nbhấndhấn sɛ̋ɛ́ndhʌ́n**
sous-sol *m* **sɛ̋ɛdhɤ̄kɔ̏gɯ́**
soutenir qn **dɔ̄ bhɛ̄n gbȁn gɔ̏**
souvenir : se souvenir **zȍ-bɤ̏**
souvent **gbɛ́, kpɛ̏ɛwō, sìʌ, yà kʌ̄ sìʌ,** pas souvent **plɛ̀-plɛ̀,** le plus souvent **ȁ gbɛ́-dhɛ̏ gɯ́**
spécialiste : il est spécialiste dans ça **ȁ là yɤ̏ ȁ gɔ̏**
spectre *m* **zȉi**
sperme *m* **gɔ̏ɔ̏n-dhɛ̏ yí**
splendide! **yɛ̋ɛdhɤ̄**
squelette *m* **bhɛ̄ngāzấŋ**
stérile : une femelle stérile **tɯ̏ʌʌ ɤ́ yáa ɤ̄ kpɔ́**
sternum *m* **kɤ̏ŋ**
stomatite *f* **dhídhɛ̏kʌ̄**
strict **dhɛ̏ɛnsɯ̏**
strident **kpɛ̋ɛ**
structure *f* **kɔ́záȁ,** il a fabriqué la structure de la maison **yȁ kɔ́ dhɯ̋ gbȁn**
stupéfaction *f* **klȉŋklīŋ̏**
stupéfait **dīnŋdhɤ̄, zītīŋdhɤ̄**
stupéfier qn **bhɛ̄n dhí dɔ̄ bōŋ ká,** je suis stupéfié **klȉŋklīŋ̏ yà yɤ̄ n̄ tȁ**
stupeur : avec stupeur *f* **gɛ̏ɛŋdhɤ̄**
stupide **bhɔ̋nbhɔ̏nsɯ̏**
stupidité : il a montré sa stupidité **yà ɤ̄ dɛ̏ kʌ̄ dɛ̏dɛ̏wō yāa**
stylo **bɛ̏nzʌ̏kápʌ̏**
subalterne **kɔ̏wlɤ̀ɤ**
subalterne *m*, *f* **kɔ̏wlɤ̀ɤ bhɛ̏n**
subitement **vɤ́ɤ̏dhɤ̄**
succéder à **dɔ̄ ȁ píɤ**
successivement **dɔ́ɔ̏ndhɤ̄**
sucer **flɛ̄ɛn, gấn, pā**
sucette *f* **bɔ̀nŋbɔ̄nŋ̏ dhɯ̋dhʌ́ndhē**
sucre *m* **sɯ̋kấdhɯ̋**
sucré **dhɛ̋ɛndhɛ̏ɛn, slʌ̋ʌnslʌ̏ʌn**
sud **síāa**
sueur *f* **fɤ̄yí**
suffire **kún, slòo**
suffisant **bhɛ̋ɛ̏, gbɛ́**
suffixe *m* **wȍkplɯ̏bhȁtàabhȁ**
suffoquer : il suffoque **ȁ tɛ̋ŋ yȁ sɯ́**
suicider : se suicider **ɤ̄ dɛ̏ zʌ̄**
suie *f* **sóŋ̏**
suinter : le sang suinte **ȁ yɔ̀ɔn yɤ̏ bhɔ̄-sīʌ**
suis-moi! **zīɤ n̄ kèŋ̏**
super! **gídhấn**
supérieur *m* **bhɛ̄ngɔ̏dhíɤbhɛ̏n**
supplier **bhɛ̋ɛ̏, gbȁn,** je te supplie **bhán gā ī dhɛ̏**
support *m* **gbȁn**
supportable : être supportable **kún**
supporter : bien supporter **gɯ́-dɔ̄,** je peux supporter la chose **wɔ́n yɤ̏ kún bhȍ n̄ gɯ́,** s'ils ne se supportent pas l'un l'autre... **bhɛ̄n sɔ̀ŋ yíi kún bhɔ̄ kó gɯ́**
sur **bhȁ, tȁ, tàa**
sûrement **dɛ̏dɛ̏wō**
surface *f* **bhȁdhɛ̏, bhȁ, tȁ,** surface du sol **síāadhɛ̏**

surgir **wɔ̀**
surmaturité *f* **glɔ̀o**
surprendre **bhán, kɑ̋n,** être surpris **kɑ̋n ɤ̄ tɑ̀,** la nuit nous a surpris en chemin **bɪ̋n yɤ̀ bhɑ̀n yī bhɑ̀ zīɑ̀an,** le jour les a surpris sur la route **dhɛ̀ yɤ̀ kʌ̄ kpœ̀œ ɑ̀-dhʊ̀n bhɑ̀ zīɑ̀an,** Tokpa a été surpris par la pluie **dhā kpîì yɑ̀ bān Tòkpɑ̀ bhɑ̀**
surprise *f* **kɑ̀nbhēŋgʊ́wɔ̀n, tīí,** sursauter de surprise **kɑ̋n ɤ̄ tɑ̀**
surveillance **kplʌ̋nŋ**
surveiller **bhɑ̀an-kʌ̄, tɤ̋ŋ-kʌ̄,** surveiller qch **tɤ̋ŋ kʌ̄ pʌ̄ gʊ́,** je le surveille **ɑ̀ tɤ̋ŋ yɤ̀ n̄ gʊ́,** se surveiller (sa santé, ses habits...) **ɤ̄ dɛ̀ kún sʌ̀**
suspendre, être suspendu **dūn**
syllabe *f* **wɔ̀gā**
sympathie *f* **tœ̋œŋ̀dhē-dhɛ̀**
syndrome *m* immunodéficitaire acquis **sɪ́dâ**

T t

tabac *m* **tɑ́ɑ̀,** tabac à chiquer **zɑ̋ŋ**
table *f* **tɑ́ɑ̀blʌ̀ʌ**
tabou **tàbû**
tabouret *m* **gblɔ̀o, yɑ̀tɑ̀glɔ̀o,** petit tabouret de cuisine **tɔ̀o kpɑ̀tɑ̀ gblɔ̀o**
tacheté **yʌ̋nŋyʌ̀nŋ**
tagadag-tagadag-tagadag **glɑ̀glɑ̀glɑ̀dhɤ̄**
taille *f* **dhɤ̀ŋdlɤ̀ɤdhɛ̀**
tailler **yʌ́n,** il a taillé son étoffe avec le couteau d'un seul mouvement brusque **yɑ̀ ɤ̄ bhā sɔ̄ pɛ̋ dhɑ̀a ká vɪ́ɔ̀odhɤ̄,** se tailler les dents **ɤ̄ sɔ̋n yʌ́n**
taire : se taire **dɔ̄ ɤ̄ dhɪ́ tʊ̋nŋ, dɔ̄ ɤ̄ tʊ̋nŋ,** je me suis tu **dhɛ̀tɑ̀ yɑ̀ gā n̄ tɑ̀,** je me tais **n̄ dhɪ́ tʊ̋uŋ, n̄ tʊ̋uŋ,** il s'est tu **dhæ̀æ yɑ̀ gā ɑ̀ tɑ̀,** taisez-vous! **kɑ̀ dɔ̄ dīnŋdhɤ̄!**
talon *m* **tɪ̋ŋ**
tambour *m* **bhɑ̀a,** jouer du tambour **bhɑ̀a zʌ̄,** tambour d'aisselle **tɑ̄ŋ̀,** tambour à fente *f* **gɔ̄, gɔ̄dhʌ́n,** tambour d'eau **kɔ̀ɔtɑ̀, yɪ́kɔ̀ɔ,** jouer du tambour d'eau **kɔ̀ɔ zʌ̄,** tambour long **fɤ̄,** jouer du tambour d'eau **kɔ̀ɔ zʌ̄,** grand tambour cylindrique **gɔ̄dhʊ̋ʊ,** espèces de tambours : **bɪ̀dhēbhɑ̀a, glɔ̀ŋ, gɔ̀ŋgɔ̄ŋ́, yɑ̋gbɑ̋**
tambourin *m* , tambourin d'aisselle **gɔ̀ŋgɔ̄ŋ́**
tamis *m* **tɛ̀nbhɛ̀n,** tamis lâche **tɛ̀nbhɛ̀n yɑ̋n gblɤ̋gblɤ̄,** tamis serré **tɛ̀nbhɛ̀n yɑ̋n sɛ̄ɛ́ndhʌ́n**
tandis que **yɑ̄ɑ̋**
tantôt **bhá bhʊ̄n**
taon *m* **wőo**
tarir **bhɤ̋ɤ**
taro *m* **kōókɔ̀o, plʌ̋ʌ̀**
tas *m* **dūuŋ, gɔ̀n,** tas de marchandises **dhɛ̋ɛ,** tas d'herbe semi-brûlée **klɑ̋a,** tas d'herbes et de bois **kɑ̋ŋ,** tas d'ordures **dʊ̋nŋ, tūŋ,** tas d'épis de maïs **kɤ̋ŋ gɔ̀n,** tas d'herbes et de bois **gɛ̋ɛ kɔ́**
taureau *m* **dù gɔ̄n**
taxi *m* **tāsî**
taximan *m* **tāsî zīɤ bhɛ̀n**
technique *f* **slʌ̋**
teigne *f* **sɔ̄blʌ̋**
teinture *f* noire **zɔ̋ŋ yɪ́**
télé *f* **tēlê**
téléphone **tīootīoo, tēlēfɔ̀n**
téléphonner à qn, appeller qn **pɪ̀ɤgā bhɑ̀n bhɛ̄n dhɛ̀**
téléviseur *m* **tēlê, tēlê gbɔ̄**
télévision *f* **tēlê**
témoin *m* **sɛ̋ɛ̀, sɛ̋ɛ̀dhɛ̀kʌ̄bhɛ̀n**
tempe *f* **tőpɪ́ɤdhɛ̀**
temps *m* **tɤ̋ŋ, yī,** cela prend du temps ... **yɤ̀ tɤ̋ŋ sʊ́-sīʌ,** en ce temps-là... **ɑ̀ tɤ̋ŋ ɤ́ bhā ɑ̀ gʊ́ kɤ̄...**
tenaille *f* **gbɛ̄ɛ̀n**

tendon *m* **sàfá,** tendon d'Achille **kèe**
tendre *(piège)* **dhi̋ɤ**
tendre **dō à gúɯ,** tendre *(vêtement)* **kpɔ́,** tendre un piège **dɤ̄ŋ dhi̋ɤ**
tendu **gɑ̋n-sɯ̀ɯ**
ténia *m* **bhīʌ́**
tenir : tenir sa parole **tó ɤ̄ wȍ tȁ,** ses jambes ne tiennent plus **ȁ gȅn yí yȁ kɑ̋n wɛ̋ɛwɛ̋ɛ**
tente ta chance! (litt.: le cabri dit: l'homme ne peut pas attendre le jour où la pierre se ramollit) **bhȍ yɤ̏ à pɤ̏: bhēn yáa gwʌ̏ zɔ̀ɔ yȉ dō**
terminaison *f* **gɔ̏**
terminer **dhi̋ɤ-pā, dhi̋ɤ-tā, gɔ̏-yɛ̋,** se terminer **yʌ̄n**
termite *m* maçon **zè**
termite *m*, espèces : **bhlʌ́, dlő o, dɔ́ɔ̏, zȕzȕ**
termitière *f* **dìʌnŋtlȍo, zèkpȉnŋdʌ̄,** termitière cathédrale **bhlʌ́tlɔ̏, tlő o,** cette termitière a perdu sa productivité **tlő o yā yà gó**
terrasser **pɔ́n**
terre *f* **sɛ̋, sɪ̋āadhȅ,** terre ferme **sɛ̋ kpǽæ tȁ**
terrible **sʌ̏, yāa gúɯ yāa**
tessons *mpl* **kɤ̀ɤ**
tête *f* **gɔ̏, gɔ̄ɔ,** tête de flambeau **gbɪ́aa gɔ̏,** tête de harpe-luth **kōnŋ sɛ̋ɛ**
tête-à-tête : ils sont allés faire un tête-à-tête **wà dhó wō gɔ̏ dūn'**
téter **flɛ̄ɛn**
têtu : personne *f* têtue **gɔ̄ɔgbɛ́ɛ̏bhȅn**
texte *m* **dhīaŋkpɤ̄**
thé *m* **téȅ,** thé en poudre **téȅ bȉ**
tibia *m* **gȅndhɯ̋ɯ, kplàa**
tic *m* nerveux : j'ai un tic nerveux de l'oeil **n̄ yɑ̋n gā yɤ̏ n̄ kún-sɪʌ klɤ̄klɤ̄dhɤ̄**
tic-tac **tɤ́tɤ́tɤ́dhɤ̄**
tiède **kpɔ́ŋ̋kpɔ̏ŋ**
tiens! **ȁhɑ̋ȁn, yàá**
tiers : un tiers de qch **ȁ pȅ-gúɯ-sɯ̀ɯ pɛ̋ɛn yȁagā-dhȁan**
tige *f* **dhɯ̋ɯ,** tige de bambou **gbœ̄œgā,** tige de manioc **bāa dhɯ̋ɯ,** tiges d'herbes non-brûlées **kɑ̋ŋ**
tilapia *m* **kòo**
timalie *f* à tête noire **zɔ̏zɔ̏dhȁ**
tinter : ses bracelets tintent **ȁ bhȁ yȁkɔ̏ɔpʌ̏-dhȕn wȍ wȅ wlɛ̋ɛnŋ̋wlȅɛnŋ̏wlɛ̋ɛnŋ̋dhɤ̄**
tique *f* **gbʌ̏ʌ**
tirer *(traîner)* **gɑ̋n, gbìɤɤ,** tirer sur *(lance-pierres)* **gɑ̋n-gúɯ**
tiroir *m* **kɛ̋ső**
tison *f* **pēŋ kpūú, sɯ̋ɤ kpūú**
tisser **sō bō**
tisserin *m* gendarme **bhȁantɛ̋ɛ, dȅbhȁan, gɔ̏plɤ́ɤ̄, pɤ̂bhȁan**
tissu *m* **sō**
tituber : en titubant **gblɔ̄ŋ̋gblɔ̏ŋgblɔ̄ŋ̋dhɤ̄**
tô *m* **tòo,** tô demi-produit **tòogā,** faire la pâte de tô **tòo bìɤɤ**
toc toc **kōkō**
toile *f* d'araignée **zìŋtőŋ dőŋ, zìŋtőŋ kɔ́**
toilettes *fpl* **gbōokɔ̏**
toiser qn des pieds à tête **ɤ̄ yɑ̋n tɑ̋ bhēn ká**
toit *m* **gbà,** toit à une ou deux pentes **gbɔ̄ŋ gbà,** toit conique **kɔ́dhēɛ̋ gbà,** toit en pente **kɔ́ gbà,** sur le toit de la maison **kɔ́ tȁ dhɯ̋ɤ́**
tôle **pȉɤdhɛ̋**
tomate *f* **tàbhàntɪ̋ȉ**
tombe *f*, tombeau *m* **būn**
tomber **bhɑ́ȁndhūn, gó, kɔ́n, pɤ̏,** *(feuilles)* **lòo, wènŋ,** *(nuit)* **dȁ, bhán,** la nuit est tombée **bɪ̋n yà bhán, dɔ̋ɔ yȁ dȁ,** lorsque la nuit tombe... **yà dō gbēŋ...,** tomber amoureux **gā,** tomber dans un piège **dȁ dɤ̄ŋ gúɯ,** tomber en avant **gblʌ̋ʌ̏dhūn,** tomber enceinte **gú**

súɪ, tomber sur **kɑ̋n … gúɪ,** la grêle est tombée **bhʌ̄nŋgā yà wɛ̀nŋ,** ma dent est tombée **n̄ sɔ́ngā yà gó bhūn,** ses fleurs sont tombées **à bɪ́n yà lòo**

ton *m* **wɔ̀dhókɔ̀,** ton bas **wɔ̀dhɔ̀sɪ́ãa-sʊ̀ɪ,** ton extra-bas **wɔ̀dhɔ̀sɪ́ãagbɛ́ɛ̀-sʊ̀ɪ,** ton haut **wɔ̀dhɔ̀dhʊ̋ɤ́-sʊ̀ɪ,** ton extra-haut **wɔ̀dhɔ̀dhʊ̋ɤ́gbɛ́ɛ̀-sʊ̀ɪ,** ton moyen **wɔ̀dhɔ̀zɪ̀nŋgúɪ-sʊ̀ɪ,** ton descendant, ton tombant **wɔ̀dhókɔ̀ ɤ́ lɔ̄ɔ-sʊ̀ɪ ká,** ton flottant **wɔ̀dhókɔ̀ ɤ́ dūn-sʊ̀ɪ ká,** ton modulé **wɔ̀dhókɔ̀ ɗàkópɪ́ɤ-sʊ̀ɪ-dhʊ̀n**

tonner : il tonne **dhā yɤ̀ wɛ́-sɪʌ**

torche *f* **sɔ̋nŋ,** torche électrique **tɔ́ɔ̀sʊ̀ɪ,** torche de raphia *m* **gbɪ́aa**

tordre **pɪ̄ɤ̀ɤ**

torrent : à torrent **zɔ̀ɔzɔ̀ɔdhɤ̀**

tort *m* **zūʌn,** avouer son tort **ɤ̄ dhɪ́ bhō wɔ́n tà, ɤ̄ dhɪ́ bhō dhīaŋ tà**

torticolis *m* **gúɪkplʊ̀ɪdhē,** j'ai le torticolis **n̄ gúɪ yà gúɪ-kplʊ̀ɪ**

tortillon *m* pour lier le fagot **wɔ̋ sʊ̀ɪ gúɪ bhɪ̄ʌ́ʌ wɔ̋ bɛ̀**

tortue *f* **bhœ̄œ,** tortue aquatique **yɪ́ à bhœ̄œ,** tortue terrestre **sɛ̋ bhœ̄œ,** il est de petite taille comme une tortue **yɤ̀ klɤ̄ɤ̀ ká dhɛ̀ bhœ̄œ dhɤ́**

tôt **pɪ́ɤ̀**

totalement **tlʌ̄ntlʌ̄ndhɤ̀**

totem *m* **kɪ́an, zʌ̀nŋ**

toucher **kɔ̀-pá, pá, vīn, zūn,** *(aborder, en conversation)* **ɗà,** *(pour signaler son choix)* **ɤ̄ kɔ̀ yɛ́ à bhà,** toucher à *(faire du mal)* **ɤ̄ kɔ̀ yɤ̄ à bhà**

touffe *f* de queue de porc-épic **sǽɛ̄ŋ**

toujours **dhɤ́dō, kpɛ̀ɛwō**

toupie *f* **dlɤ̀ŋ**

tour *m* de rôle *f* **kêdhɪ́,** faire le tour **slʌ̄ʌ, zīɤ**

Toura *(groupe ethnique et sa langue)* **Gbɪ̄ãa**

touraco *m* géant **klóɔ̀**

touraco *m* violet **glōogɪ̀aan**

tourbillon *m* **flɔ̋kpɔ̀ŋdhɛ̀**

tourmenter **sʌ̄ʌ bhō**

tourner **glʌ̄ʌn, glúɪ, klɔ̀ŋ, slʌ̄ʌ, zīɤ,** se tourner **glūʊ̀n, slʌ̄ʌ,** tourner *(autour d'un axe)* **slʌ̄ʌ ɤ̄ gúɪ ɤ̄ zʊ̀ɪ,** tourner en cercle **zīɤ,** tourner en rond **glúɪ ɤ̄ gɔ̀ zúɪ,** il tourne sur place **yɤ̀ gbœ̀œdhɛ́ kʌ̄-sɪʌ,** tourner son regard **dhɪ́ɤ-kpɔ́,** tourner *(sauce)* **kpœ̀œn,** tourner *(viande)* **fɪ̋n,** il lui a tourné le bras par derrière **yà à kɔ̀ pɪ̄ɤ̀ɤ à tà**

tourteau *m* des graines de palme **sɤ̀ dhɪ̀i,** tourteaux de graines de palmier à huile **dhɪ̀ifãa**

tourterelle tambourette **kplɛ̄ɛ̀dhɛ̀**

tous **gbàn,** tous les ans **kwɛ̀ bhà,** tous les jours **yī gbàn ká,** tous les matins **dhīɑ́ pɪ́ɤ gbàn ká,** tous sans exception **gbàn pɛ̋pɛ́**

tousser **dɔ̄n zʌ̄**

tout **gbàn, pɛ̋pɛ́,** tout à coup **wɛ́,** tout ce qui existe dans le monde **kpɔ̋ŋtàapʌ̀-dhʊ̀n,** tout de suite **dhʌ̀nwōdō, sɪ́ãabhā, ɗèe yā' gúɪ, gúɪ klɤ̄ɤ̀ bhà, yɛ́ɛ̀n gúɪ, yɛ́ɛ̀n gúɪ yā, yɛ́ɛ̀n yā' gúɪ,** tout droit **dōsēŋ, vɛ̄ɛdhɤ̀,** tout le temps *(des intervalles sont possibles)* **tɤ̋ŋgbàn ká,** tout un... **zɪ̀aanwō**

toux *f* **dɔ̄n,** il a la toux **dɔ̄n yɤ̀ à bhà**

trace *f* **glɔ̋o, pɪ́nŋ̀**

tracer **kɑ̋n,** il a tracé le plan de la maison **yà kɔ́ kplɔ̋ŋ kɑ̋n**

trahir qn **ɗà bhēn dhɛ̀ pʌ̄ pɪ́ɤ**

train *m* **tlēn**

traîner par terre **gbɪ̀ɤɤ,** en traînant **wɪ̀aadhɤ̀**

trait *m* **tlɛ̄ɛ,** trait d'union **kplʊ̀ɪtlɛɛgā, tlɛ̄ɛ**

traiter **dhɛ́-kʌ̄, kún, zīɤ**

tranchant **dhɪ́ɤsʊ̀ɪ**

tranchant *m* **gā, dhɪ́ɤ**

tranche *f* **pɛ̋n**
trancher **pɛ̋n bhō**
transe *f* chamanique **zı̏gȁ**
transformation *f* **zı̏ɤgɯ́**
transformer : se transformer **glȁ̋, kʌ̄, slʌ̄ʌ**
transgresser l'ordre **gbā bhō**
transmettre **dhı́ɤ-lòo,** transmettre ses capacités **bhō**
transparent **sɤ̋ɤŋsɤ̏ɤŋ, yȁ̋anyȁan**
transpirer : le soleil brûlant fait transpirer l'homme **yʌ́nŋ̏ gbɛ́ɛ̏ yɤ̏ fɤyı́ gā lȍo bhēn bhȁ**
trappe *f* **glūɯ̄ɯsɔ̏**
trapu **gúŋ̏gùŋ, gbʌ̂gbʌ̏**
travail *m* **bhȁ̋dhȁ̋, yʌ̄,** travail agricole **kê,** travail de bureau, travail qualifié **kwı̋ yʌ̏,** travail d'homme **yʌ̄ glȁ̋glȁ̋sɯ̏,** il fait un bon travail **ȁ pínŋ̏ yɤ̏ sʌ̏**
travailler **yʌ̄ kʌ̄**
travailleur *m* **yʌ̄kʌ̄bhɛ̏n**
travers : les roues de son vélo sont de travers **ȁ bhȁ pı̏ɤgāsòȍ gɛ̏n-dhȕn wȁ yȁ gɤ̋ŋ tȁ**
traverser **kȁ̋n,** il a traversé une rivière **yȁ yı́ kȁ̋n**
trembler **kpʌ̄nŋ, zı̀i**
trempé **yı́sɯ̏**
trépied *m* **gàŋ**
très **dɛ̏dɛ̏wō, dhɛ̀ɛ, gbɛ́ɛ̏, pɛ́ɛpɛ́dhɤ̄, yāawō,** *(blanc)* **pápádhɤ̄,** *(chaud)* **blȁblȁdhɤ̄,** *(joyeux)* **tɛ̏kpɛ̏tɛ̏kpɛ̏dhɤ̄,** *(noir)* **bhɔ́nbhɔ́n, sʌ́nsʌ́n,** très *(personne: taille grande et corpulente)* **gbȁ̋kklȁ̋agbȁkklȁa,** très *(se ressembler)* **bı́oodhɤ̄,** très bien formé **kı̏ankı̏ansɯ̏,** très doux! **dhɛ̏ɛnkɛ́ɛn,** très loin **tı̄ı́nbhɯ̄n,** très longuement **flɯ̋udhɤ̄,** très mouillé **yı́sɯ̏**
trésorier *m* **wʌ́ʌ̏yɛ̏ɛbhōbhɛ̏n**
tressaillir de surprise **kȁ̋n**
tresse *f* **wūngā,** faire des tresses longues **wūn gbɔ̋ɔ̏ bɔ̄**
tresser **bɔ̄,** tresser les cheveux **gɔ̏-lɤ̏,** tresser une natte **sɛ̄ɛ̋ bɔ̄,** on lui a tressé les cheveux *(avec des mèches artificielles)* **wȁa bhȁ wūn bɔ̄, wȁa bhȁ wūn gbɶ̋ɶ̏ bɔ̄,** on lui a tressé les cheveux *(sa propre chevelure)* **wȁ ȁ bhȁ wūn lɤ̏**
tri *m* **zʌ̏gɯ́**
tribunal *m* **zādɔ̄dhɛ̏**
trier **zʌ̏gɯ́-kʌ̄**
tringler **zɔ̄n**
triste **wʌ̏ʌsɯ̏**
tristesse *f* **wʌ̏ʌ-dhɛ̏**
trois **yȁagā**
trompe *f* *(d'éléphant)* **dhɔ̋ŋ**
trompe *f* traversière **tlɯ̋u,** jouer de la trompe **tlɯ̋u pı̏ɤ, tlɯ̋u wɛ̋**
tromper **zı̏an-kʌ̄**
tromperie *f* **zı̏an**
tronc *m* **wɔ̋ dɔ̄ŋ, dhɯ̋gā, kpʌ̀**
trop **dɛ̏dɛ̏wō, sı́nbhȁ̋nwō, gbɛ́ dɛ̏dɛ̏**
troquer **gó**
trou *m* **dhòŋ, gblɯ̀, gblɯ̀dhɛ̏, yɛ̏, yɛ̏gā,** trou d'eau **yı́gblɯ̀,** trou dans le mur **dhòŋgā,** trou de secours **dhòŋ,** trou profond **gblɯ̏gā**
troublant **yɔ̋ɔyɔ̏ɔ**
trouble *m* **zūʌ̋gı̀iwɔ̏n**
troubler **dȁ,** le poisson a troublé l'eau **yɯ́ɤ̏ɤ yȁ yı́ dūuŋ bhō,** l'eau s'est troublée **yı́ yȁ dūuŋ bhō**
troupe *f* **gblɯ̏,** troupe de lions **lāa kpɤ̏**
troupeau *m* **kpɔ̀ŋ, tɯ̏ɤ**
trouver **kpȁn, slɔ̀ɔ, yɤ̄,** se trouver **slɔ̀ɔ, wɔ̄, yɤ̄**
tubercule *m* **dhèe,** tubercule bouilli **kplɯ̀,** tubercule sauvage **bhɤ̋glɛ̋en,** tubercules de la plante bhɤ̋glɛ̋ɛn **bhɤ̋dhèe**
tuberculose *f* **fòodɔ̏n**

tuer **zʌ̄**
tumulte *m* **gbàŋ**
turbulent : personne turbulente **yáŋgúɯyāabhɛ̀n**
turque **tíukɤ̄**
tuut *(klaxon de voiture)* **pāanpāandhɤ̄**
tuyau *m* d'échappement **sīapɤ̄bháàn**

U u

ulcère à l'estomac : il souffre d'un ulcère à l'estomac **à̰ zūʌ́ yɤ̀ à̰ kʌ̀**
ulcéreux *m* **zūʌ́kʌ̄bhɛ̀n**
ululer : le grand-duc ulule **gbēŋbhàan yɤ̀ wɛ̀ ɯ́ɯ̀-ɯ̀u**
un **dō,** un à un **dōdō, dɔ́ɔ̀ndhɤ̄,** un certain **bhá ɤ́ bhūn,** un par un **flēflɛ̀flēdhɤ̄,** un seul **dōsēŋ**
unique **gādō**
unité *f* **gā**
urine *f* **wēɛ́**
uriner **ɤ̄ wēɛ́ bhō**
usé **kɛ́ɛn, kɤ̀ɤ**
user, s'user **blʌ́**
utilité **bhlʌ̀ʌ**

V v

vacances *fpl* **vàkánŋ̀sɯ̀**
vacarme *m* **gbân**
vache *f* désobéissante **dàbɯ́ɯ́dɯ̀**
vagin *m* **gwɛ́nŋ gú dhɛ̀**
vaincre **bhɔ̀ɔn, tó à̰ gbɛ́ɛ̀ ká**
vainement **wɛ́ɛwɛ́**
vairon *m* **kpéŋgā**
vaisselle *f* **pʌ̄ fíʌʌ**
valise *f* **gbʌ̀ʌ**
vallée *f* **gōo, gōogā,** vallée entre les montagnes **tɔ̀n gbɛ̀ŋ**
valoir : se valoir **slòo**
van *m* **dháà**
vanneau *m* armé **péŋ̀pɛ̀ŋ**
vanner **pɤ̀ɤ**
vantard : il est vantard **yɤ̀ dɔ̀ bhɛ̄n yán gúɯ**
varan *m* **zūɛ̀ɛ**
varicelle *f* **bhlɯ̀ɯndhíɤ, kpìʌʌkāàgúɯ**
variole *f* **bhlɯ̀ɯndhíɤ**
vaste **bōŋ**
vautour *m* **gblʌ́ʌ̀**
véhicule *m* **gɔ̄**
veillant **à̰ yáan**
veille : la veille **yāandhíɤ**
veine *f* **bhìʌʌn**
vélo *m* **pɤ̀ɤgāsɔ̀ɔ̀**
vendre **dhɔ́ɔ-dɔ̄, gó**
vendredi *m* **bháandhɔ́ɔyī, dhɔ́ɔyī**
vengeance *f* **yɔ́ɔ**
venger qn **bhlɔ̄ɔ-bhō, zɔ̀o-bhō,** se venger de qn **ɤ̄ bhà yɔ́ɔ-bhō bhɛ̄n gɔ̀**
venin *m* **bhāa,** venin de serpent **bhlɛ̀ɛn bhāa**
venir **dhūn,** *(temps)* **wɔ̀,** venir au secours **tá … dhɛ̀,** venir chez qn **zūɯn bhɛ̄n bhà, dhūn bhɛ̄n kèŋ̀,** viens chez moi **dhūn n̄ kèŋ̀**
vent *m* **tɛ́ɛ**
vente *f* **dhɔ́ɔdɔ̄**
ventilateur *m* **tɛ́ɛkʌ̄bùbù**
ventre *m* **gú, gblɯ́ɯ, gblɯ́ɯdhɛ̀**
ver *m* : ver de cola **pɛ̀n,** ver de Guinée **bhīʌ́,** ver de terre **dhìaa,** ver intestinal **bhīʌ́dhʌ́n, bhīʌ́ yùa**
véracité *f* **tæ̀æn-dhɛ̀**
verbe *m* **vēbɤ̂**
verdure *f* **blʌ̄ʌ**
verge *f* **klàa,** un verge de balai **sɛ̀nŋgā**
véritable **dèe, dèedhē, kpɛ̄ɛnŋdhɤ̄**
véritablement **dhɛ̀ɛ, kɔ̀**
vérité *f* **pɯ́u, tæ̀æn,** parole véridique **tæ̀ænwɔ̀,** il a dit la vérité **yà pɯ́u pɤ̄**
verre *m* **vɛ́dhɛ́**
vers **dhíɤ,** vers cela **à̰ pɛ́ɛn tà,** vers l'eau **bhàa**

verser **kʌ̄, lòo, wɛ̀nŋ,** verser de l'eau **yí kpɔ́**
vert *(non-mûr)* **sæ̀æ,** couleur verte **gblɛ̀eyídhē**
vertèbre *f* : vertèbres cervicales **bhɔ̄gā,** vertèbre de serpent formant une des articulations du hochet-sonnaille **yɔ̋ŋ gā**
vertex *m* **gwìnŋ̀dhɛ̀**
vertige *m* **gbœ̀œdhɛ̋,** avoir des vertiges **gúɯ-dhìʌʌn, gúɯ-zīɤ,** il a eu le vertige **gbœ̀œdhɛ̋ yà dà à gúɯ**
vésicule *f* biliaire **kʌ̋ʌ**
vessie *f* **wēɛ̋ kɔ́**
vêtement *m* **sɔ̄,** vêtement recherché **sɔ̄gā**
veuvage *m* **gɛ̀ɛn**
veuve *f* **gɛ̀ɛndhɛ̀,** elle est devenue veuve **yà gɛ̀ɛn kʌ̋n**
viande *f* **wɯ̄ɯ,** il aime trop la viande **yɤ̀ bhɯ́ɯ kʌ̀**
victime *f* immolée **sâà pʌ̄**
vide **fíʌʌ, wɛ̋ɛwɛ̋,** vide *(œuf, noix)* **flő,** les mains vides **kɔ̀ gúɯ fíʌʌ ká**
vie *f* **dhíʌŋ, kpőŋtàadhɛ̀, sìi, tɔ̀sǽæ̀,** vie en aisance *f* **bhēn-dhɛ̀**
vieillard *m* **gɔ̄ɔ̀n zīi, kwɛ̀ɛ, kwɛ̀ɛdhʌ́n,** vieillard décrépit **gbőɔ̀**
vieille *f* **dhʌ̋ndhēdhʌ́n,** vieille *f* décrépite **gbőɔ̀**
vieille femme *f* **dhɛ̋ɛndhʌ́n**
vieillesse *f* **dhɛ̋ɛndhʌ́n-dhɛ̀, kwɛ̀ɛdhʌ́n-dhɛ̀, zīi-dhɛ̀**
vieillir : il a beaucoup vieilli **yà kʌ̄ gbőɔ̀ ká, yà gbőɔ̀ kún, yà gbőɔ̀ kʌ̋n**
vierge *(forêt)* **gœ̄œ, zā,** elle s'est avérée être vierge **yà dhàagā súɯ**
vieux **zīi**
vif *(lumière)* **gbɛ̋ɛ̀,** *(rouge)* **gbàngbàn, gbàngbàndhɤ̀**
vigne *f* **dlɔ̀ɔgādhɯ̀ɯ**
vigoureux **gbɛ̋ɛ̀**
vigueur *f* **gbɛ̋ɛ̀-dhɛ̀**
vilain : il est vilain **à kpʌ̄ʌ yɤ̀ yāa,** jouer un vilain tour à qn **sɛ̄ɛ̋ kpɔ́' bhēn gɔ̀ yígblɯ̀ɯ tà**
village *m* **plɤ̀ɤdhɛ̀, pɤ̀, pɤ̀dhɛ̀, sɛ̋**
villageois *m* **pɤ̀ gúɯ bhɛ̀n**
ville *f* **kwípl ɤ̀ɤdhɛ̀, kwípɤ̀,** *(en opposition au village)* **kwí sɛ̋**
vin *m* **dlɔ̀ɔ,** vin de palme **wē, yɔ̄ yí,** vin de palmier à huile **glʌ̀ʌwē,** vin de palme que l'écorce du "gong" a servi à faire fermenter **gɔ̀ŋ wɛ̀,** vin fade **wē wɔ̋ɔ̀wɔ̀ɔ**
vinaigre *m* **vīdhênglɤ̀**
vipère *f* : vipère du Cap **gɔ̂yíbhɤ̀ɤ,** vipère du Gabon **bhɤ̀ɤ,** vipère qui saute **gɔ̂yíbhɤ̀ɤ**
virginité *f* **dhàagā**
virilité *f* **gɔ̄ɔ̀n-dhɛ̀**
visage *m* **wʌ̄, wʌ̄ʌ́, wʌ̄ʌ́dhɛ̀**
visibilité limitée : une brume est tombée **dhɛ̀ gúɯ yà yà fàadhɤ̀, dhɛ̀ gúɯ yà pű fàadhɤ̀**
visite *f* **tóɔ̀, tùaabhō,** rendre visite **wɔ̀, zūn,** aller rendre visite à qn **dhó bhēn bhà tóɔ̀ gúɯ, ɤ̄ dhɛ̀ŋ bhō bhēn tà**
visiter **lòo … píɤ**
visiteur *m* **dhɛ̀ŋ**
visqueux **dőŋsɯ̀ɯ, dɔ̋ɔndɔ̀ɔn**
vite **píɤ̀, sʌ̀, vắandhɤ̀, wìawìadhɤ̀,** vite et bref **klɤ̋ɤdhɤ̀**
vitesse *f* **bìaŋ, vìtêsɯ̀ɯ**
vitre **dhùaŋdhɛ̀**
vivaneau *m* **kòotīi**
vivant **à yắan, bhɛ̋ɛ̀, bhɛ̋ɛ̀dhɛ̀, yắandhɛ̀**
vivre **kʌ̄,** il a vécu longtemps **yɤ̀ kʌ̄ dhíʌŋ kʌ̀ dɛ̀dɛ̀wō**
voici **à gà, dhèn, kàagà,** voici mon cadeau **bhān gbœ̄œpʌ̀ dhèn,** voici un jour... **kàagà, dhɛ̀kpœ̀œyì do ká...**
voie **zìan**
voilà! **àhâàn**
voir **kpàn, yɤ̄**

voisin *m*, voisine *f* **yȁyɔ̋ɔ**
voiture *f* **gɔ̄**, voitures d'occasion **gɔ̄ kɤ̀ɤkɤ̀ɤ**
voix *f* **wȍ**, voix aiguë **wȍ sɛ̄ɛ̋ndhʌ́n**, voix grave, basse **wȍ kpȉȉ**, en voix basse **wȍ wlɤ̀ɤ**, il a perdu la voix **ȁ wȍ yà bhʌ̋nŋ**, sa voix pèse **ȁ wȍ yɤ̏ gbínŋ̏**
vol *m* *(rapt)* **kwàn**
vol *m* : au vol **bhádhɤ̏**
volant **vàláŋ̏, vòdháŋ̏**
volée *f* d'oiseaux **bhȁan kpɤ̄**
voler *(dérober)* **kwàan, sɯ́**
voler *(oiseau)* **wlɤ̏**
voleur *m* **kwànbhȅn**
vomir, faire vomir **pȅ**
voter pour **bɔ̄ ... ká**
voyage *m* **dhȉʌnŋkwʌ̋nŋ̏pɪ́ɤ, tʌ̋**, aller en voyage **dhó tʌ̋ gɯ́**
voyelle *f* **dhɪ́ɤpāwȍ**, voyelle nasale **yūngɯ̋dhɪ́ɤpāwȍ**, voyelle orale **dhɪ́gɯ́dhɪ́ɤpāwȍ**
voyou *m* **gɔ̄ɔgbɛ̋ɛ̏bhȅn**, petit voyou *m* **ɗȁbɯ̋ɗȕ**
vrai **dèedhē, kpɛ̄ɛnŋdhɤ̄**, c'est vrai! **yɤ̏ dhɤ̋ tæ̏æ̏n ká!**
vraiment **bhāa, ɗȅɗȅwō, dhɔ̀ɔ, gbáȁndhɤ̄, kɛ̀ɛ, àahʌ̋an, dhɛ̋**
vrombir : le hanneton vrombit **vūnŋdhē yɤ̏ wȅ vūuun**
vrooo **vūuun**
vue : il a une faible vue **ȁ yʌ̋n gɯ́ yɤ̏ dhɯ̋ʌʌdhȕʌʌ**, il a une bonne vue **ȁ yʌ̋n yɤ̏ dhȅ yɤ̏ sʌ̏**, il voit mal **ȁ yʌ̋n yáa dhȅ yɤ̄ sʌ̏ ká**
vulve *f* **gwɛ̋nŋ, pʌ̄ʌ, slōo, yȅgā**

W w

wawa *(un arbre)* **dhōȍ**
wèidé *(danse en rond)* **wȅɪ́dhē**
Wobé *(groupe ethnique et sa langue)* **Wɛ̂**
wouuuh **vūúvūú**

Y y

Yacouba *(groupe ethnique et sa langue)* **yàobâ**

Z z

zèle *m* **fȁan**, il travaille avec zèle **yʌ̄ kʌ̄-sɯ̏ fȁan yɤ̏ ȁ tȁ**

Liste des gloses et des abréviations

1, 2, 3 – personnes des pronoms personnels
A – fonction attributive de l'adjectif
ABSTR – suffixe de l'abstrait
AD – cas adessif (provenant de la fusion avec la postposition *tà̰*)
adj – adjectif
adv – adverbe
Ant. – antonymes
Afr. – français africain
anat. – terme anatomique
arch. – archaïque
ART – article défini
AUT – série autonome des pronoms personnels
badin – badin
bot. – mot botanique
chass. – vocabulaire des chasseurs
chr. – mot ou expression utilisé(e) dans la pratique et la littérature chrétienne
CMM – cas commun
CO – série coordinative des pronoms personnels
COM – cas comitatif (provenant de la fusion avec la postposition *kâ*)
conj – conjonction
cop – copule
DIM – diminutif
DUR – marque de duratif
dtm – déterminant
euph. – terme euphémistique
EXCL – pronom exclusif ou MPP exclusive de la 1ère personne du pluriel
EXI – série des MPP existentielles
ext. – par extension
ExtInt. – extra-intensif
f – genre féminin (du nom français)
fam. – familier
fn – nom autosémantique
FOC – marque de focalisation
foc. – forme focalisée de l'adjectif
FUT – futur

gen. – genre
GER – gérondif
gros. – grossier
(gw) – dialecte gouèta
hist. – historique
HPnym – hyponymes
HRnym – hypéronymes
imagé – imagé
IMP – série des MPP impératives
IN – cas inessif (provenant de la fusion avec la postposition *gṹ*)
INCL – pronom inclusif ou MPP inclusive de la 1ère personne du pluriel ou duel
INF – marque de l'infinitif (suffixe tonal extra-bas)
Int. – intensif
IPFV – imperfectif
iron. – ironique
itj – interjection
JNT – série conjointe des pronoms personnels ; forme verbale dans la construction conjointe
Iv. – français ivoirien
(l) – dialecte de la ville de Logoualé
lit. – littéralement
LOC – cas locatif
loc.n – nom locatif
LOG – MPP logophorique
m – genre masculin (du nom français)
(m) – dialecte de la ville de Man
MPP — marque prédicative pronominale
mrph – morphème non-autonome
MSD – marque de masdar (nom verbal)
n – nom
NEG – négatif
neol. – néologisme
NEUT – forme verbale dans la construction de l'aspect neutre
NSBJ – série des pronoms personnels non-subjectifs
num – numéral
onomat. – onomatopée
ORD – suffixe du numéral ordinaire
P – fonction prédicative de l'adjectif

pej. – péjoratif
pers. – personne
PFV – perfectif
PL – pluriel
POSS – marque du possessif ; série des pronoms personnels possessifs
PP – postposition
prev – préverbe
PRF – série des MPP du parfait
PRH – série des MPP prohibitives
pron – pronom personnel
PROS – série des MPP prospectives
prov. – proverbe
prt – particule
PST – passé
qch – quelque chose
qn – quelqu'un
Qsyn. – quasi-synonymes
rare – rare
RCI – République de Côte-d'Ivoire
REFL – pronom réfléchi
REL – conjonction relative
resp. – mot respectueux
restr – restricteur
RETR – marque du rétrospectif
rn – nom relationnel
rude – mot rude
S – fonction prédicative de l'adjectif dans la construction avec la postposition *ká*
SBJV — série des MPP subjonctives
SEQ – conjonction, indicateur des actions subsécutives
SG, sg. – singulier
sp. – espèce
spp. – espèces différentes
SUB – cas subessif (provenant de la fusion avec la postposition *bhȁ*)
SUBS – marque de l'ultérieur
SupInt. – super-intensif
Syn. – synonymes
(t) – dialecte Tɛɛ
(tp) – village du Tokpapleu (Gouèta)

v – verbe
vi – verbe intransitif (sans complément d'objet direct)
vr – verbe réfléchi
vt – verbe transitif (avec un complément d'objet direct)
vulg. – mot vulgaire
!!! – obscène
♦ – tournure idiomatique

Alphabet dan

a	**kw**
æ	**l**
ʌ	**(m)**
b	**n**
bh	**o**
d	**ɔ**
dh	**ɤ**
e	**œ**
ɛ	**p**
ɛa	**r**
f	**s**
g	**t**
gb	**u**
gw	**ɯ**
(h)	**v**
i	**w**
k	**y**
kp	**z**

Table des matières

Préface de la 2e edition (2021) 3
Préface de la première édition (2008) 4
Esquisse de grammaire du dan de l'Est (dialecte de Gouèta) 5
1. Informations générales 5
2. Phonologie 7
2.1. Phonologie segmentale 7
2.1.1. Voyelles 7
Orales 8
Nasales 8
2.1.2. Consonnes 9
2.2. Tons 10
2.3. L'organisation rythmique : pieds 11
3. Morphologie 13
3.1. Parties du discours 13
3.1.1. Critères de subdivision en parties de discours 13
3.1.2. L'inventaire des parties de discours 13
3.1.3. Conversion 14
3.2. Noms 15
3.2.1. « Noms relationnels » et « noms libres » 15
3.2.2. Pluriel 16
3.2.3. Dérivation des noms 17
3.2.4. Composition nominale 18
3.3. Noms locatifs 18
3.3.1. L'inventaire des cas 19
3.3.2. La composition de la classe des noms locatifs 20
3.3.3. Les noms locatifs relationnels et libres 21
3.3.4. Pluriel des noms locatifs 21
3.4. Marques prédicatives pronominales (MPP) 22
3.5. Pronoms personnels 26
3.6. Adjectifs 31
3.6.1. Les trois fonctions syntaxiques des adjectifs 31
3.6.2. Pluriel de l'adjectif 32
3.6.3. L'intensité de qualité 33
3.6.4. Modifications de la base adjectivale 33
3.6.5. Focalisation 34
3.6.6. Dérivation des adjectifs à partir des autres parties de discours 34
3.7. Numéraux 35
3.7.1. Numéraux cardinaux 35
3.7.2. Numéraux ordinaux 37

3.7.3. Noms des fractions....37
3.7.4. Valeur distributive....37
3.8. Verbes....38
3.8.1. Transitif, intransitif, réfléchi....38
3.8.2. « Modes impersonnels »....39
3.8.3. Aspect, temps, modalité, polarité....40
3.8.4. Dérivation et composition verbale....55
3.9. Adverbes....59
3.9.1. La syntaxe des adverbes....59
3.9.2. Les types morphologiques d'adverbes....59
3.9.3. Adverbes locatifs deïctiques....60
3.9.4. Redoublement des adverbes....62
3.10. Déterminants....62
3.10.1. Déterminants à statut pragmatique....63
3.10.2. Déterminants quantificateurs et autres....63
3.11. Postpositions....64
3.12. Conjonctions....65
3.13. Particules phrastiques....66
3.14. Interjections....66
3.15. Pronoms non-personnels....67
4. Éléments de syntaxe....67
4.1. Types de construction nominales....67
4.1.1. Construction génitivales sans connecteur....67
4.1.2. Construction génitivale à connecteur....68
4.1.3. Construction attributive....68
4.1.4. Construction superlative....68
4.1.5. Construction nominale coordinative....69
4.2. Types d'énoncés non-verbaux....69
4.2.1. Énoncé d'identification....69
4.2.2. Énoncé présentatif....70
4.2.3. Énoncé locatif....70
4.2.4. Énoncé qualitatif....70
4.3. Énoncé verbal....70
Références....71
Publications sur la langue dan....72
Introduction au Dictionnaire dan de l'Est – français.... 79
Dictionnaire dan de l'Est – français 88
Index français-dan de l'Est 337
Liste des gloses et des abréviations 405

Musical Improvisation in the Baroque Era

Specvlvm Mvsicae

Edendum Curavit
Roberto Illiano

Volume XXXIII

Publications of the Centro Studi Opera Omnia Luigi Boccherini
Pubblicazioni del Centro Studi Opera Omnia Luigi Boccherini
Publications du Centro Studi Opera Omnia Luigi Boccherini
Veröffentlichungen des Centro Studi Opera Omnia Luigi Boccherini
Publicaciones del Centro Studi Opera Omnia Luigi Boccherini
Lucca

Musical Improvisation in the Baroque Era

EDITED BY

Fulvia Morabito

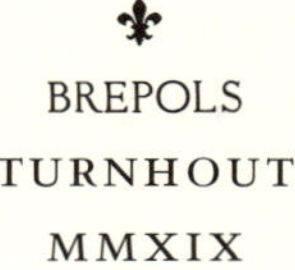

BREPOLS
TURNHOUT
MMXIX

D/2019/0095/18

ISBN 978-2-503-58369-3

Printed in Italy

To Mila,
in memoriam

Contents

Fulvia Morabito
Introduction xi

Improvisation into Composition

David Chung
French Harpsichord *doubles* and the Creative Art of the 17th-Century *Clavecinistes* 3

Massimiliano Guido
Sounding Theory and Theoretical Notes
Bernardo Pasquini's Pedagogy at the Keyboard:
A Case of Composition in Performance? 31

Javier Lupiañez – Fabrizio Ammetto
Las anotaciones de Pisendel en el Concierto para dos violines RV 507 de Vivaldi: una ventana abierta a la improvisación en la obra del 'Cura rojo' 43

Josué Meléndez Peláez
Cadenze per finali: Exuberant and Extended Cadences in the 16th and 17th Centuries 63

Marina Toffetti
Written Outlines of Improvisation Procedures in Music Publications of the Early 17th Century: The Second (1611-1623) and Third (1615-1623) Book of *Concerti* By G. Ghizzolo and the Motet *Iesu Rex Admirabilis* (1625-1627) by G. Frescobaldi 81

Issues of Performance Practice

Giovanna Barbati
«Il n'exécute jamais la Basse telle qu'elle est écrite»:
The Use of Improvisation in Teaching Low Strings 117

Anthony Pryer
On the Borderlines of Improvisation:
Caccini, Monteverdi and the Freedoms of the Performer 151

Laura Toffetti
«Sostener si può la battuta, etiandio in aria». Testi e contesti
per comprendere l'invenzione e la disposizione del discorso musicale
nel repertorio strumentale italiano fra Seicento e Settecento 175

Rudolf Rasch
Improvised Cadenzas in the Cello Sonatas Op. 5 by Francesco Geminiani 195

Contemporary Treatises,
Pedagogical Works, and Aesthetics

Valentina Anzani
Il mito della competizione tra virtuosi:
quando Farinelli sfidò Bernacchi (Bologna 1727) 223

John Lutterman
Re-Creating Historical Improvisatory Solo Practices on the Cello:
C. Simpson, F. Niedt, and J. S. Bach on the Pedagogy
of *Contrapunctis Extemporalis* 241

Francesca Mignogna
Accompagnamento e basso continuo alla chitarra spagnola.
Una cartografia della diffusione dei sistemi di notazione stenografici
in Italia, Spagna e Francia tra xvi e xvii secolo e loro implicazioni teoriche 261

Guido Olivieri
Naturalezza o artificio: riflessioni su improvvisazione
e virtuosismo italiani in Francia nel Settecento 287

Neal Zaslaw
«Adagio de Mr. Tartini. Varié de plusieurs façons différentes, très utiles aux personnes qui veulent apprendre à faire des traits sous chaque notte de l'Harmonie…» 301

The Art of Partimento

Simone Ciolfi
Cantata da camera e arte del partimento in Alessandro Scarlatti. «An Historical Link between Baroque Recitatives and Development Section of the Sonata-Form Movements?» 323

Marco Pollaci
Two New Sources for the Study of Early Eighteenth-Century Composition and Improvisation 343

Giorgio Sanguinetti
On the Origin of Partimento: A Recently Discovered Manuscript of Toccate (1695) by Francesco Mancini 353

Peter van Tour
«Taking a Walk at the Molo»: Partimento and the Improvised Fugue 371

Abstracts 383

Biographies 391

Index of Names 395

Introduction

Body and Soul

Everyone has had the experience of listening to a railway station or airport announcement. The speaker, non-human, is an aural scanner, that is, software that translates written information into sound. The total lack of expression and of cadence is striking, even though making sense. One has the same impression listening to a piece of music reproduced in one of the many music word processing programs — particularly the less sophisticated ones. The notes, all having identical 'specific gravity', are a dry sequence of sounds lacking that breath of life capable of transmitting any emotional content. Clearly the aural reception of music, whose end is the aesthetic enjoyment of a piece, is arrived at by stages that go beyond the mere sonic translation of the notes.

By way of analogy with the human body, musical notes constitute the skeleton of the composition, the responsibility of the composer. Body and soul are vouchsafed by interpretation and by improvisation, both the responsibility of the executant. Musical interpretation is a cluster of manifestations that somehow fall into the realm of predictability. A composer can expect that every executant will render the sounds of the score as he conceived it in a personal manner, including tempo nuances, dynamics, articulations, etc. Improvisation, on the other hand, implies an unpredictable, 'unrehearsed' gestural expressiveness, even if admissible by contemporary aesthetic canons. Into this realm falls a series of 'adulterations' of the score consisting of the addition of ornaments, cadenzas, and vocal and instrumental parts, as well as the alteration of the instrumental complement, etc.[1]

Composition, interpretation and improvisation render a unique and unrepeatable sounding version of every piece of music, even when it is the same piece, just as every human being is unique and unrepeatable.

Moreover, this concept must be placed in historic perspective. Musical notation, in its oldest form dating to Hellenic culture and before that to Mesopotamian culture, flourished in a context in which music was transmitted chiefly by oral tradition, having the primary function of an *aide-mémoire*. Only in the late Middle Ages did notation begin to become increasingly sophisticated, until the present day — sophistication understood

1. See Rasch, Rudolf. 'Preface', in: Rasch 2011.

as the means of fixing on paper as many parameters of musical execution as possible, the will of the composer asserting itself with more and more forcefulness and with less and less concession to the inspiration of the executant. In this interactive process, Baroque music is based on an advanced notational system that nevertheless allows an ample margin for interpretation and improvisation. In other words, the notation can indicate the sounds autonomously but requires the help of an oral tradition in order to be fully intelligible.

This is even truer if we consider that the Baroque signaled the passage from *musica mensurabilis* to accompanied monody, or rather from a musical concept focused on the mathematical relationships of sounds, to a concept based on the *affects*. Music is no longer an 'abstract game' of arithmetic relationships, but aims at interpreting the human passions, in instrumental music, and even more in vocal music. The Monteverdian aesthetic takes root, according to which the *prima prattica* gives way to the *seconda prattica*, when the texts, no longer subordinate to musical exigencies, assert their ascendancy over the music, subjecting it to their dramatic effect. Thus, the musical notation of the time is distinctly inadequate to express all the dynamic shades between loud and soft, between fast and slow, and fails to distinguish «sudden or prepared interruptions, pronunciation, declamation, syllabification or murmuring, accentuation, breathing, tranquility or excitement»[2]. Just as the alphabet, by itself, indicates the words on paper but does not suggest their expressive relationships, so the Baroque score, though indicating the pitch and the relative duration of the notes, is incapable of suggesting the nuances of tempo, the intricate linkages that give meaning to the music, infusing it with the 'breath of life' referred to above. To lend significance to a verbal or musical discourse the phenomes and sounds must be subjected to the laws of τέχνη ῥητορική of classic memory. The penalty for infraction: a kind of aphasia in which, though the words are pronounced correctly, the phrase structure and the melodic coherence of the language are altered, to the detriment of expression, and ultimately of communication.

The Form of the Ephemeral

But, musically speaking, especially in the Baroque period, of what did this *quid* consist, that signaled the divide between inexpressivity and expressivity? Many techniques were called into play. One could execute simple variations, regarding embellishments — adding or omitting them —, diminutions, harmony, rhythm, texture — to be attenuated or enriched —, tessitura — transposing up or down —, chordal figuration of the bass —

2. Quoted from the article of Laura Toffetti in this volume, p. 179: «[...] l'interruzione brusca o preparata, il pronunciare, declamare, sillabare o sussurrare, il porre accenti, il respirare, l'attendere o il concitare [...]».

broken or arpeggiated. Or one could expand a pre-existing idea by repeating notes or melodic-rhythmic patterns, and new musical material could be added, such as dissonant notes, chromaticisms, imitation, *petite reprise*, transition passages, more or less extended cadenzas, *prima volta* and *seconda volta*, refashioning of the bass etc.

It goes without saying that in such a context it is the executant that makes the difference. And the theoreticians, following with little delay the practice of performers, were also aware of this. Already in the Fifties of the sixteenth century, Vincenzo Galilei, Gioseffo Zarlino and Nicola Vicentino noted the fact that a musician who follows slavishly the written score without adding anything will be considered a sort of surveyor, a clumsy and ignorant dabbler[3]. The disparity with the past is great: music, previously esteemed among the liberal arts of the *quadrivium*, because able to embody the numerical ratios that underly all acoustical phenomena, from the most elementary to the harmony of the spheres, now descends to the 'servile' level of vocal and instrumental performance.

The phenomenon of virtuosity overflowed. Now, for the first time in the history of music, we have the exaltation of the outstanding performer, capable of ornamenting, extending and expanding a musical text, improvising *en souplesse*, that is, without stumbling when confronting *ex-tempore* what was not rehearsed. The virtuoso is a 'brand': the emotional mediator between the written text and its aural reception creates a unique and unrepeatable product, since it is the expression of the player's personal inspiration, technical ability and artistic background. From here on we have the incessant exploration for compositional/executive solutions (let us not forget that at the time there did not exist the distinction between composer and interpreter to which we have become accustomed by the history of modern and contemporary music), perpetually hovering between homage for the glorious past and succumbing to the seductiveness of the new, between restraint and excess, 'good taste' and mere athleticism, in a dialectic consummated at the personal level as well: the irregular stylistic development of Tartini is the proof[4]. Now we also have the ambivalent attitude of several virtuosos towards self-promotion: the allure of public exposure, with all that it entails, is counterpoised by the fear of revealing one's 'secret', or indeed one's own stylistic identity, which during the act of improvising exteriorizes its most tangible and genuine characteristics.

This concern manifested itself above all in the area of teaching. The attitudes of virtuosi varied from case to case, at times sharply diverging: Locatelli taught exclusively amateurs, Tartini founded the School of Nations. But it bears emphasizing that the art of improvisation, paradoxically, is learned. The elaborations of the written text are free but not anarchic, in that they benefit from pre-existing models, transmitted, in the most fortunate

[3]. See the article of Laura Toffetti inside this volume, pp. 182-183.

[4]. See the contribution of Neal Zaslaw in this volume.

cases, by the virtuosos themselves. In this sense one may speak of free composition and codified improvisation.

An essential element in the training of musicians in the Baroque and pre-Romantic era was the memorization of melodic and harmonic patterns that facilitated improvisation. Volumes of solfeggi, partimenti, *regole*, *principi*, *lezioni*, *zibaldoni* proliferated, that is, collections of melodies and basses, figured and unfigured, drawn from the repertory or not, to learn, to store up and dust off both in the act of composing and during performance, in order to develop expertise in the art of counterpoint, diminution, improvisation and accompaniment[5]. This didactic regime must also be followed by present-day musicians who undertake to execute correctly the repertory of the seventeenth and eighteenth centuries.

The actual practice of Baroque improvisation, an ephemeral art that dies at the moment of creation, is, for obvious reasons, not documented. Our understanding and reconstruction of the phenomenon comes from treatises and manuals, and from documentary testimonies. There are cases, however, in which improvisation has fortunately been preserved on paper. Albeit most of the music of the period has come down to us by way of 'approximate' notation of what can be done in the performance, certain cases, sporadic, but not exceptional, attest to a 'prescriptive' notation indicating what should be done in a performance, if not indeed 'descriptive' of what was done by a specific performer on a specific occasion. These sources are usually in manuscript, since published music is intended for a heterogenous public, and tends to be as generic as possible. Yet there are cases in which this type of music vividly evokes improvisatory practice: improvisation has become composition, as in *doubles*, cadenzas, caprices, toccatas, etc.

From what has been said thus far it is obvious that the aural realization of a Baroque piece of music cannot proceed without preliminary study of the historical context, of the theoretical and documentary evidence and of philological exegesis of the sources. Baroque music is a meeting ground between the competence of the musicologist and that of the musician, called upon by necessity to collaborate on the 'restoration' of the musical monument for which there exists no primary source (= sonic recording), but only secondary sources (= codified and written indications, mostly concise, of the aural realization).

As a musicologist, I would emphasize that the philological reconstruction of texts should be fashioned according to the peculiarity of the repertory in question. If it is true that the goal of philology is to restore a text shorn of the contaminations of tradition and as near as possible to the last wishes of the composer, it is also true that in a context in which

[5]. Van Tour 2015, p. 19.

the same piece is never played twice in the same manner, there can arise several versions of equal authority. The philologist should consider all the information potentially useful to the performer without constricting the latter's improvised inspiration. As for authorial variants, one should evaluate the nature of each, distinguishing between substitutions and alternatives, and document these last without suppressing them, thereby imposing a choice. In the case of traditional variants, a heavily interpolated text can also be of great documentary value, worth at any rate placing in an appendix.

The sonic restoration of the Baroque repertory thus necessitates musicians who are 'historically informed' and 'practically trained' in improvisation.

Inside the Volume

The contributions to the present volume, which elaborate in turn upon the themes treated in this introduction, are drawn from the talks given at an International conference entitled *Musical Improvisation in the Baroque Era*, held in Lucca from 19 to 21 May 2017, organized by the Centro Studi Opera Omnia Luigi Boccherini in collaboration with *Ad Parnassum. A Journal of Eighteenth- and Nineteenth-Century Instrumental Music*. The scholarly committee consisted of Simone Ciolfi, Roberto Illiano, Fulvia Morabito, Massimiliano Sala, Rohan H. Stewart-Macdonald (†), and the keynote speakers were Guido Olivieri, Giorgio Sanguinetti and Neal Zaslaw.

The articles have been organized into the following four thematic areas: 1) 'Improvisation into composition'; 2) 'Issues of Performance Practice'; 3) 'Contemporary Treatises, Pedagogical Works, and Aesthetics'; 4) 'The Art of *Partimento*'. This grouping should not be understood as airtight compartments as the contributions, though belonging to a distinct category, often reveal a stimulating ambivalence.

This volume is not the first on musical improvisation, nor will it be the last, as it follows a path much-trodden in the past few years. The reason without doubt lies in the fact that our present way of understanding musical notation, vitiated by the Romantic and post-Romantic eras, has accustomed us to regard the score as a form of exhaustive communication — at least in so far as the fundamental parameters are concerned — to transform on the sonic level the 'sacred' intentions of the composer, no longer a craftsman, but an artist. The approach to music in the Baroque era, as we have seen, was completely different, and it is the responsibility chiefly of musicology to throw light on the subject, often extrapolating from the repertory that kind of 'soft theory' that is confirmed and completed in the 'hard theory' of traditional treatises.

***

I would like to to thank the editorial staff of the Centro Studi Opera Omnia Luigi Boccherini, in particular, Roberto Illiano and Massimiliano Sala, for their work. As well, a warm thank goes to Warwick Lister for having translated my Introduction, and to Jennifer Walker for her careful assistance with the revision of some English texts.

This book is dedicated to Mila, who has always exhorted me to live life intensely, also for her, when without her.

Lucca, Winter 2019

Fulvia Morabito
Translation by Warwick Lister

Bibliography

Rasch 2011
Beyond Notes. Improvisation in Western Music of the Eighteenth and Nineteenth Centuries, Turnhout, Brepols, 2011 (Speculum musicae, 16)

Van Tour 2015
Van Tour, Peter. *Counterpoint and Partimento: Methods of Teaching Composition in Late Eighteenth-Century Naples*, Uppsala, Acta Universitatis Upsaliensis, 2015 (Studia musicological Upsaliansia. Nova Series, 25).

Zarlino 1558.
Zarlino, Gioseffo. *Le Istitutioni harmoniche*, Venice, Pietro da Fino, 1558.

Improvisation into Composition

French Harpsichord *Doubles* and the Creative Art of the 17th-Century *Clavecinistes*

David Chung
(Hong Kong Baptist University)

Introduction[1]

The seventeenth-century French harpsichord repertory developed from a largely improvised art in which the notation served as an *aide-mémoire* to a form with highly sophisticated notation in which the details carefully marked by the composer were expected to be observed meticulously by the performer[2]. The lack of a single, definite source for much of this repertory continues to perplex many scholars and performers[3]. Understanding the repertory's creative evolution would undoubtedly be beneficial to all those interested in 17th-century French harpsichord music.

Through an in-depth study of pieces with *doubles*, this article delves into performance practice issues pertinent to this repertory and explores the creative processes of playing and teaching by 17th-century musicians in the quasi-improvisatory tradition. Three issues will be considered in detail: (1) the art of embellishment and variation; (2) the ways in which 17th-century musicians cultivated their individual artistic voices; and (3) what concordant versions tell us about the performance of this repertory.

Definitions and Functions

Doubles, a type of variation, seem to have originated in the 17th-century *airs de cour*, with notable examples composed by Bénigne de Bacilly (1621-1690) and Michel Lambert

[1]. The author acknowledges the support of a General Research Fund (HKBU 12401714) awarded by the Research Grants Council (RGC) of Hong Kong, without which the timely completion of this article would not have been possible.

[2]. See Gustafson 1995, pp. 118-119: «French harpsichord music of the seventeenth century was to a significant extent an improvisatory art».

[3]. A major exception is music by Jean Henry D'Anglebert, which survives in both an autograph source (F-Pn Rés. 89ter) and a printed source meticulously prepared by the composer himself (Paris, 1689). See Harris 2009, vol. ii, pp. 79-102 for a discussion of the latter sources and other manuscripts containing D'Anglebert's works for the keyboard.

(1610-1696) in the decades between the 1640s and the 1660s[4]. In the *airs de cour* repertory, *doubles* are the second strophes (or couplets), in which the melody of the first verse is embroidered with diminutions and passages. Those published by Bacilly typically comprise ornamented melodies alone, without the bass[5]. The word «variation» is commonly found in English manuscripts during this period, such as in the recently rediscovered Selosse manuscript (see Leech 2008, no. 14b)[6].

In French harpsichord music, however, a *double* is usually a separate, embellished version that follows the original piece[7]. Some composers provide *doubles* of their own, but it is common practice to make a *double* from an existing piece by another composer, sometimes in homage. A piece by Marais, for example, is entitled *Rondeau redouble* in a manuscript compiled by Charles Babel[8]. In the recently rediscovered «Borel» manuscript, 10 pieces are followed by their «*redoubles*»[9].

The repertory of harpsichord *doubles* includes many courantes and menuets, as well as several bourrées, gavottes, sarabandes and other dances. Hardel's Gavotte and the C major Gavotte by Lebègue appear to have been very popular, as they were circulated in many manuscript sources.

Authorship of *doubles*

Appendix 1 provides a list of *doubles* made by the composers themselves (i.e., with both the principal piece and its *double* by the same composer). With the notable exception of those by Louis Couperin, many pieces in this category were published in collections of Chambonnières, Lebègue, D'Anglebert and Jacquet de la Guerre. Appendixes 2 and 3 list *doubles* based on works by other composers — by D'Anglebert and Louis Couperin, respectively[10]. An instrumental version of D'Anglebert's Lully Courante, for example,

4. See Gordon-Seifert 2011, pp. 1-9 for an in-depth discussion of the *airs de cour* repertory.

5. The expressive function of embellishment was emphasized by both Marin Mersenne and Bacilly. See *ibidem*, p. 115.

6. See Leech 2008, pp. v-viii and Gustafson 2018, p. 22 for a discussion of the Selosse manuscript, which is privately owned by Peter Leech.

7. In D'Anglebert 1689, the composer provided *doubles* for three courantes (G major, G minor and D minor). The shorter D minor courante and its *double* (pp. 73-74) were spread over two facing pages. For the longer G major and G minor courantes (pp. 5-8 and 41-44), the principal piece and its *double*, each engraved on two facing pages, were separated by a page turn. Similarly, the *doubles* copied by Marc Roger Normand Couperin (e.g., «Gavotte de Mr Hardel» and «Double de la Gavotte» in ff. 56^{v}-58^{r}) are clearly separated versions of the original pieces.

8. Gb-Lbl Ms Add 39569, no. 163. See Gustafson 1990 for a discussion of Babel's role in pieces he compiled.

9. See Moroney 2005, pp. 23-26 for an inventory of the «Borel» manuscript.

10. See Wilson 2013, pp. 6-25 for the argument that some of the pieces attributed to Louis Couperin in the so-called Bauyn (F-Pn Rés. Vm7 674-675) and Parville (US-BEm MS778) manuscripts could instead

survives in the 1695 'Philidor' manuscript (F-Pn Rés. F. 533). D'Anglebert's own setting, published 6 years before the date ascribed to the Philidor manuscript in his *Pieces de clavecin* (1689), is adorned with the composer's characteristic ornaments, and is probably D'Anglebert's own reworking of Lully's lost original. Apart from the Lully Courante, all of the pieces in this category survive in manuscript sources. APPENDIX 4 lists remaining pieces with *doubles* that survive in various printed and manuscript sources. In the majority of these pieces, it is impossible to assume that the *doubles* were made by the composers of the principal pieces. APPENDIX 5 lists a number of *doubles* related to keyboard arrangements of Lully's music[11].

TECHNIQUES OF MAKING *DOUBLES*

Seventeenth-century harpsichordists from Chambonnières to Jacquet de La Guerre tapped into a wide range of techniques beyond melodic diminution. Many of these techniques, such as replacing block chords with broken-chord figurations (commonly known as *brisures*), were ubiquitous in the music of the *clavecinistes*[12]. Yet by blending these conventional procedures with distinctive ideas and musical propensities, each composer created an original musical footprint.

Chambonnières

Chambonnières' *double* to the A minor Courante (1670) demonstrates conventional techniques of making keyboard *doubles*, such as diminution (treble, bass or mixed voices), changes in tessitura, alternate ornamentation and figuration, points of imitation (bars 5, 8-9) and increased rhythmic activity (see Ex. 1). Chambonnières' avoidance of mechanical, predictable patterns (e.g., in the right hand in bar 2) imparts a sense of spontaneity[13]. These techniques were skillfully combined to give shape, variety and sometimes even drama. In bar 2 of the principal piece, for example, the bass branches out into two voices, yielding an additional tenor voice above. In the *double*, the bass also separates into two voices, but this time yields a lower bass voice and a richer sonority in bars 2-3. Significantly, the figurations and diminutions in bars 9-15 are shared equally between the voices.

have been composed by his brother Charles (1632-1675); however, the evidence cited is inconclusive.

[11]. See CHUNG 2015, Introduction, pp. iv, vii for a discussion of *doubles* in the repertory of keyboard arrangements of Lully's music.

[12]. For a discussion of the *style brisé* technique frequently linked to the style of the *clavecinistes*, see LEDBETTER 1987, pp. 45-48.

[13]. See MARTIN 2009, pp. 145-149, for a rhetorical analysis of Jacquet de La Guerre's Allemande in A minor (1687), a good example of «the balance between measure and *mouvement*» characteristic of the 17th-century French harpsichord style.

Ex. 1: Jacques Champion de Chambonnières, Courante in A minor and *Double* de la Courante (*Les Pieces de clavessin, Livre Premier*, 1670, pp. 3-4), bars 1-16.

Chambonnières' *double* above brings to mind Le Gallois' observations on his playing[14].

> [...] & toutes les fois qu'il joüoit une piece il y méloit de nouvelles beautés par des ports de voix, des passages, & des agrémens differens, avec des doubles cadences. Enfin il les diversifioit tellement par toutes ces beautez differentes qu'il y faisoit toûjours trouver de nouvelles graces.

D'Anglebert

D'Anglebert's *doubles* reveal the composer's resourcefulness in combining and varying common procedures to create new shapes and effects. The opening of the G major Courante is a case in point (see Ex. 2). In the principal piece, the rhythmic characteristics of the dance are prominent from the start. The music begins with an upbeat shortened by a *détaché*, followed by a downbeat enhanced by a *tremblement appuyé*. In the *double*, D'Anglebert initiates movement with an upbeat of three quavers. Interestingly, the downbeat is stripped of the *tremblement*, possibly to yield more flow, and the *tremblement* on the third quaver propels the music forward. D'Anglebert uses diminution to create additional shapes. In the opening, a falling and rising shape is complemented by a subsequent rising and falling shape; next, a longer winding passage leads to a cadence in G in bars 3-4. In the *double*, improvisatory gestures and fluid movements take precedence over the rhythmic character of the dance, which is largely delegated to the left hand.

Ex. 2: opening of Jean Henry D'Anglebert's Courante in G major and *Double* de la Courante (*Pieces de clavecin*, 1689, pp. 5, 7).

A similar approach is evident in the D minor Courante (see Ex. 3). In the principal piece, the rhythmic quality of the dance is strongly highlighted. In the *double*, improvisatory gestures and melodic diminutions glue phrases into longer units. The composer makes

[14]. See LE GALLOIS 1680, p. 70.

ingenious use of tensions and resolutions to maintain flow. In the opening bar, for example, he adjusts the note value of the bass and tenor notes to create the expressive dissonance of a major second.

Ex. 3: opening of Jean Henry D'Anglebert's Courante in D minor and *Double* de la Courante (*Pieces de clavecin*, 1689, pp. 73-74).

D'Anglebert's propensity to recompose existing music is demonstrated in his *double* to the C major Gaillarde (Ex. 4). In the principal piece, the rhythmic character of the dance is firmly established from the outset. In the *double*, D'Anglebert creates a new gesture comprising an anacrusis (a three-note upbeat figure), a dotted rhythm, a chord and a bass note. This gesture or its elements are used to bind the piece tightly together throughout the *double*.

Ex. 4: Jean Henry D'Anglebert's Gaillarde in C major and Double (F-Pn Rés. 89ter, ff. 10v-11v), bars 1-8.

In the improvisatory tradition, alternate endings in repeats were often entrusted to the performer. In his *doubles*, however, such as the Gaillarde in C major and the Sarabande in A minor, D'Anglebert wrote out in full alternate and additional endings of increasing complexity. In his *petite reprise* of the Gaillarde in C major, the melody leaps up a fifth to *a'''*, creating a dissonance with the bass that imparts a sense of freshness and a stronger drive towards the eventual cadence (see Ex. 5). In the Sarabande in A minor, the bass is critically retouched in the penultimate bar to produce a strong cadential gesture comprising a striking subdominant seventh chord giving way to an enriched dominant sonority in which the bass leaps down dramatically by a minor ninth (see Ex. 6). Certainly, D'Anglebert's models offer very useful lessons for the modern performer seeking to construct individualized endings.

Ex. 5: endings of Jean Henry D'Anglebert's Gaillarde in C major and *Double* (F-Pn Rés. 89ter, ff. 10v-12r).

Ex. 6: endings of Jean Henry D'Anglebert's Sarabande in A minor and *Double* (US-Cn Case MS VM2.3 E58r, ff. 38ᵛ-39ᵛ).

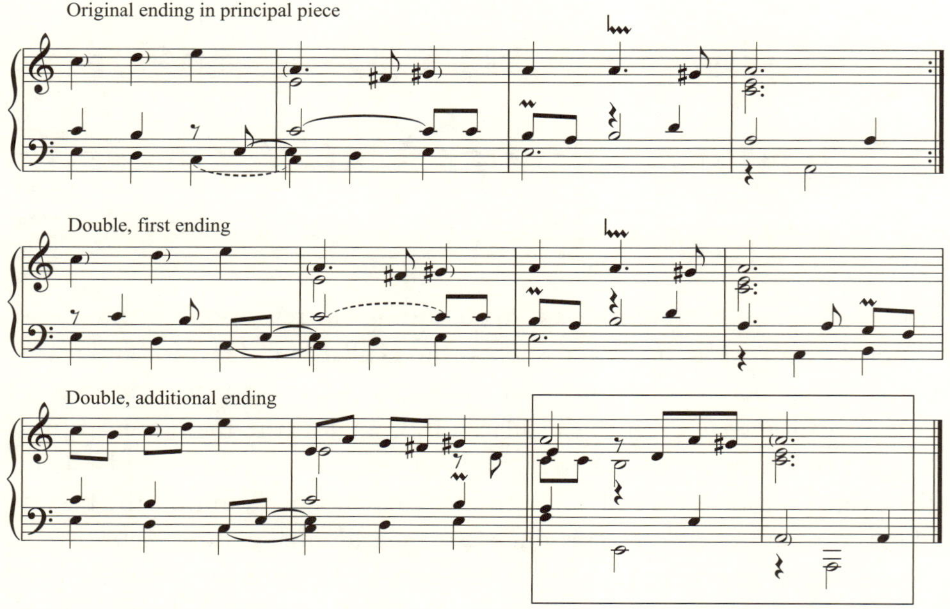

D'Anglebert's sensitivity to nuances (melodic, harmonic, rhythmic, textural) and resourcefulness in recasting existing pieces with expressive shapes and gestures is evident throughout his music. Although space does not allow a comprehensive scrutiny of his music, a few examples will suffice to indicate the palette of effects he painstakingly marked in the notation. In his *double* to Pinel's Sarabande in C major, D'Anglebert's adeptness in recasting lute-inspired textures to give effects idiomatic to the keyboard is in full display; the syncopated repeated notes in the top voice are richly supported by a sonorous accompaniment in the tenor-bass register, possibly referring to the lute's *campanella* effect (see Ex. 7)[15]. In both the principal piece and the *double*, the syncopated rhythms in bars 2-4 of the bass remove the strong accents on the first beats of bars 3-5. In bars 13-16, a quaver movement is woven throughout the texture with *brisures* and diminutions. In his *doubles* to Louis Couperin's Allemande in G and Chambonnières' Courante in G, D'Anglebert offers his signature cadential gesture of two repeated notes followed by a chord (see Ex. 8). In his *double* to Louis Couperin's Allemande, D'Anglebert's use of rhythmically enhanced texture, newly composed motivic gestures, syncopated voices and spicy dissonances add flow, fluidity and spontaneity (see Ex. 9).

[15]. In lute music, the *campanella* technique involves playing adjacent or repeated notes on different courses. The effect of *campanella* is known as «baigné». See LEDBETTER 1987, p. xi for an explanation of these two terms and pp. 79-81 for a nuanced discussion of the assimilation of these lute-originating effects into D'Anglebert's harpsichord music.

Ex. 7: Jean Henry D'Anglebert's Sarabande [de] Pinel in C major and *Double* (F-Pn Rés. 89ter, ff. 6^{v}-8^{r}), bars 1-15.

Ex. 8: cadential gesture in Henry D'Anglebert's *double* to Louis Couperin's Allemande in G major (F-Pn Rés. 89ter, ff. 69^{r}-70^{v}).

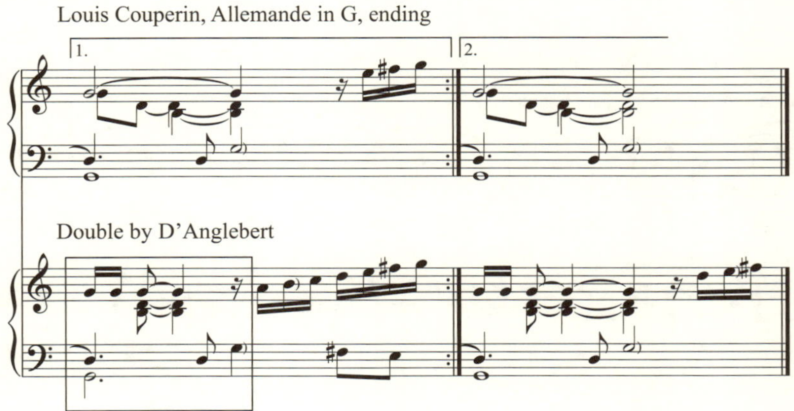

Ex. 9: Jean Henry D'Anglebert's *double* to Louis Couperin's Allemande in G major (F-Pn Rés. 89ter, ff. 68r-69v), bars 1-3.

Louis Couperin

Doubles by Louis Couperin have a strong rhythmic drive and are infused with youthfulness. Outbursts of energy and unreserved virtuosity are distinctive traits of his *doubles*, such as the *double* to Chambonnières' 'Le Moutier', whose running semiquaver passages and chains of sequences reflect a strong Italian influence (see Ex. 10). In Couperin's famous *double* to Hardel's Gavotte in A minor, the semiquaver runs extend the compass by an octave at the end of bar 1, giving clear prominence to the top voice; meanwhile, both texture and ornamentation are simplified (see Ex. 15 below). A similarly extroverted approach can be observed in the *double* to Rigaudon in C. Couperin's tendency to surprise listeners with bold gestures (bar 16) and pungent harmonic effects (bars 4-5) is clearly demonstrated in the *double* to the Menuet de Poitou (see Ex. 11)[16].

Ex. 10: Louis Couperin's *double* to Chambonnières' «Le Moutier» (F-Pn Rés.Vm7 674-675, I, ff. 1r-1v), bars 1-6.

[16]. The piece is simply entitled «de Mr Couperin» in Bauyn II (F-Pn Rés. Vm7 674-675, II, f. 68v). The title «Menuet de Poitou» comes from Parville (US-BEm MS778, p. 100). See Moroney 1985, p. 218 for a discussion of the differences between the two versions.

Ex. 11: Louis Couperin, [Menuet de Poitou] de Mr Couperin and *Double* (F-Pn Rés. Vm7 674-675, II, f. 68v), bars 1-6, 13-18.

de Mr. Couperin

Double

Other composers

Many *doubles* made by other 17th-century composers incorporate the techniques discussed above, although almost every piece offers something unique and special. *Doubles* by Lebègue contain some of the finest examples of melodic diminutions, in which the avoidance of recurrent patterns results in an improvisatory effect. In the Courante de Mr Richard, the rhythmic displacement of melody and bass notes not only gives the music more fluidity and movement, but also somewhat weakens the beat and imparts a harmonic vagueness strongly alluding to lute techniques (see Ex. 12). In bar 6, the repositioning of the melodic note *e''* creates the mild dissonance of a perfect fourth (note *f''*) over the bass, which is quickly resolved. Paradoxically, the note *e''* then creates dissonance in the subsequent dominant chord, enhancing the momentum into the cadence in C. The *double* to the G minor Menuet (1687) by Jacquet de la Guerre deserves special mention (see Ex. 13). De la Guerre varies the repeat in both strains by transferring the diminutions from the melody to the bass (first, using the same bass as the principal piece; and in the repeat, reducing the right-hand melody to either chords or single notes). The *doubles* in the 1707 book demonstrate greater sophistication: existing materials are elaborated through a complex keyboard technique to give a rich contrapuntal texture.

Ex. 12: Courante de Mr Richard and *Double* (F-Psg Ms 2356, ff. 8r-8v), bars 1-6.

Ex. 13: Jacquet de La Guerre, G minor Menuet and *Double* (1687, pp. 38-39), bars 1-8.

Summary of Techniques of Making *doubles*

Table 1 summarizes the common techniques of making *doubles* discussed above. The table reveals that 17th-century harpsichordists tapped into a wide range of techniques beyond merely the diminution of melodies. These techniques can be reduced to three main types, depending on the degree of revision of existing material: (1) variation of an idea; (2) extension and expansion of an idea; and (3) addition of new materials. These techniques can be used either in isolation or in combination to give shape and expression with endless variety, such as by forming irregular phrases and sub-phrases in the melodic line, reinforcing the tenor or bass line, injecting new expressive gestures, enhancing movement and flow by adding various degrees of dissonance and varying (usually increasing) the rhythmic energy for expressive purposes. It is in the last two types (extension/expansion of an existing idea and addition of new materials) that each composer's character and individuality are most strongly revealed; for example, in Couperin's extroverted gestures and harmonic boldness and D'Anglebert's luxuriant ornamentation and expansive textures. Significantly, *doubles* by individual composers contain a wealth of information on the composers' stylistic fingerprints and musical personalities.

Table 1: Summary of Techniques of Making *doubles*

Technique	Description
Variation of an existing idea	diminutions chords to melody block chords to *brisé* chords respaced rhythmic redistribution repositioning of melodic notes change of texture (thickening or thinning) change of tessitura (higher or lower) bass (retouched) different ornaments (including removing existing ones)
Extension/expansion of an existing idea	extending tessitura repetition of notes or musical patterns
Adding new materials	dissonant notes chromatic notes bass recomposed points of imitation new rhythms (e.g. dotted) *petite reprise* different first and second repeats linking passages new ornamentS

Concordances

Concordant versions of pieces with *doubles* contain many differences in notes, accidentals, articulation symbols and other details. Such differences, as scholars have noted, are to be expected in the manuscript tradition[17]. The late arrival of music engraving in the French harpsichord music tradition is often blamed for an imputed lack of precision in notating complex textures and sophisticated ornaments. The variant readings in concordant versions remind modern musicians of the fluidity of 17th-century notation[18].

Hardel's famous gavotte is a case in point (see Ex. 14). This gavotte has survived in more than a dozen manuscript versions, of which five stemming from sources central to the Parisian repertory have been selected for close inspection here[19]. First, the similarities

[17]. See Gustafson 1995, pp. 123-126 for a study of three versions of Chambonnières' Courante in G.

[18]. More recent editions, such as those published by the Broude Brothers, reproduce the different versions, as reproducing different versions of a piece best demonstrates «the range of ways in which a piece was understood in its own day». See Gustafson – Herlin 2017, p. xv. See also Broude 2017, pp. 284-285 for a detailed discussion of the significance of reproducing multiple texts, a procedure known as «versioning», for the 17th-century French harpsichord repertory.

[19]. The five sources are as follows: Bauyn (F-Pn Rés. Vm7 674-675), Parville (US-BEm MS778), Babell (Gb-Lbl Ms Add 39569), F-Pn Rés. F. 933 and Humeau (France, private collection of Philippe Humeau).

Ex. 14: opening of Jacques Hardel, Gavotte in A minor in Bauyn, Parville, Babell, and Humeau (see note 19).

See GUSTAFSON 1979 for inventories of Bauyn, Parville, Babell and Rés. F. 933 and GUSTAFSON 2018, pp. 31-33 for an inventory of the recently rediscovered Humeau manuscript.

in textural details suggest that all versions except the Humeau version derive from a single tradition, although a stemma cannot be established for these sources. In the opening, the melody thickens into two voices before thinning back into one, and the left-hand texture is virtually identical in the first strain in all non-Humeau versions. Given its simplified texture, the Humeau version may have been prepared for (or by) an amateur player. The differences are even more telling, and convey three types of performance practice information: (1) different notations of the same effect; (2) explicit performance information; and (3) alternate figurations or effects.

(1) Different notations of the same effect

The dotted rhythms in Bauyn, Parville and Humeau are obviously written-out *notes inégales*. The scribes of Babell and Rés. F. 933 considered the explicit notation of the dotted effect unnecessary. In bars 7-8, the so-called *tierce coulé*, effectively a grace note linking the interval of a third, is expressed in five ways, including a small note (with and without a slur), a symbol and a real note value (with and without a slur). And in bar 1, both the Bauyn and Parville versions have a 'drier' notation in the left hand than the Babell and Rés. F. 933 versions. This short piece shows us how the same (aural) effect is presented in different notations (visually) in three dimensions critical to interpretation, namely, rhythm (dotted and undotted notation), ornamentation and articulation.

(2) Explicit performance information

Of the five scribes, the Bauyn scribe uses the fewest ornament symbols. The Babell and Rés. F. 933 scribes are more generous in supplying ornaments (bars 3-4, 10-12), sometimes even writing out effects in full note values (see Ex. 14, bar 13) and links at endings and repeats.

(3) Alternate figurations/effects

Some differences appear to be connected with the character of individual musicians. In bar 3 of the *double*, for example, all versions except Babell and Humeau terminate the running passage with a trill on the note *d''* over the subdominant bass (note *F*). The continuation of the run seems to reflect the distinct creative personalities of the Babell and Humeau scribes (see Ex. 15). Both the Rés. F. 933 and Humeau scribes provide explicit links to the opening in the repeat. Whilst the idea of using continuous semiquaver movement is identical, each scribe finds a different way to accomplish this task.

Ex. 15: alternate figurations in *doubles* to Jacques Hardel's Gavotte in A minor, bars 1-4.

Evidence on the page suggests that the Rés. F. 933 scribe was particularly keen on using the *port de voix* (see Ex. 14, bars 6, 9, 13). In bars 8-9, the Babell scribe makes distinctive use of the left hand — in a manner that recalls D'Anglebert — to hold on to notes to achieve greater resonance and to create textured crescendo and diminuendo effects.

Similar observations can be made on the various versions of Chambonnières' Courante in C major, including two versions of D'Anglebert's *double* (see Ex. 16). In the opening bar of the two Roper versions, the right-hand third is staggered, and in D'Anglebert's *double* (in F-Pn Rés. 89ter), the space within the third is further filled up by a gesture that recurs later in the piece (bars 8 and 9). Performance information of particular interest includes different beaming patterns (in Rés. 89ter, quavers are uniquely beamed in pairs, not groups of four), written-out ornaments (e.g., bars 6 and 10), D'Anglebert's characteristic method of substituting a long note with a note followed by an embellished chord (bars 4 and 14), an upbeat transformed into a run (bar 7), alternative ornamentation (bar 3), different notations of the same ornament (bar 13) and the so-called 'wet' and 'dry' notation (bars 2 and 9)[20].

Ex. 16: Jacques Champion de Chambonnières, Courante in C major and *doubles* by D'Anglebert, bars 1-4.

[20]. See Ledbetter 1987, p. 68 for a discussion of the «wet» and «dry» notation.

These different notations of the same effect remind us that during the 17th century, music existed largely as sound, as notation grew out of the need to represent sound on paper. As John Butt so aptly points out (2002), notation in the manuscript tradition was sometimes an example of what could be done, sometimes a description of what had been done and sometimes a solution required by a particular musician or event[21]. Therefore, it is not surprising that different scribes took different approaches to representing music on paper[22]. These multiple versions contain various kinds of performance information (such as written-out embellishments and alternative effects), many of which are beyond the general remit of treatises and tutors. Such information provides the modern performer with an enhanced awareness of the kaleidoscopic range with which an embellished version could deviate from an existing model and more opportunities to translate the inherent richness of original notation into vivid sonic experiences.

Significance of *doubles*

Studying how a composer created an embellished version from an existing piece sheds light on the creative process. As the art of making *doubles* is closely linked to the art of embellishment, the repertory of *doubles* as a whole provides a unique window onto the hidden skills of 17th-century musicians. Without *doubles*, we would be deprived of many embellished pieces, such as the superlatively virtuosic and colouristic versions composed by Louis Couperin.

Doubles based on existing works by other composers bring to light the close relationship between imitation and creativity in 17th-century arts. In 1680, Jean le Gallois strongly promoted the idea that imitating a good model provides a solid foundation for creative development[23].

> L'on peut dire encore qu'il y en a plusieurs autres, qui ont dans leurs manieres de joüer quelque chose de particulier & de beau [...] Il suffit de dire que ces autres manieres de joüer differentes participant plus ou moins des deux premieres [celles de Chambonnières et Louis Couperin], qui sont comme les deux sources d'où les autres derivent.

For Le Gallois, Chambonnierès was unquestionably the best model for other harpsichordists[24].

---

21. Butt 2002, pp. 96-122.

22. In his edition of Hardel's harpsichord pieces, Denis Herlin (in Herlin 1991, p. 20) explains that it is not possible to work towards a single and definitive text of the composer's Gavotte in A minor.

23. Le Gallois 1680, pp. 74-75.

24. *Ibidem*, pp. 70-72.

> Et c'est ce qui a fait que chacun se l'est proposé à imiter comme un parfait modele [...] apres la mort de Chambonniere Hardelle passoit avec raison pour le plus parfait imitateur de ce grand homme [...].

Interestingly, these *doubles* most clearly reveal the composers' distinctive characteristics, such as Louis Couperin's fieriness and D'Anglebert's reflectiveness and sensitivity. Similarly, many musicians stamped their musical imprints on *doubles* with characteristic gestures and ornaments.

Conclusion

The repertory of *doubles* examined here provides insights into the creative processes of performance and teaching during the 17th century and the relationship between imitation and creativity at the core of the 17th-century musical mind. Studying the techniques of making *doubles* allows us to explore in depth the elusive art of embellishment and the resourcefulness with which 17th-century musicians cultivated their individual artistic voices. A closer examination of concordant versions reveals fascinating details of performance. By distinguishing decorative elements from those integral to the musical fabric, the modern performer can cultivate spontaneity while remaining faithful to the original spirit of the music through an increased awareness of the opportunities to fuse knowledge with creativity.

APPENDIXES

Abbreviations and sigla

RISM sigla for libraries are used. Manuscript sources are identified by the locations and call numbers. Codes for printed sources are derived from the year of publication and volume number, if there is more than one publication from the same year. For example, 1670-I (first item in APPENDIX 1) refers to Chambonnières, Jacques Champion de, *Les Pieces de clavessin* [...] *Livre Premier*, Paris, Jollain, 1670. For concordances, only information of *doubles* is included. For a comprehensive list of sources and modern editions, see GUSTAFSON 1979, GUSTAFSON – FULLER 1990, GUSTAFSON – WOLF 1999, and GUSTAFSON 2017.

Other abbreviations

G.: GUSTAFSON, Bruce. *Chambonnières: A Thematic Catalogue, JSCM Instrumenta 1*, <http://www.sscm-jscm.org/instrumenta_01>, accessed 8 October 2018.

LWV: SCHNEIDER, Herbert. *Chronologisch-Thematisches Verzeichnis sämtlicher Werke von Jean-Baptiste Lully*, Tutzing, Hans Schneider, 1981.

APPENDIX 1
DOUBLES BY ORIGINAL COMPOSERS

COMPOSER	PIECE (KEY)	DOUBLE(S)	SOURCE(S)	CONCORDANCE(S)
Chambonnières	Courante (a), G.2	Double de la Courante,	1670-I, pp. 3-6	GB Oldham, ff. 31r-31v F-Pn Rés. Vm7 674-675, I, f. 60r
Louis Couperin (?)	Menuet de Poitou (a)	Double	F-Pn Rés. Vm7 674-675, II, f. 68v, US-BEm Ms 778, p. 100	
D'Anglebert	Courante (G)	Double	1689, pp. 5-8	
D'Anglebert	Courante (d)	Double de la Courante	1689, pp. 73-74	
D'Anglebert	Gaillarde (C)	Double	F-Pn Rés. 89ter, ff. 10v-12r	
D'Anglebert	Sarabande (a)	Double	US-Cn Case MS VM2.3 E58r, ff. 38v-39v	
Gigault	Allemande par fugue (d)	[Double] La mesme allemande avec les ports de voix	1682, pp. 18-19	
Jacquet de La Guerre	Menuet (g)	Double	1687, pp. 38-39	
Jacquet de La Guerre	La Flamande [Allemande] (d)	Double	1707, pp. 1-4	
Jacquet de La Guerre	Courante (d)	Double	1707, pp. 5-7	
Jacquet de La Guerre	Gigue (d)	Double	1707, pp. 9-12	
Le Roux	Menuet (a)	Double du Menuet	1705, pp. 23-24	
Le Roux	Menuet (F)	Double du menuet Double de la Basse	1705, pp. 46-48	
Le Roux	Courante (f♯)	Double de la Courante	1705, pp. 54-55	
Lebègue	Courante (d)	Double	1677, pp. 7-10	US-BEm MS 770, p. 333 D-B Mus. Mu. 40644, f. 87r
Lebègue	Bourée (G)	Double	1677, pp. 43-44	US-Cn Case MS VM2.3 E58r, f. 27r GB-Ob MS Tenbury 1508, f. 33r Gb-Lbl Ms Add 39569, p. 63
Lebègue	2me Courante (C)	Double	1677, pp. 69-70	

Lebègue	Bourée (C)	Double	1677, pp. 73-74	
Lebègue	Gavotte (C)	Double	1677, pp. 77-78	GB-Ob MS Tenbury 1508, f. 5^{r} Gb-Lbl Ms Add 39569, p. 42 F-Psg MS 2374, ff. 8^{r}-8^{v} D-SWl Musik Hs. 619, ff. 84^{v}-85^{r} F-Pn Rés. Vm7 674-675, III, f. 40^{r} US-BEm Ms 778, p. 143 US-BEm Ms 778, pp. 276-277 F Humeau (private collection), p. 19 US-BEm Ms 1371, ff. 75^{v}-76^{r}
Lebègue	Bourée (A)	Double	1687, pp. 49-51	
Lebègue	Gavotte (G)	Double	1687, pp. 91-93	
Perrine	Courante du J.G. (a)	Double	1680, pp. 53-54, 56	
Richard	Courante (a)	Double [by Richard?]	F-Psg MS 2356, ff. 8^{r}-8^{v}	

Appendix 2

Doubles by D'Anglebert of Other Composers' Pieces

Composer	Piece (key)	Source	Concordances
Chambonnières	Courante 'Iris' (C), G.8	F-Pn Rés. 89ter, ff. 2^{v}-4^{r}	US-Cn Case MS VM2.3 E58r, ff. $8A^{v}$-$9A^{r}$ Girard, pp. 9-10 GB Oldham, ff. 17^{v}-18^{r} F-Pn Rés. Vmd. ms. 18, ff. 12^{v}-13^{r} F-Pn Rés. Vmd. ms. 18, ff. 45^{v}-46^{r} F-Pn Rés. Vmd. ms. 18, ff. $18A^{v}$-$19A^{r}$
Chambonnières	Courante 'l'Immortelle' (C), G.9	F-Pn Rés. 89ter, ff. 5^{v}-6^{r}	US-Cn Case MS VM2.3 E58r, ff. $10A^{v}$-$11A^{r}$
Chambonnières	Gigue. La Verdinguette. (C), G.35	F-Pn Rés. 89ter, ff. 9^{v}-10^{r}	GB-Cu MS. Add. 9565, p. 44 (incomplete)
Chambonnières	Courante (G), G.56	F-Pn Rés. 89ter, ff. 71^{v}-72^{r}	
Chambonnières	Courante (G), G.58	F-Pn Rés. 89ter, ff. 73^{v}-74^{r}	
Chambonnières	Sarabande 'Jeunes Zéphyrs' (G), G.59	F-Pn Rés. 89ter, ff. 75^{v}-76^{r}	
Chambonnières	Sarabande 'O beau jardin' (F), G.116	F-Pn Rés. 89ter, f. 52^{r}	
Louis Couperin	Allemande (G)	F-Pn Rés. 89ter, ff. 68^{v}-70^{r}	
Lully	Courante, Mr. de Lully (g), LWV 75/24	1689, pp. 78-80	F-Pn Rés. 89ter, ff. 87^{v}-89^{r} US-BEm Ms 778, pp. 72-73 D-Rtt Inc. IIIc/4, ff. 28^{v}-29^{r}
Pinel	Sarabande (C)	F-Pn Rés. 89ter, ff. 6^{v}-8^{r}	
Richard	Sarabande (G)	F-Pn Rés. 89ter, ff. 80^{v}-82^{r}	

Appendix 3

Doubles by Louis Couperin of Other Composers' Pieces

Composer	Piece (key)	Source(s)	Comments
Chambonnières	Le Moutier, Allemande (C), G.67	F-Pn Rés. Vm7 674-675 I, f. 1v US-BEm Ms 778, p. 118-119 Babell, pp. 148-149 US BEm Ms 1371, ff. 70v-71v	
Hardel	Gavotte (a)	F-Pn Rés. Vm7 674-675 III, ff. 38r-38v US-BEm Ms 778, p. 98-99 US-BEm MS 1372, f. 40r F Humeau, p. 28 GB-Ob MS Tenbury 1508, f. 8v E-Mn MS 1360, f. 227r GB-Ob: Ms. Mus. Sch. E. 426, f. 14v Jeans (private collection) F-Pn Rés. F. 933, f. 10r F-Pn Vm7 137321, p. 26 US-BEm Ms 1371, ff. 57v-58r D-Rtt Inc. IIIc/4, ff. 10v-11r D-Rtt Inc. IIIc/4, ff. 61v-62r F Roanne, ff. 46r-45v	See Herlin 1991, p. 20 for a list of many contemporary transcriptions for lute, flute and voice, and other instruments.
Lebègue	Gavotte (C)	F-Pn Rés. Vm7 674-675, III, f. 40r US-BEm Ms 778, p. 276	Both versions appear to have been corrupt; see Moroney 1985, p. 221.
Lully	Rigaudon, from *Acis et Galatée* (1686) (D), LWV 73/6	US-BEm Ms 778, pp. 138-141	«Double du Rigaudon fait par Mr. Couprain»; see Gustafson – Fuller 1990, p. 383 for comments on the authorship of the harpsichord version.

Appendix 4

Doubles in Other Manuscript Sources

Source(s)	Composer	Title (key)	Double	Comments
B-Bc Ms 27220, pp. 85-86		Allemande (F)	Double	
B-Bc Ms 27220, pp. 90-91		Les plaisirs derobez (d)	Double	
B-Bc Ms 50775, pp. 113-114		Gavotte (d)	Double	
D-B Lynar A-1, pp. 292-293		Courante (D)	[with interpolated variation]	Gustafson – Wolf 1999, no. 20
D-B Lynar A-1, pp. 294-295		Courante (d)	[with variations]	Gustafson – Wolf 1999, no. 21
D-B Lynar A-1, pp. 296-298		Courante (d)	Variatio	Gustafson – Wolf 1999, no. 22
D-B Lynar A-1, pp. 298-299 I-Rvat Chigi Q IV 24, ff. 47r-47v		Courante de La Barre (d)	Variatio	Gustafson – Wolf 1999, no. 6c

D-Rtt Inc. IIIc/4, ff. 17^v-19^v	Chambonnières	La Loureusse (D), (G.11b)	double de La Loureusse	*Cfr.* Gb-Lbl Ms Add 39569, pp. 136-137
D-Rtt Inc. IIIc/4, ff. 2^r-2^v		Menuet (C)	double	*Cfr.* F-Pn Rés Vmd. Ms. 18, ff. 22r, 20Ar
D-Rtt Inc. IIIc/4, ff. 67^v-69^r	Louis Couperin	Courante du vieux Couprin (d)	Double	*double* by Louis Couperin?
F Humeau, p. 3	Chambonnières or Monnard	Sarabande (C), G.150	Double	*Cfr.* Gb-Lbl Ms Add 52363, p. 154
F Roanne, ff. 44^r-43^v		Menuet (d)	[Double]	
F-Pn Rés. 1184, 1185, p. 174		Courante (d)	[with interpolated variation]	Gustafson – Wolf 1999, no. 6
F-Pn Rés. 1184, 1185, p. 337		Courante (C)	[with interpolated variation]	Gustafson – Wolf 1999, no. 3b
F-Pn Rés. Vm7 674-67, 1, f. 19^r	Chambonnières	Courante (d), G.92	Double du meme Auteur	
F-Pn Rés. Vm7 674-67, 1, f. 68^r	Chambonnières	Gaillarde (B-flat), G. 68	Double de la […] par led^r Auteur	*Cfr.* F Oldham, ff. 25^v-26^r
F-Pn Rés. Vmd. ms. 18, f. 22^r		Menuet (C)	double du Menüet (C)	F-Pn Rés. Vmd. ms. 18, f. 47^r F-Pn Rés. Vmd. ms. 18, f. 20^r
F-Pn Rés. Vmd. ms. 18, f. 47^r		menüet (C)	Double	
F-Pn Rés. Vmd. ms. 18, f. 20^r		Menüet (C)	Double	
F-Pn Vm7 6307(2), pp. 4-5		La fustanbert (g)	Double	
GB-Cu Add 9565, p. 44	Chambonnières	Guigue (C), G.35	Double	*double* by D'Anglebert, incomplete
GB-Cu Add. 9565, pp. 13-15		Gavotte (G)	Double	
Gb-Lbl Ms Add 39569, p. 76	Dieupart?	Gavotte (a)		
Gb-Lbl Ms Add 39569, p. 115	Hardel	Gavotte (a)	Double [by Louis Couperin?]	
Gb-Lbl Ms Add 39569, p. 130	Anon.	Sarabande (g)		
Gb-Lbl Ms Add 39569, p. 162	Marais	Rondeau redouble (D)		
Gb-Lbl Ms Add 39569, p. 42	Lebègue	Gavotte (C)		Copy of Lebègue
Gb-Lbl Ms Add 39569, p.63	Lebègue	Bourée (G)		Copy of Lebègue
Gb-Lbl Ms Add 39569, pp. 136-137 D-Rtt Inc. IIIc/4, ff. 18^v-19^r	Chambonnières	Allemande la loureuse (d), G.11	Le Double Double de La Loureusse	
GB-Och Mus. Ms. 1177, f. 2^r		Sarabande (e)	[with variations]	Gustafson – Wolf 1999, no. 19
GB-Och Mus. Ms. 1236, p. 10		Corant (d)	[with variation]	Gustafson – Wolf 1999, no. 6a
GB-Och Mus. Ms. 1236, pp. 11-12 US-NYp Ms. Drexel 5611, p. 103		Courante (d)	[with variation]	Gustafson – Wolf 1999, no. 14
GB-Och Mus. Ms. 378, ff. 3^v-4^v		Courante (G)	[with interpolated variation]	Gustafson – Wolf 1999, no. 15a
I-Rsc MS A/400, f. 48^r	Chambonnières or Monnard	Sarabande (C), G.150	Redoublè	
I-Rvat Chigi Q IV 24, ff. 48^r-49^r		Courante (d)	[with variation]	Gustafson – Wolf 1999, no. 27
US-BEm Ms 1365, 22^r	Brochard	Courante de Mr. brochard (a)	Suitte	
US-BEm Ms 1365, f. 11^r	La Barre	Pauane D'angleterre de Mr. De La Barre (d)	Redouble	
US-BEm Ms 1365, f. 20^v	Chambonnières	autre. Chamboniers (d), G.152	Suitte	attrib. to La Barre in D-B Lynar A-1, pp. 296-298
US-BEm Ms 1365, f. 22^v		Tricotte (d)	redouble	

US-BEm Ms 1365, f. 23^{v}	De La Barre	Courante de Monsieur de la barre organiste du Roy (F)	Redouble	
US-BEm Ms 1365, f. 24^{r}		Royale, courante (g)	Diminu[ti]on	top line only
US-BEm Ms 1365, f. 27^{v}		Sarabande avec le redouble de la main droite et de la gauche (a)	redouble	
US-BEm Ms 1365, f. 28^{r}		Sarabande (g)	redouble	top line only
US-BEm Ms 1365, f. 30^{v}		Tricottez (F)	[redouble]	
US-BEm Ms 1365, f. 9^{r}		Allemande (C)	suitte	
US-BEm Ms 1365, ff. 15^{v}-16^{r}	La Barre	Pauane D'angleterre de Monsr. de La Barre (d)	Suitte, ou redouble	*redouble* by La Barre? *Cfr.* F-Pn Rés. Vm7 674-675, III, f. 29^{v}
US-BEm Ms 1365, ff. 21^{r}-21^{v}	Chambonnières	Courante Chanbon (d), G.153	Suitte	attrib. to La Barre in D-B Lynar A-1, p. 298-299
US-BEm Ms 1371, f. 3^{r}		Sarabande	Double	
US-BEm MS 770, p. 339		Menuet (C)	Double	*Cfr.* US-Cn: Case MS VM2.3 E58r, f. 34^{r}
US-Cn Case MS VM2.3 E58r, f. 34^{r}		Menuet (C)	double	*Cfr.* US-BEm Ms 770, p. 339
US-Cn Case MS VM2.3 E58r, ff. 11^{v}-12^{r}	Lebègue	[Double to Lebègue, Gigue (C)]	Double de le gige en C sol-ut	*Cfr.* 1677, pp. 75-76
US-NYp Ms. Drexel 5611, p. 78 GB-Och Mus. Ms. 1236, p. 3		Coranto (d) [Gibbons/Tresure?]	[variation]	Gustafson – Wolf 1999, no. 6b
US-NYp Ms. Drexel 5611, pp. 104-105		Courante (G)	[with variation]	Gustafson – Wolf 1999, no. 15

Appendix 5
Doubles related to works of Lully

LWV	Work of Lully	Title (key)	Double	Source	Comments
32/7	*Ballet des Muses* (1666)	La Gauotte du ballet (G)	Double de la Gauotte du ballet	B-Bc Ms 27220, p. 42	key of Lully: B-flat
35/4	*Trios pour le coucher du Roy*	Menuet 'Dans nos bois'	2.me couplet de dans nos bois	F-Pn Rés. F. 1091, p. 17	
53/58	*Atys* (1676)	dessente de Cibelle de l'opera d'Atis | Basse Continue (a)	dessente de Cibelle de l'opera d'Atis | Basse roulante (a)	US-BEm Ms 1371, ff. 59^{v}-61^{r}	
54/12	*Isis* (1677)	Air de Trompette (C)	Double de Trompette	US-BEm Ms 1371, ff. 76^{v}-77^{r}	
54/45	*Isis* (1677)	Troisiéme Air (menuet)	Double	F-Pn Rés 476, f. 83^{v}	
57/7	*Bellérophon* (1679)	Menuet (d)	Double	B-Bc Ms 27220, pp. 150-151	incomplete
61/27	*Phaeton* (1683)	Gauotte (C)	Double	US-BEm Ms 777, ff. 2^{v}-3^{r}	
61/28	*Phaeton* (1683)	Gauotte (C)	[double]	US-BEm Ms 777, f. 3^{v}	Vocal item, *double* (bars 13-24) for harpsichord only
73/6	*Acis et Galatée* (1686)	Rigaudon	Double du Rigaudon fait par Mr. Couprain	US-BEm Ms 778, pp. 138-141	See comments in Appendix 3 above
75/24		Courante, Mr. de Lully (g)	Double	1689, pp. 78-80 F-Pn Rés. 89ter, ff. 87^{v}-89^{r} US-Bem Ms 778, pp. 72-73 D-Rtt Inc. IIIc/4, ff. 28^{v}-29^{r}	D'Anglebert/Lully (1689)

Bibliography

Broude 2017

Broude, Ronald. 'Paris *chez l'autheur*: Self-Publication and Authoritative Texts in the France of Louis xiv', in: *Early Music*, xlv/2 (2017), pp. 283-296.

Butt 2002

Butt, John. *Playing with History: The Historical Approach to Musical Performance*, Cambridge, Cambridge University Press, 2002 (Musical Performance and Reception).

Chung 2015

Keyboard Arrangements of Music by Jean-Baptiste Lully, edited by David Chung, 2 vols., Web Library of Seventeenth-Century Music, Monuments of Seventeenth-Century Music, vol. 1 (2015), <http://www.sscm-wlscm.org/monuments-of-seventeenth-century-music/volume-i>, accessed October 2018.

D'Anglebert 1689

D'Anglebert, Jean Henry. *Pieces de clavecin*, Paris, l'Auteur, 1689.

Gordon-Seifert 2011

Gordon-Seifert, Catherine. *Music and the Language of Love: Seventeenth-Century French Airs*, Bloomington-Indianapolis (IN), Indiana University Press, 2011.

Gustafson 1979

Gustafson, Bruce. *French Harpsichord Music of the 17th Century: A Thematic Catalog of the Sources with Commentary*, 3 vols., Ann Arbor (MI), UMI Research Press, 1979 (Studies in Musicology, 11).

Gustafson 1990

Gustafson, Bruce. 'The Legacy in Instrumental Music of Charles Babel, Prolific Transcriber of Lully's Music', in: *Jean-Baptiste Lully. Actes du colloque (Saint-Germain-en-Laye = Kongressbericht Heidelberg 1987)*, edited by Jérôme de La Gorce and Herbert Schneider, Laaber, Laaber-Verlag, 1990 (Neue Hidelberger Studien zur Musikwissenschaft, 18), pp. 495-516.

Gustafson 1995

Id. 'France', in: *Keyboard Music before 1700*, edited by Alexander Silbiger, New York, Schirmer Books, 1995 (Studies in Musical Genres and Repertoires), pp. 90-146.

Gustafson 2007

Id. *Chambonnières: A Thematic Catalogue: The Complete Works of Jacques Champion de Chambonnières (1601/02-1672)*, in: *Journal of Seventeenth-Century Music, JSCM Instrumenta*, vol. 1 (2007), <https://sscm-jscm.org/instrumenta/instrumenta-volumes/instrumenta-volume-1/>, accessed October 2018.

Gustafson 2018

Id. 'Four Decades after French Harpsichord Music of the Seventeenth Century: Newly Discovered Sources,' in: *Perspectives on Early Keyboard Music and Revival in the Twentieth Century*, edited by Rachelle Taylor and Hank Knox, London-New York, Routledge, 2018, pp. 7-45.

Gustafson – Fuller 1990

Id. – Fuller, David. *A Catalogue of French Harpsichord Music 1699-1780*, Oxford, Clarendon Press, 1990.

Gustafson – Herlin 2017
Chambonnières, Jacques Champion de. *The Collected Works*, edited by Bruce Gustafson and Denis Herlin, 2 vols., New York, The Broude Trust, 2017 (Art of the Keyboard, 12).

Gustafson – Wolf 1999
Harpsichord Music Associated with the Name LA BARRE, edited by Bruce Gustafson and Peter Wolf, New York, The Broude Trust, 1999 (Art of the Keyboard, 4).

Harris 2009
D'Anglebert, Jean Henry. *The Collected Works*, edited by C. David Harris, 2 vols., New York, The Broude Trust, 2009 (Art of the Keyboard, 7/1-2).

Herlin 1991
Hardel, Jacques. *Pièces de clavecin*, edited by Denis Herlin, Monaco, Éditions de l'Oiseau-Lyre, 1991 (Grand Clavier, 5).

Le Gallois 1680
Le Gallois de Grimarest, Jean-Léonor. *Lettre de Mr Le Gallois à Mademoiselle Regnault de Solier touchant la musique*, Paris, Estienne Michallet, 1680.

Leech 2008
The Selosse Manuscript: Seventeenth-Century Jesuit Keyboard Music, edited by Peter Leech, Launton, Edition HH, 2008.

Ledbetter 1987
Ledbetter, David. *Harpsichord and Lute Music in 17th-Century France*, London, Palgrave Macmillan, 1987.

Martin 2009
Martin, Margot. 'The Rhetoric of *mouvement* and Passionate Expression in Seventeenth-Century French Harpsichord Music', in: *Seventeenth-Century French Studies*, xxxi/2 (2009), pp. 137-149.

Moroney 1985
Couperin, Louis. *Pièces de clavecin*, edited by Paul Brunold, new revision by Davitt Moroney, Monaco, Éditions de l'Oiseau-Lyre, 1985.

Moroney 2005
Moroney, Davitt. 'The Borel Manuscript: A New Source of Seventeenth-Century French Harpsichord Music at Berkeley', in: *Notes: Quarterly Journal of the Music Library Association*, lxii/1 (2005), pp. 18-47.

Wilson 2013
Wilson, Glen. 'The Other Mr. Couperin', in: *Early Keyboard Journal*, xxx/30 (2013), pp. 6-25.

Sounding Theory and Theoretical Notes

Bernardo Pasquini's Pedagogy at the Keyboard: A Case of Composition in Performance?

Massimiliano Guido
(Università di Pavia)

Chi avrà ottenuta la sorte di praticare o studiare sotto la scuola del famosissimo Signor Bernardo Pasquini in Roma, o chi almeno l'avrà potuto inteso o veduto sonare, avrà potuto conoscere la più vera, bella e nobile maniera di sonare e di accompagnare; e con questo modo cosí pieno avrà sentita dal suo cimbalo una perfezione di armonia meravigliosa[1].

Francesco Gasparini fully acknowledges his teacher, praising his virtue at the keyboard. Muffat, Berardi, and Pitoni echoed Gasparini's enthusiastic words, reporting about the international students sent to Pasquini by princes from around Europe to learn the true manner of playing. Muffat's parallel between Corelli as Orpheus and Pasquini as Apollo provides a vivid picture of this outstanding couple, actually making music together on many occasions[2].

Why was Pasquini so famous as a pedagogue? What was so unique about his teaching method? To cut to the case, he connected the keyboard technique with the art of composing in a coherent unity, providing the student with all the elements to extemporize music both in the old and modern style directly at the harpsichord. Two of the most excellent teachers and practitioners of historical improvisation, Edoardo Bellotti and William Porter, conclude

[1]. «Who has had the fortune of practicing or studying at the school of the very famous Signor Bernardo Pasquini in Rome, or has had at least the chance of hearing or seeing him playing, that one is exposed to the truest, fanciest, and noblest manner of playing and accompanying. Moreover, through this way [of playing] so full, he has heard from [Pasquini's] harpsichord an astonishing perfection of harmony». Gasparini 2001, p. 62.

[2]. Berardi's passage from *Il perché musicale* is quoted in Morelli 2016, pp. 93 and 332. Muffat studied in Rome with Pasquini during 1681-1682, when he received a paid leave from Salzburg: *ibidem*, p. 98. The comparison is taken from his preface to *Außerlesene mit Ernst- und lust-gemengter Instrumnetal-Music*, Passau, Höllerin, 1701. See Morelli 2016, p. 333.

their essay on the pedagogical perspectives of Pasquini claiming that «his example can be of great value because it stands as a synthesis between theory and praxis, composition and performance, conceived as connected and complementary moments in music making»[3].

In the closing discussion of the 2013 conference on counterpoint and improvisation that I had the privilege to organize, again Porter raised the argument if improvisation were the best word for describing what the old masters were teaching and playing in the Baroque[4]. Actually, his point was more on composition, knowing from direct experience how feeble the demarcation between the two words could be. Also, I guess — we are still debating this issue today. The more we deepen our theoretical and practical understanding, the more written-out and extemporized music-making seem to be an organic, leaving entity. On the one hand, written pieces, far from being fixed once and forever, can be interpreted as traces of an ongoing process of creation. On the other hand, innocent-looking bass lines, cadences, and mechanic patterns drafted on a page and subsequently memorized might develop into a fully-fledged piece[5]. Several scholars are convincingly demonstrating that, in many and complementary ways, these two forms are condensed vehicles for knowledge transferal. Furthermore, they are also the essence of *la più vera, bella e nobile maniera di suonare* (the truest, fanciest, and noblest manner of playing), because they constituted the fundamental skills of a mature professional[6].

Bellotti and Porter draw our attention to the possibility of looking at Pasquini's music (including both didactic works and fully-composed pieces) as a coherent repository of the art of playing. They noticed how the same basic formulas presented in *basso continuo* versets, sonate, and partimenti are inserted in many toccatas, variations, and dances. They also connected a self-evident line between the cadence and progression collections and similar formulas in Pasquini. Their assumptions are also restated and discussed in the very recent work by Arnaldo Morelli, who systematizes Pasquini's biography and the thorough discussion on the sources of his music with new historical evidence. In the chapter about keyboard music, Morelli quotes the 1716 correspondence between Forzoni Accolti and his friend Giovanni Giacomo Zamboni about the music of Domenico Anglesi, suggesting that what is discussed there can be fully applicable to Pasquini: «egli non componeva

---

3. BELLOTTI – PORTER 2012, p. 209. When not otherwise indicated, translations are by the author of this essay.

4. A condensed version is incorporated in the introduction to GUIDO 2017, pp. 1-4.

5. GUIDO – SCHUBERT 2014 demonstrates how a cadential pattern can generate a sophisticated piece of contrapuntal music such as a ricercare. Furthermore, it links the harmonic idea of a cadence to its linear implications, suggesting how the basso continuo practice in Italy was intimately connected to voice leading.

6. Improvisation has never been a *per se* event; it comes out of necessity (practical use within the liturgy or during a performance) and naturally stems from the keyboard during transferal of knowledge. A historically informed approach has to deal with this characteristic adapting it to a different context. Therefore, a particular emphasis is given in the specific literature to the learning process and the benefits of using improvisation in the present-day curriculum. See SCHUBERT – GUIDO 2016, pp. 133-134.

per far mostra del suo sapere, ma solo per la lezzione che di mano in mano conosceva opportuna all'abilità dello scolare» (he did not compose for showing off his knowledge, but for teaching that gradually knew was useful for the skill of the learner)[7]. One can immediately find an echo of Gasparini's words quoted at the opening of this chapter: the absorption of knowledge happens by looking at and listening to the master; writing out pieces or sketches is only a medium for knowledge transferal.

In Pasquini's music, there are some tiny miniatures, dedicated to noblemen, students or simple admirers. They are somewhat rudimentary and look more like drafts to be continued then the shining product of the spark of genius. Morelli stresses the importance of variation settings: Pasquini provides examples and, in some cases, literally exhorts the player to continue as long as he wants or can[8]. Morelli insists on the pieces *sopra il basso*, relating them to the growing tradition of partimento, while dismisses the *Saggi di contrappunto* as a homage to the respected but old school of strict composition. Developing Bellotti's and Porter's approach, I prefer to consider the counterpoint rules as an essential part within Pasquini's pedagogical approach. The figures disseminated within the *Saggi* as a sort of commentary to the counterpoint lines are an obvious link. Furthermore, I will point out some subtler connections.

Pasquini's commitment as a teacher can be evaluated by looking at his works, especially the *Saggi di Contrappunto* (1695), the *Sonate per uno o due cembali* (1703-1704), and the *Versetti con il solo basso cifrato* (1708)[9]. They constitute a homogenous collection in which the learner is exposed to the complexity of composing at the keyboard, from the *stile osservato* to the *stile modernissimo*, as Giuseppe Ottavio Pitoni writes in his *Guida Armonica*[10]. Pasquini deals with counterpoint practically. He does not write a counterpoint treatise, but a collection of examples, *saggi*. These are exercise sketched for the student, his nephew Felice Ricordati, during private lessons, while the master sits with him at the keyboard. As different research projects have recently demonstrated, such an approach is of extreme benefit in our educational system. After more than six decades of Early Music Movement, during which we rediscovered how to deal with historical instruments as to performance practice, technique, and organology, we are finally completing our knowledge with a more historically informed way of teaching and learning counterpoint and composition. Still, the majority of classically trained musicians see composition detached from the keyboard. As a consequence, the primary function of a written out teaching collection as the *Saggi* is obliterated and its value questioned and diminished.

---

7. Morelli 2016, p. 333.

8. *Ibidem*, pp. 334-335.

9. *Saggi di Contrappunto and Regole*, in: Pasquini 2009. *Sonate a due bassi e Versetti*, in: Pasquini 2006a and Pasquini 2006b. My thanks to Armando Carideo, who shared with me his musical transcriptions for setting out the examples in this chapter.

10. Guido 2009, pp. 156-157.

In Pasquini's teaching, music speaks without words[11]. In all the collection there are only a couple of annotations, explaining the avoidance of particular intervals in invertible counterpoint because they would turn into a dissonance. We do find another descriptive text, made of continuo figures, by which Pasquini indicates both the kind of chord and the voice leading. Armando Carideo, in his critical edition, suggests that these figures are Pasquini's guidelines for his nephew[12]. The learner had to follow them and realize a three, four, or five part counterpoint that had to be checked and discussed with the master at the keyboard. Rules were eventually presented aurally, and there was no need for fixing them on paper: the music was clear enough to internalize them. The act of notating voices in a score and not as keyboard tablature is also an exercise of contrapuntal clarity. On the other side, Morelli does not believe that the *Saggi* can be the basis of composing at the keyboard, because he says that they are structured according Fux's species, and he would rather focus on the recurrent harmonic tonal schemes found in the *basso continuo* pieces[13]. More than Fux, Pasquini follows Diruta's *Breve et facile regola*, sketching the usual path from note against note to florid counterpoint. It is also true that we find advanced duos in the style of *bicinia*, modally ordered. However, the quality of the given cantus firmus is evolving throughout the collection[14].

Pasquini gives only two examples of note-against-note counterpoint. The first CF is the most awkward possible, a single note plus a cadence given by a descending fourth (Ex. 1a). This is clearly just about consonances: the student has the chance of learning and memorizing all the possibilities. The only other note-against-note example comes after a few pages, dealing with perfect and imperfect consonances, chains of thirds and sixths, and contrary motion[15]. So far, nothing exciting or particularly exotic. It is like learning to write by following the marks carved on a wax tablet: your hand learns the movement and gains confidence. By now I have memorized the CF: it is so simple that I can venture in transposition without even knowing what transposition is. The only thing I need is a new starting note. I am then so confident that I can immediately play two consonances on each note of the CF and introduce passing notes: dissonances (Ex. 1b).

So now here comes the little magic. I can play a third voice, repeating what I have just played, as long as I pair the two voices using thirds: I need to check if there is a 'hole' in my hand: 1-3 or 2-4. To make it more interesting, I can use faster note values and cross the voices (Ex. 1c). If I realize that I am coming to a unison — the distance between the parts

11. See Bellotti's remarks on 'Counterpoint, the *Seconda Prattica* and the Practice of Basso continuo', in: Pasquini 2006a, p. vi.

12. Pasquini 2009, pp. v-vi.

13. Morelli 2016, p. 340.

14. On Diruta and his integrated approach to fingering, composition, and improvisation see Guido 2012a.

15. Counterpoint xi (Pasquini 2009, p. 6).

Ex. 1a-b: counterpoints I-III.

is narrowing (3-2-1) — I can jump an octave higher and go on. In this way, the student, at the fourth exercise in his notebook, is playing a three-voice florid counterpoint with some canonic entries: this was done more intuitively than we are used to and constitutes one of the reasons for saying that Pasquini was a good teacher.

The second CF is treated precisely in the same way: in the two voice settings, Pasquini introduces some new contrapuntal devices, such as suspension or fourth species. In so doing, he provides the student with different patterns, which can be easily memorized by repetition at the keyboard. Though patterns are explicitly used in the exercises, they are never repeated mechanically[16]. The player is, therefore, guided to develop his musical

[16]. See for instance Counterpoint XIII and XIV (*ibidem*, p. 6).

invention achieving *variety*. The two *bicinia* on the ascending and descending scales, with a florid realization at the bass, are an excellent example: each bar could be repeated and work under all the CF notes[17]. Ex. 2 shows the second version, Counterpoint xviii: Pasquini mixes up the modules in coherent musical structures, usually in groups of two or three bars. Even at the early stage of a strict counterpoint exercise, we find the other fundamental principle in Pasquini's didactical approach: the variation idea. The very same concept praised by Morelli in the written out pieces.

Ex. 2: counterpoint xviii.

[17]. This learning process is a mechanical and mental rumination of patterns through finger motions. The basic idea is the step motion of the CF that is easily fillable with diminutions underneath. Once the learner possesses this skill, the sequent exercise has leaps in the CF that imply a more accurate selection of the notes in the second voice, to avoid jumping from a dissonance.

Pasquini comments upon some of the basses, providing figures. The exciting aspect is that the written out realization is always a polyphonic rendition, with great care about voice leading. Only one *Saggio* in the whole book, Counterpoint LII, has the annotation *io Bernardo*, suggesting that the master realizes the entire setting. It comes just after a three-voice version with fewer figures. Comparing the two exercises, it is evident that the first exercise has almost the identical implied figures (Ex. 3a-b). Pasquini shows how to add a fourth voice developing the same contrapuntal material used by his nephew at the alto part in *Saggio* LI. He also retains the melodic contour of the soprano — almost identical to bar 5 onwards — without changing the melodic range (highest note *g*). The tenor is the new part, to which some of the figures (*aka* contrapuntal movements) are transferred from the preexisting soprano line: the 4-3♯ used by his nephew at the second measure of the soprano in LI is used as the opening movement of the tenor and will be repeated in bar 4 in the soprano, creating an interesting polyphonic texture.

Ex. 3a-b: counterpoints LI-LII.

Figures are used in these exercises as shortcuts for memorizing several linear possibilities above the same basic idea given by the CF movement, following the Italian tradition from Diruta to Banchieri. The contrapuntal quality of the figures is even more evident in more extended exercises where the long-note CF is abandoned for a modern bass line. Once these conducts have been absorbed in this simplified (and regulated) environment, the basic movements can be extended to their real musical appearance, becoming bass lines shaped according to the modern style. The same CF is transformed and its figures almost identically repeated in the 5 voice setting of *Saggio* CVIII.

Ex. 4: counterpoints CVIII.

Before going on with the *Saggi*, I would like to present some other examples of the use of *basso continuo* as a pedagogical tool. In the other main autograph British Library Ms. Add. 31501, there are several collections of *versetti in basso continuo*[18]. They are the first examples of the famous school of Partimento, which would have developed in the Neapolitan conservatories about one generation after Pasquini[19]. This school combines the art of counterpoint with the ability to play diminutions and variations on a given music

18. Pasquini 2006a and 2006b.

19. On Pasquini and partimento see Gjerdingen 2012, Sanguinetti 2012, pp. 58-50, and Morelli 2016, pp. 335-38.

material, grounded on a set of implicit harmonic-melodic conventions, or schemata. The simplest verses are nothing but an embellished cadence, ornamented in different ways. This connects the collection on the one hand to similar works from Fattorini up to Spiridion, on the other to the same cadential patterns found in the *Saggi di contrappunto* and the written-out pieces. In their study about Pasquini's pedagogy, Bellotti and Porter identify five different categories of versetti:

a) versetto-cadenza with or without passages in the bass;

b) versetto with imitazioni;

c) versetto-sequence;

d) versetto-fugato;

e) versetto-adagio[20].

Especially the cadential and sequential types are built on repeated patterns that had to be memorized by the student. Ex. 5 shows the first 6 versets in D, all derived from the basic cadential idea of number 1.

Ex. 5: versets in D *for answering to the choir* (1-6).

If we take Pasquini's opening rubric seriously, these versetti are not only a didactic collection *per se*, but they serve a liturgical function: respond to the choir. Since 1605, the bass as a *true and specific way* for improvising verses had been introduced in Banchieri's

20. Bellotti – Porter 2012.

Organo suonarino[21]. It insisted on the contrapuntal tradition found in both counterpoint tutors such as Diruta's *Il Transilvano* and entirely composed collections like the *Musica Nova* of 1540. Responding to the choir is a set or two of entries in imitation plus a cadence on the right ecclesiastic tone. It is no surprises that a careful examination of the figures, especially in the imitative verses, suggests a contrapuntal realization. If it is so, Pasquini uses figures in a quite similar way then he does in the *Saggi*, especially the more advanced, as shown in Ex. 6.

Ex. 6: versets in G *for answering to the choir* (5-6).

Another promising comparison is between the verses and some fully written-out pieces, especially toccatas and variations settings. Again, Pasquini seems to apply the same principles of polyphonic schemes and cadences, adding the roundness of ornamental figurations to enrich the basic idea[22]. As it is written in the Noto's partimento collection: *apre gli occhi*[23]!

I would like to come back to the 'sounding theory' in the title of this article. Thomas Christensen, in his lecture 'Fragile Texts, Hidden Theory,' given at the 2012 meeting of the Society for Music Theory, talked about a discursive theory, bound to notions of authorial agency and textual representation. He then developed the idea in his chapter

21. Guido 2013.

22. Guido 2012b examines the variety of compositional schemes used in Pasquini's toccatas.

23. I-NT, *Fondo Altieri* 28, c. 89v, quoted in Morelli 2016, p. 330.

'The Improvisatory Moment' in *Studies on Historical Improvisation*[24]. He claims that, in the history of music theory, there are many examples in which theoretical knowledge is disseminated through 'fragile texts', from which the discursive part is almost eliminated. He concludes that it is possible to have music theory even without texts, a sort of 'hidden theory', transmitted within a pedagogical system centered on the direct making of music. Pasquini provides an outstanding example of this hidden praxis if we stop to question if we are dealing with improvisation within composition: theory is sounding, and notes are assuming a theoretical value.

Credo che la Fama abbia spezzate le trombe,
non avendo più voce per pubblicare i suoi applausi,
et io sospenderò la penna,
per non aver concetti adeguati per tesserae le sue lodi.
Ottavio Pitoni, *Guida Armonica*[25]

Bibliography

Bellotti – Porter 2012

Bellotti, Edoardo – Porter, William. 'Pasquini e l'improvvisazione: un approccio pedagogico', in: *Pasquini Symposium. Convegno Internazionale (Smarano, 27-30 Maggio 2010). Atti*, edited by Armando Carideo, Trento, Giunta della Provincia autonoma di Trento-Assessorato alla cultura, rapporti europei e cooperazione, 2012 (Quaderni Trentino Cultura – Cultura per il territorio, 17), pp. 195-210.

Christensen 2017

Christensen, Thomas. 'The Improvisatory Moment', in: *Studies in Historical Improvisation: From 'Cantare super Librum' to Partimenti*, edited by Massimiliano Guido, Abington-New York, Routledge, 2017, pp. 9-24.

Gasparini 2001

Gasparini, Francesco. *L'Armonico pratico al cimbalo*, (1708), Bologna, Arnaldo Forni Editore, 2001 (Bibliotheca Musica Bononiensis, iv/90).

Gjerdingen 2012

Gjerdingen, Robert. 'A Source of Pasqini Partimenti in Naples', in: *Pasquini Symposium* [...], *op. cit.*, pp. 177-194.

Guido 2009

Guido, Massimiliano. 'Lo stile come manifestazione degli affetti', in: *Storia dei concetti musicali. 3: Melodia, stile, suono*, edited by Gianmario Borio and Mario Gentili, Rome, Carocci Editore, 2009, pp. 145-159.

24. Christensen 2017, pp. 9-25.

25. «I believe that as Fame broke her trumpets, not having any more voice to praise his virtues, I shall, in the same way, drop the pen, not having adequate concepts for his eulogy».

GUIDO 2012A
ID. 'Counterpoint in the Fingers. A Practical Approach to Girolamo Diruta's *Breve & Facile Regola di Contrappunto*', in: *PhilomusicaOnline*, XI/1 (2012), pp. 63-76.

GUIDO 2012B
ID. '*Affetti cantabili* from Frescobaldi to Pasquini', in: *Pasquini Symposium* [...], *op. cit.*, pp. 154-176.

GUIDO 2013
ID. '«Con questa sicura strada»: Girolamo Diruta's and Andriano Banchieri's Instructions on How to Improvise Versets', in: *The Organ Yearbook*, no. 42 (2013), pp. 40-52.

GUIDO – SCHUBERT 2014
GUIDO, Massimiliano – SCHUBERT, Peter. 'Unpacking the Box in Frescobaldi's Ricercari of 1615', in: *Music Theory Online: A Journal of the Society for Music Theory*, XX/2 (2014), <http://www.mtosmt.org/issues/mto.14.20.2/mto.14.20.2.guido_schubert.pdf>, accessed November 2018.

MORELLI 2016
MORELLI, Arnaldo. *La virtù in corte. Bernardo Pasquini (1637-1710)*, Lucca, LIM, 2016 (ConNotazioni, 12).

PASQUINI 2006A
PASQUINI, Bernardo. *Opere per tastiera. 6: London, Bl Ms. Add. 31501. I*, edited by Edoardo Bellotti, Latina, Il Levante Libreria Editrice, 2006 (Tastata. Opere d'intavolatura d'organo e cimbalo, 18).

PASQUINI 2006B
ID. *Opere per tastiera. 7: London, Bl Ms. Add. 31501, II-III*, edited by Armando Carideo, Latina, Il Levante Libreria Editrice, 2006 (Tastata. Opere d'intavolatura d'organo e cimbalo, TA 19).

PASQUINI 2009
ID. *Opere per tastiera. 8: Saggi di contrappunto (S.B.P.K. Landsberg 214); Regole... per ben accompagnare con il cembalo (Bc, MS. D 138/2)*, edited by Armando Carideo, Latina, Il Levante Libreria Editrice, 2009 (Tastata. Opere d'Intavolatura d'organo e cimbalo, 24).

SANGUINETTI 2012
SANGUINETTI, Giorgio. *The Art of Partimento: History, Theory, and Practice*, Oxford-New York, Oxford University Press, 2012.

SCHUBERT – GUIDO 2016
SCHUBERT, Peter – GUIDO, Massimiliano. 'Back into the Classroom. Learning Music Through Historical Improvisation', in: *Improvisation and Music Education: Beyond the Classroom*, edited by Ajay Heble and Mark Laver, Abington-New York, Routledge, 2016, pp. 130-139.

Las anotaciones de Pisendel en el Concierto para dos violines RV 507 de Vivaldi: una ventana abierta a la improvisación en la obra del 'Cura rojo'

Javier Lupiáñez – Fabrizio Ammetto
(Universidad de Guanajuato, México)

La famosa colección 'Schrank ii' de la Biblioteca de la Universidad de Dresde (Sächsische Landesbibliothek – Staats- und Universitätsbibliothek Dresden) contiene unos dos mil manuscritos de música instrumental[1]. El extenso material, en el que encontramos tanto partes como partituras completas, estaba destinado a ser interpretado en la Hopfkapelle de Dresde durante la primera mitad del siglo xviii y fue reunido en su mayor parte por el violinista y compositor Johann Georg Pisendel (1687-1755).

Pisendel entró a formar parte de la orquesta de la corte de Dresde en 1712[2], y tomó el papel de concertino en 1728, aunque no fue oficialmente reconocido como tal hasta 1730[3]. Pisendel permaneció en Dresde hasta su muerte. Los manuscritos del 'Schrank ii' contienen el trabajo de recopilación y copia de Pisendel, incluyendo algunos de su colección personal compilados incluso antes de 1712 y que trajo consigo cuando ocupó su puesto en la corte[4].

La estrecha relación de Pisendel con estas partituras se hace más patente al descubrir una gran cantidad de anotaciones realizadas por él mismo sobre las mismas. Entre las anotaciones referentes a las dinámicas, o las guías de lo que hacen otros instrumentos para facilitar la labor de concertino, encontramos un tipo peculiar de anotación destinada a cambiar el discurso musical: son anotaciones destinadas a servir como ornamentación o como guía para la improvisación. Las encontramos en ciento sesenta y dos piezas. Algunas

---

1. Ver <https://hofmusik.slub-dresden.de/themen/schrank-zwei/>, visitado en Octubre 2018.
2. Köpp 2005, p. 79.
3. *Ibidem*, p. 236.
4. Entre estos manuscritos anteriores a 1712 cabe destacar la copia de la Trio Sonata RV 820 de Vivaldi (D-Dl, Mus. 2-Q-6), copiada por Pisendel durante su estancia en Ansbach, entre 1697 y 1709.

de estas anotaciones han sido comentadas y analizadas en otros estudios[5] (a partir del principio del siglo xx, con el de Arnold Schering en 1909[6]).

Este tipo de anotaciones se presentan de diversas formas, ocupando diferentes posiciones en la partitura y sirviendo para diversos propósitos. Desde simples guías para la improvisación a elaborados pasajes o, como en el caso del Concierto para violín RV 340 de Vivaldi, modificaciones sustanciales del texto musical[7]. Además es posible encontrarse en piezas de diferente naturaleza: conciertos para violín y orquesta, sonatas para violín y continuo o trio sonatas.

Podemos encontrar estas anotaciones en los más variados contextos: movimientos rápidos, lentos, como parte de cadencias en fermatas, como es el caso del siguiente ejemplo tomado del segundo movimiento de la Sinfonía para cuerdas RV 192.

Il. 1. A. Vivaldi, Sinfonía para cuerdas RV 192, ii mov., Mus.2389-N-7a.

Contextualización.
Los ornamentos de Pisendel, Vivaldi y el Concierto RV 507

Parece claro que la obra de Vivaldi ocupa un papel especial y predominante en la colección de Pisendel en Dresde[8]. De entre este corpus de manuscritos que incluyen algún tipo de anotación se posiciona en un lugar especial la obra de Antonio Vivaldi. En primer lugar por la gran cantidad de manuscritos autógrafos o en copia que incluyen anotaciones, un total de treinta y seis (más que ningún otro compositor[9]).

5. Algunas de las anotaciones de Pisendel sobre el Concierto para violín RV 340 fueron enumeradas en Landmann 1981, p. 137. Algunas otras se discuten en Heller 1976, pp. 82-83. Otro trabajo donde se analizan algunas de estas anotaciones es Fechner 1980. Algunas de las disminuciones son transcritas y atribuidas a Pisendel en Landshoff 1935, 'Preface'. El trabajo más reciente lo encontramos en Lockey 2010.

6. Schering 1905-1906. Schering realiza además una interesante transcripción de las disminuciones.

7. Lockey 2010, p. 132.

8. Heller 2010, p. 145.

9. El número de manuscritos con anotaciones es el siguiente: 36 (Vivaldi); 24 (Graun); 19 (Pisendel); 16 (Fasch); 5 (Telemann); 3 (Haendel, Quantz y Geminiani); 2 (Benda, Schreyfogel y Tartini); 1 (Tartini,

Otra de las razones que añaden interés a estas anotaciones sobre la obra de Vivaldi es que algunas de ellas fueron realizadas directamente sobre autógrafos vivaldianos, como es el caso de los conciertos para violín RV 172[10], RV 205[11], RV 237[12] y RV 340[13], o el interesante caso de la Sonata para violín y continuo RV 25[14] donde aparece un movimiento completo escrito por Pisendel insertado en una sonata autógrafa de Vivaldi.

Encontramos anotaciones de Pisendel en los siguientes manuscritos vivaldianos de Dresde (D-Dl):

- Mus. 2-O-1,1, Concierto para violín en Sol mayor, RV 326;
- Mus. 2364-O-7, Concierto para violín en Mi menor, RV 366;
- Mus. 2389-N-7a, Sinfonía en Do mayor, RV 192;
- Mus. 2389-O-42, Concierto para violín en Do mayor, RV 172;
- Mus. 2389-O-43, Concierto para violín en La mayor, RV 340;
- Mus. 2389-O-46, Concierto para violín en Re menor, RV 237;
- Mus. 2389-O-47, Concierto para violín, dos oboes, dos cornos y fagot en Fa mayor, RV 568;
- Mus. 2389-O-47a, Concierto para violín en Fa mayor compilado por Pisendel, tomando los movimientos extremos del RV 568 y el movimiento lento central del RV 202;
- Mus. 2389-O-48a, Concierto para violín en Fa Mayor, RV 571;
- Mus. 2389-O-49, Concierto para dos violines en Do mayor, RV 508;
- Mus. 2389-O-54, Concierto para dos violines en La mayor, RV 521;
- Mus. 2389-O-58, Concierto para violín en Re mayor RV 228;
- Mus. 2389-O-58b, Concierto para violín en Re mayor, RV 228;
- Mus. 2389-O-61, Concierto para violín en Re mayor, RV 213;
- Mus. 2389-O-61a, Concierto para violín en Re mayor, RV 213;
- Mus. 2389-O-67, Concierto para violín y dos orquestas en Re mayor, RV 582;
- Mus. 2389-O-74, Conciertos para violín en Re mayor, RV 205 y RV 212;
- Mus. 2389-O-92, Concierto para violín en Sol mayor, RV 298;
- Mus. 2389-O-93, Concierto para violín en Fa mayor, RV 569;
- Mus. 2389-O-93a, Concierto para violín en Fa mayor, RV 569;
- Mus. 2389-O-95, Concierto para violín en Sol mayor, RV 302;
- Mus. 2389-O-98, Concierto para dos violines en Do mayor, RV 507;
- Mus. 2389-O-105, Concierto para violín en Sol menor, RV 329;
- Mus. 2389-O-111, Concierto para violín en Mi bemol mayor, RV 259;
- Mus. 2389-O-112, Concierto para violín en La mayor, RV 343;
- Mus. 2389-O-122, Concierto para violín en Do menor, RV 202;
- Mus. 2389-O-123, Concierto para violín en Re mayor, RV 205;
- Mus. 2389-O-154, Concierto para violín en Si bemol mayor, RV 373;
- Mus. 2389-O-157, Concierto para violín en Fa mayor, RV 574;

Cattaneo, Albicastro, Somis, Torelli, entre otros).

10. D-Dl, Mus. 2389-O-42.

11. D-Dl, Mus. 2389-O-123 y D-Dl, Mus. 2389-O-74.

12. D-Dl, Mus. 2389-O-46.

13. D-Dl, Mus. 2389-O-43.

14. D-Dl, Mus. 2389-R-10,3.

- Mus. 2389-R-6,1, Sonata para violín en Sol menor, RV 28;
- Mus. 2456-R-21, Sonata para violín en Sol mayor, RV Anh. 98 (RV 776)[15];
- Mus. 2822-O-5, Concierto para violín en Sol mayor, RV 299/2[16];
- Mus. 4155-O-1, Concierto para violín en Re mayor, RV 213.

La estrecha relación establecida desde 1717[17] entre Pisendel y Vivaldi toma forma en estos manuscritos. Como alumno directo de Vivaldi, sus anotaciones y ornamentaciones sobre la obra vivaldiana conforman una importante referencia como fuente para la ornamentación sobre el repertorio vivaldiano.

Como ya señaló Kolneder[18] la cercanía de Pisendel con Vivaldi hace muy posible que las diminuciones de Pisendel estén muy cerca de la práctica del propio Vivaldi. Kolneder presenta incluso la posibilidad de que algunas de estas disminuciones fuesen escritas o elaboradas por el propio Vivaldi para el uso de sus estudiantes[19].

Sobre las fuentes de ornamentación de la época

Es posible analizar fuentes de las primeras décadas del siglo xviii que muestran cómo se improvisaba en este período y que nos servirán como comparación para las anotaciones de Pisendel.

Podemos catalogar estas fuentes en dos grupos diferentes: (a) fuentes impresas y (b) fuentes de uso particular (las anotaciones de Pisendel pertenecen a este segundo grupo).

Esta catalogación nos permite comparar las anotaciones de Pisendel con otras anotaciones similares de la época y contraponerlas con las fuentes impresas, destinadas al uso pedagógico y enfocadas a un público más general. Notamos así importantes divergencias entre las fuentes destinadas a un uso privado y las de dominio público. Estas diferencias, presentes en las disminuciones de Pisendel sobre la obra de Vivaldi son de extrema importancia para entender las diferencias entre la praxis interpretativa real de alto nivel y la interpretación llevada a cabo por el público general que consumía los métodos y ediciones del momento.

---

15. El manuscrito contiene una sonata *pasticcio* en la que el primer movimiento se corresponde con el tercer movimiento de la sonata RV 22.

16. El manuscrito contiene el segundo movimiento del concierto RV 299 de Vivaldi insertado entre dos movimientos de Visconti.

17. Heller 1997, p. 230.

18. Kolneder 1979, p. 41.

19. «[...] the Adagio of a violin concerto (Hs Dresden Cx 1091) [Concierto para violín y orquesta en Do menor, RV 202, Mus.2389-O-122] with diminutions by Pisendel is very close to the master's usage, if not indeed elaborated by himself for a pupil's usage». Kolneder 1979, p. 41.

Algo que llama la atención es la mayor variedad en función y tipología de las ornamentaciones en manuscritos destinados a un uso personal frente a las fuentes impresas. Al igual que ocurre con los manuscritos de Pisendel en Dresde, las ornamentaciones destinadas a uso personal afectan tanto a movimientos rápidos como lentos e incluyen no sólo ornamentos sino que incluso añaden variaciones y cadencias. Sin embargo, el rango de uso de la ornamentación en los ejemplos impresos es mucho más restringido y se ciñe exclusivamente a la ornamentación de movimientos lentos y ninguno incluye variaciones o pasajes con dobles cuerdas.

Acotaremos las fuentes que a continuación se enumeran a un período temporal cercano a la elaboración de las anotaciones de Pisendel en el concierto que nos ocupa.

(a) Fuentes impresas para la ornamentación:
- Johann Christoph Pez / anónimo, ornamentos sobre el Op. 5 de Corelli[20] (1707);
- Arcangelo Corelli (?), ornamentos sobre el Op. 5[21] (1710);
- William Babell, set de sonatas[22] con ornamentos en los movimientos lentos (ca. 1725);
- Georg Philipp Telemann, *Sonate metodiche* (Hamburgo, 1728);
- G.Ph. Telemann, *Trietti methodici e Scherzi*[23] (Hamburgo, 1731);
- G.Ph. Telemann, *Sonate metodiche* (II) (Hamburgo, 1732).

Il. 2. W. Babell, Sonata 1, *incipit*.

20. *A Second collection of SONATAS for two FLUTES and a BASS, by Signr Christopher Pez* […]; RISM P1689.

21. *SONATE a Violino e Violone o Cimbalo DI ARCANGELO CORELLI Da Fusignano OPERA QUINTA. Troisieme Edition ou l'on a joint les agree-mens* [*sic*] *des Adagio de cet ouvrage, composez* [*sic*] *par Mr. A. Corelli comme il les joue* […]; RISM C3812.

22. *XII Solos for a Violin or Hautboy with a Bass, figur'd for the Harpsicord. With proper Graces adapted to each Adagio* […]; RISM A/I: B 7

23. Esta obra es de especial interés por dos razones: es una de las pocas fuentes que incluyen ornamentos en dos partes al mismo tiempo y porque existe una copia manuscrita en Dresde (Mus. 2392-Q-4).

Encontramos otras fuentes muy útiles en textos de la época que nos hablan sobre la ornamentación: Scheibe[24], Tosi[25], Couperin[26], Monteclair[27], Geminiani[28], o en textos algo más tardíos como Quantz[29], L. Mozart[30] o C. Ph. E. Bach[31].

(b) Manuscritos destinados a un uso personal:

- 'Colección de Pisendel'. El archivo personal de Pisendel es quizá una de las fuentes más importantes de manuscritos con disminuciones escritas. Los ornamentos se encuentran tanto en movimientos rápidos como lentos, con uso de dobles cuerdas y con una gran variedad funcional (ornamentos, cadencias, variaciones, etc.)[32];
- 'Anónimo-Walsh'. Ornamentos sobre el Op. 5 de Corelli[33]. Ornamentos sobre movimientos lentos y rápidos (ca. 1711);
- 'BL 17,853'. Disminuciones sobre el Op. 5 de Corelli[34] (ca. 1720);
- 'Dubourg'. Disminuciones sobre el Op. 5 de Corelli[35]. Ornamentos en movimientos rápidos y lentos, incluye además variaciones y dobles cuerdas (ca. 1721);
- 'Anónimo para órgano'[36]. Ornamentos sobre la Sonata Op. 5 n. 6 de Corelli[37] (ca. 1725);
- 'Vivaldi (?)'. Ornamentos sobre el *Adagio* del Concierto para violín, RV 581[38] (ca. 1726);
- 'Festing'. Disminuciones sobre el Op. 5 de Corelli[39]. Ornamentos en movimientos rápidos y lentos, incluye además variaciones y dobles cuerdas (ca. 1736);

---

24. Carta anónima en 'Der Critische Musicus' (1737-1740) con interesantes comentarios sobre la ornamentación e improvisación llevada a cabo en orquestas (citado en SPITZER – ZASLAW 1986).

25. *Opinioni de' cantori antichi e moderni* (1723).

26. *L'Art de toucher le Clavecin* (1716).

27. *Principes de musique* (1736).

28. *Rules for Playing in a True Taste* (1748).

29. *Versuch einer Anweisung die Flöte traversiere zu spielen* (1752).

30. *Versuch einer gründlichen Violinschule* (1756).

31. *Versuch über die wahre Art das Clavier zu spielen* (1753, 1762).

32. El estudio de estos manuscritos está siendo desarrollado en estos momentos como tema de la tesis doctoral de Javier Lupiáñez (*Las anotaciones de Johann Georg Pisendel (1687-1755) en los manuscritos vivaldianos de Dresde*, Doctorado en Artes, División de Arquitectura, Arte y Diseño, Campus Guanajuato, Universidad de Guanajuato), bajo la dirección de Fabrizio Ammetto.

33. Manuscrito anónimo insertado en una re-edición de Walsh & Hare (ca. 1711); RISM C3816. Anteriormente propiedad de David Boyden, actualmente en la Biblioteca Musical de la Universidad de California, Berkeley (sin signatura).

34. GB-Lbl, Add. Ms. 17,853.

35. *Dubourg Corelli's Solos Grac'd by Doburg* [*sic*].

36. Identificado por Javier Lupiáñez en junio de 2015.

37. Gerard Cook Coll. 2/D/MISCELLANY, pp. 35-46.

38. I-Vc, Busta 55.1 (*Anna Maria Partbook*).

39. GB-Lbl, Add. Ms. 71,244, f. 30.

- 'Roman'. Ornamentos sobre el Op. 5 de Corelli[40] (ca. 1715). Ornamentos en movimientos rápidos y lentos, incluye además variaciones y dobles cuerdas;
- 'Geminiani'. Una fuente algo más tardía con ornamentos sobre el Op. 5 de Corelli[41], interesante porque incluye ornamentos en movimientos rápidos, variaciones y múltiples dobles cuerdas.

Il. 3: Michael Festing, disminuciones sobre la Sonata Op. 5 n. 5 de Corelli.

El Concierto para dos violines y orquesta en Do Mayor, RV 507

De entre todos los manuscritos que contienen anotaciones es el Concierto para dos violines en Do mayor el único que incluye anotaciones tanto para el primer solista como para el segundo solista.

Del RV 507 se conservan tres fuentes manuscritas, un autógrafo[42] y dos copias en Dresde: (a) el manuscrito D-Dl, Mus. 2389-O-98, copiado enteramente por Pisendel, en formato de partitura general y que contiene anotaciones y (b) el manuscrito D-Dl, Mus. 2389-O-98a, formado por un juego de partes mayormente copiado por Giovanni Battista Vivaldi, con partes copiadas además por Grundig y Pisendel (que añade dos oboes a la orquestación original)[43].

El concierto fue compuesto alrededor de 1716[44], coincidiendo con el viaje de Pisendel a Italia y su encuentro con Vivaldi en 1716-1717. Es justo esta fecha (1717) la datación de

40. S-Sk, Roman Collection, Mss. 61, 97.

41. El manuscrito de la Sonata Op. 5 n. 9 de Corelli elaborado por un alumno de Geminiani está perdido, pero fue posteriormente publicado en Hawkins 1776.

42. I-Tn, Giordano 35, ff. 269-278.

43. Para una descripción detallada de las fuentes, ver Ammetto 2013, pp. 67-87: 68-69 y 79.

44. *Ibidem*, p. 226.

la copia contenida en el D-Dl, Mus. 2389-O-98a[45], así como una muy posible fecha para la copia que nos ocupa y que contiene las anotaciones, el manuscrito D-Dl, Mus. 2389-O-98, es entre 1716 y 1725[46].

Análisis general de las anotaciones del RV 507

Algo que llama la atención desde el principio es que el Concierto para dos violines en Do mayor, RV 507 incluye anotaciones tanto para el primer violín como para el segundo violín solista[47]. Es posible observar dos tipos de tinta diferentes para cada una de las anotaciones, siendo la utilizada para el violín segundo de un característico color más rojizo[48]:

c. 50, Violín I

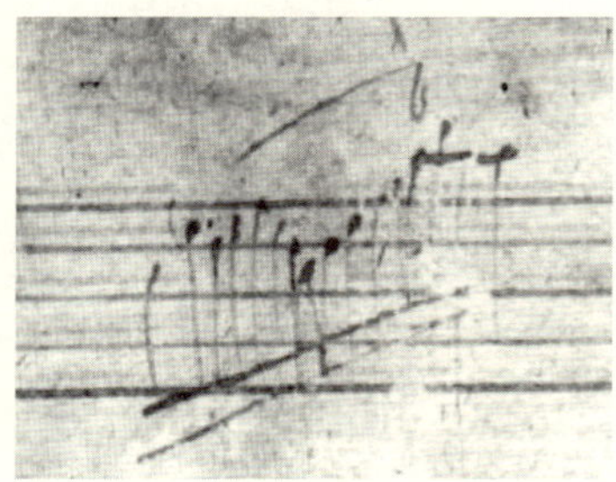

c. 74, Violín II

Las anotaciones se encuentran generalmente escritas en pentagramas adyacentes o en los lugares de la misma página donde se tuviese espacio libre, usando en muchas ocasiones los pentagramas que quedaban libres entre los sistemas o al final de la página.

Encontramos que, tanto para el violín primero como para el violín segundo, se dan en varias ocasiones diversas versiones de un mismo pasaje. En algunas ocasiones queda por determinar si se tratan de diferentes ideas con la misma validez, o una evolución, o un cambio de ideas sobre la ornamentación.

45. RISM ID no.: 212000209.

46. RISM ID no.: 212000208.

47. El hecho de encontrar anotaciones en ambas partes es bastante infrecuente, de hecho existen en el 'Schrank II' otros ejemplos de música escrita para dos solistas y que contienen ornamentaciones y anotaciones, aunque en esos casos las anotaciones se restringen al primer violín. Así encontramos en el 'Schrank II' ejemplos de importantes ornamentaciones en las siguientes obras para dos violines: Johann Friedrich Fasch, Trio Sonata para dos violines en Sol mayor, FaWV N:G4 (Mus. 2423-Q-2); Johann Gottlieb Graun, Trio Sonata para dos violines en Re mayor, GraunWV A:XV:6 (Mus. 2474-Q-9); Georg Friedrich Händel, Trio sonata para dos violines y continuo en Si bemol mayor, HWV 339 (Mus. 2410-N-5a); G.F. Händel, Trio sonata para dos violines y continuo en Fa mayor, HWV 361 (Mus. 2410-Q-20); Georg Philipp Telemann, Trio sonata para dos violines y continuo en La mayor, TWV 42:A 8 (Mus. 2392-Q-11) y Georg Philipp Telemann, Trio sonata para dos violines y continuo en Re mayor, TWV 42:D 1 (Mus. 2392-Q-6).

48. Sin embargo este hecho no nos permite afirmar que las anotaciones del segundo violín fueran hechas por una mano distinta a la de Pisendel, aunque sería una posibilidad bastante plausibile.

Ornamentos en los movimientos rápidos (i y iii)

Es interesante destacar la gran cantidad de ornamentos localizados en ambos movimientos rápidos del concierto. Si bien los métodos de ornamentación de la época se centran más en la ornamentación de los movimientos lentos, encontramos algunas referencias a la ornamentación de movimientos rápidos. Quantz, aunque se trate de una fuente más tardía, nos explica por qué: «Von willkürlichen Veränderungen leidet das Allegro nicht viel; weil es mehrenteils mit einem solchen Gesange und solchen Passagien gesetzet wird, worinne nicht viel zu verbessern ist»[49].

Podemos encontrar los ornamentos en los movimientos rápidos en las siguientes situaciones: (a) secuencias, (b) enlaces o (c) como forma de crear contraste con el otro solista.

(a) Secuencias

En secuencias formadas por patrones regulares Pisendel usa la ornamentación de dos formas distintas:

- creando un patrón diferente aunque regular (en este caso se trata de variantes para el patrón dado en la secuencia original). Pisendel escribe normalmente un solo compás con el nuevo que debería seguir como modelo para los compases siguientes[50];

Ej. 1: A. Vivaldi, Concierto RV 507, i mov., cc. 80-83.

- rompiendo una secuencia que usaba un patrón regular. En otros casos, para añadir más variedad a un pasaje articulado de forma regular, Pisendel transforma el pasaje

49. *Versuch einer Anweisung die Flöte traversiere zu spielen*, Capítulo xii, § 27.

50. El mismo procedimiento es descrito por Lockey en el las anotaciones de Pisendel sobre el concierto RV 340 (ver Lockey 2010, p. 132).

articulando la secuencia de forma desigual. En el siguiente pasaje Pisendel comienza con un movimiento melódico que desemboca en un nuevo patrón a mitad de la secuencia.

Ej. 2: A. Vivaldi, Concierto RV 507, 1 mov., cc. 49-51.

(b) Enlaces

Encontramos dos enlaces ornamentados muy idiomáticos en el primer movimiento del concierto, una interesante tirata de 14 notas del violín segundo en el compás 74 precede a la entrada del solo del primer violín.

Ej. 3: A. Vivaldi, Concierto RV 507, 1 mov., cc. 73-75.

El otro ejemplo son las varias versiones, también en el violín segundo, de una ornamentación en la cadencia que introduce el *tutti* del compás 104 en el primer movimiento.

Ej. 4: A. Vivaldi, Concierto RV 507, 1 mov., cc. 102-104.

(c) Como forma de crear contraste con el otro solista

Finalmente las encontramos con la intención de crear alguna diferencia con el otro violín solista cuando ambos repiten un mismo patrón. El primer ejemplo lo encontramos al final de la primera intervención de los solistas, donde ambos violines repiten el mismo patrón melódico de arpegios y escalas ascendentes, el segundo violín introduce una escala descendente justo al final (c. 20).

Ej. 5: A. Vivaldi, Concierto RV 507, i mov., cc. 19-22.

Otro ejemplo significativo de este recurso lo encontramos en el tercer movimiento, entre los compases 107 y 113 donde el primer y el segundo violín se responden con el mismo material melódico, en este caso el primer violín opta por una fuerte variación del motivo mientras que el segundo lo interpreta casi como está.

Ej. 6: A. Vivaldi, Concierto RV 507, iii mov., cc. 107-113.

La última ornamentación que encontramos toma la idea de un pasaje que ya apareció en el primer movimiento y lo traslada al tercer movimiento.

Ej. 7: A. Vivaldi, Concierto RV 507, i mov., cc. 63-64 y iii mov., cc. 121-122.

En la tabla que sigue se resumen los ornamentos presentes en el primer y último movimiento del Concierto RV 507.

Mov.	Compás	Solista	N. de versiones	Tipología
I	20	violín II	1	diferencia con el violín I
I	40	violín I	4	secuencia ornamentada (patrón regular)
I	50	violín I	1	secuencia ornamentada (ruptura de patrón)
I	74	violín II	1	enlace - diferencia con el violín I
I	77-80	violín I	3	secuencia ornamentada (ruptura de patrón / patrón regular)
I	81-82?	violín I	4	secuencia ornamentada (¿patrón regular?)
I	94-96	violín I	1	secuencia ornamentada (ruptura de patrón)
I	97-98	violín II	1	enlace
I	102	violín II	3	enlace (cadencia)
I	113	violín II	1	diferencia con el violín I
III	106-107	violín I	3	diferencia con el violín II
III	111	violín II	1	diferencia con el violín I
III	115-120	violín I	3	secuencia ornamentada (ruptura de patrón)
III	121-122	violín II	1	secuencia ornamentada (patrón regular)

Ornamentos en el «Largo»

Como en el caso de las anotaciones de los otros movimientos, encontramos aquí también varias versiones para el mismo pasaje, si bien aquí hay una cantidad mayor de enmiendas, tachones y otras marcas que dificultan la valorización de los ornamentos, haciendo difícil poder decir qué fragmento se conecta con qué, o qué anotaciones fueron desechadas. Véase, por ejemplo, la sección de los compases 5 y 6, donde encontramos no sólo varias versiones del mismo pasaje si no también enmiendas y líneas que parecen conectar unas ideas con otras.

Esta profusión de ornamentos y su tipología concuerda bastante bien con otras fuentes cercanas al RV 507. Encontramos, de hecho, un movimiento bastante parecido, en forma de siciliana, en el Concierto RV 340[51], también ornamentado por Pisendel, así

[51]. Mus. 2389-O-43.

como los profusos ornamentos que Pisendel añadió al Concierto RV 202[52] (transcritos ya en 1906 por Schering[53]).

Ej. 8: A. Vivaldi, Concierto RV 340 (Mus. 2389-O-43), ii mov., cc. 8-11.

Ej. 9: A. Vivaldi, Concierto RV 202 (Mus. 2389-O-122), ii mov., cc. 14-15, (fragmento de la transcripción de Schering de las disminuciones).

[52]. Mus. 2389-O-122.

[53]. Schering 1905-1906, pp. 377-385.

Merecen también especial mención las disminuciones del Concierto para violín RV 581 contenidas en el conocido como 'Libro de Anna Maria'[54]. Estas disminuciones han sido ya objeto de estudio[55], siendo una de las fuentes más cercanas a la forma de ornamentar del propio Vivaldi.

Podemos establecer algunas concordancias entre las fuentes mencionadas (los ornamentos de Pisendel en los Conciertos RV 340, 507 y 202 y los del 'Libro de Anna Maria' sobre el 581) y que se alejan de la norma corelliana, que además coinciden con los rasgos más significativos que encontramos en algunos movimientos lentos de conciertos de Vivaldi y que hacen gala de su estilo más improvisativo. Podemos citar (en una lista no exhaustiva): el *Grave* del RV 212a[56], las versiones del *Largo* del RV 279[57], el *Grave Recitativo* del RV 208, el *Adagio* del RV 195[58], el *Adagio* del 285[59], el *Largo* del RV 318[60], el *Grave* del RV 562[61]. Además, son dignos de mención los movimientos centrales de los Conciertos RV 775 y RV 771, contenidos en el 'Libro de Anna Maria'[62] que cuentan con las repeticiones ornamentadas[63].

Veamos ahora más en detalle los ornamentos del *Largo* del RV 507 y sus peculiaridades y semejanzas con otras fuentes. Encontramos ornamentaciones ya en el *tutti* de apertura, aprovechando los silencios.

EJ. 10: A. Vivaldi, Concierto RV 507, II mov., cc. 1-4.

54. I-Vc, Busta 55.1.

55. TALBOT 2007.

56. Mus. 2389-O-74.

57. El Mus. 2389-O-155 contiene dos versiones del *Largo* del Concierto, ambas presentan una escritura en un estilo improvisatorio, aunque la segunda se aleja más de la norma corelliana presentando interesantes esquemas melódicos.

58. Mus. 2389-O-117.

59. Mus. 2389-O-103.

60. Mus. 2389-O-120.

61. Mus. 2389-O-94.

62. I-Vc, Busta 55.1. El RV 775 en el f. 13 y RV 771 en los ff. 16-17.

63. Hay que decir que las disminuciones del RV 775 y del RV 771 si bien se alejan de los estándares corellianos por el uso de saltos y arpegios, pueden considerarse mucho más conservadoras si se las compara con los conciertos citados o con las ornamentaciones del Concierto RV 581 del mismo libro o las disminuciones de Pisendel sobre los conciertos de Vivaldi.

Un pasaje muy parecido se encuentra justo al final del movimiento.

Ej. 11: A. Vivaldi, Concierto RV 507, II mov., cc. 21-23.

La ornamentación de estos silencios orquestales no es algo excesivamente peculiar, encontramos un ejemplo muy parecido en los *Trietti* de Telemann para dos violines[64].

Il. 4: G. Ph. Telemann, *Trietto Secondo*, *Andante* (violín primero).

Sin embargo, existen algunas peculiaridades en nuestro concierto: Telemann mantiene un claro esquema rítmico como anacrusa hacia las notas fundamentales, usando también un patrón armónico claro: el arpegio correspondiente y el arpegio con apoyaturas cromáticas (bastante similar a las ornamentaciones de Pisendel al principio), pero Pisendel es mucho más variado rítmicamente, cambiando el patrón en sólo dos compases.

Ej. 12: A. Vivaldi, Concierto RV 507, II mov., cc. 2-3.

En el pasaje final Pisendel usa dos recursos originales y que se alejan en cierta manera de la norma: intervalos aumentados y dobles cuerdas (ver Ej. 11).

[64]. Telemann, *3 Trietti methodichi e 3 Scherzi* (Mus. 2392-Q-4). Trietto Secondo, *Andante* (final), Violino Primo.

Vemos también el uso de intervalos aumentados o disminuidos, algo bastante común al lenguaje vivaldiano[65]. Este tipo de 'difícil' interválica — que podríamos definir como un especial gusto por el uso de pasos y saltos 'duriusculus', y que se aleja de la práctica más académica — se hace bastante visible en el lenguaje pisendeliano y vivaldiano; además de los ejemplos expuestos esto incluye un característico uso del cromatismo[66].

Ej. 13: A. Vivaldi, Concierto RV 507, ii mov., cc. 6-7.

Ej. 14: A. Vivaldi, Concierto RV 581, ii mov., cc. 48-49/1[67].

Il. 5: Cadenza para el *Grave* del Concierto RV 286, 'Libro de Anna Maria'[68].

A esto podemos unir otra característica del lenguaje pisendeliano, que también se aleja de los pulcros contornos corellianos: el uso de saltos y arpegios. Juntos, los pasajes por grados conjuntos y los saltos se mezclan para crear una heterogeneidad melódica muy característica: un ejemplo lo encontramos en el uso de arpegios invertidos (comenzando por el registro agudo).

65. Talbot 1978, p. 75.
66. *Ibidem.*
67. I-Vc, Busta 55.1., f. 75^{r}.
68. I-Vc, Busta 55.1., f. 78^{v}.

Ej. 15: A. Vivaldi, Concierto RV 507, II mov., cc. 6-7.

Ej. 16: A. Vivaldi, Concierto RV 581, II mov., c. 4[69].

Se crean, de esta forma, originales pasajes con saltos y arpegios, repletos de saltos disonantes, raros en la literatura más escolástica.

Ej. 17: A. Vivaldi, Concierto RV 507, II mov., cc. 6-7.

Ej. 18: A. Vivaldi, Concierto RV 581, II mov., c. 33[70].

Todas estas disminuciones parecen alejarse del estándar corelliano predominante en los tratados y en otros ejemplos de disminuciones publicados en la época. Enrico Gatti define el estilo de Corelli de forma sucinta: «Il principio basilare è quello di collegare le note portanti della frase tramite gradi congiunti e numerose note di passaggio. I salti sono poco numerosi e ben calibrati, in modo da poter descrivere delle forme arrotondate ad arco e non squadrate come tendevano ad essere le antiche diminuzioni a cavallo fra Cinquecento e Seicento»[71].

Tanto los ornamentos de Pisendel, como los del 'Libro de Anna Maria' parecen adecuarse más a la definición que el propio Gatti otorga a la forma de ornamentar en Venecia

69. I-Vc, Busta 55.1., f. 75v.

70. I-Vc, Busta 55.1., f. 75r.

71. Gatti 2014, p. 129.

en la época de Vivaldi: «A Venezia durante l'epoca di Vivaldi lo stile dell'improvvisazione era già molto diverso, più ardito e spregiudicato, molto idiomatico e colorito rispetto all'austero ed equilibrato stile della generazione di Corelli. Purtroppo non ci sono molti documenti al riguardo, essendo questa un'arte effimera riservata ai virtuosi che improvvisavano e quindi di norma non fissata in regole precedenti»[72].

Algunas conclusiones

La estrecha relación de Pisendel con Vivaldi, la importancia y la cantidad de anotaciones de Pisendel sobre obras de Vivaldi, además del estilo de las anotaciones analizadas en este artículo hacen plausible la propuesta de Kolneder: «[...] the Adagio of a violin concerto (Hs Dresden Cx 1091) [Concierto para violín y orquesta en Do menor, RV 202, Mus. 2389-O-122] with diminutions by Pisendel is very close to the master's usage, if not indeed elaborated by himself for a pupil's usage»[73].

Las anotaciones encontradas en el RV 507 (así como, de forma general las otras anotaciones de Pisendel sobre los manuscritos vivaldianos) parecen responder a la necesidad práctica de anotar ciertas ideas surgidas en el momento de una improvisación real. Hecho por el cual se hace muy difícil comparar este tipo de anotaciones con las de otras fuentes existentes. Por lo tanto, todas estas anotaciones estarían enmarcadas dentro de un contexto interpretativo donde el intérprete improvisa y modifica el texto musical *ex tempore*: de ahí su dificultad, notada por Lockey en cuanto a la Siciliana del RV 340[74], para ser transcritas y organizadas en forma de edición moderna.

El análisis de estas anotaciones nos muestra un estilo que se aleja de los tratados contemporáneos dedicados a la ornamentación y las fuentes — académicas o no — destinadas a un público más general. En este sentido es interesante hacer notar que las mayores similitudes con otras fuentes de la época las encontramos en las ornamentaciones más 'personales' contenidas en manuscritos realizados por los propios intérpretes y que no tuvieron difusión más allá del uso personal o de un reducido círculo, como las disminuciones sobre Corelli de 'Festing' o 'Roman'.

Esto concuerda con la idea ya enunciada en 1958 por Pincherle[75] y argumentada con diversas fuentes de la época de cómo los grandes músicos evitaban en lo posible hacer público «los secretos de su estilo»: «They [composers] manifest, in a certain measure, a preoccupation with business, but at the same time, they give evidence of a desire legitimate, after all to preserve the secret of their style as much as was feasible. Indeed, ornamentation

72. *Ibidem*, p. 133.

73. Kolneder 1979, p. 41.

74. Lockey 2010, p. 135.

75. Pincherle – Cazeau 1958.

expressed, better than any other element of the art of the interpreter, his own style, his taste, his personality. He did not always like to put it within the reach of anybody at all»[76].

Referencias bibliográficas

Ammetto 2013
Ammetto, Fabrizio. *I concerti per due violini di Vivaldi*, Florencia, Olschki, 2013 (Quaderni vivaldiani, 18).

Fechner 1980
Fechner, Manfred. 'Improvisationsskizzen und ausnotierte Diminutionen von Johann Georg Pisendel, dargestellt an in Dresden handschriftlich überlieferten Konzerten von Johann Friedrich Fasch und Johann Gottlieb Graun', en: *Zu Fragen der Verzierungskunst in der Instrumentalmusik der ersten Hälfte des 18. Jahrhunderts: Konferenzbericht der 7. Wissenschaftlichen Arbeitstagung (Blankenburg/Harz, 29. Juni bis 1. Juli 1979)*, editado por Günter Fleischhauer, Blankenburg/Harz, Kultur-und Forschungsstäate Michaelstein, 1980 (Studien zur Aufführungspraxis und Interpretation der Intrumentalmusik des 18. Jahrhunderts, 11), pp. 35-55.

Gatti 2014
Gatti, Enrico. '«Però ci vole pacientia»: un excursus sull'arte della diminuzione nei secoli xvi, xvii e xviii «per uso di chi avrà volontà di studiare»', en: *Quaderni del Conservatorio 'Giuseppe Verdi' di Milano*, n.s. 2 (2014), pp. 71-188.

Hawkins 1776
Hawkins, John. *A General History of the Science and Practice of Music*, 5 vol., Londres, Payne, 1776.

Heller 1976
Heller, Karl. 'Zu einigen Aspekten der solistischen Improvisation im Instrumentalkonzert des frühen 18. Jahrhunderts', en: *Zu Fragen des Instrumentariums, der Besetzung und der Improvisation in der ersten Hälfte des 18. Jahrhunderts. Konferenzbericht der 3. Wissenschaftlichen Arbeitstagung (Blankenburg/Harz, 28.-29. Juni 1975)*, vol. ii, editado por Eitelfriedrich Thom and Renate Borman, Magdeburg, Rat des Bezirks, 1976 (Studien zur Aufführungspraxis und Interpretation von Instrumentalmusik des 18. Jahrhunderts, 2.2), pp. 80-87.

Heller 1997
Id. *Antonio Vivaldi: The Red Priest of Venice*, Portland (OR), Amadeus Press, 1997.

Heller 2010
Id. 'Pisendels Sammlung Vivaldishcher Violinkonzerte', en: *Johann Georg Pisendel – Studien zu Leben und Werk. Bericht über das Internationale Symposium vom 23. bis 25. Mai 2005 in Dresden*, editado por Ortrun Landmann y Hans-Günter Ottenberg, Hildesheim, Olms, 2010 (Dresdner Beiträge zur Musikforschung 3), pp. 145-169.

Kolneder 1979
Kolneder, Walter. *Performance Practices in Vivaldi*, Winterthur, Amadeus-Verlag, 1979.

---

[76]. *Ibidem*, p. 158.

Köpp 2005

Köpp, Kai. *Johann Georg Pisendel (1687-1755) und die Anfange der neuzeitlichen Orchesterleitung*, Tutzing, Hans Schneider, 2005.

Landmann 1981

Landmann, Ortrun. 'Katalog der Dresdner Vivaldi-Handschriften und -Frühdrucke', en: *Vivaldi-Studien. Referate des 3. Dresdner Vivaldi-Kolloquiums: mit einem Katalog der Dresdner Vivaldi-Handschriften und -Fruhdrucke*, Dresde, Sachsische Landesbibliothek, 1981, pp. 101-167.

Landshoff 1935

Landshoff, Ludwig. *Antonio Vivaldi, Violinkonzert A dur*, Berlín, Peters, 1935.

Lockey 2010

Lockey, Nicholas Scott. 'Second Thoughts, Embellishments and an Orphaned Fragment: Vivaldi's and Pisendel's Contributions to the Dresden Score of RV 340', en: *Studi vivaldiani*, x (2010), pp. 125-142.

Pincherle – Cazeau 1958

Pincherle, Marc – Cazeau, Isabelle. 'On the Rights of the Interpreter in the Performance of 17th- and 18th-Century Music', en: *The Musical Quarterly*, xliv/2 (1958), pp. 145-166.

Schering 1905-1906

Schering, Arnold. 'Zur instrumentalen Verzierungskunst im 18. Jahrhundert', en: *Sammelbande der Internationalen Musikgesellschaft*, vii (1905-1906), pp. 365-385.

Spitzer – Zaslaw 1986

Spitzer, John – Zaslaw, Neal. 'Ornamentation in Eighteenth-Century Orchestras', en: *Journal of the American Musicological Society*, xxxix/3 (1986), pp. 524-577.

Talbot 1978

Talbot, Michael. *Vivaldi*, Londres, J. M. Dent, 1978 (Master Musicians Series).

Talbot 2007

Id. "Full of Graces': Anna Maria receives Ornaments from the Hands of Antonio Vivaldi', en: *Arcangelo Corelli fra mito e realtà storica: nuove prospettive d'indagine musicologica e interdisciplinare nel 350° anniversario della nascita. Atti del Congresso internazionale di studi (Fusignano, 11-14 settembre 2003)*, a cura di Gregory Barnett, Antonella D'Ovidio y Stefano La Via, Florencia, Olschki, 2007 (Historiae Musicae Cultores, 111), pp. 253-268.

Cadenze per finali: Exuberant and Extended Cadences in the 16th and 17th Centuries*

Josué Meléndez Peláez
(University of Music, Trossingen)

We all have heard about improvised *cadenze* in classical and early romantic music, where a soloist displays her/his abilities and expressiveness towards the end of a musical piece. But do we know if this practice has antecedents in music before the classical period, and if yes, was it part of a common practice?

Extended virtuoso cadences that prolong the penultimate note of a musical piece are well documented in the second half of the sixteenth century and throughout the seventeenth. These cadences are mostly called *finale* (sometimes also *accadenza*) and their most remarkable characteristic is that they alter the length of the penultimate measure, prolonging it to provide space to add a richly ornamented cadence. Indeed, written examples of ornamented cadences[1] that are not called *finale* stay strictly to the number of beats given in their original unornamented figures, but the examples of *cadenze per finali*, the *finali diversi per diversi parti* and the *fini diversi* found in Francesco Rognoni's *Selva di varii passaggi*[2], as well as the *finali* in Johannes Andreas Herbst's *Musica moderna prattica*[3], the *cadenze finali* in the Estense manuscript (for the theorbo)[4] and the *concludendii* and *finalia* cadences in Spiridionis a Monte Carmelo's *Nuova Instructio*[5], all add extra beats to the penultimate note.

Could we imagine a classical *cadenza*-type ending in renaissance motets and madrigals or in early baroque monody?

*. A special thank to Helen Roberts and Catherine Motuz for correcting of the English language in this article.

1. For general information about cadences see Schwannberger, Sven. 'Kadenzfiguration in verschiedenen Stillen', in: Schwenkreis 2018, pp. 134-139.

2. Rognoni 1620.

3. Herbst 1653.

4. Anonymous 1995 (Estense Codex G 239).

5. Spiridionis 1670, Pars 1-2, 1670-1671.

In this article I will explain how these *cadenze per finali* were performed, written out, or just left *a suo genio* (to the performer's own genius), providing information from sources of the time that prove that this practice was common. I suggest a term to call these cadences for analytical purposes, and propose a method for inserting them in modern performances.

Already on the front page of Francesco Rognoni's *Selva di vari passaggi secondo l'uso moderno*, we read: «[here] is shown [...] the way how to *passegiar* [ornament] stepwise, with jumps of third, fourth, fifth, sixth, octave, and final cadences for all the voices, with various other examples, [...]». On the front page of the second part of his *Selva*, he addresses «Difficult *passaggi* for the instruments, [...] *cadentie finali*; examples, diminished songs [...]»[6]. In the index of both books he seems to distinguish between *cadenze* and *finali* whereby the examples called *finali* are the only ones that add extra beats or measures to the original figure. Systematically, the examples that are called simply *cadenze*, keep strictly the values of the original figures but all those that say *finale* or *fini* or *finali*, add extra beats, more or less randomly, to the penultimate note. Let us take some examples from Rognoni's page for 'Cadenze & finali sopra il basso' (Cadences & final cadences over the bass). Here we see that the first three diminutions for each cadence stays strictly within the original values of the unornamented version, but the fourth diminution of each cadence, which has an indication «per doi battuti o finali» (*per due battute o finali*, that is, for two measures or for final cadences), extends the original values by one measure. The title of the page and its contents seem to be very clear and leave us with only one possible thought: *cadenze* = cadences and *finali* = prolonged cadences for the end of a piece (see Ex. 1).

Ex. 1: Rognoni 1620, examples from 'Cadenze & finali sopra il basso'.

[6]. See Rognoni 1620.

In the several pages that Rognoni dedicates to cadences we find, again in a very systematic way, that only the cadences called *finali* alter the original figure, prolonging those that consist of one semibreve by adding two more semibreves, and those ones that are originally one breve by adding one extra semibreve (in most of the cases).

J. A. Herbst's *Musica Moderna e Prattica overo la maniera del buon canto* shows the exact same procedure, as do the *cadenze finali* from the Estense Manuscript for theorbo, although here the cadences have no original unornamented figure to refer to[7].

On the other hand, all treatises mentioning *tactus* or *battuta* in relation to *passaggi* agree that it is most important to keep the length of the original values intact. Ricardo Rognoni even recommends measuring the beat by tapping your foot «because the mind is occupied with other tasks [i.e., improvising diminutions] and without that guide, one will often find oneself lost at the end»[8]. Ludovico Zacconi dedicates almost a whole page to the importance of not converting eighths into quarters, arguing against those *suministratori del tatto* (those in charge of the tactus) that do so when a *gran copia di chrome* is to be found in the score[9]. Nevertheless, Zacconi himself, as well as Giovanni Battista Bovicelli, accepts the insertion of extra measures at the final cadence, or more precisely, at the penultimate note, in order to add more ornamentation. Criticising those musicians who, in order to accommodate *passaggi* to their own wish, hold a note that is equal to a measure for two, or even three measures, Bovicelli allows an exception by saying: «I know well that it is more praiseworthy while playing *passaggi* to stay bound to the *tempo giusto* that is to be found in the written chant, except for the end, that is, the penultimate note»[10]. Zacconi's *Prattica di Musica* dedicates a whole chapter to different ways of ending a cantilena[11]. In total he describes six final cadences; the two of them that he considers principal are — or can be — prolonged: *commune* and *soggetto*.

> After having spoken about the beginning, and the middle of a piece, it is convenient that I speak about the end; which is as important as the other two: so while beginning it is necessary [to maintain] the good way and the art; and in the middle [it is important to maintain] manners, and graces: at the end one

7. Most of the cadances in the Estense Manuscript are three semibreves long, i.e., exactly the same length as all of the sources calling for *cadenze finali*.

8. Rognoni 1592.

9. Zacconi 1592, fol. 76v.

10. Bovicelli 1594. p. 14: «Sogliono alcuni che per accomodarsi i Passaggi a modo loro, se una nota vale una battuta, tenerla due, ò tre, con che ragione, io no 'l so, so bene che è più laudabile nel Passeggiare star obligato al tempo giusto, che si trova nel Canto, fuori, che nel fine cioè nella penultima nota». Translation by Josué Mélendez.

11. Zacconi had defined cantilena as music on paper. Libro 1, chapter 3, fol. 4v: «[...] quando io vorò per Musica intendere le carte ove sono affisse et poste le figure Musicalli, ò che io le dirò cantilene, over libri da catare [...]» («when I want to understand under the term music of paper, on which musical notes are placed, [that] I call them either cantilenae or singing book»; translated in Gerhard 1968, p. 125).

needs manners and graces with art and the proper way: and if the end seems to be an easy thing, nevertheless you will find difficulties, not known to everyone.

But by demonstrating some endings here, I say that singers should be aware while singing the end of a piece, not to do like some not-very-aware singers do, that at the end cause dissatisfaction to the ears of the listeners because they don't pay attention to the final figure[12], which can be of two principal types, that is, *commune* and *soggetto*: *Commune* is the name of that ending when all parts agree on the value of such figures [presumably, how long the figure will be], as shown here [...]

Then you have to stay on the penultimate figure as long as all other parts want and are happy with; and then jump to the last figure: [the end] place where all voices agree[13].

Zacconi continues with a confusing explanation distinguishing between the *figura finale* (final figure) and the *ultima figura* (last figure), being the final figure the penultimate note of a piece. Staying (*fermare*) on the penultimate figure (note), as long as all parts want, upon an agreement on the value of that final figures seems to describe a kind of *fermata* on the penultimate note (in this case the fifth degree of a perfect cadence) to which the time values previously agreed are added. In a different chapter Zacconi tells us about soprano leading-note cadences (not necessarily cadences at the end of a piece) that can be held long: «Similarly, in cadences, that replication of sol-fa-sol; la-sol-la; fa-mi-fa; and the others can be held as long as all the time lasts that is required»[14].

Zacconi proceeds again in a very confusing way trying to explain mistakes that can be produced if a cadence is extended. Sion M. Honea has clarified that «What he [Zacconi]

---

[12]. By final figure Zacconi refers here to the penultimate note.

[13]. Zacconi 1592, libro i, chapter 70, fol. 79: «Havendo io dunque parlato del principio, e del mezzo delle cantilene, è cosa conveniente che io parli anche del fine; il quale è si d'importanza quanto che sia l'uno e l'altro: poi che se nel dar principio ci bisogna il modo, e l'arte; e nel mezzo le maniere, e le vaghezze: nel fine ci voranno le vaghezze, e le maniere, con l'arte, e il debbito modo: E se bene il fine par che sia una cosa facile: non di meno molte difficoltà vi si trovano non cosi da tutti conosciute. / Però volendone dimostrar alcune dico, che i cantori nel finir di cantare una cantilena si guardino di far quello che fanno alcuni poco accorti, che nel finir fanno mala sodisfattione alle orecchie de gli ascoltanti per non avertire alla figura finale, la quale può esser di due sorte principalmente, cioè commune, e soggetto: Commune si chiama quel fine quando le parte tutte convengano nel valore delle istesse figure, come a dire quando le parte finiscano, come qui si vede [musical example]. Allhora su la penultima figura tanto si hà da fermare quanto che tutte l'altre parte vogliano, e si contentano; e poi salire all'ultima figura; termine e l'uoco ove convengano tutte le voci sonore: [...]». I wish to thank David Yacus for revising my translation of this quote.

[14]. Honea, translation of Zacconi's libro i, part i, chapter 66, p. 16.

is describing is that some careless singers in wishing to ornament the very end of the cadence introduce pitches that can cause dissonance with the lower voices if the ornament is prolonged too far»[15].

Back to the chapter on how to finish a *cantilena*, Zacconi describes the cadence he calls *soggetto* as:

> [...] a figure on which all the other voices make, with a distinctive final voice, *quasi* like a windmill, or like turning around in an artful, lovely and pleasant way; joking [playing] around the mentioned end». [...]: «but we must know that not every time that we finish singing a cantilena, the singer should stop on the penultimate figure [note]: because on some occasions, by staying in [*fermandosi*] there could be discordance [*dissonanze*] with all the other parts, [...][16].

The singer cannot necessarily stay (*fermarsi*) on the penultimate note at the end of every *cantilena*. In the example that Zacconi provides, if the tenor were to stay on the penultimate note, a horrible, cacophonous collision would occur. Therefore, Zacconi's recommendation for this particular cadence is obviously correct. What intrigues me is that these and other observations of Zacconi confirm that it seems to have been common for singers to stop at the penultimate note of a cadence, and not necessarily only at the end of a piece, to add florid ornamentation. Other sources such as F. Rognoni and J. A. Herbst, both intended for performers to teach themselves by 'picking up' ornaments (*pigliare* or *servirsene*) and placing them into their performances, confirm that extending a cadence for a pair of beats or a pair of measures, was a common practice and that the usual term to define these cadences was *finale*[17]. Other composers, such as Giulio Caccini, associate

[15]. *Ibidem*, fn. 62.

[16]. Zacconi 1592, libro I, chapter 70, p. 79: «La figura del fine poi che è soggetto è una figura sopra la quale tutte l'altre parte con sumministratione di voce finale fanno quasi come un poco di girandola, o' torneamento: non meno artificioso che vago, e dilettevole; scherzando intorno al detto finale: [...] però è da sapere che non ogni volta che si finisce di cantare una cantilena, il cantore su la penultima figura si ha da fermare: perche fermandosi in alcune occasione faria dissonanza con tutte l'altre parte [...]».

[17]. Remarkably interesting, in that it shows the continuity of these ornamentation traditions into the nineteenth century, is Manuel Garcia's quotation of Herbst when proposing alternative musical endings to

finali with long *passaggi*[18] although he, as well as others including Francesco Severi and some examples in the Estense manuscript, often prolongs the antepenultimate note rather than the penultimate. Severi's *Salmi passaggiati* is a collection of vespers psalms (and some Misereres) in the *falso bordone* manner of improvisation. His examples provide great evidence of prolonged passages and cadences that were otherwise mostly improvised[19].

Do we have any other surviving pieces that demonstrate this practice? Surviving pieces with long final cadences that prolong their penultimate note in order to add diminutions can be found in works by Girolamo Dalla Casa, Giovanni Bassano, Ricardo Rogniono, Francesco Rognoni, Bartolomeo de Selma, Oratio (Bassani), Ascanio Mayone and Antonio Terzi, as well as in later composers including Dario Castello, Biagio Marini, Bartolomeo Barbarino, Francesco Severi, Tarquinio Merula, Giovanni Batista Fontana, Antonio Pandolfi Mealli, Vincenzo Bonizzi, Girolamo Frescobaldi, Michael Praetorius and many others. In the case of the written-out diminutions on original motets or madrigals, it is obvious that sometimes the final cadence has been prolonged (see Ex. 3, p. 69). In compositions such as the early seventeenth-century sonata or monody, we need to understand the concept of extending or prolonging a cadence to be able to call it a *finale*. However, a quick look at different bass lines gives us a very good idea of the concept. In Ex. 2 there is a simple cadence next to a *finale* cadence. Surprisingly, we could eventually prolong the first cadence, making it look like the second one, and add a florid *finale* cadence according to our own wishes; that same procedure could be done with any motet, madrigal, chanson or monody.

Ex. 2: Fontana bass lines (Fontana 1641).

the word Amen — presumably to be used at the end of a piece or a section of it (Manuel Garcia, *L'Art du chant*, 1847, p. 77). Garcia begins by copying Herbst's two first examples and continues, obviously inspired by Herbst, with his own solutions, in much the same way that Herbst himself does with the works of F. Rognoni, Bovicelli and Donati, who likewise praised the works of the older Girolamo da Udine (Dalla Casa) and Bassano (Giovanni).

18. See Gatti 2014, pp. 102-103.

19. Severi 1615.

Ex. 3: final cadence of the madrigal *Vestiva i colli* by G. P. da Palestrina. Erig 1979. The two prolonged diminutions are by F. Rognoni. The one with the indication *a cadenza* is by De Selma 1638.

*) Basso continuo

John Butt has discussed the increased tendency in the late seventeenth century for composers to include written-out embellishments in their works[20]. By comparing *cadenze finali* and other common passages included in diminution treatises to written-out music, it is possible to prove that this happens already in the early seventeenth century. Indeed, the surviving diminution pieces provide a trace of this trend also during the sixteenth century. Many compositions show a similar style to those *finali* by Francesco Rognoni, for example Castello's Sonata prima or seconda[21], the examples in the Carlo G. manuscript, or Fontana's sonata prima or seconda[22], among many others. Francesco Lomazzo writes at the end of Francesco Rognoni's second book that «the author does not deny that someone could serve himself to any kind of *passaggio* contained in the book, or of any other author, to make a cadenza, or finale, or [to place it] in any imitative passage of whatever *cantilena*, [it] being a praiseworthy thing to know how to combine them [the passages]»[23]. Musicians have always been copying works from each other to learn from them or to use or recycle specific materials in their own works. It is not surprising therefore, but nevertheless curious, that Lomazzo tells us about two or three pages of *Cadenze, ò finali* that were once stolen from his teacher (F. Rognoni).

What is surprising, though, is the artistic outpouring achieved by some sixteenth-century musicians when performing ornaments. According to Zacconi: «there are some [singers] who, at the end of a *cantilena*, desire to ornament for an hour long, and make all [their] colleagues wait for them, and even if the colleagues have waited for quite a bit, they [this singers] finish anyway after them»[24]. Likewise, more than a century later, Pier Francesco Tosi complains also about singers ornamenting too long at the final cadence. His complaint gives us a clue as to a difference in performance practice: by arguing that at the final cadence, no listener that knows about music would appreciate a cadence without a bassline, Tosi gives us a clear indication that all those not ornamenting at the end of a piece would come to a complete stop[25].

The practice of extending or prolonging a cadence might have started with the tendency of musicians to structure their works after the rhetoric discourse of the ancient Greeks. Ann Smith says that «[...] in the course of the humanist movement in the 15th century, the antique sources on rhetoric were rediscovered and soon became part of the gentle person's basic education»[26]. In this manner, «Gallus Dressler, in 1563 in his *Praecepta*

[20]. BUTT 1991.

[21]. CASTELLO 1629.

[22]. FONTANA 1641.

[23]. ROGNONI 1620, p. 76.

[24]. ZACCONI 1592, libro I, chapter 70, p. 79v: «[...] sono alcuni che nel fine delle cantilene, vogliano con le glorie tenerle un hora lunghe; e fanno che tutti gli altri compagni lo stiano ad aspettare, oltre che molte volte se bene l'hanno un pezzo aspettato, le finiscono dopo loro».

[25]. TOSI 1723, p. 89. TOSI 1967, pp. 44-45.

[26]. SMITH 2011, chapter 'The Rhetoric of Counterpoint', pp. 102ff.

Musicae Poeticae, began talking about the structure of a musical piece being similar to that of an oration»[27].

Conclusio, also called *finis*, is the part (or period) of a speech that defines the end. In his *Musical poetica* of 1606, in a chapter dedicated to musical analysis and arrangement, Joachim Burmeister divides a piece into three parts, writing that: «The ending is the principal cadence where either all the musical movement [*modulatio*] ceases or where one or two voices stop while the others continue with a brief passage called *supplementum*»[28]. Later on, analyzing Lasso's motet *In me transierunt irae tuae*, (according to Joshua Rifkin the first known analysis of a musical piece)[29] Burmeister subdivides a piece into nine rhetorical periods. «The Final, namely, the ninth, period is like the Epilog of the speech. This harmony displays a principal ending, otherwise called a *supplementum* of the final cadence, [...]»[30]. Indeed, the final cadence of this motet adds a kind of two bars supplement; the tenor concludes its final cadence and stays still holding its last note while the other four voices play around with the first and fourth degree of the mode. This is the cadence that Zacconi calls *soggetto*. Final cadences that have one or more voices holding the final note while the others continue for a couple of bars can be found in works of many renaissance and early baroque composers[31]. An extreme example of this type of cadence can be seen in the Sonata x by Gioanpietro del Buono[32] (see Ex. 4) where the tenor voice arrives at the final note at measure eleven while the other voices continue for another twenty measures.

A kind of sister of this *supplemento* or *soggetto* cadence seems to be the so called *accadenza* or *a cadenza*, an extra cadence that moves around the fourth and first degrees, which appears sometimes at the end of a piece as an *ad libitum* extra cadence. In the diminutions by Bortholomeo de Selma on Lasso's *Susane un jour*, an impressive amount of diminutions are placed in the last nine measures. These are to be repeated as many times as the soloist wants, with the request to warn the organist about the number of times this last section will be repeated. This section is followed, as if after ten repetitions it would not be enough to conclude the piece, by another four measures that play around the fourth and first degrees in the *soggetto-supplemento* manner with the indication *accadenza*[33].

---

27. *Ibidem*.

28. Burmeister 1993, p. 205.

29. See Smith 2011, chapter 'The Rhetoric of Counterpoint', pp. 102ff.

30. Burmeister 1993, p. 207.

31. For example: the chanson *Douce Memoire* by Pier Sandrin, the already mentioned *In me transierunt* by Lasso, the madrigal *Così le chiome* (the second part of Palestrina's mottet *Vestiva i colli*), Thomas Crecquillon's *Une gay bergier* and *Oncques amour*, Adrian Willaert's *Iouissance vous donneray* and *À la Fontaine du pré*, G. B. Fontana's *Sonata prima*, etc.

32. Del Buono 1641.

33. See Erig 1979, pp. 171 and 376. This same base pattern is to be found in many both vocal and instrumental 17th-century works.

Ex. 4: Gioanpietro del Buono, Sonata x sopra *Ave Maris Stella* (transcription by Lorenzo Girodo).

The recently discovered Carlo G. manuscript contains a great number of sketched diminutions added to passages and cadences that require the original figure in the score to be prolonged in order to fit. Additional ornaments for final cadences, intermediate cadences and other passages that alter the original score to add ornamentation are to be found throughout the whole manuscript. Thus, this manuscript provides enough information to understand how these cadences were performed and to confirm that this practice existed.

> An interesting feature of the Carlo G MS is the addition of optional variants for certain vocal passages. In many pieces, there are one or more *ossias*; these appear typically, but not always, on the final cadence, suggesting different variants for certain diminutions. These optional variants are not consistent in their nature; sometime they offer an easier and shorter passage, but sometime a longer and more virtuosic one. They are mostly not labeled with text, but when they are, it is along the line of: *passaggio altro* (another passage), or *per chi vuol variare* (for those who would like to vary)[34].

Ex. 6: Carlo G. ms., *Confiteor Deo*, bars 28-34.

[34]. Rotem forthcoming. Selected pieces have been edited online in <https://imslp.org/wiki/Di_Carlo_G._(Anonymous)>, accessed November 2018, by Elam Rotem. *The Carlo G Manuscript: Virtuoso Liturgical Music from the Early 17th Century*, CD, Profeti della Quinta, Glossa, 2017, GCD 922516.

Ex. 7: Carlo G. ms., *Ego Flos Campi*, bars 23ff.

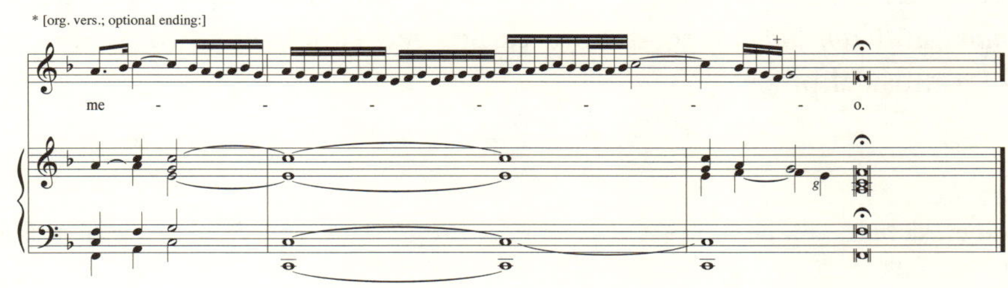

One of the first questions appearing when trying to add a *finale* cadence in modern performances is how they were to be accompanied, that is, what kind of counterpoint or harmonic patterns should be used with a prolonged cadence. The Carlo G. manuscript offers us several answers for this question. In all plagal cadences, the penultimate chord is simply held during the added embellishments. In perfect cadences sometime the chord is held long, but sometimes we find a 5/3 6/4 5/4 5/3 basso continuo pattern over the penultimate note. The *cadenze finale* from the Estense manuscript for the theorbo have mostly this kind of counterpoint pattern and, in general, the *finale* examples from Herbst and Rognoni, particularly the longest ones, seem to need that cadential pattern. I have experimented by pasting cadences requiring this pattern from both F. Rognoni's and Estense's *finali* into real pieces, with a satisfactory result[35].

Another interesting source is Spiridionis a Monte Carmelo's *Nuova instructio*[36], a series of four books intended for keyboard players to learn the practice of improvisation through memorisation and transposition of a sort of «encyclopedic collection of 1251 musical segments»[37] called *cadentiae*. Spiridione explains in the introductory letter to the reader that combining and transposing different cadences is the secret for this practice, pointing out the importance of learning how to close a musical phrase quickly (*hurtig schliessen*) with a small cadence and how to play all kinds of *finalia*[38]. In the Latin version of this text Spiridione uses the terms *concludendi* and *finalia* to denote small and large cadences. In the first pages of the first book we find 72 cadences from which a prolongation of a minim is to be found from example number 32 onwards, as well as a prolongation of a semibreve after example 42 and of two semibreves after example 57. All of these cadences present a systematic use of the 5/3 6/4 5/4 5/3 basso continuo pattern already mentioned.

Could we give a term to differentiate this cadences? It is important that, for analytical purposes, we are able to distinguish between a normal cadence and one that has been prolonged in order to add florid ornamentation, regardless of whether it is intermediate or final. It seems logical to assume that for Spiridione, a cadence that closes quickly is a *concludendi* and a prolonged cadence is a *finalia*. Considering that F. Rognoni's and Herbst's '*finalia*' add at least one semibreve, and that some intermediate prolonged cadences can be found that add only one minim, I would suggest the generic terms *finalia* and *concludendi* to denote prolonged cadences both at the end and in the middle of a musical piece.

---

35. Some examples can be heard at <www.ifedeli.org/audio>, accessed November 2018.

36. Spiridionis 1670.

37. Bellotti 2003, 'Preface'.

38. Spiridionis 1670, 'Ad Lectorem. Dem Leser', p. 3: «[...] und lernt Mann dadurch hurtig schliessen und allerhand Finalia machen».

Could prolonged cadences be related to any other type of contrapuntal *fioriture* such as *canti fermi* or pedal-like movements?

Are there any similarities between this extended Renaissance *finalia* and the classical *cadenza*, the long or double cadence, or the prolonged *cadenza finta* of the Neapolitan partimento?

Harmonic pattern relationships can be traced in between the partimento cadences, the *finalia* in Estense manuscript and Spiridioni's *Nuova Instructio*[39]. Furthermore, it is unlikely that the realisation of Durante's *Perfidia* partimento[40], which offers extremely elaborated passages and leaves the final cadence empty, with the remark *a suo genio*, would be concluded with an empty and short cadence. Instead, a majestic and well extended cadence, even for 'an hour long', could be expected.

Finally, the most clear difference between the renaissance *finalia* and the classical *cadenza* is that in the latter, the soloist is left completely alone to demonstrate their virtuosity. In the former, all other performers hold the harmony steady, for a previously agreed value, in order for the 'soloist' to add more ornamentation. The terms *a suo genio*, *col canto*, *colla parte* or *point d'orgue*, are indications that continue the renaissance *finalia* into the following centuries.

The exuberant ornamentations found in several diminution treatises of the renaissance and early baroque musical era include examples of prolonged cadences that can be added to any motet, madrigal, sonata or monody, regardless of the number of voices involved. Howard Mayer Brown, referring to sixteenth-century ornamentation, has pointed out that: «Any comprehensive view of musical life in the Renaissance would be incomplete that did not take into account these spontaneous sounds»[41]. Thus all these sources together provide a glimpse of an entirely lost practice that we are trying to recover today, and if authenticity is required in historically informed performance practice, copying ornaments form old treatises might be a good start. However, the final cadence might not be the first ornament we should add to our performance, as Zacconi warns: «In addition, the singer should take care at the end of any song not to do what many little wise and little practiced in this profession do, who make such a great mass of embellishments (*vaghezze*), because they want to show off everything at the end and have all the middle left empty and barren»[42].

---

39. For other similarities between partimento cadences and renaissance cadences see Menke, Johannes. 'Potentiale der *Cadenza doppia*', in: Schwenkreis 2018, pp. 59-66.

40. See Sanguinetti 2012, pp. 227-228.

41. Brown 1976.

42. Honea, translation of Zacconi's libro 1, part 1, chapter 66, p. 9. In Zacconi 1592, libro 1, p. 59: «In oltre si guardi il cantore nella fine di qual si voglia cantilena di non far ciò che fanno molti poco accorti, et molto poco prattici in questa professione: che fanno tanta gran copia di vaghezze, che ogni cosa vogliono mostrar nel fine, et hanno tutto il mezzo lasciato voto et secco».

Bibliography

Anonymous 1995

Anonymous. *Cadenze e passaggi diversi intavolati per tiorba dal manoscritto Estense G 239 (sec. xvii)*, edited by Tiziano Bagnati, Bologna, Ut Orpheus Edizioni, 1995 (Società italiana del liuto, 1).

Bellotti 2003

Spiridionis a Monte Carmelo. *Nova instructio pro pulsandis organis, spinettis, monuchordiis, pars prima, (Bamberg, 1670); pars seconda (Bamberg, 1671)*, edited by Edoardo Bellotti, Colledara (TE), Andromeda Editrice, 2003 (Tastature: musiche intavolate per strumenti da tasto, 11).

Bovicelli 1594

Bovicelli, Giovanni Battista. *Regole, passaggi di musica, madrigali, e motteti passeggiati* [...], Venice, G. Vincenti, 1594.

Brown 1976

Brown, Howard Mayer. *Embellishing 16th-Century Music*, London, Oxford University Press, 1976 (Early Music Series, 1).

Burmeister 1993

Burmeister, Joachim. *Musical Poetics*, (1606), translation, with introduction and notes by Benito V. Rivera, New Haven-London, Yale University Press, 1993 (Music Theory Translation Series).

Butt 1991

Butt, John. 'Improvised Vocal Ornamentation and German Baroque Compositional Theory: An Approach to "Historical" Performance Practice', in: *Journal of the Royal Musical Association*, cxvi/1 (1991), pp. 41-62.

Castello 1629

Castello, Dario. *Sonate concertate in stil moderno* [...] *a 1. 2. 3. Et 4. voci, Libro secondo*, Venice, Gardano appresso Bartolomeo Magni, 1629.

De Selma 1638

Selma y Salaverde, Bartolomé de. *Canzoni fantasie e correnti da suonar ad una 2. 3. 4. Con basso continuo, Libro primo e secondo*, Venice, Magni, 1638.

Del Buono 1641

Del Buono, Gioanpietro. *Canoni oblighi et sonate in varie maniere sopra l'Ave Maris Stella*, Palermo, Ant. Martarello et Santo d'Angelo, 1641.

Erig 1979

Italian Diminutions: The Pieces with more than One Diminution from 1553 to 1638, edited by Richard Erig and Veronika Gutmann, Zurich, Amadeus, 1979 (Prattica Musicale, 1).

Fontana 1641

Fontana, Giovanni Battista. *Sonate a 1. 2. 3. per il violino, o cornetto, fagotto, chitarrone, violoncino, o simile altro istromento*, Venice, Bartolomeo Magni, 1641.

Gatti 2014

Gatti, Enrico. '«Però ci vole pacientia»: un excursus sull'arte della diminuzione nei secoli xvi, xvii e xviii «per uso di chi avrà volontà di studiare»', in: Acciai, Giovanni – Gatti, Enrico – Tavella, Konrad. *Regole per ben suonare e cantare: diminuzioni e mensuralismo fra xvi e xix secolo*, Pisa, ETS, 2014 (Quaderni del Conservatorio 'Giuseppe Verdi' di Milano, n.s. 2/2014), pp. 71-188.

Gerhard 1968

Gerhard, Singer. *Ludovico Zacconi's Treatment of the "Suitability and Classification of All Musical Instruments" in the «Prattica di Musica» of 1592*, Ph.D. Diss., Los Angeles (CA), University of Southern California, 1968.

Herbst 1653

Herbst, Johann-Andream. *Musica moderna prattica, overo Maniera del buon canto. Das ist: Eine kurtze Anleitung wie die Knaben und andere so sonderbahre Lust und Liebe zum Singen tragen auff jetzige italienische Manier* [...] *können informirt und unterrichtet werden*, Frankfurt, A. Hummen, 1653.

Honea

Lodovico Zacconi. Prattica di Musica (1596), Part 1, Book 1, Chapter 66, 'Che stile si tenghi nel far di gorgia, & dell'uso de i moderni passaggi', translated by Sion M. Honea, at <https://www.uco.edu/cfad/files/music/zacconi-prattica.pdf>, accessed November 2018.

Rognoni 1592

Rognoni, [Rognono, Rogniono], Riccardo. *Passaggi per potersi essercitare nel diminuire*, Venice, Vincenti, 1592.

Rognoni 1620

Rognoni, Francesco. *Selva de varii passaggi* [...], (1620), edited by Alessandro Bares, Albese con Cassano (Como), Musedita, 2014.

Rotem forthcoming

Rotem, Elam. 'The Carlo G Manuscript. New Light on Early 17th-Century Accompaniment and Diminution Practices', in: *Basler Jahrbuch für historische Musikpraxis xxxix-2015*, forthcoming.

Sanguinetti 2012

Sanguinetti, Giorgio. *The Art of Partimento: History, Theory, and Practice*, Oxford-New York, Oxford University Press, 2012.

Schwenkreis 2018

Compendium Improvisation: Fantasieren nach historischen quellen des 17. und 18. Jahrhunderts, edited by Markus Schwenkreis, Basel, Schwabe Verlag, 2018 (Scripta, 5).

Severi 1615

Severi, Francesco. *Salmi passaggiati per tutte le voci* [...]. *Libro primo*, Rome, N. Borboni, 1615.

Smith 2011

Smith, Anne. *The Performance of 16th-Century Music: Learning from the Theorists*, Oxford-New York, Oxford University Press, 2011.

Spiridionis 1670
Spiridionis a Monte Carmelo. *Nova instructio pro pulsandis organis, spinettis, monuchordiis, pars prima*, Bamberg, Immel, 1670.

Tosi 1723
Tosi, Pier Francesco. *Opinione de' cantori antichi e moderni*, Bologna, Lelio dalla Volpe, 1723.

Tosi 1967
Id. *Observations on the Florid Song*, translated into English by John Ernest Galliard, London, William Reeves, 1967.

Zacconi 1592
Zacconi, Lodovico. *Prattica di musica* [...], Venice, G. Polo, 1592.

Written Outlines of Improvisation Procedures in Music Publications of the Early 17th Century

The Second (1611-1623) and Third (1615-1623) Book of *Concerti* By G. Ghizzolo and the Motet *Iesu Rex Admirabilis* (1625-1627) by G. Frescobaldi

Marina Toffetti
(Università di Padova)

And now the miracle is that this life,
presenting itself immediately, streaming forth and acting spontaneously,
expresses itself in a content given and shaped elsewhere.
Georg Simmel, *Toward the Philosophy of the Actor*[1]

Just as the script of the 'commedia dell'arte' (not by chance also called 'commedia all'improvviso', or 'commedia improvvisa', to underline its intrinsically improvisational nature) limits itself to sketching the main sequence of events and indicating the entrances and exits of the various characters, without fixing the individual lines in writing (which will be integrated extemporaneously by the actors), in the same way the musical text simply provides some of the coordinates necessary for its performance, which need to be integrated by the creative input of the performer.

While, however, all musical repertoires offer interpreters a relative freedom in terms of agogics, dynamics and expression, there are phases and repertoires in which the performer is required to provide a more significant contribution, which goes beyond the choice of how to interpret the indications provided by the composer — which are usually relatively prescriptive as far as the pitch and duration of the notes are concerned, and more indicative with regards the agogic-dynamic aspect of the performance — involving a sort of 'completion' of the compositional plan of the composer by means of extemporary integrations to the melodic texture (with an embellishing or diminutive function) and/or the harmony (with a supporting function) of the composition.

One such phase is the Baroque period, not by chance defined as the «age of the basso continuo': it comes as no surprise, then, that it is precisely the basso continuo that represents one of the elements of 17th- and 18th-century compositions which most places the performer in the dual role of performer and composer-improviser[2].

[1]. Simmel 1920-1921, p. 13.
[2]. See Gatti 2014.

The basso continuo consists in an uninterrupted melodic line (hence the adjective 'continuo'), generally set in the low register (thus the noun 'basso'), destined to be played by one or more 'fundamental' instruments and realized harmonically in an improvised manner, through the introduction of chords or variously articulated simultaneous configurations, by one or more 'ornamental' instruments (in the case of multi-voice instruments, like the organ or the harpsichord, one single instrument can carry out both functions)[3].

However, the improvisational (or more precisely elaborative) role of the performer (in this case, of the continuo player) was not limited to the mere realization of the harmonies explicitly indicated in (or simply implied by) the continuo part, but also concerned its own line, which could be played as indicated in the scores, but which was frequently re-elaborated in a variously 'articulated' manner, leaving us to suppose that, over and above what was prescribed by the composer, the continuo player tended, in fact, to perform it in a different way each time.

What most interests us here is the fact that certain traces of this usage can be found within some editions of the period, and in particular by comparing different editions of the same collection (or of the same composition). When faced with such variants, one must ask oneself whether they are the will of the composer (that is, whether the composer had changed his intentions and had deliberately made some more or less substantial changes to the continuo line in the new edition), or whether they are presumably ascribable to someone other than the composer (for example the music publisher, who may also have made the changes for extra-musical reasons). In these cases, depending on the circumstances, the most appropriate editorial strategy needs to be chosen. Moreover, one must also determine whether the variants found in the basso continuo lines might supply information useful for the modern performer and thus *if*, and if deemed appropriate, *how* they should be restituted in a modern edition.

---

[3]. On the problems posed by the realization of the basso continuo see the 18th-century treatises by Agostino Agazzari (Agazzari 1607) and Francesco Bianciardi (Bianciardi 1607). Some suggestions of a practical nature, accompanied by short musical examples, can be found in the short manual by the 'Professore della musica' Pietro Paolo Sabbatini published in Rome in the mid-17th century (see Sabbatini 1650, pp. 16-18, 'Modo per sonare il basso continuo per li principianti') and in *Li primi albori musicali* by Lorenzo Penna (Penna 1672-1679-1684). See RISM B/vi, p. 743d. The treatises of the 18th century are more copious and include those by Michael de Saint Lambert (Saint Lambert 1707), *L'Armonico pratico al cimbalo* by Francesco Gasparini (Gasparini 1708), the *Principes de l'accompagnement du clavecin* by Jean-François Dandrieu (Dandrieu 1718), the *Versuch einer Anweisung die Flote traversiere zu spielen* by Johann Joachim Quantz (Quantz 1752), *Le maitre de clavecin pour l'accompagnement* by Michel Corrette (Corrette 1753), the *Versuch uber die wahre Art das Clavier zu spielen* by Carl Philipp Emanuel Bach (Bach 1753-1762), *Li primi albori musicali* by Lorenzo Penna (Penna 1672-1679-1684), the *Pratica d'accompagnamento sopra bassi numerati e contrappunti a più voci sulla scala maggiore e minore* by Stanislao Mattei (Mattei 1788), the treatise *Thorough-bass Made Easy: Or Practical Rules for Finding and Applying Its Various Chords With Little Trouble* by Nicolò Pasquali (Pasquali 1757), while at the beginning of the 19th century it must be remembered *The Singer's Preceptor: A Treatise on Vocal Music Calculated to Teach the Art of Singing* by Domenico Corri (Corri 1810).

This article offers a reflection on the consequences that this peculiar relation between the fixed text and its extemporary realization in performance might have in editing a musical edition of compositions from the first half of the 17th century. It is an issue that has already been dealt with, first and foremost by taking into consideration the great deal of information on performance practice deducible from indirect coeval sources (manuals on realizing the basso continuo, theoretical treatises, descriptions of musical performances, iconographic sources of various kinds). The intention here is firstly to examine the information available from direct musical sources — namely the actual musical editions — focusing in particular on the information that be gleaned from a comparison of the first editions and the later reprints or re-editions. This will highlight how a new edition of a given musical collection could be transformed (and in fact this was often the case) into an opportunity to introduce corrections or to make changes to previously published works, *and in particular to the line of the basso continuo*. Setting aside the question of who was responsible for such changes, one needs to ask if, and to what extent, they might reflect aspects of coeval performance practice.

Although this peculiar relation between the written text and performance practice that was created in the 17th- and 18th-century repertoire does not bring about any radical transformation in the role of the music philologist (whose task will remain that of publishing scientifically grounded critical editions, attempting to reconstruct a text that is as close as possible to the last will of the composer) or in that of the performer (who will continue to have the task of proposing the repertoire in the context of live concerts or recordings), we nevertheless believe that it highlights the need for a closer collaboration between the editor of the edition and the 'historically informed' performer, both of whom should be intent on comprehending not only what is explicitly prescribed in the text, but also what it implies in terms of extemporary realization. We also think that this repertoire requires a greater awareness on the part of the philologist with respect to all those elements of the ancient edition which, if adequately incorporated in the modern edition, could prove useful in understanding and studying the various aspects of the performance practice of the time, as well as a greater consciousness of what should be fixed (or, on the contrary, *not* fixed) in the modern edition, making sure not to overlook any information that might be potentially useful to the performer, but at the same time not limiting his/her creative-improvisational input. In order to achieve an acceptable balance between these two requirements it could prove useful, at least in some cases, to adopt particular solutions in the presentation of the musical text that may in part be different from those commonly adopted in the restitution of other types of repertoire.

In this context any variants that come to light during the comparison of different editions of the same composition have a dual value, and will thus be examined from a dual perspective: on the one hand, we will consider what the implications might be for the way the musical text is presented in the critical edition (and therefore which elements are worth presenting to the modern user and how to present them); on the other, what impact they might have on performance practice (and therefore how to use this wide but often contradictory store of information deducible from ancient sources for the purpose of interpretation).

It will also be necessary to reflect on the nature of such variants from a strictly philological point of view. Although each case should obviously be examined in its own specific context, it can nevertheless be observed how, broadly speaking, the variants made to the vocal lines tend to be mostly a matter of substitutive variants, while those made to the basso continuo line, where the line is simply 'redesigned' in some of its rhythmic details, can be seen mostly as alternative variants and only rarely substitutive. Which suggests at least two consequences: the first is that the editor should not choose, but should limit him/herself (with appropriate strategies in presenting the text) to reporting all the solutions found in the different editions, so that the modern performer can consider and assess them one by one, drawing his/her own conclusions at an operative level. The second is that, for the purposes of performance, the presence of several alternative solutions does not imply a choice limited exclusively to *those* solutions, but should encourage the modern performer to behave like a performer of the time, that is to say like a performer-composer, able not only to choose between the solutions offered by the editions, but also to elaborate (also spontaneously) further stylistically plausible solutions.

It should be kept in mind that the composers of the early 17th century (including those we are dealing with here) were, in most cases, at the same time composers and performers-improvisers. We can thus imagine that an organist like Frescobaldi, when seated at the organ to realize the basso continuo of a motet (his or someone else's), would behave like any other continuo player of the time, and would therefore realize the part (and elaborate its line) in a different way each time, maybe growing fond of a particular solution that did not necessarily match the one fixed in the edition he was using during the performance. So it should come as no surprise if, in preparing a new edition of a motet, he had preferred to introduce the 'new' continuo line, which he had in the meantime been elaborating (and progressively fixing) under his very own fingers in the course of successive performances. In such cases the border between alternative and substitutive variants can be very flimsy; for this reason the written outlines of this process of elaboration should be reported in the edition and taken into consideration in order to study the performance practice and the creative process (which does not, in fact, mean studying just the genesis of the composition, but also its refinement)[4].

[4]. The interest of musicology in sketch-studies and authorial philology, stimulated by the debate on the usefulness of studying preparatory material for the purposes of musical analysis and/or of the critical edition, which emerged on the occasion of the anniversaries of the birth (1970) and death (1977) of Beethoven (see KERMAN 1982) and initially focused on the 19th-century repertoire, later gave way to a deeper reflection on the various aspects of the creative process, covering increasingly wider periods of time and also involving studies on ancient music. Worthy of particular mention on this matter is the pioneering book by Robert

Written Outlines of Improvisation Procedures in Music Publications

The compositions examined in this article are homogeneous both in genre (they are in any case motets, or *concerti*, for few voices and basso continuo), and in chronological range (the musical editions considered were printed in a period spanning from 1611 to 1627). Instead, the questions taken into consideration regard three aspects commonly associated with the sphere of practice: the elaboration of the basso continuo line (and, in some cases, the actual way of playing within, or accompanying a polyvocal work on the instrument), the introduction of diminutions in any vocal part, and the possible modal transposition of the compositions, mostly motivated by necessities of a practical order linked to the circumstances of the performance.

Revision Procedures in the Motets of Giovanni Ghizzolo's Second Book (1611/1623): *Full Score, Short Score* and *Basso per l'organo*

The first case examined is Giovanni Ghizzolo's *Concerti all'uso moderno*, first published in Milan by the heirs of Simon Tini and Filippo Lomazzo in 1611[5] and then reprinted in Venice by Alessandro Vincenti in 1623[6]. As I have already mentioned elsewhere, the reprinting of the collection allowed Ghizzolo to substantially revise the compositions previously published, introducing structural variants (such as to modify the form and length of the original compositions) in six motets (from a total of twenty-two)[7]. Of particular interest here are the variants found in the parts for the organist in the successive editions. In the *editio princeps* the part for the continuo player, named *Partitura*, appears as a full-score (notated on four staves) in the first eighteen compositions and as a short-score (notated on two staves) in the last four, whereas in the Venetian reprint the part for the continuo player, named *Basso per l'organo*, is notated on just one stave. Both the *Partitura* of the *princeps*, and the *Basso per l'organo* of the second edition are divided into mostly isochronic bars each with a duration of a *brevis*.

Marshall on the compositional process in the vocal music of Bach, as well as the successive work by Jessie Ann Owens on the creative process in the period from 1450 to 1600 and the recent book by Friedemann Sallis on the function of sketches and preparatory material from 1600 to today. See Marshall 1972; Owens 1997; Sallis 2015.

5. See the *Concerti all'uso moderno a quattro voci* by Giovanni Ghizzolo (Ghizzolo 1611). The collection, published in separate parts (SATB) and score, has survived in two complete copies (kept respectively in I-Bc and I-VCd) and one copy that consists only of the score (A-Wn). See RISM A/1 G 1783. Modern edition: *Giovanni Ghizzolo* 2010.

6. See Ghizzolo 1623a. The four surviving copies are all incomplete: I-Bc (S missing); I-CEc (S and organ part missing); I-Nc (T) and I-Rsc (S and organ part missing). The part-book of the soprano has not survived in any source. See RISM A/1 G 1784.

7. On Giovanni Ghizzolo's compositional process and the successive revisions of his motets see Toffetti 2018.

The comparison between the part-books of the single voices and the score of the first edition revealed a certain number of variants which could offer some indications about the various ways in which the organist could accompany the voices. See, for example, the summary of the variants between the part-book of the cantus and the cantus part of the score[8]:

Table 1: Variants between the Part-book of the Cantus and the Cantus Part of the Score (1611)[9]

N.	*Incipit*	Bars/Notes	Score	Separate part
1	*Pulchrae sunt genae tuae*	15, 4	A♯	A
2	*Domine exaudi*	16, 3	G	G♯
		38	**SB C B**	**CR C B QU C B C D**
5	*Exsurgat Deus*	28, 2-(3)	**CR A**	**QU A B**
6	*O Domine quis habitabit*	59	2 B♯ (♭ in the clef)	B natural
8	*Quemadmodum desiderat*	22	2 CR G♯ tied	Dotted CR G; QU G
		26,	G	G♯
		30, 1-(2)	F	F♯
15	*Laudate nomen Domini*	2, 4	CR G	CR rest, CR G

Although the variants are mostly of a minor entity (especially in the cases where they are simply erroneous omissions, in the score or in the separate parts, of accidentals referring to a single note), in some cases (written in bold in the Table) certain rhythmic figurations of the voice have been simplified or slightly modified in the organ score[10]. Moreover, some diminutions have been omitted in the score which are instead written out in full in the part-book of the cantus, meaning that at those points the organist should not double the voice but play a prolonged single note to sustain the more lively figuration of the voice in question. Such seemingly slight discrepancies nevertheless provide elements that can prove valuable in terms of performance practice. If, due to necessity of space or other reasons, it is decided *not* to publish the organ score in full, it would be opportune to indicate in the critical notes *all* the variants present, so as to allow a complete assessment.

Instead, on comparing the line of the bass voice of the *editio princeps* with the lowest part of the score of the same edition, one can observe how the latter mostly traces the vocal line of the bass and generally also respects the rests (when the bass voice is silent): at these points the organist, having the complete score at his disposition, could well have

---

[8]. The Table refers to the first eighteen motets of Ghizzolo's collection, with a full-score in the organ part.

[9]. Here, and in the following Tables, B = breve; SB = semibreve; M = minim; CR = crotchet; QU = quaver; SQ = semiquaver.

[10]. On this topic see also Frescobaldi 2002.

played the line that was respectively the lowest. At other points the lowest voice of the score introduces slight rhythmic modifications to the line of the bass, mostly simplifying its profile, or more simply playing a single long note where the bass voice has shorter consecutive notes of the same pitch.

In the line of the *Basso per l'organo* of the second edition things obviously change. Since the organist no longer has a score to follow, he would risk losing his place when the bass voice is silent and find it difficult to realize the continuo. Therefore, at such points the bass line of the organ part behaves prevalently as a basso seguente (tracing the profile of the lowest voice used at that moment in the polyphony, sometimes with rhythmic variants), or else as a true basso continuo (introducing elements different from those of the voice lines with a function of harmonic support), thus guaranteeing the support of the organ even in the sections where the lowest voices are silent. Furthermore, in tracing the voice that is lowest at any given moment, the organ bass line in the reprint simplifies its physiognomy more frequently than in the lowest voice of the score of the first edition, resulting in numerous differences between the two versions.

As for the possible choices for an edition, on encountering variants one would, from a purely theoretic viewpoint, be inclined to respect the version given in the second edition, since it is presumably closer to the last will of the composer (who, it should be remembered, was still alive when the second edition was published). Moreover, in the case of Ghizzolo's second book of motets a particular problem regarding the state of the sources should be kept in mind: the first edition has come down to us in three copies, two of which are complete, while the second edition has survived in four incomplete copies, all lacking the soprano part[11].

Moreover, as mentioned above, in the second edition six motets have been substantially modified on account of variants in the structure, which alter its form and modify its overall length. In these circumstances it seems inevitable that both versions should appear in the edition, given separately in their entirety: the first version taken from the *editio princeps*, the second from the reprint. The soprano part, lacking in the reprint, could simply be omitted in the modern edition; alternatively, in the portions coinciding with the version of the *princeps*, the soprano part could be borrowed from the latter, making sure not only to detail in the introduction to the critical edition the criteria for reconstruction adopted, but also to differentiate this part from the others by means of a sufficiently clear graphic expedient (for example notating it in smaller type compared to the other voices, indicating the text in italics and clearly specifying the provenance of this part at the start of the stave). In the portions where the version of the second edition differs compared to that of the first, one could consider the possibility of reconstructing the missing part by conjecture, differentiating it not only from the other parts, but also from

[11]. The four surviving copies, all incomplete, are kept in the following libraries: I-Bc (S missing); I-CEc (S and organ part missing); I-Nc (T) and I-Rsc (S and organ part missing). See RISM A/1 G 1784.

the remaining portions of the same part, which, as we have said, can be taken from the first edition (for example, placing the portions reconstructed by conjecture in square brackets, and giving an adequate account of the criterion).

In the case of the motets that did *not* undergo any structural modifications, it will be possible to recreate the text based on the only single complete edition (in this case the *princeps*), mentioning in the critical notes the sporadic variants that occur in the vocal lines of the contralto, tenor and bass in the second edition. As we have seen, though, the majority of the variants concern the bass line for the organ. In this case they are mostly alternative variants, which involve octave shifts or slight changes in the rhythmic pattern of the bass line. Variants of this type provide the organist with suggestions about how to proceed, they offer plausible alternatives in the shaping of the bass and are therefore worth including in the critical edition so that they can be adequately considered and assessed by the players. The best way to present such instances will be to reproduce both of the bass lines, one above the other, making the edition more 'transparent' by indicating their relative provenance[12].

Revision Procedures in the Motets of Giovanni Ghizzolo's Third Book (1615/1623): The Problem of Transposition

The history of the transmission of another collection of motets by the same Ghizzolo presents several analogies with that of the previous collection: the *Terzo libro delli concerti* was published first in Milan by Filippo Lomazzo in 1615[13] and was reprinted in Venice by Alessandro Vincenti in 1623[14].

Unlike in the second book, only one concerto from the third book presents a structural variant in its second edition (the motet *Omnes de Saba venient*, of which the concluding section has been modified by Ghizzolo in the 1623 version). This is the only case, then, that will require the edition of the two distinct versions (or, at least, the publication *in extenso* of both versions of the final part, to allow a comparison).

In this collection the greatest point of interest is the comparison between the organ part of the *princeps* and that of the second edition. In this case the part destined for the organist is named *Partitura* both in the *editio princeps* and in the reprint; in the first case, though, it is presented as a short-score (on two staves), while in the second it assumes the form of a basso continuo (on just one stave). Moreover, the score of the *princeps*, in which

12. An optimal solution could be to transcribe the four voices in a score, including both the organ *Partitura* of the first edition (transcribed onto a double stave), and the single line of the *Basso per l'organo* as it appears in the second edition (remembering to indicate the provenance of this line at the start of the stave).

13. Ghizzolo 1615. RISM A/1 G 1787.

14. Ghizzolo 1623b, RISM A/1 G 1788.

the bass part for the continuo player also supports the sections where the vocal bass is silent, has no numbering above the lowest line, whereas the reprint provides some numberings and indicates accidentals useful for the realization of the bass. In addition, the bass part of the reprint contains various melodic variants with respect to that of the *princeps*, similar to those found in the second edition of the motets of the second book: including the transformation of several short notes into a single longer note, the division of a long note into shorter notes, and the inversion of the trend of rising or falling intervals (see Ex. 1; in the following example lines 2 and 3 have been re-transposed *in tono*).

Ex. 1: Giovanni Ghizzolo, *Super flumina Babylonis* (from the *Terzo libro dei concerti*, 1615/1623), bars 21-32.

The most significant aspect, though, is the fact that in the organ part of the first edition all the compositions are notated *in tono* (like the vocal parts), whereas in the reprint the seven motets (out of twenty-three) notated in *chiavette* are transposed down a fourth and/or a fifth (while the vocal parts are in any case notated *in tono*).

In his article on vocal ranges, cleffing and transposition in the sacred music of Giulio Belli, Jeffrey Kurtzman investigated the «relationship between notation and sounding pitch, with regard to transposition of notated pitch levels» considering the question in terms of many interrelated aspects, such as the modes and psalm tones, the use of *mollis* signature, the vocal ranges of contemporary voices, the pitch standards of accompanying organs and other instruments, the notational conventions, and the divergent practices of individual composers[15]. «The particular significance of Giulio Belli for this study», explains Kurtzman, «resides in the fact that a number of his sacred music collections have organ part-books with specific rubrics for transposition for some of the pieces»[16].

In dealing with the «relationship between notation and sounding pitch», Kurtzman focuses not only on the usual conventions of notation, but also on the variation in their usage from one composer to another, in the awareness that «trying to make coherent sense of how composers and performers understood the notation and the issues of transposition and performance is an ongoing process, and the present study is only one further stage in that process»[17].

Considering that Giovanni Ghizzolo's *Terzo libro di concerti* includes precise indications regarding the transposition of certain compositions, it appears useful to compare them with those found in the sacred collections of Giulio Belli and examined by Kurtzman[18].

In assessing the differences between Belli's approach and that of Ghizzolo, it should be remembered that, in most cases, compositions notated in standard clefs (C_1 C_3 C_4 F_4) were usually performed *in tono* or a full step (1 tone) or a minor third downward, while compositions notated in high clefs, or *chiavi alte*, or *chiavette* (G_2 C_2 C_3 C_4 or F_3) were usually performed a fourth or a fifth lower than notated, depending on the pitch standard (according to Adriano Banchieri only a fifth below).

It is interesting to observe that in compositions notated in high clefs, while some composers of the time preferred the transposition to a fourth below, Belli shows a preference for the transposition to a fifth below, specifying on each occasion his precise choice. In the

15. Kurtzman 2014, p. 141.

16. *Ibidem*.

17. *Ibidem*.

18. It should also be remembered that both Ghizzolo and Belli belonged to the Order of Friars Minor, and that both had worked at the Veneranda Arca di Sant'Antonio in Padua: Giulio Belli between 1606 and 1608, Giovanni Ghizzolo between 1622 and 1623, leading one to suppose that Ghizzolo may have encountered Giulio Belli's sacred works during his brief period in Padua, from which the reprint of his first book dates.

second edition of Ghizzolo's third book of *concerti*, in such cases both solutions are given, thus leaving open both possibilities.

It should also be pointed out that in the organ parts of Belli's compositions we find both the version *in tono* and the transposed version, while in the organ part of the second edition of Ghizzolo's third book there are one or more transposed versions, but *not* the version *in tono*. More precisely: in the organ part the motets notated in the *cantus mollis* signature we find *only* the version transposed to a fourth below:

Ad te Domine	F *cantus mollis*	4th →	C *cantus durus*
Gaudens gaudebo	G *cantus mollis*	4th →	D *cantus durus*

while the motets notated in the *cantus durus* signature are given in versions transposed a fourth *and* a fifth below, or just a fifth below:

Super flumina	CTB	G *cantus durus* [7th]	4th → D in *cantus durus* 5th → C *in cantus mollis*
Congratulamini	CAB	G *cantus durus* [7th]	4th → D in *cantus durus* 5th → C in *cantus mollis*
Confitebor tibi	CATB	A *cantus durus* [10th]	4th → E in *cantus durus* [D♯] 5th → D in *cantus mollis*
Confitemini gentes	CATB	D *cantus durus* [1st]	4th → A in *cantus durus* 5th → G in *cantus mollis*
O Domine	CATB	C *cantus durus* [11th]	5th → F in *cantus mollis*

Table 2 summarizes the clefs used for each motet, with the relative *finalis* and realization of the bass part in the booklet of the *partitura* of the 1623 edition[19].

19. The clef is indicated with the letter and the number of the stave (e.g.: C clef in the first stave: C1). A ♭ indicates the presence of a flat in the clef. The Table is taken from Taschetti 2016.

TABLE 2: GIOVANNI GHIZZOLO, *TERZO LIBRO DI CONCERTI* (REPR. 1623): TRANSPOSITIONS

INCIPIT	VOICES	CLEFS	FINALIS	SCORE
FOR TWO VOICES				
Indica mihi	Two Cantus, or Tenors	$C_{1\flat}$, $C_{1\flat}$	F	*in tono*
Gaudete et exultate	Two Cantus, or Tenors	$C_{1\flat}$, $C_{1\flat}$	F	*in tono*
O dies infelices	Cantus and Tenor	$C_{1\flat}$, $C_{4\flat}$	G	*in tono*
Vias tuas demonstra mihi	Cantus, and Tenor, Dialogue	$C_{1\flat}$, $C_{4\flat}$	F	*in tono*
Exaudi Deus	Cantus and Bass	$C_{1\flat}$, $F_{4\flat}$	G	*in tono*
Decantabat populus Israel	Cantus and Bass	C_{1}, F_{4}	A	*in tono*
FOR THREE VOICES				
Super flumina	Cantus, Tenor and Bass	G_{2}, C_{3}, F_{3}	G	4th ↓, 5th ↓
O quam metuendus	Cantus, Tenor and Bass	C_{1}, C_{4}, F_{4}	G	*in tono*
Paratum cor meum	Cantus, Tenor and Bass	$C_{1\flat}$, $C_{4\flat}$, $F_{4\flat}$	F	*in tono*
Cantabo Domino	Two Cantus or Tenors and Basso	$C_{1\flat}$, $C_{1\flat}$, $F_{4\flat}$	F	*in tono*
Florete flores	Two Cantus or Tenors and Bass	C_{1}, C_{1}, F_{4}	G	*in tono*
Gaudete in Domino	Cantus, Alto and Bass	C_{1}, C_{3}, F_{4}	D	*in tono*
Congratulamini	Cantus, Alto and Bass	G_{2}, C_{2}, F_{3}	G	4th ↓, 5th ↓
FOR FOUR VOICES				
Confitebor tibi Domine Rex	C, A, T, B	G_{2}, C_{2}, C_{3}, F_{3}	A	4th ↓, 5th ↓
Ad te Domine clamabo	"	$G_{2\flat}$, $C_{2\flat}$, $C_{3\flat}$, $F_{3\flat}$		4th ↓
Exultate iusti in Domino	"	$C_{1\flat}$, $C_{3\flat}$, $C_{4\flat}$, $F_{4\flat}$	F	*in tono*
Iubilate deo omnis terra	"	$C_{1\flat}$, $C_{3\flat}$, $C_{4\flat}$, $F_{4\flat}$	G	*in tono*
Eripe me	"	C_{1}, C_{3}, C_{4}, F_{4}	D	*in tono*
Omnes de Saba venient	"	$C_{1\flat}$, $C_{3\flat}$, $C_{4\flat}$, $F_{4\flat}$	F	*in tono*
Gaudens gaudebo in Domino	"	$G_{2\flat}$, $C_{2\flat}$, $C_{3\flat}$, $F_{3\flat}$	G	4th ↓
Mulier quid ploras	"	C_{1}, C_{3}, C_{4}, F_{4}	F	*in tono*
O Domine semper laudabo te	"	G_{2}, C_{2}, C_{3}, F_{3}	C	5th ↓
Confitemini gentes	"	G_{2}, C_{2}, C_{3}, F_{3}	D	4th ↓, 5th ↓
Letanie B. M. Virginis	C, A, Q, T, B	C_{1}, C_{3}, C_{4}, C_{4}, F_{4}	D	*in tono*

Therefore, contrary to what occurs in the collections of most of his contemporaries, in this collection Ghizzolo not only specifies all the transpositions he considers acceptable, but provides the organist with the part *already transposed*, saving him the trouble of having to transpose it extemporaneously: this would certainly make the task easier, but at the same time would limit the possibilities of choice. On the other hand, the organ part of the 1623 edition is not given *in tono*[20]. Without going into who was responsible for such a choice — it could have been either composer or the publisher — what interests us here is how to present these compositions within the modern edition. If, in fact, we consider that the transposition of the compositions was carried out in an extemporaneous fashion, any written outlines of this procedure should be rendered in the modern edition so as not to lose any information that could be drawn from them, without however 'fixing' a single solution, given that at the time more than one would, in some cases, have been possible.

Basically, it is a question of deciding whether to present the composition *in tono*, as in the notation of the vocal parts, or in the transposed version (or else, in the case of the compositions where the organ part appears in a double version, in one of the two transposed versions, or in both). In line with the notational usages of the time, the first solution seems decidedly preferable, leaving any transpositions made necessary for contingent reasons to the practical realm (such as the comfort pitch of the choir, the instruments used for any doubling or substitutions, or even the diapason of the organ used to accompany the voices). By opting for the solution of transcription *in tono*, it will then be necessary to re-transpose the organ part and place it beneath the vocal parts in the score. Nevertheless, it would be opportune to also publish, possibly in an appendix, the transposed version (or the two different transposed versions) of the organ part.

A further issue remains to be resolved: the comparison between the organ bass line of the *editio princeps* and that of the second edition revealed a fair number of variants, mostly of an alternative nature, as if the new edition had become an opportunity to introduce different versions reflecting alternative ways of performing the same line. Moreover, in the cases where the organ part of the 1623 edition presents *two different transpositions*, these differ in numerous details not only from the version of the organ part appearing in the first edition, but also from each other. In other words, while in the case of nineteen motets we have *two different bass lines for the organ*, for the four motets where the organ part in the second edition has two possible transpositions, to the fourth and the fifth below (*Super flumina*, *Congratulamini*, *Confitebor tibi* and *Confitemini gentes*), we have as many as *three organ bass lines* that are certainly very similar, but nevertheless slightly different from one another. So which of the two (or three) versions should we choose to present in the score beneath the vocal parts? Since there appear to be no reasons to prefer one version to the other, any choice would be purely arbitrary (and still more arbitrary would be any contamination between the different versions). Given this situation, it seems reasonable to present *all* the versions of the bass in the score: the one notated *in tono* in the first edition, and the one (or ones) notated at a fourth and/or fifth below in the second edition (after re-transposition *in tono*). This solution, although quite costly in terms of space, presents the

[20]. The choice to present the organ part in this way could perhaps be ascribed to the publisher, who wished to make his edition as appealing as possible, also in virtue of these strategies aimed at simplifying the task of the organist.

no small advantage of allowing a synthetic view of all the versions available, thus making their comparison much simpler.

In such a case the potentials of an electronic edition (which the performer could also access with a tablet) could be of great help in the presentation of the musical text, making it possible to visualize *all* the solutions (*in tono*, or transposed to the fourth and/or the fifth below) in the study phase, and then being able to obscure them during the performance, without effecting the transparency criteria of the critical edition.

REVISION PROCEDURES IN THE TWO EDITIONS OF GIROLAMO FRESCOBALDI'S MOTET *IESU REX ADMIRABILIS* (1625-1627)

Revisions in the Basso Continuo Line

In the context of the issues dealt with here, a particularly interesting case is that of Girolamo Frescobaldi's motet *Iesu Rex admirabilis*, which first appeared within the *Sacri affetti*, a miscellaneous collection compiled by Francesco Sammaruco, published in Rome by Luca Antonio Soldi on the occasion of the 1625 jubilee and which survives complete[21]. The same motet reappeared two years later, with numerous modifications, in the only individual collection of motets by Frescobaldi that has survived, the *Liber secundus diversarum modulationum*, published in Rome by Andrea Fei and come down to us without the *cantus secundus*[22].

The interesting aspect of this motet is that it is the only vocal work by Frescobaldi which has reached us in two different editions, and thus the only one allowing us a glimpse into Frescobaldi's approach to writing vocal music especially in the phase of revision, which is in itself no less relevant or significant than the gestational phase of the creative process. In addition, the examination of the double version of this motet allows us to deepen

---

[21]. See *SACRI AFFETTI* 1625; RISM B/I 1625[1]. The anthology has survived in two copies, the first of which (kept in the Museo internazionale e biblioteca della musica in Bologna) is complete, while the second (kept in the Biblioteca comunale Luciano Benincasa in Ancona) contains only the Bass part.

[22]. See *LIBER SECUNDUS DIVERSARUM MODULATIONUM* 1627; RISM A/I F 1853. Partial modern edition edited by Christopher Stembridge: FRESCOBALDI 1987. The motet *Iesu Rex admirabilis* and another three motets by Frescobaldi included in three different Roman anthologies (*Peccavi super numerum*, *Angelus ad pastores* and *Ego sum panis vivus*) have been published in another modern edition edited by Lorenzo Ghielmi and Mario Valsecchi (FRESCOBALDI 1983). This collection, which survived without the *cantus secundus*, was recently published in a critical edition edited by Marco Della Sciucca and Marina Toffetti, with a complete reconstruction of the missing part, in the context of the *opera omnia* of the composer (FRESCOBALDI 2014). To avoid any undue *contaminatio* between the two versions, which present several variants, the incomplete version of 1627 was included with the other motets of the *Liber secundus*, while the complete version of 1625 was reported in its entirety in an appendix. The criteria adopted for the reconstruction of the missing part are described in TOFFETTI 2013.

our knowledge on certain aspects of Frescobaldi's technique and style as a composer of sacred vocal music, an area that remains one of the least studied within the otherwise vast literature on Girolamo Frescobaldi's output[23].

As well as *Iesu Rex admirabilis*, another three motets by Frescobaldi had appeared in Roman anthologies of the time: *Peccavi super numerum*, included in Fabio Constantino's *Selectæ cantiones* published by Bartolomeo Zannetti in 1616[24]; *Angelus ad pastores*, in *Scelta di motetti* again compiled by Constantino and published by Zannetti in 1618[25]; and *Ego sum panis vivus*, in the collection *Lilia campi* compiled and published by Giovanni Battista Robletti in 1621[26]. Why, then, does only the motet *Iesu Rex admirabilis* appear in the *Liber secundus*? We might suppose that Frescobaldi was particularly fond of this motet — the composition produces, in fact, a great impact on the listener on account of its extraordinary effectiveness in rendering the affects[27]. On the other hand, it cannot be ruled out that the other three motets, or at least some of them, had already been reprinted in the now lost 'Liber primus', which is hypothesized to have been published before 1627, when the surviving *Liber secundus* was published.

As has already been documented, the edition of the *Sacri affetti*, in which the motet *Iesu Rex admirabilis* appears for the first time, contains numerous misprints and inaccuracies in all the fascicles[28]. One reason that prompted Frescobaldi to have this particular motet reprinted may have been the simple wish to see it published in a more correct form. Whatever the case, the inclusion of this motet in his individual collection clearly became an opportunity to revise the whole composition, introducing numerous modifications of various kinds. As a result, the comparison between the two versions not only allows a deeper insight into Frescobaldi's creative process, but also raises other questions regarding the relation between the written composition and its improvised realization.

---

[23]. See Roche 1986; Luisi 1986; Stembridge 1986.

[24]. See *Selectæ cantiones* 1616; RISM B/I 1616[1]. Frescobaldi's composition is for two sopranos, tenor and basso continuo.

[25]. See *Scelta di motetti* 1618; RISM B/I 1618[3]. Frescobaldi's motet is for two voices, cantus, tenor and basso continuo.

[26]. See *Lilia campi* 1621; RISM B/I 1621[3]. Frescobaldi's composition is for two sopranos, tenor and basso continuo.

[27]. As far as the form is concerned, the motet *Iesu Rex admirabilis* has a very fragmented structure, characterized by the use of frequent cadenzas. In the opening section there is a cadenza after each word: the first after «Iesu», the second after «Rex», the third after «admirabilis». As happens in many coeval works, here too there is an alternation between different constructive techniques and ensemble combinations: the *incipit*, for example, opens with an imitative episode on the word «Iesu», and is followed by a homorhythmic passage on the words «Rex admirabilis», an imitative episode on the words «et triumphator nobilis», a passage for two cantos on the word «dulcedo», and an imitative episode based on a more sprightly motive on the words «ineffabilis». In addition, as in several motets and in many multi-instrumental canzonas by Frescobaldi, here too there are two sections in ternary mensura, using a harmonic-vertical compositional technique.

[28]. See Franchi 2006, pp. 504-506: 505.

The comparison between the surviving parts highlighted numerous variants in the basso continuo part as well as in those of the cantus and tenor. Generally speaking, the composition published in 1627 does not simply represent (as one might have expected) a 'more correct' redaction of the previous one, but introduces many slight modifications that fix certain improvisation procedures — especially in the basso continuo part — which would otherwise have remained confined to the realm of performance practice, and in so doing offers an alternative version to the one published two years before. In its double guise, this motet therefore allows us to integrate what has already been learned about Frescobaldi's *modus operandi* from the study of the multiple versions of his instrumental canzonas[29].

To the line of the studies devoted to creative process mentioned previously[30] we can add the two studies by Niels Martin Jensen and John Harper on the revision of Frescobaldi's first book of instrumental canzonas, published first in Rome in 1628 in two separate editions — that of Masotti in a score[31] and that of Robletti in separate parts[32] — and later reprinted in Venice in 1635 (1634 *more veneto*)[33]. The two essays investigate the recomposition procedure, almost certainly attributable to the same composer, which was applied to numerous canzonas[34], leading in various cases to a significant expansion of the form[35]; they also reveal how, irrespective of the type of variants introduced, the canzonas that present the greatest number of interventions are those for one or two basses and basso continuo[36], which allows us to understand that in the 1620s Frescobaldi was dedicating particular attention to the study of the relation between the lowest respective voice and the instrumental bass support, experimenting with various different solutions.

The types of revision highlighted in these studies range from structural modification (involving the addition, removal, re-working or shifting of entire sections) to the rewriting

29. See Jensen 1986; Harper 1987. See also Harper 1975.

30. See note 4.

31. See Frescobaldi 1628a; RISM A/i F 1869. The edition includes 37 canzonas.

32. See Frescobaldi 1628b; RISM A/i F 1868. The edition includes 35 canzonas, 34 of which also appear in the score printed in the same year by Masotti, while one is not present. For the contents of the three editions of the *Primo libro* see Harper 1987, p. 271, Table 1.

33. See Frescobaldi 1634; RISM A/i F 1870. The edition includes 40 canzonas, 10 of which do not appear in the score printed in 1628 by Masotti, and does not include 8 canzonas present in Masotti's score. See Harper 1987, p. 271. Critical edition by Étienne Darbellay: Frescobaldi 2002. Among the practical editions the following volumes are worthy of mention: Frescobaldi 1933; Frescobaldi 1959; Frescobaldi 1966a and Frescobaldi 1966b; Frescobaldi 1969-1970; Frescobaldi 1966a; Frescobaldi 1974-1977.

34. Among the canzonas that appear both in the score and in the 1635 edition, thirteen present only minor modifications, while seventeen have been substantially and extensively reworked. See Harper 1987, pp. 270-271.

35. See Jensen 1986, p. 323.

36. See Harper 1987, p. 277.

of one or more voices[37], the basso continuo being the part most commonly affected. Some changes show a new conception of style, no longer anchored on polyphonic writing, but oriented towards a more modern approach, with frequent echo effects and chromaticisms and a greater number of textural combinations[38]. As in the instrumental canzonas, also in the motets of the *Liber secundus diversarum modulationum* we find vestiges of late-Renaissance usages alongside a clear assimilation of more up-to-date styles[39]: this happens especially in the motets for three or four voices and basso continuo, in which the availability of a richer palette of timbres allowed the composer to try out novel textural combinations creating contrasting effects of colour.

Jensen focuses mainly on the canzonas for one voice and basso continuo and compares them with the coeval solo sonatas by the principal exponents of violin literature in the early 17th century, with particular attention to the changes made to the basso continuo line. In the 1635 edition the basso continuo is often simplified and modified on the basis of harmonic criteria, it is less linked to the other parts and, in some passages, is transposed an octave down — perhaps in view of its realization at the organ. Moreover, in the second version, the continuo often no longer acts as a basso seguente, but assumes the function of providing a harmonic support to the composition[40].

The comparison between the different versions of the canzonas highlighted elements that proved useful in understanding the nature of the interventions introduced, in the same period or in the immediately preceding years, in the second version of the motet *Iesu Rex admirabilis*. Conceived in the same period, the *Liber secundus diversarum modulationum* and *Il primo libro delle canzoni* present a similar structure, underpinned by the criterion of a progressive thickening of the texture, from one to four voices and basso continuo[41]. Despite being, still today, among the least studied and performed works of Frescobaldi[42], these two collections, both produced in a phase of experimentation and stylistic transition, are of particular historic and aesthetic interest, as testified by the musical quality of many of the compositions contained within them, including the motet *Iesu Rex admirabilis*.

37. See *ibidem*, p. 272.

38. See *ibidem*, p. 276.

39. See the concluding remarks of the introduction to the critical edition of the *Liber secundus* published in the series of Frescobaldi's *opera omnia*: «Frescobaldi's motets reveal the hand of a gifted composer, well versed in the art of imitation, and at the same time are characterized by a style that is not only modern but also decidedly original, arising from the fusion between a strictly observed counterpoint and a monodic style featuring an extensive use of diminutions and particular care for the rendering of the *affetti* evoked by the text». See FRESCOBALDI 2014, p. lxxxiii.

40. See JENSEN 1986, p. 322.

41. See STEMBRIDGE 1986, pp. 195-213.

42. This situation, which Niels Martin Jensen already noted thirty years ago, is still true today. See JENSEN 1986, p. 315.

Unlike in the different versions of the instrumental canzonas, in the motet *Iesu Rex admirabilis* Frescobaldi did not make any changes to the structure; on the contrary, the variants, often introduced in a single voice, involve passages lasting a maximum four semibreves[43]. The examination of these changes allow us to focalize on the concluding phases of the creative process, showing us a Frescobaldi intent on refining a composition that had already been published and defining it more precisely in some small details. As in the instrumental canzonas, in this motet too the part most affected by the revision what that of the basso continuo.

Out of a total of twenty-six variants found between the two versions, sixteen involve the basso continuo part, seven the cantus part and three that of the tenor; apart from these, is reasonable to imagine that Frescobaldi made some changes (which in philological terms would be defined 'compensatory variants', introduced to balance the other interventions) also to the cantus part that, in the second edition, has been lost. It should, in fact, be underlined that the lack of one part-book prevents us from assessing the overall impact of the variants made to the surviving parts, since it is impossible to establish whether they were accompanied — and possibly balanced — by further modifications in the part that has been lost.

Among the variants found, some simply involve the addition (or elimination) of figuring in the basso continuo or of accidentals (mostly in cadenzas), aimed at specifying the use of one chord instead of another; while others transform a passage in *cantus durus* to one in *cantus mollis*, and are thus interventions of a modal nature. The most significant variants are those involving the melody and/or rhythm, aimed at a greater elaboration (or, on the contrary, a simplification) of a rhythmic-melodic line.

As already observed in the motets of Giovanni Ghizzolo, also in this motet by Frescobaldi most of the variants found in the basso continuo part derive from the need to change the rhythmic profile of the supporting line.

Table 3: Frescobaldi, *Iesu Rex Admirabilis*: Variants in the Basso Continuo

Bars	1625	1627	Notes
5, i-iii [iv]	SB G; dotted M C; SM C	dotted SM G; QU G; M G; SB C	rhythmic variant (greater rhythmic articulation)
7, iv-[v-vi]	QU M	SM E; QU F G	rhythmic-melodic variant; change in the state of the chord (indicated with the number 6); passing notes added
8, ii-iii [iv-v]	M A[1]; M A[2]; dotted CR E; QU F	SB A; M E	rhythmic variant (simplification: octave shift removed); rhythmic-melodic modification (passing note removed)

43. As we have seen, it is not possible to establish whether in the version published in 1627 Frescobaldi also introduced variants in the *cantus secundus* part, which is now lost.

9, I [II]	M G^2; M G^1 M	SB G	rhythmic variant (simplification: octave shift removed); figuring removed
13, III [IV]	M C^3 M; M C^2	SB C^3	rhythmic variant (simplification: octave shift removed)
14, I–II	SB F^1; F^2	SB F^2 ; D	change of octave; melodic variant
18, I [II]	B G	dotted SB G; M G	rhythmic variant (greater rhythmic articulation)
22, I [II]	dotted B G	B G; SB G	rhythmic variant (greater rhythmic articulation)
24, III	SB A^2 SB	SB A^1 SB	octave changed (and relative numbering removed)
25, I–IV	SB A^1 ; [M D]; CR A^2 [D]	SB A^2 SB; [M D]; CR A^1 [D]	octave change
26, I	G^2	G^1	octave change (relative numbering added or removed)
31, I [II]	C C	B C	rhythmic variant: simplification (repeated note removed)
34, I [II]	F F	B F	rhythmic variant: simplification (repeated note removed)
36, I [II]	B E SB E	dotted B E	rhythmic variant: simplification (repeated note removed)
37, I–IV	SB A; CR A F	M A; dotted M A; CR F♯	rhythmic variant (repeated note added); melodic variant (accidental added); numbering removed
39, IV [V–VI]	M G^2	CR G^2 SM; QU F E	melodic variant (two passing notes added that double the tenor line)

In some cases the changes made to the bass line introduce a greater rhythmic articulation, as happens in bar 5, where the basso becomes more animated and proceeds homorhythmically with the other voices (see Ex. 2). In the same passage, however, Frescobaldi has removed the repetition on the second *brevis*, evidently satisfied with the effect created by the polyrhythmic overlapping of the upper voices.

Ex. 2: *Iesu Rex admirabilis*, bar 5.

2a (1625)

2b (1627)

In other cases the changes make the bass line more elegant, as in the following example where the bass, thanks to what we might nowadays call a different inversion of the triad, proceeds parallel to the highest voice at a distance of a tenth (see Ex. 3).

Ex. 3: *Iesu Rex admirabilis*, bar 7.

3a (1625) 3b (1627)

Considering that, throughout the composition, the bass line acts at times as a basso continuo and at others as a basso seguente, it could effectively be ruled out that this variant may have been introduced to avoid the parallel octaves (D-D C-C) between the tenor part and that of the basso continuo, even more so given that, in the second version, consecutive unisons (G-G, A-A) are created between same parts[44].

Just as in the coeval instrumental canzonas, also in the motets for 1-4 voices the bass could act both as a basso continuo and a basso seguente. In the first case it was autonomous with respect to the lowest voice and complementary to the upper voices; in the second case it doubled the lowest voice of the polyphonic texture. The passage from one approach to the other could occur not only within the same composition, but also in the same bar, and even in the space of just a few notes.

A similar situation can be observed in other motets from the *Liber secundus diversarum modulationum*. This collection includes six motets for three voices and basso continuo, one of which is divided into a *prima* and *secunda pars*[45]. On examining the relation between

44. Also in bars 39-40 the 1625 version has a succession of octaves (G-G / F-F), even though separated by two notes each lasting a quaver, while in that of 1627 there is a succession of direct octaves (E-E / F-F).

45. See the motets *O sacrum convivium* for two cantus and tenor; *Vox dilecti mei pulsantis* for two cantus and tenor, with the *secunda pars Quam pulchra es, et speciosa Virgo*; *Sic amantem diligite* for alto and two tenors; *Ego flos campi* for two cantus and bass; *Iesu Rex admirabilis* for two cantus and tenor; and *Exaudi nos Deus* for alto, tenor and basso.

the bass and the lowest line in the six motets several passages can be found where, in the space of just a few bars, the organ bass changes its function various times, behaving in a different manner also with respect to the tenor part. This happens, for example, in the opening episode of the motet *Quam pulchra es*, which makes up the *secunda pars* of the motet *Vox dilecti mei.* In the first two bars the bass assumes a complementary role with respect to the upper voices, providing a harmonic support typical of the basso continuo; in the two following bars it doubles the tenor part in unison and thus acts as a basso seguente; it then continues its role as a basso seguente, but moves parallel to the tenor at a distance of an octave; finally, at the words «et speciosa Virgo», it continues to double the tenor at the lower octave, but plays a single long note instead of the series of repeated shorter notes (see Ex. 4).

Ex. 4: *Quam pulchra es*, bars 1-7.

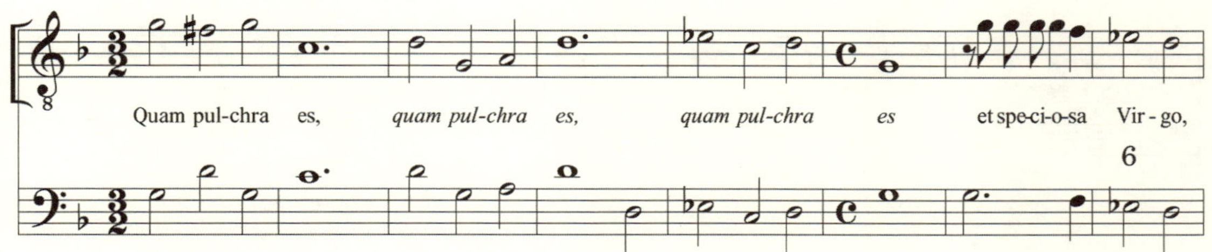

Coming back to the motet *Iesu Rex admirabilis*, the modification made in the following bars (see Ex. 5) involves the simplification of the bass line at a point where the voices have a quite lively profile and is aimed at producing a greater rhythmic contrast between the basso continuo line and those of the three vocal parts.

Ex. 5: *Iesu Rex admirabilis*, bars 8-9.

5a (1625) 5b (1627)

While it is true that, generally speaking, the variants introduced in the 1627 version, the outcome of a final careful polishing, offer mostly 'better' solutions[46], it is also true that some of them — particularly those concerning the bass line — could be considered more as alternative than substitutive variants. Examples of such *ad libitum* versions can also be identified in the passages where the revision simply consists of changes in register, frequently involving changes from one octave to the octave higher or lower (see Ex. 6). In the improvised realization of the basso continuo such octave shifts were common practice.

Ex. 6: *Iesu Rex admirabilis*, bars 24-26.

6a (1625) 6b (1627)

Also of interest are the rhythmic modifications made to the bass line in the two episodes in ternary mensura, where Frescobaldi appears inclined to adopt different approaches apparently for the sake of variety: in some cases, in fact, a long note in the 1625 version is split into two or more short repeated notes in the 1627 version, while elsewhere precisely the opposite occurs.

Such an approach to composition is by no means an isolated case: on the contrary, it can be considered paradigmatic of Frescobaldi's *modus operandi*. In the section of the motet *Sic amantem diligite* in ternary mensura, for example, a similarly erratic behavior can be observed (see Ex. 7).

Ex. 7: *Sic amantem diligite*, bars 26-31.

46. See, for example, the variants introduced in bars 31, 34 and 36, where the basso continuo is differentiated rhythmically from the vocal parts.

As we have said, the *Liber secundus diversarum modulationum* has come down to us incomplete, without the part of the *cantus secundus*. For the complete critical edition of this collection, in the context of the publication of Frescobaldi's *opera omnia*, a reconstruction was made of all the parts missing from the motets that have survived incomplete. The task raised many questions about extremely specific compositional aspects, including the function of the bass, the relation between the bass and the lowest voice at any given moment, as well as the identification of typical harmonic-melodic behaviours, especially in cadenzas. When reconstructing missing parts one tends, understandably, to look in the complete compositions — or in the surviving parts of the composer's incomplete compositions — for corresponding passages (or ones that are as similar as possible) to those to be reconstructed, so as to be able to imitate, as far as possible, the style of the composer. In the case of Frescobaldi, however, this approach did not always prove productive, since his way of working was not, at least apparently, always coherent, but on the contrary tended to approach similar passages in slightly different ways not only in different compositions but also within the same composition. In other words, the fact that at a given point he approached a passage in a certain way does not necessarily mean that he would have adopted the same solution a few bars later or in another composition. For this reason it is not only difficult to deduce 'rules' for the analysis of his works, but even when it was possible to identify them, it did not seem opportune to respect them consistently. In some ways, then, Frescobaldi's writing, being open to alternative solutions, is like the transcription of an extemporaneous improvisation, where the same passage can be played each time in a slightly different way.

In the ternary section of the motet *Sic amantem*, for example, when the voice repeats the same note, the bass tends to unite the two neighbouring notes (see Ex. 8 above). This results in a trochaic rhythm (strong-weak, or long-short), which however is not used right from the beginning: in the first bar the basso continuo doubles the voice (three breves, the first two repeating the same note). Had we found ourselves in the condition of having to reconstruct the basso continuo part, for the sake of homogeneity we would probably have introduced the long-short rhythm right from the start of the ternary episode; but in doing so we would have 'normalized' — and thus in some way betrayed — the composer's improvisatory and extemporary style.

On the other hand it should be kept in mind that whoever realizes a basso continuo always has a relatively free hand in interpreting what is written. Phenomena like the splitting of a long note into two short repeated notes, or, on the contrary, incorporating two or more short notes into a longer one, or else changing the octave, are approaches that concern performance practice and are often enacted irrespectively of what is actually fixed on the page. Every continuo player is used to making slight modifications to the rhythm of the bass line, considering what is written as an outline that can be integrated or modified according to one's tastes and taking into consideration the behavior (also spontaneous) of the voices and the specific acoustic conditions of the relative environment[47]. The analysis of Frescobaldi's works that accompanied the task of reconstructing the missing part in the incomplete motets of the *Liber secundus diversarum modulationum* certainly helped us to understand how Frescobaldi, who was used to adopting a relatively free approach when acting as an organist, maintained some of these habits also when he composed, and tended to tackle similar passages in different ways, allowing imagination to prevail over coherence and variety over uniformity.

Changes Made to the Vocal Lines

While the variants introduced in the basso continuo line are mostly alternative ones, and appear to be the result of a fixing in writing of improvisation procedures, the greatest part of the variants introduced in the vocal parts seem instead to be the result of an act of final polishing: most of the variants are improvements, offering us a photograph of the last phase of the creative process.

Let us look, then, in more detail at the discrepancies encountered between the first and second edition in the cantus and tenor parts. A comparison of the two corresponding cantus parts reveals, in the first place, that the part named *cantus secundus* in the 1625 version has become *cantus primus* in that of 1627 (and obviously *vice versa*). There seem to be no reasons for such an exchange, given that the voices are both notated in the soprano clef and have a substantially similar profile[48]. In any case, there are seven variants between the two corresponding cantus parts, of which four simply involve the addition or deletion of accidentals, two modify the rhythm and one helps to define the articulation of the phrase.

Table 4: Variants in the Part of the *Cantus secundus* (1625) / *Cantus primus* (1627)

Bars	1625	1627	Type of intervention
	Cantus secundus	*Cantus primus*	names of the two upper voices exchanged
6, ii–iii	QU G F♯	QU G♯ F	accidental moved (accidental added; accidental removed)
12, iv	CR F♯	CR F	accidental removed

47. On this matter see Westrup 1962; Borgir 1987; Carchiolo 2007. Interesting considerations can also be found in Romagnoli 2012. Manuals and teaching tools on the realization of the continuo can, in turn, offer useful points for reflection: Christensen 1992; Del Sordo 2004; Arnold 1965. For further bibliographic references see also the site <www.bassus-generalis.org>, accessed November 2018.

48. The first *cantus* part in the1625 version ranges from $C\sharp_3$ to F_4, while the second spans from D_3 to E_4.

13, viii–ix	QU E C	QU E dotted SQ C	rhythmic variant: dotted rhythm introduced
14, vi	QU F♯	QU F	accidental removed
26, iii	M F♯	M F	accidental removed
41, i–iv	QU A G A B♭	QU A-G A-B♭ slurred in pairs	two slurs introduced specifying the articulation of the phrase
42, iii–iv	QU G F	QU G dotted SQ F	rhythmic variant: dotted rhythm introduced

Some of the variants do not involve any substantial changes: see, for example, the addition of an accidental and the removal, apparently inopportune, of another accidental in an intermediate cadenza[49]. The change made in bar 12 seems instead to respond to a modal expedient: by removing the F♯ on the word «ineffabilis», the passage links more fluidly with the immediately following entry of the tenor. In the next bar there is a rhythmic variant that gives the cantus line greater impetus thanks to the introduction of the dotted figuration (a dotted quaver followed by a semiquaver in place of the two quavers of the previous version)[50].

Ex. 8: *Iesu Rex admirabilis*, bars 12-13.

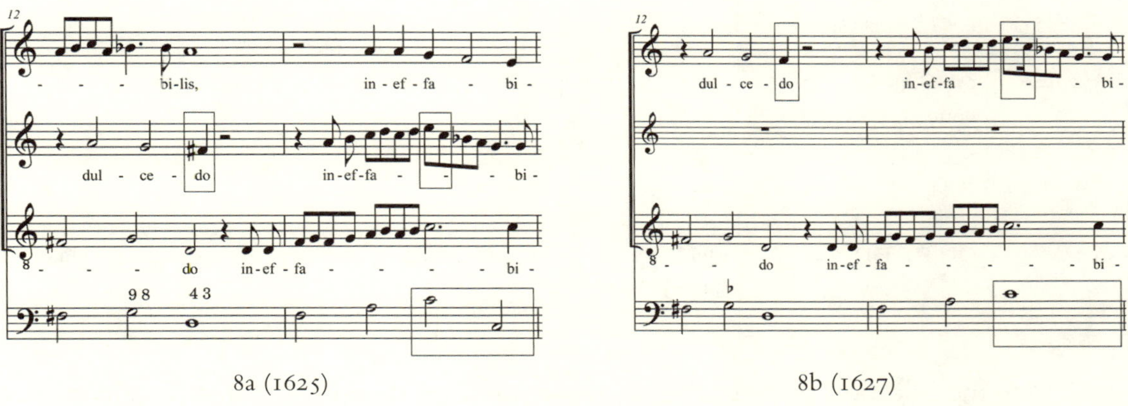

8a (1625) 8b (1627)

In a later passage Frescobaldi has added some slurs to make the articulation of a motive more precise. In this case it is not so much a modification as an integration that specifies a particular way of playing. A similar occurrence can be found in the tenor part

49. In the second version of the motet (1627) at bar 6, the first of the two Gs is given a sharp, while the sharp before the following F is not given.

50. Similar variants are found in the same part in bar 42 and in the tenor part in bar 16 (see below).

in the immediately following bar; and it is likely that slurs of the same kind were added in bar 40 of the *cantus secundus*, which is now lost (see Ex. 9).

Ex. 9: *Iesu Rex admirabilis*, bars 40-41.

9a (1625) 9b (1627)

The tenor line, which is the part that undergoes the least reworking, reveals only three variants.

Table 5: Variants in the Tenor Part

Bars	1625	1627	Type of intervention
16, viii–xi	QU dotted G; SQ A; dotted QU G; SQ A	QU G A G A	rhythmic variant: removal of a dotted rhythm
36, iv–v	M G♯ G	M G G♯	accidental moved
40, i–iv	QU F E F D	QU F-E F-D slurred in pairs	two slurs added to specify the articulation of the phrase

One modification made to the tenor part involves the moving of an accidental in a cadenza. As in a similar variant found in the cantus part[51], here too the intervention does not seem totally appropriate, since in the 1627 version a necessary accidental is missing, which is correctly marked in the previous redaction. In another passage, a rhythmic figure originally based on the dotted figuration is simplified in the new redaction and transformed into a simple group of four quavers (see Ex. 10). While the solution in the 1627 version

[51]. See note 49 above.

is in reality more homogeneous with respect to the rhythmic patterns used for the other voices, it should nevertheless be noted that the dotted rhythm present in the 1625 redaction avoided the clash of a second between the A and G in the tenor and *cantus secundus* parts[52].

Ex. 10. *Iesu Rex admirabilis*, bar 16.

10a (1625)

10b (1627)

Finally, as far as the choices to be made in a critical edition are concerned, considering that the motet *Iesu Rex admirabilis* was published twice, and that the surviving second edition is incomplete and contains variants with respect to the first edition, the most appropriate solution, and the one adopted in the *opera omnia* of Frescobaldi, seems to be that of publishing the two distinct versions separately. The presence of numerous variants (which, as we have seen, are not always simple corrections) would make every choice between the two redactions somewhat arbitrary. Given that Frescobaldi was still alive at the time of the second version, included in an individual collection of his works and thus certainly revised by the composer himself, one is inclined to opt for the publication only of the second redaction: but this is the one that has come down to us incomplete. The hypothesis of 'completing' the second version by inserting the *cantus secundus* of the previous version would give rise to a *monstrum*, a composition that never existed (and that was never performed), the outcome of the contamination between two versions that are very similar, but contain a large number of modifications of various kinds. The choice to publish only the first redaction (the only one that has survived complete) would instead deny the reader the chance to assess the nature, extent and significance of the modifications later made by the composer.

52. Moreover, the tenor part is also involved in the addition of two slurs that specify the articulation of a motive, in analogy with those introduced in the cantus part in the following bar (see Ex. 9 above).

Conclusions

The cases examined — the *concerti* from Giovanni Ghizzolo's second (1611-1623) and third book (1615-1623) and Girolamo Frescobaldi's motet *Iesu Rex admirabilis* (1625-1627) — have highlighted how the publication of a new edition could present an opportunity to review one or more compositions already printed and in particular to re-manage the basso continuo line.

The comparison between successive editions revealed some interesting elements regarding various aspects of performance practice, including the articulation of the basso continuo line and the way of accompanying the voices with the organ (and in particular the strategies to adopt at the points where the voices have diminutions or lively passages), as well as useful information about how to tackle the question of modal transposition in vocal compositions accompanied by the organ.

Taking for granted that the strategies to adopt in an edition should necessarily consider the specific history of transmission of each work (or collection of works) and the greater or lesser significance of the variants emerging from the comparison of sources, certain indispensable criteria should nevertheless be taken into account when preparing a critical edition. In particular, with regards the *restitutio textus* editors should *avoid contaminating two or more distinct versions of the same composition*, mixing parts or portions of one redaction with those of a later one. Two distinct versions of the same work should therefore be published separately, as in the case of the 'structurally' different versions of the motets of the second book — and in one case also of the third — by Giovanni Ghizzolo. Also with Frescobaldi's motet, of which we have two redactions, one complete and another incomplete, it would be opportune to produce two separate editions; though not structurally different, these two versions contain several variants in all the voices, making it impossible to combine them in order to 'recomplete' the second version, which moreover lacks the *cantus secundus*.

In the same way, editors should *avoid fixing elements that were not fixed in the 17th century edition*. Where clear indications about the transposition are specified by captions, clefs or accidentals in the key signature, or else the organ part has been rewritten a fourth and/or a fifth below, in the modern edition the composition should be written *in tono*, as in the notation of the vocal parts in the ancient edition. Moreover, all the indications contained in the ancient edition should be reported in the modern edition (possibly showing the transposed versions of the organ bass in an appendix, either in a reproduction or in a modern transcription), so as to allow the player to draw all possible information not only about the different transpositions suggested by the composer, but also about the different form assumed by the organ bass in the transposed versions. It would, in fact, be a great loss if all this information were to end up in the philologist's bin[53].

53. See Toffetti 2004.

BIBLIOGRAPHY

AGAZZARI 1607
AGAZZARI, Agostino. *Del sonare sopra 'l basso con tutti li stromenti e dell'uso loro nel conserto*, Siena, Falcini, 1607.

ARNOLD 1965
ARNOLD, Franck Thomas. *The Art of Accompaniment from a Thorough-Bass as Practised in the XVIIth & XVIIIth centuries*, 2 voll., New York, Dover, 1965 (Dover Books on Music).

BACH 1753-1762
BACH, Carl Philipp Emanuel. *Versuch uber die wahre Art das Clavier zu spielen. Zweiter Teil, in welchen die Lehre von dem Accompagnament und der freyen Fantasie abgehandelt wird*, 2 vols., Berlin, Henning-Winter, 1753, 1762.

BIANCIARDI 1607
BIANCIARDI, Francesco. *Breve Regola per imparar' a sonare sopra il Basso con ogni sorte d'Instrumento*, Siena, s.n., 1607.

BORGIR 1987
BORGIR, Tharald. *The Performance of Basso Continuo in Italian Baroque Music*, Ph.D. Diss., Ann Arbor (MI), UMI Research Press, 1987 (Studies in Musicology, 90).

CARCHIOLO 2007
CARCHIOLO, Salvatore. *Una perfezione d'armonia meravigliosa: prassi cembalo-organistica del basso continuo italiano dalle origini all'inizio del XVIII secolo*, revised edition, Lucca, LIM, 2007.

CHRISTENSEN 1992
CHRISTENSEN, Jesper Bøje. *Die Grundlagen des Generalbaßspiels im 18. Jahrhundert. Ein Lehrbuch nach zeitgenössischen Quellen*, Kassel, Bärenreiter, 1992.

CORRETTE 1753
CORRETTE, Michel. *Le maitre de clavecin pour l'accompagnement, methode theorique et pratique*, Paris, L'Auteur-Bayard-Le Clerc-Castagnère, 1753.

CORRI 1810
CORRI, Domenico. *The Singer's Preceptor: A Treatise on Vocal Music Calculated to Teach the Art of Singing*, London, Chappel, 1810 ca.

DANDRIEU 1718
DANDRIEU, Jean-François. *Principes de l'accompagnement du clavecin*, Paris, Bayard, 1718.

DEL SORDO 2004
DEL SORDO, Federico. *Il basso continuo. Una guida pratica e teorica per l'avviamento alla prassi dell'accompagnamento nei secoli XVII e XVIII*, Padua, Armelin, 2004 (Intelligere & concertare, 1).

FRANCHI 2006
FRANCHI, Saverio. *Annali della stampa musicale romana dei secoli XVI-XVII. Volume 1/1: Edizioni di musica pratica del 1601 al 1650*, in collaboration with Orietta Sartori, Rome, IBIMUS, 2006 (ASMUR-Annali della stampa musicale romana / Istituto di Bibliografia Musicale a cura di Saverio Franchi, 1/1).

Frescobaldi 1628a
Frescobaldi, Girolamo. *In partitura il primo libro delle canzoni a una, due, tre, e ouattro [sic] voci. Per sonare con ogni sorte di Stromenti. Con dui Toccate in fine, una per sonare con Spinettina sola, overo Liuto, l'altra Spinettina è Violino, ouero Liuto, è Violino del Sig. Girolamo Frescobaldi organista in S. Pietro di Roma. Date in luce da Bartolomeo Grassi organista in S. Maria in Acquirio di Roma. Con privilegio*, Rome, Paolo Masotti, 1628.

Frescobaldi 1628b
Id. *Il primo libro delle canzoni ad una, due, trè, e quattro voci. Accomodate, per sonare ogni sorte de stromenti*, Rome, Giovanni Battista Robletti, 1628.

Frescobaldi 1634
Id. *Canzoni da sonare a una due tre, et quattro voci con il basso continuo*, Venice, Alessandro Vincenti, 1634.

Frescobaldi 1933
Id. *Canzoni a due canti col basso continuo: per sonare con ogni sorte di stromenti, für zwei beliebige hohe Instrumente mit Generalbass*, edited by Hans T. David, Mainz, Schott, 1933.

Frescobaldi 1959
Id. *6 canzoni*, edited by Gustav Leonhardt, Vienna, Universal, 1959 (Classical Scores Library, 1).

Frescobaldi 1966a
Id. *Canzoni per canto solo* e *Canzoni per basso solo: Baßstimme und Generalbaß*, edited by Friedrich Cerha, Vienna-Munich, Doblinger, 1966 (Diletto musicale, Doblinger Reihe Alter Musik, 87).

Frescobaldi 1966b
Id. *Canzoni per basso solo: Baßstimme und Generalbaß*, edited by Friedrich Cerha, 2 vols., Vienna-Munich, Doblinger, 1966 (Diletto musicale, Doblinger Reihe Alter Musik, 88-89).

Frescobaldi 1969-1970
Id. *Canzonas*, London, Musica Rara, 1969-1970.

Frescobaldi 1974-1977
Id. *The Ensemble Canzonas of Frescobaldi*, edited by Bernard Thomas, 4 vols., London, Pro Musica, 1974-1977.

Frescobaldi 1983
Id. *Mottetti: a 2 e 3 voci e basso continuo*, edited by Lorenzo Ghielmi and Mario Valsecchi, Bergamo, Carrara, 1983.

Frescobaldi 1987
Id. *Mottetti a 1, 2 e 3 voci con continuo*, edited by Christopher Stembridge, Padua, Zanibon, 1987 (Capolavori musicali dei secoli xvii e xviii).

Frescobaldi 2002
Id. *Opere complete. 8: Il primo libro delle canzoni a una, due, tre e quattro voci per sonare et cantare nelle edizioni di Roma 1628 e Venezia 1635 con l'aggiunta di tre canzoni pubblicate nella raccolta Raverij 1608*, edited by Étienne Darbellay, Milan, Suvini Zerboni, 2002 (Monumenti Musicali Italiani, 22).

FRESCOBALDI 2014

ID. *Opere Complete. 11: Liber secundus diversarum modulationum singulis, binis, ternis, quaternisque vocibus* (1627), critical edition and reconstruction of the missing part by Marco Della Sciucca and Marina Toffetti, Milan, Suvini Zerboni, 2014 (Monumenti Musicali Italiani, 26).

GASPARINI 1708

GASPARINI, Francesco. *L'Armonico pratico al cimbalo*, Venice, Bortoli, 1708.

GATTI 2014

GATTI, Enrico. '«Però ci vole pacientia»: un excursus sull'arte della diminuzione nei secoli XVI, XVII e XVIII «per uso di chi avrà volontà di studiare»', in: ACCIAI, Giovanni – GATTI, Enrico – TAVELLA, Konrad. *Regole per ben suonare e cantare: diminuzioni e mensuralismo fra XVI e XIX secolo*, Pisa, ETS, 2014 (Quaderni del Conservatorio 'Giuseppe Verdi' di Milano, n.s. 2), pp. 71-188.

GHIZZOLO 1611

GHIZZOLO, Giovanni. *Concerti all'uso moderno a quattro voci. Con la partitura accomodata per suonare. Di Giovanni Ghizzolo nuovamente dati in luce. Libro secondo, et opera settima*, Milan, erede di Simon Tini e Filippo Lomazzo, 1611.

GHIZZOLO 1615

ID. *Il terzo libro delli concerti a due, 3 e quattro voci, con le Letanie della B. Vergine a cinque, et la parte per l'organo. Di Giovanni Ghizzolo Maestro di Cappella dell'eccell.mo Sig. Prencipe di Correggio. Opera XII. Nuovamente data in luce*, Milan, Filippo Lomazzo, 1615.

GHIZZOLO 1623A

ID. *Il secondo libro de concerti a quattro voci di Giovanni Ghizzolo Maestro di Capella della Veneranda Arca di Santo Antonio di Padova. Nuovamente ristampati, & dall'istesso Auttore corretti, et accomodati in varij lochi. Opera settima*, Venice, Alessandro Vincenti, 1623.

GHIZZOLO 1623B

ID. *Il terzo libro delli concerti a due tre e quattro voci, Con le litanie della Beata Vergine a 5 voci, et la parte per l'organo. Di Giovanni Ghizzolo Maestro di Cappella di Santo Antonio di Padova. Opera duodecima nuovamente ristampata et corretta dall'istesso auttore*, Venice, Alessandro Vincenti, 1623.

GIOVANNI GHIZZOLO 2010

Concerti all'uso moderno a quattro voci 1611/1623. Giovanni Ghizzolo OFMConv. (1580c.-1624c.), introduction and transcription by Daniele Gambino, Padua, Centro Studi Antoniani, 2010 (Corpus Musicum Franciscanum, 18/6).

HARPER 1975

HARPER, John Martin. *The Instrumental Canzonas of Girolamo Frescobaldi: A Comparative Edition and Introductory Study*, Ph.D. Diss., Birmingham, University of Birmingham, 1975.

HARPER 1987

ID. 'Frescobaldi's Reworked Ensemble Canzonas', in: *Frescobaldi Studies*, edited by Alexander Silbiger, Durham, Duke University Press, 1987 (Sources of Music and Their Interpretation, 1), pp. 269-283.

Jensen 1986

Jensen, Niels Martin. 'La revisione delle canzoni ed il suo significato per la comprensione del linguaggio frescobaldiano', in: *Girolamo Frescobaldi nel* IV *centenario della nascita. Atti del convegno internazionale di studi (Ferrara, 9-14 settembre 1983)*, edited by Sergio Durante and Dinko Fabris, Florence, Olschki, 1986 (Quaderni della rivista italiana di musicologia, 10), pp. 315-327.

Kerman 1982

Kerman, Joseph. 'Sketch Studies', in: *19th-Century Music*, VI/2 (Autumn 1982), pp. 174-180.

Kurtzman 2014

Kurtzman, Jeffrey. 'Vocal Ranges, Cleffing and Transposition in the Sacred Music of Giulio Belli', in: *Barocco padano e musici francescani: l'apporto dei maestri conventuali. Atti del* XVI *Convegno internazionale sul barocco padano (secoli* XVII-XVIII*) (Padova, 1-3 luglio 2013)*, edited by Alberto Colzani, Andrea Luppi and Maurizio Padoan, Padua, Centro Studi Antoniani, 2014 (Centro studi antoniani, 55. Contributi musicologici del Centro ricerche dell'A.M.I.S., 20), pp. 141-164.

Liber secundus diversarum modulationum 1627

Frescobaldi, Girolamo. *Liber secundus diversarum modulationum singulis, binis, ternis, quaternisque vocibus*, Rome, apud Andream Phæum, 1627.

Lilia campi 1621

Lilia campi binis, ternis, quaternisque vocibus concinnata cum basso ad organum. A Jo. Baptista Robletto excerta atque luce donata, Rome, apud Jo. Baptistam Roblettum, 1621.

Luisi 1986

Luisi, Francesco. 'Il *Liber secundus diversarum modulationum* (1627): proposte di realizzazione della parte mancante', in: *Girolamo Frescobaldi nel* IV *centenario della nascita* [...], *op. cit.*, pp. 163-195.

Marshall 1972

Marshall, Robert Lewis. *The Compositional Process of J. S. Bach. A Study of the Autograph Scores of the Vocal Works*, 2 vols., Princeton (NJ), Princeton University Press, 1972 (Princeton Studies in Music, 4).

Mattei 1788

Mattei, Stanislao. *Pratica d'accompagnamento sopra bassi numerati e contrappunti a più voci sulla scala maggiore e minore*, Bologna, s.n., 1788.

Owens 1997

Owens, Jessie Ann. *Composers at Work: The Craft of Musical Composition 1450-1600*, Oxford-New York, Oxford University Press, 1997.

Pasquali 1757

Pasquali, Nicolò. *Thorough-bass Made Easy: Or Practical Rules for Finding and Applying Its Various Chords With Little Trouble*, Edinburgh, Nicolò Pasquali-Bremner, 1757.

Penna 1672-1679-1684

Penna, Lorenzo. *Li primi albori musicali, libro primo, libro secondo, libro terzo*, Bologna, Monti, 1672, 1679, 1684.

QUANTZ 1752
QUANTZ, Johann Joachim. *Versuch einer Anweisung die Flote traversiere zu spielen*, Berlin, Voss, 1752.

RISM A/I
Répertoire International des Sources Musicales, Einzeldrücke vor 1800, 15 vols., Kassel [...], Bärenreiter, 1971-2003.

RISM B/I
Répertoire International des Sources Musicales, Recueils Imprimés XVI-XVII siècles, edited by François Lesure, Munich-Duisburg, Henle, 1960.

ROCHE 1986
ROCHE, Jerome. 'I mottetti di Frescobaldi e la scelta dei testi nel primo Seicento', in: *Girolamo Frescobaldi nel IV centenario della nascita* [...], *op. cit.*, pp. 153-161.

ROMAGNOLI 2012
ROMAGNOLI, Angela. '«Con varietà di bei contraponti render vaga la melodia»: The Practice of Basso Continuo with the Brain and the Hands', a panel discussion with Edoardo Bellotti, Nicola Cumer, Thérèse de Goede, Mara Galassi, and Pietro Prosser, in: *Philomusica on-line*, XII (2012), pp. 99-109.

SABBATINI 1650
SABBATINI, Pietro Paolo. *Toni ecclesiastici colle sue intonazioni, all'uso romano. Modo per sonare il basso continuo, chiavi corrispondenti all'altre chiavi generali, et ordinarie, per beneficio de' principianti, date in luce da Pietro Paolo Sabbatini professore della musica. Libro primo, opera decima ottava*, Rome, Lodovico Grignani, 1650.

SACRI AFFETTI 1625
Sacri affetti contesti da di veersi [sic] eeclentissimi [sic] autori, raccolti da Francesco Sammaruco, Rome, Luca Antonio Soldi, 1625.

SAINT LAMBERT 1707
SAINT LAMBERT, Michael de. *Nouveau traité de l'accompagnement du clavecin, de l'orgue, et des autres instruments*, Paris, Christophe Ballard, 1707.

SALLIS 2015
SALLIS, Friedemann. *Music Sketches*, Cambridge, Cambridge University Press, 2015 (Cambridge Introductions to Music).

SCELTA DI MOTETTI 1618
Scelta di motetti di diversi eccellentissimi autori, à 2, à 3, à 4 e à 5. Posti in luce da Fabio Constantini romano, Rome, Bartolomeo Zannetti, 1618.

SELECTÆ CANTIONES 1616
Selectæ cantiones excellentissimorum auctorum binis, tenir, quaternisq. vocibus concinendæ, a Fabio Constantino romano insignis Basilicæ S. Mariæ Trans Tyberim musices moderatore, simul collecta, Rome, Bartolomeo Zannetti, 1616.

SIMMEL 1920-1921
SIMMEL, Georg. 'Zur Philosophie des Schauspielers', in: *Logos: Internationale Zeitung für die Philosophie der Kultur*, IX (1920-1921), pp. 339-362. English translation by Philip Lawton, *Towards the Philosophy of the Actor*, at <https://papers.ssrn.com/sol3/papers.cfm?abstract_id=2897044>, accessed November 2018.

STEMBRIDGE 1986

STEMBRIDGE, Christopher. 'Questioni di stile nei mottetti di Frescobaldi', in: *Girolamo Frescobaldi nel IV centenario della nascita* [...], *op. cit.*, pp. 195-213.

TASCHETTI 2016

TASCHETTI, Gabriele. *Procedimenti di revisione nelle due edizioni de* Il terzo libro delli concerti *(Milano, 1615 - Venezia, 1623) di Giovanni Ghizzolo*, diss., Padua, University of Padua, 2016.

TOFFETTI 2004

TOFFETTI, Marina. 'Il cestino del filologo. Diasistema, dialisi e detriti del non autentico', in: *Hortus musicus*, V/20 (October-December 2004), pp. 216-217.

TOFFETTI 2013

EAD. 'Restoring a Masterpiece. Some Remarks on the Reconstruction of the Missing Part in Girolamo Frescobaldi's *Liber secundus diversarum modulationum* (Rome, 1627)', in: *Musica Iagellonica*, VII (2013), pp. 5-24.

TOFFETTI 2018

EAD. 'Note sul processo creativo nel primo Seicento: le due edizioni dei Concerti all'uso moderno di Giovanni Ghizzolo (Milano, 1611 - Venezia, 1623)', in: *Barocco padano e musici francescani, II. L'apporto dei maestri conventuali. Atti del XVII Convegno internazionale sul Barocco padano (secoli XVII-XVIII) (Padova 1-3 luglio 2016)*, edited by Alberto Colzani, Andrea Luppi and Maurizio Padoan, Padua, Centro Studi Antoniani, 2018 (Barocco Padano, 9), pp. 287-322.

WESTRUP 1962

WESTRUP, Jack. *The Cadence in Baroque Recitative*, in: *Natalicia musicologica: Knud Jeppesen septuagenario collegis oblata*, edited by Bjørn Hjelmborg and Søren Sørensen, Hafniae, Hansen, 1962, pp. 243-252.

Issues of Performance Practice

«Il n'exécute jamais la Basse telle qu'elle est écrite»: The Use of Improvisation in Teaching Low Strings

Giovanna Barbati
(Città Sant'Angelo, Pescara)

Historical Improvisation, Low Strings Didactic, Partimenti and Solfeggi

> Every [...] study that confines itself exclusively to the practical and theoretical sources that have come down to us in writing or print, without taking into account the improvisational element in living musical practice, must of necessity present an incomplete, indeed a distorted picture [...] For there is scarcely a single field in music that has remained unaffected by improvisation, scarcely a musical technique or form of composition that did not originate in improvisatory performance or was not essentially influenced by it[1].

The opportunity to imagine a systematic path for teaching cello or viola da gamba based on improvisation is offered to us from the rediscovery of the didactical and pedagogical practice of partimento[2]. This method was based on learning directly at the keyboard and on the progressive memorization of patterns; it rapidly developed the skill of composing, therefore of improvising, on a given bass. Since low strings have a double function, providing the continuo and *cantus*, it is very likely that also for these instruments a method similar to the partimenti was used; the traces found in the sources may confirm this hypothesis. «*Partimenti*, or instructional basses, were central to the training of European court musicians from the late 1600s until the early 1800s. [...] From seeing only one feature of a particular schema — any one of its parts — the student learned to complete the entire pattern [committing] every aspect of the schema to memory»[3]. In the baroque period besides partimenti were used *solfeggi*, or studies on melody, formed of melodic lines

1. Ferand 1961, p. 5. See also Todea 2014, p. 30. Moore 1992, p. 61: «Written documentation supports Ferand's position on the importance of improvisation in every musical era of the Western classical tradition excepting the present. Even well into the 19th century it is clear that improvisation remained an indispensable ability for most professional musicians».

2. Sanguinetti 2012; Gjerdingen 2007a; Cafiero 1993.

3. Gjerdingen 2017a.

on basses and different from those that we use nowadays. «Collections of solfeggi were thus like a lexicon of stylistically favored melodic utterances. For the future improvisor [...] solfeggi provided a storehouse of memorized material»[4]. Teaching improvisation on a given line had been already at the core of musical education: the practice of the *cantare super librum*, that is, the improvisation of other voices on the *tenor*, can be found in many sources from 1475 to 1783 and it is today well documented[5].

The central aim of this article is to look for a historical pedagogical method, a process that probably we can still use today, in the study and in the practice of baroque music, to learn creating *ex tempore* musically relevant expressions in the baroque style. To facilitate the acquisition of this skill, which we regard as fundamental and which we will discuss further in this essay, the suggestion is to supplement the didactical method, so that the interest towards improvisation is cultivated from the beginning, rather than being required at the end of a long training. Probably it is better to set from the beginning an active method based on schemes to elaborate, in which there is room also for the student's creativity within the didactical path. Moreover, we have to consider that music is a language and there are many considerations that advice to learn languages inside meaningful contexts[6]. In order to apply this approach to the pedagogy of a musical instrument, we need to contextualize the 'technical' formulas in musical structures.

During the baroque the term *exercise* had a different meaning, compared to how it is commonly understood today. Sanguinetti describes the concepts of 'exercise' and 'artistic work':

> [In] a nineteenth-century, romantic perspective, [...] every school exercise is only a preparatory work, a sort of gymnastic exercise for fingers and brain, and in no way to be confused with Art, which is inspired by the Spirit. This distinction had no real meaning for the eighteenth century music. In the pre-idealistic world there was a continuous interchange between school and art, and the boundaries between the two realms were indistinct. As W. Dean Sutcliffe writes [...] «The assumption that there is a necessary gulf between the two areas, that one either composes proper music or satisfies pedagogical demands, is creatively and historically unrealistic». [...] A great part of the music we cherish today as masterpieces — Scarlatti's *Essercizi*, Bach's *Well tempered Clavier, Klavierübungen,* l'*Orgelbüchlein* [...] originated as school works[7].

---

4. Gjerdingen 2017b.

5. Haymoz 2017; Schubert 2014; Canguilhem 2013. The complete list of the methods on *cantare super librum* has been published within the FABRICA project at the following link: <http://blogs.univ-tlse2.fr/fabrica/files/2014/01/Sources-th%C3%A9oriques-du-chant-sur-le-livre.pdf>, accessed October 2018.

6. «Figured bass could provide the vocabulary of chords — the lexicon — for filling the open-choice slots, but a master would be required to teach the large repertory of unitized phrases — the *phrasicon* — needed for fluency. Without the *phrasicon*, the result would sound like the utterances of a nonnative speaker»: Gjerdingen 2007b, p. 123. See also Strobbe – Van Regenmortel 2012; Strobbe 2014.

7. Sanguinetti 2012, p. 16.

In the baroque era, exercises were therefore intended as small pieces of different degrees of difficulty. We will follow then the traces of a didactical method in which single learning elements are always integrated in a larger musical context, for instance, a trill in a cadence or an arpeggio in a harmonic progression. First we will consider the improvisational demands of the repertoire; then we will consider some historical evidence and the traces found in documents; we will finally describe our pedagogical proposal. Before examining the sources, however, it is necessary to provide a short enquiry of the terms *composition* and *improvisation*.

The Terms *Composition* and *Improvisation*

> [According to] misguided conceptions of genius and creativity [...] today these are to be understood in terms of striking originality. [...] According to an earlier conception of musical creativity, creative composers learn from the works of their predecessors, [...] Borrowing has been a staple of musical composition since composition began[8].

The difficulty of learning how to operate on the text in accordance with the early performance practice, complying with the rules and the spirit of the baroque musical language, is increased today also by the confusion derived from the change of meaning of the terms *composition* and *improvisation* over time. As concerns composition, in Gjerdingen's opinion «the popular view of the composer — a Romantic view [...] — does not fit eighteenth-century reality [...] the galant composer lived the life of a musical craftsman, [...] who produced a large quantity of music for immediate consumption [...][9]; the schematization of courtly musical utterances was so pervasive as to constitute a dominant mode of thought [...] musicians learned, wrote, and taught this way»[10]. Such a concept of composition, as 'elaboration, variation, extension and expansion'[11] of pre-existing elements and patterns within a shared language, not only allows the development of personal formulas within the historical language, but implies a didactic that include these too. The first step in this direction lies in the learning and storage of musical patterns, collected from the repertoire and organised so that they could be later reused, following shared rules[12].

8. Young 2014, p. 23.
9. Gjerdingen 2007a, p. 6.
10. *Ibidem*, p. 448.
11. Byros 2015, p. 1.
12. For 'musical pattern' we mean a *figure*, such as for example a repeated note or a scale fragment, in relation to a chord or to a multiple chords path; combinations are endless, but each style has its own characteristic figures.

To learn to improvise Callahan suggests «a flexible and hierarchical model that draws an explicit distinction between long-range improvisational goals (*dispositio*), generic voice-leading progressions that accomplish these goals (*elaboratio*), and diminution techniques that apply motives to these progressions to yield a unique musical surface (*decoratio*)»[13]. For 'voice-leading' Callahan means a polyphonic writing, to be realized on a keyboard. However, this is not possible on a monodic instrument, except for very short sections: its typical writing is with broken or alternated voices[14], or through the accompaniment of a second instrument. The pair composition/improvisation has been investigated by scholars such as Dalhaus[15] and Canguilhem, which suggested more levels of division into parts between the two poles, as well as for the pair orality/writing[16].

Historical Improvisation Practice: Evidences and Hypotheses

> Then doubts arise, which can be summed up by this objection: how could such a simultaneous improvisation of many people happen without arousing confusion? [...] But what is remarkable is that scholars of musical matters look as if they avoid dwelling on that question [...] which is very inconvenient [...] and perhaps it being doubtful and inconvenient is the reason why they talk about it as much as scholars avoid it[17].

We do not know how baroque cello and viola da gamba players improvised, but it is recognised that it was a widespread practice, 'a solo' and in group. Pietro Della Valle provides a detailed report of the improvisation practice in the baroque orchestra[18]:

> [...] those singing and playing well in group have to give time each other, and instead of using too complicated contrapuntal artifices, they have to jest with light imitations. They will show their skill doing again and readily what others

13. Callahan 2010, p. vii.

14. *Cfr.*, *infra*, note 68.

15. «Analysed soberly, improvisation almost always relies to a large extent on formulas, tricks of the trade and models [...] The improviser must be able to fall back [...] on a store of prefabricated parts, which he may indeed modify or combine differently [...] The idea that he can commit himself entirely to the vagaries of chance is [...] an aesthetically legitimate fiction»: Dahlhaus 1987, p. 268. See also Dahlhaus 2010.

16. «While [musicology] has the tendency to define the whole musical production through the screen of the binary opposition improvisation/composition, [...] there was a great variety of solutions that the singers found to arrange writing and orality performing these music. [...] the musicologist Jean-Yves Hamelin proposed a very useful categorization [among] spontaneous, customary, and compositional practices, while these three categories aren't mutually exclusive»: Canguilhem 2010, pp. 274-275.

17. Torchi 1894, p. 8. When not otherwise indicated, translations are by the author of this essay.

18. Rose 1965. The orchestral improvisational practice is treated also in Torchi 1894.

> did before; then allowing another redoing what they did, and a proper chance, and so [...] they will show their skill among the others[19].

From the earliest sources of ornamentation practice, we find so many pleas not to diminish[20] and to observe the right rules, that we can imagine this was a habit practised not only by the most skilled musicians, but also by beginners. We will divide the subject depending on the different contexts in which the low string instrument acts: (1) 'a solo' without accompaniment; (2) as principal voice — or *cantus* — to be accompanied; as accompaniment of a *cantus* in two different ways, either (3) within a continuo group which can consist of two or more instruments[21], or (4) alone without additional instruments at the continuo (therefore without harmonic support, a documented setting, but today very seldom used in performances).

1. 'A solo' improvisation, without accompaniment, is one of the basic skills that the baroque musician had, and on which was judged[22]. If keyboard players improvised preludes, canzonas, ricercari, fantasias etc., this also happened with monodic instruments[23], including viola da gamba and cello. We find an example of what they played solo in the testimony of André Maugars, 1639:

> [...] in this worthy house [Leonora Baroni's house] I was induced for the first time to exhibit in Rome. [...] I played *studied things* very well, on the second occasion I gave them so many kinds of *preludes and fantasias* that they really granted me more appreciation than the first time. [But] the experts doubted if I were capable of *extemporising a theme and playing variations on it.* [...] The next day I was given fifteen to twenty notes, in order to make myself heard [...] with the accompaniment of a small organ. *This subject I treated with such infinite variety* that great satisfaction was shown[24].

---

19. Della Valle 1763, p. 254.

20. Esses 1992, p. 4; Collins 2001, pp. 142-146.

21. Usually with the cello or the viola da gamba we find an harpsichord and/or a theorbo, or we can add in a wider context more bass instruments like the double bass, the bassoon, or harmonic ones like harp etc.

22. «It's above all preluding that the great Musicians [...] let shine those cultivated modulations that ravish the Listeners. It's there that it's not enough to be a good Composer, nor to well dominate the Harpsichord [...] but that it is still necessary to abound in this fire of genius & this inventive spirit»: Rousseau 1768, *sub voce* 'Preluder'. «[It] is the perfection of the viol [if] a man may show the excellency both of his hands and his invention»: Simpson 1665, p. 27. *Cfr., infra*, note 24.

23. «[...] the Prélude has to be produced on the spot without any preparation, and [...] it includes a countless variety»: Hotteterre 1719, p. 3.

24. The text continues: «[in Rome] it is thought here that we are not capable of *improvising on a given theme.* In fact, whoever plays an instrument deserves no *extraordinary consideration*, unless he shows himself equal to such a demand»: Wasielewski 1894, pp. 13-15 (italics added). *Cfr.* Maugars 1672, pp. 173-175.

Still at the end of the eighteenth century, Carl Friedrich Abel, cellist and one of the last great viola da gamba players, is so described by Gerber: «With his dexterity on the gamba he also possessed the talent, like many other older virtuosi, of exciting the astonishment and admiration of his hearers by free fantasias and learned modulations [...] his cadences especially were excellent»[25].

The most common forms used to improvise in solo performance were the prelude, the toccata and the ricercare. This topic is very wide and would need a specific space.

2. As a *cantus* the low string instrument follows the same rules of the other melodic instruments and of the voices. A clarifying source is that of Bartolomeo Barbarino, who published a collection of sacred monodies with a diminished version next to an undiminished one, writing: «they will be useful to 1) singers without disposition, who can be satisfied to sing the plain version, 2) singers with disposition, but without a counterpoint knowledge, who can sing the diminutions as written and 3) singers who have both disposition and counterpoint knowledge, who can sing from the plain version, improvising their own versions»[26].

Therefore, as musicians had different dispositions towards improvisation, several possibilities of performance were considered, all valid. The performance of the plain text was considered for beginners and it was considered natural that the most skilled could develop it. For the most talented performers, besides the usual diminution and variation of the melodic line in the refrain, there were some 'musical spaces' predisposed just for improvisation. In instrumental music, besides grounds (bassi ostinati), dance forms could have a varied repetition, called *double*[27]. In various collections we also find very simple minuets and gavottes, that make you think at ready material to improvise variations; several were indeed composed that could be used as samples[28]. In vocal music,

[25]. Gerber's quote is in Wasielewski 1894, p. 33.

[26]. Barbarino 1614, quoted in Collins 2001, p. 141. Another clarifying passage is this by Luigi Zenobi, quoted in Blackburn – Lowinsky 1993, pp. 83-85: «The soprano is obliged, and has the freedom to diminish, to joke and in sum embellish a musical body [...] He must have excellent counterpoint, because without it he sings randomly, and makes thousands bad mistakes [...] Now, all or most of the mentioned conditions must be followed by a player on the Cornett, or Viola da Gamba, [...] or similar of only one voice».

[27]. Marin Marais composed many *doubles*, for exemple: *I Livre*, *Suite I*: 2 *Allemande*, 1 *Courante* and 2 *Gigue*; *Suite II*: 1 *Allemande* and 1 *Courante*; *Suite IV*: 1 *Allemande*; see Marais 1686. «There is this difference between the *Double* and the diminutions [that the musician] can make or leave when he wants, to catch the plain text up. But the *Double* can't be stopped»: Rousseau 1768, p. 175. «Variations. We mean with this term every way of embellishing and make *doubles* of an air [...] Players make often improvised or so assumed variations; but more often they write them [...] we find them also often in French songs & in short Italian airs for violin or cello»: Framery 1791, vol. II, pp. 550-551.

[28]. See Lanzetti 1750, *Gavotta*, Sonata no. 6; see also Marais 1689, p. 90, *Sujet Diversitez* (20 variazions on a bass).

instead, the space dedicated to the *ex tempore* contribution of an instrument were the refrains between the vocal verses. In some compositions they are written, in others we guess that performers are free to propose as they wish. A gorgeous model can be find in Monteverdi's aria *Et è pur dunque vero*[29] (see Ex. 1, p. 124). If in verses, for example, you have at the continuo a viola da gamba, in refrains it can take on the role of *cantus*.

The literature on melodic embellishment and variations on the *cantus* is immense; we will focus our attention instead on the less clear features of the performing practice of the low string instrument: the opportunities offered by the presence of more instruments at the continuo and the continuo function at the solo low string instrument.

3. In the continuo group instruments are classified in «two groups: as foundation and as ornament»; the low string instrument belongs to both categories, provided at least one bass line is played as foundation, as Agazzari explains[30]. Bismantova describes the difference between the *basso cantante*, a bass line rich of movement[31], and the *basso continuo*, a simpler bass with a foundation task, warning to always work out a simpler line for the continuo[32]. Therefore we can infer that if the writing of the bass line is too developed the continuo player has to simplify, when instead it is too simple, the *basso cantante* can enrich it. We find clear examples of reduction, in which simpler bass lines for the continuo are extracted from more articulated ones, in Supriani's *Sonate*, which will be treated later[33]. Improvisation on the bass was so widespread that it was often exaggerated: «We generally listen in the Music only to a thorough bass always doubled, that frequently is a kind of *battérie*, of chords, & an arpeggio [...] of those accompanying or at the harpsichord, or at the viol; it should be then that of the two instruments, there is one that plays the plain bass, & the other the *double*»[34].

We notice in this passage that bass players enriched the continuo with *battéries* and chords; these were troubling if performed by more players together, instead if one played the plain bass line and the other the *double*, they were enjoyable to listen to. The practice of adding chords at the viola da gamba is documented in Hoffmann 2010.

4. In absence of a polyphonic instrument the matter is more complicated, as it is very much debated if and how to realize the harmony, in instrumental and vocal chamber

[29]. The refrain is written in treble clef, it has been thought for a high compass, we freely infer that it is suitable for the viola da gamba. Monteverdi 1632.

[30]. Agazzari 1607, p. 3.

[31]. The movement comes from adding to the basso cantante passing notes, which connect the main harmonic notes that mostly form the basso continuo, and diminutions.

[32]. Bismantova 1677, p. 59.

[33]. See paragraph 'Solfeggi per violoncello'.

[34]. Bonnet 1715, pp. 434-435. See Bol 1973, p. 50.

Ex. 1: Claudio Monteverdi, *Et è pur dunque vero*, SV 250 (Monteverdi 1632).

music or in the recitatives. A practice somewhat documented is that of the recitatives at the cello[35]. As concerns the *recitativi secchi*, the practice of enriching the bass is attested since the earliest cello virtuosi, who realized the thorough bass together with the harpsichord or other instruments. For example «Giuseppe Jacchini was particularly famous for the way he accompanied singers in their recitatives: he seems to have made broad use of chords and melodic ornamentation in his continuo parts»[36].

In the period between the end of the eighteenth century and the first half of the nineteenth, when harpsichords disappeared from theatres, the *recitativi secchi* were instead performed mostly by the cello together with the double bass, which played the fundamental line. The use of the double bass allowed the cello to realize a good motion of the voices with some freedom in choosing the notes of the chord to use. Then it presumably consisted not of a series of chords originating by the production of simultaneous sounds 'a solo', but rather of double stop chords[37], helped by a second instrument that guaranteed the thorough bass line[38], alternated with full chords, more or less arpeggiated.

The practice of the recitatives at the cello lasted until about the middle of the nineteenth century[39]; in 1882 Amintore Galli wrote:

> [...] the cellist and the double bassist at the harpsichord were educated in the study of the figured bass, that allowed them to adorn the modulations, recurring at the end of each phrase of the recitative, with elegant embellishments [...] If singers able to perform the *recitativo secco* are rare like white flies, equally we have to say of the *violoncellisti partimentisti*. With today's instrumental polyphony, players are reduced to a merely mechanical duty, and none of them finds anymore necessary to study harmony and partimento[40].

5. We can assume what the *violoncellisti partimentisti* did when looking at some cantatas by Gaffi and Gasparini, both pupils of Pasquini, who is considered one of the founders of the didactical method based on partimenti[41]. We have for example two Cantatas by Gaffi,

---

35. For example see Bacciagaluppi 2006; Romanou 2009; Lymenstull 2014.

36. Vanscheeuwijck 1996, p. 89. About Jacchini see also Martini 1776, p. 15.

37. At the string instruments the number of the notes of chords played with simultaneous sounds corresponds to the number of the strings necessary to execute it.

38. «It is also important to note that since the Violoncellist will often omit the root due to the difficulty of the hand position, the Contra Bass is absolutely necessary; but in the absence of a Contra Bass, the Violoncellist is obliged never to omit the root»: Stiastny 1834, p. 21. *Cfr.* Lymenstull 2014, p. 18.

39. Most likely the tradition of realizing the recitatives at the cello had different features and histories depending on the places. Wasielewski says that he listened to it in Italy in 1873, and that in Germany since at least ten years it was no more practiced. Wasielewski 1894, p. 42.

40. Galli 1882, pp. 131-132 (italics added). *Cfr.* Bacciagaluppi 2006, p. 105.

41. «Yet the idea that the use of partimento as a teaching method had one of his earliest advocates in Pasquini is not without foundation», Sanguinetti 2012, p. 59.

Allor che'l vostro lume and *Dalle oziose piume*[42] (Exs. 1a and 1b) in which now and then a voice is inserted: this could be the entry of an *obbligato* cello.

Ex. 2a: excerpt from Tommaso Gaffi, *Allor che'l vostro lume* (Gaffi a).

As we see in Ex. 2a and 2b, in some passages the bass line doubles: the upper voice once follows the melody in thirds, another time creates an imitative counterpoint on the bass. These written examples, in which the bass gets 'concertante' only in a few moments, let us speculate that in vocal music a good *partimentista* could freely take the opportunity to insert a parallel voice or a countermelody.

I agree with Gjerdingen when, speaking of Cimarosa's realization of partimenti, says that the young composer «would surely have noticed an incongruity when a busy, interesting opening passage leads into a boring passage»[43], and would have got around that by filling the spaces deliberately left empty, but I would add that most likely a good musician would have always done like this. We have so many vocal compositions in which spaces are deliberately left empty, with the bass line sometimes thematic, sometimes as a simple continuo. If, for example, the continuo is realized besides the harpsichord by a cello, the latter has room to improvise.

42. Gaffi a, Gaffi b. I am grateful to Pierluigi Morelli, who kindly suggested me these cantatas.

43. «In the process of learning Durante's A-minor *partimento*, a talented boy like Cimarosa would surely have noticed an incongruity when a busy, interesting opening passage leads into a boring passage», Gjerdingen 2010, p. 46.

Ex. 2b: excerpt from Tommaso Gaffi, *dalle oziose piume* (Gaffi b).

In the prefaces of the Cantatas published in Rome by Mascardi, Gasparini and Gaffi explain that, when we find more lines at the bass, there is freedom to play everything at the harpsichord or to arrange if there is available a cello, or an archlute or a violin as well. Gasparini says: «You will find in some Arias two Basses one for convenience, or easy to accompany; as it was necessary to adapt to the Print, so that I could not fully show my intention. But where you find above the Bass some Voice or Violin keys, you will play it with the right hand like a tablature. Here still the Archlute and the Cello will be able to be satisfied»[44].

Bernardo Gaffi gives more details:

> You will find some Arias with two Basses, and that one above with key changes like Violin or Tenor, there the Violin or the Violone could be satisfied, & without these will supply the virtue of a good Harpsichord player making both Basses, i.e. the Violin key with the right hand, and the others with the left, as the Author has not the intention to present Cantatas with instruments, but only to make the Harpsichord play like as a Tablature[45].

We notice the equivalence between playing at the harpsichord and arranging with strings. Certainly cello writing until about the half of the eighteenth century largely

44. Gasparini 1695, 'A gl'amatori della Musica'. See Gialdroni 2013, p. 133.

45. Gaffi 1700, 'L'Autore a gl'Amatori della Musica'. See Gialdroni 2013, p. 133.

coincides with the one of the left hand at the harpsichord (melodic elements, arpeggios and *battéries*[46]), we hypothesize then that not only music for upper voice and bass was played at the harpsichord solo and that for harpsichord was arranged for violin and cello[47], but in general we believe quite possible that the low string instrument used techniques of the continuo line elaboration similar to those that today are common in the performance practice of polyphonic instruments.

The considerable use of the *obbligato* or *concertante* cello in Rome can be explained by the presence of a very important cello school, described by La Via in his works[48]. This arranging practice was probably widespread and also improvised in different ways, sometimes with bad taste if Benedetto Marcello says: «the cello virtuoso [...] in the arias will divide the bass whimsically, varying each evening, even if variations are not at all related with the musician's or the violins's part»[49].

6. For the realization of the continuo 'a solo' in chamber instrumental music were used the same skills of the *violoncellisti partimentisti*. We have evidence of the various tours that some duos violin-cello did: Tartini accompanied by Vandini, pupil of Jacchini; Veracini accompanied by Lanzetti; Manfredi by Boccherini[50]. What the cellist did accompanying 'a solo' it's a debated topic. Many sustain the thesis of a chordal accompaniment[51], instead the thesis suggested here, given the monodic nature of the cello and given the evidence that a good two-voices counterpoint is enough to create masterpieces, is that the cello solo accompaniment was similar to what the left hand does in a classical Sonata: sometimes it performs an Alberti bass or broken chords patterns, sometimes it accompanies the

---

46. «As concerns *battéries* [...] if the harpsichord doesn't swell its sounds, if the double beats on the same note don't work extremely well on it, it has other advantages»: Couperin 1716. From this quote in my opinion we can infer how the bass line writing was thought for different instruments, with the presence in the Sonata of passages clearly written for the low string instrument; moreover we read how features of the string sound were highly esteemed. From here we could guess that also a plain long notes accompaniment could be appreciated.

47. An example that could confirm this practice is the *Avvertissement* in the *Pièces de théorbe et de luth mises en partition*, where De Visée states: «The goal of this print is the Harpsichord, the Viol and the Violin, on which instruments they always have been arranged». We infer that it was common practice to arrange on strings score composed for polyphonic instruments. De Visée 1716.

48. During his roman stay G. F. Handel composed his Cantatas *Tra le fiamme*, with concertante viola da gamba, 1707 and *Non s'afferra d'amor il porto*, with concertante cello, 1708. *Cfr.* Hoffmann 2016; La Via 1983-1984; La Via 1987.

49. Marcello 1720, p. 53. *Cfr.* Nuti 2007, p. 110. Also Halton (Halton 2008, p. 317) draws similar conclusions: «It is possible that this division [in Scarlatti's music] of the bass part into two specialised functions [...] has its origins in improvisation practices of the new generation of violoncello virtuosi».

50. Whittaker 2012, pp. 46-47.

51. *Cfr.* Lymenstull 2014, p. 5; Whittaker 2012. We believe that the chordal realization (with simultaneous sounds) is one of the choices, but not the most idiomatic one. In our opinion a good bass realization can use various alternatives, like a theorbo does.

melody with a parallel line in thirds or sixths, sometimes it creates a countermelody, sometimes, for harmonic clarity, adds a few notes forming double stop chords or full chords. In fact, this is the kind of writing that we find in the compositions by Cervetto[52] or by other composers of the time for violin and cello. We know besides that also the violin in various contexts could add important notes to the harmony, for example with double stop chords[53].

The Historical Pedagogy

> Up to a few years ago, in almost all schools in Italy, harmony was taught more or less in the following way. Just after having learned the intervals, one studied the Rule of the Octave [...] Afterwards one went on to the study of partimento, with little or no care in the first stages [...] for knowing chords. These [...] step after step became clear[54].

The thesis suggested here is that in baroque times the teaching method was organised so that pupils could improvise, that is to say was based on patterns which could be reused in different contexts, namely based on different kind of figures. Considering the importance of arpeggios and *battéries*, it seems that these were from the beginning typical *figures* of the cello, as also François Couperin states: «as concerns *battéries*, or *arpègements* [...], whose origin comes from the Sonatas, my opinion would be that we need to limit their amount when we play them on the harpsichord. This instrument has its own features, such as the violin has its own»[55]. Towards the end of the eighteenth century, together with the decline of the harpsichord, we witness the development of figures belonging exclusively to the cello, like the special arpeggio-figures, often present in the methods.

In many sources concerning the training of a cellist or viola da gamba player, immediately after the basic instructions, we find exercises to master intervals and play arpeggios and *battéries*. For instance, in De La Borde's *Essai*, after the explanation of the left hand positions one goes directly to the *battéries*[56], and after one finds a scale harmonised in accordance with the rule of the octave, as was usual in the partimenti school. The voice

---

52. James Cervetto, pupil of his father Giacobbe, from Venice, was well known for the performance of recitatives and taught to Nochez and Robert Lindley, one of the most famous cellists at the operatic continuo.

53. Stein 2014, pp. 11-34.

54. Cav. Maestro Ettore De Champs, Sanguinetti 2012, p. 96.

55. Couperin 1716, p. 35. This could be a reference to the improvised accompaniment made of arpeggios and two-notes broken chords at the cello.

56. We infer that for *battéries* they meant many kinds of broken chords, from alternated thirds to arpeggios on three strings, all performed *détaché*, whereas *harpegés* was used only for *legato* figures. *Cfr.* De La Borde 1780, p. 314.

Ex. 3: Examples of *battéries* from De La Borde's *Essai* and the first part of a *Rondeau* by Nochez.

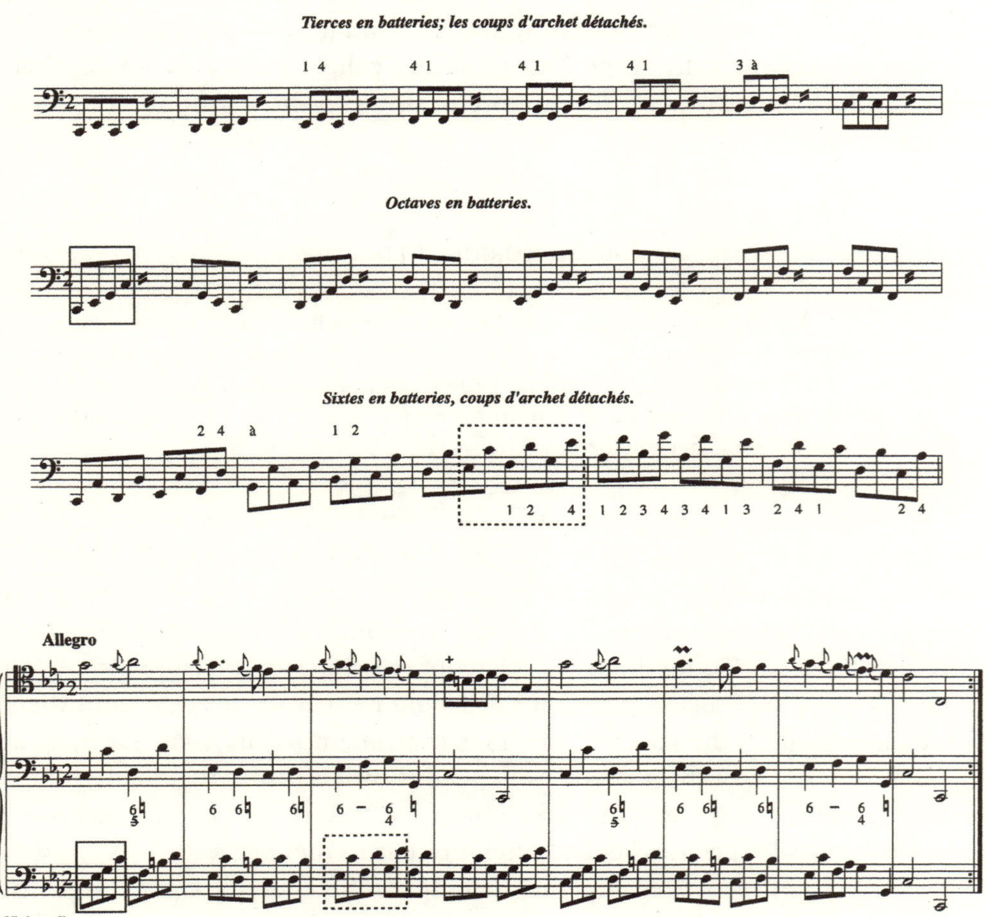

violoncelle in the *Essai* was written by Nochez, cellist at the Opera in Paris, who had studied with Cervetto and Dell'Abaco[57].

By Nochez we have also a precious bass realisation of a *Rondeau*, kindly provided by Christophe Coin (Ex. 3). The melody is written in the first stave, in the second there is a simple bass line, in the third we find an elaborated version of the latter. Analyzing the elaborated version, we notice the precise application of the figures shown by Nochez in De La Borde's *Essai*: exclusive use of arpeggios and alternated consonances of thirds and sixths (there are also occasional broken octaves) within a quavers perpetual motion, interrupted only at the cadences.

57. Wasielewski 1894, p. 93.

In various cello methods we find simple arias with the accompaniment bass line in several versions, usually in a first variant at the bass we find crotchets, then quavers, then semiquavers in different kinds of arpeggio figures. We hypothesize that these realisations work as true bass harmonisations, having already said that the cello realises chords trough its specific figures. For instance, there are many alternatives in the methods by Gunn[58] and Breval; in the latter we read: «The following Arias can be performed not only with the written bowings, but with every other we will choose among the previous examples»[59]. This let us assume that the goal was to master some chosen figures, to learn applying them later in the accompaniment of other melodies. It was therefore a matter of learning patterns that the student would later reuse in complete autonomy.

Also the interesting anonymous German viola da gamba method, probably written around 1730, edited by Bettina Hoffmann in 2014, shows the same didactic approach: a few explanations, many ready diminution patterns, arpeggios and *battérie*, with the final statement: «When a scholar has understood and put into practice these instructions, he needs no further information, and can assist himself»[60]. We interpret this expression as an exhortation to learn by heart and apply, with the implicit certainty that through experience one learns what he needs... In Ex. 4 (p. 132) we see some chords followed by a few figures, which can be used to realise those chords at the viol: slurred and separated arpeggios, simple two-notes chords, two-notes chords with repeated notes, broken thirds with an applied dotted rhythm. In other pages there are also diminutions that refer to the division — or *passaggi* — tradition. So we lie in-between the early art of ornamentation on interval basis and the art of harmonic realisation. Going back a few decades, we notice that Simpson had clearly distinguished among different kinds of *divisions*: «[We have] two kinds of divisions: a breaking of the ground and a descanting upon it: out of which two, is generated a third sort [...] to wit a mixture of those, one with the other. [...] Descant division differs from the former [because] that breaks the notes of the ground, this descant upon them [...] in any of the concords»[61]. According

58. Gunn 1789, p. 22, 63. John Gunn published also a very interesting treatise on the study and the performance of harmony at the cello: Gunn 1802. Here at pp. 35-36 there is the realisation of a scale with the rule of the octave at the cello, first with chords, then with arpeggios; at p. 39 there are examples of accompaniments of arias at the cello with arpeggios.

59. Breval 1804, pp. 121-132. Also in Duport 1840 pp. 80-87 are dedicated to arpeggio variants, with the note: «Those who practice them can vary them according to their own fantasy». It is taken for granted the practice of introducing variants to the musical text proposed.

60. Anonymous 2014, p. 30.

61. The phrase continues: «But in the main business of division, they are much the same: for all Division, whether Descant or Breaking the Bass, is but a Transition from Note to Note, or from one Concord to another, either by Degrees or by Leaps, with an Intermixture of such Discords as are allowed in Composition». Simpson 1665, p. 28. We assume that the freedom to use any of the consonances is given from the not completely tonal context.

to Simpson we have two options: to follow faithfully the bass outline, to enrich with divisions, or to create a new line above it (*descant*). To create this new line we can lean on any of the consonances (*concords*) in relation to the bass, anyway the two kind of *division* are very similar.

Ex. 4: Excerpt from Anonymous, *Instruction oder eine Anweisung auff der Violadigamba*, around 1730.

Another interesting didactical source are Sanguinazzo's sonatas for cello. In the collection we find both a whole sonata with an empty bass staff[62], probably to realise extemporaneously, and several variations on the bass[63]. This may prove the practice of the bass variation training, even at a not advanced grade of technical preparation, given the amateur level of these sonatas.

[62]. In the fourth sonata, Sanguinazzo a, pp. 15-17, the bass staff is empty, in contrast to the others sonatas, all complete.

[63]. All the variations on different basses are 230 in: Sanguinazzo b and Sanguinazzo c.

Very important sources, which can give new light to this research, turned out to be some works for cello by Lanzetti, Supriani and Caldara, already known to few specialists, but so far lacking comprehensive studies[64].

Solfeggi for Cello

Longum iter est per praecepta,
breve et efficax per exempla
Seneca

Scholars have already written on improvisation at the bass and on the continuo realisation at the cello without accompaniment of a polyphonic instrument, in recitatives and in chamber music[65], but still there is not a thorough study on the teaching methods that brought to these skills. Following the rediscovery of the didactical and pedagogical practice of partimento, we investigated the possibility of the existence of a similar historical method suited to the cello and viola da gamba characteristics. The first step is to define the specific features of the low string instruments, regarding the continuo realization: the cello and the viola da gamba are not polyphonic instruments; the cello is similar to the viola da gamba, with which shares texture and role; the two-strings chords on the cello have always a good effect, whereas three- or four-strings chords are marked by great performing troubles and by a strong character, that makes them suitable for cadences, but not to accompany long progressions or melodic phrasing; as for easiness, the three- or four-strings chords on the viol are equivalent to the two-strings chords on the cello; anyway at the cello the two-strings chords were considered already difficult to perform, as clearly indicated by Jean-Louis Duport[66]. Baumgartner suggests to harmonize at the cello often using two-strings chords instead of three «as you will be extremely embarrassed & exposed to play out of tune»[67]; when the most virtuoso players wrote music for viola da gamba and for cello often they inserted passages with double strings, limiting instead the use of three- and four-strings chords on the cello and more than three for the viol only to cadences[68].

---

[64]. Except the works of Olivieri. See Olivieri 2009.

[65]. Watkins 1996; for the realization of the recitatives see above note 35.

[66]. «Nothing more agreeable to the ears than the diatonic sequences of thirds, but unfortunately these sequences are very difficult to play on the cello, especially on the neck [...] one needs absolutely to make the hand jump every third that comes next, which makes the slurring and the sound continuity extremely difficult»: Duport 1840, p. 55.

[67]. Baumgartner 1774, p. 20.

[68]. A very important model for the cello chordal writing is the collection of J. S. Bach's *Suites*. Here three/four-strings chords are very much used only in the sarabandes, the slowest movements of the suites;

Therefore, searching for didactical works of bass realization at the string instruments and having as a reference point the partimenti, we did not look for polyphonic or chordal realizations, instead for two-voices realizations, of which one is the given bass and the other is derived from the first according to various techniques. This second voice realizes a *concertato* line, which can be a principal or a secondary voice, useful for musical ideas in 'empty' spaces of the score. The teaching goal would then exactly correspond to that of the partimento, with a specific application of the improvisation skills in the 'musical spaces' suited to the low string instrument. «A partimento is a solo piece, whose goal is teaching composition via improvisation, whereas the aim of a basso continuo playing is accompaniment»[69]. For cello the three sources which could be somehow included in the category of 'realized partimenti or solfeggi for cello' are Supriani's *Sonate*, Lanzetti's *Principes* and Caldara's *Lezioni*[70]. We could postulate that, despite the different names, the three works document three aspects of a single didactical method to the training of improvisation skills for cellists. Supriani's *Sonate*, already examined by Guido Olivieri[71], are composed on the toccatas published from the same author together with *Principij*[72], a short cello treatise. Each toccata is the foundation of a *Sonata*[73]: this last one appears in a triple staff, in the first one top line a toccata is reproduced; the staff in the middle has a version of it enriched according to various techniques; finally, in the lower staff there is a 'reduced' version of the toccata, in which a thorough bass is extracted through a reduction process[74]. Both processes, of enrichment and of reduction, are very interesting. The Fondo Noseda of the Conservatory in Milan preserves Lanzetti's *Principes ou l'application du Violoncelle par tous les tons*[75]. A meaning of *application* is 'put into practice, put into use, opposed to the

in the other movements they appear only at the beginning or at the conclusion of sections. Polyphony and harmony at the cello and at the viol alone are then obtained not with the keyboards' techniques, but rather with those described to adapt the polyphonic repertoire to the lute (VACCARO 1981, p. 131), further arranged to the string instrument. The viola da gamba has definitely a greater predisposition to the chordal writing and some viol players composed pieces in chordal style; anyway, in general, chords with more than three strings have a specific punctuation (phrase opening or closing) or accentuation role in the musical discourse.

69. SANGUINETTI 2012, p. 98.

70. SUPRIANI 2010, LANZETTI 1770, CALDARA 17--.

71. «[...] it's possible that these pieces represent written-out examples of the type of elaborations that cello players improvised when accompanying aria or recitatives, or in solo performances». OLIVIERI 2009, p. 124.

72. SUPRIANI 2008.

73. It comes naturally a comparison for example with the *Toccate* (14 for harpsichord) by Leonardo Leo, some of which have been realized by the composer himself. See SANGUINETTI 2012, p. 222.

74. A clarifying help is given by distinguishing between the bass line meant as a voice (*basso cantante*, see above note 31) and the line of the *basso continuo*. If the first has the priority of the melodic motion (prevalence of steps), the second has instead the task of making explicit the harmonic functions (presence of leaps mostly between fundamentals and thirds of the chords). In the repertoire usually the different functions are found together. Clear examples are in GUNN 1802, pp. 34-37.

75. LANZETTI 1770.

theory'. So we may interpret the title this way: 'Principles, that is the practice at the cello in all the tonalities', i.e. what the cello can do in all the tonalities. Let's see an example: the *Andante* in Ex. 5 (p. 136). The bass realization takes place through arpeggios, that keep almost always the same shape, often enriched by the addition of appoggiaturas that make the harmony more interesting[76].

Next exercise is a G major scale, first simple, then elaborated with virtuosities and figures, reusable for example in a cadence. Also in these exercises by Lanzetti, like in Supriani, we have easier realizations, with patterns repeated identical in the harmonic sequences, and further realizations more elaborated, with thematic ideas and virtuoso elements added. We presume that we are dealing with exercises to be transposed and which figures are to be learned as patterns to reuse in different contexts, as variations of arias, refrains, introductions, cadences etc. A different approach have the *Lezioni per il violoncello con il suo basso*[77] by Caldara[78] (Ex. 6, p. 137).

These are 44 lessons, each one seems to deepen one specific type of composition on the bass, that could be a model for autonomous creations by the student. One common feature among the three cellists' works is that there are not technical differences among the exercises, namely it is not a matter of single exercises dedicated for example to the study of one position, of hard bowings or strings leaps[79], even if in Supriani and Lanzetti there is a clear path towards virtuosity. Another common feature is that in all the three kind of works, figures (mostly melodic-rhythmical figures in Caldara and patterns with arpeggios, scale fragments and diminutions in Supriani and Lanzetti) are repeated through transposition and arranged to different harmonic sequences; that is we are talking about application of figures and patterns. This is exactly the didactical path for the improvisation skills that we hypothesize: the student should learn some patterns — as those we saw in the methods — and later reuse them, choosing and arranging according to the context. The three works represent three different approaches: in Supriani many elaborations can be defined divisions and the text on which they are applied are toccatas; in Lanzetti the majority of the exercises is comparable to the elaboration of figures based on scales and

[76]. Adding one note to an arpeggio has one more important result: we obtain an even number of notes, for instance, four instead of three, which allows for instance a quavers perpetual motion.

[77]. They are preserved in a manuscript belonged to Elisabeth Cowling; the original is in the Österreische Nationalbibliothek, Vienna. I'm grateful to the Library of the North Caroline University, that kindly provided a copy of the microfilm, in particular to Mrs. Stacey Krim.

[78]. «Caldara was often in Rome and besides got in touch with the Roman cello school, which featured virtuoso cellists and gave the cello a main role in the musical production within various genres [...]. Going round with Ottoboni and Ruspoli (probably also cardinal Benedetto Pamphilj and the queen of Poland) was in close contact with Corelli, Alessandro and Domenico Scarlatti, Haendel, Cesarini and Pasquini»: Kirkendale – Kirkendale 1973.

[79]. I thank Francesco Maschio for the precious help in analysing the texts and Alessandro De Marchi for his precious comments on the belongings of these works to the area of the Solfeggi.

Ex. 5: Salvatore Lanzetti, *Andante*, in: *Principes ou l'application du Violoncelle par tous les tons*, p. 1^{v}.

arpeggios, applied to the scale degrees; in Caldara the text on which the student learn to improvise thematic fragments is made of thorough bass phrases typical of arias or sonatas. The common method is nevertheless presumably that of learning directly at the instrument the improvising techniques. These lie between two poles, the division and the *discantus*, with the use of early figures, such as diminution patterns, and modern figures, connected to

Ex. 6: Antonio Caldara, *Lezione no. 1* (CALDARA 17--).

scales and arpeggios in various versions. The main difficulty, for the *violoncellista partimentista*, is not related to the instrumental technique[80], but instead concerns the *extempore* practical

[80]. Today the instrumental technique is usually undertaken in a way completely unrelated to the musical language, also because of the multiplicity of languages that the contemporary musician has to master.

application to the instrument of the harmonic and contrapuntal rules, using the figures. If in the modal system the logic of the consonances is enough to create a *discantus*, instead in the tonal system a precise harmonic reference is essential, hence the necessity of figured bass. Therefore the *violoncellista partimentista* along with the study of counterpoint, with which he learned to compose *extempore* a two-voices counterpoint on a given bass or melody, had to study harmony extensively and, above all, practice at the cello exercises like those we see in Supriani, Lanzetti and Caldara.

Updates and Research Developments

This research on solfeggi for cello has been further developed in the paper 'Un'ipotesi di ricostruzione'[81]. The main remarks[82] of this work are: in Supriani the most used enrichment techniques consist of: single notes ornaments; scale fragments or diminution patterns inserted to fill the space between notes originally approached by leaps; divisions of the rhythmic values into *battéries* (broken two-notes chords or full chords); two-notes chords or full chords additions in cadence; additions of a second alternating voice, formed by a pedal or a parallel line in consonances of thirds and sixths. The continuo line is a rare witness of the reduction practice applied to toccatas. As concerns Lanzetti, analysing all the pieces of the *Principes*, it appears that they are always composed on a scale proceeding by repeated steps, strictly following the Octave rule. A different approach, mostly based on cadence patterns, proves instead to be Caldara's *Lezioni*. Cadences, scale fragments and progressions are proposed in a large number of variants, in particular there are always progressions of fifths, from the second lesson, with numerous different figures.

Antonio Guida's «Sonate per il violoncello»

Further confirmation that the study method based on the scale and the rule of the octave was common in the Neapolitan cello didactic[83], is provided to us by Antonio

81. The final writing of this article follows the paper focused on the works by Supriani, Lanzetti e Caldara: Barbati – Maschio 2017.

82. In this paper there are also the biographical data of the three authors examined here, that witness their long collaboration in different contexts: Supriani and Lanzetti served together at the Neapolitan court musical chapel; Supriani and Caldara collaborated most probably in Barcelona, 1708, to perform Caldara's *Il più bel nome* during Charles III's wedding.

83. «The counterpoint and partimento teaching methods [...] were largely based on the scale, [...] the student spent many years training improvisation on partimento, which foundation [...] was the scale placed at the bass and accompanied according to the rule of the octave»: Sanguinetti 2009, p. 66.

Guida's manuscript[84], kindly provided to me by Guido Olivieri, who has recently confirmed the attribution. This is a collection of pieces entitled *Sonate per il violoncello*[85], which appears to be a complete course, from the first to the thumb position, formed by exercises, with no explanatory texts. After reaching an advanced skill on the four neck positions and on various bowings, we find fifteen exercises similar to those by Lanzetti, in which figures patterns are proposed according to the rule of the octave on all the scale degrees (Ex. 7). The very first exercises are simple diminution and broken chord patterns applied to the scale degrees, supporting the modular setting from the beginning of the studies.

Ex. 7: exercises from Antonio Guida, *Sonate per il violoncello* (Guida 17--).

84. Antonio Guida was string teacher at the Conservatorio di Sant'Onofrio a Capuana from 1785 to 1797; see Di Giacomo 1924, p. 138. According to Columbro – Maione 2008 he was cellist at the Tesoro di S. Gennaro in 1777-1780 and 1790-1800.

85. Guida 17--. The title *Sonate* has been probably added because there are short minuets and gavottes, but we assume that it is a complete method, which includes all the didactic path steps.

Suggestions for Using Improvisation in the Early Music Didactic

We suggest that today too it is possible to choose, in the early music training, a method based on musical elements and processes, that the students can learn and later modify. Using as a reference the tripartite plan described by Callahan[86], we can choose some figures patterns, for example diminutions or arpeggios, and arrange them in relation to the bass, according to the voice leading rules. Applying the classical terminology, it is a matter of putting the *Decoratio* on the *Elaboratio* schemes. Going a step further, even the whole structure, the *Dispositio*, would be planned by the student, who will compose short pieces like for example preludes, ricercari or minuets. Then, if on the theoretical side the order is: general structure — voice leading scheme — application of embellishment patterns, on the pedagogical side we have to start from the last level, the simplest one, to go back towards those levels that require more advanced skills in harmony, counterpoint and composition. The student will then start applying the various patterns, taken from the treatises or directly extracted from the repertoire, to harmonic sequences. At the beginning it would be highly advisable the variations on ground basses, which have been experimented also in improvisation workshops at the Frosinone Conservatory in 2015 and at the Conservatorio Regional de Ponta Delgada in 2017[87]. One can start with diminutions from the sixteenth- and seventeenth-century treatises[88], which enable to form a rich vocabulary of ready-to-use musical patterns, but it is very useful to extract patterns also directly from the general repertoire, not necessarily from that specifically for low strings. The exercises on ground basses can be carried out in groups and enable a quick and funny learning[89]. Given at the beginning the diagram of the parts[90], the rules are:

> 1) once chosen the pattern, it must be strictly used until the end of the sequence. If the student modifies the pattern, usually after two-three times he will have exhausted his inventiveness and will repeat himself;
>
> 2) the pattern can be melodic of rhythmic, it can be composed on arpeggios, or it can be a combination of these elements. The basic rule is the variety of solutions;
>
> 3) usually the ground bass includes two large phrases; it is possible to add or modify something to the pattern in the second half of the bass;

---

86. Callahan 2010.

87. Students attending to the workshops were either already trained in early music practice (Frosinone), or beginners and advanced students in a traditional academic path (Ponta Delgada).

88. A rich list of the sources around the sixteenth and seventeenth centuries can be found, with an annotated anthology, in Dongois 2014.

89. «It's more funny: then it's more useful»: Rodari 1973, p. 37. For the individual study we experimented the use of the loop station, which enables to improvise on one's own bases.

90. As we see for example in Ortiz 1553, before each *Recercada* there is the corresponding voices scheme.

4) the simplest variation is composed on one of the four voices that constitute the harmonic scheme; additional virtuoso variations can be made *alla bastarda*, that is, passing through the different voices;

5) while a colleague is improvising the task is to accompany without interfering, or add some complementary patterns.

For the whole didactic path the suggestion is to take as a model the method that Couperin explains in *L'Art de toucher le clavecin*:

> Separately from the examined embellishments, such as trills, mordents, appoggiaturas, etc., I always made my pupils make some little fingers' motions, either diminutions, or different batteries starting with the easiest, and in the most comfortable tonalities; and imperceptibly I brought them until the most nimble, and the most transposed, [...] the knowledge of intervals, of modes and their cadences, either perfect or imperfect, of chords and their *supposition*. That gives them a kind of local memory that makes them more confident, and which is useful to reset, with knowledge, when they failed[91].

We can do it also today: the student has to repeat with variations the given exercises; these consist of patterns which later will be useful as material to improvise; the first exercises are on basic embellishments (on single notes, the easiest), then one goes to study diminutions and *batteries*[92]; the study is based on transposition, starts from the nearest tones to go to the farthest and it starts from easier patterns to go to the most complex; at the same time of the technique (which consists of the clarified exercises) it is necessary to instruct pupils about intervals, modes, cadences, then about chords (starting then at two-voices to proceed with three-voices and more). This instruction has to come gradually, either from the theoretical side or from the technical one, so as to allow the student an active approach from the beginning.

We think these basic principles can be valid for all instruments. In conclusion, the exam of the sources concerning pedagogy and in particular the Solfeggi for cello brings us to the following remarks: in a path towards historical improvisation it is recommended to start with single embellishments and easy diminutions to practice with transpositions and on various schemes. If we consider the scale and the arpeggio as basic schemes, these, with a conceptual shift to an 'active technique', can be treated also as building elements, to elaborate (for example juxtaposition of scale fragments in the two directions to form endless figures, arpeggios broken and/or enriched with non-chord tones[93]). Together with

91. Couperin 1716, pp. 8-9, 34.

92. We can notice that this collection of embellishments, diminutions and batteries already forms a sort of vocabulary for the student's improvisations.

93. In Fig. 5 by Lanzetti, we can notice that the scale is used first as foundation for the exercise within the rule of the octave, and after as a compositional element, in exploring its virtuosistic potential.

the study of the first notions of harmony and counterpoint one can practice the first divisions (for example alternated consonances of parallel thirds and sixths) and *battéries* in the easiest harmonic sequences.

If enriching the bass is easier to achieve, composing a *discantus* on a bass is a true composition exercise, it is then more suitable to advanced students. Together with studying partimento directly at the keyboard, practicing directly at the instrument the works of Supriani, Lanzetti, Caldara and Guida, intended as exercises to transpose and to vary further, probably helps to develop from the beginning the skills necessary to an excellent improvisation in style.

From this point of view we interpret Ancelet's polemic statement referred to Forqueray the young («He never performs the Bass as it is written»[94]), as the observation of a common practice, but performed by a Master, who shows his ability in the continuos variation of the bass[95].

BIBLIOGRAPHY

Primary Sources

AGAZZARI 1607

AGAZZARI, Agostino. *Del sonare sopra 'l basso con tutti li stromenti*, Siena, Falcini, 1607.

ANCELET 1757

ANCELET. *Observations sur la musique, les musiciens, et les instruments*, Amsterdam, Aux dépens de la Compagnie, 1757.

ANONYMOUS 2014

ANONYMOUS. *Instruction oder eine Anweisung auff der Violadigamba*, facsimile edition edited by Bettina Hoffmann, Heidelberg, Güntersberg, 2014.

BARBARINO 1614

BARBARINO, Bartolomeo. *Secondo Libro delli Mottetti*, Venice, Magni, 1614.

BAUMGARTNER 1774

BAUMGARTNER, Johann Baptist. *Instructions de musique, théoriques et pratiques, à l'usage du violoncelle*, The Hague, D. Monnier, 1774.

BISMANTOVA 1677

BISMANTOVA, Bartolomeo. *Compendio musicale*, Ferrara, s.n., 1677.

[94]. «He never executes the bass just as it is written; he claims to greatly improve it with the great number of brilliant traits he throws at it; he fights, so to say, with the person playing the solo; and often the Composer is just as unhappy as the violinist who is playing», ANCELET 1757, *cfr.* BOL 1973, p. 50.

[95]. I am very grateful to Guido Olivieri, who helped me to use English more correctly, to Ilaria Zamuner, for her advices on editorial criteria and to Bettina Hoffmann, for her kind suggestions.

Bonnet 1715
Bonnet, Jacques. *Histoire de la Musique, et de ses effets, depuis son origine jusqu'à présent*, Paris, J. Cochart, 1715.

Breval 1804
Breval, Jean-Baptiste-Sébastien. *Traité du violoncelle*, Op. 42, Paris, Janet & Cotelle, 1804.

Caldara 17--
Caldara, Antonio. *Lezioni per il Violoncello con il suo Basso*, Vienna, Österreichische Nationalbibliothek, EM.69 Mus; Cowling box 3-2, Martha Blakeney Hodges Special Collections and University Archives, The University of North Carolina at Greensboro.

Couperin 1716
Couperin, François. *L'Art de toucher le clavecin*, Paris, Foucaut, 1716.

De La Borde 1780
De La Borde, Jean-Benjamin. 'Violoncelle', in: *Essai sur la musique ancienne et moderne. Tome Premier*, Paris, Ph.-D- Pierre, 1780, pp. 309-323.

De Visée 1716
De Visée, Robert. *Pièces de théorbe et de luth: mises en partition, dessus e basse*, Paris, Roussel, 1716.

Della Valle 1763
Della Valle, Pietro. 'Della musica dell'età nostra', in: Doni, Giovan Battista. *De' trattati di musica* [...] *tomo secondo* [...], Florence, Stamperia Imperiale, 1763.

Duport 1840
Duport, Jean-Louis. *Essai sur le doigté du violoncelle, et sur la conduite de l'archet*, Paris, Cotelle, 1840.

Framery 1791
Framery, Nicolas E. *Enciclopédie metodique. Musique*, 2 vols., Paris, Panckoucke, 1791-1818.

Gaffi 1700
Gaffi, Tommaso. *Cantate da cammera a voce sola* [...], Rome, Mascardi, 1700.

Gaffi a
Id. *Allor che il vostro lume*, manuscript, Modena, Biblioteca Estense, MO008918060, in: <www.internetculturale.it>, accessed November 2018.

Gaffi b
Id. *Dalle oziose piume*, manuscript, Modena, Biblioteca Estense, MO008918064, in: <www.internetculturale.it>, accessed November 2018.

Gasparini 1695
Gasparini, Francesco. *Cantate da camera a voce sola*, Op. 1, Rome, Mascardi, 1695.

Guida 17--
Guida, Antonio. *Sonate per il violoncello*, Berkeley (CA), University of California, Jean Gray Hargrove Music Library, MS 1016.

GUNN 1789
GUNN, John. *The Theory and Practice of Fingering the Violoncello*, London, The Author, 1789.

GUNN 1802
ID. *An Essay theoretical and practical [...] on the Application of the Principles of Harmony, Thorough Bass and Modulation to the Violoncello*, London, Preston, 1802.

HOTTETERRE 1719
HOTTETERRE, Jacques. *L'Art de préluder*, Paris, Foucault, 1719.

LANZETTI 1750
LANZETTI, Salvatore. *XII Sonate à Violoncello Solo e Basso Continuo Op. 1*, Paris, Le Clerc-Boivin, [1750].

LANZETTI 1770
ID. *Principes ou l'application du Violoncelle par tous les tons*, Amsterdam, J. J. Hummel, [1770].

MARAIS 1686
MARAIS, Marin. *Pièces de viole Livre I*, Paris, L'auteur-J. Hurel, 1686.

MARAIS 1689
ID. *Basse-Continuës des Piéces à une et à deux violes*, Paris, L'auteu-J. Hurel, 1689.

MARCELLO 1720
MARCELLO, Benedetto. *Il teatro alla moda*, (1720), Milan, Ricordi, 1883.

MARTINI 1776
MARTINI Giovanni Battista. *Serie Cronologica de' Principi dell'Accademia de' Filarmonici di Bologna*, Bologna, L. della Volpe, 1776.

MAUGARS 1672
MAUGARS, André. 'Discours sur la musique d'Italie et des opera' (1639), in: *Divers traitez d'histoire, de morale et d'éloquence. 1: La Vie de Malherbe*, Paris, C. Thiboust et E. Esclassan, 1672, pp. 154-179.

MONTEVERDI 1632
MONTEVERDI, Claudio. *Scherzi musicali*, Venice, Magni, 1632.

ORTIZ 1553
ORTIZ, Diego. *Tratado de Glosas*, Rome, Valerio e Luigi Dorico, 1553.

ROUSSEAU 1768
ROUSSEAU, Jean-Jacques. *Dictionnaire de musique*, Paris, Vve Duchesne, 1768.

SANGUINAZZO A
SANGUINAZZO, Nicolò. *Suonate à violoncello e basso*, Vienna, Österreichische Nationalbibliothek, E. M. 41, 1700-1720.

SANGUINAZZO B
ID. *Suonata violoncello solo*, Vienna, Österreichische Nationalbibliothek, E. M. 42a, 1700-1720.

Sanguinazzo c

Id. *3 Sonatas*, Vienna, Österreichische Nationalbibliothek, E. M. 43a, 1700-1720.

Simpson 1665

Simpson, Christopher. *The Division Viol*, London, W. Godbid, 1665.

Stiasny 1834

Stiastny, Bernhard. *Méthode pour le Violoncelle*, Mainz, Schott, 1834.

Supriani 2008

Supriano, (Supriani, Scipriani) Francesco P. *12 Toccate per violoncello solo; Principij da imparare à suonare il violoncello*, edited by Marco Ceccato, Albese con Cassano, Musedita, 2008 (Minghèn dal viulunzèl).

Supriani 2010

Id. *Sonate a due violoncelli*, edited by Alessandro Bares, Albese con Cassano, Musedita, 2010 (Minghèn dal viulunzèl).

Secondary Literature

Bacciagalupi 2006

Bacciagaluppi, Claudio. 'Primo violoncello al cembalo: l'accompagnamento del recitativo semplice nell'Ottocento', in: *Rivista italiana di musicologia*, xli/1 (2006), pp. 101-134.

Barbati – Maschio 2017

Barbati, Giovanna – Maschio, Francesco. 'Un'ipotesi di ricostruzione, un percorso formativo per il violoncellista improvvisatore al basso continuo', paper presented at the *xxiv Convegno annuale Sidm (Lucca 20-22 October 2017)*, unpublished.

Blackburn – Lowinsky 1993

Blackburn, Bonnie J. – Lowinsky, Edward E. 'Luigi Zenobi and His Letter on the Perfect Musician', in: *Studi musicali*, xxii/1 (1993), pp. 61-114.

Bol 1973

Bol, Hans. *La basse de viole du temps de Marin Marais et d'Antoine Forqueray*, Bilthoven, A. B. Creyghton, 1973 (Utrechtse bijdragen de muziekwetenschap, 7).

Byros 2015

Byros, Vasili. 'Prelude on a Partimento: Invention in the Compositional Pedagogy of the German States in the Time of J. S. Bach', in: *Music Theory Online*, xxi/3 (September 2015), <http://www.mtosmt.org/issues/mto.15.21.3/mto.15.21.3.byros.html>, accessed November 2018.

Cafiero 1993

Cafiero, Rosa. 'La didattica del partimento a Napoli fra Settecento e Ottocento: note sulla fortuna delle 'Regole' di Carlo Cotumacci', in: *Gli affetti convenienti all'idee, studi sulla musica vocale italiana*, edited by Maria Caraci Vela, Rosa Cafiero and Angela Romagnoli, Naples, Edizioni Scientifiche Italiane, 1993 (Archivio del teatro e dello spettacolo, 3), pp. 549-579.

Callahan 2010

Callahan, Michael. *Techniques of Keyboard Improvisation in the German Baroque and Their Implications for Today's Pedagogy*, Ph.D. Diss., Rochester (NY), University of Rochester, 2010.

Canguilhem 2010

Canguilhem, Philippe. 'Le projet FABRICA: oralité et écriture dans les pratiques polyphoniques du chant ecclésiastique (xvi-xx siècle)', in: *Journal of the Alamire Foundation*, ii/2 (2010), pp. 272-281.

Canguilhem 2013

Id. *Chanter sur le livre a la Renaissance: une édition et traduction des traités de contrepoint de Vicente Lusitano*, Turnhout, Brepols, 2013 (Epitome musical).

Collins 2001

Collins, Timothy A. 'Reactions Against the Virtuoso. Instrumental Ornamentation Practice and the Stile Moderno', in: *International Review of the Aesthetics and Sociology of Music*, xxxii/2 (2001), pp. 137-152.

Columbro – Maione 2008

Columbro, Marta – Maione, Paologiovanni. *La Cappella musicale del Tesoro di San Gennaro di Napoli tra Sei e Settecento*, Naples, Turchini, 2008 (I Turchini saggi).

Dahlhaus 1987

Dahlhaus, Carl. 'Composition and Improvisation', in: Id. *Schoenberg and the New Music: Essays by Carl Dahlhaus*, translated by Derrick Puffett and Alfred Clayton, Cambridge-New York, Cambridge University Press, 1987, pp. 265-273.

Dahlhaus 2010

Id. 'Qu'est-ce que l'improvisation musicale?', translated by Marion Siéfert and Lucille Lisack, in: *Tracés: Revue de Sciences humaines*, no. 18 (2010), pp. 181-196.

Di Giacomo 1924

Di Giacomo, Salvatore. *Il Conservatorio di Sant'Onofrio a Capuana e quello di S. M. della Pietà dei Turchini*, Palermo, R. Sandron, 1924 (Collezione settecentesca, 26).

Dongois 2014

Semplice ou passeggiato: diminution et ornementation dans l'exécution de la musique de Palestrina et du stile antico, directed by William Dongois, Droz, Geneva, 2014 (Musique & recherche).

Esses 1992

Esses, Maurice. *Dance and Instrumental Diferencias in Spain During the 17th and Early 18th Centuries. 1: History and Background, Music and Dance*, Stuyvesant (NY), Pendragon Press, 1992.

Ferand 1961

Ferand, Ernst T. *Improvisation in Nine Centuries of Western Music, an Anthology with an Historical Introduction*, Cologne, Arno Volk Verlag, 1961 (Musikwerk, 12).

Galli 1882

Galli, Amintore. 'Forme liriche. Saggio storico e tecnologico. Recitativo semplice', in: *Il teatro illustrato*, ii (1882), pp. 131-132.

Gialdroni 2013

Gialdroni, Teresa. 'La cantata a Roma negli anni del soggiorno italiano di Händel', in: *Georg Friedrich Händel Aufbruch nach Italien*, edited by Helen Geyer and Birgit Johanna Wertenson, Rome, Viella, 2013 (Venetiana / Centro tedesco di studi veneziani, 11), pp. 113-136.

Gjerdingen 2007a

Gjerdingen, Robert O. *Music in the Galant Style*, Oxford, Oxford University Press, 2007.

Gjerdingen 2007b

Id. 'Partimento, que me veux-tu?', in: *Journal of Music Theory*, li/1 (2007), pp. 85-135.

Gjerdingen 2010

Id. 'Partimenti Written to Impart a Knowledge of Counterpoint and Composition', in: Christensen, Thomas – Gjerdingen, Robert – Sanguinetti, Giorgio – Lutz, Rudolf. *Partimento and Continuo Playing in Theory and in Practice*, Leuven, Leuven University Press, 2010 (Collected Writings of the Orpheus Institute, 9), pp. 43-70.

Gjerdingen 2017a

Id. *Monuments of Partimenti*, 2017, at <http://faculty- web.at.northwestern.edu/music/gjerdingen/partimenti/aboutParti/histOverview.htm>, accessed November 2018 .

Gjerdingen 2017b

Id. *Monuments of Solfeggi*, 2017 <http://faculty-web.at.northwestern.edu/music/gjerdingen/solfeggi/index.htm>, accessed November 2018.

Halton 2008

Halton, Rosalind. 'Nicola Porpora and the Cantabile Cello', paper presented at the *Convegno Sidm. Nicola Porpora musicista europeo. Le corti, i teatri, i cantanti, i librettisti (Reggio Calabria, 2-3 October 2008)*, unpublished, online at <http://www.academia.edu/5016315/Nicol%C3%B2_Porpora_and_the_cantabile_Cello>, accessed November 2018.

Haymoz 2017

Haymoz, Jean Yves. 'Discovering the Practice of Improvised Counterpoint', in: *Studies in Historical Improvisation: from Cantare super librum to Partimenti*, edited by Massimiliano Guido, Abington-New York, Routledge, 2017, pp. 90-111.

Hoffmann 2016

Hoffmann, Bettina. ''Einige praetendiren gar einen General-Bass darauff zu wege zu bringen' – Die Gambe als akkordisches Generalbassinstrument', in: *Repertoire, Instrumente und Bauweise der Viola da gamba: xxxviii. Wissenschaftliche Arbeitstagung und 31. Musikinstrumentenbau-Symposium, Michaelstein, 19. bis 21. November 2010*, edited by Christian Philipsen, Monika Lustig and Ute Omosky, Augsburg, Wissner-Verlag; Blankenburg, Stiftung Kloster Michaelstein, 2016 (Michaelsteiner Konferenzberichte, 80), pp. 251-279.

Kirkendale – Kirkendale 1973

Kirkendale, Ursula – Kirkendale, Warren. 'Antonio Caldara', in: *Dizionario Biografico degli Italiani*, vol. xvi (1973), on line at <http://www.treccani.it/enciclopedia/antonio-caldara_%28Dizionario-Biografico%29/>, accessed November 2018.

La Via 1983-1984

La Via, Stefano. *Il violoncello a Roma al tempo del Cardinale Ottoboni*, Ph.D. Diss., Rome, Università di Roma 'La Sapienza', 1983-1984.

La Via 1987

Id. 'Un'aria di Händel con violoncello obbligato e la tradizione romana', in: *Händel e gli Scarlatti a Roma: Atti del Convegno internazionale di studi (Roma, 12-14 giugno 1985)*, edited by Nino Pirrotta and Agostino Ziino, Florence, Olschki, 1987, pp. 49-71.

Lymenstull 2014

Lymenstull, Eva. *Chordal Continuo Realization on the Violoncello*, M.Mus. Diss., The Hague, Royal Conservatory of The Hague, 2014.

Moore 1992

Moore, Robin. 'The Decline of Improvisation in Western Art Music: An Interpretation of Change', in: *International Review of the Aesthetics and Sociology of Music*, xxiii/1 (1992), pp. 61-84.

Nuti 2007

Nuti, Giulia. *The Performance of Italian Basso Continuo: Style in Keyboard Accompaniment in the Seventeenth and Eighteenth Centuries*, Aldershot, Ashgate, 2007.

Olivieri 2009

Olivieri, Guido. 'Cello Teaching and Playing in Naples in the Early Eighteenth Century: Francesco Paolo Supriani's Principij da imparare a suonare il violoncello', in: *Performance Practice: Issues and approaches*, edited by Timothy D. Watkins, Ann Arbor (MI), Steglein, 2009, pp. 109-136.

Rodari 1973

Rodari, Gianni. *Grammatica della fantasia: introduzione all'arte di inventare storie*, Turin, Einaudi, 1973 (Piccola biblioteca Einaudi, 221).

Romanou 2009

Romanou, Katy. *A Cembalo for Nabucco? - Basso Continuo Improvisation in 19th-Century Opera Performances in Italy and Corfú*, paper presented at the Biennial Euro-Mediterranean Music Conference, University of Nicosia, 18-20 September 2009, unpublished, online at <https://www.academia.edu/3256291/A_cembalo_for_Nabuco_-_Basso_continuo_improvisation_in_19th_century_opera_performances_in_Italy_and_Corf%C3%B9>, accessed November 2018.

Rose 1965

Rose, Gloria. 'Agazzari and the Improvising Orchestra', in: *Journal of the American Musicological Society*, xviii/3 (1965), pp. 382-393.

Sanguinetti 2009

Sanguinetti, Giorgio. 'La scala come modello per la composizione', in: *Rivista di analisi e teoria musicale*, xv/1 (2009), pp. 69-94.

Sanguinetti 2012

Id. *The Art of Partimento: History, Theory, and Practice*, Oxford, Oxford University Press, 2012.

Schubert 2014

Schubert, Peter. 'From Improvisation to Composition: Three 16th Century Case Studies', in: *Improvising Early Music: The History of Musical Improvisation from the Late Middle Ages to the Early Baroque*, edited by Dirk Moelants, Leuven, Leuven University Press, 2014 (Collected Writings of the Orpheus Institute, 11), pp. 93-130.

Stein 2014

Stein, Daniel. *Figure It Out: An Approach on Playing Basso Continuo on the Violin*, Ph.D. Diss., Bloomington (IN), Indiana University, 2014.

Strobbe 2014

Strobbe, Lieven. *Tonal Tools: For Keyboard Players*, Antwerpen, Garant, 2014.

Strobbe – Van Regenmortel 2012

Strobbe, Lieven – Van Regenmortel, Hans. 'Music Theory and Musical Practice: Dichotomy or Entwining?', in: *Dutch Journal of Music Theory*, xvii/1 (2012), pp. 19-30.

Todea 2014

Todea, Flavia C. *Eighteenth Century Techniques of Classical Improvisation on the Violin: Pedagogy, Practice and Decline*, Ph.D. Diss., Perth, Western Australian Academy of Performing Arts, Edith Cowan University 2014.

Torchi 1894

Torchi, Luigi. 'L'accompagnamento degl'istrumenti nei melodrammi italiani della prima metà del Seicento', in: *Rivista musicale italiana*, i/1 (1894), pp. 7-38.

Vaccaro 1981

Vaccaro, Jean-Michel. *La Musique de luth en France au xvi siècle*, Paris, CNRS, 1981.

Vanscheeuwijck 1996

Vanscheeuwijck, Marc. 'The Baroque Cello and Its Performance', in: *Performance Practice Review*, ix/1 (1996), pp. 78-96.

Wasielewski 1894

Wasielewski, Wilhelm J. von. *The Violoncello and Its History*, translated by Isobella S. E. Stigand, Novello, London, Novello, 1894.

Watkins 1996

Watkins, David. 'Corelli's Op. 5 Sonatas: "Violino e violone o cimbalo?"', in: *Early Music*, xxiv/4 (1996), pp. 645-663.

Whittaker 2012

Whittaker, Nathan H. *Chordal Cello Accompaniment: The Proof and Practice of Figured Bass Realization on the Violoncello from 1660-1850*, D.M.A. Diss., Seattle (WA), University of Washington, 2012.

Young 2014

Young, James O. 'Congetture sulle composizioni non originali', in: *Estetica. Studi e ricerche* [*Ladri di Musica, filosofia, musica e plagio*, edited by Alessandro Bertinetto, Ezio Gambia and Davide Sisto], iv/1 (2014), pp. 23-34.

On the Borderlines of Improvisation: Caccini, Monteverdi and the Freedoms of the Performer

Anthony Pryer
(Goldsmiths' College, University of London)

The Baroque in Context: Rethinking the Oral/Written Divide

Improvisation during the Baroque period stands more or less at the midpoint in the documented history of the practice. Moreover, what that history reveals is that the activities we subsume under the single term 'improvisation' comprise a complex and varied field of musical behaviour, not all elements of which are quite as spontaneous or 'in the moment' as they might appear. Improvisation is usually a 'cross-border' product arising from the interaction of both oral and written cultures, or rehearsed and spontaneous musical activity, or the routine application of performance conventions to written cues within the notation. In the middle of this activity it is sometimes difficult to distinguish between embellished compositions and *impromptu* explorations, and moments of genuine freedom often coexist alongside routine habits of decoration associated with certain genres. Moreover, there is always a framework of 'common practice' musical styles which both guide and constrain the limits of supposed 'spontaneous' creativity. To paraphrase the philosopher (and musician) Schopenhauer, musicians may do as they will, but they cannot will as they will[1] — that is, they cannot freely control or be conscious of all the forces that help to bring their apparently 'spontaneous' musical ideas, situated within a particular style, into being.

If the list above covers how, and under what circumstances, people employ improvisatory practices, then we are still left with the issue of why they pursue them at all — that is, why 'improvisation' is deemed in any society to be desirable and valuable. In fact it fulfills many functions. It can operate as a valued manifestation of technical skill and virtuosity, or as a means of producing melodic beauty, expression, and rhetorical

1. Schopenhauer 1960, p. 18.

enhancement. It may also serve to confirm a performer's understanding of style and performance conventions, and on some occasions be a symptom of a person's inspiration, spiritual possession or ecstasy. Nor is it entirely unknown for improvisation to be taken as a convenient medium of self-advertisement and individualism, or as an indicator of that artistic inspiration and creativity proper to musical geniuses. Not surprisingly, these complex factors make it difficult to know on any particular occasion what kind of 'improvisation' we are witnessing, and whether we should take the event as an unquestionable confirmation of the creativity and imagination of the performers involved. Clearly any clarification of the meaning of Baroque improvisational practices must involve some understanding of the traditions in that field and what they bequeathed to the seventeenth century. It must also re-assess the concepts under which define and judge improvisation.

The most obvious place to start is the issue of the supposed separation of oral and written cultures, a 'separation', as we shall see, that is hopelessly compromised in the Baroque period. Of course, there have been times in western history when musical cultures seem to have been almost entirely oral in nature. For example, Isidore of Seville, writing in the early seventh century of the Christian era, tells us that «unless sounds are held by the memory of man they perish because they cannot be written down»[2]. What we should notice, however, is that Isidore accepts that even in his society there is at least one possible substitute for written notation — memory, which in itself can act as a kind of 'virtual notation'. Indeed many cultures in the world still employ systems of rote learning under a 'master' (they are usually men) to train novices in the replication of traditional repertories[3]. Moreover, the identities of 'works' and their performances can sometimes be more stable under an oral system than under a written one — a phenomenon which is exemplified in modern times in the West by the tendency of some performers surreptitiously to replicate CD performance interpretations by admired artists in baroque and other repertories. The danger is that such a practice copies the musical achievement without fully understanding the knowledge and musical judgments that make that achievement possible and its procedures adaptable to new circumstances. Quantz, writing in 1752, highlights exactly this dilemma when he reports on what he clearly considers to be deceptive practices in Italy: «as it is the mode with most singers, you must keep a master constantly at hand from whom you can learn variations [...] and if you do this you will remain a student all your life and will never become a master yourself»[4].

From the point of view of defining improvisation the principle we should draw from this is that the most telling divide when it comes to 'creativity' in performance is not that between oral and written practices, but between the rehearsed and un-rehearsed elements. FIG. 1 represents this important distinction in visual form. It allows for the location of

2. ISIDORE OF SEVILLE 2006, , Book III, Section XIV, p. 95.

3. For a comparison of western and non-western practices see NETTL 1974.

4. QUANTZ 1966, Chapter XIV, Section 3, p. 163.

the 'creative' demands of different types of music by plotting them on a grid — the oral/ written divide is shown by the left hand axis and the prepared/unprepared axis runs along the top. For example, 'oral' popular music tends to have almost no written transmission of the music (though there may be of its texts), and even its apparently 'spontaneous' performance effects, are frequently learnt by rote in rehearsal, with relatively few diversions in the live event. By contrast, Baroque vocal music is deeply embedded in a notated culture but is typically open to a large number of unprepared features in performance.

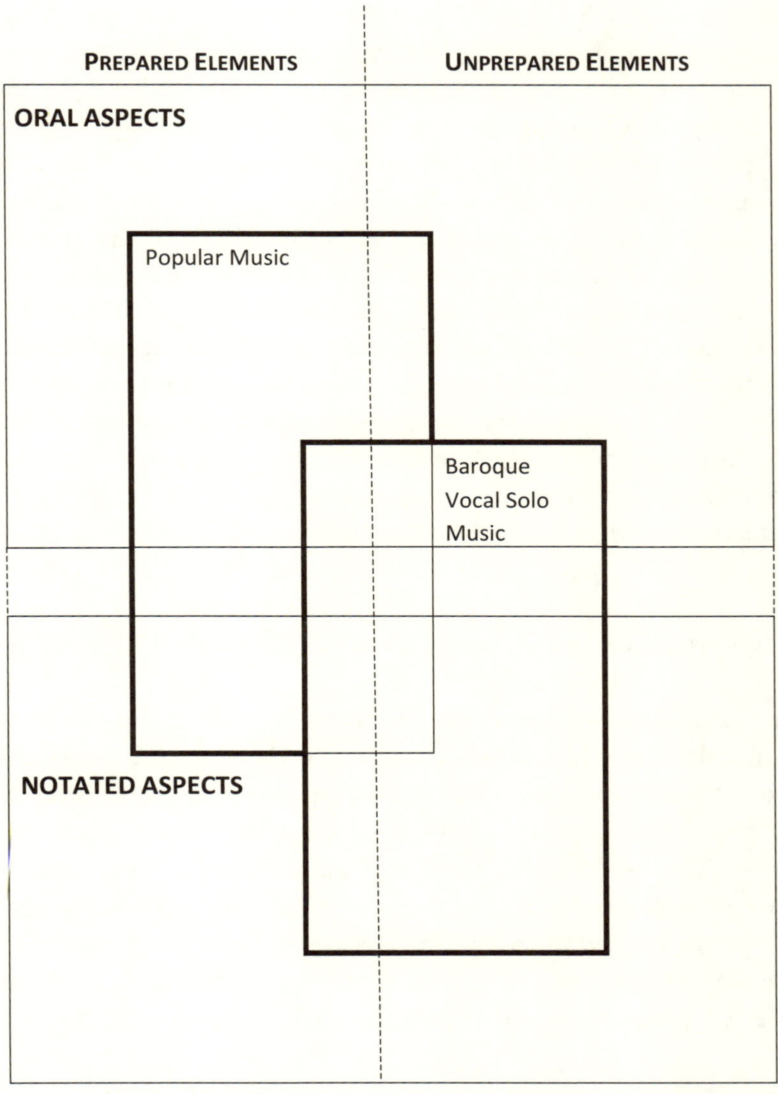

Fig. 1: Possible Notation-Culture Matrix

What Fig. 1 also suggests is that musical performances rarely derive 'purely' from one tradition or the other — the oral or the written — and history reveals some of the reasons why this might be so. For example, we know that the Ancient Greeks had musical notation (many musical fragments, including settings of the choruses of plays by Euripides, survive)[5], but some performances were certainly learnt by rote, and within those notation-free performances strong stylistic limits were placed on acceptable experimentation and embellishment. Indeed, one instance is described by Aristophanes in an episode from his play *Clouds* (lines 961-972). Village boys are rehearsing a song by ear, and the master tells us «if any of them fooled around with the tune or twisted» the mode like the composer Phrynis «he was soundly beaten for obliterating the true Muses»[6]. Clearly it was not enough that a melody might be well known, or even that a version of it might exist in a written copy; the correct approach still had to be conveyed by a person who understood the conventions of performance and the limits of style. Nineteen hundred years later in Italy a very similar approach was also in operation. A letter survives from the composer Cesare Marotta in Rome to Enzo Bentivoglio in Ferrara (3 March 1614) concerning a certain singer called Francesca. He explains that he normally «teaches Francesca by rote, and not because she cannot read music, but because the notation is insufficient to communicate the [...] monodic style»[7]. Notational systems may seem to provide independent records of music but they still require some oral transmission of the appropriate 'reading cultures' that will enable the performer to transform the signs into culturally understood music. When it comes to the performing arts, the menu is never the meal — a fact that Caccini and others struggled to compensate for when their semi-improvised music hit the cultures of print in the early seventeenth century, as we shall see shortly.

Improvisation and the Constraints of 'Common-Practice' Styles

An understanding of the boundaries of style is central for the art of improvisation. It is no accident that the Baroque, which in some ways was obsessed with the definition of styles (*stile antico*, *stile moderno*, *stile concitato*, *stile rappresentativo*, *style brisé*, *style galant*, etc.; the division of music into church, chamber or stage types; the increasing separation of instrumental styles from vocal styles; the French *clavecin* style; the Italian violin style; the distinct national styles of operatic singing; and so on), was also a period where improvisation flourished. The more secure and clear those stylistic boundaries were, the more easily could performers exercise freedoms within those boundaries and, in the moment, draw on a fully understood and accepted musical language. Moreover, the dramatic shift in

5. Sixty-one surviving examples are documented and transcribed in Pohlmann – West 2001.

6. Translation from Barker 1984, pp. 101-102.

7. Hill 1997, vol. 1, pp. 128-129.

common practice around 1600 from polyphony to melodies with harmonic accompaniment (exemplified in the pervasive use of figured bass), freed up the opportunities for performance ornamentation without endangering too much the harmonic structures of works or their textural clarity.

In those periods where common practice breaks down, as in the twentieth century for example, there tends to be a reduction in the general employment of improvisation, even if it is preserved in certain subcultures (such as Jazz, aleatoric avant-garde music, or improvised piano accompaniments to early silent films), each of which develops its own 'local' common practices with its own self-imposed limits. After all, no one would have expected Miles Davis or La Monte Young to burst into pastiche Bartók, let alone embrace Mozartian musical procedures. What this 'common-practice principle' does indicate is that 'improvised' performances are rarely completely invented or whimsically free, and this has important implications for the quality of 'spontaneity' often said to be associated with improvisations. Within a common-practice context 'spontaneity' in performance frequently turns out to be, not a compositional 'cause' (that is, not the process by which the music is 'invented'), but rather a somewhat arch 'style of presentation' — a fact evidenced, to take but one example from the Baroque period, by the care with which Giulio Caccini attempted to convey in his *Le nuove musiche* (1602) the importance in performance presentations of «a certain noble negligence of song» (una certa nobile sprezzatura di canto)[8]. Indeed, in a certain sense we may take this to mean that performers who cannot fake spontaneity cannot be successful performers at all, a precept with which many performers today would agree — it is part of the 'stylishness' of performing, even if it does on occasion offend against the claims of creativity on the part of performers. Moreover, the equivalent in compositional terms can be found in the way in which many genres — capriccios, fantasias, impromptus, rhapsodies, *etc.* — attempt to mimic the attributes of spontaneously created music despite being carefully crafted and notated.

Of course, common practice styles are frequently made manifest through, and preserved by, the notated examples of music from their culture. Hence it should not surprise us that apparently un-written 'spontaneous' improvisations have often been developed in relation to notated ideas. For example in the final chapter — on improvisation — of C. P. E. Bach's *Essay on the True Art of Playing Keyboard Instruments* he offers many notated examples of bass-lines that he will «leave to the private study of my reader» before attempts are made to elaborate them into improvised preludes and fantasias[9]. There were, long before the eighteenth century, already well-established traditions of improvised

---

8. Hitchcock 1970b, p. 44; Caccini 1602, 'Ai Lettori' (To the Readers), unnumbered p. 1. The term *sprezzatura* famously occurs in Baldassarre Castiglione's *Il Cortegiano* completed in 1521. See Saccone 1983. According to Pirrotta 1984, p. 227, its musical use added a new application to a term already used to denote «the agile suppleness of the ideal dancer».

9. Bach 1974, p. 436.

music constructed on various schematic chord sequences — such as ostinato-based pieces, variations, figurational preludes and many other types. Indeed, the pre-determined chordal basis of the figurational-prelude type is obvious in several works from Book 1 of J. S. Bach's *Well-Tempered Clavier*. For example, Preludes numbers 2 in C minor, 6 in D minor, 8 in E-flat minor, and 15 in G major all begin with embellishments of the same figured bass sequence: 5/3; 6/4; 7/4/2; and 5/3[10].

The tension between improvisatory opportunities and written or rehearsed preparation reached a kind of crisis in the seventeenth and eighteenth centuries, a crisis most easily observed in relation to what many take to be that most obvious manifestation of momentary invention — the *ad libitum* cadenza. The dilemma is best illustrated by the practices of Beethoven at the end of our period. Descriptions exist of Beethoven apparently improvising dazzling cadenzas for several of his works around 1800 — as in his First Piano Concerto, for example, or the Piano Quintet Op. 16 (a work in any case closely modeled on Mozart's Quintet, K 452) — but he none-the-less seems to have written down sketches of cadenza material for those works before their performances happened[11]. This was probably because he was trying to reconcile the traditions of *ad libitum* performance with his desire for greater compositional control, the desire to produce a perfectly formed work on the spur of the moment. He is reported as saying that no artist deserved the title of 'virtuoso' unless his improvisations could pass for written compositions[12]. His solution seems to have been partly to plan his 'improvisations' in writing before he developed them in performance, because 'pure' improvisations almost inevitably have different characteristics from written compositions. A summary of these differing tendencies can be found in Table 1, and they suggest that it is not helpful to think of improvisations as simple equivalents to compositions in un-notated form.

Free improvisations tend to be pretexts for certain kinds of event[13], rather than the primary, if virtual, texts of musical works[14], and in that sense Beethoven was not so much drawing together improvisations and compositions, as intervening in the former to such a great extent that they in fact became the latter. This impulse should be distinguished from the use of written templates to guide performers who have to insert improvisations during fluid situations to fill the time. Girolamo Frescobaldi, for example, speaking of church services in the 'Preface' to his *Fiori musicali* (1635), tells us that the pieces «may be used as one pleases», but it is «a matter of great importance» for players to refer to the scores he has provided «because this practice, like a touchstone, distinguishes and makes known the true gold of the *virtuosi* from the actions of the ignorant. Nothing else need be said except

10. Further on improvising preludes and fantasias in the Baroque see Moersch 2009, pp. 160-164.

11. See Kinderman 2008.

12. Whitmore 1991, p. 202.

13. See Cook 2017.

14. See also the discussion in Dahlhaus 1987.

that practice is the master of all»[15]. Clearly the implication here is that imaginative and worthwhile improvisations need to be built upon the study and understanding of relevant models, and are very unlikely to emerge from an unsullied field of ignorance.

Table 1: Divergent Tendencies between Compositions and Improvisations

Composition	Improvisation
1. The material is integrated before the performance. The whole, or 'idea', may be conceived in an inspired moment, but the details are then 'composed out' prior to the performance.	1. The material is integrated experientially in virtue of the performance. There is a tendency to arbitrary voice leading, isolated splashes of sound, unbalanced forms, etc. Some details may be conceived beforehand, but the 'whole' 'emerges' or has to be constructed.
2. All elements of the musical material tend to play an equal role in the composition.	2. There is a tendency to privilege only one or two parameters (melody, or rhythm, or methods of sound attack or manipulation, or harmony, etc.).
3. Style arises from the techniques employed.	3. Style tends to control the techniques employed.
4. Performers are primarily concerned with the reproduction of the music as a 'text'.	4. Performers tend to use the prepared elements as 'pretexts' for the display of individualism, virtuosity, spontaneous decision-making (characterized as 'risk'), and the presentation of unpredictable events (characterized as 'discoveries').
5. Performances are primarily characterized as presentations of a work.	5. Performances are primarily seen as a celebration of a performer or an event.

There have been several junctures in the history of Western music where oral and written cultures have clashed. Major examples include the struggle to transfer the plainsong repertory into notated form in the ninth and tenth centuries[16], the collision between improvisational practices and the cultures of print in the late sixteenth century (of which more soon), and the transformation currently taking place in the field of composition between traditional methods employing score notation and the new technologies of computer generated music and sound art. In such cases important questions arise as to how a 'composition' might emerge from the mix of oral and written cultures, and how effective a notation (or other retrieval system) might be in preserving and transmitting the necessary ingredients of the 'work' (a problematic concept in itself, especially when improvisation might be involved). Moreover, what freedoms are given to, and expected of, the performer to add to the preserved information and reconstitute it as sounding music. These issues interact in complex ways in a famous source from the early Baroque that gives us a great deal of information about the works it contains — Caccini's *Le nuove musiche* published in Florence in 1602.

15. Translation from McClintock 1979, pp. 135-136.

16. For a fascinating cultural and musicological examination of the emergence of chant compositions and their ultimate preservation in distorting notational systems, see Jeffery 1992.

Writing the Unwritable: The Case of Caccini's *Le Nuove Musiche*

The plural reference to 'new musics' in Caccini's title (the singular form would have been '*La nuova musica*') implies not only that the volume represents a decisive break with practices from the past, but also that the innovations are of more than one kind. Just exactly which types of multiple developments the collection might contain is not immediately clear. After all, Caccini himself did not invent monody nor, for that matter, its application to opera; clear traces of disputes over precedence with other protagonists in that venture survive not only in the prefaces by Jacopo Peri and himself in their respective settings of the opera *L'Euridice*, but also in a number of other sources[17]. Moreover, *Le nuove musiche* was quite probably not even the first volume of monodies published — that distinction seems to belong to Domenico Melli's *Musiche composte sopra alcuni madrigali* of 1602[18]. Again, we should recognise that it is not even Caccini's famous codification of ornaments that is especially innovative. Rather it is his holistic approach to their application[19], his insistence on linking their use to expressive intentions and detailed sensitivity to the words, and his careful calibration of the interplay between patterned, written ornaments and improvised 'characterisation' elements applied in the moment of performance by the singer with grace and nobility.

These attributes may be striking in Caccini's 'Preface', but in fact not even these were wholly his invention. His comments about demeanour, grace, nobility, ideal accompaniments, and tasteful ornamentation largely parallel those advocated in great detail some twenty years before in a document sent to him by Giovanni Bardi (a founder of the Florentine Camerata) — the *Discourse Addressed to Giulio Caccini Called the Roman, on Ancient Music and Good Singing*[20].

---

[17]. For texts and translations of the relevant documents by Jacopo Peri, Giulio Caccini, Emilio de' Cavalieri, Marco da Gagliano and Ottavio Rinuccini, see Carter – Szweykowski 1994. Also see Strunk 1998, pp. 523-525, for a letter of 1634 from Pietro de' Bardi to Giovanni Doni which retrospectively recounts the origins of the new style. On Emilio de' Cavalieri's difficulties with Caccini and Antonio Nardi (purported inventor of the *Chitarrone*), see Palisca 1994, p. 405. The attacks on Nardi provoked a fierce defence from Caccini in the final paragraph of the Preface to his 1602 print, but when the volume was reprinted in 1608 and 1615 that paragraph was omitted (see Hitchcock 1970b, p. 56.)

[18]. As reported in Fortune 1953, p. 176, n. 16.

[19]. Hitchcock 1970b, p. 48; Caccini 1602, 'Ai Lettori', [unnumbered] p. 3: «non servono solo le cose particolari, ma tutte insieme la fanno migliore».

[20]. *Discorso mandato a Giulio Caccini detto romano sopra la musica antica, e 'l cantar bene*. The original Italian with parallel translation appears complete in Palisca 1989, pp. 90-131. The shared topics and their respective page numbers in the Bardi essay (*ibidem*) and the Caccini preface (Hitchcock 1970b) include: Plato's view on music and speech (93; 43); the preference for the archlute as an accompanying instrument (117 and 125; 45 and 56); the irrelevance of counterpoint (111; 46), the singer must be guided by the words (115; 46); long syllables should not be placed on short notes (121; 46); the use of long and misplaced *passaggi* is

As for the distinction between performance elements provided by the composer and those supplied by the singer, Bardi provides an interesting metaphor. He tells us that the singer must adjust his voice «like a good cook who adds to the food that he has seasoned well a little sauce or condiment to make it pleasing to his Lord»[21]. Here Bardi seems to be suggesting that, although before the performance the work might exist together with some written in ornaments (that have 'seasoned' it well), the singer's task is to add yet further elements (the 'sauce') that make the overall presentation of the work more fitting and appetizing for its discerning recipients. This leaves us with the thought that even those works printed with ornamental runs or local embellishments in *Le nuove musiche* are open to yet further decoration and expressive enhancement. Moreover, this point is made clear in Caccini's 'Preface' addressed to the readers (*Ai Lettori*) where, after giving fully marked up examples of decoration and sung articulations in relation to 'Deh dove son fuggiti' and other compositions, he tells us «thus they may serve as models from which may be recognized similar places in the following pieces»[22] — that is, the various techniques should be adapted and added to the printed versions of works published in the body of the collection.

This requirement to transfer various types of performance articulation onto the particular poetic and musical situations of the individual works in the volume (which already contain some notated embellishments) is rarely carried through by modern singers. Indeed the relative uniformity of the many performances of one of Caccini's better-known works, 'Amarilli mia bella' demonstrates this very clearly. The performances tend to fall into one of two broad groups. The first comprises those derived from the edition in Parisotti's 1888 anthology, *Arie antiche*[23]. They can be recognised by the characteristic type of accompaniment provided, the substitution in the fifth line of the words 'Dubitar non ti vale' for the original 'Prendi questo mio strale', and the use (notated in the 1888 score) of brief anticipations of the pitches of certain notes at the end of the notes immediately preceding them (following nineteenth century vocal practice). Beniamino Gigli's 1939 recording[24] provides a clear example of a literal performance of Parisotti's edition, complete with vocal 'swoops' from note to note. There are also numerous modern singers who do not specialise in the early music but simply add the piece to their concerts for the sake of repertorial variety, and follow the Parisotti model closely. They rarely employ ornaments of any kind; instead they attempt to give the bare music import by overlaying it with a kind

distasteful (127; 46); nobility and grace are important in the demeanour of the singer (111; 43 and 47); and the enthusiasms of plebs (121, «indotta plebe»; 44, «plebi esaltati») should be ignored.

[21]. Palisca 1989, pp. 114-115.

[22]. Hitchcock 1970b, p. 55; Caccini 1602, 'Ai Lettori', [unnumbered] p. 8: «et accio[c]ché servano per esempio, in riconoscere, in esso musiche i medesimi luoghi».

[23]. Parisotti 1888, vol. ii, pp. 15-17.

[24]. Recorded on 12 May 1939 and first issued on HMV DB 3895. Now available on Naxos Historical, *The Gigli Edition*, vol. x, Naxos 8.110271, track 5.

of sub-operatic intensity, usually delivered relatively slowly and with a 'beat-counting' uniformity of pulse.

By contrast those dependent on Hitchcock's 1970b edition or a facsimile of the original print (see Ex. 1) tend to add occasional trills (which Caccini calls *gruppi*) and tremolos (which he rather confusingly calls *trilli*), but by and large they follow Caccini's score closely. However, even in this group (which includes singers such as Emma Kirkby[25] and Roberta Invernizzi[26]) it is rare for the performers to improvise those many other expressive and dramatic vocal effects related to the rhetoric of the text that Caccini recommends such as the *esclamazione* (a light, quick attack but with low intensity), the *crescere e scemare della voce* (*crescendo* followed by a *diminuendo* on long notes), the *cascata* (a cascade of notes, applied in various forms) and so on[27].

This hesitancy to go beyond the printed text, even for those with knowledge of appropriate style, may well partly be Caccini's fault. Although in the 'Preface' to *Le nuove musiche* he discuss a range of effects that might be introduced by the performer, his detailed printed examples almost inevitably give the impression that the essentials of the style can still be captured in notation. Moreover, this impression is reinforced in his 1614 publication *Nuove musiche e nuova maniera di scriverle* (New Musics and a New Manner of Writing Them)[28], which asserts on the title page that «all the delicacies of this art can be learned without having to hear the composer sing», and in the 'Preface' to 'discriminating readers' (A Discreti Lettori) where Caccini refers to his style of singing «which I *write out exactly as it is sung*» (my italics: «la quale io scrivo giustamente, come si canta»).

Given the range of vocal effects described in his publications, it is clear that Caccini's assertion cannot be completely true because: a) some effects cannot be put into exact notation; b) certain improvisatory elements are part of the performance style; and c) notation itself can have different functions. In terms of notation functions we make take the example of figured bass. Firstly it acts as an *archive* in that it records exactly what the bass line and harmonies are. However, at the same time it is also a *strategy* for allowing the performer to decide upon certain kinds of textural and voice-leading effects, as well as decorations and responses to the melodic features of the vocal part. We can see therefore that notated instructions can also imply or encapsulate improvisatory practices, not only in relation to figured bass but also elements such as cadenzas, melodic figuration (think of the mathematically suspect decorative embellishments in some of Chopin's melodies)[29], or even

[25]. Emma Kirkby, *Arie Antiche*, Columns Musica Oscura 070988 (1993), track 2.

[26]. Roberta Invernizzi and Accademia Strumentali Italiana, *Dolcissimo Sospiro*, Divox CDX 70202-6 (2005), track 9.

[27]. For a full exploration of the complete range of Caccini's suggested vocal effects (and their multiple manifestations) see HITCHCOCK 1970A.

[28]. CACCINI 1614; HITCHCOCK 1978.

[29]. For mathematically incorrect examples from Francesco Rasi's 1608 collection *Vaghezze di musica* see CARTER 2000, p. 15. Minor instances also occur in *Le nuove musiche*, for example in 'Vedrò 'l mio sol' (no. 7), and 'Io parto' (no. 14).

Ex. 1: facsimile of 'Amarilli mia bella' from Caccini's 1602 print.

13
mo re.
Fogaua con le stelle Vn infermo d'amore Sotto notturno cielo il suo do
lo re E dicea fisso in loro O o' immagini belle dell Idol mio ch'adoro si come a me mo
stra te Mētre così splendete la sua rara beltate così mostraste a lei Mentre cotanto ar
dete I viui ardo ri
miei La fareste co'l vostro aureo sembiāte Pietosa si Pieto sa si come me fa
D

the notated example of a *trillo* which Caccini gives in his 1602 'Preface'[30]. Although the *trillo* is given in a mathematically correct form (that is, its notes add up to the correct number of beats in the measure) he makes it clear that this is an exercise which he employed while teaching his wife and daughter how to execute and control a particular vocal technique. Therefore the exact notation is merely indicative and the ornament should be delivered more freely in performance[31]. Clearly we cannot discern by simply staring at an example of notated music what the subtle interplay between its strategic and archival functions might be. Moreover, those functions typically exist simultaneously in the same symbol and their implications for the improvising performer rest upon a complex field of understanding.

A more common categorisation of notation employed is that which distinguishes between its prescriptive and descriptive functions, a separation first suggested by the ethnomusicologist Charles Seeger in 1958[32]. Seeger's terms attempt to capture two distinct motivations for writing down music. In prescriptive notation the intention is to tell the performer exactly what to do in a forthcoming performance, whereas with descriptive notation the intention is to record what *was done* in a past performance.

Often early Baroque notated sources contain a complex mix not only of strategic and archival functions, but also of descriptive and prescriptive motivations. Caccini's *Le nuove musiche*, for example, presents some interesting examples among the items included from his stage work *Il rapimento di Cefalo* performed in the Uffizi palace in Florence in 1600 (items 13 a, b, and c in Hitchcock 1970b). At the head of the aria 'Muove si dolce' (item 13b) Caccini tells us «This air was sung with the passaggi as given by Melchior Palantrotti, excellent musician of Our Lord's Chapel». Thus this is a clear example of descriptive notation — it tells us what Palantrotti did — even though the figured bass and certain vocal indications (*trillo*, *esclamazione*) are of a strategic kind. A more complex case is the aria 'Qual trascorrendo' (item 13d) for which Caccini tells us: «This air was sung, with *some* of the *passaggi* as given and *some* according to his own taste, by the famous Francesco Rasi, nobleman of Arezzo, most obliging servant of His Highness, the Duke of Mantua». So the music here is descriptive in so far as it contains sections of *passaggi* performed by Rasi according to his own taste, and yet its general motivation is prescriptive since it largely offers a version of how Caccini would like it to be sung.

In terms of improvisatory freedoms on the part of the performer a complex picture is now beginning to emerge, and it seems clear that those freedoms can operate in relation to three rather different arenas. First we have the particular demeanour, characterisation and stylized attitude chosen and projected by the performer — grace, elegance, *sprezzatura*, real or simulated spontaneity, the particular display of the role of a protagonist in the narrative, and so on. Next we have a range of 'execution techniques' selected by the performer from

30. Hitchcock 1970b, p. 50.

31. See the discussion in Hitchcock 1970a, pp. 389-390.

32. Seeger 1958.

their repertory of skills and employed for articulating and underlining particular emotive or rhetorical elements in the text and/or music (in Caccini's case, *esclamazione*, *intonazione della voce*, *passaggi*, etc.). And thirdly, although less frequently mentioned by theorists, we have the use of improvised embellishment to enhance or even create the structural goals and organization of a work.

This structural use of embellishment is frequently written into the music itself (as in variations for example), or very conventionally applied (as in many performances of *da capo* arias). Its improvised application in early Baroque vocal music is less common, even when the music clearly offers the opportunity. In the case of 'Amarilli mia bella' for example, we can see from TABLE 2 that the text divides into two sections 'A' and 'B' (with the last line repeated at the end as a brief coda). In his print Caccini repeats the text and the music of the long 'B' section exactly. Only in the Coda, which appears after that repetition, and in which he repeats the last line of the text, does he then add new decoration. The long repetition of the 'B' music is almost never subjected to any kind of improvised embellishment in performance (though an interesting exception is provided by Roberta Invernizzi in the recording mentioned above).

TABLE 2: MUSICAL STRUCTURE, TEXT AND TRANSLATION OF CACCINI'S 'AMARILI MIA BELLA'

MUSIC	TEXT	TRANSLATION
A	1. *Amarilli mia bella*	1. Amarilli my love
	2. *Non credi, o del mio cor dolce desio*	2. Do you not believe, o sweet desire of my heart
	3. *D'esser tu l'amor mio?*	3. That you are my love?
B	4. *Credilo pur, e se timor t'assale*	4. Believe it indeed, and if fear torments you
	5. *Prendi questo mio strale*	5. Take this arrow of mine
	6. *Aprim'il petto, e vedrai scritto il core*	6. Open my breast, and you will see written on my heart
	7. *'Amarilli è 'l mio amore'*	7. 'Amarilli is my love'
Coda	7. *'Amarilli è 'l mio amore'* [In the 1602 printed version, after the fully written out repeat of the **B** section (Hitchcock ed., bars 28-44), Line 7 is again repeated with new music (bars 44-50) and *passaggi*. This coda is not in the early manuscript versions.]	7. 'Amarilli is my love'

This nervousness about the improvised structural use of embellishment in forms where it is not absolutely conventionally applied seems to change significantly only at the end of the Baroque period. It is interesting that C. P. E. Bach in his *Essay* keeps distinct his remarks on embellishment (which are in Part I, Chapter 2) from those on improvisation as such (in Part II, Chapter 7). He also separates embellishments into two types: the conventional (indicated by established signs); and the free (which lack signs and consist of many short notes)[33]. What we do find in C. P. E. Bach is the use of increasingly elaborate and carefully graded ornamentation to complement the structural drive of the movement. For example, in the third movement of his third Sonata from his *Sech sonaten* [...] *mit verändarten Reprisen* (Wq. 50), the published version clearly shows this tendency (bars 74-94). Moreover, in the British Library there is a copy of the print (GB-Lbl. K.10.a23) with C. P. E. Bach's additional annotated embellishments which intensify yet further the formal unfolding of the work. It is in this sense that ornamentation in the late Baroque becomes structurally integral to the music, and is not just focused on those decorative or expressive functions that we find more generally in the period[34].

Given the many complications associated with the functions and placing of improvised embellishments in Baroque works, and also the multiple functions of the notations involved, it would be difficult to take at face value the claim that Caccini's printed scores should be seen as «frozen improvisations» that require a certain «interpretative flexibility, and above all *sprezzatura*, to bring them to life»[35]. As we have seen the notation hardly functions solely as an archive of a past act of performance by Caccini or anyone else, and the term «interpretative flexibility» covers a range of complex interventions (some restricted by pattern-book formulas, performance conventions, common-practice styles, and much else besides) concerned variously with the elaboration and characterisation of the music, the elucidation of form, and with individual acts of performer display.

However, there is another sense in which we may construe the term «frozen improvisations» in relation to the works in Caccini's print. They are not records of actual (now fixed) past improvisations, but rather are tangible traces of an ongoing process through which the identity of the works continue to emerge and gain meaning — not in a straight line from oral creation to written record but from a sometimes opaque confluence of the two. 'Amarilli mia bella' for example exists in at least two manuscript versions that seem to predate the 1602 publication — Florence, Biblioteca Nazionale, I-Fn: ms. Magl. XIX. 66 (folio 18r), and Brussels, Bibliotheque du Conservatoire, B-Bc: ms. 704 (p. 46)[36]. Both

---

33. Bach 1974, p. 80.

34. It is interesting to note that when Frederick Neumann published his acclaimed study on ornamentation in the Baroque (Neumann 1978) he divided the chapters into types of ornament, but in his later work on Mozart (Neumann 1986) he treated ornamentation in relation to the different movement forms in which they were employed. This tendency to see structural musical goals as being made manifest through the intensification and embellishment of basic music material is exactly what we find in the early twentieth-century analytic methods of Heinrich Schenker. His approach was to see the goal-directed foreground and middle ground textures of a work as elaborations of a basic *Ursatz* and a proto-melodic *Urline*. It can hardly be a coincidence that Schenker did his Ph.D. on C. P. E. Bach, produced performing editions of his music, and published a pioneering study of ornamentation (see Schenker 1903).

35. Carter 1984, p. 217.

36. For a survey of the sources of 'Anima mia bella' see Carter 1988, which contains (p. 254) a facsimile of the Brussels source. The Florence source is reproduced in Donington 1981, Plate vi (between pp. 64-65).

of these provide much simplified forms of the printed version. As such they are unlikely to present actual performed improvisations at all, and we should not assume that all 'plain' versions necessarily represent an earlier stage of the conception of the work.

Ex. 2: edited musical extracts from 'Amarilli mia bella'.

a) CACCINI 1602, opening of Section A (= HITCHCOCK 1970B, bars. 1-5).

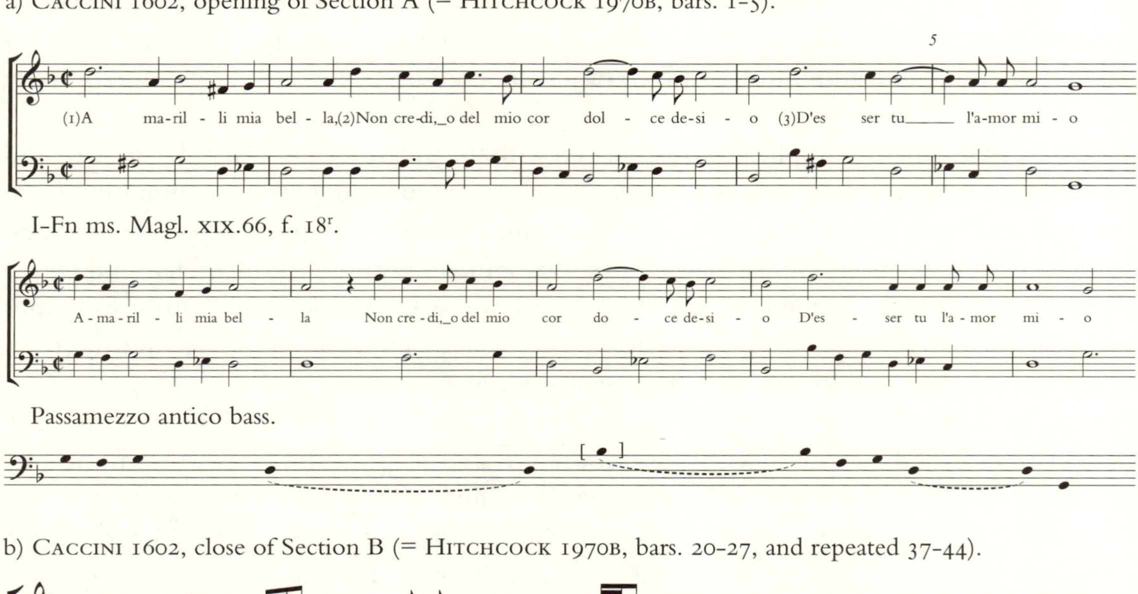

I-Fn ms. Magl. XIX.66, f. 18r.

Passamezzo antico bass.

b) CACCINI 1602, close of Section B (= HITCHCOCK 1970B, bars. 20-27, and repeated 37-44).

I-Fn ms. Magl. XIX.66, f. 18r.

c) CACCINI 1602, Coda (= HITCHCOCK 1970B, bars. 44-50).

As Ex. 2 reveals, the version in Florence is slightly 'squarer' in its rhythms (lacking the opportunity for an *esclamazione* on the first syllable of 'Amarilli' for example), and at the close of the 'B' section it lacks the small embellishments, chromaticisms and palpitating rests. Also the extensively decorated final impassioned cry of 'Amarilli è 'l mio amore' (Ex. 1c) in the Coda is entirely missing from the manuscript. It is possible that someone may have learnt the skeletal framework of the song from the Florence 'template' source but it is unlikely to preserve the details of an actual performance. It could perhaps serve for the performer as the beginning of an improvisatory process, but not the end of one; the notation comes before the improvisation not after it from this perspective. From the point of view of the composer, however, the written version might well contain the ghostly trace of genuine improvisatory exploration in relation to the creation of the song. The bass line of the 'A' music is clearly an elaboration of the passamezzo antico scheme — a scheme also adumbrated in several other items in *Le nuove musiche*, most clearly in no. 13b, 'Muove sì dolce'.

These interlocking layers of compositional exploration, notated templates and elaborations by a performer (who is sometimes also the composer) leave questions of creativity, ownership, and improvisation problematically entwined in this repertory. Another intriguing example, which I have discussed (together with music examples) in some detail elsewhere[37], is 'Possente spirto' from Monteverdi's 1607 opera *Orfeo*, an aria for which Monteverdi famously provided two versions of the vocal line sections — one 'plain' and the other decorated. The first surprise is that the 'plain' version is already decorated since this is another one of those works based on the passamezzo antico. Even more surprisingly 'Monteverdi's' elaborated version of a passamezzo antico shows a remarkable similarity to an aria contained in Caccini's 1602 *Le nuove musiche*, 'Qual trascorrendo' (no. 13d), an item originally composed for Caccini's stage work *Il rapimento di Cefalo*. We do know from the rubric in Caccini's volume that 'Qual trascorrendo' was sung by Francesco Rasi and, and, interestingly enough, it is precisely Rasi who seems to have sung the role of Orfeo in Monteverdi's opera.

There are some differences of ornamentation between Caccini's piece and those in 'Possente spirto', but we should remember that we are not looking at all the embellishments sung by Rasi in Caccini's printed version. As we have seen, Caccini tells us that Rasi sang some of the *passaggi* according to his own taste and not as written, therefore Rasi's original embellishments for Caccini's aria may have been even closer to the decorated version in Monteverdi's score than is now apparent. Also the words of 'Qual trascorrendo' are so close to the situation in Monteverdi's opera that it would be surprising if some kind of adaptation had not recommend itself to both Rasi and Monteverdi. After all, Orfeo — an offspring of the Sun God Apollo — has just embarked on an unworldly journey amongst

37. See Pryer 2007, pp. 12-14.

the shades of Hell to rescue his love. She will not in the end return to earth but will be placed to shine among the stars. And what does the text of Caccini's aria say? «As the sun brings day to the shades of night, as it proceeds on its ethereal journey, so love shines among the stars, brightening our lives and luring us with its splendour»[38]. It seems then that 'Qual trascorrendo', already composed by Caccini as a variation on the improvisatory structural model of the passamezzo antico, and enlivened and adapted in performance by Rasi's personal repertory of improvisatory *passaggi*, finally found itself embedded in Monteverdi's grand aria as it was customised for use in his opera. Clearly 'Monteverdi's' work was only the latest manifestation in a series of improvisatory adaptations that inevitably emerged from the constant interchange between the cultures of unwritten performance and written compositions during the period.

Improvisation, Authorship and Creative Freedoms

This interdependence of oral and written cultures may help to explain why definitions of the term 'improvisation' that we find in dictionaries and theoretical writings around 1600 turn out to be surprisingly brief and unhelpful. For example, the various editions of John Florio's dictionary of Italian and English, first published in 1598, says that *improvvisare* means «to sing or speake extempore»[39] — a description that was repeated in many dictionaries of the time and one that simply equates being 'out of time' or in free rhythm with any kind of spontaneous composition. We get a different emphasis from the famous Accademia della Crusca dictionary of 1612 which illustrates the word with reference to the suddenness and anti-rational nature of certain improvised actions[40]. What is particularly interesting is that neither Florio nor Crusca, nor any Italian source at all before the eighteenth century seems to contain the noun for an 'improviser' (*improvvisatore*), presumably because it was not considered a special skill distinct and separable from performance or composition.

Monteverdi's attitude is intriguing here since he seems to claim 'Possente spirto' as his own in a letter of 9 December 1616 when he tells us «*Arianna* led me to a just lament, and *Orfeo* to a righteous prayer»[41]. However, it may be that Monteverdi was implying, not ownership of the aria model, nor of the background traditions that went into it, but

---

[38]. See Hitchcock 1970b, p. 21: «Qual trascorrendo per gli eterei campi / Il sol quaggiù l'ombre notturne aggiorna / Tale amor sulle stele almo soggiorna / E cosparge fra noi fulgidi lampi / Per invogliare altrui de sol splendore».

[39]. 'Improvvisare', in: Florio 1611.

[40]. *Crusca* 1612 records *improvviso*, both as an adjective («il rumore [...] improvviso» [sudden, unexpected or unforseen noise]) and as an adverb («Il Conte Tegrino rispuose improvviso, e subito, cioè senza pensare, o premeditare» [Count Tegrino replied suddenly and hastily, which means without thinking or premeditation]). Both examples are taken from *Storia di Giovanni Villani* (Florence, 1587).

[41]. Lax 1994, p. 49: «L'Arianna mi porta ad un giusto lamento e l'Orfeo ad una giusta preghiera».

rather the 'invention' of his grand adaptation and its effects. 'Invention' (*invenzione)* is the term most often associated with creativity in his writings[42], but a word that he seems never to have used — and, indeed, it cannot be found in any Italian dictionaries of the period — is originality (*originalità*), that quality of being creatively first and unique. This should not surprise us since it was standard practice for composers of Monteverdi's time to imitate, emulate and pay homage to their colleagues through the medium of quotation, and then subtly re-work their musical material in a new ways. Moreover, it is precisely the techniques of re-combination, variation, invention, and adaptation that form the bedrock of an improvisatory process whether considered from the perspective of performance or composition[43]. These interlocking chains of intertextuality, bringing together both oral and written elements, were also common in 'literary' cultures as well, and seem to have bred few hesitations in relation to the perceived authorship and ownership of the works[44].

Throughout this article we have been attempting to differentiate between relevant and irrelevant factors in relation to our understanding of acts of improvisation. Much of our discussion comes down to the background notion of the role of freedom and its relation to creativity. In fact the difficulties we uncovered with the traditional oral/written divide discussed earlier rest on a confusion between two rather different types of freedom — what we might call 'escape' freedoms and 'fulfilment' freedoms[45]. To claim that *freedom from* notation in oral cultures automatically guarantees that we have the *freedom to* (or the capacity to) create something new is clearly not the case, most obviously in societies were the performance and transmission of music are dominated by rote learning, but also where there may be a lack of creativity to bring the desired fulfilment about. Furthermore, if fulfilment freedoms are to have a chance to operate, to play out creatively as it were, there needs to be some receptivity in at least sections of the community where those achievements can be agreed to be interesting and meaningful. This is where the importance of common-practice musical styles come into play, and why the Baroque was so successful as an 'improvising age'. Its stylistic frameworks were constantly being defined and better

42. See for example in Lax 1994, p. 28 (letter of 10 September 1609) where he praises a 'certain novel invention' («qualche invenzione nova») in the canzonas of Galeazzo Sirena; or p. 79 (letter of 1 February 1620) where he records that, in relation to his *Lamento di Apollo*, certain gentlemen were 'pleased in the manner of its invention' («piaciuto in maniera nella invenzione»).

43. On the cognitive and creative skills needed for these processes see Berkowitz 2010.

44. To take but one example, the story of Troilus and Cressida was developed out of events in Homer's tale of the Trojan war; it was elaborated in a French source, the *Roman de Trois*, by the twelfth-century poet Benoit de Sainte-Maure, which then influenced the version in Boccaccio's *Il Filostrato*. This in turn formed the basis of Chaucer's poem, which then lent inspiration to Shakespeare's play of the same name. None of this prevented Chaucer from claiming ownership of the work and fixing its identity in a written copy. Thus towards the end of the poem (Book v, line 1795) we find him pleading: «So pray I God that none mis-write thee». For the oral dimensions of Chaucer's poem see Manguel 1996, pp. 252-255.

45. See the discussion in, for example, Berlin 2009. Philosophers often refer to the two types as 'freedom from' and 'freedom to'.

understood, and therefore its musical 'liberties' entered into a more nuanced transaction than that of mere *permission*, and its improvisatory practices gained import in ways that mere *licence* or *anarchy* could not. In other words, the art world began to establish a kind of aesthetic equivalent to Rousseau's social contract (*avant la lettre*), so that communal discourses could find ways of negotiating between uniquely interesting products and merely bizarre ones, between imaginative insights with wider import, and the banal fancies of lone individuals.

These restrictions should not be seen as a dreary moral plea for compromise, or some kind of officious insistence that artistic creativity should be curtailed. Clearly composers such as Caccini and Monteverdi managed to produce interesting and enduring works, and ones that played a part in gradually enabling the musical language to evolve ('revolution' is usually too extreme and simplistic a term for cultural change). This they did by moving freely between oral and written influences, and employing a range of improvisatory mechanisms and borrowing techniques in the performance and making of musical works. As the French writer Chateaubriand said: «An original writer is not one who imitates nobody, but one whom nobody can imitate»[46].

Bibliography

Bach 1974
Bach, Carl Philipp Emanuel. *Essay on the True Art of Playing Keyboard Instruments*, (1753), translated and edited by William Mitchell, London, Eulenberg Books, 1974.

Barker 1984
Greek Musical Writings. Volume 1: The Musician and His Art, edited by Andrew Barker, Cambridge-New York, Cambridge University Press, 1984 (Cambridge Readings in the Literature of Music).

Berkowitz 2010
Berkowitz, Aaron. *The Improvising Mind: Cognition and Creativity in the Musical Moment*, Oxford-New York, Oxford University Press, 2010.

Berlin 2009
Berlin, Isaiah. 'Two Concepts of Liberty', in: *Isaiah Berlin: Liberty*, edited by Henry Hardy, Oxford-New York, Oxford University Press, 2009, pp. 166-217.

Caccini 1602
Caccini, Giulio. *Le nuove musiche*, Florence, Marescotti, 1602 [more veneto, 1601].

Caccini 1614
Id. *Nuove musiche e nuova maniera di scriverle*, Florence, Zanobi Pignoni, 1614.

[46]. Chateaubriand 1802, vol. ii, Chapter 3, p. 153: «L'écrivain original n'est pas celui qui n'imite personne, mais celui que personne ne peut imiter».

Carter 1984
Carter, Tim. 'On the Composition and Performance of Caccini's *Le nuove musiche* (1602)', in: *Early Music*, xii/2 (May 1984), pp. 208-217.

Carter 1988
Id. 'Caccini's 'Amarilli, mia bella': Some Questions (and a Few Answers)', in: *Journal of the Royal Musical Association*, cxiii/2 (1988), pp. 250-273.

Carter 2000
Id. 'Printing the "New Music"', in: *Music and the Cultures of Print*, edited by Kate van Orden, New York, Garland, 2000 (Garland Reference Library of the Humanities, 2027 / Critical and Cultural Musicology, 1), pp. 3-37.

Carter – Szweykowski 1994
Composing Opera: from Dafne to Ulisse Errante, translated and edited by Tim Carter and Zygmunt Szweykowski, Kraków, Musica Jagellonica, 1994 (Practica Musica, 2).

Chateaubriand 1802
Chateaubriand, François-Auguste René vicomte de. *Génie du christianisme*, 5 vols., Paris, Chez Migneret, 1802.

Cook 2017
Cook, Nicholas. 'Scripting Social Interaction: Improvisation, Performance and Western "Art" Music,' in: *Improvisation and Social Aesthetics*, edited by Georgina Born, Eric Lewis and Will Straw, Durham (NC), Duke University Press, 2017, pp. 59-77.

Crusca 1612
Vocabolario degli accademici della Crusca, Venice, Giovanni Alberti, 1612.

Dahlhaus 1987
Dahlhaus, Carl. 'Composition and Improvisation' in: *Schoenberg and the New Music: Essays by Carl Dahlhaus*, edited and translated by Derrick Puffett and Alfred Clayton, Cambridge-New York, Cambridge University Press, 1987, pp. 265-273.

Donington 1981
Donington, Robert. *The Rise of Opera*, London, Faber and Faber, 1981.

Florio 1611
Florio, John. Revised as *Queen Anna's New World of Words, or Dictionarie of the Italian and English tongues*, London, Edward Blount and William Barret, 1611.

Fortune 1953
Fortune, Nigel. 'Italian Secular Monody from 1600 to 1635: An Introductory Survey', in: *The Musical Quarterly*, xxxix/2 (April 1953), pp. 171-195.

Fortune 1954
Id. 'Italian 17th-century Singing', in: *Music & Letters*, xxxv/3 (July 1954), pp. 206-219.

HILL 1997

HILL, John Walter. *Roman Monody, Cantata, and Opera from the Circles around Cardinal Montalto*, 2 vols., Oxford, Clarendon Press, 1997 (Oxford Monographs on Music).

HITCHCOCK 1970A

HITCHCOCK, H. Wiley. 'Vocal Ornamentation in Caccini's *Nuove Musiche*', in: *The Musical Quarterly*, LVI/3 (July 1970), pp. 389-404.

HITCHCOCK 1970B

CACCINI, Giulio. *Le nuove musiche*, edited by H. Wiley Hitchcock, Madison, A-R Editions, 1970 (Recent Researches in the Music of the Baroque Era, 9).

HITCHCOCK 1978

ID. *Nuove musiche e nuova maniera di scriverle (1614)*, edited by H. Wiley Hitchcock, Madison, A-R Editions, 1978 (Recent Researches in the Music of the Baroque Era, 28).

ISIDORE OF SEVILLE 2006

ISIDORE OF SEVILLE. *The Etymologies*, translated by Stephen Barney, W. Lewis, Jennifer Beach and Oliver Berghof, Cambridge, Cambridge University Press, 2006 (Etymologiæ).

JEFFERY 1992

JEFFERY, Peter. *Re-envisioning Past Musical Cultures: Ethnomusicology in the Study of Gregorian Chant*, Chicago, Chicago University Press, 1992 (Chicago Studies in Ethnomusicology).

KINDERMAN 2008

KINDERMAN, William. 'A Tale of Two Quintets: Mozart's K. 452 and Beethoven's Op. 16', in: *Variations on the Canon: Essays from Bach to Boulez in Honor of Charles Rosen's Eightieth Birthday*, edited by Robert Curry, David Gable and Robert L. Marshall, Rochester (NY), Rochester University Press, 2008, pp. 55-77.

LAX 1994

Claudio Monteverdi: Lettere, edited by Éva Lax, Florence, Leo Olschki, 1994 (Studi e testi per la storia della musica, 10).

MANGUEL 1996

MANGUEL, Alberto. *A History of Reading*, London, Harper Collins, 1996.

MCCLINTOCK 1979

Readings in the History of Music in Performance, selected, edited and translated by Carol McClintock, Bloomington (IN), Indiana University Press, 1979.

MOERSCH 2009

MOERSCH, Charlotte Mattax. 'Keyboard Improvisation in the Baroque Period', in: *Musical Improvisation: Art, Education and Society*, edited by Gabriel Solis and Bruno Nettl, Urbana (IL), University of Illinois Press, 2009, pp. 150-170.

Nettl 1974
Nettl, Bruno. 'Thoughts on Improvisation: A Comparative Approach', in: *The Musical Quarterly*, lx/1 (January 1974), pp. 1-19.

Neumann 1978
Neumann, Frederick. *Ornamentation in Baroque and Post-Baroque Music*, Princeton, Princeton University Press, 1978.

Neumann 1986
Id. *Ornamentation and Improvisation in Mozart*, Princeton, Princeton University Press, 1986.

Palisca 1989
Palisca, Claude. *The Florentine Camerata: Documentary Studies and Translations*, New Haven, Yale University Press, 1989 (Music Theory Translation Series).

Palisca 1994
Id. *Studies in the History of Italian Music and Music Theory*, Oxford, Clarendon Press, 1994.

Parisotti 1888
Arie antiche ad una voce per canto e pianoforte, edited by Alessandro Parisotti, 3 vols., Milan, Ricordi, 1888.

Pirrotta 1984
Pirrotta, Nino. *Music and Culture in Italy from the Middle Ages to the Baroque: A Collection of Essays*, Cambridge (MA), Harvard University Press, 1984 (Studies in the History of Music, 1).

Pohlmann – West 2001
Documents of Ancient Greek Music: The Extant Melodies and Fragments, edited and transcribed with commentary by Egert Pohlmann and Martin L. West, Oxford-New York, Oxford University Press, 2001.

Pryer 2007
Pryer, Anthony. 'Approaching Monteverdi: His Cultures and Ours', in: *The Cambridge Companion to Monteverdi*, edited by John Whenham and Richard Wistreich, Cambridge, Cambridge University Press, 2007 (Cambridge Companions to Music), pp. 1-19.

Quantz 1966
Quantz, Johann Joachim. *On Playing the Flute*, (1752), translated by Edward R. Riley, London, Faber and Faber, 1966.

Saccone 1983
Saccone, Eduardo. '*Grazia, Sprezzatura, Affettazione* in the *Courtier*', in: *Castiglione: The Ideal and the Real in Renaissance Culture*, edited by Robert Hanning and David Rosand, New Haven, Yale University Press, 1983, pp. 45-67.

Schenker 1903
Schenker, Heinrich. *Ein Beitrag zur Ornamentik: als Einführung zu Ph. Em. Bachs Klavierwerken*, Vienna, Universal Edition, 1903.

Schopenhauer 1960
Schopenhauer, Arthur. *Essay on the Freedom of the Will*, translated by Konstantin Kolenda, New York, Bobbs-Merrill, 1960.

Seeger 1958
Seeger, Charles. 'Prescriptive and Descriptive Music Writing', in: *The Musical Quarterly*, xliv/2 (April 1958), pp. 184-195.

Strunk 1998
Strunk, Oliver. *Source Readings in Music History*, revised edition by Leo Treitler, New York, W. W. Norton, 1998 (Books that Live in Music).

Whitmore 1991
Whitmore, Philip. *Unpremeditated Art: The Cadenza in the Classical Keyboard Concerto*, Oxford, Clarendon Press, 1991 (Oxford Monographs on Music).

«Sostener si può la battuta, etiandio in aria»

Testi e contesti per comprendere l'invenzione e la disposizione del discorso musicale nel repertorio strumentale italiano fra Seicento e Settecento

Laura Toffetti
(Conservatoire de Musique H. Dutilleux, Belfort / Conservatoire de Musique H. Dreyfus, Mulhouse)

Premessa

Il dibattito sulla relazione tra musica, *ratio* logico-matematica, natura umana e soggettività ha caratterizzato la storia della musica da che se ne ha memoria e alimenta ancora oggi interessanti riflessioni in contesti scientifici diversi.

Nell'ambito di questa vasta discussione, la partitura barocca, intesa come insieme di segni appartenenti a un codice preciso, rappresenta un significativo terreno di scambio, soprattutto qualora si accetti di considerarla come un'emanazione del pensiero cristiano medievale, per cui ogni forma altro non è se non il rivestimento di un'idea che assegna all'arte in generale, come alla dottrina stessa, un carattere universale e la funzione di rappresentare il mondo nella sua globalità.

Vincenzo Galilei, figura di grande rilievo durante il periodo di affermazione della rivoluzione scientifica operatasi in Italia tra la fine del '500 e l'inizio del '600, fornisce, ad esempio, un'interessante analisi della pagina musicale barocca e, per estensione, della genesi della composizione musicale stessa. Ricalcando le orme di Leonardo da Vinci, il quale afferma che la pittura pre-esistendo al quadro nella mente del suo speculatore assurge a rango di vera scienza, nelle sue teorizzazioni Galieli afferma il sussistere, prima di tutto, dell'immagine musicale nella mente del compositore:

> Quando vorrete intavolare qual si voglia cantilena, esaminate prima molto bene qual sia stata l'intenzione del Compositore di essa, et poi cercate con il vostro sano giudizio d'intender non solo quello che dice, ma ben spesso quello che ha voluto dire[1].

Gli scritti di Leonardo chiariscono, inoltre, che la pittura non solo rappresenta l'universo, ma che essa è in grado di farlo in modo da permettere al pubblico di identificare in

[1]. Galilei 1568, p. 28.

maniera inequivocabile i soggetti rappresentati, assumendo, quindi, il ruolo di strumento di trasmissione delle idee: «l'occhio, che si dice finestra dell'anima, è la principal via donde il comune senso pò più copiosamente e magnificamente considerare le infinite opere de natura»[2].

Nel caso della musica, definita dallo stesso da Vinci quale «sorella minore della pittura» perché «si va consumando mentre ch'ella nasce» e che «s'eterna [solo] collo scriverla»[3], la comunicazione dei significati passa attraverso l'operare del 'musico prattico', incaricato della decodificazione dei segni e della conseguente comunicazione dei significati.

Le indicazioni che Vincenzo Galilei fornisce nel trattato *Fronimo, Dialogo di Vincentio Galilei fiorentino nel quale si contengono le vere et necessarie regole del intavolare la musica nel liuto*, permettono di meglio comprendere la centralità, l'importanza del ruolo e la responsabilità nella mediazione affidata alla figura che oggi chiamiamo interprete:

> [...] non vi venisse in animo volervi difendere con la sciocca scusa di alcuni, i quali dicono non essere tenuti a far più di quello che trovano stampato o scritto, perché quando ei volessero ciò osservare, non havrebbono a fare il semitono in quelle cadentie, dove rare volte per non dir mai, si trova segnato [...][4].

È importante ricordare che, nell'organizzazione medievale del sapere, solo la teoria musicale, la quale non considerava l'aspetto fisico dei fenomeni sonori, apparteneva alle arti liberali del *quadrivium*, mentre l'*ars cantus* e la *musica instrumentalis*, attività esclusivamente artigianali, erano considerate alla stregua di *artes serviles*. Vincenzo Galilei, sostenitore della nuova visione del mondo basata sull'osservazione diretta della natura come unica via capace di formulare le leggi che ordinano i fenomeni, 'sporca' l'opera teorica con le mani del 'musico prattico', legittimando, all'interno della relazione tra arte e scienza, la presenza e l'individualità dell'interprete dei segni che compongono il codice musicale.

Dal momento in cui le consonanze non sono più considerate pitagoriche manifestazioni dell'armonia del mondo ma risultato dell'interazione tra vibrazioni della corda o dell'aria con il sistema percettivo, si realizza l'importante spostamento della musica dal cielo alla terra, dalla magia dei numeri alla materialità del suono percepito dall'individuo.

Oggi un numero sempre più elevato di partiture di quest'epoca appare in pubblicazioni moderne, consegnando agli esecutori un patrimonio che, sebbene indubbiamente sempre più conosciuto, si presta ancora a esecuzioni inappropriate o monche.

L'edizione moderna, infatti, porta con sé una carica simbolica legata ad altre epoche e ad altri stili, più recenti e strettamente legati a modelli di interpretazione basati sulla fedele

---

[2]. Da Vinci 1890, parte i, i/15.

[3]. *Ibidem*, parte i, i/27.

[4]. Galilei 1568, p. 28.

riproduzione dei segni scritti, considerati, oggi, se non del tutto esaustivi del fatto sonoro, per lo meno in grado di suggerirne tutte le caratteristiche necessarie.

La scrittura musicale barocca, invece, si rivela, all'attenta lettura delle fonti, carente di indicazioni interpretative: sono rare le indicazioni dinamiche o agogiche, spesso totalmente assenti quelle relative alle articolazioni o al fraseggio. Questo aspetto, che solo a un'analisi superficiale appare effetto di un sapere primitivo o incompleto, cela, in verità, una vasta scelta di possibilità interpretative. L'apparente ambivalenza, in parte dovuta alla tecnica ancora rudimentale della stampa musicale, è conseguenza di due ragioni diverse e complementari. La prima, come già si è intuito dalle parole di Vincenzo Galilei, è legata alla prassi esecutiva barocca, che lasciava all'esecutore ampio spazio per l'arricchimento del testo scritto. La seconda, indubbiamente più importante ai fini di questa ricerca poiché direttamente connessa al processo della codificazione del pensiero musicale, è implicita alla genesi della composizione stessa, che si struttura grazie alle regole e alle consuetudini della retorica classica più che a quelle delle diverse teorie musicali.

Appare, quindi, evidente la necessità di arricchire queste musiche, la cui forma scritta è chiaramente 'non finita', con quelle informazioni che permettono la corretta comprensione del suo contenuto originario, elaborando un'ipotesi di 'ricostruzione' basata sull'analisi dettagliata non solo dei testimoni e delle teorie musicali dell'epoca, ma anche delle convenzioni editoriali ed esecutive. Situare la ricerca su questi repertori all'interno del loro contesto intellettuale e individuare le interazioni tra le diverse discipline coesistenti in quella cultura umanistica che, ancora nel primo Seicento, coniugava erudizione e oralità rappresenta quindi, a mio avviso, la chiave di volta per la comprensione della partitura di quest'epoca, al fine di poter capire e valutare i segni e restituirne i significati.

La pagina musicale diventa, così, il prezioso, anche se virtuale, luogo di incontro tra il musicologo e il musicista: dove le ricerche dell'uno assumono un assetto definitivo, inizia il percorso dell'altro e ciò non tanto per affrontare le necessità tecnico-esecutive, quanto per risolvere i quesiti posti proprio dal dover scegliere i processi adatti alla decodificazione del testo scritto.

Il procedimento di ricostruzione può considerarsi, allora, l'omologo musicale del restauro in materia d'arte o d'architettura. Purtroppo, però, se in questi ambiti la natura e l'utilità di qualsiasi intervento sono oggi facilmente comprensibili, al contrario la riflessione sulla qualità della restituzione dei monumenti musicali non è ancora altrettanto matura, concentrandosi spesso su metodologie esclusivamente pertinenti alla loro forma scritta. Inoltre, e forse proprio per questa ragione, solo un numero ristretto di addetti ai lavori è cosciente che questa forma di 'restauro musicale' è indispensabile ai fini di una corretta divulgazione della composizione del passato.

Si considerano quindi, per questa ricerca che si limita al repertorio strumentale e più precisamente violinistico delle scuole italiane tra Sei e Settecento, i risultati dei lavori di quelle discipline che, contrariamente alla musica, la quale non possiede alcuna fonte primaria (avendo per ovvie ragioni ereditato solo trascrizioni e nessuna fonte sonora), hanno la fortuna di disporre dell'oggetto della loro indagine, quali musicologia, storia dell'arte, architettura, retorica o linguistica.

La partitura barocca: chiavi di lettura

Se «l'occhio è la finestra dell'anima», come dice Leonardo, quali sono le immagini e le idee che influenzano il compositore? Qual è il contesto nel quale egli sviluppa la partitura scritta e quali sono i significati protetti da questo codice? Qual è di conseguenza il raggio d'azione del 'musico prattico', quanto può e deve, cioè, arricchire la lettura della musica, ossia quali e quanti tipi di improvvisazione devono essere considerati dall'esecutore odierno?

Si è già chiarito come la partitura barocca, primo strumento di 'registrazione' dei suoni, assolva principalmente la funzione di trasmettere la composizione allo scopo di conservarla e renderla eterna.

Questo processo si esplicita attraverso due percorsi complementari: il primo ha origine nel pensiero musicale e individua, all'interno della propria matrice culturale, i segni adatti alla trascrizione sulla pagina di altezze e durate dei suoni percepiti (percorso musica-immagine); il secondo attinge più alla sfera delle arti visive, poiché teso a sviluppare un modello di organizzazione spaziale delle figure musicali che favorisca l'evocazione del discorso attraverso un itinerario opposto al primo, ossia dalla figura all'idea musicale (percorso immagine-musica). Individuare gli archetipi di questo processo permette al musicista odierno di decodificare lo spartito in modo più pertinente e, di conseguenza, di comprenderne più in profondità il pensiero.

Confrontando la partitura con un monumento istoriato, ad esempio, è facile evincere che anche le figure musicali, come le immagini che compongono il bassorilievo, ossia i segni appartenenti al codice, possano, in contesti diversi, avere valore esclusivamente decorativo, ma anche simbolico e semantico. Sappiamo che durante tutto il Medioevo, la rappresentazione di storie, principalmente bibliche, assolve un'importante funzione non solo di ornamentazione, ma anche sociale, pedagogica e divulgativa. Questa forma d'arte rappresenta, infatti, in una società ancora profondamente influenzata da modelli di trasmissione orale, la dimensione visiva del racconto, tanto quanto la partitura ne declina la variante musicale.

Diversamente dallo spazio architettonico, però, nel caso della pagina musicale la narrazione della 'storia' necessita di un interprete in grado di decodificare le figure e veicolarne i significati. Egli, nell'assumere il ruolo di traduttore, non solo si atterrà al contenuto della composizione nel suo duplice aspetto tecnico e semantico, ma dovrà considerare tutte le variabili che riguardano il tempo necessario alla sua condivisione.

Il discorso musicale così concepito, oltre a giustificare per ogni figura la relazione con un 'momento assoluto' esprimibile in termini matematici di durata, è sostanzialmente intonazione di figure sonore, le quali acquistano valore e interesse principalmente grazie alla loro disposizione nel tempo: l'anticipare o il ritardare gli elementi di una sequenza, il dire piano, forte, veloce, lento, l'interruzione brusca o preparata, il pronunciare, declamare, sillabare o sussurrare, il porre accenti, il respirare, l'attendere o il concitare dipendono, allora, più che dalla padronanza di teorie musicali, dall'uso di tecniche declamatorie che si riferiscono a eventi semantici e a fattori psicologici.

La *Response faite à un curieux sur le sentiment de la musique en Italie*[5] di André Maugars, nella quale il famoso virtuoso di viola da gamba descrive i sentimenti suscitatigli dall'ascolto della musica eseguita durante le celebrazioni per la solennità di S. Domenico, il 6 agosto 1639 nella Chiesa della Minerva a Roma, fornisce una testimonianza di questa prassi:

> C'est sans doute dans ces sorties agréables, où consiste tout le secret de l'Art; la Musique ayant ses figures aussi bien que la Rhétorique, qui ne tendent toutes qu'à charmer et tromper insensiblement l'Auditeur[6].

Un esempio di questo doppio ruolo della scrittura musicale (computo di valori e organizzazione di distanze), più tardo ma eloquente e emblematico di questa cultura musicale, è rappresentato dall'inizio della Sonata Op. 5 n. 1 di Arcangelo Corelli.

Ex. 1: versione originale e ornata delle prime battute della Sonata Op. 5 n. 1 nell'appendice della stampa di Estienne Roger (Amsterdam 1710).

Qui minime e semiminime assumono un valore più simbolico che quantitativo (suono di apertura di un ciclo di sonate, *finalis* del *Protus*, contenitore di vaste figure ornamentali sottintese) e si prestano a esecuzioni che nulla hanno a che vedere con la durata misurabile dal moderno metronomo, soprattutto considerando l'importante dato

5. Maugars 1639.

6. *Ibidem*, p. 3 («come la retorica, la musica ha le sue figure che tendono tutte ad incantare e ingannare l'auditore, ingannandolo inavvertitamente»). Anche in Maugars 1985.

che uno strumento capace di calcolare il tempo in musica sarebbe stato realizzato solo alla fine del XVII secolo, non in Italia, ed esclusivamente allo scopo di permettere l'esecuzione, in assenza del compositore, di un brano musicale alla velocità da lui immaginata:

> Éléments ou principes de musique, [...] Avec l'estampe, la description & l'usage du chronometre ou Instrument de nouvelle invention par le moyen duquel, les compositeurs de musique pourront désormais marquer le veritable mouvement de leurs compositions & leurs ouvrages marquez par rapport à cet instrument, se pourront executer en leur absence comme s'ils en battoient eux-mesmes la mesure[7].

Da queste considerazioni si evince che l'interprete deve saper restituire il messaggio codificato secondo i criteri che erano all'origine della sua creazione. Questi criteri, per quanto riguarda il ritmo, non corrispondono alle regole del moderno solfeggio (alle quali la partitura odierna fa naturalmente riferimento), ma a quelle dell'organizzazione del discorso, ossia della retorica classica.

Teoria delle proporzioni *versus* estetica della diminuzione

Oltre alla preoccupazione di descrivere e condividere i fenomeni, il pensiero rinascimentale è pervaso dalla ricerca di un'estetica capace di conciliare aspetti ed elementi diversi di una stessa realtà. La teoria delle proporzioni, che presenta lo spazio come la dimensione della relazione tra le cose ed è fondamento del concetto umanistico di bellezza come «accordo e armonia delle parti in relazione al tutto»[8], rappresenta un ulteriore principio intorno al quale si articola il dialogo tra il mondo della musica e quello degli spazi architettonici che lo ospitano. Se nell'ambito delle arti figurative e dell'architettura questo canone estetico definisce la relazione tra le parti e il tutto come armonia delle forme[9], in musica esso stabilisce anche le basi del sistema notazionale, affermando la necessità di rispettare determinati principi aritmetici.

Così, Giovanni Maria Bononcini, ne *Il Musico prattico* ribadisce, ancora nel 1673, questo concetto: «La proporzione (lasciando altre cose, che non fanno al nostro proposito) altro non è, (secondo il Crivellati nelli suoi Discorsi Musicali Capitolo secondo) che una comparazione di numero a numero[...]»[10].

---

7. Loulié 1696, p. 1.
8. Alberti 1847, p. 239.
9. A proposito della Basilica di Santa Maria Novella a Firenze: «L'intero edificio sta rispetto alle sue parti principali nel rapporto di uno a due, vale a dire nella relazione musicale dell'ottava, e questa proporzione si ripete nel rapporto tra la larghezza del piano superiore e quella dell'inferiore [...]». Wittkower 1964, p. 48.
10. Bononcini 1673, p. 3. Crivellati 1624.

Secondo questa teoria, il 'bello' si configura come simmetria degli elementi che compongono un insieme: nella bellezza armonica, la molteplicità di questi elementi viene ricondotta a unità; un'idea, però, mai disgiunta da quella di misura fra i diversi elementi di un'opera.

Se questa teoria è universalmente accettata in ambiti quali la pittura o l'architettura, basti pensare all'attenzione portata dagli artisti allo studio della sezione aurea e al conseguente condizionamento esercitato sulla vita di tutti i giorni dal gran numero di immagini costruite secondo questo principio, meno evidente appare l'influenza esercitata sul mondo musicale. Ciò nonostante, oltre ai numerosi esempi forniti dall'analisi formale delle opere di quest'epoca e a osservazioni di tipo organologico, quali ad esempio il rilevare che Stradivari costruì il suo violino racchiudendone la forma in quattro poligoni regolari, negli scritti del teorico Gioseffo Zarlino sulla notazione l'origine filosofico-scientifica appare chiara:

> Dico adunque ch'essendo la breve madre e generatrice di qualunque altra figura cantabile, è di bisogno primieramente ragionar de tutti quelli accidenti che possono accascare intorno a lei, percioché gli antichi le attribuirono il tempo. Laonde dico che in questo luogo io non chiamo tempo quello che significa lo stato buono o la buona fortuna d'alcuno, come quando si dice: «Francesco è uomo di buon tempo», cioè mena tranquilla e lieta vita; né meno quella buona temperatura d'aria, come si suol dire: «Oggi è buon tempo», cioè oggi è giorno sereno, chiaro e lieto; neanco nomino tempo quello che 'l filosofo definisce esser numero o misura di movimento o d'alcun'altra cosa successiva; ma dico tempo, secondo la definizione degli antichi musici, essere una certa e determinata quantità de figure minori, contenute o considerate in una breve. E questo tempo è di due maniere, perfetto e imperfetto[11].

L'avvento della *musica mensurabilis* aveva, quindi, risolto già da tempo il problema della struttura ritmica, proponendo un sistema di proporzioni che permettono di stabilire, grazie a un elevato numero di segni e di combinazioni di segni, a regole, misure e alla considerazione di numerose eccezioni, il tempo dell'esecuzione e il valore proporzionale dei suoni, senza però fornire sufficienti informazioni circa la loro distanza reciproca.

Un'ulteriore considerazione per la decodificazione di questa notazione da parte del musicista odierno consiste nel riflettere sulla pratica di assumere come unità di misura per l'esecuzione il valore più piccolo, mentre risulta chiaro, alla lettura delle parole di Zarlino, che il riferimento era quello alla figura 'di contenimento', da lui identificata con la breve.

A sostegno di questa affermazione, è sufficiente osservare la struttura dei numerosi trattati di diminuzione apparsi dall'inizio del '500 e fino ai primi decenni del '600, dai quali si evince, oltre ad alcune indicazioni tecnico-stilistiche fondamentali per chiunque

11. Zarlino 1558, 'Del Tempo, del Modo, & della Prolazione', parte iii, cap. 67.

si interessi alla prassi esecutiva, l'informazione che la composizione musicale era tributaria di un'operazione di 'ricostruzione attiva' da parte dell'esecutore attraverso la pratica estemporanea dei passaggi, ossia quelle formule create per riempire, appunto, le figure estese del canto.

Senza soffermarmi, per ovvie ragioni di tempo e spazio, sull'analisi di queste opere già ampiamente discusse[12], è interessante osservare, nell'analisi delle relazioni tra la musica e il suo contesto culturale, che l'assetto editoriale e dell'impaginazione di queste opere rivelano lo sviluppo del pensiero estetico-scientifico tardo-rinascimentale dalla summa medievale, cioè quella forma chiusa e compiuta che propone una visione del mondo rassicurante davanti all'infinito, verso, la lista, ossia l'enumerazione, un concetto lineare ed estraneo, cioè, a ogni rapporto di gerarchia, che proietta il sapere, nella dimensione dell'infinito e dell'*et-cætera*[13].

Teoria degli affetti e notazione

Alle soglie della seconda pratica e dell'emergere delle esigenze di grande espressività teorizzate nell'ambito della nuova estetica sviluppatasi dopo i lavori della Camerata de' Bardi e gli scritti dei fratelli Monteverdi[14], questa notazione musicale, inizia ad andare 'stretta':

> [...] il modo di comporre in tal maniera (mensurata) non solamente non è utile ma anco dannoso, per la perdita del tempo ch'è più prezioso d'ogni altra cosa, e che i punti, le linee, i circoli, i semicircoli e altre cose simili, che si dipingono in carte, sono sottoposte al sentimento del vedere e non a quello dell'udito; e sono cose considerate dal geometra; ma i suoni e le voci (come quelli che veramente sono il proprio oggetto dell'udito, dai quali nasce ogni buona consonanza e ogni armonia) sono principalmente dal musico considerate, ancora che consideri per accidente eziandio molt'altre cose[15].

e ancora

> [...] si deve il cantore di stare attento a considerare mille chimere che cadono sotto il Modo, il Tempo, la Prolazione, le note nere, i vari tipi di punto; essendo che se facesse altrimenti, sarebbe reputato un Goffo ed un Ignorante[16].

12. A titolo di esempio si veda Gatti 2014, pp. 71-188.
13. Eco 2009, p. 18.
14. Monteverdi 1605.
15. Zarlino 1558, 'Dell'utile che apportano i mostrati accidenti nelle buone armonie', parte iii, cap. 71.
16. *Ibidem*.

Dalle parole di Gioseffo Zarlino, e nonostante le accese polemiche di cui l'Artusi si fa interprete, si evince che il dato quantitativo della notazione cinquecentesca, quella nozione di misura di cui si è parlato in precedenza, non fornisce più elementi sufficienti all'esecuzione di un repertorio nel quale si va affermando l'ideale monteverdiano di una musica che esce dal gioco astratto dei rapporti aritmetici, proponendosi invece di riprodurre e dipingere le passioni umane.

Anche Nicola Vicentino, noto compositore, ma soprattutto famoso teorico della musica, lamenta in modo ancora più esplicito l'inadeguatezza del sistema di notazione misurata, incapace di esprimere le importanti indicazioni esecutive relative alla dinamica, al carattere, ma soprattutto all'agogica:

> [...] qualche volta si usa un certo ordine di procedere nella composizione che non si può scrivere, come sono il dir piano e forte, il dir presto e tardo e, secondo le parole, muover la misura per dimostrare gli affetti delle passioni, delle parole e delle armonie [...][17].

Ex. 2: Biagio Marini, 'Sonata quarta per il violino per suonar con due corde', in: *Sonate e Symphonie a 1, 2, 3, 4, 5 e 6 voci*, Op. 8, Venezia, appresso Bartolomeo Magni, 1624.

Un riscontro pratico di questa importante affermazione si trova in due sonate di Biagio Marini, l'Op. 8 e l'Op. 22, stampate a Venezia rispettivamente nel 1629 e 1655, nelle quali i termini «presto» e «tardo» vengono aggiunti sotto le note, oltre alle più frequenti indicazioni quali «affetti» «groppo» «piano» o «forte» o «dolcemente»[18].

Sempre in ambito romano, Giovanni Battista Doni, studioso di musica, uomo di eccezionale cultura e segretario del Collegio dei Cardinali presso Francesco Barberini, afferma in modo chiaro che il violinista che suona in teatro deve far prova di un'interpretazione ritmica delle note che trascenda le ordinarie conoscenze musicali, come oggi le intendiamo:

17. Vicentino 1555, p. 89.

18. Marini 1626: nella *Sonata prima a due violini* appare il termine «affetti» (nella parte staccata del vl i); nella *Sonata quarta per suonar con due corde* appaiono i termini «presto», «tardo» e «affetti» (nella parte staccata del violino e del BC). Marini 1655: nella *Sonata per due violini* appare il termine «dolcemente» (nelle parti staccate del vl i, vl ii e BC); nella *Sonata per violino e basso* appare il termine «affetti» (nella parte staccata del vl i).

> Sopra questa base poi dovrà il violino fabricare le sue diminuzioni, come più gl'aggradirà, [...] per far spiccare massimamente le consonanze in quelle sillabe accentuate, con qualche nota un poco più lunghetta; perché anco nel parlare ordinario tali sillabe si sogliono talvolta allungare più dell'altre [...][19].

Doni descrive qui un metodo di lettura della partitura secondo una logica ritmica mutuata all'arte del discorso; un modo di procedere, cioè, in parte intuitivo, basato sull'organizzazione delle figure musicali come fossero parole e che fa riferimento al pensiero musicale quale fonte primaria, di cui la pagina scritta è l'incompleta rappresentazione.

La musica dipinge le passioni

> Il dire dunque che la battuta per se stessa formi diversità di ritmi, è fuor d'ogni ragione; come sarebbe chi dicesse che i diftongi consistino nella scrittura, e non nella pronuntia[20].

Per Doni il ritmo della recitazione, e come abbiamo visto dell'esecuzione strumentale, è un parametro molto importante al quale egli dedica, nella sua produzione, tempo e attenzione nei confronti di ogni dettaglio.

Anche Vincenzo Giustiniani, mecenate e collezionista d'arte, noto soprattutto per aver contribuito alla fama del Caravaggio, nel *Discorso sopra la musica dei suoi tempi* accorda notevole importanza alla trattazione delle tematiche relative alle esecuzioni musicali e all'interpretazione, conciliando, però, il principio della proporzione aritmetica con la descrizione del sentimento, contenuto, questo, destinato ad acquisire uno spazio sempre maggiore, nonostante l'impossibilità di misurarne i limiti. Autentico compositore è, dunque, secondo l'erudito romano, «colui che possiede tanto la conoscenza delle regole e le giuste proporzioni dei numeri», quanto «la pratica degli effetti che da queste derivano negli animi degli uomini»[21].

Ecco chiarita la nuova concezione del musicista che, come l'artista, determina d'ora in poi, in modo sempre più autonomo e soggettivo, l'orientamento culturale del proprio lavoro. In altri termini, anche la musica, come ogni attività scientifica, diventa un processo di conoscenza il cui fine ultimo è la conoscenza stessa.

Utilizzando ancora una volta il procedimento dell'analogia, proprio l'osservazione della produzione pittorica di uno degli artisti più amati da Giustiniani, Michelangelo Merisi da Caravaggio, mette in luce il passaggio, avvenuto contemporaneamente in musica e pittura, verso un'estetica che si carica di significati psicologici e drammatici.

---

19. Doni 1640a, p. 372.
20. *Ibidem*.
21. Giustiniani 1981, p. 19.

Ill. 1: Michelangelo Merisi da Caravaggio (1571-1610), *Giuditta e Oloferne* (1597), Galleria nazionale di arte antica, Palazzo Barberini, Roma.

Ill. 2: Fede Galizia (1578-1630), *Giuditta con la testa di Oloferne* (1596), John and Mable Ringling Museum of Art Sarasota, Florida USA.

L'estremo realismo e la teatralizzazione nell'uso della luce hanno un influsso evidente sul ritmo dei dipinti caravaggeschi, rendendo i contorni più malleabili, come in una frase musicale nella quale si suona «con qualche nota un po' più lunghetta»[22].

Caravaggio, a Roma, frequentava gli stessi ambienti in cui i musicisti erano soliti prodursi e nei dipinti che eseguì per i suoi committenti appare sulla tavolozza un nuovo soggetto: la musica. Egli, trascrivendo in termini pittorici le stesse tematiche che animavano i salotti e le accademie musicali, testimonia di quell'intenso dibattito interdisciplinare tra artisti e intellettuali che aveva portato ai profondi mutamenti stilistici, e quindi esecutivi, annunciati, per quanto riguarda la nuova moda musicale, dai fratelli Monteverdi[23].

22. *Ibidem*.

23. A questo proposito è interessante il volume De Pascale – Macioce 2012, che promuove un proficuo confronto tra gli studi di storia dell'arte e quelli di musicologia, in relazione alle diverse metodologie d'indagine.

Comparando la *Giuditta e Oloferne* di Caravaggio (ILL. 1) e la *Giuditta con la testa di Oloferne* di Fede Galizia (ILL. 2), due dipinti anche cronologicamente vicini, è facile cogliere la volontà caravaggesca di liberare il soggetto da ogni ornamento per fissare il fuoco sulla natura dell'uomo. Questa stessa esigenza viene espressa da Giulio Caccini nella prefazione alle *Nuove Musiche*: «I passaggi sono stati ritrovati per gli orecchi di quelli che meno intendono che cosa sia cantare con affetto […]»[24].

La produzione musicale evolve, così, dalla prassi dell'ornare e dell'abbellire con gusto a quella del descrivere, dell'esprimere con introspezione. Questa trasformazione, percepibile in modo intuitivo all'osservazione dell'opera pittorica, è registrata in modo chiaro dallo stesso Giustiniani, il quale descrive musici di entrambe la categorie, ossia gli antichi, che

> […] facevano a gare […] nell'ornamento di esquisiti passaggi tirati in opportuna congiuntura e non soverchi […] e di più col moderare e crescere la voce forte o piano, assottigliandola o ingrossandola […] ora tirando passaggi lunghi, seguiti bene, spiccati, ora gruppi, ora a salti, ora con trilli lunghi, ora con brevi […] e principalmente con azzione del viso, e de' sguardi e de' gesti che accompagnavano appropriatamente la musica e li concetti […][25].

e i moderni

> […] perché avendo lasciato lo stile passato, che era assai rozzo, et anche li soverchi passaggi con li quali si ornava, attendono ora per lo più ad uno stile recitativo ornato di grazia et ornamenti appropriate al concetto […] e sopra tutto con far bene intendere le parole, applicando ad ogni sillaba una nota or piano or forte, or adagio, or presto[26].

LA MELODIA 'ELOQUENTE'

Anche il naturalismo caravaggesco è quindi impregnato dalla progressiva tendenza a scrutare la natura, spesso quella umana, nei minimi dettagli: questo nuovo modo di concepire l'arte implica, nel caso della composizione musicale, il graduale abbandono di quella forma di improvvisazione sul testo rappresentata dall'aggiunta dei passaggi, così simili all'ordinato apparato ornamentale e simbolico di Fede Galizia, in favore di una lettura della partitura che si espleta nella libertà agogica come eco di una natura umana il cui intelletto è in continuo movimento. L'interpretazione di questa partitura non è, però, arbitraria, ma un'applicazione specifica degli insegnamenti tratti dall'*ars oratoria*.

---

24. CACCINI 1602, 'Ai lettori'.
25. GIUSTINIANI 1981, p. 22.
26. *Ibidem*, p. 31.

La nozione fondamentale che permette di studiare le caratteristiche della retorica, è contenuta nella definizione di *numerus*. Questo termine polisemantico ricorrente nei trattati dell'antichità e presso gli umanisti traduce il greco ρυθμός (ritmo, ordine) e designa qualità proprie alle arti visive, quali la proporzione e la simmetria di una statua e di una facciata, o il movimento armonioso del gesto teatrale e pittorico, ma si riferisce anche alla poesia, regolando allora il concatenarsi dei piedi o delle sillabe lunghe e brevi nel *metrum*.

È necessario, però, specificare che il rapporto tra musica e retorica è di natura duplice. Le referenze fondamentali in questo campo per il mondo latino sono senza dubbio contenute negli scritti di Cicerone e Quintiliano. Quest'ultimo ci informa che le diverse concatenazioni metriche della poesia si sono sviluppate grazie alla misura percepita dall'orecchio sensibile dei poeti. È la musica quindi, che dà origine alla poesia, e in questo atto generatore trasmette al verso le sue qualità ritmiche[27].

Il rapporto con la prosa è, invece, più complesso. Contrariamente alla poesia, infatti, in una normale sequenza di parole, prosa o discorso, il susseguirsi di sillabe lunghe e brevi è inevitabilmente irregolare; ciononostante anche in questo caso viene percepita una forma di ritmicità dovuta non agli accenti o alle durate misurate in quantità di sillabe o semiminime, ma grazie alle relazioni di spazialità che vengono messe in gioco.

Dagli scritti di Cicerone si evince che l'eloquenza degli antichi poteva perdere il suo carattere austero e acquistare piacevolezza: «solo grazie all'introduzione di pause determinate non dalla stanchezza dell'oratore, né dai segni di punteggiatura, ma dalla misura ritmica delle parole e dei pensieri»[28].

E ancora:

> [...] se unire la prosa in versi è un errore, tuttavia l'oratore deve congiungere le parole in modo armonioso affinché combacino tra loro e abbiano la necessaria completezza ritmica, poiché nessuna cosa distingue maggiormente un oratore dall'uomo inabile a parlare, quanto il fatto che l'uomo inesperto butta fuori senza alcun ordine tutto ciò che gli viene in mente e misura ciò che dice sulla base del fiato e non dell'arte, mentre il vero oratore lega il pensiero con le parole in modo da stringerlo in un ritmo che è ad un tempo libero e obbligato. Infatti, dopo averlo vincolato in una determinata maniera e ritmo, allenta il freno e lo libera, mutando l'ordine delle parole, in modo che le parole non siano né legate ad una determinata legge ritmica, né libere così da poter andare dove vogliono[...][29].

A partire dagli ultimi decenni del '500 il rapporto di dipendenza del discorso dalla musica rappresenta il fulcro di interesse nelle opere di molti eruditi, i quali, come testimonia Giustiniani, erano formati anche all'arte della musica. Questa complessa relazione è da

---

27. Sueur 2013.
28. Cicerone 2005, Libro iii, p. 173.
29. *Ibidem*, Libro iii, pp. 175-176.

considerarsi, però, reciproca. Proprio l'influenza dell'*ars oratoria* sulla musica è, infatti, riconosciuta in svariate fonti, e ciò con riferimento tanto all'opera del compositore quanto al ruolo dell'esecutore. A questo proposito, fin dai primi anni del Seicento si sviluppa, per opera di alcuni teorici fra cui Athanasius Kircher o Joachim Burmeister, un'oratoria specificamente musicale. Quest'ultimo, appoggiandosi alla teoria di Quintiliano, scrive che «ciò che conta non è tanto la qualità della composizione, ma il modo in cui la comunichiamo, poiché è ascoltando che l'uomo si commuove»[30].

La notazione musicale, fallendo come abbiamo già osservato proprio laddove si deve portare la dimensione della comunicatività all'interno della forma, libera il campo all'interprete, che assume il ruolo di medio proporzionale tra l'aspetto visivo e quello contenutistico dell'opera del compositore. In Italia questa prassi dell'improvvisare raggiunge, secondo le testimonianze di cronisti e teorici, altissimi livelli di virtuosismo. Oltralpe, invece, mentre i viaggiatori francesi rimanevano stupiti dalla grande libertà dei musici italiani, la trattatistica tedesca assegnava il ruolo di mediazione alla forma scritta, compilando cataloghi di figure retoriche specificatamente musicali. È interessante ricordare che questo termine traduce il greco *schema* o *ordine*, o anche *euritmia*, cioè *bella apparenza*, ossia l'aspetto sontuoso, coerente, eloquente che si produce quando il rapporto tra le parti e il tutto è retto dalle leggi della simmetria.

Ex. 3: Giuseppe Colombi, *Sonata da camera*, Libro settimo, Mus. F277, Modena, Biblioteca Estense Universitaria[31].

A questo stadio della riflessione, solo l'ascolto comparato di brani eseguiti in modo 'eloquente' potrebbe elucidare i concetti esposti. In mancanza di questo supporto, si propone la trascrizione di una sonata di Giuseppe Colombi tratta dal *Libro VII*, nella quale si

30. Burmeister 1601, p. 5. *Cfr.* Quintiliano 2001.

31. L'esempio è tratto da Suess 1999, p. 152.

è palesata, attraverso la spazializzazione grafica, la qualità prosodica delle figure ornamentali, ossia il ritmo della recitazione, quella forma di improvvisazione musicale basata, cioè, sulla ripartizione 'eloquente' del materiale sonoro.

Ex. 4: Giuseppe Colombi, *Sonata da camera*, Libro settimo. L'esempio trascrive la disposizione delle figure scritte e ornamentali (a cura dell'autore) delle misure 1-3[32].

In questo tipo di processo creativo a quattro mani, il compositore, secondo i dettami dell'*ars oratoria* di Quintiliano, s'incarica dell'*inventio*, ossia dell'inventare o scegliere il tema musicale, mentre il compito dell'*elocutio*, ossia dell'individuare un repertorio di moduli espressivi, è affidato all'improvvisazione dell'interprete con la precisa finalità di muovere gli affetti.

A questo proposito Giulio Caccini, nella prefazione alle *Nuove musiche* precisa:

> [...] questi intendentissimi gentiluomini m'hanno sempre confortato [...] ad attenermi a quella maniera cotanto lodata da Platone et altri filosofi, che affermarono la musica altro non essere che la favella e il ritmo et il suono per ultimo [...] a volere che ella possa penetrare nell'altrui intelletto e fare quei mirabili effetti[33].

Nell'analisi della partitura composta secondo questi criteri non basta quindi esaminare la relazione tra le note e le parole, anche se sottintese, o calcolare le durate dei suoni rispetto a quelle delle sillabe, occorre piuttosto ricercare i criteri d'organizzazione e di ripartizione del discorso musicale.

La Sonata Op. 4 n. 6 di Antonio Pandolfi Mealli, *La Vinciolina*, è esemplificativa di come la composizione musicale barocca sia fondata su nuclei linguistico-semantici diversi per natura e funzione dalle figure ritmiche alle quali siamo oggi abituati, poiché basati sull'imitazione di gesti verbali e non sull'assemblaggio matematico di valori ritmici. Quando il testo non c'è, infatti, ci si comporta come se fosse 'implicito', come chi, abituato a questa estetica vocale, ne abbia assimilato la prosodia applicandola spontaneamente al 'testo strumentale'.

La forma della Sonata Sesta, dedicata «Alla mia illustre Signora Teodora Vincioli mia signora singolarissima» si presta, inoltre, a un'esecuzione preceduta, nella tradizione retorica di questo repertorio, da un'intonazione libera e improvvisata, un'introduzione preludiata,

32. La sonata è contenuta nel CD *Duo in Rondeau, Dance Music at the Court of Francesco d'Este*, Ensemble *Antichi Strumenti*, Stradivarius, 2006, STR33764.

33. Caccini 1602.

cioè, nello stile dell'*exordium* di Quintiliano. L'uso del preludio come anticipazione è infatti, non a caso, strettamente legato alla logica del tempo inteso come spazio di esperienze (sonore) e di riflessione, di memoria e di apprendimento, in grado anche di costruire nuovi inizi.

Oltre a curarsi dell'*elocutio*, l'interprete assume, in questo caso, anche il compito della *dispositio*, cioè del predisporre il piano di svolgimento dell'opera, partecipando quindi attivamente al processo di creazione dell'opera stessa.

Pandolfi Mealli, come spesso accadeva agli strumentisti di quest'epoca, era vicino alla sfera dei cantori: lo stile vocale e recitativo delle sue sonate ne sono, infatti, una testimonianza, e la Sonata IV è un buon esempio di quanto Giovanni Battista Doni esprime nel suo *Discorso sopra il Violino Diarmonico*[34]:

> Tra tutti gli strumenti musicali, meravigliosa è veramente la voce del violino [...] e che meglio esprime la voce humana non solo nel canto, ma nella favella istessa [...] tanto più che noi udiamo talvolta esprimere col Violino alcuni accenti e parole che par proprio ch'eschino dalla bocca humana [...].

Gli elementi compositivi di questa sonata — come la figura melodica ascendente o discendente, lenta o rapida, breve o estesa e la disposizione degli intervalli — devono quindi essere considerati come strutture semantiche minime che, giustapposte nel tempo e distanziate tra loro in base al potenziale drammatico, costruiscono il discorso musicale secondo le regole della retorica.

Girolamo Frescobaldi, organista e compositore citato da Maugars nella sua cronaca per le «mille sorte d'invenzioni sopra il suo clavicembalo, sopra delle note tenute ferme dall'organo»[35], appone all'edizione delle *Toccate Libro Primo* (Frescobaldi 1616/1637) numerose indicazioni di grande aiuto per l'interprete, dalle quali si evince l'importanza da lui attribuita proprio alla prosodia nell'esecuzione anche strumentale:

> Nelle Partite quando si troveranno passaggi et affetti sarà bene di pigliare il tempo largo; il che osservarassi anche nelle toccate. L'altre non passeggiate si potranno sonare alquanto allegre di battuta, rimettendosi al buon gusto e fino giuditio del sonatore il guidar il tempo; nel qual consiste lo spirito e la perfettione di questa maniera e stile di sonare[36] [...].
>
> Primieramente che non dee questo modo di sonare stare soggetto a battuta [...] perché la perfettione di sonare principalmente consiste nell'intendere i tempi[37].

---

34. Doni 1640b, p. 337.
35. Maugars 1639, p. 6, traduzione dell'autore del presente saggio.
36. Frescobaldi 1637, 'Avvertimenti'.
37. *Ibidem*.

Conclusione

Come in tutte le forme d'espressione, è la comunicazione a svolgere, in ultima istanza, il ruolo decisivo. Roman Jakobson, in uno studio sui disturbi del linguaggio, afferma che l'atto comunicativo implica la selezione di alcune entità semantiche e la loro combinazione in unità più complesse[38]. Durante lo scambio di informazioni, prosegue, il mittente e il suo ascoltatore sono legati dall'impiego di un codice comune, costituito, appunto, da tali sequenze, il cui significato non può essere dedotto dalla semplice somma di ogni componente lessicale: il tutto non è, quindi, uguale alla somma delle parti.

Nel caso della restituzione musicale, questo codice si costruisce grazie alla relazione di contiguità dei suoni trattati come eventi semantici, alla ripartizione, cioè, della frase musicale in periodi comprensibili e non attraverso la riproduzione di valori musicali ritmati in modo matematico.

L'esecuzione che si adegua a queste regole[39] mostra come l'operazione di adattamento continuo delle durate e delle distanze del materiale sonoro sia particolarmente funzionale alla sintassi del discorso musicale.

La distanza tra le figure, paragonabili alle parole che insieme formano le frasi e i pensieri musicali, assume un'importanza predominante rispetto al valore della nota stessa. Come la sintassi lega i pensieri e permette di comprendere il messaggio, così il ritmo 'eloquente', ossia il concatenamento delle formule musicali, risulta essere il procedimento adeguato all'interpretazione della composizione barocca.

Quando, viceversa, l'approccio al repertorio si focalizza sulla scrittura in senso stretto, cioè sulla lettura dei segni piuttosto che della relazione tra di essi, si genera un fenomeno di incomprensione. I linguisti definiscono questa alterazione della facoltà di combinare unità linguistiche più semplici (le note e le figure) in unità più complesse (le frasi) con il termine di 'agrammatismo', «la malattia che si manifesta con una degenerazione della frase in semplice mucchio di parole»[40].

Bibliografia

Testi antichi

Alberti 1847

Alberti, Leon Battista. *Arte edificatoria*, in: *Opere volgari*, vol. iv, Firenze, Tipografia Galileiana, 1847.

[38]. Jakobson 1976.

[39]. Si faccia riferimento, ad esempio alla *Sonata iv a Violino e Viola* di Pietro Sorosina, contenuta nel CD *Duo in Rondeau, Dance Music at the Court of Francesco d'Este*, citato.

[40]. Jakobson 1976, p. 36.

CICERONE 2005
CICERONE, Marco Tullio. *De Oratore*, a cura di Pietro Li Causi, Rosanna Marino e Marco Formisano, Alessandria, Dell'Orso, 2005 (Culture antiche, 28).

DA VINCI 1890
DA VINCI, Leonardo. *Trattato della pittura condotto sul Cod. Vaticano Urbinate 1270*, a cura di Gaetano Milanesi, Roma, Unione cooperativa editrice, 1890.

QUINTILIANO 2001
QUINTILIANO. *Institutio Oratoria*, a cura di Adriano Pennacini, Torino, Einaudi, 2001 (Biblioteca della Pleiade, 38), Libro IX.

Trattati

BONONCINI 1673
BONONCINI, Giovanni Maria. *Il musico prattico*, Bologna, Giacomo Monti, 1673.

BURMEISTER 2007
BURMEISTER, Joachim. 'Musica Autoschédiastikè (1601)', in: ID. *Musica Poetica (1606): augmentée des plus excellentes remarques tirées de Hypomnematum musicae poeticae (1599) et de Musica autoschédiastikè (1601)*, a cura di Agathe Sueur e Pascal Dubreuil, Wavre, Mardaga, 2007 (Ars musices iuxta variorum scriptorium. 1. Reinassance et période préclassique. Domaine germanique, 1).

CACCINI 1602
CACCINI, Giulio. *Le Nuove Musiche*, Firenze, Marescotti, 1602.

CRIVELLATI 1624
CRIVELLATI, Cesare. *Discorsi musicali, nelli quali si contengono non solo cose pertinenti alla teorica, ma etiandio alla pratica*, Viterbo, Agostino Discepoli, 1624.

DONI 1640A
DONI, Giovanni Battista. 'Discorso sesto sopra il Recitare in Scena con l'accompagnamento di strumenti musicali', in: ID. *Annotazioni sopra il compendio de' generi, e de' modi della musica* [...], Roma, Andrea Fei, 1640, pp. 359-379.

DONI 1640B
ID. 'Discorso sopra il Violino Diarmonico', in: ID. *Annotazioni sopra il compendio de' generi, e de' modi della musica* [...], *op. cit.*, pp. 337-358.

GALILEI 1568
GALILEI, Vincenzo. *Il Fronimo: dialogo di Vincentio Galilei fiorentino nel quale si contengono le vere et necessarie regole del intavolare la musica nel liuto*, Girolamo Scotto, Venezia, 1568.

GIUSTINIANI 1981
GIUSTINIANI, Vincenzo. 'Discorso sopra la musica dei suoi tempi', (Lucca 1628), in: *Discorsi sulle arti e sui mestieri*, a cura di Anna Banti, Firenze, Sansoni, 1981 (Raccolta di opere inedite e rare), pp. 15-36.

Loulié 1696
Loulié, Étienne. *Éléments ou principes de musique*, Parigi, Christoph Ballard, 1696.

Maugars 1639
Maugars, André. *Response faite à un curieux sur le sentiment de la musique en Italie, Rome, 1er octobre 1639*, Parigi, BnF, RES-V-2469 e 2471.

Maugars 1985
Id. 'Risposta data a un curioso sul sentimento della musica d'Italia', a cura di Jean Lionnet, in: *Nuova rivista musicale italiana*, xix/4 (1985), pp. 681-707.

Vicentino 1555
Vicentino, Nicola. *L'antica musica ridotta alla moderna prattica*, Roma, Antonio Barre, 1555.

Zarlino 1558
Zarlino, Gioseffo. *Le Istitutioni harmoniche*, Venezia, Pietro da Fino, 1558.

Musiche

Frescobaldi 1616/1637
Frescobaldi, Girolamo. *Toccate, e partite d'intavolatura di cimbalo* [...] *libro primo*, Roma, Nicolò Borbone, 1616.

Frescobaldi 1637
Id. *Il secondo libro di toccate canzone versi d'hinni Magnificat gagliarde correnti et altre partite d'intavolatura di cimbalo et organo*, Roma, Nicolò Borbone, 1637

Marini 1626
Marini, Biagio. *Sonate, symphonie, canzoni, passemezzi, baletti, corenti, gagliarde e retornelli: per ogni sorte d'instrumenti: opera ottava*, Venezia, Bartolomeo Magni, 1626.

Marini 1655
Id. *Diverse sonate da chiesa e da camera a due, tre e quattro*, Op 22, Libro iii, Venezia, Francesco Magni, 1655.

Monteverdi 1605
Monteverdi, Claudio. *Il v libro dei madrigali*, Venezia, Ricciardo Amadino, 1605.

Rognoni 1620
Rognoni, Francesco. *Selva di vari passaggi*, Milano, Filippo Lomazzo, 1620.

Testi moderni

De Pascale – Macioce 2012
La musica al tempo del Caravaggio, a cura di Enrico De Pascale e Stefania Macioce, Roma, Gangemi, 2012.

ECO 2009
ECO, Umberto. *Vertigine della lista*, Milano, Bompiani, 2009.

GATTI 2014
GATTI, Enrico. 'Però ci vuole pacientia', in: *Regole per ben suonare e cantare: diminuzioni e mensuralismo tra 16. e 19. secolo*, Pisa, ETS, 2014 (Quaderni del Conservatorio 'Giuseppe Verdi' di Milano, n.s. 2/2014), pp. 71-188.

JAKOBSON 1976
JAKOBSON, Roman. 'Due aspetti del linguaggio e due tipi di afasia', in: *Saggi di linguistica generale*, a cura di Luigi Heilmann, Milano, Feltrinelli, [3]1976 (Sc/10, 37), pp. 22-45.

SUESS 1999
SUESS, John G. 'Giuseppe Colombi's Dance Music for the Estense Court of Duke Francesco II di Modena', in: *Marco Uccellini. Atti del Convegno Marco Uccellini da Forlimpopoli e la sua musica (Forlimpopoli, 26-7 ottobre 1996)*, a cura di Maria Caraci Vela e Marina Toffetti, Lucca, LIM, 1999 (Strumenti della ricerca musicale), pp. 141-162.

SUEUR 2013
SUEUR, Agathe. *Le Frein et l'Aiguillon: éloquence musicale et nombre oratoire (16e-18e siècle)*, Parigi, Classique Garnier, 2013 (Renaissance latine, 2).

WITTKOWER 1964
WITTKOWER, Rudolf. *Principi architettonici nell'età dell'umanesimo*, traduzione italiana a cura di Renato Pedio, Torino, Einaudi, 1964.

Improvised Cadenzas in the Cello Sonatas Op. 5 by Francesco Geminiani

Rudolf Rasch
(Utrecht University)

Improvisation always has been a standard element of the performance of early music. This must have been the case in historical times, while it applies equally to today's performance practice. No score was or is ever performed exactly as it is written down, if only because of the many elements left undefined such as tempo and much of articulation, dynamics and ornamentation. Performers must fill in what the composer or the publisher (or the copyist) has left open. These 'unforeseen' elements could be called 'improvisation', but it is more in conformity with terminological practice to reserve this term for extra notes, not provided in the score.

These extra notes can be applied in two ways. First, they can be used to adorn or embellish the melody as written down, in the way of diminutions or figuration or written-out ornamentation, either in the form of notes with exact time values or as notes with undefined values. The second way to add notes to a composition is to play short separate passages that are inserted in to places that seem appropriate for such an elaboration. Additions of the second kind are called 'cadenzas', because they most often occur as a part of the final cadence of a movement. Cadenzas play an important role in the performance of solo concertos from the Classical and Romantic periods, but they have a history that goes much further back than the second half of the eighteenth century.

Johann Joachim Quantz

There is little attention to the cadenza in early eighteenth-century music theory. By far the most comprehensive account is found in Johann Joachim Quantz's *Versuch einer Anweisung, die Flöte traversière zu spielen* (Berlin, 1752). Quantz spends an entire chapter on the subject: 'Das xv. Hauptstück: Von den Cadenzen' (pp. 151-164); it is divided into 33 numbered short sections. These sections allow us to summarize his argument point by point:

1. A cadenza consists of «embellishments produced, in concerting parts, at the end of a piece, over the penultimate note, namely, the fifth over the tonic, according to the will and pleasure of the performer».

2. Introduced by the Italians fifty years ago (that is, around 1700). First, there were a few small passages and trills in the cadence, then, from «about between 1710 and 1716», the ordinary cadenza with a prolonged bass note under it came into use.

3. Cadenzas are probably invented by performers, not by composers.

4. Unfortunately, cadenzas are often added to movements where they do not belong.

5. The aim of a cadenza is to surprise the listener just before the end of the movement.

6. Many cadenzas are bad or inappropriate.

7. There are no strict rules for cadenzas.

8. Cadenzas must match the character of the movement.

9. Describes a one-voice cadenza: «They must be short and new, and surprise the listener, as a *bon mot*. Therefore they must sound like they were conceived of at the moment they are played. Do not be wasteful with them, but treat them as a good host; in particular when you have the same listener more often before you».

10. Because cadenzas are short, they must not have too many figures.

11. The repetition of figures more than once, such as in the following example, where two figures are repeated three times, is better avoided (Tabula XX, Fig. 1):

It is better to repeat figures only once and to insert other figures between the repeated ones (Fig. 2):

This one is also better because the metre is irregular. It is meant for an *Allegro*. For an *Adagio* one must extract the main notes (Fig. 3):

12. One must avoid repeats of figures on the same pitch.

13. Dissonances (that is, alterations) must be treated properly, that is, followed by their proper resolutions (Fig. 4):

14. Cadenzas can go to neighbouring keys, but one must be cautious. An example is given in a major key (F major), where by the application of alterations modulations to the fourth (B-flat major, at [a]) and fifth (C minor, at [b]) and the return to the main key (F major, at [c]) are inserted (Fig. 5):

A similar example is given for a minor key (G minor; Fig. 6):

15. A cheerful cadence has jumps, triplets and trills (Fig. 7)…

…a sad cadence has steps and dissonances (Fig. 8):

16. Cadenzas need not obey a regular time or metre.

17. Then comes Quantz's famous advice for the length of a cadenza: when for the voice or a wind instrument it must be possible to perform the cadenza on one breath; when for a stringed instrument there is no limit, but shortness is advised.

18. He does not provide written-out examples of perfect and fully-fledged cadences.

19-31. About cadenzas for two instruments (Figs. 9-14, Tab. XXI, Figs. 1-6).

32-33. About cadenzas when the movement ends on an imperfect cadence with a seventh-sixth suspension (Figs. 7-8):

34. Cadenzas for two instruments on an imperfect cadence (Fig. 9).

35. Cadenzas on words like "vado", "parto", and so on, as a kind of tone painting (Figs. 10-11).

36. The final trill in a cadenza, with a reference to Tabula xv, Fig. 21.

Quantz's cadenzas given for a perfect authentic cadence (Tabula xx, Figs. 2-8) could serve well as practical examples for today's performers, as also the one given for an imperfect cadence (Tabula xi, Fig. 8).

Arcangelo Corelli

Although Quantz states that in Corelli's sonatas there are no cadenzas (only written-out embellishments, as in the 1710 Amsterdam edition), yet the Sonatas Op. 5 provide two written-out examples of cadenzas on the penultimate note of a movement, just as in Quantz's definition. The second movement of Sonata 1 ends with an arpeggio passage concluded by a little flourish which together can be considered as a cadenza:

Note that the first sonority of the arpeggio passage is a 6/4 chord on the dominant.

The diminished-seventh chord on G-sharp that precedes is can be considered as a chord that prepares the cadenza.

The second movement of Sonata 3 concludes with a much longer but still quasi-improvisatory passage on the penultimate note, first with broken intervals, then with broken chords, everything above the penultimate note of the bass part:

After Corelli, many composers followed suit, and soon wrote cadenzas also without an underlying bass note, thereby creating a much wider tonal space. Well-known examples of large cadenzas are the harpsichord cadenza in the first movement of the Fifth Brandenburg Concerto of Johann Sebastian Bach, just before the last repeat of the ritornello, and the Capricci that Pietro Antonio Locatelli wrote for his violin Concertos Op. 3 published as *L'arte del violino* (Amsterdam, 1733). Less known is the extensive written-out cadenza that Willem de Fesch inserted in the first movement of his Violin Concerto in A minor Op. 3 no. 6 (published in Amsterdam in 1719), just before the final ritornello.

Francesco Geminiani

The *Sonate a violino, violone e cimbalo* by Francesco Geminiani, published in London in 1716, contain two written-out cadenzas, one in Sonata 2, the other one in Sonata 3. The cadenza that is found just before the end of the second movement of Sonata 2 is of a different type than those in Corelli's sonatas. It is different in two respects. First, it is an elaboration of the diminished-seventh chord on the raised fourth degree of the key, which functions as a secondary dominant, a chord that prepares the dominant, instead of a series of sonorities that start with a 6/4 chord on the dominant. And secondly the bass note stops after the cadenza is 'launched':

The cadenza in the first movement in Sonata 3, in E minor, a movement in 'prelude style' consisting of sections in various metres and tempos, conforms to the model of the cadenza on a penultimate note that is the fundamental note of the dominant. It differs from the cadenza in Corelli's Sonata 3 mainly in the melodic figures used: instead of broken intervals and broken chords there are nearly continuously little diatonic figures:

In the reworked version of the Sonatas of 1716 that Geminiani published in 1739 under the title *Le prime sonate a violino e basso* the cadenza in Sonata 2 has disappeared, that in Sonata 3 is found there in a slightly rewritten version.

At some point between 1700 and 1739 the habit must have been established not to write out cadenzas such as the ones presented above, but to write a corona or fermata sign on the place where such a cadenza could be played. Geminiani's *Sonate a violino e basso, Opera quarta*, published in London in 1739, provide two such examples. One is towards the end of the first movement of Sonata 1:

The arrangement of this movement in the *Pièces de clavecin* (Paris and London, 1743) has an extensive written out cadenza for this passage:

This is certainly not a representation of a cadenza as played in the violin sonata.

The second cadenza example in Geminiani's Violin Sonatas Op. 4, towards the end of the first movement of Sonata 6, is somewhat problematic because the fermata is placed only in the bass part and is placed over a pause sign in the figuring, between the 6/4 suspension and the 5/3 resolution:

In a way this notation suggests that the cadenza has to be played by the continuo player, although the sketchy melodic contour of the violin part rather is also indicative of a cadenza in that part. The pause sign in the bass could simply mean that no chords are played by the continuo player for a while, until the cadenza in the violin part comes to an end.

The little flourish in *Stichnoten* in the last bar of the first movement of Sonata Op. 4 No. 3 can be considered as a very short written-out cadenza:

Interesting for this discussion is the copy of Geminiani's Op. 4 Sonatas in Ann Arbor, Michigan, USA[1]. Extra notes in pencil were written by an early possessor, either in the late eighteenth or the early nineteenth century, on various places in the main text, and several music notations can also be found in the margins. The notations in the margins appear to be cadenzas that can be played when performing the sonatas. Two examples may be given here. The third movement of Sonata 7, *Moderato*, ends in this way in the main text:

1. US-AA, M219 .G32 S71 1739.

The early owner has placed an 'X' mark above the violin part where the harmony is a 6/4 suspension of the dominant. In the upper margin a cadenza is pencilled in that can be played at the place marked by an 'X':

The fourth movement of Sonata 11, *Allegro*, is in rondeau form. In the upper margin a little cadenza is written down that can be added just before the final cadence of the refrain when it is played to conclude the movement, «zum Schluß», as the anonymous, but certainly German author of these additions, wrote next to it. The final bars of the refrain are:

The X marks the place where a cadenza can be inserted:

Note that these cadenzas are not suggested in the score; they are elaborations by an early interpreter.

Geminiani's Cello Sonatas Op. 5

Geminiani's *Sonates pour le violoncelle et basse continue, Ouvrage cinquième*, first published in The Hague, by the composer himself, early 1747, despite the year 1746 on the title page, contain more fermata signs that can be interpreted as referring to cadenzas then any of his earlier (or later) works. There are six sonatas in the set and at eight places fermata signs are found that can be interpreted as cadenzas. They occur in the following places:

	Place	Position	Suspension	Cadence	Cadence	Key	Comments
1	i/i/15	halfway	6/4 5/3	E major	PAC	A major	
2	i/i/35	final	6/4 5/3	E major	imperfect	A major	
3	ii/i/21	final	7 6	A major	imperfect	D minor	
4	iv/ii/36	halfway	6/4 5/3	D minor	PAC	B♭ major	«Fantasia ad libitum»
5	v/i/4	final	7 6	A major	imperfect	F major	
6	v/iii/9	halfway	6/4 6/5	A minor	PAC	D minor	«Cadenza al solito»
7	v/iii/24	pre-final	4 ♯3	D minor	PAC	D minor	
8	vi/i/6	final	7 6 ♯6	E major	imperfect	A minor	

This overview shows a few interesting relations. Half of the cadenzas (nos. 2, 3, 5, 8) occur on the penultimate note of an imperfect cadence that ends a slow movement. They follow the suspension note on this penultimate note and they end with the resolution of the suspension, always a note with a trill. The suspension is usually of the 7-6 type, in one case (no. 2) of the 6/4-5/3 type.

The other half of the cadenzas (nos. 1, 4, 6, 7) occur on other positions within the movement, either 'halfway' or 'pre-final'. ('Pre-final' here means 'just before the final cadence'.) These cadenzas occur as part of perfect authentic cadences (PAC). Also these cadenzas follow a suspension note and end with the resolution with a trill. Suspensions are here most often of the 6/4-5/3 type, once only 4-3. Most often they occur in slow movements, only once (no. 4) in a fast movement: it is placed just before the return to a *da capo* section. This cadenza is also exceptional because of the extra comment «Fantasia ad libitum». This may be read as an invitation to insert a cadenza that is longer than the usual one, perhaps some kind of Capriccio. The remark «Cadenza al solito» in the next Sonata (v/iii/9) may then be a reminder that this cadenza should *not* be a Fantasia, but just a regular cadence.

Most cadences with a cadenza have a trill on the note that precedes the tonic. The note before it is the note with the fermata, where there is a 6/4 or a 7 suspension in the bass, but this more often is *not* the dissonant note of which the note with the trill is the resolution. Geminiani's cadences with cadenzas often have a non-regular structure, in several cases with a rather large interval (fifth or seventh) between the note with the fermata and the note with the trill (cadenzas nos. 1, 3, 7). The cadenza can be used to bridge this interval. Sometimes it is a note which is a fourth above the bass that has the fermata, while the note with the trill that follows is a fifth above the bass (cadenzas nos. 4, 6).

Realisations of the Cadenzas

How the cadenzas of Geminiani's Cello Sonatas Op. 5 were realized in the eighteenth century we do not know. On the other hand, how they were realized during the last half century is amply documented by the LP and CD recordings that have been made of the works. Actually, Geminiani's Cello Sonatas Op. 5 are his most often recorded works, with nine complete recordings since 1976 and numerous recordings of single sonatas. The first recording was an LP, performed by Anthony Pleeth on cello, with Christopher Hogwood (harpsichord) and Richard Webb (cello) as continuo players, brought out by L'Oiseau-Lyre in 1976 and later (1991) reissued by the same label on CD. Directly on CD the sonatas were recorded by the cellists David Simpson (1984), Hidemi Suzuki (1990), Gaetano Nasillo (2001), Alison McGillivray (2005), Jaap ter Linden (2007), Bruno Cocset (2008), Enrico Bronzi (2010) and Loretta O'Sullivan (2015). More details on the recordings are given in the Appendix.

How do these nine cellists play the cadenzas in Geminiani's Cello Sonatas? Transcriptions of the cadenzas are included in the Appendix and from these transcriptions several conclusions can be drawn[2].

First of all it is clear that not all the fermata signs were interpreted in the same way. The fermata on the imperfect cadence of the first movement of Sonata 5 was never used as a starting point for a cadenza. Probably the little flourish that Geminiani inserted there himself has discouraged the performers from adding a cadenza of their own. The fermata sign near the end of the first movement of Sonata 6 has given rise to a cadenza only once (O'Sullivan) and this is a very rudimentary one at best. Here, the fermata is placed over the resolution of the suspension, which is a bit awkward, and this was probably enough reason for the performers not to play any further cadenza.

Also the final cadence of the first movement of Sonata 1 did not equally inspire the performers to insert a cadenza there. Five performers did play a cadenza there; four did not. That means that the final cadence of the first movement of Sonata 2 was the only instance of final (imperfect) cadence of a slow movement where all performers felt the need to insert a cadenza.

[2]. As a matter of fact, the transcriptions are approximate; they have done by ear. No attempts have been made to measure exactly the durations of the notes. Also there is no absolute certainty about the pitch of very short notes and notes of double stops in a low register. The transcriptions have not been checked by the players themselves.

The four fermatas on the suspension of a perfect authentic cadence, either in slow or in fast tempo, on the other hand, were always interpreted as meaning that a cadenza should be played there. The second of these is halfway through the second movement of Sonata 4, with the remark «Fantasia ad libitum». In three cases the performers indeed play a true Fantasia or Capriccio (Simpson, Nasillo, O'Sullivan); the other six play a cadenza that is either not different or hardly different from the other cadenzas and can rather be described as «al solito» than as a Fantasia.

The normal length of the cadenzas «al solito» falls somewhere between ten and twenty notes. Some are very short (three or four notes), other are long or very long (up to 37 notes) but are certainly not a Fantasia or Capriccio. The number of notes is, of course, a very crude measure of the length of a cadenza, but given the unmeasured and free structure of them, there is no better way available. The following table lists the lengths of the cadenzas expressed in the number of notes:

	PLEETH	SIMPSON	SUZUKI	NASILLO	MCGILLIVRAY	LINDEN	COCSET	BRONZI	O'SULLIVAN
1	4	10	3	7	13	4	7	4	12
2	7	18	—	—	—	—	14	13	7
3	7	21	14	5	10	8	13	9	12
4	37	145	20	96	17	12	20	17	127
5	—	—	—	—	—	—	—	—	—
6	17	43	12	17	13	10	7	13	5
7	20	17	19	15	8	11	52	9	34
8	—	—	—	—		—	—	—	3

The style of the cadenzas varies — of course — from player to player. They are all characterized by the lack of a clear metrical structure. They employ various note durations, which were transcribed as crotchets, quavers, semiquavers and demisemiquavers and their dotted variants. Triplets are very common. There is a variety of figures, among them triadic figures and scale runs, the latter both ascending and descending. Double and triple stopping is employed only occasionally (Simpson, nos. 4 and 6; O'Sullivan, no. 4). Most cadenzas can be conveniently written down with a tenor clef, the clef always used by Geminiani when writing the passage with the cadenza. Some cadences use the high register of the cello, that is, between *a1* and *e2* (Simpson, nos. 4 and 6; Cocset, no. 4); some — sometimes the same — the low register, that is, between *C* and *c* (Simpson, nos. 4 and 6; Cocset nos. 2, 4 and 7; O'Sullivan nos. 4 and 7). But in most cases the tenor register, between, say, *d* and *a1*, is preferred.

There is hardly any resemblance among the cadenzas. This probably means that all performers 'composed' their own cadenzas entirely independent of the others. Only Bruno Cocset seems to quote Anthony Pleeth with the first notes of his cadenza at the end of the first movement of Sonata 2, which must perhaps be seen as a homage rather than an imitation.

Quantz Again

To what extent do the cadenzas played by these nine performers adhere to the rules given by Johann Joachim Quantz? Not all of Quantz's points are relevant here, but some provide interesting opportunities for comparison. First of all, the cadenzas connected with perfect authentic cadences certainly conform to Quantz's basic definition that cadenzas are «embellishments produced, in concerting parts, at the end of a piece, over the penultimate note, namely, the fifth over the tonic, according to the will and pleasure of the performers» (point 1). The cadenzas connected with imperfect cadences can be connected with Quantz's points 32-33. Quantz does not acknowledge the application of cadenzas halfway through a movement. In this respect, Geminiani's cadences nos. 1, 4 and 6 fall outside the scope of Quantz's discussion.

Quantz's description of the cadenza as something «short and new, to surprise the listener, as a *bon mot*» and something «that must sound like it was conceived at the moment it was played» (point 9) can certainly be applied to the cadenzas as performed in the recordings of Geminiani's sonatas. They have little internal structure and will indeed sound as if invented on the spot, not pre-composed. Regarding the repetition of figures (Quantz's point 11), the cadenzas in principle follow Quantz's advice as well: there are few repeated figures. The application and treatment of alterations agrees with Quantz's point 13. Modulations (Quantz's point 14) are found only in the worked-out Fantasias. The main cadence there is to D minor. The Fantasias inserted there show modulations to F major and G minor, for example. In the other cases the continuing bass note on the dominant may have been a reason not to introduce any modulation to a different key.

Apart from the Fantasias for the second movement of Sonata 4, the cadenzas added to Geminiani's cello sonatas obey Quantz's rule for the length of a cadenza (point 17). The examples that Quantz gives himself vary in length mostly from sixteen to 27 notes, but two are definitely longer: his Figs. 2 (46 notes) and 7 (61 notes), and these seem to defy his own rule.

So in general 'Quantz's rules' were obeyed by the performers of Geminiani's cello sonatas. Whether that means that they have studied Quantz's text before designing their cadenzas, is impossible to tell. They may also just follow general habits that are current in the performance of early music during the last half century.

In one respect the cadenzas for Geminiani's cello sonatas do differ from the examples given by Quantz in his *Versuch*: the 'Geminiani cadenzas' are much more irregular in their figures, both regarding pitch and duration, than Quantz's examples. The latter ones always have a more compact structure and nearly always have a melodic contour that first rises to an octave above the starting note and then falls towards the note with the trill.

Conclusion

There are many more examples to study regarding the cadenzas in Geminiani's cello sonatas. The many single sonatas recorded by a variety of musicians will undoubtedly provide further examples of cadenzas. Written-out cadenzas are also provided in the editions of Sonatas 2 and 6 edited by Frank Merrick as *Sonata in D minor (A minor) for Violoncello and Piano (Harpsichord) Op. 5 No. 2 (No. 6)* (London, Schott, 1959), with cadenzas probably by Ivor James (who took care of the bowing and phrasing of the violoncello part), and of all six edited by Walter Kolneder as *Sechs Sonaten für Violoncello und Basso continuo Opus V* (Frankfurt, Peters, 1964), with cadenzas probably by Walter Schultz (who edited the cello part). In general the written-out cadenzas found in these editions are longer, more complex and technically more demanding than the cadenzas found in recordings.

Geminiani also published his cello sonatas in a version adapted to the violin, under the title *Sonates pour le violon avec un violoncelle ou clavecin* (The Hague, 1747). Recordings of these sonatas add further examples of cadenzas. Kolneder's edition of these works as *Sechs Sonaten für Violine und Basso continuo* (Frankfurt, Peters, 1965) simply transposes the cadenzas from his edition of the cello sonatas.

In short, it would not be difficult to assemble further examples of cadenzas to Geminiani's Op. 5 Sonatas for the study of improvisation as practised today as part of the performance of early music. It is, however, not to be expected that this will add any new elements to the above discussion. Whether the practice described there reflects early practice is impossible to say. Perhaps this is a question that should not be asked. Not only do we not know how representative the preserved contemporary examples of performed cadenzas 'frozen' into notation — either in practical editions or in theoretical discussions — are, there will also always have been and always will be as many ways of performing cadenzas as there are performers.

Cadenza Marks in Francesco Geminiani, *Sonates pour le violoncelle et basse continue, Ouvrage cinquième* (The Hague, Author, 1747; London, Author, 1747)

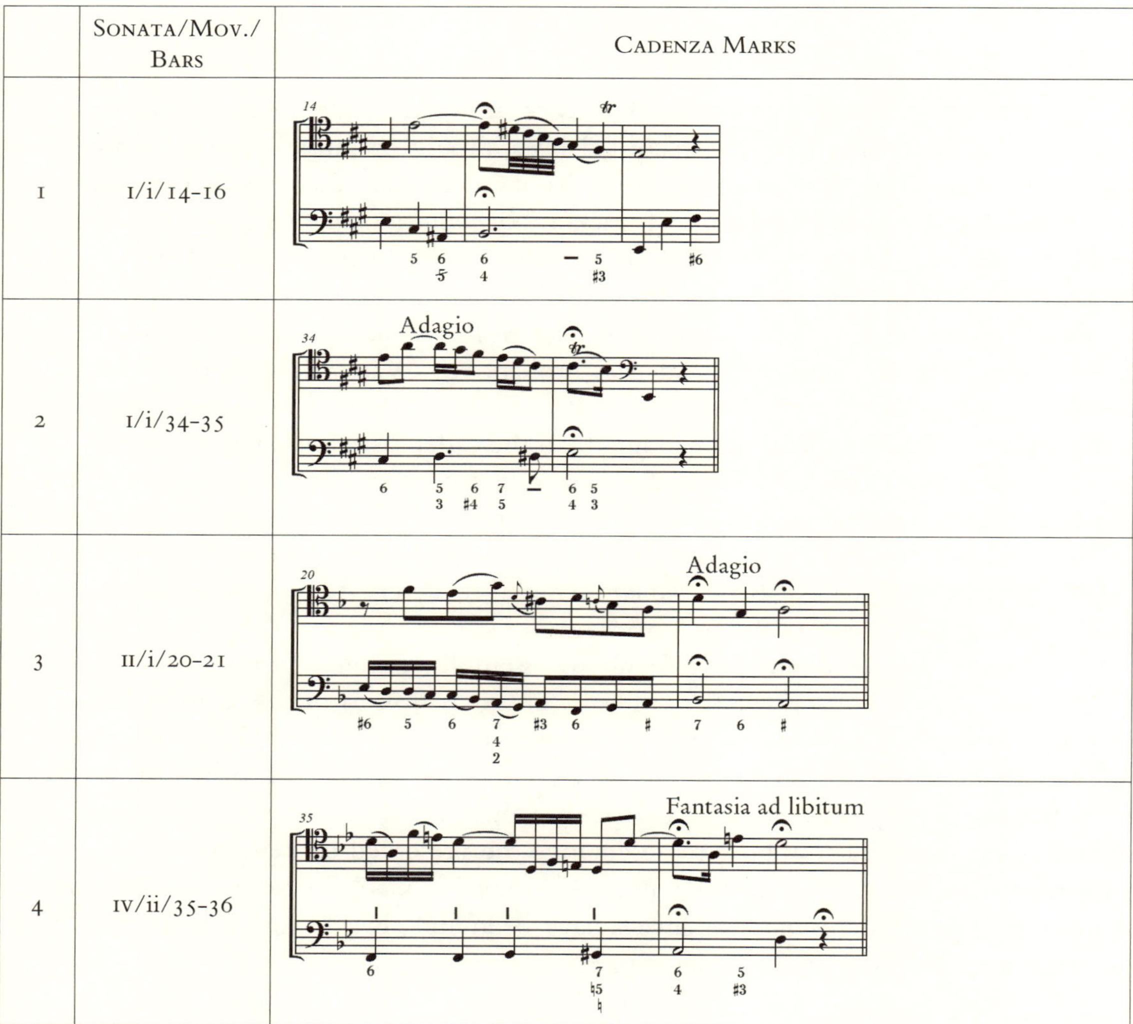

	Sonata/Mov./Bars	Cadenza Marks
1	i/i/14-16	
2	i/i/34-35	
3	ii/i/20-21	
4	iv/ii/35-36	

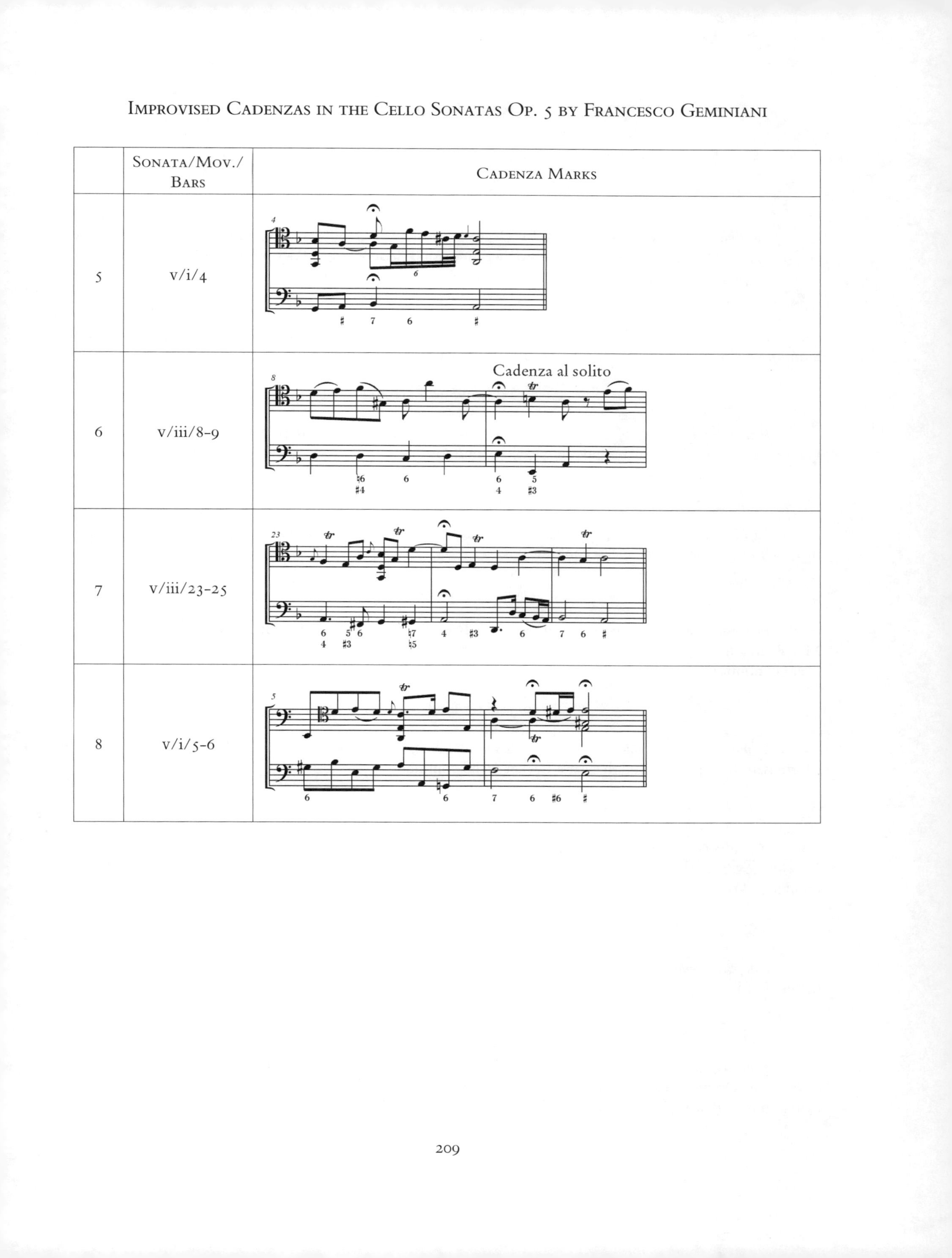

	Sonata/Mov./Bars	Cadenza Marks
5	v/i/4	
6	v/iii/8-9	Cadenza al solito
7	v/iii/23-25	
8	v/i/5-6	

Complete Recordings of Geminiani's Cello Sonatas Op. 5.

1. Anthony Pleeth (1976)

Geminiani, 6 Cello Sonatas, Op. 5, LP Decca L'Oiseau-Lyre DSLO 513, 1976. CD L'Oiseau-Lyre 433 192-2, 1992. Anthony Pleeth (cello), Christopher Hogwood (harpsichord), Richard Webb (cello continuo).

2. David Simpson (1984)

Francesco Geminiani, Les six sonates Op. 5 pour violoncello et continuo, Solstice SOCD 34, [1984]. David Simpson (cello), Noëlle Spieth (harpsichord), Claire Giardelli (cello continuo).

3. Hidemi Suzuki (1991)

Francesco Geminiani, VI Sonate di Violoncello, Ricercar RIC 095077, 1991. Hidemi Suzuki (cello), Guy Penson (harpsichord), Rainer Zipperling (cello continuo).

4. Gaetano Nasillo (2001)

Geminiani, Cello Sonatas, Pan Classics PC 10232, 2001, 2011. Gaetano Nasillo (cello), Jesper Christensen (harpsichord), Tobias Bonz (cello continuo).

5. Alison McGillivray (2005)

Francesco Geminiani, Sonatas for Violoncello & Basso Continuo, Op. 5, Linn BKD 251, 2005, 2015. Alison McGillivray (cello), David McGuinness (harpsichord), Eligio Quinteiro (also Baroque guitar), Joseph Crouch (cello continuo).

6. Jaap ter Linden (2007)

Geminiani, Cello Sonatas Op. 5, Brilliant Classics 93636, 2007. Jaap ter Linden (cello), Lars Ulrik Mortensen (harpsichord), Judith-Maria Becker (cello continuo).

7. Bruno Cocset (2008)

Francesco Geminiani, Sonates pour violoncelle avec la basse continue, Alpha 123, 2008. Bruno Cocset (cello), Luca Pianca (theorbo), Bertrand Cuiller (harpsichord), Mathurin Matharel (cello continuo), Richard Myron (double bass).

8. Enrico Bronzi (2010)

Francesco Geminiani, 6 Sonate Op. 5, Concerto CD 2061, 2010. Enrico Bronzi (cello), Michele Barchi (harpsichord).

9. Loretta O'Sullivan (2015)

Francesco Geminiani, Sonatas for Cello Continuo Op. 5a – George Fredric Handel, Suite V for Harpsichord in E Major, Orchid ORC 100049, 2015. Four Nations Ensemble: Loretta O'Sullivan (cello), Andrew Appel (harpsichord), Beilang Zhu (continuo cello), Scott Pauley (theorbo and guitar).

Cadenzas in Recordings of Geminiani's Cello Sonatas Op. 5

Anthony Pleeth (1976)

Geminiani, Cello Sonatas, Op. 5, Decca, L'Oiseau-Lyre, 1976, CD L'Oiseau-Lyre 433 192-2, 1992.

Sonata/Mov./Bar	Cadenza
i/i/15	 15 tr
i/i/35	 35 tr
ii/i/21	 21
iv/ii/36	 36 Fantasia ad libitum tr
v/i/4	none
v/iii/9	 9 Cadenza al solito tr
v/iii/24	 24 tr
vi/i/6	none

David Simpson (1984)

Francesco Geminiani, Les six sonates op. 5 pour violoncelle et continuo, Solstice SOCD 34, 1984.

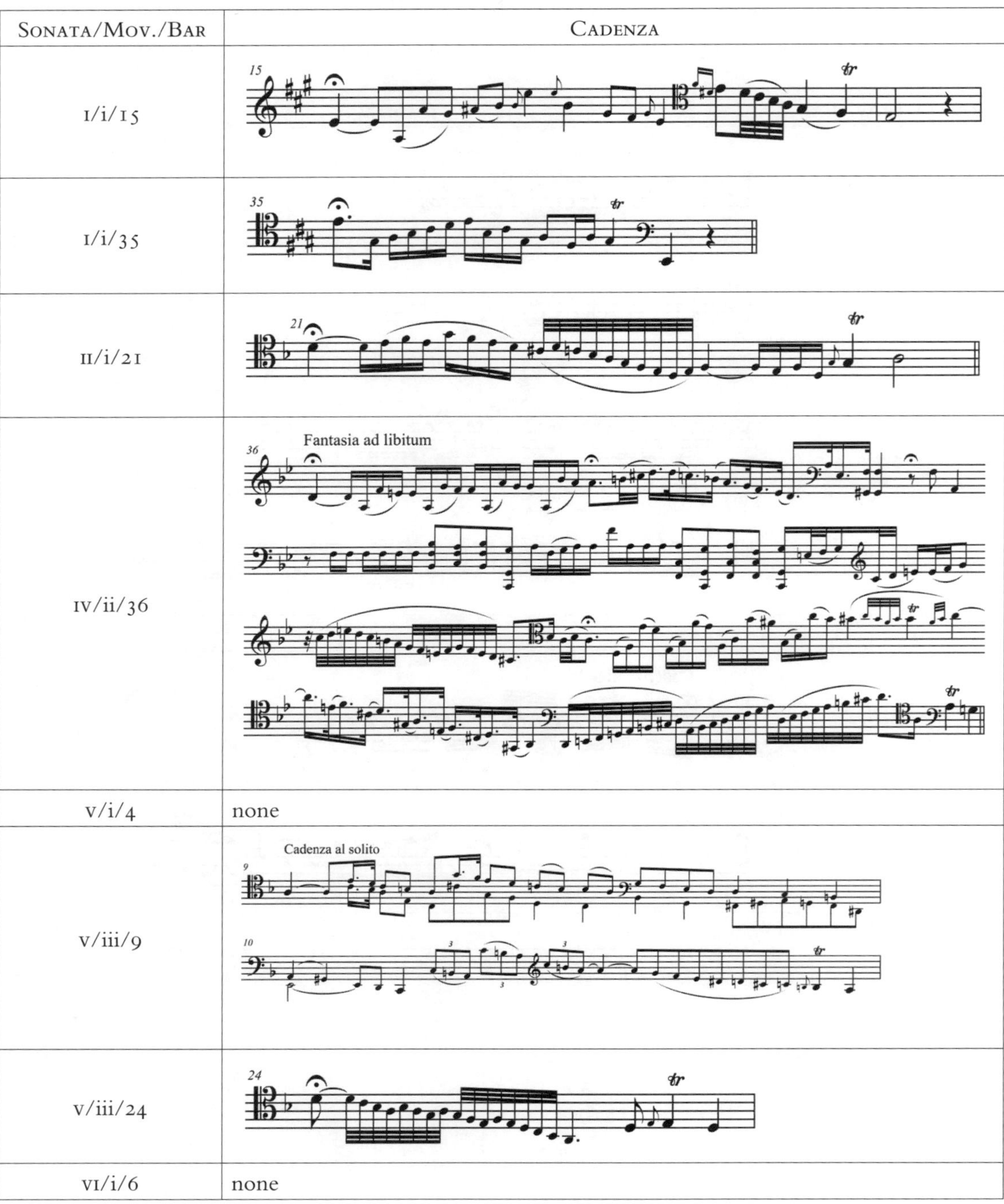

Sonata/Mov./Bar	Cadenza
I/i/15	
I/i/35	
II/i/21	
IV/ii/36	Fantasia ad libitum
V/i/4	none
V/iii/9	Cadenza al solito
V/iii/24	
VI/i/6	none

Improvised Cadenzas in the Cello Sonatas Op. 5 by Francesco Geminiani

Hidemi Suzuki (1990)

Francesco Geminiani, Sonatas for Cello and Continuo. Ricercar RIC 095077, 1990.

Sonata/Mov./Bar	Cadenza
I/i/15	
I/i/35	
II/i/21	
IV/ii/36	Fantasia ad libitum 
V/i/4	none
V/iii/9	Cadenza al solito 
V/iii/24	
VI/i/6	none

Gaetano Nasillo (2001)

Geminiani, Cello Sonatas, Pan Classics PC 10232. 2001, 2011.

Sonata/Mov./Bar	Cadenza
i/i/15	
i/i/35	none
ii/i/21	
iv/ii/36	Fantasia ad libitum
v/i/4	none
v/iii/9	Cadenza al solito
v/iii/24	
vi/i/6	none

Improvised Cadenzas in the Cello Sonatas Op. 5 by Francesco Geminiani

Alison McGillivray (2005)

Francesco Geminiani, Sonatas for Violoncello & Basso Continuo Op. 5, Linn BTK . 2005, 2015.

Sonata/Mov./Bar	Cadenza
I/i/15	 15
I/i/35	none
II/i/21	 21 tr
IV/ii/36	 Fantasia ad libitum 36 tr
V/i/4	none
V/iii/9	 Cadenza al solito 9 tr
V/iii/24	 24 tr
VI/i/6	none

Jaap ter Linden (2007)

Geminiani, Cello Sonatas Op. 5, Brilliant Classics 93636. 2007.

Sonata/Mov./Bar	Cadenza
i/i/15	 15
i/i/35	none
ii/i/21	 21
iv/ii/36	 Fantasia ad libitum 36
v/i/4	none
v/iii/9	 Cadenza al solito 9
v/iii/24	 24
vi/i/6	none

Improvised Cadenzas in the Cello Sonatas Op. 5 by Francesco Geminiani

Bruno Cocset (2008)

Francesco Geminiani, Sonates pour violoncelle avec la basse continue, Alpha 123. 2008.

Sonata/Mov./Bar	Cadenza
I/i/15	
I/i/35	
II/i/21	
IV/ii/36	 Fantasia ad libitum
V/i/4	none
V/iii/9	 Cadenza al solito
V/iii/24	 pizz. arco p pp f (35 sec)
VI/i/6	none

Enrico Bronzi (2010)

Francesco Geminiani, 6 Sonate Op. 5, Concerto CD 2061. 2010.

Sonata/Mov./Bar	Cadenza
i/i/15	15 tr
i/i/35	35 tr
ii/i/21	21 tr
iv/ii/36	Fantasia ad libitum 36 tr
v/i/4	none
v/iii/9	Cadenza al solito 9 3 tr
v/iii/24	24 3 tr
vi/i/6	none

Improvised Cadenzas in the Cello Sonatas Op. 5 by Francesco Geminiani

Loretta O'Sullivan (2015)

Francesco Geminiani, Sonatas for Cello and Continuo, Orchid ORC 100049. 2015.

Sonata/Mov./Bar	Cadenza
I/i/15	 15
I/i/35	 35
II/i/21	 21
IV/ii/36	 36 Fantasia ad libitum
V/i/4	none
V/iii/9	 9 Cadenza al solito
V/iii/24	 24
VI/i/6	 6

Contemporary Treatises, Pedagogical Works, and Aesthetics

Il mito della competizione tra virtuosi: quando Farinelli sfidò Bernacchi (Bologna 1727)

Valentina Anzani
(Università di Bologna)

Una sfida sui palchi bolognesi

Nell'estate del 1727 i castrati Antonio Bernacchi, all'epoca quarantaduenne, e Farinelli (Carlo Broschi), ventiduenne, si trovarono per la prima volta ingaggiati per una stessa opera: *Antigona, ovvero la fedeltà coronata* di Giuseppe Maria Orlandini, dramma di Benedetto Pasqualigo, dato al Teatro Malvezzi di Bologna.

Nel giugno 1727 il Teatro Malvezzi, dopo cinque anni d'inattività veniva riaperto con grande sfarzo artistico: per *Antigona* erano infatti stati scritturati alcuni tra i cantanti di maggior grido del tempo, ovvero Bernacchi, Nicola Grimaldi, Antonia Merighi e Carlo Broschi Farinelli, quest'ultimo caldamente raccomandato dal conte Sicinio Pepoli. Il nobile aveva un ruolo di primo piano nel nuovo comitato impresariale del teatro; pochi mesi prima gli era stato introdotto il giovane musico dai suoi parenti romani, il cognato don Fabrizio Colonna e il cardinale Carlo Colonna, zio della moglie: fu questa scrittura che consacrerà alla scena internazionale il giovane cantante ventiduenne, che già raccoglieva successi in patria[1].

La riapertura del teatro e lo speciale dramma per musica erano dovuti al soggiorno in città di Giacomo III Stuart (1688-1766), l'esule pretendente giacobita al trono inglese e scozzese, accolto in Italia con tutti gli onori per il suo tentativo di ripristinare il culto cattolico in Inghilterra. Di madre italiana, figlio di Giacomo II Stuart e di Maria Beatrice d'Este, considerava la musica fra i suoi passatempi più graditi. A Roma si distingueva come uno dei maggiori mecenati dei teatri d'opera: nel suo preferito, l'Alibert, gli erano assegnati eccezionalmente tre palchi e ogni allestimento era dedicato a lui o alla consorte Maria Clementina[2]. Particolari onori gli erano riservati anche quando si recava altrove,

[1]. *Cfr.* Vitali 1992, p. 2.
[2]. *Cfr.* Corp 2011, pp. 82-84.

come avvenne a Bologna, seconda città dello Stato Pontificio, dove si trattenne per diversi mesi, omaggiato lussuosamente: il 31 dicembre 1726, per il genetliaco del figlio primogenito Carlo Edoardo (1720-1788), fu dato un fastosissimo ricevimento a Palazzo Marescotti, in via Barberia 391 (oggi 4):

> In esso giorno [martedì sera], per il compleanno del principino di Galles figlio primogenito di questo re britannico, fu gran galla in sua corte, e nella sera questa nobiltà vuolle dimostrare quanto sia la stima faccino della maestà sua: sol fare per tal effetto da dodici di questi primari cavaglieri una festa di ballo nel palazzo del signore senatore Marescotti, avendo perciò nel giorno antecedente fatto dispensare polizze a bello studio stampate, colle quale invitavano tutta questa nobiltà ad intervenire a detta festa nella più sontuosa galla; come in fatti vi comparvero con superbissimi abiti, ed era illuminato detto palazzo dentro e fuori con gran quantità di lumi di cera, avendola poscia decorata la comparsa fatta di sua maestà e 'l prencipino di Galles, quali si compia[c]quero di danzare in minuetti, e contradanze, e di più la maestà sua vuole fare danzare questa nobiltà in balli all'inglese, delli quali non sapendogli fare, sua maestà ne era il maestro con gran suo contento, e vi si trattenne sino all'ore sei e mezza; e riuscì tanto più decorosa detta festa, quanto che fu fram[m]ischiata da superfluità delli più rari rinfreschi, e per certo è stata una festa delle più singolari siansi fatte mai in questa città, e tanta satisfazione ne ha riportata la maestà sua, che non si puole esprimere, conoscendo quanta parzialità, e stima abbi questa nobiltà per la reale gran casa Stuarda[3].

Come molti altri allestimenti dedicati all'esule re inglese, anche il dramma che si allestì a Bologna l'estate 1727 si prestava a interpretazioni 'giacobite': i temi trattati nella trama di *Antigona, ovvero La fedeltà coronata* erano il trionfo del bene sul male, il premio dato alla pazienza e la restaurazione di una monarchia legittima[4]. Gli *Avvisi* della città testimoniano che:

> La sera di detto giorno [2 giugno] si diede principio alle recite della grandiosa opera musicale intitolata *La fedeltà coronata* nel Teatro Malvezzi, ornata di s[c]enario di nuove invenzioni de' più celebri pennelli in simile sfera, con nobilissimo vestiario, essendo la musica del virtuoso Orlandini recitata da' primi cantanti d'Europa, fra' quali li due famosi musici Bernachi e Farinello, fatti venire di Baviera e Napoli a forza di contanti, riuscendo a meraviglia[5].

---

3. I-Bu, ms. 770 vol. xci: Ghiselli. *Memorie antiche manoscritte di Bologna, Avvisi secreti di Bologna*, 4 gennaio 1727.

4. *Cfr.* Corp 2011, pp. 89, 92.

5. I-Bu, ms. 225/iv: Barilli, Antonio. *Zibaldone, ossia Giornale di Antonio Barilli Bolognese di quanto è seguito in Bologna dal principio dell'anno 1726 per tutto l'anno 1728. Tomo quarto*. c. 139^v.

Il mito della competizione tra virtuosi: quando Farinelli sfidò Bernacchi

Narrazioni distorte, narrazioni ricche

Una tradizione diffusa vorrebbe che durante l'allestimento dell'opera Farinelli e Bernacchi avessero ingaggiato una gara: il primo incontro tra i due cantanti è narrato in numerose fonti secondarie come un momento di tensione e rivalità, in cui un borioso Farinelli avrebbe voluto dimostrare la propria superiorità all'anziano collega. Scatenata una disputa canora, entrambi si sarebbero lanciati in esecuzioni di difficilissimi passaggi, improvvisazioni estemporanee e di reciproche imitazioni, al cui termine Bernacchi non solo ebbe la meglio, ma indusse addirittura Farinelli ad accantonare la propria vanità per chiedere lezioni di canto al collega.

Il racconto iniziò a prendere questa forma nelle parole di Giovenale Sacchi, primo biografo di Farinelli (1784), che fu informato dei dettagli della sua vita da Padre Martini. Sacchi per primo affermò che quando si ritrovarono a cantare insieme, Farinelli decise di ostentare la propria abilità, che Bernacchi gli dimostrò invece di essergli superiore, e che una volta sconfitto, i due si sarebbero accordati per studiare insieme a Roma:

> Il giovine Broschi, cantando la prima volta insieme con lui privatamente, giudicò che il valore del Bernacchi non fosse uguale alla fama di cui godeva; onde con certa *animosità giovanile* cominciò a fare ostentazione della propria abilità, ciò che il più vecchio non faceva. Si accorse il Bernacchi di essere provocato, ed accesosi alquanto, fecegli sentire che egli non era ancora a tempo di uguagliarlo, non che di superarlo. Questo accidente, che avrebbe disgiunto due altri che fossero amici, congiunse questi due in amicizia che fu poi indissolubile; perché erano ambedue *di ottimo animo*, e oltre a ciò fu questa un'occasione a Farinello di farsi migliore che non era perché, compresa la superiorità del Bernacchi nell'arte del canto, lo pregò che volesse riceverlo alla sua scuola. Subito poi trasferitisi amendue a cantare a Roma, quivi ogni mattina il Broschi frequentava la casa del Bernacchi, ed apprendeva da lui quelle grazie sopraffine delle quali non era ancora abbastanza fornito[6].

Il Fétis (1860) nel suo compendio enciclopedico dedicato ai musicisti aggiunse un dettaglio sulla tipologia di duello canoro in cui i due si sarebbero confrontati: un duetto, il quale divenne sede di una vera e propria gara in cui ogni variazione proposta da Farinelli era immediatamente ripresa identica da Bernacchi, ma eseguita molto meglio. Farinelli gli aveva chiesto consiglio, e Bernacchi era stato felice di portare a compimento la formazione del cantante più talentuoso del Settecento:

> Nel 1727 [Farinelli] andò a Bologna dove doveva cantare con Bernacchi. Orgoglioso di tanto successo, fiducioso nell'incomparabile bellezza della sua voce e nella facilità prodigiosa d'esecuzione che non lo aveva mai tradito,

[6]. Sacchi 1784, pp. 13-14; corsivi aggiunti.

> temeva poco la prova cui stava per sottoporsi. L'abilità di Bernacchi era tale, tuttavia, che gli aveva fatto guadagnare l'appellativo di *Re dei cantori*; ma la sua voce non era bella, ed era solo per i mezzi dell'artificio che Bernacchi aveva trionfato sui suoi difetti. Non dubitando di una vittoria simile a quella ottenuta a Roma cinque anni prima [sul trombettiere tedesco], l'allievo di Porpora esibì tutti i tesori della sua bellissima voce, tutte le coloriture che avevano fatto la sua fama, nel duetto che cantò con Bernacchi. Il pubblico, nel delirio, rispose con applausi furiosi a ciò che aveva ascoltato. Bernacchi, per nulla turbato dalla meraviglia e dall'effetto che aveva prodotto, iniziò a sua volta la frase che doveva ripetere, e, riproducendo tutte le variazioni del giovane cantante, senza dimenticarne alcuna, mise in ogni dettaglio una perfezione così meravigliosa che Farinelli fu obbligato a riconoscere il suo maestro nel suo rivale. Dopo di che, invece di reagire con orgoglio ferito come un artista ordinario avrebbe fatto, ammise la sconfitta e chiese consiglio Bernacchi, che fu lieto di dare l'ultima rifinitura al talento del cantante più straordinario [*chanteur le plus extraordinaire*] del XVIII secolo[7].

Come sottolinea Ortkemper, il racconto suona però pericolosamente simile a un passo del trattato di Piefrancesco Tosi, tanto da far supporre che il duetto citato da Fétis non sia altro che un'aggiunta di sua mano:

> Mi sovviene, o mi sognai d'aver sentito un famoso duetto messo in pezzi minuti da due professori di grido, impegnati dalla emulazione a proporre, e vicendevolmente a rispondersi, che infine terminò in una gara a chi faceva più spropositi[8].

In un articolo pubblicato sulla *Revue des deux Mondes* del 1861, Paul Scudo riprese quasi per intero il passo di Fétis, aggiungendovi un dettaglio suggestivo: in breve, l'ultima frase ripresa da Bernacchi avrebbe conquistato il pubblico non solo perché era eseguita

---

7. «En 1727 il [Farinelli] se rendit à Bologne: il y devait chanter avec Bernacchi. Fier de tant de succès, confiant dans l'incomparable beauté de sa voix et dans la prodigeuse facilité d'execution qui ne l'avait jamais trahi, il redoutait peu l'épreuve qu'il allait subir. L'habilité de Bernacchi était telle, à-la vérité, qu'elle l'avait fait appeler *Le rois des chanteurs*; mais sa voix n'était pas belle, et ce n'était qu'a force d'art que Bernacchi avait triomphé de ses défauts. Ne doubtant pas d'une victoire semblable à celle qu'il avait obtenue à Rome cinq ans auparavant [du trompette allemande], l'élève de Porpora prodigua dans le duo qu'il chantait avec Bernacchi tous les trésors de son bel organe, tous les traits qui avaient fait sa gloire. L'auditoire, dans le délire, prodigua des applaudissements frénétiques à ce qu'il venait d'entendre. Bernacchi, sans être ému du prodige e de l'effet qu'il avait produit, commença à son tour la phrase qu'il devait répéter, et redisant tous les traits du jeune chanteur, sans en oublier un seul, mit dans tous les détails une perfection si merveilleuse, que Farinelli fut obligé de reconnaître son maître dans son rival. Alors, au lieu de se renfermer dans un orgueil blessé, comme n'aurait pas manqué de faire un *artiste ordinaire*, il avoua sa défaite et demanda des conseils à Bernacchi, qui se plut à donner la dernière perfection au talent du chanteur le plus extraordinaire du dix-huitième siècle». Fétis 1860, p. 83; corsivi aggiunti.

8. Tosi 1723, p. 96.

tanto bene quanto quella di Farinelli, ma anche perché la sua esecuzione era naturale, l'emissione semplice e l'interpretazione piena di sentimento:

> Farinelli debuttò a Bologna in un'opera in cui aveva un duetto da cantare con Bernacchi, la cui voce era sorda e mediocre [=*la voix était sourde et mediocre*]. Il brillante allievo di Porpora, che doveva solo mostrare la sua figura snella e una figura affascinante per voltare il pubblico a suo favore, cominciò sfoggiando nella frase melodica che gli fu affidata tutti i gioielli delle sue fioriture vocali, tutta l'inventiva della sua immaginazione, che gli erano così ben riusciti a Roma. Dopo lo straordinario tumulto che la prestigiosa bravura di Farinelli aveva suscitato nella sala, Bernacchi riprese con modestia il motivo già sentito, lo espose con gusto, senza il minimo artificio, e lo espresse con un tale carattere di semplicità e sentimento [=*reprit modestement le motif déjà entendu, l'exposa avec goût, sans le moindre artifice, et lui imprima un tel cachet de simplicité et de sentiment*] che anche il suo giovane rivale ne rimase commosso. Il pubblico si pronunciò a favore di Bernacchi, e Farinelli, lungi dal sentirsi umiliato da questa vittoria, si dichiarò sconfitto: chiese a Bernacchi consigli durante tutto il tempo che trascorse a Bologna[9].

Scudo fu il primo a trasformare Bernacchi in un fautore del canto patetico, e fu riproposto quasi pedissequamente nell'articolo inglese anonimo di due anni dopo 'Singing to Some Purpose'[10]. Anche Enrico Panzacchi a fine secolo narrò la propria versione dello stesso episodio in un saggio intitolato 'La musica' (1897), che appare una sua libera traduzione dei testi citati, che dunque doveva conoscere (s'inventò però l'autore dell'opera e omise ogni riferimento alla richiesta di lezioni da parte di Farinelli).

Nelle parole di Panzacchi l'esecuzione di Bernacchi fu tanto più sorprendente e inaspettata perché quest'ultimo, invece di aggiungere nuovi trilli alla frase melodica, ebbe l'ingegnosa trovata di ripresentarla al pubblico nella purezza del tema originale:

---

[9]. «Farinelli se rendit à Bologne en 1727. Il y rencontra le sopraniste Bernachi, qui devait avoir sur sa carrière d'artiste la plus salutaire influence. Bernacchi était un virtuose dèjà célèbre, que ses contamporains avaient surnommé le *roi des chantaurs*. Élève de Pistochi, qui avait fondé à Bologne une ècole de chant très estimée, Bernachi à continué avec succès l'enseignement de son maitre en formant ò son tour un grand nombre de virtuoses distingués. Farinelli débuta à Bologne dans un opéra où il avait un duo à chanter avec Bernachi, dont la voix était sourde et mediocre. Le brillant élève de Porpora, qui n'avait qu'à montrer sa taille svelte et une charmante figure pour prévenir le public en sa faveur, commença par dérouler sur la phrase mélodique qui lui était confiée tout l'écrin de ses fioritures vocales, toutes les ingéniositès de sa fantaisie, qui lui avaientsi bien réussi à Rome. Après un tumulte extraordinaire qu'avait soulevé dans la salle la bravoure prestigieuse de Farinelli, Bernachi reprit modestement le motif déjà entendu, l'exposa avec goût, sans le moindre artifice, et lui imprima un tel cachet de simplicité et de sentiment que son jeune rival en fut ému lui-même. Le public se prononça en faveur de Bernachi, et Farinelli, loin de se trouver humilié de cette victoire, s'avoua vaincu: il demanda des conseils à Bernachi pendant tout le temps qu'il passa à Bologne». Scudo 1861, p. 759.

[10]. Singing to Some Purpose 1863.

> Il Bernacchi e il Farinello divennero col tempo *rivali*, e una volta s'incontrarono a Bologna verso la metà del secolo. Il pubblico li attendeva in un duetto del maestro Hasse, detto il Sassone, dove ognuno dei due doveva dare prova del proprio talento. Raccontano che in mezzo ad una trepida aspettazione, ad un silenzio profondo i due campioni prima espressero il puro tema melodico su cui cadeva la *gara*. Il Farinello, più giovane, stupì il pubblico con variazioni audacissime, e il Bernacchi di rimando sulle prime *tenne validamente testa all'avversario*; ma poi, crescendo sempre le difficoltà inaspettate e le ardue bizzarrie del canto farinelliano, il Bernacchi ebbe l'astuzia da *vecchio lottatore*. Ad un tratto abbandonò il sistema delle variazioni e dei trilli, e ripresentò al pubblico il bel tema melodico in tutta la sua primitiva purezza e semplicità. L'entusiasmo del pubblico, a quell'effetto inatteso, non ebbe più confini. Fu domandato il bis e il Bernacchi lo concesse; ma quando fu per riprendere la sua frase, sentì nell'orchestra una certa inquietudine, una certa titubanza. Si volse a guardare, e si avvide che anche i suonatori, anche il direttore d'orchestra piangevano[11].

Panzacchi postdatò l'accaduto di un quarto di secolo («verso la metà del secolo»), forse equivocando con il *Siroe* di Hasse del 1733, con Farinelli e Caffarelli, e aggiunse dettagli romanzeschi che tradiscono la sua attitudine alla narrativa di fantasia[12]. Nella tradizione successiva questo passo venne spesso acriticamente considerato come un indizio inequivocabile del riconoscimento di Bernacchi come ultimo esponente di quello stile patetico tipico di coloro che Tosi chiama «gli antichi», contrapponendolo allo stile moderno (di cattivo gusto) di Farinelli, illustre esponente della 'scuola' napoletana.

Realtà storica

Ad uno sguardo complessivo risulta però chiaro che l'episodio tramandato dal biografo più vicino ai fatti (Sacchi 1784), subì la corruzione apologetica tipica dei biografi del XIX secolo e che una volta rielaborato da Fétis (1861), Scudo (1861) e Panzacchi (1897) la verosimiglianza storica diventa improbabile. Ognuno dei racconti riporta imprecisioni. La modalità di somministrazione delle lezioni proposta da Fétis è incongruente con la realtà dei fatti, poiché il confronto tra le carriere dei due conferma che non furono mai a Roma insieme: dopo le recite di Bologna si ritroveranno per due estati successive a Parma, dove entrambi saranno impegnati nell'allestimento del *Medo* di Frugoni/Vinci nel 1728 e nel *Lucio Papirio dittatore* di Frugoni/Giacomelli nel 1729.

---

11. La presente citazione proviene da Panzacchi 1897, pp. 522-524 (corsivi aggiunti).

12. Questa attitudine di Panzacchi è testimoniata anche dalla pubblicazione dei suoi *Racconti* (Panzacchi 1889), tra cui ve ne è anche uno, *Cantores*, dedicato ai cantanti castrati che poté udire nella Cappella Sistina.

Molto di più fu il tempo che condivideranno a Bologna: nella primavera del 1728, prima di dirigersi a Parma per le recite di *Medo*, saranno entrambi nella città felsinea, e si esibiranno in separate sedi durante le celebrazioni pasquali[13]. I due saranno di nuovo insieme a Bologna per il *Farnace* di Lucchini/Porta del 1731, estate in cui canteranno anche «in casa del Principe senator Riario, dove vi fu una nobile accademia di suono e canto»[14]; e ancora nei mesi estivi del 1732: Bernacchi arrivò in giugno[15] e Farinelli passò verosimilmente l'estate in città[16].

Sempre Fétis afferma che i due si confrontarono in un duetto; tuttavia nell'opera in scena al Teatro Malvezzi nel 1727 non ne era previsto alcuno tra loro due. Si potrebbe forse ipotizzare un'aggiunta estemporanea o non registrata da libretto o partitura, il che andrebbe a favore dell'attribuzione che Panzacchi fa del brano, dicendolo di Hasse e non dell'autore dell'opera in cartellone, che era invece Orlandini; ma all'altezza del 1727 non c'è alcun dramma per musica che contenga un duetto tra due 'primi uomini'. Si potrebbe anche immaginare che l'esibizione sia avvenuta in ambito privato («cantando la prima volta insieme con lui privatamente», come vorrebbe Sacchi), non in teatro, forse a latere dell'informale prova generale organizzata in casa Pepoli di cui parlano gli *Avvisi*, oppure in tutt'altro contesto, durante un'esecuzione di musica sacra[17].

Preso atto di tutte le inverosimiglianze presenti in questi racconti, sembra probabile che in realtà la contesa non avvenne mai, ma fu piuttosto deliberatamente inventata dai

[13]. Bernacchi cantò il 16 marzo durante un'Accademia degli alunni del Collegio dei Nobili (I-Bu, ms. 225/IV: Barilli, Antonio. *Zibaldone* [...], c. 237v); pochi giorni dopo, il 26 marzo «fu fatta grandiosa cappella a S. Petronio per la commemorazione della Risurrezione del Redentore con la presenza de' Regi Stuardi e de' signori Superiori, dove vi cantò il famoso Farinelli con gran lode, come pure il Minelli et altri accreditati musici, e la loro armonia fu accompagnata dallo sfarzo del cannone e moschettarìa svizzera su questa pubblica piazza» (*ibidem*, c. 238r).

[14]. I-Bu, ms. 225/V: Barilli, Antonio. *Zibaldone* [...]. *Tomo quinto*, c. 256r-v.

[15]. I-Bu, ms. 92, busta IV, n. 8: *Lettere 233 di Francesco Zambeccari al fratello Alessandro dal 1709 al 1745*, 2 luglio 1732.

[16]. Il diarista Barilli è prodigo di notizie a riguardo: «A dì 2 settembre: avere gl'impresari dell'opera musicale a recitarsi in Piacenza accordato a questa cantatrice signora Vittoria Tesi duecento luigi di suo onorario, oltre il regalo per la recita della medesima, la quale si dispone alla partenza, come fa il famoso musico Farinelli» (I-Bu, ms. 225/VI: Barilli, Antonio. *Zibaldone* [...]. *Tomo sesto*, 2 settembre 1732). Già in quel periodo Farinelli pensava di stabilirsi a Bologna: «A dì 22 settembre: Sèntesi che il famoso musico Farinelli sia risoluto di stabilire qui il suo soggiorno, sento in trattato di fare acquisto di decoroso stabile»; «A dì 23 ottobre: Dall'eccelso Senato è poi stato decretato della cittadinanza con il beneficio del Terminale, il famoso musico Farinelli, che fa ora un acquisto di stabili per 2800 lire di pronti contanti» (*ibidem*, 22 settembre 1732; 23 ottobre 1732).

[17]. «Da Monaco di Baviera in quattro giorni giunse in questa città il famoso musico signore Bernacchi, per la qual cosa nelli susseguenti giorni furono fatte alcune prove della nota grand'opera nel palazzo dell'eccellenza il signor conte Sicinio Pepoli. È riuscita a meraviglia, e questa sera si dovrà fare nel teatro la prova generale per dare incominciamento alle recite lunedì venturo». I-Bu, ms. 770 vol. XCI: Ghiselli. *Memorie antiche manoscritte di Bologna*, *Avvisi secreti di Bologna*, 31 maggio 1727.

biografi: è infatti altamente improbabile che proprio quegli stessi *Avvisi* (o *Zibaldoni*) che informano così diffusamente sull'arrivo dei cantanti in città, sulle loro cene e pranzi, sulle prove private e sull'andamento delle repliche non abbiano speso una riga su una disfida canora fra i due divi. Un tanto eclatante duello e l'altrettanto eclatante esito sarebbero di certo stati riportati in un tale genere di fonti che, paragonabili a moderne riviste di gossip, registravano tutte le attività degne di nota avvenute in città.

Il sonetto

L'unico documento in nostro possesso che rivela un clima di ostilità è un sonetto che circolò in città durante quell'estate[18].

In favore del musico Bernacchi e contro il Farinello

Avre ch'am dsissi cosa è mai st' gran fiach cha fâ person cun st' vostr Farinel[!] Per Crispel, av dig ch'avi pers al cervel, e s' v' sò dir ch'al canta mei Bernach[!]	*Vorrei che mi diceste cos'è mai questo gran rumore* *che la gente fa con questo vostro Farinelli!* *Per Cristo, vi dico che avete perso il cervello,* *e vi dico che canta meglio Bernacchi!*
Quest n'è spar d' raz, ne di tich tach e s' n' fâ da lusgnol, nè da franguel. L'è un capon, ch'è castrà qusi ben ugual ch'int la sò vos an spò truvar intach.	*Questo non spara né razzi né mortaretti* *e non imita né l'usignolo né il fringuello!* *È un cappone che è castrato così ben ugualmente* *che nella sua voce non si può trovare intaccatura.*
Donca, chi ha la passion la lassa andar. Es spò dir a sti tal ch'ijn in error che quand s' dis Bernach, più in là n' s' po' andar.	*Pertanto, chi ne è dispiaciuto si vada a nascondere.* *E dico a questi tali che sono in errore,* *che quando si è detto "Bernacchi", più in là non si può andare.*
Diga, chi vol Bulogna[:] n' n'a scador, qui as fâ di mustaz ch'an al cular l'in tutt l' scienzi i portin via l'unor.	*Dicano ciò che vogliono: a Bologna non danno fastidio* *e ciò alla faccia dei cani* *che disonorano tutte le scienze.*

L'anonimo autore bolognese del sonetto si schiera apertamente in favore del proprio concittadino e sostiene di non condividere l'entusiasmo di coloro che parteggiano per Farinelli; inoltre mette i due a paragone enumerando con disapprovazione le caratteristiche interpretative di Farinelli, senza però pronunciarsi su quelle di Bernacchi. Farinelli è descritto come un cantante che «spara razzi» e «mortaretti» e che «imita l'usignolo» e «il fringuello»; Bernacchi al contrario non fa nulla di tutto questo, eppure canta meglio: l'autore non

[18]. I-Bu, ms. 239, fasc. v, c. 7: *Sonetto in favore del musico Bernacchi e contro il Farinello*; trad. it. di Gabriele Musenga <http://www.haendel.it/interpreti/old/bernacchi_aneddoti.htm>, visitato nell'Ottobre 2018; *cfr.* Verdi 2008, p. 129.

aggiunge a sostegno di tale affermazione null'altro che l'assunto — non privo di humor — che egli è «castrato così bene che la sua voce non ha intaccature». Sembrerebbe insomma che il canto di Farinelli non fosse apprezzato perché implicava un'esecuzione inadeguatamente o eccessivamente ornata, una critica, questa, conforme a quanto si legge ampiamente nella letteratura coeva e successiva, a partire di nuovo da Tosi: nella contrapposizione che egli fa tra *antichi* e *moderni*, condanna i moderni di «rompere [le arie], e [...] sminuzzarle in guisa che non è possibile di poter più sentire né parole, né pensieri, né modulazioni, né discernere un'aria dall'altra a cagione di tal somiglianza, ché una che se ne senta serve per mille»; condanna inoltre l'indugiare nel «torrente de' passaggi alla moda», nelle «capricciose cadenze», nell'«artificio prodigioso di cantar come i grilli [...] dieci o dodici crome in fila», arrivando a «tritolar[l]e a una a una con un certo tremor di voce che passa da poco tempo in qua sotto nome di mordente fresco»; stigmatizza infine «l'invenzione di rider cantando, o di cantar come le galline quando han fatto l'uovo», nella «velocità continua d'una voce errante senza guida e senza fondamento»[19].

Come Tosi, molti successivi detrattori del canto ornato procedettero sulla medesima linea: Vincenzo Martinelli condanna «tutti quei voli bizzarri e poco significanti»[20] e Stefano Arteaga, contrario a quei «mille impertinentissimi gruppi di note», vorrebbe proscrivere «tutte le cadenze eseguite nello stile di *bravura*, cioè quelle cadenze arbitrarie inventate all'unico fine di far brillare una voce accumulando senza disegno una serie prodigiosa di tuoni e raggirandosi con mille *ghirigori insignificanti*»[21].

Il canto di Farinelli dunque, con i suoi «razzi e mortaretti», aveva quelle caratteristiche ritenute proprie dei *moderni*, e per questo condannate come nocive al buon gusto. Per negazione ci si aspetterebbe in Bernacchi un modo di cantare del tutto opposto (come Scudo e Panzacchi centocinquant'anni dopo vollero insinuare: «e Bernacchi *ripresentò al pubblico il bel tema melodico in tutta la sua primitiva purezza e semplicità*»). Se sul modo di cantare di quest'ultimo l'autore del sonetto non si pronuncia, è possibile però rifarsi a testimonianze relative agli stessi anni, tra cui la più esplicativa e sintetica è forse la caricatura di Antonio Zanetti risalente al 1729 in cui il cantante è impegnato in una cadenza tanto lunga da innalzarsi fin sopra il campanile di Piazza S. Marco a Venezia, ridiscendere ondeggiando sopra la libreria Sansoviniana (l'odierna biblioteca marciana) e terminare in un trillo[22].

È solo la più immediata di una serie di testimonianze che descrivono il cantante come uno degli interpreti che più indugiavano in abbellimenti, passi, cadenze e fioriture e che gli causarono le aspre critiche di alcuni detrattori del canto ornato.

---

19. Tosi 1723, pp. 67, 81-82, 105-106.

20. Martinelli 1758, p. 358.

21. Arteaga 1783, pp. 130, 122.

22. La caricatura di Antonio Bernacchi è di mano di Anton Maria Zanetti e proviene da I-Vcini, *Album di caricature di Anton Maria Zanetti e altri, appartenuto a Francesco Albergati Capacelli*, ed è pubblicata in Lucchese 2015, p. 107.

A metà Settecento Vincenzo Martinelli disapprovava Bernacchi perché era solito «voler trascorrere tutti i possibili [artifici] della musica nel breve compasso d'un'aria»[23], mentre Algarotti racconta che il maestro Pistocchi avrebbe addirittura redarguito l'allievo: «"Tristo a me, io t'ho insegnato a cantare e tu vuoi suonare", rimproverava Pistocco a Bernacchi, che si può tenere come il caposcuola, il Marini della moderna licenza» e annovera Bernacchi tra quei moderni virtuosi che «pensano in contrario, che tutta la scienza stia nello isquartar la voce, in un saltellar continuo di nota in nota, non in isceglier quello che vi ha di migliore, ma in eseguire ciò che vi ha di più straordinario e difficile»[24].

Voler associare Bernacchi, come fecero Scudo e Panzacchi, a un tipo di canto non ornato è un'evidente forzatura, poiché era anch'egli cantante che fioriva ampiamente le sue arie. Verosimilmente l'unica competizione della stagione operistica bolognese del 1727 fu quella documentata dal sonetto citato, sviluppatasi interamente tra le fazioni del pubblico, parte del quale si era schierato campanilisticamente e acriticamente a favore del concittadino: una competizione del tutto priva delle considerazioni stilistiche fatte dai biografi successivi.

A testimoniare la diffusione di situazioni di antagonismo in ambito operistico, proprio allo stesso anno risale forse il più chiacchierato litigio tra primedonne del secolo, avvenuto sui palchi londinesi durante le rappresentazioni dell'*Astianatte* di Bononcini: l'ostilità tra Faustina Bordoni (1697-1781) e Francesca Cuzzoni (1696-1778) diede luogo a racconti secondo cui le due cantanti si avventarono l'una contro l'altra in un litigio tanto violento che i commentatori lo definirono un uragano («hurricane»[25]). La risonanza di questo evento fu abbastanza ampia, seppur anche in quel caso, come sembra essere accaduto a Bologna, le narrazioni coeve (due pamphlet senza alcuna pretesa di verosimiglianza e con finalità puramente satirica[26]) abbiano di molto esagerato la realtà dei fatti, che si limitò a un astio profondo tra le due, alimentato da opposte fazioni del pubblico[27].

BERNACCHI INSEGNANTE DI CANTO

Bernacchi fu uno dei più celebrati maestri di canto del Settecento. Poter dire di aver studiato con lui era sinonimo di legittimità degli studi compiuti e un ottimo biglietto da visita per futuri ingaggi. Tra coloro che restarono sotto il suo magistero per diversi anni vi furono Ventura Rocchetti, Giovanni Tedeschi Amadori, Anton Raaff, Carlo Carlani e Tommaso Guarducci. Di Ventura Rocchetti, soprano, non si conoscono le date di nascita e morte; tuttavia quando iniziò a vivere con Bernacchi, nel 1735-1736, era attivo

23. MARTINELLI 1758, p. 358.
24. ALGAROTTI 1763, p. 46.
25. *THE DEVIL* 1727, p. 4.
26. Si vedano *THE DEVIL* 1727 e *THE CONTRE-TEMPS* 1727.
27. La questione è affrontata ampiamente in ASPDEN 2013.

nei teatri italiani da un lustro e aveva già cantato a Dresda e a Londra. Giovanni Tedeschi Amadori (1715-1787), contralto, aveva almeno 24 anni quando nel 1739 si trasferì a Bologna, e dal 1732 aveva già cantato in una decina di opere in teatri romani. Anton Raaff (1714-1797), tenore, arrivò nel 1740, essendosi esibito nei tre anni precedenti a Monaco, Firenze e Venezia.

Tutti i sopracitati avevano dunque iniziato a prendere lezioni da Bernacchi già adulti e a carriera avviata, avendo prima studiato con altri maestri, perlopiù compositori: Raaff era stato allievo di Giovanni Battista Ferrandini (ca. 1710-791), Giovanni Tedeschi di Giuseppe Amadori (1670-1730); lo stesso fecero anche altri cantanti che studiarono con Bernacchi per un più breve periodo: tra questi un certo «signor Tomasini» virtuoso della reale maestà di Portogallo, giunto da Lisbona a Bologna nel maggio del 1751 appositamente per avere lezioni da Bernacchi[28]. Nel '51 risiedevano nella sua casa anche il ventiseienne Lorenzo Memel e Antonio Ratti, trentaseienne; erano probabilmente allievi, ma non riuscirono ad avviare una carriera teatrale[29]. «In Bologna si trattenne alcuni mesi assistito dal maestro Bernacchi» anche Pietro Paolo Carnoli (1752-1802), poi al servizio dell'elettore palatino[30], e forse pure Vincenzo Caselli (1710-1799), poi alla corte di Dresda.

Altri suoi allievi furono Giuseppe Appiani detto l'Appianino (1712-1742), e Gioacchino Conti detto Gizziello (1714-1761), entrambi provenienti da scuole napoletane: il primo era stato, come Farinelli, allievo del compositore Nicola Porpora (1686-1766); il secondo del soprano Domenico Gizzi (1680-1758), da cui il soprannome artistico (talvolta storpiato in 'Egiziello'). Appiani giungeva a Bologna con una solida carriera alle spalle, nei teatri del Nord d'Italia; dal canto suo, Conti aveva già conquistato il pubblico di Londra, dove nel 1736-1737 aveva anche assistito alle esibizioni di Farinelli. Non sappiamo se, rientrando in Italia, la scelta di rivolgersi a Bernacchi sia stata suggerita da quest'ultimo; di fatto, la fiducia riposta — già famosi — nella didattica di Bernacchi venne letta da Mancini come un encomiabile segno di umiltà artistica:

> Il giovanetto Gizziello, quantunque lontano dal suo maestro [Gizzi], non lasciò di mettere in pratica tutti gli avvertimenti acquistati, e di seguire lo studio sulle regole del suo Maestro. Passò in Inghilterra per alcuni anni, dove perfezionò lo stile e si fé raro. Non ostante però l'alto nome che ivi avea alzato,

---

28. «Scrivo intanto questa per domani consegnarla in caso che partisse la detta [nave] avanti martedì, e in questa nave parte un musico di Sua Maestà per portarsi a studiare sotto la direzione del nostro famosissimo signor Antonio Bernacchi, il quale me lo potrà divertire con tutta la stima e che li sono e fui sempre suo buon amico e servitore». I-Bc, I.4.29: *Lettera di Gaetano Maria Schiassi a Giovanni Battista Martini*, Lisbona, 6 maggio 1751.

29. I-Bgd, Parrocchie Soppresse, Ss. Giacomo e Filippo de' Piatesi, *Stati delle anime*, anno 1751.

30. «Mi ricordai che avevo nella corte Palatina un mio amico chiamato Pietro Paolo Carnoli, che serve quella corte in qualità di tenore. [...] Questo giovine l'ha dovuto conoscere in Bologna, dove si trattenne alcuni mesi assistito dal maestro Bernacchi. Comunque sia, se non è morto deve rispondere». I-Bc, L.117.76: *Lettera di Giovanni Battista Mancini a Giovanni Battista Martini*, Vienna, 4 gennaio 1769.

> ritornando in Italia, quasi non contento di sé stesso, volle fermarsi in Bologna sotto la direzzione del gran Bernacchi. Fatto, che potria essere di regola e di rossore a molti, che presumono di sé stessi. Lo stesso praticò l'amabile Giuseppe Appiani detto Appianino, trattenendosi anch'esso in Bologna per studiare presso lo stesso Bernacchi. Questo studio fatto da questi due Professori fu da loro eseguito in quel medesimo tempo che ambidue erano riconosciuti ed acclamati fra il numero de' primari cantanti[31].

Vittoria Tesi era stata allieva del compositore Giovanni Redi (1685-1769) a Firenze; trasferitasi a Bologna, studiava quotidianamente con Francesco Campeggi (16??-1742), pur «non tralasciando nel medesimo tempo di frequentare la scuola di Bernacchi»[32]; aveva studiato con Bernacchi lo stesso Giovanni Battista Mancini (1714-1800): allievo di Leonardo Leo per due anni a Napoli, nel 1728 si era spostato a Bologna per perfezionarsi con quello che nei *Pensieri e riflessioni pratiche sopra il canto figurato* (1774) innalzerà poi a principe della didattica vocale.

La scuola di Bernacchi come tappa di perfezionamento

Al tempo della comparsa sulla scena bolognese, la carriera di Farinelli era in piena ascesa, tuttavia l'anno precedente questi aveva rifiutato un'importante scrittura per Londra e, secondo l'impresario inglese in esilio Owen McSwiny, non lo si sarebbe potuto convincere ad andare in Inghilterra per i successivi due o tre anni, «poiché egli ha in mente di studiare la *maniera lombarda*, che lo farà migliorare al cento per cento»[33]. Il passo testimonia in Farinelli un atteggiamento che Tosi descrive nel suo trattato come il più apprezzabile in un cantante, nonché necessario per raggiungere i più alti livelli di carriera: l'apertura continua verso nuovi studi e i consigli di nuovi mentori:

> Chi nutre però sentimenti migliori cercherà una più nobile e più ristretta compagnia. Conoscerà il bisogno che ha d'altri lumi, d'altri documenti, e d'altro

31. Mancini 1774, pp. 184-185.

32. *Ibidem*, p. 19.

33. «I am just returned from Parma where I heard ye Divine Farinelli (another blazing star) but I am sorry to tell you that I m'e affraid he'l not be p[e]rsuaded to goe for England these two or three years yet, for he has a mind to study ye Lombard Manner, which will improve him Cent per Cent: I think I told your Grace in my last letter that he was engaged to sing in one of the theatres of Rome the next winter». GB-West Sussex Record Office, Chichester, Goodwood MS 105/401, 3: *Letter by Owen McSwiny dated Venice 31 May 1726 to the Duke of Richmond*, trascritta in Llewellyn 2009, p. 228. Nel suo contributo del 2014, Anne Desler ha evidenziato l'inverosimiglianza dei testi di Sacchi e Fétis, escludendo la possibilità che i due cantanti abbiano intrapreso una gara canora, ma supportando la reale possibilità che Farinelli sia stato istruito, pur non formalmente, da Bernacchi, supportando la sua ampia argomentazione anche con questa testimonianza. *Cfr.* Desler 2014, pp. 107 e 110.

> maestro ancora. Da questo vorrà apprendere coll'arte di ben cantare quella di saper vivere, che tutta consiste nelle belle convenienze della vita civile. Unita che questa sia al merito che si farà nel canto, allora ei potrà sperare la grazia de' monarchi e la stima universale[34].

Farinelli era di certo un cantante con la piena padronanza delle proprie capacità tecniche, acquisite presso Nicola Porpora a Napoli: se avesse avuto gravi lacune non gli sarebbe stata possibile una carriera così ottimamente avviata; tuttavia, almeno già dall'anno precedente al suo incontro con Bernacchi, tutt'altro che compiaciuto di sé, desiderava migliorare il proprio stile esecutivo e rinunciava a un'importante occasione lavorativa perché aveva intenzione di imparare a cantare alla «maniera lombarda». Mancini (1774) conferma che in effetti portò a compimento il proposito:

> Nacque il Cavaliere Don Carlo Broschi nella Provincia di Bari nel Regno di Napoli. [...] I suoi *primi studi* furono diretti dal celebre Niccolò Porpora. [...] i Teatri delle primarie città d'Italia fecero a gara per averlo, e in ogni parte ov'egli cantò, ne riportò un ben meritato applauso, a tal segno che ognuno pretese di rifermarlo. Molte corti d'Europa non tardarono di farlo chiamare, e da per tutto fu ammirato, contraddistinto e ben premiato. Questo florido suo corso fu ne' primi anni della sua gioventù. Non per questo il nostro valent'uomo *cessò mai di studiare a un tanto segno che gli riuscì di cambiare in gran parte il suo primo fare, scegliendone un altro migliore; e tutto ciò fu da esso intrapreso in quel medesimo tempo che si avea già fatto il gran nome*[35].

Se Mancini non si pronuncia su cosa fece Farinelli per migliorarsi, la risposta è negli appunti manoscritti di Padre Martini, amico stretto di entrambi i soggetti coinvolti:

> 1727: [Farinelli] recitò in Bologna assieme col famoso Antonio Bernacchi, del quale è viva ancora la memoria fra' tanti scolari nel signor Giovanni Amadori, Raaff, signor Tommaso Guarducci, i quali passano fra i più eccellenti cantori de' nostri tempi. Terminato il dramma in Bologna, essendo chiamati ambedue a recitare nel teatro di Parma *ed avendo ammirata il Broschi la grand'arte del Bernacchi nel cantare, fu pregato a darle alcune istruzioni che conosceva mancargli; e infatti ogni mattina, levato dal letto lui e il Bernacchi passavano assieme al cembalo ed attendeva quelle sottigliezze che conosceva mancargli*. Da tutto ciò non è da meravigliarsi se riuscì così eccellente il cavaliere Broschi e fu ricercato dalle principali teste coronate d'Europa[36].

Dunque il giovane cantante in ascesa Farinelli, una volta avuta la fortuna di lavorare al fianco di Bernacchi, lo riconobbe come «a quel tempo il primo cantante d'Italia per

---

34. TOSI 1723, p. 90.

35. MANCINI 1774, pp. 105-107; corsivi aggiunti.

36. I-Bc, ms. H.60: MARTINI, Giovanni Battista. *Zibaldone Martiniano. Contiene notizie di musicisti, ed altre cose relative alla storia della musica*, p. 132; corsivi aggiunti. Il documento è già citato in VERDI 2008, p. 129.

gusto e sapienza»[37], ritrovò in lui un esponente di quella «maniera lombarda» diversa dalla sua 'napoletana' di cantare, e decise quindi di rivolgersi allo stimato collega per qualche consiglio, che il didatta fu pronto a dare: molto probabilmente, dopo quel primo incontro, trovarono del tempo per studiare insieme quando ebbero l'occasione di lavorare nelle stesse città e durante i frequenti soggiorni di Farinelli a Bologna.

Versioni di un mito

Avendo stabilito che in realtà non ci fu alcuna competizione, è chiaro che alcuni biografi hanno messo in atto una reinvenzione estrema, tanto estrema da suggerire che l'importanza di queste fonti 'alterate' non risieda nella loro riconduzione ad una realtà storicamente attendibile, ma nell'immagine che ci offrono della recezione postuma del personaggio Bernacchi e del rapido processo di mitizzazione cui fu sottoposto. In quest'ottica, queste diverse e successive versioni, piuttosto che essere ritenute distorte, possono essere ritenute legittime per comprendere il pensiero coevo all'autore. La chiave di lettura è dunque quella di narrazioni che possano essere esemplificative di una più ampia visione: quella del mito. Come un mito, rappresentano un episodio che possa avere caratteri universali, e per raggiungere quel grado di importanza usano come 'attori' delle figure iconiche, come erano appunto Farinelli e Bernacchi. Entrambi «di ottimo animo», il primo è l'incarnazione del virtuoso di talento (Fétis: «chanteur le plus extraordinaire») nel pieno del proprio successo e ancor giovane (Sacchi: «animosità giovanile»), l'altro è l'incarnazione del maestro di canto paterno, comprensivo, intelligente, la validità dei cui metodi d'insegnamento è confermata dal fatto che egli è a sua volta un cantante di rilievo sul piano internazionale. Il narratore attinge al repertorio di altre storie di cui dispone ed estremizza le caratteristiche di entrambi i cantanti, alterandole quanto serve perché aderiscano ai cliché che gli serve vengano impersonati: solo così il racconto mitico acquisisce adeguata forza comunicativa.

In questi racconti l'identità degli 'antagonisti' non è nemmeno troppo fondamentale per la delineazione del messaggio retorico, come dimostra una versione modificata del racconto sopracitato di Algarotti pubblicata su un giornale milanese del 1827, secondo cui Bernacchi sarebbe diventato il primo cantante d'Europa solo dopo aver rinnegato il canto ornato:

> Pistochi capo-scuola di canto del secolo passato, avendo udito dalle scene di un Teatro di Londra il suo allievo Bernachi, «Ah sciagurato!», esclamò fra il

---

37. «From Rome he [Farinelli] went to Bologna where he had the advantage of hearing Bernacchi, a scholar of the famous Pistocchi, of that city, who was then the first singer in Italy, for taste and knowledge; and his scholars afterwards rendered the Bologna school famous». Burney 1773, pp. 214-215.

> profondo silenzio del pubblico, «Io ti ho insegnato a cantare e tu vuoi suonare!». Gli inglesi applaudirono l'ardire di Pistocchi, ed il Bernacchi fu d'allora in poi il primo cantante in Europa[38].

Si vede bene un *pattern* che si ripete, invariabilmente applicabile anche su colui che in altre testimonianze è il mitico maestro salvatore e risanatore di un allievo troppo dedito alle fioriture: gli attori che impersonano l'allievo troppo audace e il maestro molto raffinato sono intercambiabili, a riprova del trattamento di mitizzazione che ricevono; ciò che viene preservata è la contrapposizione tra due generazioni in contrasto fra loro, in cui «la scuola antica si rivoltava contro le innovazioni della nuova»[39].

Nei diversi racconti le figure di Farinelli e Bernacchi assurgono dunque *ad exempla* e, come nella tradizione agiografica delle *Vite dei santi*, incarnano più di quello che furono, ovvero gli stereotipi (vuoi positivi o negativi) delle rispettive categorie. In questo modo il cantante di successo diventa vanesio, il maestro furbo ma pacato, il loro primo incontro una competizione in campo aperto e la risoluzione commovente schiude le porte per un insegnamento morale: un cantante non deve smettere di studiare e migliorarsi; un cantante più bravo di un altro non deve ostentare la propria superiorità, ma consentire all'altro di attingere in modo costruttivo dalla sua esperienza al fine di mantenere viva l'arte del canto e permetterne la trasmissione; un cantante deve essere umile e non credersi migliore di quello che è, non deve mettersi in competizione e deve comportarsi in modo rispettoso. I biografi successivi delineeranno dunque un nuovo *topos*: quello dei colleghi che si imitano in un rapporto virtuoso.

Oscurata dall'abbondanza di fonti primarie e letteratura secondaria che indugiano in forse più succulenti, pruriginosi, divertenti episodi concentrati sulla competizione, la collaborazione tra virtuosi è un aspetto della realtà di quel periodo (e di tutti gli altri) troppo spesso trascurato, sebbene non manchino altri esempi coevi che testimoniano che fosse pratica comune, come ad esempio il rapporto tra Felice Salimbeni (1712-1755) e Giuseppe Appiani (1712-1742):

> L'eccellente contraltista Giuseppe Appiani, detto Appianino, [...] aveva un timbro particolarmente bello e sapeva cantare in modo brillante e pulito. Questo suscitò in Salimbeni una lodevole ammirazione per lui che lo stimolò a imitarlo. I due erano grandi amici e studiarono insieme, con la suddetta intenzione di migliorarsi e con pari diligenza, soprattutto i duetti di Steffani[40].

---

[38]. *I teatri* 1827, p. 10.

[39]. Lemaire – Lavoix 1881, p. 388.

[40]. «[...] vortrefliche Contraltist, Giuseppe Appiani, insgemein Appianino genannt, bey seiner besonders schönen Stimme, auch viel Geschicklichkeit in der ausgehaltenen, gezogenen, doch aber auch dabei netten und brillanten Singart besaß: so erregte dies bey Salinbeni die löbliche Eifersucht, ihm es darinne gleich zu thun. Sie waren gute Freunde, und studirten, hauptsächlich in der erwähnten Absicht, die Steffanischen Duette, mit großem Fleiße, nochmals miteinander durch». Hiller 1784, p. 232.

Se improvvisazione nell'opera del Settecento significava saper applicare in un contesto quasi estemporaneo formule appropriate precedentemente apprese, la modalità di apprendimento era tanto importante quanto le potenzialità vocali dell'interprete. Senza bravi maestri, bravi esempi, stimoli al continuo miglioramento, una voce *per se* non aveva nulla di straordinario. Fondamentale dunque l'apertura del cantante/allievo ai nuovi insegnamenti, e fondamentale l'atteggiamento di accoglienza, paterno, del maestro di canto, pronto a trasmettere dalla propria voce a quella dell'allievo, come le formule melodiche e testuali delle tradizioni orali, le tecniche (o i segreti) dell'improvvisare.

Bibliografia

Algarotti 1763
Algarotti, Francesco. *Saggio sopra l'opera in musica*, Livorno, Coltellini, 1763.

Arteaga 1783
Arteaga, Stefano. *Le rivoluzioni del teatro musicale italiano dalla sua origine fino al presente*, 3 voll., Bologna, Trenti, 1783-1788, vol. i.

Aspden 2013
Aspden, Suzanne. *The Rival Sirens: Performance and Identity on Handel's Operatic Stage*, Cambridge, Cambridge University Press, 2013 (Cambridge Studies in Opera).

Burney 1773
Burney, Charles. *The Present State of Music in Germany, the Netherlands and United Provinces*, 2 voll., Londra, Beckett and Strand, 1773, vol. i.

Corp 2011
Corp, Edward. *The Stuarts in Italy, 1719-1766: A Royal Court in Permanent Exile*, Cambridge, Cambridge University Press, 2011.

Desler 2014
Desler, Anne. *"Il novello Orfeo". Farinelli: Vocal Profile, Aesthetics, Rhetoric*, Ph.D. Diss., Glasgow, University of Glasgow, 2014.

Fétis 1860
Fétis, François-Joseph. *Biographie universelle des musiciens* et *bibliographie générale de la musique. 2*, Parigi, Firmin Didot, [2]1860.

Hiller 1784
Hiller, Johann Adam. *Lebensbeschreibungen berühmter Musikgelehrten und Tonkünstler neuerer Zeit*, Lipsia, Dyk, 1784.

I teatri 1827
I teatri: giornale drammatico, musicale e coreografico, i (1827).

Lemaire – Lavoix 1881
Lemaire, Théophile – Lavoix, Henri, fils. *Le chant, ses principes et son histoire*, Parigi, Heugel, 1881.

Llewellyn 2009
Llewellyn, Timothy D. *Owen McSwiny's Letters, 1720-1744*, Verona, Scripta, 2009 (Lettere artistiche del Settecento veneziano, 4; Fonti e documenti per la storia dell'arte veneta, 14).

Lucchese 2015
Lucchese, Enrico. *L'album di caricature di Anton Maria Zanetti alla Fondazione Giorgio Cini*, Venezia, Lineadacqua-Fondazione Giorgio Cini, 2015.

Mancini 1774
Mancini, Giovanni Battista. *Pensieri, e riflessioni pratiche sopra il canto figurato*, Vienna, Ghelen, 1774.

Martinelli 1758
Martinelli, Vincenzo. 'Al signor conte di Buckinghamshire: sulla origine delle Opere in Musica', in: *Lettere Familiari e Critiche*, Londra, Giovanni Nourse, 1758, pp. 353-363.

McGeary 2005
McGeary, Thomas. 'Farinelli's Progress to Albion: The Recruitment and Reception of Opera's "Blazing Star"', in: *British Journal for Eighteenth-Century Studies*, xxviii/5 (2005).

Panzacchi 1889
Panzacchi, Enrico. *I miei racconti*, Milano, Treves 1889.

Panzacchi 1897
Id. 'La Musica', in: *La vita italiana durante la Rivoluzione francese e l'Impero. 3*, Milano, Treves, 1897, pp. 509-540.

Sacchi 1784
Sacchi, Giovenale. *Vita del Cavaliere Don Carlo Broschi*, Venezia, Coleti, 1784.

Scudo 1861
Scudo, Paul. 'Les sopranistes - Farinelli', in: *Revue des deux mondes*, xxxv/3 (1861), pp. 759-769.

Singing to Some Purpose 1863
'Singing to Some Purpose', in: *All the Year Round: A Weekley Journal Conducted by Charles Dickens*, 15 marzo 1863, pp. 21-24.

The Contre-Temps 1727
The Contre-Temps; or Rival Queens: a Small Farce, Londra, Moore, 1727.

The Devil 1727
Anonimo. *The Devil to Pay at St. James, or a Full Account of a Most Horrible and Blody Battle between Madam Faustina and Madam Cuzzoni*, Londra, s.n., 1727.

Tosi 1723

Tosi, Pier Francesco. *Opinioni de' cantori antichi e moderni o sieno Osservazioni sopra* il *canto figurato*, Bologna, Lelio dalla Volpe, 1723.

Verdi 2008

Verdi, Luigi. 'Del musico Antonio Maria Bernacchi nel 250° della morte', in: *Un anno per tre filarmonici di rango: Perti, Martini e Mozart: un principe, un definitore e un fuoriclasse da celebrare nel 2006. Atti del convegno (Bologna, Accademia Filarmonica, 3-4 novembre 2006)*, a cura di Piero Mioli, Bologna, Pàtron, 2008, pp. 125-146.

Vitali 1992

Vitali, Carlo. 'Da «schiavottiello» a «fedele amico». Lettere (1731-1749) di Carlo Broschi Farinelli al conte Sicinio Pepoli', in: *Nuova rivista musicale italiana*, n. 1 (1992), pp. 1-36.

Re-Creating Historical Improvisatory Solo Practices on the Cello

C. Simpson, F. Niedt, and J. S. Bach on the Pedagogy of *Contrapunctis Extemporalis*

John Lutterman
(University of Alaska Anchorage)

While those of us interested in historically-informed performing practices recognize that anachronistic nineteenth-century traditions have continued to influence the treatment of early music in today's conservatory and concert life, it is easy to forget that modern practices of presenting public concerts and studying at conservatories are themselves nineteenth-century inventions. We see that even *urtext* editions are often colored by nineteenth-century traditions, but often lose sight of the fact that the very idea of publishing critical editions of early music is itself a nineteenth-century invention. In light of this, it is perhaps less surprising that we rarely stop to consider the still more insidious ways in which another nineteenth-century idea about the nature of musical practices has come to govern the ways that we understand the meaning of musical notation: the idea that written compositions should be understood as fixed musical works.

The work of Roman Ingarden, Carl Dahlhaus, and Lydia Goehr[1] has prompted much of the recent scholarly writing that has questioned the ontological status of compositions before Beethoven. However, in addressing the practical concerns of performing musicians, I have found Arthur Mendel's 1957 formulation of the problem refreshingly succinct:

> Western musicians of today have such strong habits of associating a piece of music with its graphic notation that they need constant reminding, by every possible means, of the limitations of notation as applied to either old or exotic music. The hunt for the authentic version of a piece by even so recent a composer as J. S. Bach [...] is a vain one. Neither Bach nor any other good musician up to at least Bach's time probably ever played a piece exactly the same way twice. And by 'the same way' we mean nothing so narrow as the musician of today may understand. We mean that he probably never played exactly the same notes twice, or played them in exactly the same rhythm[2].

---

1. Ingarden 1986, Ingarden 1989, Dahlhaus 1989, Dahlhaus 1994, Goehr 1992.
2. Mendel 1957, pp. 10-11.

As David Schulenberg has suggested, in the course of his analysis of the three-part ricercar from *The Musical Offering* as a kind of record of Bach's improvisation on the royal theme:

> In its printed form the three-part *ricercar* might be seen in the same light as those engravings of Baroque opera scenes in which heroes rise to heaven or armies attack one another without any visible inconvenience from gravity or balky stage machinery[3].

While Bach's written music may represent an idealized portrait of practices that he was illustrating for his students and patrons, we should be able to make some educated guesses about the nature of «the inconvenient effects of gravity» and the kinds of «balky stage machinery» that may have shaped these improvisatory practices. Viewed through an analytic lens, free from the blinders of a modern work concept, the written compositions of Bach and his contemporaries may be understood as more-or-less systematically organized inventories of formal models, and as idiomatic vocabularies of motivic, harmonic and contrapuntal ideas or 'inventions', all of which are ripe for improvisatory appropriation and elaboration. Indeed, as I have argued elsewhere, I would suggest that it is these somewhat abstract, enduring 'ideas' which are best understood as Bach's contribution to the canon of musical 'works', rather than any particular instantiation of such ideas[4].

Accounts of J. S. Bach's solo performances invariably focus on his improvisatory prowess. Indeed, the only reference to his use of written music in an unaccompanied performance is found in an account by his Leipzig contemporary, Theodor Pitschel, in which Bach is said to have used organ compositions by lesser composers as a springboard for his improvisations.

> You know, the famous man who has the greatest praise in our town in music, and the greatest admiration of connoisseurs, does not get into condition, as the expression goes, to delight others with the mingling of his tones until he has played something from the printed or written page, and has [thus] set his powers of imagination in motion [...] The able man whom I have mentioned usually has to play something from the page that is inferior to his own ideas. And yet his superior ideas are the consequence of those inferior ones[5].

Recent scholarship has brought a broadening recognition of the important roles that improvisatory practices continued to play in concert life well into the nineteenth century, and this recognition poses one of the most significant challenges to the adequacy of representing historical performing practices by means of programs that consist solely of written compositions[6]. In an attempt to solve this dilemma, I often include performances of

---

3. Schulenberg 1995, p. 5.
4. Lutterman 2006.
5. Pitschel 1741.
6. Rasch 2011

unaccompanied, semi-improvised suites of pieces in my concert programs, drawing upon the written compositions by a number of eighteenth-century composers as frameworks, and employing eighteenth-century techniques and styles of improvisatory elaboration. In these programs, I have sought to re-create eighteenth-century musical practices of unaccompanied solo cello playing, rather than simply performing a fixed set of musical 'works'.

Clues to the technical means of re-creating relevant historical improvisatory practices appropriate to unaccompanied cello performance can be found in a number of sources, including Christopher Simpson's *The Divison Viol*[7], Friedrich Niedt's *Musicalische Handleitung*[8], and the earliest cello methods, which invariably included instruction in the art of chordal thoroughbass realization[9]. The rich trove of Italian partimento exercises also offer invaluable insights into historical techniques of improvisatory elaboration and development.

The particular improvisatory techniques that I have employed, and which I would like to discuss include: 1) the use of sequences of double-stops and arpeggiated patterns to create a prelude, 2) practices of thoroughbass realization on the cello and the incorporation of a basso continuo line into an unaccompanied performance of an existing work, and 3) the use of «points of division» or «inventions» over a bass framework to generate complete movements in particular genres.

Clues to the employment of sequences of double-stops and arpeggios for preluding can be found in several of the early cello methods, starting with Baumgartner[10], whose treatise was the first to provide explicit instruction in chordal thoroughbass realization, but the most systematic treatment is Duport[11]. Fingerings of double-stops in the early cello treatises is invariably arranged in patterns designed to facilitate the performance of common contrapuntal sequences, which may be easily memorized and employed as a kind of vocabulary when preluding. In my experiments, I frequently adapt this vocabulary to harmonic patterns derived from Bach's preludes as a framework to provide a large-scale formal structure for my improvisations.

Duport (see Ex. 1, p. 244) begins with sequences of 2-3 suspensions, and then expands this treatment by adding a 6th as preparation for each suspension. This is followed by circle-of-5^{ths} sequences, using alternating 6^{ths} and 3^{rds}, sequences of diminished 5^{ths} and 3^{rds}, and then examples of sequences of augmented 4^{ths} resolving to 6^{ths} which conclude with various 4-3 and 7-6 cadential formulas. After this, we get sequences of 5-6 progressions. At the end come sequences with 7^{ths}: 7-6 suspensions, a rising-4th sequence of alternating 7ths and 3^{rds}, and finally, diminished 7^{ths} alternating with 5^{ths}.

---

7. SIMPSON 1659.
8. NIEDT 2003.
9. LUTTERMAN 2011.
10. BAUMGARTNER 1774.
11. DUPORT 1806.

Ex. 1: Duport Sequences.

2-3 Suspensions
Sequence of 2-3 Suspensions and 6ths
Circle of 5ths sequence in 6ths and 3rds
Sequences of diminished-5ths resolving to 3rds
Sequences with augmented 4ths resolving to 6ths with cadences of 4-3 or 7-6 suspensions
Sequences of 5-6 patterns
Sequences of 7-6 suspensions
Sequences of 7ths resolving to 3rds

While Baumgartner's treatise was the first to offer explicit instruction in chordal thoroughbass realization on the cello, it is clear from his text that he is documenting an established practice. His written examples included idiomatic realizations of common cadential patterns in which octave placement and inversions are treated quite freely. Written examples of figured bass realizations in the other cello treatises also frequently treat inversions (including 2nd inversion) interchangeably. The most thorough treatment of figured bass realization on the cello is found somewhat later in a treatise by John Gunn[12], who illustrates several idiomatic 'rule of the octave' progressions, with a number of alternative cadences (see Ex. 2, p. 246). Gunn also illustrates the application of thoroughbass treatment to unaccompanied playing with examples of arpeggiated realizations of two well-known eighteenth-century «standards»: the folk-song *Ah! Vous dirai-je maman* and *La Folia* (or, as Gunn puts it: «a Spanish melody from Corelli's Opera 5ta»).

At this point, before continuing my discussion of thoroughbass realization, I would like to briefly consider a set of six pieces by Boismortier, entitled *Suite de pieces qu'on peut jouer seul*, found as an *addendum* to his Op. 40 Sonatas, which are often held up as early examples of unaccompanied works[13] (see Ex. 3, p. 247).

These pieces, which are somewhat more idiomatic for bassoon than cello, do in fact work reasonably well in an unaccompanied performance, but the textures are not substantially different from the accompanied continuo sonatas which make up the bulk of the Op. 40 collection (see Ex. 3, A). Indeed, unaccompanied performance is much more effective for several movements from Boismortier's Op. 50[14], in which he incorporates the basso line as well as its chordal realization into the solo part to a degree that frequently makes a basso accompaniment superfluous (see Ex. 3, B).

This observation supports my hypothesis that thoroughbass training would have played an essential role in unaccompanied solo practices of the eighteenth century. In my experiments with chordal realization of figured bass on the cello, I have discovered that I often find myself incorporating the solo part into my own part when preparing a thoroughbass realization of an aria or solo sonata. By the same token, when practicing a solo concerto or sonata, I have frequently found myself incorporating a realization of the basso into the solo part. And this is what I often attempt to do when generating unaccompanied versions of several of the 'framework' compositions in my little fantasy suites. Here, you can see two small samples from my experiments: the first, a *Largo* in ritornello form from Boismortier's Op. 50 Sonatas (see Ex. 3, C1 and C2); the second an *Adagio* in the form of a *da capo* aria, from Vivaldi's G minor Cello Concerto, RV 416 (see Ex. 3, D1 and D2).

---

12. Gunn 1802.

13. Boismortier 1732.

14. Boismortier 1734.

Ex. 2: John Gunn, examples of thoroughbass realization on the cello.

Ex. 3: Excerpts from works by Boismortier and Vivaldi that may be realized and performed by an unaccompanied cello.

The next step would be to improvise an entirely new solo part above such a realization, much as Kirnberger suggests in his charming tract entitled, *Methode Sonaten aus'm Ermel zu Schüdeln*[15] (How to shake a sonata out of one's sleeve), in a process which I view as 'dialogic' in a Bakhtinian sense. This dialogic sense has also informed my experiments in improvising complete movements by employing motivic ideas ('inventions') drawn from historical sources to elaborate contrapuntal frameworks that I have extracted from Bach's unaccompanied works. As for the working out of 'inventions' or 'points of division', I would like to consider Christopher Simpson's and Friedrich Niedt's pedagogical methods, and offer two (written-out) samples of my experiments in a partimento-style of improvisation, in which I have employed a number of strategies outlined by Simpson and Niedt.

Christopher Simpson's *The Division Viol* is one of the most comprehensive treatises on improvisation ever written, offering valuable clues to the nature of a number of historical improvisatory practices, particularly his method of teaching the art of extemporaneous implied polyphony, which Simpsons terms a 'mixt' style of divisions. While the importance of Simpson's treatise for understanding the practices of seventeenth-century British musicians is well known, *The Division Viol* had a greater influence on the continent than has generally been recognized. The popularity of the *Division-Viol* led to the printing of a second edition with a parallel Latin translation in 1667, in order «that it might be understood in Foreign Parts», and this edition found its way into a number of continental collections[16]. Demand for copies of *The Division-Viol* was strong enough to warrant additional printings of the second edition, and a third edition was published in 1712[17]. Mattheson discusses Simpson's work in his *Critica Musica* of 1722-1725[18] and *The Division Viol* remained influential enough to be mentioned in Walther's *Musicalisches Lexicon* as late as 1732[19].

Simpson's approach to counterpoint is more harmonically conceived than has generally been recognized (he anticipates Rameau in demonstrating the inversional equivalence of triads), and the organization of his treatise shows interesting parallels to Niedt's *Musikalische Handleitung*, which itself appears to reflect Italian partimento practices. While I would not posit a causal link of influence between these three important approaches to the pedagogy of improvisation in the seventeenth century, I do suggest that a better understanding of the similarities between them can offer valuable insights into the mechanics and the underlying grammatical and syntactical structures of the elusive improvisatory practices that they were meant to teach. My discussion here will focus primarily on Simpson's contributions, in large part because his work has received less scholarly attention than Niedt's treatise or the partimento tradition has in recent years.

15. Kirnberger 1783.
16. Simpson 1667
17. Simpson 1712.
18. Mattheson 1722-1725.
19. Walther 1732.

The *Division-Viol* is divided into three parts, preceded by a glossary of terms that gives translations in Latin, French and Italian. The set of translations for the English term 'Descant' that Simpson presents in his glossary is of particular interest, suggesting several shades of meaning to the improvisatory process of contrapuntally elaborating an idea: Latin - *Contrapunctus ex-temporalis*; French - *Contrepoint a première veüe*; and Italian - *Contrapunto a mente*.

Part III of the treatise contains perhaps the most valuable insights into Simpson's approach to teaching improvised counterpoint, in particular chapters three, four and five, which introduce three broad approaches to elaborating a bass line: 'Breaking the Ground', 'Descant Division', and 'Mixt Division'. These chapters elaborate three fundamental categories of skills that a student was expected to develop: 1) ornamenting a bass line, 2) improvising a new contrapuntal line, and 3) using real or implied polyphony to project several lines at once. These skills are interdependent, and each would have been an essential component of earlier improvisatory practices, but Simpson's decision to treat them systematically is surely one of his most important contributions to the pedagogy of improvisation.

Friedrich Niedt employs a similar organization of topics in the *Musicalische Handleitung*. Methods of varying the bass (the left hand) are presented first, followed by instructions for creating a new part above the bass (varying the right hand realization in various ways). As for the 'mixt' style, while Niedt doesn't explicitly label this as an individual category of variation, several of his later examples clearly demonstrate the realization of an underlying contrapuntal texture as a compound melody.

Simpson's chapter three, 'Breaking the Ground', gives detailed and systematically ordered instructions for varying a bass line. He outlines five progressive steps for learning this style of divisions: 1) simple rhythmic division of each note of the ground, 2) examples of simple turns and short linear ornamental passages that begin and end on each note of the ground before moving on, 3) examples in which the end of each point of division makes a smooth stepwise transition to the following pitch without returning to the pitch being divided, 4) examples which, as in the second, begin and end on each note of the bass, but make use of intermediate skips to consonant pitches, and 5) examples in which the arpeggiations introduced in part four are filled in with scalar passages to create smoother transitions.

After systematically describing these five procedures, Simpson offers three general guidelines for improvising an effective «broken ground»:

> First, That it be harmonious to the holding Note. Secondly, That it come off so, as to meet the next Note of the *Ground* in a smooth and natural passage. Thirdly, Or if it pass into Discords, that they be such as are aptly used in Composition[20].

[20]. Simpson 1667, p. 30.

Simpson then gives several examples in which the connection is rather mechanically made smooth «by making the last three, or more of the Minute Notes (at least two of them) ascend or descend by degrees, unto the next succeeding Note»[21]. This last point is followed by an admonishment that «this requires not only a Notion but a Habit also, which must be got by practice»[22].

As further illustration of the above points, and in order to provide more material for practice, Simpson then gives an example of divisions over a longer ground bass line. The student's attention is called to several new points here: the appropriate use of accidentals, the inversional equivalence of 2nds and 7ths, 3ds and 6ths, etc., and the need to sharpen the leading tone in minor ('flat') keys and at internal 'closes'. Simpson also uses this opportunity to introduce several examples in which a point of division begins on a pitch other than the one given in the ground. This pitch must be consonant with the ground, of course, which provides a nice segue to his discussion of descant division in chapter four.

Descant division is defined as «that which makes a Different-concording-part unto the *Ground*». This is distinguished from breaking the ground by the fact that the latter «takes the liberty to wander sometimes beneath the *Ground*», while descant «(as in its proper sphere) moves still above it»[23]. In breaking the ground one «meets every succeeding Note […] in the *Unison* or *Octave*», while in descant one may proceed to any of the concords. Simpson's discussion of descant is surprisingly concise. As justification, he argues that the skills involved in improvising descant division are much the same as breaking the ground:

> For all *Division*, whether *Descant* or *Breaking the Bass*, is but a Transition from Note to Note, or from one Concord to another, either by Degrees or Leaps, with an intermixture of such Discords as are allowed in Composition[24].

Simpson's chapter on 'mixt' division, which is of great importance to understanding the heritage of Bach's solo music, is still more concise. His description touches on both the desired effect, and the means to achieve this end:

> *Mixt Division* which mixeth *Descant* and *Breaking the Ground*, one with the other […] presents to our Ears the Sounds of *Two* or more Parts moving together: And, this is expressed either in single Notes, by hitting first upon One String and then upon an Other; or in double Notes, by touching two or more Strings at once with the Bow. This is more excellent than the single ways […] so it is more intricate, and requires more of judgement and skill in Composition; by reason of the Bindings and intermixtures of Discords, which are as frequent in This as in any other *Figurate Musick*[25].

21. *Ibidem*, p. 31.
22. *Ibidem*.
23. *Ibidem*.
24. *Ibidem*.
25. *Ibidem*, p. 36.

As in his introduction to descant, Simpson's examples are left to the later chapters, which also serve to broach other considerations of effective improvisation. While the explanation of descant and 'mixt' division is confined to simple general rules, the remainder of the treatise provides an inventory of concrete, systematically organized practical examples of their application.

In fact, chapters six through eleven each present numerous short, easily memorized examples of breaking the ground, descant and 'mixt' division over various common short bass patterns. These patterns include 4-3 and 7-6 contrapuntal cadences, rising and falling scales, and scales in broken thirds. In the process of introducing these patterns, he also discusses the treatment of accidentals, and of thirds, sixths, fifths and octaves in descant division. Each type of ground that he illustrates begins with the ground bass, followed by examples of breaking the ground, examples of descant and then examples of his two types of 'mixt' division: 1) broken-chord jumping between voices of an implied polyphony and 2) multiple-stop chordal progressions.

Since he is always careful to identify these short passages of divisions as examples, it is clear that Simpson means for them to be memorized as a kind of vocabulary to be drawn on in extemporaneous performance. This is made explicit in chapter eleven:

> It now only remains that I give you some little assistance, by taking you (as it were) by the Hand, and leading you into the easiest way of Playing *Ex tempore* to a *Ground*.
>
> First, you are to make choice of some *Ground* consisting of *Semibreves* or *Minims*, or a mixture of these two [...]
>
> Next, you ought to be provided of ten, twelve, or more points of *Division* (the more the better) each consisting of a *Semibreve* or *Minim* [...]
>
> Being thus prepared, take one of the said Points, and apply it first to One Note, and then to another, and so through the whole *Ground*. When you can do this, take another Point, and do the like with it, and so after another so many as you please[26].

At this point he lists 24 'points of division', which are short motivic ideas, closely related to seventeenth-century German theorists' treatment of 'inventions' or *Manieren*, each with a distinctive melodic/rhythmic profile. Next, he proceeds to systematically apply each 'point of division' to a ground bass. Apart from the fact that the metric and rhythmic profile of Simpson's ground remains more-or-less constant, the procedures which he employs are strikingly similar to those employed in Niedt's examples showing how to generate a suite of dances from a common figured bass line. Simpson's treatment of 'points of division' is similar to Niedt's suggestion that once a figure has been chosen «the whole bass can then be worked out in the same way» and is also closely related to Forkel's definition of an invention:

[26]. *Ibidem*, p. 53.

> A musical subject which was so contrived that, by imitation and transposition of the parts, the whole of a composition might be unfolded from it was called an invention. The rest was only elaboration, and if one but knew properly the means of development, did not need to be invented[27].

Here is an example in which I have employed one of Niedt's simple motivic ideas to create a prelude, using a bass line which I have extracted from the corresponding movement of Bach's Suite for Solo Cello in G Major, BWV 1007 (Ex. 4):

Ex. 4: Method for improvising a prelude by applying one of Friedrich Niedt's 'inventions' to a framework abstracted from the prelude of BWV 1007.

[27]. FORKEL 1998, p. 467.

While many of Simpson's examples seem rather mechanical and tedious, it should be kept in mind that they are presented as steps in a didactic method — they are clearly not meant to be considered finished musical works. On the other hand, while he is keenly aware of the pedagogical value of varied repetition, Simpson does not rigidly maintain a single point of division for each variation, and the change from one idea to another does not always coincide with repetitions of the ground. He does point to the unifying aesthetic value of carrying an idea through, but this notion of a single unifying affect should not be unduly stressed. In the complete sets of divisions with which Simpson concludes his treatise, as in so much seventeenth-century instrumental music, there is often a strong contrast in character between individual variations, but a degree of freedom is allowed in extemporaneously carrying a point of division through each repetition of the ground. Indeed, a given point of division will often require modification to allow for smooth connection and appropriate voice leading.

> This driving or carrying on of a *Point*, doth much ease the Invention, which hath no further trouble, so long as the *Point* is continued, but to place and apply it to the several Notes of the *Ground*: Besides, it renders the *Division* more uniform and more delightful also; provided you do not cloy the Ear with too much repetition of the same thing; which is easily avoided with a little variation, as you can see I have done in carrying on some of the foregoing *Points*. Also you have liberty to change your *Point* in the middle or in any other part of the *Ground*: or you may mingle one *Point* with another, as best shall please your fancy[28].

Chapters twelve through fourteen give advice on various ways of structuring a set of divisions. Chapter twelve is primarily concerned with divisions as variations over a basso ostinato. The performer is advised to begin with a performance of the ground itself, followed by a slow point of division. The speed of divisions should gradually increase, but slow divisions should be interspersed, and variety should be sought through the use of suspensions, alternation between leaping and scalar motion, and dynamic and rhythmic

[28]. Simpson 1667, p. 56.

variation. «You must so place and dispose your *Division*, that the change of it from one kind to another may still beget a new attention»[29].

Most of Simpson's divisions make use of relatively short bass patterns, but his suggestion to use a longer «continued ground», such as «the Through-Bass of some Motet or Madrigal», as a framework for improvising divisions foreshadows the exercises found in Niedt's treatise and the Italian partimento sources. While Simpson does not give written-out examples of longer pieces, following his advice to use a bass from a pre-existent composition as a formal schema would result in a structured approach to improvisation similar to that which German and Italian partimento practices were designed to cultivate. Here is an example of an allemande which I have created by using one of Simpson's 'points of division' over a bass line that I have extracted from the corresponding movement of Bach's Suite for Solo Cello in G Major, BWV 1007 (Ex. 5).

Ex. 5: Method for improvising an allemande by applying one of Christopher Simpson's 'points of division' to a framework abstracted from the allemande of BWV 1007.

[29]. *Ibidem.*

Chapters fourteen through sixteen are concerned with arranging divisions for various combinations of viols and continuo. Simpson's discussion of divisions for a single viol is quite short, but does make an important point about contemporary attitudes toward the compositions of other musicians, which were regarded as examples, as inventories of musical ideas or inventions to be learned and deployed when improvising. Simpson directs his students to «peruse the *Divisions* which other men have made upon *Grounds* [...] observing and noting in their *Divisions*, what you find best worthy to be imitated»[30]. This point is reinforced in the concluding paragraph of the treatise, which also points to financial constraints that limited Simpson's ability to provide further illustrations of his improvisatory practices.

> Myself, amongst others more eminent, have made divers Compositions, which perhaps might be useful to young Musicians, either for their Imitation or Practice; but the Charge of Printing *Divisions* (as I have experienced in the *Cuts* of the *Examples* in this present Book) doth make that kind of Musick less communicable[31].

Chapter fifteen concerns the performance of extemporaneous divisions by two viols, and is of particular interest because of the historical evidence it offers of sophisticated improvisatory skills similar to the jazz practices of 'trading fours' and 'cutting contests'. Simpson suggests arranging divisions for two viols into four large sections. At the beginning, the performers are to take turns playing the ground and improvising divisions, each player continuing in their role until a new repetition of the ground begins. He also gives advice on effective ordering of these solos.

30. *Ibidem*.

31. *Ibidem*, p. 61.

> The *Ground* thus Play'd over, *C.* may begin again, and Play a Strain of quicker *Division*; which ended, let *B.* answer the same with something like it, but of a little more lofty Ayre: for the better performance whereof, if there be any difference in the Hands or Inventions, I would have the better Invention *lead*, but the more able Hand still *follow*, that the Musick may not seem to flaccess or lessen, but rather increase in the performance[32].

After trading choruses in this manner for as long as they like, perhaps with the continuo player taking a turn, comes a passage in which the two soloists improvise simultaneously. This is managed by having one violist break the ground in such manner that his divisions begin and end on each note of the bass before moving on to the next. The other violist is then free to improvise descant above the ground. In the third section, the two viols alternate roles as in the opening section, but this time each plays a shorter passage, the pace of dialogue quickens and the performance becomes a contest:

> *C.* may begin some Point of *Division*, of the length of a *Breve* or *Semibreve*, naming the said work, that *B.* may know his intentions; which ended, let *B.* answer the same upon the succeeding Note or Notes to the like quantity of Time [...].
>
> This contest in *Breves*, *Semibreves*, or *Minims* being ended, they may give the Signe to *A.* [the continuo player] if (as I said) he have ability of Hand, that he may begin his Point as they had done one to another; which point may be answered by the *Viols*, either singly or jointly[33].

In the final section, the viols are to:

> [...] joyn together in a Thundering Strain of *Quick* Division; with which they may conclude; or else with a Strain of slow and sweet Notes, according as may best sute the circumstance of time and place[34].

This kind of extemporaneous performance requires highly developed skills, and Simpson speaks of having «some experimental knowledge» of it. It is perhaps not likely that many musicians of his day were capable of successfully performing this kind of group improvisation, but clearly some were. Simpson recalled:

> I have known this kind of *Extemporary* Musick, sometimes (when it was performed by Hands accustomed to Play together) pass off with greater applause, than those Divisions which had been most studiously composed[35].

---

32. *Ibidem*, p. 58.
33. *Ibidem*, p. 59.
34. *Ibidem*.
35. *Ibidem*.

The examples of fully formed («studiously composed») solo preludes and divisions over repeated bass patterns with which Simpson's treatise concludes are meant to be studied and imitated. They contain new points of division, which we can extract and use in our own improvisations. They also illustrate his advice for pacing and structuring a set of divisions effectively, and can serve as models for framing large-scale structures. Finally, for performers who are capable of facing the considerable technical challenges which they present, but lack the necessary skills of invention, written examples such as Simpson's may be performed «as if» extemporized, «though less to be admired, as being more studied».

> He that hath it *not* in so high a measure as to play *ex tempore* to a *Ground*, may, notwithstanding give both himself and hearers sufficient satisfaction in playing such Divisions as himself or others have made for that purpose; in the performance whereof he may deserve the Name of an excellent Artist; for here the excellency of the Hand may be shewed as well as in the Other, and the Musick perhaps better, though less to be admired, as being more studied[36].

Bibliography

Baumgartner 1774

Baumgartner, Johann Baptist. *Instructions de musique theorique et pratique: a l'usage du violoncello*, The Hague, Monnier, 1774.

Boismortier 1732

Boismortier, Joseph Bodin de. *6 Sonates suives d'un nombre de pieces qu'on peut jouer seule, Op. 40*, Paris, l'Auteur, 1732.

Boismortier 1734

Id. *6 Sonates don't la dernier est en trio, Op. 50*, Paris, l'Auteur, 1734.

Dahlhaus 1989

Dahlhaus, Carl. *Geschichte der Musiktheorie. 11. Die Musiktheorie im 18. und 19. Jahrhundert. 2: Deutschland*, edited by Ruth E. Müller, Darmstadt, Wissenschaftliche Buchgesellschaft, 1989.

Dahlhaus 1994

Id. 'Das Musikalische Kunstwerk als Gegenstand der Soziologie', in: *The International Review of the Aesthetics and Sociology of Music*, xxv/1-2 (1994), pp. 115-130.

David – Mendel 1998

David, Hans T. – Mendel, Arthur. *The New Bach Reader: A Life of Johann Sebastian Bach in Letters and Documents*, revised edition by Christoph Wolf, New York, W. W. Norton, 1998.

[36]. *Ibidem.*

Duport 1806
Duport, Jean-Louis. *Essai sur le doigté du violoncelle, et sur la conduite de l'archet*, Paris, Imbault, 1806.

Forkel 1998
Forkel, Johann Nikolaus. *Ueber Johann Sebastian Bachs Leben, Kunst und Kunstwerke* (Leipzig, Hoffmeister und Künet, 1802), English translation by Hans T. David in: David – Mendel 1998.

Goehr 1992
Goehr, Lydia. *The Imaginary Museum of Musical Works: An Essay in the Philosophy of Music*, Oxford-New York, Clarendon Press, 1992.

Gunn 1802
Gunn, John. *An Essay Theoretical and Practical, with Copious and Easy Examples on the Application of the Principles of Harmony, Through Bass, and Modulation to the Violoncello*, London, Preston, 1802.

Ingarden 1986
Ingarden, Roman. *The Work of Music and the Problem of its Identity*, English translation by Adam Czerniawski, edited by Jean G. Harrell, Berkeley (CA), University of California Press, 1986.

Ingarden 1989
Id. *Ontology of the Work of Art: The Musical Work, the Picture, the Architectural Work, the Film*, Athens (OH), Ohio University Press, 1989 (Series in Continental Thought, 12).

Kirnberger 1783
Kirnberger, Johann Philipp. *Methode Sonaten aus'm Ermel zu schüdeln*, Berlin, F. W. Birnstiel, 1783.

Lutterman 2006
Lutterman, John Kenneth. *Works in Progress: J. S. Bach's Suites for Solo Cello as Artifacts of Improvisatory Practices*, Ph.D. Diss., Ann Arbor (MI), UMI Research Press, 2006.

Lutterman 2011
Id. '«Cet art est la perfection du talent». Chordal Thoroughbass Realization and Improvised Solo Performance on the Viol and Cello in the Eighteenth Century', in: Rasch 2011, pp. 111-128.

Mattheson 1722-1725
Mattheson, Johann. *Critica Musica*, 2 vols., Hamburg, the Author, 1722-1725.

Mendel 1957
Mendel, Arthur. 'The Services of Musicology to the Practical Musician', in: *Some Aspects of Musicology*, edited by Arthur Mendel, Curt Sachs and Carroll C. Pratt, New York, Liberal Arts Press, 1957.

Niedt 2003
Niedt, Friedrich Erhard. *Musikalische Handleitung. Teil I-III in Einem Band (1710, 1721, 1717)*, facsimile reprint, Hildesheim, Olms, 2003.

Pitschel 1741
Pitschel, Theodor Leberecht. 'Letter' (1741), in: Schulze 1969, p. 397; English translation by Hans T. David, in: David – Mendel 1998, pp. 333-334.

Rasch 2011
Beyond Notes: Improvisation in Western Music of the Eighteenth and Nineteenth Centuries, edited by Rudolf Rasch, Turnhout, Brepols, 2011 (Speculum Musicae, 16).

Schulenberg 1995
Schulenberg, David. 'Composition and Improvisation in the School of J. S. Bach', in: *Bach Perspectives. 1*, edited by Russell Stinson, Lincoln-London, University of Nebraska Press, 1995, pp. 1-42.

Schulze 1969
Bach-Dokumente. Supplement zu Johann Sebastian Bach neue Ausgabe Samtlicher Werke. 2: Fremdschriftliche und Gedruckte Dokumente zur Lebensgeschichte Johann Sebastian Bachs, 1685-1750, edited by Werner Neumann and Hans-Joachim Schulze, Leipzig, Bärenreiter, 1969.

Simpson 1659
Simpson, Christopher. *The Division-Violinist: or, The Art of Playing Ex-Tempore Upon a Ground*, London, W. Godbid, 1659.

Simpson 1667
Id. *Chelys, Minuritionum Artificio Exornata, Sive, Minuritiones ad Basin, Etiam Ex Tempore Modulandi Ratio in Tres Partes Distributa / The Division-Viol, or, The art of Playing Ex Tempore Upon a Ground, Divided into Three Parts, Early English Books, 1641-1700*, London, W. Godbid for Henry Brome, [2]1667.

Simpson 1712
Id. *Chelys, Minuritionum Artificio Exornata* [...] *The Division-Viol* [...]*: Prioribus Longe Auctior*, London, William Pearson for Richard Mears, [3]1712.

Walther 1732
Walther, Johann Gottfried. *Musikalisches Lexikon; oder Musicalische Bibliothec*, Leipzig, W. Deer, 1732.

Accompagnamento e basso continuo alla chitarra spagnola

Una cartografia della diffusione dei sistemi di notazione stenografici in Italia, Spagna e Francia tra xvi e xvii secolo e loro implicazioni teoriche

Francesca Mignogna
(Université de Paris-Sorbonne/IReMus)

La questione riguardante il rapporto tra orizzontalità e verticalità — quello che oggi definiamo armonia funzionale — prima della teorizzazione del sistema tonale coinvolge numerosi aspetti della pratica e della teoria della musica. Come sottolineato da Massimo Preitano in un articolo apparso nel 1994 sulla *Rivista Italiana di Musicologia*[1] e che ancora oggi resta uno dei rari studi in lingua italiana consacrati al ruolo della chitarra barocca spagnola nell'evoluzione del linguaggio tonale, le significative evoluzioni della pratica musicale avvenute nel periodo di tempo che va dalle *Istituzioni Harmoniche* di Zarlino[2] al *Traité* di Rameau[3] non trovano reale corrispondenza nelle opere di speculazione teorica coeve, ma sono piuttosto da ricercare nella manualistica[4]. La (apparente) netta distinzione tra musica pratica e musica teorica risulta ancora radicata nel pensiero del musico negli anni della teorizzazione del basso continuo; ciò nonostante, le vere origini di quest'ultimo non sono rintracciabili in un trattato propriamente teorico e la sua formulazione risulta essere una sistematizzazione a posteriori di una pratica preesistente. Come sottolineato da John Walter Hill, a proposito delle origini dello stile recitativo:

---

1. Preitano 1994.
2. Zarlino 1558.
3. Rameau 1722.
4. «Se è lecito considerare le date di pubblicazione di questi due trattati [*Istituzioni Harmoniche* di Zarlino e *Traité* di Rameau, n.d.a.] come due ideali capisaldi di altrettante distinte concezioni musicali in una fase di acquisita consapevolezza dei rispettivi orizzonti stilistici, risulta un lasso di tempo piuttosto ampio all'interno del quale il passaggio dall'una all'altra è, in pratica, avvenuto, ma mai direttamente testimoniato da una formulazione teorica compiuta: nell'ambito strettamente speculativo, difatti, la trattatistica secentesca non si discosta in maniera significativa dalla tradizione zarliniana, evidenziando però un progressivo scollamento dalla prassi musicale, intorno alla quale le informazioni più attendibili sono desumibili, piuttosto, dalla letteratura specifica di tipo 'manualistico'». Preitano 1994, pp. 27-28.

> Si tratta, almeno in parte, del seguente problema più generale: se nel mutamento dello stile musicale siano da considerarsi più importanti le cause interne (musicali) o esterne (intellettuali) e, di questo problema più specifico, se l'ultima fase della storia della musica protomoderna — spesso indicata come l'età barocca — si originasse dalla fissazione in forma di notazione musicale di precedenti tradizioni non scritte, o solo parzialmente scritte. Finché non si giunge alla comprensione dello stile recitativo, non si potrà comprendere pienamente come è potuta cominciare l'età barocca[5].

L'interesse musicologico relativo alla realizzazione del basso continuo è stato per lungo tempo rivolto quasi esclusivamente agli strumenti a tastiera; un numero di studi comunque rilevante ha portato l'attenzione sul ruolo degli strumenti a corde pizzicate in questa pratica. Tali studi, tra i quali l'eccellente articolo di Thomas Christensen che pone il continuo barocco come una delle applicazioni più importanti della tecnica chitarristica spagnola del *rasgueado*[6], hanno mostrato il sorgere, tra XVI e XVII secolo, di sistemi stenografici di notazione per tale strumento, le cui caratteristiche permettono di considerarli non solo un primo esempio di notazione 'aleatoria' dal punto di vista armonico ma anche un primitivo tentativo di cifrare il basso. Tali sistemi sono basati sulla corrispondenza di un numero o una lettera con ciascun agglomerato armonico verticale che, sovrapposti al testo o al basso, servono da soli a realizzare l'accompagnamento senza rispondere alle regole di condotta delle parti. Benché questi sistemi sopravvivano — in progressivo declino — fino al 1800, verrà qui proposta una cartografia corrispondente al periodo compreso tra i due trattati sopracitati, dunque tra il 1558 e il 1722, considerando queste date come punti di apertura e di chiusura della lunga elaborazione del concetto teorico di accordo. Ci si riferirà esclusivamente alle opere spagnole, italiane e francesi, a stampa o manoscritte, nelle quali vengono fornite 'istruzioni' riguardo ai sistemi stenografici; tra di queste, solo alcune sono definibili trattati (o manuali), mentre nella maggior parte dei casi l'apporto teorico è costituito solamente da tavole esplicative anteposte alle raccolte di musica. Le raccolte di musica nelle quali sono utilizzati tali sistemi di notazione ma che sono prive di qualunque istruzione sono invece numerosissime: basti pensare che solo in Italia, tra il 1610 e il 1665, ne vengono pubblicate circa 100[7]. In questo articolo, che vede come punto di partenza le riflessioni proposte da Christensen e Preitano nei due articoli sopracitati, non sarà proposta una descrizione dettagliata di tutti i manuali, né tantomeno un confronto sistematico tra di essi; verranno estrapolate le caratteristiche chiave di questo tipo di notazione per metterle in relazione all'evoluzione della notazione e della teoria tonale. Soltanto i dettagli del primo sistema in esame, quello di Amat, saranno proposti, a titolo rappresentativo.

5. Hill 2003, pp. 35-36.
6. Christensen 1992, p. 20.
7. *Cfr.* Gavito 2006.

Per comprendere il contesto nel quale questi sistemi si collocano e la loro importanza dal punto di vista teorico, risulta necessaria qualche riflessione sulla notazione, in particolare sulla notazione per strumenti a corde pizzicate. L'evoluzione della musica 'a suoni simultanei'[8] si accompagna in maniera indissolubile all'evoluzione della notazione musicale; i differenti stadi evolutivi di quest'ultima sono al tempo stesso rivelatori della concezione musicale di un determinato periodo storico e catalizzatori nel processo di ideazione di nuove forme musicali, in particolare di nuove forme polifoniche: l'introduzione dei modi ritmici (scuola di Notre Dame) e la conseguente precisione nella notazione ha reso possibile l'evoluzione di una scrittura polifonica più articolata[9]. La più precisa sovrapposizione di suoni che questo sistema ha generato non può non aver avuto influenza sull'evoluzione di una scienza esatta della verticalità in musica. In questo senso, il passo fondamentale arriverà circa quattro secoli più tardi, con la riapparizione della notazione in forma di partitura[10]. La questione è stata oggetto di ampia discussione: l'avanzamento degli studi e la scoperta di nuove fonti sembra anticipare progressivamente l'avvento di questa pratica. Se per William Apel la disposizione in parti separate è da considerarsi l'unica utilizzata fino al XVII secolo (eccezion fatta per alcune composizioni in stile di conductus del XIV e XV secolo[11] e il motteto *Laus Domino*[12]) gli studi di Kinkeldey, Schwartz, Haas, Smijers e Lowinsky[13] hanno provato l'esistenza di musica notata in partitura già nel XVI secolo. Il concetto di partitura, al suo primo stadio[14], non concerne in modo diretto il processo compositivo. Tra le partiture del XVI secolo identificate da Lowinsky, sono identificabili tre tipologie che differiscono in base alla loro funzione: si potrebbero identificare con i nomi di 'false partiture' (sovrapposizioni casuali di parti, dovute a questioni editoriali), 'partiture di esecuzione' (trascrizioni in partitura preparate dagli strumentisti per agevolare l'esecuzione)[15] e 'partiture di elaborazione' (la partitura è utilizzata nell'atto compositivo)[16]. La pratica di trascrivere in partitura le composizioni polifoniche in vista di un'esecuzione

---

8. Il termine, utilizzato per indicare le musiche armoniche e polifoniche in un'ottica storicizzante, è preso da Coussemaker 1852, p. 1.

9. *Cfr.* Apel 1998, p. 196.

10. Fatto interessante rispetto a l'ipotesi, da me sostenuta, di una progressiva orizzontalizzazione della polifonia nel corso del medioevo, una disposizione definibile 'in partitura' caratterizzava le prime composizioni polifoniche (*Musica enchiriadis* — notazione dasiana —, il *Micrologo* di Guido d'Arezzo, i manoscritti di San Marziale, di Compostela e di Notre Dame; *cfr. ibidem*, p. 14).

11. *Ibidem*, p. 241.

12. *Ibidem*, p 14.

13. *Cfr.* Lowinsky 1948, p. 17.

14. Ci si riferisce solamente al percorso evolutivo della partitura in era moderna, non considerando in questa affermazione le forme di 'notazione sovrapposta' utilizzate per la notazione teorica durante il medioevo.

15. La stessa espressione è usata da Jean-Michel Vaccaro in relazione alla tablatura (*cfr.* Vaccaro 1981, p. 121).

16. Le espressioni non sono di Lowinsky. *Cfr.* Lowinsky 1960.

alla tastiera o al liuto, corrispondente alla seconda tipologia di partiture individuata da Lowinsky, rivela il fatto che la concezione orizzontale delle voci come entità autonome è perdurata, in quanto «apparent maintenance of the old order»[17], meno presso i compositori che presso i teorici, e ancor meno presso gli strumentisti. Come sottolineato da Apel, uno dei criteri fondamentali di classificazione della notazione per la musica a suoni simultanei concerne il numero di esecutori coinvolti: una distinzione di base è istituita tra musica per *ensemble* e musica per un solo strumentista (strumenti a tastiera o a corde pizzicate)[18]. La pratica di trascrivere la musica polifonica vocale per uno strumento a corde pizzicate rappresenta, in qualche maniera, una conciliazione tra le due categorie identificate da Apel, ed è origine di un riallineamento verticale che vede la pratica musicale — e non la riflessione teorica — come principale propulsore dell'evoluzione di una coscienza armonica verticale. Il XVI secolo vede il fiorire della musica strumentale amatoriale, sotto la spinta dei precetti dell'umanesimo italiano del Quattrocento: l'ideale platonico dell'uomo in equilibrio, che pratica la ginnastica e la musica, trova la sua manifestazione più ricca nelle corti italiane, prima fra tutte la corte di Isabella d'Este a Mantova. In questo contesto dall'*allure* popolare, ispirato all'arte dei menestrelli, la pratica di uno strumento musicale diventa elemento imprescindibile per il buon cortigiano. In *Il libro del Cortegiano*, Baldesar Castiglione si riferisce al liuto (alla viola, più precisamente) mostrando le ragioni per le quali questo strumento è da preferire agli altri:

> Bella musica [...] parmi il cantar bene a libro sicuramente e con bella maniera; ma ancor molto più il cantare alla viola perché tutta la dolcezza consiste quasi in un solo e con molto maggior attenzion si nota ed intende il bel modo e l'aria non essendo occupate le orecchie in più che in una sol voce, e meglio ancor vi si discerne ogni piccolo errore; il che non accade cantando in compagnia perché l'uno aiuta l'altro. Ma sopra tutto parmi gratissimo il cantare alla viola per recitare; il che tanto di venustà ed efficacia aggiunge alle parole, che è gran maraviglia[19].

In questa breve affermazione sono messi in evidenza due concetti importanti. In primo luogo, Castiglione osserva che il liuto permette a un solo individuo di riprodurre tutta la ricchezza armonica della polifonia, sottolineando così la capacità del liuto di 'sintetizzare'

---

17. «When harmonic phenomena [...] are explained as contrapunctually conceived, it is little wonder that the author of this explanation finds it necessary to consider the bass progressions that are fundamental to cadential structures in tonal music as nonstructural and nonessential in the cadence formulas of fifteenth- and sixteenth-century. [...] [This position] ignores a fundamental and delicate historic process: the transition from an old mode of artistic conception to a new one within the apparent maintenance of the old order. This is what we are in fact witnessing in the phenomena of harmony and incipient tonal orientation emerging within the contrapuntal and modal matrix of fifteenth-century music». Lowinsky 1989, pp. 889-890.

18. *Cfr.* Apel 1998, p. 14.

19. Castiglione 1528, libro II, cap. XIII.

le voci che, nella polifonia propriamente detta, costituiscono degli elementi distinti; tale osservazione sembra preconizzare il concetto di accordo in quanto entità integra. In secondo luogo, Castiglione sottolinea che suonare il liuto permette di eseguire al canto una sola voce, estrapolata dal complesso polifonico; il testo di questa voce sarà quindi più intelligibile che nel contesto polifonico. Il nuovo interesse a donare priorità al testo che è tipico del pensiero rinascimentale marca l'inizio di un processo che avrà grande influenza sul sistema musicale: dare priorità al testo comporterà la prevalenza di forme dotate di uno schema armonico fisso, in contrapposizione alla *varietas* musicale che governava le leggi del contrappunto. La diffusione del liuto si accompagna alla nascita di un sistema di notazione appositamente ideato, la tablatura, che resterà per secoli l'unico sistema utilizzato per notare la musica per strumenti a corde pizzicate. L'ideazione della tablatura è senza dubbio da ricondurre in primo luogo alla necessità di semplificare la lettura della musica polifonica[20]. La semplificazione non riguarda solamente l'essere accessibile a un pubblico che non conosce le regole della notazione mensurale — in altre parole, l'amatore — ma coinvolge anche un altro fattore importante, ben sintetizzato nella seguente definizione di tablatura: «A score in which the voice-parts are 'tabulated' or written so that the eye can encompass them»[21]. Questa problematica — ossia che tutte le voci possano essere comprese in un solo sguardo — troverà risoluzione generale nella realizzazione in partitura della musica polifonica; ma, nel caso specifico degli strumenti a corde pizzicate, si aggiunge una seconda problematica, di carattere tecnico: le voci della composizione polifonica devono poter essere comprese non solamente in un solo sguardo, ma anche in una stessa posizione della mano (sinistra) dello strumentista. Si potrebbe così riformulare la frase citata: la tablatura per strumenti a corde pizzicate è una partitura nella quale le differenti voci sono intavolate in maniera da poter essere comprese in un solo sguardo e da poter essere suonate, verticalmente, con un'unica posizione della mano. Questa necessità genera inevitabilmente un *découpage* della linearità temporale del contrappunto in blocchi verticali dalla durata variabile, durata che corrisponde al tempo in cui una stessa posizione della mano è mantenuta. Alcuni elementi riscontrabili nelle intavolature per liuto del XVI secolo testimoniano questo fenomeno. Come sintetizzato da Howard Mayer Brown:

---

[20]. «Bermudo [*Declaracion des instrumentos musicales*, 1555, fol. 83, n.d.a.] offers three reasons for the use of tablature: (1) convenience in preparing an "improvised" rendering of a motet; (2) economy in paper, since a score takes four times as much space as a tablature; (3) simplicity, since even a beginner can use with ease a tablature in which every key on the harpsichord is designated by a number. He censures those who, "ignorant of counterpoint, are yet desirous to compose through mere calculation of consonances: they bar the music paper so as not to get lost in their calculation. Although this method is crude, I give an example for those who need and wish to use it" [*ibidem*, fol. 134, n.d.a.]. The example is a score — this time the meter is alla breve and hence the unit a breve per bar — and the music is so primitive an example of three-part harmony, almost completely homophonic, as to be without either melodic or rhythmic interest». Lowinsky 1960, pp. 146-148, nota.

[21]. Dart – Moren – Rastall 2001.

> The evident attempt of the lutenists to reproduce literally the vocal polyphony succeeds in spite of small variants of a sort we can expect from all lute music: ties are broken; some long notes are divided into notes of smaller value, or more rarely the reverse; a few rhythms are dotted or undotted; and the polyphony is occasionally rearranged slightly in order to make it fit better under the instrumentalist's hand[22].

Vaccaro analizza tali modificazioni del modello nel passaggio da notazione mensurale a tablatura in termini di «réduction de l'espace vocal à l'espace du luth»[23] e identifica otto parametri interessati da questa riduzione: altezza, durata, timbro, intensità, articolazione (di suoni e frasi), struttura polifonica, rapporto intensità-durata, rapporto struttura polifonica-timbro. Tre di queste categorie risultano di particolare interesse nell'evoluzione del sistema contrappuntistico e in direzione di una coscienza dell'accordo e della tonalità. Prima fra tutte, la categoria delle altezze: la riorganizzazione del materiale dallo spazio vocale a quello strumentale comporta talvolta la trasposizione e condiziona la tonalità — fittizia — dell'intavolatura sulla base di questioni pratiche (a questo proposito, bisogna ricordare che esistevano strumenti di differenti dimensioni e dal tipo di accordatura differente); inoltre, tale riorganizzazione corrisponde anche, inconsapevolmente, a una trasposizione da un sistema non temperato a un sistema temperato[24]. Al livello della struttura polifonica, sono le relazioni di comunicazione interna tra le voci a essere stravolte: se nella polifonia vocale si sviluppano in modo orizzontale, nella tablatura diventano verticali (la relazione tra una nota di una voce e la nota successiva della stessa voce è meno forte che la relazione tra una nota di una voce e quella emessa simultaneamente da un'altra voce); questo comporta un indebolimento dell'identità di ogni voce e la polarizzazione delle parti esterne, oltre che un aumento di variabilità dello spazio polifonico (il raddoppio o l'aggiunta di suoni non alterano lo svolgimento logico della struttura musicale)[25]. L'identità di ogni voce è

22. Brown 1973-1974, p. 55.

23. Vaccaro 1981, pp. 131-138.

24. «[...] l'accordatura et la tasteggiatura de l'instrument établirent nécessairement ce tempérament égal (gamme tempérée) que le génie du grand Bach appliqua plus tard au clavier pour mettre en œuvre toutes les tonalités, en détruisant définitivement toutes traces de l'ancien système des modes ecclésiastiques. Il est curieux de voir qu'au xvie siècle on discutait avec passion [*cfr.* Galilei, Vincentio. *Della musica antica e della moderna*, 1581] sur la manière de plier la gamme naturelle aux exigences de l'évolution que subissait l'art musical, tandis que dans la pratique le seul moyen propre était déjà en usage sur le luth, sans qu'on s'en fût aperçu». Chilesotti 1912, p. 637. Si veda anche Lindley 1984.

25. «[...] l'espace vocal [de la polyphonie, n.d.a.] peut être qualifié de "pluri-linéaire". Il est engendré par la superposition de plusieurs "lignes" indépendantes ayant leurs déroulements spécifiques: les voix. Ces lignes sont, si l'on peut dire, parallèles [...]. Il n'existe entre elles aucune communication possible. À cause de cette individualité irréductible, elles engendrent un espace de caractère discontinu. À cette discontinuité en quelque sorte "verticale" (dans la simultanéité) s'oppose, organiquement, une continuité "horizontale" (dans la succession). L'espace sonore du luth, comme d'ailleurs celui de tout instrument polyphonique soliste, se caractérise par l'opposition inverse. L'émission sonore est unifiée; la polyphonie s'élabore dans un

ulteriormente indebolita dal nuovo rapporto struttura polifonica-timbro: nel contesto del contrappunto del xvi secolo, che abbonda di incroci e imitazioni, la condotta di ogni voce, sul liuto, diventa ambigua a causa della mancanza del differenziale timbrico[26]. Questo tipo di trasformazioni sono peculiari delle tablature per strumenti a corde pizzicate. È quanto dimostrato da uno studio comparativo condotto da Wolfgang Boetticher sulle intavolature per organo e per liuto delle opere di Lasso comprese nel periodo tra 1566 e 1603. Tale studio ha rivelato che:

> 1) le déroulement harmonique semble fixé avec plus de précision dans les transcriptions pour luth que dans celles pour instruments à clavier de la même époque; 2) le Fingerfall de l'orgue, le suspirium, est remplacé la plupart du temps, dans les transcriptions pour luth, par des accords brisés de grande amplitude; 3) la polyphonie factice du luth tend souvent à simplifier la basse en tant que soutien harmonique et fait ainsi partiellement disparaître l'exécution en legato des parties inférieures; 4) les diminutions enveloppant les notes principales des petits intervalles qui correspondaient à un vieux principe fondamental du style des instruments à clavier cède de plus en plus le pas, dans les pièces pour instruments à cordes pincées à la main, au jeu par amples accords; 5) les fausses relations latentes du modèle vocal sont largement compensées [...] par la fugacité des sons; 6) le riche travail figuratif de la basse se conforme moins aux lois du contrepoint vocal qu'au broderies et aux retards de la partie supérieure, contrairement à ce qui se passait pour les tablatures d'orgue restées plus fidèles à l'original [...][27].

Inoltre, l'intavolatura della musica polifonica vocale comporta un'altra conseguenza significativa: considerato che la tablatura non è una rappresentazione astratta della musica ma la descrizione dell'azione fisica necessaria alla produzione del suono[28], la *musica*

---

geste unique et une communication peut s'établir à tout moment entre les différentes parties créant ainsi une continuité "verticale". [...] Les voix n'ont plus qu'une existence virtuelle [...]. Cette transformation entraîne nécessairement une discontinuité "horizontale" caractéristique. Unifié du grave à l'aigu, le champ des hauteurs se dessine en fonction des seuls contours extérieurs, les parties extrêmes. La polyphonie se polarise autour d'un axe supérius-basse; l'autonomie et la continuité des parties intermédiaires s'effacent. C'est en ce sens que le contrepoint du modèle vocal tend à se transformer en harmonie». Vaccaro 1981, p. 136.

26. «Lorsque les parties polyphoniques ne sont opposées ni par leurs régimes de valeurs de durée ni par leurs registres comme dans le cas d'un croisement passager d'imitations ou d'un canon à l'unisson, le mouvement contrapuntique se fige en ostinato. Les voix fusionnent entre elles pour ne laisser émerger que leurs contours combinés. Le mouvement en avant des imitations se transforme en piétinement rythmique et harmonique; la mélodie, fixée dans ses superpositions successives, s'immobilise en sonorité harmonique». *Ibidem*, p. 138.

27. Boetticher 1958, pp. 147-148.

28. «The term 'tablature' generally signifies a notational system using letters of the alphabet or other symbols not found in ordinary staff notation, and which generally specifies the physical action required to

ficta vi è obbligatoriamente notata. Questo fenomeno ha senza dubbio contribuito alla sistematizzazione dell'uso e della funzione delle alterazioni[29].

Tutto quanto evidenziato fino a questo momento appartiene comunque al dominio della musica scritta. Benché delle modificazioni avvengano rispetto al modello polifonico, non c'è discrepanza — se non per quanto riguarda la fioritura — tra la musica scritta in tablatura e il prodotto risultante dall'esecuzione. Tutto quello che è scritto in tablatura (sebbene non risponda più, come abbiamo visto, alle regole che reggevano la costruzione contrappuntistica originale) non contempla ulteriori interventi da parte dell'esecutore per quello che riguarda la struttura armonico-polifonica; semmai, il contrario: la tablatura non è che la descrizione dell'azione fisica necessaria alla produzione del suono ed è dunque un mero sistema semiografico che non rimanda ad alcun sistema teorico. Inoltre, anche se la tablatura, in quanto sistema di notazione distinto dal sistema mensurale, sancisce in un certo senso l'indipendenza della musica strumentale[30], è nella musica originale per strumenti a corde pizzicate che le caratteristiche idiomatiche e stilistiche di questi ultimi emergono in maniera più evidente. Come sottolineava circa un secolo fa Chilesotti:

> [...] la transformation de la tonalité ancienne dans nos modes majeur et mineur a été favorisée ou, mieux encore, presque déterminée d'une manière décisive par la musique originale du luth, dont le caractère absolument mélodique fait de l'accord un élément essentiel de l'art, et non un fait accidentel dans la rencontre des diverses parties de la polyphonie. [...] Il faut encore noter que dans la musique originale du luth fonctionne évidemment ce basso continuo dont l'invention, selon les histoires de l'art, appartiendrait au père Lodovico Grossi de Viadana. Celui-ci donc, au lieu de découvrir un nouveau moyen de structure pour la composition, aurait seulement appliqué aux voix la basse instrumentale naturelle sur laquelle la musique de luth était déjà basée[31].

La notazione in tablatura è idealmente destinata all'esecuzione *punteado*: è la tecnica che è propria all'esecuzione di musiche polifoniche al liuto, e che permette,

---

produce the music from a specific instrument, rather than an abstract representation of the music itself». Bent 2001.

29. «De cette évolution enfin [l'identificazione del rapporto tonica-dominante, n.d.a.], au cours de laquelle on employait des altérations chromatiques, qui faisaient perdre à la tonalité antique la caractéristique de ses divers modes, nous pouvons suivre les phases dans les compositions polyphoniques transportées sur les cordes du luth. Ici, en efffet, la notation (tablature) pour l'instrument était établie [...] de façon à représenter l'exécution matérielle de la musique sur les touches; de sorte qu'il n'y a point de doute au sujet des notes altérées que les chanteurs, guidés par le sentiment artistique qui devinait l'art nouveau, employaient en faveur de la transformation de la tonalité, et que les joueurs de luth marquaient naturellement dans leurs tablatures». Chilesotti 1912, p. 637. Si veda anche Brown 1973-1974.

30. «Y es más lógico, para destacar su independencia y emancipación frente a la música vocal, aplicar un sistema casi completamente distinto del de la notación mensural». Schmitt 1997, p. 182.

31. Chiesotti 1912, p. 637.

grazie all'utilizzazione indipendente di ogni dito della mano destra, di eseguire melodie e di escludere determinate corde nell'esecuzione di agglomerati armonici. Tale tecnica sembrerebbe la logica derivazione della tecnica liutistica a plettro del XV secolo[32]; inoltre, è recentemente stato mostrato che già all'epoca coesistevano la tecnica del plettro (utilizzata per i passaggi accordali) e quella delle dita (utilizzata per i passaggi melodici)[33]. Ma l'evoluzione del linguaggio accordale e di un proto basso continuo alla chitarra spagnola è ascrivibile a un altro stile esecutivo, comunemente noto come *rasgueado* (ma anche come battuto — in Italia — e *golpeado* — in Spagna) e pertinente all'ambito della danza e dell'accompagnamento della canzone popolare. Tecnicamente, il *rasgueado* prevede la sollecitazione simultanea di tutte le corde della chitarra, senza la possibilità di escludere l'una o l'altra. *Nella Declaracion des intrumentos* del 1555[34], Bermudo testimonia l'esistenza dello stile *golpeado* sulla chitarra a 4 corde[35], ma è sulla chitarra a 5 corde che tale stile si sviluppa in modo più sistematico. Lex Eisenhardt sottolinea che l'aggiuta della quinta corda potrebbe essere vista non soltanto come la naturale evoluzione dello strumento, ma come un avanzamento tecnico necessario a migliorare l'esecuzione del *rasgueado*: uno strumento a quattro corde, infatti, generalmente non permetteva l'esecuzione di armonie complete; in questo senso, è fortemente influente anche il tipo di accordatura dello strumento[36]. In quest'ottica, estendendo la riflessione di Eisenhardt, si può affermare che è lo sviluppo della chitarra a cinque corde a permettere l'evoluzione di un sistema di notazione per il *rasgueado* che, come era stato per la tablatura, riposa su un sistema di relazioni tra semiografia e prodotto musicale proprio e distinto dal sistema mensurale. Un sistema di notazione completamente dedicato al *rasgueado* sancisce, in un certo senso, l'affrancamento di quest'ultimo, come aveva fatto la tablatura per la musica per liuto.

In base alle fonti a noi pervenute, il primo sistema di notazione stenografica del *rasgueado*, detto 'catalano', appare in Spagna nel manuale *Guitarra española* di Juan Carles Amat; sebbene l'esemplare più antico a noi pervenuto sia un'edizione del 1626 (Lérida, Anglada & Llorens), l'*imprimatur* data al 1596. Brown[37] riporta l'ipotesi di una prima edizione del 1586, secondo quanto indicato da Fray Leonardo de San Martin in una lettera ad Amar datata 30 aprile 1639 e riportata nell'edizione di Barcellona del 1639; considerato che nel 1586 Amat avrebbe avuto solamente quattordici anni, l'ipotesi di un errore nella lettera di Fray Leonardo sembrerebbe la più realistica[38]. Il trattato di Amat, diviso in nove

32. *Cfr.* Danner 1972.

33. Ivanoff 2005.

34. Bermudo 1555.

35. *Ibidem*, pp. xcixv e xxviiiv.

36. Eisenhardt 2015, pp. 13-14.

37. Brown 1965, p. 343.

38. Riguardo a questa data, si veda: Esses 1992, p. 117; Hall – Tyler 1976, pp. 227-229; Pujol 1950.

capitoli, è esplicitamente consacrato al *rasgueado*[39]. Il secondo capitolo è completamente dedicato al concetto di accordo, che per l'autore è il primo argomento da dover trattare, una volta terminata la descrizione tecnica della chitarra: «Pues tienes la gúitarra ya téplada y puesta a punto de tañer, rason es agora enseñarte que cosa es punto, quátos son, y como se llaman»[40]. Nel descrivere quello che è un accordo (*punto*), Amat non fa alcun riferimento al sistema intervallare contrappuntistico; inoltre, ci lascia dedurre che l'idea di accordo in quanto entità integra era già affermata all'epoca, poiché esistevano già diversi termini per indicare l'accordo[41]. Nel terzo capitolo, in cui descrive le diteggiature degli accordi previsti nel suo sistema, non fa alcun riferimento ai nomi delle note (descrive solamente il gesto strumentale) ma identifica, di ogni accordo, quale siano la fondamentale, la terza e la quinta. È nel completamento della descrizione della diteggiatura, nel quinto capitolo, che la descrizione del gesto strumentale finisce per diventare sistema: gli accordi, con la loro diteggiatura e una cifra corrispondente, sono disposti in un cerchio (i maggiori — *naturales* — nella metà superiore, i minori — *mollados* — nella metà inferiore) in successione di quarte in senso orario.

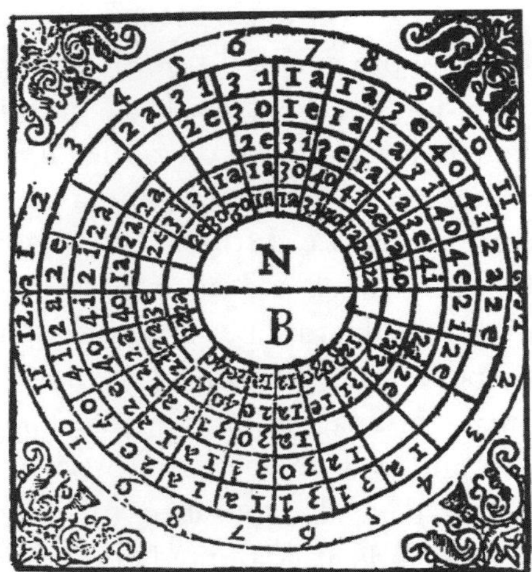

Ill. 1: Amat 1627, quinto capitolo, descrizione della diteggiatura.

[39]. «Considerando pues yo la falta que havia en toda esta tierra por nó haver algú auctor tartado desto (alomenos que yo fepa) le querido escrivir, con este estilo el modo de templar y tocar rasgado. esta guitarra de cinco, llamada Española por ser mas recibida en esta tierra que en las otras, y el modo de poner en ella, qualquier tono, paraque sirua de maestro, y tambien para que los dicipulo della no esten sujetos a tanta miseria como es la que nos da este humor». Amat 1627, f. [2v].

[40]. *Ibidem*, f. [6r].

[41]. «Llamanse estos pútos de muchas maneras como es cruzado mayor y cruzado menor, vacas altas, y vacas baxas, puente, y de otras infinitas suertes que los muficos, unos y otros les han puestos nombres diferentes; pero yo aqui no las ıllamare sino primero, segundo, tercero, y quarto, &c.y estos o naturales,o b, mollados», *Ibidem*, f. [6v].

Questa rappresentazione grafica è alla base del riconoscimento dell'enarmonia proclamato implicitamente nel capitolo successivo:

> En la susodicha tabla estan puestos todos los puntos que se pueden hazer en esta guitarra, y si alguno dize que y ay otros, como son aquellos que se hazen en el quinto, sexto, septimo, y en los otros trastes, buelvo por mi, y digo, que todos aquellos tienen la mesma consonancia, y 1a misma boz que tienen estos que havemos trahido: porque, el punto treze, que es el que viene despues del doze, tiene la misma consonancia y bos que tiene el primero [...][42].

In questo capitolo, Amat fa riferimento alla solmizzazione e spiega come il sistema — che noi definiremmo temperato — dei 12 semitoni della chitarra permetta di superare il sistema degli esacordi. Il settimo capitolo si apre con un'immagine che conferma che è l'accordo, e non il singolo intervallo, l'elemento di base della composizione in stile *rasgueado*:

> Todo lo que se ha tratado hasta aqui, es como la materia, de la qual se puede hazer muchas formas. El bueno y platico pintor tiene aparejadas todas las colores que son neccessarias para pintar, de las quales està a su alvedrio si quiere pintar, o un hombres, o un Leon, o un buey, del a mesma manera, nosotros hasta aqui havemos aparejados todos los puntos, que son como materia, y como las colores del pintor, de los quales, se pueden formar toda manera y suerte de tonos, saltando del uno al otro[43].

Sulle basi di tale osservazione, Amat mostra come sia semplice trasportare qualsiasi successione armonica senza dover ricorrere alla solmizzazione[44]: «[...] y lo que es de maravillar (lo que a muchos parecera ímpossible) que cóestos puntos, puede qualquier ajuntar,o acomodar, por las dichas doze partes, todo lo que se tañe; y puede tañer, có qualquier instruméto de musico [...]»[45]. L'utilità di poter trasporre in tutti i 12 toni sembra evidente per Amat: non soltanto si potrà accompagnare qualsiasi registro vocale, ma sarà possibile suonare con strumenti accordati in modo differente: «Desta manera se pueden tocar doze guitarras juntas cada una por sus puntos, y todas haran una misma consonancia»[46]. Nell'ottavo capitolo si trova una vera e propria 'istruzione' per poter improvvisare una riduzione di qualsiasi composizione polifonica, secondo una tecnica di invenzione dell'autore (questo ci fa dedurre che tale pratica non fosse già diffusa prima di allora)[47]. Il sistema che Amat propone si basa sull'identificazione del basso della

42. *Ibidem*, f. [13^{v}].
43. *Ibidem*, f. [15^{r}].
44. Anche in questo caso, Amat si avvale di un grafico.
45. *Ibidem*, f. [15^{r}-15^{v}].
46. *Ibidem*, f. [17^{r}].
47. *Ibidem*, f. [17^{v}-18^{r}].

composizione polifonica e corrisponde a una vera e propria — seppur rudimentale — armonizzazione della scala diatonica: una volta individuato l'esacordo al quale le note del basso della composizione polifonica appartengono, si faranno corrispondere a ogni 'grado' gli accordi corrispondenti individuati da Amat e riportati, ancora una volta, in una tabella. Come sottolineato da Christensen:

> In most cases this will be a "root-position" major or minor triad determined by the numbers found intabulated in the circle printed earlier in his treatise. If, however, the chord does not seem to fit well with any of the upper parts, one can find a chord that does fit by means of the letters ciphered above mi, ut-sol, and la-mi, and match these with other chords through an algorithm that Amat describes. The net result of Amat's table is that the third, fifth and seventh scale degrees of the major and minor diatonic scales can support one of four different triads: the root-position consonant triad, first inversion (6) major and minor triads, and a second inversion (6) major triad. Evidently Amat did not find it necessary to offer inversional substitutes on the remaining scale degrees (which consequently permit only root-position triads)[48].

Amat afferma addirittura di essere riuscito a improvvisare la riduzione di opere di Palestrina grazie al suo sistema[49]. Sebbene tale affermazione sia da circostanziare alla retorica autocelebrativa dell'epoca e nonostante il sistema preveda una reale corrispondenza tra armonie scritte e armonie ridotte solo statistica e adattabile solo a procedimenti armonici elementari[50], l'idea di partire della sola lettura del basso per sviluppare le armonie ci permette di definire tale sistema come il primissimo esperimento di basso cifrato.

La chitarra spagnola, e con essa lo stile *rasgueado*, trovano rapidissima diffusione in Italia. In un articolo del 2002, John Walter Hill[51] mette in relazione il rasgueado allo stile recitativo fiorentino, presentendoci l'evidenza che l'accompagnamento ad accordi lunghi fosse noto non solo in Spagna, ma anche a Napoli, già intorno agli anni '50 del Cinquecento, e di come questi fosse in possesso di tutte le caratteristiche accordali riscontrate in una serie di accompagnamenti fiorentini in intavolatura per liuto degli anni '90 del Cinquecento. È in Italia che la notazione stenografica degli accordi per chitarra troverà la più ampia diffusione, secondo un sistema differente ma fondato sullo stesso principio di base: la rappresentazione di un accordo per mezzo di un unico simbolo. Nel caso dell'Italia, sono le lettere dell'alfabeto a essere utilizzate, ed è 'alfabeto' il nome attribuito al sistema. La paternità del sistema alfabetico italiano viene comunemente attribuita al manuale di Girolamo Montesardo del 1606[52]; in realtà, la notazione alfabetica è riscontrabile in due

48. Christensen 1992, p. 26.
49. Amat 1627, f. [18v].
50. A questo proposito, si veda: O'Donnell 2011, pp. 134-136.
51. Hill 2003.
52. Montesardo 1606.

opere del 1599, una conservata alla biblioteca vaticana e una (spagnola) nella biblioteca privata di Szayas[53]. Il sistema montesardiano, dal quale gli altri derivano, sostituisce i numeri del sistema di Amat con le lettere ma si regge sugli stessi principi fondamentali; pur non utilizzando il sistema a cerchio, gli elementi fondanti restano gli stessi: equivalenza dei rivolti, enarmonia e assenza di condotta contrappuntistica delle parti. La Francia manterrà una posizione per lo più di importazione rispetto ai sistemi stenografici. Il primo ad apparire è il sistema alfa-numerico detto castigliano, a opera di Luis de Briçeno, nel 1626[54]; il fatto che sia edito a Parigi da Ballard è testimonianza di una diffusione non secondaria. È francese, inoltre, l'unica apparizione dei sistemi in esame in un trattato teorico: il sistema numerico spagnolo, come quello alfabetico italiano, fanno apparizione nel terzo volume dell'*Harmonie Universelle* di Marin Mersenne[55]. L'avvento dell'alfabeto italiano nella pratica francese è tardivo, e di autore italiano: Corbetta, *La guitarre royale*[56]; sarà ripreso poi da Derosier nel 1696[57]. Il sistema italiano è quello che conoscerà la diffusione più ampia. Per questo studio, una distinzione netta tra questi tre sistemi non è rilevante; si farà dunque riferimento agli 'alfabeti' per riferirci ai tre sistemi, e le riflessioni proposte saranno basate sulle caratteristiche comuni a essi. Una cartografia della diffusione di manuali o raccolte contenenti istruzioni per gli alfabeti è proposta nella Tavola 1 (p. 283).

In Italia, il sistema alfabetico diviene strumento di preferenza per l'accompagnamento della monodia sulla chitarra, principalmente a causa dell'immediatezza e facilità di lettura per l'amatore; la presenza della notazione alfabetica nelle raccolte di monodie è, come già accennato, quantitativamente significativa. Molto spesso, però, gli accordi indicati dalle lettere dell'alfabeto risultano essere addirittura incompatibili con un'armonizzazione corretta del basso. Questo ha suscitato l'ipotesi, oggi ritenuta valida, che spesso fossero gli editori ad aggiungere l'alfabeto per ragioni commerciali; a supporto di ciò, osserviamo che circa la metà delle raccolte apparse tra il 1610 e il 1660 sono edite a Venezia, e la maggior parte di esse da un solo editore, Vincenti[58]. In ogni caso, l'accompagnamento tramite alfabeto è da considerarsi come tipicamente chitarristico e, come evidenziato da Natasha Miles, come l'incontro della tradizione popolare di accompagnamento e la realizzazione del continuo[59]; a questo si può aggiungere, per le ragioni brevemente investigate qui sopra, l'eredità liutistica dalla pratica della riduzione. L'elemento di collegamento tra l'alfabeto e il basso continuo sono le cosiddette 'scale di musica', paradigmi di armonizzazione solitamente proposte nei manuali in due versioni, per B quadro e per B molle, e che

---

53. I-Rvat Chigi L.vi.200; E-Szayas A.iv.8, *Cancionero de Matheo Bezón* (Napoli).
54. Briçeno 1626.
55. Mersenne 1636.
56. Corbetta 1671.
57. Derosiers 1696.
58. O'Donnell 2011, p. 130.
59. Miles 2013, p. 105.

rappresentano degli antecedenti alla regola dell'ottava di Campion del 1716. Già in Amat abbiamo visto esistere una tabella contenente un sistema per armonizzare il basso nei dodici toni; in un manoscritto italiano del 1613 (I-Bc Ms. Q. 34, f. 94^{v}) è rappresentata una scala di musica armonizzata con alfabeto, nella quale è interessante notare non solo un'armonizzazione quasi diatonica dell'intervallo fa-fa, ma anche che le note alterate sono armonizzate come un primo rivolto. Questa sarà una costante in tutte le scale di musica: non tutte le note del basso sono considerate come fondamentali. Foscarini, nella sua regola per suonare sopra la parte del 1640[60], propone addirittura una scala cromatica nella quale tutte le note alterate con un diesis sono armonizzate in 3/6. La scala che ha avuto il maggior successo è quella proposta da Milanuzzi[61] nel 1622, e verrà sistematicamente riutilizzata, anch'essa, dall'editore Vincenti di Venezia. Nell'armonizzazione di queste scale non è comunque individuabile alcun tipo di funzionalità tonale né tantomeno una vera identificazione dei modi maggiore/minore. Tale armonizzazione non si discosta molto dai precetti per suonare sopra la parte di Bianciardi e degli altri teorici del basso continuo, aderendo alla visione 'probabilistica' del basso continuo proposta da Preitano: l'aggiunta delle lettere dell'alfabeto si basava sul fatto che le probabilità che l'esecutore avrebbe suonato il giusto accordo sul basso erano molte[62]. A partire dalla metà del secolo, i limiti del sistema alfabetico nella realizzazione del basso continuo cominciano a farsi evidenti. Si comincia a quest'epoca ad aggiungere cifrature supplementari per precisare meglio le note da suonare sul basso e rendere l'esecuzione più coerente dal punto divista dei ritardi e delle dissonanze. L'alfabeto decadrà progressivamente a partire dalla metà del secolo, in favore di una notazione mista costituita da alfabeto e tablatura. Inoltre, è di particolare rilevanza il fatto che, a partire dal 1640 (Foscarini) si assiste all'uso sistematico delle cosiddette 'lettere false' e, in seguito, delle 'lettere tagliate', forme di accordi dissonanti e che cercano, in un certo senso, di reintrodurre le tensioni melodiche proprie al contrappunto, con lo scopo — presumibilmente — di ottenere una più realistica corrispondenza tra il modello polifonico e l'esecuzione accordale.

Nonostante non sia assolutamente adeguato parlare di armonia funzionale riferendosi a tali sistemi, la messa in evidenza delle loro caratteristiche fondanti fa scaturire delle riflessioni che possono legittimamente essere relazionate ai concetti di armonia e funzionalità, considerati individualmente[63]. Uno degli aspetti più interessanti dei sistemi

60. Foscarini 1640.

61. Milanuzzi 1622.

62. Preitano 1994, p. 29.

63. «We use the term "functional harmony" so often that we say "functionalharmony" — one word with the accent on the fourth syllable. We forget that there are two words with two different meanings; that there might be "non-functional harmony", or even "function" in the absence of "harmony". Now it seems clear that "function", since Riemann, refers to relationships between triadic chords, relationships that may be actual or implied. Armed with a more comprehensive view of history, we can proceed cautiously to speak of functions between two-note entities instead of between triads. [...] The formulas of the 15th century, then,

alfabetici è che non solo viene individuato, implicitamente, l'accordo in quanto unità integra, ma viene anche censita formalmente l'equivalenza dei rivolti: già in Amat, nonostante vengano indicate la fondamentale, terza e quinta di ogni triade, si sottolinea che la disposizione di esse non è importante. Tale affermazione appare in Amat ben in anticipo rispetto al trattato di Lippius del 1612 nel quale appariva, secondo Dahlhaus, la primissima teorizzazione del concetto di rivolto[64] (derivante, in Lippius, dalla divisione aritmetica della quinta). L'individuazione di questa equivalenza deriva da una questione strumentale: nella tecnica del *rasgueado* le corde vengono suonate tutte simultaneamente (o quasi) in un unico movimento della mano, dunque la nota che si trova 'al basso' non è determinata da nient'altro che dalla corda più grave. Questa contingenza tecnico-strumentale ci fa immaginare che la corrispondenza dei rivolti fosse una realtà di fatto esistente nella pratica chitarristica già prima della stesura del trattato di Amat. Un discorso analogo è applicabile ai raddoppi. I sistemi alfabetici prevedono un principio di sostituzione tra accordi equivalenti, tra i diversi rivolti: questo vuol dire che sono riconosciute delle caratteristiche alle quali applicare la variazione in base a caratteristiche comuni; agli accordi, che diventano entità autonome giustapponibili liberamente e che non rispondono più alla condotta delle parti (si veda il paragone fatto da Amat tra il pittore e il compositore, riportato più in alto), è riconosciuta un'identità di 'funzione', a prescindere delle disposizioni intervallari al loro interno. Quello che è interessante del sistema alfabetico, che da mero veicolo didattico finisce, attraverso il principio di sostituzione degli accordi, per essere linguaggio compositivo estemporaneo, non è tanto il fatto che sia fondato su delle sonorità triadiche ma che, seppur estraneo a un sistema di funzionalità tonale, esclude ogni legame col pensiero intervallare. Nel motetto *Sicut lilium* di Antoine Brumel (ca. 1500), ad esempio, che secondo Lowinsky costituisce un paradigma dell'armonia tonale a causa delle armonie di terza e quinta risultanti dal contrappunto, queste armonie triadiche non erano, come sottolinea Dahlhaus, il punto di partenza ma il risultato della composizione, aspetto estetico esteriore[65]; nell'alfabeto, invece, si assiste al fenomeno inverso: gli accordi costituiscono il punto di partenza del processo creativo. Il contrappunto, per definizione, riposa su due elementi fondamentali: la condotta melodica delle parti e l'opposizione tra consonanze e dissonanze[66]. Il sistema alfabetico, considerato nella sua forma iniziale puramente triadica, si distacca dall'idea che reggeva il contrappunto non soltanto perché non è gestito dalla legge della condotta delle parti, ma ancor di più perché non prevede l'alternanza consonanza/dissonanza; in questo senso, è da

are indeed functional: they depend upon the two-note progressions of discant. They also sound like the familiar progressions of "functionalharmony", which simply means that triadic functions and progressions develop in unbroken continuity out of discant. The difference between discant and "functionalharmony" has to do not with "function" (although the specific functions are slightly different in the two systems) but with harmony». Crocker 1962, p. 16.

64. *Cfr.* Dahlhaus 1993, p. 116.

65. *Ibidem*, p. 111.

66. *Ibidem*, p. 128.

considerarsi più simile alla diafonia parallela medievale. La sopracitata introduzione di accordi dissonanti a partire dagli anni '40 del Seicento e l'avvento della notazione mista di alfabeto e tablatura alla metà del secolo sono sintomo che il semplicismo di un sistema costituito solo di triadi maggiori e minori comincia a essere percepito come un limite. La scrittura chitarristica risponde così, nuovamente, alla chiamata del movimento melodico, restando però legata agli stilemi idiomatici (accordali) di cui la scrittura alfabetica è stata veicolo e catalizzatore.

Interessante è la questione concernente l'ordine di presentazione degli accordi nei sistemi alfabetici. Nel cerchio di Amat sono avanguardisticamente disposti in un circolo di quarte, in senso orario. Quello di Amat può essere largamente ritenuto il primo caso di circolo 'armonico'[67]. Il primissimo circolo di quinte in un trattato teorico appare solamente alla fine degli anni '70 del Seicento, nel trattato di contrappunto del russo Nikolai Diletskii *Idea Grammatiki Musikiiskoi*. Anche in questo trattato, l'idea del circolo sembra essere originata dalla volontà di semplificare il lavoro compositivo dello studente:

> The second part of the treatise covers composition. Diletskii lays out a series of rules designed to help the student compose sections of a *kontsert*. In one passage he describes two series of progressions by fifths, using first major and then minor triads, illustrated on circular staves to show how each series begins and ends on the same pitch[68].

Nell'alfabeto italiano, gli accordi non sono presentati secondo un ordine scalare ma secondo un ordine apparentemente casuale che mostra avere una relazione con le strutture armoniche tipiche delle danze spagnole (le stesse danze per le quali il *rasgueado* era lo stile di elezione)[69]: nei sistemi italiano e castigliano sono individuabili raggruppamenti corrispondenti alla successione I-IV-V, corrispondente allo schema tipico della passacaglia spagnola. Un altro aspetto fondamentale dei sistemi di armonizzazione proposti (già presente in Amat) è interessante: il mi e il si, e in seguito anche le note alterate, sono armonizzati in 3/6 per evitare il tritono, fatto che per Dahlhaus rappresenta il primo passo verso l'organizzazione del sistema di accordi in gradi principali e secondari[70]. Se a questo si aggiunge il fatto che non solo la passacaglia, ma tutte le danze tipiche del *rasgueado* sono generalmente basate su soli 3 o 4 accordi di base sostituibili in base al principio di 'equivalenza funzionale'[71], in Amat si assiste all'inizio del processo di individuazione dei gradi forti della scala diatonica, processo che culminerà in quello che per Dahlhaus è il principio fondante dell'armonia tonale, ossia la dipendenza del III e VI grado dal I[72].

---

67. *Cfr.* Preitano 1994, p. 76.
68. Jensen 1992, p. 307.
69. *Cfr.* Hudson 1970.
70. *Cfr.* Dahlhaus 1993, pp. 123-124.
71. *Cfr.* Hudson 1970.
72. *Cfr.* Dahlhaus 1993, p. 124.

Un'altra questione importante, che emerge già in Amat, è quella concernente la trasposizione. Già dal sistema di Amat, e in tutti i sistemi a venire, si rende possibile — grazie al riconoscimento dell'enarmonia degli accordi — la trasposizione sui 12 toni senza dover ricorrere alla solmizzazione: una certa cifra o lettera corrispondente alla posizione dell'accordo deve solamente essere spostata sul manico della chitarra di un dato numero di tasti. Questo è strettamente legato alla fisionomia della chitarra che, in quanto strumento dotato di tasti, beneficia di un sistema quasi temperato e si presta dunque a fare da propulsore al temperamento equabile. Certamente, il fatto che un proto sistema temperato esista sugli strumenti a corde non rivela, di per sé, l'esistenza di un sistema tonale:

> Lindley considère un tempérament égal acquis en ce qui concerne les années 1550-1650 [Lindley 1984, p. 19] soit la période qui me concerne; il signale d'ailleurs qu'une des toutes premières sources musicales faisant preuve du tempérament égal est un morceau destiné aux instruments à frettes. [*Ibidem*, p. 22. Il s'agit d'un morceau de Valderrábano 1547, pp. 48-50] En effet, ces instruments ont alors un rapport particulier avec la transposition, en raison du tempérament quasi-égal qui fait que la transposition par *n* nombre de demi-tons correspond au déplacement par *n* nombre de frettes sur le manche. [...] La présence d'un tempérament quasi-égal a permis aux musiciens et théoriciens d'établir un système chromatique sous-jacent, sans pour autant susciter derechef un nouveau système musical. Un système tonal n'advient pas nécessairement une fois le tempérament égal admis. Il est simplement dès lors plus envisageable[73].

In ogni caso, gli espedienti grafici utilizzati da Amat e Doizi de Velasco[74] ci rimandano ancora al trattato di Diletskii. In Doizi de Velasco sono proprio dei cerchi il sistema grafico utilizzato per la trasposizione[75] e in Amat, come si è visto, è il cerchio rappresentante gli accordi ad essere lo strumento di base per la trasposizione. Il circolo delle quinte di Diletskii è presentato come funzionale all'idea di 'trasposizione', intesa in un senso più ampio:

> The circles of fifths appear in the Grammatika's long final chapter, a miscellany appropriately headed 'On Things I Forgot to Write about Earlier'. The circles are part of a section called 'On Amplification', which describes ways of expanding or spinning out a musical idea and is one of several rhetorically-inspired sectional headings in the work. [...] The circles of fifths (Diletskii calls them musical circles) represent yet another way to expand a composition. Diletskii takes a brief melody and shows how it might pass through all of the musical letters and wind up back in its original position. The author explains

73. O'Donnell 2011, pp. 77-78.
74. Doizi 1640.
75. *Ibidem*, p. 61.

> his musical circles in terms already familiar to his readers: the circles are labelled "happy" or "sad" and each statement of the melody as it moves around the circle is identified by its *kliuch*[76].

A differenza del sistema di Amat, in Diletskii il riferimento alla teoria dell'esacordo è ancora esplicitamente presente, anche se si è ipotizzato che l'autore lo abbia utilizzato solo in riferimento al canto e che nel suo pesiero teorico fosse invece già ben definito il concetto di bimodalità:

> Diletskii's division of music into happy and sad and his illustrations of these categories in the musical circles raise the important and difficult question of his understanding of the evolving system of major/minor tonality. Protopopov [Diletskii 1979, pp. 584-586] believes that the *Grammatika* refers unambiguously to the two-mode system and that Diletskii's references to the hexachordal syllables are included only as practical aids for singers and have no part in his overall theoretical scheme[77].

Quello che emerge da questa riflessione è che la ragione per la quale il sistema di Amat ci appare più avanzato dal punto di vista della bimodalità risiede nel fatto che quest'ultimo è basato su un tipo di notazione che, come si è visto, non intrattiene alcun legame con un sitema astratto quale è quello mensurale. In Amat (nel suo sistema di base, astrazion fatta dalla sua tecnica di 'armonizzazione del basso') decade ogni vestigia dell'antico sistema di solmizazione; i due sistemi non sono relazionabili direttamente, in quanto basati su codici 'linguistici' completamente differenti[78].

Quest'ultima osservazione di carattere particolare ci conduce ad una conclusione generale. A pochi decenni di distanza dal tempo in cui Sánchez de Lima, nella sua *Arte poetica en romance castellano* (Alcala de Henares, 1580) osservava che «[e]verything that is usually sung and played nowadays is in the strummed fashion and nothing is sung or played with understanding»[79], il rapporto tra 'causa ed effetto' (e, con esso, tra teoria e pratica) nella nascita di un linguaggio armonico chitarristico si mostra ambiguo. Se è vero che, come si è dimostrato, la nascita di un sistema di notazione indipendente si rivela essere la «conseguenza di un'idea»[80], è allo stesso tempo vero che sono la particolarità e, in un certo senso, il confinamento subito dal linguaggio

[76]. Jensen 1992, p. 319.

[77]. *Ibidem*, p. 320.

[78]. *Cfr.* Preitano 1994, pp. 86-87.

[79]. Citato in Eisenhardt 2015, p. 12.

[80]. Si è presa in prestito l'espressione usata da Schmitt in riferimento alla tablatura: «[...] fenómeno histórico que vamos a considerar no tanto como evento estático [...] sino más bien como algo que ocurrió en los siglos xv y xvi como consecuencia de algo, quizá como consecuencia de una idea». Schmitt 1997, p. 177.

chitarristico ad averlo reso propulsore dell'evoluzione teorica del linguaggio musicale. Citando Thomas Christensen: «Paradoxically, one might say that it was precisely the wide gulf separating the conservative Spanish traditions of received music theory from the empirical practice of the guitarists (to say nothing of the social distinctions) that freed the latter to reconceptualize harmony so radically»[81].

BIBLIOGRAFIA

AMAT 1627
AMAT, Joan Carles. *Guitarra Española* [...] *de cinco ordenes* [...], Lérida, Viuda Anglada y Andres Lorenço, 1627.

APEL 1998
APEL, Willi. *La notation de la musique polyphonique. 900-1600*, traduzione francese di Jean-Philippe Navarre, Sprimont, Mandraga, 1998 (Musique-musicologie).

BENT 2001
BENT, Ian D. *et alii*. 'Notation', in: *Grove Music Online*, <http://www.oxfordmusiconline.com>, visitato nell'ottobre 2018.

BERMUDO 1555
BERMUDO, Fray Juan. *Declaración de instrumentos musicales*, Osuna, s.n., 1555.

BOETTICHER 1958
BOETTICHER, Wolfgang. 'Œuvres de Lassus mises en tablature de luth', in: *Le luth et sa musique: Neuilly sur Seine, 10-14 sept. 1957*, a cura di Jean Jaquot, Parigi, CNRS, 1958 (Colloques internationaux du Centre de la recherche scientifique, 12), pp. 143-153.

BRICEÑO 1626
BRICEÑO, Luis de. *Metodo mui facilissimo para aprender a tañer la guitarra a lo Español*, Parigi, Pierre Ballard, 1626 (fac-simile, Ginevra, Minkoff Reprint, 1972).

BROWN 1965
BROWN, Howard Mayer. *Instrumental Music Printed before 1600. A Bibliography*, Cambridge (MA), Harvard University Press, 1965.

BROWN 1973-1974
ID. 'Embellishment in Early Sixteenth-Century Italian Intabulations', in: *Proceedings of the Royal Musical Association*, C (1973-1974), pp. 49-83.

CASTIGLIONE 1528
CASTIGLIONE, Baldassarre. *Il libro del Cortegiano*, Firenze, per li heredi di Philippo Giunta, 1528.

81. CHRISTENSEN 1992, pp. 11-16.

CHILESOTTI 1912

CHILESOTTI, Oscar. 'Notes sur les tablatures de luth et de guitare – XVIe et XVIIe siècles', in: *Encyclopédie de la Musique et Dictionnaire du Conservatoire. 1.1: Histoire de la Musique: Antiquité, moyen age*, fondato da Albert Lavignac e diretto da Lionel de la Laurencie, Parigi, Delagrave, 1912, pp. 636-684.

CHRISTENSEN 1992

CHRISTENSEN, Thomas. 'The Spanish Baroque Guitar and Seventeenth-Century Triadic Theory', in: *Journal of Music Theory*, XXXVI/1 (1992), pp. 1-42.

CORBETTA 1671

CORBETTA, Francesco. *La guitare royalle dediée Au Roy de la Grande Bretagne*, Parigi, Bonneuil, 1671 (fac-simile Ginevra, Minkoff, 1975).

COUSSEMAKER 1852

COUSSEMAKER, Charles Edmond Henri de. *Histoire de l'harmonie au moyen* âge, Parigi, V. Didron, 1852.

CROCKER 1962

CROCKER, Richard L. 'Discant, Counterpoint, and Harmony', in: *Journal of the American Musicological Society*, XV/1 (1962), pp. 1-21.

DAHLHAUS 1996

DAHLHAUS, Carl. *La tonalité harmonique. Étude des origines*, tradotto dal tedesco da Anne-Emmanuelle Ceulemans, Liegi, Madraga, 1993.

DANNER 1972

DANNER, Peter. 'Before Petrucci: the Lute in Fifteenth Century', in: *Journal of the Lute Society of America*, n. 5 (1972), pp. 4-17.

DART – MOREN – RASTALL 2001

DART, Thurston – MOREHEN, John – RASTALL, Richard. 'Tablature', in: *Grove Music Online*, <http://www.oxfordmusiconline.com>, visitato nell'ottobre 2018.

DEROSIERS 1696

DEROSIERS, Nicolas. *Les principes de la guitarre*, Amsterdam, Antoine Pointel, ca. 1696.

DILETSKII 1979

DILETSKII, Nikolai. *Idea Grammatiki Musikiiskoi*, a cura di Vladimir Protopopov, Mosca, Muzyka, 1979 (Pamiatniki russkogo muzykal'nogo iskusstva, 7).

DOIZI 1640

DOIZI DE VELASCO, Nicolás. *Nuevo modo de cifra para tañer la guitarra con variedad, y perfección, y se muestra ser instrumento perfecto, y abuntantissimo*, Napoli, [Egidio Longo], 1640.

EISENHARDT 2015

EISENHARDT, Lex. *Italian Guitar Music of the Seventeenth Century: Battuto and Pizzicato*, Rochester, University of Rochester Press, 2015 (Eastman Studies in Music).

Esses 1992

Esses, Maurice. *Dance and Instrumental «Diferencias» in Spain during the 17th and Early 18th Centuries. Vol. 1: History and Background, Music and Dance*, Stuyvesant (NY), Pendragon, 1994 (Dance and Music Series, 2).

Foscarin 1640

Foscarini, Giovanni Paolo. *Li cinque libri della chitarra alla spagnola* [...] *con il modo di sonare sopra la parte*, Roma, s.n., 1640 [fac-simile Firenze, Studio per edizioni scelte, 1979 (Archivum musicum. Collana di testi rari, 20)].

Gavito 2006

Gavito, Cory Michael. *The Alfabeto Song in Print, 1610 - ca. 1665: Neapolitan Roots, Roman Codification, and «il Gusto Popolare»*, Ph.D. Diss., Austin (TX), University of Texas at Austin, 2006.

Hall – Tyler 1976

Hall, Monica – Tyler James. 'The 'Guitarra Española', in: *Early Music*, iv/2 (1976), pp. 227, 229.

Hill 2003

Hill, John Walter. 'L'accompagnamento rasgueago di chitarra: un possibile modello per il basso continuo dello stile recitativo?', in: *Rime e suoni alla spagnola. Atti della Giornata internazionale di studi sulla chitarra spagnola (Firenze, Biblioteca Riccardiana, 7 febbraio 2002)*, Firenze, Alinea, 2003 (Secoli d'oro, 33).

Hudson 1970

Hudson, Richard. 'The Concept of Mode in Italian Guitar Music during the First Half of the Seventeenth-Century', in: *Acta Musicologica*, xlii/3-4 (1970), pp. 163-183.

Ivanoff 2005

Ivanoff, Vladimir. 'An Invitaton to the Fifteenth-century Plectrum: the Pesaro Manuscript', in: *Performance on Lute, Guitar and Vihuela: Historical Practice and Modern Interpretation*, a cura di Victor Coelho, Cambridge (UK), Cambridge University Press, 2005 (Cambridge Studies in Performance Practice, 6).

Jensen 1992

Jensen, Claudia R. 'A Theoretical Work of Late Seventeenth-Century Muscovy: Nikolai Diletskii's 'Grammatika' and the Earliest Circle of Fifths', in: *Journal of the American Musicological Society*, xlv/2 (1992), pp. 305-331.

Lindley 1984

Lindley, Mark. *Lutes, Viols & Temperaments*, Cambridge, Cambridge University Press, 1984.

Lowinsky 1948

Lowinsky, Edward E. 'On the Use of Scores by Sixteenth-Century Musicians', in: *Journal of the American Musicological Society*, i/1 (1948), pp. 17-23.

Lowinsky 1960

Id. 'Early Scores in Manuscript', in: *Journal of the American Musicological Society*, xiii/1-3 (1960), pp. 126-173.

Lowinsky 1989
Id. 'Canon Technique and Simultaneous Conception in the Fifteenth-Century Music: A Comparison of North and South', in: Id. *Music in the Culture of the Renaissance & Other Essays*, a cura di Bonnie J. Blackburn, 2 voll., Chicago, University of Chicago Press, 1989, vol. ii, pp. 884-910.

Mersenne 1636
Mersenne, Marin. *Harmonie universelle*, 3 voll., Parigi, S. Cramoisy, 1636 (fac-simile Parigi, CNRS, 1963).

Milanuzzi 1622
Milanuzzi, Carlo. *Primo scherzo delle ariose vaghezze* [...], Venezia, Bartholomeo Magni, 1622.

Miles 2013
Miles, Natasha Frances. *Approaches to Accompaniment on the Baroque Guitar c. 1590 - c.1730*, 2 voll., Ph.D. Diss., Bimingham, University of Bimingham, 2013.

Montesardo 1606
Montesardo, Girolamo. *Nuova inventione d'Intavolatura: per sonare li Balletti sopra la chitarra spagnuola, senza numeri e note; per mezzo della quale da se stesso ogn'uno senza maestro potrà imparare*, Firenze, Christofano Marescotti, 1606.

O'Donnell 2011
O'Donnell, Aidan. *Le rôle de l'alfabeto dans le développement de la pensée harmonique en Italie, 1600-1650*, Ph.D. Diss., Parigi, Université de Paris-Sorbonne, 2011.

Preitano 1994
Preitano, Massimo. 'Gli albori della concezione tonale: aria, ritornello strumentale e chitarra spagnola nel primo Seicento', in: *Rivista Italiana di Musicologia*, xxix/1 (1994), pp. 27-88.

Pujol 1950
Pujol, Emilio. 'Significación de Joan Carlos Amat, 1572-1644, en la historia de la guitarra', in: *Anuario musical*, v (1950), pp. 125-146

Rameau 1722
Rameau, Jean-Philippe. *Traité de l'harmonie*, Parigi, Ballard, 1722 (fac-simile [Parigi], Fondation Singer-Polignac, 1986).

Schmitt 1997
Schmitt, Thomas. 'Sobre la necesidad de las tablaturas', in: Bordas Ibañez, Cristina – Vicente, Alfonso de. *Los instrumentos musicales en el siglo xvi. Primer encuentro Tomás Luis de Victoria y la Música Española del Siglo xvi. Ávila, mayo de 1993*, Avila, Fundación Cultural Sta. Teresa, 1997, pp. 177-185.

Vaccaro 1981
Vaccaro, Jean-Michel. *La musique de luth en France au xvie siècle*, Parigi, CNRS, 1981 (Chœur des muses. Corps des luthistes français).

Zarlino 1558
Zarlino, Gioseffo. *Le istitutioni harmoniche*, Venezia, Pietro da Fino, 1558.

Tavola 1: trattati e raccolte contenenti istruzioni o tavole per alfabeto/cifras

	Spagna	Italia	Francia
[1596]	[J. C. Amat, *Gvitarra Española*]		
1599		I Rvat Chigi L.VI.200 E Szayas A.VI.8, *Cancionero de Matheo Bezón* (Napoli)	
1606		G. Montesardo, *Nuova inventione d'Intavolatura* (Firenze, Christofano Marescotti, 1606)	
1608		Pico, *Nuova scelta di sonate* (Napoli, Giovaanni Francesco Paci, 1608)	
1609		Anon, I-Fr Ms. 3145, *Intavolatura della chitarra spagniola* (1609)	
		Palumbi, F-Pn Ms. Esp. 390, *Libro de villanelle spagnuol' et italiane* [...] (ca. 1610-1620) F. Palumbi, I-Fr Ms. 2804 (ca. 1610-1620) F. Palumbi, I-Fr Ms. 2849 (ca. 1610-1620) Anon, I-Fr Ms. 2973/3, *Canzonette musicali spagnoli e Italiane* (ca. 1610-1620) Anon, I-Fl Ashb 791 (inizi Seicento)	
		Petrus Jacobus Pedruil, I-Bc Ms. V.280, *Libro de sonate diverse alla chitarra spagnola* (1614-1625)	
1616		F. Corradi, *Le stravaganze d'amore* (Venezia, Giacomo Vincenti, 1616) B. Sanseverino, *El segundo libro de los ayres, villançicos, y cancioncillas* (Milano, Filippo Lomazzo, 1616) A. Falconieri, *Libro primo di villanelle* (Roma, Giovanni Battista Robletti, 1616)	
1618		F. Corradi, *Le stravaganze d'amore* (Venezia, Giacomo Vincenti, 1618) R. Romano, *Prima raccolta* (Vicenza, Angelo Salvadori, 1618; rist. 1622; rist. Torino, F. Cavaleri, 1624)	
1619		G. G. Kapsberger, *Libro secondo di villanelle* (Roma, Giovanni Battista Robletti, 1619) G. G. Kapsberger, *Libro terzo di villanelle* (Roma, s.n., 1619)	
	I:Fl Ashb 791 (inizio Seicento)	Anon, F-Pn Res Vmc. Ms. 59 (ca. 1620-1630) Anon, I-Fr Ms. 2951 (ca. 1620-1630) Anon, I-Fr Ms. 2952 (ca. 1620-1630) I-Fr Ms. 2868 vol. II (ca. 1620-1640) Anon, I-Fr MS 2774, *Intavolatura della chitarra spagnola* (ca. 1620)	
1620		G. A. Colonna, *Intavolatura di chitarra alla spagnuola* (Milano, eredi di G. B. Colonna, 1620) G. A. Colonna, *Il secundo libro d'intavolatura di chitarra alla spagnuola*, Milano B. Sanseverino, *Intavolatura facile* (Milano, Filippo Lomazzo, 1620)	
1621		G. Stefani, *Affetti amorosi* (Venezia, Alessandro Vincenti, 1621)	
1622		G. Stefani, *Scherzi amorosi* (Venezia, Alessandro Vincenti, 1622) B. Marini, *Scherzi, e canzonette* (Parma, Anteo Viotti, 1622) B. Sanseverino, *Il primo libro d'Intavolatura per la chitarra spagnuola* (Milano, Filippo Lomazzo, 1622) C. Milanuzzi, *Primo scherzo delle ariose vaghezze* (Venezia, Bartholomeo Magni, 1622)	

		C. Milanuzzi, *Secondo scherzo delle ariose vaghezze* (Venezia, Alessandro Vincenti, 1622) R. Romano, *Prima raccolta* ([Vicenza], Angelo Salvadori, 1618, rist.)	
1623		G. Stefani, *Concerti amorosi* (Venezia, Alessandro Vincenti, 1623) C. Milanuzzi, *Terzo scherzo delle ariose vaghezze* (Venezia, Alessandro Vincenti, 1623) G. Ghizzolo, *Frutti d'amore* (Venezia, Alessandro Vincenti, 1623) D. Manzolo, *Canzonette* (Venezia, Alessandro Vincenti, 1623) G. A. Colonna, *Il terzo libro d'intavolatura*, (Milano, erede di G. B. Colonna, 1623)	
1624		C. Milanuzzi, *Quarto scherzo delle ariose vaghezze* (Venezia, Alessandro Vincenti, 1624) G. P. Berti, *Cantade et arie* (Venezia, Alessandro Vincenti, 1624)	
1625		R. Romano, *Prima raccolta* (Pavia, G. B. de Rossi, 1625) C. Milanuzzi, *Secondo scherzo delle ariose vaghezze* (Venezia, Alessandro Vincenti, 1625)	
1626	J. C. Amat, *Gvitarra Española* (Lerida, Viuda Anglada y Andres Lorenço, 1626)	A. Grandi, *Cantade et arie* (Venezia, Alessandro Vincenti, 1626)	L. de Briceño, *Metodo mui facilissimo* (Parigi, Pierre Ballard, 1626)
1627		G. P. Berti, *Cantade et arie* (Venezia, Alessandro Vincenti, 1627) D. Obizzi, *Madrigali et arie a voce sola* (Venezia, Alessandro Vincenti, 1627) P. Millioni, *Seconda impressione del Quarto libro d'intavolatura* (Roma, Guglielmo Facciotti, 1627) P. Millioni, *Prima impressione del Quinto Libro d'Intavolatura* (Roma, Guglielmo Facciotti, 1627) G. B. Abatessa, *Corona di vaghi fiori* (Venezia, Bartholomeo Magni, 1627) M. Aldigatti da Cesena, *Gratie et affetti amorosi* (Venezia, s.n., 1627) F. Costanzo, *Fior novello* (Bologna, Nicolò Tebaldini, 1627) G. Miniscalchi, *Arie di Guglielmo Miniscalchi Libro Primo* (Venezia, Alessandro Vincenti, 1627) G. Miniscalchi, *Arie di Guglielmo Miniscalchi Libro Secondo* (Venezia, Alessandro Vincenti, 1627)	
1628		C. Milanuzzi, *Sesto libro delle ariose vaghezze* (Venezia, Alessandro Vincenti, 1628)	
1629		G. P. Foscarini, *Intavolatura di chitarra spagnola, libro secondo* (Macerata, Gio. Battista Bonomo, 1629)	
		Anon. I-Fc Ms. B. 2556 (=CF.108), *Sonate di chitarra spagniola* (metà Seicento) Anon, I-Fr Ms. 3121 (metà Seicento)	
1630		G. Miniscalchi, *Arie di Guglielmo Miniscalchi Libro Terzo* (Venezia, Alessandro Vincenti, 1630) C. Milanuzzi, *Settimo libro delle ariose vaghezze* (Venezia, Alessandro Vincenti, 1630) G. P. Foscarini, *Il primo, secondo e terzo libro della chitarra spagnola* (s.l, s.n., [1630])	
1632		G. P. Foscarini, *I quattro libri della chitarra spagnola* (s.l., s.n., [1632])	
1633		Anon, I-Fn Ms. Magl.VII.894 (1633)	
1635		G. B. Abatessa, *Cespuglio di varii fiori* (Orvieto, Gio. Battista Robletti, 1635) C. Milanuzzi, *Ottavo Libro delle Ariose Vaghezze* (Venezia, Alessandro Vincenti, 1635) P. Millioni, *Quarto libro d'intavolatura di chitarra spagnola* (Roma, Paolo Masotti, 1635)	

1636		P. Millioni, *Corona del primo, secondo, e terzo libro d'intavolatura* (Roma e Torino, Giovanni Manzolino & Domenico Roveda, 1635; rist. Milano, Filippo Ghidolfi, G. B. Cerri & C. Ferrardi, 1636) M. Pesenti, *Arie a voce sola* (Venezia, Alessandro Vincenti, 1636) L. Monte, *Vago fior di virtù* (Venezia, Angelo Salvadori, ca. 1636) G. F. Sances, *Il quarto libro delle cantate* (Venezia, Alessandro Vincenti, 1636)	M. Mersenne, *Harmonie universelle* (Parigi, Sebastien Cramoisy, 1636)
1637		G. A. Colonna, *Intavolatura di chitarra spagnuola del primo, secondo, terzo, & quarto Libro* (Milano, Dionisio Gariboldi, 1637) P. Millioni – L. Monte, *Vero e facil modo d'imparare a sonare* (Roma e Macerata, eredi di Salvioni & Agostino Grisei, 1637) G. B. Abatessa, *Cespvglio di varii fiori* (Firenze, Zanobi Pignoni, 1637)	
1638		C. Busatti, *Arie a voce sola* (Venezia, Alessandro Vincenti, 1638)	
1639	J. C. Amat, *Gvitarra Española* (Barcellona, Lorenço Dèu, 1639)	F. Corbetta, *De gli scherzi armonici trouati* (Bologna, Giacomo Monti, 1639) A. Trombetti, *Intavolatura di sonate* [...] *Libro Primo, et secondo* (Bologna, Nicolò Tebaldini, 1639)	
1640		Anon, I-Fn Ms. Magl.XIX.143 (ca. 1640) A. M. Bartolotti, *Libro P.° di chitarra spagnola* (Firenze, s.n., 1640) G. P. Foscarini, *Li cinque libri della chitarra alla spagnola* (Roma, s.n., 1640) A. Carbonchi, *Sonate di chitarra spagnola* (Firenze, Amador Massi e Lorenzo Landi, 1640) N. Doizi de Velasco, *Nuevo modo de cifra* (Napoli, Egidio Longo, 1640)	
		A. Carbonchi, *Sonate per chitarra spagnola*, I-PEc Ms H72 (metà Seicento)	
1643		A. Carbonchi, *Le dodici chitarre spostate* (Firenze, Francesco Sabatini, 1643) F. Corbetta, *Varii capricii per la ghittara spagnuola* (Milano, Bianchi, 1643)	
1646		F. Valdambrini, *Libro primo d'intavolatura di chitarra* (Roma, s.n., 1646) G. B. Granata, *Capricci armonici sopra la chittarriglia spagnola* (Bologna, Giacomo Monti, 1646) C. Calvi, *Intavolatura di chitarra* (Bologna, Giacomo Monti, 1646)	
1647		P. Millioni – L. Monte, *Vero e facil modo d'imparare a sonare, et accordare da se medesimo la Chitarra Spagnola* (Roma e Macerata, Agostino Grisei, 1647)	
1648		S. Pesori, *Lo scrigno armonico* (Verona, s.n., 1648) S. Pesori, *Galeria Musicale* (Verona, Gio. Battista, & Fratelli Merli, 1648)	M. Mersenne, *Harmonicorum libri* (Parigi, Guillaume Baudry, 1648)
1650	F. Corbetta, *Guitarra española y sus differencias de sonos* (Madrid, s.n., ca. 1650)	D. Pellegrini, *Armoniosi concerti sopra la chitarra* (Bologna, Giacomo Monti, 1650) G. B. Abatessa, *Ghirlanda di varii fiori* (Milano, Lodovico Monza, ca. 1650)	
1655		A. M. Bartolotti, *Secondo Libro di chitarra* (Roma, s.n, ca. 1655)	
1660		T. Marchetti, *Il primo libro d'intavolatvra della chitarra spagnola* (Roma, Francesco Moneta, 1660) S. Pesori, *I Concerti Armonici di Chitarriglia* (Verona, Andrea Rossi, ca. 1660)	

1661		P. Millioni, *Nuova corona d'intavolatura di chitarra spagnola* (Roma, eredi di Mancini, 1661)	
1666		P. Millioni – L. Monte, *Vero e facil modo d'imparare a sonare* (Venezia, Giacomo Bortoli, 1666) Anonimo, *Novissime canzonette musicali de diversi auttori* (Venezia, Camillo Bortoli, 1666)	
1671			F. Corbetta, *La guitarre royalle* (Parigi, H. Bonneuil, 1671)
1674	G. Sanz, *Instruccion de musica sobre la guitarra española* (Saragozza, eredi di Diego Dormer, 1674)		F. Corbetta, *La guitarre royalle* (Parigi, H. Bonneuil, 1674)
1675		S. Pesori, *Ricreationi armoniche* (s.l., s.n., ca. 1675)	
1677	L. Ruiz de Ribayaz, *Lvz, y norte mvsical* (Madrid, Melchor Alvarez, 1677)	G. P. Ricci, *Scuola d'intavolatura* (Roma, Paolo Moneta, 1677)	
1678		P. Millioni – L. Monte, *Vero e facil modo d'imparare a sonare* (Venezia, Giacomo Zini, 1678) Anonimo, *Novissime canzonette musicali* (Venezia, il Zini, 1678)	
1680		A. Micheli, *La nuova chitarra di regole* (Palermo, P. Coppula, 1680)	
1696			[N. Derosier, *Les principes de la guitarre* (Amsterdam, Antoine Pointel, ca. 1696)]
1697	G. Sanz, *Instruccion* (Saragozza, eredi di Diego Dormer, 1697)		
1698		F. Pico, *Nuova scelta di sonate per la chitarra* (Napoli, Giovan. Francesco Paci, 1698)	
1699	A. de Santa Cruz, E-Mn Ms. M.2209, *Livro donde se veran […] escribia y asia Dn. Antonio de Santa Cruz, para D. Juan de Miranda* (ca. 1699)		Derosier, *Nouveaux principes pour la guittare* (Parigi, Christophe Ballard, 1699)
			[Anon, CZ-Pu Ms. II.Kk.77, *Pièces composee par le Conte Logis* (1700-1725)]
1717	S. de Murcia, *Resumen de acompañar la parte con la guitarra* (Madrid, s.n., 1717)		

Naturalezza o artificio: riflessioni su improvvisazione e virtuosismo italiani in Francia nel Settecento

Guido Olivieri
(University of Texas, Austin, TX)

Il termine 'improvisar' è puramente italiano[1]. Questa categorica definizione, apparsa nel 1768 nel *Dictionnaire de musique* pubblicato da Jean-Jacques Rousseau, è anche una delle prime relative all'uso di questo termine che diverrà di uso comune in Francia solo verso la fine del secolo.

È certamente sorprendente incontrare, ancora nella seconda metà del Settecento, una definizione della pratica dell'improvvisazione musicale così circoscritta e, in fondo, limitata. Sebbene alcuni studiosi abbiano di recente messo in guardia da un'estensione e un'applicazione indiscriminata del concetto di improvvisazione a qualsiasi fenomeno di produzione musicale spontanea[2], l'improvvisazione è tuttavia oggi considerata un fenomeno complesso e presente praticamente in tutte le culture musicali, seppure a diversi livelli e con diverse modalità di attuazione.

La voce del *Dictionnaire* sembra volutamente ignorare questa complessità e connette, invece, l'improvvisazione a una pratica percepita come appartenente esclusivamente alla tradizione musicale italiana contemporanea. Si tratta, dunque di una definizione molto distante da quella che siamo soliti fornire modernamente e che ha poco a che fare con lo sviluppo dell'improvvisazione considerata — ben prima del Settecento — come cifra caratterizzante del virtuosismo vocale e strumentale.

La definizione del *Dictionnaire* mostra evidentemente che in Francia il termine improvvisazione era ancora praticamente sconosciuto e che il suo uso si limitava a indicare una pratica diversa da quella francese. Ovviamente l'approccio all'improvvisazione non era sconosciuto alla musica francese che applicava da tempo la pratica dell'ornamentazione. Già alla fine del Seicento un altro Rousseau, Jean, nel suo *Traité de la viole* del 1686 affermava — in quello che è forse uno dei primi esempi della metafora del gusto riferita alla musica — che

1. Rousseau 1768, p. 255. «Le mot *improvisar* est purement Italien». Se non è ulteriormente specificato, le traduzioni italiane sono dell'autore del presente saggio.

2. Treitler 2015.

> [...] gli ornamenti sono un sale melodico che condisce il canto e che gli dona il gusto (goût), senza i quali esso sarebbe scialbo e insipido; e come il sale dev'essere usato con prudenza, cosicché non ne serve né troppo, né troppo poco, e come esso occorre più nel condimento di alcune carni e meno in altre, così bisogna far un uso moderato degli ornamenti e saper discernere dove ne siano necessari di più e dove meno[3].

Nell'estetica francese, dunque, l'ornamentazione è governata dal gusto e controllata dalla moderazione. Ma si tratta di aggiunte, ornamenti appunto, al testo scritto che hanno la funzione di abbellire e rendere interessante la pagina musicale, senza stravolgerne la struttura e travisare le intenzioni del compositore.

Lo ribadisce Michel Pignolet de Montéclair qualche anno più tardi, a proposito delle diminuzioni, i *Passages*:

> I *Passaggi* sono arbitrari, ciascuno può farne più o meno a seconda del proprio gusto e della propria disposizione. Si praticano meno nella musica vocale che in quella strumentale, soprattutto adesso che gli strumentisti, per imitare il gusto degli italiani, sfigurano la nobiltà delle melodie semplici, con delle variazioni spesso ridicole[4].

Per comprendere meglio i motivi per i quali Rousseau indica l'improvvisazione come prassi tipicamente italiana occorre leggere fino in fondo la definizione che appare nel *Dictionaire*. Per Rousseau l'improvvisazione consiste nel «fare e cantare all'improvviso delle canzoni, arie e parole che vengono accompagnate di solito da una chitarra o altro strumento simile». Il filosofo francese sottolinea come non ci sia «nulla di più comune in Italia del vedere due maschere incontrarsi, sfidarsi, attaccarsi e replicare con coppie di versi sulla stessa Aria con una vivacità di dialogo, di canto, di accompagnamento cui bisogna aver assistito per poterlo comprendere»[5].

---

3. Rousseau 1687, p. 75: «[...] les Agrémens sont un Sel Melodique qui assaisonne le Chant, & qui luy donne le goût, sans lequel il seroit fade & insipide, & comme le Sel doit estre employé avec prudence, en sorte qu'il n'en faut ny trop, ny trop peu, & qu'il en faut plus dans l'assaisonnement de certaines viandes, & moins en autres: Ainsi dans l'usage des Agrémens il faut les appliquer avec moderation, & sçavoir discerner où il en faut plus, & où il en faut moins».

4. Monteclair 1736, p. 86: «Le Passages sont arbitraire, chacun peut en faire plus ou moins suivant son goût et sa disposition. Ils se pratiquent moins dans la Musique vocale que dans l'instrumentale, sur tout à present que les joüeurs d'instruments, pour imiter le goût des Italiens, defigurent la noblesse des chants simples, par des variations souvent ridicules».

5. Rousseau 1768, p. 255: «C'est faire & chanter impromtu des Chansons, Airs & paroles, qu'on accompagne communément d'une Guitarre ou autre pareil Instrument. Il n'y a rien de plus commun en Italie, que de voir deux Masques se rencontrer, se désier, s'attaquer, se riposter ainsi par des couplets fur le même Air, avec une vivacité de Dialogue, de Chant, d'Accompagnement dont il faut avoir été témoin pour la comprendre».

L'improvvisazione di stampo italiano appare dunque cosa ben diversa dalla pratica di ornamentazione alla francese e si caratterizza già in queste descrizioni come creazione spontanea che nasce al di fuori delle regole e di ogni moderazione. Se nei confronti del testo musicale l'improvvisazione opera a diversi livelli — come libera creazione, ri-creazione (o completamento), oppure elaborazione (ornamentale) — si può affermare che la tradizione musicale francese coltivi prevalentemente l'ultima, mentre in Italia si preferivano le prime due.

È evidente che l'improvvisazione descritta nel *Dictionnaire* coinvolge anche altre manifestazioni artistiche e letterarie, non esclusivamente musicali. La prassi improvvisativa va ricondotta all'aspetto linguistico oltre che quello musicale e si identifica almeno in parte con un fenomeno di natura letteraria. L'improvvisazione italiana è per Rousseau invenzione spontanea e immediata condotta su testi posti in musica. Inoltre il riferimento alle maschere incluso nella definizione fa senza dubbio riferimento alla tradizione della commedia dell'arte e all'espressione musicale che di quella cultura teatrale era erede, ovvero l'intermezzo. Sarà opportuno notare che la voce del *Dictionnaire* venne pubblicata a distanza di appena una quindicina di anni dalla famosa *Querelle des Bouffons* (1752-1754), controversia in cui lo stesso Rousseau ebbe un ruolo centrale. Una *querelle*, com'è noto, centrata sulla performance della *Serva padrona* di Pergolesi e di altri intermezzi, e sulle abilità improvvisative della compagnia teatrale della commedia dell'arte di Eustachio Bambini[6].

In realtà, questa consuetudine improvvisativa ha un momento di rinascita e rivalutazione nell'Italia del XVII secolo; poeti quali Giovan Battista Zappi, Paolo Rolli, Metastasio, Vincenzo Monti furono celebri improvvisatori. È già nell'ambito dell'Accademia dell'Arcadia che si riprendono ideali presenti nei circoli letterari e intellettuali italiani che risalgono almeno a due secoli prima:

> Ai nostri tempi l'improvvisare si è avanzato di stima e di reputazione [...] ci ha di nobilissimi personaggi e di Letterati nulla meno eccellenti che sovente godono di esercitarlo [...] anzi il glorioso Principe Cardinal Pietro Ottoboni Vice Cancelliere di Santa Chiesa, il cui ingegno, e la cui prontezza è mirabile in ogni cosa, e particolarmente nelle materie letterarie, istituì gli anni passati una conversazione privata di lettere, la quale ogni Lunedì si adunava nel suo Palagio, e talora in altri luoghi di sua giurisdizione, e in essa si operava improvvisamente con eruditi discorsi e con poesie d'ogni genere, tessendosi anche, talora col suono, e talora senza, poemetti d'ottave, capitoli, catene di sonetti, di canzoni, di canzonette, e arrivandosi infine a comporvi corone perfette, e a stendersi le disfide degli improvvisatori per quattro, sei ore continue[7].

6. Sulla *Querelle des Bouffons* si veda Sacaluga 1968.

7. Crescimbeni 1731, p. 220. Nella sua *Storia dell'Accademia degli Arcadi*, Crescimbeni ribadisce la partecipazione dei più eminenti letterati alle adunanze dell'accademia, facendo anche un accenno all'uso di 'maschere': «Per maggiormente coltivare lo studio delle scienze, e risvegliare in buona parte d'Italia il buon gusto nelle lettere umane, ed in particolare nella Poesia Volgare, alquanto addormentato, fu da alcuni

In Arcadia l'improvvisazione poetica si coltiva come parte della ricerca di una nuova armonia classica fra naturalezza e artificio: «La poesia doveva ritrovare l'equilibrio tra cultura e ispirazione, tra tecnica e spontaneità, e le sfide tra gli improvvisatori ricreavano l'illusione di tornare nell'età dell'oro, quando i pastori si sfidavano in tenzoni poetiche, lasciandosi guidare dal fiume rapido e senza indugi dell'estro»[8].

È Crescimbeni, fra i fondatori dell'Arcadia e acceso sostenitore del valore dell'improvvisazione poetica, a riferirci delle gare poetico-musicali che avevano luogo in Arcadia, in particolare frutto della collaborazione fra Terpandro — Alessandro Scarlatti — e Tirsi — l'avvocato e poeta Giovan Battista Felice Zappi. In una occasione, invitato da Scarlatti a prestare i suoi versi per un'improvvisazione musicale, Zappi risponde:

> 'Deh per grazia, Terpandro, toglietene d'altrui; e lasciate star me; sapendo voi molto bene, che simili componimenti, fatti solamente in grazia della Musica, poco sono confacevoli al delicato gusto de' cospicui letterati, quali sono i Pastori di questo congresso: e massimamente ciò dee dirsi de' miei, che da me si producono senza alcuno studio all'improvviso, e per lo più al tavolino medesimo del Compositor della Musica, come più volte avete voi stesso e veduto e sperimentato; e particolarmente quando eravamo nelle Campagne della deliziosa Partenope'. 'Egli è il vero, allora Terpandro; ma ciò rende più mirabile il vostro ingegno, dappoiché all'improvviso producete voi ciò che altri con comodo studio mal sa produrre'. [...] Restava intanto ognuno soprafatto in vedere, come mai gareggiassero que' due sì eccellenti Maestri, l'uno di Poesia, l'altro di Musica; ed il loro gareggiamento giunse a tal segno, che appena ebbe l'uno terminato di replicare l'ultimo verso della novella Aria, che l'altro chiuse l'ultima riga della sua Musica[9].

L'abilità improvvisativa degli italiani, non solo in musica e poesia, ma in ogni espressione artistica, provoca stupore e ammirazione, soprattutto presso i viaggiatori stranieri. La scrittrice Anne-Marie Fiquet du Boccage, in visita a Roma nel 1757 descrive un'improvvisazione di Orazio Arrighi Landini: «Il Signor Landini prese il suo mandolino e, con melodie varie, seguendo il loro uso, cantò su un soggetto propostogli dei versi spesso straordinari. Questo talento, sconosciuto presso di noi, ci stupisce»[10].

---

letterati instituita in Roma l'anno 1690 a' 5 d'Ottobre una Conversazione letteraria in forma di repubblica democratica, che abbraccia quasi tutti i Letterati d'Italia, e non pochi anche di là da i monti, e per togliere ogni riguardo di preminenza e precedenza tra i personaggi, che la dovevano formare, e anche per allettare coll'amenità e novità, si stabilì d'andar tutti mascherati sotto la finzione de' Pastori dell'antica Arcadia, dalla quale la Conversazione prese il nome; e i suggetti che la compongono Pastori Arcadi s'appellarono, e s'appellano». Crescimbeni 1806, p. 5.

8. Finotti 2003, p. 31.

9. Crescimbeni 1708, pp. 289-293.

10. 'Recueil des œuvres de madame Du Boccage', vol. iii, p. 157, citato in Giuli 2009, p. 304.

Lo stupore dell'uditorio nasce, naturalmente, non solo dalla maestria, dall'essere gli improvvisatori e improvvistrici «mostri d'ingegno»[11], ma soprattutto dall'abilità di celare ogni sforzo e artificio. Il fine ultimo degli Arcadi improvvisatori è quello di unire la cultura e tecnica derivanti da una lunga tradizione letteraria a un potere creativo apparentemente spontaneo e naturale, quasi una nuova *sprezzatura*, «che nasconda l'arte e dimostri ciò che si fa e dice venir fatto senza fatica e quasi senza pensarvi»[12].

Il momento più alto di ispirazione si manifesta quindi non tanto nell'elaborazione testuale, ma anche, e forse soprattutto, nella fase della *performance*, genuina espressione della transitorietà dell'improvvisazione poetico-musicale: «Non erano solo i testi, ma la recitazione, il tono della voce, gli atteggiamenti, e persino gli sguardi dell'improvvisatore a conquistare l'uditorio»[13]. Saverio Bettinelli fornisce una dettagliata enumerazione delle fasi dell'ispirazione poetica che va dalla «immaginazione» alla «trasfusione», passando per la «visione» e la «passione»:

> Un eccellente poeta estemporaneo più volte considerai nel più forte accesso dell'estro poetico per buona mia sorte, e il vidi in prima cheto e pensoso incominciare con difficoltà, urtando or colla rima or colla frase quasi ancor si restasse nel basso e terra terra; ed eccolo a un punto raccendersi, ed elevarsi quasi a volo spiegando l'ale. Gli brillano gli occhi, serena il volto, guarda alto ed astratto dagli oggetti presenti, e il più spesso esprime questa elevazione dicendo ove sono? chi mi leva sopra di me? sdegno l'umili cose, il basso suolo, sorgiamo, o musa etc. Tali sono gli esordi più frequenti.
>
> [...] Onde affrettasi e affolla concetti ed immagini, s'incalzano i versi, e trae seco il suonatore fuor di tempo; spesso tronca e finisce per tal violenza. [...] Giubila ed arde affezionandosi a quelle viste ed attrattive di grandi oggetti, e belli, l'anima tutta s'affaccia, e commosso anche fuori da quel fuoco, che gli serpe entro le vene, onde gli occhi s'infiammano, arrossan le guance, sorridon le labbra, e freme la persona. [...]
>
> Il qual fremito e fuoco diffondesi negli uditori, che gridan per gioia tratto tratto, e s'alzan dal luogo, e applaudono, e paiono in lui assorti, e trasformati, e trasportati con lui, ripercotendosi come palla da lui a loro, da loro a lui l'entusiasmo[14].

---

11. Un secolo più tardi Ugo Foscolo rimarca l'importanza dell'improvvisazione e il ruolo delle poetesse italiane: «Il dono dell'improvvisazione, che può essere definito innato in quel paese [Italia], diede celebrità a due o tre poetesse e sembra invero che la dolcezza delle voci femminili, la mobilità della loro fantasia e la scioltezza delle loro lingue le rendano più adatte degli uomini alla poesia estemporanea. Ma le donne che godono di tanta celebrità sono rare in Italia, e sono considerate non tanto con rispetto, quanto con meraviglia, come mostri d'ingegno; né vanno immuni dalle pene e dai tormenti del ridicolo». Foscolo 1826.

12. Castiglione 1528, vol. xxvi, p. 44.

13. Finotti 2003, p. 35.

14. Bettinelli 1799, p. 48.

Non è difficile accostare questa animata descrizione dell'ispirazione poetica a quella dell'espressività esecutiva del musicista virtuoso, ispirato e quasi posseduto dalla potenza creatrice dell'improvvisazione: «Non ho mai incontrato nessuno soffrire delle proprie passioni nel suonare il violino da esserne quasi trasfigurato quanto il famoso Arcangelo Corelli, i cui occhi diventavano talvolta rossi come il fuoco; il suo aspetto si altera, i suoi occhi roteano come in agonia, ed egli è così preso da ciò che esegue che non sembra quasi la stessa persona»[15].

L'abilità improvvisativa, la potenza del genio creativo si connettono in ambiente italiano con l'idea del virtuosismo e ne divengono cifra caratterizzante. Nei primi anni del Settecento emerge e si afferma la figura del virtuoso moderno, una figura che diverrà centrale per lo sviluppo della musica francese e europea nel corso del secolo.

È proprio negli anni dell'incontro della cultura francese con la tradizione musicale italiana che troviamo una delle prime definizioni del virtuoso in ambito musicale; è un altro dizionario francese, il *Dictionnaire de musique* compilato da Sébastien de Brossard nel 1703, a fornircela:

> *VIRTÙ* vuol dire in italiano non soltanto quella predisposizione dell'anima che ci rende graditi a Dio e che ci fa agire secondo le regole della giusta ragione; ma anche quella *Superiorità di genio, di destrezza*, o *di abilità*, che ci fa *eccellere* sia nella *Teoria* che nella *Pratica* delle *belle arti*, al di sopra di quelli che vi si applicano tanto quanto noi. Da questo gli Italiani hanno creato l'aggettivo *VIRTUOSO* o *VIRTUDIOSO*, al femminile *Virtuosa*, da cui ottengono anche spesso dei sostantivi per appellare o per lodare coloro cui la Provvidenza ha voluto donare questa *eccellenza* o questa *superiorità*. Dunque secondo loro un eccellente *Pittore* o un *Architetto* di talento etc. è un *Virtuoso*; ma danno più comunemente e più specificamente questo bel Epiteto ai *Musicisti eccellenti* e tra questi piuttosto a quelli che si applicano alla *Teoria*, o alla *Composizione* della musica, che a quelli che eccellono nelle altre arti, tanto che nel loro linguaggio dire semplicemente che un uomo è un *Virtuoso* significa quasi sempre che è un *eccellente Musicista*. Il nostro linguaggio non ha che la parola *Illustre* che possa in qualche modo corrispondere a *Virtuoso* degli Italiani; quanto a *Vertueux*, l'uso non gli ha ancora dato lo stesso significato[16].

---

[15]. L'originale si trova nelle glosse anonime a RAGUENET 1709, pp. 20-21: «I never met with any man that suffered his passions to hurry him away so much whilst he was playing on the violin as the famous Arcangelo Corelli, whose eyes will sometimes turn as red as fire; his countenance will be distorted, his eyeballs roll as in an agony, and he gives in so much to what he is doing that he doth not look like the same man». Il testo che viene commentato, fa riferimento anch'esso all'intensa espressività della tradizione esecutiva dei virtuosi italiani: «A symphony of furies shakes the soul; it undermines and overthrows it in spite of all its care; the artist himself, whilst he is performing it, is seized with an unavoidable agony; he tortures his violin; he racks his body; he is no longer master of himself, but is agitated like one possessed with an irresistible motion».

[16]. «*VIRTU.* veut dire en Italien non seulement cette habitude de l'ame qui nous rend agréables à Dieu & nous fait agir selon les regles de la droute raison; mais aussi cette *Superiorité de genie*, *d'adresse* ou *d'habilité*,

Se per Brossard il termine sembra applicarsi a quei musicisti che si dedicano alla teoria e alla composizione, piuttosto che alla 'pratica' della musica, occorre ricordare come l'autore scriva in un periodo in cui è ancora lontana la separazione fra esecutore e compositore e che, particolarmente nel caso dell'improvvisazione, il confine fra composizione ed esecuzione è sempre molto evanescente.

Non è un caso che questa definizione avvenga nell'ambiente culturale francese. Anche in questa circostanza è l'incontro della prassi musicale italiana con la tradizione francese a determinare la necessità di una definizione. La cultura musicale italiana gioca un ruolo fondamentale nello sviluppo dell'improvvisazione musicale e soprattutto nel legame fra questo fenomeno e quello del virtuosismo 'internazionale' sia vocale che strumentale. Appena due anni dopo la pubblicazione del *Dictionaire* di Brossard, il termine 'virtuoso' riappare, questa volta con connotazioni negative, in uno dei pamphlet che alimenta la famosa controversia sui rispettivi meriti della musica italiana e di quella francese. La *querelle* si sviluppa a partire dalla contrapposizione fra i difensori della musica italiana, il cui portavoce, l'abbate François Raguenet, pubblica nel 1702 il *Paralèle des italiens et des françois, en ce qui regarde la musique et les opéra*, e i sostenitori della tradizione francese, capeggiati da Jean Laurent Lecerf de la Viéville che risponde con la *Comparaison de la musique italienne et de la musique Françoise*, pubblicata in tre parti fra il 1704 e il 1706.

Le opposte visioni vengono efficacemente sintetizzate in un articolo (probabilmente attribuibile a Monsieur de La Tour) apparso nel *Mercure galant* nel novembre 1713: «Un [partito] ammiratore eccessivo della musica italiana, disprezza completamente la musica francese in quanto piatta e priva di gusto; l'altro, fedele al gusto della propria patria [...] tratta la Musa italiana come bizzarra e capricciosa»[17].

Il dibattito non coinvolge certo esclusivamente la dimensione estetico-musicale, ma riflette il momento di profondo cambiamento politico e sociale che investe la capitale francese all'inizio del secolo. Al tramonto dell'*ancien régime*, la musica italiana diventa il vessillo della nuova cultura proclamata e sostenuta da un'aristocrazia non più di stampo

qui nous fait *exceller* soit dans la *Théorie*, soit dans la *Prattique* des *beaux Arts* au dessus de ceux qui s'y apliquent aussi bien que nous. C'est de-là que les Italiens ont formé les Adjectifs *VIRTUOSO*, ou *VIRTUDIOSO*, au feminin *Virtuosa*, dont même ils sont souvent des Substantifs pour nommer, ou pour loüer ceux à qui la Providence a bien voulu donner cette *excellence* ou cette *superiorité*. Ainsi selon eux un excellent *Peintre*, un habile *Architecte*, &c. est un *Virtuoso*; mais ils donnent plus communément & plus specialement cette belle Epithete aux *excellens Musiciens*, & entre ceux là, plûtôt à ceux qui s'apliquent à la *Théorie*, ou à la *Composition* de la Musique, qu'à ceux qui excellent dans les autres Arts, en sorte que dans leur langage, dire simplement qu'un homme est un *Virtuoso*, c'est presque toûjours dire que c'est un *excellent Musicien*. Nôtre langue n'a que le mot *Illustre* qui puisse en quelque maniere répondre au *Virtuoso* des Italiens, car pour celuy de *Vertueux*, l'usage ne luy a pas encore donné cette signification, du moins en parlant serieusement». 'Virtu', in: Brossard 1703, p. 71.

17. L. T. M. de [La Tour?]. 'Dissertation sur le bon gout et la musique italienne et de la musique françoise, et sur ses opéras', in: *Mercure galant*, novembre 1713, pp. 3-62: 7-8.

ereditario, ma basata sul censo. I nuovi banchieri, ricchi mercanti e finanzieri che controllano le leve del potere, si distanziano gradualmente dalla politica del Re: dalle lussuose residenze di Parigi favoriscono e sponsorizzano gli artisti italiani e impongono in Francia una moderna visione estetica. Nascono in tal modo le serie di concerti pubblici, che culmineranno nel 1725 con l'istituzione dei *Concerts Spirituels* e si assiste alla creazione di un pubblico che applaude e accoglie criticamente le esecuzioni dei virtuosi internazionali.

Nei suoi scritti in difesa della tradizione francese, Le Cerf riafferma la contrapposizione fra natura e artificio, fra semplicità e «mostruosità d'ingegno»: «Da un lato il naturale e la semplicità, dall'altro l'affettazione e la brillantezza. Qui il vero, abbellito con proprietà, lì il falso, mascherato da mille raffinatezze, e carico degli eccessi di una scienza mostruosa»[18].

L'aderenza alle regole di imitazione della natura determina il buon gusto in musica e rende le composizioni musicali intelligibili e razionali:

> La musica francese è dunque saggia, uniforme e *naturale*, e non sopporta che di tanto in tanto e alla lontana i toni inusuali e gli ornamenti troppo ricercati. La musica italiana, al contrario, sempre forzata, sempre al di fuori dei confine della natura, senza unità, senza coerenza, rifiuta i nostri abbellimenti dolci e semplici. Non è sorprendente che gli italiani trovino la nostra [musica] scialba e insipida[19].

All'origine di questa contrapposizione c'è l'incontro con la tradizione virtuosistica e improvvisativa italiana. È di nuovo Le Cerf che nel 1705 dichiara apertamente la sua avversione e scagliandosi contro certi «*Virtuosi* de l'Italie» che si curano solo di «un'abilità folle e futile»[20]. Il virtuosismo esasperato è dunque percepito in Francia come una cifra caratteristica degli esecutori italiani. I commenti alle esecuzioni dei virtuosi italiani sottolineano gli elementi di sorpresa, ammirazione, ma anche sconcerto e opposizione a un tipo di esecuzione che viene sempre definita come al di fuori dei limiti stabiliti dalla natura, in altri termini 'artificiale' e innaturale. Ciò che provoca l'entusiasmo o l'aspra critica è precisamente lo stupore di fronte a musicisti che eccellono nell'esecuzione densa di passaggi virtuosistici, padroni di una tecnica di improvvisazione brillante e del tutto sconosciuta in terra francese. Per i virtuosi italiani, sia vocali che strumentali, la pagina scritta non è

---

18. Le Cerf 1705-1706, vol. i, p. 183. «D'un côté le naturel & la simplicité: de l'autre l'affectation & le brilliant. Là le vrai, embelli avec justesse: ici le faux, masqué par mille raffinemens, & chargé des excés d'une science monstrueuse».

19. *Ibidem*, vol. ii, pp. 34-35. «La Musique Françoise est donc sage, unie et naturelle, et ne souffre que de tems en tems, et à loin les tons extraordinaires et les agrémens si recherchés. La Musique Italienne, au contraire, toujours forcée, toujours hors des bornes de la nature, sans liaison, sans suite, rejette nos agrémens doux et aisés. Il n'est pas étonnant que les Italiens trouvent la notre fade et insipide».

20. *Ibidem*, pp. 118-119.

che una traccia sempre e in modo variabile trasformata dall'aggiunta di improvvisazioni, abbellimenti e articolazioni idiomatiche. La natura estemporanea dell'esecuzione porta l'esecutore in un ruolo di primo piano rispetto al compositore — qualora le due figure siano effettivamente diverse — e, stabilendo un'equivalenza fra esecutore e virtuoso, esalta la figura del musicista professionista.

Che tra i musicisti che diffusero questa prassi in Francia vi fossero in una prima fase soprattutto strumentisti di origine e formazione napoletana non sorprende. Nei quattro antichi Conservatori napoletani già dalla metà del Seicento un approccio sistematico all'insegnamento formava musicisti professionisti, dotati di un'avanzata tecnica esecutiva e di una specifica abilità nell'elaborazione improvvisativa applicata alla composizione.

I nomi dei virtuosi che Le Cerf include nella sua critica sono quelli dei violinisti che si erano mossi in quegli anni da Napoli e che avevano incontrato fama e successo nella capitale francese. Virtuosi quali Giovanni Antonio Piani e Giovanni Antonio Guido che insieme a Michele Mascitti erano autori di collezioni che influenzano lo sviluppo della musica strumentale francese e fra i protagonisti delle *soirées* musicali organizzate dai più illustri mecenati di Parigi[21]. Se già nei suoi *Petits motets* pubblicati nel 1707 Giovanni Antonio Guido aveva inserito passaggi solistici per il violino con l'uso di doppie corde, nella sua collezione di Sonate per violino e basso continuo, pubblicata nel 1726, il violinista napoletano fa ricorso a un evidente virtuosismo, includendo successioni di accordi e arpeggi ed estesi passaggi di agilità che dimostrano, come afferma Moser, che Guido doveva essere «un violinista molto abile»[22].

Quanto a Giovanni Antonio Piani, la sua collezione di 12 Sonate stampata nella capitale francese già nel 1712 si apre con un'inusuale premessa nella quale il compositore fornisce la spiegazione di segni e colpi d'arco che vanno utilizzati per dare «brillantezza all'esecuzione». È evidente che con queste spiegazioni — scritte in francese, mentre la dedica è in italiano — l'autore intendeva illustrare tecniche espressive e virtuosistiche che facevano certamente parte del bagaglio professionale dei virtuosi italiani, ma che erano evidentemente ancora poco note e diffuse in ambito francese.

La formazione professionale dei musicisti realizzata nei conservatori napoletani favoriva evidentemente lo sviluppo di un'abilità improvvisativa, trasmessa oralmente da allievo a maestro — e dunque di per sé evanescente — e sistematicamente applicata alla prassi e alla creazione musicale. Ne resta traccia nella pratica del partimento, metodologia al confine fra improvvisazione e creazione estemporanea, basata sull'elaborazione di modelli compositivi[23]. Non diversamente dai poeti improvvisatori dell'Arcadia, questa metodologia

---

21. Su Antonio Guido si veda Olivieri 1996, Nestola 2004; su Mascitti e più in generale sull'influenza dei violinisti napoletani sulla scuola francese si veda Olivieri *in corso di stampa*.

22. «Ohne Zweifel muß Guido ein sehr tüchtiger Geiger gewesen sein». Moser 1923, p. 171.

23. Sui partimenti e sulla loro relazione con l'improvvisazione si veda Sanguinetti 2012 e la sezione sui partimenti in questo volume.

si muoveva fra artificio e spontaneità, forniva al virtuoso i modelli e le tecniche per un'elaborazione improvvisativa che apparisse spontanea, estemporanea e libera.

Questa pratica e lo sviluppo di una superiore abilità improvvisativa come bagaglio del virtuoso veniva tuttavia esercitato in modo particolare dagli strumentisti. In aggiunta ai partimenti, fra i mezzi didattici con cui veniva trasmessa questa tradizione vi erano i duetti e le variazioni su basso ostinato. Di questo approccio didattico rimane qualche traccia in alcuni manoscritti napoletani: da un lato un relativamente ampio repertorio di duetti, genere da sempre deputato principalmente a scopi didattici (si vedano per esempio le Sonate per due violini di Francesco ed Emanuele Barbella, che tuttavia elevano il genere a risultati di alto livello artistico)[24]; dall'altro le raccolte di variazioni per due violoncelli in cui il compositore-esecutore elabora e esperimenta le potenzialità virtuosistiche e di supporto armonico dello strumento[25]. Basti ricordare le Sonate per due violoncelli di Francesco Paolo Supriani, in cui undici Toccate originariamente parte del suo metodo per lo strumento diventano la base per un'ulteriore elaborazione virtuosistica che espande i limiti tecnici dello strumento[26].

Un esempio significativo della combinazione dei due approcci didattici sembra essere un manoscritto risalente al 1699 che include duetti per violoncelli basati su elaborazioni del basso di Passacaglia o su temi liturgici, attribuiti rispettivamente a Gaetano Francone e da Rocco Greco[27]. Anche in questo caso la scelta di due strumenti uguali, anche se non sempre impiegati allo stesso livello tecnico, suggerisce una destinazione didattica del manoscritto. La presenza e organizzazione sistematica della variazioni sulla Passacaglia e i riferimenti ai versetti liturgici rafforzano questa impressione, particolarmente evidente nelle indicazioni di improvvisazione e persino di elaborazione estemporanea presenti in alcune Sinfonie di Rocco Greco. Sono queste fonti che ci permettono di gettare uno sguardo sui metodi didattici del tempo, di chiarire alcuni aspetti della prassi esecutiva e di valutare quanto l'improvvisazione fosse parte integrante della formazione del musicista di stampo italiano.

Non c'è dubbio che in un'epoca in cui gli approcci esecutivi peculiari di una tradizione potevano circolare e diffondersi quasi esclusivamente grazie a esecutori che ne padroneggiassero le tecniche e i principi, la presenza dei musicisti italiani in Francia contribuì in modo determinante allo sviluppo di una nuova estetica e un nuovo linguaggio.

---

24. Una delle numerose collezioni di duetti di Emanuele Barbella è apparsa nel CD *A Due Viole*, esecutori: Stefano Marcocchi e Simone Laghi, Passacaille, 2018 (PAS 1046).

25. Sulla didattica del violoncello e sul repertorio di duetti si veda anche il saggio di Giovanna Barbati in questo volume.

26. Su questa collezione e in generale sull'attività di Supriani, si veda Olivieri 2009.

27. Ho presentato uno studio preliminare di questo manoscritto, conservato presso la biblioteca del Conservatorio di Napoli, alla *16th International Baroque Conference* tenutasi a Salisburgo nel 2014. Ho in preparazione un contributo dedicato a questo manoscritto e alla sua importanza nell'ambito della tradizione violoncellistica napoletana.

Naturalezza o artificio

Negli anni centrali del xviii secolo si sviluppa la figura del musicista virtuoso che fa dell'arte improvvisativa uno dei cardini dell'avanzamento tecnico e del successo presso un più ampio pubblico. L'incontro di questa tradizione tutta italiana con l'ambiente culturale francese e la sua apertura a fenomeni sociali e di promozione musicale che erano invece in gran parte sconosciuti in Italia contribuiranno alla trasformazione del linguaggio musicale verso i *goûts réunis* e verso gli esiti dello stile galante, e produrranno nel secolo successivo la straordinaria fioritura della figura del solista virtuoso. È di fronte al sorgere e all'inarrestabile sviluppo di questo fenomeno e a partire dalle considerazioni sulle peculiarità dello stile strumentale italiano, che intellettuali e musicisti francesi del xviii secolo avanzano le prime riflessioni sui caratteri costitutivi dell'improvvisazione e sul suo legame con il virtuosismo musicale.

Bibliografia

Bettinelli 1799
Bettinelli, Saverio. *Dell'entusiasmo delle belle arti*, 24 voll., Venezia, Adolfo Cesare, vol. i, 1799.

Brossard 1703
Brossard, Sébastien de. *Dictionaire de musique*, Parigi, Ballard, 1703.

Castiglione 1528
Castiglione, Baldassarre. *Il libro del Cortegiano*, Firenze, per li heredi di Philippo Giunta, 1528.

Crescimbeni 1708
Crescimbeni, Giovan Mario. *Arcadia*, Roma, 1708.

Crescimbeni 1731
Id. *Dell'istoria della volgar poesia*, vol. i, lib. iii, Venezia, Basegio 1731.

Crescimbeni 1806
Id. *Storia dell'Accademia degli Arcadi, Istituita in Roma l'anno 1690 per la coltivazione delle scienze delle lettere umane e della poesia... pubblicata l'anno 1712 d'ordine della medesima adunanza*, Londra, Thomas Becket, 1804.

Finotti 2003
Finotti, Fabio. 'Il canto delle Muse: improvvisazione e poetica della voce', in: *Corilla Olimpica e la poesia del Settecento europeo. Atti del convegno tenuto in occasione delle celebrazioni del secondo centenario della morte di Maria Maddalena Morelli (Pistoia, Antico Palazzo dei Vescovi, 21-22 ottobre 2000)*, a cura di Moreno Fabbri. Pistoia, M&m, 2003, pp. 31-42.

Foscolo 1826
Foscolo, Ugo. 'The Women of Italy', in: *London Magazine*, vi/22 (ottobre 1826), pp. 204-219.

Giuli 2009
Giuli, Paola. 'Monsters of Talent: Fame and Reputation of Women Poets in Arcadia', in: *Italy's*

Eighteenth-Century Gender and Culture in the Age of the Gran Tour, a cura di Paula Findlen, Wendy Wassyng Roworth e Catherine M. Sama, Stanford (CA), Stanford University Press, 2009.

Le Cerf 1705-1706
Le Cerf de la Viéville, Jean-Laurent. *Comparaison de la musique italienne et de la musique françoise*, (1705-1706), ripr. facs., Ginevra, Minkoff Reprint, 1972.

Monteclair 1736
Monteclair, Michel Pignolet de. *Principes de musique*, Parigi, s.n., 1736.

Moser 1923
Moser, Andreas. *Geschichte des Violinspiels*, Berlino, Max Hesse, 1923.

Nestola 2004
Nestola, Barbara. 'Giovanni Antonio Guido e il *petit motet* all'inizio del Settecento: dal *dessus* al violino solo', in: *Florilegium Musicae*, a cura di Patrizia Radicchi e Michael Burden, 2 voll., Pisa, ETS, 2004, vol. ii, pp. 737-755.

Olivieri 1996
Olivieri, Guido. '«Si suona a Napoli!» I rapporti fra Napoli e Parigi e i primordi della Sonata in Francia', in: *Studi Musicali*, xxv/1-2 (1996), pp. 409-427.

Olivieri 2009
Id. 'Cello Playing and Teaching in Eighteenth-Century Naples: F. P. Supriani's *Principij da imparare a suonare il violoncello*', in: *Performance Practice: Issues and Approaches*, a cura di Timothy D. Watkins, Ann Arbour (MI), Steglein Publishing, 2009, pp. 109-136.

Olivieri *in corso di stampa*
Id. 'Forgotten Virtuosi: The Violin Tradition in 17th- and 18th-Century Naples', in: *The Italian Violin Tradition: 1650-1850*, a cura di Simone Laghi, Bologna, Ut Orpheus Edizioni, in preparazione (Ad Parnassum Studies, 13).

Piani 1975
Piani, Giovanni Antonio. *Sonatas for Violin Solo and Violoncello with Cembalo. Opera Prima*, a cura di Barbara Garvey Jackson, Madison (WI), A-R Editions, 1975 (Recent Researches in the Music of the Baroque Era, 20).

Raguenet 1709
Raguenet, Francois. *A Comparison between the French and Italian Musick and Operas, Translated from the French with some Remarks*, (1709), edizione in facsimile, Farnborough, Gregg International Publishers, 1968.

Rousseau 1687
Rousseau, Jean. *Traité de la viole*, Parigi, Christoph Ballard, 1687.

Rousseau 1768
Rousseau, Jean-Jacques. *Dictionnaire de musique*, Parigi, Duchesne, 1768.

Sacaluga 1968
Sacaluga, Servando. 'Diderot, Rousseau, et la querelle musicale de 1752: nouvelle mise au point', in: *Diderot Studies*, x (1968), pp. 133-173.

Sanguinetti 2012
Sanguinetti, Giorgio. *The Art of Partimento: History, Theory and Practice*, Oxford, Oxford University Press, 2012.

Treitler 2015
Treitler, Leo. 'Speaking of the I-Word', in: *Archiv für Musikwissenschaft*, lxxii/1 (2015), pp. 1-18.

Adagio de Mr. Tartini. Varié de plusieurs façons différentes, très utiles aux personnes qui veulent apprendre à faire des traits sous chaque notte de l'Harmonie...

Neal Zaslaw
(Cornell University, Ithaca, NY)

Giuseppe Tartini was perhaps the most influential teacher of violinists of the mid-eighteenth century. Violinists traveled to Padua from around Europe to apprentice at his so-called Scuola degli nazioni. During five decades of training violinists, Tartini developed an arsenal of teaching materials, which (with the exception of his *L'arte del arco*[1]) neither he nor anyone else published during his lifetime. Some of the pedagogical materials circulated in manuscript, as attested to by Leopold Mozart's unacknowledged borrowings from Tartini's *Regole per arrivare a saper ben suonar il violino* in his *Versuch einer gründlichen Violinschule* (1756)[2]. After Tartini's death in 1770, a few of his former students did publish, or allow to be published, things they possessed from their time with him. Two such posthumous publications are well known: the *Lettera alla signora Maddalena Lombardini*[3], dated «Padova li 5. Marzo 1760» and published in 1770, as well as

[1]. Pinelli 174?; RISM T 277 (17 variations). An expanded, separate edition of *L'arte del arco* — Paris, Leclerc, [1758]; RISM T 278 (38 variations) — can be consulted at <http://imslp.org/wiki/L'arte_del_arco_%28Tartini%2C_Giuseppe%29>, accessed November 2018. An even more expanded, posthumous edition (Rome, Mareschalchi, 178?; RISM T 279) contains 50 variations. For details see Seletsky 1989.

[2]. Petrobelli 1968, pp. 1-17.

[3]. The *Lettera alla signora Maddalena Lombardini* attracted international interest, judging by frequent republications and translations: Tartini 1770; *Una importante lezione per i suonatori di violino* (Bologna, Sassi, 1770); *Una importante lezione per i suonatori di* violino (Milan, Galeazzi, 1770); *Una importante lezione per i suonatori di* violino (Venice, Colombani, 1770); *A Letter from the Late Signor Tartini to Signora Lombardini* [...] , translated by Charles Burney (London, Bremner, 1771); 'Lettre de Feu Tartini à Madame Madeleine Lombardini [...]', translated by Antoine-Léonard Thomas, in: *Journal de Musique*, II (1771), pp. 15ff.; *A Letter from the Late Signor Tartini to Signora Lombardini* [...], translated by Charles Burney (London, Bremner, 1779); *Brief des Joseph Tartini an Magdalena Lombardini* [...], translated by Johann Adam Hiller (Leipzig, Dykische Buchhandlung, 1784); *Brief an Magdalena Lombardini, enthaltend eine wichtige Lection für*

a French translation of the *Regole* as *Traité des agrémens de la musique*, the following year[4]. A third instructional item, which was and has remained controversial at least in part because it was believed to have been published for the first time only in 1798, provides the impetus for this essay. This is the

> ADAGIO de Mr. TARTINI. Varié de plusieurs façons différentes, très utiles aux personnes qui veulent apprendre à faire des traits sous chaque notte de l'Harmonie. On pourra remplir les lacunes qui se trouvent dans les variations par une des lignes au dessus et au dessous et par des traits arbitraires. [( ]Prix 5tt.)
> Celle Seconde Édition est Gravé D'après les soins de J. B. CARTIER. Chez Decombe, Editeur. Luthier, Facteur d'Instruments en tout genre, M[aît]r[e] de Musique et Professeur, Successeur de Salomon. Place de l'École près le Pont-neuf No. 45 à Paris.
> Gravé Par Melle. Potel Fem. Callaudaux[5].

This text, presented above as if transcribed from an ordinary title page, is in fact spread across the tops of the four pages of a folio-size, gatefold score inserted in J. B. Cartier's *L'Art du violon*[6] (see ILLS. 1a-d).

In the nearly two-and-a-half centuries since the first edition of the «Adagio varié» was published, its reception has been almost entirely negative. Paul Brainard, the formidable cataloguer of Tartini's sonatas, believed it most likely inauthentic[7] and many other violinists and scholars have agreed. Questions have been raised not only about the publication's authenticity but also about its possible utility. Here are four such questions.

---

die Violinspieler, translated by Leopold Rohrmann (Hannover, Pochwitz, 1786); *Un'importante lezione per i suonatori di violino* (Venezia, Paolo Marescalchi, 1799); 'Tartini's Brief an Madame B** [*sic*] seine Schülerin', in: *Allgemeine musikalische Zeitung*, VI/9 (30 November 1803), cols. 134-138. See BERDES 1994 and TENI 2007, p. 124.

4. TARTINI 1771.

5. Missing diacritical marks supplied by N.Z. «Adagio by Mr. Tartini. Varied in several different fashions, most useful to persons who wish to learn to make variations upon each note of the harmony. One can fill in the blank spaces found in the variations from the staves above and below, and by arbitrary variations. This second edition is engraved through the good offices of J. B. Cartier. Available at the premises of [Jacques-François] Decombe, publisher, luthier, maker of every sort of musical instrument, music-master and professor, in succession to [Jean Baptiste Dehaye] Salomon. Place de l'École near the Pont-neuf, No. 45, Paris. Engraved by Mlle. Potel, wife of Callaudaux». <http://hz.imslp.info/files/imglnks/usimg/b/bc/IMSLP333435-PMLP538968-lartduviolonoucoocart_cartier.pdf>, last 4 images, accessed November 2018.

6. «L'Art du violon, ou Collection choisie dans les sonates des écoles italienne, françois et allemande, précédée d'un abrégé des principes pour cette instrument» (1st ed.: Paris, Decombe, [1798]); RISM, Series BII, p. 100).

7. BRAINARD 1975, p. xl and 58: «La tesi di Arnold Schering, che considerava tali variazioni come spurie, è probabilmente corretta»; *cfr. Sammelbände der Internationalen Musikgesellschaft*, VI (1905-1906), pp. 365ff.

Adagio de Mr. Tartini

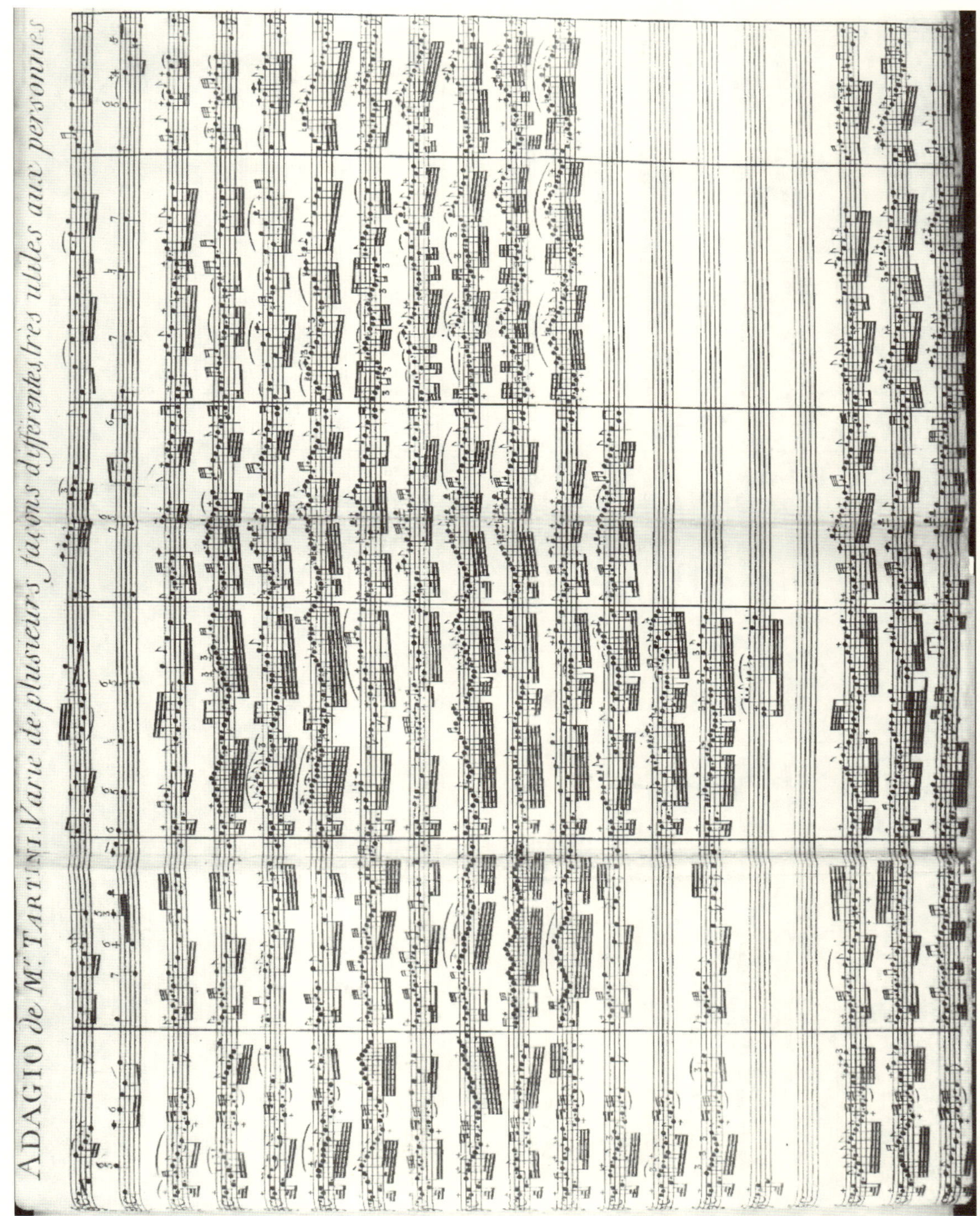

Ills. 1a-d: Tartini, *Adagio varié* from Cartier, *L'Art du violon*.

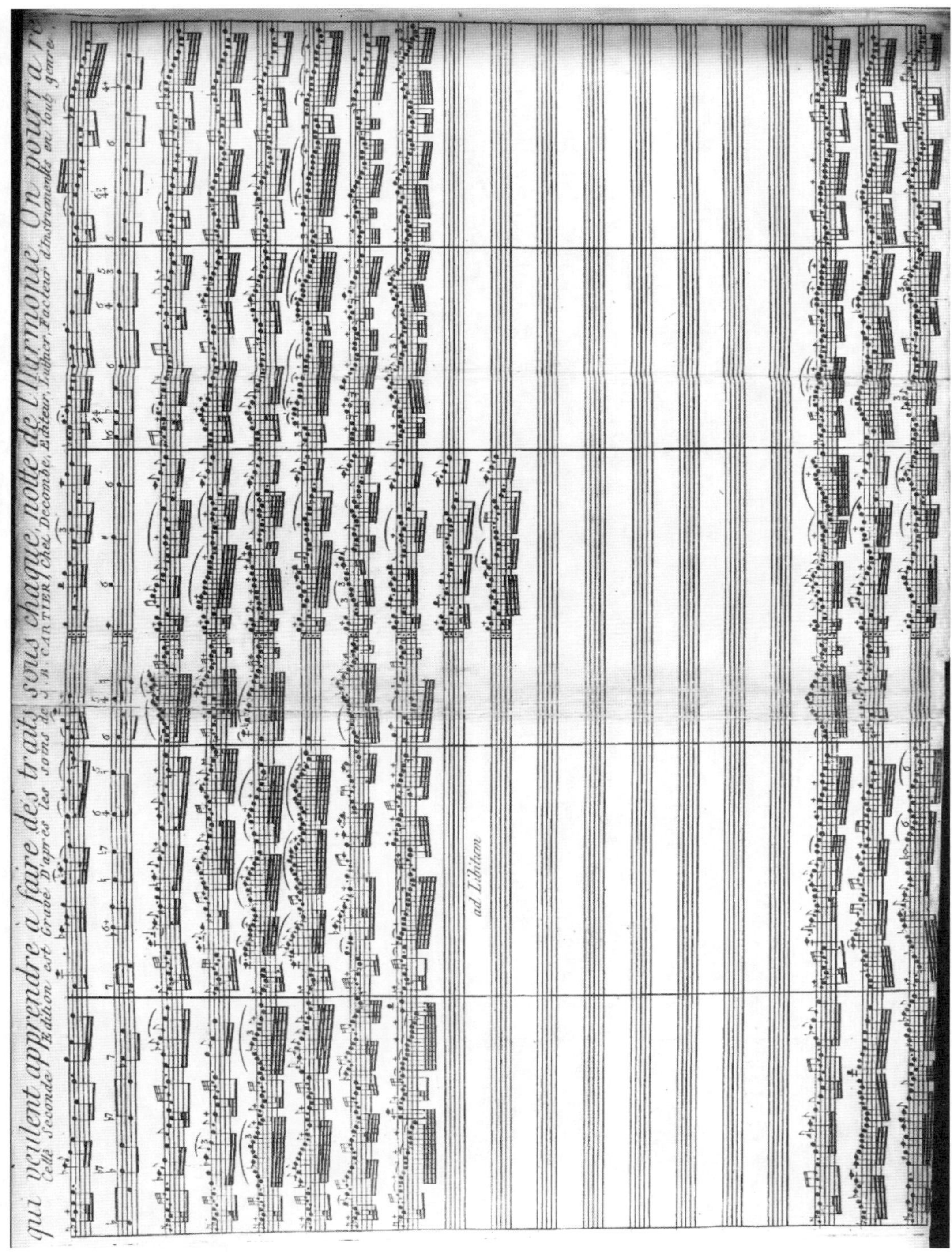
qui veulent apprendre à faire des traits sous chaque notte de l'Harmonie On pourra
Cette Seconde Edition est Gravé D'après les sons de J. B. CARTIER chez Decombe, Editeur, Luthier, Facteur d'Instruments en tout genre
ad Libitum

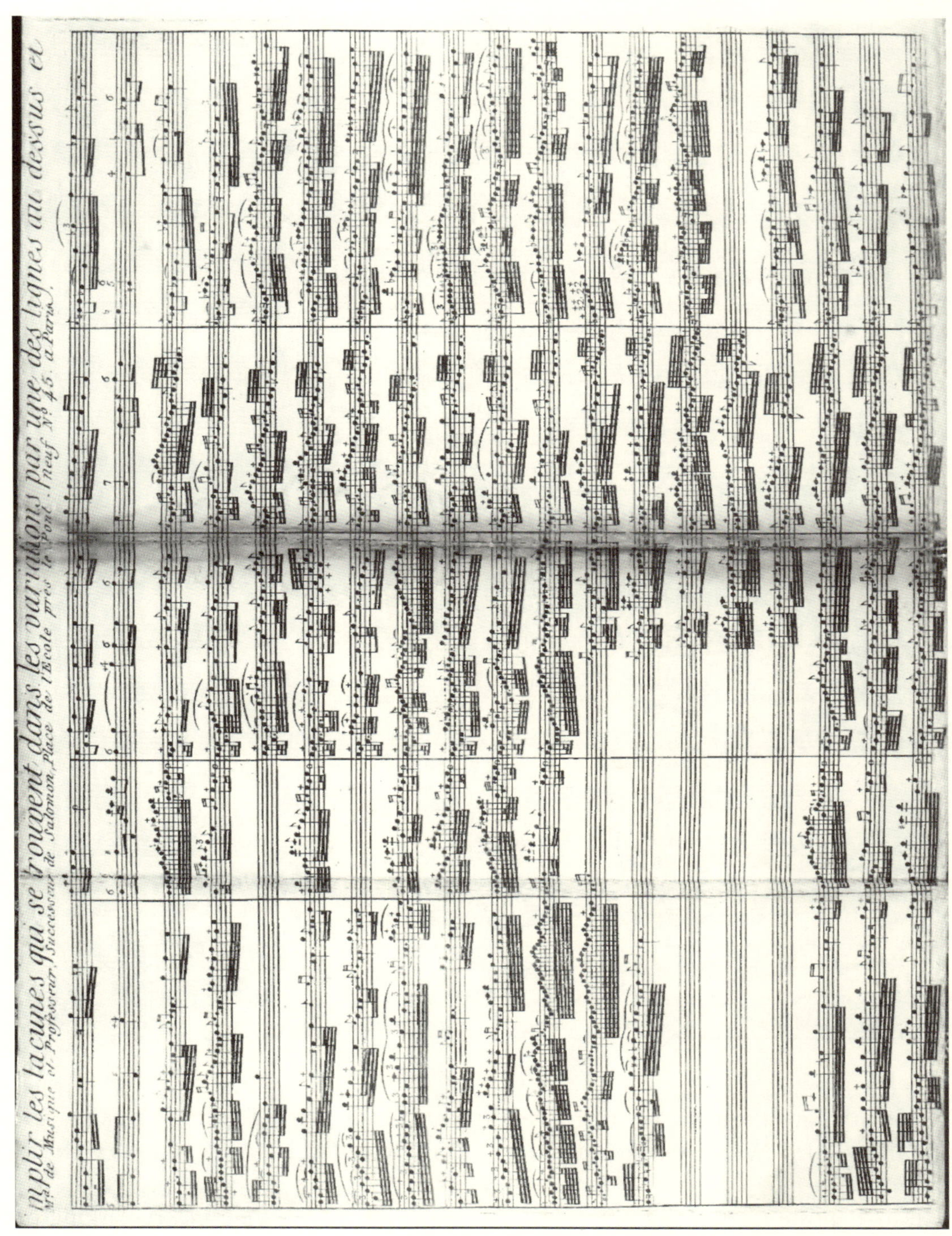
mplir les lacunes qui se trouvent dans les variations par une des lignes au dessus et
de Musique et Professeur, Successeur de Salomon, Place de l'Ecole pres le Pont Neuf Nº 45. à Paris.

Why Should a Publication that Appeared 26 Years after Tartini's Death, and for Which There Were Apparently No Earlier Sources, Be Accepted as Genuine?

Jean-Baptiste Cartier did not reveal his source for the *Adagio varié*, remarking only that, «Ce Recueil contient surtout une pièce que j'ai le Bonheur d'avoir sauvé d'une perte presque certaine: c'est le chef-d'oeuvre appellé la feuille de Tartini»[8]. Yet the *Adagio varié* did have an earlier publication history, one that can be documented to a few years after Tartini's death — in other words, to the period when Tartini's students made available their maestro's *Lettera alla signora Maddalena Lombardini* and his *Traité des agréments*. Tracing earlier sources of the *Adagio varié* is the concern of the rest of this essay.

Given that the *Adagio varié* as inserted into Cartier's *L'Art du violon* bears the indication 'second edition', there presumably was a first edition. Robert Eitner[9] believed that he had located a reference to that item, for sale at the antiquarian dealer Leo Liepmannssohn. Eitner's imprecise reference can be traced to number 616 of a Liepmannssohn catalogue of 1872[10], which reads:

> Tartini. Adagio de M. Tartini, varié de plusieurs façons différentes, très-utiles aux personnes qui veulent apprendre à faire des traits sous chaque note de l'harmonie. Gravé par Mlle Potel, f^em Callaudaux. *Paris, s.d.* (vers 1750).
>
> 5 fr.
>
> Quatre feuilles in-fol. oblong, qui sont collées ensemble pour former un seul tableau de plus de deux mètres de longueur. Chaque variation (elles sont au nombre de 17), est contenue dans une seule ligne. Elles sont places les unes sous les autres, mesure par mesure, «pour qu'on puisse remplir les lacunes qui se trouvent dans les variations par une des lignes au-dessus ou au-dessous». *Fort rare.*

Liepmannssohn's «vers 1750» is mistaken: «Melle Potel, wife of Monsieur Callaudaux» was active as an engraver in Paris no earlier than the mid-1780s[11].

A copy of the *Adagio varié* reproduced in Alberto Bachmann's *Les Grands violonistes du passé*[12] on which the notation 'second edition' is absent was certainly printed from the same Cartier/Potel engraved plates, however in this exemplar the texts in the upper margin were applied in a free calligraphic hand, and Potel's name is nowhere to be seen. I suspect that Bachmann's facsimile may have been tampered with in production and is unreliable, although unfortunately I have not yet been able to investigate this. Bachmann's exemplar was probably not the putative 'first edition' implied by Cartier's 'second edition'[13].

As Cartier's publisher Decombe prepared to issue *L'Art du violon*, he solicited subscriptions in the press. Among the publication's principal attractions Decombe chose

8. CARTIER 1798, p. i. «Above all, this collection contains an item that I have had the good fortune to save from almost certain loss: the masterpiece known as 'Tartini's Sheet'».

9. 'Tartini', in: EITNER 1904-1916.

10. LIEPMANNSSOHN 1872, p. 43.

11. RISM, Series A/I, index of engravers, pp. 237-238: Mme Callaudaux *née* Potel died in 1811.

12. BACHMANN 1913, 2 unnumbered folded leaves between pp. 316 and 317.

13. BACHMANN indicates that the source for his facsimile of the *Adagio varié* was «B. Conserv. de Paris» (= F-Pc); according to RISM, vol. BII *Recueils*, F-Pc owns two copies of Cartier's anthology, which I have not yet been able to examine.

to single out «[...] le fameux *Adagio*, connu sous le nom de *Feuille de Tartini* [...]. Cet Ouvrage [Cartier's entire volume], qui paroîtra dans le courant du mois prochain, coûtera 20 liv., y compris le *Feuille de Tartini*. Les personnes qui souscriront jusqu'au moment où il paroîtra, ne paieront le tout que 12 liv.»[14].

A possible clue to the earlier origin of the *Adagio varié* emerges from an edition published in 1802 in Vienna by Giovanni Cappi (RISM T 289). The beginning of the violin part of Cappi's *Caprices, ou Étude du violon dediés aux Amateurs par Tartini* is labeled: «Adagio. Con Variazioni. Del Sig: Tartini»[15]. Unlike Cartier's edition, where the 17 sets of ornaments are stacked vertically below Tartini's original melody and bassline, Cappi's is organized as a traditional set of 17 variations, presented sequentially. Assuming (as I do) that Cartier's vertical arrangement reproduced Tartini's original concept, the horizontal one reproduced by Cappi can be seen as following Cartier's instructions «remplir les lacunes qui se trouvent dans les variations par une des lignes au dessus et au dessous», even if not actually by «des traits arbitraires».

Knowing that Cappi acquired the musical holdings of the Viennese publisher Artaria & Comp. in 1801[16], I thought to investigate Artaria's music catalogues, where I discovered in his firm's supplement to its 1779 music catalogue the following item[17]:

> *Tartini*. Adagio. Varié de plusieurs façons differentes, tres utiles aux personnes qui veulent apprendre à faire des traits sous chaque note de l'Harmonie. On pourra remplir les lacunes qui se trouvent dans les variations, par une des lignes au dessus & au dessous ou par des traits arbitraries.
>
> Paris Op. — / 1 fl. / 48 kr.

This item reveals that Artaria's offering was derived from a Paris edition that, unlike Cappi's but like Cartier's, presented the 17 variations stacked up one below

14. *Journal typographique et bibliographique*, no. 4 (9 brumaire an VI [= 30 October 1797]), pp. 31-32: «[...]the famous *Adagio*, known by the name *Tartini's Leaf* [...]. This work [*L'Art du violon*], which will appear next month, will cost 20 pounds, including *Tartini's Leaf*. Those who subscribe before the volume's appearance, will pay only 12 pounds for all of it». Decombe subsequently (in the same journal [no. 18, 28 Pluviôse, an 6 = 16 February 1798, pp. 143-144]), informed his subscribers that Cartier's volume would be ready in a fortnight. Decombe subsequently (in the same journal [no. 18, 28 Pluviôse, an 6 = 16 February 1798], pp. 143-144), informed his subscribers that Cartier's volume would be ready in a fortnight.

15. RISM T 289 and TT 289a. <http://imslp.org/wiki/Caprices_%28Tartini%2C_Giuseppe%29>, accessed November 2018. Cappi advertised this edition in the *Wiener Zeitung*, XLI (22 May 1802), p. 1927: «Tartini, Caprices ou Etude du Viol. 1 fl. 30».

16. Weinmann 1967, pp. iii-viii.

17. Biba – Fuchs 2006, p. 45; Ridgewell 2007. I thank Rupert Ridgewell for his kind assistance in the preparation of this article.

another[18]. So far I haven't found a Paris edition of the *Adagio varié* from 1779 or earlier. Note, however, that between the late 1750s and 1768 the publisher Le Duc advertised otherwise unidentified 'Variations' by Tartini[19]. Given that Tartini's *L'arte dell'arco* was readily available from other Parisian publishers and that some years later Le Duc published his own edition of *L'arte dell'arco*, clearly identified as such (RISM T 279), these unidentified variations published between the late 1750s and 1768 may have been what Artaria offered for sale in 1779.

TABLE 1 proposes a timeline for the *Adagio varié* that, if correct, traces the work's earliest dissemination to no later than 1779 — in other words, to the decade during which Tartini's students published two other items of their maestro's pedagogical materials[20].

TABLE 1: A HYPOTHETICAL PUBLICATION HISTORY OF TARTINI'S *ADAGIO VARIÉ*[21]

late 1750s-1768	Paris: Le Duc advertises unidentified 'Variations' by Tartini (no copy known)
1779	Vienna: Artaria advertises a Paris edition of the *Adagio varié* (no copy known)
ca. 1796	Paris: Decombe's 1st printing of the *Adagio varié*, sold separately (RISM TT 262a)
1798	Paris: 2nd printing of same, a separate gatefold folio inserted in Cartier's *L'Art du violon*
1802	Vienna, Cappi, 1802 (RISM T 289)

WAS THE UNORNAMENTED VERSION OF THE *ADAGIO* REALLY BY TARTINI?

This question was raised only prior to the publication of Paul Brainard's catalogue of Tartini's sonatas[22]. Had the skeptics been more diligent, they could have satisfied themselves that the unornamented movement was to be found in Tartini's readily available Op. 2, as the first movement of a Sonata in F major, No. 5 in the Paris edition (Le Cène, [1743];

---

18. As an aside, I wonder if Tartini associated the number 17 with a particular symbolic or mystical meaning, given that the first edition of his *L'arte del arco* also contained 17 variations.

19. DEVRIÈS – LESURE 1979, plates 131-133.

20. Tartini pupils active in Paris in the 1770s included Pierre La Houssaye, André Noël Pagin, the no-given-name Petit, and possibly also Pietro Denis, responsible for the French translation of Tartini's treatise on ornamentation.

21. RISM Series A/1 T 290 bears a passe-partout title page: «Caprices ou étude du violon, Paris, Auguste Le Duc & Co.». This served in the early 19th century as the title page for sonata movements excerpted from Cartier's *L'Art du violon*, not however for the *Adagio varié*, whose engraved plates were too large to be used in that format. The passe-partout's annotation, «gravé d'après l'édition originale d'Amsterdam de J. J. Hummel», refers to Hummel's much earlier editions of Tartini's Opp. 1 and 2 violin sonatas (RISM T 242, T 252); Hummel never published the *Adagio varié* (JOHANSSON 1972). The Sidney Cox Library of Music and Dance at Cornell University, holds an exemplar of the passe-partout title identical to that cited as RISM T 290; it contains movements from Tartini's Opp. 1 and 2.

22. For instance, by BACHMANN 1913.

RISM T 251) and No. 4 in the London edition (Walsh, [1746] RISM T 256). While Brainard of course knew that the movement itself was genuine, he remained among those who questioned the authenticity of the 17 ornamented versions[23].

Don't the Bizarrely Dense Variations of the *Adagio varié* Seem more a Parody of Late-baroque Ornamentation than a Potential Rosetta Stone Intended to Convey and Preserve a Fading Tradition?

Cartier's *Traité du violon* was an attempt to honor his forebears by means of a grand anthology of 18th-century violin music from around Western Europe. His motivation was to provide a resource for young violinists, especially those whose teachers lacked access to a large music collection. That motivation may have been intensified by concern that the French Revolution was sweeping away some good old things along with the bad old ones, inflicting injury upon French musical culture. He was certainly announcing to the world a belief that the Paris Conservatoire was then the center of Europe's musical universe. Perhaps he regarded Tartini's ornaments as an instructive 'blast from the past'.

In any case, surviving ornamentation for many 18th-century adagios are just as dense as those for Tartini's *Adagio varié* — for instance, some of the ornamented versions of the adagios of Corelli's Op. 5 violin Sonatas[24]. The same can be said for a stand-alone instruction manual for ornamenting adagios by the Italian violinist and composer Carlo Zuccari[25]. And perhaps most tellingly, dozens of manuscripts containing a wealth of just-as-elaborately-ornamented adagios from Tartini's own sonatas and concertos survive in his hand and the hands of his students[26]. In some musical circles north of the Alps, Italian adagios were much valued, even if the training required for their idiomatic performance was not as easy to come by there as it was on the Italian peninsula. This is revealed, for instance, by the fact that most surviving notated sets of ornaments for Corelli's adagios originated in the north, as did the already-mentioned instruction manual for adagios by Italian violinist Carlo Zuccari. Consider, too, a rather defensive letter from one of Tartini's most successful students, Pietro Nardini (1722-1793), writing to his own former pupil Joseph Otter (1760-1836), whose patrons had rejected copies of Nardini's string quartets:

---

[23]. See note 7. Tartini's autograph manuscript of Op. 2 is in F-Pn, non-autograph manuscripts are in D-B, I-AN, I-Rsc, I-Vnm, and B-Bc; published editions are available in many libraries. The movement is labeled *Grave* in some 18th-century sources, *Adagio* in others.

[24]. Zaslaw 1996, pp. 95-115; Zaslaw 2015, pp. 179-192. See also Hogwood – Mark 2013.

[25]. Zuccari 1760.

[26]. For the largest collection of manuscripts containing ornaments for Tartini's violin sonatas see Duckles – Elmer 1963, especially pp. 380-384; also Brainard 1975. For ornamented concerto movements see Canale 2011.

> When I promised my quartets, I didn't specify how many movements they would have, because that decision is the composer's prerogative; and you know very well that my adagios aren't suitable for quartets, since they belong to another genre. Therefore, that excuse [lack of adagios] from those who promised to buy them [the quartets] doesn't seem reasonable to me. Maybe they didn't like them [the quartets], or maybe they didn't know how to perform them. [I reject their excuses] because I've sent many copies to Italy, Germany, England and other countries, and no-one raised this problem with me[27].

But Wasn't Tartini Understood to Have Rejected this Elaborate Style of Ornamentation When, after Long Exploration and Experimentation, He Believed that He Had Discovered 'Truth and Beauty' in a Simplified, Cantabile Approach to Composition and Performance?

The most frequently cited accounts of Tartini's reforms of his aesthetic date from after his death, from obituaries, reminiscences and tributes to Tartini written by people who had known him. There is, however, an account from his lifetime, which is, in effect, an extended interview of him at age 66 written down as it took place — that is, a dozen years before he died. This account was recorded in the travel diary of Achilles Ryhiner-Delon (1731-1788), a Swiss violinist who spent three weeks in Padua in the summer of 1758[28].

Table 2: Tartini's Artistic Evolution as Reported in Ryhiner-Delon's Diary
with words rendered in bold-face font by NZ

Key to numbers added by NZ
[1] = extreme technical difficulties the principal goal
[2] = impasse
[3] = rebellion against technical difficulties, and opting for radical simplicity
[4] = simplicity overloaded with ornaments
[5] = realization that full success requires aspects of **1** and **2**

[27]. Pietro Nardini, Letter to Joseph Otter, 27 May 1783, Paris, BNF, Richelieu VM BOB 21584. Laghi 2017, pp. 62-63: «Quando io ho promesso i miei quartetti non ho specificato di quanti tempi dovevano essere, perché ciò appartiene alla volontà del compositore, ed ella sà molto bene, che i miei adagj non sono proprj per i quartetti, essendo questi di altro genere; onde questa scusa non mi pare a proposito per quelli che Le hanno promesso di pigliarli: potrebbe darsi che non piacessero, o potrebbe anche darsi che ciò dipendesse dal non li sapere eseguire, perché avendone dati tanti fuori, sì in Italia come in Germania[,] in Inghilterra ed in altri Luoghi, nessuno mi ha fatto queste difficoltà». English translation by Simone Laghi.

[28]. Translated from Staehelin 1978, pp. 251-274.

I [Rhyner] formed [...] a personal acquaintanceship [...] with the famous violinist, Mr. Tartini. I visited him several times to discuss music. He assured me that, even though he had, during his lifetime and right up to the present, continually investigated the **[5] True Manner** of violin-playing, he nonetheless succeeded only recently; that in his youth he had believed **[1] Beauty inhered in difficulties**, but that he discovered he had been wrong; that he had fallen into a manner **[1] overloaded with ornaments**; that [he discovered] much later that that had led to **[2] Falsehood**, that thereafter he had for some time **[2] truly been stuck, not knowing what to do**. He had thought about the idea of trying the **[3] totally simple and completely unified manner**, but it hadn't seemed to him worthy or capable of sustaining his reputation.

Finally, [however,] not having a better idea of what to do, he undertook to put it to the test by trying **[3]** [the **totally simple and completely unified manner]**, and he quickly perceived that not only did the **[3] Truly Beautiful** and **Good Taste** reside therein, but also that **[3] this simplicity, this unity**, was deceptive; that it was even more difficult than any other manner; that for those who played **[1] technically difficult pieces**, difficulties excused other defects; that everyone judged such a person a great violinist, but that they pleased only a very small number of people — and perhaps no-one; that on the other hand, those who, **[4] without creating extremely difficult things, had overloaded the piece with embellishments**, had taken the work's meaning and obscured it to such an extent that one no longer knew what it meant; that he had compared such people to authors who filled their writings with parentheses to such a degree that one lost the meaning of the text.

«These sorts of musicians **[4]** have yet another advantage over the first **[3]**», he continued, «They **conceal many of their weaknesses with ornaments**, and earn more applause. But neither of these two sorts of people **[3 or 4]** is capable of playing consistently [in a simple manner], which they consider unworthy of them».

«In the end I believe that the one and only **[5] true Good Taste** comprises a unified, clear tone, **instrumental** [«sonant»] **in one passage and singing** [«chantant»] **in another.** A sigh, a trill, a passing tone, a detached bow stroke, another slurred, a mordent; finally, all those different manners of varying the sounds that can be employed in the proper time and place; and even though that is necessary to impart expression to what one plays, it is [likewise] necessary to make use of it [the instrumental style] only in spots where absolutely required in order to relieve the simplicity of the unified, cantabile sounds».

«There are some movements in which **[5]** it is absolutely necessary to play in an **instrumental style**, and others in a **singing style**; the latter, more flattering to the ear than the previous, is consequently judged yet finer in **Good Taste**. This is the very reason that instruments with fixed pitches — like the harpsichord, lute, harp, zither, guitar, mandolin, and others — are considered inferior to others that are not so fixed. You cannot play **cantabile** on the former instruments, since creating cantabile is possible only during sustained sounds that you can hold as long as you please while nuancing them a bit; on the harpsichord, etc., you aren't able to sustain and are forced to repeat notes».

«Once I had discovered **[5] Good Taste**, I studied it with the utmost patience; it gave me more trouble than any other [study], and at the present moment I cannot say that I am satisfied with myself» [...]

To return to Signore Tartini: here is how I [Ryhiner] spent my time with him. He's a bit of a philosophe, but one of those likeable philosophes, gentle, obliging and very sociable. He doesn't object if you beg him to play. He plays best especially in the adagios. It is true that he's no longer in his prime, but that doesn't prevent him from being the most capable and the best suited person in the world for teaching. His method is excellent; he has a surprising amount of patience and attention. He doesn't seek to advance himself, but he strives to bring honor to his students. I don't know what about me merited a personal acquaintanceship with this man; he was pleased to instruct me. He had me play an entirely easy solo for him without accompanying me. He wanted to hear me all alone. He followed every note with his eyes. Once I had played in as unified and neat manner as I could, he had the graciousness to praise the good disposition that I had for this instrument and even, as far as he had seen, for music in general.

Dounias's foundational catalogue of Tartini's concertos argued at length for a division of Tartini's career into an apprenticeship followed by three canonical, Beethovenian biographical periods[29], and many other writers have followed suit. If one superimposes on Dounias's tripartite schema what Tartini told Achilles Ryhiner in 1758, something like Table 3 results. However, even though Ryhiner's account can readily be mapped onto three imagined biographical periods, real lives as lived seldom (perhaps almost never?) sort themselves into such tidy Trinitarian patterns.

Table 3: Hypothetical Progression of Tartini's Artistic Development

Youth
Short 'Corelli' bow/difficulties valued
Suonabile

***

Crisis 1: encounter with Francesco Maria Veracini (July 1716) leading to a retreat to reformulate his technique
First flowering = long 'Tartini' bow/simplicity rejected
Suonabile[30]

***

29. Dounias 1935, pp. 33-232.
30. Durante 2017, p. 23.

Crisis 2: Self doubt
«Lacking a better idea of what to do…»
Truth and Beauty/Imitation of Nature
Cantabile

***

Crisis 3: Injury to bow arm
Suonabile and Cantabile both essential

Tartini's own binary formulations of his ideas about musical styles and concepts are also troubling; these are matters for which mixtures, permeable boundaries and continua are what one requires (see TABLE 4). Thankfully, Sergio Durante has recently provided a finely-nuanced debunking of such historiographical tactics[31].

Some light may be shed on Tartini's self-fashioning during the period when he favored suonabile, from remarks he made in 1739 or 1740 to the French amateur musician Charles de Brosses. According to de Brosses, Tartini complained about

> […] [an] abuse in which the composers of instrumental music want to meddle in creating vocal music and *vice versa*. «These two species», he said to me, «are so different that music proper to one can hardly be proper to the other; each person must remain within the bounds of his talent. I have», he said, «been asked to work for the theaters of Venice, and I never wanted to do it, knowing that a throat is not the neck of a violin»[32].

Do Tartini's binaries may reflect something about the culture of his time or about his idiosyncratic ways of thinking? Does the prevalence of binary thinking reveal something behind the opaque prose style of his non-performance-oriented theoretical writings? Or could these binaries be a manifestation of his well-documented fascination with Platonic reasoning? After all, the best-known likeness of Tartini portrays him in an oval hovering above his symbolic attributes: violin, bow, score by Corelli, and learned tomes by Zarlino and Plato (ILL. 2).

TABLE 4: TARTINI'S BINARIES
(ALSO KNOWN AS FALSE DICHOTOMIES)

Allegro	Adagio
Artifice	Nature
Ugliness	Beauty
Bad taste	Good taste

[31]. *Ibidem*, pp. 70-74.

[32]. BROSSES 1858, vol. II, pp. 360-361.

Suonabile	Cantabile
Difficulty	Simplicity
Early style	Late style
False	True
Inferior (harpsichord)	Superior (violin)

Ill. 2: engraving by Carlo Calcinotto (Padua, 1761) after an anonymous oil painting in the Conservatorio musicale G. B. Martini, Bologna.

In Tartini's defense, however, he did in the end conclude (at least according to Ryhiner) that «the one and only true Good Taste comprises a unified, clear tone, instrumental [*sonant*] in one passage and singing [*chantant*] in another», in that way adumbrating in a flexible manner the fading of baroque notions of unified affect and the concomitant rise of a style that is more favorable to juxtaposing contrasting elements in the same movement.

***

In a program note about Tartini's *Adagio varié*, the baroque violinist Patrick Oliva wrote something that captures, as well as anything I've read on the subject, my understanding of the Maestro's ideas about ornamentation in general and the *Adagio varié* in particular:

> Giuseppe Tartini's ornamentation [...] combines Corelli's Italian diminutions [actually «free ornamentation», not diminutions] with the application of agréments to notes pushed to the extreme [...]. «L'Adagio orné de plusieurs manières différentes» [...] is subjected to seventeen sets of ornamentation, one more exuberant than another. Mordents, trills, appoggiaturas literally invade the melodic line. Behind this overabundance one notices a certain logic in the manner of varying the different passages. Like his contemporaries, Tartini employs a rich system of ornamentation. Certain characteristic figures appear in a recurrent manner [...][33].

As one example of what might be learned about 18th-century ornamentation from close study of Tartini's teaching materials, I gloss the final sentence of this excerpt from Oliva's note. Early in my own musical apprenticeship, I understood from remarks and performances by leading performers of 18th-century music that the norm when it came to ornamenting the three iterations of a rising melodic sequence was this: leave the first «come sta», ornament the second modestly, and then ornament the third more intensely. On the contrary, judged by his notated ornamentations, Tartini more often preferred to characterize the first iteration with a notable ornamental pattern, which he re-applied *verbatim* twice more, transposed[34]. This can be confirmed in many slow movements for which Tartini and his students have left us (sometimes multiple) ornamented versions.

---

[33]. «L'ornementation de Giuseppe Tartini [...] allie l'héritage des diminutions [recte: ornamentation libre] italiennes de Corelli et une agrémentation des notes poussée à l'extrême [...]. L'Adagio orné de plusieurs manières différentes [...] extrait d'une des sonates du maître soumis à dix-sept ornementations toutes plus exubérantes les unes que les autres. Les mordants, les trilles, les appoggiatures envahissent littéralement la ligne mélodique. Derrière ce foisonnement, on observe une certaine logique dans la manière de varier les différents passages. Tartini, à l'instar de ses contemporains, utilise un riche système ornemental. Certaines figures caractéristiques apparaissent de manière récurrente [...]». Oliva 2012, p. 4.

[34]. I owe this *aperçu* to my former student, Hannah Krall.

Therefore, what I had previously understood about ornamenting melodic sequences offers an illustration of an anachronistic, *ad hoc* «rule of thumb» hardened into an inviolable and misleading commandment.

The manuscripts of ornamented movements from Tartini's 'Scuola delle nazioni' (of which the *Adagio varié* is but a singularly curious example) preserve a large reservoir of patterns to be dipped into, mixed, matched and imitated, as occasions warrant. These idiomatic patterns ('riffs') can serve as models for decorating characteristic openings, middles and endings of phrases — especially cadences, of course — of late baroque music, to be learned by ear, by musical notation, by verbal suggestions, and incorporated into performers' conscious knowledge and muscle memory, thereby providing a mass of raw materials for spontaneous ornamentation and improvisation.

Bibliography

Bachmann 1913
Bachmann, Alberto. *Les Grands violonistes du passé*, Paris, Fischbacher, 1913.

Berdes 1994
Berdes, Jane L. 'L'ultima allieva di Tartini: Maddalena Lombardini Sirmen', in: *Tartini, il tempo e le opere*, edited by Andrea Bombi and Maria Nevilla Massaro, Bologna, Il Mulino, 1994 (Temi e discussioni), pp. 213-225.

Biba – Fuchs 2006
Biba, Otto – Fuchs, Ingrid. *Die Sortimentskataloge der Musikalienhandlung Artaria Comp. in Wien aus dem Jahren 1779, 1780, 1782, 1785 und 1788*, Tutzing, Hans Schneider, 2006 (Veröffentlichungen des Archivs der Gesellschaft der Musikfreunde in Wien, 5).

Brainard 1975
Brainard, Paul. *Le sonate per violino di Giuseppe Tartini: catalogo tematico*, translated by Claudio Scimone, Padua, Accademia Tartiniana, 1975.

Brosses 1858
Brosses, Charles de. *Le president De Brosses en Italie: lettres familiéres écrit d'Italie en 1739 et 1740*, second edition edited by Romain Colomb, 2 vols., Paris, Dider, 1858.

Canale 2011
Canale, Margherita. *I concerti solistici di Giuseppe Tartini: testimoni, tradizione e catalogo tematico*, 2 vols. and 1 DVD_ROM, Ph.D. Diss., Padua, Università di Padova, 2011.

Cartier 1798
Cartier, Jean-Baptiste. *L'Art du violon, ou Division des écoles choisies dans les sonates itallienne, françoise et allemande, précédée d'un abrégé de principes pour cet instrument*, Paris, Decombe, 1798 [RISM Series Bvi[1], p. 209].

Devriès – Lesure 1979

Devriès, Anik – Lesure, François. *Dictionnaire des éditeurs de musique français: des origins à environ 1820. 1.2: des origins à environ 1820: catalogues*, Geneva, Minkoff, 1979 (Archives de l'édition musicale française, 4/1).

Dounias 1935

Dounias, Minos. *Die Violinkonzerte Giuseppe Tartinis als Ausdruck einer Künstlerpersönlichkeit und einer Kulturepoche*, Munich, Salesianischen Offizin, 1935.

Duckles – Elmer 1963

Duckles, Vincent – Elmer, Minnie. *Thematic Catalog of a Manuscript Collection of Eighteenth-Century Italian Instrumental Music*, Berkeley-Los Angeles, University of California Press, 1963.

Durante 2017

Durante, Sergio. *Tartini, Padova, l'Europa*, Leghorn, Sillabe, 2017.

Eitner 1904-1916

Eitner, Robert. *Biographisch-bibliographisches Quellen-Lexikon der Musiker und Musikgelehrten der christlichen Zeitrechnung bis zur Mitte des neunzehnten Jahrhunderts*, 11 vols., Leipzig, Breitkopf & Härtel, ^{2}1904-1916.

Hogwood – Mark 2013

Hogwood, Christopher – Mark, Ryan. *Corelli: Sonaten für Violine und Basso continuo, Op. 5, mit zeitgenössischen Verzierungen sowie einer Aussetzung für Tasteninstrument von Antonio Tonelli (1686-1765)*, 2 vols. Kassel, Bärenreiter, 2013 (Bärenreiter Urtext).

Johansson 1972

Johansson, Cari. *J. J. & B. Hummel. Music-Publishing and Thematic Catalogues*, 3 vols., Stockholm, Almquist & Wiksell, 1972.

Laghi 2017

Laghi, Simone. *Italian String Quartets and Late Eighteenth-Century London: Publication and Production. With a Critical Edition of the Quartets, Opp. 2 and 7 by Venanzio Rauzzini (1746-1810)*, Ph.D. Diss., Cardiff, Cardiff University, 2017.

Liepmannssohn 1872

Liepmannssohn, Leo. *Catalogue No. 37 de la Librairie ancienne et moderne*, Paris, s.n., [1872].

Oliva 2012

Oliva, Patrick. 'L'imaginaire galant. Aperçu de l'ornementation pour violon en Europe au milieu du xviiie siècle', 2012, <http://www.conservatoiredeparis.fr/fileadmin/user_upload/Voir-et-Ententre/jeunes_solistes/CREC_JS_livret_PatrickOliva_1712.pdf>, accessed November 2018.

Petrobelli 1968

Petrobelli, Pierluigi. *Giuseppe Tartini: le fonti biografiche*, Vienna, Universal, 1968 (Studi di musica veneta, 1).

Petrobellli 1992

Id. *Tartini, le sue idee e il suo tempo*, Lucca, LIM, 1992 (Musicalia, 5).

Pinelli 174?

Pinelli, Petronio. *Nouvelle étude pour le violon, ou Maniere de varier et orner un pièce dans le goût du cantabile italien, augmenté d'une Gavotte de Corelli, travailez et doublez par Mr. Giuseppe Tartini*, Paris, Boivin et al., [174?].

Ridgewell 2007

Ridgewell, Rupert. Review of Biba – Fuchs 2006, in: *The Library: The Transactions of the Bibliographical Society*, viii/3 (September 2007), pp. 345-347.

Seletzky 1989

Seletzky, Robert Eric. *Improvised Variation Sets for Short Dance Movements in Violin Repertory, circa 1680-1800, Exemplified in Period Sources for Corelli's Violin Sonatas, Opus 5*, D.M.A. Diss., Ithaca (NY), Cornell University, 1989 <https://newcatalog.library.cornell.edu/catalog/1666315>, accessed November 2018.

Staehelin 1978

Staehelin, Martin. 'Giuseppe Tartini über seine künstlerische Entwicklung. Ein unbekanntes Selbstzeugnis', in: *Archiv für Musikwissenschaft*, xxxv/4 (1978), pp. 251-274.

Tartini 1770

Tartini, Giuseppe. 'Lettera del Defunto Sig. G. T. alla Signora Maddalena Lombardini', in: *Europa Letteraria*, iv/1 (1 June 1770), pp. 70ff.

Tartini 1771

Id. *Traité des agrémens de la musique*, French translation by Pietro [Pierre] Denis. Paris, l'auteur, 1771 [RISM Series Bvi[2], p. 820].

Teni 2007

Teni, Maria Rosaria. *Una donna e la sua musica: Maddalena Laura Lombardini Sirmen e la Venezia del xviii secolo*, Novoli, Bibliotheca Minima, 2007 (Scriptorium, 36).

Weinmann 1967

Weinmann, Alexander. *Verlagsverzeichnis Giovanni Cappi bis A. O. Witzendorf*, Vienna, Universal, 1967 (Beiträge zur Geschichte des alt-Wiener Musikverlages, 2/11).

Zaslaw 1996

Zaslaw, Neal. 'Ornaments for Corelli's Violin Sonatas, Op. 5', in: *Early Music*, xxiv/1 (1996), pp. 95-115 [reprinted in *Baroque Music*, edited by Peter Walls, Farnham-Burlington, Ashgate, 2011 (The Library of Essays on Music Performance Practice), pp. 325-345].

Zaslaw 2015

Id. '"Graces" and "Vermin": Problems with the Ornaments for Corelli's Opus 5', in: *Basler Jahrbuch für historische Musikpraxis*, xxxix (2015), pp. 179-192.

Zuccari 1760

Zuccari, Carlo. *The True Method of Playing an Adagio, Made Easy by twelve Examples, First, in a Plain Manner with a Bass, Then with all their Graces. Adapted for those who Study the Violin*, London, R. Bremner, [ca. 1760] [RISM Z 354].

The Art of Partimento

Cantata da camera e arte del partimento in Alessandro Scarlatti

«An Historical Link between Baroque Recitatives and Development Section of the Sonata-Form Movements?»

Simone Ciolfi
(Conservatorio 'Arcangelo Corelli' di Messina)

Il mito di Alessandro Scarlatti iniziatore o codificatore di una tradizione nonché compositore 'ricercato', ha origine all'epoca di Scarlatti stesso ed echeggia ancora oggi in varie pubblicazioni. Eccone alcuni esempi, settecenteschi e contemporanei, riguardanti la forma dell'aria e il carattere stilistico del repertorio scarlattiano. All'inizio del Capitolo IV della sua *General History of Music*, Burney cita il fatto che «it has been said that the *Da Capo* is a new invention; that [...] was first used by Alessandro Scarlatti, in his *Theodora*, 1693; and that in 1715 there was no an air without it in Gasparini's opera of *Il Tartaro alla China*». Lo stesso Burney, poco dopo, confuta questa affermazione erronea, ma essa prova la fama di Scarlatti nel Settecento come iniziatore di una tradizione[1]. Alberto Basso ritiene Scarlatti il codificatore dell'aria col da capo non l'inventore, anche se la codificazione è una forma di paternità[2].

Nell'ambito della cantata da camera, di cui Scarlatti fu prolifico autore, si riporta, in relazione con l'aria di cui il nostro compositore dovrebbe essere stato 'inventore' o 'codificatore', l'opinione di Helen T. Harris che concorda con Malcolm Boyd sul fatto che il «1697 represents a significant stylistic break in the style of Alessandro Scarlatti's cantatas [...]. After 1697 Scarlatti's cantatas illustrate the supremacy of the *da capo* aria [...]»[3]. Si deve specificare però che nelle cantate e nelle opere scarlattiane a cavallo tra Seicento e Settecento, l'aria col da capo conviveva con forme più aperte, e con diverse forme dello

[1]. Burney 1789, vol. IV, p. 169.

[2]. Basso 1991, p. 11. Jack Westrup scrive che la codificazione dell'aria col da capo «certainly does not have the connection with Alessandro Scarlatti that many writers, mainly out of a limited knowledge of the repertory, have suggested». Westrup 2001.

[3]. Harris 2001, p. 64.

stesso 'da capo'[4]. Per i molti lusinghieri apprezzamenti fatti sui recitativi delle cantate da camera di Scarlatti, rimando ad altre mie pubblicazioni[5]. Il loro stile è retrospettivo: le soluzioni altamente cromatiche e dissonanti di certi recitativi li apparentano a una scuola del ricercato e dell'estroso prettamente seicentesca.

Tuttavia, l'analisi del repertorio delle cantate scarlattiane rivela che soluzioni stilisticamente retrospettive potrebbero occultare strumenti compositivi nuovi. Alessandro Scarlatti si colloca infatti all'inizio di un'altra importante tradizione: quella del partimento. «It was only with Alessandro Scarlatti's surviving partimenti collections that an unmistakable pedagogical project is clearly visible», scrive Giorgio Sanguinetti in *The Art of Partimento*[6]. Se dunque Scarlatti si pone all'inizio di una tradizione, questa fu sicuramente quella del 'partimento'. Il presente scritto ha la finalità di evidenziare come le regole del partimento siano presenti nella musica delle cantate scarlattiane, e di sottolineare come, una volta mutati i gusti del pubblico da metà Settecento in poi, le cantate acquisirono valore didattico anche in virtù del loro legame con il partimento.

Clausole prearmoniche e regole del partimento nella cantata

La produzione di cantate di Alessandro Scarlatti inizia nell'alveo della libertà formale della cantata secentesca, continua con un'utilizzazione sempre più frequente dell'aria col da capo, ed è emblematica di quella standardizzazione della forma che si ebbe a cavallo tra Seicento e Settecento anche in questo genere. Tuttavia, all'interno di questa produzione,

---

4. Si usa qui come riferimento la matura aria col da capo, quella che segue il modello AA'BAA' con la doppia ripetizione di A, e non dei modelli precedenti nei quali è assente la doppia ripetizione di A (ABA), o ve ne è una tripla (ABABA). La tripla ripetizione di A nelle arie delle cantate di Scarlatti è riscontrata da Laura Damuth, che sottolinea come la forma ABABA possa talvolta costituirsi anche come ABACA oppure come ABCA. A seguito di un'accurata casistica sul tipo di arie presenti nelle cantate di Scarlatti, la Damuth evidenzia come la forma bipartita AB possa costituirsi anche senza la ripetizione di B e di A, e non necessariamente come $A^1B^2B^1$ o $A^1A^2B^2B^1$. Inoltre, nella forma ABCA, la C può essere ripetuta secondo il modello A(a1a2)BC(c1c2)A(a1a2). Nelle forme col da capo, la studiosa individua poi quattro possibilità: ABA semplice senza ripetizione di alcuna sezione; A(a1a2)BA(a1a2), con doppia ripetizione di A secondo il modello che diverrà predominante nell'aria col da capo del Settecento maturo; il modello AB(b1b2)A dove solo la parte B è ripetuta in una differente tonalità. Infine, è reperibile lo schema di aria col da capo dove le tre sezioni sono tutte ripetute A(a1a2)B(b1b2)A(a1a2). DAMUTH 1993, pp. 166-189. Nel suo volume su Scarlatti, Edward Dent sostiene che: «the irregularity of form is one of the distinguishing characteristics of Scarlatti's early cantatas [...]. To the early period also belong airs in binary form, airs on a ground bass, and all airs, in whatever form, that have two stanzas». Dent afferma di aver reperito nelle prime cantate soprattutto arie in forma bipartita del tipo $A^1B^2B^1$, $A^1A^2B^2B^1$, oppure forme come $A^1B^2B^1C^2C^1$ e, con più rarità, i tipi $A^1B^2A^1B^1$ e $A^1B^2A^2B^1$ (si riporta qui la sua grafia nella quale la lettera rappresenta il testo e i numeri la differente tonalità). DENT 1905, p. 12 per la citazione e p. 21 per il tipo di arie. *Cfr.* anche STROHM 1976, pp. 22-32, 72-87.

5. CIOLFI 2012, pp. 3-5.

6. SANGUINETTI 2012, p. 15.

Scarlatti non rinunciò mai alla qualità e alla sorprendente fattura dei recitativi e delle arie. Anzi, secondo Laura Damuth, nelle cantate di Scarlatti «there are more instances of tonal surprise and unusual modulations [...] from 1704-1705»[7].

Per iniziare con il caso dei recitativi, i movimenti cadenzali tipici dello stile recitativo compaiano nei trattati teorici attribuiti a Scarlatti, di cui alcuni probabilmente autografi. Egli, dunque, aveva piena coscienza dei moduli armonici di base di tali movimenti, sebbene l'indagine sui recitativi ha fatto emergere come tali formule subiscano elisioni e trasferimenti di risoluzione ispirati dal testo anche nelle cantate della maturità. I moduli cui si fa cenno si trovano nei *Principi del sig.re Cavaliere Alessandro Scarlatti* (d'ora in poi *Principi*) che contengono quelle «series of rules» sulle quali si accordano, come Sanguinetti afferma, i partimenti presenti nello stesso volume, 'rules' che vedremo fra poco. I *Principi* non sono l'unica pubblicazione di natura teorica attribuita a Scarlatti: vi sono anche manoscritti di *Regole*, sull'analisi delle quali rimando ad altre mie pubblicazioni[8].

Lo sforzo di chiarificazione didattica necessaria a Scarlatti per redigere queste trattazioni lo ha portato a evidenziare modelli compositivi di base (utili per scrivere recitativi ma non solo), soprattutto porzioni di basso continuo, che sono in sostanza regole del partimento. È necessario sottolineare subito che, all'interno di una partitura scarlattiana, la dialettica tra il modello e la sua trasgressione può essere innescata all'uopo dal compositore, quando un destinatario esigente, un testo particolare, o altro, lo richiedono. Questi fenomeni armonici arricchiscono e variano la natura musicale di un recitativo che è lungi dalla noia ed è ricco di soluzioni interessanti.

Si prenda, per esempio, l'inizio della cantata attribuito ad Alessandro Scarlatti, *Crudo amor empie stelle iniqua sorte*, contenuta nell'edizione che Etienne Roger ha stampato ad Amsterdam nel 1701[9]. Il tragico testo iniziale che dà il titolo alla cantata ispira al compositore l'uso di un tetracordo discendente collegato al primo verso. Tale formula, anche in versione cromatica, è frequente all'inizio dei recitativi per cantata di Scarlatti, ed è una strategia d'esordio ispirata al secentesco tetracordo di lamento. Col suo percorso dalla tonica al V grado, il tetracordo dissipa l'energia collocata nella fase iniziale del recitativo facendola giungere a una stasi sulla dominante, stasi adatta a mimare disperazione e abbandono. Tale soluzione è reperibile in celebri cantate di Scarlatti come *Andate o miei sospiri* (H53), *Amor Mitilde è morta* (H49), *Al fin m'ucciderete* (H21), *D'altr'uso serbate* (H12).

L'uso del tetracordo dà un tocco di tradizionalismo al recitativo di Scarlatti. Tale soluzione d'apertura è reperibile nei recitativi delle cantate di Atto Melani, scritte intorno al 1650. Il richiamo alla forma dell'aria lamento, dove il tetracordo diatonico o cromatico era utilizzato per arie di sconforto, testimonia il valore espressivo che Scarlatti conferiva al

7. Damuth 1993, p. 122.

8. Ciolfi 2011, pp. 84-88 e Ciolfi 2014, pp. 195-199.

9. *CANTATE / a I & II voci / col basso continuo / del Sig. SCARLATI / opera prima*, A Amsterdam, chez Estienne Roger, Marchand Librerie, [1701].

recitativo, in una visione di parità tra questo e l'aria. Tale esordio si ricollega alla tradizione seicentesca anche per un altro genere: quello del lamento recitativo da camera[10]. In questa forma dalle ampie potenzialità drammatiche non era di norma usato il tetracordo discendente, ma la situazione dipinta dal testo era patetica e psicologicamente cangiante, come accade nei testi delle cantate (talvolta basate anche su temi di famosi lamenti, come la cantata *Arianna*, H209, dello stesso Scarlatti).

Quando il testo poetico ha i caratteri dell'abbattimento tragico, Scarlatti predilige dunque una forma ibrida dove il vecchio lamento recitativo da camera ha assorbito i tratti ariosi del tetracordo discendente, trasformandosi con probabilità nell'esordio-lamento del repertorio in questione. Il recitativo di Scarlatti è infatti erede del recitativo affettuoso, animato da salti, contrasti di registro, ritardi, dissonanze e sorprese nell'armonia, che già nelle prime favole per musica si affiancava a quello che riprendeva il parlare ordinario, più lineare e armonicamente stabile rispetto al precedente[11].

Viene spontaneo collegare il genere del lamento e del tetracordo discendente che lo contraddistingue, alla tradizione letteraria e teatrale del Seicento[12]. Riguardo al fatto musicale, il tetracordo discendente è imparentato con la clausola prearmonica ⑧⑥⑤, ampiamente diffusa al basso come formula d'apertura nella musica madrigalistica nonché nel recitativo barocco, e mostrata come movimento armonico da molti trattatisti, per esempio da Lorenzo Penna (che la connette al recitativo), e dallo stesso Scarlatti nelle *Regole* e nei *Principi* (Ess. 1 e 2)[13]. È stato qui usato il termine clausola, frequente ormai nella moderna letteratura analitica e mutuato dalla trattatistica musicale prebarocca e barocca, perché evidenzia la tendenza di alcuni movimenti armonici a punteggiare il discorso più che a chiuderlo, un potere che spetta solo al salto V-I, l'unico per il quale si mantiene la terminologia di cadenza[14]. La clausola ⑧⑥⑤ circoscrive infatti un verso, ne punteggia la struttura, ma non esaurisce mai il potenziale espressivo di un intero periodo del testo. Tale

10. Si veda Porter 1995, pp. 73-110, in particolare pp. 96-107, dove Porter evidenzia l'uso del tetracordo cromatico discendente negli autori di cantate d'ambiente romano. Il rapporto fra recitativo in stile cromatico e scena di lamento nel secondo Seicento è evidenziato anche in Murata 1979, pp. 45-73: 68-73 (si veda anche Murata 1981, pp. 161-176). Per il rapporto tra lamento polifonico e lamento monodico si veda Caraci Vela 1993, pp. 339-383.

11. Staffieri 2014, p. 41.

12. Su Monteverdi come modello per il genere del lamento monodico si veda Tomlinson 1981, pp. 60-108. Sul tetracordo discendente si veda Rosand 1979, pp. 346-59; Rosand 1991, pp. 361-386; Rosand 2007, pp. 224-248; Bianconi 1991, pp. 219-235. Per approfondimenti sulla versione parodistica del lamento si veda Gialdroni 1987, pp. 125-150: 132-134. Sul tetracordo cromatico discendente in ambito sacro si veda Marx 1971, pp. 1-23: 9-10.

13. Penna 1684, pp. 180-181 (facsimile: Bologna, Forni, 1996). Per gli esempi di Scarlatti si vedano le note seguenti. Per la comprensione dei simboli sia detto che i numeri arabi racchiusi nel cerchio (①, ②, ③, ecc.) indicano i gradi della scala nel basso. I numeri romani (I, II, III...) indicano il grado armonico.

14. Sui termini 'clausula' e 'cadenza' si veda Meier 2015, p. 79. Si veda poi il capitolo 'Clausulae' in Gjerdingen 2007, pp. 139-176.

esaurimento avviene solo con una cadenza perfetta. Nel tetracordo ⑧⑦⑥⑤ utilizzato nel recitativo in questione, l'aggiunta del ⑦ deriva probabilmente da un processo di rilettura della ⑧⑥⑤ (come di molte altre clausole prearmoniche) nei processi tonali della Regola dell'ottava, la scala armonizzata ascendente e discendente che tanto successo ha avuto nella teoria del partimento già dal primo Settecento[15].

Nell'esempio n. 3 viene mostrato l'inizio del recitativo della cantata *Crudo amor empie stelle iniqua sorte*, dopo una selezione di clausole presenti nel trattato *Principi* di Scarlatti (Ess. 1 e 2)[16].

Es. 1: A. Scarlatti, *Principi*, sequenza di clausole ⑧⑥⑤.

Es. 2: A. Scarlatti, *Principi*, 'arpeggio di cembalo' in Do minore (di cui viene mostrato solo l'iniziale tetracordo ⑧⑦⑥⑤).

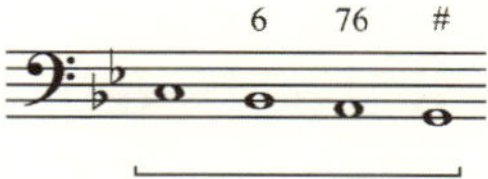

Es. 3: A. Scarlatti, tetracordo discendente dal primo recitativo (bb. 1-3) della cantata *Crudo amor empie stelle iniqua sorte*.

Nel passaggio fra Seicento e Settecento, infatti, la Regola dell'ottava si prestò a inglobare e organizzare in un pensiero coerentemente tonale una serie di formule contrappuntistiche che avevano avuto origine nella pratica precedente. La sovrapposizione tra schemi preesistenti e Regola dell'ottava, attestata in quasi tutti i trattati di fine Seicento e inizio Settecento (quelli di Scarlatti compresi), portò a una convivenza tra antiche clausole e porzioni di detta Regola. Infatti, per fare un esempio, l'antica regola di armonizzazione del semitono ascendente o discendente, chiamata '*mi-fa*' (la regola prescriveva che se due

15. Le numerose attestazioni della Regola dell'ottava in manoscritti e pubblicazioni del primo Settecento sono elencate in Christensen 1992, pp. 91-117. Per un riassunto delle varie attestazioni reperibili nelle 'regole' manoscritte italiane del Settecento riguardanti l'uso parziale della Regola dell'ottava si consulti Sanguinetti 2012, pp. 114-116. Alla storia del tetracordo cromatico dal tardo Cinquecento alla modernità è dedicato il testo di Williams 2006, che tocca il tema del recitativo e del lamento alle pp. 51-76.

16. Scarlatti [1715-1716], f. 4^{v} per l'Es. 1 e f. 70^{r} per l'Es. 2.

suoni salgono di semitono il primo porterà l'accordo di 6/3 e il secondo di 5/3, mentre se due suoni scendono di semitono accadrà il contrario), che nella versione ascendente costituisce la clausola ⑦①, può comparire in serie oppure acquisire elementi di definizione tonale più pronunciati grazie a una cadenza che ne conferma la triade. Ancora, alcune clausole antiche, presenti nei trattati e assai utilizzate come la ①⑦① (in cui il ⑦ porta l'accordo di 6/3, 6/5 o 7-6/3) o la ①②① (in cui il ② porta l'accordo di 6/3, 7-6/3 o 6/5), possono benissimo manifestarsi al basso come tali[17]. Seguono alcuni esempi di clausole tratte dai *Principi* scarlattiani[18].

Es. 4: A. Scarlatti, *Principi*, regola del semitono ascendente ('*mi-fa*' ascendente) ovvero clausola ⑦①.

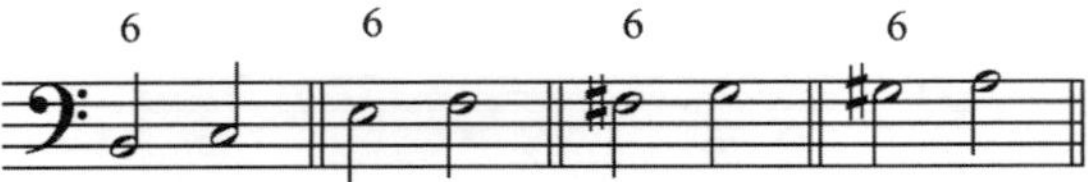

Es. 5: A. Scarlatti, *Principi*, esempi di clausole ⑧⑥⑤, ①②① e ①⑦①.

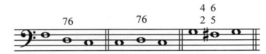

Nel recitativo scarlattiano la formula ①⑦① ha spesso il ruolo di armonizzare il *topos* retorico dell'evocazione del nome dell'amata o dell'amato. Tale formula ha una funzione d'esordio confermata da numerosi studi nonché dalla sua facile reperibilità nel repertorio settecentesco, sia nell'ambito strumentale sia in quello vocale[19]. La novità non è il suo uso in forma d'esordio né la sua natura musicale. Ciò che si sottolinea è che, nel repertorio in questione, formule armoniche assai semplici si prestano a costituire l'ambientazione sonora per versi dal contenuto ricorrente, nell'ambito di una tradizione in cui luoghi letterari e luoghi musicali, che potremmo definire *topoi* retorici, si integrano catalizzando il senso del testo e materializzando le suggestioni antiche che la natura letteraria della cantata comportava. Suggestioni antiche che appartennero al recitativo fin dalla sua origine, essendo questo stile la ricreazione di una prosa musicale, di un'arte retorica a cavallo tra parola e canto, stile composto da versi sciolti evocanti la prosa oratoria, che per gli antichi non era poesia, non era prosa, ma una 'cosa mezzana' tra le due.

Tuttavia, l'analisi del primo recitativo di *Crudo amore empie stelle iniqua sorte* rivela anche altro (l'analisi si può seguire nell'Es. 7). In connessione al secondo endecasillabo 'che pretendete più da questo core' compare una clausola discendente di due suoni, anch'essa assai diffusa nella trattatistica di fine Seicento: al basso troviamo infatti *re-do*♯ (un semitono

[17]. La sovrapposizione e nuova lettura delle clausule prearmoniche con porzioni della Regola dell'ottava sono approfonditamente discusse in Ciolfi 2012, pp. 45-57.

[18]. Scarlatti [1715-1716], f. 41^{v} per l'Es. 4 e ff. 6^{r} e 10^{v} per l'Es. 5.

[19]. Gjerdingen 2007, pp. 77-88.

discendente) che sono rispettivamente i gradi melodici ④③ della scala discendente di La maggiore (Es. 7, battuta 4). In questa formula il ④ porta sempre l'accordo di quarta aumentata e scende al ③ in 6/3, stabilizzando una triade in consonanza imperfetta. Sebbene non si tratti della nota cadenza frigia (che dal ⑥ abbassato scende al ⑤, unica clausola sopravvissuta come tale a secoli di tonalità), l'effetto prodotto dal semitono è quello dello stupore patetico perché corrisponde nel testo a una domanda retorica («Amore, stelle, che pretendete più da questo core?»).

Il terzo verso, un settenario, recita «di Doriste infelice», ed è inizialmente sostenuto al basso da due suoni, *si* e *do*♯, che costituiscono rispettivamente il ② e il ③ grado melodico della scala di La maggiore, triade che verrà tonicizzata dal ⑤① (v-i) successivo. Si tratta qui di altre due clausole assai note: la ②③ con la sesta aumentata sul ② che termina sul terzo grado della scala in consonanza imperfetta (6/3), e il movimento cadenzale ⑤① che diventerà il punto culminante della progressione cadenzale iv-v-i (Es. 7, battute 5 e 6).

La parola 'infelice' ben si sposa alla forza conclusiva del salto ⑤①, dove accentua la costatazione d'infelicità dell'io narrante e gli dona inesorabilità. Si tratta, però, di un movimento non preceduto da un iv grado, e dunque tale cadenza è 'inaspettata', tipica dell'apertura formale dello stile recitativo, sebbene armonicamente preparata dalle clausole ④③ e ②③ nella stessa tonalità. L'assenza del iv grado ci porta a considerare ②③ e ⑤① come due entità separate, non riconducibili a una progressione cadenzale pienamente tonale.

Prima di proseguire il discorso, nell'esempio successivo compaiono, in una versione standard in Do maggiore, le principali clausole utilizzate nella musica recitativa. Non sono altro che le clausole prearmoniche utilizzate nel sistema modale (*cantizans*, *altizans* e *tenorizans*, cioè i movimenti cadenzali tipici delle voci d'ambito polifonico) rilette, all'inizio del Settecento, alla luce del sistema tonale, per il quale poi la clausola con il salto v-i, ovvero la *basizans* ⑤① (non mostrata nell'Es. 6) è diventata la cadenza per eccellenza[20]. Nell'Es. 7 esse vengono mostrate all'interno del recitativo in questione, divise da una linea tratteggiata.

Es. 6: Principali clausule prearmoniche di due suoni e loro condotta delle voci.

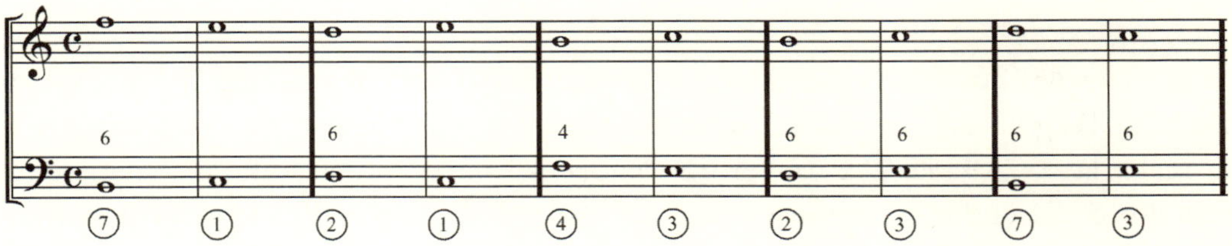

[20]. Sanguinetti 2007, p. 67: «Furno describes four bass motions that may induce a scale mutations, two ascending and two descending [...]. When the bass moves up a semitone, the two notes a minor second apart become ⑦ and ① of the new scale. When the bass moves up a whole tone, the two notes a major apart become ④ and ⑤ if the new scale. When the bass moves down a semitone, the two notes a minor second apart become ⑥ and ⑤ of the new scale. When the bass moves down a whole tone the two notes a major second apart become ② and ① of the new scale».

Es. 7: A. Scarlatti, cantata *Crudo amore, empie stelle, iniqua sorte*, primo recitativo (con clausole).

Le clausole ④③ con l'accordo di 6/4 con la quarta aumentata e la ②③, sono entrambe porzioni di Regola dell'Ottava sia se appartenenti a scale diverse sia se appartenenti alla stessa scala; la ①⑦①, la ⑦① ovvero la regola del *mi-fa* (utilizzabile anche in sequenza ascendente o discendente, oppure come ①⑦), la ①②①, la ②①, sono tutti movimenti cadenzali ricorrenti nella teoria del partimento, alcune delle quali potevano anche assumere il nome di «terminazioni di tono»[21]. Anche il tetracordo cromatico discendente fa parte del

[21]. Per le 'terminazioni di tono' si veda Sanguinetti 2012, p. 159. Per un inquadramento storico generale delle clausole e della cadenza perfetta si veda Meier 2015, pp. 79-93. Per un approfondimento sulle caratteristiche della cadenza autentica si veda Neuwirth – Bergé 2015, pp. 287-307.

gruppo di regole del partimento. Tutte queste regole includevano una loro condotta delle voci, specificata da Sanguinetti in *The Art of Partimento*[22].

Nel mondo del recitativo scarlattiano questi moduli armonici hanno una collocazione sequenziale. Tali moduli sono facilmente reperibili anche nei partimenti attribuiti allo stesso. Le clausole ④③ e ②③ sono tipiche formule che nel recitativo di Scarlatti seguono la fase d'esordio (dove si prediligono moduli che prolungano una tonica come la ①⑦① o la ①②①) appartengono a una fase successiva definibile come 'narrazione', fase seguita e conclusa da una figura cadenzale vera e propria, che si può chiamare 'epilogo' (dove troviamo cadenze perfette col salto ⑤①). Sebbene nelle prime 5 battute del primo recitativo di *Crudo amor, empie stelle* si trovino tutte apparentate alla stessa triade (La maggiore, si veda Es. 7), la sensazione è che questi movimenti armonici scandiscano il testo poetico come entità autonome. L'autonomia tonale delle formule l'una dall'altra è infatti la vera peculiarità dello stile recitativo.

La musica successiva lo conferma, perché una nuova clausola ④③ (*sol-fa♯*) tonicizza la triade di Re maggiore in 6/3 sul settenario 'siete troppo tiranna' (Es. 7, b. 6), e ancora la stessa formula (clausola ④③, Mi-Re) tonicizza la triade di Si minore in 6/3 sui versi 'se dopo tanti affanni ancor volete / con barbaro rigor condurla a morte', per poi cadenzare in Fa♯ minore sulla parola 'morte', la cui inesorabilità richiama la cadenza perfetta (⑤①).

Nella ripetizione finale del verso d'apertura ('crudo amor empie stelle iniqua sorte') abbiamo ancora una clausola ④③ e una cadenza ⑤① (non preceduta dal IV grado) sulla parola 'sorte', la cui inesorabilità, ricordata anche dalla sua rima con 'morte', si accompagna alla cadenza perfetta. Tale verso di cornice è musicato con due clausole (④③ e ⑤①) nella stessa tonalità di Do♯ minore (c'è dunque qui una coerenza tonale simile a quella dei primi tre versi del recitativo), che è, tuttavia, una tonalità assai lontana da quelle toccate in precedenza (Es. 7, bb. 10-12).

La relazione tra queste tonalità non può essere giustificata, infatti, dal circolo delle quinte, ma da una concezione locale dell'armonia, dove ogni clausola si lega a un verso, più raramente a due o a una parola specifica, innescando un peregrinare armonico in cui la musica, qui davvero serva dell'orazione, dona sfumature sempre diverse al susseguirsi dei versi e dei loro affetti[23].

La tripartizione del 'periodo recitativo' e le clausole nell'aria

Riepilogando, il recitativo (almeno quello del repertorio di Scarlatti) è costituito da una sequenza di moduli specifici legati a un periodo di senso compiuto (la concezione antica di periodo non è quella in due proposizioni come nel periodo moderno, ma poteva essere composto anche da una sola proposizione) nei quali la tensione delle formule si regola sia sul

[22]. Sanguinetti 2012, pp. 105, 112-123 (p. 114 per l'uso parziale della Regola dell'ottava, p. 117 per le clausole ①⑦① e ①②①), pp. 159-163 (§ 'Bass Motion Inducing a Scale Mutation').

[23]. Per il rapporto tra clausole e affetti si veda Ciolfi 2012, pp. 243-266.

senso del testo sia sulla sua scansione metrica, per cui le clausole musicali combaciano con le clausole metriche, cioè con il piede finale del verso. In questo tipo di periodo letterario musicato verso per verso con formule ordinate in sequenze c'è tutta la logica di questo stile. Si tratta, in estrema sintesi, di una serie di clausole e porzioni di Regola dell'ottava, armonicamente indipendenti e collocate all'esordio, al centro e all'epilogo del periodo[24].

Come si può vedere negli esempi, nel primo recitativo di *Crudo amor, empie stelle, iniqua sorte* è presente l'armatura di chiave. Talvolta ciò accade nei recitativi più antichi di Scarlatti. Si tratta di un elemento destinato a scomparire nei primi anni del Settecento, che illumina un momento ambiguo nella vita dello stile recitativo. Ci fu, talvolta, la volontà di organizzare il recitativo, principalmente sostenuto da clausole prearmoniche eredi della tradizione modale, in un quadro tonale più coerente? Potrebbe sembrare così per i primi tre versi del recitativo in questione, ma la soluzione adottata nel resto del brano vede le stesse formule vagare in tonalità lontane. Sarà questa la strada che prenderà il recitativo nel repertorio di Scarlatti e in quello della maggior parte dei compositori: assenza dell'armatura e libertà armonica in un quadro di rispetto per il testo poetico e per la correlazione dei versi con le clausole, organizzate, come detto, in una sequenza che va dal prolungamento di una tonica (esordio) alla rapida mutazione di triade (narrazione) fino alla cadenza perfetta (epilogo).

Ecco, in sintesi, le formule recitative organizzate secondo la sequenza standard, da me definito 'periodo recitativo' reperita durante l'analisi del repertorio:

PERIODO RECITATIVO[25]

1.	ESORDIO	Prolungamento di una tonica: ①⑦①, ①②①, pedale di tonica (5/3, 6/4, 7/5, 5/3), ⑧⑥⑤, ⑧⑦⑥⑤ (tetracordo cromatico e diatonico), ①②③④⑤ (Regola dell'ottava ascendente).

[24]. La sequenza di formule del periodo nel recitativo, poiché ha la possibilità di eliminare una o più funzioni, manifesta le stesse caratteristiche che William Caplin reperisce nei temi subordinati delle forme classiche, caratteristiche da lui definite *looser sentential functions*. Mi riferisco soprattutto alla «omission of an initiating function» («a subordinate theme can acquire formal loosening by giving the impression of starting in medias res»), che porta il tema a iniziare con una funzione di continuazione «by means of sequential harmonic progressions» o addirittura con una funzione cadenzale («a subordinate theme occasionally begins directly with a cadential progression»). Particolarmente importante per le funzioni formali nel sequenza di formule del periodo nel recitativo è l'affermazione di Caplin sulla «capacity for a passage to express the sense of beginning middle, or end indipendent of the passage's actual temporal location. Because formal functions are so conventionalized, because they are so well defined by specific characteristics, we can sometimes identify a given function without necessarily taking into account its position». CAPLIN 1998, pp. 111 e 113, e in generale, pp. 99-119.

[25]. CIOLFI 2011, pp. 90-93, CIOLFI 2012, pp. 123-151. CIOLFI 2014, pp. 203-213. Per una categorizzazione delle formule recitative dal punto di vista melodico si veda: SHERRILL – BOYLE 2015, pp. 1-61.

2.	Narrazione	Rapida mutazione di triade: ②①, ⑦①, (⑤)④③, ⑦③, ②③, ⑥⑤.
3.	Epilogo	Cadenze perfette: ④⑤①, ③⑤①, ⑥⑤①.

Proseguendo nell'analisi della cantata *Crudo amor, empie stelle, iniqua sorte*, dopo il primo recitativo si incontra un'aria monostrofica su questi versi: «ma sprezza la morte / si ride del fato / un'anima forte / un core sdegnato». La rima alternata, il verso senario, sono caratteristiche che spettano all'aria, in questo caso sentenziosa. Tuttavia, quest'aria (anche per via della congiunzione iniziale 'ma') sembra sgorgare dal recitativo precedente, quasi come una conseguenza concettuale. La differenzia dal recitativo, però, il piglio energico che si deve a un'affermazione del genere, in contrapposizione con l'ambientazione languida del recitativo. Legame e separazione, dunque, il primo evidenziato dalla presenza della stessa tonalità iniziale del recitativo (La maggiore), dalla stessa armatura di chiave, dalla natura breve dell'aria che è in sostanza in forma AA con la ricomparsa di A variata e condensata (elementi che ne fanno quasi un'appendice ariosa al recitativo, pur non essendo il brano un arioso), dallo stesso andamento di quartine discendenti per grado congiunto, che ricorda la discesa del tetracordo iniziale del recitativo.

La separazione è invece evidenziata dalla dinamicità del basso continuo, dal ritornello introduttivo e finale nonché dalla dizione melismatica dei versi (molto contenuta) e dalla loro ripetizione (frequente). Da notare come l'inizio del ritornello prolunghi la tonica La tramite un movimento con nota di volta inferiore (*la – sol♯ – la)* simile alla clausola ①⑦① d'esordio che, con le sue tipiche armonie, compare all'inizio del canto e all'inizio di ogni mutazione di tono fra le due enunciazioni della strofa (entrambe nella tonalità di impianto).

Es. 8: A. Scarlatti, cantata *Crudo amore, empie stelle, iniqua sorte*, aria 'Ma sprezza la morte' (bb. 1-12).

Le clausole sembrano essere dunque un elemento comune tra recitativo e aria. La loro funzione di apertura, narrazione e chiusura, in generale si potrebbe dire di 'punteggiatura', si dispiega nel recitativo in forma esclusiva e preponderante, ma è necessaria anche all'aria, sebbene qui vengano inserite in un discorso armonico strutturato. Tuttavia, contrariamente a quanto accade nel recitativo, nell'aria il circolo delle quinte diventa normativo e dunque guida i processi modulanti senza la libertà reperibile nel recitativo, il quale è libero di vagare di triade in triade.

La 'modulazione circolare' per terze

Sebbene non possa essere involontaria la similarità fra la tonalità dell'aria e quella iniziale del recitativo, il compositore ha separato la fine del recitativo dall'inizio dell'aria con uno spostamento di terza dalla triade di Do♯ minore a quella di La maggiore. Si tratta di una delle strategie più diffuse nel passaggio tra recitativo e aria, all'epoca cosciente, e di cui oggi si sono perse le tracce. È una strategia di modulazione neutra, cioè libera dalla consequenzialità tonale delle quinte; è spesso presente anche fra i periodi di un recitativo e come strategia di connessione fra aria e recitativo e fra recitativo e aria[26]. Tracce di questa tecnica si trovano in un'osservazione di Johann David Heinichen contenuta nei

[26]. Tali osservazioni trovano conferma nell'analisi della Damuth, che afferma come «Recitatives/aria pairs for major-key arias from later years show an increasing use of third relationships. In 1701-1705 the most common relationship is that of iii-I (with the occasional III-I)». E anche per la relazione tra aria e recitativo «some kind of third relationship is the most common choice» (DAMUTH 1993, pp. 112 e 114. Si vedano le tabelle delle pp. 115-116).

paragrafi 840 e 841 del suo *Der General-Bass in der Composition*, stampato a Dresda nel 1728. Egli racconta come, in gioventù, volendo passare da una tonalità maggiore a una tonalità minore che non fosse la relativa, i precetti del suo insegnante Kuhnau non lo avessero soddisfatto e «che nulla ancora sapevo all'epoca della modulazione circolare per terze»[27]. Si potrebbe a ragione ipotizzare che, poiché non ne aveva avuto notizia durante il suo apprendistato in Germania, Heinichen ne fosse venuto a conoscenza in Italia (Francesco Gasparini fa cenno nell'*Armonico pratico al cimbalo* alla «mutazione di tono per terza»)[28]. Inoltre, troviamo una descrizione di questo tipo di modulazione anche nel *Musicalische Handleitung* di Friderich Erhard Niedt, stampato ad Amburgo nel 1700. Nel capitolo IX, 'Wie man manierlich aus einem Thon in den andern fallen sol' ('Come passare elegantemente da una tonalità a un'altra') egli sostiene che la modulazione per terze si può realizzare discendendo alternativamente di una terza maggiore e di una minore, oppure ascendendo alternativamente di una terza maggiore e di una minore[29]. Tuttavia, Neidt, negli esempi che dà di questa pratica, non rispetta l'alternanza tra maggiore e minore, e passa, per esempio, da Si♭ maggiore a Sol minore e da Sol minore a Mi maggiore (invece che a Mi♭). Ebbene il passaggio di terza in terza era prescritto nelle regole del partimento come strategia tonale neutra[30]. Di questa tecnica di modulazione la storia della teoria musicale sembra aver perso traccia, almeno fino alla riscoperta operata in recenti studi sull'opera ottocentesca[31].

Clausole prearmoniche in alcuni partimenti scarlattiani

Passiamo ora a osservare alcuni esempi di partimenti scarlattiani. Come si può vedere nell'Es. 9, le modalità di inizio con clausola con nota di volta ①⑦① e prosecuzione con due clausole, una ④③ (preceduta da ⑤, eventualità frequente) e una cadenza frigia, sono esattamente quelle che ritroviamo nei bassi dei recitativi. Anche la loro struttura sequenziale è simile: all'inizio viene prolungata la triade di tonica ed essa è poi seguita da due clausole più brevi. La fermata sul ③ e sul ⑤ accentua l'indipendenza armonica delle clausole brevi, pur essendo qui collocate in un contesto tonalmente coerente e non all'interno di un recitativo.

---

27. Citato in Buelow 1992, p. 286.

28. Gasparini 1708, p. 44.

29. Per approfondimenti sul *Musicalische Handleitung* di Niedt si veda Arnold 1965, vol. I, pp. 213-236. L'argomento della modulazione per terze è toccato a p. 235.

30. Sanguinetti 2012, p. 158.

31. Tale pratica è frequentemente reperibile fra le tecniche di modulazione dell'opera italiana di primo Ottocento. Si veda Rothstein 2008, cap. IV, § 17: «[...] the characteristically Rossinian move of a major third downward, from one major triad to another, was far from unknown in eighteenth-century music».

Es. 9: A. Scarlatti, *Principi*, partimento (bb. 1-4)[32].

Stesso discorso per il partimento che segue (Es. 10), dove l'inizio è ancora effettuato con una clausola con nota di volta, questa volta superiore, nella triade di Sol, seguita da due tetracordi discendenti alle tonalità di Re minore e di La minore, realizzate tramite due gruppi di due clausole (④③ + ②①). Pur trattandosi qui di un basso tonalmente coerente, la cifratura ci indica sequenze armoniche simili che ci permettono di considerare queste formule anche come elementi indipendenti, in modo simile alla concezione locale dell'armonia che troviamo in un recitativo (nella seconda battuta, la comparsa dell'accordo di 4/2 con la quarta alterata trasforma il ① in ④ della triade di Re).

Es. 10: A. Scarlatti, *Principi:* partimento (bb. 1-5).

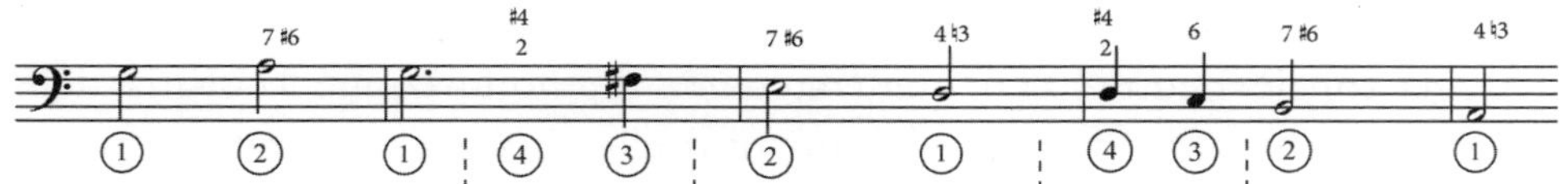

«An Historical Link between Baroque Recitatives and the Development Sections of the Sonata-Form Movements»?

Constatata la neutralità di queste formule del partimento per il fatto che esse viaggiano tra generi diversi, si prenda ora in considerazione la seguente osservazione di Michael Talbot: «[...] althought there is no historical link between Baroque recitatives and the development sections of the sonata-form movements of the Classical period and later, one cannot help noticing of the advanced techniques of modulations employed. Would it be too bold to suggest that recitatives in chamber cantatas (and, of course, in dramatic genres) served as a useful laboratory, during the first half of the eighteenth century, for harmonic and tonal processes that became widely applied to closed forms only in the second?»[33].

Per tentare di rispondere a questa stimolante domanda proviamo a procedere per gradi. Abbiamo constatato che alcune regole del partimento sono comuni agli esercizi del partimento così come alla musica della cantata. Mentre nelle arie esse sono immerse nella coerenza tonale delle forme chiuse, nei recitativi sono usate in forma indipendente, peregrinando da triade e a triade al fine di sottolineare porzioni di testo. Si noti poi che in

32. Scarlatti [1715-1716], f. 41r per l'Es. 12 e 46r per l'Es. 13.

33. Talbot 2009, p. 272.

vari trattati, come per esempio i *Principi* di Scarlatti (si veda sopra), appaiono vari recitativi o bassi di recitativo presentati come esercizi. Il peregrinare armonico tipico del recitativo faceva forse parte di un training che potremmo definire come appartenente a quello del partimento. L'instabilità tonale, il viaggio di triade in triade in effetti caratterizza anche la sezione di sviluppo della forma-sonata. Osserviamo ora la riduzione sintetica delle battute 7-19 dello sviluppo nel primo movimento della Sonata per pianoforte in Do maggiore Op. 2 n. 3 di Beethoven (Es. 11).

Es. 11: Beethoven, Sonata Op. 2 n. 3, riduzione delle batt. 7-19.

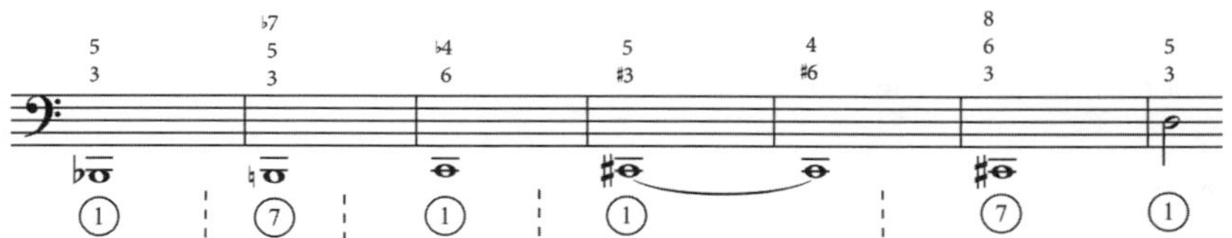

Il basso di questo esempio è in semibrevi come nella composizione originale di Beethoven (la presenza della stessa figurazione in due battute è stata ridotta a una sola battuta), gli accordi spezzati alla mano destra sono qui trasformati in cifre del basso. Nel processo armonico è possibile leggere le caratteristiche di un basso per recitativo: l'inizio prevede una tonica momentanea in *si*♭, *si*♭ che poi diventa naturale e sostiene una settima diminuita che evita di risolvere a *do* (una 'catacresi', ovvero una elisione della risoluzione). Nel successivo accordo è però implicita la risoluzione a *do*, perché l'accordo che compare è il tipico secondo *step* di quelle figure iniziali di recitativo che aprono con la triade e, tenendo il pedale di tonica, si spostano alla 6/4 per poi approdare alla settima e tornare in 5/3 (gli ultimi due passi eliminati sempre per catacresi). Ciò accade proprio nei due *do*♯ successivi, il primo sostenente la triade perfetta, il secondo l'accordo di 6/4. Anche qui manca il completamento della figura (accordo di settima e ritorno all'accordo in 5/3 sono elisi). La figura finale è un semplice '*mi-fa*'.

In sostanza un basso del genere potrebbe benissimo comparire in un recitativo, perché ne ha la classica peregrinazione armonica a tonalità lontane (Si♭ maggiore, Do♯ maggiore, Re maggiore), perché ne possiede le clausole, perché ne usa i procedimenti cromatici (come l'elisione della risoluzione), perché la concezione dell'armonia è locale, come in un recitativo. L'ipotesi di Talbot ha dunque un suo fondamento, anche se l'indagine è tutta da compiere: è molto probabile che nell'apprendistato di un compositore i processi armonici del recitativo siano serviti da modello per la conduzione di uno sviluppo nella forma-sonata (almeno nel primo classicismo viennese), ed è dunque possibile che i recitativi delle cantate, dove sono evidenti formule del partimento, abbiano costituito un banco d'esercizio per compositori poi dedicatisi ad altro. Dietro questi fenomeni l'arte del partimento giace come processo fondativo le cui potenzialità si applicano a genere diversi e talvolta apparentemente lontani tra loro.

Bibliografia

Arnold 1965

Arnold, Franck Thomas. *The Art of Accompaniment from a Thorough-Bass as Practised in the* xvii*th* & xviii*th centuries*, 2 voll., New York, Dover, 1965 (Dover Books on Music).

Basso 1991

Basso, Alberto. *Storia della musica. 6: L'Età di Bach e di Händel*, nuova edizione riveduta e ampliata, Torino, EdT, 1991 (Biblioteca di cultura musicale).

Bianconi 1991

Bianconi, Lorenzo. *Storia della musica. 5: Il Seicento*, nuova edizione riveduta e ampliata, Torino, EdT, 1991 (Biblioteca di cultura musicale).

Buelow 1992

Buelow, George J. *Thorough-Bass Accompaniment According to Johann David Heinichen*, edizione riveduta, Lincoln, University of Nebraska Press, 1992.

Burney 1789

Burney, Charles. *A General History of Music, from the Earliest Ages to the Present Period*, 4 voll., Londra, The Author, 1776-1789, vol. iv (1789).

Caplin 1998

Caplin, William E. *Classical Form: A Theory of Formal Functions for the Instrumental Music of Haydn, Mozart and Beethoven*, Oxford, Oxford University Press, 1998.

Caraci Vela 1993

Caraci Vela, Maria. 'Lamento polifonico e lamento monodico da camera all'inizio del Seicento: affinità stilistiche e reciprocità di influssi', in: *Seicento inesplorato. Atti del* iii *convegno internazionale sulla musica in area lombardo-padana del secolo* xvii *(Lenno-Como, 23-25 giugno 1989)*, a cura di Alberto Colzani, Andrea Luppi e Maurizio Padoan, Como, Antiquae Musicae Italicae Studiosi, 1993 (Contributi musicologici del Centro ricerche dell'A.M.I.S., 7), pp. 339-383.

Christensen 1992

Christensen, Thomas. 'The *Régle de l'Octave* in Thorough-Bass Theory and Practice', in: *Acta Musicologica*, lxiv/2 (1992), pp. 91-117.

Ciolfi 2011

Ciolfi, Simone. 'Formule e improvvisazione nei recitativi delle cantate di Alessandro Scarlatti', in: *Beyond Notes: Improvisation in Western Music of the Eighteenth and Nineteenth Centuries*, a cura di Rudolf Rasch, Brepols, Turnhout, 2011 (Speculum musicae, 16), pp. 83-96.

Ciolfi 2012

Id. *Il recitativo semplice nelle cantate di Alessandro Scarlatti: aspetti formali e funzionali*, tesi di dottorato, Roma, Università degli studi di Tor Vergata, 2011-2012.

Ciolfi 2014

Id. 'L'espressione degli 'affetti' nei recitativi delle cantate di Alessandro Scarlatti. Nuovi elementi per una teoria del recitativo', in: *Devozione e Passione: Alessandro Scarlatti nella Napoli e Roma Barocca*, a cura di Luca Della Libera e Paologiovanni Maione, Napoli, Turchini, 2014, pp. 191-213.

Damuth 1993

Damuth, Laura. *Alessandro Scarlatti's Cantatas for Soprano and Basso Continuo (1693-1705)*, Ph.D. Diss., New York (NY), Columbia University, 1993.

Dent 1905

Dent, Edward Joseph. *Alessandro Scarlatti: His Life and Works*, Londra, E. Arnold, 1905.

Gasparini 1708

Gasparini, Francesco. *L'Armonico pratico al cimbalo*, Venezia, Antonio Bortoli, 1708.

Gialdroni 1987

Gialdroni, Teresa Maria. 'Francesco Provenzale e la cantata a Napoli nella seconda metà del Seicento', in: *La musica a Napoli durante il Seicento. Atti del convegno internazionale di studi, Napoli (11-14 aprile 1985)*, a cura di Domenico Antonio D'Alessandro e Agostino Ziino, Roma, Torre d'Orfeo, 1987 (Miscellanea musicologica, 2), pp. 125-150.

Gjerdingen 2007

Gjerdingen, Robert. *Music in the Galant Style*, Oxford, Oxford University Press, 2007.

Harris 2001

Harris, Ellen T. *Handel as Orpheus: Voice and Desire in the Chamber Cantatas*, Cambridge (MA), Harvard University Press, 2001.

Marx 1971

Marx, Hans Joachim. 'Monodische Lamentationen des Seicento', in: *Archiv für Musikwissenschaft*, xxviii/1 (1971), pp. 1-23.

Meier 2015

Meier, Bernard. *I modi della polifonia vocale classica descritti secondo le fonti*, edizione italiana a cura di Alberto Magnolfi, Lucca, LIM, 2015 (Teorie musicali, 1).

Murata 1979

Murata, Margaret. 'The Recitative Soliloquy', in: *Journal of the American Musicological Society*, xxxii/1 (1979), pp. 45-73.

Murata 1981

Ead. *Operas for the Papal Court (1631-1668)*, Ann Arbor (MI), UMI Research Press, 1981 (Studies in Musicology, 39).

Neuwirth – Bergé 2015

'Towards a Syntax of the Classical Cadence', in: *What is a Cadence? Theoretical and Analytical Perspectives on Cadences in the Classical Repertoire*, a cura di Markus Neuwirth e Pieter Bergé, Lovanio, Leuven University Press, 2015.

Porter 1995
Porter, William E. 'Lamenti recitativi da camera', in: *'Con che soavità'. Studies in Italian Opera, Song, and Dance, 1580-1740*, a cura di Iain Fenlon e Tim Carter, Oxford, Clarendon Press, 1995.

Penna 1684
Penna, Lorenzo. *Li primi albori musicali per li principianti della musica figurata*, Bologna, Giacomo Monti, 1684.

Rosand 1979
Rosand, Ellen. 'The Descending Tetrachord: An Emblem of Lament', in: *The Musical Quarterly*, lxv/3 (1979), pp. 346-359.

Rosand 1991
Ead. *Opera in Seventeenth-Century Venice: The Creation of a Genre*, Berkeley (CA), University of California Press, 1991.

Rosand 2007
Ead. *Monteverdi's Last Operas: A Venetian Trilogy*, Berkeley (CA), University of California Press, 2007.

Rothstein 2008
Rothstein, William. 'Common-Tone Tonality in Italian Romantic Opera: An Introduction', in: *Music Theory Online*, xiv/1 (2008), <http://www.mtosmt.org/issues/mto.08.14.1/mto.08.14.1.rothstein.html>, visitato nel novembre 2018.

Sanguinetti 2007
Sanguinetti, Giorgio. 'The Realization of Partimenti: An Introduction', in: *Journal of Music Theory*, li/1 (2007), pp. 51-83.

Sanguinetti 2012
Id. *The Art of Partimento*, Oxford, Oxford University Press, 2012.

Scarlatti [1715-1716]
Scarlatti, Alessandro. *Principi della musica del Sig.re Cavaliere Alessandro Scarlatti*, GB-Lbl Add. 14244.

Sharrill-Boyle 2015
Sharrill, Paul – Boyle, Matthew. 'Galant Recitative Schemas', in: *Journal of Music Theory*, lix/1 (2015), pp. 1-61.

Staffieri 2014
Staffieri, Gloria. *L'opera italiana: dalle origini al secolo dei Lumi (1590-1790)*, Roma, Carocci, 2014 (Frecce, 171).

Strohm 1976
Strohm, Reinhard. *Italienische Opernarien des Frühen Settecento (1720-1730). 1: Studien*, Colonia, Volk Verlag H. Gerig KG, 1976 (Analecta Musicologica, 16/1).

Talbot 2009

Talbot, Michael. 'Patterns and Strategies of Modulation in Cantata Recitatives', in: *Aspects of the Secular Cantata in Late Baroque Italy*, a cura di Michael Talbot, Aldershot, Asghate, 2009, pp. 255-272.

Tomlinson 1981

Tomlinson, Gary. 'Madrigal, Monody, and Monteverdi's «Via naturale alla immitatione»', in: *Journal of the American Musicological Society*, xxxiv/1 (1981), pp. 60-108.

Westrup 2001

Westrup, Jack. 'Aria', in: *The New Grove Dictionary of Music and Musicians*, seconda edizione, a cura di Stanley Sadie, 29 voll., Londra, Macmillan, 2001, vol. 1, p. 889.

Williams 2006

Williams, Peter. *The Chromatic Fourth during Four Centuries of Music*, Oxford, Clarendon Press, 2006 (Oxford Monographs on Music).

Two New Sources for the Study of Early Eighteenth-Century Composition and Improvisation

Marco Pollaci
(Nottingham University)

In recent years, the role of musical improvisation has increasingly interested both musicians and scholars, together with the revival of a keyboard repertoire from the seventeenth and the eighteenth centuries[1]. The Romantic idea of creative genius being inspired by virtue of the sheer power of creativity in the composer is being steadily eclipsed by the study of pedagogic traditions that more specifically emphasise the role of musical improvisation in composition teaching[2]. In fact, until the beginning of the nineteenth century, composition was taught almost entirely through practice and indeed improvisation at the keyboard[3].

Recent studies dedicated to improvisation in history highlight a close link between improvisation, composition pedagogy, and practical musicianship[4] to re-establish the inextricably entwined nature of theory and practice through examples from the past[5]. Significant data, derived from eighteenth century primary sources preserved in European libraries, attest to this legacy of improvisation, which undoubtedly held much significance for most composers of the period. Beyond proving that improvisation and composition were interwoven in musical training, these sources also testify to the importance of the main pedagogic tool in the compositional practice of the eighteenth century: the partimento tradition and its rules.

This work does not intend to explore the history and the rules of the partimento tradition and the Neapolitan school[6]; rather, it seeks to describe two manuscript

---

1. Among other works, see Christensen 2017.
2. Mann 2013, Lester 1994.
3. Guido 2017.
4. Erhardt 2013.
5. These aspects are investigated in the significant work by Bernstein – Hatch 1993.
6. The essential result of the *partimento* research studies has been the publication by Sanguinetti 2012. See also Gjerdingen 2007, Gjerdingen 2009, Van Tour 2015, Cafiero 1993, Cafiero 2007, Cafiero 2009. See also Van Tour 2014a— and Van Tour 2014b—.

sources preserved in the Staatsbibliothek zu Berlin Preussischer Kulturbesitz: *Regole per accompagnare nel Cimbalo ò vero Organo*[7] and *Principi di Cembalo*[8] and their reflections on this pedagogic tool.

The art of partimento has become increasingly prominent in recent musicological literature. Noteworthy studies have been dedicated to the centrality of the Neapolitan school and indeed the solfeggi traditions in the eighteenth century[9]. Although the partimento derives from the teaching and practice of the thoroughbass, it differs from the latter in certain musical aspects and compositional purposes. Collections of partimenti show exercises written on a bass line, figured or not, and intended to develop and refine one's ability to improvise and to compose at the keyboard. Settled on one voice, they can have key changes and provide thematic proposals for the extemporaneous processing and elaboration of the music itself.

Naples and its four conservatories (Santa Maria di Loreto, Santa Maria della Pietà dei Turchini, Sant'Onofrio a Capuana, and I Poveri di Gesù Cristo)[10], became the *fulcrum* of what may be seen as a response to the considerable demand of musicians and of the teaching of composition, in which partimento was a useful tool. From at least the end of the seventeenth to the beginning of the nineteenth century, through the teaching methods of musicians such as Francesco Durante (1684-1755), Leonardo Leo (1694-1744) and Nicola Porpora (1686-1768), *inter alia*, the partimento technique became an essential skill and its importance in musical improvisation an essential lesson for any student seeking to become a professional musician regardless of specialisation, assuring a gateway to widespread exposure.

Recent debates on the genesis of partimento have given rise to new hypotheses[11]. It is speculated that the technique's origins may lie in Roman ecclesiastical circles, where the production of organ music necessitated keyboard improvisation skill[12]. This milieu would have unknowingly supported the incorporation of partimento into music teaching methodologies. Such approaches would view either possession or assimilation of thoroughbass and liturgical music as essential requisites for seventeenth-century musicians involved in ecclesiastic expression. Therefore, the two contexts in which our partimento sources are examined are the aforementioned Neapolitan conservatories and the Roman institutions.

---

7. D-Bsb Mus.ms.theor. 1483.

8. D-Bsb Mus.ms.theor. 1417.

9. See Baragwanath 2014. Baragwanath is currently working on the first book-length study regarding solfeggi's theory and practice, titled *The Solfeggio Tradition: A Forgotten Art Melody in the Long Eighteenth Century* (Baragwanath forthcoming)

10. More details in Sanguinetti 2012, pp. 29-40.

11. See Cipriani, forthcoming and Giorgio Sanguinetti's article in this volume.

12. This aspect has been discussed in Sanguinetti 2012, pp. 20-23.

Two New Sources

Sources referring to this Roman circle are scarce since the teaching of music was, at that time, restricted to religious, welfare or charitable entities or private institutions, which were not driven to preserve or transmit pedagogical traditions like the Neapolitan conservatoires were. In fact, the teaching of composition in the Rome of the time generally operated from musically inclined chapels and religious institutions, and often involved private teaching from teacher to pupil rather than formalized groups like in the conservatoires of Naples with established cultures of musical instruction. This deficiency of source data is noted but does not undermine the interest of the Roman *milieu*.

This work includes an initial, but not exhaustive, investigation of the sources; it will introduce us to two manuscripts that remain unexplored in scholarship. It should be noted that it is not always possible to attribute, with certainty, the sources relating to the partimento as they are often *Principi*, *Lezioni*, *Regole* or *Zibaldoni*, aggregated collections of autographs or of material for didactic use from various copyists. The styles and ink found therein indicate content that cannot be regarded as homogeneous or attributable to a single master. As Sanguinetti argues:

> With perhaps the exception only of the chamber cantatas, no other repertoire is affected by such great uncertainty about authorship as are partimenti. This uncertainty is most clearly discernible in the several anonymous manuscripts and zibaldoni [...][13].

For this reason, I attribute the manuscripts described in this article to the Roman circle without certitude, given some indicative, but still not exhaustive, detailing in the reconstruction of the collections. This study aims to inspire scholars to further investigate such unexplored sources in the hope that firmer knowledge of the Roman circle may be uncovered, by means of anonymous manuscripts like these two partimenti sources.

This work highlights the improvisational aspects of the partimento tradition and its rules. What emerges from the analysis of the collections under the spotlight here is certain stylistic characteristics that confirm the importance of improvisation and inspiration for students to improvise accordingly. Let us examine the two in succession.

The first of the two, the anonymous manuscript 1417 entitled *Principi di Cembalo*, may be dated around the seventeenth century or early eighteenth century, although this remains an estimation. The collection of rules and musical examples includes 36 partimenti without realizations. Following the modalities typical of Neapolitan school sources, which inform the transmission of musical elements without extensive prescriptive and written treatise, the manuscript begins with a brief introduction to the first elements with musical examples. What follows is a series of examples of harmonised ascending scales, following

[13]. Sanguinetti 2012, p. 63.

the Rule of the Octave[14]. This is one of the prototypical Neapolitan school pedagogical instruments for instructing on harmonising a scale[15]. In fact, the approach to harmonising each note of the diatonic scale reflects the common practice of accompaniment of a scale and can have several variants with different chords. The RDO was described by Sanguinetti as having a range of variants as employed by the likes of Alessandro Scarlatti (1660-1725), Giacomo Tritto (1733-1824), Giovanni Paisiello (1740-1816), and the renowned Fedele Fenaroli (1730-1818)[16].

Ex. 1 shows the RDO presented in manuscript 1417, but an interesting and new detail concerns the harmonisation of the ascending scale. The schema does not entirely correspond with other such chord successions generally. It is similar to Francesco Durante's and Fedele Feranoli's version, following Sanguinetti's synoptic view of the different versions of the RDO[17]. Yet, it does not correspond entirely to those versions either. The second degree is prescribed to use a 3/6 chord instead of 3/4/6.

Ex. 1: the Rule of the Octave according to the anonymous manuscript D.Bsb Mus.ms.theor.1417, folio 4r.

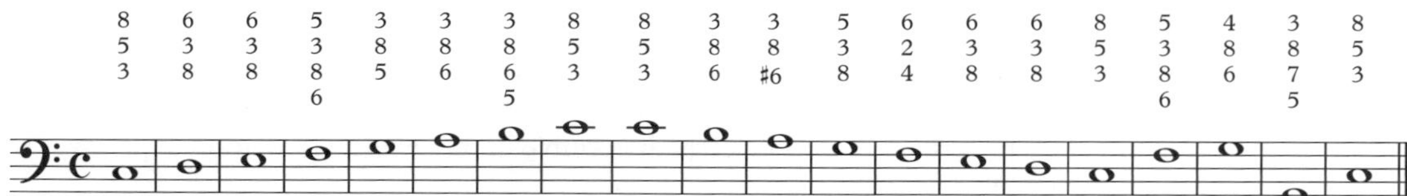

Following this first part dedicated to the scales, a larger section then presents the series of 36 partimenti that do not correspond with other sources, as far as current literature is able to inform us. The partimenti are presented progressively by complexity, from the simplest patterns to the most difficult. Each of the more or less figured partimenti suggests examples to practice the study of cadences, suspensions, RDO, sequences, and schematic bass. Ex. 2 shows two examples of these partimenti at the beginning of the source from the collection 1417. The manuscript does not trace the date of composition, and therefore links with any musical institute cannot be identified. Following my investigation, I can assert that this is the only copy of these partimenti in existence.

Ex. 2: two partimenti from the manuscript Mus.ms.theory 1417, folio 10r.

[14]. Hereafter abbreviated as RDO (= *Regola dell'Ottava*).

[15]. Holtemeier 2007.

[16]. Sanguinetti 2012, pp. 113-125.

[17]. *Ibidem*, p. 123.

One more detail might be interesting about the origin of this source. The last partimento, at the end of the manuscripts, is presented as a bass written by Signor Cavalieri Alessandro Scarlatti (Ex. 3). Located across other sources for comparison and verification, this partimento is included in the collection entitled *Principi del Sig.re Cavaliere Alessandro Scarlatti*, preserved in the British Library as Ms. Add. 14244.

Ex. 3: *Basso del Signor Cavaliere Allesandro Scarlatti*, from the manuscript Mus.ms.theory 1417, folio 18r.

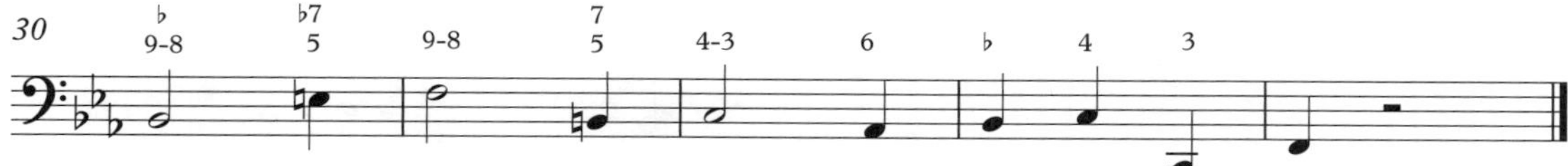

The presence of this particular partimento might be a detail suggesting links with the Roman circle, in which Alessandro Scarlatti was himself a protagonist. The handwriting looks consistent throughout the manuscript; there is no difference in the paper or ink between the last page and the rest of partimenti collection.

The second manuscript to be examined is preserved at the Staatsbibliothek zu Berlin Preussischer Kulturbesitz as well as in the manuscript 1483. It contains rules and partimento for keyboard accompaniment; it is entitled *Regole per accompagnare nel Cimbalo ò vero Organo*. This source is certainly one of the earliest manuscripts to exhibit a collection of partimenti and it is dated 1696[18]. It presents a brief and general introduction to the music languages, the names of the notes, keys, and cadences. Similarly, in only five pages, including musical examples themselves, the rules appear as short written explanations directing the reader to consistent musical examples. The largest part presents only partimenti, to assist the student in practising and improvising accordingly to late seventeenth-century partimenti function.

These anonymous partimenti are often presented as unfigured bass lines, and they exhibit changes in texture and clef, following the partimento rules found in Neapolitan compositional practice. It should be noted that all these partimenti present typical contrapuntal patterns, showing a tight link to pedagogic exercises that help students improvise and practice at the keyboard. Students could rehearse the ascending 5-6 technique sequences on bass motions, diminution techniques, descending 5-6 motion bass and ascending chromatic motions, segments of RDO, as shown in one example from the collection 1483 (Ex. 4).

Ex. 4: partimento from the anonymous manuscript D.Bsb Mus.ms.theor.1438m folio 8r.

[18]. This document has been mentioned by Sanguinetti with a short description: «As the title makes clear, it is a series of rules and precepts for through bass interspersed with exercises and more demanding pieces in partimento notation, such as organ versets». *Ibidem*, p. 20.

A second section of this source is an explanation on harmonising scales, *Regole per accompagnare i Toni*. On close inspection, we can observe a link with the Roman chapel master Raimondo Lorenzini, whose *Grammatica per il Bassetto* (1787) is preserved at the Biblioteca Casanatense in Rome[19]. The second section of the manuscript 1438 appears to be a replication of Lorenzini's rules. It seems clear that this section from the manuscript is related to but not written by the same author, perhaps nor in the same period. This second part presents scales as a principal contrapuntal tool in studying elementary counterpoint. For each scale and example, a small collection of partimenti follows, of which some are completely original, however, and do not exhibit such correlations with Lorenzini's sources, nor with any others.

Once again, the presence of musical examples, rather than of written rules and theoretical guidelines, testify to the will to steer student proficiency towards improvisation though actual practice of partimento methods at the keyboard. As mentioned before, detailed instructions and long descriptions of theory were less important in the partimento art. What was crucial was practising; the conceptual frameworks simply served to briefly support and ultimately empower the internalising of such exercises, which gradually enable the art of improvising. This practical transmission, as mentioned in the introduction, resonates with oral pedagogical traditions; the fundamental idea is that of physical guidance through spoken instruction. Over time, the teacher aids the student in creating a space in their competence for fluid improvisation, a skill essential for the latter to graduate as professional musicians.

Indeed, the conceptual and instructive components that do exist can also be lent to this idea. Manuscript 1483 contains some written guidance mandating that a composer's

[19]. Lorenzini 1787.

core idea should be variability in the music and that this is what makes a real musician, especially when combined with a good voice leading. They steer the reader to focus on the experiential nature of what the musician plays or hears[20]. They comment that even rules themselves are inherently inclined to give rise to more specific rules, depending on the composer's thinking in the moment.

This needs to be seen in a broader context. The series of tips and exercises on how to learn music and improvise at the keyboard, derived from expanding on such models as these, inspired generations of students and professional musicians throughout the baroque period and thereafter. Yet currently, even specialist senior musicians would seldom consider these notions of improvisation when playing or singing eighteenth century music. They often consider such repertoires to be untouchable, even inviolable in a sense, as written and transmitted, thereby needing to be preserved as faithfully as possible. The paradigmatic shift away from the Romantic ideal that music should be original — that is, born from the inspiration of genius — did not undermine the importance of improvising in the eighteenth century. Furthermore, improvisation did not mean avoiding repeating oneself. On the contrary, repetitions, the art of diminution, varied sequences, and partimenti patterns such as those evident in the described sources, all these can serve to heighten the students' and audience's depth of engagement as well as the musician's own proficiency, through the layers of familiarity — even intimacy — with the patterns to produce them instinctively.

Music improvisation and the strong connection between theory and practice, between the composition and pedagogic methods of teaching partimenti and solfeggi, existed side by side at least from the late seventeenth until the early nineteenth century. All these aspects stimulated and inspired one another.

Bibliography

Baragwanath 2014

Baragwanath, Nicholas. 'Giovanni Battista de Vecchis and the Theory of Melodic Accent from Zarlino to Zingarelli', in: *Music & Letters*, xcv/2 (2014), pp. 157-182.

Baragwanath forthcoming

Id. *The Solfeggio Tradition: A Forgotten Art Melody in the Long Eighteenth Century*, forthcoming.

Bernstein – Hatch 1993

Music Theory and the Exploration of the Past, edited by David W. Bernstein and Christopher Hatch, Chicago, The University of Chicago Press, 1993.

[20]. See the suggestions from the Ms.1438 such as «La prattica in ciò fa divenir capace», f. 26v; «[...] secondo l'idea del compositore che la pratica lo fará vedere», f. 33r.

Cafiero 1993

Cafiero, Rosa. 'La didattica del partimento a Napoli fra Settecento e Ottocento: note sulla fortuna delle Regole di Carlo Cotumacci', in: *Gli affetti convenienti all'idee: studi sulla musica vocale italiana*, edited by Maria Caraci Vela, Rosa Cafiero and Angela Romagnoli, Naples, Edizioni scientifiche italiane, 1993 (Archivio del teatro e dello spettacolo, 3), pp. 549-580.

Cafiero 2007

Ead. 'The Early Reception of Neapolitan Partimento Theory in France: A Survey', in: *Journal of Music Theory*, li/1 (2007), pp. 137-159.

Cafiero 2009

Ead. 'La formazione del musicista nel xviii secolo: il "modello" dei conservatori napoletani', in: *Composizione e improvvisazione nella scuola napoletana del Settecento*, edited by Gaetano Stella, Lucca, LIM, 2009 (= *Rivista di analisi e teoria musicale*, xv/1 [2009]), pp. 5-25.

Christensen 2017

Christensen, Thomas. 'The Improvisatory Moment', in: Guido 2017, pp. 9-24.

Cipriani forthcoming

Cipriani, Benedetto. 'La didattica musicale del partimento: la situazione del contesto romano tra figure chiave e nuove fonti', in: *Music, Individuals and Contexts: Dialectical Interactions*, edited by Nadia Amendola, Alessandro Cosentino and Giacomo Sciommeri, Rome, Societá Editrice di Musicologia-Universitalia, forthcoming.

Erhardt 2013

Erhardt, Martin. *Upon a Ground: Improvisation on Ostinato Basses from the Sixteenth to the Eighteenth Centuries*, translated by Milo Machover, Magdeburg, Edition Walhall-Verlag Franz Biersack, 2013.

Gjerdingen 2007

Gjerdingen, Robert O. *Music in the Galant Style*, Oxford-New York, Oxford University Press, 2007.

Gjerdingen 2009

Id. 'The Perfection of Craft Training in the Neapolitan Conservatories', in: *Composizione e improvvisazione nella scuola napoletana del Settecento*, *op. cit.*, pp. 26-51.

Guido 2017

Studies in Historical Improvisation: From 'Cantare super Librum' to Partimenti, edited by Massimiliano Guido, Abington-New York, Routledge, 2017.

Holtemeier 2007

Holtemeier, Ludwig. 'Heinichen, Rameau and the Italian Thoroughbass Tradition: Concepts of Tonality and Chord in the Rule of the Octave', in *Journal of Music Theory*, li/1 (2007), pp. 5-49.

Lester 1994

Lester, Joel. *Compositional Theory in the Eighteenth Century*, Cambridge (MA), Harvard University Press, 1994.

Lorenzini 1787

Lorenzini, Raimondo. *Grammatica per il bassetto composta dal Sig. Raimondo Lorenzini fatto Maestro di Cappella della Basilica di S. Maria Maggiore l'ann.87 copiata in quest'an. med da me e per uso di me Gio. Nicoletti*, [1787], I-Rc Ms 2546.

Mann 2013

Mann, Alfred. *Teoria e pratica della composizione: i grandi compositori come maestri e come allievi*, edited by Giorgio Sanguinetti, Rome, Astrolabio, 2013 (Adagio).

Sanguinetti 2012

Sanguinetti, Giorgio. *The Art of Partimento in Naples: History, Theory and Practice*, Oxford-New York, Oxford University Press, 2012.

Van Tour 2014a—

Van Tour, Peter. *UUPart: The Uppsala Partimento Database*, Uppsala, 2014—, <https://www2.musik.uu.se/UUPart/UUPart.php>, accessed November 2018.

Van Tour 2014b—

Id. *UUSolf: The Uppsala Solfeggio Database*, Uppsala, 2014—, <https://www2.musik.uu.se/UUSolf/UUSolf.php>, accessed November 2018.

Van Tour 2015

Id. *Counterpoint and Partimento: Methods of Teaching Composition in Late Eighteenth-Century Naples*, Uppsala, Acta Universitatis Upsaliensis, 2015 (Studia musicologica Upsaliensia, Nova Series, 25).

On the Origin of Partimento: A Recently Discovered Manuscript of Toccate (1695) by Francesco Mancini

Giorgio Sanguinetti
(Università di Roma 'Tor Vergata')

In my book, *The Art of Partimento*, which was published in 2012, I attempted to build a narrative on the origin of partimento based on the evidence available at that time[1]. My narrative is mainly based (but not exclusively) on the fact that the earliest known collection of partimenti with an author's name was found in the manuscript by Bernardo Pasquini in the British Library, presumably compiled between 1703 and 1708, for the education of Pasquini's nephew, Bernardo Felice Ricordati[2]. Pasquini, together with Alessandro Scarlatti and Arcangelo Corelli, formed a circle of elite musicians who gathered in Rome around Queen Christina of Sweden in the earliest years of the eighteenth century. This, and other evidence — such as an anonymous manuscript, which dates back to 1696 in the Berlin library[3], but clearly originated in Rome as evident from the watermarks on the paper — led me to speculate about the Roman origin of the partimento tradition and its subsequent move to Naples, following Alessandro Scarlatti's appointment as maestro di cappella at the royal court.

Only three years later, Peter van Tour, in his 2015 doctoral dissertation, made the existence of the manuscript dated 1695 and containing a large partimenti collection by Francesco Mancini public; this manuscript represents the earliest known document attesting the usage of partimenti as teaching material[4]. The Mancini manuscript — currently preserved in the National Library of Paris (F-Pn Rés. 2315), bearing the title *Regole o vero Toccate di studio del Sig. Abb[at]e Fran[cesc]o Mancini 1695* — is a large collection of (mainly) keyboard music: it probably arrived in Paris with the 'Selvaggi collection' and

1. Sanguinetti 2012.

2. London (GB-Lbl) MS Add. 31501, Facsimile edition: Pasquini 1988. Modern editions: Pasquini 1968; Pasquini 2006a; Pasquini 2006b.

3. *Regole per accompagnare nel Cimbalo ò vero Organo*, Berlin (D-Bsb) Mus.ms.theor. 1483.

4. Van Tour 2015.

was bought by the conservatoire in 1812[5]. The manuscript — whose existence Florimo suspected, which can be inferred from an oblique allusion in volume two of his history of the Naples conservatories — adds substantially to the meagre catalogue of the hitherto known keyboard music of Mancini[6]. The keyboard music in this manuscript includes titled works (a series of 21 *Toccate di studio*, 8 *Sonate*, 12 *Lettioni di sonare* and three isolated pieces) and untitled works, almost all notated as partimenti (the complete list is given in Table 1). Noteworthy is the fact that the toccate and the sonate are multi-movement pieces — a very unusual circumstance in later partimenti — and that they offer a remarkable amount of performance directions: hence, this manuscript can shed light both on the origin of partimento and on its early performance practice.

As it often happens with partimenti codices, the title and the author's name do not necessarily correspond to the actual content, which might not be entirely the work of Francesco Mancini. Rés. 2315 is in fact a *zibaldone* — a haphazard collection of material coming from different sources and authors. We cannot even be sure that all the material contained in the codex was composed in the year 1695. In fact, the dates on *zibaldoni* often indicate the year in which the manuscript was copied, or when it came into possession of the owner. Therefore, the content may have been composed earlier.

Before examining the content of the manuscript, I would like to spend a few words on Francesco Mancini. He was born in 1672 in Naples and entered the Pietà dei Turchini conservatory in 1688. In 1695, (the date on our manuscript) Francesco Mancini was 23 years old. He had been a student of the conservatory for seven years, having teachers such as Francesco Provenzale and Gennaro Ursino (more about Ursino later)[7]. In 1694, he began his six-year tenure as an organist at La Pietà dei Turchini conservatory; therefore, when the date 1695 was written on the manuscript, he had just started his duty as an organist. As one of the most outstanding composers of his generation, and one who worked as an organist for most of his life, very little is known of his keyboard works. As Angela Romagnoli had put it, «only a few traces are left of his keyboard toccate, written for pedagogical purposes, which must have been part of a larger corpus, given Mancini's long teaching career»[8]. This passage echoes Florimo's complaint, «Of all his other musical compositions that he, as a teacher of the conservatory, no doubt made in great quantity, nothing is known [...] perhaps they were lost»[9]. Florimo's source is probably Giuseppe Sigismondo's *Apotheosis of the Music in the Kingdom of Naples* (now available in a modern bilingual Italian-English

5. On the Selvaggi collection: see Cafiero 2007 and Fabris 2015.

6. See footnote 8.

7. The most complete biographical account on Francesco Mancini is Romagnoli 2018.

8. «È rimasta solo qualche traccia delle toccate per tastiera (scritte a scopo didattico), che dovevano far parte di un *corpus* più ampio dato il lungo impegno del M. nell'insegnamento». *Ibidem*.

9. «Di tutte le altre sue composizioni musicali, che, come maestro del Conservatorio, molte ne dovette fare, nulla si sa, salvoché di quelle esistenti nel Real Collegio di Napoli. Forse andarono disperse per trascurataggine di chi dovea aver cura di conservarle». Florimo 1882, p. 308.

edition)[10]. The discovery of this manuscript solves the mystery of the disappearance of Mancini's didactical toccate.

The manuscript has an oblong format and consists of eighty folios, or 161 pages. It contains 109 pieces (the content of the manuscript is shown in Table 1). As we can see, the content of this manuscript is composite in many ways. First, there is more than one hand involved in the physical making of the manuscript. The alternation in three different hands creates five groups, arranged in a rondo-like form.

Table 1: Content of Manuscript F-Pn Rés. 2315

Group	Folio	Copyist
21 *Toccate*	1^{r}-21^{v}	copyist A
Una sincopa	21^{v}	
8 *Sonate*	22^{r}-31^{v}	
15 partimenti [no title]	32^{r}-35^{v}	copyist B
26 partimenti [no title]	36^{r}-48^{v}	copyist A
1 cantata «del Sig. Bononcini 1695»	49^{r}-49^{v}	
12 *Lettioni di sonare del sig. Francesco Mancini*	50^{r}-77^{v}	copyist C
1 intavolatura [no title]	78^{r}-80^{r}	
6 partimenti [no title]	80^{v}-84^{v}	
3 examples of diminutions [no title]	84^{v}	
1 partimento [no title]	85^{r}-85^{v}	copyist A
16 lessons [no title]	85^{r}-97^{v}	
Fantasia di capriccio	97^{v}-99^{r}	
Capriccio	99^{r}-99^{v}	
Cantata «Del Sig. Bononcini 1695»	100^{r}	
Cantata «Del Sig. Gio. Nardelli»	100^{v}	

Most of the content is keyboard music, with the addition of three short cantatas[11]. There are also differences in the notation of the keyboard pieces: most are notated as partimenti — on a single staff with continuo figures — and some are written as *intavolature* (the standard two staves notation). Yet, the two-staves notation is far from being thoroughly written out. In fact, the notation of the left hand often consists of a sketch of the bass, which needs to be further elaborated and composed. In this aspect,

10. Sigismondo 2016.

11. The textual incipits of the cantatas are: 'Ritorno Aquila amante' (Bononcini, cc. 49^{r}-49^{v}); 'Non sa che sia costanza' (Bononcini, c. 100^{r}); 'Se i tuoi sguardi furon dardi' (Nardelli, c. 100^{v}).

Neapolitan intavolature have much in common with partimenti, since they share a different kind of incomplete notation[12].

Multiple authorship is another problem with partimenti. Sometimes, the same piece is found in several different manuscripts with the attribution to different authors. So, how can we be sure that Francesco Mancini was the author of the entire manuscript? I immediately nurtured doubts on the authenticity of the *Sonate*, since several movements in this series open with long rests. This makes no sense in a partimento. In fact, the eight sonates are actually the continuo part of Corelli's Church Trio Sonatas Op. iii[13]. Interestingly, the continuo part of Op. iii appears in a manuscript in the Doria Pamphilj archive in Rome with the title «Bassetti», a synonym for partimenti used in Rome (in general, the term 'partimento' was hardly used outside the kingdom of Naples)[14]. This confirms that bass parts extracted from Corelli's works were used for teaching purpose, such as *bassetti*, or partimenti (a use also attested in Emanuele Muzio's studies in composition with Giuseppe Verdi in the third decade of the nineteenth century)[15].

Mancini's authorship is openly stated for two series only: the 21 *Toccate* and the 12 *Lezioni di Sonare*. But what about the rest? Today, we have tools at our disposal that were not available only a decade ago. I refer in particular at the UUPart — the Uppsala partimento database, freely available on the web — founded by Peter van Tour[16]. UUPart allows a string search of a single partimento, building instantly a table of concordance for each string. This feature is crucial, because it helps in analysing one of the biggest questions in partimento research: multiple attribution, namely the attribution of the same partimento to several authors. Thanks to the UUPart database, I found some concordances: nos. 63, 68 and 71 (all fugues) appear in other manuscripts with attribution to Durante and Leo (no. 71 appears in *seventeen* manuscripts)[17]. No. 79 (f. 80v) is a special case: it is incomplete in the Mancini manuscript, but complete in only one other source. This other manuscript is I-Nc 33.2.3, a collection of partimenti, intavolature and more with a clear attribution to Rocco Greco (ca. 1650-before 1718), who taught violin at the Poveri di Gesù Cristo

[12]. On this subject: see Sanguinetti 2017.

[13]. I owe this information to Peter van Tour. Corelli's Op. iii was first published in Rome by Gio. Girolamo Komarek in 1689 (six years earlier than 1695) and in separate parts.

[14]. *Bassetti del Sig. Arcangelo Corelli*, Rome (I-Rdp) 276/B.

[15]. Emanuele Muzio described in great detail his studies with Verdi in his letters to Giuseppe Barezzi: see Garibaldi 1931 and Marvin 2010.

[16]. <http://www2.musik.uu.se/UUPart/UUPart.php>, accessed October 2018.

[17]. The numbering I am using is provisional, as Mancini's partimenti still does not have GJ numbers. When I am referring to a single partimento, I always give the folio indication as well. No. 63 (f. 47v): D-MÜs SANT HS 1430, GB-Cfm MU.MS 709, I-Nc Roche A.5.6; no. 68 (f. 50v) D-MÜs SANT HS 1430, GB-Cfm MU.MS 709, I-Nc Roche A.5.6, I-Mc Noseda Th.c.107, I-Nc 22.2.6/5, I-PESc Rari Ms.c.12: no. 71 (f. 52v) D-MÜs SANT HS 1430, GB-Cfm MU.MS.709, I-Bc EE.171, I-MC 7-A-28, I-Mc Noseda Th.c.107, I-Mc Noseda Th.c.123, I-Mc Noseda Th.c.133, I-Nc 22.1.14, I-Nc 34.2.3, I-Nc 34.2.4, I-Nc Oc 3.40, I-Nc Roche A.5.6, I-PESc Rari Ms.c.13/1 and 13/2, I-Ria Misc.Mss.Vess. 283.

conservatory between 1678 and 1695 (the date on the Mancini manuscript). Rocco was the elder brother of Gaetano Greco, the teacher of Domenico Scarlatti and Nicola Porpora, who taught Haydn. Another significant concordance is with a manuscript counterpoint treatise whose author is probably (but not certainly) Gennaro Ursino, one of the teachers of Mancini (I will discuss this point later).

The 21 *Toccate di Studio*

The most distinctive series in the Mancini manuscript are the 21 Toccate, which also give their name to the manuscript. The title, translated, is: 'Rules, or Instructional Toccatas'. Two things are immediately evident in this title: first, if we mean by 'Rule' a written (verbal) instruction about some aspect of the theory, then in the whole manuscript there are no rules, not even the concise instructions offered by Furno, Durante, or Cotumacci. Second, the title suggests that partimenti, even at this very early stage, were already being used for teaching purposes.

The *Toccate di studio*, in comparison with the partimenti written by the later generations of maestri, are quite unique. They are generally longer that the standard Neapolitan partimento: the first toccata is 111-bar long, that is, from two to three times the average length of a Durante's *Numerato*. More importantly, they are multi-movement pieces whose style is close to the organ toccata, which was practiced in Naples during the first half of the seventeenth century, with authors such as Giovanni Maria Trabaci and Ascanio Mayone. Finally, these toccate are among the few partimenti having performance directions (other than tempo indications). Table 2 shows a list of these directions:

Table 2: Performance Directions in the *Toccate di studio*

Toccata 1:	«dolce; camina; pia[no]»
Toccata 2:	«piano, tasto solo»
Toccata 5:	«tirata di tasti»
Toccata 6:	«camina»
Toccata 7:	«staccato»
Toccata 8:	«tirata di tasti»
Toccata 9:	«tirata di tasti»
Toccata 21:	«tirata di tasti»

While most of the terms are self-explanatory, the term 'tirata di tasti' needs perhaps some clarification. According to Sébastien de Brossard, this term was used by the Italians to designate «all stepwise succession of several notes of the same value, ascending or descending. The *Tirata Aucta* or *Excedens* is the musical note achieved when it exceeds the borders of the octave, going one third, or one fourth, or even one fifth above or below the octave»[18].

As one can see in Ex. 1, the notated music already shows two *Tirate Auctae*: but why did the author (or the scribe) pen down what is already evident on the score? Is this a performance direction like *camina*, or *staccato*? Or has the sign a didactic intent, as to tell the student, «You see? This is a tirata»? Or perhaps, its purpose is to suggest the performer a specific accompaniment, such as a parallel run in the right hand by thirds or tenths?

Ex. 1: directions «tirata di tasti» in *Toccata nona* (f. 11^{r}).

The length and the variety of the 21 Toccate in this manuscript do not allow to focus on a single technical problem, as is the case with most mid-to-late eighteenth century partimenti, such as those by Durante or, even more, by Fenaroli. However, some of them do seem to focus on some specific issues.

The first toccata stands out for its bold modulations. The complete transcription of this piece in its original partimento notation is given in Ex. 2.

Ex. 3 reproduces the first 25 bars of the *Toccata prima* with analytical annotations. The home key is clearly E major, but with a key signature of two sharps only. The Toccata opens with a syncopated octave descent accompanied with alternating 4/2 and 6 chords and closed by a cadence — a standard partimento technique. An ascending fourth by stepwise motion, accompanied with the *Regola dell'ottava*, leads to A (in bar 5). This note sets in motion a descending progression by minor thirds, confirmed by a strong cadenza doppia on F sharp in bars 6-7 (indicated with the sign CD in Ex. 3) This progression

18. 'Tirata', in: Brossard 1703, pages not numbered.

Ex. 2: *Toccata prima*, transcription in the original partimento notation.

Dolce
Camina
Pia:
Andante

repeats one minor third lower (on D sharp) and again one minor third below, on B sharp, thus delineating an overall motion by diminished seventh. The B sharp is then brought an octave higher (bar 10) and then sets in motion a passage with four notes a whole tone apart (bar 13), leading to a cadenza doppia in the key of A-sharp minor; the modulation is further confirmed by two progressions, the latter ending with a cadenza composta (CC) in the same key. The A sharp is again brought an octave higher (bar 19), and then a new pattern begins: a bass motion by 'third down, second up' six steps long. The pattern in itself is not unusual at all, but the scale in use actually is: the first five steps delineate again a whole tone scale A sharp - G sharp – F sharp – E natural – D natural, and finally C sharp as dominant of the new key, F-sharp minor (bar 25): this arrival point is emphasized by an expanded cadenza doppia.

Ex. 3: first 25 bars of *Toccata prima* with analytical annotation added.

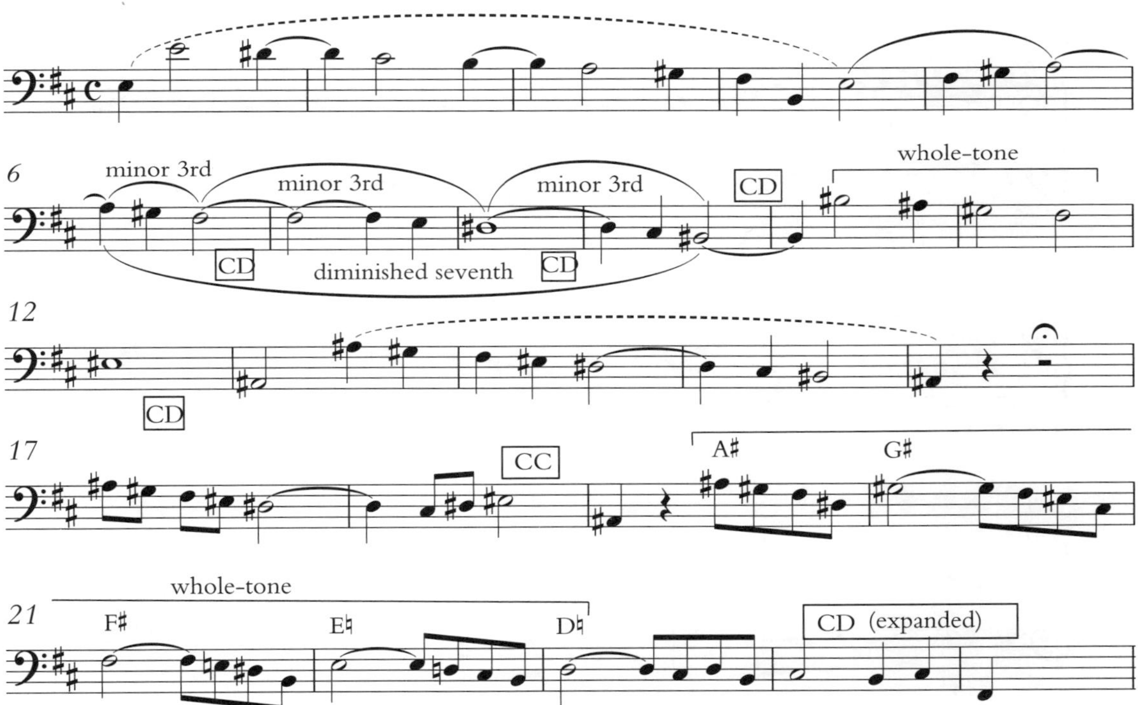

In the remainder of the *Toccata*, the bass line briefly touches F major and C major before returning to the sharp side passing through G minor, E minor and B minor (in this notation the flat has a double meaning: as a real flat and as a natural, depending on the context). Ex. 4a and 4b show two sections of the *Toccata prima*, bars 1-15 and 57-79, respectively in my essential realisation of these bars. By 'essential realisation' I mean a realisation that gives the essential harmonic and contrapuntal contour, leaving aside idiomatic passages and embellishments.

Ex. 4: essential realisation of bars 1-25 and 57-79 of *Toccata prima*.

57
61
Dolce
66
72
Camina
76

The Toccata features repeated modulatory patterns, which seem to indicate that it was intended as an exemplar, that is, a work written as a model for imitation and speculation: in other words, a theoretical work, but one that ought to be played too. But how could a single piece written in the second half of the seventeenth century modulate so many and such distant keys? My conjecture is that this toccata in particular (more than the other twenty, which do not modulate so boldly) was written with an enharmonic instrument in mind, such as the sambuca lincea, or the tricembalo. The sambuca lincea was invented and described by the Neapolitan musician, naturalist and botanic, Fabio Colonna (ca. 1567-1640), a scientist much admired by Linnaeus. Tricembalo was created by the priest and organist, Scipione Stella (ca. 1558-1622), who in his youth was at the service of Gesualdo da Venosa. In the seventeenth century Naples, together with Ferrara, was apparently affected by an enharmonic madness, at the point that even the famous Bolognese painter Domenico Zampieri, called the Domenichino, built his own archicembalo during his Neapolitan period[19].

According to Patrizio Barbieri, the sambuca lincea could modulate to 31 keys, and the tricembalo to 21, allowing the performance of music to 'circulate' through all the keys before returning home[20]. The daring modulations of the *Toccata prima* — something that disappeared with the onset of galant style during the eighteenth century — may be reminiscent of the fashion of harmonically 'circulating' music that permeated Naples during the early seventeenth century. Further, my evidence showed that the collection was actually composed in the seventeenth century, and perhaps much earlier than the date written on the manuscript.

Earlier, I briefly mentioned Gennaro Ursino with reference to another seventeenth century manuscript. A manuscript in the Naples conservatory library entitled *Lezzioni di contropunto*, dated 1677, contains a complete course in counterpoint, (from species to invertible to imitative) which apparently took many years to complete[21]. On the first page of the manuscript, the sign «Di Gennaro» indicated the owner/scribe of the manuscript, perhaps Gennaro Ursino (ca. 1650-1715). The first date in the frontispiece is 1677, but the owner marked the completion of the different sections with the respective dates: June 1679 is the date of a study of imitation, and August 1681 refers to the first, second and fourth species of (Fuxian) counterpoint. July 1688 marks a study on fugue. Then, a single partimento appears (f. 58ᵛ), followed by other fugues (this partimento is shown in Ex. 5). On the last pages of the manuscript, there are examples of cadences, including the 'cadenza lunga' progression.

19. Barbieri 1987.

20. A transcription of an anonymous 'circulating' toccata is given by *ibidem* pp. 194-196.

21. Gennaro Ursino, *Lezzioni di Contropunto*, 1677, Naples (I-Nc 34.2.7).

Ex. 5: *Lezzioni di contropunto*, f. 58ᵛ.

The only partimento in the Ursino manuscript appears also in the Mancini manuscript at c. 32ʳ, as no. 1 of the 15 partimenti written by copyist B (section 4 in Table 1). Since the Ursino is a very clean manuscript, with almost no erasures and corrections, it was probably conceived as an exemplar: a collection of examples written by a maestro as guide to the student's work. This hypothesis agrees with the dates and the presumed author, who in 1677, was already an assistant professor of Francesco Provenzale at the conservatory of La Pietà dei Turchini. If this assumption is correct, the Ursino partimento could be the oldest partimento known, and also in the Ursino manuscript there is evidence of the use of partimenti at La Pietà as soon as in 1688. Therefore, the date 1695 in the Mancini manuscript does not necessarily refer to the year of composition of the material therein contained.

Earlier, I mentioned the Rocco Greco manuscript (I-Nc 33.2.3). This manuscript's title (*Intavolature per cembalo e partimenti di Rocco Greco*) was probably added by a librarian and misrepresents the content. There are indeed partimenti and intavolature for keyboard, but there are also five very unusual pieces written on a two-staff system, both with a bass clef, such as the one shown in Ex. 6[22].

22. The manuscript is acephalous: the first of the five pieces appears on the second page (f. 1ᵛ), in what seems to be a very old handwriting, the number 12, but afterwards the page numbering becomes erratic. The series interrupts after nine folios.

Ex. 6: Excertps from *Intavolature per cembalo e partimenti di Rocco Greco.*

It consists of two bass lines: the lowest is simple and schematic, the upper one is essentially the same, but more complex. What is interesting, in my opinion, is that the upper line is not only a diminution of the lower but is also a complete realisation of its harmonic implications. So, it was indeed possible for a bass instrument player (in this case, a cello) to realise a partimento with no keyboard, using a single, polyphonic melody[23]. This answers a common question among theory teachers who want to introduce partimenti in their syllabus: how can I teach this to non-keyboard students? One possibility is using an ensemble with different instruments playing different voices of the texture. The possibility shown by Rocco Greco is perhaps more challenging because one should not only master simultaneously continuo realisation and diminution; but also stimulating, because by using this technique, a non-keyboard player can create a solo realisation.

In conclusion, we can say that today we know much more about partimenti than we did ten of fifteen years ago. But, much more is still to be discovered. I am sure that many other exciting developments will take place in the future.

Bibliography

Barbieri 1987

Barbieri, Patrizio. 'La 'Sambuca Lincea' di Fabio Colonna e il 'Tricembalo' di Scipione Stella', in: *La musica a Napoli durante il Seicento. Atti del convegno internazionale di studi (Napoli, 11-14 aprile 1985)*, edited by Domenico Antonio D'Alessandro and Agostino Ziino, Rome, Torre d'Orfeo, 1987, pp. 167-236.

[23]. On cello teaching methods in Naples: see Olivieri 2009.

Brossard 1703

Brossard Sébastien de. 'Tirata', in: *Dictionnaire de Musique*, Paris, Ballard, 1703.

Cafiero 2007

Cafiero, Rosa. 'The Early Reception of Neapolitan Partimento Theory in France: A Survey', in: *Journal of Music Theory*, LI/1 (2007), pp. 137-159.

Fabris 2015

Fabris, Dinko. 'L'art de disperser da collection: Le cas du napolitain Gaspare Selvaggi' (1763-1856), in: *Collectionner la musique: Erudits collectionneurs*, edited by Denis Herlin, Catherine Massip and Valérie De Wispelaere, Turnhout, Brepols, 2015 (Collectionner la musique, 3), pp. 359-394.

Florimo 1882

Florimo, Francesco. *La scuola musicale di Napoli e i suoi conservatorii: con uno sguardo sulla storia della musica italiana. 2: La scuola musicale di Napoli e i suoi conservatorii, con le Biografie dei maestri usciti dai medesimi*, Naples, Morano, 1882.

Garibaldi 1931

Garibaldi, Luigi Agostino. *Giuseppe Verdi nelle lettere di Emanuele Muzio ad Antonio Barezzi*, Milan, Treves, 1931 (Grandi musicisti italiani e stranieri).

Marvin 2010

Marvin, Roberta Montemorra. *Verdi the Student – Verdi the Teacher*, Parma, Istituto Nazionale di Studi Verdiani, 2010 (Premio internazionale Rotary Club di Parma 'Giuseppe Verdi', 5).

Olivieri 2009

Olivieri, Guido. 'Cello Teaching and Playing in Naples in the Early Eighteenth Century: Francesco Paolo Supriani's *Principij da imparare a suonare il violoncello*', in: *Performance Practice: Issues and Approaches*, edited by Timothy D. Watkins, Ann Arbor (MI), Steglein, 2009, pp. 109-136.

Pasquini 1968

Pasquini, Bernardo. *Collected Works for Keyboard*, edited by Maurice Brooks Haynes, American Institute for Musicology, 1968.

Pasquini 1988

Id. *London, British Library, MS Add. 31501*, Facsimile edition edited by Alexander Silbiger, New York-London, Garland, 1988 (17th Century Keyboard Music, 8).

Pasquini 2006a

Id. *Opere per tastiera: vol. VI*, edited by Edoardo Bellotti, Latina, Il Levante 2006.

Pasquini 2006b

Id. *Opere per tastiera: vol. VII*, edited by Armando Carideo, Latina, Il Levante 2006.

Romagnoli 2018

Romagnoli, Angela. 'Mancini, Francesco', in: *Dizionario Biografico degli Italiani*, <http://www.treccani.it/enciclopedia/francesco-mancini_%28Dizionario-Biografico%29/>, accessed October 2018

Sanguinetti 2012

Sanguinetti, Giorgio. *The Art of Partimento: History, Theory and Practice*, Oxford-New York, Oxford University Press, 2012.

Sanguinetti 2017

Id. 'Partimento and Incomplete Notation in Eighteenth-Century Keyboard Music', in: *Studies in Historical Improvisation: From 'Cantare super Librum' to Partimenti*, edited by Massimiliano Guido, Abington-New York, Routledge, 2017, pp. 149-171.

Sigismondo 2016

Apoteosi della musica del Regno di Napoli: Giuseppe Sigismondo, edited by Claudio Bacciagaluppi, Giulia Giovani and Raffaele Mellace, with an introduction by Rosa Cafiero, Rome, Società Editrice di Musicologia, 2016 (Saggi, 2).

Van Tour 2015

Van Tour, Peter. *Counterpoint and Partimento: Methods of Teaching Composition in Late Eighteenth-Century Naples*, Uppsala, Acta Universitatis Upsaliensis, 2015 (Studia musicologica Upsaliensia. Nova Series, 25).

«Taking a Walk at the Molo»: Partimento and the Improvised Fugue

Peter van Tour
(Norwegian Academy of Music)

During the last few decades, the partimento repertoire and its pedagogical functions have been discussed in an increasing number of books, articles, and dissertations[1]. Although there is general agreement among scholars that partimenti were used in the Neapolitan conservatories for developing improvisational fluency at the keyboard, it has not been entirely clear exactly *when* students carried out their studies in partimento in relation to their studies in counterpoint. Were partimenti studied prior to the study of written counterpoint, or was it rather a certain part of this repertoire that had that function?

In recent years it has become increasingly clear that partimento, solfeggio, and counterpoint were applied as integral parts of the curriculum in the Neapolitan conservatories to teach composition through vocal improvisation, composition at the keyboard[2], and through written counterpoint and composition. It was necessary to have some basic skills in partimento playing before one could advance to the counterpoint class. The educational context has helped us to further define the term 'partimento', showing its double pedagogical function: on the one hand partimenti were used for developing musical imagination through the realization of figured or unfigured basses at the keyboard, on the other hand partimenti were used for developing fluency in written composition. In other words, the term 'partimento' can be understood as «a notational device, commonly written on a single staff in the F clef, either figured or unfigured, applied both in playing and in writing activities, and used for developing skills in the art of accompaniment, improvisation, diminution, and counterpoint»[3]. Partimento and

[1]. Borgir 1987; Christensen 1992; Renwick 1995; Renwick 2001; Gjerdingen 2007; Gingras 2008; Callahan 2010; Sanguinetti 2012; Van Tour 2015; Bellotti 2017, among others.

[2]. For a brief reflection on this term, see Bellotti 2017, p. 115.

[3]. See also Van Tour 2015, p. 19.

composition were fully complementary, in similar ways as was the case with thoroughbass and composition in German compositional theory[4].

A first account regarding the relationship between partimento and counterpoint is found in one of the counterpoint notebooks that describe Fedele Fenaroli's (1713-1818) teaching in counterpoint, entitled *Studio di Contrapunto del Sig.r D. Fedele Fenaroli* (I-Nc 22-2-6/2), in which Fenaroli leaves no doubt about the propedeutical function of his first three books of partimenti:

> For those who want to learn counterpoint, it is necessary first to thoroughly study the first and second books of partimenti, and then the moti del basso of the third book[5].

At the Conservatorio di Santa Maria della Pietà de' Turchini, hereafter called the Pietà, counterpoint was taught according to a more conservative method of teaching counterpoint, in which partimenti were used to prepare students for their lessons in written counterpoint and fugue[6]. In the two other Neapolitan conservatories, the Onofrio and the Loreto, the writing of fugues had already declined, probably as a result of an increased interest for melodic writing, which evidently was esteemed to be greater important for writing of dramatic music.

In his *Biographie* of 1848, the Bohemian composer Adalbert Gyrowetz (1763-1850) gives some interesting anecdotal evidence of how students were mentally prepared for their future work as a composer. In this autobiography (because that is what it is)[7], Gyrowetz describes the path taken in counterpoint lessons with his teacher Nicola Sala (1713-1801) at the Pietà:

> *Maestro* Sala was in this subject [counterpoint] the most famous teacher and likewise, he was *maestro* in counterpoint at *La Pietà*, the most distinguished of the musical conservatories, of which there were three in Naples. Maestro Sala had already reached an advanced age and was happy to take care of a young German student who already had a good reputation in the field of instrumental music. The study of counterpoint started with exercises on the scale, and since Gyrowetz already had considerable experience combining chords, he proceeded with dispositions for two, three and four parts, then moving on with canons and fugues, etc. etc., in which art maestro Sala was an excellent teacher[8].

---

4. For the relationship between thoroughbass and composition in German eighteenth-century compositional theory, see: LESTER 1992, pp. 65-68.

5. I-Nc 22-2-6/2, fol. 1v: «Quelli che desiderano apprendere il Contropunto è necessario che prima studiassero bene il primo e secondo libro numerico, ed ancora li movimenti del Basso del terzo libro [...]». .

6. For a description of the contrapuntal training at the Pietà, see VAN TOUR 2015, pp. 169-207.

7. RENWICK 1995, p. 10.

8. GYROWETZ 1848, p. 26: «Kapellmeister Sala war in diesem Fach in Neapel der berühmteste und auch zugleich Meister des Contrapunctes im Conservatorium della Pietà, welches unter den andern Conservatorien,

Adalbert Gyrowetz' lessons with Nicola Sala must have taken place at the Pietà within the time span between 1787 and 1789 (most probably in 1788 and 1789) and contain several interesting details. The lessons started with contrapuntal exercises written over and under the scale. This method of working is also known from Sala's printed counterpoint treatise the *Regole del contrappunto pratico* (Naples, 1794), where such exercises dominate the greater part of the first volume, and appears likewise in Benedetto Neri's counterpoint notebook written in 1796 (see Ex. 1)[9]:

Ex. 1: Benedetto Neri, 'Quarta specie a due' (1796) (I-NOd, Fondo cappella musicale 3387, fols. 7r).

After these exercises, Gyrowetz's biography tells us that the counterpoint student advanced to what he terms «zwei, drei, und vierstimmigen Satz», that is dispositions (*disposizioni*) for two, three, and four voices. A great number of such dispositions are found in Sala's *Regole del contrappunto pratico*[10].

Finally, Gyrowetz's biography reports that the counterpoint studies led to the training of canon and fugue, «in which art Maestro Sala was an excellent teacher» (see the quotation above). After having expressed his admiration for his former counterpoint teacher, Gyrowetz gives us a few details about Sala's pedagogy:

> He had the habit of taking a walk at the Molo or near Mount Vesuvius together with Gyrowetz, after finishing the class in counterpoint and during the walk Gyrowetz was obliged to repeat orally what he had learnt; since the

deren es in Neapel drei gab, das vorzüglichste war. Meister Sala war bereits in einem hohen Alter, und freute sich, einen deutschen jungen Schüler zu übernehmen, welcher sich bereits in der Instrumental-Musik einen erfreulichen Namen erworben hatte. Der Anfang des Unterrichtes im Contrapunct wurde dann mit Ausübung einer regelmäßigen echten Tonleiter gemacht, und weil Gyrowetz in den Accorden-Fügung ohnedies bereits erfahren war, so wurde sogleich zum zwei, drei und vierstimmigen Satz und sodann zu Verfertigung von Fugen und Canons etc. etc. geschritten, in welcher Musikgattung Meister Sala ein ausgezeichneter, vorzüglicher Lehrer war. Er hatte die Gewohnheit, nach beendigter Lehrstunde immer mit Gyrowetz einen Spaziergang am Molo, oder in die Nähe vom Vesuv zu machen, und im Gehen mußte Gyrowetz das Erlernte ihm mündlich wiederholen; als der Unterricht bereits schon zu den Fugen gekommen war, mußte Gyrowetz ihm sämmtliche Bestandtheile einer Fuge, nämlich Thema, Umkehrung, Modulation, Imitationen, Verdopplung, Verengung etc. etc. bis zur Coda auswendig lernen, und mündlich vorrecitiren; das war eine sehr gute Methode, welche einem jeden Schüler in der Composition besonders anzuempfehlen ist».

9. Benedetto Neri (1771-1841), «Studio di contrappunto incominciato da me Benedetto Neri nell'anno 1796 alli 12. di Decembre 1796» (I-NOd, Fondo cappella musicale 3387).

10. See also Brandenburg 2003.

> teaching already had come to the fugues, Gyrowetz had to memorize all the different components of a fugue, such as the theme, its inversion, modulation, imitation, augmentation, stretti, etc. etc. up to the coda and to recite these loudly; this was a very good method, which particularly may be recommended to any student in composition[11].

This quotation suggests that the extensive series of fugues that Gyrowetz wrote during his lessons with Sala had a pedagogical function reaching beyond the mere skills of putting a fugue together. As becomes clear, Sala demanded quite a remarkable level of mental skills in his contrapuntal teaching, urging Gyrowetz to vocally reproduce all components of the fugue, while taking a walk after their lesson in counterpoint.

In addition to this, an anonymous counterpoint notebook (F-Pn Ms. 8223) from about the same year (1789), which I recently identified as deriving from Sala's contrapuntal instruction, may here serve as an example of how the various components of the fugue were labeled.

I presume that the scribe of this counterpoint notebook may have been a certain Louis Julien Castels de Labarre (1771-?) who studied with Sala between 1788 and 1789[12]. The following two-part fugue from Louis Julien Castels de Labarre's notebook of fugues shows an example of how Sala introduced his students in the various components of the two-part fugue. Similar to what can be seen in a great number of counterpoint notebooks, de Labarre marked the start of these lessons on the first page of his notebook: «Du Dimanche 11 Janvier 1789, 1[e] Leçon de fugue a 2» (see Ex. 2):

---

[11]. Gyrowetz 1848, p. 26: «Er hatte die Gewohnheit, nach beendigter Lehrstunde immer mit Gyrowetz einen Spaziergang am Molo, oder in die Nähe vom Vesuv zu machen, und im Gehen mußte Gyrowetz das Erlernte ihm mündlich wiederholen; als der Unterricht bereits schon zu den Fugen gekommen war, mußte Gyrowetz ihm sämmtliche Bestandtheile einer Fuge, nämlich Thema, Umkehrung, Modulation, Imitationen, Verdopplung, Verengung etc. etc. bis zur Coda auswendig lernen, und mündlich vorrecitiren; das war eine sehr gute Methode, welche einem jeden Schüler in der Composition besonders anzuempfehlen ist».

[12]. Since the author of F-Pn Ms. 8223 also left two partimento collections with partimenti by Nicola Sala and Leonardo Leo, it seems likely that this author must have been known to Alexandre-Étienne Choron, and that he thus should appear in Choron's *Dictionnaire historique des musiciens*, published in 1810. At that time Choron had done extensive research in Sala's pedagogical writings, published and translated Sala's entire *Regole del contrapuntto pratico*. We know also, that Choron was aware of at least one other French student who studied at the same conservatory with Nicola Sala, in 1776: Étienne-Joseph Floquet (1748-1785). Floquet owned an autograph collection of Sala's partimenti which were reprinted in Choron's *Principes de Composition des Écoles d'Italie*. Given these circumstantial facts, it seems reasonable to assume that the author of F-Pn Ms. 8223 should appear in Choron's *Dictionnaire*. Investigation of this matter shows indeed that Sala did have a French student around 1790 by the name of Louis-Julien Castels de Labarre, who studied at the same conservatory with exactly the same teacher. However, Choron gives a slightly later date for de Labarre's studies: 1791 until 1793, instead of 1788 and 1789. Although we cannot be entirely sure about this, I assume that Choron did give incorrect dates for de Labarre's time of study. See Choron 1810, p. 383.

Ex. 2: Louis Julien Castels de Labarre (?), Fuga No. 1, bars 1-20 (F-Pn Ms. 8223, fols. 1[r]).

Even though it may seem clear that students wrote extensive series of fugues, the question remains how all this is related to the practice of partimento? Were the partimenti generally studied before these two-part written exercises and were partimenti intended to prepare the student for his studies in written counterpoint? And how could we possibly know this, when the partimenti in most cases survive in notebooks different from the counterpoint notebooks?

Luckily, in the case of Louis Julien Castels de Labarre's materials, there is a clear answer to this question: both his partimento notebooks and his counterpoint notebook were dated by de Labarre on the front covers: his first partimento collection is entitled «1.er Cayé de Partimenti de Basses d'accompagnement Del Signor D. Nicola Sala, Premier Maitre de composition du conservatoire de la Pieta a Naples a 15 Juillet 1788» (F-Pn 4° c[2] 343/1), while his counterpoint notebook is dated «Du dimanche 11 Janvier 1789» (F-Pn Ms. 8223), about six months later. The fact that both the partimento collections and the counterpoint notebook are written by the same scribal hand, suggests that this French student, who almost certainly belonged to the group of the paying boarder students, the *pensionaristi*, engaged himself for at least half a year of intensive partimento studies before advancing to the class of counterpoint.

In addition to this, it is revealing to take a closer look at the partimenti in the two partimento notebooks of De Labarre. The first 'cahier' of partimenti contains thirty-

Ex. 3: The front covers of two notebooks, the first containing partimenti, the second containing counterpoint exercises, both dated and written in the same hand (F-Pn 4° c^2 343/1 and F-Pn Ms. 8223).

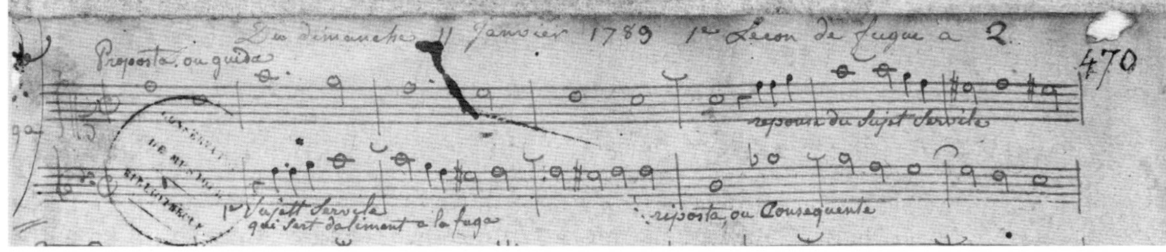

two partimenti by Nicola Sala and twenty partimenti by Leonardo Leo (1694-1744)[13]. All thirty-two partimenti by Sala in the first collection F-Pn 4° c^2 343/1 are pieces of low to moderate level, all in F-clef and without any use of clef changes. This section is followed by twenty partimenti by Leonardo Leo that are slightly more difficult, containing clef changes and more elaborate imitative counterpoint[14]. The start of Leonardo Leo's partimento may here serve to exemplify how the course in counterpoint and fugue was prepared through the practicing of imitative partimenti (see Ex. 4):

[13]. The partimenti by Sala are those that are numbered nos. 143-176, and 178. I here use the numbering system used in Van Tour 2017b. The collection F-Pn 4° c^2 343/2 ends with Nicola Sala's partimento no. 178. For the identification of the partimenti by Leonardo Leo in F-Pn 4° c^2 343/1 and F-Pn 4° c^2 343/2, see: Van Tour 2014—.

[14]. The attribution to Leonardo Leo of these pieces merit particular credibility, since the attribution to Leo is written under the authority of Nicola Sala, who was Leonardo Leo's successor as a teacher of counterpoint at the Pietà between the 1740s and 1799.

Ex. 4: Leonardo Leo, Fuga No. 1, bars 1-14, (F-Pn 4° c² 343/1, p. 39).

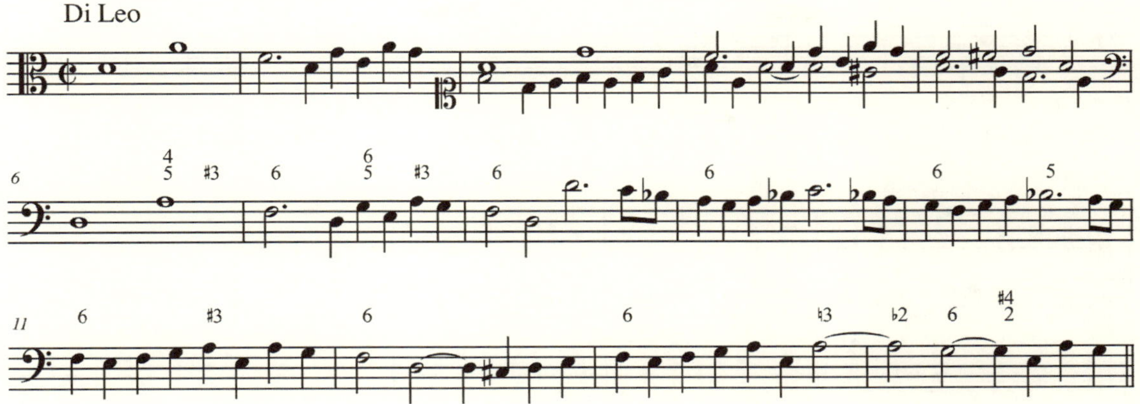

Louis Julien Castels de Labarre's two partimento collections F-Pn 4° c² 343/1 and F-Pn 4° c² 343/2 merit attention also for a second reason: they give no less than twelve *bassi seguenti*, which I have been able to identify in sacred vocal works by Leonardo Leo[15]. Eleven of these have been listed previously in my doctoral dissertation. In addition to these, only recently I was able to identify yet another partimento in F-Pn 4° c² 343/2 (no. 62 in this collection) as being a *basso seguente*[16]. The corresponding mass movement is the final *Cum Sancto Spiritu* at the end of the *Gloria* of Nicola Sala's Mass *Kyrie e Gloria intero* (I-BGc Mayr Fald. 53/4)[17]. Let us take a closer look at this basso seguente and its vocal counterpart (see Exs. 5 and 6):

Ex. 5: Leonardo Leo, *basso seguente* to the *Cum Sancte Spiritu* in G major, bars 1-24, (F-Pn 4° c² 343/1, p. 39).

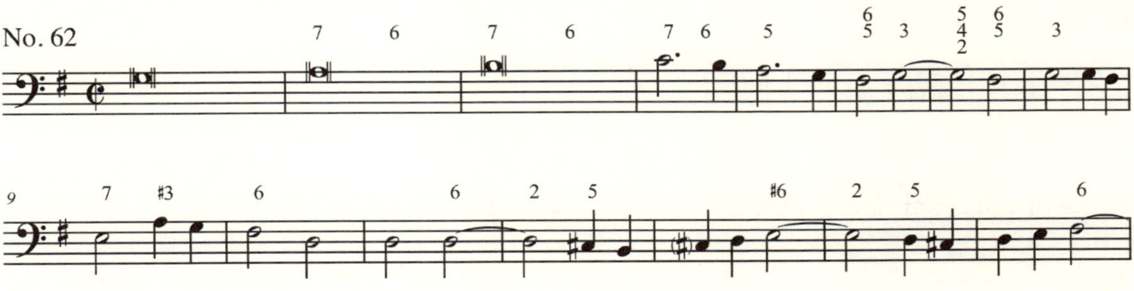

[15]. See Van Tour 2015, pp. 279-289.

[16]. For the argumentation why these pieces should be called *bassi seguenti*, see *ibidem*, pp. 208-226.

[17]. It should be mentioned, at this point, that Nicola Sala's Mass *Kyrie e Gloria intero* (I-BGc Mayr Fald. 53/4), in which I identified this partimento (or *basso seguente*, to be precise) contains two fugal mass sections for which Nicola Sala used fugues by his teacher Leonardo Leo. These both fugues appear originally in Leonardo Leo's Mass in G major. For a list of concordant sources of this mass by Leo, see: Krause 1987, p. 30. As can be noticed from the concordance list in this book, Krause does not mention this particular source for Leo's G major Mass, I-BGc Mayr Fald. 53/4.

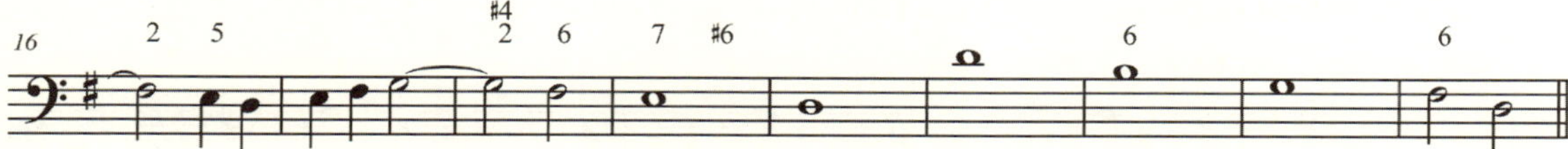

Ex. 6: Leonardo Leo, *Cum Sancte Spiritu* from the Mass in G major, bars 1–24, (I-BGc Mayr Fald. 53/4, fol. 61r).

The content of the two partimento collections F-Pn 4° c² 343/1 and F-Pn 4° c² 343/2 also raise a few other questions: 1) Why did Sala not use any of his partimenti that we know from two autographs I-Nc 46-1-34 and F-Pn 4° c² 344? 2) Why are Sala's partimenti followed by those of Leo? 3. And why did Sala include no less than twelve *bassi seguenti* by Leonardo Leo in these two collections?

It should be noted that these two partimento collections were written relatively late, in 1788. At that time, Sala appears to have abandoned the 131 partimenti that he had written in the 1750s and 1760s[18]. I suspect that the series of 131 partimenti had become too complicated for most of the students in the 1780s and 1790s, a time when there were many complaints about the decreasing standard of teaching at the Neapolitan conservatories[19].

It may seem somewhat surprizing that Sala in his partimento instruction used partimenti by his teacher Leonardo Leo from the 1730s and 1740, that is some 40 or 50 years later. It is not impossible that the reintroduction of Leo's partimenti represented a kind of 'nostalgia' for the 1740s and 1750s, the time when the Neapolitan conservatories had been in full bloom. Also in the case of Durante's partimenti it is possible to see such changes of stylistic orientation. As I have shown elsewhere, the twenty old-style fugues that commonly appear at the end of Durante's partimenti in early nineteenth-century collection, were almost certainly added to Durante's partimenti somewhere around the 1790s, probably with the aim of restoring some of the skills and knowledge that had been lost[20]. These fugues are compositions by early eighteenth-century composers. The twelve *bassi seguenti* by Leonardo Leo were introduced in the late 1780s, possibly for similar reasons. Also here, Sala may have had the ambitions to restore some important skills that had been the very essence of the contrapuntal tradition of the *Pietà* in the early eighteenth century.

Additionally, the two partimento notebooks of Louis Julien Castels de Labarre F-Pn 4° c² 343/1, F-Pn 4° c² 343/2, and the counterpoint notebook F-Pn Ms. 8223 shed new light on the content of a student's studies in partimento and counterpoint at the Pietà in the years around the French Revolution. A note added to the two-part fugue no. 12

[18]. This set of 131 partimenti have appeared as part of my complete edition with critical commentary, Van Tour 2017a, nos. 1-131.

[19]. See Sigismondo 1820, vol. iv, p. 173: «Cafaro se ne morì e Sala rimpiazzò il suo luogo. Introdotti nel *Collegio* i partimenti e solfeggi di Leo, poscia di Cafaro, egli non volle far uso de' suoi» («Cafaro died and Sala replaced him in his role. As he had introduced the partimenti and solfeggi by Leo and later by Cafaro in the *collegio*, he would not make use of his own»). Translation according to Bacciagaluppi 2016, 269. These circumstances are confirmed through the solfeggio collection I-Nc Solfeggio 250, containing Leo's solfeggi, not in the hand of Pasquale Cafaro, as the title page suggests, but in fact in the hand of Nicola Sala. The collection 'I-Nc Solfeggio 250' was probably used as teaching material at the *Pietà*.

[20]. None of the partimenti in F-Pn 4° c² 343/1 and F-Pn 4° c² 343/2 appears in the earlier collections of Sala's partimenti, such as I-Nc 46-1-34 or F-Pn 4° c² 344. Sala's partimenti in F-Pn 4° c² 343/1, F-Pn 4° c² 343/2, and in I-Nc S-1-94 were written rather late in his career and may have served to replace the previous collection of the 131 partimenti. See also Van Tour 2017b, vol. 1, introduction without pagination.

in Labarre's counterpoint notebook F-Pn Ms. 8223, reveals Nicola Sala's answer to De Labarre's supposed question:

> The way to become skilled in constructing operas: after the fugues a 4, one must write 8 to 10 arias, five or six duos, five or six trios, five or six quartets, after that recitatives, and then the opera[21].

These notebooks show only the very start of this process, displaying a strong focus on counterpoint and fugue. At some point, De Labarre must have wondered how many more such fugues he would need to write, before he finally would be allowed to write any dramatic music. Sala's curriculum started quite rigorously with this «hard nut of counterpoint», to paraphrase Heinrich Schütz' expression in the forward of the *Geistliche Chormusik 1648*. The abrupt ending in the middle of one of the three-part fugues raises the question, whether De Labarre perhaps did end his counterpoint studies prematurely: the fourth three-part fugue was left unfinished, and the rest of the notebook remained empty too. From similar counterpoint notebooks we know that more three-part fugues normally would have been added, and after that even a similar set of four-part fugues. Probably the «hard nut of counterpoint» was somewhat too hard for De Labarre.

The partimento notebooks of 1788 by De Labarre and his counterpoint notebook of 1789 remind us of the fact that partimenti were not only used to develop skills in thoroughbass realization, but also, and most specifically, to prepare the student for his forthcoming studies in counterpoint. As such they enrich our present understanding of the educational function of partimenti.

Bibliography

Bacciagaluppi 2016

Apotheosis of Music in the Kingdom of Naples: Giuseppe Sigismondo, edited by Claudio Bacciagaluppi, Giulia Giovani and Raffaele Mellace, Introduction by Rosa Cafiero, Rome, Società Editrice di Musicologia, 2016 (Saggi, 3).

Bellotti 2017

Bellotti, Edoardo. 'Composing at the Keyboard: Banchieri and Spiridion, Two Complementary Methods', in: *Studies in Historical Improvisation: From 'Cantare super Librum' to Partimenti*, edited by Massimiliano Guido, Abington-New York, Routledge, 2017.

Borgir 1987

Borgir, Tharald. *The Performance of the Basso Continuo in Italian Baroque Music*, Rochester (NY), University of Rochester Press, 1987 (Studies in Musicology, 90).

[21]. F-Pn Ms. 8223, fols. 16r: «Marche pour se mettre en état de faire des operas: Apres les fugues a 4. Il faut faire 8. ou 10 ariettas, cinq ou six duos, 5 ou six trios, 5 ou 6 quartetto, après les recitatifs, ensuitte l'opéra».

Brandenburg 2003
Brandenburg, Daniel. 'Reisende Musiker in Neapel im späten 18. Jahrhundert: Adalbert Gyrowetz, Michael Kelly, Giacomo Gottifredo Ferrari', in: *Le Musicien et ses voyages: pratiques, réseaux et représentations*, edited by Christian Meyer, Berlin, BWV Berliner Wissenschafts, 2003 (Musical Life in Europe 1600-1900. Circulation, Institution Representation), pp. 113-126.

Callahan 2010
Callahan, Michael. *Techniques of Keyboard Improvisation in the German Baroque and Their Implications for Today's Pedagogy*, Ph.D. Diss., Rochester (NY), University of Rochester, 2010.

Choron 1810
Choron, Alexandre-Étienne. *Dictionnaire historique des musiciens, artistes et amateurs, morts ou vivants* [...], 2 vols., Paris, Valade et Lenormant, 1810-1811, vol. 1????OK????, 1810.

Christensen 1992
Christensen, Thomas. 'The 'Règle de l'Octave' in Thorough-Bass Theory and Practice', in: *Acta Musicologica*, lxiv/2 (1992), pp. 91-117.

Gingras 2008
Gingras, Bruno. 'Partimento Fugue in Eighteenth-Century Germany: A Bridge between Thoroughbass and Fugal Composition', in: *Eighteenth-Century Music*, v/1 (2008), pp. 51-74.

Gjerdingen 2007
Gjerdingen, Robert. *Music in the Galant Style*, Oxford-New York, Oxford University Press, 2007.

Gyrowetz 1848
Gyrowetz, Adalbert. *Biographie des Adalbert Gyrowetz*, Vienna, Mechitaristen-Buchdruckerei, 1848.

Krause 1987
Krause, Ralf. *Die Kirchenmusik von Leonardo Leo (1694-1744). Ein Beitrag zur Musikgeschichte Neapels im 18. Jahrhunderts*, Regensburg, Gustav Bosse Verlag, 1987 (Kölner Beiträge zur Musikforschung, 151).

Lester 1992
Lester, Joel. *Compositional Theory in the Eighteenth Century*, Cambridge (MA), Harvard University Press, 1992, pp. 65-68.

Renwick 1995
Renwick, William. *Analyzing Fugue: A Schenkerian Approach*, Stuyvesant (NY), Pendragon Press, 1995 (Harmonologia, 8).

Renwick 2001
The Langloz Manuscript: Fugal Improvisation Through Figured Bass, edited by William Renwick, Oxford, Oxford University Press, 2001 (Early Music Series).

Sanguinetti 2012
Sanguinetti, Giorgio. *The Art of Partimento: History, Theory and Practice*, Oxford-New York, Oxford University Press, 2012.

Sigismondo 1820

Sigismondo, Giuseppe. *Apoteosi della Musica del Regno di Napoli in tre ultimi transundati secoli*, 4 vols. D-B Mus. ms. autogr. theor. Sigismondo, G.I., 1820.

Van Tour 2014—

Van Tour, Peter. *UUPart: The Uppsala Partimento Database*, Uppsala, 2014—, <http://www2.musik.uu.se/UUPart/UUPart.php>, accessed November 2018.

Van Tour 2015

Id. *Counterpoint and Partimento: Methods of Teaching Composition in Late Eighteenth-Century Naples*, Uppsala, Acta Universitatis Upsaliensis, 2015 (Studia musicological Upsaliansia. Nova Series, 25).

Van Tour 2017a

Id. 'Partimento Teaching according to Durante, Investigated through the Earliest Manuscript Sources', in: *Studies in Historical Improvisation: From Cantare super Librum to Partimenti*, *op. cit.*, pp. 131-148.

Van Tour 2017b

The 189 Partimenti of Nicola Sala: Complete Edition with Critical Commentary, 3 vols., edited by Peter van Tour, Uppsala, Acta Universitatis Upsaliensis, 2017 (Studia musicologica Upsaliensia. Nova Series, 27).

Abstracts

David Chung, *French Harpsichord «doubles» and the Creative Art of the 17th-Century «Clavecinistes»*

The seventeenth-century French harpsichord repertory developed from a largely improvised art in which notation served as an *aide-mémoire* to a form in which details carefully marked by the composer were expected to be observed meticulously by the performer. Through an in-depth study of the repertory of pieces with *doubles*, this paper delves into performance practice issues and explores the creative processes of how seventeenth-century French musicians in the quasi-improvisatory tradition played and taught. This paper considers three key issues in detail: (1) the possible variants (melodic, rhythmic, textural) between performances; (2) the role of improvisation; and (3) the ways how seventeenth-century musicians cultivated their individual artistic voices. A dozen concordant manuscript versions of Hardel's Gavotte, which inspired Louis Couperin's famous *double*, provide valuable materials for exploring the close relationship between imitation and creativity, as espoused by Jean Le Gallois (1680) and other seventeenth-century writers. The *double* by Louis Couperin has survived in multiple versions in a variety of manuscript sources, and virtually no two versions are cut from the same cloth. Although some of the differences among the manuscript sources could be explained as the inevitable result of aural transmission, it is clear that seventeenth-century scribes did not restrict their role to that of a faithful or mechanical copyist. Instead, they felt quite ready to impose their copying habits, musical tastes and their personalities during the process of writing out ornaments, rhythms, cadences, and other effects. In this context, the notation serves sometimes as an example of what could be done and sometimes as what had been done – a case in which many elements of the notation are not at all binding on the part of the performer. By identifying elements of the music that are decorative and those that are structural and integral to the musical fabric, this paper aims to encourage modern performers to nurture ways to be spontaneous yet stay faithful to the original spirit of the music through an increased awareness of the creativity embedded in the performance.

Massimiliano Guido, *Sounding Theory and Theoretical Notes Bernardo Pasquini's Pedagogy at the Keyboard: A Case of Composition in Performance?*

In a recent essay, Thomas Christensen calls for an 'improvisatory moment' and proposes the coexistence of two heretofore competing facets of music theory. Almost the entirety of our discipline is rooted in 'hard theory' and consists of prolix prose and myriad rules and corollaries. Music examples within this tradition only serve the words and do not reach a status of independence. On the other hand, we are slowly rediscovering a semi-forgotten tradition of 'soft theory': 'fragile texts' arising out of the aural-mnemonic praxis of Antiquity, exemplified in the 'artisanal' apprenticeship of music in which students had to 'analyze' didactic examples. The latter approach has been rejected for some time as 'real theory' because of the lack of surrounding discourse. In many cases music stands alone, and readers might not grasp its 'sounding theoretical' value. The concept of 'soft theory' is intimately connected to the Italian tradition of *suonar di fantasia* at the keyboard; this has been discussed by several scholars in recent years. Here I consider the didactic works of one of the most influential musicians in seventeenth-century Rome: Bernardo Pasquini. His *Saggi di Contrappunto* (1695), the *Sonate per uno o due cembali* (1703-1704), and the *Versetti con il solo basso cifrato* (1708) constitute a homogenous collection in which the learner is exposed to the complexity of composing at the keyboard. Pasquini's oeuvre stands in between the Renaissance tradition of improvised counterpoint and Neapolitan partimenti. Its pedagogical value derives from the pleasantness of making music combined with the authority of theory. Why was Pasquini so famous as a pedagogue? What was so unique about his teaching method? I demonstrate how he connected keyboard technique with the art of composing in a coherent unity, providing the student with all the elements necessary to extemporize music at the harpsichord in the modern style.

Javier Lupiáñez – Fabrizio Ammetto, *Las anotaciones de Pisendel en el Concierto para dos violines RV 507 de Vivaldi: una ventana abierta a la improvisación en la obra del 'Cura rojo'*

The famous 'Schrank II' collection of the Sächsische Landesbibliothek – Staats- und Universitätsbibliothek (SLUB) in Dresden contains about two thousand music manuscripts, most of which were collected by the violinist and composer Johann Georg Pisendel (1687-1755), concertmaster of the Dresden court orchestra in the first half of the eighteenth century; he was also a personal pupil of Antonio Vivaldi. A careful analysis of these manuscripts reveals the presence of a large number of annotations by Pisendel that, for the most part, provide guidance for ornamentation and/or improvisation. Within this large corpus of manuscripts, Vivaldi's works are the most copiously annotated. Pisendel's copy of Vivaldi's Concerto in C major for two violins and orchestra (RV 507; D-Dl, Mus.2389-O-98) is particularly interesting by virtue of the fact that it contains annotations and ornamentation for both soloists. An analysis of these markings reveals a style that moves away from the one presented in contemporary treatises on ornamentation that generally adhere to the Corellian language predominant at the time. The style of ornamentation found in RV 507 shows significant similarities both with other Vivaldi works annotated by Pisendel (RV 202 and RV 340) and with certain slow movements in his concertos that adopt a particularly improvisatory language (*Adagio* in RV 195, *Grave Recitativo* in RV 208, *Grave* in RV 212a, *Largo* in RV 279, *Adagio* in RV 285, *Largo* in RV 318, *Grave* in RV 562). Additionally, there are similarities in the diminutions for the Concerto for violin and double orchestra, RV 581 (I-Vc, busta 55), written for another of Vivaldi's pupils, the famous violinist Anna Maria (1696-1782), a «figlia di coro» at the Ospedale della Pietà in Venice. These particularities of the ornamentation notated in the Dresden version of RV 507 appear to show that these annotations belong to a performative context in which the performer improvised and modified the musical text *ex tempore*. Moreover, they reflect the hypothesis advanced by numerous scholars that the works, given the similarities, may be Vivaldi's own.

Josué Meléndez Peláez, *«Cadenze per nali»: Exuberant and Extended Cadences in the 16th and 17th Centuries*

The influence of humanism led composers of the sixteenth and seventeenth centuries to structure their works after the rhetorical processes of the ancient Greeks. *Conclusio*, also known as *finis*, is the part (or 'period') of a speech that defines its end. Joachim Burmeister subdivides a piece into nine rhetorical periods: «The Final, namely, the ninth, period is like the epilogue of a speech. This harmony displays a principal ending, otherwise called a *supplementum* of the final cadence [...]» (*Musica poetica*, 1606). The technique of extending a final cadence by prolonging its original time values can be found in compositions of the sixteenth and seventeen centuries. Extending the final note seems to have been common in polyphony of the early sixteenth century but as the century progressed and the thirst for rhetorical expressiveness grew, this musical epilogue was extended further by adding extra measures onto the penultimate – or, in some cases, also the antepenultimate – note. Late sixteenth- and seventeenth-century sources, such as those by L. Zacconi, G. B. Bovicelli, B. Barbarino, F. Severi F. Rognoni, H. A. Herbst, the Anonymous manuscript G239 (Estense Codex), the manuscript 'Carlo G', and the treatises of Spiridionis a Monte Carmelo show that this practice was originally improvised by performers. Other sources, such as notated diminutions, monodies and instrumental music by composers such as Caccini, Mayone, Frescobaldi, Monteverdi, Castello, Marini and many others, appear to begin notating florid ornamentation on prolonged basslines at final (and sometimes intermediate) cadences. The vast documentation of this practice, both in notated musical examples and theoretical treatises of the time, gives us a glimpse of the interpretive skills that performers were expected to possess in the Renaissance and Baroque periods and encourages modern performers to study them and to include them in historical performances.

MARINA TOFFETTI, *Written Outlines of Improvisation Procedures in Music Publications of the Early 17th Century: The Second (1611-1623) and Third (1615-1623) Book of «Concerti» By G. Ghizzolo and the Motet «Iesu Rex Admirabilis» (1625-1627) by G. Frescobaldi*

Procedures such as diminution, the realization (and 'articulation') of the basso continuo, and modal transposition have been entrusted to the practice of improvisation for centuries. The information provided on the written page did not resolve all the problems that could arise in performance; such solutions could only be achieved by calling on the skills and experience of the performers. Therefore, musical sources that allow us to shed light on these procedures assume a great value and need to be examined with care. The cases examined here – the *concerti* from Giovanni Ghizzolo's second (1611-1623) and third book (1615-1623) and Girolamo Frescobaldi's motet *Iesu Rex admirabilis* (1625-1627) – reveal that the publication of a new edition could present an opportunity to review one or more previous published compositions, allowing us to focus on such issues as the articulation of the basso continuo line and its fixing on the written page, the modal transposition of compositions notated in *chiavette* and the possible presence of written indications referring to this practice, and the presence of diminutions written out in full in one or more voices. Each of these three aspects has been dealt with from two different angles, which consider both the consequences of these written outlines of improvisation procedures on performance practice and the implications they have on the practice of publishing. Taking for granted that the strategies to adopt in an edition should consider the specific history of each work's transmission, certain indispensable criteria should nevertheless be taken into account when preparing a critical edition. In particular, editors should avoid contaminating two or more distinct versions of the same composition, mixing parts or portions of one version with those of a later version. In the same way, editors should avoid fixing elements that were not fixed in the 17th-century edition. Moreover, all the indications contained in the ancient edition should be reported in the modern edition, so as to allow the player to glean all possible information from the different aspects of performance practice.

GIOVANNA BARBATI, *«Il n'exécute jamais la Basse telle qu'elle est écrite»: The Use of Improvisation in Teaching Low Strings*

The opportunity to imagine a method of teaching for cello or viola da gamba based on improvisation is offered to us from the rediscovery of the didactical and pedagogical practice of *partimento*. This method was based on learning directly at the keyboard and on the progressive memorization of patterns; from there, it rapidly led to composing or improvising on a given bass line. Given that low strings perform the double function of providing the continuo and the *cantus*, I investigated the possibility that a similar historical method that was suited to the cello and viola da gamba might exist; evidence found in the sources may confirm this hypothesis. I believe that historical improvisation was based on elaborations of pre-existing elements and patterns within a shared language that allowed for the development of individual formulae within the historical language. Here I suggest that, during the Baroque era, teaching methods were organised such that pupils could improvise based on patterns which could later be reused in different contexts. It was therefore a matter of teaching and learning patterns that the best students would later reuse with complete autonomy. First we consider the improvisational demands of the repertoire, depending on different the bass instrument's different performative contexts: as a 'solo', as the principal voice, or as accompaniment. I then examine historical documentary evidence; I conclude by describing my pedagogical proposal, which suggests that the didactical method should be supplemented with schemes on which to elaborate from the beginning, while still leaving room for the student's creativity. Indeed, I believe that one can find a valid way to enrich one's skills on low string instruments while learning how to interpret and perform Baroque music more accurately with this approach.

Anthony Pryer, *The Borderlines of Improvisation: Caccini, Monteverdi, and the Freedoms of the Performer*

Improvisation during the Baroque period stands more or less at the mid-point in the documented history of the practice. This study draws on those traditions to illuminate the contexts in which improvisation might take place, and what its attributes and procedures might be. The argument proceeds in four stages. First, it suggests that the traditional division between oral and written cultures is rather unhelpful because a) most Western musical communities consist of a mixture of both, and b) the more important distinction seems to be found between 'prepared' and 'unprepared' musical activity. A 'Notation-Culture' grid is constructed onto which repertories combining improvisational and written features can be mapped. I then examine the role of 'common practice' styles. Since the Baroque period spent more time than most on defining its styles, that seems to have provided a particularly fertile framework for improvisational practices. Third, I look at Caccini's *Le nuove musiche* (1602) in detail as an attempt to 'write the un-writable' and to examine how it uses various types of notational function (archival, strategic, prescriptive, and descriptive) to capture the confluence between improvisatory performance practices and written compositional structures. Finally, I examine Caccini's 'Amarilli mia bella' and Monteverdi's 'Possente spirto' to show how they emerged via the essentially improvisational techniques of adaptation, re-combination and variation. Just where 'creative freedom' should be located in that process is a complex question. It is why and how people improvise that points to its social and artistic significance.

Laura Toffetti, *«Sostener si può la battuta, etiandio in aria». Testi e contesti per comprendere l'invenzione e la disposizione del discorso musicale nel repertorio strumentale italiano fra Seicento e Settecento*

The perception of the score as an unfinished work is the centre of this research. Since Baroque notation does not provide details for exact execution through interpretive signs commonly found in most modern musical writings, the examination of contemporary theoretical sources is necessary in order to understand and perform the musical text. The works of composers such as Girolamo Frescobaldi, of theorists such as Vincenzo Galilei, or of intellectuals such as Vincenzo Giustiniani clarify that Baroque composition is based on precise idiomatic formulations, arranged and adjusted according to rules inherited from classical rhetoric. These items or figures are comparable to semantic structures, which, linked together, build the musical statements. Identifying these gestures in the score and performing them, through the consideration of some important didactic works, introductory notes of music editions, and analyses of their cultural contexts, is the first objective of this research. I then focus on the evolution of musical terms such as 'tempo', 'figure' or 'numerus' as evidence of the analogy between musical language, rules of rhetoric and prosody, and the considerations of the communicative function of musical practice. Improvisation, a necessary step to realizing the unfinished score, thus acquires a new meaning. Broadened by different elements such as agogics, text organisation, or eloquence, this technique becomes a vehicle for expressive and semantic gestures: simultaneously *ex tempore* and rooted in an extremely precise cultural and aesthetic system.

Abstracts

Rudolf Rasch, *Improvised Cadenzas in the Cello Sonatas Op. 5 by Francesco Geminiani*

During the eighteenth century, composers developed the habit of creating room in their compositions for freely improvised passages; this practice was extensively described by Johann Joachim Quantz in his *Versuch einer Anweisung* (1752). These passages were called cadenzas because they were often connected with the final cadence of a movement within a larger work. Examples of notated cadenzas can be found in Corelli's Sonatas Op. 5 (1700) and Geminiani's Sonatas Op. 1 (1716, 1739) and Op. 4 (1739); they provide examples for performing such cadenzas where others are only suggested by a fermata. This article investigates how present-day performers perform the cadenzas that are indicated in eight places in the Cello Sonatas Op. 5 by Geminiani (1747). The cadenzas were transcribed from nine complete recordings of these sonatas, released from 1976 to 2015, and were then compared with the 'rules' given in Quantz's *Versuch*. Not surprisingly, the cadenzas as performed by these nine cellists vary greatly in length and style. Nevertheless, Quantz's suggestions are clearly recognizable.

Valentina Anzani, *Il mito della competizione tra virtuosi: quando Farinelli sfidò Bernacchi (Bologna 1727)*

In the summer of 1727, Farinelli, a rising star, and Antonio Maria Bernacchi, an older virtuoso and famous teacher, shared the same stage in Bologna. According to numerous versions of the event, Farinelli apparently challenged the older colleague in a contest of variations. The two engaged in improvisations and reciprocal imitations: Bernacchi got the better of Farinelli, and Farinelli was led to ask his competitor for voice lessons. This story has been important in establishing the relevance of Bernacchi's school and its notability in being a place for virtuosos' improvement in our collective imaginations. In reality, accounts of the meeting multiplied until the early nineteenth century, and the degrees of truth contained within them should be considered on a case-by-case basis. However, they share one aspect in common: they each describe the two virtuosos rising to *exempla*, one, the embodiment of the musical and human characteristics that being a virtuoso required and the other, the ideal representative of the good singing teacher. This essay aims to reconstruct (with archival foundation) what really happened between the two singers. It clarifies the ways in which the event has been changed in subsequent literature and also reveals how the event can be read as a representation of a diametrically opposite *topos* – and a positive one at that: that of two colleagues who imitate themselves in a virtuous relationship rather than as another negative commentary on the deistic attitudes of castrati.

John Lutterman, *Re-Creating Historical Improvisatory Solo Practices on the Cello: C. Simpson, F. Niedt, and J. S. Bach on the Pedagogy of «Contrapunctis Extemporalis»*

Clues to the technical means of re-creating the improvisatory practices of Bach's world can be found in a great number of sources, including Christopher Simpson's *The Divison Viol*, Friedrich Niedt's *Musicalische Handleitung*, and the rich trove of Italian *partimento* exercises. Viewed through an analytic lens, free from the blinders of a modern work concept, the written compositions of Bach and his contemporaries may be understood as inventories of formal models and as idiomatic vocabularies of motivic, harmonic, and contrapuntal ideas ripe for improvisatory appropriation and elaboration. *The Division Viol* is one of the most comprehensive treatises on improvisation, offering valuable clues to the nature of a number of historical improvisatory practices, including instruction in the art of extemporaneous implied polyphony, which Simpsons calls the 'mixt' style of divisions. The importance of Simpson's treatises for understanding the practices of seventeenth-century British musicians is well known, and copies of *The Division Viol* can be found in important musical archives throughout Europe. Indeed, the treatise remained popular enough to justify the printing of a third edition in 1712. Simpson's approach is more harmonically conceived than has been generally recognized, and the organization of *The*

Division Viol shows interesting parallels to Niedt's treatise, which Bach is known to have used in his own teaching, and which in turn appears to be indebted to Italian partimento practices. Although Simpson's treatise does not offer written-out examples of longer pieces, following his advice to use a bass from a pre-existent composition as a formal schema would result in a structured approach to improvisation similar to that which German and Italian *partimento* practices were designed to cultivate.

Francesca Mignogna, *Accompagnamento e basso continuo alla chitarra spagnola. Una cartogra a della diffusione dei sistemi di notazione stenogra ci in Italia, Spagna e Francia tra* xvi *e* xvii *secolo e loro implicazioni teoriche*

Interest in thoroughbass has long been nearly exclusively confined to its practice on keyboard instruments. Nevertheless, a considerable number of studies, all published during the 20th century, brought attention to thoroughbass as it would be performed on instruments with plucked strings. These studies, among them Thomas Christensen's excellent article that identifies Baroque thoroughbass practice as one of the most important applications of *rasgueado*, a Spanish guitar technique, have dated the appearance of stenographic systems of notation for plucked-string instruments to the turn of the 17th century. These systems consisted of a synthetic representation of the accompaniment that was notated by letters of the alphabet on a melody, bass, or text. They were derived from Spanish *rasgueado* handbooks and were subsequently used in the practice of thoroughbass, especially in Italy. The *alfabeto* Italian system, along with the French and Spanish systems, displays techniques of chordal variation that include, in some cases, dissonant sounds. These stenographic systems – looking to the past in the practice of reduction and toward the future theorization of Campion's *règle de l'octave* (1716) – allow for a realization of thoroughbass on the Spanish Baroque guitar that is strongly idiomatic yet free from predetermined schemes at the same time. Such systems aim to simplify concepts (such as transposition) that were considered abstract and complex at that time by using the gestures and the physical characteristics of the guitar itself to their advantage. These systems were not only a means of synthetic notation. They also functioned as non-intellectual didactical works that were aimed toward an amateur public who wanted to learn quickly. Their significance lies in their role in the evolution of music theory toward functional harmony (other than in the concept of fundamental bass). The goal of this essay is to offer an extensive list of the handbooks and songbooks containing instructions for *alfabeto* systems that appeared during the 16th and 17th centuries in Italy, France and Spain so as to undertake an analysis of their role in the evolution of the thoroughbass practice and the transition between counterpoint and the tonal system.

Guido Olivieri, *Naturalezza o artificio: riflessioni su improvvisazione e virtuosismo italiani in Francia nel Settecento*

Improvisation was perceived as a trait typical of the Italian tradition in 18th-century France. Connected to poetic and literary practices, improvisation became a distinctive characteristic of the style of the Italian virtuosi who moved to Paris at the beginning of the century and influenced the development of French music. This style rose from a performance practice that was transmitted from teachers to students, cultivated in particular by the teaching methods used in the Neapolitan conservatories. It is not surprising, therefore, to find that the virtuosi who introduced the Italian virtuosic approach to France came mostly from Neapolitan training. With their brilliant performance practice and flair for improvisation they helped establish the new image and career path of the international virtuoso.

Neal Zaslaw, *«Adagio de Mr. Tartini. Varié de plusieurs façons différentes, très utiles aux personnes qui veulent apprendre à faire des traits sous chaque notte de l'Harmonie...»*

A Parisian publication, the *Adagio de Mr. Tartini. Varié de plusieurs façons différentes*, widely known from its inclusion in J. B. Cartier's *L'Art du violon* (Paris, 1798), has been readily available since its re-publication in facsimile by Alberto Bachmann in 1913 and by Hans-Peter Schmitz in 1955. (Subsequently, at least three more facsimile editions have appeared.) Because of its late date, apparent absence of an established pedigree, and dense notation, the *Adagio varié* has been received almost universally negatively by violinists and scholars. How could something this dense have come from Tartini, who was understood to have radically simplified his musical style in the context of the evolving aesthetics of the mid-eighteenth century? Uninvestigated in the negative critiques of the *Adagio varié* is an indication that its 1798 version was a «Seconde Édition». By investigating other known and putative editions, the earliest publication of the *Adagio varié* can be dated to no later than the 1770s, the decade during which his students published posthumously two other of his pedagogical works. Returning Tartini's *Adagio varié* to his canon re-opens questions about how he performed slow movements and how he trained his students to do likewise.

Simone Ciolfi, *Cantata da camera e arte del partimento in Alessandro Scarlatti. «An Historical Link between Baroque Recitatives and Development Section of the Sonata-Form Movements?»*

The partimento as pedagogical project begins with Alessandro Scarlatti's surviving partimenti. This article aims to examine basic elements of partimento theory, including the introduction of scale mutations as standard bass formulas (called here 'clausolas' because they are heritage of previous pre-harmonic clausolas), portions of the Rule of the Octave, and basses falling by thirds. These elements are found in Scarlatti's recitatives, arias and partimento exercises. Michael Talbot has written of a possible «historical link between Baroque recitatives and development sections of the sonata-form». Here I suggest that elements of the partimento technique, in combination with components of different musical genres, form the probable link between Baroque recitatives and sonata-form development sections. In fact, the composition of recitatives likely formed part of every Classical composer's training.

Marco Pollaci, *Two New Sources for the Study of Early Eighteenth-Century Composition and Improvisation*

The study of partimento traditions has revealed a strong connection between the compositional practice of the eighteenth century and improvisational techniques. Pedagogical exercises, musical treatises, and other primary sources clearly indicate that improvising and learning the rules of partimento were essential aspects of musicians' training and study. Unsurprisingly, many European libraries contain a large number of manuscript sources related to partimento pedagogical traditions – a testament to the importance of improvisation and the knowledge of the pillars of Neapolitan counterpoint in musical practice at the end of the seventeenth century. To understand these methods of teaching counterpoint, studying musical sources such as the *regole*, *lezioni*, partimenti, and many other notebooks that demonstrate the relevant principles connected to the art of improvisation help us realize the importance of being skilled in the peculiar nature of these rules to every musician during that period. The Staatsbibliothek zu Berlin holds volumes of anonymously-written counterpoint exercises (D-B Mus. Ms theor.1483 and 1417) that have not yet been analysed. This study investigates the importance of these manuscript sources in connection with the compositional practices outlined in the texts *Principi di Cembalo* and *Regole per accompagnare nel Cimbalo ò vero Organo.*

Giorgio Sanguinetti, *On the Origin of Partimento: A Recently Discovered Manuscript of Toccate (1695) by Francesco Mancini*

When dealing with the difficult issue of determining when and where partimenti came into use, one can speculate about a Roman origin. Indeed, during the early years of the eighteenth century, Rome was considered to be the most advanced musical center in Europe; the earliest partimenti manuscript collection, signed by Bernardo Pasquini, originated here in approximately 1707. Later, following Alessandro Scarlatti's move from Rome to Naples, a migration occurred. After my book *The Art of Partimento* was published, things became complicated. Newly discovered sources, such as the *Regole o vero Toccate di studio del Sig. Abb[at]e Fran[cesc]o Mancini 1695* (F-Pn Rés. 2315) prove that partimenti were in use in Naples already at the end of the seventeenth century – and possibly earlier. In fact, the Mancini manuscript, and in particular the *21 Toccate* for harpsichord, display an impressive level of sophistication and virtuosity. Other manuscripts, such as the coeval Rocco Greco manuscript (I-Nc 33.2.3) show that bass string players studied partimenti at the keyboard, but also learned how to improvise diminutions on standard bass patterns *harmonically* on their instruments. Musicological research thus gives us a better understanding of the origins of the practice and also helps us find a solution for the problem we face today when teaching partimenti to non-keyboard majors.

Peter van Tour, *«Taking a Walk at the Molo»: Partimento and the Improvised Fugue*

In this article I focus on the relationship between partimento studies and studies of counterpoint and composition. Were partimenti studied before students advanced to writing counterpoint and composition, and if so, it is possible to reveal more about how partimento prepared the student for studies in written counterpoint and composition? A biographical anecdote by Adalbert Gyrowetz (1763-1850) suggests that Nicola Sala demanded quite a remarkable level of aural skills from his students. Gyrowetz, who studied in Naples between 1787 and 1789, was invited to talk after his lessons in counterpoint, during which he was supposed to recapitulate the lesson by singing the theme, the countersubject, and the other components of the fugue. This article focusses further on how such aural skills were prepared through practical exercises, such as solfeggi and partimenti. In addition, I introduce a newly identified counterpoint notebook that is written in exactly the same handwriting as previously known partimento collections (F-Pn 4° c² 343/1 and F-Pn 4° c² 343/2); it is preserved in the Bibliothèque nationale de France (F-Pn Ms. 8223), The partimento collections are dated «15 July 1788», while the counterpoint notebook bears the date «Sunday 11 January 1789». These materials give a unique insight into how partimenti were used in preparation for counterpoint studies. The second partimento collection merits special attention as it contains no less than twelve *bassi seguenti* that I have identified in sacred vocal works by Leonardo Leo (1684-1744).

Biographies

Fabrizio Ammetto is a Full Professor in the Music Department of the University of Guanajuato, Mexico. He is a member of the 'Mexican Academy of Science' and the 'Mexican National Researchers System'. He holds degrees in violin, viola, and electronic music, and he received his Ph.D. in musicology from the University of Bologna. As a violinist, violist, and conductor, he has performed over 700 concerts in Europe and America, and has produced numerous critical editions and recordings of eighteenth- and nineteenth-century instrumental music. He has published several books, chapters and articles. He is a member of the international Editorial Committee of the Istituto Italiano Antonio Vivaldi (Fondazione Giorgio Cini), Venice.

Valentina Anzani is completing her Ph.D. at Bologna University with a dissertation on the castrato Antonio Bernacchi (1685-1756) and his pupils. Her research concerns castrati and the production of opera theatre. Her first publications are about castrati: 'Un soggetto equivoco al crepuscolo degli dèi castrati' (with Marco Beghelli, in *L'equivoco stravagante*, Fondazione Rossini, 2014), 'Castrato per amore: Casanova, Salimbeni, Farinelli e il misterioso Bellino' (in *Il Farinelli ritrovato*, LIM, 2015), 'Pseudonimi all'opera: un soprannome per la celebrità' (in *Il nome nel testo*, EdT, 2015). She was awarded the 'Handel Award' by the Handel Institute (UK) in 2017.

Giovanna Barbati (cellist and viola da gamba player) is a performer of early, contemporary, and improvised music. Her work as a researcher focuses on improvisation in early music and on historical didactics. She prepared a critical edition of Riccardo Broschi's opera *La Merope* for the Innsbrucker Festwochen der alten Musik in 2018. She was a pupil of Siegfried Palm (cello) and she studied the early practice with Christophe Coin and Jesper Christensen at the Schola Cantorum Basiliensis. She has been the principal cellist and viola da gambist of the baroque orchestra *Academia Montis Regalis* under Alessandro De Marchi for many years. She performed in the same role with many well-known European Baroque orchestras and groups in prestigious theatres and halls in Europe. She has recorded dozens of CDs, many of which are winners of awards and she has personally received rapturous praise from critics.

David Chung completed his musicological studies at Cambridge University and has published articles and reviews in *Early Music*, *Early Keyboard Journal*, *Journal of Eighteenth-Century Music*, *Journal of Seventeenth-Century Music*, *Music and Letters*, and *Revue de musicologie*. His edition of nearly 250 keyboard arrangements of Jean-Baptiste Lully's music has recently been published by the *Web Library of Seventeenth-Century Music* (<www.sscm-wlscm.org>). Chung maintains an active schedule as harpsichordist and has performed in cities across Europe, North America and Asia. Chung is currently Professor of Music at Hong Kong Baptist University.

Simone Ciolfi obtained his Master's degree (*laurea*) at the University 'La Sapienza' and his Ph.D. at the University of Rome 'Tor Vergata'. He has written articles on early nineteenth-century music, on Dallapiccola, on the programming of nineteenth-century Italian musical organizations, and on contemporary music. His areas of interest include the evolution of the concept of tradition in the music of the eighteenth and nineteenth centuries and the relationships between music theory and composition around 1700. He has worked on the artistic management of the Accademia Filarmonica Romana and has collaborated with *Concerto Italiano*, under the direction of Rinaldo Alessandrini for many years. He teaches Music History at Saint Mary's College (Notre Dame - Indiana, Rome program) and at the Conservatorio statale 'Arcangelo Corelli' di Messina.

MASSIMILIANO GUIDO is a Senior Researcher in the Department of Musicology and Cultural Heritage of Pavia University, where he teaches courses in the history of music theory and history of musical instruments. He previously served as a Banting Post-Doctoral Fellow at the Schulich School of Music, McGill University, where he worked with Peter Schubert on a project about the art of memory at the keyboard as a tool for teaching counterpoint (2012-2014). He was the principal investigator of the research project *Improvisation in Classical Music Education: Rethinking our Future by Learning our Past*, funded by the Social Sciences and Humanities Research Council of Canada (2013-2014). He holds degrees in musicology (Pavia University, doctorate and *laurea*, Göteborg University, Master of Music Research), organ (Parma Conservatory, Italy), and harpsichord (Como Conservatory, Italy). He combines musicological research with organ teaching and performance.

JAVIER LUPIÁÑEZ holds, among other diplomas, a Master's (with distinction) from The Royal Conservatory of The Hague in Baroque violin, and a Master's in musicology from Salamanca University. As a performer, he has won six international awards and has recorded for Harmonia Mundi, Ayros, France Musique, Musiqu3, Concertzender, and Radio Klara. His work as a researcher led to the identification of new works by Antonio Vivaldi. He is currently a Ph.D. student at the University of Guanajuato, Mexico, where he is working on a dissertation entitled *Las anotaciones de Johann Georg Pisendel (1687-1755) en los manuscritos vivaldianos de Dresde*.

JOHN LUTTERMAN is currently an Associate Professor at the University of Alaska, having previously served on the faculty of Whitman College, the University of California, Davis, the University of the Pacific, Lawrence University, and the San Francisco Conservatory He holds a Ph.D. in musicology from the University of California, Davis, and a DMA in cello performance from Stony Brook University. He has given solo performances throughout Europe and America, and has performed with a number of prominent early-music ensembles. His research focuses on the relationship between notation, compositional theory, and historical improvisatory practices.

JOSUÉ MELÉNDEZ PELÁEZ (cornetto and recorder player) studied music in Costa Rica, Guatemala, Mexico, Holland and Switzerland. He founded the first early music festival of Mexico, *Festival Santo Domingo de Música Antigua*. He is the founder and director of the ensemble *I Fedeli*, and has performed and recorded CDs with some of the most recognized European ensembles. He is a specialist in Renaissance and Baroque musical improvisation. He teaches Diminution/Improvisation at the University of Music, Trossingen, Germany and in various summer courses.

FRANCESCA MIGNOGNA is an Italian musician and musicologist who is currently a doctoral candidate at Sorbonne University in Paris. She studied saxophone and music composition at the State Conservatory of Campobasso (Italy). She obtained a Bachelor's degree and a Master of Music and Musicology at Sorbonne University of Paris. Her academic activities and research focuses on Renaissance and Baroque music theory and counterpoint. She collaborates with the IReMus (Institut de Recherche en Musicologie) on the publication of a critical edition of the works of Pierre-Louis Pollio (1724-1796).

GUIDO OLIVIERI is an Associate Professor of Musicology at the University of Texas at Austin, where he also directs the early music ensemble *Austinato*. He edited the collective volume *Arcomelo 2013. Studi in occasione del terzo centenario della nascita di Arcangelo Corelli* (Lucca, LIM, 2015), and the edition of A. Corelli, *Sonate da camera di Assisi* (Lucca, LIM, 2015). He has authored entries in *The New Grove Dictionary of Music*, *MGG*, and *Dizionario Biografico degli Italiani* and has published articles in journals and collected volumes on the developments of the string sonata in Naples and also on violin and cello repertories and performance practices in the 17th and 18th centuries. He is currently preparing the critical edition of D. Cimarosa *Il matrimonio segreto* for Bärenreiter.

Following his studies as a pianist, Marco Pollaci graduated from the University of Tor Vergata in Rome. In 2018, he obtained a Ph.D. from Nottingham University. He specialises in diverse topics including music theory and music history – especially Italian – spanning the sixteenth to nineteenth centuries. He is also interested in music analysis and nineteenth-century opera.

Anthony Pryer is a Reader in Historical Musicology and Aesthetics at Goldsmiths College, University of London. He has edited Monteverdi's three earliest publications (*Sacrae cantiunclae*, *Madrigali spirituali*, and *Canzonette a tre voci*) for the new Collected Works published in Cremona, and has written widely on other aspects of his output. Recent publications on aesthetics include articles on Hanslick's *Vom musikalisch-Schönen*, Japanese concepts of Nature, and the challenge of performance to the ontology of music. For many years he served on the executive committee of the British Society of Aesthetics. He currently holds a Research Fellowship at Seian University in Japan.

Rudolf Rasch studied musicology at the University of Amsterdam and was affiliated with the Institute of Musicology, later the Department of Media and Culture Studies, of Utrecht University from 1977 to 2010. His research focuses on temperament and the works of composers including Corelli, Vivaldi, Geminiani and Boccherini. He has published a number of articles, books and editions in these areas, including *Music Publishing in Europe 1600-1900* (an edited collection of essays, 2005), *Driehonderd brieven over muziek* (letters about music written by and to Constantijn Huygens, 2007), *Understanding Boccherini's Manuscripts* (an edited collection of essays, 2014), *Music and Power in the Baroque Era* (an edited collection of essays, 2014) and *Muziek in de Republiek* (about musical life in the Dutch Republic, 2018). He has also contributed to several volumes in the critical editions of the works of Luigi Boccherini and Francesco Geminiani. He has been the general editor of the Opera Omnia Francesco Geminiani since 2015.

Giorgio Sanguinetti is Associate Professor of Music Theory at the University of Rome 'Tor Vergata'. He has published extensively on the history of Italian music theory, Schenkerian analysis, form, and opera analysis. In 2011 he organized the seventh Euromac conference in Rome. He is a member of the scientific committee of the Istituto Nazionale di Studi Verdiani. His book *The Art of Partimento: History, Theory and Practice* (Oxford University Press, 2012) received the Wallace Berry Award of the Society for Music Theory in 2013.

Laura Toffetti is a Professor of Baroque Violin at the Conservatories of Belfort and Mulhouse. After she graduated from the Conservatory of Milan with a degree in Modern Violin, she obtained a Master of Music in Performance Practice (Baroque Violin) from the Royal College of Music (London) and the «Certificat d'Aptitude en Musique Ancienne» from the Ministère de la Culture Française. As a member of several Baroque orchestras in Europe, she founded the *Antichi Strumenti* Ensemble (Music Award of Académie Rhénane 2011), and she has directed «Un Vendredi au Musée» at the Musées Historique des Beaux-Arts in Mulhouse. Her discography includes several cd and musical prizes, and she has published for Ortus Verlag (Germany).

Biographies

Marina Toffetti is an Assistant Professor of Music Theory at the University of Padua. She has won musicological competitions and scholarships, has given lectures, masterclasses, and seminars at different institutions, and has read papers at international conferences in Italy and abroad (including England, Germany, France, Poland, Slovenia, Slovakia, Czech Republic, Croatia, Sweden, and USA). She coordinates international research projects on the dissemination of Italian music in central-eastern Europe in the Baroque period. In 2013 she was awarded the 'Italian Heritage Award' international prize for 'Research, education and innovation in the protection of cultural heritage' for the restoration of the incomplete score of G. C. Ardemanio's *Musica a più voci*. Her main research interests concern the history of music and musical institutions (16th-18th century), music reception, assimilation and adaptation, musical philology, and musical analysis.

Peter van Tour is a Lecturer in Music Theory and Aural Training at the Norwegian Academy of Music in Oslo. As a scholar of musicology he has specialized in counterpoint pedagogy and historic composition. He studied Music Pedagogy at Brabant Conservatory in Tilburg (MA), Musicology at the University of Utrecht (MA), and obtained a Master in Music Theory at the Royal College of Music in Stockholm (MA). His Ph.D. dissertation *Counterpoint and Partimento* (Uppsala 2015) highlights the practical teaching strategies at the Neapolitan Conservatories during the late eighteenth century. In 1995, Peter co-founded the Gotland School of Music Composition, where he taught music theory from 1995 to 2014.

Neal Zaslaw is the Herbert Gussman Professor of Music at Cornell University, where he has taught since 1970. He is the author or editor of nine books and more than 75 articles on early music, historical performance practice, and the history of the orchestra. Zaslaw's revision of Köchel's venerable catalogue of Mozart's works will be published in 2019, as a book in German and online in English. His current research involves Italian music of the Baroque period.

A

Abel, Carl Friedrich 122
Acciai, Giovanni 79, 111
Agazzari, Agostino 82, 109, 123, 142
Alberti, Leon Battista 180, 191
Albicastro, Giovanni Henrico 45
Algarotti, Francesco 232, 236, 238
Amadori [Giovanni Tedeschi] 232-233
Amadori, Giuseppe 233
Amat, Joan Carles 262, 269-272, 274-279, 283-285
Amendola, Nadia 351
Ammetto, Fabrizio 43, 49, 61
Anglesi, Domenico 32
Anzani, Valentina 223
Antonio da Padova, Saint 90
Apel, William 263-264, 279
Appel, Andrew 210
Appiani, Giuseppe 233, 237
Arezzo, Guido d' 263
Arnold, Franck Thomas 104, 109, 335, 338
Arteaga, Stefano 231, 238
Artusi, Giovanni Maria 183
Aspden, Suzanne 232, 238

B

Babel, Charles 4
Babell [Babel], William 16-20, 47
Bacciagaluppi, Claudio 125, 145, 369, 379-380
Bach, Carl Philipp Emanuel 48, 82, 109, 155, 164-165, 170
Bach, Johann Sebastian 133, 155-156, 165, 199, 241-243, 250, 252, 254
Bachmann, Alberto 307, 309, 317
Bagnati, Tiziano 78
Banchieri, Adriano 37
Banti, Anna 192
Baragwanath, Nicholas 344, 350
Barbarino, Bartolomeo 68, 122, 142
Barbati, Giovanna 117, 138, 145
Barbella, Emanuele 296
Barbella, Francesco 296
Barberini, Francesco 183
Barbieri, Patrizio 364, 367
Barchi, Michele 210
Bardi, Giovanni 158-159
Bares, Alessandro 79, 145
Barezzi, Giuseppe 356
Barilli, Antonio 224, 229
Barker, Andrew 154, 170
Barnett, Gregory 62
Barney, Stephen 172
Baroni, Leonora 121
Bartók, Béla 155

BASSANI, Oratio 68
BASSANO, Giovanni 68
BASSO, Alberto 323, 338
BAUMGARTNER, Johann Baptist [Jean Baptiste] 133, 142, 243, 245, 257
BEACH, Jennifer 172
BECKER, Judith-Maria 210
BEETHOVEN, Ludwig van 84, 156, 241, 337
BELLI, Giulio 90, 91
BELLOTTI, Edoardo 31-34, 39, 41-42, 76, 78, 113, 368, 371, 380
BENDA, Franz 44
BENT, Ian D. 279
BENTIVOGLIO, Enzo 154
BERARDI, Angelo 31
BERDES, Jane L. 302, 317
BERGÉ, Pieter 330, 339
BERGHOF, Oliver 172
BERKOWITZ, Aaron 169-170
BERLIN, Isaiah 169-170
BERMUDO, Fray Jua 269, 279
BERNACCHI, Antonio Maria 223, 225-237
BERNSTEIN, David W. 343, 350
BERTINETTO, Alessandro 149
BETTINELLI, Saverio 291, 297
BIANCIARDI, Francesco 82, 109
BIANCONI, Lorenzo 326, 338
BIBA, Otto 308, 317, 319
BISMANTOVA, Bartolomeo 123, 142
BLACKBURN, Bonnie J. 122, 145, 282
BOCCACCIO, Giovanni 169
BOCCAGE, Anne-Marie Fiquet du 290
BOCCHERINI, Luigi 128
BOETTICHER, Wolfgang 267, 279
BOISMORTIER, Joseph Bodin de 245, 247, 257
BOL, Hans 142, 145
BOMBI, Andrea 317
BONIZZI, Vincenzo 68
BONNET, Jacques 123, 143
BONONCINI, Giovanni 232, 355
BONONCINI, Giovanni Maria 180, 192
BONZ, Tobias 210
BORDAS IBAÑEZ, Cristina 282
BORDONI, Faustina 232
BORGIR, Tharald 104, 109, 371, 380
BORIO, Gianmario 41
BORMAN, Renate 61
BORN, Georgina 171
BOVICELLI, Giovanni Battista 65, 68, 78
BOYD, Malcolm 323
BOYLE, Matthew 332, 340
BRAINARD, Paul 302, 310, 317
BRANDENBURG, Danie 373, 381
BREVAL, Jean-Baptiste-Sébastien 131, 143
BRIÇEÑO, Luis de 273, 279
BRONZI, Enrico 204, 210, 218
BROSSARD, Sébastien de 292-293, 297, 357-358, 368
BROSSES, Charles de 314, 317
BROUDE, Ronald 28
BROWN, Howard Mayer 77-78, 265-266, 268-269
BRUMEL, Antoine 275
BUELOW, George J. 335, 338
BURDEN, Michael 298
BURMEISTER, Joachim 71, 78, 188, 192
BURNEY, Charles 236, 238, 301, 338
BUTT, John 21, 28, 70, 78
BYROS, Vasili 119, 145

C

CACCINI, Giulio 67, 151, 154-155, 157-161, 163-168, 170, 172, 186, 189, 192
CAFFARELLI [Gaetano Majorano] 228
CAFIERO, Rosa 117, 145, 343, 351, 354, 368-369, 380
CALCINOTTO, Carlo 315
CALDARA, Antonio 133-138, 142-143
CALLAHAN, Michael 120, 140, 146, 371, 381
CAMPEGGI, Francesco 234
CAMPION, Thomas 274
CANALE, Margherita 310, 317
CANGUILHEM, Philippe 118, 120, 146
CAPLIN, William E. 332, 338
CAPPI, GIOVANNI 308-309
CARACI VELA, Maria 145, 194, 326, 338, 351
CARAVAGGIO, Michelangelo Merisi da 184-185
CARCHIOLO, Salvatore 104, 109
CARIDEO, Armando 33-34, 41-42, 368
CARLANI, Carlo 232

Charles Edward, Stuart, Prince 224
Carnoli, Pietro Paolo 233
Carter, Tim 158, 160, 165, 171, 340
Cartier, Jean-Baptiste 302-303, 306-310, 317
Caselli, Vincenzo 233
Castello, Dario 68, 78
Castiglione, Baldassarre [Baldassar o Baldesar] 264-265, 279, 291, 297
Cattaneo, Giacomo 45
Cavalieri, Emilio de' 158, 347
Cazeau, Isabelle 60, 62
Ceccato, Marco 145
Cerha, Friedrich 110
Cervetto, Giacobbe Basevi 129
Cervetto, James 129-130
Cesarini, Carlo Francesco 135
Chambonnières, Jacques Champion de 4-7, 12, 16, 20-21, 29
Chateaubriand, François-Auguste René, vicomte de 170-171
Chaucer, Geoffrey 169
Chilesotti, Oscar 266, 268, 280
Choron, Alexandre-Étienne 374, 381
Christensen, Jesper Bøje 104, 109, 210
Christensen, Thomas 41, 147, 262, 272, 279-280, 327, 338, 343, 351, 371, 381
Christina [Kristina], Queen of Sweden 353
Chung, David 3, 5, 28
Cicero 187, 192
Cimarosa, Domenico 126
Ciolfi, Simone xv, 323-325, 328, 331-332, 338-339
Cipriani, Benedetto 344, 351
Clayton, Alfred 146, 171
Cocset, Bruno 204, 206, 210, 217
Coelho, Victor 281
Coin, Christophe 130
Collins, Timothy A. 121-122, 146
Colomb, Romain 317
Colombi, Giuseppe 188-189
Colonna, Fabio 364
Columbro, Marta 139, 146
Colzani, Alberto 112, 114
Constantino, Fabio 95
Conti, Gioacchino 233
Cook, Nicholas 156, 171
Corbetta, Francesco 273, 280, 285
Corelli, Arcangelo 31, 47-49, 59-60, 135, 179, 198-199, 292, 310, 314, 353, 356
Corp, Edward 223-224, 238
Corrette, Michel 82, 109
Corri, Domenico 82, 109
Cosentino, Alessandro 351
Cotumacci, Carlo 357
Couperin, François 48, 128, 141, 143
Couperin, Louis 4, 10-13, 21-22, 29
Couperin, Marc Roger Normand 4
Coussemaker, Charles Edmond Henri de 263, 280
Cowling, Elisabeth 135
Crecquillon, Thomas 71
Crescimbeni, Giovan Mario 289-290, 297
Crivellati, Cesare 180, 192
Crocker, Richard L. 275, 280
Crouch, Joseph 210
Cuiller, Bertrand 210
Cumer, Nicola 113
Curry, Robert 172
Cuzzoni, Francesca 232
Czerniawski, Adam 258

D

Dahlhaus, Carl 120, 146, 156, 171, 241, 257, 275-276, 280
D'Alessandro, Domenico Antonio 339, 367
Dalla Casa, Girolamo 68
Damuth, Laura 325, 334, 339
Dandrieu, Jean-François 82, 109
D'Anglebert, Jean Henry 3-5, 7-12, 15, 20, 22, 28-29
Danner, Peter 269, 280
Darbellay, Étienne 96, 110
Dart, Thurston 265, 280
David, Hans T. 110, 257, 258
Davis, Miles 155
De Champs, Ettore 129
Decombe, Jacques-François 302, 307
Del Buono, Gioanpietro 71, 78
Dell'Abaco, Evaristo Felice 130

Della Libera, Luca 339
Della Sciucca, Marco 94, 111
Della Valle, Pietro 120-121, 143
Del Sordo, Federico 104, 109
De Marchi, Alessandro 135
Denis, Pietro 302, 309
Dent, Edward Joseph 324, 339
De Pascale, Enrico 185, 193
Derosiers, Nicolas 273, 280
Desler, Anne 234, 238
Devriès, Anik 309, 318
De Wispelaere, Valérie 368
Di Giacomo, Salvatore 139, 146
Diletskii, Nikolai 276-278, 280
Diruta, Girolamo 34, 37, 40, 42
Doizi de Velasco, Nicolás 277, 280
Donati, Ignazio 68
Dongois, William 140, 146
Doni, Giovanni Battista 183-184, 190, 192
Donington, Robert 165, 171
Dounias, Minos 313, 318
D'Ovidio, Antonella 62
Dubreuil, Pascal 192
Duckles, Vincent 310, 318
Duport, Jean-Louis 131, 133, 143, 243-244, 258
Durante, Francesco 77, 344, 346, 356-358, 379
Durante, Sergio 112, 313-314, 318

E

Eco, Umberto 182, 194
Eisenhardt, Lex 269, 278, 280
Eitner, Robert 307, 318
Elmer, Minnie 310, 318
Erhardt, Martin 343, 351
Erig, Richard 71, 78
Esses, Maurice 121, 146, 269, 281
Euripides 154

F

Fabbri, Moreno 297
Fabris, Dinko 112, 354, 368
Farinelli [Carlo Broschi] 223, 225, 227-231, 233-237
Fasch, Johann Friedrich 44
Fechner, Manfred 44, 61
Fei, Andrea 94
Fenaroli, Fedele 346, 358, 372
Fenlon, Iain 340
Ferand, Ernst T. 117, 146
Ferrandini, Giovanni Battista 233
Fesch, Willem de 199
Fétis, François-Joseph 225-226, 228-229, 236, 238
Findlen, Paula 298
Finotti, Fabio 290-291, 297
Fleischhauer, Günter 61
Florimo, Francesco 368
Florio, John 168, 171
Fontana, Giovanni Battista 68, 70-71, 78
Forkel, Johann Nikolaus 251, 258
Formisano, Marco 192
Forqueray, Antoine 142
Fortune, Nigel 158, 171
Forzoni Accolti 32
Foscarini, Giovanni Paolo 274, 281
Foscolo, Ugo 291, 297
Framery, Nicolas Étienne 122, 143
Franchi, Saverio 95, 109
Francone, Gaetano 296
Frescobaldi, Girolamo 68, 81, 84, 86, 94-99, 102-105, 107-108, 110-112, 156, 190, 193
Fuchs, Ingrid 308, 317, 319
Fuller, David 28
Furno, Giovanni 357
Fux, Johann Joseph 34

G

Gable, David 172
Gaffi, Bernardo 127
Gaffi, Tommaso 125-127, 143
Galassi, Mara 113
Galilei, Vincenzo xiii, 175-177, 192, 266
Galizia, Fede 185-186
Galli, Amintore 125, 146
Galliard, John Ernest 80
Gambia, Ezio 149
Garcia, Manuel 67-68
Garibaldi, Luigi Agostino 356, 368

Gasparini, Francesco 31, 33, 41, 82, 111, 125, 127, 143, 323, 335, 339
Gatti, Enrico 59, 61, 68, 79, 81, 111, 182, 194
Gavito, Cory Michael 262, 281
Geminiani, Francesco 44, 48, 195, 199-208, 210-219
Gentili, Mario 41
Gerber, Ernst Ludwig 122
Gerhard, Singer 65, 79
Gesualdo, Carlo, Prince of Venosa 364
Geyer, Helen 147
Ghielmi, Lorenzo 94, 110
Ghiselli, Francesco 224, 229
Ghizzolo, Giovanni 81, 85-86, 88-92, 98, 108, 111
Giacomelli, Geminiano 229
Gialdroni, Teresa Maria 127, 147, 326, 339
Giardelli, Claire 210
Gigli, Beniamino 159
Gingras, Bruno 371, 381
Giovani, Giulia 369, 380
Giuli, Paola 290, 297
Giustiniani, Vincenzo 184, 186, 192
Gizzi, Domenico 233
Gjerdingen, Robert O. 38, 41, 117-119, 126, 147, 326, 328, 339, 343, 351, 371, 381
Goede, Thérèse de 113
Goehr, Lydia 241, 258
Gordon-Seifert, Catherine 4, 28
Graun, Carl Heinrich 44
Greco, Gaetano 357
Greco, Rocco 296, 356-357, 365, 367
Grimaldi, Nicola 223
Guarducci, Tommaso 232
Guida, Antonio 139, 142-143
Guido, Giovanni Antonio 295
Guido, Massimiliano 31-32, 40-42, 343, 351, 369, 380
Gunn, John 131, 134, 144, 245-246, 258
Gustafson, Bruce 3-4, 16-17, 28-29
Gyrowetz, Adalbert 372-374, 381

H

Hall, Monica 269, 281
Halton, Rosalind 128, 147
Hamelin, Jean-Yves 120
Handel, George Frideric 44, 135
Hanning, Robert 173
Hardel, Jacques 4, 16-17, 19, 21, 29
Hardy, Henry 170
Harper, John Martin 96, 111
Harris, C. David 3, 29
Harris, Helen T. 323, 339
Hasse, Johann Adolf 228-229
Hatch, Christopher 343, 350
Hawkins, John 49, 61
Haymoz, Jean Yves 118, 147
Heble, Ajay 42
Heilmann, Luigi 194
Heinichen, Johann David 334
Heller, Karl 44, 46, 61
Herbst, Johannes Andreas 63, 65, 67-68, 79
Herlin, Denis 16, 21, 29, 368
Hill, John Walter 154, 172, 261-262, 272, 281
Hiller, Johann Adam 237-238, 301
Hitchcock, H. Wiley 155, 158-160, 163, 166, 168, 172
Hjelmborg, Bjørn 114
Hoffmann, Bettina 128, 131, 142, 147
Hogwood, Christopher 204, 210, 310, 318
Holtemeier, Ludwig 346, 351
Homer 169
Honea, Sion M. 66, 77, 79
Hotteterre, Jacques 121, 144
Hudson, Richard 276, 281
Humeau, Philippe 16-18
Hummel, Johann Julius 309

I

Illiano, Roberto xv-xvi
Ingarden, Roman 241, 258
Invernizzi, Roberta 160
Isabella d'Este, Marchioness of Mantua 264
Isidore of Seville 152, 172
Ivanoff, Vladimir 269, 281

J

Jacchini, Giuseppe Maria 125, 128
Jackson, Barbara Garvey 298
Jakobson, Roman 191, 194

James, Ivor 207
James ii [and vii], King of England, Ireland and Scotland 223
James Francis Edward, [James iii] Stuart, Prince of Wales 223
Jaquot, Jean 279
Jeffery, Peter 157, 172
Jensen, Claudia R. 276, 278, 281
Jensen, Niels Martin 96-97, 112
Johansson, Cari 309, 318

K

Kerman, Joseph 84, 112
Kinderman, William 156, 172
Kinkeldey, Otto 263
Kircher, Athanasius 188
Kirkby, Emma 160
Kirkendale, Ursula 147
Kirkendale, Warren 135, 147
Kirnberger, Johann Philip 248, 258
Knox, Hank 28
Kolenda, Konstantin 174
Kolneder, Walter 46, 60-61, 207
Komarek, Giovanni Girolamo 356
Köpp, Kai 62
Krall, Hannah 316
Krause, Ralf 377, 381
Kuhnau, Johann 335
Kurtzman, Jeffrey 90, 112

L

Labarre, Louis Julien Castels de 374-375, 377, 379-380
La Borde, Jean-Benjamin de 129-130, 143
Laghi, Simone 296, 298, 311, 318
La Gorce, Jérôme de 28
La Guerre, Jacquet de 4-5, 14-15
La Houssaye [Housset], Pierre(-Nicolas) 309
Lambert, Michael de Saint 82
Landini, Orazio Arrighi 290
Landmann, Ortrun 44, 61-62
Landshoff, Ludwig 44, 62
Lanzetti, Salvatore 122, 128, 133-136, 138-139, 141-142, 144
Lasso [Lassus], Orlando di [Roland, Orlande de] 71, 267
Laver, Mark 42
La Via, Stefano 62, 128, 148
Lavigna, Albert 280
Lavoix, Henri, fils 237, 239
Lawton, Philip 113
Lax, Éva 168-169, 172
Le Cerf de la Viéville, Jean-Laurent 293-295, 298
Ledbetter, David 5, 10, 20, 29
Leech, Peter 4, 29
Le Gallois de Grimarest, Jean-Léonor 7, 21, 29
Lemaire, Théophile 237, 239
Leo, Leonardo 344, 356, 376-379
Leonardo da Vinci, 175-176, 178, 192
Leonhardt, Gustav 110
Lester, Joel 343, 351, 372, 381
Lesure, François 113, 309, 318
Lewis, Eric 171
Lewis, W. 172
Li Causi, Pietro 192
Liepmannssohn, Leo 307, 318
Linden, Jaap ter 204, 210, 216
Lindley, Mark 266, 281
Lindley, Robert 129
Linnaeus, Pietro 364
Lionnet, Jean 193
Lippius, Johannes 275
Lisack, Lucille 146
Lister, Warwick xvi
Llewellyn, Timothy D. 234, 239
Locatelli, Pietro Antonio xiii, 199
Lockey, Nicholas Scott 44, 51, 60, 62
Lomazzo, Filippo 85, 88
Lomazzo, Francesco 70-71
Lorenzini, Raimondo 349, 352
Loulié, Étienne 180, 193
Lowinsky, Edward E. 122, 145, 263-264, 275, 281
Lucchese, Enrico 231, 239
Luisi, Francesco 95, 112
Lully [Lulli], Jean-Baptiste [Giovanni Battista] 4-5
Lupiáñez, Javier 43, 48
Luppi, Andrea 112, 114
Lustig, Monika 147

Lutterman, John Kenneth 241-243, 258
Lutz, Rudolf 147
Lymenstull, Eva 125, 128, 148

M

Machover, Milo 351
Macioce, Stefania 185, 193
Maione, Paologiovanni 139, 146, 339
Mancini, Francesco 353-356, 365
Mancini, Giovanni Battista 233-235, 239
Manfredi, Filippo 128
Manguel, Alberto 157, 169, 172
Mann, Alfred 343, 352
Marais, Marin 4, 122, 144
Marcello, Benedetto 128, 144
Marcocchi, Stefano 296
Marescalchi, Paolo 302
Maria Beatrice, d'Este [Mary of Modena], Queen of England, Ireland and Scotland 223
Maria Klementyna, Sobieska, Princess 223
Marini, Biagio 68, 183, 193, 232
Marino, Rosanna 192
Mark, Ryan 310, 318
Marotta, Cesare 154
Marshall, Robert Lewis 84-85, 112, 172
Martin, Margot 5, 29
Martinelli, Vincenzo 231-232, 239
Martini, Giovanni Battista, Padre 125, 144, 225, 235
Marvin, Roberta Montemorra 356, 368
Marx, Hans Joachim 326, 339
Mascardi, Agostino 127
Maschio, Francesco 135, 138, 145
Mascitti, Michele 295
Massaro, Maria Nevilla 317
Massip, Catherine 368
Mathurin Matharel 210
Mattei, Stanislao 82, 112
Mattheson, Johann 243, 248, 258
Maugars, André 121, 144, 179, 190, 193
Mayer Brown, Howard 279
Mayone, Ascanio 68, 357
McClintock, Carol 172
McGeary, Thomas 239
McGillivray, Alison 204, 210, 215
McGuinness, David 210
McSwiny, Owen 234
Meier, Bernard 326, 330, 339
Melani, Atto 325
Mélendez Peláez, Josué 63, 65
Mellace, Raffaele 369, 380
Melli, Domenico 158
Memel, Lorenzo 233
Mendel, Arthur 241, 257-258
Merighi, Antonia 223
Merrick, Frank 207
Mersenne, Marin 4, 273, 282
Merula, Tarquinio 68
Metastasio, Pietro 289
Meyer, Christian 381
Mignogna, Francesca 261
Milanuzzi, Carl 274, 282
Miles, Natasha Frances 273, 282
Minelli, Giovanni Battista 229
Mioli, Piero 240
Moelants, Dirk 149
Moersch, Charlotte Mattax 156, 172
Monteclair, Michel-Pignolet de 48, 288, 298
Montesardo, Girolamo 272, 282
Monteverdi, Claudio 123-124, 144, 151, 167-169, 182, 193
Monti, Vincenzo 289
Moore, Robin 117, 148
Morabito, Fulvia xv-xvi
Morehen, John 280
Morelli, Arnaldo 31-34, 36, 38, 40, 42
Moroney, Davitt 4, 12, 29
Mortensen, Lars Ulrik 210
Moser, Andreas 295, 298
Motuz, Catherine 63
Mozart, Leopold 48, 301
Mozart, Wolfgang Amadeus 156, 165
Muffat, Georg 31
Müller, Ruth E. 257
Murata, Margaret 326, 339
Musenga, Gabriele 230
Muzio, Emanuele 356
Myron, Richard 210

N

Nardi, Antonio 158
Nardini, Pietro 310-311
Nasillo, Gaetano 204-205, 210, 214
Navarre, Jean-Philippe 279
Neri, Benedetto 373
Nestola, Barbara 295, 298
Nettl, Bruno 152, 172, 173
Neumann, Frederick 165, 173
Neumann, Werner 259
Neuwirth, Markus 330, 339
Niedt, Friedrich Erhard 243, 248-249, 251-252, 258, 335
Nuti, Giulia 128, 148

O

O'Donnell, Aidan 272-273, 277, 282
Oliva, Patrick 316, 318
Olivieri, Guido xv, 133-134, 139, 148, 287, 295-296, 298, 367-368
Omosky, Ute 147
Ortiz, Diego 140, 144
Ortkemper, Hubert 226
O'Sullivan, Loretta 204-205, 210, 219
Ottenberg, Hans-Günter 61
Otter, Joseph 310, 311
Ottoboni, Pietro, Cardinal 135, 289
Owens, Jessie Ann 85, 112

P

Padoan, Maurizio 112, 114
Pagin, André Noël 309
Palestrina, Giovanni Pierluigi da 69
Palisca, Claude 158-159, 173
Pamphilj, Benedetto 135
Pandolfi Mealli, Giovanni Antonio 68, 189-190
Panzacchi, Enrico 227-228, 231-232, 239
Parisotti, Alessandro 159, 173
Pasquali, Nicolò 82, 112
Pasquini, Bernardo 31-42, 125, 135, 353, 368
Pauley, Scott 210
Pedio, Renato 194
Penna, Lorenzo 82, 112, 326, 340
Penson, Guy 210
Peri, Jacopo 158
Petrobelli, Pierluigi 301, 318
Pez, Johann Christoph 47
Philipsen, Christian 147
Pianca, Luca 210
Piani, Giovanni Antonio 295, 298
Pincherle, Marc 60, 62
Pinelli, Petronio 301, 319
Pirrotta, Nino 148, 155, 173
Pisendel, Johann Georg 43-52, 54-57, 59-60
Pistocchi, Francesco Antonio Mamiliano 227, 232, 236
Pitoni, Giuseppe Ottavio 31, 33, 41
Pitschel, Theodor Leberecht 242, 258
Plato 158, 314
Pleeth, Anthony 204, 206, 210-211
Pohlmann, Egert 154, 173
Pollaci, Marco 343
Porpora, Nicola 227, 233, 235, 344, 357
Porter, William E. 31-33, 39, 41, 326, 340
Praetorius, Michael 68
Pratt, Carroll C. 258
Preitano, Massimo 261, 274, 276, 278, 282
Prosser, Pietro 113
Protopopov, Vladimir 280
Provenzale, Francesco 354, 365
Pryer, Anthony 151, 167, 173
Puffett, Derrick 146, 171
Pujol, Emilio 269, 282

Q

Quantz, Johann Joachim 44, 48, 113, 152, 173, 195, 197-198, 206-207
Quinteiro, Eligio 210
Quintilianus, Marcus Fabius 187-190, 192

R

Raaff, Anton 232-233
Radicchi, Patrizia 298
Raguenet, François 292, 293, 298
Rameau, Jean-Philippe 248, 261, 282
Rasch, Rudolf xi, svi, 195, 242, 259, 338
Rasi, Francesco 163, 167
Rastall, Richard 265, 280

Ratti, Antonio 233
Raupach, Christoph 243, 258
Redi, Giovanni 234
Renwick, William 371-372, 381
Ricordati, Bernardo Felice 33, 353
Ridgewell, Rupert 308, 319
Riemann, Hugo 274
Rifkin, Joshua 71
Riley, Edward R. 173
Roberts, Helen 63
Robletti, Giovanni Battista 95
Rocchetti, Ventura 232
Roche, Jerome 95, 113
Rodari, Gianni 140, 148
Roger, Estienne 179, 325
Rogniono, Ricardo 68
Rognoni, Francesco 63-65, 67-70, 79, 193
Rognoni, Riccardo 79
Rohrmann, Leopold 302
Rolli, Paolo 289
Romagnoli, Angela 104, 113, 145, 351, 354, 368
Romanou, Katy 125, 148
Rosand, David 173
Rosand, Ellen 326, 340
Rose, Glori 120, 148
Rotem, Elam 74, 79
Rothstein, William 335, 340
Rousseau, Jean 298
Rousseau, Jean-Jacques 121-122, 144, 170, 287-289, 298
Roworth, Wendy Wassyng 298
Ruspoli, Bartolomeo 135
Ryhiner-Delon, Achilles 311, 313

S

Sabbatini, Pietro Paolo 82, 113
Sacaluga, Servando 289-299
Sacchi, Giovenale 225, 236, 239
Saccone, Eduardo 155, 173
Sachs, Curt 258
Sadie, Stanley 341
Sainte-Maure, Benoit de 169
Saint Lambert, Michael de 113
Sala, Massimiliano xv, xvi
Sala, Nicola 373-377, 379-380
Salimbeni, Felice 237
Sallis, Friedemann 85, 113
Salomon, Jean Baptiste Dehaye 302
Sama, Catherine M. 298
Sammaruco, Francesco 94
Sánchez de Lima, Miguel 278
Sandrin, Pier 71
Sanguinazzo, Nicolò 132, 144-145
Sanguinetti, Giorgio xv, 38, 42, 77, 79, 117-118, 125, 129, 134, 138, 147-148, 295, 299, 324-325, 327, 329-331, 335, 340, 343-346, 348, 352-353, 356, 369, 371, 381
Scarlatti, Alessandro 135, 290, 323-328, 330, 332-333, 336-337, 346-348, 353
Scarlatti, Domenico 135, 357
Scheibe, Johann Adolph 48
Schenker, Heinrich 165, 173
Schering, Arnold 44, 55, 62
Schmitt, Thomas 268, 278, 282
Schneider, Herbert 28
Schopenhauer, Arthur 151, 174
Schreyfogel, Johan Friedrich 44
Schubert, Peter 32, 42, 118, 149
Schulenberg, David 242, 259
Schultz, Walter 207
Schulze, Hans-Joachim 258-259
Schütz, Heinrich 380
Schwenkreis, Markus 63, 77, 79
Scimone, Claudio 317
Sciommeri, Giacomo 351
Scudo, Paul 227-228, 231-232, 239
Seeger, Charles 163, 174
Seletzky, Robert Eric 301, 319
Selma y Salaverde, Bartolomé de 68-69, 71, 78
Seneca, Lucius Annaeus 133
Severi, Francesco 68, 79
Sharrill, Paul 332, 340
Siéfert, Marion 146
Sigismondo, Giuseppe 354-355, 379, 382
Silbiger, Alexander 28, 111, 368
Simmel, Georg 81, 113
Simpson, Christopher 121, 132, 145, 243, 248-251, 253-257, 259

SIMPSON, David 204-205, 210, 212
SIRENA, Galeazzo 169
SISTO, Davide 149
SMITH, Anne 70-71, 79
SOLDI, Luca Antonio 94
SOLIS, Gabriel 172
SOMIS, Giovanni Battista 45
SØRENSEN, Søren 114
SOROSINA, Pietro 191
SPIETH, Noëlle 210
SPIRIDIONIS A MONTE CARMELO, father 63, 76-78, 80
SPITZER, John 62
STAEHELIN, Martin 311, 319
STAFFIERI, Gloria 326, 340
STEFFANI, Agostino 237
STEIN, Daniel 129, 149
STELLA, Gaetano 351
STEMBRIDGE, Christopher 95, 110, 114
STEWART-MACDONALD, Rohan H. xv
STIASTNY, Bernhard 125, 145
STIGAND, Isobella S. E. 149
STINSON, Russell 259
STRAW, Will 171
STROBBE, Lieven 118, 149
STROHM, Reinhard 340
STRUNK, Oliver 158, 174
SUESS, John G. 188, 194
SUEUR, Agathe 187, 192, 194
SUPRIANI, Francesco Paolo 296
SUPRIANO, Francesco P. 133-135, 138, 142, 145
SUZUKI, Hidemi 204, 210, 213
SZWEYKOWSKI, Zygmunt 158, 171

T

TALBOT, Michael 56, 58, 62, 336-337, 341
TARTINI, Giuseppe xiii, 44, 128, 301-303, 306-314, 316-317, 319
TASCHETTI, Gabriele 91, 114
TAVELLA, Konrad 79, 111
TAYLOR, Rachelle 28
TELEMANN, Georg Philipp 44, 47, 57
TENI, Maria Rosaria 319
TERZI, Antonio 68
TESI, Vittoria 229
THOM, Eitelfriedrich 61
THOMAS, Antoine-Léonard 301
THOMAS, Bernard 110
TINI, Simon 85
TODEA, Flavia C. 117, 149
TOFFETTI, Laura xii-xiii, 175
TOFFETTI, Marina 81, 85, 94, 108, 111, 114, 194
TOMLINSON, Gary 326, 341
TORCHI, Luigi 120, 149
TORELLI, Giuseppe 45
TOSI, Piefrancesco 226, 231, 234-235, 240
TOSI, Pierfrancesco 70, 80
TOSI, Pier Francesco 48
TRABACI, Giovanni Maria 357
TREITLER, Leo 174, 287, 299
TRITTO, Giacomo 346
TYLER James 269, 281

U

URSINO, Gennaro 354, 357, 364

V

VACCARO, Jean-Michel 134, 149, 263, 266-267, 282
VALSECCHI, Mario 110
VAN REGENMORTEL, Hans 118, 149
VANSCHEEUWIJCK, Marc 125, 149
VAN ORDEN, Kate 171
VAN TOUR, Peter xiv, xvi, 343, 352-353, 356, 369, 371-372, 376-377, 379, 382
VERACINI, Francesco Maria 128
VERDI, Giuseppe 356
VERDI, Luigi 230, 235, 240
VIADANA [GROSSI DA VIADANA], Lodovico 268
VICENTE, Alfonso de 282
VICENTINO, Nicola xiii, 183, 193
VINCENTI, Alessandro 85
VINCENTI, Giacomo 273-274
VINCIOLI, Teodora 189
VISÉE, Robert de 128, 143
VITALI, Carlo 223, 240
VIVALDI, Antonio 43-46, 48-49, 51-53, 55-60, 245

W

Walker, Jennifer xvi
Walls, Peter 319
Walther, Johann Gottfried 248, 259
Wasielewski, Wilhelm J. 121-122, 125, 130, 149
Watkins, David 133, 149
Watkins, Timothy D. 148, 298, 368
Webb, Richard 204, 210
Weinmann, Alexander 308, 319
Wertenson, Birgit Johanna 147
West, Martin L. 154, 173
Westrup, Jack 104, 114, 323, 341
Whenham, John 173
Whitmore, Philip 156, 174
Whittaker, Nathan H. 128, 149
Willaert, Adrian 71
Williams, Peter 327, 341
Wilson, Glen 4, 29
Wistreich, Richard 173
Wittkower, Rudolf 180, 194
Wolf, Christoph 257
Wolf, Peter 29

Y

Yacus, David 66
Young, James O. 119, 149
Young, La Monte Thornton 155

Z

Zacconi, Ludovico 65-67, 70-71, 77, 80
Zamboni, Giovanni Giacomo 32
Zampieri, Domenico 364
Zanetti, Antonio 231
Zanetti, Anton Maria 231
Zannetti, Bartolomeo 95
Zappi, Giovan Battista Felice 289-290
Zarlino, Gioseffo xiii, xvi, 181-183, 193, 261, 282, 314
Zaslaw, Neal xiii, xv, 62, 301, 310, 319
Zhu, Beilang 210
Ziino, Agostino 148, 339, 367
Zipperling, Rainer 210
Zuccari, Carlo 310, 319